Lecture Notes in Computer Science   9256

Commenced Publication in 1973
Founding and Former Series Editors:
Gerhard Goos, Juris Hartmanis, and Jan van Leeuwen

More information about this series at http://www.springer.com/series/7412

George Azzopardi · Nicolai Petkov (Eds.)

Computer Analysis of Images and Patterns

16th International Conference, CAIP 2015
Valletta, Malta, September 2–4, 2015
Proceedings, Part I

Springer

Editors
George Azzopardi
University of Malta
Msida
Malta

Nicolai Petkov
University of Groningen
Groningen
The Netherlands

ISSN 0302-9743   ISSN 1611-3349 (electronic)
Lecture Notes in Computer Science
ISBN 978-3-319-23191-4   ISBN 978-3-319-23192-1 (eBook)
DOI 10.1007/978-3-319-23192-1

Library of Congress Control Number: 2015946746

LNCS Sublibrary: SL6 – Image Processing, Computer Vision, Pattern Recognition, and Graphics

Springer Cham Heidelberg New York Dordrecht London

Printed on acid-free paper

Springer International Publishing AG Switzerland is part of Springer Science+Business Media
(www.springer.com)

Preface

This book constitutes one part of the two-part volume of proceedings of the 16th International Conference on Computer Analysis of Images and Patterns, CAIP 2015, held in Valletta, Malta, during September 2–4, 2015.

CAIP is a series of biennial international conferences devoted to all aspects of computer vision, image analysis and processing, pattern recognition and related fields. Previous conferences were held in York, Seville, Münster, Vienna, Paris, Groningen, Warsaw, Ljubljana, Kiel, Prague, Budapest, Dresden, Leipzig, Wismar, and Berlin.

CAIP 2015 featured three plenary lectures by the invited speakers Patrizio Campisi from the Università degli Studi Roma Tre, Bart ter Haar Romenij from the Eindhoven University of Technology, and Mario Vento from the University of Salerno. CAIP 2015 aimed to extend the scope of the series by allowing also submissions in pattern recognition of non-image data, machine learning and brain-inspired computing. Each submission was reviewed by at least three members of the international Program Committee and only high-quality papers were selected for inclusion in these proceedings.

We thank the Steering Committee of CAIP for giving us the honor of organizing this reputable conference in Malta. We also thank the Maltese Ministry of Finance, the Malta Council for Science and Technology, the Malta Tourism Authority, Springer, and the Jülich Supercomputing Center for sponsorships. Last but not least, we thank Charles Theuma, principal of Saint Martin's Institute of Higher Education (Malta), for coordinating the local arrangements.

September 2015

George Azzopardi
Nicolai Petkov

Organization

Program Committee

Enrique Alegre	University of Leon, Spain
Muhammad Raza Ali	Vision Research Division, InfoTech, Rawalpindi, Pakistan
Furqan Aziz	Institute of Management Sciences, Pakistan
George Azzopardi	University of Malta, Malta
Andrew Bagdanov	Computer Vision Center, Barcelona, Spain
Donald Bailey	Massey University, New Zealand
Antonio Bandera	University of Malaga, Spain
Ardhendu Behera	Edge Hill University, UK
Gyan Bhanot	Rutgers University, USA
Michael Biehl	University of Groningen, The Netherlands
Adrian Bors	University of York, UK
Henri Bouma	TNO, The Netherlands
Kerstin Bunte	University of Birmingham, UK
Ceyhun Burak Akgül	Boğaziçi University, Turkey
Kenneth Camilleri	University of Malta, Malta
Patrizio Campisi	University of Rome Tre, Italy
Mateu Sbert Casasayas	University of Girona, Spain
Andrea Cerri	University of Bologna, Italy
Kwok-Ping Chan	The University of Hong Kong, Hong Kong, SAR China
Rama Chellappa	University of Maryland, USA
Dmitry Chetverikov	Hungarian Academy of Sciences, Hungary
Marco Cristani	Università degli Studi di Verona, Italy
Gabriel Cristobal	Instituto de Optica (CSIC), Spain
Guillaume Damiand	LIRIS/Université de Lyon, France
Carl James Debono	University of Malta, Malta
Joachim Denzler	University of Jena, Germany
Mariella Dimiccoli	Universitat Politècnica de Catalunya, Spain
Junyu Dong	Ocean University of China, China
Pieter Eendebak	TNO, The Netherlands
Hakan Erdogan	Sabanci University, Turkey
Francisco Escolano	University of Alicante, Spain
Taner Eskil	IŞIK University, Turkey
Alexandre Falcao	University of Campinas, Brazil
Giovanni Maria Farinella	University of Catania, Italy
Reuben Farrugia	University of Malta, Malta
Gernot Fink	Dortmund University of Technology, Germany

Patrizio Frosini	University of Bologna, Italy
Laurent Fuchs	Université de Poitiers, France
Edel García	Advanced Technologies Applications Center (CENATAV), Cuba
Eduardo Garea	Advanced Technologies Applications Center (CENATAV), Cuba
Daniela Giorgi	ISTI-CNR, Pisa, Italy
Javier Gonzalez	University of Malaga, Spain
Rocio Gonzalez-Diaz	University of Seville, Spain
Cosmin Grigorescu	European Patent Office, The Netherlands
Miguel Gutiérrez-Naranjo	University of Seville, Spain
Michal Haindl	Institute of Information Theory and Automation, Czech Republic
Edwin Hancock	University of York, UK
Yo-Ping Huang	National Taipei University of Technology, Taiwan
Atsushi Imiya	IMIT Chiba University, Japan
Xiaoyi Jiang	Universität Münster, Germany
Maria-Jose Jimenez	University of Seville, Spain
Martin Kampel	Vienna University of Technology, Austria
Vivek Kaul	Facebook, USA
Nahum Kiryati	Tel Aviv University, Israel
Reinhard Klette	Auckland University of Technology, New Zealand
Gisela Klette	Auckland University of Technology, New Zealand
Andreas Koschan	University of Tennessee Knoxville, USA
Walter Kropatsch	Vienna University of Technology, Austria
Pascal Lienhardt	Université de Poitiers, France
Guo-Shiang Lin	Da-Yeh University, Taiwan
Agnieszka Lisowska	University of Silesia, Poland
Josep Llados	Computer Vision Center, Universitat Autonoma de Barcelona, Spain
Rebeca Marfil	University of Malaga, Spain
Manuel Marin	Universidad de Córdoba, Spain
Thomas Martinetz	University of Lübeck, Germany
Phayung Meesad	King Mongkuts University of Technology North Bangkok, Thailand
Heydi Mendez	Advanced Technologies Applications Center (CENATAV), Cuba
Eckart Michaelsen	Fraunhofer IOSB, Germany
Mariofanna Milanova	University of Arkansas at Little Rock, USA
Majid Mirmehdi	University of Bristol, UK
Matthew Montebello	University of Malta, Malta
Rafael Muñoz Salinas	University of Córdoba, Spain
Adrian Muscat	University of Malta, Malta
Radu Nicolescu	Auckland University of Technology, New Zealand
Mark Nixon	University of Southampton, UK

Laurens van der Maaten	Delft University of Technology, The Netherlands
Mario Vento	University of Salerno, Italy
Thomas Villman	University of Applied Sciences Mittweida, Germany
Michael Wilkinson	University of Groningen, The Netherlands
Richard Wilson	University of York, UK
David Windridge	University of Surrey, UK
Christian Wolf	Université de Lyon, France
Xianghua Xie	Swansea University, UK
Wei Qi Yan	Auckland University of Technology, New Zealand
Hongbin Zha	Peking University, China
Zhao Zhang	Soochow University, China

Local Organizing Committee

| Charles Theuma | Saint Martin's Institute of Higher Education, Malta |

Steering Committee

Edwin Hancock	University of York, UK
Reinhard Klette	Auckland University of Technology, New Zealand
Xiaoyi Jiang	Universität Münster, Germany
Nicolai Petkov	University of Groningen, The Netherlands
George Azzopardi	University of Malta, Malta

Contents – Part I

On-The-Fly Handwriting Recognition Using a High-Level Representation . . .   1
  C. Reinders, F. Baumann, B. Scheuermann, A. Ehlers, N. Mühlpforte,
  A.O. Effenberg, and B. Rosenhahn

What Is in Front? Multiple-Object Detection and Tracking with Dynamic
Occlusion Handling. 14
  Junli Tao, Markus Enzweiler, Uwe Franke, David Pfeiffer,
  and Reinhard Klette

Correlating Words - Approaches and Applications. 27
  Mario M. Kubek, Herwig Unger, and Jan Dusik

ExCuSe: Robust Pupil Detection in Real-World Scenarios 39
  Wolfgang Fuhl, Thomas Kübler, Katrin Sippel, Wolfgang Rosenstiel,
  and Enkelejda Kasneci

Textured Object Recognition: Balancing Model Robustness
and Complexity 52
  Guido Manfredi, Michel Devy, and Daniel Sidobre

Review of Methods to Predict Social Image Interestingness
and Memorability 64
  Xesca Amengual, Anna Bosch, and Josep Lluís de la Rosa

Predicting the Number of DCT Coefficients in the Process of Seabed
Data Compression. 77
  Paweł Forczmański and Wojciech Maleika

Recognition of Images Degraded by Gaussian Blur. 88
  Jan Flusser, Tomáš Suk, Sajad Farokhi, and Cyril Höschl IV

Rejecting False Positives in Video Object Segmentation 100
  Daniela Giordano, Isaak Kavasidis, Simone Palazzo,
  and Concetto Spampinato

Ground Truth Correspondence Between Nodes to Learn Graph-Matching
Edit-Costs 113
  Xavier Cortés, Francesc Serratosa,
  and Carlos Francisco Moreno-García

Recognising Familiar Facial Features in Paintings Belonging
to Separate Domains 125
  Wilbert Tabone and Dylan Seychell

Content Based Image Retrieval Based on Modelling Human Visual
Attention   137
  Alex Papushoy and Adrian G. Bors

Tensor-Directed Spatial Patch Blending for Pattern-Based Inpainting
Methods.   149
  Maxime Daisy, Pierre Buyssens, David Tschumperlé,
  and Olivier Lézoray

A Novel Image Descriptor Based on Anisotropic Filtering   161
  Darshan Venkatrayappa, Philippe Montesinos, Daniel Diep,
  and Baptiste Magnier

A Novel Method for Simultaneous Acquisition of Visible and Near-Infrared
Light Using a Coded Infrared-Cut Filter.   174
  Kimberly McGuire, Masato Tsukada, Boris Lenseigne, Wouter Caarls,
  Masato Toda, and Pieter Jonker

Scale-Space Clustering on a Unit Hypersphere   186
  Yuta Hirano and Atsushi Imiya

Bokeh Effects Based on Stereo Vision.   198
  Dongwei Liu, Radu Nicolescu, and Reinhard Klette

Confidence Based Rank Level Fusion for Multimodal Biometric Systems . . .   211
  Hossein Talebi and Marina L. Gavrilova

Optical Flow Computation with Locally Quadratic Assumption.   223
  Tomoya Kato, Hayato Itoh, and Atsushi Imiya

Pose Normalisation for 3D Vehicles   235
  Trevor Farrugia and Jonathan Barbarar

Multimodal Output Combination for Transcribing Historical Handwritten
Documents.   246
  Emilio Granell and Carlos-D. Martínez-Hinarejos

Unsupervised Surface Reflectance Field Multi-segmenter   261
  Michal Haindl, Stanislav Mikeš, and Mineichi Kudo

A Dynamic Approach and a New Dataset for Hand-Detection in First
Person Vision.   274
  Alejandro Betancourt, Pietro Morerio, Emilia I. Barakova,
  Lucio Marcenaro, Matthias Rauterberg, and Carlo S. Regazzoni

Segmentation and Labelling of EEG for Brain Computer Interfaces.   288
  Tracey A. Camilleri, Kenneth P. Camilleri, and Simon G. Fabri

Wood Veneer Species Recognition Using Markovian Textural Features   300
  Michal Haindl and Pavel Vácha

Performance Analysis of Active Shape Reconstruction of Fractured,
Incomplete Skulls   312
  Kun Zhang, Wee Kheng Leow, and Yuan Cheng

Content Extraction from Marketing Flyers   325
  Ignazio Gallo, Alessandro Zamberletti, and Lucia Noce

Puzzle Approach to Pose Tracking of a Rigid Object in a Multi Camera
System   337
  Sönke Schmid, Xiaoyi Jiang, and Klaus Schäfers

Adaptive Information Selection in Images: Efficient Naive Bayes Nearest
Neighbor Classification   350
  Thomas Reineking, Tobias Kluth, and David Nakath

The Brightness Clustering Transform and Locally Contrasting Keypoints. . . .   362
  J. Lomeli-R. and Mark S. Nixon

Feature Evaluation with High-Resolution Images.   374
  Kai Cordes, Lukas Grundmann, and Jörn Ostermann

Fast Re-ranking of Visual Search Results by Example Selection   387
  John Schavemaker, Martijn Spitters, Gijs Koot, and Maaike de Boer

Egomotion Estimation and Reconstruction with Kalman Filters
and GPS Integration   399
  Haokun Geng, Hsiang-Jen Chien, Radu Nicolescu, and Reinhard Klette

Bundle Adjustment with Implicit Structure Modeling Using a Direct Linear
Transform   411
  Hsiang-Jen Chien, Haokun Geng, and Reinhard Klette

Efficient Extraction of Macromolecular Complexes from Electron
Tomograms Based on Reduced Representation Templates   423
  Xiao-Ping Xu, Christopher Page, and Niels Volkmann

Gradients and Active Contour Models for Localization of Cell Membrane
in HER2/neu Images   432
  *Marek Wdowiak, Tomasz Markiewicz, Stanislaw Osowski,
  Janusz Patera, and Wojciech Kozlowski*

Combination Photometric Stereo Using Compactness of Albedo
and Surface Normal in the Presence of Shadows and Specular Reflection. . . .   445
  *Naoto Ienaga, Hideo Saito, Kouichi Tezuka, Yasumasa Iwamura,
  and Masayoshi Shimizu*

Craniofacial Reconstruction Using Gaussian Process Latent Variable
Models 456
  Zedong Xiao, Junli Zhao, Xuejun Qiao, and Fuqing Duan

A High-Order Depth-Based Graph Matching Method. 465
  Lu Bai, Zhihong Zhang, Peng Ren, and Edwin R. Hancock

On Different Colour Spaces for Medical Colour Image Classification 477
  Cecilia Di Ruberto, Giuseppe Fodde, and Lorenzo Putzu

SIFT Descriptor for Binary Shape Discrimination, Classification
and Matching 489
  Insaf Setitra and Slimane Larabi

Where Is My Cup? - Fully Automatic Detection and Recognition
of Textureless Objects in Real-World Images 501
  Joanna Isabelle Olszewska

Automatic Differentiation of u- and n-serrated Patterns in Direct
Immunofluorescence Images. 513
  Chenyu Shi, Jiapan Guo, George Azzopardi, Joost M. Meijer,
  Marcel F. Jonkman, and Nicolai Petkov

Means of 2D and 3D Shapes and Their Application in Anatomical Atlas
Building. 522
  Juan Domingo, Esther Dura, Guillermo Ayala, and Silvia Ruiz-España

Optimized NURBS Curves Modelling Using Genetic Algorithm for Mobile
Robot Navigation 534
  Sawssen Jalel, Philippe Marthon, and Atef Hamouda

Robust Learning from Ortho-Diffusion Decompositions 546
  Sravan Gudivada and Adrian G. Bors

Filter-Based Approach for Ornamentation Detection and Recognition
in Singing Folk Music. 558
  Andreas Neocleous, George Azzopardi, Christos N. Schizas,
  and Nicolai Petkov

Vision-Based System for Automatic Detection of Suspicious Objects
on ATM 570
  Wirat Rattanapitak and Somkiat Wangsiripitak

Towards Ubiquitous Autonomous Driving: The CCSAD Dataset. 582
  Roberto Guzmán, Jean-Bernard Hayet, and Reinhard Klette

Discriminative Local Binary Pattern for Image Feature Extraction 594
  Takumi Kobayashi

A Homologically Persistent Skeleton Is a Fast and Robust Descriptor
of Interest Points in 2D Images................................... 606
    Vitaliy Kurlin

A *k*-max Geodesic Distance and Its Application in Image Segmentation..... 618
    Michael Holuša and Eduard Sojka

Ground Level Recovery from Terrestrial Laser Scanning Data with the
Variably Randomized Iterated Hierarchical Hough Transform............. 630
    Leszek J. Chmielewski and Arkadiusz Orłowski

U3PT: A New Dataset for Unconstrained 3D Pose Tracking Evaluation...... 642
    Ngoc-Trung Tran, Fakhreddine Ababsa, and Maurice Charbit

Characterization and Distinction Between Closely Related South Slavic
Languages on the Example of Serbian and Croatian 654
    Darko Brodić, Alessia Amelio, and Zoran N. Milivojević

Few-Views Image Reconstruction with SMART and an Allowance
for Contrast Structure Shadows.................................... 667
    Vitaly V. Vlasov, Alexander B. Konovalov, and Alexander S. Uglov

Gaussian Mixture Model Selection Using Multiple Random Subsampling
with Initialization 678
    Josef V. Psutka

Vectorisation of Sketched Drawings Using Co-occurring Sample Circles 690
    Alexandra Bonnici and Kenneth P. Camilleri

Robust Contact Lens Detection Using Local Phase Quantization and Binary
Gabor Pattern 702
    Lovish, Aditya Nigam, Balender Kumar, and Phalguni Gupta

Low-Dimensional Tensor Principle Component Analysis 715
    Hayato Itoh, Atsushi Imiya, and Tomoya Sakai

Empirical Study of Audio-Visual Features Fusion for Gait Recognition 727
    Francisco M. Castro, Manuel J. Marín-Jimenez, and Nicolás Guil

Web User Interact Task Recognition Based on Conditional Random Fields... 740
    Anis Elbahi and Mohamed Nazih Omri

Tree Log Identification Based on Digital Cross-Section Images of Log Ends
Using Fingerprint and Iris Recognition Methods 752
    *Rudolf Schraml, Heinz Hofbauer, Alexander Petutschnigg,
    and Andreas Uhl*

Detecting Human Falls: A Vision-FSM Approach..................... 766
    Roger Trullo and Duber Martinez

Trademark Image Retrieval Using Inverse Total Feature Frequency
and Multiple Detectors.   778
    Minoru Mori, Xiaomeng Wu, and Kunio Kashino

Adaptive Graph Learning for Unsupervised Feature Selection.   790
    Zhihong Zhang, Lu Bai, Yuanheng Liang, and Edwin R. Hancock

Shot and Scene Detection via Hierarchical Clustering for Re-using
Broadcast Video.   801
    Lorenzo Baraldi, Costantino Grana, and Rita Cucchiara

Locally Adapted Gain Control for Reliable Foreground Detection.   812
    *Duber Martinez, Alessia Saggese, Mario Vento, Humberto Loaiza,
    and Eduardo Caicedo*

Fourier Features for Person Detection in Depth Data.   824
    Viktor Seib, Guido Schmidt, Michael Kusenbach, and Dietrich Paulus

Author Index   837

Contents – Part II

Texture and Mathematical Morphology for Hot-Spot Detection in Whole
Slide Images of Meningiomas and Oligodendrogliomas 1
    Zaneta Swiderska, Tomasz Markiewicz, Bartlomiej Grala,
    and Wojciech Kozlowski

Scale Estimation in Multiple Models Fitting via Consensus Clustering 13
    Luca Magri and Andrea Fusiello

Writer Identification and Retrieval Using a Convolutional Neural Network . . . 26
    Stefan Fiel and Robert Sablatnig

Optical Truck Tracking for Autonomous Platooning 38
    Christian Winkens, Christian Fuchs, Frank Neuhaus,
    and Dietrich Paulus

Combination of Air- and Water-Calibration for a Fringe Projection Based
Underwater 3D-Scanner 49
    Christian Bräuer-Burchardt, Peter Kühmstedt, and Gunther Notni

Calibration of Stereo 3D Scanners with Minimal Number of Views
Using Plane Targets and Vanishing Points 61
    Christian Bräuer-Burchardt, Peter Kühmstedt, and Gunther Notni

Spatially Aware Enhancement of BoVW-Based Image Retrieval Exploiting
a Saliency Map 73
    Zijun Zou and Hisashi Koga

An Edge-Based Matching Kernel for Graphs Through the Directed Line
Graphs 85
    Lu Bai, Zhihong Zhang, Chaoyan Wang, and Edwin R. Hancock

The Virtues of Peer Pressure: A Simple Method for Discovering
High-Value Mistakes 96
    Shumeet Baluja, Michele Covell, and Rahul Sukthankar

Binarization of MultiSpectral Document Images 109
    Fabian Hollaus, Markus Diem, and Robert Sablatnig

Parallel 2D Local Pattern Spectra of Invariant Moments for Galaxy
Classification 121
    Ugo Moschini, Paul Teeninga, Scott C. Trager,
    and Michael H.F. Wilkinson

Automatic Detection of Nodules in Legumes by Imagery in a Phenotyping
Context   134
  Simeng Han, Frédéric Cointault, Christophe Salon,
  and Jean-Claude Simon

Human Skin Segmentation Improved by Saliency Detection   146
  Anderson Santos and Helio Pedrini

Disparity Estimation for Image Fusion in a Multi-aperture Camera   158
  Janne Mustaniemi, Juho Kannala, and Janne Heikkilä

Optimizing the Accuracy and Compactness of Multi-view Reconstructions . . .   171
  Markus Ylimäki, Juho Kannala, and Janne Heikkilä

Multiframe Super-Resolution for Flickering Objects   184
  Atsushi Fukushima and Takahiro Okabe

Entropy-Based Automatic Segmentation and Extraction of Tumors
from Brain MRI Images.   195
  Maria De Marsico, Michele Nappi, and Daniel Riccio

Multiple Hypothesis Tracking with Sign Language Hand Motion
Constraints   207
  Mark Borg and Kenneth P. Camilleri

Combining Features for Texture Analysis.   220
  Anca Ignat

A Novel Canonical Form for the Registration of Non Rigid 3D Shapes   230
  Majdi Jribi and Faouzi Ghorbel

A New One Class Classifier Based on Ensemble of Binary Classifiers.   242
  Hamed Habibi Aghdam, Elnaz Jahani Heravi, and Domenec Puig

Real-Time Head Pose Estimation Using Multi-variate RVM on Faces
in the Wild.   254
  Mohamed Selim, Alain Pagani, and Didier Stricker

A Verification-Based Multithreshold Probing Approach to HEp-2 Cell
Segmentation   266
  Xiaoyi Jiang, Gennaro Percannella, and Mario Vento

Precise Cross-Section Estimation on Tubular Organs   277
  Florent Grélard, Fabien Baldacci, Anne Vialard,
  and Jacques-Olivier Lachaud

Materials Classification Using Sparse Gray-Scale Bidirectional Reflectance
Measurements.   289
  Jiří Filip and Petr Somol

Multiscale Blood Vessel Delineation Using *B*-COSFIRE Filters 300
  Nicola Strisciuglio, George Azzopardi, Mario Vento, and Nicolai Petkov

Progressive Blind Deconvolution. 313
  Rana Hanocka and Nahum Kiryati

Leaf-Based Plant Identification Through Morphological Characterization
in Digital Images 326
  Arturo Oncevay-Marcos, Ronald Juarez-Chambi,
  Sofía Khlebnikov-Núñez, and César Beltrán-Castañón

Cutting Edge Localisation in an Edge Profile Milling Head 336
  Laura Fernández-Robles, George Azzopardi, Enrique Alegre,
  and Nicolai Petkov

Recognition of Architectural and Electrical Symbols by COSFIRE Filters
with Inhibition 348
  Jiapan Guo, Chenyu Shi, George Azzopardi, and Nicolai Petkov

Improving Cross-Domain Concept Detection via Object-Based Features. 359
  Markus Mühling, Ralph Ewerth, and Bernd Freisleben

Deep Learning for Feature Extraction of Arabic Handwritten Script. 371
  Mohamed Elleuch, Najiba Tagougui, and Monji Kherallah

Automatic Summary Creation by Applying Natural Language Processing
on Unstructured Medical Records 383
  Daniela Giordano, Isaak Kavasidis, and Concetto Spampinato

Bilateral Filtering of 3D Point Clouds for Refined 3D Roadside
Reconstructions. 394
  Bradley Moorfield, Ralf Haeusler, and Reinhard Klette

Can Computer Vision Problems Benefit from Structured Hierarchical
Classification? 403
  Thomas Hoyoux, Antonio J. Rodríguez-Sánchez, Justus H. Piater,
  and Sandor Szedmak

A Multiple Classifier Learning by Sampling System for White Blood Cells
Segmentation 415
  Cecilia Di Ruberto, Andrea Loddo, and Lorenzo Putzu

TECA: Petascale Pattern Recognition for Climate Science 426
  Prabhat, Surendra Byna, Venkatram Vishwanath, Eli Dart,
  Michael Wehner, and William D. Collins

Visualization of Regression Models Using Discriminative Dimensionality
Reduction   437
   Alexander Schulz and Barbara Hammer

Evaluation of Multi-view 3D Reconstruction Software.   450
   Julius Schöning and Gunther Heidemann

Sample Size for Maximum Likelihood Estimates of Gaussian Model.   462
   Josef V. Psutka and Josef Psutka

Projective Label Propagation by Label Embedding   470
   *Zhao Zhang, Weiming Jiang, Fanzhang Li, Li Zhang, Mingbo Zhao,
   and Lei Jia*

Simplifying Indoor Scenes for Real-Time Manipulation on Mobile Devices. . . .   482
   Michael Hödlmoser, Patrick Wolf, and Martin Kampel

Image Contrast Enhancement by Distances Among Points in Fuzzy
Hyper-Cubes   494
   Mario Versaci, Salvatore Calcagno, and Francesco Carlo Morabito

Iris Recognition Using Discrete Cosine Transform and Relational Measures . . .   506
   Aditya Nigam, Balender Kumar, Jyoti Triyar, and Phalguni Gupta

3D Texture Recognition for RGB-D Images.   518
   Guoqiang Zhong, Xin Mao, Yaxin Shi, and Junyu Dong

Detection and Classification of Interesting Parts in Scanned Documents
by Means of AdaBoost Classification and Low-Level Features Verification . .   529
   Andrzej Markiewicz and Paweł Forczmański

Speed Parameters in the Level-Set Segmentation.   541
   Luigi Cinque and Rossella Cossu

Bayesian Networks-Based Defects Classes Discrimination in Weld
Radiographic Images.   554
   *Aicha Baya Goumeidane, Abdessalem Bouzaieni, Nafaa Nacereddine,
   and Salvatore Tabbone*

Feature Selection in Gait Classification Using Geometric PSO Assisted
by SVM.   566
   *Tze Wei Yeoh, Saúl Zapotecas-Martínez, Youhei Akimoto,
   Hernán E. Aguirre, and Kiyoshi Tanaka*

Automatic Images Annotation Extension Using a Probabilistic Graphical
Model   579
   Abdessalem Bouzaieni, Salvatore Tabbone, and Sabine Barrat

An Improved ANOVA Algorithm for Crop Mark Extraction from Large
Aerial Images Using Semantics   591
    R. Marani, V. Renò, E. Stella, and T. D'Orazio

An Electronic Travel Aid to Assist Blind and Visually Impaired People
to Avoid Obstacles   604
    Filippo L.M. Milotta, Dario Allegra, Filippo Stanco,
    and Giovanni M. Farinella

Cellular Skeletons: A New Approach to Topological Skeletons with
Geometric Features   616
    Aldo Gonzalez-Lorenzo, Alexandra Bac, Jean-Luc Mari, and Pedro Real

Model-Free Head Pose Estimation Based on Shape Factorisation
and Particle Filtering   628
    Stefania Cristina and Kenneth P. Camilleri

Plane-Fitting Robust Registration for Complex 3D Models   640
    Yuan Cheng, Shudong Xie, Wee Kheng Leow, and Kun Zhang

Incremental Fixed-Rank Robust PCA for Video Background Recovery   652
    Jian Lai, Wee Kheng Leow, and Terence Sim

Sperm Cells Segmentation in Micrographic Images Through Lambertian
Reflectance Model   664
    Rosario Medina-Rodríguez, Luis Guzmán-Masías, Hugo Alatrista-Salas,
    and Cesar Beltrán-Castañón

Interactive Image Colorization Using Laplacian Coordinates   675
    Wallace Casaca, Marilaine Colnago, and Luis Gustavo Nonato

LBP and Irregular Graph Pyramids   687
    Martin Cerman, Rocio Gonzalez-Diaz, and Walter Kropatsch

Fusion of Intra- and Inter-modality Algorithms for Face-Sketch
Recognition   700
    Christian Galea and Reuben A. Farrugia

View-Independent Enhanced 3D Reconstruction of Non-rigidly Deforming
Objects   712
    Hassan Afzal, Djamila Aouada, François Destelle, Bruno Mirbach,
    and Björn Ottersten

Automated Fast Marching Method for Segmentation and Tracking
of Region of Interest in Scintigraphic Images Sequences   725
    Yassine Aribi, Ali Wali, and Adel M. Alimi

Adaptive Saliency-Weighted 2D-to-3D Video Conversion   737
  Hamed Taher, Muhammad Rushdi, Muhammad Islam,
  and Ahmed Badawi

Variational Multiple Warping for Cardiac Image Analysis   749
  Shun Inagaki, Hayato Itoh, and Atsushi Imiya

Facial Expression Recognition Using Learning Vector Quantization   760
  Gert-Jan de Vries, Steffen Pauws, and Michael Biehl

Learning Vector Quantization with Adaptive Cost-Based Outlier-Rejection. . .   772
  Thomas Villmann, Marika Kaden, David Nebel, and Michael Biehl

Tensorial Orientation Scores.   783
  Jasper J. van de Gronde

Author Index   795

On-The-Fly Handwriting Recognition Using a High-Level Representation

C. Reinders[1]([✉]), F. Baumann[1], B. Scheuermann[1], A. Ehlers[1], N. Mühlpforte[2], A.O. Effenberg[2], and B. Rosenhahn[1]

[1] Institut für Informationsverarbeitung (TNT),
Leibniz University Hanover, Hanover, Germany
reinders@tnt.uni-hannover.de
[2] Institute of Sports Science, Leibniz University Hanover, Hanover, Germany

Abstract. Automatic handwriting recognition plays a crucial role because writing with a pen is the most common and natural input method for humans. Whereas many algorithms detect the writing after finishing the input, this paper presents a handwriting recognition system that processes the input data during writing and thus detects misspelled characters on the fly from their origin.

The main idea of the recognition is to decompose the input data into defined structures. Each character can be composed out of the structures point, line, curve, and circle. While the user draws a character, the digitized points of the pen are processed successively, decomposed into structures, and classified with the help of samples. The intermediate classification allows a direct feedback to the user as soon as the input differs from a given character.

1 Introduction

Handwriting is an ability unique to humans. It is the most natural method of storing and transmitting information. Due to its variability, handwriting as an input method for electronic devices is superior to a keyboard which offers only a limited character set. Therefore, researchers are working on automatic handwriting recognition for more than 40 years [6,8].

Until now, handwriting recognition has remained an unsolved problem because of the insufficient quality, as the large number of different writing styles cause difficulties [11]. There are two basic approaches: Off-line and on-line handwriting recognition [8]. Off-line methods recognize writing on a paper or a similar medium. First they digitize the medium and then process the recognition on the image [2]. The results are sufficient for specialized applications like recognition of mailing addresses on envelopes [12] or reading of bank checks [5]. Because of that, the enabled automation of activities gives these algorithms a significant economic value [10].

This work has been partially funded by the ERC within the starting grant Dynamic MinVIP.

© Springer International Publishing Switzerland 2015
G. Azzopardi and N. Petkov (Eds.): CAIP 2015, Part I, LNCS 9256, pp. 1–13, 2015.
DOI: 10.1007/978-3-319-23192-1_1

On-line methods use another way of capturing the writing. The writing movements on the input medium (e.g. a tablet with a pen) are digitized immediately. Thus additional information like the writing direction and the order of the strokes can be taken into consideration and can be used to recognize structures. Because of the additional information achieved, on-line methods have better results than off-line methods [4, 7, 9].

Interactivity is another advantage that makes on-line methods interesting. While off-line methods scan and process the writing only after the user has finished the input, on-line methods are able to recognize it simultaneously to the input. This allows the application to respond to the user input [7, 13]. The disadvantage of on-line methods is that, in contrast to off-line methods, the data cannot be recorded through a scanner afterwards [4, 13].

Contribution: We propose a novel handwriting recognition system which is based on a concept described by Chan and Yeung [1]. According to that, characters consist of structures (like points, lines, curves, and circles) and differ in the number, kind, and orientation of the structures. Due to the lack of concrete algorithms that are required for an implementation, we present fundamental algorithms to decompose an input into structures and develop such a handwriting recognition system.

After giving an overview of the system (Section 2), we describe how the system decomposes the input into structures (Section 3 and 4). Subsequently, we present the classification which compares the decomposition to known samples (Section 5 and 6). The system is specialized on recognizing whether an input corresponds to a given word. Its particular characteristic is that the recognition is done in real-time during the input to detect errors as early as possible. Finally, we present the experimental results and conclude the paper (Section 7 and 8).

Related Work: Connell summarized the different on-line handwriting recognition technique categories identified by Bellegarda et al. [2]. For instance, elastic matching calculates the similarity between two sequences using dynamic programming. The category that is most similar to our approach is primitive decomposition. The difference between all these techniques and our approach is that they need the whole input for the classification whereas we classify after every new point.

2   Foundations

Figure 1 shows a structural overview of the handwriting recognition system. The system is divided into two phases: a training phase and a recognition phase. In the training phase, the characters from the training data are decomposed into structures through the structure recognition system. Afterwards, the constraints are calculated for each sample which describe the connection between the structures. The result is a database with training samples. In the recognition phase, the system is ready to process user input. The input is decomposed into structures through the structure recognition system in the same way as in the training

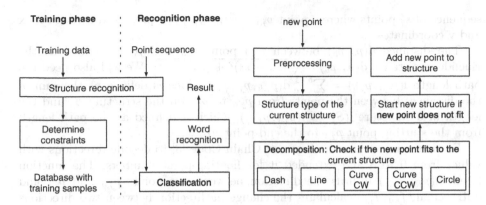

Fig. 1. High-level system architecture. In the training phase at the beginning of the system the database with training samples is created. In the recognition phase the input can be processed.

Fig. 2. The structure recognition procedure. Every time the position of the pen changes, the procedure decides if the new point belongs to the current structure or is the start of a new structure.

phase. Subsequently, the decomposition is used to classify the input with samples out of the training database. The word recognition system processes the given word letter by letter and returns a result indicating whether the input corresponds to the expected word.

An important part of the system is the structure recognition system. The procedure receives sequences of points as input and decomposes them into the structures point, line, curve clockwise (CW), curve counterclockwise (CCW), and circle [1]. The special characteristic is that, instead of performing the decomposition into structures only after the input is finished, it is performed immediately during writing. For every new point the structure recognition system decides whether: (1) the point belongs to the current structure or (2) a new structure begins.

Figure 2 shows a schematic overview of the proposed procedure. Every time a pen motion happens, the illustrated algorithm is executed with the new position of the pen. First, a preprocessing of the points is performed. Next, we determine the structure type of the current structure to specialize the following decomposition algorithm which decides whether a point belongs to the current structure. If the new point does not fit to the current structure, the structure is finished and a new structure is started. As a last step, the new point is added to the current structure.

2.1 Formal Representation

Characters are drawn through one or more strokes. The system decomposes each stroke into structures so that we can represent a character $C = \{S_1, \ldots, S_n\}$ as a sequence of n structures. A structure $S_j = \{p_{j,1}, \ldots, p_{j,s_j}\}$ is defined as a sequence of s_j points where a point $p_{j,i} = (x_{j,i}, y_{j,i})$ is represented through its x and y coordinates.

The distance $d(p_a, p_b)$ between two points p_a and p_b is defined as the Euclidean distance $d(p_a, p_b) = \sqrt{(x_a - x_b)^2 + (y_a - y_b)^2}$. We will also need the path length $l(p_{j,a}, p_{j,b}) = \sum_{k=a}^{b-1} d(p_{j,k}, p_{j,k+1})$, which is defined as the sum of the distances between the points from $p_{j,a}$ to $p_{j,b}$ on the structure S_j and the length of a structure $l(S_j) = l(p_{j,1}, p_{j,s_j})$, which is defined as the path length from the starting point $p_{j,1}$ to the end point p_{j,s_j}.

Furthermore, we use the Freeman Chain Code [3] to decode directions with values from 0 to 8 and extended it for floating-point numbers. The function $freeman(p_{j,a}, p_{j,b})$ returns the direction between two points $p_{j,a}$ and $p_{j,b}$ and diffFreeman($f_{j,a}, f_{j,b}$) calculates the change in direction between two directions $f_{j,a}$ and $f_{j,b}$.

In the following sections, we introduce a couple of constraints and provide a recommended value for each that worked best for our system. Some of them depend on the resolution where our capital letters have an approximate height of 90. According to that, the constraints can be rescaled for other applications.

3   Determination of the Structure Type

In this section we introduce three functions, f_{Line}, f_{Curve}, and f_{Circle}, which serve as metrics to determine the structure type. The structure type is used for two different purposes: the specialization of the decomposition and the classification. Because both applications require slightly different definitions, we split the decision in section 3.1 into the two functions, structuretype$_d(S_j)$ ($d \stackrel{\wedge}{=}$ decomposition) and structuretype$_c(S_j)$ ($c \stackrel{\wedge}{=}$ classification).

Line or Circle. The function $f_{Line}(S_j)$ calculates the bulge of a structure $S_j = \{p_{j,1}, \ldots, p_{j,s_j}\}$ to decide whether it is a line or curve. Therefore we define a line g that runs through the starting point $p_{j,1}$ and the end point p_{j,s_j} and calculate for each point $p \in S_j$ the minimal distance $dist(p, S_j)$ to g. The bulge is defined as the maximum of the minimum distances over all points of the structure, see Eq. (3). To calculate the minimal distance $dist(p, S_j)$ between a point $p \in S_j$ and the line g we apply an orthogonal projection $P(p, S_j)$ of p on g. $\boldsymbol{u}$ is the direction vector of g ($\boldsymbol{u} = p_{j,s_j} - p_{j,1}$). Sought is the length of the vector $\boldsymbol{v} = P_v(p, S_j)$, which runs from p to $P(p)$ (see Figure 3a):

$$P_v(p, S_j) = P(p, S_j) - p = p_{j,1} + \frac{(p - p_{j,1}) \cdot \boldsymbol{u}}{\boldsymbol{u} \cdot \boldsymbol{u}} \cdot \boldsymbol{u} - p \qquad (1)$$

$$dist(p, S_j) = \|P_v(p, S_j)\| \qquad (2)$$

$$f_{Line}(S_j) = \max_{p \in S_j} dist(p, S_j) \qquad (3)$$

If the starting and end point are equal ($p_{j,1} = p_{j,s_j}$), we cannot calculate an orthogonal projection because $\boldsymbol{u}$ is zero and define $f_{Line}(S_j) = \infty$. This might occur, for example, with circles.

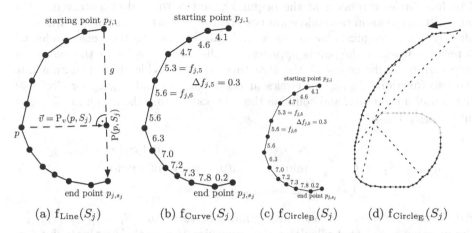

(a) $f_{Line}(S_j)$ (b) $f_{Curve}(S_j)$ (c) $f_{Circle_B}(S_j)$ (d) $f_{Circle_E}(S_j)$

Fig. 3. (a) The function f_{Line} calculates the bulge of a structure to distinguish between a line and a curve by determining the point that is farthest away from the line that runs through the starting point and the end point. (b) The function f_{Curve} calculates the curvature to decide whether a curve is clockwise or counterclockwise by averaging the changes in direction between the points. (c) To recognize circles at the beginning, for every point that does not lie at the beginning of the structure the approximation to the starting point is calculated. (d) Recognizing circles at the end works in the same way with the only difference that we use the end point instead of the starting point for the calculations (see Section 3 for details).

Curve CW or CCW. To distinguish between a curve clockwise and a curve counterclockwise, the following function $f_{Curve}(S_j)$ calculates the curvature of a structure $S_j = \{p_{j,1}, \ldots, p_{j,s_j}\}$ (see Figure 3b):

$$f_{j,k} = \text{freeman}(p_{j,k-1}, p_{j,k})$$
$$\Delta f_{j,k} = \text{diffFreeman}(f_{j,k}, f_{j,k+1})$$
$$f_{Curve}(S_j) = \frac{1}{l(S_j)} \sum_{k=2}^{s_j-1} \Delta f_{j,k} \cdot d(p_{j,k}, p_{j,k+1}) \qquad (4)$$

At first we determine the change in direction $\Delta f_{j,k}$ by regarding the direction $f_{j,k}$ from $p_{j,k-1}$ to $p_{j,k}$ and the direction $f_{j,k+1}$ from $p_{j,k}$ to $p_{j,k+1}$. Afterwards, we multiply $\Delta f_{j,k}$ by $d(p_{j,k}, p_{j,k+1})$ to weight the change in direction with the length of the segment. Finally, we add up the value for each $k \in [2, s_j - 1]$ and divide it by the length of the structure $l(S_j)$.

The resulting average change in direction indicates the curve type. If $f_{Curve}(S_j)$ is greater than zero, the directions from the starting point to the end point increase and the curve turns counterclockwise (and vice versa for $f_{Curve}(S_j) < 0$). If $f_{Curve}(S_j)$ is equal to zero, the changes in direction are balanced.

Circle. Circles can occur at the beginning and at the end of a structure. For our system, circles in the middle are not possible because the structure will have already been recognized as having a circle at the end. To recognize circles we determine whether the points approximate the starting point or the end point respectively in the course of the structure [1]. We divide the calculation into the two functions, $f_{\mathrm{Circle_B}}$ for circles at the beginning and $f_{\mathrm{Circle_E}}$ for circles at the end of a structure, and combine them by calculating the minimum $f_{\mathrm{Circle}} = \min(f_{\mathrm{Circle_B}}, f_{\mathrm{Circle_E}})$.

$$f_{\mathrm{Circle_B}}(S_j) = \begin{cases} \infty & \text{if } l(S_j) < d_{\mathrm{Circle_{Path}}} \\ \min_{\substack{p_{j,k} \in S_j \\ l(p_{j,1}, p_{j,k}) \geq d_{\mathrm{Circle_{Path}}}}} \mathrm{d}(p_{j,1}, p_{j,k}) & \text{otherwise} \end{cases} \quad (5)$$

For the recognition of circles at the beginning of a structure $S_j = \{p_{j,1}, \ldots, p_{j,s_j}\}$ the function $f_{\mathrm{Circle_B}}(S_j)$ calculates the approximation to the starting point (see Figure 3c). This is done by calculating for each point $p_{j,k} \in S_j$ the distance $\mathrm{d}(p_{j,1}, p_{j,k})$ from the starting point $p_{j,1}$ to $p_{j,k}$ and picking the minimum out of it. Additionally, we have to add a constraint that forces a minimum path length $d_{\mathrm{Circle_{Path}}}$ for the path between the starting point and $p_{j,k}$. Otherwise, each time the starting point $p_{j,1}$ would have a minimum distance of zero. Through this minimum path length, only points that are not located directly at the beginning of a structure will be taken into account for the calculation. Thereby we ensure that the minimum is a follow-up approximation and the structure forms a circle. If the length of a structure is shorter than $d_{\mathrm{Circle_{Path}}}$, we define $f_{\mathrm{Circle_B}}(S_j) = \infty$. $f_{\mathrm{Circle_E}}(S_j)$ is calculated in the same way with the only difference that we use the end point p_{j,s_j} instead of the starting point $p_{j,1}$ (see Figure 3d).

3.1 Decision

The determination of the structure type is utilized specifically for decomposition and classification. The structure decomposition uses the structure type to optimize the decomposition algorithm for the respective structure type. For this, the decision analyzes the current metrics to forecast the trending structure type. To make more reliable forecasts, we wait until a structure has a certain length and classify it at first as 'dash'.

The classification uses structure types to compare structures with each other. Because of that, the classification into structure types should be as clear as possible. For this we classify very short structures as 'point'. Both structure type determinations $\mathrm{structuretype}_d(S_j)$ and $\mathrm{structuretype}_c(S_j)$ are defined as follows:

$$\mathrm{structuretype}_{d/c}(S_j) = \begin{cases} \text{Dash/Point} & \text{if } l(S_j) \leq d_{\mathrm{Dash/Point}} \\ \begin{cases} \text{Circle} & \text{if } f_{\mathrm{Circle}}(S_j) \leq d_{\mathrm{Circle}} \\ \begin{cases} \text{Line} & \text{if } \mathrm{isLine}_{d/c}(f_{\mathrm{Line}}(S_j), l(S_j)) \\ \begin{cases} \text{Curve CW} & \text{if } f_{\mathrm{Curve}}(S_j) < 0 \\ \text{Curve CCW} & \text{otherwise} \end{cases} \end{cases} \end{cases} \end{cases} \quad (6)$$

where we set $d_{\text{Dash}} = 30$, $d_{\text{Point}} = 10$, $d_{\text{Circle}} = 15$, and

$$
\text{isLine}_{d/c}(c, l) = \begin{cases}
\text{true} & \text{if } l \leq 40 \text{ and } c < 1 \text{ resp. } c < 3 \text{ (for classification)} \\
\text{true} & \text{if } 40 < l \leq 50 \text{ and } c < 2 \text{ resp. } c < 6 \\
\text{true} & \text{if } 50 < l \leq 70 \text{ and } c < 3 \text{ resp. } c < 9 \\
\text{true} & \text{if } 70 < l \leq 110 \text{ and } c < 5 \text{ resp. } c < 15 \\
\text{true} & \text{if } l > 110 \text{ und } c < 8 \text{ resp. } c < 24 \\
\text{false} & \text{otherwise}
\end{cases} \tag{7}
$$

4   Structure Decomposition

The next step of the structure recognition procedure is the structure decomposition, which recognizes when a structure is completed. After determining the structure type for the current structure $S_j = \{p_{j,1}, \ldots, p_{j,s_j}\}$, the algorithm decides whether a new point p_{new} belongs to the current structure or a new structure has started.

To make the decomposition more robust against outliers we introduce a filter that checks if the new point p_{new} has a minimum distance $d_{\text{min}}(= 2.0)$ to the last point p_{last} ($d(p_{\text{last}}, p_{\text{new}}) \geq d_{\text{min}}$) and processes the point only if this condition is satisfied. Otherwise, the point will be bypassed.

In the following sections, we present the specialized decomposition algorithms for each structure type which define a tolerance range in which the new point must be located to be added to the current structure.

Dash. The decomposition checks whether the location of the new point fits to the current structure, i.e. the change in direction is not too large. Therefore we compare the direction from the last two points $f_{\text{last}} = \text{freeman}(p_{j,s_j-1}, p_{j,s_j})$ with the direction from the last point to the new point $f_{\text{new}} = \text{freeman}(p_{j,s_j}, p_{\text{new}})$. If the difference $\Delta f = \text{diffFreeman}(f_{\text{last}}, f_{\text{new}})$ is within the tolerance range $|\Delta f| \leq t_{\text{Dash}}(= 2.0)$ the new point belongs to the current structure (see Figure 4a).

Line. We use a similar approach to decompose lines. Unfortunately, it is possible that we miss a decomposition if too many points are spaced closely together. If each of them is just within the tolerance range, there is no strong change in direction.

To solve this problem, we modify the algorithm by using the information that all points of a line are located closely to the line which runs from the starting point to the end point. New points have to be approximately on the same line. Thus we calculate the last direction between the starting point and the end point $f_{\text{last}} = \text{freeman}(p_{j,1}, p_{j,s_j})$ and use a stricter tolerance range $|\Delta f| \leq t_{\text{Line}}(= 1.0)$ (see Figure 4b).

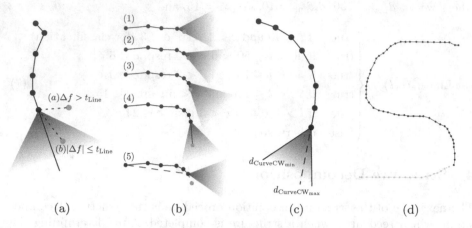

Fig. 4. (a) The algorithm to decompose dashes decides on the basis of the change in direction (between the last two points and the new point) if the new point fits to the current structure. (b) Using exactly the same approach to decompose lines leads to the problem that a structure might not have a strong change in direction and we miss a decomposition (1-4). Hence we calculate the last direction between the starting and the end point (5). (c) The tolerance area for curves is rotated according to the direction of the curvature. (d) The basic algorithm might decompose two successive curves too late because there is no bend. To avoid this, we have to add an additional calculation step (see Section 4 for details).

Curve. For curves, we use the information of the rotation direction and rotate the tolerance range accordingly. The tolerance range is now defined as $(-2.0 =) \, t_{\mathrm{CurveCW_{min}}} \leq \Delta f \leq t_{\mathrm{CurveCW_{max}}} (= 1.0)$ for clockwise curves and $(-1.0 =) \, t_{\mathrm{CurveCCW_{min}}} \leq \Delta f \leq t_{\mathrm{CurveCCW_{max}}} (= 2.0)$ for counterclockwise curves (see Figure 4c). Unfortunately, that does not work for two consecutive curves. Because there is no strong change in direction, the algorithm might decompose too late or not at all (see Figure 4d).

To solve this problem we add an additional calculation step which determines the curvature of the last part of the structure to see whether it is reversed. The length of this part is set to $d_{\mathrm{Curve_{Part}}} (= 30)$.

$$t \qquad = \min\left\{ k \,\middle|\, 1 \leq k \leq s_j \text{ and } \mathrm{l}(p_{j,k}, p_{j,s_j}) < d_{\mathrm{Curve_{Part}}} \right\} \qquad (8)$$

$$\mathrm{f}_{\mathrm{Curve_{Last}}}(S_j) = \frac{1}{\mathrm{l}(p_{j,t}, p_{j,s_j})} \sum_{k=t+1}^{s_j-1} \Delta f_{j,k} \cdot \mathrm{d}(p_{j,k}, p_{j,k+1}) \qquad (9)$$

First, we determine the index t of the first point of this part, see Eq. (8). The calculation is done in the same way as for the whole structure (see Eq. (4)) but we use only the points from $p_{j,t}$ to the end point. Also, we consider $\mathrm{f}_{\mathrm{Curve_{Last}}}(S_j)$ only when the absolute value is greater than a threshold $t_{\mathrm{Curve_{Curvature}}} (= 0.2)$ to avoid outliers. If the curvature is different from the curvature of the whole structure, a shift in direction is detected. In this case, we cut off the current structure in the middle of the last part because the shifts in direction are recognized with a slight delay and begin a new structure from that point.

Circle. When recognizing a circle, the structure is not decomposed immediately because more points might belong to the circle. For that reason, we check if the new point closes the circle.

Circles at the Beginning. The function f_{Circle_B} (see Section 3) calculates the approximation to the starting point. To check whether the new point p_{new} closes the circle, we calculate this approximation for p_{new}: $f_{Circle_{B_{new}}}(S_j) = d(p_{new}, p_{j,1})$. After adding a tolerance $t_{Circle}(= 1.5)$ to avoid causing premature decompositions by outliers, we compare both functions. If the condition $f_{Circle_{B_{new}}}(S_j) \leq t_{Circle} \cdot f_{Circle_B}(S_j)$ applies, the new point closes the circle and belongs to the current structure.

Circles at the End. To recognize circles at the end of a structure we use f_{Circle_E} (see Section 3) to calculate the approximation to the end point. If the new point fits to the circle, it would be the new end point. We simulate this by calculating the approximation to the new point to check whether it closes the circle:

$$f_{Circle_{E_{new}}}(S_j) = \begin{cases} \infty & \text{if } l(S_j) < d_{Circle_{Path}} \\ \min_{\substack{p_{j,k} \in S_j \\ l(p_{j,k}, p_{new}) \geq d_{Circle_{Path}}}} d(p_{j,k}, p_{new}) & \text{otherwise} \end{cases} \tag{10}$$

If $f_{Circle_{E_{new}}}$ is smaller than f_{Circle_E}, the new point is closer to the structure than the last one and it closes the circle. To be robust against outliers we also allow a tolerance so that the new point belongs to the current structure if $f_{Circle_{E_{new}}}(S_j) \leq t_{Circle} \cdot f_{Circle_E}(S_j)$ applies.

While drawing a circle, the structure first forms a curve. If a circle at the end is detected, we have to cut off the first part from the circle. Because the dividing point depends on the continuing course of the structure we cannot immediately cut off after detecting a circle. Instead, we cut off as soon as the circle is completed meaning when (1) we find a point that does not belong anymore to the structure or (2) the input ends. The division point is the starting point of the circle. It is defined by the point which has the shortest distance to the end point in the calculation of $f_{Circle_E}(S_j)$. With the aid of the dividing point we divide the structure into the section before the dividing point and the circle.

5   Training Database

To be able to compare the input, training data is needed. We use a self-recorded training data set consisting of character samples from different persons. In the

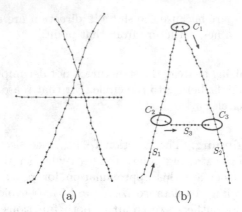

(a)   (b)

Fig. 5. (a) Comparing only the structures does not consider the connection between the structures and this example would be accepted in comparison with a normal 'A'. (b) To avoid this problem we introduce constraints which store the additional information when two structures come close to each other ($C_1 = (1, 2, 1.0, 0.0), C_2 = (1, 3, 0.42, 0.0), C_3 = (2, 3, 0.61, 1.0)$) (see Section 5 for details).

training phase at the beginning the recognition system reads in the training data and decomposes every character sample into a set of structures $C = \{S_1, \ldots, S_n\}$.

As shown in Figure 5a, the introduction of constraints is necessary to check the connection between the structures. Therefore, we determine for every structure pair S_i and S_j for $1 \le i < j \le n$, the pair of points where the structures are closest to each other:

$$(p_{i,a}, p_{j,b}) = \arg\min_{(p_{i,a}, p_{j,b}) \in S_i \times S_j} \mathrm{d}(p_{i,a}, p_{j,b}) \tag{11}$$

If the distance $\mathrm{d}(p_{i,a}, p_{j,b})$ between both structures is less than a threshold $d_{\text{Constraint}} (= 12)$ they are positioned closely together at a certain point. To save this property, a constraint $C = (i, j, r_i, r_j)$ is created which contains the index of both structures i and j and the relative position of $p_{i,a}$ and $p_{j,b}$ ($r_i = \mathrm{l}(p_{i,1}, p_{i,a})/\mathrm{l}(S_i)$) (see Figure 5b). We use relative positions to be independent of the structure length. Finally, we add each decomposition and its corresponding constraints to the training database.

6   Classification

After creating the training database the system is ready for user input. To recognize misspelling as fast as possible, the system classifies the input each time a structure is completed.

6.1   The Process

For the classification all samples of the same character as the expected character are fetched from the training database and each is compared to the input. The aim is to check if one of them is similar to the input.

The comparison between a sample and the input is done in two steps. At first we determine all possible assignments from the input structures to similar sample structures without multiple assignments to the same sample structure (see Section 6.2). In the second step we check the constraints for each assignment (see Section 6.3).

As a result, the classification returns a 'complete match' if it finds an assignment for one sample so that every sample structure is assigned by a structure from the input, an 'incomplete match' if it finds an assignment but the input has less structures than the sample, or 'no match' if there is no possible assignment for any sample.

6.2   Similar Structures

The comparison of the input with a sample is dependent upon the structures. We introduce different conditions that have to be fulfilled in order for two structures S_a and S_b to be similar. First of all, the structure types have to be the same: $\text{structuretype}_c(S_a) = \text{structuretype}_c(S_b)$. For every other structure type except for a point we also compare the length and vertical position. The length of S_a must not exceed the length of S_b by more than a factor $d_{\text{Length}}(= 0.5)$, see Eq. (12). Also, the vertical position of the lowest (see Eq.(13)) and highest (see Eq. (14)) points have to be about the same except for a tolerance $d_{\text{Vertical}}(= 20)$.

$$(1 - d_{\text{Length}}) \cdot l(S_a) \leq l(S_b) \leq (1 + d_{\text{Length}}) \cdot l(S_a) \tag{12}$$

$$\left| \min_{(x_{a,j}, y_{a,j}) \in S_a} y_{a,j} - \min_{(x_{b,j}, y_{b,j}) \in S_b} y_{b,j} \right| \leq d_{\text{Vertical}} \tag{13}$$

$$\left| \max_{(x_{a,j}, y_{a,j}) \in S_a} y_{a,j} - \max_{(x_{b,j}, y_{b,j}) \in S_b} y_{b,j} \right| \leq d_{\text{Vertical}} \tag{14}$$

When the structure type is a line or a curve we also compare the directions. These are measured from the starting point to the end point and have to be about the same for both structures:

$$\left| \text{diffFreeman}(\text{freeman}(p_{a,1}, p_{a,n_a}), \text{freeman}(p_{b,1}, p_{b,n_b})) \right| \leq d_{\text{Direction}}(= 0.3) \tag{15}$$

6.3   Checking Constraints

If a constraint between two structures of the sample exists, the constraint has to be fulfilled by the corresponding assigned structures from the input. Therefore, we convert the relative positions back to the closest points on the structures and measure whether the distance between both is also less than $d_{\text{Constraint}}$. If this is not the case for any constraint, the assignment is not valid.

6.4 Word Recognition

Our recognition system works letter by letter. To handle given words we introduce a word recognition which detects the boundaries between the characters of the input and switches to the next character every time a complete match is found. The word recognition system is only described for completeness because it is used in a larger context.

7 Experimental Results

We evaluate the system by examining the characters 'A', 'M', 'O', 'T', and 'U'. The training database consists of eleven samples per character. In this experiment, we first ignore all structures from the structure type 'point' because we use a simple pen without palm rejection which result in accidental input.

Recognition Rate. The system expects a given character and checks the input for accordance. Ideally, it accepts each input of the same character and declines every other character. To measure the quality of the system we do leave-one-out cross-validation and take one sample at a time out of the training database to simulate its input and classify it against all other samples. An input is recognized if the system finds at least one complete match with a sample of the same character. For this case we achieve an average recognition rate of 74.7% ('A': 63.6%, 'M': 63.6%, 'O': 72.7%, 'T': 90.9%, 'U': 81.8%). Additionally, we measure if the system declines input of another character (e.g. we input a 'M' when an 'A' is expected). For this case the system achieves optimal results, which means that no sample has any match with a sample of another character. We have to mention that we use a very small database which results in a worse recognition rate because of less variability in the training data.

Speed. To measure the performance of the system we use an iPad 4 with iOS 7.1.2 as testing device and raise the number of training samples to 318. The speed of two methods is of particular significance because they are performed during input: processing a point in the structure recognition system (see Figure 2) and classifying the input (see Section 6). On average, a new point arrives every 56.3 ms and both methods have to be fast enough to be real-time capable. We measure on average 0.205 ms to process a new point and 11.46 ms per classification with 317 samples.

8 Conclusions

In this paper, we propose a novel handwriting recognition system that detects faulty characters and misspelled words immediately. The basic idea is to decompose the input into structures and to classify the input based on that. We developed fundamental algorithms to determine the structure type from a sequence of points and to decompose the input into structures. The main advantage of our system is the instantaneous feedback after every new point. The results indicate that the system perfectly detects confused characters and achieves an average recognition rate of 74.7%. The experiments illustrate that not all different writing styles were covered. Raising the number of training samples lead to a significantly higher recognition rate.

In this paper, we specialized our handwriting recognition system to detect faulty characters but basically the system is not limited to this case. In future work, it could be possible to compare the input against all training samples and thus detect the character.

References

1. Chan, K.F., Yeung, D.Y.: Recognizing on-line handwritten alphanumeric characters through flexible structural matching (1999)
2. Connell, S.D., Jain, A.K.: Template-based online character recognition. Pattern Recognition 34(1), 1–14 (2001)
3. Freeman, H.: Computer processing of line-drawing images. ACM Comput. Surv. 6(1), 57–97 (1974)
4. Fujisaki, T., Chefalas, T.E., Kim, J., Tappert, C.C., Wolf, C.G.: On-line run-on character recognizer: Design and performance. International Journal of Pattern Recognition and Artificial Intelligence 5(01n02), 123–137 (1991)
5. Impedovo, S., Wang, P., Bunke, H.: Automatic Bankcheck Processing. Series in machine perception and artificial intelligence. World Scientific (1997)
6. Jäger, S.: Recovering Dynamic Information from Static, Handwritten Word Images. Fölbach (1998)
7. Santosh, K.C., Nattee, C.: A comprehensive survey on on-line handwriting recognition technology and its real application to the Nepalese natural handwriting. Kathmandu University Journal of Science, Engineering, and Technology 5(I), 31–55 (2009). https://hal.inria.fr/inria-00354242
8. Liwicki, M., Bunke, H.: Recognition of Whiteboard Notes - Online, Offline and Combination. Series in Machine Perception and Artificial Intelligence, vol. 71. World Scientific (2008)
9. Niels, R., Vuurpijl, L.: Using dynamic time warping for intuitive handwriting recognition. In: Proc. IGS 2005, pp. 217–221. Press (2005)
10. Plamondon, R., Srihari, S.N.: On-line and off-line handwriting recognition: A comprehensive survey. IEEE Trans. Pattern Anal. Mach. Intell. 22(1), 63–84 (2000)
11. Schomaker, L.: User-interface aspects in recognizing connected-cursive handwriting. In: Proceedings of the IEE Colloquium on Handwriting and Pen-Based Input (1994)
12. Srihari, S.N.: Handwritten address interpretation: A task of many pattern recognition problems. IJPRAI 14(5), 663–674 (2000)
13. Tappert, C.C., Suen, C.Y., Wakahara, T.: The state of the art in online handwriting recognition. IEEE Trans. Pattern Anal. Mach. Intell. 12(8), 787–808 (1990). http://dx.doi.org/10.1109/34.57669

What Is in Front? Multiple-object Detection and Tracking with Dynamic Occlusion Handling

Junli Tao[1]([✉]), Markus Enzweiler[2], Uwe Franke[2], David Pfeiffer[2], and Reinhard Klette[3]

[1] Department of Computer Science,
The University of Auckland, Auckland, New Zealand
jtao076@aucklanduni.ac.nz
[2] Image Understanding, Daimler AG, Boeblingen, Germany
[3] Auckland University of Technology, Auckland, New Zealand

Abstract. This paper proposes a multiple-object detection and tracking method that explicitly handles dynamic occlusions. A context-based multiple-cue detector is proposed to detect occluded vehicles (occludees). First, we detect and track fully-visible vehicles (occluders). Occludee detection adopts those occluders as priors. Two classifiers for partially-visible vehicles are trained to use appearance cues. Disparity is adopted to further constrain the occludee locations. A detected occludee is then tracked by a Kalman-based tracking-by-detection method. As dynamic occlusions lead to role changes for occluder or occludee, an integrative module is introduced for possibly switching occludee and occluder trackers. The proposed system was tested on overtaking scenarios. It improved an occluder-only tracking system by over 10% regarding the frame-based detection rate, and by over 20% regarding the trajectory detection rate. The occludees are detected and tracked in the proposed method up to 7 seconds before they are picked up by occluder-only method.

1 Introduction

Multiple-object detection and tracking is a main subject in computer vision. Examples of considered objects are pedestrians [9] or vehicles [15]. Tracking-by-detection methods are developed for, e.g., surveillance, robotics, or autonomous driving [1,9,15]. These methods are mainly focusing on data association[1,7,21]. Occlusions pose difficulties for data association due to appearance changes. Because of occlusions, detection results (i.e. bounding boxes) for the occluded objects are noisy, containing partially their *occluders*. An occluder is a fully-visible vehicle; some fully-visible vehicles may not have any occludee but we still call them occluders in this paper.

By *occludee* we denote any partially occluded vehicle. Heavily occluded objects are often not detected at all, as the object model is designed or learned to detect non-occluded objects. Instead of taking occludees as exceptions, this paper proposes to detect occludees explicitly. The visible part of an occludee is obtained for further tracking, which is considered as being separated from its

© Springer International Publishing Switzerland 2015
G. Azzopardi and N. Petkov (Eds.): CAIP 2015, Part I, LNCS 9256, pp. 14–26, 2015.
DOI: 10.1007/978-3-319-23192-1_2

Fig. 1. *Left:* A sample frame with a tracked occluder (the filled pink rectangle). *Middle:* A partially-visible car. *Right:* Zoom-in view on an occludee (the yellow rectangle).

occluder. In this way, noise introduced by detection is suppressed in subsequent tracking. There are already methods [5,10] aiming at a detection of occludees separated from their occluders.

For a heavily occluded object, only weakly visible evidence complicates the detection task. Consider the scenario shown in Fig. 1. Without context knowledge it is even challenging for a human observer to recognize the partially-visible vehicle. But by identifying a vehicle as a (possible) occluder, it is more likely that we can also recognize occludees. Occludees act as valuable context information in a traffic scenario; they support the analysis of the behavior of their occluders. An occluder behaves possibly differently with or without an occludee. On the other hand, a visible vehicle, being potentially an occluder, also defines context for scanning for occludees. Simple as is, each occludee has at least one occluder. In this paper, we propose to detect occludees, using the occluders as priors.

We propose an integrated occluder-occludee object detection and tracking method Input sequences are recorded from a mobile binocular system. Occluders are detected and tracked independently. Occludees are explicitly detected and tracked, adopting occluders as priors. Finally, we integrate the occluder and occludee tracking systems. Figure 2, top row, shows three consecutive frames from

Fig. 2. *Top:* Input frames (intensity channel). *Middle:* A tracked vehicle acts as occluder (pink rectangles). *Bottom:* Tracked occludees (green rectangles) and occluders (pink rectangles).

a test sequence. The figure illustrates the following scenarios: An occluder switches to be an occludee (shown in the left and middle frames); an occludee is about to switch into an occluder (shown in the middle and right frames). The middle row illustrates results for occluder detection and tracking, shown by red filled rectangles; the bottom row shows detection and tracking results from the proposed system, with occluders and occludees shown by filled pink and green rectangles, respectively. In this paper we propose a context-based occludee detector, detecting occludees with occlusion portions up to 80%; we also apply the proposed occludee detector in an integrated occluder-occludee detection and tracking system to handle dynamic occlusions. Finally, we demonstrate the potential assistance for avoiding collisions in critical highway driving scenarios.

This paper is structured as follows. Section 2 provides a brief review of related work on occludee detection. Section 3 introduces our occluder detection and tracking method, followed by a proposed occludee detection and tracking method in Section 4. Section 5 describes the integration of both the occluder and occludee tracking systems. Experimental results and evaluations are given in Section 6. Section 7 concludes.

2   Related Work

Occlusions cause appearance changes and pose difficulties for data association in tracking. We review papers regarding occludee detection methods. Approaches used for fully-visible vehicles cannot be simply adapted for partially occluded vehicles. For example, Haar-like features, horizontal edges, visual symmetry, and corner density are properties used in [16] for detecting fully-visible vehicles. The visual appearance of partially occluded vehicles varies, edges might be too short to be identifiable. We cannot assume visual symmetry. This section reviews detection methods for occluded or general objects based on context information.

Single Object Model Occlusion Handling. [3] introduces a rich object representation for a deformable part model, extensively studied for object detection and pose estimation. For handling occlusion, [4] proposes to introduce a binary variable for each bounding box fragment, denoting whether it is from object or background; structured SVM and inference methods are used for learning and testing. In [5], a hierarchical deformable part model is proposed to explicitly handle occluded objects. Each part is further divided into subparts, and a modified structure SVM is adopted for learning. [20] discusses the training of two detectors (global bounding box-based or part-based); an occlusion map is generated by the global detector, and used for the part-based detector.

Occluder-occludee Pair Model. Occluders are often modelled together with occludee for detection. [17] proposes to train a pairwise object detector to detect occluder-occludee pairs explicitly. In [14], occluder-occludee occlusion patterns are explored for detection. A clustering method is adopted to obtain the occlusion patterns from a training set of pairs. Two joint deformable part models are proposed for learning those occlusion patterns. [11, 12] adopt an *and-or* graph model to couple the occluders and occludees based on structure SVM. The occluder-occludee models are manually designed for specific occlusions, e.g. on a parking lot.

Context-Based Methods. Contextual information, adopted for object class recognition tasks, leads to performance improvement [2,8,13,23]. [13] proposes to adopt a visual-cue surround to improve individual pedestrian detection. [2] adopts co-occurrence context evolution in a deformable part model. In [23], touch-codes are explored to model the interaction between two people in a photo.

Single model methods focus on occludees separately from their occluders. In order to handle dynamic occlusion patterns, designed occluder-occludee-pair models are not suitable. With promising results achieved by adopting contextual information, this paper proposes a context-based multiple-cue occludee detector. It uses occluders for extracting the context cue, the visible part for exploring appearance information, and stereo pairs for obtaining depth information. The combined verification of threes cues, context, appearance, and depth, is sufficient for robust occludee detection.

We handle dynamic occlusions by applying an occludee detector in a vehicle-detection and tracking system. Occluders are detected and tracked independently, and subsequently used as priors for occludee detection. Due to dynamic occlusions, occludees and occluders may change their roles. Thus, we propose an integrative module to switch occluder-occludee detection and tracking systems while processing an image sequence. The proposed integrated occluder-occludee tracking system handles dynamic occlusions efficiently; see Section 6 for experiments.

3 Occluder Detection and Tracking

Vehicles may appear fully visible (occluders) or partially occluded (occludees). Occluder detection and tracking is done independently from occludees. We use a stereo pair as input at each time step. A sliding window generates initial hypotheses $\mathcal{H}^\circ = \{h_i^\circ : 1 \leq i \leq N\}$, with $h_i^\circ = (x_i, y_i, W_i, H_i)$, where (x_i, y_i) are the top-left coordinates, and W_i and H_i the width and height of the bounding box of hypothesis h_i°.

Two layers of classifiers are adopted for classification. The first layer uses a cascaded AdaBoost classifier as commonly used for face, pedestrian, or vehicle classification [18, 19]. We adopt it for rejecting 'easily' identifiable false hypotheses. Remaining hypotheses are fed into a small convolutional network. For details see [22]. Verified hypotheses define the subset $\mathcal{B}^\circ \subseteq \mathcal{H}^\circ$; they are passed on for tracking. We note that our overall approach is independent from the actual type of classifiers used.

We assign a tracker T_j^{er} (using tracking-by-detection; superscript "er" for "occluder", j denotes the tracker ID) to each verified hypothesis $b_j^\circ \in \mathcal{B}^\circ$, $1 \leq j \leq M \leq N$, which uses a Kalman filter for tracking the vehicle 3D position (X_j, Z_j). X denotes the lateral position, Z the longitudinal position, and (X_j, Z_j) is the mid-point at the bottom of the vehicle, assuming vertical position $Y = 0$ (vehicles are not flying). The 3D location is provided by a disparity map generated by a semi-global matching technique [6]. We assume that disparity values inside b_j° are all identical (i.e. we use the mean disparity). To calculate the initial state $\mathbf{x}_j^{er} = (X_j, Z_j)^T$, we use the mean disparity and the mid-bottom point coordinates (x_j, y_j) of the vehicle bounding box.

The sketched detection-by-tracking method uses the trackers $\mathcal{T}^{er} = \{T_j^{er} : 1 \leq j \leq M\}$ for generating hypotheses, denoted by $\mathcal{H}^{er}$. $\mathcal{H}^{er}$ are verified by occluder classifiers. In this way we include the trackers' capabilities into the detection process which improves the detection rate. The process is robust with respect to jittering and small scale changes.

By verification we obtain a subset $\mathcal{B}^{er} \subseteq \mathcal{H}^{er}$ of hypotheses, where each $b_j^{er} \in \mathcal{B}^{er}$ is flagged with its tracker ID j. Thus, data association can be done by matching tracker IDs. Currently active trackers are updated by detections obtained in initial (detected) hypotheses $\mathcal{B}^\circ$ or in tracked hypotheses $\mathcal{B}^{er}$ when applying the occluder trackers. Some detected bounding boxes b_j° may overlap with some tracked boxes b_g^{er}. Mean-shift based non-maximum suppression is used to merge multiple detection responses. New trackers are initialized if there are unmatched boxes b_j°. Overall, our approach effectively combines the tracking-by-detection and detection-by-tracking paradigms.

4 Occludee Detection and Tracking

This section describes a new occludee detection and tracking method. We employ multiple cues, occlusion context, appearance, and disparity. Each cue poses individually a weak constraint which is not yet sufficient for detecting a vehicle in general based on a small fragment of its rear side.

Detected occludees, denoted by b_{kj}^{ee}, are tagged with their occluder track ID. Let j denote the occluder tracker ID, and k the index of the occludee (superscript "ee" for "occludee"). We assume that each occluder has a maximum of two occludees, with $k = l$ if on the left, or $k = r$ if on the right. We adopt again the tracking-by-detection method to track detected occludees. Different to occluders, where we apply detection-by-tracking, occludees are detected by our proposed context-based multiple-cue detector. We do not use tracking of predictions in this case. The prediction from occludee trackers may not be as reliable, due to small visible regions. The appearance may change considerably caused by dynamic occlusions. For occluder j, the occludee trackers T_{kj}^{ee} define a set $\mathcal{T}_j^{ee}$ (of up to two elements).

Context-Based Multiple-cue Occludee Detector. Occludees do not appear everywhere in the image. The occluder gives hints for scanning for its occludees. Assuming a (nearly) planar road surface, the occludees are located further away (in longitudinal direction), and the occludee is occluded by this occluder in the image plane. The bounding box of an occludee b_{kj}^{ee} and that of its occluder b_j^{er} are expected to be overlapping, or adjacent to each other. Considering real-world applications (e.g. autonomous driving), a range of possible positions of an occludee can be estimated according to the position of its occluder. Given a candidate occludee position (X_i, Z_i) in a defined 3D region, the corresponding

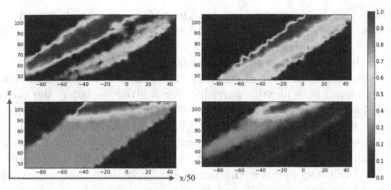

Fig. 3. Multiple-cue responses shown in heat-color maps. The corresponding 3D top-view is shown in Fig. 4. A more reddish color denotes large response values, meaning more likely a 3D position (X, Z) of an occludee. The combined response map (shown on the bottom, right) denotes that there is possibly an occludee at a distance of about 100 m ahead. *Top, left*: Quarter-width classifier response. *Top, right*: Half-width classifier response. *Bottom, left*: Disparity response. *Bottom, right*: Combined multiple-cue response.

occludee hypothesis h_i^{ee} in the image plane is obtained with a defined vehicle size. The context, i.e. occlusion with its occluder in the image plane, is adopted as context cue. More context cues, e.g. lane detection results, could be included to further improve the robustness.

Intuitively, since the occludees are partially-visible vehicles, we propose to train partial-vehicle classifiers. Those classifiers are applied for recognising that the occluded object is a vehicle, instead of, for example, a traffic sign or any other object in a traffic scene. We train a quarter- and a half-width classifier. Both classifiers' training data are cropped from a fully-visible vehicle training set used for training of the occluder classifier.

Using an occlusion check, the classifier can be applied to various occlusion patterns. Adopting occluders as priors, with a given candidate occludee at 3D position (X_i, Z_i), the visible part of the occludee is known by occlusion check in the image plane as mentioned above. When the occludee's bounding box h_i^{ee} is visible more than half of the usual width, both the quarter- and the half-width classifier are adopted to classify a quarter or half of h_i^{ee} in the intensity image.

We apply a local convolutional neural network; it could be replaced by any bounding-box-based classifier. The quarter- or the half-width classifiers' responses are taken as appearance cues.

Given a candidate occludee's 3D position (X_i, Z_i), assuming the disparity value for a vehicle (considered to be a vertically planar object), the measured disparity value within the corresponding h_i^{ee} region should be aligned with the expected disparity value. We model disparities by a Gaussian distribution with respect to differences between expected disparity and measured disparity values.

So far we have multiple weak cues, context priors, classifiers, and disparities. Multiple cues are combined in a particle filter framework. Each particle is the 3D location of a candidate occludee. The confidence for each particle presents those multiple cues. A higher confidence value denotes a larger likelihood of an existing occludee. The most confident particle is selected as an occludee detection. Left and right occludees are detected independently.

Let N denote the number of particles (3D locations around an occluder); see Fig. 4. Colored dots identify particles. For a given occluder, the occludees are located in a range further away with valid occlusion to their occluder. The particles are denoted by $\{(X_{ij}, Z_{ij}) : 1 \leq i \leq N\}$. Each position (X_{ij}, Z_{ij}), identifying the middle-bottom point of a candidate occludee, can be projected into a hypothesis h_{ij}^{ee} in the image plane with a defined 3D size (width and height). The occlusion between the candidate hypothesis and its occluder is valid if their bounding boxes h_{ij}^{ee} and b_j^{er} are non-disjoint. In other words, the candidate occludee is actually occluded by its occluder. Non-valid hypotheses are excluded from further processing, formally represented by

$$C_i^{cont} = \begin{cases} 1 \text{ if } \tau_1 > f(h_{ij}^{ee}, b_j^{er}) > \tau_2 \\ 0 \text{ otherwise} \end{cases} \tag{1}$$

where $f(h, b)$ is a function which returns an overlap-ratio for input boxes h and b, and τ_1 and τ_2 are upper and lower thresholds for the overlapping ratio.

The appearance of the visible part is verified by a quarter- or half-vehicle classifier. According to occlusion patterns, we derive a visible part of an candidate occludee from the occluder. Two partial vehicle classifiers are applied to obtain classifier responses C_{quar} and C_{half}. The appearance cue is defined by

$$C_i^{class} = \begin{cases} \omega_1 C_{quar} + \omega_2 C_{half} \text{ if } f(h_{ij}^{ee}, b_j^{er}) < \tau_3 \\ C_{quar} \qquad\qquad\qquad\quad \text{ otherwise} \end{cases} \tag{2}$$

Fig. 4. *Left, top*: Intensity image with tracked occluder (the pink filled rectangle). *Left, bottom*: Corresponding disparity map, with close to far away encoded by red to green. *Right*: Top view of the shown 3D scene with disparity map shown in lower-left. The zoom-in region (the light-grey rectangle) shows two sample regions overlaid with colored dots. Each colored dot denotes a sample. The region highlighted in orange denotes the same 3D position as show in Fig. 3.

If more than half of the width of a candidate occludee appears, we adopt the half-width classifier along with the quarter-width classifier. The ratio threshold τ is constant. Weights ω_1 and ω_2 define the applied contributions of the two classifiers.

If there is an occludee then the measured disparity value from hypothesis h_{ij}^{ee} is aligned to the expected disparity value. Even if being verified by context prior and classifiers, hypotheses with high scores are still shattered across different distances, which corresponds to different scaled bounding boxes in the image plane; see Fig. 3.

Given a candidate occludee (X_{ij}, Z_{ij}), the expected disparity d_i^{exp} for the occludee is obtained by assuming a vertical position $Y = 0$. The measured disparity d_i^{mea} is obtained by averaging disparity values in the central subregion of h_{ij}^{ee}. A Gaussian distribution is adopted to model the disparity cue with respect to the difference between d_i^{mea} and d_i^{exp}. The value of σ is obtained by measuring the uncertainty of disparity in a statistical manner. The disparity-cue response is defined by

$$C_i^{disp} = \frac{1}{\sqrt{2\sigma\pi}} \exp^{-\frac{(d_i^{mea} - d_i^{exp})^2}{2\sigma^2}} \tag{3}$$

Each sample (X_{ij}, Z_{ij}) is measured with context, classifier response, and disparity cues, obtaining responses C_i^{cont}, C_i^{class}, and C_i^{disp}. The higher the responses value, the more likely that there is an occludee located at the sample position. The *confidence* (i.e. combined response) of a sample (X_{ij}, Z_{ij}) that contains an occludee is defined by

$$C_i = C_i^{cont} C_i^{class} C_i^{disp} \tag{4}$$

All cues are required for a response with high confidence, as just individual cues are insufficient. The occludee is detected by a greedy selection of that sample which has the highest confidence, formally

$$b_{kj}^{ee} = arg \max_{h_{ij}^{ee}} C_i \tag{5}$$

A low-pass filter is employed to reduce false positives. Figure 3 shows multiple-cue responses of an occludee candidate; a corresponding 3D top-view is shown in Fig. 4. The intensity image with a tracked occluder (the pink rectangle) and a disparity map are shown in Fig. 4. In Fig. 3, the more reddish color denotes large response values, meaning a larger likelihood of an occludee at that position. The combined response map (bottom, right) indicates that there is possibly an occludee at distance 100 m ahead.

Occludee Tracking. We detected occludees in $\mathcal{B}^{ee} = \{B_j^{ee} : 1 \leq j \leq M\}$. A Kalman filter-based tracking-by-detection method is adopted for occludee tracking. Similar to occluder tracking, the middle-bottom 3D position of an occludee is defined as tracking state (X, Z). A constant-velocity assumption is adopted. The detections from a multiple-cue detector are used for updating the state.

Using the proposed context-based occludee detector, occludee detections are tagged with their occluder tracker IDs. Instead of doing data association for each occludee against the occludee trackers, an occludee detection, b_{kj}^{ee}, is associated with occludee tracker T_{kj}^{ee}. The occluder tracker ID j and occludee tracker ID k specify the corresponding occludee detection to its tracker.

5　Integration of Occluder-Occludee Tracking

In real world scenarios, a vehicle was fully visible (occluder) may be partially occluded (occludee) in a few seconds. On the other hand, a partially-visible vehicle may become fully visible. We introduce the proposed integration of occluder-occludee tracking.

Case 1: An occluder is gradually occluded by another occluder. The detection-by-tracking method will fail to verify the predicted bounding box, due to occlusion. This vehicle is lost even if it is still partially visible. *Case 2*: A tracked occludee is shifting away to another lane and becomes gradually more visible. The occludee tracker can generate a hypotheses for the occluder classifier for verification.

To interactively integrate occluder and occludee tracking systems, we propose to switch occludee and occluder trackers when conditions apply.

Occluders Switch to Occludees. To switch an occluder tracker T_j^{er} to an occludee tracker T_{kg}^{ee}, the occluder has a valid occluder T_g^{er} that causes the occlusion. The occluder j is located further away from its potential occluder. The overlap in image plane between b_j^{er} and b_g^{er} is over a given threshold. We conclude an occludee detection from having occluder g matched to occluder j, with b_{kg}^{ee} overlapped by b_j^{er}. The conditions are formulated as

$$T_j^{er} \Rightarrow T_{kg}^{ee}, \quad \text{s.t. } f(b_j^{er}, b_g^{er}) > \tau_4, \quad \exists b_{kg}^{ee}, f(b_j^{er}, b_{kg}^{ee}) > \tau_5, \quad z_j > z_g \quad (6)$$

Occludees Switch to Occluders. To switch an occludee tracker T_{kj}^{ee} to an occluder tracker T_g^{er}, the occludee is tracked for a while and overlap ratio with its occluder are low, defined by

$$T_{kj}^{ee} \Rightarrow T_g^{er}, \quad \text{s.t. } g(T_{kj}^{ee}) > \tau_6, \quad f(b_{kj}^{ee}, b_g^{er}) < \tau_4 - \varepsilon \quad (7)$$

where $g(T)$ denotes the tracked frames for the tracker T, and ε is a positive constant, adopted to prevent a switching loop between occluders and occludees.

6　Experiments

The proposed system is evaluated on two types of sequences, Dynamic and Dense; see Tab. 1. Dynamic contains four sequences of 1650 frames, approximately one minute each. 6259 vehicles (occluder and occludees), 992 occludees, and 188 trajectories, are labelled frame by frame. The Dynamic sequences contain scenarios with dynamic occlusions, recorded with regular driving style. To evaluated

Fig. 5. A frame with labelled vehicles. Red rectangles denote the occluders; green rectangles denote occludees.

the proposed occluder-occludee integrative system, there are scenarios occluders changing lane with their occludees becoming fully visible, or with occluders on fast lane driving pass the ego-vehicle becoming occludees. The Dense sequence contains 8300 frames with every 100 frames labelled (approx. 5.5 minutes). 343 vehicles and 67 occludees are labelled. The number of objects at the first glance seems limited, but those 83 frames are randomly sampled from thousands of frames. This sequence is adopted to estimate the proposed system on dense highway traffic, a more general evaluation. Both Dynamic and Dense sequences are recorded at 25 fps, from stereo cameras mounted behind the windscreen of an ego-vehicle.

One example frame with object labels shown in Fig. 5. The occluders and occludees are explicitly labelled respectively, denoted with different color rectangles. The occludee labels (green rectangles) are overlapped with their occluders. The proposed integrated system and occludee detector output the visible part exclusive to its occluder. Thus, the overlap ratio for measuring is set relatively low 0.25. A zoom-in region shown on top left corner illustrates what the perfect system is expected to detect. There are occluded vehicles appear further away from occludees. We will focus on those situations in future work.

6.1 Integrated System *vs* Occluder System

We begin the evaluation with comparing the proposed integrated system with the baseline system (occluders detection and tracking system). The frame-wise detection rate and precision are adopted. Since tracking is involved, the recall

Table 1. The test sequences.

Sequences	Frames	Objects	Occludees	Trajectories
Dynamic	1,650	6,259	992	188
Dense	8,300	343	67	-

curve is not applicable. The trajectory detection rate is used to evaluate tracking performance. A trajectory is counted as detected if 50% frames over the trajectory length are detected.

For Dynamic sequences, both frame-wise detection and trajectory measures are shown in Tab.2, left. 'Integrated' denotes the proposed integrated system. 'Occluder' denotes the occluder detection and tracking system. The proposed system fires more false positives, but improves both the detection rate and trajectory detection rate by significant margins 11% and 27.9% respectively. The proposed system detects and tracks occludees with occlusion portion up to 80%. The detection rate is improved due to the occludee detection and tracking system, and the integration between occluder and occludee trackers. The evaluation results on Dense sequence are illustrated in Tab. 2, right. Similar performance is observed. 'Integrated' outperforms 'Occluder' by a large margin 17.8%.

6.2   Application Scenario

Different levels of autonomous driving on highways are available in serial production cars, e.g auto-brake, distance keeping, lane keeping etc.. In order to enable more advanced autonomous driving, better understanding the environment offers better foundation for that purpose. Driving environment in real world is dynamic. Vehicles changing from one lane to the other, because of the vehicle in front (their occludees) driving slow, or even, suddenly broken down. The occludees affects the behavior of their occluders. If the ego-vehicle observes a bit further away (the occludees), a more advanced reaction could be made, instead of just braking abruptly.

Using occluder detection and tracking system, the occludees are not picked up due to occlusion, although they are visible, partially. The proposed integration system detects and tracks the occludees with the occlusion portion up to 80%. Four Dynamic sequences are adopted to measure the time (frame) difference between the proposed system and the occluder system picking up the previously heavy occluded then fully-visible vehicles. The evaluation results are shown in Tab. 3.

In the first three Dynamic sequences, the proposed system picks up the occludees $30-40$ frames ahead of the occluder. With recording frame rate 25 fps, the proposed system 'sees' the occludee $1.2-1.6$ seconds before the occluder system. With high speed, even a few milliseconds make a difference. In 'sequence 4', the occludee is partially visible for 7 s before appearing fully visible. This

Table 2. Performance measured on the Dynamic sequences (*left*) and on the Dense sequence (*right*).

	Detection rate	Precision	Trajectory detection rate		Detection rate	Precision	Trajectory detection rate
Occluder	59.9	88.9	44.2	Occluder	55.7	89.2	-
Integrated	76.9	79.7	72.1	Integrated	73.5	80.3	-

Table 3. Frames ahead of occluder tracker by the integrated system picked up the occluded car in front of a leading car.

	Frames	Time(s)
Sequence 1	40	1.6
Sequence 2	35	1.4
Sequence 3	29(27,32)	1.2
Sequence 4	191	7.64

information can be used for higher level decision making, e.g regarding changing lane for the ego-vehicle.

7 Conclusions

We proposed a vehicle detection and tracking system for handling dynamic occlusions. The proposed method integrates detection and tracking of occludees and occluders. We proposed a context-based multiple-cue method for occludee detection. The applied classifiers for occluders and occludees may be replaced by other bounding-box-based classifiers. A tracking-by-detection method is used for tracking occludee and occluder respectively. The proposed integrated occluder-occludee tracking system shows promising results on handling dynamic occlusions. The proposed system improves detection rate and trajectory detection rate by significant margins, compared with the occluder-only system. The proposed context-based multiple-cue occludee detector detects the immediate occludees for left and right sides of an occluder. It detects slightly to heavily occluded vehicles, occlusion portion up to 80%. The proposed system contributes to handle emergency situations in highway autonomous driving. Generally, instead of focusing on the target-object, e.g occludees in isolation, adopting the contextual information improves the performance.

References

1. Brendel, W., Amer, M.R., Todorovic, S.: Multiobject tracking as maximum weight independent set. In: CVPR (2011)
2. Chen, G., Ding, Y., Xiao, J., Han, T.X.: Detection evolution with multi-order contextual co-occurrence. In: CVPR (2013)
3. Felzenszwalb, P.F., Girshick, R.B., McAllester, D., Ramanan, D.: Object detection with discriminatively trained part-based models. TPAMI **32**(9), 1627–1645 (2010)
4. Gao, T., Packer, B., Koller, D.: A segmentation-aware object detection model with occlusion handling. In: CVPR (2011)
5. Girshick, R.B., Felzenszwalb, P.F., Mcallester, D.A.: Object detection with grammar models. In: NIPS (2011)
6. Hirschmüller, H.: Accurate and efficient stereo processing by semi-global matching and mutual information. In: CVPR (2005)

7. Huang, C., Li, Y., Nevatia, R.: Multiple target tracking by learning-based hierarchical association of detection responses. TPAMI **35**(4), 898–910 (2013)
8. Karlinsky, L., Dinerstein, M., Harari, D., Ullman, S.: The chains model for detecting parts by their context. In: CVPR (2010)
9. Leal-Taix, L., Fenzi, M., Kuznetsova, A., Rosenhahn, B., Savarese, S.: Learning an image-based motion context for multiple people tracking. In: CVPR (2014)
10. Li, B., Hu, W., Wu, T., Zhu, S.C.: Modeling occlusion by discriminative and-or structures. In: ICCV (2013)
11. Li, B., Wu, T., Zhu, S.-C.: Integrating context and occlusion for car detection by hierarchical and-or model. In: Fleet, D., Pajdla, T., Schiele, B., Tuytelaars, T. (eds.) ECCV 2014, Part VI. LNCS, vol. 8694, pp. 652–667. Springer, Heidelberg (2014)
12. Li, B., Song, X., Wu, T., Hu, W., Pei, M.: Coupling-and-decoupling: A hierarchical model for occlusion-free object detection. PR **47**(10), 3254–3264 (2014)
13. Ouyang, W., Wang, X.: Single-pedestrian detection aided by multi-pedestrian detection. In: CVPR (2013)
14. Pepikj, B., Stark, M., Gehler, P., Schiele, B.: Occlusion patterns for object class detection. In: CVPR (2013)
15. Pirsiavash, H., Ramanan, D., Fowlkes, C.C.: Globally-optimal greedy algorithms for tracking a variable number of objects. In: CVPR (2011)
16. Rezaei, M., Klette, R.: Look at the driver, look at the road: no distraction! no accident! In: CVPR (2014)
17. Tang, S., Andriluka, M., Schiele, B.: Detection and tracking of occluded people. IJCV **110**(1), 58–69 (2009)
18. Viola, P., Jones, M.: Rapid object detection using a boosted cascade of simple features. In: CVPR (2001)
19. Klette, R.: Concise Computer Vision. Springer, London (2014)
20. Wang, X., Han, T.X., Yan, S.: An HOG-LBP human detector with partial occlusion handling. In: ICCV (2009)
21. Wen, L., Li, W., Yan, J., Lei, Z., Yi, D., Li, S.Z.: Multiple target tracking based on undirected hierarchical relation hypergraph. In CVPR, 2014
22. Wöhler, C., Joachim, K.A.: An adaptable time-delay neural-network algorithm for image sequence analysis. IEEE Trans. Neural Networks **10**(6), 1531–1536 (1999)
23. Yang, Y., Baker, S., Kannan, A., Ramanan, D.: Recognizing proxemics in personal photos. In: CVPR (2012)

Correlating Words - Approaches and Applications

Mario M. Kubek[✉], Herwig Unger, and Jan Dusik

Chair of Communication Networks, FernUniversität in Hagen, Hagen, Germany
kn.wissenschaftler@fernuni-hagen.de
http://www.fernuni-hagen.de/kn/en/

Abstract. The determination of characteristic and discriminating terms as well as their semantic relationships plays a vital role in text processing applications. As an example, term clustering techniques heavily rely on this information. Classic approaches for this means such as statistical co-occurrence analysis however usually only consider relationships between two terms that co-occur as immediate neighbours or on sentence level. This article presents flexible approaches to find statistically significant correlations between two or more terms using co-occurrence windows of arbitrary sizes. Their applicability will be discussed in detail by presenting solutions to improve the interactive and image-based search in the World Wide Web. Moreover, approaches to determine directed term associations and applications for them will be explained, too.

Keywords: Word correlations · Co-occurrence analysis · N-term co-occurrences · Term associations · Co-occurrence graphs

1 Introduction

In many text processing applications, the extraction of semantic relationships between words or terms plays an important role. For instance, query expansion techniques such as [1][2] strongly rely on them. Term clustering techniques based on e.g. the k-means [3] algorithm or the Chinese Whispers [4] algorithm to identify semantically connected groups of words or word forms make use of them, too. The flat visualisation of term relations in form of semantic graphs (Fig. 1) is another use case.

In recent years, many approaches have been introduced for uncovering those relationships. The so-called statistical co-occurrence analysis for doing so is a popular means as this technique is very effective and can be easily implemented. Co-occurrences are word pairs that occur together in any order in a predefined window of n words. The most prominent kinds of co-occurrences are word pairs that appear as immediate neighbours or together in a sentence. Word pairs that co-occur with a higher probability than expected stand in a syntagmatic relation [5] to each other and are also known as significant co-occurrences. However, the obtained relationship of the co-occurrents involved (the words that significantly

© Springer International Publishing Switzerland 2015
G. Azzopardi and N. Petkov (Eds.): CAIP 2015, Part I, LNCS 9256, pp. 27–38, 2015.
DOI: 10.1007/978-3-319-23192-1_3

co-occur) is unspecific as it is only possible to make a statement in the form "word A has something to do with word B" (and vice versa) about them.

There are several well-established measures to calculate the statistical significance of co-occurrences by assigning them a significance value. If this value is greater than a pre-set threshold, the co-occurrence can be regarded as significant and a semantic relation between the words involved can often be derived from it. Rather simple co-occurrence measures are, e.g. the frequency count of co-occurring terms and the similar Dice [6] and Jaccard [7] coefficients. More advanced formulae rely on the expectation that the appearance of two words in close proximity is statistically independent (a usually inadequate hypothesis). With this hypothesis, however, the deviations between the number of observed and expected co-occurrences of real corpus data can be calculated. Therefore, a significant deviation leads to a high co-occurrence value. Co-occurrence measures based on this hypothesis are, for instance, the mutual information measure [8], the Poisson collocation measure [9] and the log-likelihood ratio [10]. Stimulus-response experiments have shown that co-occurrences found to be significant by these measures correlate well with term associations by humans [11]. The significant co-occurrences of a text can be represented as a graph of semantically related words (with the words as the vertices and the edges representing the found relation between two words), a so-called co-occurrence graph or co-occurrence network. An example graph can be seen in Fig. 1. Co-occurrence graphs are generally undirected and are suitable for the flat visualisation of term relations and for applications like query expansion via spreading activation techniques.

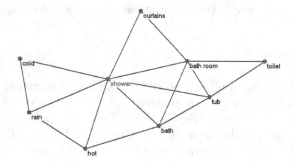

Fig. 1. A Co-occurrence graph for the word "shower"

As said before, detecting the relationship of word pairs by statistical means is very effective. However, there are further approaches to enhance this detection and to correct wrongly detected relations. One possible way is to consult manually created semantic networks such as WordNet [12], a large lexical database containing semantic relationships for the English language that covers relations like polysemy, synonymy, antonymy, hypernymy and hyponymy (i.e. more general and more specific concepts), as well as part-of-relationships. If two co-occurring terms are, e.g. synonyms, then it is sensible to merge their respective vertices of the co-occurrence graph, or to add this relationship information to their interconnecting edges as an additional feature or, at least, to draw an undirected edge with a high weight between the vertices of the terms. If one term A is a hyponym of another co-occurring term B, or if it is in a part-of-relationship with that term B, then a directed and accordingly annotated edge should be drawn from the vertex of term A to term B, whereby the weight depends on the distance of these terms in the WordNet graph. Another way to build directed term graphs is the usage of dependency parsers [13]. After a part-of-speech tagging is applied, they identify syntactic relationships among words in the text and generate dependency trees of them for each sentence. Detecting term relations using lexico-syntactic patterns is another well-known approach [14] for this task. Hereby, interesting patterns of parts of speech and/or word forms in a specified order are defined and searched for in the texts. This way, part-of- and is-a-relationships can be detected easily. A pattern like "[NN] like [NN] and [NN]" can be used to uncover hyponyms and hypernyms and, thus, determine the direction of the relation between the terms referred to.

Although, there is no broader use of co-occurrence relations in the search process of the big web search engines, e.g. for suggesting related query terms or the grouping of similar search results (which are applications for co-occurrences), tools such as the Google Ngram Viewer [15] or Google Autocomplete [14] extract phrases (a special form of co-occurrences) from books, web contents and user queries in order to visualise trends in the usage of n-grams over the years and to suggest query terms that often appear in the immediate neighbour-hood of entered search words. However, it might be sensible to also consider co-occurrences that do not only contain terms which are immediate neighbours or appear on sentence level and that are not limited to two words only.

For this purpose, in the next section, a novel approach to flexibly determine statistically significant correlations between two words using co-occurrence windows of arbitrary sizes is introduced and evaluated against two well-known co-occurrence measures. Section three discusses the mentioned generalisation of co-occurrences which allows them to consist of n terms/words ($n \geq 2$) that do not need to appear directly next to each other in a text fragment (the order of their occurrence does not play a role). They may be used like word frequency vectors (bag-of-words model) to determine content differences in large corpora. In section four, a previously introduced solution [17] to calculate directed term associations and derive influential topics from texts using them is presented and compared to another similar approach, called TermsNet [19], to determine non-obvious terms for low-cost search engine advertising. The benefits of using term associations are discussed as well. Section five concludes the article and provides future research directions that deal with or make use of term relations.

2   Correlating Two Words

As mentioned in the introduction, classic approaches for co-occurrence analysis count the occurrence of word pairs that appear as immediate neighbours or occur on sentence level. Herein, however, this lack of flexibility is addressed by using a co-occurrence window of arbitrary size represented by the neighbourhood τ ($\tau \geq 1$) which determines the number of words (and therefore their positions) before and after a word of interest (punctuation marks will be ignored) that will be considered co-occurrents. As an example, for the phrase "the quick brown fox jumps over the lazy dog", the word of interest being "fox" and $\tau = 2$ the list of co-occurrents would contain the words "quick", "brown", "fox", "jumps", "over" from which all term combinations/co-occurrences (e.g. "quick brown", "quick fox", "quick jumps" and so on) can be determined. The size of the co-occurrence window will therefore be $2 \times \tau + 1$. To evaluate the correlation between two words A and B from the set of all words T_C in a text corpus C, the number of times a specific co-occurrence is found, must be counted. In formula 1, function $f_\tau(A, B)$ therefore returns the number of times the words A and B with their respective positions P_A and P_B in the text co-occurred given τ:

$$f_\tau(A, B) := |\{B \in T_C| \ \exists A \in T_C : B \in K(A, \tau)\}| \tag{1}$$

The environment $K(A, \tau)$ is defined by formula 2:

$$K(A, \tau) := \{W \in T_C| \ |P_A - P_W| \leq \tau\} \tag{2}$$

The following applies $A \in K(B, \tau) \Leftrightarrow B \in K(A, \tau)$ and $f_\tau(A, B) = f_\tau(B, A)$. Then, the correlation of two words A and B can be calculated as follows:

$$Corr_\tau(A, B) := \frac{f_\tau(A, B)}{\max_{t \in T_C} f(t)} \tag{3}$$

Here, $\max_{t \in T_C} f(t)$ denotes the frequency of the most frequent word t in C.

For all words and A and B the correlation value can be easily calculated this way. Afterwards, a ranking should be applied in order to obtain a list of co-occurrences that is ordered by the correlation values whereby each co-occurrence is assigned a rank according to its correlation value. The co-occurrence with the lowest possible rank (1) has the highest correlation value. Co-occurrences with the same correlation value will receive the same rank. This makes it possible to compare the rankings of different co-occurrence measures that usually return significance values of incomparable value ranges. However, for this purpose, these co-occurrences must be ranked in the same way, too.

In order to show the validity of the correlation approach presented, several experiments have been conducted. Significant co-occurrences obtained from the renowned log-likelihood measure and the equally important Poisson collocation measure are generally considered to be relevant. Therefore, the idea is to compare their ranks with the ranks obtained from the correlation measure. Here, the goal was to show that the ranks from the three co-occurrence measures do not differ greatly. As an example, the rank of a specific co-occurrence "car, BMW" might be 1 according to the log-likelihood measure, yet, its rank according to the correlation might be 3. The difference (distance) of these two values is 2.

These distances have been calculated for all co-occurrences determined in the experiments. In Fig. 2 and Fig. 3, the average of those rank differences for 10 corpora each consisting of 10 topically homogeneous texts from the German news magazine "Der Spiegel" is depicted for the first 120 co-occurrences. To make the results more meaningful (in these tests, the log-likelihood measure and the Poisson collocation measure determine co-occurrences on sentence level) the parameter τ for the correlation measure has been set to 8. The co-occurrence window size is therefore 17 (the window acts as an artificial sentence), which is a good estimation for the average number of words per sentence [20].

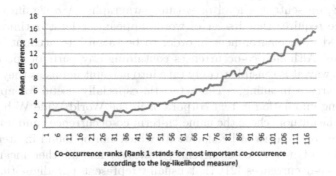

Fig. 2. Average of rank differences (log-likelihood measure vs. correlation measure)

It is easy to see, that especially among the first 50 most important co-occurrences found by the log-likelihood measure, the correlation measure regards those co-occurrences as significant, too. Their rank values do not differ much from the values assigned by the log-likelihood measure.

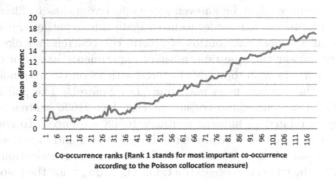

Fig. 3. Average of rank differences (Poisson colloc. measure vs. correlation measure)

For the less significant co-occurrences, however, these ranks differ increasingly. This is not surprising as the probability that less frequently co-occurring words receive the same rank using different measures decreases. The same applies to the comparison of the Poisson collocation measure with the correlation measure. Also, although not depicted here, the curves for different values of τ such as 6, 7, 9 and 10 look similar. This shows that the same co-occurrences are regarded as significant by all three measures.

3 N-term Co-occurrences

The previous approaches to determine co-occurrences can applied to find n-term co-occurrences, too. An n-term co-occurrence can be defined as an unordered set of n terms $n \geq 2$ appearing together within a co-occurrence window of specified size, on sentences level or within paragraphs. A σ-significant n-term co-occurrence requires that its set of words appears at least σ times together in the selected word environment in order to be taken into account for further considerations. Although co-occurrences containing any parts of speech can be detected this way, it is sensible to only take into account nouns as they represent terms that carry a meaning, a characteristic especially useful for applications such as finding infomation in text corpora or in the World Wide Web (WWW). This is why the authors chose the name "n-term co-occurrence" and not "n-word co-occurrence" or "multi-word collocation" which can be found in literature [9].

The notion of n-term co-occurrence, however, has another meaning than higher-order co-occurrences [21] that usually represent paradigmatic relations of word forms that in turn can be derived by comparing the semantic contexts (e.g. vectors of significantly co-occurring words) of word forms. Higher-order co-occurrences cannot be directly extracted by parsing the mentioned text fragments. N-term co-occurrences, however, represent important syntagmatic relations between two or more word forms and can be easily extracted in the process of parsing text. Significant n-term co-occurrences can also be found using the approaches presented in the previous section to determine and rank 2-term co-occurrences. As 2-term co-occurrences can be used for query expansion purposes, n-term co-occurrences might be an even more effective means to filter out documents in search processes. In order to investigate this hypothesis, it is sensible to find out what a typical distribution of n-term co-occurrences looks like?

In order to answer this question, a set of experiments has been conducted using different corpora with topically clustered articles on German politics, cars and humans of the German news magazine "Der Spiegel". The politics corpus consists of 45984 sentences, the corpus on cars has 21636 sentences and the corpus on topics related to humans contains 10508 sentences. To conduct the experiments, stop words have been removed, only nouns and names as the only allowed parts of speech have been extracted and base form reduction has been applied prior to the co-occurrence extraction. The value τ for the co-occurrence neighbourhood has been set to 8 as in the previous section. The n-term co-occurrences must have appeared at least twice in the corpus (in two different τ neighbourhoods) in order to be called significant. In Fig. 4, the power-law distributions of 2-, 3-, 4-, 5-, 6-, 7-, and 8-term co-occurrences for the German politics corpus are presented (logarithmic scale on X-axis). The distributions for the two other corpora mentioned look alike.

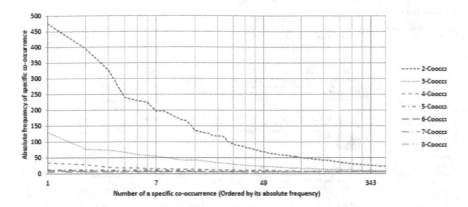

Fig. 4. Distribution of n-term co-occurrences (logarithmic scale on X-axis)

It can be clearly seen, that the most frequent co-occurrence is a 2-term co-occurrence and was found 476 times. This specific co-occurrence ("Euro, Milliarde") appeared more than three times more often than the most frequent 3-term co-occurrence ("Euro, Jahr, Milliarde") that was found 130 times. This observation is interesting as it shows that by taking into account just one additional term (in this case "Jahr", German for "year") the semantic context of a 2-term co-occurrence can be specified much more precisely. This is particularly true for co-occurrences that appear very frequently and therefore in many different semantic contexts in the used corpus.

By adding another co-occurring term such as "Bund" to the most frequent 3-term co-occurrence, the absolute frequency of this 4-term co-occurrence is again drastically reduced to 12. However, the frequency of specific 5-term, 6-term, 7-term or 8-term co-occurrences is generally much lower than the frequency of 2-term, 3-term or 4-term co-occurrences. When using five or more terms in a query, it is therefore likely that only a very low number of results will be returned, or even no results at all. However, the effort to determine such types of n-term co-occurrences will rise significantly due the increased number of possible term combinations. Even so, for the effective refinement of queries, 3-term or 4-term co-occurrences hold, as assumed in the hypothesis, valuable expansion terms and can be used to effectively filter out documents. Therefore, in [17] the interactive search application "DocAnalyser" (Fig. 5) has been presented that uses by default four highly relevant keywords from analysed text documents as query terms in order to find more similar and related documents in the WWW. Additionally, "PDSearch" (Picture-Document-Search) [18], an extension for "DocAnalyser", has been realised that can be used to search for similar web documents using images. In order to do so, "PDSearch" takes an initial query, returns matching results from Google's image search and allows users to select one or more of these images (Fig. 6) to refine the query and find more matching images or documents.

Fig. 5. DocAnalyser's result page

In the query refinement process, "PDSearch" analyses the web documents the selected images are embedded in (the images' contexts), extracts their four most relevant keywords and uses them as query terms.

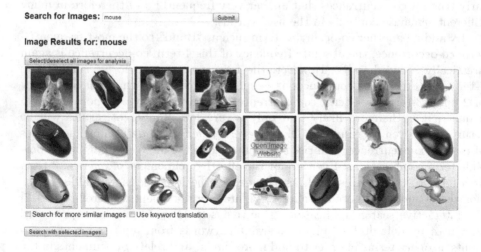

Fig. 6. PDSearch: query refinement using images

This solution is especially useful to determine the correct sense of a query when dealing with ambiguous terms such as bank and mouse. Moreover, in order to cluster (group) related terms in texts, the usage of n-term co-occurrences is a natural way for doing so and does not involve additional calculations of term similarities at all.

4 Finding Term Associations

While the classic co-occurrence measures mentioned return the same significance value for the relation of a term A with another term B and vice versa, an undirected relation of such kind often does not represent real-life relationships very well. As an example, one might instantly and strongly associate the term BMW with the term car, but not vice versa. The strength of the association of car with BMW might be much lower. Thus, it is sensible to deal with directed and therefore more specific term relations instead. To determine the strength of such an association of term A with term B on sentence level in a text corpus C, the authors propose the usage of formula 4 as a measure of confidence known from the field of association rule mining.

$$Assn(A \rightarrow B) = \frac{|S_A \cap S_B|}{|S_A|} \tag{4}$$

Here, S_A and S_B denote the sets of sentences containing term A or term B respectively, $|S_A|$ is the number of sentences term A occurred in and $|S_A \cap S_B|$ is the number of times term A and B co-occurred on sentence level.

A relation of term A with term B obtained this way can be interpreted as a recommendation of A for B when the association strength is high. Relations gained by this means are more specific than undirected relations between terms because of their direction. They resemble a hyperlink on a website to another one. In this case, however, this link has not been manually and explicitly set and carries an additional weight that indicates the strength of the term association.

The set of all such relations obtained from a text or text corpus also represents a directed co-occurrence graph that can be analysed by e.g. the extended HITS algorithm [17] to find the main topics and their sources (important inherent, influential aspects / basics). Topical sources of documents can be iteratively used to track topics they exhibit to their roots by e.g. using them as query terms which leads to further documents that in turn primarily deal with these topical sources. In order to gain a much clearer discriminability between the returned lists of main and source topics (less overlap is wished-for), an association should be taken into account only when its strength is greater or equal to the strength of the reverse association. The authors therefore propose formula 5 that accounts for this requirement.

$$Assn(A \rightarrow B) = \begin{cases} \frac{|S_A \cap S_B|}{\max_{t \in T_C} |S_t|}, & \text{if } \frac{|S_A \cap S_B|}{|S_A|} \geq \frac{|S_A \cap S_B|}{|S_B|} \\ 0, & \text{otherwise} \end{cases} \tag{5}$$

In addition to the previous expressions, $|S_B|$ is the number of sentences term B occurred in and $\max_{t \in T_C} |S_t|$ stands for the maximum number of sentences any (but a fixed term) term t from the set of all terms T_C in corpus C has occurred in. The resulting weight $\frac{|S_A \cap S_B|}{\max_{t \in T_C} |S_t|}$ of the directed link from A to B is derived by multiplying $\frac{|S_A \cap S_B|}{|S_A|}$ that indicates the basic association strength of A with B by $\frac{|S_A|}{\max_{t \in T_C} |S_t|}$ that accounts for the relative frequency of A (on sentence level) in the text as a measure for A's overall importance.

Table 1 presents for the article "Financial crisis of 2007–08" from the English Wikipedia the two lists of main and source topics extracted by the extended HITS algorithm, whereby the following parameters have been used: removal of stop words, part-of-speech restriction to nouns and names, base form reduction and phrase detection.

Table 1. Terms with high authority (main topics) and hub values (source topics) from the Wikipedia-Article "Financial crisis of 2007–08":

Term	Main topic score	Term	Source topic score
bank	0.57	system	0.20
crisis	0.42	institution	0.19
US	0.34	lending	0.19
market	0.27	house	0.18
mortgage	0.25	loan	0.18
credit	0.18	risk	0.18
institution	0.17	market	0.17
house	0.16	investment	0.17
price	0.15	mortgage	0.16
system	0.13	credit	0.15

Another graph-based approach to find non-obvious terms for search engine advertising, called TermsNet, has been presented in [19].

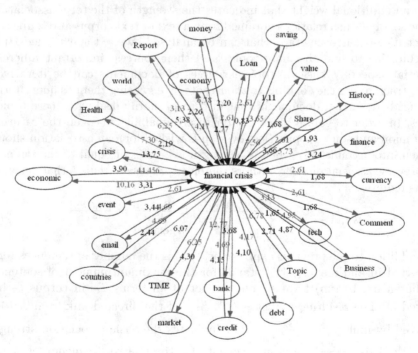

Fig. 7. TermsNet's graph for the query "financial crisis"

This method calculates term associations using text snippets from Google's Top-50 search hits. It was shown that TermsNet can identify highly relevant keywords that are non-obvious and therefore can be used to lower advertising costs. An example graph built by TermsNet for the query term "financial crisis", from which those term suggestions are derived, can be seen in Fig. 7. Although, the authors of [19] suggest a specific formula to score the relevance of terms to an initial query, it is possible to analyse the gained graph using the extended HITS algorithm in order to extract its authorities and hubs (main and source topics) while taking into account its structure and associations weights, too. This way, the quality of TermsNet's keyword suggestion could be further improved. In future articles, the authors will compare these two approaches in more detail.

5   Conclusion

In this article, flexible approaches to uncover relationships and associations between two or more words by statistical means have been introduced and evaluated. One of the main findings was that n-term co-occurrences, especially those containing 3 and 4 terms, can be used to effectively filter out documents from text corpora which is why this approach has been implemented in the interactive search application "DocAnalyser" and its extension for image-based document search "PDSearch". Another interesting observation was that documents containing the same n-term co-occurrences are semantically similar or related. As this finding would propose a natural way to cluster documents, it is subject of further research. It was also shown that term associations are more meaningful than undirected co-occurrences and can be used to detect non-obvious and topically influential terms. Those terms are especially of interest for low-cost search engine advertising and for topic tracking purposes. In order to detect even more useful term associations and therefore topical relationships in texts, the inclusion of higher-order associations might be a sensible approach. The terms involved in such kind of associations do not co-occur in texts within co-occurrence windows, yet, they appear in the semantic contexts of specific terms. A term's semantic context in this sense is represented by its set of first-order associations obtainable by the approaches presented in section four. In future articles, the usefulness of higher-order associations will therefore be evaluated.

References

1. Timonen, M., Silvonen, P., Kasari, M.: Modelling a query space using associations. In: Proceedings of the 2011 Conference on Information Modelling and Knowledge Bases XXII, pp. 77–96. IOS Press (2011)
2. Kubek, M., Witschel, H.F.: Searching the web by using the knowledge in local text documents. In: Proceedings of Mallorca Workshop 2010 Autonomous Systems. Shaker Verlag Aachen (2010)
3. MacQueen, J.B.: Some methods for classification and analysis of multivariate observations. In: Proceedings of 5th Berkeley Symposium on Mathematical Statistics and Probability, vol. 1, pp. 281–297. University of California Press (1967)

4. Biemann, C.: Chinese whispers: an efficient graph clustering algorithm and its application to natural language processing problems. In: Proceedings of the HLT-NAACL-06 Workshop on Textgraphs-06, pp. 73–80. ACL, New York City (2006)
5. de Saussure, F.: Cours de Linguistique Générale. Payot, Paris (1916)
6. Dice, L.R.: Measures of the Amount of Ecologic Association Between Species. Ecology **26**(3), 297–302 (1945)
7. Jaccard, P.: Étude comparative de la distribution florale dans une portion des alpes et des jura. Bulletin del la Société Vaudoise des Sciences Naturelles **37**, 547–579 (1901)
8. Büchler, M.: Flexibles Berechnen von Kookkurrenzen auf strukturierten und unstrukturierten Daten. Masters thesis, University of Leipzig (2006)
9. Quasthoff, U., Wolff, C.: The poisson collocation measure and its applications. In: Second International Workshop on Computational Approaches to Collocations. IEEE, Vienna (2002)
10. Dunning, T.: Accurate methods for the statistics of surprise and coincidence. Computational Linguistics **19**(1), 61–74. MIT Press, Cambridge (1993)
11. Heyer, G., Quasthoff, U., Wittig, T.: Text Mining: Wissensrohstoff Text: Konzepte, Algorithmen, Ergebnisse. W3L-Verlag, Dortmund (2006)
12. Fellbaum, C.: WordNet and wordnets. In: Brown, K., et al. (eds.) Encyclopedia of Language and Linguistics, 2nd edn, pp. 665–670. Elsevier, Oxford (2005)
13. McDonald, R., et al.: Non-projective dependency parsing using spanning tree algorithms. In: Byron, D., Venkataraman, A., Zhang, D. (eds.) Proc. of the Joint Conf. on Human Language Technology and Empirical Methods in Natural Language Processing (HLT/EMNLP), pp. 523–530. ACL, Vancouver (2005)
14. Riloff, E., Jones, R.: Learning dictionaries for information extraction by multi-level bootstrapping. In: Proc. of the Sixteenth National Conference on Artificial Intelligence, Orlando, pp. 474–479 (1999)
15. Michel, J., et al.: Quantitative Analysis of Culture Using Millions of Digitized Books. Science **331**(6014), 176–182 (2011)
16. Website of Google Autocomplete (2015). https://support.google.com/websearch/answer/106230?hl=en
17. Kubek, M.: Interaktive Anwendungen Kontextbasierter Suchverfahren. In: Fortschritt-Berichte VDI, Reihe 10 Nr. 839, VDI-Verlag Düsseldorf (2014)
18. Sukjit, P., Kubek, M., Böhme, T., Unger, H.: PDSearch: using pictures as queries. In: Boonkrong, S., Unger, H., Meesad, P. (eds.) Recent Advances in Information and Communication Technology. AISC, vol. 265, pp. 255–262. Springer, Heidelberg (2014)
19. Joshi, A., Motwani, R.: Keyword generation for search engine advertising. In: Sixth IEEE International Conference on Data Mining Workshops, Hong Kong, pp. 490–496 (2006)
20. Cutts, M.: Oxford Guide to Plain English. Oxford University Press (2013)
21. Biemann, C., Bordag, S., Quasthoff, U.: Automatic acquisition of paradigmatic relations using iterated co-occurrences. In: Proc. of the 4th International Conference on Language Resources and Evaluation (LREC 2004), Lisbon, Portugal, pp. 967–970 (2004)

ExCuSe: Robust Pupil Detection in Real-World Scenarios

Wolfgang Fuhl$^{(\boxtimes)}$, Thomas Kübler, Katrin Sippel, Wolfgang Rosenstiel, and Enkelejda Kasneci

Eberhard Karls Universität Tübingen, 72076 Tübingen, Germany
wolfgang.fuhl@uni-tuebingen.de
http://www.ti.uni-tuebingen.de/

Abstract. The reliable estimation of the pupil position is one the most important prerequisites in gaze-based HMI applications. Despite the rich landscape of image-based methods for pupil extraction, tracking the pupil in real-world images is highly challenging due to variations in the environment (e.g. changing illumination conditions, reflection, etc.), in the eye physiology or due to variations related to further sources of noise (e.g., contact lenses or mascara). We present a novel algorithm for robust pupil detection in real-world scenarios, which is based on edge filtering and oriented histograms calculated via the Angular Integral Projection Function. The evaluation on over 38,000 new, hand-labeled eye images from real-world tasks and 600 images from related work showed an outstanding robustness of our algorithm in comparison to the state-of-the-art. Download link (algorithm and data): https://www.ti.uni-tuebingen.de/Pupil-detection.1827.0.html?\&L=1.

1 Introduction

Eye-tracking technology has helped us getting a deeper understanding of human cognition, answering questions from psychology, medicine, marketing research, and many other disciplines. With the development of mobile, head-mounted eye trackers the number of studies conducted in real-world scenarios, such as in sports, while driving a car, or shopping are increasing. Such eye trackers consist of two or more cameras, recording the subject's eyes from close-up and the scenery from the ego-perspective. The most essential step of the analysis of data recorded by such devices is the accurate identification of the center of the pupil in the camera image. In 2000, Schnipke and Todd [13] reported several difficulties arising in eye-tracking applications, e.g., changing illumination conditions, intersection of eyelashes with the image of the pupil, glasses, etc. Frequent illumination changes are often caused by the ego motion and rotation, especially when moving fast, e.g. while driving. Reflections are caused by a variety of light sources on the subject's eye itself or on glasses or contact lenses. Another factor that may negatively affect the pupil detection rate is the position of the camera that records the subject's eye. For best pupil detection the camera should be positioned directly in front of the subject's eye. Since this would influence the

© Springer International Publishing Switzerland 2015
G. Azzopardi and N. Petkov (Eds.): CAIP 2015, Part I, LNCS 9256, pp. 39–51, 2015.
DOI: 10.1007/978-3-319-23192-1_4

natural viewing behavior, the camera is usually positioned at the borders of the visual field and, consequently, the images recorded are highly off-axial. While in the meantime several of the above problems have been solved for pupil detection under laboratory conditions [3, 6–8, 10, 12, 15, 19, 21], studies employing eye tracking in real-world scenarios regularly report low pupil detection rates [5,9]. Thus, the data collected from such studies has to be processed post-experimentally and the pupil has to be manually labeled in the recorded images. A popular and robust algorithm is *Starburst* by Li et al. [7], which is based on the calculation of edges along rays from an initial guess of the pupil position in the image. Areas of high intensity change along these rays are then used as possible pupil border features. Finally, an ellipse is fitted to these features using RANSAC. In 2012, Swirski et al. [15] proposed a robust pupil tracking algorithm for highly off-axis images. Their approach is based on an initial approximation of the pupil position using Haar Wavelets and a refinement step with RANSAC-based ellipse fitting. Another approach introduced by Goni et al. [3] is based on the bright-pupil technique. In [6] and [8] the algorithm searches for the corneal reflection on IR images. The pupil is expected close to the corneal reflection and extracted using histograms and thresholds-based techniques [6]. In Long et al. [10] IR images are thresholded using a symmetric mass center algorithm. Image thresholding and mass center calculation is also performed in [12], whereas Valenti et al. [19] use isophotes curvature estimation and select the maximum isocenter as pupil center. In [21] the image is thresholded and the curvature of the threshold border is calculated. Despite the above approaches, most eye tracking vendors employ their own pupil detection algorithms, which are specifically tailored for their devices and mostly unpublished. To the best of our knowledge, the above approaches have been evaluated on rather small data sets.

We propose a novel algorithm, **Ex**clusive **Cu**rve **Se**lector or *ExCuSe* for short that is well suited for real-world eye-tracking applications, providing high detection rates and robustness in images where other algorithms fail. Our algorithm is based on oriented histograms calculated via the Angular Integral Projection Function [11]. The coarse pupil center estimation is then refined by ellipse estimation similar to Starburst [7]. The algorithm is evaluated on the Swirski data set [15] as well as nine other data sets that were collected during an on-road driving experiment [5] and eight data sets that were collected during a supermarket study [14]. The evaluation data set consists of overall 38,401 images, where the pupil position was labeled manually on each image. Thus, despite our algorithmic contribution we provide an enormous evaluation data set that may serve as ground truth data for further research.

2   Method

Input to our algorithm are 8-bit gray-scale images. The work-flow of the algorithm for pupil detection is depicted in Figure 1. Each step is described in detail in the following subsections. Furthermore, this paper is accompanied by a supplementary video, which demonstrates the main idea behind each step of ExCuSe and the processing result on real-world eye videos of different subjects.

2.1   Normalization and Histogram Analysis

The peripheral regions of the input image (i.e., 10% in our application) are excluded from further processing in order to avoid the frame of eyeglasses. Furthermore, we assume that on images with an overall bright intensity and similar gray values a reflection on eyeglasses or a bright illumination spot is present. Using an intensity threshold approach to extract the pupil is hard in such cases, since the pupil can not be expected to appear dark and is likely to contain a broad range of intensity values.

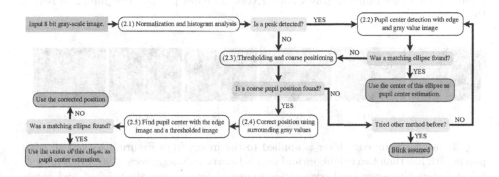

Fig. 1. The algorithmic work-flow in ExCuSe. Light gray boxes represent decisions, dark gray boxes stand for termination points, and white boxes represent processing steps.

Thus, in a first step, the input image is normalized (range 0 to 255) and a histogram of the image is calculated. Then the algorithm checks whether the histogram contains a peak in the bright area (Figure 2(d)) with a gray value above a threshold th_1 (i.e., $th_1 = 200$ chosen empirically). The peak is detected if a bin in the histogram is higher than a multiple mu_1 of the average image intensity (we chose $mu_1 = 10$ empirically). If such a peak was detected, the pupil can be found based on edge-filtering.

2.2   Pupil Center Detection on Edge and Gray Value Image

We assume that the pupil appears as a curved edge encapsulating the darkest intensity values of the image. To find such an edge, four processing steps are performed on the Canny-edge-filtered image, Figure 3.

2.2.1   Filtering the Edge Image

Figure 3(a) shows the edge-filtered image from Figure 2(b), which appears cluttered and contains many edges that are not relevant for pupil detection. The pupil edges are difficult to detect since they are crossed by the eyelashes. In a

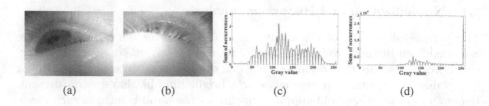

(a)   (b)   (c)   (d)

Fig. 2. Figures 2 (a) and (b) show two images from a dataset introduced by Swirski et al. [15] and their corresponding intensity histograms in (c) and (d). Figure 2 (b) shows a pupil with a high range of gray values. Eyelashes cover parts of the pupil and reflect the light.

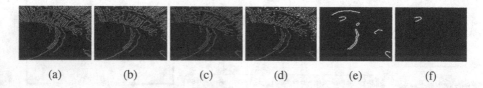

(a)   (b)   (c)   (d)   (e)   (f)

Fig. 3. (a) A Canny edge filter is applied to the image from Figure 2(b). (b) all edge pixels with less than two neighbors and angels between all neighbors ≤ 90° are removed. (c) the remaining connected edge pixels represent lines. They are thinned and pixels connecting two lines orthogonally are removed. (d) for each line the centroid (shown as white point) is inspected and lines close to their centroid are removed (e). (f) the longest line which contains the darkest pixels is assumed to encapsulate the pupil.

first filtering step, thin edge lines (i.e., 1 pixel thickness) and pixels of small rectangular surfaces (2 × 2 pixels) are removed. More specifically, the above criterion is fulfilled by neighboring pixels which (considered as vectors) have angels greater than 90° between each other. The remaining edge pixels represent lines which are straight, curved, or consist of both straight and curved parts. The separation step is here of particular interest, e.g., the edge of the eyelashes in the pupil are straight and connected to the curved edge of the pupil. To distinguish between connected line parts that have to be separated and those that do not, the connection point between such parts has to be examined in detail. The assumption is that line parts that have to be separated are orthogonal to each other at the connection point.

To separate lines consisting of curved and straight parts into the corresponding curved and straight segments, the morphologic operations shown in Figure 4 are applied. If one of these patterns matches to the edge pixels (shown in gray), that pixel is deleted. Pixels marked black in the Figure are added. After thinning, lines can be separated into segments by deletion of just one pixel. However, there are still pixels which prevent the patterns from Figure 4(d), (e), or (f) to match. Therefore, lines are straightened using the patterns shown in Figure 4(b) and (c). Now the connection points of line parts which are orthogonal to each

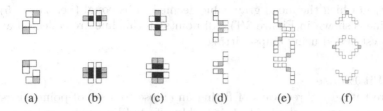

Fig. 4. Morphologic pixel manipulation patterns. White and gray boxes represent pixels that were detected as edges in the image. If the pattern matches an edge segment, gray pixels are removed and black pixels are added to the edge image. Operand (a) thins lines. Operands (b) and (c) are used to straighten lines. (d), (e) and (f) separate straight parts of a line from curved parts.

other can be separated using the patterns in Figure 4(d),(e), and (f). The result of this step is shown in Figure 3(c).

2.2.2   Remove Straight Lines

The next step is to detect and remove straight lines. Since the pupil is expected to be encapsulated in a curved line, straight lines are of no interest. Therefore, all remaining edge pixels are combined to lines based on their connection to neighboring edge pixels. The steps that are performed to calculate lines from the edge image are the following:

1. Find edge pixels that do not belong to any line yet
2. Create a new line with the edge pixel
3. Add all direct neighbor edge pixels to the line
4. Repeat Steps 3 + 4 for all added neighbor pixels

Calculate the line centroid for each line. If the pixel distance between the centroid and at least one point of the line segment is smaller than a threshold di_1, the line is assumed to be straight (in our application we chose $di_1 = 3$ empirically). Figure 3(d) shows all lines with their centroid (white point) and Figure 3(e) shows the remaining, curved lines after the removal of straight segments. We expect that one of the remaining lines belongs to the pupil.

2.2.3   Choose Curved Line

We assume the pupil to be a dark spot in the intensity image. Therefore, the pupil candidate with the darkest area contained in it is most likely to be the pupil. To calculate an intensity value for the contained area we choose the pixel with a distance of di_2 pixels for each line point which have the smallest euclidean distance to the line's centroid (i.e., $di_2 = 2$ chosen empirically). For these pixels, the mean gray value is calculated. It is possible that there is more than one curved line belonging to the pupil. We choose the longest line found with the darkest inboard area. To ensure that larger lines are not discarded, we choose a range ra_1 in which the mean gray value deemed to be equal (i.e., $ra_1 = 5$). The chosen line is shown in Figure 3(f). All points on this line are collected and the center is estimated using ellipse fitting.

2.2.4   Fit Ellipse

There are basically three ways of fitting an ellipse to a set of points. First, the direct least squares method, which is highly affected by pixels not belonging to the border of the ellipse [2]. The other two possibilities are vote- and search-based (e.g., RANSAC [1]). These are more robust to in- and outliers, yet computationally expensive [20]. We fit the ellipse based on the direct least squares method. It is fast to calculate and also used as abort criterion on failure for the step (2.2) Figure 1.

2.3   Thresholding and Coarse Positioning

If the gray value histogram does not contain a peak (Figure 2(c)), we extract the pupil based on a threshold th_2. Each pixel with a gray value lower than th_2 is set to 255 as shown in Figure 5(b). In highly scattered images the pupil may consist of a range of different intensity values. The threshold th_2 is chosen dependent on the scattering in the image as half the standard deviation of the image intensity. In this step we aim at determining a coarse pupil position. It is not necessary to extract the whole pupil. Therefore a conservative threshold that reduces noise at the potential cost of cutting part of the pupil is preferable. The coarse pupil position is estimated utilizing the Angular Integral Projection Function (AIPF) [11] on the thresholded image. The AIPF allows the calculation of the Integral Projection Function (IPF) for any specified angle.

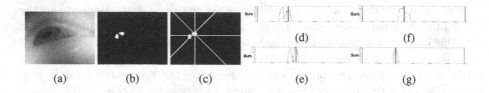

Fig. 5. (a) An image from the Swirski et al. [15] data set and (b) its corresponding thresholded image. In (c) the coarse positioning (white lines) of the four orientations from the Angular Integral Projection Function (AIPF) [11] are shown. The results of the AIPF calculated on the threshold image for the orientations 0°, 45°, 90° and 135° are shown in the histograms (d), (e), (f), and (g) in corresponding order. The chosen positions are shown as red lines and correspond to the white lines in (c) with (d) defining the vertical white line in (c), (e) the line from the right bottom to the top left corner, (f) to the horizontal line and (g) to the line from the left bottom to the top right corner.

$$IPF_h(y) = \int_{x_1}^{x_2} I(x,y) \; dx \tag{1}$$

$$IPF_v(x) = \int_{y_1}^{y_2} I(x,y) \; dy \tag{2}$$

With $I(x,y)$ as the gray value at the location (x,y) equation (1) (as found in [11]) defines the IPF$_h$ (Integral Projection Function horizontally) for the interval $[x_1, x_2]$ and equation (2) define the IPF$_v$ (Integral Projection Function vertically) for the interval $[y_1, y_2]$. The IPF calculates the sum of the intensity values of an image in one direction. For example, outgoing form the x-axes for each row (pixel line from the bottom of the image to the top) the pixel values are summed up and represent one bin in the resulting histogram. Those histograms do not rely on shape and our assumption is that the region with the highest response is the pupil. We used the AIPF because it allows to calculate IPFs for different orientations, it is known to be robust and is fast to calculate. Two well known IPFs are the horizontal (IPF$_h$) and the vertical (IPF$_v$) IPF. The IPF$_v$ corresponds to the AIPF with angle $0°$ and the IPF$_h$ corresponds to the AIPF with angle $90°$ [11].

With $I(x,y)$ as the gray value at location (x,y) equation (3) (as found in [11]) defines the AIPF. Θ is the angle of the line to the x-axis from which the integration rotated by $90°$ takes place, p is the position on the line or the bin of the corresponding histogram, h is the number of pixels to be integrated and (x_0, y_0) is the position of the start point of the line along which the integration rotated by $90°$ takes place. We used the orientations $0°$, $45°$, $90°$ and $135°$ for the AIPF to calculate the histograms shown in Figure 5(d),(e),(f), and (g).

$$AIPF(\Theta, p, h) = \frac{1}{h+1} * \int_{j=-\frac{h}{2}}^{\frac{h}{2}} I\Big((x_0 + p \cos \Theta)$$
$$+ (j \cos (\Theta + 90°)), (y_0 + p \sin \Theta) \tag{3}$$
$$+ (j \sin (\Theta + 90°)) \Big) \; dj$$

In these four histograms the coarse pupil location is assumed at a wide and high response area. The minimum length of the area is specified by ar_1 and the number of consecutive bins allowed to be low is specified by ar_2 (in our application we chose $ar_1 = 7$ and $ar_2 = 5$ empirically). This is done to eliminate single high responses in the histogram.

Areas of high response are defined by a threshold th_3 which is a percentage of the maximum of the histogram (in our application we chose $th_3 = 0.5$ empirically). If there is more than one acceptable area in a histogram, our assumption is that the pupil can be found at the center of the image. Therefore, the midpoint of the area which is closest to the bin in the histogram corresponding to the center of the image is chosen as the pupil position. The white lines in

Figure 5(c) represent the angle of the AIPF for each histogram rotated by 90°
(angle of the integration) and are the chosen positions. Therefore, these white
lines correspond to the red lines from Figures 5(d), (e), (f), and (g) drawn to the
threshold image shown in Figure 5(b). The pupil position is estimated based on
the intersection of these lines. Our assumption is that the intersection of those
lines orthogonal to each other are close to or hit the pupil. This way, up to two
intersection points are considered. The pupil position is assumed as the point
between these intersections. In the case that no intersection was found, branch
2.2 of the algorithm will take over. If this branch fails to detect the pupil as
well, a blink is assumed.

2.4   Correct Position Using Surrounding Gray Values

Once a coarse pupil center estimation has been established, it has to be improved
because it is possible that the coarse position lays outside or on the boarder of
the pupil. It can be refined within a small area ar_3 around the estimation without
being dependent on the shape or color of the pupil (in our application we chose
$ar_3 = 0.1$ empirically, which represents 10% of the width and height of the
image in each direction). The only assumption made is that pixels belonging
to the pupil are surrounded by brighter or equally bright pixels. This step is
important for images in which the pupil is especially hard to detect.

$$PS(x,y) = \sum_{x_i=x_1}^{x_2} \sum_{y_i=y_1}^{y_2} \begin{cases} I(x,y) - I(x_i,y_i), I(x_i,y_i) < I(x,y) \\ 0, I(x_i,y_i) >= I(x,y) \end{cases} \tag{4}$$

For each pixel the sum $PS(x,y)$ of gray value differences to its neighbors is calculated. Only gray values lower than the value of the pixel under consideration
are taken into account. For the neighborhood area the square root of the diagonal of the area specified by ar_3 is used. The mean of the pixel positions with
the lowest sum value is the new corrected position. In equation (4) $PS(x,y)$
is the sum calculated for the pixel at position (x,y), $[x_1,x_2]$ is the interval on
the x-axis of the neighborhood area, $[y_1,y_2]$ is the interval on the y-axis and
$I(x,y)$ is again the gray value at position (x,y).

2.5   Find Pupil Center with the Edge and Threshold Image

This step does not require the corrected position to be the accurate pupil center,
however it is required to lie inside of the pupil. The concept of using a threshold image to improve the edge image and refine finding the pupil edges with
rays outgoing from this position is described in the following chapter. Only the
region ar_4 around the corrected point is of interest for finding the pupil (in our
application we chose $ar_4 = 0.2$ empirically, which means 20% of the width and
height of the image in each direction). We use only eight rays because for too
many rays it is more likely that rays hit edges not belonging to the pupil if the
edges belonging to the pupil are not consistently present. Therefore rays missing
the pupil edges can hit other edges that do not belong to the pupil thus making
the pupil center detection incorrect.

2.5.1   Improve Edge Image with Threshold Image

First, an edge-filter of the image region is calculated, as shown in Figure 6(a). The calculated threshold image from step *2.3* is not useful here because the threshold chosen was for coarse positioning and there was no need to extract the whole pupil. In this step, the threshold th_2 (chosen as half the standard deviation) is increased to the full standard deviation to calculate the new threshold image (Figure 6(b)). In this step it is important that no part of the pupil gets cut off by a too conservative threshold. Edges of the edge image are preselected by overlay with the threshold image. Only edges close to the border of the threshold region (Figure 6(c)) are considered relevant. This border is calculated by accepting only white pixels in the threshold image which have black direct neighbors. Only edges close to the border region are considered, see Figure 6(d). To calculate this the surrounding area ar_5 of each threshold border pixel is inspected (in our application we chose $ar_5 = 5$ empirically which means 5 pixels in each direction outgoing from the threshold border pixel). If an edge pixel lies within the ar_5 region of a threshold border pixel it is accepted. Then the border refinement steps described in *2.2.1* and *2.2.2* are carried out (the result is shown in Figure 6(e)).

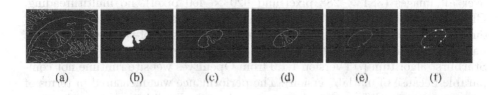

(a)   (b)   (c)   (d)   (e)   (f)

Fig. 6. The edge-filtered eye image (a) of the region where the pupil is expected. A threshold image (b) is calculated to determine the threshold border (c). Only edge pixels close to this border are used for further calculations (d). After the edge refinement steps explained in *2.2.1* and *2.2.2* the remaining edges are used for edge selection (e): rays are sent out from the corrected point (white point in the middle of (f)) into all directions with an angle step of 45°. If a ray hits an edge (white points on the ellipse in (f)) the line belonging to this edge is supposed to belong to the pupil.

2.5.2   Find Edges that Represent the Pupil Border

In the resulting edge image, rays from the corrected position (small white point in the middle of Figure 6(f)) are sent in all directions with an angle step of 45° until they hit an edge (white points on the elliptic line in Figure 6(f)), similar to the method used by the Starburst algorithm [7]. The intersection points between the rays and the edges are used to collect points. All edge pixels connected to a hit edge pixel and iteratively all that are connected to those pixels are used to fit an ellipse.

3   Experimental Evaluation

3.1   Data

We evaluated our approach on eighteen data sets. The first data set was published by Swirski et al. [15]. Nine data sets were recorded during an on-road driving experiment [5] using a head-mounted camera system (Dikablis Mobile Eye Tracker by Ergoneers GmbH). The remaining eight data sets were recorded during a supermarket search task [14]. These data sets are highly challenging, since illumination conditions change often and rapidly. Furthermore reflections on eyeglasses and contact lenses occur. The data reflect the results of standard eye-tracking experiments out of the laboratory and was recorded for other studies that did not focus on pupil detection. Pupil position was hand labeled for all of the above data sets. The data is available for download under https://www.ti.uni-tuebingen.de/Pupil-detection.1827.0.html?&L=1.

3.2   Results

The runtime of ExCuSe (C++ implementation) was 7ms per image (averaged over all images (384 × 288 pixel and 620 × 460 pixel), no multithreading, CPU: i5-4570 3.2GHz). We compared the performance of our algorithm (without changing any parameter for all data sets) to two state-of-the-art approaches, namely Swirski et al. [15] (Version June 1st, 2014 runtime:14ms) and to the Starburst algorithm [7] (Version 1.1.0 from OpenEyes website runtime not comparable because of matlab version). The performance was measured in terms of detection rate for different pixel errors based on the Euclidean distance between the hand-labeled ground-truth and the pupil center as reported by each algorithm. Table 1 shows the results for each algorithm on each data set with a pixel error up to 5.

Note that the performance of the pupil tracking software provided by the eye-tracker manufacturer (Ergoneers GmbH) was very poor on all the above data sets (without Swirski data) with a detection rate of less than 0.027 % for 15 error pixels. Therefore, the results of the manufacturer software will not be

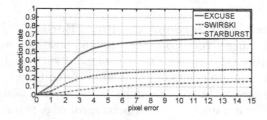

Fig. 7. Average pupil detection rates for different pixel errors achieved by ExCuSe (solid), the Swirksi et al. algorithm (dashed), and Starburst (double dashed) on all data sets from Table 1.

presented here. In addition, Figure 7 shows the average performance of all three algorithms over the entire evaluation data, i.e., on about 39,000 hand-labeled images. As shown in the Figure, ExCuSe outperforms the competitor algorithms with detection rates nearly twice as good as the Swirski et al. algorithm and is therefore a suitable choice for pupil detection on such difficult data.

Table 1. Detection rate of Starburst, Swirski et al. and ExCuSe on each evaluation data set. For each data set, the table shows the number of hand-labeled images and a description of the challenges faced by the image processing as seen by the authors. The last three columns are the results up to an pixel error of 5.

Data Set	Images	Challenges	Starburst	Swirski et al.	ExCuSe
Swirski	600	Highly off axis, eyelashes	21%	78%	**86%**
I	6.554	Reflections	5%	5%	**70%**
II	505	Reflections, bad illumination	2%	24%	**34%**
III	9.799	Reflections, recording errors, bad illumination	1%	6%	**39%**
IV	2.655	Contact lenses, bad illumination	4%	34%	**81%**
V	2.135	Shifted contact lenses	14%	**77%**	**77%**
VI	4.400	Bad illumination, Mascara	18%	19%	**53%**
VII	4.890	Bad illumination, mascara, eyeshadow	2%	39%	**46%**
VIII	630	Bad illumination, Eyelashes	8%	41%	**56%**
IX	2.831	Reflections, additional black dot	12%	23%	**74%**
X	840	Bad illumination, pupil at image boarder	53%	29%	**79%**
XI	655	Reflections, bad illumination, additional black dot	26%	20%	**56%**
XII	524	Bad illumination	61%	70%	**79%**
XIII	491	Bad illumination, Eyelashes	43%	61%	**70%**
XIV	469	Bad illumination	21%	52%	**57%**
XV	363	Shifted contact lenses	8%	**62%**	52%
XVI	392	Mascara, eyelashes	8%	18%	**49%**
XVII	268	Bad illumination, eyelashes	0%	68%	**78%**

4   Conclusions

We presented a pupil detection algorithm, ExCuSe, for application in real-world eye-tracking experiments. The focus was primarily on the robustness of the algorithm with respect to frequently and rapidly changing illumination conditions, off-axial camera position, and other sources of noise. We evaluated our algorithm on a total of 39,001 eye images in comparison with two state-of-the-art approaches. Our method showed high robustness and clearly outperformed the competitor algorithms. Since robust pupil position tracking under real-world illumination conditions is a crucial prerequisite towards online analysis of eye-tracking data in different applications, e.g., driving, where such information can be used to determine the visual attention focus of the driver [4,16,17], we encourage the application of ExCuSe in such tasks. In our future work, we will integrate ExCuSe in visual search tools (e.g., Vishnoo [18]) to make it available for pupil detection in search tasks under laboratory conditions.

References

1. Fischler, M.A., Bolles, R.C.: Random sample consensus: a paradigm for model fitting with applications to image analysis and automated cartography. Communications of the ACM **24**(6), 381–395 (1981)
2. Fitzgibbon, A., Pilu, M., Fisher, R.B.: Direct least square fitting of ellipses. IEEE Transactions on Pattern Analysis and Machine Intelligence **21**(5), 476–480 (1999)
3. Goni, S., Echeto, J., Villanueva, A., Cabeza, R.: Robust algorithm for pupil-glint vector detection in a video-oculography eyetracking system. In: Pattern Recognition. ICPR 2004, vol. 4, pp. 941–944. IEEE (2004)
4. Kasneci, E.: Towards the Automated Recognition of Assistance Need for Drivers with Impaired Visual Field. Ph.D. thesis, University of Tübingen, Wilhelmstr. 32, 72074 Tübingen (2013)
5. Kasneci, E., Sippel, K., Aehling, K., Heister, M., Rosenstiel, W., Schiefer, U., Papageorgiou, E.: Driving with Binocular Visual Field Loss? A Study on a Supervised On-road Parcours with Simultaneous Eye and Head Tracking. Plos One (2014). doi:10.1371/journal.pone.0087470
6. Keil, A., Albuquerque, G., Berger, K., Magnor, M.A.: Real-time gaze tracking with a consumer-grade video camera
7. Li, D., Winfield, D., Parkhurst, D.J.: Starburst: a hybrid algorithm for video-based eye tracking combining feature-based and model-based approaches. In: IEEE Computer Society Conference on Computer Vision and Pattern Recognition-Workshops, 2005. CVPR Workshops, pp. 79–79. IEEE (2005)
8. Lin, L., Pan, L., Wei, L., Yu, L.: A robust and accurate detection of pupil images. In: 2010 3rd International Conference on Biomedical Engineering and Informatics (BMEI), vol. 1, pp. 70–74. IEEE (2010)
9. Liu, X., Xu, F., Fujimura, K.: Real-time eye detection and tracking for driver observation under various light conditions. In: IEEE Intelligent Vehicle Symposium, 2002, vol. 2, pp. 344–351. IEEE (2002)
10. Long, X., Tonguz, O.K., Kiderman, A.: A high speed eye tracking system with robust pupil center estimation algorithm. In: 29th Annual International Conference of the IEEE on Engineering in Medicine and Biology Society. EMBS 2007, pp. 3331–3334. IEEE (2007)
11. Mohammed, G.J., Hong, B.R., Jarjes, A.A.: Accurate pupil features extraction based on new projection function. Computing and Informatics **29**(4), 663–680 (2012)
12. Peréz, A., Cordoba, M., Garcia, A., Méndez, R., Munoz, M., Pedraza, J.L., Sanchez, F.: A precise eye-gaze detection and tracking system
13. Schnipke, S.K., Todd, M.W.: Trials and tribulations of using an eye-tracking system. In: CHI 2000 extended abstracts on Human factors in computing systems, pp. 273–274. ACM (2000)
14. Sippel, K., Kasneci, E., Aehling, K., Heister, M., Rosenstiel, W., Schiefer, U., Papageorgiou, E.: Binocular Glaucomatous Visual Field Loss and Its Impact on Visual Exploration - A Supermarket Study. PLoS ONE **9**(8), e106089 (2014)

15. Świrski, L., Bulling, A., Dodgson, N.: Robust real-time pupil tracking in highly off-axis images. In: Proceedings of the Symposium on Eye Tracking Research and Applications, pp. 173–176. ACM (2012)
16. Tafaj, E., Kasneci, G., Rosenstiel, W., Bogdan, M.: Bayesian online clustering of eye movement data. In: Proceedings of the Symposium on Eye Tracking Research and Applications, ETRA 2012, pp. 285–288. ACM (2012)
17. Tafaj, E., Kübler, T.C., Kasneci, G., Rosenstiel, W., Bogdan, M.: Online classification of eye tracking data for automated analysis of traffic hazard perception. In: Mladenov, V., Koprinkova-Hristova, P., Palm, G., Villa, A.E.P., Appollini, B., Kasabov, N. (eds.) ICANN 2013. LNCS, vol. 8131, pp. 442–450. Springer, Heidelberg (2013)
18. Tafaj, E., Kübler, T., Peter, J., Schiefer, U., Bogdan, M., Rosenstiel, W.: Vishnoo - an open-source software for vision research. In: Proceedings of the 24th IEEE International Symposium on Computer-Based Medical Systems, CBMS 2011, pp. 1–6. IEEE (2011)
19. Valenti, R., Gevers, T.: Accurate eye center location through invariant isocentric patterns. Transactions on pattern analysis and machine intelligence **34**(9), 1785–1798 (2012)
20. Yuen, H., Illingworth, J., Kittler, J. Ellipse detection using the hough transform. In: Alvey Vision Conference, pp. 1–8 (1988)
21. Zhu, D., Moore, S.T., Raphan, T.: Robust pupil center detection using a curvature algorithm. Computer methods and programs in biomedicine **59**(3), 145–157 (1999)

Textured Object Recognition: Balancing Model Robustness and Complexity

Guido Manfredi[1,2]([✉]), Michel Devy[2], and Daniel Sidobre[1,2]

[1] LAAS CNRS, F-31400 Toulouse, France
[2] Univ. de Toulouse, UPS, Toulouse, France
gmanfred,michel,daniel@laas.fr

Abstract. When it comes to textured object modelling, the standard practice is to use a multiple views approach. The numerous views allow reconstruction and provide robustness to viewpoint change but yield complex models. This paper shows that robustness with lighter models can be achieved through robust descriptors. A comparison between various descriptors allows choosing the one providing the best viewpoint robustness, in this case the ASIFT descriptor. Then, using this descriptor, the results show, for a wide variety of object shapes, that as few as seventeen views provide a high level of robustness to viewpoint change while being fast to process and having a small memory footprint. This work concludes advocating in favour of modelling methods using robust descriptors and a small number of views.

Keywords: Object modelling · Object recognition · Multiple views · Robust descriptors

1 Introduction

For textured objects recognition, current modelling methods rely on hundreds of views to build models containing tens of thousands of local descriptors. In object recognition problems, an image is compared to known models to identify objects present in the scene. The objects of interest can have any pose, i.e. the object-to-image transform can be of any type, see the transform types Table 1. To ensure recognition under any transform, current modelling methods aim for viewpoint invariant models. This is generally achieved by including numerous views of the object and produces complex models. The drawback of such approach is that complex models are harder to build, slower to process and their many descriptors increase the chances of confusion. Though solutions exists to reduce the processing time through efficient matching [13,18], these methods do not solve the loading time, disc access, storage or confusion issues. We believe that, for many applications, full invariance is excessive and some blind spots in the model are acceptable. Moreover, this paper advocates in favour of using robust descriptors to reduce the number of views required to achieve a given level of viewpoint robustness.

© Springer International Publishing Switzerland 2015
G. Azzopardi and N. Petkov (Eds.): CAIP 2015, Part I, LNCS 9256, pp. 52–63, 2015.
DOI: 10.1007/978-3-319-23192-1_5

Table 1. List of transforms that the image of an object can undergo depending on the viewpoint. The variables t_x, t_y, $r_{i,j}$, s, $a_{i,j}$ and $h_{i,j}$ are respectively translation, rotation, scale, affine and homography coefficients.

Name	Matrix	Figures
Euclidean	$\begin{pmatrix} r_{1,1} & r_{1,2} & t_x \\ r_{2,1} & r_{2,2} & t_y \\ 0 & 0 & 1 \end{pmatrix}$	
Similarity	$\begin{pmatrix} sr_{1,1} & sr_{1,2} & t_x \\ sr_{2,1} & sr_{2,2} & t_y \\ 0 & 0 & 1 \end{pmatrix}$	
Affine	$\begin{pmatrix} a_{1,1} & a_{1,2} & t_x \\ a_{2,1} & a_{2,2} & t_y \\ 0 & 0 & 1 \end{pmatrix}$	
Projective	$\begin{pmatrix} h_{1,1} & h_{1,2} & h_{1,3} \\ h_{2,1} & h_{2,2} & h_{2,3} \\ h_{3,1} & h_{3,2} & t_{3,3} \end{pmatrix}$	

Indeed, robustness to viewpoint change can be achieved through two different paradigms.

- Multiple Views: The model can be made robust to a given transform type by including multiple views of the object, under a wide variety of the given transform. For example, to achieve in-plane rotation invariance, the model should include multiple images of the object with different in-plane rotation angles. This method requires numerous views and creates a complex model.
- Robust Descriptors: Some image descriptors already carry their own invariance to given transforms. By using these descriptors, the resulting model acquires the descriptor's invariance. For example, Harris cornerness descriptors [5] are invariant to in-plane rotation. Thus, a model using Harris descriptors is invariant to object rotation in the camera plane. Usually, a descriptor robust to complex transforms has higher dimensionality.

Though the multiple views paradigm is the most popular, this paper shows that a correct balance between both paradigms produces light models with high robustness to viewpoint change.

The contribution of this work is twofold. First, a methodology to assess the robustness of a recognition model is proposed in Section 3. Scanning an object observation half-sphere allows finding the blind spots positions and size. Then, this methodology is put to use on 272 models to get an insight into the balance between number of views and viewpoint robustness. Results presented in Section 4 suggest that as few as seventeen views provide high robustness while keeping complexity low.

The next section describes the multiple view and robust descriptors paradigms in more detail and covers the corresponding literature.

2   Previous Works

Few works have tackled the specific problem of modelling for recognition [12,16]. In a notable effort, Waibel et al. [21] created a tool to build models by scanning objects. But it is hard to control the complexity of the resulting models which tend to be large and complex. The previous works rely on the multiple views paradigm, described hereafter. However, the modelling can also rely on the robust features paradigm. This section presents the two main paradigms used when modelling for recognition and their state of the art.

2.1   Multiple Views Paradigm

The general idea is to build an object's 3-D model, from pictures or a video stream. Then, synthetic views of the 3-D model are generated by moving a virtual camera around it under various transforms. Descriptors are extracted from each view and added to the model. More different views imply more robustness to viewpoint change. The aim is to have numerous views for all type of image-to-object transform. To the best of our knowledge, few works tried to merge the 3-D modelling and recognition modelling processes [16].

To build the 3-D model, the object recognition community relies on techniques originating both from photogrammetry [20] and Structure from Motion [14]. These methods allow building a 3-D model of the observed scene from a large set of overlapping images. By matching point features on two images and using multiple view geometry [6], one can compute the motion between the two cameras. The motion information allows triangulating [7] the matched features to get 3-D points, i.e. the structure information. The idea can be applied offline or online.

The offline methods use a fixed set of images, or views, to create a model. Such algorithm selects two initial images to compute a baseline, the first motion, according to some criterion. This is often done by adding a known pattern to the scene in order to set the scale factor. Then, the other images are added to the model one by one. Finally, a bundle adjustment algorithm is run on the model. As an example, the software Bundler allows accurate reconstruction of large scenes, like a city [19], in the form of a point cloud. It can be combined with the work from Ponce and Furukawa [4] which allows turning this point cloud into a full 3-D model. The main drawback is that the views must be taken carefully to have enough overlap and cover the scene properly. Recently, Autocad released 123DCatch [2], a software which allows creating a textured model of an object from a limited set of views. The modelling itself is made offline, in the cloud. Then, the user retrieves a textured 3-D model. To facilitate access for non experts, the software guides the user in finding good views for the model. But even with this help, getting a precise 3-D model requires expertise and understanding of the underlying techniques.

The online methods build a model incrementally by adding new views as they are taken, usually from a video stream. The overlap between views is computed automatically and a new view is added when the overlap is not sufficient for precise motion estimation. Usually, while modelling is under way, a bundle adjustment algorithm enforces coherence within the data. The work from [12] shows an online object modelling program using the 3-D model under construction to help further modelling. They also regularly run a bundle adjustment for increased precision. Royer et al. [17] proposed a similar method for modelling but the bundle adjustment is only run on the most recent parts of the reconstructed model.

All these methods share the same defect, they need numerous images to cover all possible transforms. This yields large and complex models.

2.2   Robust Descriptors Paradigm

Instead of capturing views of the object under different transforms, the robust descriptors paradigm relies on descriptors robust to these transforms. As the descriptors handle the robustness to transforms, a smaller amount of views is required. The following goes over some of the most popular descriptors.

The cornerness descriptor [5] captures the structure of the local neighbourhood with an auto-correlation matrix. It is robust to translations and rotations. The SIFT descriptor [9] relies on histograms of gradients and a multi-scale simulation to achieve high degree of robustness against translation, rotation and scale. The authors of the SURF descriptor [3] use Haar wavelets to approximate the Hessian over a local image patch. The integral image technique allows fast computation. These approaches are robust to translation, rotation and scale. Recently, Yu et al. proposed the ASIFT descriptor [22], an extension of the SIFT descriptor which handles affine transforms. The image being described is simulated under different affine transforms, providing robustness to affine transforms.

These descriptors have high discriminative power at the cost of a high dimensionality. Inspired by the CENSUS transform [23], various works have tackled this problem by focusing on binary descriptors. The ORB descriptor [18] uses differences of pixels to form a binary vector. Proposed by Alahi et al. and inspired by the retina, the FREAK descriptor [1] uses differences of Gaussians to create a binary string.

Finally, the so-called Calonder descriptor [11] is created through a learning process. This descriptor learns, on a set of images, how to be robust against different transforms that are present in the training set. Though having showed good results, it is seldom used. For a detailed comparison of local descriptors performances, see the work from Mikolajczyk et al. [10].

This Section has introduced the two main paradigms available when modelling an object. They are complementary, but finding a right balance between the number of views and strength of features while keeping the model complexity low is a hard task.

In the next section, a robust descriptor is chosen for our experiments. Then various models are compared, with different number of views, to provide an insight about how to find a right balance between robustness to viewpoint change, model complexity and processing time.

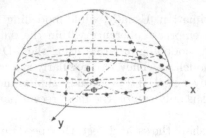

Fig. 1. The observation half-sphere around an object sampled with angular steps θ and ϕ.

3   Comparing Models

The general idea is to build a model with a given number of views and a descriptor type. Then scan the observation half-sphere around a test object and find out from how many points of view the object is correctly recognized. Scanning the full observation half-sphere in a continuous way is not possible, so it is sampled discretely as illustrated in Figure 1. This sampling method tend to over-represent the sphere's poles. In this work, care is taken to keep some distance between the sampling points and the pole. In the experiments, the minimum θ angle is 30°.

3.1   Comparison Method

Consider a set of RGB views of an object, these views form the object set. To create a model, one selects D, a descriptor type, and N views from the object set. These N views form the model set. The model set is for training and the object set is for testing.

Each view in the object set is compared with each view of the model set, using the descriptors D. For each couple of object-model views, matches are extracted and filtered using the fundamental matrix.

For a given object view, the best matching model view is the one with the maximum number of remaining matches. A percentage is obtained by dividing the number of matches by the total number of descriptors in the object view. If the percentage of matches is superior to a threshold, fixed for the whole experiment, then the recognition is considered as successful for this pose. As will be explained later, the dataset provides views with an approximately 9° spacing, so there is no data for some angles. In this case, the number of matches is interpolated by computing a mean between the closest informative points.

3.2   Comparison Metrics

When building a model for recognition, three properties are desirable: robustness to viewpoint changes, low size and low processing time. Viewpoint robustness is measured by quantifying the size of the model's blind regions. The blind regions are the angles from which a camera would not be able to recognize the object, for a given model. The blind region size is measured with the total blind region, i.e. the sum of all blind regions, expressed in degrees. The smaller the total blind region, the higher the viewpoint robustness. The size of a model has no direct impact on the recognition performances but it is crucial when scaling up the number of objects. Models weighting various gigabytes will be hard to store when becoming numerous. It can even come to the point where disc access speed may slow down the overall process. The model size is measured in megabytes. Finally, the complexity of a model impacts the processing speed. It depends on the number of views incorporated in the model, and the dimensionality of the descriptors used to characterise these views. The processing speed is computed in seconds.

The next section describes two experiments to help select a robust descriptor and assess the viewpoint robustness, size and processing time of models depending on the number of views used to create them.

4   Experiments and Results

Some descriptors provide high robustness to viewpoint change but at the cost of longer processing time and/or higher model complexity. Before comparing models, the dataset is presented and the choice of the ASIFT descriptor for this experiment is justified.

4.1   Dataset: Washington RGB-D

This dataset comes from the work of Lai et al. [8]. It has been acquired by rotating an object on a turntable in front of a couple of sensors equivalent to a RGB-D camera.

For a given object, the camera samples the observation half-sphere with an approximate step of 9° around the vertical axis (pan); and at positions of 30°, 45° and 60° above the horizontal plan (tilt), see Figure 2. The resulting dataset contains RGB and depth pictures for 300 objects from 51 categories. Only the

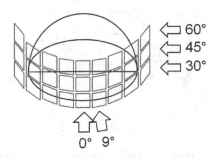

Fig. 2. The horizontal sampling is approximately 9° with three tilt position, 30°, 45° and 60°.

RGB pictures are used for this experiment. There are roughly 250 pictures per object, though approximately 160 pictures are labelled with an angular pose. Because texture is necessary for this experiment, only the following categories are considered: cereal box, food bag, food box, food can, food jar, instant noodles, soda can, water bottle. This makes a total of 68 objects from 8 categories, see Figure 3. The goal when using various objects is to account for different objects geometries. In this dataset, objects in the same categories have similar geometry. For this reason, the results shown are the mean over the objects from each categories.

Fig. 3. An example for each of the considered categories. From left to right: cereal box, food can, instant noodles, soda can, food box, food bag, food jar, water bottle.

4.2 Preliminary Experiment

The goal of this preliminary experiment is to select the best descriptor for the rest of the experiments. An object is matched with a simplified model made of two views, chosen arbitrarily at 90° and 270°, see Figure 4. Five descriptors are compared: ASIFT, SIFT, SURF, ORB and FREAK. Each one is computed on key points obtained with their classically associated detectors, respectively SIFT, SIFT, SURF, Oriented FAST and FAST [15] detectors.

The model and the object contain two identical views, the 90° and 270° views, two peaks in the percent of matches are expected, corresponding to these identical views being matched, and few matches away from the peaks. Because the objects are not perfectly aligned, at most three successive small peaks are visible, one for each tilt position (30°, 45° and 60°). Note that the curve reaches 100% matches when all points from the three tilt positions match.

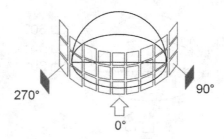

Fig. 4. The framed squares represent the views from the object set. The plain squares are the views selected to build the model set. In this experiment, the model views are located at 90° and 270°.

To quantify the descriptors performance, a model curve is constructed. This curve is equal to one around $90° \pm 20°$ and $270° \pm 20°$, and zero otherwise. Ideally, the descriptor's curves should look like the model. The Frechet distance from each curve to the model is computed to obtain an error measure. The Frechet distance between two curves A and B is defined as,

$$F(A, B) = \inf_{\alpha,\beta} \max_{t \in [0,1]} \{d(A(\alpha(t)), B(\beta(t)))\}$$

A small distance means that the descriptor produces a curve close to the model. The distances for each descriptor and category are summarised Table 2. According to the overall mean, ORB and FREAK exhibit high error. The SIFT descriptor has medium error. On the other hand, ASIFT and SURF have the lowest errors, though ASIFT error is lower than SURF's.

Table 2. Frechet distances between the curve generated with the ASIFT, SIFT, SURF, ORB and FREAK descriptors and a model curve. Values are multiplied by 10^{-3} for clarity.

	ASIFT	SIFT	SURF	ORB	FREAK
cereal box	0.73	0.70	0.75	0.72	0.71
food can	0.69	0.95	0.74	0.91	0.85
instant noodles	0.72	0.80	0.73	0.74	0.96
soda can	0.73	0.89	0.78	1.07	0.91
food box	0.69	0.69	0.70	0.63	0.89
food bag	0.74	0.72	0.74	0.78	0.81
food jar	0.71	0.91	0.77	1.09	0.84
water bottle	0.74	0.83	0.75	0.81	0.87
mean	**0.72**	**0.81**	**0.74**	**0.84**	**0.85**

To gain further understanding, the curves for the food box category are shown Figure 5. As can be seen, ORB, and FREAK descriptors show numerous peaks and find many matches independent of the angle, thus false matches. These descriptors are binary descriptors, fast to match but with lower dimensionality, thus lower discriminative power. The SURF curve tend to have a high match percentage where there are no training images, thus false matches. For their part, ASIFT and SIFT descriptors behave similarly showing peaks around the training images positions and low percent of matches elsewhere, but ASIFT tend to fit better the model. ASIFT uses an affine approximation of the object to account for affine transforms. As noted by Lowe in [9], for a given affine transform, the approximation error can be bounded by the projected diameter of the object's circumscribing sphere times a constant. It seems reasonable to believe that SIFT and ASIFT giving similar results hints to the fact that this affine approximation is not valid for objects of this size. Nevertheless, because of its lower error score, ASIFT is chosen to perform the next experiment.

4.3   Models Comparison

Given the descriptor type and an object, successive models are created using more and more views. The models are compared with the comparison metrics described

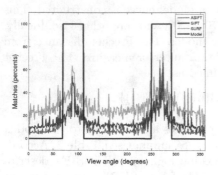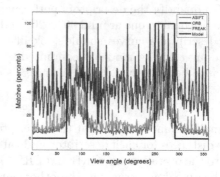

Fig. 5. Results for the food box category two views model. ASIFT is provided in both curves for comparison.

in the previous section in order to look for the best compromise between model robustness, model size and processing speed. There are 40 views per tilt position, so four models are built using 4, 8, 17 and 33 views uniformly distributed, with tilt 45°. As noted earlier, the ASIFT descriptor is used in this experiment. Each model is then matched to the full object. Two views are considered as matching if at least 30% of their key points are matching, this threshold is chosen empirically. Key points are matched with a nearest neighbour approach and Lowe's distance ratio is used to discard unlikely matches. Moreover, a RANSAC scheme with a Perspective-N-Point algorithm allows removing matches which are not consistent with a rigid motion.

The results are presented in Table 3. In terms of blind spots, one should account for the number of views in the model and the fact that there are three tilt positions. Indeed, a sum of blind spots of 100° is likely to mean a $100/3 = 33°$ sum per tilt position. Moreover, the blind spots are in all probability distributed between the model views. So if the model has 30 views, it is likely that there is a 1° blind spot between two views. This seems low enough to be acceptable, especially for application where moving the camera is possible. Overall, the gain for going from 4 or 8 views to 17 views is higher than going from 17 to 33 views. Plus, using 17 views seems to produce models quite robust as in the worst case the blind spot sum is 224°, which is means about 4° between each view. If robustness is to be favoured, using 33 views in the model provides a high degree or robustness, with a minimum sum of 19°, which is 0.19° between two views, to a maximum of 171°, 1.7° between two views. For the particular case of the food can category, a model with 8 views is sufficient for recognition with 3.3° of blind spots between two views. This may be due to the cylindrical shape which provide features appearance changing smoothly.

With regard to the matching time, it should be as low as possible to allow recognition of various objects simultaneously and at high frame rate. Note that the results shown Table 3 have been obtained with a brute-force nearest neighbour. The matching speed scales directly with the number of views in the model. Though matching various objects with a model made from four views is tractable

Table 3. For each considered category, this Table shows the number of views in the model, total sum of blind spots, mean matching time and mean size of the model. The rounded mean and standard deviation over all categories are provided at the bottom row. This experiment considers 360° pan positions and 3 tilt positions.

Category	Views	Blind spots (degs)	Time (s)	Size (Mb)
cereal box	4	243	0.30	2.96
	8	165	0.64	6.59
	17	123	1.36	14.03
	33	99	2.70	26.67
food can	4	216	0.07	0.24
	8	80	0.16	0.48
	17	27	0.33	1.03
	33	19	0.65	2.00
instant noodles	4	323	0.10	0.55
	8	274	0.21	1.39
	17	217	0.45	2.98
	33	170	0.88	5.83
soda can	4	283	0.08	0.28
	8	220	0.16	0.56
	17	188	0.34	1.18
	33	171	0.67	2.28
food box	4	253	0.13	1.27
	8	160	0.28	2.99
	17	100	0.57	6.32
	33	75	1.12	12.26
food bag	4	327	0.21	2.04
	8	295	0.47	4.79
	17	224	0.88	10.31
	33	163	0.58	20.12
food jar	4	205	0.06	0.25
	8	102	0.14	0.51
	17	41	0.30	1.09
	33	33	0.60	2.13
water bottle	4	326	0.10	0.55
	8	286	0.21	1.13
	17	219	0.45	2.41
	33	155	0.87	4.68
mean / std-dev	**4**	**272/47**	**0.13/0.08**	**1.01/0.94**
	8	**198/78**	**0.28/0.16**	**2.30/2.14**
	17	**142/76**	**0.58/0.34**	**4.91/4.58**
	33	**111/59**	**1.0/0.66**	**9.49/8.76**

it quickly becomes time consuming when using more views in the models. With seventeen views it is possible to have a recognition time inferior to the second. The high variances in time processing comes from the varying number of key points extracted for each category.

Concerning the size of the resulting model, it is proportional to the number of views. Once again the high variance can be explained by the number of key points extracted for each object. If models of one megabytes with 4 views are acceptable, it becomes ten times heavier when using 33 views and thus impractical.

5   Conclusion

This work shows that seventeen views are sufficient to create models robust to out of plane rotation. Added to the translation invariance, in plane rotation robustness and scale invariance of the ASIFT descriptor, it yields models highly robust to viewpoint change. The small image set compensate for the complexity of the descriptors and overall the models are light and fast to process when compared with models using hundreds of views. Though creating light models seems to be the way to go, most modelling methods rely on overlapping images and does not allow to do so. Future work involves developing methods to create light yet robust models in a simple fashion.

References

1. Alahi, A., Ortiz, R., Vandergheynst, P.: Freak: fast retina keypoint. In: 2012 IEEE Conference on Computer Vision and Pattern Recognition (CVPR), pp. 510–517. IEEE (2012)
2. Autodesk: 123d catch (2014). http://www.123dapp.com/catch (accessed: September 30, 2010)
3. Bay, H., Ess, A., Tuytelaars, T., Van Gool, L.: Speeded-up robust features (surf). Computer Vision and Image Understanding 110(3), 346–359 (2008)
4. Furukawa, Y., Ponce, J.: Accurate, dense, and robust multiview stereopsis. IEEE Transactions on Pattern Analysis and Machine Intelligence 32(8), 1362–1376 (2010)
5. Harris, C., Stephens, M.: A combined corner and edge detector. In: Alvey vision conference, vol. 15, p. 50. Manchester, UK (1988)
6. Hartley, R., Zisserman, A.: Multiple view geometry in computer vision. Cambridge University Press (2003)
7. Hartley, R.I., Sturm, P.: Triangulation. Computer Vision and Image Understanding 68(2), 146–157 (1997)
8. Lai, K., Bo, L., Ren, X., Fox, D.: A large-scale hierarchical multi-view rgb-d object dataset. In: 2011 IEEE International Conference on Robotics and Automation (ICRA), pp. 1817–1824. IEEE (2011)
9. Lowe, D.G.: Distinctive image features from scale-invariant keypoints. International Journal of Computer Vision 60(2), 91–110 (2004)
10. Mikolajczyk, K., Schmid, C.: A performance evaluation of local descriptors. IEEE Transactions on Pattern Analysis and Machine Intelligence 27(10), 1615–1630 (2005)
11. Ozuysal, M., Calonder, M., Lepetit, V., Fua, P.: Fast keypoint recognition using random ferns. IEEE Transactions on Pattern Analysis and Machine Intelligence 32(3), 448–461 (2010)

12. Pan, Q., Reitmayr, G., Drummond, T.: Proforma: probabilistic feature-based on-line rapid model acquisition. In: BMVC, pp. 1–11 (2009)
13. Papazov, Chavdar, Burschka, Darius: An efficient RANSAC for 3D object recognition in noisy and occluded scenes. In: Kimmel, Ron, Klette, Reinhard, Sugimoto, Akihiro (eds.) ACCV 2010, Part I. LNCS, vol. 6492, pp. 135–148. Springer, Heidelberg (2011)
14. Pollefeys, M., Koch, R., Vergauwen, M., Van Gool, L.: Flexible acquisition of 3d structure from motion. In: Proc. IEEE workshop on Image and Multidimensional Digital Signal Processing. Citeseer (1998)
15. Rosten, Edward, Drummond, Tom W.: Machine learning for high-speed corner detection. In: Leonardis, Aleš, Bischof, Horst, Pinz, Axel (eds.) ECCV 2006, Part I. LNCS, vol. 3951, pp. 430–443. Springer, Heidelberg (2006)
16. Rothganger, F., Lazebnik, S., Schmid, C., Ponce, J.: 3d object modeling and recognition using local affine-invariant image descriptors and multi-view spatial constraints. International Journal of Computer Vision 66(3), 231–259 (2006)
17. Royer, E., Lhuillier, M., Dhome, M., Chateau, T.: Localization in urban environments: monocular vision compared to a differential gps sensor. In: IEEE Computer Society Conference on Computer Vision and Pattern Recognition. CVPR 2005, vol. 2, pp. 114–121. IEEE (2005)
18. Rublee, E., Rabaud, V., Konolige, K., Bradski, G.: Orb: an efficient alternative to sift or surf. In: 2011 IEEE International Conference on Computer Vision (ICCV), pp. 2564–2571. IEEE (2011)
19. Snavely, N., Seitz, S.M., Szeliski, R.: Modeling the world from internet photo collections. International Journal of Computer Vision 80(2), 189–210 (2008)
20. Sturm, Peter: A historical survey of geometric computer vision. In: Real, Pedro, Diaz-Pernil, Daniel, Molina-Abril, Helena, Berciano, Ainhoa, Kropatsch, Walter (eds.) CAIP 2011, Part I. LNCS, vol. 6854, pp. 1–8. Springer, Heidelberg (2011)
21. Waibel, M., Beetz, M., Civera, J., D'Andrea, R., Elfring, J., Galvez-Lopez, D., Haussermann, K., Janssen, R., Montiel, J.M.M., Perzylo, A., Schiessle, B., Tenorth, M., Zweigle, O., van de Molengraft, R.: Roboearth. IEEE Robotics Automation Magazine 18(2), 69–82 (2011)
22. Yu, G., Morel, J.M.: ASIFT: an algorithm for fully affine invariant comparison. Image Processing On Line 2011 (2011)
23. Zabih, R., Woodfill, J.: A non-parametric approach to visual correspondence. In: IEEE transactions on pattern analysis and machine intelligence. Citeseer (1996)

Review of Methods to Predict Social Image Interestingness and Memorability

Xesca Amengual$^{(\boxtimes)}$, Anna Bosch, and Josep Lluís de la Rosa

DEEEA, Centre Easy, Agents Research LAB, Universitat de Giroan, Girona, Spain
{xesca.amengual,peplluis}@silver.udg.edu, annabosch@easyinnova.com

Abstract. An entire industry has developed around keyword optimization for ad buyers. However, social media landscape has shift to a photo driven behavior and there is a need to overcome the challenge to analyze all this large amount of visual data that users post in internet. We will address this analysis by providing a review on how to measure image and video interestingness and memorability from content that is tacked spontaneously in social networks. We will investigate current state-of-the-art of methods analyzing social media images and provide further research directions that could be beneficial for both, users and companies.

Keywords: Interestingness · Memorability · Image · Video · Review

1 Introduction

The total number of internet users around the world was stated up to three billion in 2014[1] whereas the number of social network users worldwide from 2010 to 2014 has grown from 0.97 billion users to 1.79. In 2016, it is estimated that there will be around 2.13 billion social network users around the globe, up from 1.4 billion in 2012[2]. The amount of users generated data is huge and there is a need to provide tools to automatically process it.

To date, internet data and specifically social networks generated data have been monetized primarily by text-based applications. In fact, an entire industry has developed around keyword optimization for ad buyers, text analysis for opinion [1] and sentiment discovery [2], brand positioning [3], user behavior [4] and so on. Words drive economy of the web. However, it appears that Social Networks are now more show than tell. The shift to a personal newspaper-style format with larger and more prominent photo displays is a response to photo driven behavior that has rapidly changed the social media landscape. Machines that monetize the internet need to keep up with the times to analyze the large amount of uploaded photographs and video to internet.

The motivation of this work is twofold. First, it is well known that some images/videos get much more views than others so there is a need to understand what makes an image or a video more interesting/popular/memorable[3]

---

[1] http://www.internetlivestats.com/internet-users/
[2] http://www.statista.com/statistics/278414/
[3] In this paper we consider interesting and popular as synonyms

© Springer International Publishing Switzerland 2015
G. Azzopardi and N. Petkov (Eds.): CAIP 2015, Part I, LNCS 9256, pp. 64–76, 2015.
DOI: 10.1007/978-3-319-23192-1_6

Fig. 1. Images ranked by their interestingness (top row) and memorability (bo0ttom row). Images are sortd form high (left) to low (right) score. [5,6]

than others from a computer vision perspective (Fig. 1). Some works have recently started to address this theme with different techniques and methodologies, so a review to state best methodologies and further directions is needed. Second, text is no longer enough to provide monetization tools over the current internet behavior, there is a need to include knowledge from images in this process. We will provide here some clues on how this information could be considered. The rest of the paper is organized as follows. Since interestingness and memorability have different objectives, we provide, in Section 2 and 3, an overview of the most relevant research works respectively. The used datasets are detailed in Section 4. Finally, in Section 5 we give the conclusions and future work.

2   Interestingness

Interestingness is said to be the power of attracting or holding ones attention. This property has been object of study with several goals, such as knowledge discovery [7], association patterns [8] or Wikipedia data [9]. In this survey we focus on image and video interestingness. For years, psychological researchers have proposed several variables that affect interestingness measures. Berlyne [10] considered novelty, uncertainty, conflict and complexity, whereas Chen et al. [11] identified novelty, challenge, instant enjoyment and demand for attention as the most relevant cues. According to [12] high pleasantness was the major aspect of interestingness and [13] supported the presence of polygons and painting.

Although interestingness is clearly a subjective property and depends on personal preferences and experiences, there exists a significant agreement among users about which images are considered more interesting than others, and this has encouraged researches from psychology and now from computer vision to learn more about this topic. In addition, video interestingness research has also been addressed by the computer vision field for different applications such as video retrieval or video summarization by selecting the most interesting scenes.

2.1 State-of-the-Art

To the best of our knowledge, the study of image interestingness is a novel research line and there are only a few papers addressing this topic from a computer vision perspective. Some studies compare their predictions with crowdsourcing results [14–16] whereas others prefer to compare them with the actual interestingness or popularity raised by images in social networks [5,17–19]. In addition to image features, the usefulness of social cues is studied for the latter choice.

Grabner et al. [14] investigate how different features perform to determine which events are considered of interest in image sequences recorded by a static video camera. They highlight emotion (depending on brightness an saturation), complexity (bytes of encoded image) and novelty (outlier detection) of images, as well as, an interestingness score learned directly from gist features using a ν-SVR. Performance of individual features states that novelty is the best cue for this task, however best results are obtained when combining all of them by training a simple linear model with a ν-SVR. Even though the proposed cues are of interest, the context of image sequences plays an important role on the performed experiments and one may think that this method cannot be extended to other less contextualized image datasets.

In [15] authors study the correlation of interestingness with aesthetics and memorability. They find that interestingness is really correlated with aesthetics but, contrary to the popular belief, the correlation with memorability is very low. They train a ν-SVR to build a predictor using several cues, some of them taken from previous work [14] and other novel features for the purpose of interestingness prediction (see Table 1 for the specific features used). These attributes are selected to emphasize aspects such as unusualness, aesthetics and other general preferences. The method is applied over three datasets (the Webcam dataset (WD) used in [14] of strong context, the Scene Categories dataset (SCD) [20] of weak context and the Memorability dataset (MD) [6] of arbitrary photos) and predictions are compared with the ground truth obtained by crowdsourcing tools. Results show that unusualness is the most useful cue to predict interestingness for strong context, whereas general preferences are more relevant for weaker contexts. These experiments highlight the importance of the image type, layout and context when estimating its interestingness.

Recently, crowdsourcing tools are employed to obtain less subjective and more reliable annotations of the datasets. However, it brings new problems such as sparse and outliers annotations. While above approaches [14,15] prune the annotation outliers by majority voting, a new approach to globally detect outliers is proposed in [16]. They propose a Unified Robust Learning to Rank (URLR) framework to identify annotation outliers and, simultaneously, to build an interestingness ranking. This method is applied in WD [14,15] and in a YouTube dataset [21] for image and video interestingness respectively (details of video results in Section 2.2). The experiments of image ranking prediction outperforms [15], proving the efficiency of the novel outlier detection model.

In contrast with [14–16], Dhar et al. [5] use the actual interestingness in social networks (number of views, popularity of user, etc.) to obtain the ground truth in order to avoid the crowdsourcing drawbacks and compare predictions with real behavior since, usually, the users concept of interestingness is not consistent with their behavior on social networks when selecting images to share or like. They study how aesthetic cues may be useful to predict image interestingness over Flickr photos, becoming a benchmark for most of the subsequent works on this research branch. The studied cues, referred as *high level describable attributes*, are: compositional attributes (layout of images), content attributes (presence of specific objects, categories of objects) and Sky-illumination attributes (natural outdoor illumination). They train a SVM to predict both image aesthetic and interestingness. Precision-Recall curves show good performance using high level attributes and better results when combining with low level features.

Some other approaches are focused on the prediction of image interestingness using social platforms information such as the number of views, likes or shares an image receives as a complement of visual cues. In [17], authors distinguish between Visual Interestingness (VI) and Social Interestingness (SI) since an image could be considered interesting due to its visual content or its social context. The VI score of each image is related to the crowdsourcing results whereas the SI score is provided by the photo sharing services Flickr and Pinterest and depends on statistics such as the number of likes, comments or number of users sharing the image. Hsieh et al. [17] investigate the correlation between VI, SI, and image aesthetics. Results show, more formally than [5,15], a high correlation between VI and image aesthetics. It is also exposed the small or null correlation between VI and SI indicating that beautiful images are not the more likely to be shared by users in social networks. They also build a predictor using low level features such as color, edge, texture and saliency. Results show that texture and color are the best features to estimate VI and SI respectively, although the experiments only use low level features which does not allow the comparison with [5] that, in contrast with this work, obtains the best results with high level features.

In [18], they explore more in depth the social cues (amount of followers, number and content of tags, uploaded time, etc.) related to SI, referred as popularity, over Instagram. They also consider semantic concepts of images that refer to the objects depicted on the images and image categories. Experiments show: (i) the most correlated cue with popularity is the number of followers. This is not a surprising result since the more followers a user has the more people will view and share its images; (ii) low correlation between the image semantic concept and its popularity in the social network. They compare popularity on Instagram with crowdsourcing scores and results show that images depicting people, stadiums, baseball or amusement parks are the most popular on Instagram whereas the least popular contain buildings, fountains or cityscapes. In contrast, the user study selects images containing cityscapes, animals, restaurants or fountains as the most popular and people and buildings images as the least popular.

These conflicting results evidence the importance to consider SI to predict if an image will be interesting or popular in social networks. With this aim [19] investigates how image content and social context affect image popularity. They use features based on image content such as simple image features (hue, saturation and value), low level features (gist, texture, color patches, gradient and a learned interestingness score) and high level features (objects), whereas the features to highlight social cues are the number of views, total images uploaded by the user, number of contacts, etc. Used images are extracted from Flickr, which provides all the required social information. A SVR is trained to predict image interestingness using the aforementioned features. Results show social cues are better to estimate the number of views of an image and these are improved when social context features are complemented with image content features. They also build popularity maps of images to visualize which image regions are more influential and better understand image interestingness. Similar approaches investigate which parts of images humans look at [22] or which words are the most dominant to describe an image [23–25]. These methods can be used to generate textual descriptions of images or sort retrieved results, on image search, depending on the dominance of the attributes provided in the query.

In Table 1 we compare the best results of the studied method. We also detail their contribution and the attributes, training methods and datasets used.

2.2   What About Video?

In addition to image, the issue of how to measure video interestingness on internet is addressed from the computer vision community. Due to the subjectivity of interestingness, many papers use social cues for video popularity prediction [29–32]. However, video content is also relevant and image and audio features can be used. Thus, from the computer vision perspective, some papers have been published [16,21,33] since the first approach in 2009 [34].

The method proposed in [34] leverages Flickr images to obtain the interestingness of each frame for YouTube videos with the key point that frames similar to interesting images should also be interesting. The similarity between images depends on the scene content (SIFT features) and composition (similar content in similar location). Although preliminary results are encouraging, the experiment is restricted to travel videos that contain well-known places and only the frames similar to these famous scenes are considered interesting. With these constraints, results may not be extendable to other less bounded experiments. Another drawback of this method is that the selected images from Flick need to be manually clustered depending on the depicted scene.

Actually, Liu et al. [34] only take into account the similarity between the video frames and interesting images, what is, in fact, the same as image interestingness prediction. On the other hand, Jiang et al. [21] proposes an entire video-level prediction using visual (SIFT, HOG, SSIM and GIST), audio (Mel-Frequency Cepstral Coefficients (MFCC), Spectrogram SIFT and six basic audio

Table 1. Comparison of image interestingness methods in 5 top rows of the table. Comparison of image memorability methods in 4 top rows of the table.

Authors	Contribution	Attributes	Training	Dataset[a]	Result
Dhar et al. 2011 [5]	- High level describable attributes - Predictor of aesthetics - Predictor of interestingness	Compositional (salient objects, rule of thirds, depth of field and opposing colors), content (presence of people or animals, portrait, indoor-outdoor and scene type) and sky-Illumination (clear, cloudy or sunset).	SVM	FD	Prec-Recall curves
Grabner et al. [14]	- Predictor of interestingness in image sequences	Emotion (depending on brightness an saturation), complexity (bytes of encoded image), novelty (outlier detection) and learned interestingness score.	ν-SVR	WD	0.36[c]
Gygli et al. 2013 [15]	- Predictor of interestingness in different image context.	Unusualness (global outliers and composition of parts), aesthetics (color, arousal, complexity, contrast and edge distribution) and general preferences.	ν-SVR	WD SCD MD	0.42[c] 0.83[c] 0.77[c]
Hsieh et al. 2014 [17]	- Comparison of visual and social interestingness and aesthetics. - Predictor of VI and SI separately.	- **Color** - Texture - Saliency - Edge	Adaboost	PD	0.73[bd]
Khosla et al. 2014 [19]	- Importance of image content and social cues for popularity. - Predictor of image popularity. - Visualization of popularity of image regions.	- Image content: simple image features (hue, saturation, value and intensity), low-level features (gist, texture, color patches, gradient and a learned score) and high-level features (objects). - Social cues: mean views, photo count, contacts, groups, group members, member duration, is pro, tags, title length and description length.	SVR	VSOD UMD USD	0.81[e] 0.72[e] 0.48[e]
Isola et al. 2011 [6]	- Analysis of relevant features for image memorability. - Predictor of image memorability. - Memorability map.	Simple image features (hue, saturation, value and intensity), non-semantic object statistics (object counts and areas), **semantic object statistics** (labeled object counts and areas), **scene category and global features** (GIST, SIFT, HOG2x2 and SSIM).	SVR	MD	0.54[be]
Isola et al. 2011 [26]	- More understandable features for image memorability. - Predictor of image memorability	- General attributes: spatial layout (enclosed /open, empty/cluttered), aesthetics (dull/ attractive, pleasant), emotions (Funny?, frightening?), actions, location and people. - People attributes: visibility, gender, age, hair length and color, clothing, activities, accessories, subject and scenario. - Global features and Object and Scene annotation from [6]	SVR	MD	0.55[e]
Khosla et al. 2012 [27]	- Memorability maps - Predictor of image memorability.	- Gradient - Saliency - Color - Shape - Texture - Semantic	SVM-Rank	MD	0.50[e]
Kim et al. 2013 [28]	- Two spatial features: Weighted Object Area (WOA) and Relative Area Rank (RAR)	WOA, RAR, global features and Scene annotations from [6] and attribute annotation from [26]	ε-SVR	MD	0.58[e]

[a] Databases are detailed in Section 4   [b] Best results uses only the attributes in bold
[c] Average precision value   [d] Classification rate   [e] Spearman's rank correlation (ρ)

descriptors) and high level semantic features (object, scenes and photographic style). Authors propose a model to rank the videos instead of predicting an interestingness score. To evaluate this model they construct two benchmark datasets of Flickr and YouTube videos whose ground-truth is collected by crowdsourcing. Individual results show that videos are better ranked with visual and audio features, and their combination provides the best results. Otherwise, in contrast to [5] for image, high level attributes give the worst performance.

The approach for global outliers detection of the crowdsourcing annotations detailed in the previous section [18] also provides results for video interestingness prediction. Fu et al. apply their method (URLR) to rank videos from the dataset built by Jiang et al. [21](YTD). Comparing both methods, URLD is superior and extends its good results, not only for image, but also for video prediction.

In [33] a different approach to measure video interestingness is proposed relating interestingness to how appealing or curious is a scene. With this insight, several features to highlight affectivity, aesthetics and semantic content are extracted to find appealing scenes in a video. They train two frameworks: a binary (positive/negative labels) and a graded (multiple degrees of annotations) relevance systems, the latter yields the best results when combining all the features.

In contrast with the above reviewed work, other approaches consider video interestingness as a subjective property and tackle the prediction issue using social information such as users patterns and current tendencies on video sharing services. A benchmark work is [29] that analyze the popularity distribution and evolution of videos from YouTube and Daum Videos (popular Korean platform). Moreover, duplicated and illegal content is posed as potential problems for accurate video popularity ranking. The growth patterns of video popularity are studied in [30] over three video datasets: (i) the top lists videos, (ii) removed videos due to copyright violation and (iii) random queries videos. In addition, the mechanisms to attract users towards a video are specified finding that the internal web systems are the most relevant. Later, Figueiredo [31] present a methodology to predict trends and hits in user generated videos and Pinto et al. [32] propose to predict video popularity using early view patterns.

2.3   Conclusions

Studied papers from state-of-the-art aim to better understand which visual features make an image interesting and build predictors to estimate if an image will be shared or liked in social platforms. Studied features evidence that high level features are more useful than low level features and the high importance of social cues to predict image interestingness, and especially, when results are compared with the users behavior on social networks. They also find a low correlation between social interestingness in the net and visual interestingness and aesthetics. Combining social accounts information with low and high level features gives the best predictions of the user's behavior in photo sharing platforms.

Research on video encourage the study of visual and audio features for video retrieval that appears to be, contrary to image, more useful than high level features. As for image, aesthetic features are related with video interestingness.

3   Memorability

Image memorability has been studied by psychologists since the 70s. L. Standing [35,36] was one of the first to study the capacity of people memorizing images. Results evidenced the large memory of human being and posed the need to continue investigating. In the past 10 years, psychological researches of visual short- and long-term memory (VSTM and VLTM) have presented important results. The role of VSTM and VLTM in natural scenes perception and visual search is studiend in [37]. Other studies have focused on the amount and precision of details humans can remember in VLTM [38–40]. Contrary to the assumption that large amount of images can be remembered but with few details, results from [38] indicate that VLTM can store a large amount of image details.

Over the past few years, not only in the psychological domain, but also computer vision researchers have shown interest for the study of visual memory [6,26–28,41,42]. Image memorability is considered an intrinsic property of images that do not depend on the observer and can be explained in terms of image features. Several recent works [8, 42, 43] aim to explain why some pictures are more memorable than others finding out the most relevant features to predict image memorability. Most authors analyze the whole image, whereas few of them are focused on analyzing which image regions are more memorable [27,41].

3.1   State-of-the-Art

To the best of our knowledge, the earliest paper is from 2011 [6] and is a benchmark for the subsequent works [26–28,41]. Isola et al. [6] introduce the insight of memorability as an intrinsic property of images highly independent of the user context. This statement is supported by a user study to build a benchmark dataset (MD) that shows a high agreement between participants when memorizing images. To study which features are more significant, several are considered and they conclude that best results are obtained with object and scene semantics features, achieving the best results when combining both of them. For memorability prediction they train a SVR to map from features to memorability scores and the best prediction is performed when combining all global features (GIST [20], SIFT [43], HOG2x2 [44–46] and SSIM [47]) with object and scene semantics features. As expected, results support the use of high level features, like [5] for interestingness, since they contribute with more image information and are closer to the attributes used by human when evaluating an image.

As an extension of [6], a deeper study of relevant features is found in [26]. They complement the dataset MD from [6] with more attribute annotations referred to spatial, content and aesthetic image properties. An information-theoretic approach is used to select a set of non-redundant features and calibrate them by maximizing mutual information with memorability. Experiments with the extended annotations outperform [6] that uses only object and scene annotations. Furthermore, the information-theoretic approach provides the relevance of each feature showing that images of enclosed spaces containing people with visible faces are memorable while landscapes and peaceful images are not. Moreover, contrary to popular belief, unusualness and aesthetic attributes are not related to high image memorability. Finally, they also propose an automatic prediction using learned annotations that outperforms previous work in [6].

Kim et al. [28] consider that, although unusualness is not related to memorability [26], unusualness of the expected object size or location could be relevant and introduce two novel spatial features. One takes into account the size and location of objects supporting the hypothesis that central objects are more likely to be remembered. The second captures the unusualness of each object size depending on the object class coverage size. They obtain similar results to [6,26], but the main advantage is that these two features together perform better than object statistics from [6] and they do not required a high level human annotation.

In contrast to previous approaches, the image memorability research can be addressed by estimating which image regions may be forgotten [27] modeling automatic memorability maps and combining both local and global features with no required human annotations. Results with gradient, color, texture, saliency, shape and semantic meaning outperform state-of-the-art results [6].

As a complete novel point of view, [41] introduces the idea of visual inception that refers to the possibility of modifying the memorability of images. Experiments describe how different images with similar structure can be identified as the same image. They also pose the issue of how an image can be changed while still making people believe they have seen it. However, the experiments are not enough detailed to show consistent results. A similar approach for face photos is [42] that manipulates traits of faces to make more memorable images.

In Table 1 we compare the best predictions of the studied method. We also detail their contribution and the attributes, training methods and datasets used.

3.2 Conclusions

The publications reviewed aim to understand and predict automatically image memorability. As for interestingness, features analysis reveal the relevance of high level features due to their high contribution of image information, and find images of enclosed spaces containing people with visible faces are memorable while landscapes and peaceful images are not. Moreover, contrary to popular belief, unusual and beautiful images are not necessarily memorable, unlike for interestingness where these attributes are influential. These assumptions are supported by memorability maps generated to visualize the memorable and forgettable regions. Good prediction results support the idea that memorability is a property independent of the user context and can be predicted in terms of image features.

4 Image and Video Datasets

We detail below the different datasets used for the experiments described above:

- **Flickr dataset (FD):** 40,000 images from Flickr. It is used in [5] for image interestingness prediction.
- **Webcam dataset (WD):** 20 sequences of 159 images each, from different public webcams. It is used in [14–16] for image interestingness prediction.
- **Scene categories dataset (SCD) [23]:** 2,688 images from 8 scene categories. It is used in [15] for image interestingness prediction.
- **Memorability dataset (MD):** 2,222 images. It is used in [6, 26–28] for memorability prediction and in [15] for image interestingness prediction.
- **Pinterest dataset (PD):** 989 images from Pinterest. It is used in [17] for image interestingness prediction.
- **Visual Sentiment Ontology dataset (VSOD):** 930k images collected from 400k users of Flickr. In [19], it is referred as one-per-user dataset and used to predict image interestingness.
- **User-mix dataset (UMD):** 1.4M images of a subset of user from VSOD. It is created by selecting 100 users from VSOD that have between 10k and 20k shared images. It is used in [19] to predict image interestingness.
- **User-specific dataset (USD):** independent datasets with the images of each user from UMD. It is used in [19] for image interestingness prediction.
- **YouTube Travel dataset (YTTD):** 3 videos for each of the 10 queries from YouTube travel category. It is used for video interestingness in [34].
- **Flickr Video dataset (FVD):** 400 videos for each search (15 queries). It is used in [21] for video interestingness prediction.
- **YouTube dataset (YTD):** 30 videos for each query (14 queries). It is used in [16, 21] for video interestingness prediction.

5   Conclusions and Future Work

A review of image interestingness and memorability research has been presented. Although these properties have been studied from psychologists since the 70s, they are new on the computer vision area, the first paper is from 2011. For image interestingness, experiments show a need to differentiate between visual and social interestingness since the interesting images collected by crowdsourcing are not the same than the interesting images in social platforms. They conclude that: (i) high level features are the most useful to predict visual interestingness; (ii) image aesthetics are highly correlated with it; (iii) for social interestingness, the social features are the most relevant and their combination with image features gives the best results. Similar conclusions can be found for memorability where high level features perform the best results. However, in contrast to interestingness, memorability has a low correlation with aesthetics and unusualness.

Some of these findings can be extended to video such as the correlation between interestingness and aesthetics and the effectiveness of social context based methods. In contrast with image, low level image and audio features work better than high level features. Future work on video analysis should address the interestingness prediction combining image and audio features with social cues.

Memorability is an objective property and image features provide good results, while interestingness is more subjective and depends largely on social context.

Most works consider all users have the same context assuming the interestingness objetivity. Future research should be addressed to find common image features of most interesting images from a single user. Image features from the whole social network should also be studied to find similarities between images.

Further research on how to monetize the large amount of visual data uploaded in internet should be addressed. Interestingness and memorability scores will be used to appraise images, thus, companies will be provided with the most socially interesting and memorable images. Images owners that allow their use are rewarded with profitable assets. Also, the presence of brands could be considered to compute different image appraisal depending on each company.

Acknowledgments. This work was supported in part by VISUAL AD, RTC-2014-2566-7 and GEPID, RTC-2014-2576-7, as well as the consolidated research group CSI ref.2014 SGR 1469, and the grant of industrial PhD with expedient number 2014 DI 007.

References

1. Pang, B., Lee, L.: Opinion mining and sentiment analysis. Found. Trends Inf. Retr. **2**(1–2), 1–135 (2008)
2. Bifet, A., Frank, E.: Sentiment knowledge discovery in twitter streaming data. In: Pfahringer, B., Holmes, G., Hoffmann, A. (eds.) DS 2010. LNCS, vol. 6332, pp. 1–15. Springer, Heidelberg (2010)
3. Liu, B., Hu, M., Cheng, J.: Opinion observer: analyzing and comparing opinions on the web. In: 14th int. conf. on World Wide Web, pp. 342–351. ACM (2005)
4. Mitrović, M., Paltoglou, G., Tadić, B.: Quantitative analysis of bloggers' collective behavior powered by emotions. J. Stat. Mech: Theory Exp. (02), P02005 (2011)
5. Dhar, S., Ordonez, V., Berg, T.L.: High level describable attributes for predicting aesthetics and interestingness. In: CVPR, pp. 1657–1664. IEEE (2011)
6. Isola, P., Xiao, J., Torralba, A., Oliva, A.: What makes an image memorable? In: CVPR, pp. 145–152. IEEE (2011)
7. Silberschatz, A., Tuzhilin, A.: On subjective measures of interestingness in knowledge discovery. In: KDD, pp. 275–281 (1995)
8. Tan, P.N., Kumar, V., Srivastava, J.: Selecting the right interestingness measure for association patterns. In: ACM SIGKDD, pp. 32–41. (2002)
9. Schaul, T., Pape, L., Glasmachers, T., Graziano, V., Schmidhuber, J.: Coherence progress: a measure of interestingness based on fixed compressors. In: Schmidhuber, J., Thórisson, K.R., Looks, M. (eds.) AGI 2011. LNCS, vol. 6830, pp. 21–30. Springer, Heidelberg (2011)
10. Berlyne, D.E.: Conflict, arousal, and curiosity (1960)
11. Chen, A., Darst, P.W., Pangrazi, R.P.: An examination of situational interest and its sources. British Journal of Educational Psychology **71**(3), 383–400 (2001)
12. Smith, C.A., Ellsworth, P.C.: Patterns of cognitive appraisal in emotion. Journal of Personality and Social Psychology **48**(4), 813 (1985)
13. Turner Jr, S.A., Silvia, P.J.: Must interesting things be pleasant? a test of competing appraisal structures. Emotion **6**(4), 670 (2006)
14. Grabner, H., Nater, F., Druey, M., Van Gool, L.: Visual interestingness in image sequences. In: ACM Int. Conf. Multimed., pp. 1017–1026 (2013)

15. Gygli, M., Grabner, H., Riemenschneider, H., Nater, F., Gool, L.V.: The interestingness of images. In: ICCV, pp. 1633–1640. IEEE (2013)
16. Fu, Y., Hospedales, T.M., Xiang, T., Gong, S., Yao, Y.: Interestingness prediction by robust learning to rank. In: Fleet, D., Pajdla, T., Schiele, B., Tuytelaars, T. (eds.) ECCV 2014, Part II. LNCS, vol. 8690, pp. 488–503. Springer, Heidelberg (2014)
17. Hsieh, L.C., Hsu, W.H., Wang, H.C.: Investigating and predicting social and visual image interestingness on social media by crowdsourcing. In: ICASSP IEEE (2014)
18. Fiolet, E.: Analyzing image popularity
19. Khosla, A., Das Sarma, A., Hamid, R.: What makes an image popular? In: World Wide Web, pp. 867–876 (2014)
20. Oliva, A., Torralba, A.: Modeling the shape of the scene: a holistic representation of the spatial envelope. Int. J. Comput. Vis. **42**(3), 145–175 (2001)
21. Jiang, Y.G., Wang, Y., Feng, R., Xue, X., Zheng, Y., Yang, H.: Understanding and predicting interestingness of videos. In: AAAI. (2013)
22. Judd, T., Ehinger, K., Durand, F., Torralba, A.: Learning to predict where humans look. In: Computer Vision, pp. 2106–2113. IEEE (2009)
23. Spain, M., Perona, P.: Measuring and predicting importance of objects in our visual world. Tech. Rep. (2007)
24. Berg, A.C., Berg, T.L., Daume, H., Dodge, J., Goyal, A., Han, X., et al.: Understanding and predicting importance in images. In: CVPR, pp. 3562–3569. IEEE (2012)
25. Turakhia, N., Parikh, D.: Attribute dominance: what pops out? In: ICCV, pp. 1225–1232. IEEE (2013)
26. Isola, P., Parikh, D., Torralba, A., Oliva, A.: Understanding the intrinsic memorability of images. In: NIPS, pp. 2429–2437 (2011)
27. Khosla, A., Xiao, J., Torralba, A., Oliva, A.: Memorability of image regions. In. Advances in Neural Information Processing Systems, pp. 305–313. (2012)
28. Kim, J., Yoon, S., Pavlovic, V.: Relative spatial features for image memorability. In: ACM Multimedia, pp. 761–764 (2013)
29. Cha, M., Kwak, H., Rodriguez, P., Ahn, Y.Y., Moon, S.: Analyzing the video popularity characteristics of large-scale user generated content systems. IEEE/ACM Transactions on Networking (TON) **17**(5), 1357–1370 (2009)
30. Figueiredo, F., Benevenuto, F., Almeida, J.M.: The tube over time: characterizing popularity growth of youtube videos. In: ACM WSDM, pp. 745–754 (2011)
31. Figueiredo, F.: On the prediction of popularity of trends and hits for user generated videos. In: ACM WSDM, pp. 741–746 (2013)
32. Pinto, H., Almeida, J.M., Gonçalves, M.A.: Using early view patterns to predict the popularity of youtube videos. In: ACM WSDM, pp. 365–374 (2013)
33. Redi, M., Merialdo, B.: Where is the beauty?: Retrieving appealing videoscenes by learning flickr-based graded judgments. In: ACM Multimedia, pp. 1363–1364 (2012)
34. Liu, F., Niu, Y., Gleicher, M.: Using web photos for measuring video frame interestingness. In: IJCAI, pp. 2058–2063 (2009)
35. Standing, L., Conezio, J., Haber, R.N.: Perception and memory for pictures: Single-trial learning of 2500 visual stimuli. Psychonomic Science **19**(2), 73–74 (1970)
36. Standing, L.: Learning 10000 pictures. Q. J. Exp. Psychol. **25**(2), 207–222 (1973)
37. Hollingworth, A.: Constructing visual representations of natural scenes: the roles of short-and long-term visual memory. J. Exp. Psychol.: Hum. Percept. Perform. **30**(3), 519 (2004)

38. Brady, T.F., Konkle, T., Alvarez, G.A., Oliva, A.: Visual long-term memory has a massive storage capacity for object details. Nat. Acad. Sci. 14325–14329 (2008)
39. Konkle, T., Brady, T.F., Alvarez, G.A., Oliva, A.: Scene memory is more detailed than you think the role of categories in visual long-term memory. Psychological Science 21(11), 1551–1556 (2010)
40. Konkle, T., Brady, T.F., Alvarez, G.A., Oliva, A.: Conceptual distinctiveness supports detailed visual long-term memory for real-world objects. Journal of Experimental Psychology: General 139(3), 558 (2010)
41. Khosla, A., Xiao, J., Isola, P., Torralba, A., Oliva, A.: Image memorability and visual inception. In: SIGGRAPH Asia 2012 Technical Briefs, pp. 35. ACM (2012)
42. Khosla, A., Bainbridge, W.A., Torralba, A., Oliva, A.: Modifying the memorability of face photographs. In: ICCV, pp. 3200–3207. IEEE (2013)
43. Lazebnik, S., Schmid, C., Ponce, J.: Beyond bags of features:spatial pyramid matching for recognizing natural scene categories. In: CVPR, pp. 2169–2178. IEEE (2006)
44. Felzenszwalb, P.F., Girshick, R.B., McAllester, D., Ramanan, D.: Object detection with discriminatively trained part-based models. In: IEEE PAMI, pp. 1627–1645 (2010)
45. Dalal, N., Triggs, B.: Histograms of oriented gradients for human detection. In: CVPR, vol. 1, pp. 886–893. IEEE (2005)
46. Xiao, J., Hays, J., Ehinger, K.A., Oliva, A., Torralba, A.: Sun database: Large-scale scene recognition from abbey to zoo. In: CVPR, pp. 3485–3492. IEEE (2010)
47. Shechtman, E., Irani, M.: Matching local self-similarities across images and videos. In: CVPR, pp. 1–8. IEEE (2007)

Predicting the Number of DCT Coefficients in the Process of Seabed Data Compression

Paweł Forczmański[✉] and Wojciech Maleika

Faculty of Computer Science and Information Technology, West Pomeranian University of Technology, Żołnierska Str. 52, 71-210 Szczecin, Poland
{pforczmanski,wmaleika}@wi.zut.edu.pl

Abstract. The paper presents Discrete Cosine Transform-based compression method applied to data describing seabed topography. It is an improvement over the previously developed and described algorithms capable of variable compression ratio and a possibility to limit the maximal reconstruction error. The main objective is to find an optimal number of DCT coefficients representing a surface with an acceptable reconstruction accuracy. In the original approach the compression was performed in an iterative manner, where successive values were tested, yielding high computational cost and time overhead. The algorithm presented in this paper allows to predict a number of DCT coefficients based on characteristics of specific input surface. Such characteristics are statistical measures describing a complexity of the surface. The classification using simple, fast and easy to learn classifiers does not introduce additional computational overhead. Presented experiments performed on real data gathered by maritime office gave encouraging results. Developed method can be employed in modern data storage and management system handling seabed topographic data.

1 Introduction

The knowledge of the physical structure of oceans, seas, lakes and rivers is essential and finds many applications in different fields of science and industry. Nowadays, the most common area of application is maritime cartography, where seabed topography measurement is the one and only source for creating maps and charts for safe navigation. The gathered information is also used in offshore industry (underwater construction plants, deep-sea exploration, hydrography, environmental protection and mineral exploitation).

It should be noted, that the use of water areas requires the detailed knowledge of precise bathymetric data. During the process of making a seabed model one should remember that the accuracy depends mostly on the volume of scanned data and the required scale of the output map. The more complex is the surface and the bigger the scale, the more points should be measured and stored.

There are several types of devices used to make hydrographic measurements in water environment. The most commonly used are single and multibeam echosounders [1,2]. Nowadays, sounding that employs multibeam echosounder

© Springer International Publishing Switzerland 2015
G. Azzopardi and N. Petkov (Eds.): CAIP 2015, Part I, LNCS 9256, pp. 77–87, 2015.
DOI: 10.1007/978-3-319-23192-1_7

(MBES) is one of the most effective and accurate methods of depth measurements. In most cases, MBES data recordings consist of an enormous number of measurement points, often irregularly distributed in two-dimensional space. Hence, due to large quantity and irregular distribution, such data are not suitable for direct processing, such as analysis or visualization [3,4]. Let us assume that each point of the seabed is represented in by a triple (X, Y, Z) assigned to its longitude, latitude and depth. To perform numerical operations or to visualise these points, they should be processed in a special way depending on the purpose. The process of creating digital terrain model (DTM) [5–7] involves among others the transformation of each point from the irregular grid to the regular one (often defined as a regular square network) through interpolation of measurement data [5,8,9].

For example, a rather small area of one square kilometer with a resolution of grid equal to one meter gives one million of data points (real values), occupying 3.8 Megabytes of memory. In practice we collect and process much larger areas (of several hundreds of square kilometers) e.g. approach channels to the harbours, harbours basins, anchorage areas, bays etc.

The continuous increase in data volume, often driven by new technology, makes the problem of compression very up-to-date [10]. It should be noted that any algorithm of compression should meet specific requirements such as high compression ratio and exact reconstruction [11]. Hence, the most important features of the developed method are determined by the properties of input data and their volume. To be applicable it should meet some minimal requirements, namely it should be a lossy compression (giving higher compression ratios), provide known, fixed, maximal reconstruction error in any grid node (the depth difference between original and decompressed data), assure adaptive and variable compression ratio in small sub-regions (maximal compression for requested accuracy), implement fast searching and reconstruction stage for small sub regions.

The papers is organized as follows. First, we review related works aimed at elevation data compression. Then, we present a base algorithm that employs iterative searching for optimal number of spectral components used for representing a surface. Next, we introduce a prediction stage using surface characteristics. Finally, we present some experimental results and conclude our work.

1.1   Previous Works

The literature survey shows that there is a certain number of works aimed at general compression of elevation data. In case of land data, often gathered using the Light Detection And Ranging (LIDAR) systems, processed elevation data (represented by Digital Terrain Model) are often stored as grayscale raster bitmaps. Hence, in [12] different methods of DEM compression were compared. In [13,14] authors described surface compression using Overdetermined Laplacian Partial Differential Equation (ODETLAP). In [15] the authors proposed the Triangulated Irregular Network DEM compression using second generation wavelets. In [16] an approach to the compression of elevation data based on JPEG-LS algorithm was presented. In [17] a compression of hyperspectral imagery using the 3-D DCT and hybrid DPCM/DCT is proposed.

Although the problem of handling measurement data has been presented in the literature [17–19], an issue discussed in this paper, related to seabed data processing, is still interesting. In fact, some dedicated methods have been proposed, but they work under restricted conditions [20, 21] (e.g. do not support floating-point values) or are inadequate for modern requirements [22–25]. To the best knowledge of the authors, even up-to-date software used in maritime business does not provide any acceptable data compression.

As it was shown, most of scientific works deal with compressing elevation data stored in raster images (bitmaps), which is motivated by practical aspects of gathering, storing, and transmitting such data. In our previous works we have investigated the possibility of compressing seabed data by means of Discrete Cosine Transform [26], Discrete Wavelet Transform [27] and Karhunen-Loeve Transform [28]. Proposed algorithms dealt also with raster images and the compression was performed using straightforward procedure involving iterative way of finding compression parameters based on reconstruction accuracy evaluation. Although such an approach is not optimal in terms of computing overhead, it gave acceptable performance for small data volumes.

Hence, this article is focused on increasing the speed of computations by means of predicting initial compression factor using a set of simple statistical measures and a classifier learned on ground-truth compression coefficients calculated for reference surfaces. It is especially important in case of large volumes of measurements. This approach is inspired by a general-purpose method applied for natural images, described in [29], yet the features are slightly different and the classification does not employ a linear model.

2   Algorithm Description

2.1   Assumptions

In the process of depth measurements compression we have to process data denoted with real values (floating-point representation of depth), which is different from typical image/video domain. The main objective in case of such data is to obtain the highest compression factor while not exceeding pre-defined reconstruction error. These assumptions are especially important, in order to satisfy International Hydrographic Organization standards [11]. Hence, during compression based on DCT, we select only the minimal number of spectral coefficients satisfying criteria related to compression factor and reconstruction accuracy.

2.2   Base Algorithm

The compression algorithm that uses an iterative way of finding DCT coefficients consists of the following steps (see Fig. 1):

1. Decompose data matrix into non-overlapping, square blocks D of $N \times N$ elements,

2. For each block D:
   (a) perform two-dimensional Discrete Cosine Transform;
   (b) set components number M in each direction to 1;
   (c) extract a square submatrix of $M \times M$ form upper-left corner of DCT spectrum of D;
   (d) perform inverse two-dimensional Discrete Cosine Transform for spectrum with $M \times M$ components (the rest is set to zero);
   (e) evaluate the difference (reconstruction error E between original block D and reconstructed one);
   (f) if error E is greater than a set threshold (according to given IHO norm) increment M (while $M < N$) and go to (2c);
   (g) otherwise store $M \times M$ components of DCT spectrum for analysed block D,
3. Save all DCT components for all blocks describing whole surface.

We employed Discrete Cosine Transform as it has been successfully applied for compression of digital images of natural origin. If we assume a seabed surface being an image, then the application of DCT is rather straightforward. Moreover, the basis functions of DCT seem to capture all the diversity of natural structures of seafloor. This approach to the surface compression assumes also that data are placed in a regular grid and from this point of view differs from vector-based methods [30]. As it was noted, in order to preserve adequate accuracy, depth data are stored on real (double precision) values.

The reconstruction error is calculated on a basis of a maximal absolute difference between original surface and the reconstructed one. It is compared to predefined threshold (in terms of appropriate surface class [11]).

In the previous works [26] we found $N = 32$ being an optimum square block size in terms of compression efficiency versus computational overhead.

2.3   Modified Algorithm

As it can be clearly seen, the proposed algorithm is rather naive in terms of looking for final M value for each block. The decompression and error evaluation steps (2c,2d,2e) are executed many times, making the search for optimal compression factor a typical linear search problem. Our experience shows that in most cases, those steps are repeated more than 10 times, which is far from optimum. Hence, the obvious solution is a binary search, which will reduce the number of searches. The binary search halves the number of items to check with each iteration, so locating proper M value takes logarithmic time. For a block of $N = 32$ we perform maximum $log_2(N) = 5$ searches. It is performed for each block not taking into consideration its content. On the other hand, it is also obvious than the more complex the block is, the less it can be compressed (hence the number of DCT components is larger).

Hence, our proposal is to increase the speed of computations (in terms of decreasing the number of reconstruction/error estimation stages) by means of predicting M value on a base of surface characteristics. In the modified version

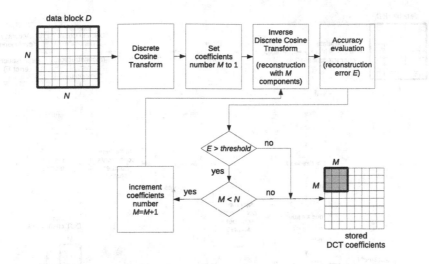

Fig. 1. Base compression algorithm with linear search

of the compression algorithm (see Fig. 2) we calculate the characteristics of each processed block and based on them predict M value. Unfortunately, the prediction of M can not be 100% error-free, so we introduce a stage of local search (increasing and decreasing M according to the error E changes) in the neighborhood of predicted M value. In order to protect the algorithm from being endlessly looped, we introduce a flag dcc which is responsible for a proper termination.

2.4 Surface Features

We assume, that there is a direct association between surface complexity and reconstruction accuracy, which can be represented by a number of DCT coefficients needed for a successful reconstruction. Some exemplary surfaces together with reference DCT coefficient number (M) for an error $E \leq 1$cm and block size $N = 32$ are presented in Fig. 3.

In order to capture surface characteristic we investigated several typical scalar measures that describe the complexity level of surface (represented as a square matrix). Some of them have been successfully applied to other pattern recognition tasks, e.g. stamps detection [31] and proved their usefulness. The following measures calculated for each block independently have been considered: variance,standard deviation, entropy, contrast, autocorrelation, features derived from Gray-Level Coocurrence Matrix (contrast, correlation, energy, homogenity) calculated for horizontal and vertical directions in two-pixel neighborhood.

In our investigations we considered two variants of feature vector calculated for each block, namely the long representation consisting of all 13 elements and a reduced one, having only 4 features. The short vector contains standard

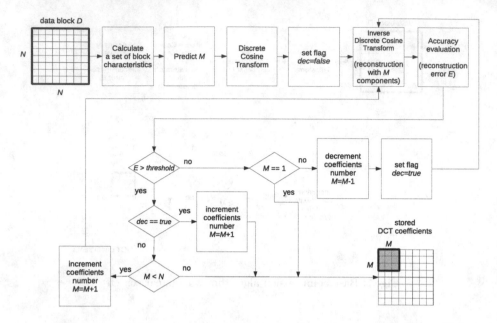

Fig. 2. Modified compression algorithm with prediction and local search

deviation, entropy, contrast, and autocorrelation. These measures were selected as a compromise between complexity and discrimination ability.

3   Experiments

During the experiments we evaluated the performance of several classifiers used to predict the number of DCT coefficients thus decreasing the number of iterations at the compression stage. Employed benchmark database consists of processed measurements representing seabed profiles collected from Szczecin Lagoon and Pomeranian Bay. They were gathered by Maritime Office in Szczecin, Poland. We selected three particular areas (the details are given in Tab. 1) in order to cover most representative types of seabed. While the seabed in most areas in the world is not so variable, the results of the experiments should give good approximation of projected efficiency of the method. Thus, in the benchmark database we included a surface of quite high and uniform complexity ("rotator") and surfaces featuring high local depth variance ("wrecks" and "gate") and large areas of near-constant depth. The "gate" represents measurements of route gate, "wrecks" – an area containing car wrecks left on the seabed, while the "rotator" is a place where ships can rotate. After decomposition of tree surfaces, the benchmark database consists of 3875 blocks of 32×32 elements. The visualizations of selected surfaces in 3D perspective are shown in Fig. 4.

Each sample in the database contains a feature vector (4- or 13-element long, depending on the variant) and a value of M (the number of decompression/error

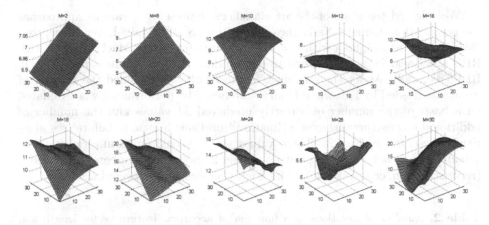

Fig. 3. Exemplary surfaces (blocks) taken from benchmark dataset labeled with numbers of DCT coefficients in each dimension

Table 1. Characteristics of benchmark surfaces

No.	Name	Grid resolution [meters]	Grid size [nodes]	No. points [thousands]	Filesize [MBytes]
1.	gate	0.5	1888 × 1888	3081	23.51
2.	rotator	0.75	2464 × 1760	4336	33.09
3.	wrecks	0.01	1856 × 672	1247	9.52

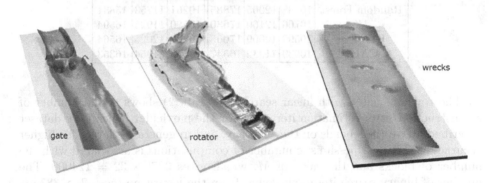

Fig. 4. Benchmark surfaces visualized in 3D

evaluation iterations) calculated for each test block using above mentioned linear search. To make the results objective, we divided the dataset into learning and testing parts according to the typical 10-fold cross validation technique.

As a measure of accuracy, we investigated three reconstruction errors, namely 1, 5 and 10 centimeters. It should be stressed that they are much more strict than IHO-suggested accuracies for that kind of areas (which is equal to 30 centimeters).

We selected ten state-of-the-art classifiers, representing various approaches to classification, namely: Naive Bayes Classifier (NBC), Multi-Layer Perceptron (MLP), Nearest Neighbor with $k = 1$ (1NN), Support Vector Machine (both with RBF and linear kernels), decision trees (Random Tree, Random Forest, CART, REPTree, J48). As for the reference, in the results we included the number of iterations needed by linear and binary searches. The performance was evaluated on a basis of the number of correctly predicted M values and the number of additional reconstruction/error estimation iterations in case of failure (see algorithm presented in Fig. 2). These values were taken from confusion matrices calculated for each classifier's output. Table 2 shows the numbers of iterations (reconstruction/error estimation) for each classifier and expected accuracy.

Table 2. Number of iterations as a function of accuracy, feature vector length and classifier for benchmark surfaces

	4-el. feature vector			13-el. feature vector		
Accuracy (error)	10 cm	5 cm	1 cm	10 cm	5 cm	1 cm
Linear Search	18683	25546	52359	18683	25546	52359
Binary Search	19375	19375	19375	19375	19375	19375
NBC	11446	13307	18445	11967	13864	19552
MLP	10485	12027	16941	10401	11890	16471
1NN	11777	14010	21172	12499	14980	22928
SVM (RBF)	11144	13142	19411	11742	14026	21858
SVM (Linear)	10926	12927	18456	10930	12823	18115
Random Tree	11130	13039	19421	10944	12513	17820
Random Forest	10538	12065	17835	10261	11753	15831
J48	10766	12160	17630	10580	11925	16594
REPTree	10599	12009	17008	10601	12025	16564
CART	10539	11982	16547	10533	11954	16353

The row associated with linear search (see Tab. 2) shows actual number of reconstruction/error estimation iterations for the particular benchmark dataset described above (it depends on the accuracy, and in general, is larger for higher accuracy). The most pessimistic number of computations is associated with the number of blocks and the value of M, which gives $3875 \times 32 = 124000$. The number of binary search iterations comes from the logarithm $log_2(32) \times 3875 = 19375$ and it does not depend on the accuracy. It is worth noticing also, that the binary search approach gives computation savings only in case where block size is equal or larger than 32×32 elements for accuracies higher than 5 cm (5 cm and 1 cm in our experiments).

As it can be seen, the proposed algorithm is able to predict the number of DCT components used at the compression stage and, hence, decrease the number of computations (of more then 40%). It has been proved also that the usage of full, 13-element feature vector is not justified, since it does not give any significant improvement. In most cases, the best results was observed for

Multi-Layer Perceptron, but we have to remember that it is quite complex in training. The performance of tree-based classifiers is similar.

The results show that the algorithm efficiency (in terms of a boost in computations speed in comparison to binary search) depends on the requested accuracy, namely it gives 46% less reconstruction/error estimation operations for accuracy of 10 centimeters, while 38% for 5 centimeters and 15% for 1 centimeter, respectively.

It should be also stressed that a total computational overhead depends not only on the number of reconstruction/error estimation iterations but also on the features calculation and classification. However, those operations are quite fast and their influence on the total computations time is not significant. The cost of training the classifier can be also omitted.

To summarize, when we forget the cost of computations related to calculating four simple features, a rather unsophisticated tree-based classifier (e.g. CART or J48) can give significant improvement in the performance of the compression algorithm.

4   Summary

A novel approach for increasing the speed of DCT-based seabed data compression was presented. It is founded on the classification of surfaces on a basis of their complexity, which is later employed to predict a compression factor. The experiments on real measurement data proved its efficiency. In a comparison to direct (iterative) methods presented previously it features the same compression ratio without the loss in quality together with a significant decrease in computational overhead. The performed experiments showed that even by employing much lower number of surface features (4 out of 13) we can preserve a significant reduction of the number of operations needed while retaining high reconstruction accuracy and compression rate. Future investigations should be aimed at two directions. The first one is related to the development of a general system, which can be based on different transformations (e.g. PCA/KLT, Wavelets) depending on the properties of the surface being compressed. In the second direction, one could investigate saliency areas (i.e. by means of methods presented in [32]) in order to group them according to their characteristics.

References

1. Maleika, W.: Development of a Method for the Estimation of Multibeam Echosounder Measurement Accuracy, Przeglad Elektrotechniczny (Electrical Review), R. 88 No. 10b/2012, pp. 205–208 (2012)
2. Wawrzyniak, N., Hyla, T.: Managing depth information uncertainty in inland mobile navigation systems. In: Kryszkiewicz, M., Cornelis, C., Ciucci, D., Medina-Moreno, J., Motoda, H., Raś, Z.W. (eds.) RSEISP 2014. LNCS, vol. 8537, pp. 343–350. Springer, Heidelberg (2014)

3. Zhao, J., Yan, J., Zhang, H.: A new method for weakening the combined effect of residual errors on multibeam bathymetric data. Marine Geophysical Research **35**(4), 379–394 (2014)
4. Maleika, W.: Moving average optimization in digital terrain model generation based on test multibeam echosounder data. Geo-Marine Letters **35**(1), 61–68 (2015)
5. Gaboardi, C., Mitishita, E.A., Firkowski, H.: Digital Terrain Modeling generalization with base in Wavelet Transform. Boletim de Ciencias Geodesicas **17**(1), 115–129 (2011)
6. Hamilton, E.L.: Geoacoustic modeling of the sea floor. Journal of the Acoustical Society of America **68**(5), 1313–1340 (1980)
7. Maleika, W.: The influence of the grid resolution on the accuracy of the digital terrain model used in seabed modeling. Marine Geophysical Research **36**(1), 35–44 (2015)
8. Łubczonek, J., Stateczny, A.: Concept of neural model of the sea bottom surface. Neural Networks and Soft Computing Book Series: Advances in Soft Computing 861–866 (2003)
9. Maleika, W., Palczynski, M., Frejlichowski, D.: Interpolation methods and the accuracy of bathymetric seabed models based on multibeam echosounder data. In: Pan, J.-S., Chen, S.-M., Nguyen, N.T. (eds.) ACIIDS 2012, Part III. LNCS, vol. 7198, pp. 466–475. Springer, Heidelberg (2012)
10. Stateczny, A., Wlodarczyk-Sielicka, M.: Self-organizing artificial neural networks into hydrographic big data reduction process. In: Kryszkiewicz, M., Cornelis, C., Ciucci, D., Medina-Moreno, J., Motoda, H., Raś, Z.W. (eds.) RSEISP 2014. LNCS, vol. 8537, pp. 335–342. Springer, Heidelberg (2014)
11. IHO standards for hydrographic surveys, Publication No. 44 of International Hydrographic Organization, 5th edn (2008). http://www.iho.int/iho_pubs/standard/S-44_5E.pdf
12. Franklin, W.R., Said, A.: Lossy compression of elevation data. In: Seventh International Symposium on Spatial Data Handling, Delft, pp. 29–41 (1996)
13. Xie, Z., Franklin, W., Cutler, B., Andrade M., Inanc, M., Tracy, D.: Surface compression using over-determined Laplacian approximation. In: Proceedings of SPIE, Advanced Signal Processing Algorithms, Architectures, and Implementations XVII, vol. 6697, San Diego, CA. International Society for Optical Engineering (2007)
14. Stookey, J., Xie, Z., Cutler, B., Franklin, W., Tracy, D., Andrade, M.: Parallel ODETLAP for terrain compression and reconstruction. In: GIS 2008: Proceedings of the 16th ACM SIGSPATIAL International Conference on Advances in Geographic Information Systems, pp. 1–9 (2008)
15. Pradhan, B., Mansor, S.: Three dimensional terrain data compression using second generation wavelets. In: 8th International Conference on Data, Text and Web Mining and Their Business Applications. Book Series: WIT Transactions on Information and Communication Technologies, vol. 38 (2007)
16. Rane, S.D., Sapiro, G.: Evaluation of JPEG-LS, the new lossless and controlled-lossy still image compression standard, for compression of high-resolution elevation data. IEEE Transactions on Geoscience and Remote Sensing **39**(10), 2298–2306 (2001)
17. Abousleman, G.P., Marcellin, M.W., Hunt, B.R.: Compression of Hyperspectral Imagery Using the 3-D DCT and Hybrid DPCM/DCT. IEEE Trans. on Geoscience and Remote Sensing **33**(1), 26–34 (1995)
18. Klimesh, M.: Compression of Multispectral Images. TDA Progress Report, pp. 42–129 (1997)

19. Cao, W., Li, B., Zhang, Y.: A remote sensing image fusion method based on PCA transform and wavelet packet transform. Neural Networks and Signal Processing **2**, 976–981 (2003)

20. Fowler, J.E., Fox, D.N.: Wavelet based coding of three dimensional oceanographic images around land masses. In: Proceedings of the IEEE International Conference on Image Processing Vancouver, Canada, pp. 431–434 (2000)

21. Kazimierski, W., Zaniewicz, G.: Analysis of the possibility of using radar tracking method based on GRNN for processing sonar spatial data. In: Kryszkiewicz, M., Cornelis, C., Ciucci, D., Medina-Moreno, J., Motoda, H., Raś, Z.W. (eds.) RSEISP 2014. LNCS, vol. 8537, pp. 319–326. Springer, Heidelberg (2014)

22. Bruun, B.T., Nilsen, S.: Wavelet representation of large digital terrain models. Computers & Geosciences **29**, 695–703 (2003)

23. Stateczny, A., Łubczonek, J.: Radar sensors implementation in river information services in Poland. In: 15th International Radar Symposium (IRS), Book Series: International Radar Symposium Proceedings, pp. 1–5 (2014)

24. Wessel, P.: Compression of large data grids for Internet transmission. Computers & Geosciences **29**, 665–671 (2003)

25. Wright, D.J., Goodchild, M.F.: Data From the Deep: Implications for the GIS Community. The International Journal of Geographical Information Science **11**(6), 523–528 (1997)

26. Maleika, W.: Adaptive compression of real data describing sea bottom using DCT. In: Proceedings of 8th International Conference Advanced Computer Systems, Szczecin (2001)

27. Forczmański, P., Maleika, W.: Wavelets in adaptive compression of data describing sea bottom. In: Proc. 9th International Multi-conference Advanced Computer Systems ACS 2002, Miedzyzdroje, pp. 381–388 (2002)

28. Maleika, W.: Compression of sea floor data by means of Principal Component Analysis. In: 10th Marine Traffic Engineering Conference, pp. 189–197. Szczecin (2003) [in Polish]

29. Forczmański, P., Mantiuk, R.: Adaptive and quality-aware storage of JPEG files in the web environment. In: Chmielewski, L.J., Kozera, R., Shin, B.-S., Wojciechowski, K. (eds.) ICCVG 2014. LNCS, vol. 8671, pp. 212–219. Springer, Heidelberg (2014)

30. Maes, J., Bultheel, A.: Surface Compression With Hierarchical Powell Sabin B Splines. International Journal of Wavelets, Multiresolution and Information Processing 177–196 (2004)

31. Forczmański, P., Markiewicz, A.: Low-level image features for stamps detection and classification. In: 8th International Conference on Computer Recognition Systems (CORES). Advances in Intelligent Systems and Computing, vol. 226, pp. 383–392 (2013)

32. Choras, R.S., Andrysiak, T., Choras, M.: Integrated color, texture and shape information for content-based image retrieval. Pattern Analysis and Applications **10**(4), 333–343 (2007)

Recognition of Images Degraded
by Gaussian Blur

Jan Flusser, Tomáš Suk[✉], Sajad Farokhi, and Cyril Höschl IV

Institute of Information Theory and Automation of the CAS,
Pod Vodárenskou věží 4, 182 08 Praha 8, Czech Republic
{flusser,suk,fsajad2,hoschl}@utia.cas.cz

Abstract. We introduce a new theory of invariants to Gaussian blur. The invariants are defined in Fourier spectral domain by means of projection operators and, equivalently, in the image domain by means of image moments. The application of these invariants is in blur-invariant image comparison and recognition. The behavior of the invariants is studied and compared with other methods in experiments on both artificial and real blurred and noisy images.

Keywords: Blurred image · Object recognition · Blur invariant comparison · Gaussian blur · Projection operators · Image moments · Moment invariants

1 Introduction

Image recognition/classification in general is an extremely broad area which apparently cannot be resolved by a single always-optimal method. This is why numerous specific formulations of the problem have appeared which consequently have resulted in many particular algorithms or classes of algorithms. Some of them have already become an established discipline of image analysis while some others are still undergoing initial development. One of the representatives of the latter group are methods for recognition of images which are degraded by a uniform Gaussian blur.

The mathematical formulation of the problem is well known in image processing. Capturing an ideal scene f by an imaging device with the point-spread function (PSF) h, the observed image g is a convolution of both

$$g(x,y) = (f * h)(x,y). \tag{1}$$

This linear space-invariant image formation model, even if it is very simple, is a reasonably accurate approximation of many imaging devices and acquisition scenarios. In this paper, we concentrate our attention to the case when the PSF is a Gaussian (with unknown parameters).

Gaussian blur appears whenever the acquisition was accomplished through a turbulent medium and the acquisition/exposure time is by far longer than

© Springer International Publishing Switzerland 2015
G. Azzopardi and N. Petkov (Eds.): CAIP 2015, Part I, LNCS 9256, pp. 88–99, 2015.
DOI: 10.1007/978-3-319-23192-1_8

the period of Brownian motion of the particles in the medium. Ground-based astronomical imaging through the atmosphere, taking pictures through a fog, fluorescence microscopy, and underwater imaging are three typical examples of such situation (in these cases, the blur may be coupled with a contrast decrease). Gaussian blur is also introduced into the images as the sensor blur which is due to a finite size of the sampling pulse; this effect is, however, mostly of low significance. Moreover, Gaussian kernel is often used as an approximation of some other blurs which are too complicated to work with them exactly. Gaussian blur is sometimes even introduced intentionally, for instance to suppress additive noise, to "soften" the image or before the image down-scaling and building the image pyramid. So, we can see there is actually a demand for having the tools designed particularly for processing Gaussian-blurred images.

Let us imagine a classification problem, when we need to classify a blurred image g against a database of clear images. (The database typically consists of images acquired under good imaging conditions, so their blur can be considered much smaller than the blur of the query image or even negligible. In template matching, when the template has been extracted from the blurred image, the term "database" may refer to a single clear image of a scene in which the template should be located.) We have basically three options. The most time-expensive one is to generate all possible blurred versions of all templates (i.e. blurring with Gaussians the variances of which fill a reasonable, properly sampled interval) and incorporate them into the database. This brute-force approach is not practically feasible.

Another approach relies on the solution of the inverse problem, when the blur is removed from the input image and the deblurred image is then classified by any standard technique. This process contains semi-blind image deconvolution (the term "semi-blind" is used because we know the parametric form of the kernel but its parameter(s) are unknown), which is in the case of a Gaussian kernel an unstable, ill-posed problem. Unlike motion blur and out-of-focus blur, Gaussian blur does not introduce any zero patterns into the spectrum of the image, which are in the other cases employed for parameter estimation. Only few semi-blind deconvolution methods w.r.t. Gaussian blur have been published. They first try to estimate the size (variance) of the blur and then to perform a non-blind deconvolution [6] [1], [2], [11], [10]. All these methods are sensitive to variance overestimation and relatively time-consuming.

The third and the most promising approach is based on the idea that for blur-insensitive recognition we do not need to restore the query image, we only need its representation which might be lossy but robust w.r.t. the Gaussian blur. Such a representation should describe those features of the image, which are not affected by the degradation. Since the classification is mostly performed by minimum distance rule in some (usually Euclidean) feature space, the task of finding a proper representation is always coupled with the task of defining a blur-robust distance measure. Technically speaking, we are looking for a distance measure d between two images such that

$$d(f_1, f_2) = d(f_1 * h, f_2) \tag{2}$$

for any Gaussian kernel h. Instead of an explicit definition of blur-invariant distance d, we may look for a blur-invariant feature descriptor I such that

$$I(f) = I(f * h) \tag{3}$$

and then use one of standard vector metrics for evaluating the distance between $I(f)$ and the same representation of the database templates.

Several authors have tried to derive invariants (3) w.r.t. Gaussian blur. Tianxu [7] realized without a deeper analysis that the complex moments of the image, one index of which is zero, are invariant to Gaussian blur. Xiao [9] seemingly derived invariants to Gaussian blur but he did not employ the parametric Gaussian form explicitly. He only used the circular symmetry property which lead to an incomplete invariant system. Gopalan et al. [5] derived another invariant set without assuming the knowledge of the parametric shape of the kernel but imposed a limitation of its support size. Flusser et al. derived blur invariants for centrosymmetric kernels [3] and later for arbitrary N-fold symmetric kernels [4]. All the methods mentioned above do not use the parametric form of the PSF at all. Although they can be applied to Gaussian blur, too, because the Gaussian kernel is a particular case of symmetric kernels, they do not reach the maximum discrimination power. Specific invariants to Gaussian blur providing an optimal discriminabilty cannot be obtained as a special case of these methods (even if the idea of projection operators we employ in this paper is similar to that we proposed in [4]).

The most promising approach so far was proposed by Zhang et al. [13], [12], who employed Gaussian parametric form to derive a blur-invariant similarity measure between two images of the type (2), without deriving blur invariants explicitly. The method looks elegant and the authors reported a good performance. However, a serious weakness of the Zhang's method is its high complexity and sensitivity to noise in the images to be compared, as will be demonstrated in the experimental part of this paper.

2   Gaussian Blur Invariants in the Spectral Domain

In this section we present an approach which is based on the *invariant descriptors* of the type (3). The basic conceptual difference from the Zhang's method is that these invariants are defined for a single image, while the Zhang's distance always requires a pair of images. So, we can calculate the invariant representations of the templates only once and store them in the database, which leads to much faster recognition.

2.1   Projection Operators in 1D

The new invariants are based on the projection of the image onto a space of unnormalized Gaussian functions, which preserves the image moments of the zero, the first, and the second orders. The separability of the 2D Gaussian function allows us to create a 1D theory (which is more transparent and easy to explain) first and then to generalize it to the 2D case.

Let us consider a 1D "image" f with a finite non-zero integral and a finite second-order central moment. The projection operator P_G is defined as

$$P_G(f)(x) = m_0 G_s(x), \tag{4}$$

where

$$G_s(x) = \frac{1}{\sqrt{2\pi}\sigma} e^{-\frac{x^2}{2s^2}},$$

$$s^2 = m_2/m_0$$

and

$$m_p = \int (x-c)^p f(x) dx \tag{5}$$

is the p-th central moment of f (with c being the centroid of f). Hence, P_G assigns each f to a multiple of a centralized Gaussian such that the central moments up to the second order of f and $P_G(f)$ are the same. In other words, $P_G(f)$ is the "closest" unnormalized Gaussian to f in terms of the moment values. In this sense, P_G can be considered a projector onto the set of all unnormalized Gaussian functions. In particular, $P_G(G_\sigma) = G_\sigma$. An important property of P_G, which will be later used for construction of the invariants, is its relationship to a convolution with a Gaussian kernel

$$P_G(g)(x) \equiv P_G(f * G_\sigma)(x) = m_0 G_{\sqrt{(s^2+\sigma^2)}}(x) \equiv \frac{m_0}{\sqrt{2\pi(s^2+\sigma^2)}} e^{-\frac{x^2}{2(s^2+\sigma^2)}}.$$

Finally, we show how the operator P_G behaves under the Fourier transform. Since the Fourier transform of a Gaussian G_σ is an (unnormalized) Gaussian $G_{1/\sigma}$

$$\mathcal{F}(G_\sigma)(u) = e^{-2\pi^2\sigma^2 u^2},$$

we have

$$\mathcal{F}(P_G(f))(u) = \mathcal{F}(m_0 G_s)(u) = m_0 e^{-2\pi^2 s^2 u^2}$$

and

$$\mathcal{F}(P_G(g))(u) \equiv \mathcal{F}P_G(f * G_\sigma)(u) = m_0 e^{-2\pi^2(s^2+\sigma^2)u^2} = \mathcal{F}(P_G(f))(u) \cdot \mathcal{F}(G_\sigma)(u).$$

2.2 1D Gaussian Blur Invariants in the Fourier Domain

Now we can formulate the central theorem of this paper.

Theorem 1. *Let f be an image function. Then*

$$I_G(f)(u) = \frac{\mathcal{F}(f)(u)}{\mathcal{F}(P_G(f))(u)}$$

is an invariant to Gaussian blur, i.e. $I_G(f) = I_G(f * G_\sigma)$ for any blur parameter σ.

The proof follows immediately from the assertions introduced in the previous section. Note that I_G is invariant also to the contrast stretching, $I_G(f) = I_G(af)$.

$I_G(f)$ can be viewed as a Fourier transform of the *primordial image*

$$f_r = \mathcal{F}^{-1}(I_G(f)).$$

However, f_r is not an image in a common sense because the existence of $\mathcal{F}^{-1}(I_G(f))$ is not generally guaranteed and even if f_r exists, it may contain negative values.

This is a kind of normalization w.r.t. Gaussian blurring of unknown extent. The primordial image plays the role of a canonical form of f, which actually is its "maximally deconvolved" non-Gaussian part.

The operator I_G decomposes the image space into classes of equivalence. Fortunately, this decomposition is exactly the same as that one induced by the following relation: two functions f_1 and f_2 are equivalent if and only if there exists $\sigma \geq 0$ such that $f_1 = f_2 * aG_\sigma$ or $f_2 = f_1 * aG_\sigma$. This is an important observation, saying that $I_G(f)$ is a *complete* description of f up to a convolution with a Gaussian and a multiplicative contrast change. In other words, $I_G(f)$ defines an *orbit*[1] of images equivalent with f. Thanks to the completeness, I_G discriminates between the images from different orbits but obviously cannot discriminate inside an orbit. In particular, I_G cannot discriminate between two Gaussians since all Gaussians lie on the orbit the root of which is the delta function.

2.3   1D Gaussian Blur Invariants in the Image Domain

In principle, we can use directly $I_G(f)$ as the invariant feature vector of the same size as f but working in the Fourier domain brings two practical difficulties. Since $I_G(f)$ is a ratio, we possibly divide by very small numbers which requires an appropriate numerical treatment. Moreover, high frequencies of $I_G(f)$ use to be sensitive to noise. This can be overcome by suppressing them by a low-pass filter, but this procedure requires additional time and introduces a user-defined parameter which should be set up with respect to the particular noise level. That is why in most cases we prefer to work directly in the image domain, where invariants equivalent to $I_G(f)$ can be constructed.

To obtain the link between the Fourier and image domains, we use a Taylor expansion of the harmonic functions and a term-wise integration

$$\mathcal{F}(f)(u) \equiv \int_{-\infty}^{\infty} f(x) \cdot e^{-2\pi i u x} dx = \sum_{k=0}^{\infty} \frac{(-2\pi i)^k}{k!} m_k u^k. \tag{6}$$

The above formula tells us that the moments of the image are Taylor coefficients (up to a constant factor) of its Fourier transform. Analogous formula for $\mathcal{F}(P_G(f))$ is

$$\mathcal{F}(P_G(f))(u) = m_0 \sum_{k=0}^{\infty} \frac{(-2\pi^2)^k}{k!} \left(\frac{m_2}{m_0}\right)^k u^{2k}. \tag{7}$$

---

[1] The term "orbit" was introduced by Zhang in [12] in this context.

If the Taylor expansion of $I_G(f)$ is

$$I_G(f)(u) = \sum_{k=0}^{\infty} \frac{(-2\pi i)^k}{k!} a_k u^k, \tag{8}$$

where a_k are the moments of the primordial image, we can rewrite Theorem 1 as

$$\sum_{k=0}^{\infty} \frac{(-2\pi i)^k}{k!} m_k u^k = m_0 \sum_{k=0}^{\infty} \frac{(-2\pi^2)^k}{k!} \left(\frac{m_2}{m_0}\right)^k u^{2k} \cdot \sum_{k=0}^{\infty} \frac{(-2\pi i)^k}{k!} a_k u^k.$$

Comparing the terms with the same power of u we obtain, after some manipulation, the recursive expression for each a_p

$$a_p = \frac{m_p}{m_0} - \sum_{\substack{k=2 \\ k \text{ even}}}^{p} (k-1)!! \cdot \binom{p}{k} \left(\frac{m_2}{m_0}\right)^{k/2} a_{p-k}. \tag{9}$$

The symbol $k!!$ means a double factorial, $k!! = 1 \cdot 3 \cdot 5 \cdots k$ for odd k. Since the primordial image itself (more precisely, its Fourier transform) was proven to be blur invariant, each its moment must be also a blur invariant. If we restrict ourselves to a brightness-preserving blurring, then m_0 itself is an invariant and we obtain from (9) the simplified final form of Gaussian blur invariants

$$B(p) \equiv m_0 a_p = m_p - \sum_{\substack{k=2 \\ k \text{ even}}}^{p} (k-1)!! \cdot \binom{p}{k} \left(\frac{m_2}{m_0}\right)^{k/2} B(p-k). \tag{10}$$

As we already said, $B(p)$ is actually a p-th moment of the primordial image of f. Regardless of f, $B(1) = 0$ because we work with central moments because the second-order moment was used to eliminate the unknown blur parameter σ. Hence, $B(1)$ and $B(2)$ should not be used in the feature vector since they do not carry any information.

In addition to higher robustness, using the image-domain features (10) is also faster than using I_G. In practice, we do not need a complete representation of the images in question. Usually a few invariants provide a sufficient discrimination power, so we use the $B(p)$'s up to the certain order Q only. This Q is a user-defined parameter the determination of which should be based on a discrimination analysis of the database images. The choice of Q is always a compromise between the discriminative power and the complexity of the method.

2.4 Gaussian Blur Invariants in Two Dimensions

Now let us assume the image domain is a subset of R^2. The centralized 2-D Gaussian function has the form

$$G_C(\mathbf{x}) = \frac{1}{2\pi\sqrt{|C|}} \exp\left(-\frac{1}{2}\mathbf{x}C^{-1}\mathbf{x}'\right), \tag{11}$$

where $\mathbf{x} \equiv (x_1, x_2)$ and C is the covariance matrix which determines the shape of the Gaussian. Provided that the covariance matrix of the blur kernel is diagonal, we define the projection operator as

$$P_G(f)(\mathbf{x}) = m_{00} G_\Sigma(\mathbf{x}), \tag{12}$$

where

$$\Sigma = \text{diag}(m_{20}/m_{00}, m_{02}/m_{00}).$$

Then

$$I_G(f)(\mathbf{u}) = \frac{\mathcal{F}(f)(\mathbf{u})}{\mathcal{F}(P_G(f))(\mathbf{u})}$$

is a blur invariant and after applying the Taylor expansion, we end up with the following moment invariants analogous to (10)

$$B(p,q) = m_{pq} - \sum_{\substack{k+j=2 \\ k,j \text{ even}}}^{p,q} (k-1)!! \cdot (j-1)!! \cdot \binom{p}{k}\binom{q}{j}\left(\frac{m_{20}}{m_{00}}\right)^{k/2}\left(\frac{m_{02}}{m_{00}}\right)^{j/2} B(p-k, q-j).$$

$$\tag{13}$$

Note that we are not limited to circularly symmetric Gaussian blur kernels but we allow different extent of the blur in x_1 and x_2 directions. This may be useful when the horizontal and vertical resolutions of the sensor differ from each other.

3   Experiments and a Comparison to the Zhang's Method

The aim of this section is not only to demonstrate the performance of the proposed method but also to compare it with the method by Zhang et al. [12]. To make the comparison as fair as possible, we asked the authors of [12] for providing all necessary codes. Then we implemented our method using the same version of Matlab (R2013a) and always run both on the same computer (Dell Notebook, VOSTRO 1510, Intel, Core2 Duo CPU, 4GB RAM, Windows 8, 32-bit) and on the same test images. Since the Zhang's method can compare only images of the same size, we kept this condition in all experiments.

3.1   Blur Invariance Property

As we expected, both methods actually exhibit high invariance w.r.t. a "perfect" (i.e. computer generated) Gaussian blur (see Table 1). We changed the blur parameter σ from 0 to 7 and calculated both the invariant distance (ID) and the Zhang's distance (ZD) between the blurred image and the original. Both are reasonably small although not zero. The non-zero values appear because the sampled Gaussian does not fulfil exactly the assumption. For comparison, we also calculated the distances between several *different* originals of the same size, which is by many orders higher.

Table 1. The values of ZD and ID in case of simulated Gaussian blur

Filter size	Sigma	ZD	ID
1	0	0	0
9	1	0.112	2e-19
17	2	0.005	1e-19
25	3	0.009	3e-19
33	4	0.012	4e-19
41	5	0.014	6e-19
49	6	0.016	2e-19
57	7	0.017	2e-19

(a)   (b)   (c)

Fig. 1. Test image "windmills": (a) original, (b) blurred, (c) blurred with noise.

3.2 Matching of Blurred Templates - Simulated Blur

In this experiment we tested the performance in the template matching, which is a particular classification problem we often face in practice. Assuming that we have a large clear image of a scene and a blurred template, the task is to localize this template in the clear image. For non-blurred templates, cross-correlation has been traditionally used to resolve this task. For blurred templates, we again tested both ID and ZD and for a comparison we included also the cross-correlation. Since the testing of each possible template location is very time consuming, we used all three methods in a hierarchical coarse-to-fine implementation. On the coarse level, we shifted the template by the step of 4 pixels in both directions. On the fine level, we searched a 9×9 neighborhood of the "best" location found in the coarse level. Provided that the horizontal and vertical localization errors are independent and both have the same normal distribution, the absolute localization error has a Rayleigh distribution. We estimated the mean values and standard deviations of the localization error of all three methods, which illustrates the accuracy. Since these parameters might be influenced by few big errors, we also calculated the number of "correct hits", which may serve as another accuracy measure. We marked the position of the template found by the algorithm as a hit, if its localization error was less or equal to one pixel in each direction.

Note that in template matching, when the blurred templates have been extracted from a large scene, we always face a boundary effect. This means there is a strip along the template boundary where the convolution model is not valid (even if the blur has been introduced artificially) because the pixels laying outside the template also contribute to the intensity values inside this strip due to the blurring kernel. The boundary effect is the main source of errors in a noise-free case.

We used a simulated blur. We took a clear image of the size 256×256, blurred it by a 13×13 Gaussian of $\sigma = 2$ and randomly selected 30 templates of the size 32×32. These templates were searched in the clear image. We used the invariants up to the order six. The results of the matching in terms of the accuracy and computational time are summarized in Table 2. We can see that the accuracy of both ID and ZD are excellent, so both methods are stable w.r.t. the boundary effect. The ZD yields even better localization error than ID because it uses a complete information about the template while the invariants work with highly compressed information. On the other hand, ID is more than 20 times faster than ZD. The cross-correlation was much faster than ID but its accuracy was very low because of the blurring. The time measurement for one template includes a complete "scan" of the scene including invariant and distance calculation for each tested position and search for the minimum distance. Overheads (reading of the images, generating blur kernel, blurring the image, template selection, etc.) are common for all methods and were not included into the measurement.

Table 2. Matching of blurred templates

Methods	Mean error	Std	Mean time complexity(s)	Correct hits
Cross-correlation	42.53	22.22	1.29	23
ZD	0.16	0.08	831.54	30
ID	0.39	0.20	34.55	30

Table 3. Matching of blurred and noisy templates

Methods	Mean error	Std	Mean time complexity(s)	Correct hits
Cross-correlation	41.24	21.55	1.31	20
ZD	43.99	22.98	825.11	15
ID	0.90	0.47	33.11	28

Then we repeated the same experiment with the same setting and with the same templates but we added a Gaussian white noise of SNR = 10 dB into the blurred image (see Fig. 1). As can be seen from Table 3, the results changed dramatically. The ID still provides 28 correct hits and the mean error less than one, while the ZD was even worse than the cross-correlation. The invariant method is robust because the moments are defined as integrals, which basically "averages" the noise and decreases its impact on the feature values. On the other hand, the Zhang distance is very sensitive. This is because in this method the image blur level is estimated by measuring the energy in the high-pass band. The noise dominates the image on high frequencies and contributes a lot to this measure. Hence, the blurred image with a noise may often be considered "sharper" than the clear image, which leads to a wrong estimate of the blur level and to incorrect distance calculation. The time complexity is basically the same as in the first experiment.

3.3 Matching of Blurred Templates - Real Blur

We repeated the same experiment with a real blur. We employed two images of the spot in the solar photosphere taken by a telescope with a CCD camera in a visible spectral band (venue: Observatory Ondřejov, Czech Republic; wavelength: $\lambda \doteq 590$ nm). Since the time interval between the two acquisitions was only a few minutes, the scene can be considered still and the images are almost perfectly registered. As the atmospheric conditions changed between the acquisitions, the first image is relatively sharp while the other one is noticeably blurred by the atmospheric turbulence (see Fig. 2). The blur kernel is believed to be approximately Gaussian (an experimental validation of this assumption can be found for instance in [8]). Mild additive noise is present in both images. By the same algorithm as in the previous case, we matched 20 randomly chosen templates extracted from the blurred image against the "clear" image. The size of the images was 175×175, the template size was 32×32, and the maximum order of the invariants used was six. As one can see from Table 4, the results are consistent with those we achieved on simulated blurring: ZD performs insignificantly better localization than ID on the expense of the time complexity.

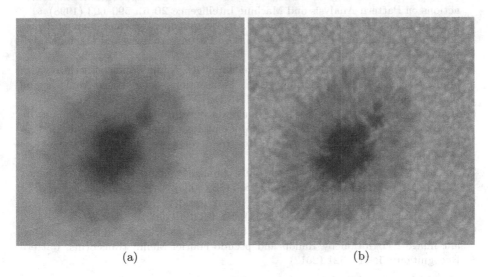

(a)   (b)

Fig. 2. Detail of solar photosphere (a) with higher blur, (b) with lower blur.

Table 4. Template matching in astronomical images

Methods	Mean error	Std	Mean time complexity(s)	Correct hits
Cross-correlation	11.83	6.18	0.47	16
ZD	0.74	0.38	329.72	20
ID	0.81	0.42	15.74	20

4   Conclusion

We proposed new invariants w.r.t. Gaussian blur, both in frequency and image domains. We showed the performance of the new method in matching of blurred and noisy templates. Comparing to the Zhang's method [12], which has been the only Gaussian-blur invariant metric, the proposed method is significantly faster and more robust to additive noise.

Acknowledgments. The authors express their gratitude to the Czech Science Foundation for financial support of this work under the grant No. GA15-16928S. Thanks to Observatory Ondřejov for their help with accessing the images of the solar photosphere.

References

1. Carasso, A.S.: The APEX method in image sharpening and the use of low exponent Lévy stable laws. SIAM Journal on Applied Mathematics **63**(2), 593–618 (2003)
2. Elder, J.H., Zucker, S.W.: Local scale control for edge detection and blur estimation. IEEE Transactions on Pattern Analysis and Machine Intelligence **20**(7), 699–716 (1998)
3. Flusser, J., Suk, T.: Degraded image analysis: An invariant approach. IEEE Transactions on Pattern Analysis and Machine Intelligence **20**(6), 590–603 (1998)
4. Flusser, J., Suk, T., Boldyš, J., Zitová, B.: Projection operators and moment invariants to image blurring. IEEE Transactions on Pattern Analysis and Machine Intelligence **37**(4), 786–802 (2015)
5. Gopalan, R., Taheri, S., Turaga, P., Chellappa, R.: A blur-robust descriptor with applications to face recognition. IEEE Transactions on Pattern Analysis and Machine Intelligence **34**(6), 1220–1226 (2012)
6. Honarvar Shakibaei, B., Flusser, J.: Image deconvolution in moment domain. In: Papakostas, G.A. (ed.) Moments and Moment Invariants - Theory and Applications Gate to Computer Science and Research, vol. 1, pp. 111–125. Science Gate Publishing (2014)
7. Liu, J., Zhang, T.: Recognition of the blurred image by complex moment invariants. Pattern Recognition Letters **26**(8), 1128–1138 (2005)
8. Šroubek, F., Flusser, J.: Multichannel blind iterative image restoration. IEEE Transactions on Image Processing **12**(9), 1094–1106 (2003)
9. Xiao, B., Ma, J.F., Cui, J.T.: Combined blur, translation, scale and rotation invariant image recognition by Radon and pseudo-Fourier-Mellin transforms. Pattern Recognition **45**, 314–321 (2012)

10. Xue, F., Blu, T.: A novel SURE-based criterion for parametric PSF estimation. IEEE Transactions on Image Processing **24**(2), 595–607 (2015)
11. Zhang, W., Cham, W.K.: Single-image refocusing and defocusing. IEEE Transactions on Image Processing **21**(2), 873–882 (2012)
12. Zhang, Z., Klassen, E., Srivastava, A.: Gaussian blurring-invariant comparison of signals and images. IEEE Transactions on Image Processing **22**(8), 3145–3157 (2013)
13. Zhang, Z., Klassen, E., Srivastava, A., Turaga, P., Chellappa, R.: Blurring-invariant riemannian metrics for comparing signals and images. In: IEEE International Conference on Computer Vision, ICCV 2011, pp. 1770–1775 (2011)

Rejecting False Positives in Video Object Segmentation

Daniela Giordano, Isaak Kavasidis, Simone Palazzo,
and Concetto Spampinato[✉]

Department of Electrical, Electronics and Computer Engineering,
University of Catania, Viale Andrea Doria 6, 95125 Catania, Italy
{dgiordan,kavasidis,simone.palazzo,cspampin}@dieei.unict.it,
http://www.dieei.unict.it/eng

Abstract. False-positive removal is a necessary step for robust video object segmentation because of the presence of visual noise introduced by unavoidable factors such as background movements, light changes, artifacts, etc. In this paper we present a set of generic visual cues that enable the discrimination between true positives and false positives detected by a video object segmentation approach. The devised object features encode real-world object properties, such as shape regularity, marked boundaries, color and texture uniformity and motion continuity and can be used in a post-processing layer to reject false positives.

A thorough performance evaluation of the employed features and classifiers is carried out in order to identify which visual cues/classifier allow for a better separability between true and false positives. The experimental results, obtained on three challenging datasets, showed that a post-processing layer exploiting the devised visual features is able a) to reduce the false alarm rate by about 10% to 20%, while keeping the number of true positives almost unaltered, and b) to generalize over different object classes and application domains.

1 Introduction

Video object segmentation is a fundamental task for many computer vision problems from object tracking to behaviour understanding. One of the most common approaches for object segmentation is through background modeling [7], which aims at estimating a model of the scene without objects of interest; this model is then compared to each video frame to extract *foreground* objects. Assuming static cameras, much of the difficulty of these methods lies in the characteristics of the background: for example, moving background elements (e.g. trees in the wind) or light changes may be erroneously segmented as objects of interest, thus leading to a performance decrease. Traditionally, background modeling has been addressed by density-based methods, where the distribution of each background pixel in time is modeled by a probability density function (e.g. Gaussian) [20,23]. Motion analysis [3,17], object ranking [13,25] and clustering point track [6,19] methods have been also proposed, but the problem of false positives is still

© Springer International Publishing Switzerland 2015
G. Azzopardi and N. Petkov (Eds.): CAIP 2015, Part I, LNCS 9256, pp. 100–112, 2015.
DOI: 10.1007/978-3-319-23192-1_9

Fig. 1. Example results of the video object segmentation algorithm in [4] on the I2R Dataset: (left) input frame, (right) output mask. The algorithm is able to segment well the object of interest, however, it also detects part of the curtain, i.e. a false positive, as its pixel distribution does not fit with the background model, previously computed.

unsolved (see Fig. 1). This becomes more evident in particularly challenging scenarios featured by high object appearance variability, background movements and sudden light changes and, operating only at the pixel-level (or superpixel level [15,18]) might be not enough to solve the problem, while methods working at blob-level are necessary.

The identification of the visual features able to support this process is the subject of the work presented in this paper. The basic concept is to analyze each blob (detected by a video object segmentation approach) and to compute a set of low-level features inspired to real-world object properties (such as shape regularity and color/motion differences with respect to the surrounding region) which allow to discriminate between actual objects of interest and false alarms.

The main contributions of our paper are: 1) identification of the suitable object features (and their combination) for discriminating objects of interest from background objects, thus improving the video object segmentation performance without the need of heavy pixel-wise post-processing steps (e.g., Markov Random Fields); 2) a systematic evaluation of the devised features and classifiers in order to identify the most meaningful object descriptors and the most promising classifier to be used in a post-processing layer; and 3) the evaluation of such post-processing layer in several scenarios, from people walking in urban environments to fish freely swimming in an underwater unconstrained environments, thus proving the generalization capabilities of proposed object descriptors.

The paper is organized in the following sections: Section 2 presents an overview of the state of the art on the topic of this paper; Section 3 describes the devised features from both a mathematical and a motivational point of view; Section 4 shows all the obtained results, from individual feature analysis to overall classification performance, in terms of misclassification rate and ROC curves. Discussion on the achieved results and conclusions are given also in Section 4.

2   Related Works

The problem of false positives in video object segmentation is an old one, it has been often tackled by employing morphological operators, e.g. erosion, dilation, connected components removal [24], etc. More recently, methods, e.g. Markov Random Fields [20] exploiting the inherent spatial coherency of real-world objects have been successfully applied to remove false positives instead of using ad hoc heuristics. However, these methods suffer from two main shortcomings: 1) they operate at single pixel level and do not consider the detected blob (output of video segmentation approach) as a whole, and 2) they are sometimes applied indistinctly to all the image pixels (generally to probabilities maps), thus worsening algorithms' performance.

From a general point of view, the subject of this paper is a bit different: in fact it aims at analyzing a blob/segment deciding whether it is an object of interest according to specific features of real-world objects. To the best of our knowledge, in the literature there exist few works dealing with this topic. Alexe *et al.* [2] define the notion of "objectness" as the likeliness that an image window contains an object of any class. Since no hypothesis is provided on the classes of objects, this approach defines a criterion for *saliency* analysis in images, based on the extraction of several cues describing contrast, segmentation, presence of edges, etc. One of the aspects highlighted in this work is that segmentation information plays an important role in objectness analysis. In fact, a well-detected contour typically coincides with curves in the image laying on the boundary between two different regions, in terms of differences in color and texture. The problem of the objectness-based approach is that it does not take into account any real-world object features and the visual cues are identified only according to some intuitive principles without an exhaustive evaluation of them.

A method that, instead, takes object structural properties into consideration is presented by Cheng *et al.* [8], and it enhances the output of a superpixel-based segmentation algorithm [11] with a perceptual organization framework inspired by the application of Gestalt laws in images [16]. Starting from a relatively grained segmentation, this approach allows to join together those image regions which are likely to represent individual parts of a larger structured object.

Another application of object likeliness is in the performance evaluation of video object segmentation algorithms without ground truth data. Erdem *et al.* [10] proposed a method for evaluating segmentation algorithms without the availability of ground-truth data. Similarly to [2], this approach consists in computing a set of contrast- and motion-based features which are linearly combined to provide an overall goodness score.

The work described in this paper extends a previous work by the same authors [21], where a Naive Bayesian Classifier was used to identify false positives by exploiting some of the visual cues proposed in [2,8,10]. In this work, we carry out a more detailed and systematic analysis of a) the visual cues adopted to reflect real-world object features, and b) the most suitable classifiers for a better class separability.

3 Method

The idea behind this work is that the same intuitive principles, according to which people are able to distinguish objects, can be mathematically encoded into a set of features: for example, a well-marked and regular boundary, a consistent and uniform internal structure, and motion continuity and rigidity in time are properties which real-world objects satisfy and can therefore be used to identify them. Of course, none of these features is sufficient by itself: for example, in cases of mimicry, visual cues based on the contrast might be useless.

The features used by our approach are categorized in: shape and size, contrast and boundary, internal and on-boundary homogeneity. They are described in the next subsections, explaining the idea behind them, their implementation and parameterization.

In the notation used in formulas and descriptions, the symbols $I(x, y)$ and $M(x, y)$ indicate, respectively, the processed video frame and the output mask containing the detected segments/blobs. Pixel coordinates (x, y) may be substituted by a generic pixel index p. Coordinate indexes are removed when unnecessary. The output of a video segmentation approach is often referred to either as segments or blobs.

3.1 Shape and Size

Only one cue has been taken into consideration to describe geometrical properties of blob's shape: i.e., contour complexity.

- **Boundary complexity** (bc)
  This visual cue is able to provide information on the complexity of a shape, which is obviously strongly correlated to the quality of a contour. The computation of this score consists in scanning a contour by shifting a fixed-size "window" (in this case, a section of the contour) and analyzing the degree of curvature C (by comparing the distance between the segment's end-points and the segment's actual length) and the presence of notches (i.e. non-convex corners) P within the window:

$$bc(M, s, k, s_n) = \frac{1}{N} \sum_{d=1}^{N} C_{M,d}(s, k) \cdot P_{M,d}(s, k, s_n) \tag{1}$$

$$C_{M,d}(s, k) = 1 - \frac{\|p_{d+ks} - p_d\|}{\sum_{c=1}^{k} \|p_{d+cs} - p_{d+(c-1)s}\|} \tag{2}$$

$$P_{M,d}(s, k, s_n) = 1 - 2 \cdot \left| 0.5 - \frac{n}{N-3} \right| \tag{3}$$

  where k is the length of the sliding window measured in pixel "steps" (i.e. a sequence of a small number of consecutive pixels), s is the number of pixel included in a step for the curvature analysis, s_n is number of pixels included in a step for the notch analysis, N is the length of the contour, p_d is the location of the d-th point in the contour, and n is the number of notches in the window.

According to this formula, an absolutely convex shape (i.e. without notches) will have a boundary complexity equal to 0, whereas the more irregular a shape is, the higher its complexity score will be.

3.2   Contrast on Boundary

A straightforward way to check the quality of a segmentation, when knowing an object's real contour, is to verify that the segment boundaries actually divide an area into regions characterized by markedly different visual and motion properties. This is the purpose of the following visual cues.

– **Color contrast** (*cc*)

The color contrast score on the boundary is inspired by [10]. Given the current mask M, we apply θ cycles of morphological dilation to compute the enlarged mask $M_{\theta,\text{out}}$; similarly, we apply erosion to compute the shrunk mask $M_{\theta,\text{in}}$. Two corresponding histograms from a given color space are then computed from the points belonging to $M_{\theta,\text{out}}$'s and $M_{\theta,\text{in}}$, namely $H_{\theta,\text{in}}$ and $H_{\theta,\text{out}}$. Finally, the χ^2 distance is applied to compute the similarity between the two histograms.

In other words: given n-th channel from the color space CS (grayscale, RGB, HSV, CIELAB), we define $H_{\theta,\text{in}}(b)$ as the relative frequency of histogram bin b, computed over the points in the contour of the shrunk mask $M_{\theta,\text{in}}$; similarly we compute $H_{\theta,\text{out}}(b)$.

The color contrast score cc is then computed as:

$$cs_C(\theta) = \frac{1}{2}\sum_{b=0}^{N}\frac{(H_{\theta,\text{out}}(b) - H_{\theta,\text{out}}(b))^2}{H_{\theta,\text{out}}(b) + H_{\theta,\text{out}}(b)} \tag{4}$$

where C indicates the channel on the chosen color space and N the number of histogram bins.

– **Superpixel straddling** (*ss*). Superpixel segmentation [11] divides an image into small regions having uniform color or texture, which directly implies that superpixels typically preserve object boundaries. This property allows us to define a boundary correctness cue based on the evidence that the boundary of a "good" blob should contain all of its superpixels; on the contrary, in a "bad" blob, superpixels may be located partly inside and partly outside of its boundary.

The *superpixel straddling* score is computed by evaluating the area of the intersection between the blob's mask M (i.e. the output of the video object segmentation) and each overlapping superpixel S_i; if the boundary of the object is close to the boundary between superpixels, the intersection area will be small, compared to the areas of both the mask and the S_i patch. Summing up the contributions from all $\{S_i\}$, the final score is computed as:

$$ss\,(M, S) = 1 - \sum_{S_i \in S} \frac{min\,(|S_i \setminus M|, |S_i \cap M|)}{|M|} \tag{5}$$

where S is the superpixel segmentation (i.e. the set of segments $\{S_i\}$) of the area surrounding the target blob. Each region S_i keeps the score high if it is mainly inside or outside of the object's boundary.

- **Motion on boundary** (mc). The previously described features can all be computed on a single image, since they involve only spatial variations. However, motion information is extremely important to evaluate if a blob's contour has been correctly extracted [10]. In theory, for a correct segmentation we should find that the motion of pixels on its inner border should be larger than zero and roughly uniform, whereas outside of it the motion should be zero (when the object moves against background) or different in modulus and/or direction (for example, in the case of occlusions).

   This idea is expressed numerically in the same way as for the color contrast score, with the only difference that the histogram is computed over the modulus or phase of the motion vector computed by optical flow [5], and that two distinct values are used as number of cycles for dilation and erosion. This distinction is due to the fact that optical flow may mark pixels immediately outside of the boundary of the object as moving even if they belong to the background, so it may be useful to choose a larger number of cycles for dilation than for erosion:

$$mc_C\,(\theta_{\text{in}}, \theta_{\text{out}}) = \frac{1}{2} \sum_{b=0}^{B-1} \frac{(H_{\theta_{\text{out}},\text{out}}\,(b) \quad H_{\theta_{\text{in}},\text{in}}\,(b))^2}{H_{\theta_{\text{out}},\text{out}}\,(b) + H_{\theta_{\text{in}},\text{in}}\,(b)} \tag{6}$$

C is either the modulus or phase of the motion vector, from which histograms are computed, B is the number of bins of the histogram, and θ_{out} and θ_{in} are respectively the number of cycles applied from dilation and erosion.

- **Edge density** (ed). The edge density score [2] assesses the density of edges (computed by a Canny edge detector) close to the object's boundary. The computation of the scores consists of counting the number of *edgels* (edge pixels) just inside of the contour – that is, on the boundary of a $M_{\theta,\text{in}}$ mask, as defined previously – and normalizing the count by the perimeter of the inner boundary.

3.3   Internal Homogeneity

Apart from checking for the visual and motion properties in the proximity of contours, a good blob should also be featured by a relative internal homogeneity of the same properties, which is what the following two features are meant to evaluate.

- **Color homogeneity** (ch). Color homogeneity is computed on a per-color-space (grayscale, RGB, HSV CIELAB) and per-channel basis, and consists in evaluating the distribution properties of the relevant histogram (e.g. the red channel for RGB, or the saturation channel for HSV). The computation depends on the histogram moments: mean, variance, skewness and kurtosis:

$$ch_C = f(H_C) \tag{7}$$

where $f(\cdot)$ computes the specified distribution property on the given histogram.

Motion homogeneity (mh). The duality of the *color contrast* score and the *motion contrast* score appears again in the homogeneity evaluation. Therefore, the *motion homogeneity* is computed as the internal homogeneity score – the only difference is that the C channel is either the modulus or the phase of the motion vector.

In this section, we have defined the set of features used to decide whether a blob/segment detected by a video object segmentation algorithm actually is an object of interest according to the specific task. This selection was meant to include several different aspects through which such a decision could be made, from a visually intuitive point of view. However, not all of them can be always significant:

- contrast-based scores may fail in scenes with low contrast or dark lighting;
- boundary analysis may fail if the segmented contour for an object is too large or too irregular, yet roughly correct;
- internal homogeneity may not be meaningful for structured objects made up of distinct and different parts;

These limitations show how each single feature does not provide enough information to perform the classification by itself. Moreover, some of them, in spite of the apparent intuitive significance, might reveal unnecessary. Furthermore, many of the above-described scores have several parameters on which they depend and which can critically influence the success or failure in the adoption of those scores.

For these reasons, a thorough analysis of each score contribution (also in combination to the others) is necessary in order to verify the discrimination capability of the overall approach and maximize its accuracy.

4   Experiments and Results

4.1   Datasets

For experimental evaluation we used three datasets consisting of good and bad detections (manually annotated) in different scenarios. Each sample in the datasets consists of three images: the video frame at time t where the object was detected, the object's binary mask and the frame at time $t+1$ (used for the optical flow computation).

- **Dataset 1**: 530 images taken from underwater videos, equally divided between good, i.e. showing fish, and bad samples, i.e., showing background objects or noise. This dataset was used for feature analysis and for training and testing the classifiers;
- **Dataset 2**: 501 images the I2R dataset [14], divided between 243 good samples and 258 bad samples. This dataset was used for testing the classifier in a different domain than the one it was trained for.
- **Dataset 3**: consisting of 154 manually-labeled ground-truth frames (only true positives are labeled) from 3 underwater videos, for a total of 322 objects. This dataset was used to evaluate the false-positive removal capability of the proposed approach when used for post-processing of a background modeling approach.

4.2   Feature Selection

Given the large number of parameters in the computation of the scores in Section 3, our first tests were aimed at selecting, for each of those scores, a small number (up to 3) of best parameter sets. Such parameter sets were chosen according to the class separation capability of the corresponding score, which was evaluated by analyzing the overlap of the probability density functions built from the values obtained for the "good" and the "bad" samples as shown in Fig. 2.

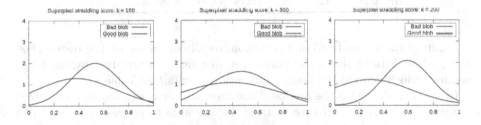

Fig. 2. Distributions of the superpixel straddling score in case of "good" (green line) and the "bad" (red line) blobs as the number of superpixels (k) per image varies. We chose the values for which the separation between the two classes was the highest (rightmost)

After performing this optimization, we analyzed the combinations between the chosen candidate features. Since each feature can have several values for each parameter, we built as many classifiers as the number of combinations (*configurations*) between the different parameters of the features; in our case, the number of possible configurations was 5832. The evaluation proceeded independently for each one of the 5832 configurations, in order to find which one yielded the best classification results. For a given configuration, before training and testing the corresponding classifier, sequential feature selection [1] was performed, so that only significant features where used for the computation. The need for feature selection was not related to the high number of features (in fact, there are only seven of them), but to consideration on computation time, since some of those features (e.g. those exploiting optical flow) could take a considerable amount of time.

4.3 Classification

After feature selection was performed for each configuration, a binary classifier was trained and tested using the samples from Dataset 1 (containing fish images). The classifiers tested were: Support Vector Machines with a Radial Basis Function kernel (SVM-RBF), Naive Bayes Classifier, Linear, Quadratic and Mahalanobis.

Table 1 shows the average misclassification rate (MCR, i.e. the ratio of misclassified samples over the total size of the test set) for the best configuration of each classifier, obtained through a 5-fold cross validation on Dataset 1.

Table 1. Average misclassification rate (MCR) obtained with a 5-fold cross-validation for each classifier, with the corresponding selected features.

Classifier	MCR	Features
SVM-RBF [9]	4.34%	bc, cc, ch, ed, ss, mc, mh
Naive Bayes classifier [12]	7.17%	bc, cc, ch, ed, ss
Linear [12]	6.98%	bc, cc, ed, ss
Quadratic [12]	6.33%	bc, cc, ch, ed, ss
Mahalanobis [12]	7.03%	bc, cc, ch, ed, ss

Figure 3 shows the ROC and precision/recall curves for all the tested classifiers, while Table 2 shows the parameters for each feature used by the SVM classifier, which achived the best classification results (see Table 1).

In order to show that the proposed features, although selected and optimized on a given dataset (in our case Dataset 1), are able to generalize over object classes, we tested the best-performing classifier on a set of images taken from a human video-surveillance datasets (dataset 2, as described in paragraph 4.1) and the results are reported in Table 3. It can be noticed that also in this case the algorithm was able to obtain satisfactory results.

4.4 Post-Processing Layer for Video Object Segmentation

Our final test concerned the application of the overall system for the suppression of false positives in a video object segmentation framework. In detail, we added the classifier previously trained as the downstream module for blob analysis (with the goal to discard false positives) of two classic background modeling algorithms, namely, ViBe [4] and GMM [22]. We tested the application of the proposed false-positive filtering system on Dataset 3, and the results, in terms of false alarm rate (FAR), precision, recall and F-measure, are given in Table 4. Fig. 4 shows some example results of the proposed approach.

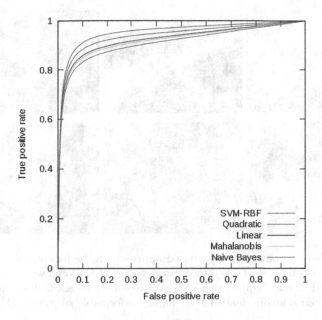

Fig. 3. ROC curves of the classifiers in Table 1.

Table 2. Feature configuration for the SVM classifier which yields the best classification accuracy.

Feature Configuration	
bc	s: 5, k: 8, s_n:5
cc	θ: 3, color channel: H (HSV)
ch	color channel: H (HSV), statistic: mean
ed	Canny lower threshold: 0.1
ss	σ: 0.5, k: 200, minimum size: 50
mc	Lucas-Kanade [5] parameters: window: 10, max. level: 0, iterations: 5, type: modulus; θ_{in}: 3, θ_{out}: 7
mh	Lucas-Kanade parameters: window: 20, max. level: 0, iterations: 5, type: modulus, statistic: mean

Table 3. Average misclassification rate (MCR) obtained with a 5-fold cross-validation using either dataset as training set and dataset 2 as test set.

Training dataset	Test dataset	MCR
Dataset 2	Dataset 2	6.8%
Dataset 1	Dataset 2	9.3%

4.5 Discussion

The results show how the application of the presented approach reduces significantly false positives, while at the same time keeping the recall high. Video 3 exemplifies a case in which the algorithm filters out many true positives, however the much larger decrease in the false alarm rate still allows to obtain an increase in the F-measure value.

Fig. 4. Example of outputs of the proposed approach on the fish image dataset (first row) and the I2R dataset (last row). False positives are red-colored while true positives are green-colored. It may happen that true positives are misclassified as false positives especially in those domains featured by highly deformable objects and with many occlusions.

Table 4. Comparison between the performance of ViBe [4] and GMM [22] without and with the application of false-positive removal layer.

| Alg. | Video | Original | | | | With post-processing | | | |
		FAR	Precision	Recall	F-measure	FAR	Precision	Recall	F-measure
ViBe	1	18.7%	81.3%	77.6%	79.4%	10.5%	89.5%	76.2%	82.3%
	2	42.2%	57.8%	74.2%	65.0%	25.8%	74.2%	70.2%	72.5%
	3	25.0%	75.0%	74.9%	75.0%	11.9%	88.1%	67.3%	76.3%
GMM	1	22.0%	78.0%	76.9%	77.4%	11.2%	88.8%	74.3%	80.9%
	2	51.4%	48.6%	69.4%	57.2%	30.9%	69.1%	67.0%	68.0%
	3	24.7%	75.3%	74.5%	74.9%	19.9%	80.1%	70.1%	75.0%

Furthermore, the results presented in Table 3 show that the features employed are actually representative of real-world object properties, independently of the specific domain they are applied to. This is a very interesting result; in fact, apart from the possibility of using the same classifier in different contexts (e.g. if no training data is available), this is also a further confirmation of the generalization capabilities of the proposed visual cues over object classes.

Finally, the proposed features can be also employed for object detection in still images if leaving out motion cues.

4.6 Materials

The Matlab source code for the features used in this work and the datasets used to carry out the training and performance evaluation is available online at http://perceive.dieei.unict.it (Papers section).

References

1. Aha, D.W., Bankert, R.L.: A comparative evaluation of sequential feature selection algorithms, vol. 206, pp. 1–7. SpringerVerlag New York (1995)
2. Alexe, B., Deselaers, T., Ferrari, V.: Measuring the Objectness of Image Windows. IEEE Transactions on Pattern Analysis and Machine Intelligence, PP(c), 1–14 (2012)
3. Bai, X., Wang, J., Sapiro, G.: Dynamic color flow: a motion-adaptive color model for object segmentation in video. In: Daniilidis, K., Maragos, P., Paragios, N. (eds.) ECCV 2010, Part V. LNCS, vol. 6315, pp. 617–630. Springer, Heidelberg (2010)
4. Barnich, O., Van Droogenbroeck, M.: ViBe: a universal background subtraction algorithm for video sequences. IEEE transactions on image processing : a publication of the IEEE Signal Processing Society 20(6), 1709–24 (2011)
5. Bouguet, J.-Y.: Pyramidal Implementation of the Lucas-Kanade Feature Tracker Description of the algorithm (2000)
6. Brox, T., Malik, J.: Object segmentation by long term analysis of point trajectories. In: Daniilidis, K., Maragos, P., Paragios, N. (eds.) ECCV 2010, Part V. LNCS, vol. 6315, pp. 282–295. Springer, Heidelberg (2010)
7. Brutzer, S., Hoferlin, B., Heidemann, G.: Evaluation of background subtraction techniques for video surveillance. In: 2011 IEEE Conference on Computer Vision and Pattern Recognition (CVPR), pp. 1937–1944, June 2011
8. Cheng, C., Koschan, A., Chen, C.-H., Page, D.L., Abidi, M.: Outdoor scene image segmentation based on background recognition and perceptual organization. IEEE Transactions on Image Processing 21(3), 1007–1019 (2012)
9. Cortes, C., Vapnik, V.: Support-vector networks. Machine Learning 20(3), 273–297 (1995)
10. Erdem, C.E., Sankur, B., Tekalp, A.M.: Performance measures for video object segmentation and tracking. IEEE Transactions on Image Processing 13(7), 937–951 (2004)
11. Felzenszwalb, P., Huttenlocher, D.: Efficient graph-based image segmentation. International Journal of Computer Vision 59(2), 167–181 (2004)
12. Krzanowski, W.J.: Principles of Multivariate Analysis: A User's Perspective. Oxford University Press, New York (1988)
13. Lee, Y. J., Kim, J., Grauman, K.: Key-segments for video object segmentation. In: Proceedings of the 2011 International Conference on Computer Vision, ICCV 2011, pp. 1995–2002 (2011)
14. Li, L., Huang, W., Gu, I.Y.H., Tian, Q.: Foreground object detection from videos containing complex background. In: Proceedings of the Eleventh ACM International Conference on Multimedia MULTIMEDIA 2003, vol. 3, p. 2 (2003)
15. Lim, J., Han, B.: Generalized background subtraction using superpixels with label integrated motion estimation. In: Fleet, D., Pajdla, T., Schiele, B., Tuytelaars, T. (eds.) ECCV 2014, Part V. LNCS, vol. 8693, pp. 173–187. Springer, Heidelberg (2014)

16. Liu, Z., Jacobs, D.W., Basri, R.: The role of convexity in perceptual completion: beyond good continuation. Vision Research **39**(25), 4244–4257 (1999)
17. Ochs, P., Malik, J., Brox, T.: Segmentation of moving objects by long term video analysis. IEEE Transactions on Pattern Analysis and Machine Intelligence **36**(6), 1187–1200 (2014)
18. Papazoglou, A., Ferrari, V.: Fast object segmentation in unconstrained video. In: 2013 IEEE International Conference on Computer Vision, pp. 1777–1784, December 2013
19. Ochs, P., Brox, T.: Object segmentation in video: a hierarchical variational approach for turning point trajectories into dense regions. In: IEEE International Conference on Computer Vision (ICCV) (2011)
20. Sheikh, Y., Shah, M.: Bayesian object detection in dynamic scenes. In: 2005 IEEE Computer Society Conference on Computer Vision and Pattern Recognition CVPR 2005, vol. 1, pp. 74–79 (2005)
21. Spampinato, C., Palazzo, S.: Enhancing object detection performance by integrating motion objectness and perceptual organization. In: 2012 21st International Conference on Pattern Recognition (ICPR), pp. 3640–3643, November 2012
22. Stauffer, C., Grimson, W.: Adaptive background mixture models for real-time tracking. In: Proceedings of 1999 IEEE Computer Society Conference on Computer Vision and Pattern Recognition (Cat. No PR00149), pp. 246–252 (1999)
23. Stauffer, C., Grimson, W.E.L.: Adaptive background mixture models for real-time tracking. In: IEEE Computer Society Conference on Computer Vision and Pattern Recognition, vol. 2, pp. 246–252 (1999)
24. Stauffer, C., Grimson, W.E.L.: Learning patterns of activity using real-time tracking (2000)
25. Zhang, D., Javed, O., Shah, M.: Video object segmentation through spatially accurate and temporally dense extraction of primary object regions. In: 2013 IEEE Conference on Computer Vision and Pattern Recognition, pp. 628–635 (2013)

Ground Truth Correspondence Between Nodes to Learn Graph-Matching Edit-Costs

Xavier Cortés, Francesc Serratosa[✉], and Carlos Francisco Moreno-García

Universitat Rovira i Virgili, Tarragona, Spain
{xavier.cortes,francesc.serratosa}@urv.cat,
carlosfrancisco.moreno@estudiants.urv.cat

Abstract. The Graph Edit Distance is the most used distance between Attributed Graphs and it is composed of three main costs on nodes and arcs: Insertion, Deletion and Substitution. We present a method to learn the Insertion and Deletion costs of nodes and edges defined in the Graph Edit Distance, whereas, we define the Edit Cost Substitution data dependent and without parameters (for instance the Euclidean distance). In some applications, the ground truth of the correspondence between some pairs of graphs is available or can be easily deducted. The aim of the method we present is the learning process depends on these few available ground truth correspondences and not to the classification set that in some applications is not available. To learn these costs, the optimisation algorithm tends to minimise the Hamming distance between the ground truth correspondences and the automatically extracted node correspondences. We believe that minimising the Hamming distance makes the matching algorithm to find a good correspondence and so, to increase the recognition ratio of the classification algorithm in a pattern recognition application.

Keywords: Graph edit distance · Learning edit costs · Hamming distance · Continuous optimisation

1 Introduction

In Pattern Recognition, there are so many applications that work with data types of very different kind and nature, like images [1], fingerprints [2], handwritten symbols [3], chemical structures [4], social networks [5], biological structures [6] and many more. In many cases these data types need to represent the relationships between local parts. For this reason, Attributed Graphs are commonly used in Structural Pattern Recognition.

Graphs are a collection of nodes and edges that connect pairs of nodes. Attributed Graphs are graphs in which some attributes are added on nodes and edges to represent local information or characterisation. Attributes on the nodes and edges represent unary and binary relations of local parts of the objects.

This research is supported by Spanish projects DPI2013-42458-P & TIN2013-47245-C2-2-R.

G. Azzopardi and N. Petkov (Eds.): CAIP 2015, Part I, LNCS 9256, pp. 113–124, 2015.
DOI: 10.1007/978-3-319-23192-1_10

Pattern recognition methods based on graphs consist on a process that extracts Graphs from raw data (images, structures…) and another process that compares Graphs through evaluating the structural similarity of graphs, in a process called Error-Tolerant Graph Matching. Graph Matching Methods consist on finding the correspondence (also called labelling) between different parts of the graphs. Typically, this problem is mathematically formulated as a quadratic assignment problem, which has been demonstrated to be an NP problem. For this reason, some sub-optimal algorithms have been presented [8]. Probably the most well known distance between graphs is the graph edit distance [7], [8], [9] and [10]. The latest algorithm computes the correspondence and distance in cubic cost respect the number of nodes [21], [22]. This distance measure is defined as the minimum amount of required distortion to transform one graph into the other. To this end, a number of distortion or edit operations, consisting of insertion, deletion and substitution of both nodes and edges are defined. To quantitatively evaluate the degree of distortion, edit cost functions are introduced. The basic idea is to assign a penalty cost to each edit operation according to the amount of distortion that it introduces in the transformation. An interesting question arises in this context: given the attributed graphs that represent some objects, how we gauge the importance of each edit operation? That is, how we decide the penalty cost?

Usually, edit costs are estimated in a naïve way or they are learned by trial and error method. The works presented in [11] and [12] have the aim of automatically estimate these costs, but their method minimises an energy related to the recognition ratio in a pattern recognition framework without considering the goodness of the correspondence of the involved graphs. Note that the option to find the costs to minimize the recognition ratio impose that graphs have to be classified or clustered, which it is not always the case, for instance, in image retrieval applications. On the other hand, works presented in [13] and [14], minimize the distance between the automatic obtained labelling and the oracles labelling, but they only estimate the substitution costs and do not contemplate the possibility of having null nodes. Null nodes appear in the edit distance when the node correspondence does not map the whole set of nodes from one of the graphs to the whole set of nodes to the other graph, that is, the application considers the existence of outlier nodes. Finally, the work presented in [15] estimates costs considering the possibility of null nodes and minimizing the distance respect oracles labelling but they do so by a brute-force approach that requires a considerable computation effort and there is no guarantee to explore the best solution, because the space of costs have to be limited.

Given two graphs several correspondences between nodes can be deducted if different costs are presented to the error-tolerant graph-matching algorithm. In this case, a consensus algorithm can be useful to find the final correspondence [16].

The aim of this work is to present a new supervised learning method [17] to automatically learn the insertion and deletion edit costs for Graph Matching such that the distance between the automatic obtained labelling and the oracles labelling is minimised whereas null nodes are considered. An extended version of this paper has been published in [26].

2   Error-Tolerant Graph Matching Based on Edit Operations

One of the most widely used methods for error-tolerant graph matching is the graph edit distance. The basic idea behind the graph edit distance is to define dissimilarity measure between two graphs by the minimum amount of distortion required to transform one graph into the other [7], [9]. To this end, a number of distortion or edit operations ε, consisting of insertion, deletion and substitution of both nodes and edges must be defined. Then, for every pair of graphs (G and G'), there exists a sequence of edit operations, or edit path $(G, G') = (\varepsilon_1, ..., \varepsilon_k)$ (where each ε_i denotes an edit operation) that transforms one graph into the other. In general, several edit paths may exist between two given graphs. This set of edit paths is denoted by $\vartheta(G, G')$. To quantitatively evaluate which is the best edit path, edit cost functions are introduced. The basic idea is to assign a penalty cost C to each edit operation ε_i according to the amount of distortion that it introduces in the transformation. The edit distance between two graphs G and G', denoted by $dist_{K_nK_e}(G, G')$, is defined as the minimum cost of edit path that transforms one graph into the other given parameters K_n (cost of node insertion or deletion) and K_e (cost of edge insertion or deletion). More formally, the edit distance is defined by,

$$dist_{K_nK_e}(G, G') = \underset{(\varepsilon_1, ..., \varepsilon_k) \in \vartheta(G, G')}{min} \left\{ \sum_{i=1}^{k} C(\varepsilon_i) \right\}$$

Optimal [18] and approximate algorithms [19], [20] and [21] for the graph edit distance computation have been presented so far, which are out of the scope of this paper. These algorithms obtain the distance value $dist_{K_nK_e}(G, G')$ as well as a labelling $f_{[K_n K_e]}$ from vertices and arcs of the first graph to vertices and arcs of the second graph. Given an edit path, $path(G, G')$, a labelling $f(G, G')$, can be defined univocally.

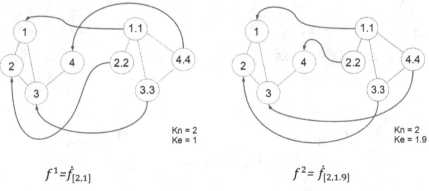

$$f^1 = \dot{f}_{[2,1]} \qquad\qquad f^2 = \dot{f}_{[2,1.9]}$$

Fig. 1. 11 possible optimal labellings $\dot{f}_{[K_n, K_e]}$ (green arrows) depending on K_n and K_e between graph G (red colour) and G' (blue colour). The nodes of the graphs are represented by circles and edges by lines between them.

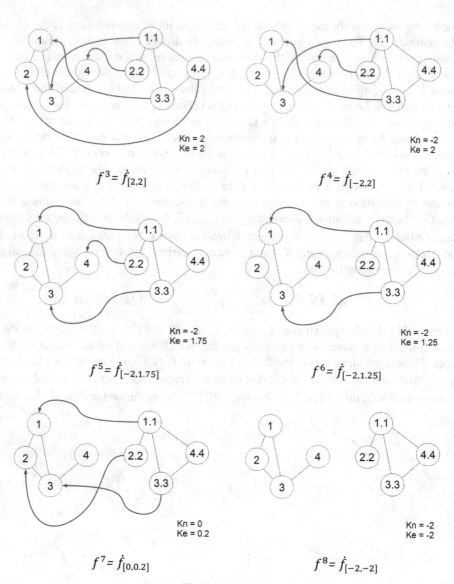

$$f^3 = \dot{f}_{[2,2]}$$

$$f^4 = \dot{f}_{[-2,2]}$$

$$f^5 = \dot{f}_{[-2,1.75]}$$

$$f^6 = \dot{f}_{[-2,1.25]}$$

$$f^7 = \dot{f}_{[0,0.2]}$$

$$f^8 = \dot{f}_{[-2,-2]}$$

Fig. 2. (*Continued*)

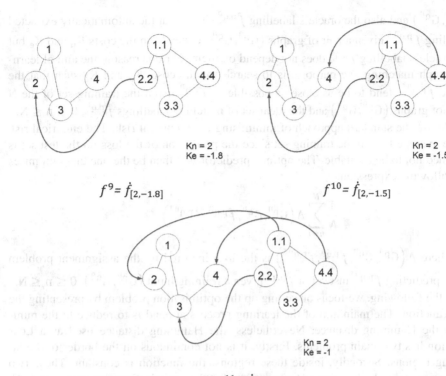

Fig. 3. (*Continued*)

The cost of this labelling is,

$$Cost_{K_n K_e}(G, G', f) = \sum_{i=1}^{k} C(\varepsilon_i) \text{ being related } f \text{ to path } (G, G') = (\varepsilon_1, \ldots, \varepsilon_k)$$

Figure 1 shows 11 possible optimal labellings between two graphs, depending on K_n and K_e. Note that all of them are optimal since, given the specific values of K_n and K_e, they obtain the minimum cost.

In the next section, we present a method to automatically estimate edit costs K_n and K_e through an optimisation method that minimizes the Hamming distance between the optimal labelling and the ideal one.

3   Learning K_n and K_e Costs

Similarly to [14], we approach the problem of learning the costs K_n and K_e for graph matching as a supervised learning problem [23], [24], [25] [26]. The training set is composed of N observations. Each observation is composed of a pair of graphs

$\left(G^{p^n}, G^{q^n}\right)$ and also the oracle's labelling $\hat{f}^{p,q^n}$. Note that the automatically extracted labelling $f^{p,q^{n*}}$ given a pair of graphs $\left(G^{p^n}, G^{q^n}\right)$ depends on the costs K_n and K_e but the oracle's labelling $\hat{f}^{p,q^n}$ does not depend on them. For this reason, the aim of learning graph matching, we purpose, is to search for the costs K_n and K_e such that the whole $f^{p,q^{n*}}$ tend to be as close as possible to $\hat{f}^{p,q^n}$ given the training set of the N pairs of graphs $\left(G^{p^n}, G^{q^n}\right)$ and the ideal set of matching labellings $\hat{f}^{p,q^n}, 0 \le n \le N$.

We use the standard approach of minimising the empirical risk. The empirical risk is the average loss in the training set since the prediction of the loss on the test set is assumed not to be available. The optimal predictor will then be the one that minimises the following expression,

$$\frac{1}{N} \sum_{n=1}^{N} \Delta\left(G^{p^n}, G^{q^n}, \hat{f}^{p,q^n}, f^{p,q^{n*}}\right)$$

Where $\Delta\left(G^{p^n}, G^{q^n}, \hat{f}^{p,q^n}, f^{p,q^{n*}}\right)$ is the loss incurred by the assignment problem when predicting $f^{p,q^{n*}}$ instead of $\hat{f}^{p,q^n}$ given a training input $\left(G^{p^n}, G^{q^n}\right), 0 \le n \le N$.

In the following, we focus on setting up the optimisation problem by presenting the loss function. The main aim of the learning process at hand is to reduce to the minimum the Hamming distance. Nevertheless, the Hamming distance used as a Loss function has two main problems. Firstly, it is not continuous on the border of the labelling regions. Secondly, inside these regions, the function is constant. These two properties make the function not appropriate for the optimisation algorithms. In [14], they suppose the node and edge attributes are real numbers and they present a method to learn the weights that have to be applied to each of the attributes while comparing two nodes. Due to the nature of the method, node insertions and deletions are not possible. The Loss function they propose is based on the end-point error since nodes represent salient points in images. They method has three main drawbacks. The first one is that it is strongly dependent on the regularisation term. The second one is that they need the attributes to be real number and the nodes to represent positions in a given space. And the third one is that nodes cannot be inserted or deleted and so, it supposes there is always a bijective labelling between the original graphs (there are no outliers).

We have named our Loss function Edit-Cost Error Loss because it gauges how far we are to obtain the cost generated by the ideal matching matrix.

$$\Delta\left(G^{p^n}, G^{q^n}, \hat{f}^{p,q^n}, f^{p,q^{n*}}\right) =$$
$$\left(EditCost(G^{p^n}, G^{q^n}, \hat{f}^{p,q^n}) - EditCost\left(G^{p^n}, G^{q^n}, f^{p,q^{n*}}\right)\right)^2$$

Clearly, we assume that two labellings that are close to each other (small Hamming distance) tend to achieve similar costs $EditCost(\cdot)$. Although this relation is not true for all graphs and labellings, the empirical evaluation shows that it is true for most of the graphs and labellings in the datasets. Moreover, in cases where there are symmetries on the graphs, labellings $\hat{f}^{p,q^n}$ and $f^{p,q^{n*}}$ can be completely different but represent a similar mapping between graph nodes. In these cases, our Loss function obtains better results than the Hamming distance function. Figure 2 shows the edit costs of Figure 1 example a) the oracle's labelling and b) the automatically obtained labelling and c) shows our Loss function.

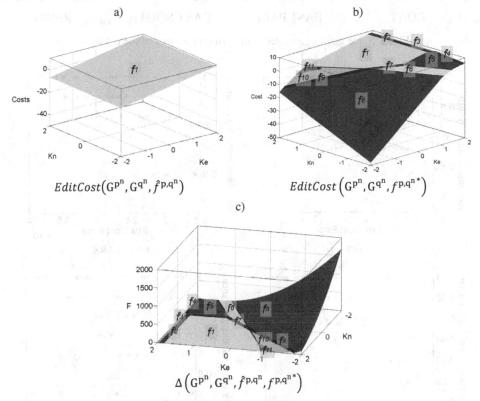

Fig. 2. Following the example of Figure 1, a) Cost of labelling f^1 b) Costs of optimal labelling c) Edit-Cost Error, when oracle labelling is f^1, (each colour represents a different optimal labelling corresponding to that region).

4 Experimental Validation

To empirical validate our proposal; we present some experiments using four databases: BOAT, EAST PARK, EAST SOUTH and RESID [27]. They consist of images taken from different outdoor scenarios across different zooms and rotations and also the homography matrix from the first image to the other ones. From each image, we have extracted salient points using Speeded Up Robust Features detector [28] keeping the 50 points with highest scales. Edges have been determined using Delaunay triangulation [29] (figure 3). Attributes on nodes are the features extracted from the detector [28] and edges do not have attributes. The node substitution cost, K_{ns}, is de normalised Euclidean distance between features, $K_{ns} \in [0,1]$. The edge substitution cost, K_{es}, is 0 if both arcs exist or do not exist. Otherwise $K_{es} = 1$.

BOAT   EAST PARK   EAST SOUTH   RESID

Fig. 3. Some graphs generated from different images of the databases.

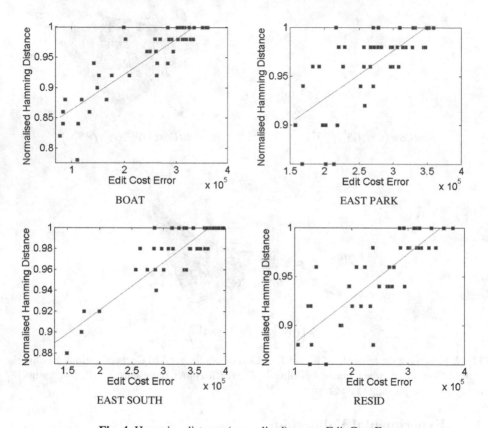

Fig. 4. Hamming distance (normalised) versus Edit Cost Error

Given two images of the same database, the ground truth correspondence is composed of the pairs of points of both images such that the points of one of the images projected to the points of the other image becomes closer than 6 pixels. The non-mapped points are considered outliers and so nodes that have to be inserted or deleted in the ground truth correspondence. The training set (test set) of each database consists of the even (odd) images of the databases' sequences.

We divide the experimental evaluation in two sections, firstly we shown the correlation between Edit Cost Error and the Hamming Distance and secondly we show the increase of accuracy when learned edit costs are used.

Figure 4 shows the relation between the Edit Cost Error and the Hamming distance (normalised by the order of the graph) in all pairs of graphs in the databases. We have taken arbitrarily costs $K_v = 1$ and $K_e = 1$. We can deduct a positive linear relation although in some of the sequences there is a high linear approximation error. We show these scatters to empirically validate our initial assumption that when the Edit Cost Error increases, the Hamming distance so it does.

BOAT   EAST PARK

EAST SOUTH   RESID

Fig. 5. Some examples of correspondences. Upper images: $K_n = 1$ and $K_e = 1$. Below images: Learned costs. Yellow lines: missing mappings. Green lines: correct mappings. Red lines: incorrect mappings.

The aim of the practical evaluation is to show the increase of accuracy when the learned edit costs are used respect four different usual combinations of edit costs. We used all combinations of image pairs of the training set (test set) in the learning process (validation process). The accuracy is defined as the normalised number of nodes that have been mapped in the same node than the ground truth correspondence. In both, the learning process and the validation process, we have used the Fast Bipartite algorithm [21]. Moreover, the optimisation algorithm has been the Nelder-Mead method [30]. Table 1 shows the obtained average accuracies in the four databases.

The first Accuracy column has been obtained using the initial costs (no learning process is performed). The second Accuracy column has been obtained using the learned costs. Note that, given a database, the learning algorithm converges at the same costs independently of the initial costs and the Accuracy drastically increases. The first two combinations of initial costs are the usual ones considering that $C_{ns} \in [0,1]$ and $C_{es} \in \{0,1\}$. The last two combinations are considered to know if edges or nodes are useful.

Figure 5 shows some examples of correspondences given the initial costs $K_n = 1$ and $K_e = 1$ and the learned costs.

Table 1. Accuracy results obtained after and before learning given different initializations.

Databases	Initial Costs			Learned Costs		
	K_n	K_e	Accuracy	K_n	K_e	Accuracy
BOAT	1	1	**0.0340**	0. 0487	-0. 0021	**0. 7480**
	0.5	0.5	**0.0340**	0. 0487	-0. 0021	**0. 7480**
	1	0	**0.0900**	0. 0487	-0. 0021	**0. 7480**
	0	1	**0.0340**	0. 0487	-0. 0021	**0. 7480**
EAST PARK	1	1	**0.0260**	0. 0190	-0.0017	**0.8160**
	0.5	0.5	**0.0280**	0. 0190	-0.0017	**0.8160**
	1	0	**0.0680**	0. 0190	-0.0017	**0.8160**
	0	1	**0.0260**	0. 0190	-0.0017	**0.8160**
EAST SOUTH	1	1	**0.0200**	0. 0135	0	**0. 8560**
	0.5	0.5	**0.0200**	0. 0135	0	**0. 8560**
	1	0	**0.0300**	0. 0135	0	**0. 8560**
	0	1	**0.0200**	0. 0135	0	**0. 8560**
RESID	1	1	**0.0440**	0. 0157	-0.0003	**0.8360**
	0.5	0.5	**0.0440**	0. 0157	-0.0003	**0.8320**
	1	0	**0.0820**	0. 0157	-0.0003	**0.8320**
	0	1	**0.0440**	0. 0157	-0.0003	**0.8320**

5   Conclusions

This paper presents a method to learn the insertion and deletion costs of nodes and edges defined on the Graph Edit Distance. It is based on a continuous optimisation function that its aim is to minimise the difference between the costs of the ground truth correspondence and the automatically obtained correspondence. The practical evaluation shows that while minimising this cost difference, the Hamming distance between their correspondences is also minimised and so the correspondence accuracy is maximised.

References

1. Jouili, S., Tabbone, S.: Hypergraph-based image retrieval for graph-based representation. Pattern Recognition 45(11), 4054–4068 (2012)
2. Neuhaus, M., Bunke, H.: A graph matching based approach to fingerprint classification using directional variance. In: Kanade, T., Jain, A., Ratha, N.K. (eds.) AVBPA 2005. LNCS, vol. 3546, pp. 191–200. Springer, Heidelberg (2005)
3. Serratosa, F., Cortés, X., Solé-Ribalta, A.: Component retrieval based on a database of graphs for Hand-Written Electronic-Scheme Digitalisation. Expert Syst. Appl. 40(7), 2493–2502 (2013)
4. Mahé, P., Vert, J.-P.: Graph kernels based on tree patterns for molecules. Machine Learning 75(1), 3–35 (2009)
5. Fan, W.: Graph pattern matching revised for social network analysis. In: ICDT 2012, pp. 8–21
6. Qi, X., Wu, Q., Zhang, Y., Fuller, E., Zhang, C.-Q.: A novel model for DNA sequence similarity analysis based on graph theory. Evolutionary Bioinformatics 7, 149–154 (2011)
7. Sanfeliu, A., Fu, K.S.: A Distance measure between attributed relational graphs for pattern recognition. IEEE Trans. on Systems, Man, and Cybernetics 13(3), 353–362 (1983)
8. Gao, X., et al.: A survey of graph edit distance. Pattern Analysis and Applications 13(1), 113–129 (2010)
9. Bunke, H., Allermann, G.: Inexact graph matching for structural pattern recognition. Pattern Recognition Letters 1(4), 245–253 (1983)
10. Solé, A., Serratosa, F., Sanfeliu, A.: On the Graph Edit Distance cost: Properties and Applications. Intern. Journal Pattern Recognition & Artificial Intelligence 26(5) (2012)
11. Neuhaus, M., Bunke, H.: Self-organizing maps for learning the edit costs in graph matching. IEEE Trans. on Sys., Man, and Cybernetics, Part B 35(3), 503–514 (2005)
12. Neuhaus, M., Bunke, H.: Automatic learning of cost functions for graph edit distance. Information Sciences 177(1), 239–247 (2007)
13. Leordeanu, M., Sukthankar, R., Hebert, M.: Unsupervised Learning for Graph Matching. International Journal of Computer Vision 96(1), 28–45 (2012)
14. Caetano, T., et al.: Learning Graph Matching. Transaction on Pattern Analysis and Machine Intelligence 31(6), 1048–1058 (2009)
15. Serratosa, F., Solé-Ribalta, A., Cortés, X.: Automatic learning of edit costs based on interactive and adaptive graph recognition. In: Jiang, X., Ferrer, M., Torsello, A. (eds.) GbRPR 2011. LNCS, vol. 6658, pp. 152–163. Springer, Heidelberg (2011)
16. Moreno, C., Serratosa, F.: Consensus of Two Sets of Correspondences through Optimisation Functions, Pattern Analysis and Applications (2015)
17. Mohri, M., Rostamizadeh, A., Talwalkar, A.: Foundations of Machine Learning. The MIT Press (2012). ISBN: 9780262018258
18. Cortés, X., Serratosa, F.: Learning Graph-Matching Edit-Costs based on the Optimality of the Oracle's Node Correspondences. Pattern Recognition Letters 56, 22–29 (2015)
19. Lladós, J., Martí, E., Villanueva, J.J.: Symbol Recognition by Error-Tolerant Subgraph Matching between Region Adjacency Graphs. IEEE Trans. Pattern Anal. Mach. Intell. 23(10), 1137–1143 (2001)
20. Gold, S., Rangarajan, A.: A Graduated Assignment Algorithm for Graph Matching. IEEE TPAMI 18(4), 377–388 (1996)
21. Riesen, K., Bunke, H.: Approximate graph edit distance computation by means of bipartite graph matching. Image Vision Computing 27(7), 950–959 (2009)

22. Serratosa, F.: Fast Computation of Bipartite Graph Matching. Pattern Recognition Letters **45**, 244–250 (2014)
23. Serratosa, F.: Speeding up Fast Bipartite Graph Matching trough a new cost matrix. International Journal of Pattern Recognition and Artificial Intelligence **29**(2) (2015)
24. Cortés, X., Moreno, C., Serratosa, F.: Improving the correspondence establishment based on interactive homography estimation. In: Wilson, R., Hancock, E., Bors, A., Smith, W. (eds.) CAIP 2013, Part II. LNCS, vol. 8048, pp. 457–465. Springer, Heidelberg (2013)
25. Serratosa, F., Cortés, X.: Interactive Graph-Matching using Active Query Strategies. Pattern Recognition **48**, 1360–1369 (2015)
26. Cortés, X., Serratosa, F.: An Interactive Method for the Image Alignment problem based on Partially Supervised Correspondence. Expert Systems with Applications **42**(1), 179–192 (2015)
27. http://www.featurespace.org
28. Bay, H., Ess, A., Tuytelaars, T., Van Gool, L.: SURF: Speeded Up Robust Features. Comp. Vision and Image Unders. **110**(3), 346–359 (2008)
29. Delaunay, B.: Sur la sphère vide. Izvestia Akademii Nauk SSSR, Otdelenie Matematicheskikh i Estestvennykh Nauk **7**, 793–800 (1934)
30. Nelder, J.A., Mead, R.: Computer Journal **7**, 308–313 (1965)

Recognising Familiar Facial Features in Paintings Belonging to Separate Domains

Wilbert Tabone[(✉)] and Dylan Seychell

St. Martin's Institute of Higher Education, Hamrun, Malta
{wtabone,dseychell}@stmartins.edu

Abstract. We present a system[1] that detects faces in various paintings and subsequently recognise and points out any similarities that a certain face in one painting may have to another on a different artwork. The results would be ranked up according to similarity in a bid to produce an output that may assist art researchers to discover new links between different works which pertain to the same or different artist. Through various tests conducted, we have proved that our method was successful in exposing new links of similarity in various scenarios including cases where the human visual system failed to pinpoint any.

1 Introduction

Face detection and recognition systems have been developed for numerous applications which span across different areas of research. However we have noticed that there is a lack of published research which apply such techniques for such a purpose in the area of fine art. Our system allows a user to input a photograph or scan of a painting and receive a result that ranks other paintings according to a similar face detected within. There are cases where systems try to identify where a portrait has been featured across different mediums. Our research differentiates from this as it aims to find this face exclusively on the painted media, whilst also returning other similar faces. The latter would aid in establishing new links between the human models and the artists. We also aim to target museum displays with this system.

For the purpose of this research, we have chosen paintings from the Baroque period, specifically focusing on works by Francesco Zahra, a Maltese artist of that era. It is noted that there are several occurrences in Zahra's work in which the same or very similar faces are found on different artworks pertaining to the same or different character being portrayed [15]. This rendered the evaluation of such a domain, that is difficult to evaluate, possible. Furthermore, the results obtained were directly compared to the human visual system in order to assess the accuracy and success of the rankings.

The first part of this paper will discuss the research background, followed by the methods implemented in order to design an artefact that would aid in assessing the thesis explored. The last part will present the results and subsequently a discussion, followed by the conclusion.

This work is based on a report submitted in partial fulfilment of the B.Sc. (Hons.) Creative Computing, offered by the University of London International Programmes.

G. Azzopardi and N. Petkov (Eds.): CAIP 2015, Part I, LNCS 9256, pp. 125–136, 2015.
DOI: 10.1007/978-3-319-23192-1_11

2   Research

In this section, research areas that were drawn upon in order to develop our system are discussed. Research was spread over various areas such as classifiers, edge detection and face detection and recognition techniques. The first three areas were explored as preparation to the various classifiers and image similarity methods explored in the face detection and recognition section, since various combinations of the three are utilised.

2.1   Classifiers

A classifier can be expressed as a function that takes a value of a feature and subsequently predicts the class that that example belongs to [10]. In preparation for research on classifiers utilised for face detection and recognition, linear classifiers were researched. These are defined by [5] as being classifiers that use feature functions $\mathbf{f}(x) = (f_1(x), \ldots, f_m(x))$ and feature weights $\mathbf{w} = (w_1, \ldots, w_m)$ to assign $x \in X$ to class $c(x) = \text{sign}(\mathbf{w}. \mathbf{f}(x))$, where $\text{sign}(y) = +1$ if $y > 0$ and -1 if $y < 0$. In the preceding notation, $x \in X$ defines an example whilst the classifier is defined by the mapping of the example to a binary class $c(x) \in -1, 1$.

2.2   Edge Detection

Some of the most prominent edge detection techniques were researched since edges extracted from an image may facilitate in the detection and classification of faces. The general edge detection method is given as a system that smoothens the image and subsequently enhances and thresholds the edges to produce a binary edge map. There exist two categories of detectors: first order and second order, where each refers to the application of first or second order differentiation [9].

The Sobel edge detector calculates the magnitude and direction of the gradients in an image by the utilisation of the Euclidean distance for magnitude and the *arctan* of the angle for the orientation (direction) [13]. On the other hand, the Canny edge detector utilises five steps [6] that enable it to produce clearer results by following the criteria outlined by Canny in [4] which include having a low error rate, having well localised edge points and giving only one response to a single edge. The last method to be explored was the Laplacian second order edge detector. In order to alleviate the problem of its sensitivity to noise, the detector employs Gaussian smoothing beforehand [16]. This detector highlights the zero crossing of the image (the points at which its second derivative equates to zero) in order to produce the edge map [6]. In conclusion it is noted that the Canny edge detector handles noisy images better than its counterparts discussed here. This is ideal for paintings as they are intrinsically noisy.

2.3   Face Detection

Various image-pre-processing methods such as histogram equalisation were explored as precedents to face detection techniques. It was decided that from the different detector classes, the appearance-based methods would be the most suitable for the system since these probabilistic-methods classify a random variable x as a *face* or *non-face* [19]. This is basically what is wanted in the context of what is to be achieved.

The chosen detector from this category was the Viola-Jones Haar classifier [17]; this produces an integral image, which is an array that contains the sum of the pixel intensities of the pixel at location (x,y) and its neighbours through which it eliminates false positives [7]. Furthermore, through the use of Haar features (wavelets), rectangular groups of pixels are formed based on the intensity value and hence the facial features are found [8, 12].

2.4 Face Recognition

Although research was conduced on the eigenfaces approach (principal component analysis), fisherfaces approach (linear discriminant analysis), support vector machines (SVM) and Gaussian naive Bayes (GNB), it was later discovered that these were nonoptimal for the purpose of what was to be achieved, due to the limited amount of training examples that paintings provide. Therefore, a different approach was taken and image similarity measurements were researched instead, as similarities between faces can still be assessed through such methods. Even though some of these methods were created to be applied on video data, they were still utilised as internally these are operating on image frames.

The first method to be explored was the Wilkie, Stonham and Aleksander's Recognition Device (WiSARD) which is a collection of RAM-discriminates. In general, the WiSARD classifier has a collection of RAM units (neurons) each of which are trained on a particular pattern [2]. When it receives an input pattern, each neuron outputs a 0 if there is no match or 1 if there is a match in the pattern area assigned to it. The WiSARD sums up the result to produce the total value, which may be expressed as a percentage of recognition [3,7]. The architecture of such a system is presented in Figure 1.

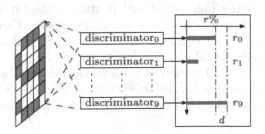

Fig. 1. A representation of a 10 RAM- discriminator WiSARD (Source: [1]).

Two further methods explored were the PSNR (peak signal-to-noise ratio) and SSIM (structural similarity index) measurements which may be used as a crosscheck for the WiSARD. While PSNR measures the change in the signal between two frames, SSIM correlates to how humans visually perceive a scene and therefore it measures similarity on the basis of luminance and contrast amongst others [18].

3   Methods

We chose OpenCV[1] as the programming framework.

Detection

In order to prepare the paintings for detection, transformation from the 3D to 2D colour space was performed, followed by histogram equalisation. Choosing the detector involved various experiments that first identified the most optimal classifier and secondly enhanced the latter further. For the purposes of this work, a pre-trained classifier was chosen over training.

The two pre-trained cascades provided by OpenCV: LBP (Local Binary Patterns) and Haar (Viola-Jones detector) were tested. Each of these detectors were executed on a test set made up of eleven paintings and one photograph. While the LBP detector was found to be more efficient in execution time, with a difference of 22.92 ms, the Haar classifier had a higher success rate (by 4%) together with 100% precision and was therefore deemed the ideal cascade to utilise for the face detector. In order to find the best possible way to enhance the success rate of the Haar detector, various tests were conducted on the Haar detector with different minimum neighbour parameter values, switching between having histogram equalisation or not and utilising different edge detection techniques in order to enhance the edges (by superimposing the produced edge image onto the original).

From the conducted experiments, it was discovered that the most efficient method is the Haar detector using histogram equalisation, a minimum neighbour parameter value of one (how many detections in a particular area is allowed) and utilising no edge detector whatsoever. It was noted that when the recommended default value of three (for min. neighbour) is utilised, the Precision is excellent (100%), however the Recall rate is not satisfactory enough. Furthermore, it was noted that while histogram equalisation improves the results, edge detection does not. These results are tabulated below in Figure 2.

Now that the best combination of parameters for the Haar classifier was found, the next problem to be tackled was the detection of faces having a slightly rotated pose in order to aim for a rotation-robust face detection process.

Head pose

One of the various challenges attributed to face detectors is the head pose of the subject [20]. In order to aim for a rotation-robust detection process, an automated rotation system that attempted to detect a face at each ten degree interval

---

[1] OpenCV: http://opencv.org/ (programming library for real-time computer vision applications)

Comparison of Results

HistEq	minNeighbour	Edge	Recall	Precision	Failure Rate
Yes	1	N/A	59%	97%	41%
Yes	2	N/A	53%	87%	47%
Yes	3	N/A	51%	100%	49%
No	1	N/A	55%	87%	45%
No	2	N/A	53%	93%	47%
No	3	N/A	51%	96%	49%
Yes	1	Canny	46%	82%	53%
No	1	Canny	49%	92%	51%
Yes	1	Sobel	29%	74%	71%
No	1	Sobel	33%	94%	67%
Yes	1	Laplacian	29%	88%	71%
No	1	Laplacian	37%	86%	63%

Fig. 2. Comparison of Haar experiment results.

was created. This resulted in a large number of false positives being recorded. Therefore, since the focus of the conducted research was on the recognition of faces, a simpler system that utilises basic coordinate geometry was developed.

In this system, a line is first constructed between the two eyes and another straight horizontal line is constructed from the topmost eye to the position where the bottommost eye should be if the face was properly aligned. This is demonstrated in Figure 3.

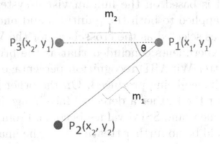

Fig. 3. Mathematical principle behind the head pose rectification solution.

Both gradients, m_1 and m_2 are calculated and subsequently, the angle θ between the two lines is found. The image is rotated by θ following complimentary angle laws. This process greatly improved the number of detections and TPs in paintings containing tilted faces, as evidenced by Figure 4.

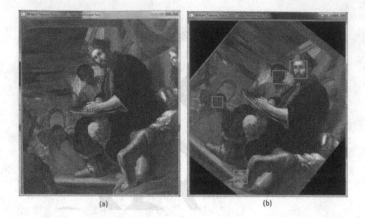

Fig. 4. Improvement of results once head is correctly aligned. (a): Detection without alignment; (b): detection after alignment.

Recognition:

As the commodity of having several images of the same face at different angles is not provided by paintings, it was not possible to train any classifiers and therefore there was no need for the vector space model to be utilised. Image similarity measurements were employed instead. The WiSARD classifier, which is applied on bi-level images was utilised as the main discriminator. There was also a need for a crosscheck since the system needed to be automated. Therefore, the list of outputted similar faces would have to be filtered in order to only allow the most accurate results to be displayed. Both SSIM and PSNR was tested, together with the WiSARD classifier on a second test set containing similar photographs and paintings. Since SSIM is based on the human visual system, it gave the most positive results when applied to both the paintings and photographs.

Therefore, SSIM was selected as the crosscheck for the WiSARD in the final application. Further experiments concluded that as the brightness of the input images increases, a better WiSARD recognition percentage is achieved due to a higher quality binary image being produced. On the other hand, it was noticed from a further test that the further a detected face image is cropped, the lower the WiSARD measurement and SSIM values become. From this observation, we decided that there would be no further treatment to the images produced by the detector once created.

Application

Through the use of the partitioning software development approach [11], all test applications were amalgamated into a final UI application that would prove the concept of this research.

In this application, a set of pre-selected images are presented as part of the test set selection module and the query window. First the user constructs a test set made up of six images to be used by the WiSARD and SSIM and consequently the system allows the user to select one of twelve query images. Each of the query images may be rotated, if necessary, before being processed for ranking. Once the detection is completed, each detection area is processed through the WiSARD classifier which determines, through a threshold of 20.0, which detected faces will go on for ranking. Subsequently, the SSIM, which is given by Equation 1, is calculated between the detected face and each previously selected test image.

$$S(x, y) = f(\mathbf{l}(x, y), \mathbf{c}(x, y), \mathbf{s}(x, y)). \tag{1}$$

Where, l is luminance, c is the contrast and s is the structure.

A ranking window containing the WiSARD value, together with the three most similar faces to the detected face (containing the highest SSIM value) are displayed. Next to each face, a link to the source paining is presented. This is shown below in Figure 5.

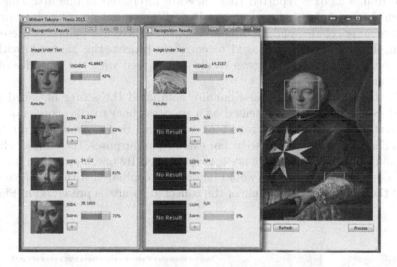

Fig. 5. The rank window for each detection containing the similarity results. Note how the false postitive returned no result due to the thresholds put in place.

As a way to compare the results that were obtained with a fixed questionnaire, a score system was created. The utilised formula returns a score $\mathbf{S}(\%)$ that is based on both the WiSARD and SSIM values, which are both normalised and subsequently the resultant value is divided by two (for the average) and multiplied by 100 for the percentage value as per Equation 2:

$$S = \left(\frac{\left(\frac{WiSARD}{55} \right) + \left(\frac{SSIM}{40} \right)}{2} \right) \times 100 \tag{2}$$

The values for normalisation, i.c. 55 and 40 were obtained through results of experiments conducted to determine the best possible combination.

4 Results

Several results given by the detector and ranking windows were obtained under different circumstances. Overall, the detector gave positive results, with only a minimal number of FPs. Moreover, positive results were obtained by the WiS-ARD and SSIM recognition system (ranker). In order to better evaluate the system, a fixed questionnaire that aimed to collect both quantitative and qualitative data was devised. The quantitative sections of the questionnaire assessed the human visual system (represented by the respondents) against various components of the developed system described in the previous section. On the other hand, the qualitative data sections required text-input answers from the public.

The majority of the hundred and ten respondents belong to the 19-25 age bracket, with females being the major gender group. Following the demographics, the respondents were asked about their interest in art; a question that returned positive results as 51% reported that they are interested in fine art. The next part, which assessed the detector, required the respondents to point out the amount of non-occluded and prominent faces in the five five paintings presented to them. The application managed to correctly process the paintings with no FPs in four of the five paintings; a result that agreed with the majority of the respondents.

A further section in the questionnaire compared the scores obtained from the rank result window (represented as a progress bar) to the score chosen by respondents on a Likert scale from 1-10, where one denotes minimal similarity and ten denotes maximal similarity. For evaluation purposes, the number chosen by the majority of the respondents was multiplied by one hundred in order to obtain a percentage value that would be directly compared with the percentage score of the application. A sample of the collected results is presented in Figures 6 and 7.

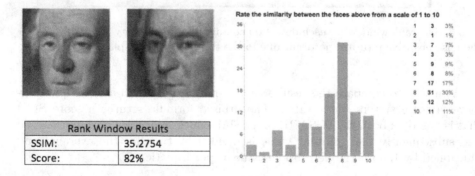

Fig. 6. A sample from the results. Notice how the system developed has returned a value of 82% whilst the HVS (majority of respondents) chose a score of 80%.

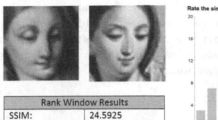 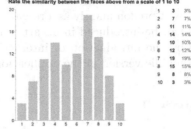

Rank Window Results	
SSIM:	24.5925
Score:	71%

Fig. 7. A further sample from the results. Although a more subjective comparison is presented in this case, the respondents reported a 70% similarity score whilst the application returned a score of 71%.

The first part of this section contained side-by-side comparisons of query faces to faces from the test set, which were deemed similar by us through our personal analysis and were ranked as the topmost result by the application. On the other hand, in the second part of this section, the second and third ranked results of the software were presented next to the query face. These latter results are interesting as although they are deemed similar by the software application, they would not look similar on immediate examination by the observers, however prolonged analysis would prove otherwise.

From the tests in the first part, where the first result of the rank window was presented to the respondents, there was agreement between the system and the scores of the respondents ($\pm$ 10%) in five from the six eligible side-by-side comparisons. Hence, an 83 % success rate was obtained. On the other hand in the second part, these disagreements were more frequent as only in four from thirteen tests did the respondents and ranker agree on an equal score; yet a close score was observed in the majority of results. These disagreements were expected in this case, since as previously mentioned, subjectivity came into place in non-obvious similarity exercises.

Once this data was collected, we presented our findings, together with the developed application to art researchers in a semi-structured interview. With regards to the application and results obtained, the interviewees had positive comments. It was asserted that as the current application stands, it would be mainly useful for research. Furthermore, our application will provide researchers in the area of the history of art a tool that will perform multiple tests that would aid them in gauging if the same human model was used in works of different artists. This is something that very few researchers have done as usually the study is on models that featured in multiple works of the same artist.

The curator of a National fine arts museum stated that in such a setting, the application may be used to link works from such museums to those found in churches across the country/ world (e.g: commissioned by the Church during the Baroque period). Another interesting application would be to genealogically connect pieces in portrait galleries through the recognition system presented here.

Overall, the interviewees were intrigued by the application, asserting that while they see it predominantly as a research tool, there could be various variants of it which can be introduced in an art museum/gallery setting to enhance the experience by the introduction of interactive elements through the use of, for example, a mobile version of the application.

5   Discussion

The system was successful in detecting facial features in the input paintings whilst also correctly utilising its primary recognition system: the WiSARD weightless neural network in order to assess if any similar faces exist in the test set and subsequently utilising the SSIM measurement to pinpoint and rank the actual similar faces by their structural similarity value. We believe that the pre-trained Viola Jones Haar classifier that was utilised provided overall satisfactory results for what we were aiming for, with minimal resource use and efficient execution time.

Moreover, from our analysis we deem the recognition results obtained by the system as satisfactory. Although there were some small discrepancies between the HVS and the system when comparing the second and third rank results, we believe that since the results were still in the region of the application's score and since a high number of agreeable results between the HVS and rank window primary results were attained, it can be concluded that the ranking system is working as expected as a high enough success rate was achieved.

The shortcomings of the system at its current state are that it requires an input of a scan or quality photograph of the painting to be queried in order to produce satisfactory results. Moreover, the current facial rotation system is not automated due to the problem outlined above in Section 3. This is not presently an issue due to the nature of the application being created to run on desktop computers. However, if the system is to be exported to a mobile device, an alternative solution would be utilised.

5.1   Enhancements

From a further question in the questionnaire, it was discovered that people find it easier to discover any similarities between faces when presented with the whole painting. This fact may be exploited further so that more information may be extracted from the painting making it ripe to implement multiple information extractors such as those presented in the work of [14]. Therefore, a system which recognises familiar facial features, links faces to artists and influence between artists can be produced. The final product would be a network that links faces, models and artists in the same or different time periods.

6   Conclusion

In conclusion, we believe that such a system is possible to be applied to a wider range of different artworks and media. In the future, we plan to adapt the system in order to support different art forms and pinpoint similarities in both facial and artistic features. Moreover, a system that creates clusters of paintings according to the artist and the characters portrayed may be implemented. These clusters would contain paintings from various sources across the globe, such as museums and private collections. Each item in the collection would have embedded meta-data that would allow the user to search by artist or discover new ones upon examining the meta-data included with the similarity results.

We strongly believe that such a system would help art researchers in amassing collections of links in similarity between works of the same or different artists. This will aid in building upon or commencing new research in their respective areas.

References

1. Aleksander, I., De Gregorio, M., França, F.M.G., Lima, P.M.V., Morton, H.: A brief introduction to weightless neural systems. In: ESANN. Citeseer (2009)
2. Aleksander, I., Morton, H.: An introduction to neural computing, vol. 3. Chapman & Hall, London (1990)
3. Beham, M.P., Roomi, S.M.M.: Face recognition using appearance based approach: a literature survey. In: Proceedings of International Conference & Workshop on Recent Trends in Technology, Mumbai, Maharashtra, India, pp. 24–25 (2012)
4. Canny, J.: A computational approach to edge detection. IEEE Transactions on Pattern Analysis and Machine Intelligence 6, 679–698 (1986)
5. Johnson, M.: A brief introduction to kernel classifiers (2009)
6. Maini, R., Aggarwal, H.: Study and comparison of various image edge detection techniques. International Journal of Image Processing (IJIP) 3(1), 1–11 (2009)
7. Medioni, G., Kang, S.B.: Emerging topics in computer vision. Prentice Hall PTR (2004)
8. Nilsson, M.: Face detection. Presentation by the Mathematical Imaging Group, Centre for Math ematical Sciences, Lund University (2014)
9. Nixon, M.: Feature extraction & image processing. Academic Press (2008)
10. Pereira, F., Mitchell, T., Botvinick, M.: Machine learning classifiers and fmri: a tutorial overview. Neuroimage 45(1), S199–S209 (2009)
11. Pressman, R.S.: Software engineering: a practitioners approach. McGrow-Hill International Edition (2005)
12. Rabbani, M., Chellappan, C.: A different approach to appearance-based statisti-cal method for face recognition using median. International Journal of Computer Science and Network Security 7(4), 262–267 (2007)
13. Fisher, R., Perkins, S., Walker, A., Wolfart, E.: Sobel Edge Detector. HPR2 (2004)
14. Saleh, B., Abe, K., Arora, R.S., Elgammal, A.M.: Toward automated discovery of artistic influence (2014). CoRR abs/1408.3218
15. Sciberras, K.: Francesco Zahra: His life and art in mid-18th century Malta 1710–1773. Midsea Books (2010)
16. Shrivakshan, G., Chandrasekar, C.: A comparison of various edge detection tech-niques used in image processing. IJCSI International Journal of Computer Science Issues 9(5), 269–276 (2012)
17. Viola, P., Jones, M.: Rapid object detection using a boosted cascade of simple features. In: Proceedings of the 2001 IEEE Computer Society Conference on Com-puter Vision and Pattern Recognition, CVPR 2001, vol. 1, pp. I-511. IEEE (2001)

18. Wang, Z., Bovik, A.C., Sheikh, H.R., Simoncelli, E.P.: Image quality assessment: from error visibility to structural similarity. IEEE Transactions on Image Processing **13**(4), 600–612 (2004)
19. Yang, M.H., Ahuja, N.: Face detection and gesture recognition for human-computer interaction, vol. 1. Springer (2001)
20. Yang, M.H., Kriegman, D., Ahuja, N.: Detecting faces in images: A survey. IEEE Transactions on Pattern Analysis and Machine Intelligence **24**(1), 34–58 (2002)

Content Based Image Retrieval
Based on Modelling Human Visual Attention

Alex Papushoy and Adrian G. Bors[✉]

Department of Computer Science, University of York, York YO10 5GH, UK

Abstract. In this paper we propose to employ human visual attention models for content based image retrieval. This approach is called query by saliency content retrieval (QSCR) and considers visual saliency at both local and global image levels. Each image, from a given database, is segmented and specific features are evaluated locally for each of its regions. The global saliency is evaluated based on edge distribution and orientation. During the retrieval stage, the most similar images are retrieved by using an optimization approach such as the Earth Moving Distance (EMD) algorithm. The proposed method ranks the similarity between the query image and a set of given images based on their similarity in the features associated with the salient regions.

Keywords: Content based image retrieval · Human visual attention models · Earth moving distance · Local and global saliency

1 Introduction

Given the wide availability of image acquisition and storage, searching and retrieving useful information has become a necessity for many activities, including in forensics search and security applications. Content-based image retrieval (CBIR) employs a user-provided image as a query, whose visual information is processed and used for content-based search [4,15]. Modeling of human perception of images is very important not only for searching and retrieving images based on their content, but also for modeling the human intent in a certain situation. CBIR is based on the notion that visual similarity implies semantic similarity, which is not always the case, but is a valid assumption. The main challenge in CBIR systems is the ambiguity in the high-level (semantic) concepts extracted from the low-level (pixels) features of the image [16]. The second obstacle is the sensory gap which can be interpreted as the incompleteness of the object information captured by an imaging device. Generally, it is difficult for CBIR systems to search for broad semantic concepts because it is hard to limit the feature space without broadening the semantic gap.

There are four categories of CBIR methods, [4]: bottom-up, top-down, relevance feedback and based on image classification. Those that rely purely on the information contained in the image are bottom-up approaches such as [12], while top-down approaches consider the prior knowledge for image retrieval.

© Springer International Publishing Switzerland 2015
G. Azzopardi and N. Petkov (Eds.): CAIP 2015, Part I, LNCS 9256, pp. 137–148, 2015.
DOI: 10.1007/978-3-319-23192-1_12

In image classification approaches, the system is presented with training data from which it learns a query [2]. Systems involving the user in the retrieval process via relevance feedback mechanisms are a mixture of bottom-up and top-down approaches [14].

This paper proposes a new query by similarity content retrieval (QSCR) method which is based on human visual attention models. During the first stage, the image is segmented into regions and feature vectors characterizing color, contrast, texture, the region centroid, and the contrast with respect to the neighbourhood, are extracted for each region. Saliency is then considered at two levels: the regional level by assessing the level of saliency in each region and at the general image level by using the salient edges detected from the image [11]. An optimization procedure called Earth Mover's Distance (EMD) [13] is used together with the energy of salient edges for evaluating the similarity between the query image and a given retrieved image. The proposed QSCR methodology and the visual attention model is described in Section 2 while the similarity-based ranking procedure is detailed in Section 3. Experimental results are provided in Section 4 and the conclusions of this research study are outlined in Section 5.

2 Using Visual Attention Models in Content Based Image Retrieval

The proposed methodology consists of three main processing stages as shown in the diagram from Figure 1. Image segmentation is performed using the mean-shift algorithm [3]. For each image region we calculate a characteristic feature vector with entries corresponding to: color, contrast, texture information, the region neighbourhood information and region centroid. These features are used for calculating the similarity distance between two images, region by region.

In this research study, saliency is represented locally by extracting salient regions, while globally is determined by the salient edges. Regions provide a good local saliency measure, while the salient edges are associated with global image saliency. The human visual system is attracted to specific image regions coinciding with the fixation points chosen by saccades (random eye movements) at the pre-attentive stage for foveation (conscious acquisition of detail). Such image regions are characterized by local discontinuities and relevant features that make them stand out from the rest. There are two ways to detect salient regions in images: bottom-up and top-down attention. Bottom-up attention is instinctive and involuntary corresponding to a human reflex. It is entirely driven by the low-level image information. Top-down attention on the other hand, is driven by memory and prior experiences.

The Itti-Koch saliency model [7–9] is a well-known biologically plausible method designed for fast bottom-up scene analysis which employs the model of neurological processes occurring in primates' brains. Graph-Based Visual Saliency (GBVS) [6] is the graph-based normalization of the Itti-Koch model. Other approaches, loosely based on the visual attention model of Itti-Koch, are the Saliency Using Natural statistics (SUN) [17] and the Frequency-Tuned

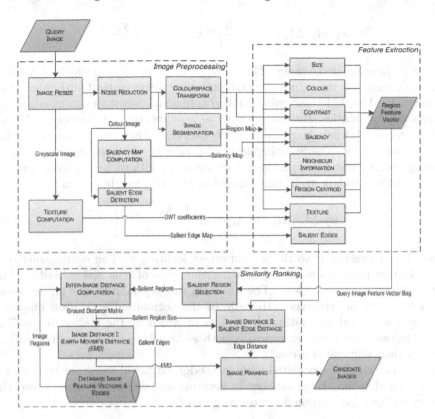

Fig. 1. Query by similarity content retrieval (QSCR) image retrieval.

Saliency (FTS) [1]. SUN is a hybrid biologically-plausible and computational attention model based on the Bayesian framework using the *a priori* information from natural images collected off-line [17], while FTS uses a bank of Gabor filters at different orientations for extracting orientation features [1].

GBVS [6] was chosen in this study for calculating the saliency map in images due to its ability to clearly identify the most salient objects and image regions. Generally, saliency maps are created in three steps: feature vectors are extracted for every pixel to create feature maps, then, activation maps are computed, and finally the activation maps are normalized and combined. GBVS employs dyadic Gaussian pyramids for the image scales of 2:1, 3:1 and 4:1. These are applied for each channel of the physiologically derived D*K*L* color space. Orientation maps are created after applying Gabor filters at $\{0, 45, 90, 135\}$ degrees at every scale of each color channel. Unlike the Itti-Koch model that computes activation maps by center-surround differences of image features [8], GBVS applies a graph-based approach [6]. The adjacency matrix is constructed by connecting each pixel of the map to all the other pixels, excluding itself, by using the following similarity function $w(\mathbf{M_x}, \mathbf{M_y})$ between feature vectors corresponding to the pixels located at $\mathbf{x}$ and $\mathbf{y}$:

$$w_1(\mathbf{M_x}, \mathbf{M_y}) = \left| \log \frac{\mathbf{M_x}}{\mathbf{M_y}} \right| \exp\left[-\frac{\|\mathbf{x} - \mathbf{y}\|^2}{2\sigma^2} \right] \tag{1}$$

where σ is the scale, in the range of $[0.1, 0, 2]$ from the given map width. A Markov chain is defined over this adjacency matrix, where the weights of outbound edges are normalized to 1, by assuming that graph nodes are states, and edges are transition probabilities. By computing the equilibrium distribution yields an activation map $\mathcal{A}$, where large values are concentrated in areas of high activation and thus are salient. The resulting activation map is smoothed and normalized. A new graph is constructed on the activation map, with each node connected to all the others including itself, and which has the edge weights given by:

$$w_2(\mathbf{M_x}, \mathbf{M_y}) = A(\mathbf{y}) \exp\left[-\frac{\|\mathbf{x} - \mathbf{y}\|^2}{2\sigma^2} \right] \tag{2}$$

where $A(\mathbf{y})$ corresponds to the activation at location $\mathbf{y}$. The normalization of the activation maps leads to emphasizing the areas of true dissimilarity, while suppressing non-salient regions. The resulting saliency map for the entire image is denoted as $\mathbf{S}$ and represents the sum of the normalized activation maps for each color and local orientation channel as provided by the Gabor filters. The salient regions are decided, empirically, as those that have more than 20 % salient pixels in their segmented areas.

A saliency value is associated with each edge extracted using the well known Canny edge detector. Edge saliency is determined by the edge length and the saliency in the edge surrounding area as given by:

$$\mathcal{S}_e = \lambda_L L_e + \lambda_N \mathcal{N}_e \tag{3}$$

where $\mathcal{S}_e$ represents the saliency of edge e, L_e represents the length of the edge, $\mathcal{N}_e$ is the saliency in the edge neighbourhood, and where $\lambda_L = 0.3$ and $\lambda_N = 0.7$ are weighting factors. The saliency in the neighbourhood of the edge is calculated by averaging over a small neighbourhood. Salient edges are those that have their saliency as 0.25 from the maximum saliency. The statistics of the edges are grouped in edge histogram descriptors (EHD) as in the representation of the edge information by the MPEG-7 image compression standard. Salient edges are counted for each orientation from the entire image, resulting in the vector EHD(θ, I), where $\theta = \{0, \pi/2, \pi, 3\pi/4, \text{non-directional}\}$.

3   Image Ranking

The procedure of segmentation, feature extraction and saliency extraction described in the previous section is applied to all the retrieval candidate images as well as to the query image. Given a query image, we rank all the available candidate images according to their similarity with the query image. Let us consider that both the query image Q and a given image I from the database are segmented into several regions Q_i, $i = 1, \ldots, M$ and I_j, $j = 1, \ldots, N$, respectively. The similarity ranking becomes a many-to-many region matching problem which takes into account the salient edges as well.

The similarity-based image ranking procedure is outlined in the lower part of the diagram from Figure 1 and consists of a similarity measure between the query image Q and a given image I, represented as the weighted sum of the EMD matching cost function and the global image saliency measure as given by its salient edges:

$$S(Q, I) = 0.7 \frac{EMD(Q, I)}{\alpha_{EMD}} + +0.3 \frac{\sum_\theta |\text{EHD}(\theta, Q) - \text{EHD}(\theta, I)|}{5\,\alpha_E} \qquad (4)$$

where $\text{EMD}(Q, I)$ is the EMD metric between images Q and I, $\text{EHD}(\theta, Q)$ represents the average salient edge energy in the direction of $\theta = \{0, \pi/2, \pi, 3\pi/4,\text{non-directional}\}$ for the image Q. α_{EMD} and α_E represent the robustness factors which are set as the 95th percentile of the cumulative distribution function of the EMD and the EHD measures, respectively, calculated using a statistically significant image sample set. The robustness factors are used for normalizing whilst eliminating outliers. EMD represents a measure of similarity in the local salient regions between the images Q and I, while EHD represents the similarity in the salient edge distributions and is extracted as described in the previous section. An inter-region distance measure $D(Q_i, I_j)$ is calculated between each region $i = 1, \ldots, M$ from the query image Q and each region $j = 1, \ldots, N$ from the candidate retrieval image I as:

$$D(Q_i, I_j) = \psi(S_i, S_j)D(\mathbf{F}) \qquad (5)$$

where $\psi(S_i, S_j)$ denotes the joint saliency weight for Q_i and I_j and $D(\mathbf{F})$ represents a distance in the feature space depending on the color, texture, contrast vectors, neighbourhood colour consistency and region location, whose weights are provided in the experimental results section. The following weight corresponding to the joint saliency of the image regions Q_i and I_j is considered in equation (8):

$$\psi(S_i, S_j) = \max\left(1 - \frac{S_i + S_j}{2}, 0.1\right) \qquad (6)$$

where S_i is the saliency of the query image region Q_i and S_j is the saliency of the a candidate image region I_j, where the regions saliency represent the ratios of salient pixels, calculated as described in the previous section. It can be observed that the distance $D(Q_i, I_j)$ is smaller when the two regions Q_i and I_j are salient. EMD algorithm [13] is an optimization algorithm with constraints representing the normalized cost of transforming the query image signature into the signature of the candidate retrieval image. The corresponding weights only add up to unity when all image regions are used. We are filtering out non-salient regions and consequently the weights will add up to a value less than one. Such signatures enable partial matching which is essential in image retrieval where there is a high likelihood of occlusion in the salient regions [11].

4   Experimental Results

We have applied the proposed query by saliency content retrieval (QSCR) methodology to various image databases including Corel 1000, SIVAL and Flickr. Corel 1000 consists of 10 semantic categories of natural scenes, each containing 100 images showing distinct objects. Flickr database consists of 20 categories with 100 highly diverse images in each, while another 2000 images do not have any specific concept. Images are ranked based on their similarity to the query, thus producing an ordered set of results. The rank-weighted average precision (WPR) is given by, [16]:

$$\text{WPR} = \frac{1}{N} \sum_{k=1}^{N} \frac{n_k}{k}, \tag{7}$$

where N is the total number of retrieved images and n_k is the number of matches in the first k retrieved images. Receiver Operating Characteristic (ROC) plots the true positive rate versus false alarms. We also use the area under the ROC curve (AUC), which corresponds to the Wilcoxon-Mann-Whitney statistics [12].

In Figure 2 we provide a comparison of saliency maps produced by four saliency algorithms: Itti-Koch (IK) [8], graph-based visual saliency (GBVS) [6], saliency using natural statistics (SUN) [17], and frequency-tuned saliency

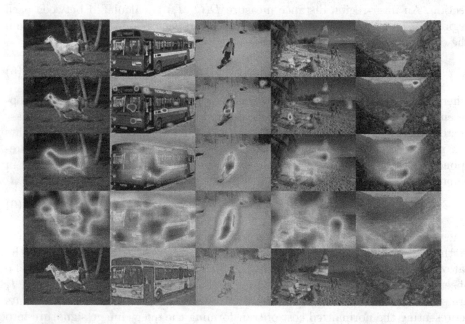

Fig. 2. Comparison of saliency maps. Original images are in the first row, Itti-Koch saliency maps are in the second row, GBVS maps are in the third row, SUN maps are in the fourth row, and FTS maps are in the fifth row. Saliency maps, pseudo-colored from red to blue depending on the visual attention intensity, are overlaid.

(FTS), [1].From these results it can be seen that IK produces small highly focused peaks in saliency that tend to concentrate on small areas of the object which are insufficient for representing the semantic concept of the image. The large amount of false positives, bias, and lack of precision makes SUN an unsuitable choice for retrieval in the broad image domain. FTS algorithm works well only when there is a salient color object in the image. GBVS produces the most useful maps for the purposes of image retrieval as it can be observed from Figure 2.

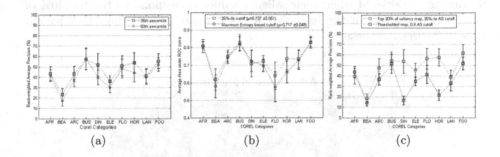

(a)   (b)   (c)

Fig. 3. Selecting salient regions. (a) Rank-weighted average precision when selecting salient regions based on the percentile of salient pixels. (b) Area under ROC curve measure. (c) WPR when comparing with salient region extraction using a thresholded saliency map.

In the following we evaluate the segmented image region saliency by considering only those salient pixels which are among the top 20% salient pixels, which we found based on empirical study as being a reliable saliency measure. We define the saliency of a region as the percentage of salient pixels calculated from all pixels in the image. After forming the cumulative distribution function (cdf) of all salient regions from the COREL 1000 database with respect to their saliency we choose the 35% percentile as a cut-off threshold because it represents the location of significant change in the cdf's gradient. Experimentally, we have observed that this saliency region selection threshold removes most of the regions with small saliency content, whilst retaining some regions with relevant background information. In Figure 3(a) we compare the proposed salient region selection method with the approach which considers the regions with 50% salient pixels as salient using the WPR measure from (7). In Figure 3(b) we compare, by using the AUC measure, the proposed saliency selection approach with a method using the maximization of the entropy for the average region saliency values, proposed in [5], when using 100 saliency levels. The method based on the maximization of entropy for the average region saliency values is not suitable for retrieving the images from Flower (FLO) and Horse (HOR) categories because it does not select enough background regions to distinguish the red and yellow flowers from buses. In Figure 3(c) we provide the comparison with the method which selects salient regions by binarizing the saliency map using Otsu's method [10] and then choosing the salient regions as those which have at least 80% salient pixels. The proposed approach is clearly better when categories have a well-defined salient object because it selects some outlying areas defining the context of the salient object. Meanwhile, the method based on Otsu's approach selects just the salient object creating confusions due to the semantic gap. The proposed method considers for the retrieval the top 65% salient regions from the image for general-purpose image data sets, such as Corel and Flickr. However, in the SIVAL database, which consists entirely of distinctive objects, salient regions are considered when their saliency values correspond to the top 40% of most salient regions in the image, which is consistent with the cdf of salient regions for this database.

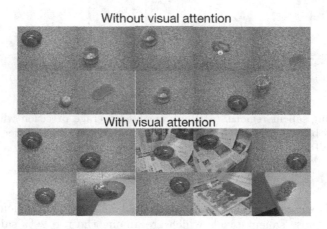

Fig. 4. Retrieving a translucent bowl image from SIVAL database. The query image is the first right-top image on each row followed by the retrieved images without and with modelling the visual attention.

When applying the visual attention to retrieval, after segmenting the images, we estimate a series of parameters and in equation (8) we use the following inter-region distance measure:

$$D(\mathbf{F}) = \sqrt{0.9(5d_{cl}^2(i,j) + 2.6d_{te}^2(i,j) + 0.5d_{co}^2(i,j)) + 0.1(0.4d_{nn}^2(i,j) + 0.4d_{cd}^2(i,j))} \qquad (8)$$

where d_{cl}, d_{te} and d_{co} are the Euclidean distances characterizing features such as color, texture and contrast vectors, while d_{nn} and d_{cd} are the Euclidean distances between the secondary features characterizing the colors of the nearest neighbouring regions and the centroids of the regions Q_i and I_j. Each distance component is normalized to the interval $[0,1]$ and is weighted according to its significance for retrieval with an empirically estimated weight. The color distance d_{cl} is calculated as the average distance of the normalized $\Delta E2000$ distance, which conforms with the minimal perceptual color difference according to CIE.

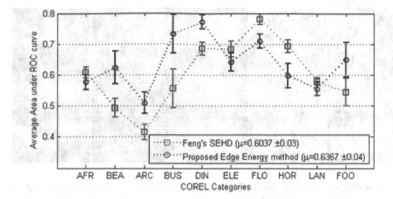

Fig. 5. Retrieval using salient edges on COREL 1000 database subset. μ indicate the average area under ROC curve.

The texture distance d_{te} corresponds to the Euclidean distance between the average of the horizontal, vertical and oblique absolute value of the Discrete Wavelet Transform coefficients for the regions Q_i and I_j divided by their corresponding standard deviations, calculated across the entire image database. The contrast difference d_{co} is represented by the normalized Euclidean difference of the contrast features for the two regions. The neighbourhood characteristic difference d_{nn} is calculated as the average of the resulting twelve color space distances to the four nearest neighbouring regions from above, below, left and right. The centroid distance d_{cd} is the Euclidean distance between the coordinates of the regions centers.

In Figure 4 we present an example of retrieving the translucent bowl image in SIVAL database without visual attention models and with visual attention models. As it can be observed in this figure when using visual attention models, all first six retrieved images correspond to its category. When not using the visual attention models, only the seventh image is from the correct category. Salient edges are extracted and used in the final image ranking evaluation measure from (4). Unlike in SEHD approach [5], the method proposed in this paper decouples the edge histogram from its spatial domain by considering the edge energy, corresponding to a specific image feature orientation, calculated from the entire image. In Figure 5 we compare the proposed salient edge retrieval approach (the proposed method considering only the global image saliency and not the local saliency) and SEHD image retrieval method, [5], using AUC. The mean AUC value for SEHD is 0.6037 while for the proposed method, is 0.6367. Thus, performing a two-tailed Students t-test at the highly significant 1% level with 598 degrees of freedom yields a p-value of 0.0022 which shows that the difference is statistically significant. In Figure 6 we provide the results for segmentation, saliency map extraction, salient edges and the salient region selection for three images from three distinct image categories of COREL 1000 database.

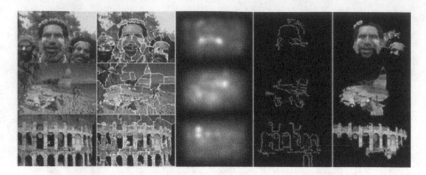

Fig. 6. Extracting query information. Each column indicates from left to right: original image, segmented regions, GBVS saliency map, salient edges and salient regions.

Fig. 7. Retrieval of "Checkered Scarf" images from SIVAL database.

Images are ranked according to the similarity measure $\mathcal{S}(Q, I)$ from (4), between the query image Q and a candidate retrieval image I. In Figure 7 we provide the images retrieved for a query image from "Checkered Scarf" images from SIVAL database. This category of images has a large degree of ambiguity due to the fact that the object in this case can have a variety of shapes and be located in a large variety of surroundings.

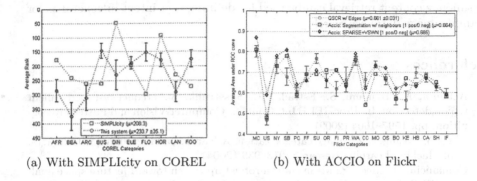

(a) With SIMPLIcity on COREL   (b) With ACCIO on Flickr

Fig. 8. Comparison results with other methods for COREL and Flickr databases.

Quantitative tests are performed by evaluating the average performance of the QSCR system across the whole of each database considering 300 queries for COREL 1000 and 600 queries for Flickr. In Figure 8(a) we provide the results for QSCR and SIMPLIcity [16], on the entire COREL 1000 database, using the average rank. QSCR unlike SIMPLIcity provides rather uniform results for all image categories. In Figure 8(b) we compare the results of QSCR, with the two retrieval methods proposed in [12], on Flickr database when using AUC. The results of QSCR and ACCIO are broadly similar while outperforming the ACCIO segmentation with neighbors method from [12]. Moreover, ACCIO involves feedback from human intervention, while the proposed approach is completely automatic. The salient edge information provides better performance when the category has limited variation among its salient objects, which are distinctive. The semantic gap is most evident in Flickr database, because its images and ground truths were obtained by performing keyword search.

5   Conclusion

In this paper we propose to model visual attention for content based image retrieval. The proposed method is bottom-up and unsupervised and consists of the following processing stages: image segmentation, feature extraction, saliency evaluation and image ranking. After segmenting each image, we calculate the feature vectors for each region characterizing color, contrast, texture, region centroid location. The visual saliency is defined at both local and global image levels. A graph-based implementation of the Itti-Koch visual saliency model is used for identifying image regions that drive human attention. The global saliency is modelled by the statistical distribution of edge orientation calculated for the entire image. A matching procedure is used for fitting characteristics of images, using the region saliency, from two different images. Consequently, a given image set is ranked based on both their similarity with respect to image features as well as by considering the attention that they would attract from a viewer. Image query by saliency content retrieval can be used for defining user intent in general as for example image database search.

References

1. Achanta, R., Hemami, S., Estrada, F., Susstrunk, S.: Frequency-tuned salient region detection. In: Proc. IEEE Int. Conf. on Computer Vision and Pattern Recognition, pp. 1597–1604 (2009)
2. Chen, Y., Wang, J. Z.: Image categorization by learning and reasoning with images. J. of Machine Learning Research, 913–939 (2004)
3. Comaniciu, D., Meer, P.: Mean shift: a robust approach toward feature space analysis. IEEE Trans. on Pattern Analysis and Machine Intelligence 24(5), 603–619 (2002)
4. Datta, R., Joshi, D., Li, J., Wan, J.Z.: Image retrieval: Ideas, influences, and trends of the new age. ACM Computing Surveys 40(2), 5:1–5:60 (2008)
5. Feng, S., Xu, D., Yang, X.: Attention-driven salient edge(s) and region(s) extraction with application to CBIR. Signal Processing 90(1), 1–15 (2010)
6. Harel, J., Koch, C., Perona, P.: Graph-based visual saliency. In: Proc. Advances in Neural Information Processing Systems (NIPS), vol. 19, pp. 545–552 (2007)
7. Itti, L., Koch, C.: Computational modelling of visual attention. Nature Reviews Neuroscience 2(3), 194–203 (2001)
8. Itti, L., Koch, C., Niebur, E.: A model of saliency-based visual attention for rapid scene analysis. IEEE Transactions on Pattern Analysis and Machine Intelligence 20(11), 1254–1259 (1998)
9. Itti, L., Ullman, S.: Shifts in selective visual attention: Towards the underlying neural circuitry. Human Neurobiology 4(4), 219–227 (1985)
10. Otsu, N.: A threshold selection method from gray-level histograms. IEEE Trans. on Syst., Man and Cyber. 9(1), 62–66 (1979)
11. Papushoy, A., Bors, A.G.: Image retrieval based on query by saliency content. Digital Signal Processing 36, 156–173 (2015)
12. Rahmani, R., Goldman, S.A., Zhang, H., Cholleti, S.R., Fritts, J.E.: Localized content-based image retrieval. IEEE Transactions on Pattern Analysis and Machine Intelligence 30(11), 1902–1912 (2008)
13. Rubner, Y., Tomasi, C., Guibas, L.J.: The earth mover distance as a metric for image retrieval. Int. Journal of Computer Vision 40(2), 99–121 (2000)
14. Rui, Y., Huang, T., Ortega, M., Mehrotra, S.: Relevance feedback: A power tool in interactive content-based image retrieval. IEEE Trans. on Circuits and Systems for Video Technology 8(5), 644–655 (1998)
15. Smeulders, A., Worring, M., Santini, S., Gupta, A., Jain, R.: Content-based image retrieval at the end of the early years. IEEE Trans. on Pattern Analysis and Machine Intelligence 22(12), 1349–1380 (2000)
16. Wang, J., Li, J., Wiederhold, G.: Simplicity: Semantics-sensitive integrated matching for picture libraries. IEEE Trans. on Pattern Analysis and Machine Intelligence 23(9), 947–963 (2001)
17. Zhang, L., Tong, M.H., Marks, T.K., Shan, H., Cottrell, G.W.: SUN: A Bayesian framework for saliency using natural statistics. Jour. of Vision 8(7), 32.1–32.20 (2008)

Tensor-Directed Spatial Patch Blending
for Pattern-Based Inpainting Methods

Maxime Daisy[✉], Pierre Buyssens, David Tschumperlé, and Olivier Lézoray

GREYC CNRS UMR6072, Image Team, 6 Bd Maréchal Juin, 14000 Caen, France
maxime.daisy@ensicaen.fr

Abstract. Despite the tremendous advances made in recent years, in the field of patch-based image inpainting algorithms, it is not uncommon to still get visible artefacts in the parts of the images that have been resynthetized using this kind of methods. Mostly, these artifacts take the form of discontinuities between synthetized patches which have been copied/pasted in nearby regions, but from very different source locations. In this paper, we propose a generic patch blending formalism which aims at strongly reducing this kind of artifacts. To achieve this, we define a tensor-directed anisotropic blending algorithm for neighboring patches, inspired somehow from what is done by anisotropic smoothing PDE's for the classical image regularization problem. Our method has the advantage of blending/removing incoherent patch data while preserving the significant structures and textures as much as possible. It is really fast to compute, and adaptable to most patch-based inpainting algorithms in order to visually enhance the quality of the synthetized results.

Keywords: Patch · Blending · Tensor-directed · Geometry-aware · Anisotropy

1 Introduction and Context

Image inpainting is an image processing task aiming at completing missing, corrupted, and/or undesired data inside an image. It is commonly used in a professional way to remove scratches or microphones in a video, or in a more amateur way, to remove undesired peoples or objects from photographs for example. As wisely described in [15], plenty of inpainting methods exist in the literature. They can be mainly categorized in two kinds of methods:

• Geometry-based methods [3,4,6,19,21] try to extend the local geometry inside the area to complete in order to reconstruct image structures as better as possible. These methods show impressive results in term of geometry synthesis, but mainly fail at building complex textures.

• Pattern-based methods have their origins in works on texture synthesis [2,14]. Based on the *self-similarity principle*, they use known parts of the image as

Maxime Daisy—This research was supported by French national grant *Action 3DS*.

G. Azzopardi and N. Petkov (Eds.): CAIP 2015, Part I, LNCS 9256, pp. 149–160, 2015.
DOI: 10.1007/978-3-319-23192-1_13

(a) Inpainting without blending.   (b) With isotropic blending.   (c) With tensor-based blending.

Fig. 1. Effect of our anisotropic blending where the inpainted region is highlighted

potential sources to reconstruct the missing part. These methods can be clustered into three main groups: 1) The *greedy* methods [5, 9, 10, 17] that copy/paste patch chunks in a greedy manner until the hole is filled. Efficient for texture synthesis, these methods can fail at reconstructing structures, and exhibit typical block-effect artifacts. 2) The *hybrid* methods [8, 16] that incorporate geometry-based methods to first continue the main structures before inpainting the textures. These methods are quite slow in practice, and require a segmentation of the image to separate structures from textures, which is an ill-posed problem. 3) The *energy-based* methods try to minimize coherence energy function via a multi-resolution [22] or variational framework [1]. While the solution in [22] tends to produce blurry textures due to the mix of patches used for the reconstruction, [1] incorporates a Poisson variant derived from [20] to smooth the transitions between pasted chunks.

In this paper we focus on the greedy *pattern-based* inpainting methods for their ability at reconstructing large portions of textures. Especially, we are interested in enhancing the perceptual quality of the results they provide. Our main **contribution** is the proposal of a novel tensor-guided spatial blending algorithm that strongly reduces the typical block-effect artifacts, while preserving the sharpness of synthesized structures and textures.

Notations: In the following, we define by $I : p \in \mathcal{I} \mapsto I(p) \in \mathbb{R}^3$ a multi-valued image. The known domain of this image is denoted Ω while unknown one (often called *mask* or *hole*) is denoted $\bar{\Omega}$, with $\Omega \cup \bar{\Omega} = \mathcal{I}$. We define by $\mathcal{N}_p$ a square neighbourhood domain of size $N \times N$ centered at p, and by, $\psi_p : q \in \mathcal{N}_p \subset \mathcal{I} \mapsto \psi_p(q) \in \mathbb{R}^3$ a patch value function. In the sequel, uppercase bold letters will stand for matrices while those in lowercase are for vectors.

Structure Tensors: Introduced in [23], *structure tensors* are a natural extension of gradient notion for multi-valued images. They represent the local image color changes: the value of the variations, and their directions. In this paper, we deal with two-dimensional RGB images, so structure tensors reduce to 2×2 matrices defined as follows:

$$\mathbf{S} = \sum_{c \in \{R,G,B\}} \overrightarrow{\nabla I^c} . \overrightarrow{\nabla I^c}^T$$
$$= \lambda_1 . \mathbf{u} . \mathbf{u}^T + \lambda_2 . \mathbf{v} . \mathbf{v}^T \quad \text{with} \quad \lambda_1 > \lambda_2$$

with $\lambda_{\{1,2\}}$ the eigen values of $\mathbf{S}$ and $\mathbf{u}, \mathbf{v}$ the eigen vectors associated to λ_1 and λ_2 respectively. The eigen vector associated to the biggest eigen value is oriented along the major image color change direction while the one associated to the smaller eigen value is oriented along the smallest image variation direction. In the following, tensors are represented with ellipses whose diameters and orientation are given by the eigen values and eigen vectors respectively.

Since they define a robust and accurate local geometry model, structure tensors have been used for years in image processing, as for image regularization [21], geometry-based [7,21] or pattern-based [11,18] image inpainting.

Spatial Patch Blending: In our previous works [12,13], we proposed a patch blending method that tries to reduce block effect artifact in pattern-based image inpainting results. The core of the method is to mix the data of several patches in a way that the reconstruction seems more continuous than with blocky patch chunks. This algorithm is mainly composed of two main consecutive steps:

1. **Artifact detection** tries to locate and estimate the strength of the possible artifacts present in the image. To locate artifacts, two hypotheses are made a) there are sharp variations of image intensity, and b) the source patches used for the reconstruction come from very different locations. The output of this artifact detection pipeline is a blending amplitude map that indicates, for each pixel, the bandwidth of blending to be applied locally.
2. **Patch blending** step uses the previously computed blending amplitude map as a model. Figure 2 illustrates the principle: for each $p \in \Omega$, the spatial blending performs a linear combination of all the pixels $\{p_1, \ldots, p_n\}$ overlapping p from the set of reconstructed patches $\{\psi_{p_1}, \ldots, \psi_{p_n}\}$.

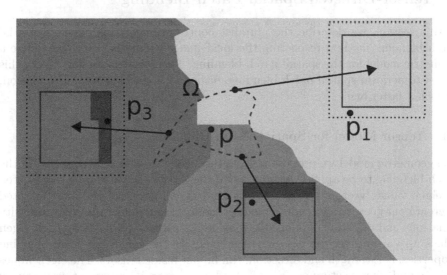

Fig. 2. Illustration of the spatial patch blending principle

(a) Pure patch-based inpainting result without patch spatial blending.

(b) Result (a) with the application of isotropic patch blending [12].

Fig. 3. Example of damaged textures with isotropic blending

Despite great improvements to the final visual quality of the inpainted image, this method suffers from a significant flaw: the spatial blending is performed through isotropic Gaussian weights, that do not respect enough the image structures. Figure 3 shows an inpainting result of a textured image (left) and its blended result (right) with this algorithm. Since the blending is applied in all directions (isotropic), some joints between bricks are too blurry. Such a flaw in fact damages both structures and textures, and that is the point we try to solve in this paper.

In the following of this paper, we propose a spatial patch blending method that is much more careful about the local image structures and textures. We first define a geometric model for patch blending, and then explain how we use it to apply a patch blending aware of local image geometry.

2   Tensor-Directed Spatial Patch Blending

In this section, we describe the pluralist contribution of this paper: a spatial patch blending method respecting the local image geometry. First, we define a geometric model for the spatial patch blending. Then we explain how to use this model to perform spatial patch blending, either with the elemental formulation, or with a faster one.

2.1   Tensor Model for Spatial Patch Blending

The geometric model we propose reflects the strength and the orientation of the patch blending to be applied locally. As all these information can be represented by eigen values/vectors of tensors, this kind model is one of the most adapted to create our geometric blending model. The local amount of the color intensity variations and directions are encoded inside a structure tensor $\mathbf{S}$ by their eigen values $\lambda_{\mathbf{S}\{1,2\}}$ and vectors $\mathbf{e}_{\mathbf{S}\{1,2\}}$ respectively. In the same way, local blending properties, i.e. strength and direction, can be put inside tensors. The eigen values $\lambda_{\mathbf{B}\{1,2\}}$ and eigen vectors $\mathbf{e}_{\mathbf{B}\{1,2\}}$ of blending tensors $\lambda_{\mathbf{B}}$ represent respectively the bandwidth and the direction of the spatial patch blending to be applied locally. As structure tensors already provide a good local geometry analysis, we propose to use them as a basis for building our *blending tensor* model. Transformation on eigen values and vectors of structure tensors is performed in a way that the final tensor fit our model. For flat area, patch blending must be omnidirectional, strong enough to remove small reconstruction artifacts, and highly smooth sharp variations. In this case, blending tensors keep the isotropic shape of structure tensors, but are much bigger. The textures are very important inside an image and should be preserved. In this case, blending tensors have the same properties of structure tensor, namely a small and isotropic shape. Finally, for sharp image structures, blending is able to preserve them while smoothing small breaks. Hence, they are oriented along the smallest variation direction, orthogonally to structure tensors. From this description of our tensorial blending model, we propose the following steps to build it. As computed using image gradient, structure tensors have eigen values that are fully dependent of the image value range, which is not be the case of blending tensors. Hence, the first step of the blending tensor construction is to normalize structure tensor eigen values:

$$\hat{\lambda}_{\mathbf{S}(p)i} = \frac{\lambda_{\mathbf{S}(p)}}{\max\limits_{p \in \mathcal{I}} \lambda_{\mathbf{S}(p)i}}$$

The local blending bandwidth, and so the eigen values of blending tensors, highly depends on the local image geometry which is given by the ratio between the smallest and the biggest eigen values of structure tensors. The less the ratio, the more anisotropic the tensor. At the contrary, the more the ratio, the more isotropic the tensor. Therefore, the next step is to modify eigen values $\hat{\lambda}_{\mathbf{S}(p)i}$ depending on this ratio in order to have new eigen values $\lambda_{\mathbf{B}i}$. The proposed function is inspired by partial differential equations for diffusion [21] and is defined as the following:

$$\lambda_{\mathbf{B}i} = \frac{1}{\left(1 + \hat{\lambda}_{\mathbf{S}1} + \hat{\lambda}_{\mathbf{S}2}\right)^{\gamma_i}} \tag{1}$$

where γ_i $(i \in \{1, 2\})$ are parameters controlling overall tensor isotropy. Examples of the effect of different configurations of γ_i are provided in Fig. 4.

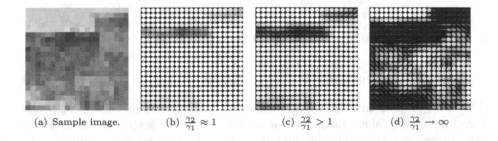

(a) Sample image.   (b) $\frac{\gamma_2}{\gamma_1} \approx 1$ (c) $\frac{\gamma_2}{\gamma_1} > 1$ (d) $\frac{\gamma_2}{\gamma_1} \to \infty$

Fig. 4. Illustration of the effect of the values of parameters γ_i

The final step is to build the blending tensor itself. As a symmetric and positive definite matrix, it can be expressed using the following composition:

$$\mathbf{B} = \lambda_{\sigma B1} \mathbf{e}_{\mathbf{S}1}^{\perp}{}^{T} \mathbf{e}_{\mathbf{S}1}^{\perp} + \lambda_{\sigma B2} \mathbf{e}_{\mathbf{S}2}^{\perp}{}^{T} \mathbf{e}_{\mathbf{S}2}^{\perp} \qquad (2)$$

where $\lambda_{\sigma Bi} = \sigma_{\mathbf{B}} \lambda_{Bi}$, are the eigen values of the blending tensors.

The above description gives a blending tensor configurations depending on the local geometry (see Table 1). The tensor model proposed in this section

Table 1. Correspondence between types of image areas and how patch blending should apply on these areas

Type of image area	Blending strength	Direction
flat area	strong	all
textured area	small	all
structured area	weak	structure

provides all local information needed to apply a spatial patch blending aware of image structure and texture. In the next section, we describe how to use this model to perform spatial patch blending on patch-based inpainting results.

2.2   Elemental Tensor-Directed patch blending

The first proposed scheme is the elemental formulation of our geometry-guided patch blending process. This scheme aims at applying patch blending in a pixel-wise fashion using the proposed tensor model $\mathbf{B}(p)$. Our approach is to compute a linear combination of pixels coming from several patches overlapping one another, using the local geometry. For each $p \in \Omega$ in each image channel k, the following formula is applied:

$$J^k(p) = \frac{\sum\limits_{\psi_q \in \Psi_p} w_{\mathbf{B}}(p,q) \, \psi_q^k(p - q)}{\varepsilon + \sum\limits_{\psi_q \in \Psi_p} w_{\mathbf{B}}(p,q)} \qquad (3)$$

where $\Psi_p = \{\psi_0, \ldots, \psi_n\}$ is the set of source patches overlapping p, and $w_{\mathbf{B}}$ is an anisotropic Gaussian weight function defined as follows:

$$w_{\mathbf{B}}(p,q) = e^{\frac{X^T \mathbf{B}(p)^{-1} X}{2\sigma_{\mathbf{B}}^2}} \qquad \text{with } X = q - p \qquad (4)$$

The effect is to blend very strongly flat areas such that no seams appear, while blending slightly along image contours. This allows to keep the strong image structures reconstructed during inpainting and also the complex textures.

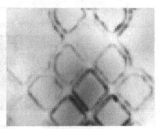

Fig. 5. Illustration of the difference between summed patch blending weights using isotropic weights (middle), and anisotropic geometry-aware weights (right) on a sample image (left)

2.3   Faster Tensor-Directed patch blending

The elemental formulation of the spatial patch blending, as pointed out in [12], is slow to compute and does not allow to use it easily. In this section, we propose an adaptation of the work of [12] to the geometric model proposed in this paper.

The proposed algorithm remains quite the same that those in [12]. The first difference lies in the Gaussian weights used to apply patch blending at each scale of the blending amplitude map. While these weights are isotropic in [12], in this version we use anisotropic Gaussian weights based on the geometric model described in 2.1 (see Fig. 5). As previously described, proposed geometric model describes the way to blend patches locally. Therefore, there is no need to compute patch blending at multiple scale since it is done per se with proposed tensor model. In this faster blending method, geometry of reconstructed patches are approximate using regularized blending tensor on their center. The computation time of this method is really smaller than those of elemental method. While in the elemental formulation there are as many weight functions as patches overlapping the position a specified pixel to compute, in the faster formulation only one weight function is computed per patch. Table 2 summarizes the computation times for some of the images of this paper. One can notice that compared to the elemental formulation, the faster one is more stable with respect to inpainting patch size. It is also fast with high resolution images.

Table 2. Comparison of computation times (in sec) between elemental and fast anisotropic patch blending method

Size	Missing	Patch size	Elemental	Fast
500 × 375	7%	9	0.85	0.6
-	-	21	5.5	0.6
-	-	43	33.5	0.65
1024 × 768	12%	9	5.2	2.6
-	-	21	29	2.2
-	-	43	33.5	2.74

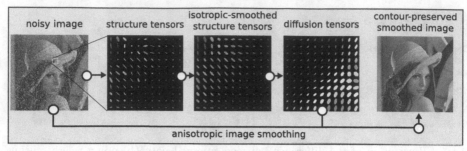

(a) Anisotropic image smoothing process.

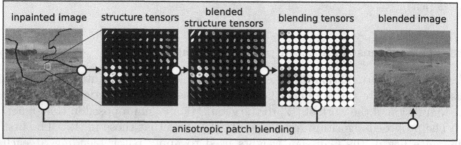

(b) Geometry-guided patch blending process.

Fig. 6. Analogy between anisotropic image smoothing and proposed geometry-guided spatial patch blending

2.4 High Level Process

The proposed process for tensor-directed patch blending is similar to anisotropic image smoothing, as described in Fig. 6. In the latter case, in image denoising for example, the structure tensor field is first extracted from the input image. This field is then smoothed using an isotropic Gaussian kernel. The effect is to regularize the tensor field and to get a more continuous version of it. Finally, the regularized structure tensor field is used to apply anisotropic smoothing on the input image.

In the case of the proposed tensor-directed spatial patch blending algorithm, the process is very similar with the isotropic one. This algorithm contains four main consecutive steps (see Fig. 6):

1. The blending tensor field is computed on the masked version of the image. This step is quite thorny since the image domain is not defined on Ω. However, image gradient at the boundary of Ω can be estimated using finite differences schemes depending on the known neighborhood of a pixel.
2. In order to obtain a complete tensor field, the structure tensor field is reconstructed simultaneously with the input image during inpainting. Also, it can be reconstructed from the warping map, after the inpainting.
3. Once the tensor field is reconstructed, it is blended in an isotropic fashion using the method of [12]. The effect is to smooth the tensors that are

induced by the reconstruction seams between patches. In this way, they do not interfere in the anisotropic patch blending step.

4. Finally, patch blending is performed on the inpainted image with the previously described scheme (see. Eq. (3,4)).

3   Results, Comparisons and Discussions

Fig. 7 compares our approach with the one of [1]. On the tiles image (first row), the result of [1] is a little blurry while the edges with our apporach are slightly more preserved. On the yellow texture image (second row), one can see that our method brings more geometric coherence. Finally on the dots image (third row), one can notice that the effect of our anisotropic blending is near of the effect of [1]. In Fig. 8 we show comparisons of our method results (right column) with those of [12] (middle column). In a common way, one can see that the results of [12] present some structure superposition effect due to the blending of structures and flat areas, like between the rocks (rows 2-4). Also, one can clearly notice that the structures of the rocks (third row) are more preserved with our method, than with the method of [12] that presents more evanescent structures. Through these results, one can see that the geometric model we propose for patch blending algorithm really reduces the smoothing effect present in [12], and provides similar or better results than state-of-the-art methods. In addition, proposed method frees users from choosing a scheme depending on the

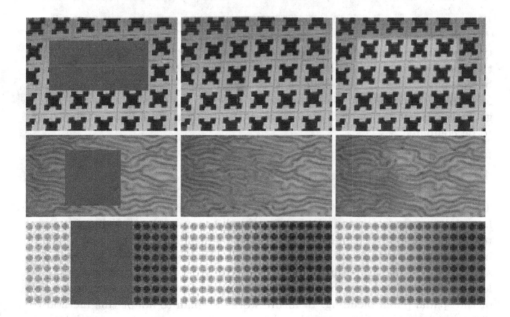

Fig. 7. Comparison between results of state-of-the-art method [1] (middle column) and proposed method (right column)

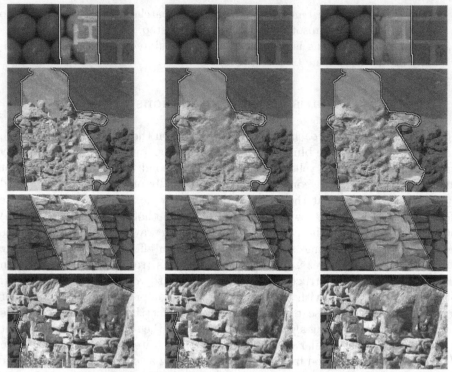

(a) Inpainting without blending. (b) Using blending method of [12]. (c) Proposed blending method.

Fig. 8. Comparison of results of the blending our method with the method of [12]

type of image. Concerning the computation time, proposed method is longer than isotropic one. This is because for isotropic method, Gaussian weights can be computed once at each scale, and reused for every patches. In the case of anisotropic blending, the Gaussian weight function depends on the local patch geometry. Hence, as many Gaussian weight function as number of patches have to be computed.

4   Conclusions and Future Work

This paper presents a structure and texture preservative method to reduce arti-facts in image inpainting methods using patch-based synthesis. Using structure tensors, we compute "blending" tensors that aim at directing the patch blend-ing along the structures, flattening the nearly placid area, and damage texture as less as possible. Experiments and comparisons were made on several chal-lenging cases. They show that the proposed method really improves the quality of the spatial patch blending. In future works we plan to adapt this method to video inpainting by fully integrating the temporal dimension to our spatial patch blending geometric model.

References

1. Arias, P., Facciolo, G., Caselles, V., Sapiro, G.: A variational framework for exemplar-based image inpainting. International Journal of Computer Vision **93**(3), 319–347 (2011). http://dx.doi.org/10.1007/s11263-010-0418-7
2. Ashikhmin, M.: Synthesizing natural textures. In: Proceedings of the 2001 Symposium on Interactive 3D Graphics, pp. 217–226. ACM (2001)
3. Ballester, C., Bertalmio, M., Caselles, V., Sapiro, G., Verdera, J.: Filling-in by joint interpolation of vector fields and gray levels. IEEE Transactions on Image Processing **10**(8), 1200–1211 (2001)
4. Bertalmio, M., Sapiro, G., Caselles, V., Ballester, C.: Image inpainting. In: Proceedings of the 27th Annual Conference on Computer Graphics and Interactive Techniques, pp. 417–424 (2000)
5. Bornard, R., Lecan, E., Laborelli, L., Chenot, J.H.: Missing data correction in still images and image sequences. In: Proceedings of the Tenth ACM International Conference on Multimedia, pp. 355–361 (2002)
6. Bornemann, F., März, T.: Fast image inpainting based on coherence transport. Journal of Mathematical Imaging and Vision **28**(3), 259–278 (2007)
7. Bugeau, A., Bertalmio, M., et al.: Combining texture synthesis and diffusion for image inpainting. In: Combining Texture Synthesis and Diffusion for Image Inpainting, pp. 26–33 (2009)
8. Cao, F., Gousseau, Y., Masnou, S., Pérez, P.: Geometrically guided exemplar-based inpainting. SIAM Journal on Imaging Sciences **4**(4), 1143–1179 (2011)
9. Criminisi, A., Pérez, P., Toyama, K.: Region filling and object removal by exemplar-based image inpainting. IEEE Transactions on Image Processing **13**(9), 1200–1212 (2004)
10. Criminisi, A., Perez, P., Toyama, K.: Object removal by exemplar-based inpainting. In: Computer Vision and Pattern Recognition, vol. 2, pp. II-721. IEEE (2003)
11. Daisy, M., Buyssens, P., Tschumperlé, D., Lézoray, O.: A smarter exemplar-based inpainting algorithm using local and global heuristics for more geometry coherence. In: Internation Conference on Image Processing, Paris, France (2014)
12. Daisy, M., Tschumperlé, D., Lézoray, O.: A fast spatial patch blending algorithm for artefact reduction in pattern-based image inpainting. In: SIGGRAPH Asia 2013 Technical Briefs (2013)
13. Daisy, M., Tschumperlé, D., Lézoray, O.: Spatial patch blending for artefact reduction in pattern-based inpainting techniques. In: Wilson, R., Hancock, E., Bors, A., Smith, W. (eds.) CAIP 2013, Part II. LNCS, vol. 8048, pp. 523–530. Springer, Heidelberg (2013)
14. Efros, A.A., Leung, T.K.: Texture synthesis by non-parametric sampling. In: International Conference on Computer Vision, vol. 2, pp. 1033–1038. IEEE (1999)
15. Guillemot, C., Le Meur, O.: Image inpainting: Overview and recent advances. Signal Processing Magazine, IEEE **31**(1), 127–144 (2014)
16. Jia, J., Tang, C.K.: Inference of segmented color and texture description by tensor voting. IEEE Transactions on Pattern Analysis and Machine Intelligence **26**(6), 771–786 (2004)
17. Le Meur, O., Ebdelli, M., Guillemot, C.: Hierarchical super-resolution-based inpainting. IEEE Transactions on Image Processing **22**(10), 3779–3790 (2013)
18. Le Meur, O., Gautier, J., Guillemot, C.: Examplar-based inpainting based on local geometry. In: International Conference on Image Processing, Brussel, Belgium, pp. 3401–3404 (2011). http://hal.inria.fr/inria-00628074

19. Masnou, S., Morel, J.M.: Level lines based disocclusion. In: International Conference on Image Processing (3), pp. 259–263 (1998)
20. Pérez, P., Gangnet, M., Blake, A.: Poisson image editing. ACM Transactions on Graphics **22**(3), 313–318 (2003)
21. Tschumperlé, D., Deriche, R.: Vector-valued image regularization with pdes: A common framework for different applications. IEEE Transactions on Pattern Analysis and Machine Intelligence **27**(4), 506–517 (2005)
22. Wexler, Y., Shechtman, E., Irani, M.: Space-time completion of video. IEEE Transaction on Pattern Analysis and Machince Intelligence **29**(3), 463–476 (2007)
23. Di Zenzo, S.: A note on the gradient of a multi-image. Computer Vision, Graphics, and Image Processing **33**(1), 116–125 (1986). http://www.sciencedirect.com/science/article/pii/0734189X86902239

A Novel Image Descriptor Based on Anisotropic Filtering

Darshan Venkatrayappa$^{(\boxtimes)}$, Philippe Montesinos, Daniel Diep,
and Baptiste Magnier

LGI2P - Ecole des Mines D'Ales, Nimes, France
{darshan.venkatrayappa,philippe.montesinos,daniel.diep,
baptiste.magnier}@mines-ales.fr

Abstract. In this paper, we present a new image patch descriptor for object detection and image matching. The descriptor is based on the standard HoG pipeline. The descriptor is generated in a novel way, by embedding the response of an oriented anisotropic derivative half Gaussian kernel in the Histogram of Orientation Gradient (HoG) framework. By doing so, we are able to bin more curvature information. As a result, our descriptor performs better than the state of art descriptors such as SIFT, GLOH and DAISY. In addition to this, we repeat the same procedure by replacing the anisotropic derivative half Gaussian kernel with a computationally less complex anisotropic derivative half exponential kernel and achieve similar results. The proposed image descriptors using both the kernels are very robust and shows promising results for variations in brightness, scale, rotation, view point, blur and compression. We have extensively evaluated the effectiveness of the devised method with various challenging image pairs acquired under varying circumstances.

Keywords: Anisotropic half derivative gaussian kernel · Anisotropic half derivative exponential kernel · Image descriptor · HoG · Image matching

1 Introduction

Currently, most of the promising method for image content description use local features as their basis. Thus, image feature extraction has become an important and active research topic in the field of computer vision. Local image features form the foundation for many real time applications such as object detection and tracking, panorama stitching, video surveillance and image based retrieval. In addition to feature description these applications require invariance to rotation, scale, viewpoint and illumination changes. Many image description algorithms have been proposed to incorporate all these characteristics. To name a few: SIFT[1], GLOH[2], SURF[3], LIOP[4], ASIFT[5], DAISY[6] and many more. Most of these descriptors are based on Histogram of Oriented Gradients (HoG)[7]. SIFT, SURF and GLOH are robust to rotation and scale invariance characteristics. ASIFT improves on these descriptors by exhibiting good affine

© Springer International Publishing Switzerland 2015
G. Azzopardi and N. Petkov (Eds.): CAIP 2015, Part I, LNCS 9256, pp. 161–173, 2015.
DOI: 10.1007/978-3-319-23192-1_14

invariance properties. LIOP has succeeded in handling both the geometric distortions and monotonic changes in illumination. Some of these descriptors and their variants are compared and reviewed in detail in [2].

Another category of feature descriptors use filter response as their basis. Schmid and Mohr [8] use differential invariant responses to compute new local image descriptors. Differential invariant responses are obtained from a combination of Gaussian derivatives of different orders, which are invariant to 2-dimensional rigid transformations. Koenderink et al. [9] formulate a methodology based on Gaussian function and its derivatives to capture the local geometry of the image. Larsen et al. [10] follow a new approach for the construction of an image descriptor based on local k-jet, which uses filter bank responses for feature description. Palomares et al.[11] have come up with a local image descriptor issued from a filtering stage made of oriented anisotropic half-Gaussian smoothing convolution kernels. They achieve euclidean invariance in the matching stage. However, most of the descriptors based on filter response vaguely capture the geometry of the region around key-points, as a result they fail to compete with the HoG based descriptors.

Some researchers capture the geometry of the image patch using curvature information, and various edge related information. Monroy et al. [12] use descriptor based on curvature histograms for object detection. This descriptor gives good results for images with strong line segments. Authors in [13] use location, orientation and length of the edges to construct an image patch descriptor. Here, the descriptor encodes the presence or absence of edges using a binary value for a range of possible edge positions and orientations. Eigenstetter et al. [14] have proposed an object representation framework based on curvature self-similarity. This method goes beyond the popular approximation of objects using straight lines. However, like all descriptors using second order statistics, this approach also exhibits a very high dimensionality.

In our method rotation and affine normalized gray level image patch is extracted as in [19]. Then, we construct our descriptor on this image patch. Thus obtained descriptor is completely different than the above mentioned descriptors. It can be seen as a combination of all the above three approaches. In the remaining of this paper for simplicity we refer to anisotropic half Gaussian derivative kernel as AHGDK and anisotropic half exponential derivative kernel as AHEDK. In our descriptor :

1. The response of a rotating AHGDK or AHEDK around pixels is used to construct signatures.
2. The orientation of the edges and the anisotropic gradient directions are extracted from the signatures, thus capturing the geometry/curvature of the image patch.
3. These orientations are binned separately in different ways as in HoG to form different descriptors.
4. Additionally, we construct a faster variant of our descriptor by replacing the AHGDK with a computationally inexpensive AHEDK.

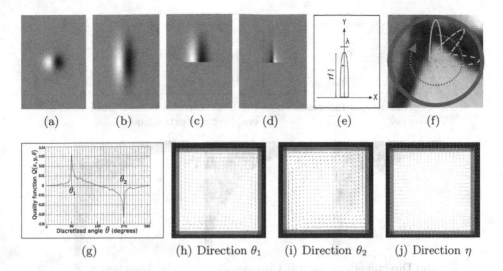

Fig. 1. (a) Isotropic gaussian kernel (b) Anisotropic gaussian kernel (c) AHGDK (d) AHEDK with $\alpha_\mu = 1$ and $\alpha_\lambda = .2$ (e) A thin Gaussian derivative half-filter. (f) AHGDK applied to a keypoint (x_p, y_p) in the image patch. (g) Extrema of a function $\mathcal{Q}(x_p, y_p, \theta)$. and $\Delta\theta = 2°$. Note that the initial orientation of the filter is vertical, upwardly directed and steerable clockwise. ((h),(i),(j)) Synthetic square illustrating the image geometry captured by AHGDK. All the figures in this paper are best when viewed in color.

2 Filtering Stage

2.1 Anisotropic Half Gaussian Derivative Kernel (AHGDK)

When compared to isotropic filters (Fig.1(a)), anisotropic filters (Fig.1(b)) have an advantage in detecting large linear structures. For anisotropic filters, at the corners the gradient magnitude decreases as the edge information under the scope of the filter decreases (Fig.2(a)). Consequently, robustness to noise, when dealing with tiny geometric structures weakens. This weakness can be nullified by using AHGDK [16]. In addition to this, thanks to the elongated and oriented half kernels (Fig.1(c), Fig.1(e)), we are able to estimate the two edge directions as in Fig.2(b). As illustrated in Fig.1(f), at the pixel coordinate (x, y), a derivative kernel is applied to obtain a derivative information $\mathcal{Q}(x, y, \theta)$ in a function of orientation $\theta \in [0; 360°[$:

$$\mathcal{Q}(x, y, \theta) = I_\theta * C \cdot H(-y) \cdot x \cdot e^{-\left(\frac{x^2}{2\lambda^2} + \frac{y^2}{2\mu^2}\right)}, \tag{1}$$

where I_θ corresponds to a rotated image of orientation θ, C is a normalization coefficient [17] and (μ, λ) represent the standard deviation of AHGDK. Only the causal part of this filter along the Y axis is used, this is obtained by cutting the

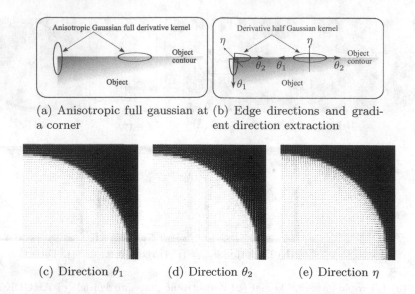

(a) Anisotropic full gaussian at a corner

(b) Edge directions and gradient direction extraction

(c) Direction θ_1 (d) Direction θ_2 (e) Direction η

Fig. 2. Synthetic quarter circle used to illustrate the image geometry captured by AHEDK. Enlarge the image to get a proper view of the orientations.

kernel in the middle, in an operation that corresponds to the Heaviside function H. As in [16], we have chosen to rotate the image instead of filter, thereby reducing the algorithmic complexity by making use of a recursive Gaussian filter [17].

2.2   Anisotropic Half Exponential Derivative Kernel (AHEDK)

We modify the Shen Castan filter [18] to imitate the AHGDK. We call this modified filter as anisotropic half exponential derivative kernel (AHEDK). AHEDK shows similar characteristics and produces similar results as that of the above explained AHGDK. We use the recursive implementation of half exponential kernel which is of order 1. So, it is approximately 5 times faster than the recursive implementation of anisotropic half derivative kernel. By construction AHEDK exhibits derivative characteristics along the X direction and smoothing characteristics along the Y direction.

$$\mathcal{E}(x, y, \theta) = I_\theta * C_1 \cdot H(y) \cdot e^{(-\alpha_\mu \cdot y)} \cdot sign(x) \cdot e^{(-\alpha_\lambda \cdot |x|)} \tag{2}$$

The derivative information $\mathcal{E}(x, y, \theta)$ in Eq.2 is obtained by spinning the AHEDK around a pixel (x, y), C_1 is a normalization coefficient and $(\alpha_\mu, \alpha_\lambda)$ the height and width of the anisotropic half exponential kernel (see Fig.1(d)).

Similar to Eq.1 only the causal part of this filter along the Y axis is used by cutting the kernel in the middle, in an operation that corresponds to the Heaviside function H.

2.3   Anisotropic Gradient Magnitude and Direction Estimation

We construct the signature $\mathcal{Q}(x_p, y_p, \theta)$ by considering the response of the above described rotating filter at a pixel location (x_p, y_p) as in Fig.1(f). Fig.1(g) shows a sample signature obtained by applying the AHGDK at the the pixel location (x_p, y_p) in steps of $2°$. Anisotropic gradient magnitude $\|\nabla I\|_a$ and its associate direction η for the key-point at location (x_p, y_p) are obtained by considering the global extrema G_{max} and G_{min} of the function $\mathcal{Q}(x_p, y_p, \theta)$ along with θ_1 and θ_2. The two angles θ_1 and θ_2 define a curve crossing the pixel (an incoming and outgoing direction) thus representing the two edge directions. Two of these global extrema are combined to maximize the gradient $\|\nabla I\|_a$, i.e:

$$\begin{cases} G_{max} = \max_{\theta \in [0,360°[} \mathcal{Q}(x_p, y_p, \theta) \quad \text{and} \quad \theta_1 = \arg\max_{\theta \in [0,360°[} (\mathcal{Q}(x_p, y_p, \theta)) \\ G_{min} = \min_{\theta \in [0,360°[} \mathcal{Q}(x_p, y_p, \theta) \quad \text{and} \quad \theta_2 = \arg\min_{\theta \in [0,360°[} (\mathcal{Q}(x_p, y_p, \theta)) \\ \|\nabla I\|_a = G_{max} - G_{min} \\ \eta \quad = \dfrac{\theta_1 + \theta 2}{2} \end{cases} \quad (3)$$

By construction, our filter naturally detects curvature information with θ_1 and θ_2 using only 1st order derivatives. The arrows on the circle in Fig.2 and on the square in Fig.1 illustrates this property. We follow the same procedure to obtain the signature $\mathcal{E}(x_p, y_p, \theta)$ and extract the edge and gradient directions using the AHEDK.

3   Descriptor Construction

Descriptor construction process is shown in Fig.3. As in [19], we follow the standard procedure to obtain the rotation and affine normalized gray level image patch. This standard procedure is followed in the construction of all the descriptors (SIFT, DAISY, GLOH) used in our experiments. As in Fig.3, for each pixel in the image patch, we spin the AHGDK and obtain a signature (for simplicity and proper viewing, in Fig.3 signatures are not shown). From this signature we extract : i) Angle at the maxima, θ_1 and the response G_{max} at θ_1. ii) Angle at the minima, θ_2 and the response $\|G_{min}\|$ at θ_2. iii) Anisotropic gradient angle η and its magnitude $\|\nabla I\|_a$. The next step is to construct 3 intermediate descriptors by forming the HoG of all the 3 angles separately. The angle θ_1 is weighed by G_{max}, θ_2 by $\|G_{min}\|$, η by $\|\nabla I\|_a$ and binned as in Eq.4.

$$\begin{cases} HoG_{\theta_1} = \{\theta_{1_{bin1}}, \theta_{1_{bin2}}, \theta_{1_{bin3}}, \theta_{1_{bin4}} \ldots \theta_{1_{bin128}}\} \\ HoG_{\theta_2} = \{\theta_{2_{bin1}}, \theta_{2_{bin2}}, \theta_{2_{bin3}}, \theta_{2_{bin4}} \ldots \theta_{2_{bin128}}\} \\ HoG_{\eta} = \{\eta_{bin1}, \eta_{bin2}, \eta_{bin3}, \eta_{bin4} \ldots \ldots \eta_{bin128}\} \end{cases} \quad (4)$$

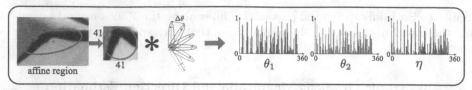

Fig. 3. Histogram construction process using 3 directions θ_1, θ_2 and η obtained using anisotropic half Gaussian kernel.

Finally, we combine the three intermediate descriptors in 4 different ways, i) DESCT1-theta1-eta : A 256 dimension(length) descriptor obtained by concatenating HoG_{θ_1} and HoG_η. ii) DESCT2-theta2-eta : A 256 dimension descriptor obtained by concatenating HoG_{θ_2} and HoG_η. iii) DESCT3-theta1-theta2 : A 256 dimension descriptor obtained by concatenating HoG_{θ_1} and HoG_{θ_2}. iv) DESCT4-theta1-theta2-eta : A 384 dimension descriptor obtained by concatenating HoG_{θ_1}, HoG_{θ_2} and HoG_η. We follow the same procedure to construct the descriptors using AHEDK and call them EXP-DESCT1-theta1-eta, EXP-DESCT2-theta2-eta, EXP-DESCT3-theta1-theta2 and EXP-DESCT4-theta1-theta2-eta.

4   Experiments and Results

4.1   Dataset and Evaluation

The entire code was implemented on Matlab platform. Harris affine key points [19] were used for image patch extraction. Key points obtained from other detectors can also be used for extracting the image patches. We evaluate and compare the performance of our descriptor against the state of the art descriptors on the standard dataset using the standard protocol provided by Oxford group. The binaries and dataset are obtained from website linked to [2] (http://www.robots.ox.ac.uk/ vgg/research/affine/). The dataset used in our experiments has different geometric and photometric transformations such as change of scale and image rotation (boat), viewpoint change (graf), image blur (bike), JPEG compression (compression) and illumination change (Leuven). For each type of image transformation there is a set of six images with established ground truth homographies.

We use the evaluation criterion as proposed by [2]. The evaluation criteria is based on the number of correspondences, number of correct matches and the number of false matches between two images. Here, we test the descriptors using Similarity based method and Nearest neighbour method. Due to lack of space we restrain from going in to the details of these methods. A detailed description of these methods can be found in [2]. The results are presented using the recall vs 1-precision curves. As in eq.5, recall is defined as the total number of correctly matched regions over the number of corresponding regions between two images of the same scene. From eq.6, 1-precision is represented by the number of false matches relative to the total number of matches. In all our experiments, Euclidean distance is used as the distance measure.

$$\text{recall} = \frac{\text{Total No of correct matches}}{\text{No of correspondences}} \tag{5}$$

$$\text{1-precision} = \frac{\text{No of false matches}}{\text{No of correct matches + No of false matches}} \tag{6}$$

Our descriptors depends on 4 different parameters: $\Delta\theta$, $No-of-bins$, height and width (μ, λ for AHGDK and α_μ, α_λ for AHEDK). The rotation step $\Delta\theta$ is fixed to 10°. Increasing the rotation step results in loss of information. The image patch is divided into 16 blocks. All blocks are of size 10x10(Since we are using a patch of size 41x41 the blocks in the extreme right and bottom have 11x11 size). The number of bins ($No-of-bins$) is fixed to 8 per block, resulting in a $8 * 16 = 128$ bins for 16 blocks. Increasing the number of bins results in almost the same performance but, increases the dimensionality of the descriptor. AHGDK height μ and width λ is fixed to 6 and 1 respectively. AHEDK height α_μ and width α_λ is fixed to 1 and 0.2 respectively. Width and height parameters are chosen to have a ratio sharpness length suitable for robust edge detection [16], which generally gives good results in most cases. This ratio is compatible with the angle filtering step.

4.2   Descriptor Performance

The performance of descriptors obtained using both AHGDK and AHEDK are compared against SIFT, GLOH and DAISY. For SIFT and GLOH, the descriptors are extracted from the binaries provided by Oxford group (http://www.robots.ox.ac.uk/~vgg/research/affine/)[2]. DAISY descriptor for patches is extracted from the code provided by [6]. We have compared our descriptor on all the images in the dataset. Due to lack of space, we omit showing the quantitative results for the image pair (1-6). Qualitative results using nearest neighbour approach for the image pair (1-4) using descriptors obtained from both AHGDK and AHEDK is shown in Fig.7.

1. Rotation changes (boat).
   Using similarity matching strategy, all of our descriptors obtained from both AHGDK and AHEDK have a clear advantage over SIFT, GLOH and DAISY. This can be seen from the 1st row of Fig.4 and Fig.5. When the descriptors obtained using AHGDK and AHEDK are compared against each other they exhibit similar results as shown in the 1st row of Fig.6. The same can be said, when experimented with nearest neighbour matching strategy. Due to lack of space, for all the dataset we omit showing the quantitative results using nearest neighbour matching method.
2. Viewpoint changes (graff).
   For image pair (1-2), (1-3) and (1-4), using similarity approach our descriptors and its variants performs similar to or better than that of SIFT, DAISY and GLOH. Image pair (1-5) is very challenging and all the descriptors including SIFT, DAISY and GLOH fail. The results can be seen from the

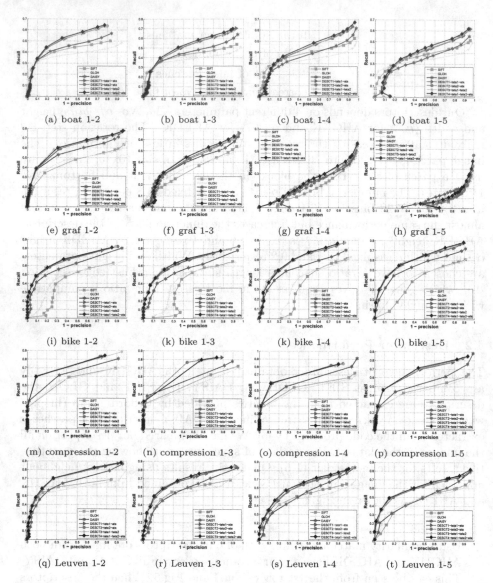

Fig. 4. Recall vs 1-Precision curves for SIFT, GLOH, DAISY and 4 descriptors obtained using AHGDK. Similarity matching is used for evaluation.

graphs in the 2nd row of Fig. 4 and Fig. 5. When the descriptors obtained using AHGDK and AHEDK are compared against each other they exhibit similar results as shown in the 2nd row of Fig. 6.

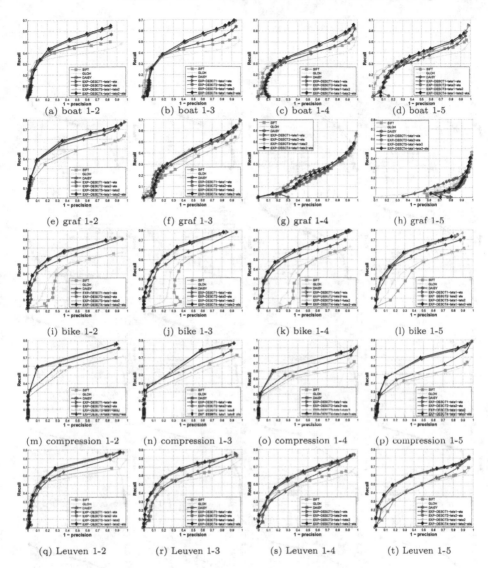

Fig. 5. Recall vs 1-Precision curves for SIFT, GLOH, DAISY and 4 descriptors obtained using AHEDK. Similarity matching is used for evaluation.

3. Variations in blur, compression and brightness.

For the blur (bike), compression, and brightness (Leuven) changes, using similarity approach all our descriptors outperform SIFT, DAISY and GLOH. The performance can be seen in the third, fourth and fifth rows of Fig. 4 and Fig. 5 respectively. When the descriptors obtained using AHGDK and AHEDK are compared against each other they exhibit similar results as shown in the 3rd, 4th and 5th row of Fig. 6.

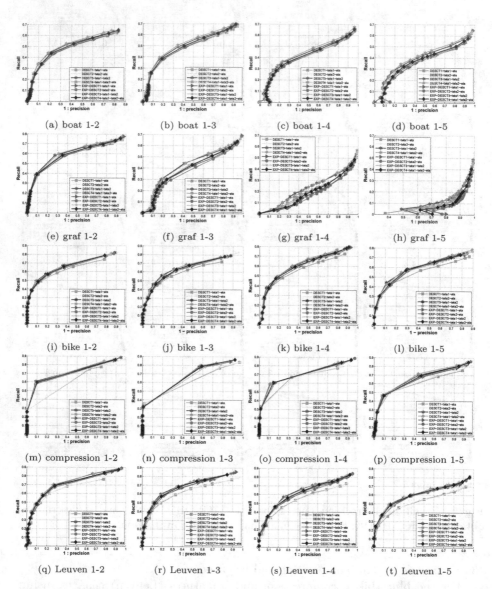

Fig. 6. Recall vs 1-Precision curves for all descriptors obtained using both AHGDK and AHEDK. Similarity matching is used for evaluation.

(a)DESCT4-theta1-theta2-eta (boat 1-4)   (b)EXP-DESCT4-theta1-theta2-eta (boat 1-4)

(c)DESCT4-theta1-theta2-eta (Graf 1-4)   (d)EXP-DESCT4-theta1-theta2-eta (Graf 1-4)

(e)DESCT4-theta1-theta2-eta (bike 1-4)   (f)EXP-DESCT4-theta1-theta2-eta (bike 1-4)

(g)DESCT4-theta1-theta2-eta (comp 1-4)   (h)EXP-DESCT4-theta1-theta2-eta (comp 1-4)

(i)DESCT4-theta1-theta2-eta (leuven 1-4)   (j)EXP-DESCT4-theta1-theta2-eta (leuven 1-4)

Fig. 7. Qualitative matching results for the Oxford dataset using the nearest neighbour matching method. Matches in the Left column are obtained using AHGDK and the matches in the right column are obtained using AHEDK.

5   Conclusion

This paper proposes novel image patch descriptors based on anisotropic half Gaussian derivative kernel (AHGDK) and anisotropic half exponential derivative kernel (AHEDK). The originality of our method is that it captures the geometry of the image patch by embedding the response of the AHGDK or AHEDK in a HoG framework. Our method incorporates edge direction as well as anisotropic gradient direction for generating the descriptor and its variations. On the standard dataset provided by the Oxford group our descriptor and its variants outperform SIFT, GLOH and DAISY. In the future, we would like to learn the parameters by introducing a learning stage. We would also like to use this approach for object classification and image retrieval purpose. The speed of the descriptor generation can be boosted by parallel programming.

Acknowledgments. This work is funded by L'institut mediterraneen des metiers de la longevite (I2ML), Nimes, France.

References

1. Lowe, D.G.: Distinctive Image Features from Scale-Invariant Keypoints. International Journal of Computer Vision (IJCV) **60**, 91–110 (2004)
2. Mikolajczyk, K., Schmid, C.: A Performance Evaluation of Local Descriptors. IEEE Trans. Pattern Anal. Mach. Intell., 1615–1630 (2005)
3. Bay, H., Ess, A., Tuytelaars, T., Van Gool, L.J.: Speeded-up robust features. In: Computer Vision and Image Understanding, vol. 110, pp. 346–359 (2008)
4. Wang, Z., Fan, B., Wu, F.: Local intensity order pattern for feature description. In: IEEE International Conference on Computer Vision (ICCV), pp. 603–610, November 2011
5. Morel, J.M., Yu, G.: ASIFT: A New Framework for Fully Affine Invariant Image Comparison. Journal on Imaging Sciences **2**, 438–469 (2009)
6. Tola, E., Lepetit, V., Fua, P.: DAISY: An Efficient Dense Descriptor Applied to Wide Baseline Stereo. TPAMI **32**, 815–830 (2010)
7. Dalal, N., Triggs, T.: Histograms of oriented gradients for human detection. In: Computer Vision and Pattern Recognition (CVPR), pp. 886–893 (2005)
8. Schmid, C., Mohr, R.: Local Gray-value Invariants for Image Retrieval. IEEE Trans. Pattern Anal. Mach. Intell. **9**, 530–535 (1997)
9. Koenderink, J.J., Van Doorn, A.J.: Representation of local geometry in the visual system. Biological Cybernetics **55**, 367–375 (1987)
10. Larsen, A.B.L., Darkner, S., Dahl, A.L., Pedersen, K.S.: Jet-based local image descriptors. In: Fitzgibbon, A., Lazebnik, S., Perona, P., Sato, Y., Schmid, C. (eds.) ECCV 2012, Part III. LNCS, vol. 7574, pp. 638–650. Springer, Heidelberg (2012)
11. Palomares, J.L., Montesinos, P., Diep, D.: A new affine invariant method for image matching. In: 3DIP Image Processing and Applications, vol. 8290 (2012)
12. Monroy, A., Eigenstetter, A., Ommer, B.: Beyond straight lines - object detection using curvature. In: ICIP, pp. 3561–3564 (2011)
13. Zitnick, C.L.: Binary coherent edge descriptors. In: Daniilidis, K., Maragos, P., Paragios, N. (eds.) ECCV 2010, Part II. LNCS, vol. 6312, pp. 170–182. Springer, Heidelberg (2010)

14. Eigenstetter, A., Ommer, B.: Visual Recognition using Embedded Feature Selection for Curvature Self-Similarity, Curran Associates, Inc. (2012)
15. Magnier, B., Montesinos, P.: Evolution of image regularization with PDEs toward a new anisotropic smoothing based on half kernels. In: SPIE, Image Processing: Algorithms and Systems XI (2013)
16. Montesinos, P., Magnier, B.: A new perceptual edge detector in color images. In: Blanc-Talon, J., Bone, D., Philips, W., Popescu, D., Scheunders, P. (eds.) ACIVS 2010, Part I. LNCS, vol. 6474, pp. 209–220. Springer, Heidelberg (2010)
17. Deriche, R.: Recursively implementing the gaussian and its derivatives. In: ICIP, pp. 263–267 (1992)
18. Shen, J., Castan, S.: An optimal linear operator for step edge detection. Graphical Model and Image Processing (CVGIP) 54, 112–133 (1992)
19. Mikolajczyk, K., Schmid, C.: Scale & Affine Invariant Interest Point Detectors. International Journal of Computer Vision (IJCV) 60, 63–86 (2004)

A Novel Method for Simultaneous Acquisition of Visible and Near-Infrared Light Using a Coded Infrared-Cut Filter

Kimberly McGuire[1]($\boxtimes$), Masato Tsukada[2], Boris Lenseigne[1], Wouter Caarls[3], Masato Toda[2], and Pieter Jonker[1]

[1] Technical University of Delft, Delft, The Netherlands
{k.n.mcguire,b.a.j.lenseigne,p.p.jonker}@tudelft.nl
[2] NEC Corporation, Kawasaki, Japan
m-tsukada@cj.jp.nec.com, m-toda@ap.jp.nec.com
[3] Federal University of Rio de Janeiro, Rio de Janeiro, Brazil
wouter@caarls.org

Abstract. This paper presents a novel image sensing method to enhance the sensitivity of a camera. Most image sensors used in commercial digital cameras are sensitive for both visible and infrared light. An IR-cut filter, that obstructs the infrared component of natural light, is used in such cameras to realize a similar color reproduction as for the human visual system. However, recent studies have shown that the near infrared light contains useful information to further enhance the visible image. This paper introduces a new sensing method by using a coded IR-cut filter to enable simultaneous capturing of NIR and visible light on a single image sensor. The coded IR-cut filter lets a fraction of the near infrared light pass and blocks out the rest. Both visible and near infrared light images can be separated from the sensor output when taking the diffraction of the NIR light into account. Experiments, using a synthesized image sensor output, demonstrate the validity of the method.

Keywords: Coded IR-cut filter · Near-infrared · Sensitivity

1 Introduction

Infrared light (IR) is an electromagnetic radiation with a longer wavelength than visible light and is impossible for the human eye to perceive. However, it contains useful information, and hence used for a vast number of applications, such as thermography, astronomy, art history and many more [1][2]. Most image sensors used in digital cameras are sensitive to near infrared light (NIR), the closest in the IR spectrum to visible light. NIR radiation will cause the resulting images to look unnatural. Every digital camera for the consumer market, therefore, possesses an IR-cut filter to prevent this.

Recent studies showed that NIR light can enhance the quality of digital photography. For instance, it can be used for dehazing images [3] because of its

© Springer International Publishing Switzerland 2015
G. Azzopardi and N. Petkov (Eds.): CAIP 2015, Part I, LNCS 9256, pp. 174–185, 2015.
DOI: 10.1007/978-3-319-23192-1_15

better ability to travel through fog. Zhoa et al. [4] use it to eliminate noise in pictures taken of under-illuminated scenes. NIR can be used for improving object and material recognition. Li et al. [5] have implemented NIR images for facial recognition as it is illumination invariant. These applications show the interest of capturing both visible and NIR light.

The simultaneous acquisition of visible and infrared light is a new problem. Before this came to the attention, two multi-spectral images were captured sequentially, but camera shifts or objects moving in the scene causes artifacts in the final result. To prevent this, Zhuo et al. used a hybrid camera set-up which splits the visible light and NIR light into two separate beams, captured by two separate cameras [4]. However, implementing such a system into a consumer product will cause a bulky and expensive camera.

Lu et al. [6] have proposed to use a different color filter array (CFA) than the conventional red-green-blue Bayer array. It can be used without an IR-cut filter since the CFA's filter is optimized in the positioning and wavelength transmittance for separating visible and NIR images. Another patented CFA [7] is more like the conventional Bayer CFA, however, half of the green color filters are replaced with an IR-only filter. Sadephipoor et al. [8] proposed another modified Bayer CFA, where half of the green color filters have a different transmittance than the other half. The joint NIR and visible light on the sensor are represented as an under-determined set of linear equations. They assume that the set is within a close neighborhood with eachother, so it can be solved by sparse representation.

The above solutions focused on capturing both visible and NIR light on the same sensor. Nevertheless, they need a modified CFA, which involves modifying the sensor itself. Considering production costs and implementability, this should be avoided. We propose a solution that can be used with any conventional Bayer CFA image sensor existing today. The only modification is to replace the digital camera's IR-cut filter with a coded IR-cut filter (CIRCF). In section 2 this CIRCF is explained in detail together with the methods for validation. The experimental results are shown in section 3 and the CIRCF, the results and its future possibilities are discussed in section 4 and 5.

2   Coded IR-Cut Filter

A digital camera has an IR-cut filter together with the image sensor to capture natural images as perceived by the human eye. Without this filter, the resulting image contains both visible and NIR light, which cannot be separated from each other and gives an unnatural color reproduction. The CIRCF, is an IR-cut filter which has apertures (circular holes) that let some NIR pass and blocks out the rest (Fig. 1(a)). This results in a camera output which still contains both visible and NIR light, but these can be separated. This is done by using the surrounding pixels that exclusively contain visible light as references. However, the apertures in the CIRCF will be tiny and inevitably the NIR light will spread out. It is crucial to understand this phenomenon. An important issue is to reproduce each

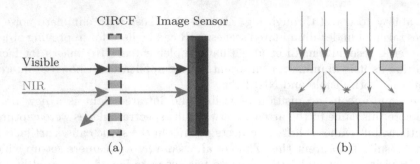

Fig. 1. (a) The assembly with a CIRCF and (b) occurring diffraction due to the filter

image considering the diffraction by the CIRCF as illustrated in Fig. 1(b). This section will go into this phenomenon and we will propose several separation strategies to further validate the CIRCF.

2.1 Diffraction of NIR

Diffraction is a phenomenon that occurs when light encounters an obstruction. In photography, optics, astronomy, microscopy etc. diffraction is a known enemy which poses limits to the quality of high resolution recordings. To simulate the behavior of NIR light when it passes through a coded aperture comparable to the CIRCF, we built an optical setup. A gray scale CMOS image sensor captures with a pixel size of 4 μm. Two of the recordings from this setup are shown in Fig. 2(a & b), using a laser with two different wavelength 780 nm and 850 nm within the NIR region. NIR light diffraction patterns are caused by a metal plate of a grid of apertures (circular holes of 4 μm and pitch of 24 μm). The resulting diffraction pattern with the coded aperture is positioned at 0.5 mm from the image sensor. It shows that even at this distance diffraction is severe enough to complicate the visible and NIR image extraction.

To predict the behavior of the diffraction, many approximations are developed [9]. The complexity of these approximations depends on the parameters of the optical setup: the size of the aperture, the wavelength of the light and the distance between the aperture and the image plane. Usually the IR-cut filter is positioned at a distance of about 0.5-2.5 mm from the image sensor. A near-field diffraction approximation is needed to calculate the diffraction pattern. A grid of apertures will create many wave fronts which will interfere with each other. This interference is one reason an approximation should be used that is close to the original wave behavior equations.

The Rayleigh Sommerfeld integral, derived in the paper of Gillen [10] is one formula that possesses these qualities. This integral is derived to calculate near-field diffraction and can be used for any aperture. Since in this paper circular apertures are considered, the integral is transformed from Cartesian to circular coordinates. The modified Rayleigh Sommerfeld integral (RS), expressed as a convolution, is as follows:

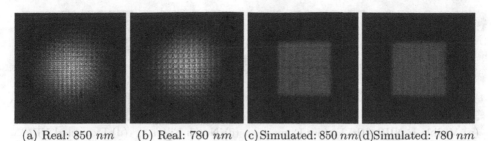

(a) Real: 850 nm (b) Real: 780 nm (c)Simulated: 850 nm(d)Simulated: 780 nm

Fig. 2. The recorded diffraction pattern caused by a grid of circular apertures using two wavelengths of 850 nm (a) and 780 nm (b). This was simulated by using the Rayleigh Sommerfeld integral for the same grid and wavelengths 850 nm (c) and 780 nm (d).

$$U_2(r_2) = U_1(r_1) * H \tag{1}$$

where

$$H = \frac{kz}{i2\pi} \frac{e^{ik\rho_c}}{\rho_c^2} \left(1 - \frac{1}{ik\rho_c}\right) \tag{2}$$

$$\rho_c = \sqrt{r_2^2 + z^2}, \quad k = \frac{2\pi}{\lambda} \tag{3}$$

Where U_2 is the wave amplitude distribution at a distance z from the coded aperture plane U_1 and with a wavelength λ. r_1 and r_2 are the aperture plane and image plane coordinates, starting from the axis of the circular aperture. z is the distance of the aperture plane and the image sensor.

The coded aperture image $U_1(r_1)$ should first be resized to match the Nyquist frequency (twice the frequency of the light). After convolving it by the kernel H, the diffracted CIRCF image is resized back to match the original pixel size. This is done by taking the mean of all values within the boundaries of one image sensor pixel. After resizing, the intensity is given by taking the squared magnitude of the complex wave amplitude distribution $U_2(r_2)$: the value captured by the image sensor (Fig. 2(c)and(d)). The results are verified with the computational wave optics library, which uses the angular spectrum method to calculate the diffraction [11].

2.2   Visible and NIR Light Separation

If the NIR diffraction pattern by the CIRCF is small enough to be contained within the boundaries of one pixel, separation of the NIR and visible light can be easy. If the CIRCF distributes the NIR light separation can be done in the spatial domain by using bilinear interpolation [12]. This functions as a conventional method for demosaicking of CFA to a RGB image, however, a modified version

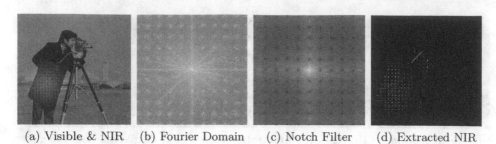

(a) Visible & NIR   (b) Fourier Domain   (c) Notch Filter   (d) Extracted NIR

Fig. 3. (a)The recorded NIR diffraction patterns from Fig. 2(a) with a visible image with (b) the magnitude of its Fourier domain giving on a logarithmic scale. In (c) the notch filter is applied and (d) shows the resulted normalized extracted NIR patterns.

can be used for the NIR extraction. This is done for the green pixels within the Bayer CFA, assuming that the CIRCF's holes are positioned on top of half of them. The demosaicking procedure is:

$$I_{vis} = \frac{1}{4}(I_{vis,[-1-1]} + I_{vis,[+1-1]} + I_{vis,[-1+1]} + I_{vis,[+1+1]}) \tag{4}$$

where I_{vis} is the value of the visible light of the green color pixel, approximated at the location which also contains NIR, which is right underneath of a CIRCF's aperture. $I_{vis,[x,y]}$ is the value of the green pixel surrounding it, where x and y are the coordinates of those values relative to I_{vis}. To obtain the intensity of NIR (I_{NIR}) of that pixel, I_{vis} is subtracted from the pixels original value I ($I_{NIR} = I - I_{vis}$). This is done for the entire image until all the NIR values have been extracted. If the I_{NIR}'s are replaced by the I_{vis}'s in the camera output, the visible image CFA can be demosaicked using the conventional bilinear method.

The dimensions of the CIRFC and its assembly will cause diffraction to be severe enough to complicate the visible and NIR image separation as seen in the experiments of the optical setup in Fig. 2. If the NIR light contaminates the surrounding pixels underneath the CIRCF aperture, separation in the spatial domain is difficult, however, one can consider looking at the frequency domain. In Fig. 3(a), the recorded diffraction patterns of Fig. 2(a) is put on top of a visible image. If that image is transformed to the Fourier domain, one can see that peaks appear in the Fourier domain's magnitude (Fig. 3(b)). This inspired us to treat the diffraction patterns as structured noise on top of the visible image, which is easy to remove in the frequency domain [13].

The diffraction pattern of the NIR will manifest itself in the Fourier transform's magnitude image as noise peaks, which can be removed by a notch filter. To apply it, the positions of the noise peaks are determined first. These peaks are removed by cutting out those sections from the frequency domain [14]. To avoid any ringing effect in the spatial domain, caused by too sharp a cut-off of the peaks, a Butterworth transfer function is used. This transfer function is as follows:

$$Bw(\omega) = 1 - \frac{1}{1 + (\omega/\omega_c)^2} \tag{5}$$

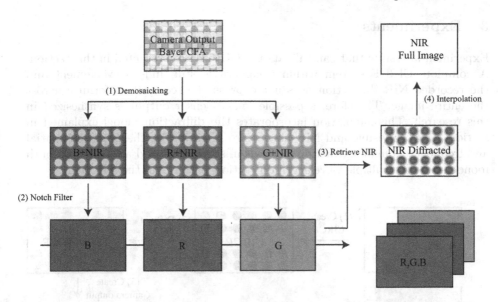

Fig. 4. The flowchart for the extraction of the visible and NIR image

where ω is the spatial frequency in the image, and ω_c is the cut-off frequency. This can be done for each magnitude noise peak within the Fourier domain (see Fig. 3(c)). Since the apertured grid causes the diffraction noise peaks to be evenly distributed from each other, only the distance from the main peak (which should not be removed) to the first noise peak has to be determined to locate the others. Transforming the image back to the spatial domain results in the diffraction pattern free image, which can be subtracted from the original image to obtain NIR diffraction patterns (Fig. 3(d)).

To summarize, the flowchart in Fig. 4 shows the proposed procedure to separate the visible and NIR light for a Bayer CFA in the Fourier domain:

1. The camera output from the simulation is demosaicked to a three color channel image.
2. The notch filter is applied to all color channels.
3. The noise peaks are removed by applying the Butterworth filter on their positions. Since the green channel dominates the CFA, it is subtracted from the camera output, to retrieve the diffracted NIR image.
4. The extracted NIR image is retrieved by removing diffraction patterns not located underneath the CIRCF's apertures.

These proposed separation method and with the whole concept, is for now too specific to compare to any other work. To show the advantage of this notch filtering technique, it is compared with the spatial separation method based on bilinear interpolation.

3   Experiments

Experimental results that can validate the CIRCF are presented in this section. A complete CIRCF system within a camera is still under development and the recorded NIR diffraction does not express the required uniformity across the entire image. Therefore, a possible image sensor output is synthesized in this research. This simulation incorporates the diffraction model explained in section 2.1. The visible and NIR images are retrieved by the proposed spatial and frequency domain extraction methods in section 2.2 and are tested on both monochrome as multiple wavelength diffraction patterns of the NIR light.

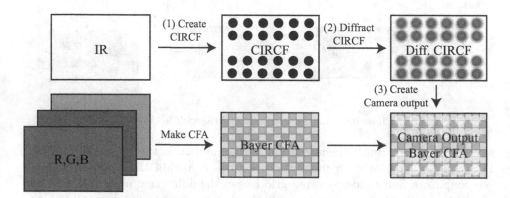

Fig. 5. Flowchart of the simulation of the camera output

3.1   Simulated Camera Output

Two images are taken by a Pentax 645D camera with an external IR-cut filter which can be attached and removed. The visible image (RGB) is taken with the IR-cut filter mounted on the camera and the visible plus NIR image (RGB+NIR) is taken without the filter. RGB and RGB+NIR images start as the demosaicked raw images, which then are resized to 1350 x 1600 pixels and cropped to a specific region of 290 x 290 pixels, with no other post-processing afterwards. The RGB image is subtracted from the RGB+NIR image to retrieve the NIR only image (Fig. 6(a & b)).

The simulated image sensor output is created as shown by the flowchart given in Fig. 5. The camera output is synthesized by inserting a visible color image (RGB) and NIR image into the simulation to create a CIRCF image from the NIR image (1) and calculating its diffraction by the RS integral of Eq 1 (2). It is added on top of the Bayer CFA visible image (3) and the apertures of the CIRCF are aligned with the green pixels.

From the NIR image, the CIRCF image is created where all pixels, presumably blocked by the filter, are removed. The pixel size of the simulated image sensor is 4 μm for the entire experiment. The apertured grid patterns of the

(a) Visible Scene   (b) NIR scene

Fig. 6. The 1350 x 1600 px images used for simulating a scene of (a) the visible light and (b) the NIR light.

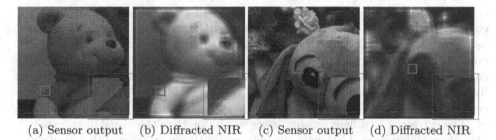

(a) Sensor output   (b) Diffracted NIR   (c) Sensor output   (d) Diffracted NIR

Fig. 7. These are the simulated image sensor output and expected extracted NIR with the CIRCF for a single wavelength of 800 nm (a & b) and for multiple wavelengths (c & d). The expected NIR image, is the diffracted CIRCF, cropped with only the values remaining underneath the apertures.

CIRCF image has a diameter of 4 μm and a pitch of 8 μm (every 2 pixels). Using the RS method, the CIRCF's diffraction patterns are calculated. To approximate the NIR light diffraction patterns, a wavelenght is used of 800 nm. The camera outputs from the single diffraction pattern are shown in Fig. 7(a) and (c). The calculated diffraction pattern is cropped to contain exclusively the values that should be underneath the CIRCF, so providing a ground truth to evaluate the extracted NIR images (Fig. 7(b) and (d)).

However, since natural light does not contain just a single wavelength, combined wavelengths (700, 800 and 900 nm) are simulated as well to validate the extraction method's generality. The same sample images are used for this simulation, however, since visually the result is very similar to the single wavelength it is not shown is this paper. It is used evaluate the extracted images. It is expected that the same notch filter used for the monochrome 800 nm NIR light, can be used for the multi-spectral NIR light. This is as long the noise peaks stay on the same position.

3.2   Extracted Visible and NIR Images

As said in section 2.2, the visible and NIR light can be separated in both the spatial and frequency domain. The spatial separation is done by bilinear interpolation, given in Eq. 4, which will not need any further explaining. The separation in frequency domain has more sub steps shown in the flowchart of Fig. 4. As in Fig. 3(b), the Fourier domain of the synthesized sensor output also has distinctive noise peaks evenly distributed throughout the frequencies. Here the cut-off frequency ω_c of the Butterworth filter (Eq. 5) is set at a radius of 5 pixels around those noise peaks.

In Fig. 8, the extracted RGB and NIR images from the simulated image sensor output from Fig. 7(a) can be seen. Fig. 8(a) and (b) shows the results of the spatial filtering with bilinear interpolation and Fig. 8(c) and (d) are obtained by the proposed frequency filtering. These images are compared to their ground truth with the peak-signal-to-noise ratio (PSNR) for the extracted NIR and the color PSNR (cPSNR) for the entire extracted RGB.[1][2] Comparing this with the values of the extracted images reveal differences in quality, which gives the preference to the frequency filtering for this occasion. This can visually be confirmed since much of the NIR diffraction patterns still exist in the spatially filtered visible image. The RGB image obtained by the notch filter (Fig. 4(c)), does not contain much of these patterns anymore.

The extracted NIR light images, lower resolution than the visual light images, also show differences. The spatially obtained NIR image (Fig. 8(b)) contains many textures included from the RGB image, as they are non existent in the NIR ground truth pictures. The extracted NIR image by frequency filtering, also show more similarities with the simulated NIR image (Fig. 7(b)). By these

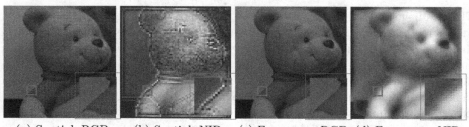

(a) Spatial: RGB   (b) Spatial: NIR   (c) Frequency: RGB   (d) Frequency: NIR

Fig. 8. The extracted RGB (a&c) and NIR (b&d) images from the simulated image sensor output with a single wavelength of 800 nm. (a) and (b) are extracted with bilinear interpolation in the spatial domain and (c) and (b) with the notch filter in the frequency domain. Their PSNR and cPSNR values with the ground truth are 23.78 dB, 16.33 dB, 25.42 dB and 20.64 dB respectively (l.t.r.).

---

[1] Note that a cPSNR show a lower value than single color channel PSNR.

[2] The cPSNR of sensor's output (Fig. 7(a)) to the ground truth RGB image is 22.87 dB.

(a) Extracted RGB   (b) Extracted NIR   (c) Extracted RGB   (d) Extracted NIR

Fig. 9. The extracted RGB (a & c) and NIR (b & d) from the simulated image sensor output, regarding multiple wavelengths of 700, 800 and 900 nm and using a frequency filter. The PSNR and cPSNR values with their ground truth are 20.78 dB, 25.33 dB, 23.69 dB and 18.54 dB from left to right. As comparison, the values in case of spatial domain extraction is 19.17 dB, 18.45 dB, 22.13 dB and 11.73 dB respectively.

observations and the differences in PSNR values, one can see that the frequency filter is more suitable to separate with these diffraction patterns.

As said before, the spectrum of NIR light does not contain only one wavelength, but a range of them. Therefore, a simulated image sensor output with diffracted NIR light of multiple wavelengths is created.[3] Fig. 9 show the extraction results of the frequency filtering for two separate scene samples. The exact same notch filter used on the single wavelength, is used to extract the NIR and visible light here. The diffraction peaks in the Fourier domain are located in approximately the same location, therefore were all able to get eliminated by the same notch filter as for the single wavelength. This could imply that the noise peaks within the frequency domain should be relatively on the same position as the single wavelength. The PSNR values of these extracted images, can also be compared to the case if they are extracted by bilinear interpolation. This indicates that the frequency filter performed better for this occasion for both scene samples. This difference in quality can especially be noticed in the extracted NIR image.

4   Discussion

We have showed several experimental results to validate the CIRCF. An important aspect of these results, is to separate the visible and NIR light. We showed that diffraction will occur, but by simulation we found a solution which uses this phenomenon as an advantage. Repeatability of the diffraction pattern enables that both the visible and NIR image can be separated by removing the peaks in the frequency domain. The NIR light is transformed in such a way it can be extracted by a notch filter, making it a robust separation method.

Diffraction causes the extracted NIR to be blurred, but unavoidable if the CIRCF should stay implementable for current existing image sensor assemblies.

---

[3] The cPSNRs of the sensor outputs used to the ground truth are 19.32 dB and 22.14 dB respectively.

For applications as intelligent video surveillance system it will still be useful to increase the sensitive of the camera since the outline of the NIR scene is obtained. To further increase the quality of the NIR image, a special deblurring algorithm can be developed. This should base on the diffraction model presented in this paper where the NIR image can be deconvolved to a sharper image.

Several simplifications are made to make the diffraction simulation feasible for the validation. One simplification is the monochrome light based simulation, however, the continuity is these wavelengths is of the essence too. The form of this continues range of wavelengths is very dependable on the material in the captured scene, therefore unfeasible to simulate without this extra knowledge. Another simplification is that the difference in transmittance within the Bayer CFA is not taken into account. However, we believe that it will lead to the conclusion to use a different color channel for separation than the green channel we have used.

5 Conclusion

The CIRCF method provides a convenient solution for the simultaneous acquisition of visible and NIR light on the same sensor implementable into most commercial cameras. This provides a low cost solution to increase the spectral sensitivity of the image sensor. There are aspects to take into consideration for future research. For the simulation, we recommend to implement a more continuous range of wavelengths instead of combining several monochrome lights. The separation procedure and post-processing will be further developed to ensure sharper NIR images. Future research of these improvements, will further substantiate the validation of the CIRCF as a novel sensing method to enhance the spectral sensitivity of image sensors.

References

1. Rieke, G.H.: History of infrared telescopes and astronomy. Experimental Astronomy **25**(1–3), 125–141 (2009)
2. Daffara, C., Pampaloni, E., Pezzati, L., Barucci, M., Fontana, R.: Scanning multispectral ir reflectography smirr: an advanced tool for art diagnostics. Accounts of Chemical Research **43**(6), 847–856 (2010)
3. Schaul, L., Fredembach, C., Süsstrunk, S.: Color image dehazing using the near-infrared. In: Proc. IEEE International Conference on Image Processing (ICIP), Number LCAV-CONF-2009-026 (2009)
4. Zhuo, S., Zhang, X., Miao, X., Sim, T.: Enhancing low light images using near infrared flash images. In: 2010 17th IEEE International Conference on Image Processing (ICIP), pp. 2537–2540. IEEE (2010)
5. Li, S.Z., Chu, S.R., Liao, S., Zhang, L.: Illumination invariant face recognition using near-infrared images. IEEE Transactions on Pattern Analysis and Machine Intelligence **29**(4), 627–639 (2007)
6. Lu, Y.M., Fredembach, C., Vetterli, M., Süsstrunk, S.: Designing color filter arrays for the joint capture of visible and near-infrared images. In: 2009 16th IEEE International Conference on Image Processing (ICIP), pp. 3797–3800. IEEE (2009)

7. Wu, F., Mou, S., Shan, J.: Visible and infrared dual mode imaging system, April 2, 2013. US Patent 8,408,821
8. Sadeghipoor, Z., Lu, Y.M., Susstrunk, S.: A novel compressive sensing approach to simultaneously acquire color and near-infrared images on a single sensor. In: 2013 IEEE International Conference on Acoustics, Speech and Signal Processing (ICASSP), pp. 1646–1650. IEEE (2013)
9. Goodman, J.W.: Introduction to Fourier optics. Roberts and Company Publishers (2005)
10. Gillen, G.D., Guha, S.: Modeling and propagation of near-field diffraction patterns: a more complete approach. American Journal of Physics 72(9), 1195–1201 (2004)
11. Shimobaba, T., Weng, J., Sakurai, T., Okada, N., Nishitsuji, T., Takada, N., Shiraki, A., Masuda, N., Ito, T.: Computational wave optics library for c++: Cwo++ library. Computer Physics Communications 183(5), 1124–1138 (2012)
12. Gribbon, K.T., Bailey, D.G.: A novel approach to real-time bilinear interpolation. In: Proceedings of the 2004 IEEE International Conference on Field-Programmable Technology, pp. 126–131. IEEE (2004)
13. Jain, P., Tyagi, V.: Spatial and frequency domain filters for restoration of noisy images. IETE Journal of Education 54(2), 108–116 (2013)
14. Department of Computer Science, University of Regina: Image Processing: Frequency Domain Processing

Scale-Space Clustering on a Unit Hypersphere

Yuta Hirano[1] and Atsushi Imiya[2]($\boxtimes$)

[1] School of Integrated Sciences, Chiba University, Chiba, Japan
[2] Institute of Management and Information Technologies, Chiba University,
Yayoi-cho 1-33, Inage-ku, Chiba 263-8522, Japan
imiya@faculty.chiba-u.jp

Abstract. We present an algorithm for the scale-space clustering of a point cloud on a hypersphere in a higher-imensional Euclidean space. Our method achieves clustering by estimating the density distribution of the points in the linear scale space on the sphere. The algorithm regards the union of observed point sets as an image defined by the delta functions located at the positions of the points on the sphere. As numerical examples, we illustrate clustering on the 3-sphere $\mathbb{S}^3$ in four-dimensional Euclidean space.

1 Introduction

Linear scale-space theory [1,2] provides a dimension-independent observation theory of input data [3,4]. As an extension of the scale-space clustering of a point cloud on a plane and a curved manifold [7], we develop a framework to extract the clusters in a point cloud [5] on a unit hypersphere. Regarding the density function as a greyscale image [4,5,7], we can estimate the density function in the scale space and identify the point correspondences by scale-space analysis of image structure. The principal advantage of scale-space-based analysis for point-set analysis is that deterministic features of the point set can be observed at higher scales even if the positions of the points are stochastic. This property can be qualitatively explained using an image of dots.

For the n-dimensional Gaussian distribution $G(\boldsymbol{x}, \sigma) = \frac{1}{\sqrt{2\pi}^n \sigma} \exp\left(-\frac{|\boldsymbol{x}|^2}{2\sigma^2}\right)$ where $\boldsymbol{x}$ is an n-dimensional vector, events for $G(\boldsymbol{x}, \sigma) = \sigma$ are distributed on the hypersphere $|\boldsymbol{x}|^2 = 2\sigma^2 \log \frac{1}{\sqrt{2\pi}^n \sigma^2}$. Figure 1 shows that a level-set slice of the two-dimensional homogenous Gaussian in (a) derives a distribution on a circle (b). Furthermore, since we deal with normalised vectors $\hat{\boldsymbol{x}} = \frac{\boldsymbol{x}}{|\boldsymbol{x}|}$, which are elements in a collection of pattern vectors lying on the unit hypersphere as shown in Fig. 1 (c), for pattern recognition, classification of the normalised pattern vectors is achieved on the unit hypersphere. Therefore, for the precise analysis of events, clustering on the sphere is desired.

There are two types of clustering methodology: (i) supervised clustering and (ii) unsupervised clustering. Furthermore, there are metric-based and non-metric-based clustering methods. In this paper, we focus on unsupervised metric-based clustering by scale-space analysis of a point cloud. Although in typical

G. Azzopardi and N. Petkov (Eds.): CAIP 2015, Part I, LNCS 9256, pp. 186–197, 2015.
DOI: 10.1007/978-3-319-23192-1_16

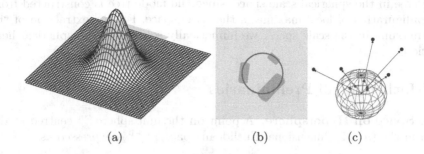

Fig. 1. Collection of unit vectors. (a) Two-dimensional homogenous Gaussian. (b) Distribution on a circle derived from a level-set slice of the two-dimensional homogenous Gaussian. (c) Collection of normalised vectors.

metric-based clustering, algorithms are designed assuming that a point cloud lying in a flat space, point clouds sometimes lie on a curved manifold as shown in Fig. 1(b) and Fig. 1(c). The graph-Laplacian-based method is a powerful method to deal with data on a manifold expressing data as an undirected weighted graph using a metric in the data space. On the other hand, scale-space clustering [3,4,6] estimates the number of clusters from a hierarchical expression of the data derived by scale-space analysis of a point cloud.

In our previous paper [10], we introduced the scale-space clustering on the unit sphere in three-dimensional Euclidean space. In the method, we used the heat kernel on the sphere in three-dimensional Euclidean space [9] for the computation of hierarchy of a point cloud. The heat kernel for the sphere is constructed using spherical harmonics. For a higher dimensional sphere, the heat kernel is constructed as

$$K(p, p') = \sum_{l_1=0 l_2=0 \cdots l_{n-1}=0}^{\infty} Y_{l_1 l_2 \cdots l_{n-1}}(p) Y_{l_1 l_2 \cdots l_{n-1}}(p') \tag{1}$$

where $p = (\theta_1, \theta_2, \cdots, \theta_{n-1})$ and $p' = (\theta'_1, \theta'_2, \cdots, \theta'_{n-1})$ express the spherical corrdinate in a n-dimensional Euclidean space, using the Jacobi polynomials

$$Y_{l_1 l_2 \cdots l_{n-1}}(\theta_1, \theta_2, \cdots, \theta_{n-1}) \frac{1}{\sqrt{2\pi}} e^{i l_1 \theta_1} \prod_{j=2}^{n-1} {}_j \bar{P}_{l_j}^{l_{n-2}}(\theta_j), \tag{2}$$

where

$$_j \bar{P}_L^l(\theta) = \sqrt{\frac{2L + j - 1}{2} \frac{(L + l + j - 2)!}{(L - l)!}} \sin^{\frac{2-j}{2}} P_{L + \frac{i-2}{2}}^{-(L + \frac{i-2}{2})}(\cos \theta) \tag{3}$$

is the Legendre function. In this paper, we deal with spherical scale space without the heat kernel on a hypersphere. For scale-space clustering, we deal with a mode tree in the spherical scale space, since the mode tree is constructed from the configuration of local maxima in the scale space. For the extraction of the local maxima in the scale space, we numerically solve the hyperspherical heat equation.

2　Mathematical Preliminaries

Scale Space on Hypersphere. A point on the unit sphere $\mathbb{S}^n$ centred at the origin in the $(n+1)$-dimensional Euclidean space $\mathbb{R}^{n+1}$ is expressed as

$$
\begin{aligned}
\omega_1 &= \sin\theta_{n-1}\sin\theta_{n-2}\cdots\sin\theta_2\sin\theta_1\cos\phi \\
\omega_2 &= \sin\theta_{n-1}\sin\theta_{n-2}\cdots\sin\theta_2\sin\theta_1\sin\phi \\
\omega_3 &= \sin\theta_{n-1}\sin\theta_{n-2}\cdots\sin\theta_2\cos\theta_1
\end{aligned}
\tag{4}
$$

$$
\vdots
$$

$$
\begin{aligned}
\omega_n &= \sin\theta_{n-1}\cos\theta_{n-2} \\
\omega_{n+1} &= \cos\theta_{n-1},
\end{aligned}
$$

where $0 \le \theta_i < \pi$ and $0 \le \phi < 2\pi$ for $\boldsymbol{\omega} = (\omega_1, \ldots, \omega_{n+1})^{\top}$.

The scale-space function $f(\boldsymbol{\omega}, \tau)$ of a function $f(\boldsymbol{\omega})$ on $\mathbb{S}^n$ is the solution of the linear spherical heat equation

$$
\frac{\partial}{\partial\tau}f(\boldsymbol{x},\tau) = \Delta_{\mathbb{S}^n}f(\boldsymbol{x},\tau),
\tag{5}
$$

for $\tau > 0$. For the linear heat equation, the relationship

$$
\Delta_{\mathbb{S}^n}f = \Gamma_n f \frac{1}{(\sin\theta_{n-1})^2}\Delta_{\mathbb{S}^{n-1}}f
\tag{6}
$$

$$
\Gamma_n f = \frac{1}{(\sin\theta_{n-1})^{n-1}}\frac{\partial}{\partial\theta_{n-1}}\left((\sin\theta_{n-1})^{n-1}\frac{\partial f}{\partial\theta_{n-1}}\right), \; n > 2,
$$

$$
\Delta_{\mathbb{S}^1}f = \frac{\partial^2}{\partial\phi^2}f
\tag{7}
$$

is satisfied.

Since $\mathbb{S}^1 = \{\theta, | -\pi \le \theta \le \pi\}$, we deal with scale-space analysis on the unit circle such that

$$
\frac{\partial}{\partial\tau}f(\theta,\tau) = \frac{\partial^2}{\partial x^2}f(\theta,\tau), \; f(\theta,0) = f(\theta)
\tag{8}
$$

with the cyclic condition $f(\theta + 2\pi, \tau) = f(\theta, \tau)$.

Scale Space Tree and Mode Tree. For the solution of

$$
\frac{\partial}{\partial\tau}f(\boldsymbol{x},\tau) = \Delta f(\boldsymbol{\omega},\tau), \; f(\boldsymbol{\omega},0) = f(\boldsymbol{\omega})
\tag{9}
$$

for $\boldsymbol{\omega} \in \mathbb{S}^n$ and $\tau > 0$, the mode tree M corresponding to f is defined as follows.

- Each node in M has three values: the node ID i, a scale value τ and a location vector ω, which are denoted by a triplet (τ, i, ω).
- M has N leaf nodes. Each node has a unique ID in $\{0, \ldots, N-1\}$. The scale values of all the leaf nodes are 0 and each location is defined by $\mathcal{P}$.
- The parent of a node whose scale is τ_i is a node whose scale is τ_{i+1} for $i < M - 1$.
- A node whose scale and location are τ and p, respectively, is one of the local maxima of the function $f(\omega, \tau)$ at $\omega = \sigma$.

Figure 2 shows the mode tree for a two-dimensional function defined on a plane. (a) is a topographical map of the function on the plane. (b) is the mode tree. (c) is the scale space tree. (d) is the distribution of extremals and the figure field $F = \nabla f$ on the grey scale topography, where red, green and blue points are local minimal, saddle and local maximal points, respectively. (e) is the distribution of maximal points. (f) is the distribution of extremals.

Definition 1. *An element of an edge set* E *connects a local maximum* $f(\omega(\tau), \tau)$ *and a collection of local maxima* $f(\omega(\tau'), \tau')$ *for* $\tau' < \tau$ *as*

$$\omega(\tau') = \arg\min d(\omega(\tau'), \omega(\tau)), \quad d(\omega(\tau'), \omega(\tau)) = \left| \int_{\omega(\tau')}^{\omega(\tau)} \nabla_{\mathbb{S}^n} f ds \right|. \tag{10}$$

For a function on the unit sphere $\mathbb{S}^n$, the figure field is computed as $F = \nabla_{\mathbb{S}^n} f$ for the function f defined on $\mathbb{S}^n$, where $\nabla_{\mathbb{S}^n}$ is the gradient operation.

Figure 3 illustrates the clustering procedure of a point cloud using a multi-scale expression of a point cloud on a plane. Using the mode tree in (b) constructed from the hierarchical expression of a point cloud in the scale space (a), the hierarchical property of the point cloud is extracted as shown in (c).

3   Structural Simplification and Mode Tree Construction

The trajectory of the stationary point [8]

$$s(\tau) = \left\{ \omega(\tau) \in \mathbb{S}^2 \mid \nabla_{\mathbb{S}^n} f(\omega, \tau) = 0 \right\} \tag{11}$$

in the scale space is called the stationary curve in scale-space theory. Since $\nabla_{\mathbb{S}^n} f = 0$ and $f_\tau = \Delta_{\mathbb{S}^n} f$, we have the relationship

$$\nabla_{\mathbb{S}^n} \nabla_{\mathbb{S}^n}^\top \frac{d}{d\tau} f(\omega(\tau), \tau) = -\nabla_{\mathbb{S}^2} \Delta_{\mathbb{S}^n} f(\omega(\tau), \tau), \tag{12}$$

where $\nabla_{\mathbb{S}^n} \nabla_{\mathbb{S}^n}^\top$ is the Hessian on $\mathbb{S}^n$.

For the clustering of point sets, the trajectory of the maximal points

$$m(\tau) = \left\{ \omega(\tau) \mid \nabla_{\mathbb{S}^n} f(\omega, \tau) = 0 \; D_{\mathbb{S}^n}^2 f < 0 \right\}, \tag{13}$$

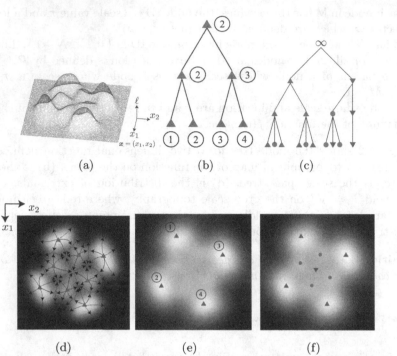

(a)   (b)   (c)

(d)   (e)   (f)

Fig. 2. Scale-space tree and mode tree. (a) Greyscale topographical map of a function. (b) Mode tree constructed from (a). (c) Scale space tree constructed from (a). (d) Figure field connecting extremal on greyscale topographical map of a function in (a). (e) Distribution of maxima. (f) Distribution of extremals.

where $D^2_{\mathbb{S}^n} f$ is the second-order directional derivative on the sphere, is re-expressed as

$$m(\tau) = \{\, \boldsymbol{\omega}(\tau) \mid \nabla_{\mathbb{S}^n} f(\boldsymbol{\omega}, \tau) = 0, \mid f(\boldsymbol{\omega}(\tau), \tau) > f(\boldsymbol{\omega}'(\tau), \tau)\; \boldsymbol{\omega}'(\tau) \in \Omega(\boldsymbol{\omega}(\tau)) \,\} \tag{14}$$

where $\Omega(\boldsymbol{\omega}(\tau), \tau))$ is a neighbourhood of $\boldsymbol{\omega}(\tau)$.

Assuming that for a scale τ_k, the number of maxima is n_{τ_k}, we set the collection of the maxima as $V_{\tau_k} = \{v(l)\}_{l=0}^{\tau_k - 1}$. Furthermore, we express the collection of edges connecting vertices in V_{τ_k} and $V_{\tau_{k+1}}$ as $E(k)$ for $k \geq 0$, where $\tau_0 = 0$.

If $v_{\tau_k}(l_1) = v_{\tau_{k+1}}(l_2)$, we add an edge $e_{\tau_{k+1}}(l_1) = \overline{v_{\tau_k}(l_1) v_{\tau_{k+1}}(l_2)}$ to M. Otherwise, we add an edge $e_{\tau_{k+1}}(l_1) = \mathrm{arc}(v_{\tau_k}(l_1), v_{\tau_{k+1}}(l_2))$ for $v(\tau_{k+1}(l_1)) = \arg d(v(\tau_k), v(\tau_{k+1})$.

Setting $M(\tau)$ to be the number of maxima of the scale-space function $f(\boldsymbol{\omega}, \tau)$ on $\mathbb{S}^3$, $M(\tau)$ satisfies the following property.

Property 1. If $\tau \leq \tau'$, $M(\tau)$ satisfies the relation $M(\tau) \leq M(\tau')$.

Using this property, we introduce the following definitions.

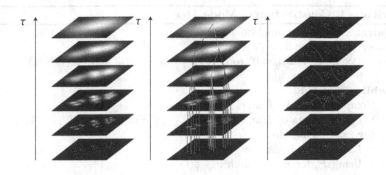

Fig. 3. Scale-space structure of a function. (a) Hierarchical expression of a point cloud. (b) Mode tree of the point cloud. (c) Hierarchical property of the point cloud in (a).

Property 2. For $\tau < \tau' < \tau''$, if $M(\tau) = M(\tau') = M(\tau'')$, the estimated number of segments of the point cloud $f(\omega)$ is $M(\tau)$.

Since an element of vertex set V corresponds to a local maximum of $f(\omega, \tau)$, we have the following definition.

Definition 2. *A collection of points whose sub-root satisfies property 2, is referred as a cluster in a point cloud.*

Definition 2 implies that by backtracking the edges on the mode tree constructed from the input point cloud to the leaves, we achieve clustering.

4   Numerical Experiments

Numerical Scheme. Setting $\theta_{1(i)} = i\Delta_{\theta_1}, \phi_{(j)} = j\Delta_\phi$, $\Delta_{\theta_1} = \frac{\pi}{N_{\theta_1}}, \Delta_\phi = \frac{2\pi}{N_\phi}, f(\theta_{1(i)}\phi_{(j)}) = f_{(i,j)}$, for $\mathbb{S}^2$, we first have

$$\frac{f_{(i,j)}^{(\tau+1)} - f_{(i,j)}^{(\tau)}}{\Delta_\tau} = (\Delta_{\mathbb{S}^2} f^{(\tau+1)})_{(i,j)}$$

$$= \frac{1}{\sin\theta_{1(i)}} \left(\sin\theta_{1(i+1)} \frac{f_{(i+1,j)}^{(\tau+1)} - f_{(i,j)}^{(\tau+1)}}{\Delta\theta_1} - \sin\theta_{1(i-1)} \frac{f_{(i,j)}^{(\tau+1)} - f_{(i-1,j)}^{(\tau+1)}}{\Delta\theta_1} \right)$$

$$+ \frac{1}{\sin^2\theta_{1(i)}} \left(\frac{f_{(i,j+1)}^{(\tau+1)} - 2f_{(i,j)}^{(\tau+1)} + f_{(i,j-1)}^{(\tau+1)}}{2\Delta_\phi} \right), \tag{15}$$

Algorithm 1. Construction of Mode Tree

Require: :Scale space function $f(\tau)$
Ensure: : Mode tree $\mathsf{M} = (\mathsf{V}, \mathsf{E})$
1: Set maxima of $f(\boldsymbol{\omega}\tau_0 = 0)$ to be $\{\mathcal{V}_{\tau_0}\} = v_{\tau_0}(l_0)(l_0 = 0, \ldots, N-1)$
2: $k \leftarrow 0$
3: **while** $n_{\tau_k} \neq 1$ **do**
4:    Compute $\boldsymbol{F} = \Delta_{\mathbb{S}^n} f(\boldsymbol{\omega}, \tau_{k+1})$
5:    Set the maxima of $f(\boldsymbol{\omega}, \tau_{k+1})$ to $\{\mathcal{V}_{\tau_{k+1}}\} = v_{\tau_{k+1}}(l_{k+1})(l_{k+1} = 1, \ldots, n_{\tau_i})$
6:    **for** $i = 1$ to n_{τ_k} **do**
7:       For $f(\boldsymbol{\omega}\tau_{k+1})$, mark $v_{\tau_k}(i)$
8:       Using $\boldsymbol{F}$, for τ_{k+1}, search $v_{\tau_{k+1}}(l)$
9:       Construct edges
10:   **end for**
11:    $\tau_{k+1} = \tau_k + \delta_k$
12: **end while**

---

and second we have

$$\frac{f_{(i,j)}^{(\tau+1)} - f_{(i,j)}^{(\tau)}}{\Delta_\tau}$$

$$= (\Delta_{\mathbb{S}^2} f^{(\tau+1)})_{(i,j)}$$

$$= \frac{1}{\sin \theta_{1(i)}} \left(\sin \theta_{1(i+1)} \frac{f_{(i+1,j)}^{(\tau+1)} - f_{(i,j)}^{(\tau+1)}}{\Delta\theta_1} - \sin \theta_{1(i-1)} \frac{f_{(i,j)}^{(\tau+1)} - f_{(i-1,j)}^{(\tau+1)}}{\Delta\theta_1} \right)$$

$$+ \frac{1}{\sin^2 \theta_{1(i)}} \left(\frac{f_{(i,j+1)}^{(\tau+1)} - 2f_{(i,j)}^{(\tau+1)} + f_{(i,j-1)}^{(\tau+1)}}{2\Delta_\phi} \right). \tag{16}$$

Therefore, we have

$$\left\{ 1 + \frac{\Delta_\tau \left(\sin \theta_{1(i+1)} + \sin \theta_{1(i-1)} \right)}{\Delta_{\theta_1} \sin \theta_{1(i)}} + \frac{\Delta_\tau}{\Delta_\phi \sin^2 \theta_{1(i)}} \right\} f_{(i,j)}^{(\tau+1)}$$

$$- \frac{\Delta_\tau \sin \theta_{1(i+1)}}{\Delta_{\theta_1} \sin \theta_{1(i)}} f_{(i+1,j)}^{(\tau+1)} - \frac{\Delta_\tau \sin \theta_{1(i-1)}}{\Delta_{\theta_1} \sin \theta_{1(i)}} f_{(i-1,j)}^{(\tau+1)}$$

$$- \frac{\Delta_\tau}{2\Delta_\phi \sin^2 \theta_{1(i)}} \left(f_{(i,j+1)}^{(\tau+1)} - f_{(i,j-1)}^{(\tau+1)} \right)$$

$$= f_{(i,j)}^{(\tau)}. \tag{17}$$

For $n = 3$, equations (5) and (6) imply that

$$\boldsymbol{\omega} = (\sin \theta_2 \sin \theta_1 \cos \phi, \sin \theta_2 \sin \theta_1 \sin \phi, \sin \theta_2 \cos \theta_1, \cos \theta_2)^\top \tag{18}$$

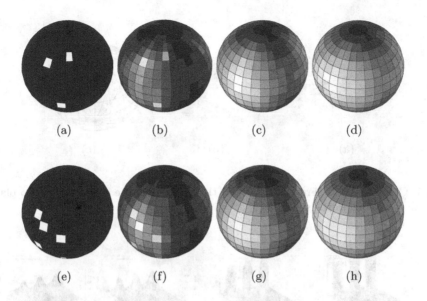

(a)   (b)   (c)   (d)

(e)   (f)   (g)   (h)

Fig. 4. Scale-space functions of a point cloud on a hypersphere. The top and bottom images show spheres for $\theta_2 = \frac{8\pi}{16}$ and $\theta_2 = \frac{9\pi}{16}$, respectively. From left to right, for $\tau = 0, 1, 2, 3$, the scale-space functions are expressed. These spheres are parameterised by ϕ and θ_1 by fixing θ_2.

and that

$$
\Delta_{\mathbb{S}^3} f = \frac{1}{\sin^2 \theta_2} \frac{\partial}{\partial \theta_2} \left(\sin^2 \theta_2 \frac{\partial f}{\partial \theta_2} \right)
$$
$$
+ \frac{1}{\sin^2 \theta_2} \left(\frac{1}{\sin \theta_1} \frac{\partial}{\partial \theta_1} \left(\sin \theta_1 \frac{\partial f}{\partial \theta_1} \right) + \frac{1}{\sin^2 \theta_1} \frac{\partial^2 f}{\partial \phi^2} \right). \tag{19}
$$

For numerical computation, setting $\theta_{2(i)} = i\Delta_{\theta_2}$, $\Delta_{\theta_2} = \frac{\pi}{N_{\theta_2}}$, we have

$$
(\Delta_{\mathbb{S}^3} f^{(\tau+1)})_{(i,j,k)}
$$
$$
= \frac{1}{\sin^2 \theta_{2(i)}} \left(\sin^2 \theta_{2(i+1)} \frac{f_{(i+1,j,k)} - f_{(i,j,k)}}{\Delta\theta_2} - \sin^2 \theta_{2(i-1)} \frac{f_{(i,j,k)} - f_{(i-1,j,k)}}{\Delta\theta_2} \right)
$$
$$
+ \frac{1}{\sin^2 \theta_{2(i)}} \frac{1}{\sin \theta_{1(j)}}
$$
$$
\times \left(\sin \theta_{1(j+1)} \frac{f_{(i,j+1,k)} - f_{(i,j,k)}}{\Delta\theta_1} - \sin \theta_{1(j-1)} \frac{f_{(i,j,k)} - f_{(i,j-1,k)}}{\Delta\theta_1} \right)
$$
$$
+ \frac{1}{\sin^2 \theta_{2(i)}} \frac{1}{\sin^2 \theta_{1(j)}} \left(\frac{f_{(i,j,k+1)} - 2f_{(i,j,k)} + f_{(i,j,k-1)}}{2\Delta_\phi} \right) \tag{20}
$$

From this expression, we have the iteration form

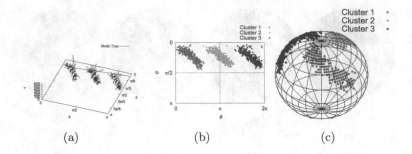

(a)   (b)   (c)

Fig. 5. Clustring on $\mathbb{S}^2$. From left to right, the mode tree, the clustering on θ-ϕ plane and the clustering on the sphere $\mathbb{S}^2$.

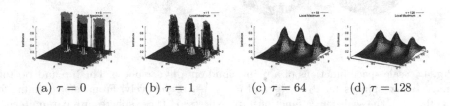

(a) $\tau = 0$ (b) $\tau = 1$ (c) $\tau = 64$ (d) $\tau = 128$

Fig. 6. Hierarchical expressions of point cloud in spherical scale space. From left to right, for $\tau = 0, 1, 64, 128$, scle-space functions are shown. These expressions indicate that the number of clusters is three.

$$F(i,j,k)f_{(i,j,k)}^{(\tau+1)} - \frac{\Delta_\tau \sin^2\theta_{2(i+1)}}{\Delta_{\theta_2}\sin^2\theta_{2(i)}}f_{(i+1,j,k)}^{(\tau+1)} - \frac{\Delta_\tau \sin^2\theta_{2(i-1)}}{\Delta_{\theta_2}\sin^2\theta_{2(i)}}f_{(i-1,j,k)}^{(\tau+1)}$$

$$-\frac{\Delta_\tau \sin\theta_{1(j+1)}}{\Delta_{\theta_1}\sin^2\theta_{2(i)}\sin\theta_{1(j)}}f_{(i,j+1,k)}^{(\tau+1)} - \frac{\Delta_\tau \sin\theta_{1(j-1)}}{\Delta_{\theta_1}\sin^2\theta_{2(i)}\sin\theta_{1(j)}}f_{(i,j-1,k)}^{(\tau+1)}$$

$$-\frac{\Delta_\tau}{2\Delta_\phi \sin^2\theta_{2(i)}\sin^2\theta_{1(j)}}\left(f_{(i,j,k+1)}^{(\tau+1)} - f_{(i,j,k-1)}^{(\tau+1)}\right)$$

$$= f_{(i,j,k)}^{(\tau)} \tag{21}$$

where

$$F(i,j,k) = 1 + \frac{\Delta_\tau\left(\sin^2\theta_{2(i+1)} + \sin^2\theta_{2(i-1)}\right)}{\Delta_{\theta_2}\sin^2\theta_{2(i)}}$$

$$+\frac{\Delta_\tau\left(\sin\theta_{1(j+1)} + \sin\theta_{1(j-1)}\right)}{\Delta_{\theta_1}\sin^2\theta_{2(i)}\sin\theta_{1(j)}}$$

$$+\frac{\Delta_\tau}{\Delta_\phi \sin^2\theta_{2(i)}\sin^2\theta_{1(j)}} \tag{22}$$

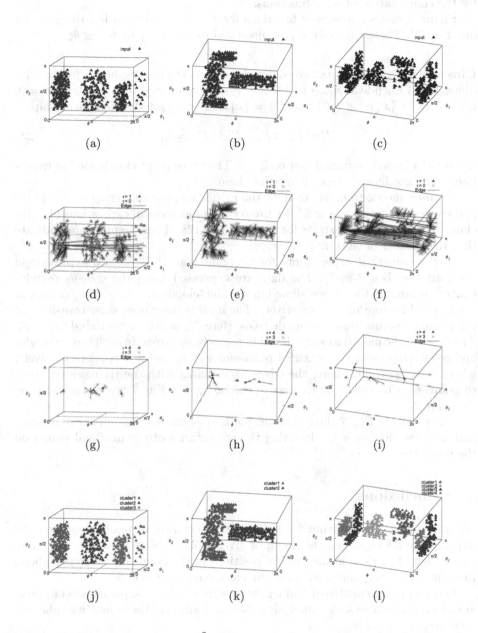

Fig. 7. examples of clustering on $\mathbb{S}^3$. From top to bottom, the input, the edges for $\tau = 0$, the edges for $\tau = 9$ and the clustering results are shown, respectively. In each box, triangles and crosses represent the maximal points for $\tau = \tau_k$ and $\tau = \tau_{k+1}$, respectively, where $\tau_k < \tau_{k+1}$.

for the computation of scale functions.

Figure 4 shows scale-space functions for $\tau = 0, 1, 2, 3$ from left to right. for input on $\mathbb{S}^3$. These spheres are parameterised by ϕ and θ_1 by fixing θ_2.

Clustering Experiments. For point cloud P on the hypersphere $\mathbb{S}^n$ in $(n+1)$-dimensional Euclidean space $\mathbb{R}^{n+1}$, if P can be separated by a plane $\boldsymbol{n}^\top \boldsymbol{x} = 0$, that is, $P_+ = \{x \mid \boldsymbol{n}^\top \boldsymbol{x} > 0\}$ and $P_- = \{x \mid \boldsymbol{n}^\top \boldsymbol{x} < 0\}$ satisfy the relationships

$$P = P_+ \cap P_-, \quad P_+ \cup P_-, = \emptyset, \tag{23}$$

we call P a linearly separable set on $\mathbb{S}^{n-1}$. The three point clouds used in experiments are not linearly separable point clouds.

Figure 5 shows, from left to right the mode tree, the clustering on θ-ϕ plane and clustering on the sphere $\mathbb{S}^2$. Figure 6 shows hierarchical expressions of point cloud in spherical scale space for $\tau = 0, 1, 64, 128$. These expressions indicate that the number of clusters is three.

In the numerical experiments for $\mathbb{S}^3$ points on $\mathbb{S}^3 \subset \mathbb{R}^4$ are expressed in the Cartesian box ϕ-θ_1-θ_2. The data are expressed using the ϕ-θ_1-θ_2 pseudo-Cartesian box. In Fig. 7, we show input point clouds and clustering results in the top and bottom rows, respectively. The middle three rows show transition of the maximal points along the mode trees. Here $N_\phi = 30, N_{\theta_1} = 15 and N_{\theta_2} = 15$. The edges of the mode trees are shown in the ϕ-θ_1-θ_2 boxes. In each box, triangles and crosses represent the maximal points for $\tau = \tau_k$ and $\tau = \tau_{k+1}$, respectively, where $\tau_k < \tau_{k+1}$. Therefore, the edges from points with the triangles converge to points shown cross. The clusters in the bottom of Fig. 7 are extracted using Property 2.

The results in Fig. 7 show that our method estimates the number of clusters and achieves clustering by detecting the trajectories of the maximal points on the mode tree.

5   Conclusions

We introduced an algorithm for scale-space clustering of point clouds on the hypersphere $\mathbb{S}^n$ regarding the union of given point sets as an image of a finite sum of delta functions located at the positions of the points on the hypersphere. In numerical experiments, we show the clustering results on $\mathbb{S}^3$.

Our method is capable of finding the deterministic correspondences of points and clusters at stable scales, analysing the distribution of the points in a spherical scale space.

References

1. Iijima, T.: Pattern Recognition. Corona, Tokyo (1976). (in Japanese)
2. Witkin, A.P.: Scale space filtering. In: Proc. 8th IJCAI, pp. 1019–1022 (1983)

3. Griffin, L.D., Colchester, A.: Superficial and deep structure in linear diffusion scale space: Isophotes, critical points and separatrices. Image and Vision Computing **13**, 543–557 (1995)
4. Nakamura, E., Kehtarnavaz, N.: Determining number of clusters and prototype locations via multi-scale clustering. Pattern Recognition Letters **19**, 1265–1283 (1998)
5. Leung, Y., Zhang, J.-S., Xu, Z.-B.: Clustering by scale-space filtering. IEEE Trans. PAMI **22**, 1396–1410 (2000)
6. Loog, M., Duistermaat, J.J., Florack, L.M.J.: On the behavior of spatial critical points under gaussian blurring (a folklore theorem and scale-space constraints). In: Kerckhove, M. (ed.) Scale-Space 2001. LNCS, vol. 2106, pp. 183–192. Springer, Heidelberg (2001)
7. Sakai, T., Imiya, A.: Unsupervised cluster discovery using statistics in scale space. Engineering Applications of Artificial Intelligence **22**, 92–100 (2009)
8. Zhao, N.-Y., Iijima, T.: A theory of feature extraction by the tree of stable viewpoints. IEICE Japan, Trans. D **J68–D**, 1125–1135 (1985). (in Japanese)
9. Chung, M.K.: Heat kernel smoothing on unit sphere. In: Proc. 3rd IEEE ISBI: Nano to Macro, pp. 992–995 (2006)
10. Mochizuki, Y., Imiya, A., Kawamoto, K., Sakai, T., Torii, A.: Scale-space clustering on the sphere. In: Wilson, R., Hancock, E., Bors, A., Smith, W. (eds.) CAIP 2013, Part I. LNCS, vol. 8047, pp. 417–424. Springer, Heidelberg (2013)

Bokeh Effects Based on Stereo Vision

Dongwei Liu[1]([⊠]), Radu Nicolescu[1], and Reinhard Klette[2]

[1] Department of Computer Science,
The University of Auckland, Auckland, New Zealand
[2] School of Engineering, Auckland University of Technology,
Auckland, New Zealand
dliu697@aucklanduni.ac.nz

Abstract. Bokeh, a sought-after photo rendering style of out-of-focus blur, typically aims at an aesthetic quality which is not available to low-end consumer grade cameras due to the lens design. We present a bokeh simulation method using stereo-vision techniques. We refine a depth map obtained with stereo matching with a little user interaction. A depth-aware bokeh effect is then applied with user-adjustable apertures sizes or shapes. Our method mainly aims at the visual quality of the bokeh effect rather than time efficiency. Experiments show that our results are natural-looking, and can be similar to the bokeh effect of a real-world bokeh-capable camera system.

1   Introduction

Bokeh (a word of Japanese origin) refers to the rendering style of out-of-focus blur in a photo, typically aiming at aesthetic quality. Such a phenomenon is an important composition factor in photography, especially for portrait photos. Using a bokeh effect properly is typically identified with blurring non-essential elements in the foreground or background, thus simplifying the frame and guiding a viewer's visual attention to the main object in the scene.

The bokeh effect is also widely used in 3D rendering to achieve natural-looking scenes [2]. Image-based bokeh simulation is an emerging area. Previous research emphasises also on time efficiency, which is important for online video editing [1,19]. Our novel method focuses on the visual quality of the bokeh effect.

A large-aperture lens and a large-size sensor are normally required to ensure a sufficient degree of blur. Such equipment is normally expensive and also (still) voluminous. In photography, the particular aesthetic quality of bokeh is affected by optical aberrations of a lens (e.g. spherical, coma, or chromatic). Such requirements may define further constraints on the used optics equipment.

A simulated bokeh effect by computerised postprocessing is a way for making things easier. Bokeh is a depth-aware photo effect. Single image based bokeh simulation methods [17,20] try to "guess" the depth information of the input image (normally according to the contrast of object edges), and then apply a blur effect. Since a single image cannot provide enough depth cues, results of such methods often show an inconsistent spatial logic and look artificial, accordingly.

G. Azzopardi and N. Petkov (Eds.): CAIP 2015, Part I, LNCS 9256, pp. 198–210, 2015.
DOI: 10.1007/978-3-319-23192-1_17

Stereo-vision techniques and products became popular these years (from IMAX 3D movies to 3D TV or monitors, and then to consumer level stereo cameras). Depth hints contained in a *stereo pair* (i.e. a base image and a match image) provide a possibility to synthesize a natural-looking bokeh effect. In this paper we present a stereo-based bokeh simulation method which takes a stereo pair as input, estimates depth information from the stereo pair, and then applies a depth-aware bokeh effect on the base image. See Fig. 1 for a brief workflow of our method. The input stereo pair can be obtained from a consumer-level binocular camera (i.e. a calibrated pair of monocular cameras), or, for a statical scene, by moving one monocular camera on a platform.

A proper depth map is the key towards a high-quality bokeh effect. From our observation, absolutely accurate depth information is not required for depth-aware photo effects. The essential requirement is a consistency of the depth map with the geometric features of the original image (e.g. at occlusion edges of objects). Depth maps generated by a stereo matcher tend to involve not-available pixels (due to occlusion or low confidence in matching) or coarse object edges (due to a smoothing term in the stereo matcher). From our experiments, such issues may lead to disturbing bokeh effects.

Inpainting techniques [13] fill unavailable pixels in a depth map; this will not revise invalid object edges. A *joint bilateral filter* [1,14,15,19] can fill those unavailable pixels and improve the quality of object edges using color information of the original image. The revising ability of a joint bilateral filter is quite limited, especially on large-size occlusions caused by close-up objects (e.g. people). Such limitations are illustrated in Section 5. In order to achieve a proper depth map for the image editing purpose, we present a novel depth refinement method. First, we remove obviously incorrect depth information in the left-side region by a simple pre-filter. Then, we employ an interactive alpha-matting method [12] to extract the main object of the photo. Later, we remove possibly incorrect depth information around the main object. Finally, we run a joint bilateral filter on the main object and the surroundings separately, and merge results according to the alpha value. Experiments show that our depth refinement method can achieve a better quality of a depth map than simply running a joint bilateral filter.

Such improvements on the depth map lead to visible advances in bokeh quality. With the refined depth map, we present a novel image-based bokeh simulation method. We map each point of the base image into a *circle of confusion*

Fig. 1. Brief workflow of our method. From left to right: given a stereo pair as input, we calculate a raw depth map by stereo matching, then refine the depth map, and finally apply a depth-aware bokeh effect on the base image of the stereo pair.

according to a user defined *aperture f-number* and some camera parameters, and then merge those circles of confusion considering partial occlusion. The aperture shape of a real-world lens is not always a circle. The light distribution in a circle of confusion depends on the optical design of specific lenses, which is, normally, nonuniform. Such features have an important impact on the visual effect of bokeh. We build an aperture and distribution model from the input texture.

Existing stereo-based bokeh simulation research [1,15,19] uses a synthesized light field to render bokeh, which is similar to the workflow of accumulation-buffer methods [8,18]. Without knowledge of occluded structures, these methods degenerate into an approximation of a scattering method. These papers also place its emphasis on time efficiency, which is important for online video editing, but generate only a small number of buffer views (e.g. 36 to 48 in [19]), which may lead to artifacts due to undersampling. In comparison, our method does dense pixel scattering which achieves a high visual quality of the bokeh effect.

Main contributions in this paper include depth refinement for improved photo editing, an image-based depth-aware bokeh simulation method considering aperture shape and light distribution, and a convenient bokeh control interface.

2 Basics and Notations

This section lists notation and techniques used. RGB color images I are defined on a rectangular set Ω of pixel locations, with $I(p) = (R, G, B)$ for $p \in \Omega$ and $0 \leq R, G, B \leq G_{\max}$. Let N_{cols} and N_{rows} be width and height of Ω, respectively, and $|\Omega| = N_{\text{cols}} \times N_{\text{rows}}$. The left image of a stereo pair is the base image.

Stereo Matching. Stereo matching techniques [3,4] take a rectified stereo pair (i.e. a base image I_b and a match image I_m) as input. For each pixel p in I_b, a stereo matcher aims at identifying a corresponding pixel p_m in I_m (i.e. p and p_m are projections of the same point in the 3D scene). The shift between p and p_m identifies the disparity $d(p) = d_p$, where d is a *disparity map* defined on Ω. Stereo matching typically aims at minimizing an error function

$$E(d) = \sum_{p \in \Omega} \left[E_{\text{data}}(p, d_p) + \sum_{q \in W_p \wedge p \neq q} E_{\text{smooth}}(d_p, d_q) \right] \tag{1}$$

where E_{data} and E_{smooth} are data and smoothness cost functions, respectively, and W_p is a pixel neighbourhood of p. Then, depth information can be calculated by triangulation:

$$D(p) = \frac{f \cdot b}{d_p + \Delta} \tag{2}$$

where Δ is a small positive number to avoid a division by zero, f is the *focal length*, and b is the *base distance* between both cameras.

Joint Bilateral Filter. A *bilateral filter*, also known as "surface blur", is a selective mean filter for image smoothing or noise reduction. The *joint bilateral* *filter* [6,14] is a variation of a bilateral filter for depth refinement. This filter uses the original color image I to refine the corresponding disparity map d:

$$d_{j\_bilateral}(p) = \frac{1}{\omega_p} \sum_{q \in W_p} d_q \cdot f_c(\|I(q) - I(p)\|_2) \cdot f_s(\|q - p\|_2)$$

$$\omega_p = \sum_{q \in W_p} f_c(\|I(q) - I(p)\|_2) \cdot f_s(\|q - p\|_2)$$

(3)

where f_c is the kernel for color distances of pixels, and f_s is the kernel for the spatial distance of pixels.

Some pixels in I_b do not have a corresponding pixel in I_m because of occlusion. Thus, depth in such a region cannot be calculated by stereo matching. Close-up objects, such as people in a portrait photo, cause large occlusions on the left side of the object silhouette. Because of the smoothness error term E_{smooth} in Equ. (1), a matcher tends to produce coarse object silhouettes, especially on the occlusion side. Due to the lack of correct depth information in occlusion regions, a joint bilateral filter would spread such false information instead of removing it. We need a special strategy to handle such false information.

Out-of-focus Rendering. Distributed ray tracing methods [9,16] can achieve high accurate bokeh effect by casting rays from a lens model instead of a "pin-hole". Recent methods that go beyond thin-lens models can also simulate several kinds of optical aberrations. Accumulation-buffer methods [8,18] approximate distributed ray tracing by generating multiple buffer views on the lens plane of a thin-lens model, and then simulate bokeh by blending those buffer views. These methods cannot be applied on photos, since 2D photos lack enough information about occluded structures. A layered model [7] or gathering-based methods [10] are designed for GPU computing; they are time-efficient but suffer from several kinds of artifacts [2]. Scattering-based methods [11] map a pixel in the source image to a *circle of confusion* on the destination image and provide a high-quality bokeh effect; our method follows this workflow.

3   Extract Depth Information

Scattering-based bokeh simulation techniques in the 3D rendering area suppose an RGB-D input image; RGB-D cameras are currently limited for indoor scenes.

Given a stereo pair I_b and I_m, we run a semi-global stereo matcher (SGM) [3] and obtain a disparity map d defined on the carrier Ω of I_b. Then, d is pre-filtered to remove large-scale incorrect information in the left-edge occlusion, defining a modified depth map $d^{(1)}$. The main object, which should be in focus (e.g. a person in a portrait photo), is extracted by an interactive alpha-matting. Object and surrounding define two, possibly overlapping subsets $d_o^{(1)}$ and $d_s^{(1)}$ of disparity map $d^{(1)}$, with $d_o^{(1)} \cup d_s^{(1)} = d^{(1)}$. Unreliable disparity values near the silhouette of the object are removed from $d_o^{(1)}$ and $d_s^{(1)}$, defining sets $d_o^{(2)}$ and $d_s^{(2)}$. We run a joint bilateral filter on both $d_o^{(2)}$ and $d_s^{(2)}$, and then merge them according to alpha values, and obtain a refined disparity map $d_{refined}$. The rest of this section describes the details of our depth refinement process.

Left-side Occlusion. Disparity map d may involve large-scale false information close to the left border of Ω, defining set Ω_{left}. This is due to visibility in the left image I_b but not in the right image I_m (making it impossible that a correct disparity is generated by stereo matching at such pixels). In general, a usual practice is to discard a part of I_b (or of d-values) on the left-hand side, e.g. about 10% of the image's width. For photography such a cut-off is unwelcome since it might damage the composition of an artwork. Thus, we try to repair such missing d-data in Ω_{left} based on the given information.

We remove invalid information from d in Ω_{left} for future repair. We identify outliers in Ω_{left} by using the calculated disparity map d, since cases of occlusions can be understood in terms of estimated distances to objects. First we consider a pixel location $p = (x_p, y_p)$ to be in Ω_{left} if

$$x_p < \frac{1}{N_{\text{cols}}} \cdot \sum_{x=1}^{N_{\text{cols}}} d(x, y_p) + C_{\text{relax}} \tag{4}$$

i.e., the mean disparity value in a row specifies how far Ω_{left} goes in this row. We used $C_{\text{relax}} = 0.02 \cdot N_{\text{cols}}$. Next we identify $d(p)$ as being an outlier if this value deviates too much from the mean disparity in its row. We set $d(p) = \text{NA}$ (i.e. "not available") if $p \in \Omega_{\text{left}}$ and

$$\left| d(p) - \frac{1}{N_{\text{cols}}} \cdot \sum_{x=1}^{N_{\text{cols}}} d(x, y_p) \right| > T_{\text{outlier}} \tag{5}$$

We use $T_{\text{outlier}} = 0.3 \cdot d_{\max}$, where $d_{\max}$ is the maximum disparity in d. Let $d^{(1)}$ be the (so far) pre-processed disparity map.

Object and Surroundings. As we discussed in Section 2, a stereo matcher may produce false depth information in an occlusion zone of the main object. Such false depth information may lead to weird artifacts in bokeh, and they are hard to remove by a joint bilateral filter.

We employ closed form matting [12] on I_b to extract the main object, and then remove unreliable depth information around its silhouette. Resulting gaps in disparity maps are fixed in the following joint bilateral filter process. Here, the matting technique can be seen as a segmentation method adapted to complex geometries, e.g. to people's hair.

The matting method needs a few user strokes to indicate the object and surroundings. An alpha map $\alpha : \Omega \to [0, 1]$ is then generated from color information of I_b. See Fig. 2 for an intuitive example. Such an alpha map defines two (maybe overlapping) subsets of Ω, the object Ω_o and surroundings Ω_s:

$$\Omega_o = \{p \in \Omega : \alpha(p) > 0\} \quad \text{and} \quad \Omega_s = \{p \in \Omega : \alpha(p) < 1\} \tag{6}$$

Accordingly we generate disparity maps $d_o^{(1)}$ and $d_s^{(1)}$ from $d^{(1)}$ (see Fig. 3, left):

$$d_o^{(1)}(p) = \begin{cases} d^{(1)}(p), & p \in \Omega_o \\ \text{NA}, & \text{otherwise} \end{cases} \qquad d_s^{(1)}(p) = \begin{cases} d^{(1)}(p), & p \in \Omega_s \\ \text{NA}, & \text{otherwise} \end{cases} \qquad (7)$$

Here the main object is not defined as foreground because some objects in surroundings may be closer. Let $\overline{d}_o^{(1)}$ be the mean disparity of the main object. Regions close to the silhouette are defined by a dilation operation [5] on both inside Ω_{eo} and outside Ω_{es} the silhouette.

$$\begin{aligned} \Omega_{eo} &= \{p \in \Omega_o : \exists q \, [\, q \in \Omega_s \wedge \|p - q\|_2 < T_{\text{fringe}} \,]\} \\ \Omega_{es} &= \{p \in \Omega_s : \exists q \, [\, q \in \Omega_o \wedge \|p - q\|_2 < T_{\text{fringe}} \,]\} \end{aligned} \qquad (8)$$

Threshold $T_{\text{fringe}} = 1.1 \cdot \overline{d}_o^{(1)}$ defines the maximum possible occlusion size. Unreliable disparity values are then removed from Ω_{eo} and Ω_{es} (see Fig. 3, middle). Consider a pixel location $p = (x_p, y_p) \in \Omega$ and let

$$d_o^{(2)}(p) = \begin{cases} \text{NA}, & p \in \Omega_{eo} \wedge \left\| d_o^{(1)}(p) - \overline{d}_o^{(1)} \right\|_2 > 3 \cdot \sigma_o \\ d_o^{(1)}(p), & \text{otherwise} \end{cases}$$

$$d_s^{(2)}(p) = \begin{cases} \text{NA}, & p \in \Omega_{es} \wedge \left\| d_s^{(1)}(p) - \overline{d}_o^{(1)} \right\|_2 < 3 \cdot \sigma_o \\ & \wedge \left\| d_s^{(1)}(p) - \mu_s^{line}(y_p) \right\|_2 > \sigma_s^{line}(y_p) \\ d_s^{(1)}(p), & \text{otherwise} \end{cases} \qquad (9)$$

$$\mu_s^{line}(y_p) = \frac{1}{\triangle} \cdot \sum_{(x, y_p) \in \Omega_s} d_s^{(1)}(x, y_p)$$

$$\sigma_o = \sqrt{\frac{1}{|\Omega_o|} \sum_{q \in \Omega_o} d_o^{(1)}(q)^2 - \left[\frac{1}{|\Omega_o|} \sum_{q \in \Omega_o} d_o^{(1)}(q)\right]^2} \qquad (10)$$

$$\sigma_s^{line}(y_p) = \sqrt{\frac{1}{\triangle} \sum_{(x, y_p) \in \Omega_s} d_s^{(1)}(x, y_p)^2 - \left[\frac{1}{\triangle} \sum_{(x, y_p) \in \Omega_s} d_s^{(1)}(x, y_p)\right]^2}$$

Fig. 2. Alpha matting. Given an input color image (left), and a few user strokes (middle) as hints, an alpha map (right) is calculated by closed form matting [12].

using $\triangle = N_{\text{cols}}(\Omega_s, y_p)$, $\mu_s^{line}(y_p)$ is the mean disparity value on $d_s^{(1)}$ on the same line of p, $\sigma_s^{line}(y_p)$ is the standard deviation of disparities on $d_s^{(1)}$ on the same line of p, and σ_o is the standard deviation of disparities on $d_o^{(1)}$.

Layered Joint Bilateral Filter. We run a joint bilateral filter, as defined in Eq. (3), separately on both layers $d_o^{(2)}$ and $d_s^{(2)}$ of the disparity map, in order to avoid depth bleeding. In this case, both color information I_b and matting result α are involved for enhancing depth information.

The $(2m+1) \times (2m+1)$ window W_p is defined according to the size of the input image. We use $m = N_{col}/30$ and Gaussian kernels for both f_c and f_s. The spatial scale parameter σ_s depends on the size of W_p:

$$f_c(\|I(q) - I(p)\|_2) = \frac{1}{\sigma_c \sqrt{2\pi}} \exp\left(-\frac{\|I(q) - I(p)\|_2^2}{2\sigma_c^2}\right)$$

$$f_s(\|q - p\|_2) = \frac{1}{\sigma_s \sqrt{2\pi}} \exp\left(-\frac{\|q - p\|_2^2}{2\sigma_s^2}\right)$$

$$\sigma_c{}^2 = \frac{1}{|\Omega|} \sum_{q \in \Omega} \|I(q)\|_2^2 - \left(\frac{1}{|\Omega|} \sum_{q \in \Omega} \|I(q)\|_2\right)^2$$

$$\sigma_s = \frac{1}{3} \cdot (m + 0.5)$$

(11)

We iteratively run such a joint bilateral filter for three times on both $d_o^{(2)}$ and $d_s^{(2)}$. We denote the result by $d_o^{(3)}$ and $d_s^{(3)}$, respectively (see Fig. 3, right).

Finally, we merge these two disparity layers according to α, and obtain the refined disparity map $d_{refined}$:

$$d_{refined}(p) = \alpha(p) \cdot d_o^{(3)} + [1 - \alpha(p)] \cdot d_s^{(3)}$$

(12)

A depth map $D_{refined}$ can then be calculated by triangulation following Eq. (2).

4   Simulated Bokeh Effect

We use a scattering-based method for simulating a bokeh effect. For each pixel location p in I_b, we map it into a *circle of confusion* on a destination image I_{bokeh}. Partial occlusion is considered according to pixel depth information. Inaccuracies around object edges caused by occlusion are compensated. By default, the *on focus distance*, D_{focus}, is the mean depth of the matting-out main object; however, this value can be adjusted by the user. The degree of blur can be controlled by a single *aperture f-number* parameter F (so familiar to photographers). Users can try different bokeh styles by simply inputting a texture.

Circle of Confusion. In a thin lens model, an out-of-focus point p distributes into a *circle of confusion* (CoC), denoted by $c(p)$. The diameter $\phi(p)$ of $c(p)$ is determined by the following formula:

$$\phi(p) = \left| A \, \frac{f \cdot (D_{\text{focus}} - D(p))}{D(p) \cdot (D_{\text{focus}} - f)} \right| \tag{13}$$

Here, $D(p)$ is the distance of p from the lens plane, f is the lens' *focal length*, A is the diameter of aperture, and $F = f/A$.

For computational purposes, we need to measure the circle of confusion by pixels. To be intuitive, we convert the camera system into a "full-frame" system, where the equivalent focal length $f_{\text{fullframe}} = f \cdot w_{\text{fullframe}}/w_{\text{sensor}}$. Here, w_{sensor} is the width of real camera sensor, and $w_{\text{fullframe}} = 36$ mm is the width of a full-frame sensor. Thus, we adapt Eq. (13) into the following form:

$$\hat{\phi}(p) = \left| \frac{N_{\text{cols}} \cdot w_{\text{sensor}} \cdot f_{\text{fullframe}}^2 \cdot (D_{\text{focus}} - D_{refined}(p))}{w_{\text{fullframe}} \cdot F \cdot D_{refined}(p) \cdot (D_{\text{focus}} \cdot w_{\text{fullframe}} - f_{\text{fullframe}} \cdot w_{\text{sensor}})} \right| \tag{14}$$

Assume that the light spreads uniformly in a circle. The *intensity* $\alpha_c(q) \in [0,1]$ is distributed on a pixel q in circle $c(p)$ [i.e. $\|q - p\|_2 < \hat{\phi}(p)$] as $\alpha_c(q) = 4/\hat{\phi}^2(p)$. Here, $\hat{\phi}(p)$ can be a real number. Pixels on the border of $c(p)$ need to be treated in a resampling process.

Gathering. For a pixel location $p \in \Omega$ in the destination image I_{bokeh}, assume p is impacted by a set C_p of CoCs. We sort the CoCs in C_p according to the corresponding depth, from close to far, and obtain $C_p = \{c(q_1), c(q_2), ..., c(q_n)\}$. We discard those CoCs after index k, if we have such a k, $1 \le k \le n$, defined by

$$\sum_{i=1}^{k-1} \alpha_c(q_i) < 1 \wedge \sum_{i=1}^{k} \alpha_c(q_i) \ge 1 \tag{15}$$

Fig. 3. Object and surroundings refinements. Two sets of the original depth map, object and surroundings, are obtained according to an alpha map (left). Unreliable disparity values close to the object silhouette are then removed (middle). A joint bilateral filter is iteratively applied to refine object and surrounding (right).

Then we do gathering:

$$I_{\text{bokeh}}(p) = \frac{1}{\omega_\alpha(p)} \cdot \sum_{i=1}^{k} [I_b(q_i) \cdot \alpha_c(q_i)] \quad \text{with} \quad \omega_\alpha(p) = \sum_{i=1}^{k} \alpha_c(q_i) \qquad (16)$$

Actual bokeh effects in *partial occlusions* cannot be calculated in an image-based bokeh simulation, since some of the rays, which would correspond to a large-aperture lens model, do not appear in our input image. Our gathering method assumes that partial occlusions have similar textures with their visible adjacent regions. Experiments show that our results are not affected by artifacts and look similar to real bokeh photos.

Lens Aperture and Distribution Model. Aperture shape and light distribution are important characteristics of real-world lenses, which can impact the visual style of bokeh, but cannot be simulated by thin lens models.

We simulate lens aperture and distribution by replacing a circle of confusion with a diffuse model α_t defined by an $N_{\text{texture}} \times N_{\text{texture}}$ input texture. Here, α_t is a transmission map normalized to $[0, 1]$, with its origin at the center.

For a CoC $c(p)$ with diameter $\hat{\phi}(p)$, we calculate the width $w(p) \in \mathbb{R}$ of a corresponding diffuse model and its mean transmission, $\overline{\alpha}_t$:

$$w(p) = \hat{\phi}(p) \cdot \sqrt{\frac{\pi}{4 \cdot \overline{\alpha}_t}} \quad \text{with} \quad \overline{\alpha}_t = \frac{1}{N_{\text{texture}}^2} \cdot \sum_{p \in \Omega_t} \alpha_t(p) \qquad (17)$$

Now Equ. (16) can be transformed into

$$I_{\text{bokeh}}(p) = \frac{1}{\hat{\omega}_\alpha(p)} \cdot \sum_{i=1}^{k} [I(q_i) \cdot \alpha_c(q_i) \cdot \alpha_t^{q_i}(q_i - p)]$$

$$\hat{\omega}_\alpha(p) = \sum_{i=1}^{k} \alpha_c(q_i) \cdot \alpha_t^{q_i}(q_i - p) \qquad (18)$$

Here $\alpha_t^{q_i}$ is a scaled diffuse model with width $w(q_i)$.

5   Experiments

Implementation is on a 3.30 GHz PC with 8.00 GB RAM and no graphics card. We run our program on photos of 800×600 resolution. The run time for each example is about 2 to 3 minutes depending on the amount of blurring. Our method aims mainly at the visual quality of the bokeh effect, instead of time efficiency. (There are obvious ways for speed-up, not yet followed at the time being.) Figure 4 shows some results. Taking advantage of depth information, our method produces a natural-looking bokeh effect without artificiality.

Figure 5 demonstrates bokeh styles obtained using different aperture and distribution models. Gaussian distribution (Fig. 5, left) achieves a very smooth

Fig. 4. Three results. *Top*: Original image. *Bottom*: Corresponding bokeh effect.

Fig. 5. Various bokeh styles by using different aperture and distribution models. From left to right: Gaussian distribution, round aperture with uniform distribution, and pentagon aperture with a nonuniform distribution.

bokeh, which normally is ideal for photography with an aesthetic meaning. Only special lenses with a *defocus image control* (e.g. Nikon 135mm f/2 DC) can obtain similar effects. The largest aperture setting of a lens normally leads to a round bokeh (see Fig. 5, middle), while using aperture settings other than the largest may cause a polygon bokeh (see Fig. 5, right) due to the impact of aperture blades. Polygon bokeh effects are less smooth than Gaussian or round bokeh, but are individualistic. The energy distribution of bokeh depends on the specific optical design of a lens, which is hard to calculate in ray-tracing but can be simulated by our model. Artists can choose different bokeh styles according to specific creative intentions using our method.

As pointed out in Section 1, a high-quality depth is the key to avoid artificiality. Figure 6 compares the results of our refinement against those obtained by (just) joint bilateral refinements proposed in [1, 15, 19]. Black pixels in Fig. 6, top left, denote pixel locations where depth is not available. In Fig. 6, bottom left, pixels without depth value are not blurred. Besides those black pixels, the original depth map obtained from an SGM stereo matcher involves false depth information, especially around the silhouette of the boy. Such false information causes invalid artificial-looking bokeh. Simply using joint bilateral filters

Fig. 6. How the quality of a depth map affects the bokeh effect. Top, left to right: Original depth map from an SGM stereo matcher, joint bilateral refinement result, an our refinement result. Bottom line: Corresponding bokeh effects.

Fig. 7. The role of depth information in bokeh simulation. Left to right: Bokeh effect by our method, bokeh simulation without depth information, real bokeh effect taken by Canon 5D2 camera body and 50mm F/1.8 lens (i.e. the "ground truth").

cannot completely remove such false information, or may even spread this (to some extent), thus the corresponding bokeh effect may still look artificial. Our method is able to remove such false depth information, and thus leads to natural-looking bokeh effect. Taking advantage of image matting, our refinement works well on regions with complex geometry; see the hair of the boy in Fig. 6, right.

Figure 7 compares bokeh with depth information, without depth, and bokeh from a real-world camera and lens (i.e. our "ground truth"). In this example, the book is the object to focus on. Here, Fig. 7, middle, is processed by Gaussian blur with an alpha matting result of the book as a mask. The bokeh effect without depth information looks flat, lacking any special feeling. The bokeh of our method transits naturally from close to far, and looks similar to the real bokeh example photo.

6 Conclusions

In this paper, we present a bokeh simulation method using stereo-vision techniques. Our method takes a stereo pair as input. A raw depth map is calculated by stereo matching. We then refine such raw depth map with a little user interaction to identify the main object. A depth aware bokeh effect is then applied to the base image. Users can control the degree of blur by setting an aperture f-number, and control the style of bokeh by simply inputting a texture that indicate the aperture shape and the light distribution of blur. Experiments show that our results are natural-looking, similar to the bokeh of real-world bokeh-capable camera systems. Future work might evaluate the bokeh results with some cognitive-based methodology, since the quality of bokeh is subjective.

Acknowledgment. The authors thank Tim Banyar for kindly being the model of Fig. 6. This paper is supported by China Scholarship council.

References

1. Abbott, J., Morse, B.: Interactive depth-aware effects for stereo image editing. In: Proc. 3DTV-Conf., pp. 263–270 (2013)
2. Demers, J.: Depth of field: a survey of techniques. In: Fernando, R. (ed.) GPU Gems, pp. 375–390. Addison Wesley (2004)
3. Hirschmüller, H.: Accurate and efficient stereo processing by semi-global matching and mutual information. In: Proc. CVPR, pp. 807–814 (2005)
4. Klette, R.: Concise Computer Vision: An Introduction into Theory and Algorithms. Springer, London (2014)
5. Klette, R., Rosenfeld, A.: Digital Geometry: Geometric Methods for Digital Picture Analysis. Morgan Kaufmann, San Francisco (2004)
6. Kopf, J., Cohen, M.F., Lischinski, D., Uyttendaele, M.: Joint bilateral upsampling. ACM Tran. Graphics **26**, no. 96 (2007)
7. Kraus, M., Strengert, M.: Depth-of-field rendering by pyramidal image processing. Computer Graphics Forum **26**(3), 645–654 (2007)
8. Lee, S., Eisemann, E., Seidel, H.P.: Depth-of-field rendering with multiview synthesis. ACM Trans. Graphics **28**(5), No. 134 (2009)
9. Lee, S., Eisemann, E., Seidel, H.P.: Real-time lens blur effects and focus control. ACM Trans. Graphics **29**(4), No. 65 (2010)
10. Lee, S., Kim, G.J., Choi, S.: Real-time depth-of-field rendering using anisotropically filtered mipmap interpolation. IEEE Trans. Visualization Computer Graphics **15**(3), 453–464 (2009)
11. Lee, S., Kim, G.J., Choi, S.: Real-time depth-of-field rendering using point splatting on per-pixel layers. Computer Graphics Forum **27**(7), 1955–1962 (2008)
12. Levin, A., Lischinski, D., Weiss, Y.: A closed-form solution to natural image matting. IEEE Trans. PAMI **30**(2), 228–242 (2008)
13. Liu, J., Gong, X., Liu, J.: Guided inpainting and filtering for kinect depth maps. In: Proc. ICPR, pp. 2055–2058 (2012)
14. Matsuo, T., Fukushima, N., Ishibashi, Y.: Weighted joint bilateral filter with slope depth compensation filter for depth map refinement. In: Proc. VISAPP, pp. 300–309 (2013)

15. Wang, Q., Yu, Z., Rasmussen, C., Yu, J.: Stereo vision based depth of field rendering on a mobile device. J. Electronic Imaging **23**(2), No. 023009 (2014)
16. Wu, J., Zheng, C., Hu, X., Wang, Y., Zhang, L.: Realistic rendering of bokeh effect based on optical aberrations. The Visual Computer **26**, 555–563 (2010)
17. Xue, W., Zhang, X., Sheng, B., Ma, L.: Image-based depth-of-field rendering with non-local means filtering. In: Proc. ICMEW, pp. 1–6 (2013)
18. Yu, X., Wang, R., Yu, J.: Real-time depth of field rendering via dynamic light field generation and filtering. Computer Graphics Forum **29**(7), 2099–2107 (2010)
19. Yu, Z., Yu, X., Thorpe, C., Grauer-Gray, S., Li, F., Yu, J.: Racking focus and tracking focus on live video streams: a stereo solution. The Visual Computer **30**(1), 45–58 (2014)
20. Zhang, W., Cham, W.K.: Single image focus editing. In: Proc. ICCV Workshops, pp. 1947–1954 (2009)

Confidence Based Rank Level Fusion for Multimodal Biometric Systems

Hossein Talebi$^{(\boxtimes)}$ and Marina L. Gavrilova

University of Calgary, 2500 University Dr. NW, Calgary T2N 1N4, Canada
{htalebi,mgavrilo}@ucalgary.ca

Abstract. Multimodal biometric systems have proven advantages over single biometric systems as they are using multiple traits of users. The intra-class variance provided by using more than one trait results in a high identification rate. Still, one of the missing parts in a multimodal system is inattention to the discriminability of each rank list for each specific user. This paper introduces a novel approach to select a combination of rank lists in rank level so that it provides the highest discrimination for any specific query. The rank list selection is based on pseudo-scores lists that are created by combination of rank lists and resemblance probability distribution of users. The experimental results on a multimodal biometric system based on frontal face, profile face, and ear indicated higher identification rate by using novel confidence based rank level fusion.

Keywords: Multimodal biometrics · Rank level fusion · Rank list selection · Resemblance probability distribution

1 Introduction and Background

The undeniable need for higher security has resulted in a tremendous growth in biometric systems. The integration of biometric system with government identity management systems as well as consumer products has created the demand for more accurate systems.

Biometric systems can be categorized into unimodal and multimodal systems [1]. Although single biometric systems have been widely used in access control and identity management systems, there are some issues regarding their performance. The low inter-class and high intra-class variance caused by the use of one biometric as well as the non-universality, sensitivity to noise and data quality issues have shifted the attention toward multimodal biometric systems [2]. In a multimodal biometric system, different biometrics of a person are captured in order to provide uncorrelated information about the identity. These multiple evidences help the system to infer about the identity of the query with higher confidence [1].

One of the important aspects of a multimodal biometric system is the fusion of information from different biometric traits. The fusion can be done in pre-mapping stage where biometric traits have not matched against the training

© Springer International Publishing Switzerland 2015
G. Azzopardi and N. Petkov (Eds.): CAIP 2015, Part I, LNCS 9256, pp. 211–222, 2015.
DOI: 10.1007/978-3-319-23192-1_18

samples as well as post-mapping stage where the comparison is done and the recognition results need to be fused [3].

Post-mapping fusion can take place on three levels: score level, decision level, and rank level [1]. Score level deals with systems that provide score values to show the proximity of a query to the samples in the database. On decision level, each biometric classifier independently provides the final decision about the identity of the user. These levels of fusion are mostly used in commercial biometric systems which solely provide the final decision [4]. Unlike score level and decision level, some biometric devices provide a ranking of users as their output. The output of such systems is similar to the scores in case that it contains a list of possible identities, although it only provides a ranking of identities and lacks the rich score information. The lack of scores obscures the information on how confident each classifier is about the results. On the other hand, rank level fusion does not require normalization of scores which can be computationally expensive and also the inappropriate selection of normalization method can degrade the recognition rate [2]. Rank level fusion is a relatively new approach which has not been studied much compared to others. Several rank-level fusion methods have been proposed and developed in the past decade using different fusion techniques and biometric traits [5–7].

Lee et al. [8] compared rank-level methods, such as Borda count and Bayes fuse, and score level, such as sum rule and binary classification, based on fingerprint and face biometric traits. They concluded that the binary classification outperforms other methods and in case of lack of scores, Bayes fusion has an advantage over Borda count. Monwar et al. [9] showed that using more sophisticated approaches with rank information can result in a higher recognition rate than score level. They proposed a fuzzy rule based inference system for rank fusion. The comparison of fuzzy rank fusion with other rank, score, and decision level fusions demonstrated not even a better accuracy but a faster system performance.

The quality of biometric data can significantly impact the classifiers confidence and the recognition result, especially when there is a possibility that image quality degrades due to ambient conditions and acquisition device. Marasco et al. [10] investigated the stability of rank-level fusion and analyzed the performance of rank-level and score level fusion in presence of biometric data with low quality. Their experiments with low quality face images and syntactically degraded fingerprints revealed that both rank and score are unstable while the degradation is significant, although rank is more stable than scores in case of small degradations. Abaza and Ross [11] proposed a modification for highest rank and Borda count fusion by incorporating a quality factor. Alam et al. [12] utilized a quality measure which did not require any prior modeling of the noise and degradation factors of input data. They tried to extract the quality measure by considering a measure of deviation of scores from the mean and then utilizing this confidence measure for highest rank and Borda count methods. They developed a multimodal system for face and voice biometrics and validated the improvement impact of confidence measure by comparing their proposed method against highest rank and Borda count.

Previous works tried to improve the accuracy of the rank level fusion by considering different factors and using different approaches. Aiming at a same goal, this paper introduces a novel approach to user based rank list selection based on the confidence of rank lists. The main contribution of this paper is an adaptive selection of rank lists for any queries based on the rank lists performance for that specific query. This approach does not require score information to evaluate the confidence of classifiers. It calculates the confidence by recovering pseudo-score lists using the similarity of each user's resemblance probability distribution with the rank lists. The most important feature of this approach is the adaptive selection of rank lists based on their performance for each user. This system is advantageous since it can be adopted for different queries based on how different rank lists are performing. By modifying the rank lists using the novel confidence based rank list selection (CBRLS) approach, the fusion method is able to select the most confident rank lists and reach a higher identification rate.

This paper is organized as follows: Section 2 introduces the novel confidence based rank list selection by explaining the resemblance probability distributions, rank list confidence, and the whole cascade rank list selection approach. Section 3 validates the applicability of the confidence based rank list selection by providing experimental results. Section 4 concludes the paper.

2   Methodology

This section details the novel confidence based rank list approach. Fig. 1 shows a flowchart of the novel confidence based rank level fusion method. The fusion starts with rank lists that are created by the classifiers. Each rank list is converted to a pseudo-score list using the resemblance probability distributions. For each biometric, the confidence of the pseudo-score list is calculated and a fraction of each list is selected based on its confidence. Then, the algorithm finds the next rank list that provides the most confidence value for each of the restricted lists. The algorithm continues until some stopping criteria is met. This procedure results in a cascade of rank lists working together to provide the highest confidence to the list of users. This approach is novel in terms of confidence calculation from rank lists and also rank list selection to improve the confidence of rank lists. The rest of this section explains the detail of the proposed multimodal biometric system and the novel fusion approach.

2.1   Feature Extraction

The importance of a discriminative feature extraction in any machine learning systems is undeniable. Without features that provide discrimination between different classes of objects, it is impossible to reach a high recognition rate. Fisher Linear Discriminant Analysis (FLDA) [13] is a feature extraction and dimensionality reduction approach. In its essence, it projects data to a linear subspace that provides high inter-class variance as well as low intra-class similarity. It also

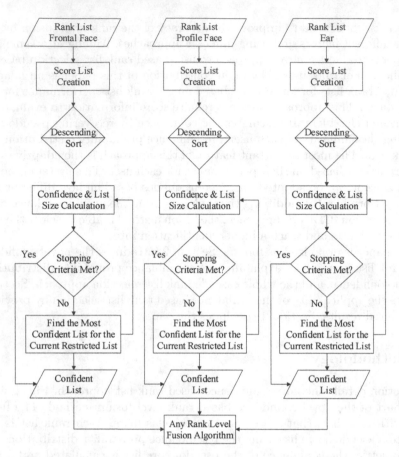

Fig. 1. Flowchart of the confidence based rank list selection (CBRLS) approach.

reduces the computation time by dimensional reduction with the least effect on the discriminatory information.

The FLDA [13] subspace for each biometric is created using the vectorised images of biometric traits accompanied with their corresponding classes. The FLDA algorithm provides the basis for the subspace and each biometric sample can be projected as a point to the FLDA subspace. The similarity of the samples can be considered as the Euclidean distance between FLDA feature vectors.

2.2 Resemblance Probability Distribution (RPD)

The FLDA projects training data into a feature space where each biometric sample becomes a point. For a specific biometric trait, each user's samples cluttered in this subspace. The configuration of all data points in the feature space creates the training data set. Based on the distances between data points of different classes, there are different probabilities to misclassify each class during the test phase. Formally speaking, if there are n different classes, namely $c_1, ..., c_n$ and each class c_i contains m training samples $s_{i,1}, ..., s_{i,m}$, then the distance from class c_i to c_j is defined as:

$$D_{b_j}(c_i, c_{i'}) = \begin{cases} 1/m \sum_{k=1}^{m} \min_{l \in \{1,...,m\}} \|(f_{s_k^{c_i,b_j}} - f_{s_l^{c_{i'},b_j}})\|, & \text{if } i \neq i' \\ 1/m \sum_{k=1}^{m} \min_{l \in \{1,...,m\}-\{k\}} \|(f_{s_k^{c_i,b_j}} - f_{s_l^{c_{i'},b_j}})\|, & \text{if } i = i' \end{cases}$$

(1)

The distance of class c_i to all the classes in the training data set can be used to create the Resemblance Probability Distribution (RPD) [14] as follows:

$$PRD(c_i) = \frac{\max(D_{c_i,b_j}) \times 1 - D_{c_i,b_j}}{\| \max(D_{c_i,b_j}) - D_{c_i,b_j} \|}$$

(2)

where D_{c_i,b_j} is a vector representing the distance of c_i from all the other classes and 1 is a vector of ones, the same size as D_{c_i,b_j}. The Resemblance Probability Distribution (RPD) [14] for each class shows how different classes resemble that specific class and manifests the probability of misclassifying a certain class with other classes.

Fig. 2 demonstrates the resemblance probability distribution for three biometrics of two users with identity 30 and 60. The RPDs for all three biometrics have their maximum values for the identity 30 or 60 which demonstrates the fact that they have the most resemblance to their actual identities. The RPDs have different values for other identities which demonstrates the independence of different biometrics [15].

2.3 Confidence Based Rank List Selection (CBRLS)

A rank list only provides a relative ordering of users based on their similarities to the queried sample. A rank list does not provide any information about how confident is the classifier about the ranking. On the other hand, score list can provide information about how confident is the classifier based on the scores assigned to each user. In order to calculate the confidence of each classifier about the rank list, there is a need to recover scores information. Here, we propose a novel method to convert rank lists to pseudo-score lists using the resemblance probability distributions. The confidence of each classifier can be calculated based on its pseudo-score list. Then, the novel rank list selection is used to create a cascade of rank lists and increase the confidence of rank lists.

Converting from Rank List to Pseudo-score List. Since the rank list and resemblance probability distributions are both generated from a same feature space and samples, it can be considered that the rank list should be similar to the resemblance probability distribution of its true identity or its neighbors in the feature space. In order to find how similar the rank list is to each resemblance probability distribution, we consider the rank list as a probability distribution and used the Bhattacharyya distance[16] to find the similarity of two probability

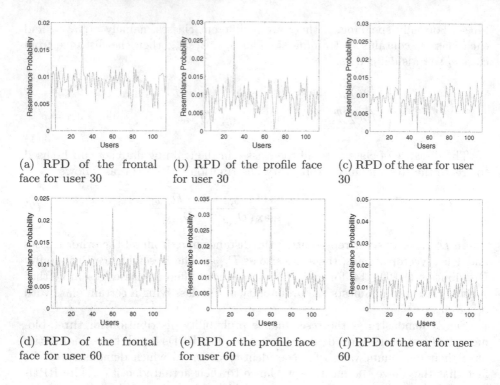

(a) RPD of the frontal face for user 30

(b) RPD of the profile face for user 30

(c) RPD of the ear for user 30

(d) RPD of the frontal face for user 60

(e) RPD of the profile face for user 60

(f) RPD of the ear for user 60

Fig. 2. Resemblance probability distribution for three biometrics of two users.

distributions. The Bhattacharyya distance of two discrete probability distributions P_1 and P_2 over a same domain X is defined as:

$$D_B(P_1, P_2) = -ln(BC(P_1, P_2)) \qquad (3)$$

where,

$$BC(P_1, P_2) = \sum_{x \in X} \sqrt{P_1(x)P_2(x)} \qquad (4)$$

The similarity measure based on the Bhattacharyya distance is defined as:

$$S_B(P_1, P_2) = 1 - D_B(P_1, P_2) \qquad (5)$$

The rank list of each classifier can be converted to a probability distribution by dividing each element by the sum of all the ranks.

The transformation of a rank list to a pseudo-score list is done using algorithm 1. The algorithm calculated the Bhattacharyya similarity of the rank list with all the resemblance probability distributions and then multiply the similarity of each RPD of each user to the rank of that user in the rank list to create a pseudo-score list (PSL). At last, the pseudo-score list (PSL) is normalized by dividing by each pseudo-score by the sum of all the pseudo-scores.

> **for** *each normalized rank list* NL_j **do**
> > **for** *each enrolled identity* I_i **do**
> > > $PSL_i^j = (N - Rank_i^j) * S_B((1 - NL_j), RPD_i^j)$
> >
> > **end**
> > $NPSL^j$=Normalize(PSL^j)
>
> **end**

Algorithm 1. The process of creating pseudo-score list from rank list containing N users using resemblance probability distributions.

Confidence of Lists. The confidence measure is considered as how probable is that the current list misclassifies the actual user as its neighbors. For the normalized pseudo-score list $NPSL^j$ of biometric j, the confidence measure is defined as:

$$CM(NPSL^j) = \sum_{i=1}^{N-1} e^{\frac{-(i-1)^2}{N}} (SortedNPSL_i^j - SortedNPSL_{i+1}^j) \qquad (6)$$

where N is the number of users registered to the system and $SortedNPSL^j$ is the decreasing sorted list of $NPSL^j$. This equation considers the confidence of each list as a weighted sum of differences of consecutive sorted pseudo-scores. The more the distance between the consecutive users' normalized sorted pseudo-scores, the higher is the confidence of that list. The weighting factor has larger values for score difference of users at the top of the list and the value decreases as it reaches to less probable identities. This weighting makes sense, since users at the beginning of the sorted list have more effect on the final decision. The confidence measure ranges from 0 to 1. The confidence measure is equal to 1, when the probability of first user is 1 and the rest is equal to 0. In this case, rank list is completely confident about its choice. The confidence measure is equal to 0 when the probabilities of all users are equal to a same number. In this case, the rank list cannot distinguish between users.

Restricted List Creation. The restricted lists are created based on the confidence of each list. If a list has a low confidence value, it means that more users should be on the restricted list. If a list is confident about its ranking, then we can consider a less number of users can be on the restricted list. The number of users in the restricted list of a rank list with N users and the confidence measure of CM is defined as:

$$k = \max\{(1 - CM)(N - 1) + 1, n\} \qquad (7)$$

where n is the minimum number of users that the restricted list should maintain. Using threshold value n protects the algorithm from losing the actual user during the restricted list creation due to accidental wrong confidence measure.

Increasing Lists Confidence Using Confidence Based Rank List Selection. For each biometric trait, the rank list is first converted to a pseudo-score list using resemblance probabilities. Then, for each list, the confidence level and the restricted list size are calculated. For each list, based on the restricted list size, the first k users are kept and then the confidence level of all the rank lists for these k users are calculated. The rank list, which provides the highest confidence for the current restricted list is used for the next round. The algorithm continues the same process for all the lists till there is no more changes in the lists and the confidence levels reach to its highest values. In this situation, any rank level fusion approach can be applied to the lists to create the consensus list.

3   Experimental Results

The performance evaluation of the proposed system is essential in order to assure its effectiveness for real-world scenarios. Even though the confidence based rank list selection algorithm is not dependent on any particular biometrics and is able to work with any sets of biometric traits, it has its best performance in case there is the least correlation between selected biometric traits. In order to demonstrate the performance of the system in case of correlated traits, we have selected frontal face and profile face as two of correlated biometric traits and ear as the third one.

Due to inherit cost associated with creating a real multimodal biometric database, most multimodal biometric systems are evaluated based on virtual databases. A virtual database is constructed by pairing of users from different biometrics databases and creating a virtual user that borrows each biometric from a specific database. In this work we have created a virtual database using frontal face, profile face and ear.

Facial Recognition Technology (FERET) database [17] is used for both frontal and profile faces. The collection of this database in done by researchers at George Mason University sponsored by The U.S. Department of Defense. FERET is a widely used database due to the collection of facial images with various positions, illuminations, and expressions. Since we were only interested to frontal and profile faces, we exclude images that were not taken from these angles. The database consist of 1199 subjects with multiple images of each subject. Among all the subjects there are only 974 subjects with profile face images.

For ear, the USTB ear database [18] is used. All the subjects were students from University of Science and Technology Beijing. They gathered three different databases based on three different conditions and configurations. In total there are 216 subjects among 1276 ear images that were taken in different illumination and orientation.

In order to create the virtual database, a user from the FERET database (which consists of frontal and profile faces) is selected and randomly paired with a user from the USTB ear database to form a virtual person. Enrollment and identification databases are created by randomly selecting one or two image(s)

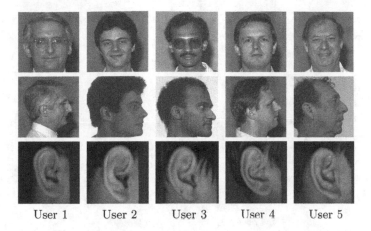

User 1   User 2   User 3   User 4   User 5

Fig. 3. Samples of virtual multimodal database.

Table 1. First rank identification rates of rank level fusions for k=1 and k=2

Fusion Method	Identification % for k=1	Identification % for k=2
Highest rank	88.32%	88.51%
Confidence based highest rank	93.42%	93.79%
Borda count	90.92%	91.35%
Confidence based Borda count	95.71%	96.12%
Logistic regression	92.32%	92.74%
Confidence based logistic regression	96.89%	97.41%

(depending on the availability) from each biometric of a virtual users for enrollment and taking the rest for the identification phase. Fig. 3 shows five samples of virtual users created using this approach. By following this approach, we have created 2,210 virtual persons in 10 different virtual databases where each database contains 216 individuals. Test queries for identification phase are created by pairing of test images from biometrics of each virtual person. For the performance evaluation of proposed method 98,500 test queries have been created.

Rank lists are created using the k-nearest neighbors classifier [19] for k equals 1 and 2. Table 1 demonstrates that there is a minor improvement in identification rate by using $k = 2$. Since there is not much differences between the identification rates for $k = 1$ and $k = 2$, we have considered $k = 1$ for the rest of experiments.

To demonstrate the performance of our fusion method, we used cumulative match characteristic (CMC) curve, which is a commonly used metric for evaluation of biometric systems. CMC is used to show the identification rate of the system at different ranks. The identification rate is the portion of times the system recognizes the true identity of the users. The CMC value for rank k is the

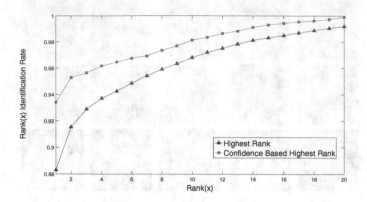

(a) CMC curves for highest rank with and without CBRLS.

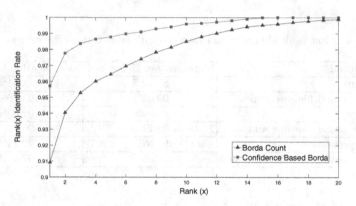

(b) CMC curves for Borda count with and without CBRLS

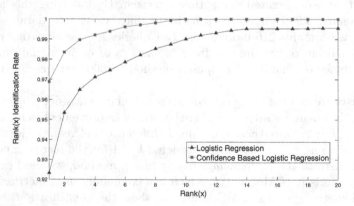

(c) CMC curves for logistic regression with and without CBRLS

Fig. 4. CMC curves for multimodal biometrics rank fusion with and without the use of confidence based rank list selection.

portion of times the true identity is among the first k users listed as the final result of the system.

Fig. 4 shows the CMC curves for highest rank, Borda count, and logistic regression with and without confidence based rank list selection (CBRLS). The comparison of three CMC curves for fusion without CBRLS reveal that logistic regression outperforms Borda count and highest rank while Borda count performs better than highest rank. The comparison of CMC curves in each sub-figure shows that CBRLS increases the first rank identification rate of highest rank by 5.1%, Borda count by 4.8%, and logistic regression by 4.6%. The highest first rank identification rate obtained using the system is 96.9% for CBRLS with logistic regression.

The experimental results are indicator of improvement of rank level fusions by incorporating confidence based rank list selection (CBRLS). The usage of CBRLS is not limited to the experimented fusion methods and it can be applied to any rank level fusion approach to improve the identification rate.

4 Conclusion

In this paper, a novel user based rank list selection for fusion of biometrics in rank level was introduced. The proposed algorithm recovered scores information by combining the rank list and the resemblance probability distribution of users. It calculated the confidence of each list based on pseudo-scores and selects rank lists based on the confidence they provide for any specific test query. The most important features of this approach are recovering the scores which are valuable information and also selecting the rank lists based on their performance for each user. The experimental results show the ability of the confidence based rank list selection to improve the identification rate for three well-known rank level fusions, i.e. highest rank, Borda count, and logistic regression. The highest first rank identification rate of the system was 96.9% for logistic regression with confidence based rank list selection which had improved the solo logistic regression by 4.6%. The confidence based rank list selection can be used with any rank level fusion method.

Acknowledgments. The authors would like to thank NSERC DISCOVERY program grant RT731064, URGC, NSERC ENGAGE and Alberta Ingenuity for partial support of this project.

References

1. Ross, A.A., Nandakumar, K., Jain, A.K.: Handbook of multibiometrics. Springer Science & Business Media (2006)
2. Jain, A.K., Flynn, P., Ross, A.A.: Handbook of biometrics. Springer Science & Business Media (2007)
3. Revett, K.: Behavioral biometrics: a remote access approach. John Wiley & Sons (2008)

4. Prabhakar, S., Jain, A.K.: Decision-level fusion in fingerprint verification. Pattern Recognition **35**(4), 861–874 (2002)
5. Mowar, M., Gavrilova, M.L.: Multimodal biometric system using rank-level fusion approach. IEEE Transactions on Systems, Man, and Cybernetics, Part B: Cybernetics **39**(4), 867–878 (2009)
6. Bhatnagar, J., Kumar, A., Saggar, N.: A novel approach to improve biometric recognition using rank level fusion. In: IEEE Conference on Computer Vision and Pattern Recognition, CVPR 2007, pp 1–6. IEEE (2007)
7. Kumar, A., Shekhar, S.: Personal identification using multibiometrics rank-level fusion. IEEE Transactions on Systems, Man, and Cybernetics, Part C: Applications and Reviews. **41**(5), 743–752 (2011)
8. Lee, Y.-J., Lee, K.-H., Jee, H., Gil, Y.H., Choi, W., Ahn, D., Pan, S.B.: Fusion for multimodal biometric identification. In: Kanade, T., Jain, A., Ratha, N.K. (eds.) AVBPA 2005. LNCS, vol. 3546, pp. 1071–1079. Springer, Heidelberg (2005)
9. Monwar, M.M., Gavrilova, M., Wang, Y.: A novel fuzzy multimodal information fusion technology for human biometric traits identification. In: 2011 10th IEEE International Conference on Cognitive Informatics & Cognitive Computing (ICCI* CC), pp. 112–119. IEEE (2011)
10. Marasco, E., Abaza, A., Cukic, B.: Why rank-level fusion? and what is the impact of image quality?
11. Abaza, A., Ross, A.: Quality based rank-level fusion in multibiometric systems. In: IEEE 3rd International Conference on Biometrics: Theory, Applications, and Systems, BTAS 2009, pp. 1–6. IEEE (2009)
12. Alam, M.R., Bennamoun, M., Togneri, R., Sohel, F.: Confidence-based rank-level fusion for audio-visual person identification system. In: 3rd International Conference on Pattern Recognition Applications and Methods, 2014, pp. 608–615 (2014)
13. Belhumeur, P.N., Hespanha, J.P., Kriegman, D.: Eigenfaces vs. fisherfaces: recognition using class specific linear projection. IEEE Transactions on Pattern Analysis and Machine Intelligence **19**(7), 711–720 (1997)
14. Talebi, H., Gavrilova, M.: Prior resemblance probability of users for multimodal biometrics rank fusion. In: IEEE International Conference on Identity, Security and Behavior Analysis (ISBA 2015). IEEE (2015)
15. Monwar, M., Gavrilova, M.: Fes: a system for combining face, ear and signature biometrics using rank level fusion. In: Fifth International Conference on Information Technology: New Generations, 2008, pp. 922–927. IEEE (2008)
16. Bhattacharyya, A.: On a measure of divergence between two multinomial populations. Sankhyā: The Indian Journal of Statistics, 401–406 (1946)
17. Phillips, P.J., Wechsler, H., Huang, J., Rauss, P.J.: The feret database and evaluation procedure for face-recognition algorithms. Image and Vision Computing **16**(5), 295–306 (1998)
18. USTB ear database, china. http://www.ustb.edu.cn/resb/ (accessed May 11, 2008)
19. Cover, T., Hart, P.: Nearest neighbor pattern classification. IEEE Transactions on Information Theory **13**(1), 21–27 (1967)

Optical Flow Computation with Locally Quadratic Assumption

Tomoya Kato[1], Hayato Itoh[1], and Atsushi Imiya[2(⊠)]

[1] School of Advanced Integration Science, Chiba University, Chiba, Japan
[2] Institute of Management and Information Technologies,
Chiba University, Yayoi-cho 1-33, Inage-ku, Chiba 263-8522, Japan
imiya@faculty.chiba-u.jp

Abstract. The purpose of this paper is twofold. First, we develop a quadratic tracker which computes a locally quadratic optical flow field by solving a model-fitting problem for each point in its local neighbourhood. This local method allows us to select a region of interest for the optical flow computation. Secondly, we propose a method to compute the transportation of a motion field in long-time image sequences using the Wasserstein distance for cyclic distributions. This measure evaluates the motion coherency in an image sequence and detects collapses of smoothness of the motion vector field in an image sequence.

1 Introduction

In this paper, we develop a method to compute a locally quadratic optical flow field. Furthermore, we propose a method to evaluate the global smoothness and continuity of motion fields and detect collapses of smoothness of the motion fields in long-time image sequences using the Wasserstein distance for cyclic distributions [2,7,10].

In ref. [13], using the local stationarity of visual motion, a linear method for motion tracking was introduced. The Lucas-Kanade (LK) method was proposed as an image-matching and -registration method assuming that the deformation field between images is locally constant. Subsequently, the method has been widely used for fast optical flow computation [11].

It is possible to extend the local assumption on the optical flow field to higher-order constraints on the motion field. In this paper, we assume that optical flow fields are locally quadratic. This local property of the optical flow field allows us to decompose an optical flow computation scheme to a collection of systems of linear equations defined in the neighbourhood of each point. The size of the system-matrix of each system of linear equations is 14×14, where 14 is the number of parameters used to describe a locally quadratic vector field on a plane. Furthermore, this decomposition property also allows us to select regions of interest for the optical flow computation and to construct a parallel method which computes the optical flow vectors of all points simultaneously.

For the computation of the three-dimensional scene flow from a stereo image sequence [4,5,6], we are required to solve four image-matching problems and

© Springer International Publishing Switzerland 2015
G. Azzopardi and N. Petkov (Eds.): CAIP 2015, Part I, LNCS 9256, pp. 223–234, 2015.
DOI: 10.1007/978-3-319-23192-1_19

their deformation fields. Two of them are optical flow computations for left and right image sequences. The other two of them are stereo matching for two successive stereo pairs. The displacements between stereo pairs are at most locally affine transformations caused by perspective projections based on the camera geometry. The displacement between a pair of successive images in left and right sequences, however, involves higher-order transformations caused by camera motion if a pair of cameras is mounted on a mobile vehicle. Therefore, since we are required to adopt different-order constraints on the optical flow computation and stereo matching for a stereo pair sequence, we develop a method with locally higher-order constraints for the fast computation of the optical flow field.

The Wasserstein distance defines a metric among probability measures [10]. In computer vision and pattern recognition, the 1-Wasserstein [2] distance is known as the earth movers' distance (EMD). We deal with the distribution of optical flow vectors as directional statistics [3]. Then, using the Wasserstein distance for cyclic distributions [7], we evaluate the temporal total transportation between a pair of successive optical flow fields. If the motion in an image sequence has a constant speed, this transportation measure between a pair of successive images is zero. Therefore, we use this temporal transportation of the flow fields as a measure to evaluate motion smoothness and continuity. Ustundag-Unel [15] and Chaudhry et. al. [16] analysed human motion using the orientation histogram of the optical flow field. There histogram is based on the histogram of oriented gradient (HoG) method [14] although we deal with the directional statistics to compute the temporal transportation of the optical flow fields.

Although classical optical flow computation methods [1,12] are based on least-squares optimisation, the total variation (TV) of the solution as a prior [20,17] and the L_1-constraint allow us to deal with the sparsity of images. The TV-L_1 minimisation for optical flow computation is solved by the primal-dual method [19]. There are a number of numerical schemes for (TV-L_1)-based image analysis [21,22]. These methods minimise a criterion defined over the whole image [19].

On the other hand, by dividing the region of interest into windowed areas and assuming that the optical flow field is locally quadratic in each region, our method solves a large system of diagonal linear equations. Furthermore, the local method allows us to select a region of interest for the optical flow computation, because the method computes the optical flow for each point in its local neighbourhood with a local constraint on the optical flow field [18].

2   Local Optical Flow Computation

For $f(x, y, t)$, the optical flow vector [12] $\boldsymbol{u} = \dot{\boldsymbol{x}} = (\dot{x}, \dot{y})^\top$, where $\dot{x} = u = u(x, y)$ and $\dot{y} = v = v(x, y)$, of each point $\boldsymbol{x} = (x, y)^\top$ is the solution of the singular equation

$$f_x u + f_y v + f_t = \nabla f^\top \boldsymbol{u} + \partial_t f = \boldsymbol{J}^\top \boldsymbol{u} + f_t = 0. \tag{1}$$

Assuming u to be constant in the neighbourhood $\Omega(x)$ of point x [12], the optical flow vector is the minimiser of the criterion

$$E_0 = \frac{1}{2|\Omega(x)|} \int_{\Omega(x)} |J^\top u + f_t|^2 dx = \frac{1}{2} uGu + a^\top u + \frac{1}{2} c, \qquad (2)$$

where $J = (f_x, f_y)^\top$, for

$$G = \frac{1}{|\Omega(x)|} \int_{\Omega(x)} J^\top J dx, \qquad (3)$$

$$a = \frac{1}{|\Omega(x)|} \int_{\Omega(x)} f_t \nabla f dx, \quad c = \frac{1}{|\Omega(x)|} \int_{\Omega(x)} |f_t|^2 dx. \qquad (4)$$

If the displacement is locally affine such that $u = Dx + d$, where D and d are a 2×2 matrix and a two-dimensional vector, we estimate D and d which minimise the criterion [1]

$$E_1 = \frac{1}{2} \cdot \frac{1}{|\Omega(x)|} \int_{\Omega(x)} |J^\top (Dx + d) + f_t|^2 dy$$

$$= \frac{1}{2} \cdot \frac{1}{|\Omega(x)|} \int_{\Omega(x)} |(J, (x^\top \otimes J)) + f_t|^2 d, \ v_{(1)} = \begin{pmatrix} d \\ vecD \end{pmatrix} \qquad (5)$$

as an extension of eq. (2). From the relation $\frac{\partial E_1}{\partial v_{(1)}} = 0$, we have the system of linear equations

$$A_{(1)} v_{(1)} + b_{(1)} = 0 \qquad (6)$$

for

$$A_{(1)} = \begin{pmatrix} G, & x^\top \otimes G \\ x \otimes G, & (xx^\top) \otimes G \end{pmatrix}, \ v_{(1)} = \begin{pmatrix} d \\ vecD \end{pmatrix}, \ b_{(1)} = \begin{pmatrix} a \\ x \otimes a \end{pmatrix} \qquad (7)$$

for the point x which is the centre point of the windowed area $\Omega(x)$.

The piecewise quadratic optical flow field is expressed as

$$u = \begin{pmatrix} x^\top Px \\ x^\top Qx \end{pmatrix} + Dx + d = (e \otimes x)^\top Diag(P, Q)(e \otimes x) + Dx + d \qquad (8)$$

for 2×2 symmetric matrices P and Q, a 2×2 matrix D and a two-dimensional vector d. Therefore, the minimiser of the criterion

$$E_2 = \frac{1}{2|\Omega(x)|} \int_{\Omega(x)} \left| J^\top \left(\begin{pmatrix} x^\top Px \\ x^\top Qx \end{pmatrix} + Dx + d \right) + f_t \right|^2 dy \qquad (9)$$

is the the matrix equation

$$G_{(2)} v_{(2)} + b_{(2)} = 0 \qquad (10)$$

---

[1]   The matrix equation $AXB = C$ is replaced to the linear system of equations $(B^\top \otimes A)vecX = vecC$.

at each point x, for

$$G_{(2)} = \begin{pmatrix} G, & x^\top \otimes G, & x_\otimes^\top \otimes GX_\otimes^\top \\ x \otimes \bar{G}, & (xx^\top) \otimes G, & (xx_\otimes^\top) \otimes GX_\otimes^\top \\ x_\otimes \otimes X_\otimes G, & (x_\otimes x^\top) \otimes X_\otimes G, & (x_\otimes x_\otimes^\top) \otimes X_\otimes GX_\otimes^\top \end{pmatrix}$$

$$v_{(2)} = \begin{pmatrix} d \\ vecD \\ vecC \end{pmatrix}, \quad b_{(2)} = \begin{pmatrix} a \\ x \otimes a \\ ((xx_\otimes^\top) \otimes X)a \end{pmatrix}, \tag{11}$$

where $e = (1,1)^\top$, $C = Diag(P, Q)$, $x_\otimes = e \otimes x$, $X_\otimes = I \otimes x$ and I is the 2×2 identity matrix. This matrix equation is used for the computation of the piecewise quadratic field as an extension of the LK method. For numerical experiment, we set $\Omega(c) = \{x \mid |x - c|_\infty \leq k\}$, for a positive integer k, where $|x|_\infty$ is the l_∞ norm on the plane $\mathbf{R}^2$. Therefore, in eq. (11), we set $x := x - c$ for the computation of the optical flow vector of point c.

3 l_2^2-l_2 Optimisation

For the computation of the local optical flow field, we deal with the minimisation of the functional

$$J_{2221}(x) = \frac{1}{2}|Ax + b|_2^2 + \lambda|x|_2, \tag{12}$$

where we set $A := G \backslash G_{(2)}$, $x := u \backslash v_{(2)}$ and $b := b \backslash v_{(2)}$. Since the functional derivative of J_{2221} with respect to x is

$$\frac{\delta J_{2221}(x)}{\delta x} = A^\top (Ax + b) + \lambda \frac{x}{|x|_2}, \tag{13}$$

the minimiser of eq. (12) is the solution of

$$(A^\top A + \frac{\lambda}{|x|_2} I)x = A^\top b. \tag{14}$$

We compute the solution of eq. (14) using the iteration form

$$A^\top A x^{(n)} = b^{(n)}, \quad b^{(n)} = A^\top b - \frac{\lambda}{|x^{(n-1)}|_2} x^{(n-1)} \tag{15}$$

until $|x^{(n+1)} - x^{(n)}|_2 < \epsilon$, where

$$x^{(n)} = (A^\top A - \lambda^{(n)} I)^{-1} A^\top b, \quad \lambda^{(n)} = \frac{\lambda}{|x^{(n-1)}|} \tag{16}$$

This procedure is performed in Algorithm 1. In this algorithm, $x(i)$ expresses the ith element of vector x.

Algorithm 1. $l_2^2 - l_2$ Minimisation

Data: $x^0 := 1$, $k := 0$, $0 \leq \delta \ll 1$, $0 < \epsilon$
Result: minimiser of $\frac{1}{2}|Ax - b|_2^2 + \lambda|x|_2$
while $|x^{(k)} - x^{(k-1)}|_2 > \delta$ **do**
$\quad$ $\lambda^{(k-1)} := \frac{\lambda}{|x^{(k-1)}|_2}$;
$\quad$ solve $(A^\top A + \lambda^{(k)} I)x^{(k)} = A^\top b$;
$\quad$ **if** $x^{(k)}(i) = 0$ **then**
$\quad\quad$ $x^{(k)}(i) := x^{(k)}(i) + \epsilon$;
$\quad$ **end**
$\quad$ $k := k + 1$
end

We call this method of the optical flow computation the $l_2^2 - l_2$ quadratic Kanade-Lucas-Tomasi tracker (2221QKLT tracker). Moreover, to ensure stable and robust computation, we use the pyramid-transform-based [8,9] multiple resolution method described in Algorithm 2. We call the method based on Algorithm 2 the pyramid-based 2221QKLT (2221PQKLT) tracker.

Algorithm 2. Quadratic-Optical-Flow Computation with Gaussian Pyramid

---

Data: $u^{L+1} := 0$, $L \geq 0$, $l := L$
Data: $f_k^L \cdots f_k^0$
Data: $f_{k+1}^L \cdots f_{k+1}^0$
Result: optical flow u_k^0
while $l \geq 0$ **do**
$\quad$ $f_{k+1}^l := f_{k+1}^l(\cdot + E(u_k^{l+1}), k + 1)$;
$\quad$ compute C_k^l, D_k^l and d_k^l ;
$\quad$ $u_k^l := x_1^{l\top} C_k^l x_1^l + D_k^l x^l + d_k^l$;
$\quad$ $l := l - 1$
end

---

4   Transportation of Motion Direction

We define the coherency of motion along the time axis and in a scene. Then, we introduce a measure for the evaluation of the coherency of motion in an image sequence.

Definition 1. *If a vector field on an image generated by the motion of a scene and moving objects is spatially and temporally smooth, we call this property of the field motion coherency.*

Therefore, rapid changes in the spatial direction of motion causes collapses of motion coherency on the imaging plane, even if the spatial motion of the object is smooth. Moreover, the sudden halting of a moving object destroys motion smoothness and causes the collapses of the motion coherency.

The p-Wasserstein distance between a pair of distributions $f(x)$ and $g(y)$ for $x \in X$ and $y \in Y$ is

$$W_p(f,g) = \left(\min_c \int_X \int_Y |f(x) - g(y)|^p c(x,y) dx dy \right)^{\frac{1}{p}}. \tag{17}$$

For discrete probabilistic distributions $F = \{f_i\}_{i=1}^n$ and $G = \{g_j\}_{j=1}^n$ such that $\sum_{i=1}^n f_i = 1$ and $\sum_{i=1}^n g_i = 1$, setting $d_{ij} = |f_i - g_j|^p$, the distance between distributions F and G is computed as

$$DW_p(F,G) = \min_{x_{ij}} \left(\sum_{i=1}^n \sum_{j=1}^n d_{ij} x_{ij} \right) \tag{18}$$

subject to the conditions $\sum_{i=1}^n x_{ij} = f_i$, $\sum_{j=1}^n x_{ij} = g_j$ and $x_{ij} \geq 0$. The minimisation is achieved by solving the linear programming for transportation problem. DW_1 is called the earth mover's distance in computer vision and pattern recognition.

Setting $f(t) \geq 0$ and $g(t) \geq 0$ to be cyclic distributions on $[0, 2\pi]$, the Wasserstein distance for the cyclic distributions $f(s + 2\pi) = f(x)$ and $g(t + 2\pi) = g(t)$ is

$$CW_p(f,g) = \left(\min_{c,\theta} \int_0^{2\pi} \int_0^{2\pi} |f(t) - g(s - \theta)|^p c(t,s) dt ds \right)^{\frac{1}{p}}, \tag{19}$$

where $\int_0^{2\pi} f(t) dt = 1$ and $\int_0^{2\pi} g(t) dt = 1$. For the discrete cyclic distributions $F_c = \{f_i\}_{i=0}^{N-1}$ and $G_c = \{g_i\}_{i=0}^{N-1}$, such that $f_{i+N} = f_i$ and $g_{j+N} = g_j$, eq. (19) becomes

$$DCW_p(F_c, G_c) = \left(\min_{c_{ij}, k} \sum_{i=0}^{N-1} \sum_{j=0}^{N-1} |p_i - q_{j-k}|^p c_{ij} \right)^{\frac{1}{p}}. \tag{20}$$

Therefore, setting

$$D_k = \sum_{i=0}^{N-1} \sum_{j=0}^{N-1} d_{ijk} c_{ij}, \quad d_{ijk} = |f_i - g_{j-k}|^p, \tag{21}$$

we have the relation

$$DCW_p(F_c, G_c) = (\min_k D_k)^{\frac{1}{p}}. \tag{22}$$

We apply $CDW_p(F, G)$ to compute the transportation distance between the directional statistics F and G.

For a vector-valued function $f(x)$ such that $x \in \mathbf{R}^n$, setting $d = \hat{f}(\omega; x)$ $\omega \in S^{n-1}$, to be the spherical expression of f at point x, we construct the directional statistics of f at the point $a \in \mathbf{R}^n$ as

$$h(\omega; \boldsymbol{a}, \alpha) = d, \ \boldsymbol{x} \in \Omega_{\alpha,r}(\boldsymbol{a}) \tag{23}$$

for $\Omega_{\alpha,r}(\boldsymbol{a}) = \{\boldsymbol{x} | \ |\boldsymbol{x} - \boldsymbol{a}|_\alpha \leq r\}$, where $|\boldsymbol{x}|_\alpha$ is the l_α-norm.

From the temporal optical flow field $\boldsymbol{u}(\boldsymbol{x}, t)$, we define

$$u^d(\theta; \boldsymbol{a}, t, \alpha) = \sqrt{u(x,y)^2 + v^2(x,y)}, \ \theta = \tan^{-1} \frac{v(x,y)}{u(x,y)} \tag{24}$$

for $\boldsymbol{x} = (x, y)^\top \in \Omega_{\alpha,r}(\boldsymbol{a})$. For the evaluation of motion coherency, we define

$$W(t, k) = \frac{1}{|\mathbf{A}|} \int_{\boldsymbol{y} \in \mathbf{A} \subset \mathbf{R}^2} \int_{\Omega_{r,\alpha}(\boldsymbol{y})} CW_p(u^d(\theta; \boldsymbol{x}, t+1, \alpha), u^d(\theta; \boldsymbol{x}, t, \alpha)) d\boldsymbol{x} d\boldsymbol{y}. \tag{25}$$

If the motion along an image sequence has a constant speed, the transportation of the optical flow field between a pair of successive images is zero. We use this transportation computed as the Wasserstein distance along flow fields as a measure to evaluate the motion smoothness along an image sequence.

In our numerical examples, we set $\alpha = \infty$ on $\mathbf{R}^2$ and 2. Furthermore, for the sampled optical flow fields, $\Omega_{1,r}(\boldsymbol{a})$ is the 7×7 neighbourhood of each point. Figure 1 shows the procedure for the construction of the directional statistics. Moreover, we set $N = 16$ for cyclic histograms, that is, we devide the $0 \leq \theta < 2\pi$ to $\frac{\pi}{8}i \leq \theta < \frac{\pi}{8}(i+1)$ for $i = 0, 1, \cdots, 15$.

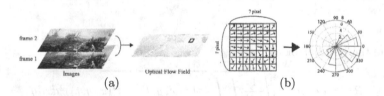

Fig. 1. Construction of directional statistics from optical flow field. (a) The optical flow field is computed from a pair of successive images from an image sequence. (b) For each point, directional statistics is constructed from flow vectors in the 7×7 neighbourhood of the point.

5   Numerical Examples

5.1   Effects of Window Size and Pyramid Hierarchy Level

Before the frame-wise evaluation, we evaluated the effects of the regularisation parameter, the size of the windows and the level of the pyramid hierarchy using the temporal continuity of the optical flow fields. For the evaluation of temporal continuity, we use the warp error (RMS error) and the temporal derivative. For the flow vector $\boldsymbol{u}(x, y, t) = (u, v)^\top$, setting

$$f'(x, y, t) = f(x - u, y - v, t + 1), \tag{26}$$

Table 1. RMS error of 2221PQKLT tracker for Motorway sequence. These experiments imply that the preferred window size and the pyramid hierarchy level for accurate and stable computation of the optical flow are 7×7 and 6. The preferred regularisation parameter λ is 0.5.

	Pyramid Level	2			4			6		
		Window Size			Window Size			Window Size		
	λ	3×3	7×7	11×11	3×3	7×7	11×11	3×3	7×7	11×11
	0.2	37.8	34.5	33.2	32.1	31.7	31.7	33.8	33.2	33.1
	0.5	37.8	34.5	33.2	32.1	31.7	31.7	33.8	33.2	33.1
	0.7	37.8	34.5	33.2	32.1	31.7	31.7	33.8	33.2	33.1
	1.0	37.8	34.5	33.2	32.1	31.7	31.7	33.8	33.2	33.1
KLT	2.0	37.8	34.5	33.2	32.1	31.7	31.7	33.8	33.2	33.1
	10.0	37.8	34.5	33.2	32.1	31.7	31.7	33.8	33.2	33.1
	Pyramid Level	2			4			6		
		Window Size			Window Size			Window Size		
	λ	3×3	7×7	11×11	3×3	7×7	11×11	3×3	7×7	11×11
	0.2	35.5	33.7	33.3	31.8	31.4	31.3	32.2	31.8	31.8
	0.5	35.5	33.7	33.3	31.8	31.4	31.3	32.2	31.8	31.8
	0.7	35.5	33.7	33.3	31.8	31.4	31.3	32.2	31.8	31.8
	1.0	35.5	33.7	33.3	31.8	31.4	31.3	32.2	31.8	31.8
QKLT	2.0	35.5	33.7	33.3	31.8	31.4	31.3	32.2	31.8	31.8
	10.0	35.5	33.7	33.3	31.8	31.4	31.3	32.2	31.8	31.8

we define the RMS error as

$$RMS\ error = \sqrt{\frac{1}{|A|} \int\int_{x \in A} (f(x,y,t) - f'(x,y,t))^2 dxdy} \qquad (27)$$

in the region of interest A at time t, where $|A|$ is the area measure of region A.

Tables 1 and 2 list the least mean errors and angle errors, respectively, for several window sizes and pyramid levels for the Motorway sequence. These results indicate that for all window sizes and pyramid levels, the performance of the 2221PQKLT tracker is superior to that of KLT tracker. These results imply the the preferred window size and pyramid hierarchy level for accurate and stable computation of the optical flow field are 7×7 and 6, respectively. Moreover, the preferred regularisation parameter λ is 0.5.

5.2   Performance of Motion Recognition

In the top row of Fig. 2, from left ot right, single images from the Crazy turn, Motorway and CloseObject sequences, respectively, are shown. The second and third rows of Fig. 2, colour charts of the optical flow fields and radar charts of the directional statistics, respectivey, are shown. Figure 3 shows the result for the

Table 2. Motorway Angle error of 2221QKLT tracker ($\lambda = 0.5$). These experiments imply that the preferred window size and the pyramid hierarchy for accurate and stable computation of the optical flow are 7×7 and 6, respectively.

		Window Size		
	Pyramid Level	3×3	7×7	11×11
KLT	2	1.72×10^{-1}	1.67×10^{-1}	1.67×10^{-1}
	4	1.58×10^{-1}	1.52×10^{-1}	1.52×10^{-1}
	6	1.47×10^{-1}	1.44×10^{-1}	1.43×10^{-1}
		Window Size		
	Pyramid Level	3×3	7×7	11×11
QKLT	2	1.66×10^{-1}	1.52×10^{-1}	1.50×10^{-1}
	4	1.53×10^{-1}	1.45×10^{-1}	1.44×10^{-1}
	6	1.42×10^{-1}	1.41×10^{-1}	1.41×10^{-1}

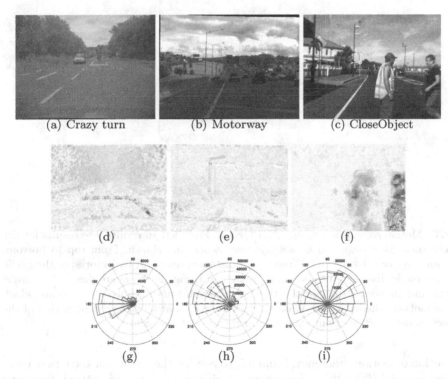

(a) Crazy turn   (b) Motorway   (c) CloseObject

(d)   (e)   (f)

(g)   (h)   (i)

Fig. 2. Images from Crazy turn, Motorway and CloseObject data sets. In the first row, From left ot right, single images from the Crazy turn, Motorway and CloseObject sequences, respectively. In the second and third rows, colour charts of the optical flow fields and radar charts of the directional statistics, respectivey.

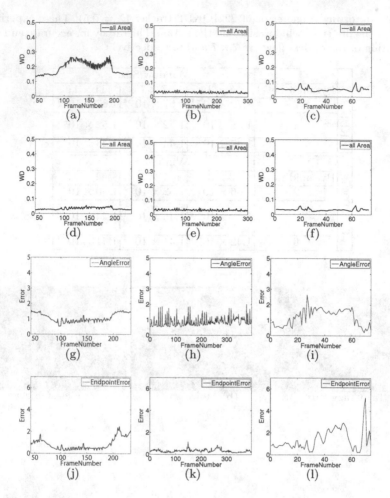

Fig. 3. Motion recognition using 2221PQKLT. From left to results, the results for the Crazy turn, Motorway and CloseObject sequences are shown. From top to bottom, temporal trajectories of the 2-Wasserstain distance, temporal trajectories of the cyclic 2-Wasserstain distance, the end point errors and the angle errors are shown. The angle errors and endpoint errors in the third and fourth rows do not detect events which brake motion coherency. The Wasserstein distance evaluates the transportation of the allows to detect events from transition of the optical flow field.

detection of motion coherency. From left to results, the results for the Crazy turn, Motorway and CloseObject sequences are shown. From top to bottom, temporal trajectories of the 2-Wasserstain distance, temporal trajectories of the cyclic 2-Wasserstain distance, the end point errors and the angle errors are shown. The window size and hierarchy of pyramid transform are 7×7 and 6, respectively.

If the motion displacement in a sequence of images is coherent, the transportation of directions of flow vectors is small, and the Wasserstein distance of the flow fields between a pair of successive images is small.

For the Crazy turn, Motorway and CloseObject sequences the optical flow fields and the radar charts of 184th, 127th and 35th frames, respectively are shown on the first in Fig. 2. In the Crazy turn and CloseObject sequences turn of a car and motion of men are captured around 184th and 34th frames, respectively.

In the Crazy turn sequence, a car with a mounted camera system turns to the left. This event is detected as a mode stated around 100th frame in trajectory of the Wasserstein distance. However, trajectory of the cyclic Wasserstein distance processes any modes. This statistical property implies that in a sequence object turns with a constant speed. The cyclic Wasserstein distance removes the appearance motion on an image screen. as shown in Fig. 3. Therefore, the transportation of the direction statics of optical flow fields allows us to detect the collapses of motion coherency on a screen in a sequence of images. In the Motorway sequence, cars in the opposite lane periodically moves toward the car-mounted camera then disappear, and cars in the same lane periodically move in front of the car-mounted camera. The temporal trajectory of the Wasserstein distance allows us to detect the temporal transportation of the optical flow fields as small periodic peaks in the temporal trajectory. In the CloseObject sequence, two men cross in front of a car. This event is detected as a peak of the temporal trajectory around 20th frame as shown in Fig. 3(c).

The angle errors and endpoint errors in the third and fourth rows in Fig. 3 do not detect events which brake motion coherency, since these errors evaluate the pointwise accuracy of the computed optical flow vectors. On the other hand, since the Wasserstein distance evaluates the transportation of the optical flow field, the distance allows to detect events from transition of the optical flow field. These results show that the Wasserstein distance of the directional statistics of an optical flow field sequence is an effective measure for the evaluation of motion coherency and its collapses in a sequence of images.

6   Conclusions

In this paper, by extending the KLT tracker, we develop a locally quadratic tracker for the motion analysis of long-time image sequences. The method computes locally quadratic optical flow fields using a model-fitting scheme. Furthermore, the method can select a region of interest for the optical flow computation.

References

1. Horn, B.K.P., Schunck, B.G.: Determining optical flow. Artificial Intelligence **17**, 185–204 (1981)
2. Rubner, Y., Tomasi, C., Guibas, L.J.: A metric for distributions with applications to image databases. In: Proceedings of ICCV 1998, pp. 59–66 (1998)

3. Fisher, N.I.: Statistical Analysis of Circular Data. Cambridge University Press (1993)
4. Wedel, A., Cremers, D.: Stereo Scene Flow for 3D Motion Analysis. Springer (2011)
5. Vogel, Ch., Schindler, K., Roth, S.L.: Piecewise rigid scene flow. In: Proceedings of ICCV 2013, pp. 1377–1384 (2013)
6. Vogel, Ch., Schindler, K., Roth, S.: 3D scene flow estimation with a rigid motion prior. In:`Proceedings of ICCV 2011, pp. 1291–1298 (2011)
7. Rabin, J., Delon, J., Gousseau, Y.: Transportation distances on the circle. JMIV 41, 147–167 (2011)
8. Hwang, S.-H., Lee, U.-K.: A hierarchical optical flow estimation algorithm based on the interlevel motion smoothness constraint. Pattern Recognition 26, 939–952 (1993)
9. Amiaz, T., Lubetzky, E., Kiryati, N.: Coarse to over-fine optical flow estimation. Pattern Recognition 40, 2496–2503 (2007)
10. Villani, C.: Optimal Transport, Old and New. Springer (2009)
11. Baker, S., Matthews, I.: Lucas-Kanade 20 years On: A unifying framework. IJCV 56, 221–255 (2004)
12. Lucas, B.D., Kanade, T.: An iterative image registration technique with an application to stereo vision. In: Proceedings of IJCAI 1981, pp. 674–679 (1981)
13. Shi, J., Tomasi, C.: Good features to track. In: Proceedings of CVPR 1994, pp. 593–600 (1994)
14. Dalal, N., Triggs, B.: Histograms of oriented gradients for human detection. In: Proceedings of CVPR 2005 (2005)
15. Ustundag, B.C., Unel, M.: Human action recognition using histograms of oriented optical flows from depth. In: Bebis, G., et al. (eds.) ISVC 2014, Part I. LNCS, vol. 8887, pp. 629–638. Springer, Heidelberg (2014)
16. Chaudhry, R., Ravichandran, A., Hager, G.D., Vidal, R.: Histograms of oriented optical flow and binet-cauchy kernels on nonlinear dynamical systems for the recognition of human actions. In: Proceedings of CVPR 2009, pp. 1932–1939 (2009)
17. Mileva, Y., Bruhn, A., Weickert, J.: Illumination-robust variational optical flow with photometric invariants. In: Hamprecht, F.A., Schnörr, C., Jähne, B. (eds.) DAGM 2007. LNCS, vol. 4713, pp. 152–162. Springer, Heidelberg (2007)
18. Bruhn, A., Weickert, J., Schnörr, C.: Lucas/Kanade meets Horn/Schunck: Combining local and global optic flow methods. IJCV 61, 211–231 (2005)
19. Zach, C., Pock, T., Bischof, H.: A duality based approach for realtime TV-L^1. In: Hamprecht, F.A., Schnörr, C., Jähne, B. (eds.) DAGM 2007. LNCS, vol. 4713, pp. 214–223. Springer, Heidelberg (2007)
20. Papenberg, N., Bruhn, A., Brox, T., Didas, S., Weickert, J.: Highly accurate optic flow computation with theoretically justified warping. IJCV 67, 141–158 (2006)
21. Shin, Y.-Y., Chang, O.-S., Xu, J.: Convergence of fixed point iteration for deblurring and denoising problem. Applied Mathematics and Computation 189, 1178–1185 (2007)
22. Chambolle, A.: An algorithm for total variation minimization and applications. JMIV 20, 89–97 (2004)

Pose Normalisation for 3D Vehicles

Trevor Farrugia[✉] and Jonathan Barbarar

Saint Martin's Institute of Higher Education, Hamrun, Malta
{tfarrugia,jbarbara}@stmartins.edu

Abstract. This study[1] investigates the various pose normalisation techniques that can be used for 3D vehicle models. A framework is built on which the pose normalisation performance of four PCA based techniques are tested on a database of 335 3D vehicles. The evaluation is performed using two methods. In the first method a silhouette view of each pose normalised vehicle is rendered from a consitent point in the 3D space. The pose consitency of each vehicle is then compared to the silhouettes of the vehicles in the same category. The second method compares the direct influence of the four techniques on the final precision and recall results of a search algorithm based on a simple scan-line feature descriptor. Results from both methods show that Center-of-Gravity PCA and Continous-PCA performed noticably better then PCA and Normal-PCA. The superiority of Continous-PCA over Center-of-Gravity PCA was negligible.

Keywords: Pose normalisation · Principal component analysis · Normal PCA · Centre of gravity PCA · Continous PCA · 3D vehicle · 3D model alignment · Vehicle recognition · Vehicle classification · Symmetry normalisation

1 Introduction

Recent advances in 3D technologies have prompted a huge surge in the number of available digital 3D models. This has in turn led to an increase in interest for new algrithms that can sort, retrieve and normalise the pose of 3D models. 3D Model processing algorithms, such as those used in 3D model retrieval, are often more efficient when applied on a pose normalised set of models. Although several algorithms have been proposed for pose normalisation on inter-class 3D model databases, few researchers have focused on the problem of pose normalisation for Intra-class 3D models.

3D vehicles are amongst the most popular types of 3D models and are used in various domains such as gaming, animation, vehicle design and vehicle recognition. The rest of this paper focuses on comparing the various algorithms that can be used to normalise the pose of an Intra-class 3D vehicle database.

---

[1] This work is based on a report submitted in partial fulfilment of the BSc (Hons) Creative Computing in the University of London International Programmes.

© Springer International Publishing Switzerland 2015
G. Azzopardi and N. Petkov (Eds.): CAIP 2015, Part I, LNCS 9256, pp. 235–245, 2015.
DOI: 10.1007/978-3-319-23192-1_20

A database of 3D models is commonly compiled from different sources and can therefore contain models of different scale, position and rotational orientation. Pose normalisation can be defined as the process which aligns all models to a common canonical orientation. It also ensures that the models are consistently scaled and positioned. While scale and translation normalisation can be easily computed with reliable results, as outlined in the next section, rotation normalisation is still a much researched problem.

2   Literature Review

Rotation normalisation techniques can be classified into two main categories. The first category consists of techniques based on the Principal Component Analysis algorithm while in the second category, rotation invariance is attained by computing the symmetrical planes of a 3D object.

2.1   Principal Component Analysis Based Techniques

Principal Component Analysis (PCA) is a technique used in various fields of computer science. Its use for the purpose of 3D mesh pose normalisation involves building a covariance matrix in which the element (i, j) represents the mesh's covariance between axes i and j. Since mesh representation is 3-dimensional, the covariance matrix is a 3 X 3 matrix. The three eigenvectors and eigenvalues of the covariance matrix are used to build a frame matrix which when cross multiplied with the 3D model's vertices will align the model to a canonical orientation. The frame matrix is composed of the eigenvectors sorted (highest to lowest) according to their corresponding eigenvalues. The eigenvector with the highest eigenvalue represents the direction at which the highest vertex variance (spread) occurs and is hence chosen as the principal component.

The coordinate values of the vertices in most 3D vehicle models have a predominant variance along three directions (shown in Fig. 1 below). This suggests that the Principal Component Analysis method is an adequate technique to align 3D vehicles to a canonical orientation.

Although the main concepts of the PCA technique indicate that it can be used for 3D mesh pose normalisation, various studies have shown that the technique

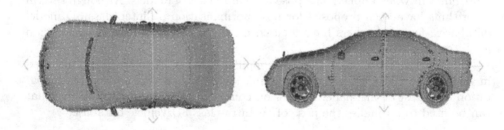

Fig. 1. Vertex coordinates of a 3D vehicle vary predominantly along 3 main directions.

in its raw form has deficiencies that may lead to inconsistent results. In [1] the authors affirm that since PCA does not take into account the distance between two neighbouring vertices, it is inefficient when aligning models in an intra-class database. Wei and Yuanjun [2] use PCA for rotation normalisation in their 3D model retrieval system and acknowledge that its performance is subject to the uniformity of the mesh's vertex point distribution. Finer detail in certain local areas results in a concentration of vertices in that area. That local part will therefore have an undesired dominant influence on the calculation of the principal components. Pears et al. [3] point out that another deficiency of PCA is that it does not provide reflection invariance.

These deficiencies in the PCA technique have prompted researchers to study modifications that can enhance the adequateness of PCA for 3D mesh pose normalisation. All variances of PCA described below differ from the original PCA only in the computation of the covariance matrix.

In [4] each vertex is weighted by the total area of the mesh triangles that have the same vertex as one of their points. Another method is to calculate the PCA over the Centre of Gravity of each mesh face rather than the actual vertices (CoG PCA) [5]. Each centre of gravity is then weighted by the area of the face it represents. In Normal-PCA (NPCA) technique [6], the principal axes are identified from the covariance of the mesh face normals rather than the vertex points. As in the CoG PCA method, each normal is weighted by the area of the triangle it represents. Napoleon and Sahbi [7] investigate rotation normalisation using both the NPCA and CoG PCA techniques. They present their global results in a table which shows that on their inter-class database of 3D models, CoG PCA has a slightly better performance than NPCA.

In the context of 3D vehicles, although the normal variance direction of a vehicle is fairly consistent, as shown in Fig. 2, models with more rounded shapes may be erroneously aligned.

The Continuous-PCA (CPCA) method is proposed by Vranic [8]. To overcome the issue of unbalanced point distribution Vranic applies PCA to an infinite continuous point set instead of the traditional discrete point set. This is done by using integrals of the mesh's triangular faces. Papadakis et al. [9] test CPCA against NPCA by adding different levels of noise to their 3D models database and conclude that NPCA is more robust to mesh noise than CPCA. Tangelder

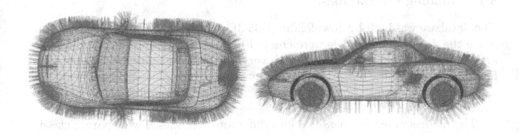

Fig. 2. Face normals of a Porsche Boxster.

and Veltkamp [10] rate CPCA as a better option than both conventional PCA and weighted PCA. Chaouch and Verroust-Blondet [11] claim that CPCA is the most complete and stable pose normalisation method compared to the ones they have studied. Axenopoulos et al. [12] present a table which shows the percentage of perfect alignment for different pose normalisation methods on the SHREC 2009 Generic shape benchmark [13]. The results are presented by classes of 3D models and the table shows that CPCA obtains 100 percent perfect alignment for the cars category.

2.2 Symmetry Based Techniques

Rotation normalisation can also be achieved by exploiting the symmetrical properties of the 3D shape. In such methods, the axes that best segment the model into two reflecting parts are used as principal axes. In their research on an intra-class retrieval system, Atmosukarto et al. [14] obtain pose normalisation of a human head by using the head's and face's symmetrical properties.

Axenopoulos et al. [12] obtain rotation normalisation through a combination of CPCA and reflective symmetry based methods. They point out that the calculation of the symmetry is a computational intensive process and is hence time inefficient. Sfikas et al. [15] outline another issue of symmetry based techniques. They state that such methods may detect symmetry in local parts of a 3D model and are hence inadequate for shapes which contain both global and local symmetrical properties.

The fact that 3D vehicles contain symmetrical properties would justify an investigation on the use of such methods for 3D vehicle pose normalisation. However, it must be noted that only one symmetrical plane can be precisely identified from the shape of a vehicle.

The vertex distribution of a 3D vehicle, substantiates this researchs rationale that PCA based techniques are the most appropriate pose normalisation methods for 3D vehicle models. On this basis, this research experimentally investigated which PCA based technique is most suitable to normalise the pose of 3D vehicles.

3   Method

3.1   Building the Database

The database was built by downloading 335 3D vehicles from DMI's website [16]. Since the downloaded models were created by a substantial number of different artists, the meshes vary from those with very fine detail to more simple ones with few vertices. The pose of the downloaded models was randomised by generating random scaling, translation and rotation matrices and applying them to the models.

The models were then classified into different categories. Two separate classifications were built individually by two adult human evaluators. After studying these two classifications, a third classification was built as a means of balance between them. This third classification was used as a base for the evaluation of the pose normalisation techniques. This method of classification is similar to the method used by Shilane et al. [17]. The final classification is illustrated in Table 1 of section 4.

3.2 Building the Evaluation Framework

The algorithm for each of the four evaluated pose normalisation techniques was implemented and applied to all the 3D models in the database. The resultant pose normalised models were then evaluated for each technique using two independent methods:

- Method 1 : In the first method the silhouettes of the normalised vehicles were visually examined and a statistical table was built, recording for each normalisation technique, the number of models consistently aligned with the other models in the same category.
- Method 2: The second method analyses the efficiency of the four techniques by comparing their direct influence on the final precision and recall results of a search algorithm based on a simple scan-line feature descriptor.

The utility tools presented by Shilane et al. [17] were used for the evaluation described in method 2 above. These tools take as input a distance matrix populated with similarity distances between all pairs of models in the database and automatically output precision/recall results.

An algorithm was developed which calculates the distance between two 3D objects based on a simple scan-line feature descriptor. This algorithm renders a silhouette image of each vehicle from a fixed angle in a 3D space in which the pose normalised 3D vehicle is placed. The silhouette image is then transformed into a 2D array representing the bitmap of the image. The bitmap images are then sampled along the x axis and the difference between the minimum and maximum y pixel positions that have a value of 0 (black) is calculated. These values are used as feature descriptors on which the difference between two models is calculated. Scale normalisation is obtained by dividing each sampled feature by the average value of all sampled features in the model. The distance matrix is then compiled by iteratively applying the developed alogirthm to all pair-wise combinations of models in the database.

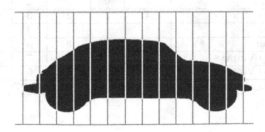

Fig. 3. Scan Line Feature Descriptor

4 Results

Table 1 was compiled by visually inspecting the silhouette rendering of the four pose normalisation techniques while Figure 4 illustrates the effect of each pose normalisation technique on the final Precision and Recall results

Table 1. Pose Normalisation Consistency Table

Class Name Level 1	Class Name Level 2	Total No. of Models	Max no. of models aligned with the other models in the same class			
			PCA	NPCA	CoG PCA	CPCA
Bus	Large Bus	4	4	2	2	2
	Mini Bus	4	4	2	2	2
Convertible	Classic Convertible	5	3	3	4	4
	Contemporary Convertible	12	5	10	9	9
HatchBack	90's HatchBack	6	4	4	6	6
	City Car HatchBack	3	2	3	3	3
	Classic HatchBack	8	5	7	8	8
	Contemporary HatchBack	28	14	26	26	26
Pick Up	Commercial Pickup	9	6	5	5	6
	Large Pickup	2	0	0	2	2
	Military Pickup	4	2	2	2	2
Sedan	90's Sedan	24	18	23	23	23
	Classic Sedan	4	2	3	4	4
	Contemporary Sedan	25	13	22	22	22
	Muscle Car Sedan	18	16	14	14	14
Sports Car	Classic Coupe	3	2	3	3	3
	Coupe	40	20	33	35	35
	Formula 1	10	7	10	10	10
	Rally Style	19	13	19	19	19
	Super Car	25	8	13	20	20
Station Wagon	Classic StationWagon	4	4	4	4	4
	Contemporary Station Wagon	7	5	7	7	7
SUV	Commercial Suv	18	9	18	18	18
	Military SUV	14	12	13	11	11
Truck	Box Truck	3	0	3	2	2
	Cab Over Engine Tractor	4	2	0	3	4
	Dump Truck	2	0	0	2	2
	Long Nose Tractor	4	3	2	3	3
Van	Large Van	8	8	4	4	4
	Small Van	4	3	3	3	3
Vintage	Hard Top Vintage	8	4	7	7	7
	Roof Less Vintage	6	3	3	5	5
	% of aligned models	**335**	**60**	**80**	**85.97**	**86.27**

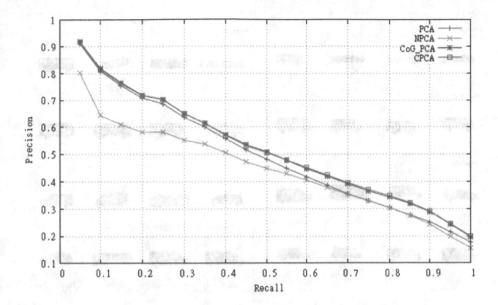

Fig. 4. Comparison of the normalisation techniques in Terms of Precision & Recall

5   Discussion

5.1   Method 1 - Pose Normalisation Consistency Table

The results in Table 1 show that, PCA was by far the most inconsistent technique. However, it performed better than the other three techniques for vehicles which had a high but narrow shape as in the case of buses and vans. This is demonstrated by the silhouette images in Fig. 5.

Overall, NPCA performed better PCA. NPCAs greatest inconsistency was in the Super Car category where vehicles have a very low but wide form. It managed to perform better than CoG PCA and CPCA in three classes namely, Contemporary Convertible, Military SUV and Box Truck although in all these three classes, the difference was only of 1 to 2 models.

CoG PCA performed better than both PCA and NPCA but obtained very similar results to CPCA. In actual fact, rather surprisingly, CPCA and CoG PCA produced exactly the same poses for all 3D vehicles except vehicle 307 Volvo FH12. This is illustrated in Fig. 6 below.

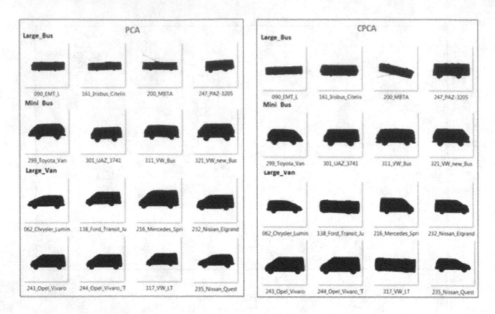

Fig. 5. PCA perfectly aligned the bus & van categories as opposed to CPCA

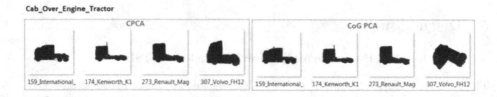

Fig. 6. The pose of model 307 was the tnly difference between CPCA and CoG PCA

5.2   Method 2 - Precision and Recall Results

As shown in Fig. 4 the final implemented system managed to obtain better results with PCA than with NPCA. This is contrasting with the results shown in the Pose Normalisation Consistency Table however, it is however explained by the fact that the results in the Pose Normalisation Consistency Table present a general analysis of the pose normalisation techniques on a 3D vehicle database and hence do not consider any pose invariance obtained by the feature descriptors implemented in method 2.

While compiling the Pose Normalisation Consistency table it was observed that most of the deficiencies of PCA consisted of incorrect reflection normalisation along the x and y axes. In this case the vehicle was still rendered as a side view but some were rendered from the left side while others projected the right side. In cases where the sides of the Y axis were inverted, the vehicles appeared capsized. As shown in Fig. 7 the feature descriptor and matching algorithms chosen for this research are invariant to inconsistencies of this type.

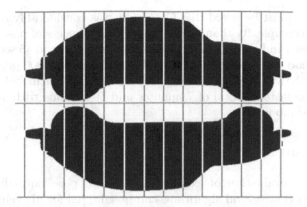

Fig. 7. Invariance to incorrect reflection normalisation along the Y axis. The lengths or the white lines in the top image are the same as those of the capsized image.

On the other hand as shown in Fig. 8, NPCA suffered from incorrect identification of the three axes. The scan-line feature descriptors used in this research is not invariant to this type of inconsistency.

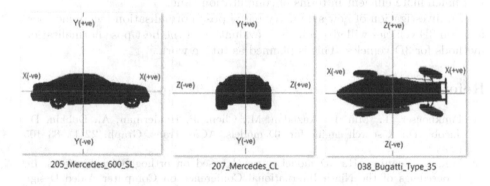

Fig. 8. Inconsistency in identifying the three axes.

Since it was claimed that the implemented system is invariant to the second category of inconsistencies mostly experienced by the PCA technique, it must be asked why PCA was not able to get equal or better Precision and Recall than CPCA and CoG PCA. The answer for this lies in the fact that PCA also suffered from inconsistent pitch rotation around the Z axis. This was much less of a problem for CPCA and CoG PCA.

The Precision and recall results of CoG PCA and CPCA confirm that for these two techniques, the observations made on the Pose Normalisation Consistency Table are also true in the context of the the scan-line 3D model retrieval algorithm. In fact, the optimal Precision and Recall was obtained using these two techniques and both techniques performed equally well.

Ultimately, it must be noted that CoG PCA was considerably more efficient in terms of time complexity than CPCA. In fact, the process of pose normalising all the 335 vehicles and saving them to disk took 6 minutes and 45 seconds for the CoG PCA method on a laptop with an Intel Core 2 Quad Q9000 processor and a 6GB DDR2 SDRAM. This is an average of 1.21 seconds per model. For CPCA, the same process lasted a total of 7 minutes and 59 seconds with an average of 1.43 seconds per model.

6   Conclusion

In this paper an evaluation of existing research on pose normalisation techniques suggested that several algorithms can be adapted for 3D vehicle retrieval however, PCA based algorithms were considered as the most appropriate. Four different PCA-based techniques were tested on a 3D vehicle database using two independent methods. Experimental results showed that PCA was inefficient when it comes to reflection normalisation along the x and y axes. Normal-PCA on the other hand suffered from incorrect identification of the three axes. Both Center of Gravity-PCA and Continous-PCA performed noticeably better than PCA and Normal-PCA. Continous-PCA had the best performance but its superiority over Center of Gravity-PCA was negligible. In addition, Center of Gravity-PCA was much more efficient in terms of computation time.

An investigation of how symmetry-based pose normalisation techniques perform on 3D vehicles will give a holistic evaluation of the best pose normalisation methods for 3D vehicles. This is planned as future work.

References

1. Funkhouser, T., Min, P., Kazhdan, M., Chen, J., Halderman, A., Dobkin, D., Jacobs, D.: A search engine for 3D models. ACM Trans. Graph. **22**(1), 83–105 (2003)
2. Wei, L., Yuanjun, H.: 3D model retrieval based on orthogonal projections. In: Proceedings of the Ninth International Conference on Computer Aided Design and Computer Graphics, CAD-CG 2005, pp. 157–162. IEEE Computer Society, Washington, DC (2005)
3. Pears, N., Heseltine, T., Romero, M.: From 3D point clouds to pose-normalised depth maps. Int. J. Comput. Vision **89**(2–3), 152–176 (2010). doi:10.1007/s11263-009-0297-y
4. Vranic, D., Saupe, D.: 3D model retrieval. In: Proc. Spring Conference on Computer Graphics and its Applications, pp. 89–93. Budmerice Manor, Slovakia (2000)
5. Paquet, E., Rioux, M., Murching, A., Naveen, T., Tabatabai, A.: Description of shape information for 2-D and 3-D objects. Signal Processing: Image Communication **16**(1–2), 103–122 (2000)
6. Papadakis, P., Pratikakis, I., Perantonis, S., Theoharis, T.: Efficient 3D shape matching and retrieval using a concrete radialized spherical projection representation. Pattern Recogn. **40**(9), 2437–2452 (2007)
7. Napoléon, T., Sahbi, H.: From 2D silhouettes to 3D object retrieval: Contributions and benchmarking. J. Image Video Process., 1:1–1:22, January 2010

8. Vranic, D.: 3D Model Retrieval. Ph.D. thesis, University of Leipzig (2004)
9. Papadakis, P., Pratikakis, I., Theoharis, T., Perantonis, S.: Panorama: A 3D shape descriptor based on panoramic views for unsupervised 3D object retrieval. International Journal of Computer Vision **89**(2–3), 177–192 (2010)
10. Tangelder, J.W., Veltkamp, R.C.: A survey of content based 3D shape retrieval methods. Multimedia Tools Appl. **39**(3), 441–471 (2008)
11. Chaouch, M., Verroust-Blondet, A.: 3D model retrieval based on depth line descriptor. In: 2007 IEEE International Conference on Multimedia and Expo., pp. 599–602, July 2007
12. Axenopoulos, A., Litos, G., Daras, P.: 3D model retrieval using accurate pose estimation and view-based similarity. In: Proceedings of the 1st ACM International Conference on Multimedia Retrieval, ICMR 2011, pp. 41:1–41:8. ACM, New York (2011)
13. NIST: Results for shrec 2009 - shape retrieval contest on a new generic shape benchmark. http://www.itl.nist.gov/iad/vug/sharp/benchmark/shrecGeneric/results.html
14. Atmosukarto, I., Wilamowska, K., Heike, C., Shapiro, L.G.: 3D object classification using salient point patterns with application to craniofacial research. Pattern Recogn. **43**(4), 1502–1517 (2010)
15. Sfikas, K., Theoharis, T., Pratikakis, I.: Rosy+: 3D object pose normalization based on pca and reflective object symmetry with application in 3D object retrieval. International Journal of Computer Vision **91**(3), 262–279 (2011)
16. DMI: Dmi car 3D models. http://www.dmi-3d.net/
17. Shilane, P., Min, P., Kazhdan, M., Funkhouser, T.: The princeton shape benchmark. In: Proceedings of the Shape Modeling Applications, pp. 167–178, June 2004

Multimodal Output Combination for Transcribing Historical Handwritten Documents

Emilio Granell[✉] and Carlos-D. Martínez-Hinarejos

Pattern Recognition and Human Language Technology Research Center,
Universitat Politècnica de València, Camino de Vera s/n, 46022 Valencia, Spain
{egranell,cmartine}@dsic.upv.es

Abstract. Transcription of digitalised historical documents is an interesting task in the document analysis area. This transcription can be
achieved by using Handwritten Text Recognition (HTR) on digitalised
pages or by using Automatic Speech Recognition (ASR) on the dictation
of contents. Moreover, another option is using both systems in a multimodal combination to obtain a draft transcription, given that combining
the outputs of different recognition systems will generally improve the
recognition accuracy. In this work, we present a new combination method
based on Confusion Network. We check its effectiveness for transcribing
a Spanish historical book. Results on both unimodal combination with
different optical (for HTR) and acoustic (for ASR) models, and multimodal combination, show a relative reduction of Word and Character
Error Rate of 14.3% and 16.6%, respectively, over the HTR baseline.

Keywords: Document analysis and transcription · Handwritten text
recognition · Automatic speech recognition · Confusion Networks combination · Recognition outputs combination

1 Introduction

Document analysis and recognition is a popular field of application of image
analysis. This field includes several interesting applications in real tasks, such as
the automatic transcription of forms or the transcription of handwritten documents. This last application is of particular interest for recovering the contents
of ancient manuscripts available in many historical libraries. Transcribing the
handwritten text of these manuscripts would allow to access their contents in a
more comfortable manner, which can be interesting for historical, cultural, and
even legal purposes.

In this context, transcription of these documents could benefit of the use of
image analysis and natural language processing techniques, and more specifically
of Handwritten Text Recognition (HTR) techniques [14]. The basic idea is to
provide paleographers (expert people in transcribing ancient documents) with
an initial draft transcription that they can properly ammend, decreasing the

© Springer International Publishing Switzerland 2015
G. Azzopardi and N. Petkov (Eds.): CAIP 2015, Part I, LNCS 9256, pp. 246–260, 2015.
DOI: 10.1007/978-3-319-23192-1_21

effort in the global transcription task. Moreover, these systems can use feedback from transcribers in order to speed up the transcription process [15]. The high interest in this task within the field of Digital Humanities is reflected in projects such as IMPACT[1] or tranScriptorium[2].

As an alternative to HTR systems, many paleographers asked for dictation systems based on Automatic Speech Recognition (ASR) engines, since many of them claim that it is more comfortable for them to dictate the document contents. Since HTR and ASR systems share most part of the technology related to the recognition process (they are usually based on Hidden Markov Models -HMM- with N-grams recognition systems using regular or tandem features), the possibility of combining both types of systems arises immediately. This combination would take advantage from two different data sources.

Systems combination is not restricted to different modalities (image and speech) systems, but it can be also applied to the combination of different systems of the same modality (unimodal system combination). In this case, many techniques have been proposed [2,10,7]. In the case of bimodal combination, [18] presents a technique that can be applied for isolated words. However, bimodal combination in continuous decoding is a hard problem because of time asynchrony between the two signals, i.e., the sequence of feature vectors for each modality differs in length and it is not easy to find the time points where the same elements (words in this case) are synchronised. An initial approximation for this case was presented in [1].

In this work, a new technique of recognition output combination is presented. This technique is based on the combination of Confusion Networks [19] derived from the outputs of two recognition systems, of the same or different modality. Furthermore, this technique can be used sequentially to combine the outputs of more than two recognition systems, by using hierarchical combination.

Results show that several errors can be corrected on the resulting unimodal Confusion Network. Nevertheless, the greatest improvements are reached with the multimodal combination. Moreover, results show that the combined Confusion Networks store better quality recognition hypotheses than those of the plain systems. These hypotheses can be used to speed up the transcriber task.

The paper is organised as follows: Section 2 presents the combination technique; Section 3 details the experimental framework (data, conditions, and assessment); Section 4 shows the results of the different experiments; Section 5 offers the final conclusions and future work lines.

2   Confusion Network Combination

As an output format for handwriting and speech recognisers, Confusion Networks (CN) reduce the complexity of Word Graph (WG) lattices without losing important information [19]. Figure 1 provides an example of WG and its corresponding CN. A CN is a weighted directed graph, in which each hypothesis

---

[1] http://www.impact-project.eu/
[2] http://transcriptorium.eu

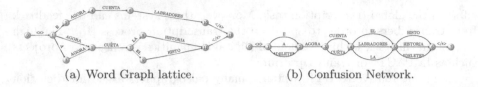

      (a) Word Graph lattice.   (b) Confusion Network.

Fig. 1. Word Graph lattice and Confusion Network.

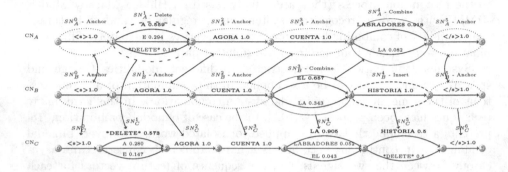

Fig. 2. Bimodal combination example, reference sentence: $<s>$ *AGORA CUENTA LA HISTORIA* $</s>$.

goes through all the nodes. The words and their probabilities are stored in the edges, and the total probability of the words contained in a subnetwork (all edges between two consecutive nodes) sum 1.

The first step of our CN combination technique aligns by similarity the subnetworks of both CN, marking the selected subnetworks as immovable anchors. In the second step, a new CN is composed from the base of the first CN, by using combination, insertion and deletion of subnetworks.

2.1 Subnetworks Based Alignment

Due to the fact that outputs of different recognition systems may have different errors, it is necessary to find some reference subnetworks that serve as anchors between the CN to combine. The search of anchor subnetworks is performed in both directions (from left to right and vice versa) simultaneously, taking as anchor subnetworks only those where the search on both directions coincide. This search can be adjusted by several parameters, such as:

- Searching unigrams, bigrams or skip-bigrams.
- Searching only in the most probable word or in all the words contained in the subnetworks.
- Setting a gram matching error threshold ϵ between words.

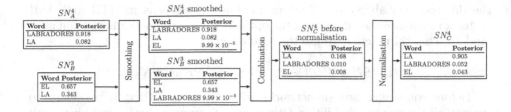

Fig. 3. Example of subnetwork combination with $\alpha = 0.5$ and $\Theta = 10^{-4}$. The Smoothing block represents the use of Equation (4), and the Combination block the use of Equation (3).

As words can be decomposed on characters (basic unit for HTR) and phonemes (basic unit for ASR), the quadratic mean of the Character Error Rate (CER) and the Phoneme Error Rate (PER) was used to assess the gram matching error between words of both CN:

$$E(w_A, w_B) = \sqrt{\frac{\text{CER}(w_A, w_B)^2 + \text{PER}(w_A, w_B)^2}{2}} \qquad (1)$$

Where the words of the first and the second CN are represented by w_A and w_B respectively. CER and PER are Levensthein distances between the words of both CN. CER is the distance at character level, and PER at phoneme level, by using the phonetic transcriptions of the recognised words. E represents the gram matching error.

In Figure 2 a complete example of the performance of our technique is shown. In this example, CN_A and CN_B represent the two CN to combine, and CN_C the resulting CN. When searching for anchor subnetworks on bigrams and unigrams with $\epsilon = 0$, it would find the following anchor subnetwork pairs: $SN_A^0 - SN_B^0$, $SN_A^2 - SN_B^1$, $SN_A^3 - SN_B^2$, and $SN_A^5 - SN_B^5$.

2.2 Composing a New Confusion Network

The final goal of the CN combination is to compose a new CN with a higher accuracy than the two original CN. The edit operations used to compose the new CN are: combination, insertion and deletion of subnetworks.

Combination. Combination of subnetworks allows to maximise the probability of the correct word, if it is present on both subnetworks (SN_A and SN_B). Based on the Bayes theorem and assuming a strong independence on $\Pr(w \mid SN_A, SN_B)$, we get:

$$\Pr(w \mid SN_A, SN_B) \simeq \Pr(w \mid SN_A) \Pr(w \mid SN_B) \qquad (2)$$

However, in practice it is usual to employ a weighted version of Equation (2) in which the weight factor α permits to balance the relative reliability between the different probability distributions models (as happens in HTR and ASR systems to balance the influence of the optical/acoustic models and the language model). Thus, in practice we use the following:

$$\Pr(w \mid SN_A, SN_B) \simeq \Pr(w \mid SN_A)^\alpha \Pr(w \mid SN_B)^{1-\alpha} \tag{3}$$

Before combining two subnetworks with Equation (3), it is necessary to smooth all the word probabilities. Otherwise, uncommon words would have null probabilities. Equation (4) permits to smooth the word probabilities of all words ($n = common + uncommon$) in both subnetworks. This equation is based on Laplacian smoothing [21]. However, here the word counts are obtained by dividing the word probabilities by a defined granularity Θ.

$$\Pr{}_{smoothed}(w \mid SN) = \frac{\Pr(w \mid SN) + \Theta}{1 + n\Theta} \tag{4}$$

Finally, the word probabilities on the resulting subnetwork are normalised.

In the example (Figure 2), SN_A^4 and SN_B^3 are selected for combination. In this case, the correct word (LA) is not the most probable word in either subnetwork. However, it becomes the most probable word when combining both subnetworks with $\alpha = 0.5$ and $\Theta = 10^{-4}$, as can be seen in SN_C^4 (in Figure 3 this combination process is shown in detail).

Insertion and Deletion. Insertion and deletion of subnetworks allows to reach a compromise when there is a disagreement between the CN on whether a particular position between two words should or should not be another word. Specifically, insertion occurs when the second CN subnetwork presents a word with a probability greater than a threshold γ and which is not present in the same position of the first CN subnetwork. Deletion occurs similarly, when the second CN considers that a word is not necessary in a specific position of the first CN, and the most probable word of the first CN subnetwork to delete does not reach a threshold δ.

Both operations use the same procedure. First, we halve the probability of all the words of the subnetwork to insert or delete, and then, we increase in a 50% the probability of deleting this subnetwork. As an example, the subnetworks SN_B^4 and SN_A^1 (see Figure 2) are inserted and deleted, respectively.

Composition of the New Confusion Network. The first step on the composition of the new CN is to combine the subnetworks labeled as anchor. Thereby between consecutive anchored subnetworks a series of aligned fragments appear in both CN. Each fragment can contain from none to several subnetworks. In the example in Figure 2, two fragments appear, the first one between anchors $SN_A^0 - SN_B^0$ and $SN_A^2 - SN_B^1$, and the second one between anchors $SN_A^3 - SN_B^2$, and $SN_A^5 - SN_B^5$. We use these fragments sizes to decide what to do with each subnetwork. Comparing the sizes of two aligned fragments, we can find the following cases, when both fragment sizes are not null:

1. If both fragment sizes match, all subnetworks are combined one by one.
2. If the fragment size of only one CN is null, we must choose whether to insert or to delete (as explained above) for all the subnetworks contained in the fragment of the other CN. This is the case of the first fragment in the example of Figure 2, which is composed only by SN_A^1. It is deleted, since the probability of the first word does not reach the δ threshold (in this case, $\delta = 0.75$ was chosen).
3. If both fragment sizes are different and none is null, we must find every additional anchor subnetworks in a relaxed search, and decide whether to insert or delete for the rest of subnetworks. This is the case of the second fragment in the example of Figure 2, which is formed by SN_A^4 on a side, and by SN_B^3 and SN_B^4 on the other. When searching for unigrams on the whole subnetworks, it is found that SN_A^4 can be combined with SN_B^3, and given that SN_B^4 exceeds the threshold γ (in this case, $\gamma = 0.25$ was taken), it is inserted.

Finally, a new CN is obtained as a result of this process. In Figure 2, CN_C is the resulting CN; it can be seen that several errors have been corrected, and the correct sentence ($<s>AGORA\ CUENTA\ LA\ HISTORIA\ </s>$) has the highest probability.

3 Experimental Framework

3.1 Corpora

The historical handwritten text corpus used for this work is RODRIGO [16]. It is composed of a set of 853 pages written by a single writer in 1545, entitled "Historia de España del arçobispo Don Rodrigo". The topic of the book is historical chronicles of Spain. Most pages form a single block with well separated lines (usually 25 lines per page), written in calligraphical text. The corpus is available with the lines separated, which are the source of feature extraction (Figure 4 shows an example of a separated line). The corpus has a total of 20,356 lines in PNG format. Some standard partitions were defined for baseline experiments, by using a training set of 5000 lines (about 205 pages). The test set for multimodal experiments is a set of 50 lines (pages 515 and 579). The set of symbols present in this corpus gets modelled by 106 HMM, which take into account lowercase and uppercase letters, numbers, punctuation marks, special symbols, and blank spaces.

Fig. 4. Example of an extracted line from the RODRIGO corpus.

For the training of the ASR acoustic models we used a partition of the Spanish phonetic corpus Albayzin [12]. This corpus consists of a set of three subcorpus recorded by 304 speakers using a sampling rate of 16 kHz and a 16-bit quantisation. The training partition used in this work includes 4800 phonetically balanced utterances. Specifically, 200 utterances were read by four speakers and 25 utterances were read by 160 speakers, with a total length of about 4 hours. A set of 25 HMM (23 monophones, short silence, and long silence) was estimated from this corpus. For the multimodal test we recorded 7 different speakers who read the 50 handwritten test lines (those of pages 515 and 579), giving a total set of 350 utterances (about 15 minutes).

3.2 Features

HTR Features. Handwritten text features are computed in several steps. First, we perform a bright normalisation by using the pnmnorm tool of Netpbm [13], with -bvalue 150 -wvalue 200. After that, we apply a median filter of size 3×3 pixels to the whole image. Next, we perform slant correction by using the maximum variance method and a threshold of 92%. Then, we perform a size normalisation and scale the final image to a height of 40 pixels. Finally, features are extracted by using the method described in [5]. Final regular feature vectors are composed of 60 dimensions.

ASR Features. Mel-Frequency Cepstral Coefficients (MFCC) are extracted from the audio files. The Fourier transform is calculated every 10ms over a window of 25 ms of a pre-emphasised signal. Next, 23 equidistant Mel scale triangular filters are applied and the filters outputs are logarithmised. Finally, to obtain the MFCC, a discrete cosine transformation is applied. We use the first 12 MFCC and the log frame energy with the first and second order derivatives as regular ASR features, resulting in a 39 dimensional vector.

Tandem Features. In the tandem feature extraction scheme, two Multi-Layer Perceptrons (MLP) with 2000 neurons at the hidden layer and a softmax transfer function at the output layer were trained to estimate symbol-phoneme posterior probabilities. On the one hand, for HTR, a MLP with 60 neurons at the input layer and 106 neurons at the output layer was trained with Torch [4]. On the other hand, for ASR, the MLP had 39 neurons at the input layer and 25 neurons at the output layer and it was trained using QuickNet [8]. The final tandem features are constituted by the log posteriors probabilities of the MLP.

Both MLP's were trained by backpropagation with a mean-squared error criterion. The frame-level labelling required to train the MLP's can be generated from a forced alignment decoding by a previously trained recognition system [6]. For this work, the forced alignment decoding and the model training were repeated several times until the convergence of the frame labels.

3.3 Models

Optical and acoustic models were trained by using HTK [20]. On the one hand, symbols on the optical model are modelled by a continuous density left-to-right

HMM with 6 states and 32 gaussians per state. On the other hand, phonemes on the acoustic model are modelled as a left-to-right HMM with 3 states and 64 gaussians per state.

In order to test the influence of the speaker adaptation in the acoustic models, the speaker independent acoustic models were adapted to each speaker and page using HTK's Maximum Likelihood Linear Regression global adaptation [20]. For each independent acoustic model (regular and tandem), two adapted models were obtained per speaker, since we got the adapted models for decoding one page by using the audio samples of the other page, and vice-versa.

The lexicon models for both systems are in the HTK lexicon format, where each word is modelled as a concatenation of symbols for HTR or phonemes for ASR.

The language model was estimated directly from the transcriptions of the 5000 lines included in the HTR training set by using the SRILM *ngram-count* tool [17]. The model was a 2-gram with the Kneser-Ney back-off smoothing [9]. The test baseline language model presents a 6.2% of Out Of Vocabulary words and a perplexity of 298.4. Although language models could be enriched with external sources, the antiquity and the topic of the book makes it difficult to find representative texts to enhance the language model.

3.4 Evaluation Metrics

The Levensthein distance was used to assess our system at the word level with the Word Error Rate (WER) and at the character level with the Character Error Rate (CER). These measures calculate the error between the best hypothesis from decoding processes and the reference. CER is especially interesting within this framework, since transcription errors are usually corrected at character level. For both measures, confidence intervals at 95% were calculated by using the bootstrapping method with 10,000 repetitions [3]. Similarly, oracle WER and oracle CER are the best WER and best CER, respectively, that can be obtained from the hypotheses present in a Confusion Network. In this work, the search of oracle values was limited to the 2000-best.

The statistical dispersion of the position of the n-best values that allow to obtain the oracle permits to estimate the difficulty of obtaining this oracle. The interquartile range (IQR), the median, and the median absolute deviation (MAD) were used to measure this statistical dispersion.

3.5 Experimental Setup

The recognition systems were implemented by using the iATROS [11] recogniser, and the SRILM *lattice-tool* [17] utility was used to obtain CN from the n-best WG recognition outputs.

In the experiments, the anchor subnetworks search was performed several times, looking for skip-bigrams (allowing only one wrong word in the gap) and unigrams, throughout the whole hypothesis in the subnetworks. Specifically, we started with a perfect matching search of skip-bigrams, followed by a perfect matching search of unigrams. Next, we made a relaxed matching search of skip-bigrams, and a relaxed matching search of unigrams, setting the matching error threshold to $\epsilon = 2^{-\frac{1}{2}}$. A relaxed search with this threshold would allow to align words like *3* and *TRES* that coincide in their phonetic transcription (['tres]), since it is the same word written differently.

4 Experimental Results

In order to check the performance of our technique we used six different recognition systems; two HTR systems (regular and tandem), and four ASR systems: regular and tandem, with (A) and without speaker adaptation. As a first step, the reference values for each recognition system were obtained. As a second step, the unimodal combination was performed. Finally, the multimodal combination was conducted. With regard to the order of the combinations, the best results were obtained with the order represented in Figure 5. However, the differences were not significant with respect to the rest of possible combination orders.

The values of the main variables were tuned, in order to optimise the experimental results. We used a weight factor of $\alpha = 0.5$, a granularity for smoothing of $\Theta = 10^{-4}$, and $\gamma = 0.25$ and $\delta = 0.75$ as thresholds for insertion and deletion, respectively.

4.1 Baseline Experiments

The reference values obtained for each one of the six recognition systems are shown in Table 1 and Table 2. As can be observed, the HTR reference values are better than the ASR reference values.

As to the baseline HTR results (Table 1), the tandem system produces lower error rates. Therefore, we take these values as a baseline reference, namely 32.9% for WER and 15.7% for CER. Regarding the oracle baseline results, the lower bounds were obtained in the HTR modality, specifically 24.9% for WER and 11.6% for CER. Both are also from the tandem system.

The baseline ASR results (Table 2) are quite poor because of the difficulty of the corpus. In RODRIGO we faced with text images containing hyphenated words (e.g., *REYNA*, where a part of the word *RE* is at the end of a line and the second part *YNA* is at the beginning of the following line), abbreviations (e.g., *NRÕ*) that are pronounced as the whole word (*NUESTRO* ['nwes tro]), and words written in multiple forms (e.g., *XPIÃNOS* and *CHRISTIANOS*, or numbers as *5* and *V*) but that are pronounced in the same way ([kris 'tja nos], ['θiŋ ko]). In spite of these facts, speaker adaptation and tandem features provide improvements for ASR when compared to the regular baseline. Specifically, the best results were obtained with the regular model with speaker adaptation (A). Regarding the WER, a value of 51.0% was obtained, while the value of CER reached 26.4%. In terms of the oracle, the ASR oracle values are worse than the HTR baseline values.

Table 1. HTR baseline results, along with the average decoding times for each sample (in seconds).

Model	1-best WER	Oracle WER	1-best CER	Oracle CER	Time per sample
Regular	39.3% ± 4.1	28.0% ± 3.1	20.6% ± 2.5	14.0% ± 2.1	36.7 s
Tandem	**32.9% ± 5.3**	**24.9% ± 5.6**	**15.7% ± 4.9**	**11.6% ± 4.9**	**15.4 s**

Table 2. ASR baseline results, along with the average decoding times for each sample (in seconds).

Model	1-best WER	Oracle WER	1-best CER	Oracle CER	Time per sample
Regular	62.9% ± 2.2	44.9% ± 2.1	35.4% ± 1.4	25.1% ± 1.4	55.2 s
Regular (A)	**51.0% ± 2.2**	**33.7% ± 2.0**	**26.4% ± 1.3**	**17.2% ± 1.2**	43.2 s
Tandem	58.6% ± 2.2	41.1% ± 2.0	31.3% ± 1.3	21.9% ± 1.3	30.7 s
Tandem (A)	55.5% ± 2.2	38.4% ± 2.1	28.9% ± 1.3	19.7% ± 1.1	**29.4 s**

Concerning the average decoding times per sample, we take as a reference 55.2 s, which is the time of the slower decoding system (ASR regular), because it represents the average time required to decode a sample by all the systems in parallel.

4.2 Unimodal Combination Experiments

In these experiments, the output of the different systems of the same modality were combined. The input signals to each recognition system are the same. Therefore, the combination of these outputs does not present the difficulty of asynchrony.

On the one hand, in the case of the HTR unimodal combination (Figure 5), once the image signals were processed through each HTR system, the n-best WG outputs were transformed into CN. Then, these CN were processed by our CN combination technique, which returned a new CN by combining the information from both HTR systems.

On the other hand, for the ASR unimodal combination, as our technique allows to combine only two CN and we used four ASR systems, it was necessary to use the CN combination technique three times as described in Figure 5. First, the voice signals were processed through each ASR system, and its n-best WG outputs were transformed in CN. Secondly, these CN were processed by our CN combination technique by pairs, in order to obtain two combined CN. Finally, the two combined CN were processed by our CN combination technique, thereby we got a new CN that combines the information from the four ASR systems.

As shown in Table 3, the HTR unimodal combination reduced the error with respect to the baseline HTR system at both the WER and CER level, 1.8% and 2.4% respectively. Meanwhile, the combination introduced new information in the new CN that reduced the oracle levels, being of special interest the case of the oracle CER since it presents 32.8% of relative reduction over the HTR oracle CER baseline reference. In the case of the ASR unimodal combination, only a

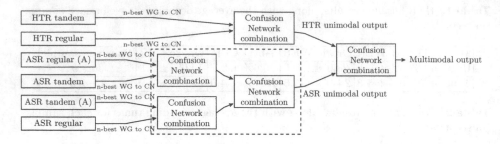

Fig. 5. Unimodal - Multimodal combination diagram.

small improvement is produced at the WER level when compared to the ASR baseline.

The time required for combining two CN is related to its density. The average time per sample used in the unimodal combinations was 457.1 ms for HTR and 596.9 ms for ASR. Nevertheless, due to the two combination levels for ASR, the actual average time used for ASR was 1.2 s.

4.3 Multimodal Combination Experiment

In the multimodal combination experiment, the unimodal CN were combined with the aim of obtaining a multimodal CN (Figure 5). The multimodal CN combination produced improvements compared with the results obtained by the unimodal combinations; despite the high error values obtained by the ASR unimodal combination. As can be seen in Table 3, a relative WER improvement of 9.3% is achieved when compared to the HTR unimodal combination, and this relative improvement increases to 14.3% when compared to the baseline reference as well. Furthermore, in terms of the CER a relative improvement of 1.5% is produced when compared to the HTR unimodal combination; besides, the relative improvement over the baseline reached 16.6%.

The oracle WER level presents a statistically significant relative improvement of 33.3% when compared to the oracle WER baseline, while the statistically significant relative improvement presented by the oracle CER level when compared with the oracle CER baseline attained 46.6%.

The average time per sample was 596.2 ms, considering the necessary the time to obtain the unimodal combinations this value increases to 1.8 s, which means that the required time for the multimodal combination represents 3.3% of relative increase of extra time to the decoding processes.

4.4 Difficulty of Reaching the Oracle Values

The difficulty of reaching the oracle values from the information contained in each confusion network was estimated by means of a statistical study of the dispersion of the n-best positions that allowed to achieve those oracle values.

Table 3. Combination results, along with the average combination times for each pair of samples (in miliseconds).

Combination	1-best WER	Oracle WER	1-best CER	Oracle CER	Time per sample
HTR unimodal	31.1% ± 3.7	20.6% ± 3.2	13.3% ± 1.9	7.8% ± 1.4	457.1 ms
ASR unimodal	50.4% ± 2.0	34.9% ± 1.9	28.6% ± 1.3	18.5% ± 1.2	596.9 ms
Multimodal	**28.2% ± 1.3**	**16.6% ± 1.3**	**13.1% ± 0.7**	**6.2% ± 0.5**	596.2 ms

Table 4. Statistical dispersion of the n-best positions that allow to obtain the oracle values.

Confusion network	Oracle WER			Oracle CER		
	IQR	Median	MAD	IQR	Median	MAD
HTR regular	423	62	61	1041	415	409
HTR tandem	50	2	2	119	17	16
ASR regular	967	412	398	1242	906	617
ASR regular (A)	897	365	359	1230	756	601
ASR tandem	866	334	329	1164	796	591
ASR tandem (A)	728	263	260	1300	831	658
HTR unimodal combination	137	26	25	594	144	142
ASR unimodal combination	567	129	127	1161	625	573
Multimodal combination	166	29	28	510	100	99

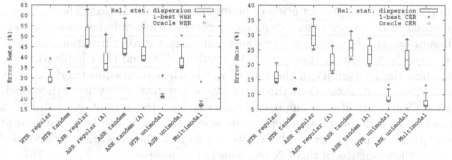

(a) Statistical dispersion relative to 1-best WER and oracle WER.

(b) Statistical dispersion relative to 1-best CER and oracle CER.

Fig. 6. Relative statistical dispersion in the set of the positions of the n-best that obtain the oracle values.

In Table 4 the statistical dispersion obtained for each CN is outlined, for oracle WER and oracle CER. Regarding the CN obtained from the recognition systems, the CN obtained from the tandem model of the HTR offered the narrowest IQR, side by side with the lowest median and MAD values. On the opposite side, all the CN of the ASR presented a wide IQR with high median and MAD values. As to the CN acquired from the combinations, the depth of the search is reduced because of the increase in the amount of information and the word probability correction resulting from the combination.

To show the importance of these statistical dispersions it is necessary to represent them with their related error values, as in Figure 6. In Figures 6(a) and 6(b), the statistical dispersions are plotted as box plots, where the positions are normalised, the range of values is set to the difference between the 1-best error value and the oracle error value, and the minimum value is set to the oracle error value. In the box plots, the IQR, the median, the minimum and the maximum values of the statistical dispersions are represented. The smaller the box plot, the easier it will be to reach the oracle error value. Therefore, the better systems present the lower values.

Regarding the oracle WER (Figure 6(a)), in the CN of the reference system (HTR tandem) it is very easy to reach the oracle WER value (24.9%) from the WER value (32.9%), whereas in the CN from the different ASR systems it is not easy to reach the oracle WER value. With the combination, the difficulty of reaching the oracle values is reduced, especially in the CN obtained from the multimodal combination where it is quite easy to reach the oracle WER value (16.6%) from the WER value (28.2%). In the oracle CER (Figure 6(b)), a similar behaviour is observed.

5 Conclusions

In this study, we have confirmed the benefits of combining multiple recognition outputs for the transcription of handwritten historical text. The technique presented in the paper takes advantage of the fact that different systems make different errors; thus, editing operations can correct errors. Insertion and deletion create new bigrams than enrich the resulting CN, and the combination can maximise the probability of the correct word, when both subnetworks contain the correct word, even when this word has a low probability in both subnetworks. Conversely, if only one subnetwork contains the correct word and both subnetworks contain the same erroneous word, this error will be maximised at the expense of the correct word. Despite of this fact, the experiments performed confirm the strengths of this CN combination technique.

The obtained results show that there is still room for improvement. For example, one of the improvements that could be made is to extend the technique in order to combine the outputs of more than two recognition systems simultaneously. Moreover, we propose for future studies the use of more robust methods of optical and acoustic modelling, such as the use of Recurrent Neural Networks with Long Short-Term Memory features on the tandem approach. From the ASR point of view, the possibility of using not lines but whole sentences of the handwritten text corpus could make multimodality more natural. Eventually, integrating the technique presented in this paper in an interactive transcription system could reduce the time and the workload for transcribing historical books, due to the increased recognition accuracy and the facility of achieving the oracle values on the resulting CN, without a significant increase of processing time.

Acknowledgments. Work partially supported by European Union - 7th FP, under grant 600707 (tranScriptorium), and by the Spanish MEC under projects STraDA (TIN2012-37475-C02-01), Active2Trans (TIN2012-31723), and SmartWays (RTC-2014-1466-4).

References

1. Alabau, V., Martínez-Hinarejos, C.D., Romero, V., Lagarda, A.L.: An iterative multimodal framework for the transcription of handwritten historical documents. Pattern Recognition Letters **35**, 195–203 (2014)
2. Bertolami, R., Halter, B., Bunke, H.: Combination of multiple handwritten text line recognition systems with a recursive approach. In: Proc. Int. Conf. Frontiers Handwriting Recognition, pp. 61–65 (2006)
3. Bisani, M., Ney, H.: Bootstrap estimates for confidence intervals in ASR performance evaluation. In: Proc. of Int. Conf. on Acoustics, Speech and Signal Processing, vol. 1, pp. 409–412 (2004)
4. Collobert, R., Bengio, S., Mariéthoz, J.: Torch: a modular machine learning software library. Tech. rep., IDIAP-RR 02–46, IDIAP (2002)
5. Dreuw, P., Jonas, S., Ney, H.: White-space models for offline Arabic handwriting recognition. In: Proc. of Int. Conf. on Pattern Recognition, pp. 1–4 (2008)
6. Hermansky, H., Ellis, D.P., Sharma, S.: Tandem connectionist feature extraction for conventional HMM systems. In: Proc. of Int. Conf. Acoustics, Speech and Signal Processing, vol. 3, pp. 1635–1638 (2000)
7. Ishimaru, S., Nishizaki, H., Sekiguchi, Y.: Effect of confusion network combination on speech recognition system for editing. In: Proc. of APSIPA Annual Summit and Conf., vol. 4, pp. 1–4 (2011)
8. Johnson, D.: ICSI Quicknet soft package (2004). http://www1.icsi.berkeley.edu/Speech/qn.html
9. Kneser, R., Ney, H.: Improved backing-off for m-gram language modeling. In: Proc. of Int. Conf. Acoustics, Speech and Signal Processing, vol. 1, pp. 181–184 (1995)
10. Krishnamurthy, H.K.: Study of algorithms to combine multiple automatic speech recognition (ASR) system outputs. Master's thesis, Department of Electrical and Computer Engineering (2009). http://hdl.handle.net/2047/d10019273
11. Luján-Mares, M., Tamarit, V., Alabau, V., Martínez-Hinarejos, C.D., Pastor i Gadea, M., Sanchis, A., Toselli, A.H.: iATROS: a speech and handwritting recognition system. In: V Jornadas en Tecnologías del Habla (VJTH2008), pp. 75–78 (2008)
12. Moreno, A., Poch, D., Bonafonte, A., Lleida, E., Llisterri, J., Mariño, J.B., Nadeu, C.: Albayzin speech database: design of the phonetic corpus. In: Proc. of EuroSpeech 1993, pp. 175–178 (1993)
13. Netpbm home page. http://netpbm.sourceforge.net/
14. Plamondon, R., Srihari, S.N.: On-Line and Off-Line Handwriting Recognition: A Comprehensive Survey. IEEE Transactions on Pattern Analysis and Machine Intelligence **22**(1), 63–84 (2000)
15. Romero, V., Leiva, L.A., Toselli, A.H., Vidal, E.: Interactive multimodal transcription of text images using a web-based demo system. In: Proc. of Conf. on Intelligent User Interfaces, pp. 477–478 (2009)
16. Serrano, N., Castro, F., Juan, A.: The RODRIGO Database. In: Proc. of Language Resources and Evaluation Conference, pp. 2709–2712 (2010)

17. Stolcke, A.: SRILM - an extensible language modeling toolkit. In: Proc. Interspeech, pp. 901–904 (2002)
18. Woodruff, P., Dupont, S.: Bimodal combination of speech and handwriting for improved word recognition. In: Proc. of EUSIPCO 2005, pp. 1918–1921 (2005)
19. Xue, J., Zhao, Y.: Improved confusion network algorithm and shortest path search from word lattice. In: Proc. of Int. Conf. in Acoustics, Speech and Signal Processing, vol. 1, pp. 853–856 (2005)
20. Young, S., Evermann, G., Gales, M., Hain, T., Kershaw, D., Liu, X., Moore, G., Odell, J., Ollason, D., Povey, D., et al.: The HTK book (for HTK version 3.4). Cambridge university Eng. Dept. (2006)
21. Zhai, C., Lafferty, J.: A study of smoothing methods for language models applied to information retrieval. Transactions on Information Systems 22(2), 179–214 (2004)

Unsupervised Surface Reflectance Field Multi-segmenter

Michal Haindl[1]([✉]), Stanislav Mikeš[1], and Mineichi Kudo[2]

[1] The Institute of Information Theory and Automation of the Czech Academy
of Sciences, Prague, Czech Republic
{haindl,xaos}@utia.cz
[2] Graduate School of Engineering, Hokkaido University, Sapporo, Japan
mine@main.eng.hokudai.ac.jp

Abstract. An unsupervised, illumination invariant, multi-spectral, multi-resolution, multiple-segmenter for textured images with unknown number of classes is presented. The segmenter is based on a weighted combination of several unsupervised segmentation results, each in different resolution, using the modified sum rule. Multi-spectral textured image mosaics are locally represented by eight causal directional multi-spectral random field models recursively evaluated for each pixel. The single-resolution segmentation part of the algorithm is based on the underlying Gaussian mixture model and starts with an over segmented initial estimation which is adaptively modified until the optimal number of homogeneous texture segments is reached. The performance of the presented method is extensively tested on the Prague segmentation benchmark both on the surface reflectance field textures as well as on the static colour textures using the commonest segmentation criteria and compares favourably with several leading alternative image segmentation methods.

Keywords: Unsupervised image segmentation · Textural features · Illumination invariants · Surface reflectance field · Bidirectional texture function

1 Introduction

Segmentation is the fundamental process which partitions a data space into meaningful salient regions. Image segmentation essentially affects the overall performance of any automated image analysis system thus its quality is of the utmost importance. Image regions, homogeneous with respect to some usually textural or colour measure, which result from a segmentation algorithm are analysed in subsequent interpretation steps. Texture-based image segmentation is area of intense research activity in recent years and many algorithms were published in consequence of all this effort. These methods are usually categorised

© Springer International Publishing Switzerland 2015
G. Azzopardi and N. Petkov (Eds.): CAIP 2015, Part I, LNCS 9256, pp. 261–273, 2015.
DOI: 10.1007/978-3-319-23192-1_22

[18] as region-based, boundary-based, or as a hybrid of the two. Different published methods are difficult to compare because of lack of a comprehensive analysis together with accessible experimental data, however available results indicate that the ill-defined texture segmentation problem is still far from being satisfactorily solved. Spatial interaction models and especially Markov random fields-based models are increasingly popular for texture representation [4,18], etc. Several researchers dealt with the difficult problem of unsupervised segmentation using these models see for example [10,15,17] or [5,7,12]. The concept of decision fusion [14] for high-performance pattern recognition is well known and widely accepted in the area of supervised classification where (often very diverse) classification technologies, each providing complementary sources of information about class membership, can be integrated to provide more accurate, robust and reliable classification decisions than the single classifier applications.

Similar advantages can be expected and achieved [12] also for the unsupervised segmentation applications. However, a direct unsupervised application of the supervised classifiers fusion idea is complicated with unknown number of data hidden classes and consequently a different number of segmented regions in segmentation results to be fused. This paper exploits above advantages by combining several unsupervised segmenters of the same type but with different feature sets. It introduces a novel eight-directional generative multispectral texture representation and invariant features capable to discriminate surface reflectance field type of textures, i.e., bidirectional texture function (BTF) textures with a fixed or small range of viewing angle.

2   Combination of Multiple Segmenters

The proposed method (MW3AR8^i) combines segmentation results from different resolution. We assume to down-sample input image Y into M different resolutions $Y^{(m)} = \downarrow^{\iota_m} Y$ with sampling factors ι_m $m = 1, \ldots, M$ identical in both horizontal and vertical directions and $Y^{(1)} = Y$. Local surface reflectance field texture for each pixel $Y_r^{(m)}$ in resolution m is represented the 3D simultaneous causal autoregressive random field model (CAR) parameter space $\Theta_r^{(m)}$ (5) and modeled by the Gaussian mixture model (6),(7).

2.1   Single-Resolution Texture Model

Static smooth multi-spectral textures require three dimensional models for adequate representation. We assume that single multi-spectral textures can be locally modelled using a 3D simultaneous causal autoregressive random field model (CAR). This model can be expressed as a stationary causal uncorrelated noise driven 3D autoregressive process [11]:

$$Y_r = \gamma X_r + e_r \ , \tag{1}$$

where $\gamma = [A_1, \ldots, A_\eta]$ is the $d \times d\eta$ parameter matrix, $A_i \forall i \in I_r^c$ are $d \times d$ parametric matrices, d is the number of spectral bands, I_r^c is a causal neighborhood index set with $\eta = card(I_r^c)$ and e_r is a white Gaussian noise vector with zero mean and a constant but unknown covariance, X_r is a corresponding vector of the contextual neighbours Y_{r-s} where $s \in I_r^c$ and $r, r-1, \ldots$ is a chosen direction of movement on the image index lattice I. The selection of an appropriate CAR model support ($I_r^c \subset I$) is important to obtain good texture representation but less important for segmentation. The optimal neighbourhood as well as the Bayesian parameters estimation of a CAR model can be found analytically under few additional and acceptable assumptions using the Bayesian approach (see details in [11]). The recursive Bayesian parameter estimation of the CAR model is [11]:

$$\hat{\gamma}_{r-1}^T = \hat{\gamma}_{r-2}^T + \frac{V_{x(r-2)}^{-1} X_{r-1} (Y_{r-1} - \hat{\gamma}_{r-2} X_{r-1})^T}{(1 + X_{r-1}^T V_{x(r-2)}^{-1} X_{r-1})} , \qquad (2)$$

where $V_{x(r-1)} = \sum_{k=1}^{r-1} X_k X_k^T + V_{x(0)}$. Local texture for each pixel is represented by eight parametric vectors. Each vector contains local estimations of the CAR model parameters. These eight models have identical contextual neighbourhood I_r^c but they differ in their major movement direction ($\downarrow, \uparrow, \rightarrow, \leftarrow, \searrow, \nwarrow, \nearrow, \swarrow$), i.e.,

$$\tilde{\gamma}_r^T = \left\{ \hat{\gamma}_r^t, \hat{\gamma}_r^b, \hat{\gamma}_r^r, \hat{\gamma}_r^l, \hat{\gamma}_r^d, \hat{\gamma}_r^{-d}, \hat{\gamma}_r^a, \hat{\gamma}_r^{-a} \right\}^T . \qquad (3)$$

The parametric space $\tilde{\gamma}$ (Section 2.2) is subsequently smooth out, rearranged into a vector and its dimensionality is reduced using the Karhunen-Loeve feature extraction ($\bar{\gamma}$).

2.2   Illumination Invariant Textural Features

We assume that two images $\tilde{Y}, Y$ of the same texture and view position differing only in illumination can be linearly transformed to each other:

$$\tilde{Y}_r = B Y_r ,$$

where $\tilde{Y}_r, Y_r$ are multispectral pixel values at position r and B is some transformation matrix dependent on an illumination. This linear formula is valid for changes in brightness and illumination spectrum, with surfaces including both Lambertian and specular reflectance. We have proven [20] that the following features are illumination invariant for each CAR model:

1. trace: $\qquad\qquad tr\{A_m^j\} \qquad m = 1, \ldots, \eta, \; j \in \{t, b, r, l, d, -d, a, -a\}$,
2. A_m eigenvalues: $\qquad \nu_{m,k}^j \qquad k = 1, \ldots, C$.

The illumination invariant feature vector (3) for every pixel r has the form:

$$\tilde{\gamma}_r^T = \left\{ tr\{A_1^t\}, \nu_{1,1}^t, \ldots, \nu_{1,C}^t, \ldots, tr\{A_\eta^{-a}\}, \ldots, \nu_{\eta,1}^{-a}, \ldots, \nu_{\eta,C}^{-a} \right\}^T . \qquad (4)$$

2.3   Mixture Based Segmentation

Multi-spectral texture segmentation is done by clustering in the CAR parameter space Θ defined on the lattice I where

$$\Theta_r = [\bar{\gamma}_r, \zeta_r]^T \tag{5}$$

is the modified local parameter vector (3) computed for the lattice location r. The vector ζ_r contains both spatial coordinates r_1, r_2 and local colour values. We assume that this parametric space can be represented using the Gaussian mixture model (GM) with diagonal covariance matrices due to the previous CAR parametric space decorrelation. The Gaussian mixture model for CAR parametric representation at the m-th resolution $(m = 1, \ldots, M)$ is as follows:

$$p(\Theta_r^{(m)}) = \sum_{i=1}^{K^{(m)}} p_i^{(m)}\, p(\Theta_r^{(m)} \,|\, \nu_i^{(m)}, \Sigma_i^{(m)}) \ , \tag{6}$$

$$p(\Theta_r^{(m)} \,|\, \nu_i^{(m)}, \Sigma_i^{(m)}) = \frac{|\Sigma_i^{(m)}|^{-\frac{1}{2}}}{(2\pi)^{\frac{d}{2}}}\, e^{-\frac{(\Theta_r^{(m)} - \nu_i^{(m)})^T (\Sigma_i^{(m)})^{-1} (\Theta_r^{(m)} - \nu_i^{(m)})}{2}} \ . \tag{7}$$

The mixture model equations (6),(7) are solved using a modified EM algorithm.

Initialization. The algorithm is initialised using $\nu_i^{(m)}, \Sigma_i^{(m)}$ statistics for each resolution m estimated from the corresponding thematic maps in two subsequent steps:

1. refining direction
   $$\nu_i^{(m-1)} \left(\forall \Theta_r^{(m-1)} \,:\, r \in \uparrow \Xi_i^{(m)} \right) , \qquad\qquad \Sigma_i^{(m-1)} \left(\forall \Theta_r^{(m-1)} \,:\, r \in \uparrow \Xi_i^{(m)} \right)$$
   $$m = M+1, M, \ldots, 2 \qquad\qquad i = 1, \ldots, K^{(m)} \ ,$$

2. coarsening direction
   $$\nu_i^{(m)} \left(\forall \Theta_r^{(m)} \,:\, r \in \downarrow \Xi_i^{(m-1)} \right) , \qquad\qquad \Sigma_i^{(m)} \left(\forall \Theta_r^{(m)} \,:\, r \in \downarrow \Xi_i^{(m-1)} \right)$$
   $$m = 2, 3, \ldots, M \qquad\qquad i = 1, \ldots, K^{(m)} \ ,$$

where $\Xi_i^{(m)} \subset I$ $\forall m, i$, and the first initialisation thematic map $\Xi_i^{(M+1)}$ is approximated by the rectangular subimages obtained by regular division of the input texture mosaic. All the subsequent refining step are initialised from the preceding coarser resolution up-sampled thematic maps. The final initialisation results from the second coarsening direction where the gradually coarsening segmentations are initialised using the preceding down-sampled thematic maps. For each possible couple of components the Kullback-Leibler divergence

$$D\left(p(\Theta_r \,|\, \nu_i, \Sigma_i) \,\|\, p(\Theta_r \,|\, \nu_j, \Sigma_j)\right) = \int_\Omega p(\Theta_r \,|\, \nu_i, \Sigma_i) \, \log \left(\frac{p(\Theta_r \,|\, \nu_i, \Sigma_i)}{p(\Theta_r \,|\, \nu_j, \Sigma_j)} \right) d\Theta_r$$

is evaluated and the most similar components, i.e.,

$$\{i, j\} = \arg\min_{k,l} D\left(p(\Theta_r \,|\, \nu_l, \Sigma_l) \,\|\, p(\Theta_r \,|\, \nu_k, \Sigma_k)\right)$$

are merged together in each initialisation step. This initialisation results in K_{ini} subimages and recomputed statistics ν_i, Σ_i. $K_{ini} > K$ where K is the optimal number of textured segments to be found by the algorithm. Two steps of the EM algorithm are repeating after initialisation. The components with smaller weights than a fixed threshold $(p_j < \frac{0.02}{K_{ini}})$ are eliminated. For every pair of components we estimate their Kullback-Leibler divergence. From the most similar couple, the component with the weight smaller than the threshold is merged to its stronger partner and all statistics are actualised using the EM algorithm. The algorithm stops when either the likelihood function has negligible increase $(\mathcal{L}_t - \mathcal{L}_{t-1} < 0.01)$ or the maximum iteration number threshold is reached.

2.4 Resulting Mixture Probabilities

Resulting mixture model probabilities are mapped to the original fine resolution image space for all $m = 1, \ldots, M$ mixture sub-models ((6)(7)). The M cooperating segmenters deliver their class response in the form of conditional probabilities. Each segmenter produces a preference list based on the mixture component probabilities of a particular pixel belonging a particular class, together with a set of confidence measurement values generated in the original decision-making process.

Single-Segmenters Correspondence. Single-resolution segmentation results cannot be combined without knowledge of the mutual correspondence between regions in all different-resolution segmentation probabilistic mixture component maps $(K^1 \times \sum_{m=2}^{M} K^m$ combinations). Mutual assignments of two probabilistic maps are solved by using the Munkre's assignment algorithm [12] which finds the minimal cost assignment

$$g : A \mapsto B, \quad \sum_{\alpha \in A} f(\alpha, g(\alpha))$$

between sets $A, B, |A| = |B| = n$ given the cost function $f(\alpha, \beta), \alpha \in A, \beta \in B$. α corresponds to the fine resolution probabilistic maps, β corresponds to down-sampled probabilistic maps and $f(\alpha, \beta)$ is the Kullback-Leibler divergence between probabilistic maps. The algorithm has polynomial complexity instead of exponential for the exhaustive search.

Final Parametric Space. The parametric vectors representing texture mosaic pixels are assigned to the clusters based on our modification of the sum rule according to the highest component probabilities, i.e., Y_r is assigned to the cluster ω_{j*} if [9]

$$\pi_{r,j*} = \max_j \sum_{s \in I_r} w_s \left(\sum_{m=1}^{M} \frac{p^2(\Theta_{r-s}^{(m)} \mid \nu_j^{(m)}, \Sigma_j^{(m)})}{\sum_{i=1}^{M} p(\Theta_{r-s}^{(i)} \mid \nu_j^{(i)}, \Sigma_j^{(i)})} \right) ,$$

where w_s are fixed distance-based weights, I_r is a rectangular neighbourhood and $\pi_{r,j*} > \pi_{thre}$ (otherwise the pixel is unclassified). The area of single cluster blobs is evaluated in the post-processing thematic map filtration step. Regions with similar statistics are merged. Thematic map blobs with area smaller than a given threshold are attached to its neighbour with the highest similarity value.

3   Experimental Results

The algorithm was tested on natural wooden bidirectional texture function (BTF) mosaics from the Prague Texture Segmentation Data-Generator and Benchmark (http://mosaic.utia.cas.cz) [6]. The benchmark test mosaics layouts and each cell texture membership are randomly generated and filled with BTF textures from the large UTIA BTF database. The BTF wood measurements are mapped on the randomly generated spline surface. These tested BTFs have 3 spectral bands ($d = 3$) but the segmenter can handle any number of bands.

The benchmark ranks segmentation algorithms according to a chosen criterion. There are implemented twenty seven most frequented evaluation criteria categorised into four criteria groups – region-based [6], pixel-wise [6], clustering comparison criteria, and consistency measures [6]. The region-based [6] performance criteria mutually compare ground truth (GT) image regions with the corresponding machine segmented regions (MS). The pixel-wise criteria group contains the most frequented classification criteria such as the omission and commission errors, class accuracy, recall, precision, etc. Finally the last two criteria sets incorporate the global and local consistency errors [6] and three clustering comparison criteria.

Table 1 compares the overall benchmark performance of the proposed algorithm MW3AR8^i with the Voting Representativeness - Priority Multi-Class Flooding Algorithm (VRA-PMCFA) [8,16], Segmentation by Weighted Aggregation (SWA) [19], Efficient Graph-Based Image Segmentation (EGBIS) [3], Factorization-based texture SEGmenter (FSEG) [21], HGS [13], Edge Detection and Image SegmentatiON (EDISON) [1], JSEG [2], Deep Brain Model (DBM) [8], respectively. The table criteria are averaged over 10 experimental mosaics.

MW3AR8^i ranks second (average rank 3.05) over all benchmark criteria, slightly worse than the overall winner of the ICPR 2014 Unsupervised Image Segmentation Contest [8] - the VRA-PMCFA method.

These results illustrated in Figs. 1-3 and Table 1 demonstrate very good pixel-wise, correct region segmentation, missed error, noise error, and undersegmentation properties of our method. For most the pixel-wise criteria our method is among the best ones while. Our oversegmentation value is the second worst from all the compared methods what offers a large space for further improvement by better future post-processing.

Figs. 2,3 and show five selected 1024×1024 experimental benchmark mosaics created from four to twelve natural BTF textures. The last four or five rows on these figures demonstrate comparative results from the eight alternative algorithms. Three methods (VRA-PMCFA, FSEG, DBM) participated in the ICPR contest.

Table 1. BTF wood benchmark results for VRA-PMCFA, MW3AR8^i, SWA, EGBIS, FSEG, HGS, EDISON, JSEG, DBM. (Benchmark criteria: CS = correct segmentation; OS = over-segmentation; US = under-segmentation; ME = missed error; NE = noise error; O = omission error; C = commission error; CA = class accuracy; CO = recall - correct assignment; CC = precision - object accuracy; I. = type I error; II. = type II error; EA = mean class accuracy estimate; MS = mapping score; RM = root mean square proportion estimation error; CI = comparison index; GCE = Global Consistency Error; LCE = Local Consistency Error; dD = Van Dongen metric; dM = Mirkin metric; dVI = variation of information; $\bar{f}$ are the performance curves integrals; $\bar{F}$ = F–measure curve; small numbers are the corresponding measure rank over the listed methods.)

	VRA-PMCFA (2.19)	MW3-AR8^i (3.05)	SWA (3.33)	EGBIS (4.90)	FSEG (5.14)	HGS (5.38)	EDISON (6.14)	JSEG (7.19)	DBM (7.67)
↑CS	**59.55** [1]	49.78 [2]	44.87 [4]	45.41 [3]	36.87 [6]	42.79 [5]	29.25 [7]	20.15 [8]	*17.86* [9]
↓OS	16.10 [2]	53.96 [8]	19.97 [5]	34.19 [7]	*58.03* [9]	**11.92** [1]	19.68 [4]	17.83 [3]	23.80 [6]
↓US	29.22 [5]	11.58 [2]	26.60 [3]	45.90 [7]	**10.31** [1]	30.01 [6]	61.32 [8]	27.53 [4]	*62.59* [9]
↓ME	6.00 [3]	4.51 [2]	8.76 [6]	**1.13** [1]	9.36 [7]	23.62 [8]	8.20 [5]	*40.30* [9]	8.06 [4]
↓NE	6.33 [3]	4.90 [2]	9.15 [5]	**2.81** [1]	9.52 [7]	26.06 [8]	8.10 [4]	*38.68* [9]	9.49 [6]
↓O	16.15 [3]	12.87 [2]	**12.79** [1]	35.79 [6]	26.86 [5]	23.34 [4]	49.92 [8]	47.89 [7]	*70.86* [9]
↓C	**16.98** [1]	91.10 [6]	30.30 [2]	96.43 [8]	91.47 [7]	40.85 [3]	90.00 [4]	*100.00* [9]	90.33 [5]
↑CA	**72.28** [1]	70.07 [2]	68.01 [3]	57.47 [6]	59.75 [5]	59.83 [4]	45.29 [7]	45.08 [8]	*36.39* [9]
↑CO	**80.25** [1]	75.02 [3]	75.61 [2]	68.06 [5]	64.74 [6]	71.29 [4]	60.40 [7]	57.99 [8]	*52.64* [9]
↑CC	81.30 [3]	**93.72** [1]	80.28 [4]	78.42 [5]	91.07 [2]	72.97 [7]	72.74 [8]	75.16 [6]	*55.90* [9]
↓I.	**19.75** [1]	24.98 [3]	24.39 [2]	31.94 [5]	35.26 [6]	28.71 [4]	39.60 [7]	42.01 [8]	*47.36* [9]
↓II.	2.78 [2]	3.25 [4]	3.07 [3]	8.22 [6]	**1.51** [1]	6.21 [5]	*15.38* [9]	9.28 [7]	14.99 [8]
↑EA	78.35 [2]	**78.71** [1]	75.08 [3]	63.05 [6]	71.04 [4]	69.24 [5]	51.74 [8]	55.19 [7]	*44.70* [9]
↑MS	**73.17** [1]	70.92 [2]	66.63 [3]	54.77 [6]	60.04 [4]	59.77 [5]	41.81 [8]	42.56 [7]	*32.19* [9]
↓RM	6.37 [4]	**4.09** [1]	5.76 [3]	6.83 [6]	4.37 [2]	7.09 [7]	8.47 [8]	6.53 [5]	*11.83* [9]
↑CI	79.51 [2]	**80.56** [1]	76.46 [3]	66.14 [6]	74.19 [4]	70.54 [5]	54.98 [8]	59.16 [7]	*47.92* [9]
↓GCE	**6.27** [1]	7.20 [3]	9.50 [5]	8.46 [4]	13.41 [7]	19.74 [8]	6.77 [2]	*23.23* [9]	12.72 [6]
↓LCE	3.77 [4]	4.38 [5]	3.52 [3]	2.85 [2]	7.44 [6]	*14.02* [9]	**1.92** [1]	12.20 [8]	7.58 [7]
↓dD	**11.45** [1]	14.21 [3]	13.82 [2]	16.81 [4]	20.41 [6]	19.06 [5]	20.90 [7]	25.05 [8]	*26.01* [9]
↓dM	**7.75** [1]	10.16 [3]	8.79 [2]	20.33 [6]	12.27 [4]	12.34 [5]	30.58 [8]	20.98 [7]	*33.07* [9]
↓dVI	14.53 [4]	16.56 [8]	14.87 [6]	13.97 [3]	*18.29* [9]	14.85 [5]	**12.66** [1]	15.51 [7]	13.57 [2]
↑$\overline{CS}$	**57.12** [1]	46.35 [3]	49.84 [2]	44.89 [4]	32.85 [6]	37.65 [5]	29.48 [7]	22.94 [8]	*16.37* [9]
↓$\overline{OS}$	**13.40** [1]	48.90 [8]	20.55 [4]	36.41 [7]	*51.65* [9]	14.32 [2]	22.22 [6]	21.11 [5]	20.33 [3]
↓$\overline{US}$	26.27 [6]	10.75 [2]	24.26 [4]	36.16 [7]	**8.27** [1]	25.92 [5]	*57.14* [9]	23.92 [3]	53.86 [8]
↓$\overline{ME}$	11.91 [2]	13.97 [5]	13.14 [4]	12.16 [3]	21.50 [6]	33.95 [8]	**11.59** [1]	*42.40* [9]	22.36 [7]
↓$\overline{NE}$	11.89 [2]	14.04 [5]	13.07 [3]	13.39 [4]	21.94 [6]	35.50 [8]	**11.83** [1]	*41.59* [9]	24.00 [7]
↑$\overline{F}$	79.19 [2]	**80.11** [1]	76.07 [3]	65.22 [6]	73.28 [4]	70.17 [5]	54.34 [8]	57.95 [7]	*47.00* [9]

VRA-PMCFA

MW3AR8^i

SWA

EGBIS

FSEG

HGS

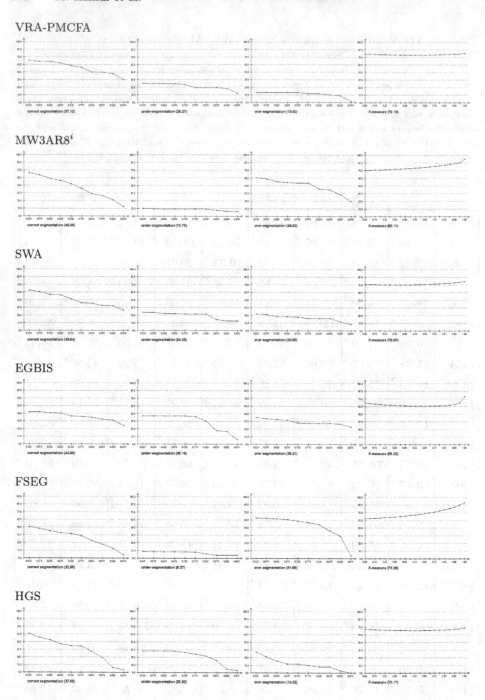

Fig. 1. Performance curves (vertical axis - $f(threshold)$), horizontal axis - threshold, details in http://mosaic.utia.cas.cz) of correct segmentation, undersegmentation, over-segmentation, and F-measure, respectively.

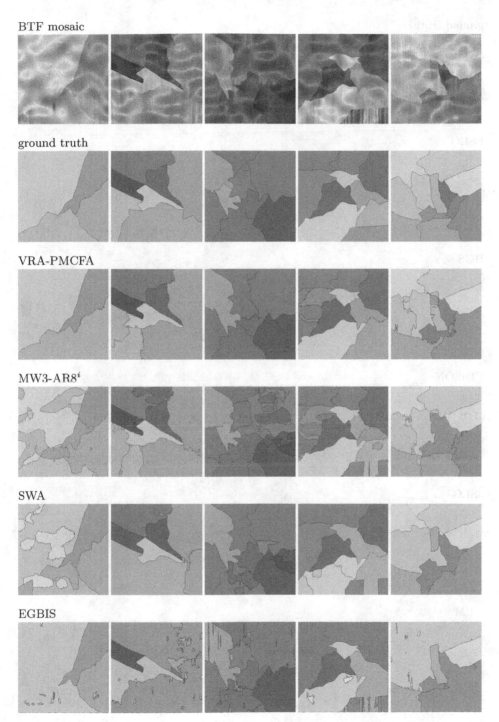

Fig. 2. BTF mosaic, ground truth, and segmentation results, respectively.

ground truth

FSEG

HGS

EDISON

JSEG

DBM

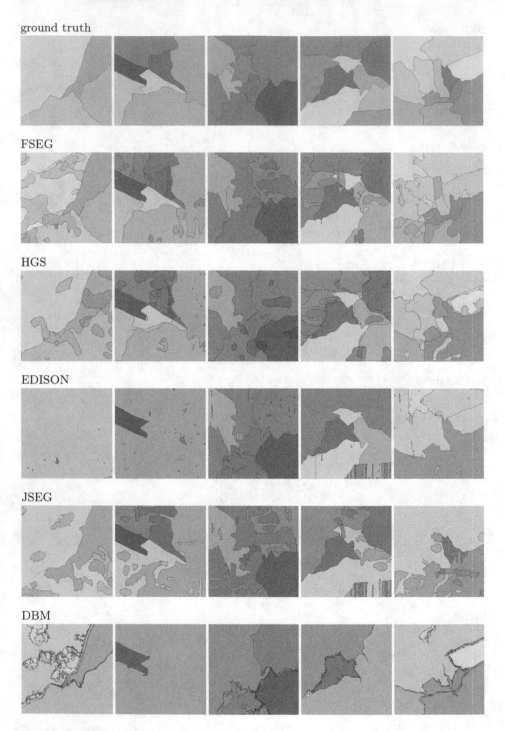

Fig. 3. Ground truth, and segmentation results, respectively.

The contest used the large size (80 textural mosaics) unsupervised *Colour* benchmark without noise degradation and with linear region borders. The contest criterion was the average rank over all benchmark criteria.

Hard natural BTF textures were chosen rather than synthesised (for example using Markov random field models) ones because they are expected to be more difficult for the underlying segmentation model. The fourth row on Fig. 2 demonstrates solid behaviour of our $MW3AR8^i$ algorithm but also infrequent algorithm failures producing the oversegmented thematic map for some textures. Such failures can be reduced by a more elaborate post-processing step.

The SWA [19], EGBIS [3], FSEG [21], HGS [13], EDISON [1], JSEG [2], and DBM algorithms on these data performed mostly worse as can be seen in their corresponding rows on Figs. 2,3 some areas are undersegmented while other parts of the mosaics are oversegmented. The best six method's performance is illustrated also on Fig. 1.

4   Conclusions

We proposed a significant improvement of our previously published unsupervised multi-segmenter [9]. The $MW3AR8^i$ segmenter is computationally efficient and robust method for unsupervised textured image segmentation with unknown number of classes based on the underlying CAR and GM texture models. The algorithm is reasonably fast, despite of using the random field type data representation, due to its efficient recursive parameter estimation of the underlying models and therefore is much faster than the usual Markov chain Monte Carlo estimation approach required for the Markovian image representations. Usual drawback of most segmentation methods is their application dependent parameters to be experimentally estimated. Our method requires only a contextual neighbourhood selection and two additional thresholds. The method's performance is demonstrated on the extensive benchmark tests on both natural texture mosaics as well as on BTF mosaics. It performs favourably compared with eight alternative segmentation algorithms. Detailed experimental results are available in http://mosaic.utia.cas.cz.

Acknowledgments. This research was supported by the Czech Science Foundation project GAČR 14-10911S.

References

1. Christoudias, C., Georgescu, B., Meer, P.: Synergism in low level vision. In: Kasturi, R., Laurendeau, D., Suen, C. (eds.) Proceedings of the 16th International Conference on Pattern Recognition, vol. 4, pp. 150–155. IEEE Computer Society, Los Alamitos (2002)
2. Deng, Y., Manjunath, B.: Unsupervised segmentation of color-texture regions in images and video. IEEE Transactions on Pattern Analysis and Machine Intelligence **23**(8), 800–810 (2001)

3. Felzenszwalb, P., Huttenlocher, D.: Efficient graph-based image segmentation. IJCV **59**(2), 167–181 (2004)
4. Haindl, M.: Texture synthesis. CWI Quarterly **4**(4), 305–331 (1991)
5. Haindl, M., Mikeš, S.: Unsupervised texture segmentation using multispectral modelling approach. In: Tang, Y., Wang, S., Yeung, D., Yan, H., Lorette, G. (eds.) Proceedings of the 18th International Conference on Pattern Recognition, ICPR 2006, vol. II, pp. 203–206. IEEE Computer Society, Los Alamitos (2006)
6. Haindl, M., Mikeš, S.: Texture segmentation benchmark. In: Lovell, B., Laurendeau, D., Duin, R. (eds.) Proceedings of the 19th International Conference on Pattern Recognition, ICPR 2008, pp. 1–4. IEEE Computer Society, Los Alamitos (2008)
7. Haindl, M., Mikeš, S.: Model-based texture segmentation. In: Campilho, A.C., Kamel, M.S. (eds.) ICIAR 2004. LNCS, vol. 3212, pp. 306–313. Springer, Heidelberg (2004)
8. Haindl, M., Mikeš, S.: Unsupervised image segmentation contest. In: Proceedings of the 22nd International Conference on Pattern Recognition, ICPR 2014, pp. 1484–1489. IEEE Computer Society CPS, Los Alamitos, August 2014. http://mosaic.utia.cas.cz/icpr2014/
9. Haindl, M., Mikeš, S., Pudil, P.: Unsupervised hierarchical weighted multisegmenter. In: Benediktsson, J.A., Kittler, J., Roli, F. (eds.) MCS 2009. LNCS, vol. 5519, pp. 272–282. Springer, Heidelberg (2009)
10. Haindl, M.: Texture segmentation using recursive Markov random field parameter estimation. In: Bjarne, K.E., Peter, J. (eds.) Proceedings of the 11th Scandinavian Conference on Image Analysis, pp. 771–776. Pattern Recognition Society of Denmark, Lyngby (1999)
11. Haindl, M.: Visual data recognition and modeling based on local markovian models. In: Florack, L., Duits, R., Jongbloed, G., Lieshout, M.C., Davies, L. (eds.) Mathematical Methods for Signal and Image Analysis and Representation, Computational Imaging and Vision, chap. 14, vol. 41, pp. 241–259. Springer, London (2012). doi:10.1007/978-1-4471-2353-8_14
12. Haindl, M., Mikeš, S.: Unsupervised texture segmentation using multiple segmenters strategy. In: Haindl, M., Kittler, J., Roli, F. (eds.) MCS 2007. LNCS, vol. 4472, pp. 210–219. Springer, Heidelberg (2007)
13. Hoang, M.A., Geusebroek, J.M., Smeulders, A.W.: Color texture measurement and segmentation. Signal Processing **85**(2), 265–275 (2005)
14. Kittler, J., Hojjatoleslami, A., Windeatt, T.: Weighting factors in multiple expert fusion. In: Proc. BMVC, pp. 41–50. BMVA (1997)
15. Manjunath, B., Chellapa, R.: Unsupervised texture segmentation using markov random field models. IEEE Transactions on Pattern Analysis and Machine Intelligence **13**, 478–482 (1991)
16. Panagiotakis, C., Grinias, I., Tziritas, G.: Natural image segmentation based on tree equipartition, bayesian flooding and region merging. IEEE Transactions on Image Processing **20**(8), 2276–2287 (2011)
17. Panjwani, D., Healey, G.: Markov random field models for unsupervised segmentation of textured color images. IEEE Transactions on Pattern Analysis and Machine Intelligence **17**(10), 939–954 (1995)

18. Reed, T.R., du Buf, J.M.H.: A review of recent texture segmentation and feature extraction techniques. CVGIP-Image Understanding **57**(3), 359–372 (1993)
19. Sharon, E., Galun, M., Sharon, D., Basri, R., Brandt, A.: Hierarchy and adaptivity in segmenting visual scenes. Nature **442**(7104), 719–846 (2006)
20. Vacha, P., Haindl, M.: Image retrieval measures based on illumination invariant textural mrf features. In: CIVR 2007: Proceedings of the 6th ACM international conference on Image and video retrieval, pp. 448–454. ACM Press, New York (2007)
21. Yuan, J., Wang, D.: Factorization-based texture segmentation. Tech. Rep. OSU-CISRC-1/13-TR0, The Ohio State University, Columbus (2013)

A Dynamic Approach and a New Dataset for Hand-detection in First Person Vision

Alejandro Betancourt[1,2][✉], Pietro Morerio[1], Emilia I. Barakova[2],
Lucio Marcenaro[1], Matthias Rauterberg[2], and Carlo S. Regazzoni[1]

[1] Department of Naval, Electric, Electronic and Telecommunications Engineering,
University of Genoa, Genoa, Italy
a.betancourt@tue.nl
[2] Designed Intelligence Group, Department of Industrial Design,
Eindhoven University of Technology, Eindhoven, The Netherlands

Abstract. Hand detection and segmentation methods stand as two of
the most most prominent objectives in First Person Vision. Their popularity is mainly explained by the importance of a reliable detection and
location of the hands to develop human-machine interfaces for emer-
gent wearable cameras. Current developments have been focused on hand
segmentation problems, implicitly assuming that hands are always in the
field of view of the user. Existing methods are commonly presented with
new datasets. However, given their implicit assumption, none of them
ensure a proper composition of frames with and without hands, as the
hand-detection problem requires. This paper presents a new dataset for
hand-detection, carefully designed to guarantee a good balance between
positive and negative frames, as well as challenging conditions such as
illumination changes, hand occlusions and realistic locations. Additionally, this paper extends a state-of-the-art method using a dynamic filter
to improve its detection rate. The improved performance is proposed as
a baseline to be used with the dataset.

1 Introduction

Videos recorded from head-mounted cameras are becoming popular due to the
increasing availability of wearable devices such as smart glasses and action cameras. The idea of a wearable computer recording what the user is looking at, and
giving him relevant feedback and assistance is nowadays technically possible.
As expected, this emerging technology is increasingly capturing the interest of
computer scientists and software developers to create methods to process videos
recorded with head or chest mounted cameras. This video perspective is commonly referred as First Person Vision (FPV) or Egocentric-vision [9]. In fact,
FPV video analysis is not a new research field. It is possible to state that modern
devices are highly influenced by the academic research of the late 1990s [29].

This work was supported in part by the Erasmus Mundus joint Doctorate in Interactive and Cognitive Environments, which is funded by the EACEA, Agency of the
European Commission under EMJD ICE.

G. Azzopardi and N. Petkov (Eds.): CAIP 2015, Part I, LNCS 9256, pp. 274–287, 2015.
DOI: 10.1007/978-3-319-23192-1_23

Existing literature points out several promising applications of this video perspective. Among them, hand-based methods stand as the most explored ones, aiming to exploit the conscious or unconscious hands movements for performing higher inference about the user [7] as in activity recognition [14,23] and user-machine interaction [27]. A common practice in FPV is to assume that hands are always recorded by the camera and, as a consequence, they can be located and tracked to infer more complex information. As it can be concluded after a quick scan of uncontrolled datasets like Disney [13] or UTE [15], this assumption is not entirely true. In fact, the predominance of one or the other type of frames (with/without hands) in a video sequence is not a consequence of the advantageous camera location but also of the activity performed e.g. hands are more frequent when the user is cooking than when he is walking in the street.

Despite the practical advantages of assuming full time hands presence, this fact introduces important issues when the proposed methods are applied on uncontrolled videos, for example wasted computational resources or noisy signals in the hand-segmentation stage, that could be propagated to other levels of the system. The authors in [6] propose a characterization of the two distinct problems, namely *hand-detection* and *hand-segmentation*, and combine them in a sequential structure to improve the overall system performance. Following the definition of [6], the *hand-detection* level answers the yes-or-no question of the hands' presence in the frame using global features and classifiers, while the *hand-segmentation* level locates and outlines the hands' region in a positive frame using low level features like color under an exhaustive pixel by pixel classification framework [19,21,27].

Regarding data availability, there are several FPV datasets available for research purposes. In general the technical characteristics of these datasets are similar and the videos are carefully recorded to guarantee the basic requirements identified by Schiele in 1999 [26]: i) Scale and texture variations, ii) Frame resolution, iii) Motion blur and iv) Hand occlusions. Undoubtedly, these requirements are important, but, under the light of the recent technological trends, some extra characteristics must be taken into account. An example is the necessity of balanced datasets in terms of hands presence as described by [6] and [8], to face the *hand-detection* problem under a classification framework. A balanced dataset is a realistic assumption for wearable devices and could lead to important improvements in the battery life, as well to the performance of higher-level methods like hand-based activity-recognition[12] and user-machine interaction [27]. It is worth to mentions that, as shown in section 2, existing datasets does not guarantee this condition, which makes them inappropriate to face the classification problem of the *hand-detection* level.

This work focuses indeed on *hand-detection*, and its contributions are three-folded: i) It presents the UNIGE-HANDS dataset for *hand-detection*, which guarantees a balanced number of frames with and without hands in 5 realistic locations, as well as changes in illumination, camera motion and hands occlusions. [1] ii) Multiple *hand-detectors* (feature-classifier) are evaluated over the dataset,

---

[1] [Dataset:] http://www.isip40.it/resources/UNIGEhands

following [6], without considering the temporal dimension of the data. iii) The best *hand-detector* (HOG-SVM) is extended using a Dynamic Bayesian Network (DBN), which is tuned to smooth the decision process. The presented method improves the performance of [6], taking advantage of the temporal dimension of the video, and of [8], tuning the parameters through an heuristic optimization. The computational complexity of the proposed approach is taken into account by filtering the classification certainty of the SVM directly, instead of a generic *multidimensional* array of features. Namely, we perform the filtering step at a higher hierarchical level in the estimation process as depicted in Figure 1.

The remainder of this paper is organized as follows: Section 2 summarizes the evolution of *hand-detection and segmentation* methods and shows why the existent datasets are not suitable to solve the *hand-detection* problem. Section 3, presents the UNIGE-HANDS dataset and evaluates multiple frame by frame *hand-detectors* (combinations of image features and classifiers). Later, section 4 extends the state-of-the-art method using a DBN and briefly describes each of its components. Section 5 tunes the DBN using a classic Genetic Algorithm (GA) and the Nelder-Mead simplex (NM) algorithm in a cooperative fashion. Subsequently, the performance of the DBN is evaluated, and under the light of the results, the challenges offered by the UNIGE-HANDS dataset are presented. Finally, in section 6 conclusions are drawn and some lines for future research are proposed.

2   State of the Art

In the recent years, thanks to the growing availability of FPV recording devices, the number of methods to process related videos, as well as datasets, has increased quickly. To the best of our knowledge a total of 16 datasets have been published between 2005 and 2014, each of them especially designed to face a particular objective, i.e. Object recognition and tracking, activity recognition, computer machine interaction, video summarization, physical scene reconstruction, and interaction detection. Table 1 summarizes the existent datasets and their basic characteristics. The table also highlights the evolution of the camera location, moving from shoulder, to

Table 1. Current datasets and sensors availability [9].

			# Objects			C. Location		
	Year	Objective	Activities	Objects	Num. of People	Shoulder	Chest	Head
Mayol05 [20]	2005	O1		5	1	✓		
Intel [23]	2009	O1		42	2	✓		
Kitchen. [28]	2009	O2	3		18		✓	
GTEA11 [12]	2011	O2	7		4		✓	
VINST [2]	2011	O2			1	✓		
UEC Dataset [16]	2011	O2		29	1			✓
ADL [24]	2012	O2		18	20	✓		
UTE [15]	2012	O4	4			✓		
Disney [13]	2012	O6			8			✓
GTEA gaze [14]	2012	O2	7		10			✓
EDSH [18]	2013	O1	-	-	-			✓
JPL [25]	2013	O6	7		1			✓
Virtual Museum [27]	2013	O3	5		1			✓
BEOID [11]	2014	O2	6		5			✓
EGO-GROUP [4]	2014	O6			19			✓
EGO-HPE [3]	2014	O1			4			✓

*__Objectives:__ [O1] Object Recognition and Tracking. [O2] Activity Recognition. [O3] User-Machine Interaction. [O4] Video Summarization. [O5] Phisical Scene Reconstruction. [O6] Interaction Detection.

head-mounted. This trend can be explained by the interest of technology companies to develop smart glasses and action cameras.

Existing datasets can be divided in two main groups: datasets where hands are almost always present, and datasets where hands barely appear. The first group has been used for object recognition (Mayol05, Intel), activity recognition (Kitchen, GTEA11, GTEA12) and user-machine interaction (Virtual-Museum). These datasets are usually recorded in fixed locations, like a kitchen or the office, while the user performs different tasks. Regarding the *hand-detection* problem, these datasets are not suitable because it is not possible to extract a set of negative samples in the same location and light conditions as the positive ones to train binary classifiers. The second group of datasets are frequently used for activity recognition (VINST, UEC, ADL), video segmentation (UTE, BEOID), Interaction Detection (Disney, JPL, Bristol, EGO-GROUP, EGO-HPE). In general these datasets are large and contain sequences of the user moving through several realistic locations. The number of frames with hands is low compared with the length of the videos, and the locations with frames with hands are sparse, making impossible to extract a large enough balanced training set with similar locations. It is worth to highlight the importance of having frames with and without hands in the same location. This would lead the classifiers to learn patterns related with the hands presence and not from the changes in the location.

According to [20], known for being the first public dataset in FPV for object recognition, *hand-detection/segmentation* methods can be grouped in two: model-driven and data-driven. The former uses a computerized model of the hands to recreate the image of the videos [30], while the latter exploit image features to infer about hand location, shape and position [19,21,27].

Regarding *hand-detection*, a data-driven sequential classifier is proposed in [6], which in a first stage detects hands, and in a second stage finds the hands silhouette at a pixel level *only for positive frames*. In their experiments, the authors report the performance of multiple classifiers and image features, to finally conclude that the best-performing combination is HOG plus SVM achieving 90% of true-positives and 93% of true-negatives. The authors in [31] follow a color-based approach in the same line of [19] which, as is shown in [6], could introduce noise in the results under large illumination changes. To conclude the overview, [17] proposes a probabilistic approach to detect if the hands in the video belongs to the user or to another person.

3 UNIGE-HANDS: Hand-detection Dataset

The UNIGE-HANDS dataset for *hand-detection* is a set of FPV videos, carefully recorded to guarantee a good balance between frames with hands and without hands, and offers challenging characteristics such as changes in illumination, camera motion and hand occlusions. The UNIGE-HANDS dataset, videos and ground truth, is distributed for public use. The dataset contains videos recorded in 5 uncontrolled locations (1. Office, 2. Coffee Bar, 3. Kitchen, 4. Bench, 5. Street). Each location in the dataset is in turn divided in training and testing videos. Table 2 shows some examples of the frames in each location.

Table 2. Examples of the dataset frames.

		Office	Street	Bench	Kitchen	Coffe Bar
Training	Hands					
	No Hands					
Testing	Hands					
	No Hands					

To record the dataset we used a *GoPro hero3+* head mounted camera with a resolution of 1280×720 *pixels* and 50 *fps*. The whole dataset, including training and testing videos, contains one-hour and thirty eight minutes of video. In total, the training videos have 37.21 and 37.63 minutes of positives and negative sequences, respectively. The training videos for each location are formed by 2 positives and 2 negatives videos approximately 3.34 minute-long each (10020 frames). Regarding the testing videos, they comprise 12.6 minutes of positive and 12.7 minutes of negative segments. The testing video of each location lasts approximately 4 minutes (12000 frames), changing from positive to negative in intervals of about one minute.

Following the procedure described in [6], multiple combinations of classifiers and video features are evaluated over the new dataset. The classifiers are: Support Vector Machine (SVM), Decision Tree (DT), and Random Forest (RF). The video features are: Histogram of Oriented Gradients (HOG), the global scene descriptor GIST, three color spaces (RGB, HSV, LAB) and its concatenation (RHL). The SVM uses a linear kernel with a regularization parameter $C = 1$. To compute the features, each frame is compressed to 200×112 *px*. The HOG extractor uses a block size of $16px$, a cell size of $8px$, and 9 directional bins, while color features are estimated over a grid of 25×14 cells (which are indeed $8 \times 8px$ cells).

Table 3. Performance of the proposed *hand-detectors*.

		True Positives			True Negatives		
		SVM	DT	RF	SVM	DT	RF
10-fold	HOG	**0.89**	0.77	0.81	**0.90**	0.76	0.88
	GIST	0.78	0.75	0.72	0.79	0.74	0.88
	RGB	0.77	0.72	0.73	0.77	0.73	0.86
	HSV	0.72	0.76	0.78	0.72	0.78	0.88
	LAB	0.75	0.85	**0.89**	0.75	0.85	**0.90**
	RHL^1	0.78	0.85	0.86	0.77	0.85	0.91
Training	HOG	**0.93**	0.80	0.83	**0.91**	0.80	0.91
	GIST	0.83	0.81	0.80	0.82	0.80	0.91
	RGB	0.82	0.76	0.78	0.82	0.78	0.90
	HSV	0.77	0.80	0.83	0.78	0.82	0.92
	LAB	0.80	0.88	**0.92**	0.79	0.88	**0.93**
	RHL^1	0.81	0.87	0.88	0.81	0.87	0.93
Testing	HOG	**0.76**	0.72	0.70	**0.84**	0.75	0.83
	GIST	0.51	0.51	0.43	0.67	0.58	0.70
	RGB	0.57	0.60	0.57	0.72	0.64	0.68
	HSV	0.60	0.65	0.65	0.66	0.67	0.75
	LAB	0.56	0.75	**0.74**	0.69	0.73	**0.77**
	RHL^1	0.57	0.74	0.71	0.68	0.71	0.78

[1] *RHL* is the concatenation of RGB, HSV and LAB.

Table 3 reports the performance of each feature-classifier combination under three different evaluation strategies: i) *Cross-validation:* 10-fold validation performed using the training frames as described in [6]. This procedure requires to train each classifier 10 times using 90% of the sampled frames for training and 10% for testing. The reported performances are computed using as training data 2203 frames with hands and 2233 without hands. These frames are gathered by sampling the training videos once every second. ii) *Frame by frame in the training videos:* The classifier is trained using the sampled frames, and tested in the remaining frames of the training videos. This approach only requires to train the classifiers once, which is particularly useful for the tuning procedure explained in section 4. iii) *Frame by frame in the testing videos:* The classifier is trained in the sampled frames but tested in the testing videos. This approach is the more realistic to test the classifier because, despite being recorded in the same locations, the testing videos are completely independent of the training stage.

The first finding in the table is that the performance reported in the 10-fold is slightly lower that the reported by the authors in the original paper. This reduction is explained by the challenges intentionally introduced in the dataset, namely the illumination changes and the number of locations. The 10-fold performance validates the conclusion of [6], where HOG-SVM stands as the best performing combination, although here the LAB-RF achieve a similar performance. In general the first (10-fold) and second group (Training) of performances are similar, which validates the use of the second strategy to tune the DBN in a computationally efficient way. To evaluate the performances in a dynamic perspective (video sequences), each frame of the testing videos is classified using the already trained *hand-detectors*. In general, these performances are lower than the first and second group, showing the importance of the testing videos. The optimistic performance reported by the cross-validation method is extensively explained in the literature and is known as the bias in the cross validation procedure [5].

It is worth to note that HOG-SVM is the best performing combination in all the evaluation strategies, particularly in the third one (*testing videos*), where it achieves 76% of true-positives and 84% of true-negatives. Noteworthy is also the performance of LAB-RF, which despite of being lower than HOG-SVM in the testing case, could offer important cues for to improve computational efficiency of the hand-detector. In addition to the outstanding classification rate, the HOG-SVM combination shows an extra advantage, given by its theoretical formulation, which naturally provides could provide a real valued confidence measurement of hands presence. The latter is particularly important in the dynamic approach as explained in the next section. The remainder of this paper is focused on the HOG-SVM detector and the dynamic strategy to improve its results.

4   Hand-detection DBN

In this section, a SVM-based detector is extended with dynamic information using the DBN proposed in
Figure 1. The figure sketches a multi-
level Bayesian filter for state estimation where the bottom level contains the raw images and the upper
level the filtered decision. In general,
the measurement (z_k) is a real valued representation of the SVM classifier applied to set of features F_k
extracted from the kth frame I_k. The
state $x_k \in R^2$ is the filtered SVM
confidence enriched with its speed:
$x_k = [f(F_k), \dot{f}(F_k)]$. Finally, h_k is the
binary decision based on the filtered

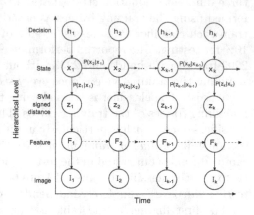

Fig. 1. Dynamic Bayesian Network for
smoothing the decision process.

value of the state: $h_k = sign(x_k[0] + t_h)$. The latter allows t_h to take values
different from 0, in order to capture the effects of the dynamic filter to the decision threshold of the SVM. The dotted line of Figure 1 is drawn to illustrate
the possible filtering at features level, as discussed in section 1. However, in our
case only the state of the system is filtered. The remaining part of this section
briefly introduces the SVM notation, the dynamic filtering, and the heuristic
tuning of the DBN parameters. See [8] for extra details about the mathematical
formulation of the SVM and the dynamic filter.

i) **Support Vector Machine:** Let's assume a dataset composed by N pairs
of training data: $(F_1, y_1), (F_2, y_2), \ldots, (F_N, y_N)$, with $F_i \in R^p$ and $y_i \in \{-1, 1\}$.
Equation (1) defines a classification hyperplane and equation (2) its induced
classification rule, where β is a unit vector. Assuming that the classes are not
separable then the values of β and β_0 are the solution of the optimization problem
given by (3), where $\xi = (\xi_1, \xi_2, \ldots, \xi_N)$ are referred to as the slack variables, and
K is constant.

$$\{F : f(F) = F^T\beta + \beta_0 = 0\} \tag{1}$$
$$G(F) = sign(f(F)) = sign(F^T\beta + \beta_0) \tag{2}$$

$$\min_{\beta,\beta_0} ||\beta|| \text{ subject to: } y_i(F_i^T\beta + \beta_0) \geq 1 - \xi_i, \forall i, \tag{3}$$

$$\xi_i \geq 0, \sum \xi_i \leq K$$

For the *hand-detection* problem we use the signed distance to the classification hyperplane, $f(F_k)$, as the measurement ($f(F_k)$ is denoted as z_k in the
DBN diagram, using the common notation for measurements in Bayesian filtering), where F_k is a global feature extracted from the k-th frame. It is important
to note that the signed distance to the decision boundary $f(F)$ gives both a

description of the result $G(F)$ of the classification (i.e. $sign(f(F))$) as well as its level of certainty. In addition, augmenting the state with the speed ($\dot{f}(F)$) would allows us to control sudden variations of such confidence. In some sense the DBN is thus self-aware of how good the classification is evolving, and can introduce some feedback mechanism to compensate for poor classification.

ii) Kalman Filter: Once the certainty level from the SVM is extracted, we address the problem of transferring and stabilizing that measurement from time to time. This strategy aims to reduce the number of wrong decisions caused by little variations in the features between frames. For this purpose we use a discrete linear Kalman filter. In general notation, the process and measurement model is given by (4), where $x_k \in \mathbb{R}^n$ is the state and $z_k \in \mathbb{R}^m$ is the measurement. The matrix $A_{n \times n}$ relates the state at previous step, x_{k-1}, with the state at current step, x_k. The matrix $H_{m \times n}$ relates the state with the measurement. Finally, w and v are the process and measurement noise respectively, which are assumed Gaussian with zero mean and covariances $Q_{n \times n}$ and $R_{m \times m}$ respectively. In our case $n = 2$ and $m = 1$, x_k is then a two dimensional vector, whose first component contains the decision certainty and the second its changing speed. At this point the binary decision, h_k, is calculated using $sign(x_0 + t_h)$, which as already mentioned, is equivalent to allow changes in the original SVM decision threshold.

$$x_k = Ax_{k-1} + w_k, \qquad z_k = Hx_k + v_k \qquad (4)$$

iii) Tuning the DBN: Within the general framework presented above, there are two sets of parameters to be estimated. The first set are the parameters defining the classification hyperplane of the SVM, namely β and β_0. These parameters are estimated using the training dataset and the SVM implementation of sklearn library [22] for python . The second set are the Kalman filter parameters and the decision threshold, namely Q, R and t_h. The tuning of the parameters of a dynamic filter is a widely explored field, and different approaches are usually followed according to the requirements of the system, restrictions in the measurements, and the ground truth availability.

Following the work of [1] the main idea behind the tuning procedure is to decompose the joint distribution of the system $p(z_{0:T}, x_{0:T}, h_{0:T})$, using the Bayesian notation, and, given the data availability and characteristics of the marginal distributions, find the optimal values of the parameters. In our case the more appropriated approach, taking advantage of the ground truth, and given the non-differentiability the binary decision boundary, is to minimize the residual prediction error in an heuristic way. With this in mind we look to minimize the squared error of the DBN decisions, defining the optimization problem as (5).

$$< Q, R, t_h >= \arg\min_{Q, R, t_h} \sum_{k=0}^{T} (h_k - \hat{h}_k)^2 \qquad (5)$$

This optimization problem is usually faced using a method like the Nelder-Mead simplex (NM) algorithm to find a optimal solution close to an initial solution. Under the absence of intuition about the initial point, the authors in [10] suggest to use a combination of a basic Genetic Algorithm (GA), to find some initial points, and later improve them using NM. In our case we design a classical GA where each genome is an instance of the parameters to be optimized, and each generation contains 100 genomes. The algorithm starts with an initial population of 100 random genomes to select the best 4, named parents. The subsequent generation is then composed by two parts. The first 64 genomes are crossovers: combinations of the parents, and the remaining 36 genomes are mutations: random modifications of the parents. In the mutation stage, the parents are selected randomly, and each element is modified with a probability of 0.5. Once the algorithm achieved an acceptable decaying rate of the objective function, the 4 best genomes among all the generations are used as initial points in NM. The best of the NM results is selected as the optimal combination.

5   Results

The results presented in this section are two-fold. First, we introduce two different optimization cases for the proposed filter. Second, we show how the DBN approach considerably improves the performance of the naive HOG-SVM detector (detailed results are presented for the best optimization problem only, but they enhancement is significant even in the worst case).

The Kalman filter is formulated as a kinematic model of the "position" (distance to the separation hyperplane) enriched with the speed, and a sampling rate Δ_t. Equation (6) shows the process and measurement model, where $w_k \sim \mathcal{N}(0, Q)$ and $v_k \sim \mathcal{N}(0, r)$. There is not exact knowledge of the differential equation regulating the dynamic process, thus it is not possible to precisely state the law that moves the decision back and forth the decision boundary. Actually, it is not known if such differential equation exists or can be solved in closed form. For this reason, we borrow from physics a constant force model, which we think is a good starting point. This is equivalent to suppose there is some constant (oscillating) force that keeps the features away from the decision hyper-surface or make them cross it, with a constant acceleration a.

$$\begin{bmatrix} x_k \\ \dot{x}_k \end{bmatrix} = \begin{bmatrix} 1 & \Delta_t \\ 0 & 1 \end{bmatrix} \begin{bmatrix} x_{k-1} \\ \dot{x}_{k-1} \end{bmatrix} + w_k, \text{ and } z_k = [1, 0] \begin{bmatrix} x_k \\ \dot{x}_k \end{bmatrix} + v_k \qquad (6)$$

More in detail, the first equation in (6) models an exact constant acceleration, where a is the *effect* of a control input which generates exactly the time-dependent noise term. On the other hand, employing a state augmented with the second derivative as well, would allow small variations of a, accounted for in the noise term w_k. In our optimization framework, this is equivalent to parametrize each of the elements of Q. In this case the genomes are given by instances of $[Q_{1,1}, Q_{1,2}, Q_{2,1}, Q_{2,2}, r, t_h]$, and the elements of each crossover are selected randomly from one of the current parents. In the second optimization case, we suppose instead that the acceleration is constant, and the matrix Q is factorized isolating the sampling rate as in (7). In this case the genomes are of the form $[q, r, t_h]$ and the crossovers are all the possible combinations of the current parents. To keep control of the search space we bound the elements of Q as well as q and r to move between 0 and 1000. The decision criteria t_h is bounded between -0.5 and 0.5. The number of iterations is set to 20. To evaluate the objective function for each combination we merge the testing videos and calculate the overall accuracy under the second strategy of Table 3. We point out that the second strategy is used because of computational advantages and to keep the training and tuning process independent of the testing videos.

$$Q = q * \begin{bmatrix} \frac{\Delta_t^4}{4} & \frac{\Delta_t^3}{2} \\ \frac{\Delta_t^3}{2} & \Delta_t^2 \end{bmatrix} \tag{7}$$

From the tuning process of the two cases presented above we found that the best accuracy is achieved for the genome $[+1.15e^{-9}, +1.39e^{-7}, +8.72e^{-8}, +2.07e^{-5}, +60.78, -7.63e^{-2}]$ and $[+0.039, +32.54, -0.151]$ for the general and factorized case respectively. The final number of frames misclassified by each case are 3505 and 3391 over a total of 220610. As a comparison, the total of misclassified frames using naive HOG-SVM is 18211. It is remarkable the fact that both optimization scenarios reach a similar value in the objective function, validating the use of the constant acceleration model to reduce the flickering in the decision. The remaining of this section present more in detail the results achieved by the factorized case over the testing videos. Figure 2 shows, in red line, the measurement z_k and, in blue line, the filtered state

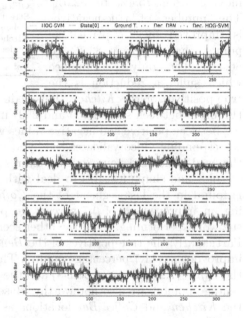

Fig. 2. Performance of the DBN in each of the locations in the UNIGE-HANDS . dataset.

x_k. The horizontal axis is the decision threshold. Taking the value of 4, 5, 6 (-4, -5, -6) the figure shows the ground truth, the decision of the HOG-SVM method and DBN, respectively. These decisions takes positive values if there are hands and negative if not. The noisy movements of z_k confirm the dependence of the measurement to little changes between frames. As it is intended, the Kalman filter reduces the noise and preserve the trend of z_k.

It can be noted from the pointwise decisions of HOG-SVM (Dec. HOG-SVM) that it is difficult to obtain continuous segments of the video with or without hands. This effect is the consequence of the measurement noise changing frequently the sign of z_k. Once the noise is reduced using the DBN, the decisions stabilizes and continuous segments appear. It is particularly remarkable the performance of the DBN in the *Office* and the *Bench* sequences. However, because of the poor performance of the HOG-SVM, the DBN misclassifies long segments in the *Kitchen* and the *Coffee bar* sequences. The poor performance of the HOG-SVM in these sequences can be explained by the 3D perspective created by the table, which creates lines in the same positions and directions of those created by the hands.

Table 4 summarizes the performance for each location of the dataset. In total the DBN improves the number of true-positives by 5.6 percentage points, moving from 76.4% to 82.0%. The number of true-negatives is improved by 2.7 percentage points, changing from 83.7% to 86.4%. The only performance which suffer a reduction is the

Table 4. Comparsion of the performance of the HOG-SVM and the proposed DBN.

	True positives		True negatives	
	HOG-SVM	DBN	HOG-SVM	DBN
Office	0.893	0.965	0.929	0.952
Street	0.756	0.834	0.867	0.898
Bench	0.765	0.882	0.965	0.979
Kitchen	0.627	0.606	0.777	0.848
Coffee bar	0.817	0.874	0.653	0.660
Total	0.764	0.820	0.837	0.864

true-positives of the *Kitchen*. This reduction is explained by a long segment (Figure 2 between second 150 and 250) in which the measurements are switching between positive and negative values with no trend. An extra analysis of the corresponding video validates the hypothesis of the 3D perspective created by the used table, and points out an interesting research idea regarding the fusion of color and shape features to deal with this kind of scenarios. A similar case is found in the last segment of the *Coffee Bar* location, which despite showing an improvement of 0.7 percentage points in the true-negatives, is one of the worst performing. In all the other scenarios the improvement is remarkable. Particularly, the true-positives of the *Bench* location is the one with the largest improvement (11.7 percentage points). The improvement in the true-positives of the *Office* (7.2 percentage points) and the true-negatives of the *Kitchen* (7.1 percentage points) are also noteworthy. Based on these improvements we validate the *Kitchen* and *Coffee Bar* locations as the more challenging in the UNIGE-HANDS dataset.

6   Conclusions and Future Research

This paper presents the UNIGE-HANDS dataset for *hand-detection* and extends a state-of-the-art method proposed in [6] incorporating a dynamic perspective. The dataset is recorded in 5 different locations and guarantees realistic conditions like, changes in the illumination, occlusions and fast camera movements. Additionally, the dataset is divided in training and testing videos to guarantee fair comparisons of coming methods.

To validate the consistence of the dataset with previous studies we evaluate the state-of-the-art method using cross validation, as suggested in [6,8], and using the testing videos of the dataset. Three conclusions arises from the results: i) The dataset is challenging enough, and the testing videos are a good approach to avoid the bias in the cross validation results, ii) Little variations between frames highly affects the performance of the existing frame-by-frame *hand-detectors*, iii) The performances reported validates the results of previous studies on which SVM-HOG is the best combination for *hand-detection*.

The HOG-SVM frame by frame approach is extended using a Dynamic Bayesian Network where the dynamic part is carried by a Kalman filter with a constant acceleration model. The parameters of the KF, as well as the decision threshold, are tuned using a genetic algorithms and the Nelder-Mead simplex algorithm. The DBN is evaluated in each of the dataset locations and its performance is presented as the baseline to be used with the UNIGE-HANDS dataset. We highlight the model selection as an interesting research line that could lead to further improvements in the performance of the classifier.

References

1. Abbeel, P., Coates, A.: Discriminative training of Kalman filters. In: Robotics: Science and Systems, pp. 1–8. Cambridge, MA, USA (2005)
2. Aghazadeh, O., Sullivan, J., Carlsson, S.: Novelty detection from an ego-centric perspective. In: Computer Vision and Pattern Recognition, pp. 3297–3304. IEEE, Pittsburgh, June 2011
3. Alletto, S., Serra, G., Calderara, S., Cucchiara, R.: Head pose estimation in first-person camera views. In: International Conference on Pattern Recognition, p. 4188. IEEE Computer Society (2014)
4. Alletto, S., Serra, G., Calderara, S., Solera, F., Cucchiara, R.: From ego to nos-vision: detecting social relationships in first-person views. In: Computer Vision and Pattern Recognition, pp. 594–599. IEEE, June 2014
5. Bengio, Y., Grandvalet, Y.: No Unbiased Estimator of the Variance of k-fold Cross-Validation. The Journal of Machine Learning Research **5**, 1089–1105 (2004)
6. Betancourt, A.M.L., Rauterberg, M., Regazzoni, C.: A sequential classifier for hand detection in the framework of egocentric vision. In: 2014 IEEE Conference on Computer Vision and Pattern Recognition Workshops, vol. 1, pp. 600–605. IEEE, Columbus, June 2014
7. Betancourt, A., Morerio, P., Marcenaro, L., Barakova, E., Rauterberg, M., Regazzoni, C.: Towards a unified framework for hand-based methods in first person vision. In: IEEE International Conference on Multimedia and Expo (Workshops). IEEE, Turin (2015)
8. Betancourt, A., Morerio, P., Marcenaro, L., Rauterberg, M., Regazzoni, C.: Filtering SVM frame-by-frame binary classification in a detection framework. In: International Conference on Image Processing. IEEE, Quebec (2015)
9. Betancourt, A., Morerio, P., Regazzoni, C., Rauterberg, M.: The Evolution of First Person Vision Methods: A Survey. IEEE Transactions on Circuits and Systems for Video Technology **25**(5), 744–760 (2015)
10. Chelouah, R., Siarry, P.: Genetic and NelderMead algorithms hybridized for a more accurate global optimization of continuous multiminima functions. European Journal of Operational Research **148**(2), 335–348 (2003)

11. Damen, D., Haines, O.: Multi-user egocentric online system for unsupervised assistance on object usage. In: European Conference on Computer Vision (2014)
12. Fathi, A., Farhadi, A., Rehg, J.: Understanding egocentric activities. In: International Conference on Computer Vision, pp. 407–414. IEEE, November 2011
13. Fathi, A., Hodgins, J., Rehg, J.: Social interactions: a first-person perspective. In: Computer Vision and Pattern Recognition, pp. 1226–1233. IEEE, Providence, June 2012
14. Fathi, A., Li, Y., Rehg, J.: Learning to recognize daily actions using gaze. In: European Conference on Computer Vision, pp. 314–327. Georgia Institute of Technology, Florence (2012)
15. Ghosh, J., Grauman, K.: Discovering important people and objects for egocentric video summarization. In: Computer Vision and Pattern Recognition, pp. 1346–1353. IEEE, June 2012
16. Kitani, K., Okabe, T.: Fast unsupervised ego-action learning for first-person sports videos. In: Computer Vision and Pattern Recognition, pp. 3241–3248. IEEE, Providence, June 2011
17. Lee, S., Bambach, S., Crandall, D., Franchak, J., Yu, C.: This hand is my hand: a probabilistic approach to hand disambiguation in egocentric video. In: Computer Vision and Pattern Recognition, pp. 1–8. IEEE Computer Society, Columbus (2014)
18. Li, C., Kitani, K.: Pixel-level hand detection in ego-centric videos. In: Computer Vision and Pattern Recognition, pp. 3570–3577. IEEE, June 2013
19. Li, Y., Fathi, A., Rehg, J.: Learning to predict gaze in egocentric video. In: International Conference on Computer Vision, pp. 1–8. IEEE (2013)
20. Mayol, W., Murray, D.: Wearable hand activity recognition for event summarization. In: International Symposium on Wearable Computers, pp. 1–8. IEEE (2005)
21. Morerio, P., Marcenaro, L., Regazzoni, C.: Hand detection in first person vision. In: Information Fusion, pp. 1502–1507. University of Genoa, Istanbul (2013)
22. Pedregosa, F., Varoquaux, G., Gramfort, A., Michel, V., Thirion, B., Grisel, O., Blondel, M., Prettenhofer, P., Weiss, R., Dubourg, V., Vanderplas, J., Passos, A., Cournapeau, D., Brucher, M., Perrot, M., Duchesnay, E.: Scikit-learn: Machine Learning in Python. Research, Journal of Machine Learning **12**, 2825–2830 (2011)
23. Philipose, M.: Egocentric recognition of handled objects: benchmark and analysis. In: Computer Vision and Pattern Recognition, pp. 1–8. IEEE, Miami, June 2009
24. Pirsiavash, H., Ramanan, D.: Detecting activities of daily living in first-person camera views. In: Computer Vision and Pattern Recognition, pp. 2847–2854. IEEE, June 2012
25. Ryoo, M., Matthies, L.: First-person activity recognition: what are they doing to me? In: Conference on Computer Vision and Pattern Recognition, pp. 2730–2737. IEEE Comput. Soc, Portland (2013)
26. Schiele, B., Oliver, N., Jebara, T., Pentland, A.: An interactive computer vision system DyPERS: dynamic personal enhanced reality system. In: Christensen, H.I. (ed.) ICVS 1999. LNCS, vol. 1542, pp. 51–65. Springer, Heidelberg (1998)
27. Serra, G., Camurri, M., Baraldi, L.: Hand segmentation for gesture recognition in ego-vision. In: Workshop on Interactive Multimedia on Mobile & Portable Devices, pp. 31–36. ACM Press, New York (2013)

28. Spriggs, E., De La Torre, F., Hebert, M.: Temporal segmentation and activity classification from first-person sensing. In: Computer Vision and Pattern Recognition Workshops, pp. 17–24. IEEE, June 2009
29. Starner, T., Schiele, B., Pentland, A.: Visual contextual awareness in wearable computing. In: International Symposium on Wearable Computers, pp. 50–57. IEEE Computer Society (1998)
30. Sun, L., Klank, U., Beetz, M.: Eyewatchme3d hand and object tracking for inside out activity analysis. In: Computer Vision and Pattern Recognition, pp. 9–16 (2009)
31. Zariffa, J., Popovic, M.: Hand Contour Detection in Wearable Camera Video Using an Adaptive Histogram Region of Interest. Journal of NeuroEngineering and Rehabilitation 10(114), 1–10 (2013)

Segmentation and Labelling of EEG for Brain Computer Interfaces

Tracey A. Camilleri$^{(\boxtimes)}$, Kenneth P. Camilleri, and Simon G. Fabri

Department of Systems and Control Engineering,
University of Malta, Msida MSD 2080, Malta
tracey.camilleri@um.edu.mt

Abstract. Segmentation and labelling of time series is a common requirement for several applications. A brain computer interface (BCI) is achieved by classification of time intervals of the electroencephalographic (EEG) signal and thus requires EEG signal segmentation and labelling. This work investigates the use of an autoregressive model, extended to a switching multiple modelling framework, to automatically segment and label EEG data into distinct modes of operation that may switch abruptly and arbitrarily in time. The applicability of this approach to BCI systems is illustrated on an eye closure dependent BCI and on a motor imagery based BCI. Results show that the proposed autoregressive switching multiple model approach offers a unified framework of detecting multiple modes, even in the presence of limited training data.

1 Introduction

Electroencephalographic (EEG) signals recorded non-invasively from a subject using a brain computer interface (BCI) system are known to be non-stationary. This can be considered to reflect the switching dynamics across states of the underlying neurons, matching with the generic definition of temporal multimodal systems [3] whose dynamics may switch from one mode of operation to another in an abrupt and arbitrary fashion. Denoting a mode of operation as a mental state, the brain activity recorded through EEG can thus be modelled as a sequence of transitions between one mental state and another, with each state having distinct temporal, spectral and spatial properties which allow for their differentiation.

Various approaches of representing or modelling EEG data have been documented to obtain more insight on brain behaviour [10]. Switching between different brain patterns is generally accomplished by looking for statistical differences across local stationary segments, assuming adaptive modelling techniques such as the adaptive autoregressive model, or considering a divide and conquer approach where distinct brain patterns are represented by individual expert models.

Parametric approaches such as the adaptive autoregressive model and its variants have been successfully applied to model EEG data [8] but their extension to a switching multiple modelling framework has been limited. This work thus proposes the use of such a framework, referred to as an autoregressive switching multiple modelling (AR-SMM) framework, for the automatic segmentation and

© Springer International Publishing Switzerland 2015
G. Azzopardi and N. Petkov (Eds.): CAIP 2015, Part I, LNCS 9256, pp. 288–299, 2015.
DOI: 10.1007/978-3-319-23192-1_24

labelling of EEG data typical in BCI systems. The advantage of the proposed method is that it can be used in real-time, requires very limited training data and offers a unified framework for detecting different brain patterns.

2   Theory of Autoregressive Switching Multiple Models

In multiple modelling, it is assumed that the data is well represented by a set of N models, each representing one specific mode of operation, which in this context is a mental state. Each model M^i for $i = 1, 2, ..., N$, is characterised by a set of parameters Θ^i. The goal is to find which of these candidate models best represents the data.

In this work a linear Gaussian State Space Model [4] is assumed for each mode, represented by the following state and measurement equations:

$$\mathbf{x}_t = \boldsymbol{\Phi} \mathbf{x}_{t-1} + \mathbf{w}_t \tag{1}$$

$$y_t = \mathbf{H}_t \mathbf{x}_t + v_t \tag{2}$$

where y_t represents the EEG voltage recorded from one particular channel at time t, $\mathbf{x}_t$ represents a latent variable called the state vector, $\mathbf{H}_t$ is the observation vector, $\boldsymbol{\Phi}$ represents the state transition matrix and $\mathbf{w}_t$ and v_t are two independent Gaussian noise processes with zero mean and covariance $\mathbf{Q}$ and variance R, respectively. For autoregressive models, the state vector consists of the p unknown autoregressive parameters, $\mathbf{x}_t = [a_1, a_2, ..., a_p]$ and the observation vector is made up of the p past observations, i.e. $\mathbf{H}_t = [y_{t-1}, y_{t-2}, ..., y_{t-p}]$, where p is the autoregressive model order.

Apart from the unknown state vector $\mathbf{x}_t$, each model consists of a set Θ of five unknown system parameters given by:

$$\Theta = [R, \mathbf{Q}, \boldsymbol{\Phi}, \boldsymbol{x_0}, \boldsymbol{\Sigma}] \tag{3}$$

Parameter $\boldsymbol{x_0}$ represents the initial hidden state vector and $\boldsymbol{\Sigma}$ its corresponding covariance. Following the approach in [4], in order to find an estimate of this set of system parameters, the Expectation Maximisation algorithm [2] is used.

In a multimodal system that is not subject to temporal switching, the model M^i from the candidate set which best represents the data can be evaluated using Bayes' rule. In this case, the posterior probability of model M^i given the data history $\mathbf{Y}^t = [y_t, y_{t-1}, ..., y_1]$ is given by [3]:

$$\begin{aligned} Pr(M^i | \mathbf{Y}^t) &= Pr(M^i | y_t, \mathbf{Y}^{t-1}) \\ &= \frac{p(y_t | M^i, \mathbf{Y}^{t-1}) Pr(M^i | \mathbf{Y}^{t-1})}{\sum_{j=1}^{N} p(y_t | M^j, \mathbf{Y}^{t-1}) Pr(M^j | \mathbf{Y}^{t-1})} \end{aligned} \tag{4}$$

For a state space model with linear and Gaussian dynamics, the Kalman filter [6] can be used to calculate the mean square estimate of state $\mathbf{x}_t$ according to model M^i, denoted as $\hat{\mathbf{x}}^i_{t|t-1}$ and the corresponding covariance of the estimation error denoted as $\mathbf{P}^i_{t|t-1}$. Linearity and Gaussianity give the likelihood function:

$$p(y_t|M^i, \mathbf{Y}^{t-1}) = -\frac{1}{(2\pi)^{\frac{1}{2}}|C^i_t|^{\frac{1}{2}}} \exp^{-\frac{1}{2}(y_t-\hat{y}^i_t)'(C^i_t)^{-1}(y_t-\hat{y}^i_t)} \tag{5}$$

where the mean estimate of the observation y_t, denoted as $\hat{y}^i_t$, and the corresponding variance C^i_t attributed to model M^i are estimated as follows [3]:

$$\hat{y}^i_t = \mathbf{H}^i_t \hat{\mathbf{x}}^i_{t|t-1} \tag{6}$$

$$C^i_t = \mathbf{H}^i_t \mathbf{P}^i_{t|t-1} \mathbf{H}^{i'}_t + R^i \tag{7}$$

and $(y_t - \hat{y}^i_t)$ in equation (5), referred to as the residual, represents the difference between the observation y_t and its mean estimate $\hat{y}^i_t$. The most suitable model from the candidate set of models at every time instant is taken to be the one that has the maximum *a posteriori* (MAP) probability calculated by (4). To extend the use of (4) to the temporal switching case, the lower bounding method [3] was applied. This bounds all model probabilities to some specific non-zero, small, positive value so that the models remain possible candidates if a switch in dynamics occurs. Thus, if $Pr(M^i|\mathbf{Y}^t)$ calculated in (4) is smaller than a chosen lower bound δ, the value of $Pr(M^i|\mathbf{Y}^t)$ is reset to δ. This approach offers a simple pragmatic solution for switching systems when compared to other more theoretically rigorous, but more computationally demanding, approaches such as the Interacting Multiple Model (IMM) and the Generalized Pseudo Bayes (GPB) techniques [3]. The lower bounding approach, despite being a pragmatic solution, has been shown to give good results on data other than EEG [5, 7]. This work thus investigates the applicability of an Autoregressive Switching Multiple Model (AR-SMM) framework with lower bounding approximations to EEG data typical in BCI systems. More details on the algorithm and its application to sleep EEG data can be found in [1].

3   AR-SMMs Applied to EEG Data

This section shows the segmentation and labelling results of the AR-SMM framework when applied to EEG data recorded during i) an eye-closure dependent BCI and ii) a motor imagery based BCI.

3.1   Eye-Closure Dependent BCI

EEG data recorded during an eyes-open (EO) eyes-closed (EC) test was used to identify whether the AR-SMM approach is able to identify the two states (EO and EC). It is known that the alpha activity recorded from the occipital region of the scalp is blocked or attenuated when eyes are open [11], thus allowing for their differentiation in principle. This dataset is also used to investigate whether the approach can be extended to detect eye blinks.

Data. The dataset consists of 11 eyes open and 11 eyes closed trials, recorded from one subject who was taking part in a larger BCI experiment. The data was recorded over channel O2 with a sampling frequency of 256Hz and band pass filtered between 0.5-60Hz. Each trial was 7.25s long, with a visual cue presented between 3 and 4.25s to indicate whether to close the eyes or to keep them open. Trials were separated with random periods ranging between 1 and 2 seconds.

Supervised Learning. Adopting a 10 by 2-fold cross validation scheme, the system parameters of the EO and EC states were first learnt using the EM algorithm. Specifically, six windows of 1s length, denoting visually clear state characteristics, were selected from the training data and supplied to the EM algorithm which was allowed to go through 100 recursions to estimate the unknown system parameters Θ.

Figure 1 shows the smoothed segmentation and labelling results of 10 trials in the first cross validated set, using a mode filter of 0.5s and an AR model order of 6. The latter was based on the result of a one-way analysis of variance test which showed that there is no statistically significant difference in results for model orders between 2 and 10. From Figure 1 it is observed that when the alpha rhythm emerges, model switching to the EC model, which captures this characteristic, occurs. Measuring performance on a sample by sample basis over the 4.25s-7.25s window and taking an average over the 10 cross validated sets showed that 65.85% of this window for EC trials and 83.59% for EO trials was labelled as an eyes closed state. The lower percentage for the EC trials is a result of inter-trial variability of the actual eye closure of the subject.

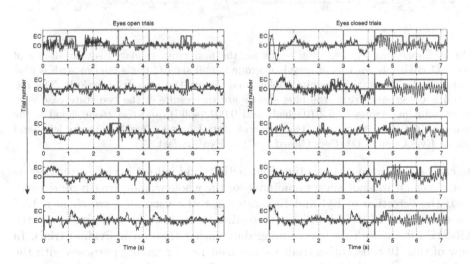

Fig. 1. Segmentation and labelling result (shown in red) for 5 eyes open (left) and 5 eyes closed (right) trials. The green lines show the period from 3-4.25s during which the visual cue was displayed.

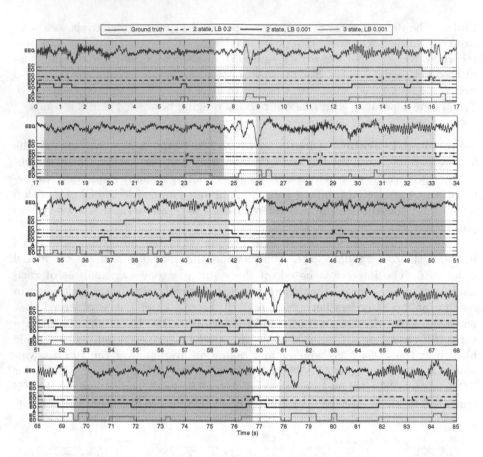

Fig. 2. Supervised segmentation result for the first cross validated set consisting of four EO trials (shown with a grey background) and six EC trials (shown with a blue background). Areas with a white background denote the inter-trial periods. The red signal is the ground truth, the blue signals are the results of the two state case with lower bounding values of 0.2 (dashed) and 0.001 (solid), and the green signal is the result for the three state case. The different state labels are marked on the left hand side as Eyes Open (EO), Eyes Closed (EC) or Eye Artifact (A).

As can be seen, in most trials the alpha activity did not set in right after the cue at 4.25s and it was not always dominant for the whole window length considered.

If the detection of EO and EC states is to be used as a switch in a BCI system as done in [12], it will be interesting to analyse the performance of the AR-SMM framework on free running data rather than on individual trials. In view of this, 10 consecutive trials were considered for testing purposes with the training phase remaining the same as before. Performance was measured against a ground truth signal assuming the subject to be in an EO state throughout the whole recording except for the 3-7.25s windows of EC trials in which that data was assumed to be in an EC state.

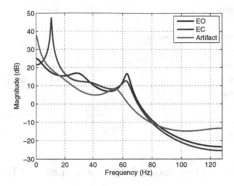

Fig. 3. Spectra for the eyes open (EO), eyes closed (EC) or eye artifact models.

Figure 2 shows the segmentation and labelling result of one of the 10 validated sets having 4 EO and 6 EC trials. The signal in red shows the ground truth signal while those in blue show the results of the AR-SMM using a mode filter of 0.5s and a lower bound δ of 0.2 (dashed line) and 0.001 (solid line) respectively. This result shows that during EC events, the AR-SMM framework correctly switches to an EC state. Although the switched interval does not always correspond entirely to the window marked as EC in the ground truth signal, it is clear that it does capture the alpha activity dominant in the EEG signal during this time. Some false positives do occur, especially during noisy periods such as from 0-3s and around the 28th second, but these are generally less than half a second in duration and can possibly be filtered out at a later stage.

The results for the two considered δ values showed very minor differences but as expected a high δ increases the likelihood of switching between states. A multiple comparison test showed that the labelling performance of the AR-SMM is insensitive to the choice of lower bounding threshold value as long as $\delta < 0.3$.

Eye Artifact Detection. Given a number of eye artifacts visually detectable in the recorded EEG data, the AR-SMM framework was extended to a three model case to investigate whether it could distinguish between EO, EC and eye artifact (A) states. Supervised learning of the three modes was carried out but this time training of the eyes open and eye blink states was done on six 0.5s windows rather than 1s windows. The reason behind the use of shorter windows was i) to restrict the EO model from capturing low frequencies well and hence having eye blinks being labelled as EO and ii) to take into consideration the short duration of eye blinks and ensure that the A model reflects only its characteristics. Figure 3 shows the resulting spectra for the three different states where it is clear that the EC model has dominant alpha activity (10-12Hz) while the eye artifact model has dominant low frequency activity which is distinct from the EO model.

For comparison purposes, the results for the three model case are shown in green on Figure 2. In this case a mode filter of 0.25s was used instead of 0.5s to avoid having the eye blink periods filtered out due to their short duration.

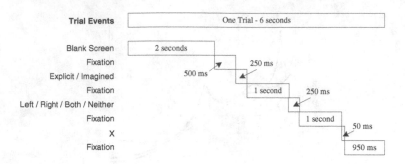

Fig. 4. Experimental protocol of the motor imagery EEG data [9].

The new results show that the periods denoting eye closure are still well captured as in the two mode case but now a switch to artifact mode is also detected at each inter-trial period and in periods of low frequency activity occurring prior to seconds 36 and 39 which can also possibly be eye artifacts. This shows that training on pre-defined artifact signals can be incorporated within the switching framework such that apart from detecting events used as control signals in the BCI system, artifact detection can also be accomplished.

3.2 Motor Imagery Based BCI

This section analyses EEG data recorded in a BCI system based on somatosensory rhythms generated during left and right hand motor imagery. The event related desynchronisation and synchronisation, synonymous with motor imagery, are considered to represent switching dynamics within the EEG signal which can be captured through an autoregressive switching multiple modelling framework.

Data. For this analysis the EEG data of 8 subjects made available for the NIPS2001 Brain-Computer Interface Workshop was used [9], with the experimental protocol as shown in Figure 4. Left and right mental tasks were considered where a total of 90 trials were available per subject. Given that event related EEG responses are predominant on the hand motor cortical area, only the EEG data recorded at channels C3 and C4, at a sampling frequency of 100Hz, were analysed. As a pre-processing step the data was pre-filtered between 0.5Hz and 30Hz and spatially filtered using Hjorth Laplacian.

Supervised Learning. Although the experimental protocol of this dataset was based on a cued experiment, in this study an asynchronous BCI simulation as done in [13] is considered by assuming the first part of each trial to represent a No Control (NC) background state and the second part an Intentional Control (IC) state. The transition from one state to another is expected to occur close to the preparation cue shown at 3.75s. Spectrogram analysis showed that ERD

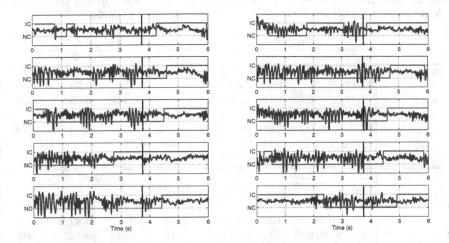

Fig. 5. Data segmentation and labelling (in red) of 10 right trials from Subject 1.

occurs after cue onset but the challenge lies in identifying such transitions on a single trial basis where these ERD patterns may not be consistent.

Using a 10 by 2-fold cross validation scheme, the training data for the EM algorithm was extracted by taking the 1 to 1.5 second window from each trial to represent the NC state and the 4.75 to 5.25 second window to represent the IC period. These windows were chosen as visually they exhibited clear ERD in the alpha band which would allow the two states to be differentiated.

Table 1. Quantitative measures and their description.

Measure	Description
$Switch_{NC \longrightarrow IC}$	The percentage number of trials in which a transition from a NC to an IC state occurred within the 3.75s to 6s window.
T_s	The average time taken to switch from NC to IC in those trials where a switch within the 3.75s to 6s time window was detected.
$NC_{[0-3.75s]}$	The percentage of this 3.75s window in which each trial was correctly labeled as being in a NC state. This measure is equivalent to the True Negative Rate (TNR).
$IC_{[3.75-6s]}$	The percentage of this 2.25s window in which each trial was correctly labeled as being in an IC state. This measure is equivalent to the True Positive Rate (TPR).
NC_{Switch}	The number of false switches per trial occurring in the NC period, taken over the 0-3.75s window.
IC_{Switch}	The number of false switches (>2) from the NC to IC state per trial, in the IC period, taken over the 3.75-6s window.
MSE	The mean squared difference between a ground truth label considering from 0-3.75s as NC and from 3.75-6s as IC, and the true label given by the AR-SMM approach.

Table 2. Quantitative measures of the single trial classification results on right and left hand trials, for all 8 subjects, recorded on contralateral channels.

	Subject 1		Subject 2	
	Right	Left	Right	Left
$Switch_{NC \longrightarrow IC}$	$76.67 \pm 2.62\%$	$76.22 \pm 4.92\%$	$56.00 \pm 5.72\%$	$63.56 \pm 5.46\%$
T_s	$0.64 \pm 0.07s$	$0.64 \pm 0.11s$	$0.87 \pm 0.11s$	$0.70 \pm 0.10s$
$NC_{[0-3s]}$	$72.00 \pm 5.10\%$	$64.68 \pm 2.31\%$	$65.86 \pm 6.44\%$	$66.52 \pm 4.62\%$
NC_{Switch}	1.63 ± 0.25	2.20 ± 0.31	1.49 ± 0.23	1.74 ± 0.13
$IC_{[4.5-6s]}$	$71.55 \pm 2.60\%$	$71.00 \pm 5.60\%$	$49.42 \pm 5.38\%$	$59.01 \pm 5.66\%$
IC_{Switch}	0.52 ± 0.12	0.66 ± 0.08	0.64 ± 0.18	0.90 ± 0.05
MSE	0.28 ± 0.02	0.33 ± 0.02	0.40 ± 0.03	0.36 ± 0.02

	Subject 3		Subject 4	
	Right	Left	Right	Left
$Switch_{NC \longrightarrow IC}$	$11.11 \pm 3.14\%$	$22.89 \pm 6.87\%$	$47.33 \pm 7.41\%$	$56.47 \pm 7.86\%$
T_s	$0.89 \pm 0.31s$	$1.11 \pm 0.15s$	$0.59 \pm 0.07s$	$0.89 \pm 0.09s$
$NC_{[0-3s]}$	$42.59 \pm 10.90\%$	$40.10 \pm 6.72\%$	$49.94 \pm 8.20\%$	$66.22 \pm 6.50\%$
NC_{Switch}	0.84 ± 0.16	1.34 ± 0.16	1.96 ± 0.25	1.56 ± 0.26
$IC_{[4.5-6s]}$	$66.85 \pm 10.29\%$	$62.75 \pm 9.98\%$	$81.77 \pm 3.13\%$	$66.06 \pm 4.44\%$
IC_{Switch}	0.09 ± 0.04	0.16 ± 0.07	0.43 ± 0.13	0.50 ± 0.06
MSE	0.48 ± 0.03	0.51 ± 0.02	0.38 ± 0.04	0.34 ± 0.03

	Subject 5		Subject 6	
	Right	Left	Right	Left
$Switch_{NC \longrightarrow IC}$	$57.33 \pm 3.89\%$	$49.33 \pm 6.61\%$	$76.00 \pm 7.75\%$	$80.00 \pm 4.56\%$
T_s	$0.79 \pm 0.07s$	$0.99 \pm 0.06s$	$0.63 \pm 0.08s$	$0.57 \pm 0.03s$
$NC_{[0-3s]}$	$47.74 \pm 5.42\%$	$59.82 \pm 12.48\%$	$79.73 \pm 7.45\%$	$77.71 \pm 3.00\%$
NC_{Switch}	1.82 ± 0.20	1.57 ± 0.12	1.54 ± 0.57	1.59 ± 0.13
$IC_{[4.5-6s]}$	$70.93 \pm 5.96\%$	$52.73 \pm 14.41\%$	$68.40 \pm 8.07\%$	$69.812 \pm 2.64\%$
IC_{Switch}	0.69 ± 0.11	0.47 ± 0.09	0.7 ± 0.1	0.65 ± 0.08
MSE	0.43 ± 0.03	0.43 ± 0.04	0.25 ± 0.02	0.26 ± 0.01

	Subject 7		Subject 8	
	Right	Left	Right	Left
$Switch_{NC \longrightarrow IC}$	$36.67 \pm 7.28\%$	$55.56 \pm 6.37\%$	$59.11 \pm 8.84\%$	$25.56 \pm 15.26\%$
T_s	$0.67 \pm 0.07s$	$0.84 \pm 0.08s$	$1.01 \pm 0.08s$	$0.84 \pm 0.39s$
$NC_{[0-3s]}$	$62.78 \pm 3.15\%$	$66.27 \pm 4.91\%$	$50.12 \pm 8.48\%$	$55.08 \pm 14.24\%$
NC_{Switch}	1.84 ± 0.22	1.71 ± 0.12	1.52 ± 0.21	1.34 ± 0.29
$IC_{[4.5-6s]}$	$74.40 \pm 4.46\%$	$61.77 \pm 5.54\%$	$65.01 \pm 5.37\%$	$54.76 \pm 27.61\%$
IC_{Switch}	0.54 ± 0.10	0.60 ± 0.12	0.26 ± 0.09	0.23 ± 0.11
MSE	0.33 ± 0.01	0.35 ± 0.01	0.44 ± 0.05	0.45 ± 0.03

The segmentation result of the AR-SMM approach when using a model order of 7 and a δ of 0.001 is shown in Figure 5 for ten right hand trials of Subject 1. A model order of 7 was chosen as it provides enough poles to represent the spectral characteristics of the EEG data. The segmentation result in red shows a clear transition to the IC state close to the cue onset, represented by the vertical black line, with the different transition instants reflecting inter-trial variability.

To obtain better insight on the performance of the AR-SMM framework on single trials, a set of quantitative measures, defined in Table 1, were evaluated for all 8 subjects. Table 2 shows the average results over the 10 cross validated sets. The great inter-subject variability is highlighted where the best performing Subjects 1 and 6 have over 76% of the training trials switching from a NC to an IC state, some time after the preparation cue shown at 3.75s, whilst Subject 7, for example, has a switch for right trials in only 36% of the cases. Another interesting result is the trend observed across all subjects for the number of false switches in the NC and IC periods. Specifically, in the IC period there is typically 1 false switch every 2 trials while in the NC period false switches range from 1.5 to 2 per trial. This could reflect a possibly higher non-stationary NC period which could be the result of the various cues being presented.

Sensitivity to Lower Bound δ. The results for the motor imagery data were obtained with a lower bound $\delta = 0.001$, allowing all models to remain possible candidates and at the same time avoiding excessive switching across the two states which is not typical of the data being analysed. To evaluate the sensitivity of the AR-SMM approach to the δ value, the right trials of Subject 1 were re-evaluated for $1 \times 10^{-10} \leq \delta \leq 0.4$. The True Positive Rates (TPR) and False Positive Rates (FPR) averaged over the 10 cross validated sets are plotted as a Receiver Operating Characteristic (ROC) curve in Figure 6 where the best compromise can be seen to correspond to a threshold of 1×10^{-3}, giving an averaged TPR of 71.6% and an averaged FPR of 27.5%.

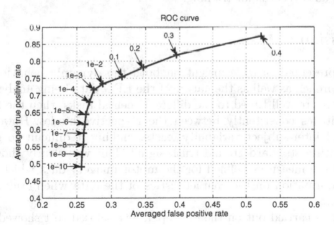

Fig. 6. ROC curve showing the averaged AR-SMM performance for the right trials of Subject 1 when varying the lower bounding threshold value between 1×10^{-10} and 0.4.

Sensitivity to the Amount of Training Data. To evaluate the difference in AR-SMM performance when training data is limited, a test was carried out varying the number of 0.5s training windows from 45 down to 15, in steps of 10. Figure 7 shows that performance deteriorated only for the case with 15 samples.

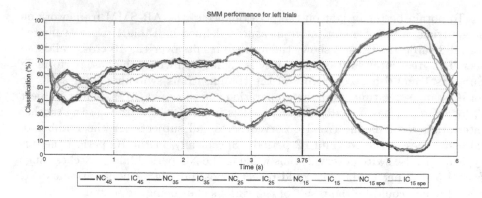

Fig. 7. AR-SMM performance for left hand trials of Subject 1 as the number of trials in the training set is varied from 15 to 45 windows in steps of 10.

To test the hypothesis that this decrease in performance was due to a poorly tuned model resulting from training data with unclear state characteristics, the test was carried out again, this time choosing the 15 windows manually to ensure that the NC sample windows had high alpha activity and the IC sample windows had clear ERD. The new results, denoted as NC_{15spe} and IC_{15spe} in Figure 7, show that the performance is again comparable to that obtained with 45 samples. Thus, if the characteristics of the distinct states are well captured, there is no need for long data records for training.

4   Discussion

The results presented provide insight on both the dynamic behaviour of the AR-SMM approach as well as the nature of the EEG data being analysed. Once the AR models are well tuned to the different mental tasks, then the AR-SMM approach switches consistently between the respective modes. However clear inter-trial and inter-subject variability exists, making it difficult to generalise the results with a standard ground truth signal. This was clearly shown in the evaluation of the measures defined for the motor imagery data which provided interesting information on the characteristics of the data when evaluated on a single trial basis.

The analysis carried out on the eyes-open, eyes-closed test showed that the AR-SMM approach offers a unified framework of identifying i) mental states which can be used as control signals and ii) artifact periods which can be reliably differentiated from the mental states of interest. This is important for the use of BCIs in everyday life. Further tests could be done to incorporate more artifacts and other distinct modes. The advantage of the proposed framework in this case is that it can accomodate different model types and model orders within the same framework, thus catering for the characteristics of the various modes present in the data.

Another intrinsic advantage of the AR-SMM approach is that it requires very little training data which is important for the practicality of BCI systems. Furthermore, since it provides continuous automatic labelling of the data, it can be readily used in real-time.

References

1. Camilleri, T., Camilleri, K., Fabri, S.: Automatic detection of spindles and K-complexes in sleep EEG using switching multiple models. Biomedical Signal Processing and Control **10**, 117–127 (2014)
2. Dempster, A.P., Laird, N.M., Rubin, D.B.: Maximum Likelihood from Incomplete Data via the EM Algorithm. J. R. Stat. Soc. **39**(1), 1–38 (1977)
3. Fabri, S.G., Kadirkamanathan, V.: Functional Adaptive Control - An Intelligent Systems Approach. Springer (2001)
4. Ghahramani, Z., Hinton, G.E.: Parameter Estimation for Linear Dynamical Systems. Technical report CRG-TR-96-2, Department of Computer Science, University of Toronto (1996)
5. Hoffman, G.S.: A Novel Electocardiogram Segmentation Algorithm using a Multiple Model Adaptive Estimator. Master's thesis, Air Force Institute of Technology, Graduate School of Engineering and Management, Ohio (2002)
6. Maybeck, P.S.: Stochastic Models, Estimation and Control. Mathematics in Science and Engineering. Academic Press Inc., London (1979)
7. Maybeck, P., Stevens, R.: Reconfigurable flight control via multiple model adaptive control methods. IEEE Trans. on Aerosp. and Electron. Syst. **27**(3), 470–480
8. Pardey, J., Roberts, S., Tarassenko, L.: A Review of Parametric Modelling Techniques for EEG Analysis. Med. Eng. Phys. **18**, 2–11 (1996)
9. Sajda, P., Gerson, A., Muller, K.R., Blankertz, B., Parra, L.: A data analysis competition to evaluate machine learning algorithms for use in brain-computer interfaces. IEEE Trans. Neural Syst. Rehabil. Eng. **11**(2), 184–185 (2003)
10. Sanei, S., Chambers, J.: EEG Signal Processing. John Wiley & Sons, Inc. (2007)
11. Schomer, D.L., Lopes da Silva, F.H. (eds.): Niedermeyer's Electroencephalography: Basic Principles, Clinical Applications, and Related Fields, 6th edn. Lippincott Williams & Wilkins (2010)
12. Thuraisingham, R.A., Tram, Y., Boord, P.A.C.: Analysis of eyes open, eye closed EEG signals using second-order difference plot. Medical and Biomedical Engineering and Computing **45**, 1243–1249 (2007)
13. Townsend, G., Graimann, B., Pfurtscheller, G.: Continuous EEG classification during motor imagery-simulation of an asynchronous BCI. IEEE Trans. Neural Syst. Rehabil. Eng. **12**(2), 258–265 (2004)

Wood Veneer Species Recognition Using Markovian Textural Features

Michal Haindl$^{(\boxtimes)}$ and Pavel Vácha

The Institute of Information Theory and Automation,
Czech Academy of Sciences, Prague, Czech Republic
{haindl,vacha}@utia.cz

Abstract. A mobile Android application that can automatically recognize wood species from a low quality mobile phone photo under varying illumination conditions is presented. The wood recognition is based on the Markovian, spectral, and illumination invariant textural features. The method performance was verified on a wood database, which contains veneers from sixty-six varied European and exotic wood species. The Markovian features improvement of the correct wood recognition rate is about 40% compared to the best alternative - the Local Binary Patterns features.

Keywords: Wood recognition · Textural features · Illumination invariants · Surface reflectance field · Bidirectional texture function

1 Introduction

Each type of wood has its own specific physical, aesthetic and economic properties; thus correct identification of wood species is required in numerous practical applications, from construction industry, manufacturing, furniture design, and restoration to pricing evaluation of wooden items. Fast, reliable, and practical recognition of wood species is therefore important, having potential impacts in a range of areas, including: the intended application, construction safety, and detecting illegal logging of endangered species. The traditional method of identifying wood species involves manual browsing through digital wooden veneer catalogues and making a subjective judgement. This is labour intensive, and concentration problems can lead to errors. Additionally, gradual changes and changing shades due to variable light conditions are confusing and difficult for humans to detect.

Several wood recognition systems using grey-scale textural features and laboratory measurement setups were proposed. A wood recognition system using macroscopic camera setup, neural networks classifier and grey-level co-occurrence matrix features is specified in [6]. This system requires large number (≈ 100) of training images per wood class. Papers [2,12] report similar systems using also grey-level or rotational invariant grey-level co-occurrence matrix

© Springer International Publishing Switzerland 2015
G. Azzopardi and N. Petkov (Eds.): CAIP 2015, Part I, LNCS 9256, pp. 300–311, 2015.
DOI: 10.1007/978-3-319-23192-1_25

features and correlation based classifier. A comparative study [11] reports better performance of the Gabor features over the co-occurrence matrix features. Finally, [15] combines the Gabor and the co-occurrence matrix features for the neural networks classifier. All these systems ignore textural spectral information, use obsolete textural features, and require good quality visual measurements with fixed illumination conditions.

As an alternative, we have developed an application to identify wood species using a smartphone camera, which returns the resulting species name and a corresponding high quality database wood specimen image. This computer-aided wood identification system retrieves a wood template from a digital wood database, selecting that which most closely resembles the query sample. A wooden surface is captured by a smartphone camera with the developed Android application, and the image is transmitted to the server side which computes the advanced multispectral Markovian textural features and finds the most similar wood species from its database. The Markovian features are not only very efficient, compacting the representation of visual wood properties, but they are simultaneously invariant to illumination colour, robust to illumination heterogeneity, and illumination direction, therefore the retrieval result is not influenced by the unknown and variable illumination properties. Thus we assume that the wooden texture can be approximated by a surface reflectance field model [4], i.e., bidirectional texture function with fixed or small viewing angle changes. The recognized wood species together with its high quality database pattern is sent back to the user so he or she can verify the classifiers result. The challenging part of the method is to compare poor quality smartphone images taken under variable illumination and resolution conditions with high quality high resolution matte wooden textures stored in the wood database.

2   Markovian Textural Features

Our texture analysis is based on spatial and multimodal relations modelling by a wide-sense Markovian model. We employ a Causal Autoregressive Random (CAR) model, because it allows very efficient analytical estimation of its parameters. Subsequently, the estimated model parameters are transformed into illumination/colour invariants, which characterize the corresponding wooden texture. These colour invariants encompass inter-spectral (in the case of full 3D CAR model) and spatial relations in the texture which are bounded to a selected contextual neighbourhood (see Fig. 1). Wood veneers with similar structure and spectral properties produce similar features.

Texture Model
Let us assume that multispectral texture image is composed of C spectral planes (usually $C = 3$ for colour images). $Y_r = [Y_{r,1}, \ldots, Y_{r,C}]^T$ is the multispectral pixel at location r, where the multiindex $r = [r_1, r_2]$ is composed of r_1 row and r_2 column index, respectively. The spectral planes are modelled using a set of C 2-dimensional CAR models. The set of 2D models is used instead of full 3D

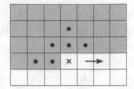 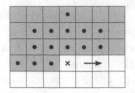

Fig. 1. Examples of contextual neighbourhood I_r. From the left, it is the unilateral semi-hierarchical neighbourhood of third and sixth order. X marks the current pixel, the bullets are pixels in the neighbourhood, the arrow shows movement direction, and the grey area indicates acceptable neighbourhood pixels.

model, because images from smarthone cameras had degradated interspectral relations.

The CAR representation assumes that the multispectral texture pixel Y_r can be modelled as a linear combination of its neighbours:

$$Y_r = \gamma Z_r + \epsilon_r \ , \qquad Z_r = [Y_{r-s}^T : \forall s \in I_r]^T \qquad (1)$$

where Z_r is the $C\eta \times 1$ data vector with multiindices r, s, $\gamma = [A_1, \ldots, A_\eta]$ is the $C \times C\eta$ unknown parameter matrix with square sub-matrices A_s. Some selected contextual causal or unilateral neighbour index shift set is denoted I_r and $\eta = cardinality(I_r)$, see Fig. 1. A unilateral neighbourhood I_r (the left upper orientation) is defined as $I_r \subset I_r^U = \{s : s_1 < r_1 \ or \ (s_1 = r_1, s_2 < r_2)\}$ and similarly ([3]) its subset - the causal neighborhood. The neighborhood order is based on the Euclidean distance from r. The white noise vector ϵ_r has normal density with zero mean and unknown diagonal covariance matrix, same for each pixel. In the case 2D CAR models stacked into the model equation (1) the uncorrelated noise vector components ϵ_r are assumed and the parameter matrices A_s are diagonal.

The texture is analysed in a chosen direction, where multiindex t changes according to the movement on the image lattice. Given the known history of CAR process $Y^{(t-1)} = \{Y_{t-1}, Y_{t-2}, \ldots, Y_1, Z_t, Z_{t-1}, \ldots, Z_1\}$ the parameter estimation $\hat{\gamma}$ for the given pixel position can be computed using statistics [3]:

$$\hat{\gamma}_{t-1}^T = V_{zz(t-1)}^{-1} V_{zy(t-1)} \ ,$$

$$V_{t-1} = \begin{pmatrix} \sum_{u=1}^{t-1} Y_u Y_u^T & \sum_{u=1}^{t-1} Y_u Z_u^T \\ \sum_{u=1}^{t-1} Z_u Y_u^T & \sum_{u=1}^{t-1} Z_u Z_u^T \end{pmatrix} + V_0 = \begin{pmatrix} V_{yy(t-1)} & V_{zy(t-1)}^T \\ V_{zy(t-1)} & V_{zz(t-1)} \end{pmatrix} \ , \qquad (2)$$

$$\lambda_{t-1} = V_{yy(t-1)} - V_{zy(t-1)}^T V_{zz(t-1)}^{-1} V_{zy(t-1)} \ ,$$

where the positive definite matrix V_0 represents a prior knowledge, see [3] for details. Moreover, the parameter estimate can be efficiently computed for all pixel positions using a numerically robust recursive formula [3], which is advantageous for texture segmentation applications. Finally, the optimal contextual neighbourhood I_r can be found analytically by maximising the corresponding posterior probability [3].

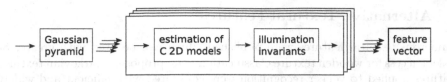

Fig. 2. The texture analysis algorithm flowchart using a set of 2D random field models.

Colour Invariant Features

Colour invariants are computed from the CAR parameter estimates to make them independent on changes of illumination intensity and colours. Moreover, our invariants are approximately invariant to infrequent changes of local illumination intensity and experiments show their robustness to variation of illumination direction (see [13, 14] for details). For 2D models, their definition is the following:

1. trace: $\operatorname{tr} A_s$, $\forall s \in I_r$,
2. diagonals: $\nu_s = \operatorname{diag} A_s$, $\forall s \in I_r$.
3. α_1: $1 + Z_r^T V_{zz}^{-1} Z_r$,
4. α_2: $\sqrt{\sum_r (Y_r - \hat{\gamma} Z_r)^T \lambda^{-1} (Y_r - \hat{\gamma} Z_r)}$,
5. α_3: $\sqrt{\sum_r (Y_r - \mu)^T \lambda^{-1} (Y_r - \mu)}$, μ is the mean value of vector Y_r ,

where the invariants $\alpha_1 - \alpha_3$ are computed for each spectral plane separately. The model parameters $\hat{\gamma}$, λ are estimated using formula (2), we omit subsctripts for simplicity. Feature vectors are formed from these illumination invariants, which are easily evaluated during the CAR parameters estimation process.

Algorithm

The texture analysis algorithm starts with factorisation of texture image into K levels of the Gaussian down-sampled pyramid and subsequently each pyramid level is modelled by the CAR model. The pyramidal factorization is used, because it enables model to easily capture larger spatial relations. We usually use $K = 4$ levels of the Gaussian pyramid, if the image size is sufficient (at least 400×400) it is possible to improve performance with the additional pyramid level ($K = 5$).

Although the optimal neighbourhood of the CAR model can be optimally selected, practically, we use the 6-th order semi-hierarchical neighbourhood (cardinality $\eta = 14$), see Fig. 1 for details. This neighbourhood size provides good combination of sufficient support and stable model parameters, which do not varies for similar textures. Finally, the estimated parameters for all pyramid levels are transformed into the colour invariants and concatenated into a common feature vector. The algorithm scheme is depicted in Fig. 2.

The dissimilarity between two feature vectors of two textures T, S is computed using fuzzy contrast [10] in its symmetrical form FC_3.

3   Alternative Textural Features

Numerous textural features were published which can be used with greater or lesser success for wooden texture classification. The proposed Markovian textural features applied to veneer recognition were compared with efficient and widely used alternative Local Binary Patterns (LBP) [8] and Gabor textural features [1,7,9]. Results of the Opponent Gabor features [5] were inferior, so that they are not included in the paper.

3.1   Local Binary Patterns

Local Binary Patterns [8] are histograms of texture micro patterns. For each pixel, a circular neighbourhood around the pixel is sampled, P is the number of samples and R is the radius of circle. The sampled point values are thresholded by the central pixel value and the pattern number is formed:

$$LBP_{P,R} = \sum_{s=0}^{P-1} \text{sgn}\,(Y_s - Y_c)\,2^s, \tag{3}$$

where sgn is the sign function, Y_s is the grey value of the sampled pixel, and Y_c is the grey value of the central pixel. Subsequently, the histogram of patterns is computed. Because of the thresholding, the features are invariant to any monotonic grey-scale change. The multiresolution analysis is done by growing of the circular neighbourhood size. All LBP histograms were normalised to have unit L_1 norm. The similarity between LBP feature vectors is measured by means of Kullback-Leibler divergence as the authors suggested.

We have tested features $LBP_{8,1+8,3}$, which are combination of features with radii 1 and 3. They were computed either on gray images or on each spectral plane of color image and concatenated. We also tested uniform version $LBP^u_{16,2}$, but their results were inferior.

3.2   Gabor Features

The Gabor filters [1,7,9] can be considered as orientation and scale tunable edge and line (bar) detectors and statistics of Gabor filter responses in a given region are used to characterize the underlying texture information. A two dimensional Gabor function $g(r_1, r_2) : \Re^2 \to \mathcal{C}$ can be specified as

$$g(r_1, r_2) = \frac{1}{2\pi\sigma_{r_1}\sigma_{r_2}} \exp\left[-\frac{1}{2}\left(\frac{r_1^2}{\sigma_{r_1}^2} + \frac{r_2^2}{\sigma_{r_2}^2}\right) + 2\pi i W r_1\right], \tag{4}$$

where $\sigma_u = \frac{1}{2\pi\sigma_{r_1}}$, $\sigma_v = \frac{1}{2\pi\sigma_{r_2}}$, and $\sigma_{r_1}, \sigma_{r_2}$ are filter parameters. $\sigma_{r_1}, \sigma_{r_2}$ are variances in r_1, r_2 directions and W is a modulation frequency parameter. Gabor wavelet transform is defined as

$$W_{mn}(r_1, r_2) = \int Y(s_1, s_2) g^*_{mn}(r_1 - s_1, r_2 - s_2) ds_1 ds_2, \tag{5}$$

where $*$ indicates the complex conjugate. The Gabor features are defined as the mean μ_{mn} and the standard deviation σ_{mn} of the magnitude of transform coefficients.

4 Experiments

The performance of our application was verified on the wood database, which contains veneers from varied European and exotic wood species, each with two sample images only. The training set included images of 66 wood species acquired by a colour scanner device, while the test set was composed of images of 59 wood species acquired by two different smartphones (HTC Desire S and Samsung Galaxy S3). The training set was acquired with controlled condition (stable illuminations source, aligned position) provided by the scanning machine. On the contrary, the test set was captured from a hand without controlled conditions, however, the images were taken from approximately the same distance and with orientation approximately with the material sample to limit unnecessary variations. All images were resized to 767×1024 pixels aspect ratio were maintained and redundant pixels were discarded. Lanczos interpolation was employed in image resize.

We have performed three wood veneers recognition experiments. Naturally, the proposed textural features and the alternatives were compared in the exactly same conditions. The computed feature vectors were compared with author suggested distances and classified using the Nearest Neighbour (1-NN) classifier.

4.1 Experiment 1

In the first experiment, we tested recognition of whole images captured by two mobile phones against training database acquired by the scanner. Separately, we tested images acquired by the mobile phones with the internal flash ON and OFF, see examples in Fig. 3. Each of these four setups included 59 test images.

Tab. 1 displays the results, where the recognition accuracy of the images without flash were worse for all features. The reason is that (a) the images captured without flash were more blurry (caused by small smartphones lenses and sensors) (b) additionally, CAR features cancel uneven illumination present in images with flash. Worse results of the HTC smartphone were caused probably by its very aggressive JPEG compression, which cannot be adjusted in the used device model.

Figs. 4–7 illustrate the systems typical performance applied to European (Figs. 4, 5) and exotic wood (Figs. 6, 7) samples. Fig. 4 illustrates retrieval results of our method - the most probable results were both apple samples, which is correct, and the third result was the closest pear wood specimen. In the same figure, the LBP features retrieved wrongly all three most probable results (twice a bamboo sample and the macassar wood).

Scanner   HTC no flash   HTC flash   Samsung no flash   Samsung flash

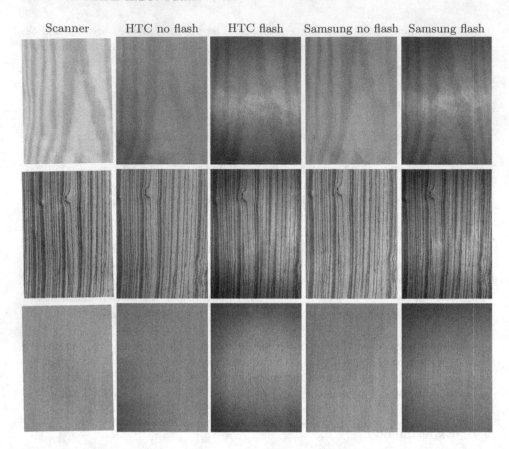

Fig. 3. Images of the following veneer samples: pine, zebrano, and beech, respectively. The columns correspond to different acquisition setups.

Table 1. Experiment 1, recognition accuracy [%] of whole veneers by both smartphones.

	HTC flash	HTC	Samsung flash	Samsung
Gabor colour	28.6	8.1	36.7	26.5
LBP gray	24.5	8.2	34.7	16.3
LBP colour	20.4	8.2	38.8	18.4
2D CAR	59.2	30.6	79.6	63.4
2D CAR ($K = 5$)	**65.3**	40.8	**81.6**	67.7

4.2 Experiment 2

In the second experiment, we tested ability of textural features to generalize and to recognize different parts of material sample. The setup was almost the same as in the Experiment 1 with the exception that both test and training set was

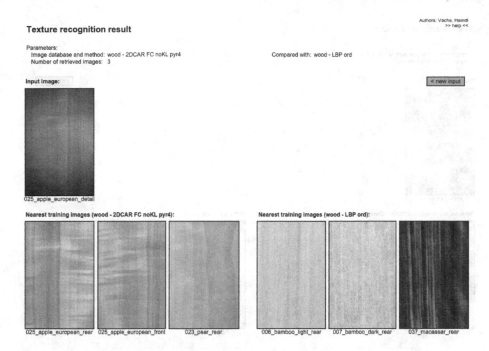

Fig. 4. An apple wood sample taken by a smartphone camera and the three closest query results using either Markovian or LBP textural features.

composed of upper half and lower half of the original images. The recognition was performed "across" halfs, i.e., in two sub-experiments: (a) trained on upper halfs from the scanner, tested on the lower halfs from a mobile; (b) trained on the lower halfs from the scanner, tested on the upper halfs from a mobile. The results of these two sub-experiments, each with 59 test images, were averaged.

The results are summarized in Tab. 2, where the recognition accuracy of images without flash were excluded as they were inferior for all tested features (consistently with the Experiment 1).

4.3 Experiment 3

In the third experiment, we tested classification of upper against lower parts similarly as in the Experiment 2, however, both training and test images were from the same acquisition device. Again, the recognition accuracy was evaluated for 2×59 test images. The purpose of this experiment was to asses, what is the cause of the performance degradation.

The results are displayed in Tab. 3. Recognition accuracy 100%, in the upper left corner, means that 2D CAR features extract important textural properties as they are able to perfectly recognise different parts of the same veneer sample. In fact, this is true for all tested features as the recognition accuracy was always between 99% and 100%. When compared with the results in Experiment 2,

308   M. Haindl and P. Vácha

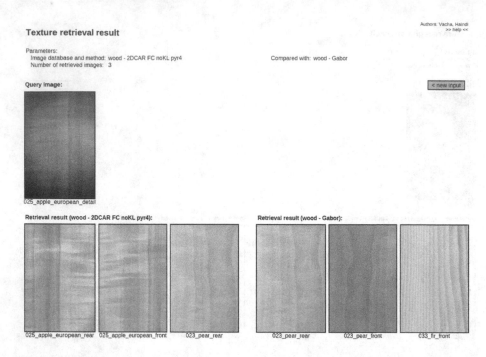

Fig. 5. The apple wood sample taken by a smartphone camera and the three closest query results using either Markovian or Gabor textural features.

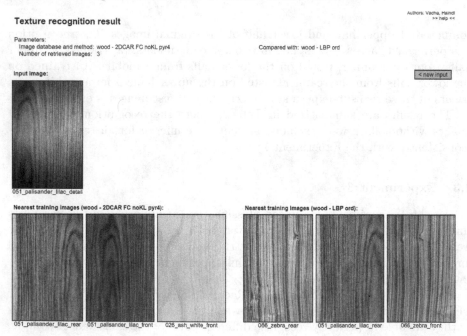

Fig. 6. A palisander wood retrieval results comparison between the Markovian and LBP features.

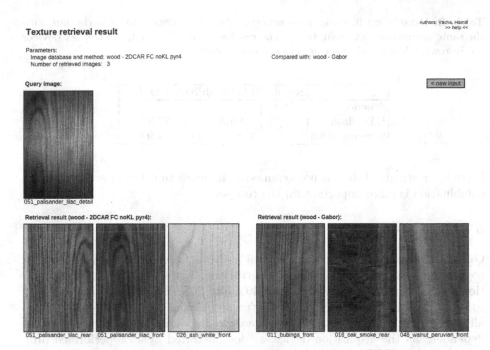

Fig. 7. The palisander wood retrieval results comparison between the Markovian and Gabor features.

Table 2. Experiment 2, recognition accuracy [%] of different veneer parts by the smartphones.

	HTC flash	Samsung flash
LBP gray	29.6	40.8
LBP colour	29.6	48.0
2D CAR	46.9	69.4
2D CAR ($K = 5$)	**49.0**	**66.3**
Gabor color	18.3	27.5

it implies that about 30% of recognition accuracy for 2D CAR features were lost, probably, by combination of two factors: (a) poor quality of smartphone cameras, (b) scale and other variations introduced by acquisition from hand. (For the simplicity, the rest of the first column is left empty, since the results are included in the Experiment 2.)

To examine more carefully the previous claim about performance lost, the rest of the table displays results with changing training and testing combinations of the smartphones (still different half of the veneer sample was used for test and training). Very good results on the diagonal (89.9% and 94.9%) implies that degradation by smartphone cameras are consistent. We can speculate that remaining 7–10% of performance was lost due to image acquisition from hand.

Table 3. Experiment 3, recognition accuracy [%] of different veneer parts, but with the same acquisition device (in bold). The results are for 2D CAR, the test set devices are in rows, while training set devices are in columns.

	Scanner	HTC flash	Samsung flash
Scanner	**100**		
HTC flash		**89.8**	78.6
Samsung flash		83.7	**94.9**

More interestingly, Tab. 3 is not symmetric, it seems that better sensor/camera combination is more important for the test set.

5 Conclusion

Our colour invariant Markovian textural features were successfully applied for recognition of wood veneers using a smartphone. The method's correct recognition accuracy improvements are about 40% and 20% (Experiment 2), compared to the Local Binary Patterns (LBP) features, which is the best alternative from all tested standard textural features. However, the actual performance is highly dependent on the acquisition device, as demonstrated by 15% performed drop for camera in HTC Desire S compared to Samsung Galaxy S3. In general, smartphone cameras have sufficient resolution (up to 10 mega pixels), however, their poor quality lenses and aggressive JPEG compression result in inferior image quality and thus a more demanding recognition task. Nevertheless, our high correct recognition rate (82%), suggests that the proposed method can be successfully used in various practical wood recognition applications.

The results can be reviewed in an online demonstration[1], which shows retrieval using images from mobile phones as queries.

Acknowledgments. This research was supported by the Czech Science Foundation project GAČR 14-10911S.

References

1. Bovik, A.: Analysis of multichannel narrow-band filters for image texture segmentation. IEEE Trans. on Signal Processing **39**(9), 2025–2043 (1991)
2. Bremananth, R., Nithya, B., Saipriya, R.: Wood species recognition using glcm and correlation. In: International Conference on Advances in Recent Technologies in Communication and Computing. ARTCom 2009, pp. 615–619. IEEE (2009)
3. Haindl, M.: Visual data recognition and modeling based on local markovian models. In: Florack, L., Duits, R., Jongbloed, G., Lieshout, M.C., Davies, L. (eds.) Mathematical Methods for Signal and Image Analysis and Representation, Computational Imaging and Vision, chap. 14, vol. 41, pp. 241–259. Springer, London (2012). doi:10.1007/978-1-4471-2353-8_14. http://dx.doi.org/10.1007/978-1-4471-2353-8_14

---

[1] http://cbir.utia.cas.cz/veneers/

4. Haindl, M., Filip, J.: Visual Texture. Advances in Computer Vision and Pattern Recognition. Springer-Verlag London, London (January 2013)
5. Jain, A., Healey, G.: A multiscale representation including opponent colour features for texture recognition. IEEE Transactions on Image Processing **7**(1), 124–128 (1998)
6. Khalid, M., Lee, E.L.Y., Yusof, R., Nadaraj, M.: Design of an intelligent wood species recognition system. International Journal of Simulation System, Science and Technology **9**(3), 9–19 (2008)
7. Manjunath, B.S., Ma, W.Y.: Texture features for browsing and retrieval of image data. IEEE Transactions on Pattern Analysis and Machine Intelligence **18**(8), 837–842 (1996)
8. Ojala, T., Pietikäinen, M., Mäenpää, T.: Multiresolution gray-scale and rotation invariant texture classification with local binary patterns. IEEE Transactions on Pattern Analysis and Machine Intelligence **24**(7), 971–987 (2002)
9. Randen, T., Husøy, J.H.: Filtering for texture classification: A comparative study. IEEE Transactions on Pattern Analysis and Machine Intelligence **21**(4), 291–310 (1999)
10. Santini, S., Jain, R.: Similarity measures. IEEE Transactions on Pattern Analysis and Machine Intelligence **21**(9), 871–883 (1999)
11. Tou, J.Y., Tay, Y.H., Lau, P.Y.: A comparative study for texture classification techniques on wood species recognition problem. In: Fifth International Conference on Natural Computation. ICNC 2009, vol. 5, pp. 8–12. IEEE (2009)
12. Tou, J.Y., Tay, Y.H., Lau, P.Y.: Rotational invariant wood species recognition through wood species verification. In: First Asian Conference on Intelligent Information and Database Systems. ACIIDS 2009, pp. 115–120. IEEE (2009)
13. Vacha, P., Haindl, M.: Image retrieval measures based on illumination invariant textural MRF features. In: Sebe, N., Worring, M. (eds.) Proceedings of ACM International Conference on Image and Video Retrieval, CIVR 2007, pp. 448–454. ACM, July 9–11, 2007
14. Vácha, P., Haindl, M.: Texture recognition using robust Markovian features. In: Salerno, E., Çetin, A.E., Salvetti, O. (eds.) MUSCLE 2011. LNCS, vol. 7252, pp. 126–137. Springer, Heidelberg (2012)
15. Yusof, R., Rosli, N.R., Khalid, M.: Using gabor filters as image multiplier for tropical wood species recognition system. In: 2010 12th International Conference on Computer Modelling and Simulation (UKSim), pp. 289–294. IEEE (2010)

Performance Analysis of Active Shape Reconstruction of Fractured, Incomplete Skulls

Kun Zhang, Wee Kheng Leow$^{(\boxtimes)}$, and Yuan Cheng

Department of Computer Science,
National University of Singapore, Singapore, Singapore
{zhangkun,leowwk,cyuan}@comp.nus.edu.sg

Abstract. Reconstruction of normal skulls from deformed skulls is a very important but difficult task in practice. Active shape model (ASM) is among the most popular methods for reconstructing skulls. To apply ASM to skull reconstruction, it is necessary to establish shape correspondence among the training and testing samples because wrong correspondence will introduce unwanted shape variations in ASM reconstruction. Despite the popularity of ASM, the accuracy of ASM skull reconstruction has not been well investigated in existing literature. In particular, it is unclear how to estimate the reconstruction error of skulls without ground truth. This paper aims to investigate the source of error of ASM skull reconstruction. Comprehensive tests show that the error of accurate correspondence algorithm is uncorrelated and small compared to reconstruction error. On the other hand, ASM fitting error is highly correlated to reconstruction error, which allows us to estimate the reconstruction error of real deformed skulls using ASM fitting error. Moreover, ASM fitting error is correlated to the severity of skull defects, which places a limit on the reconstruction accuracy that can be achieved by ASM.

1 Introduction

Practitioners in surgery, forensics, and anthropology often encounter subjects whose skulls are incomplete and fractured due to impact injury, criminal acts, or natural processes. An important task in these practices is to reconstruct normal, complete skulls from the subjects' deformed (incomplete, fractured) skulls, in the absence of their original complete skull models. The reconstruction process has to predict the skulls' normal shapes from the normal parts of the deformed skulls. Although human skulls have the same global structure, they differ greatly in shape details among people with different races, genders, and ages. Therefore, reconstructing normal skulls from deformed skulls is a very difficult task.

Active shape model (ASM) is among the most popular methods for reconstructing skulls [10,15,21]. To build an ASM of the skull from a set of training samples, it is necessary to first establish the shape correspondence among the training samples. Wrong correspondences will introduce unwanted shape variations in ASM. During skull reconstruction, correspondence between the target skull and the ASM needs to be established before ASM can be fitted to the

© Springer International Publishing Switzerland 2015
G. Azzopardi and N. Petkov (Eds.): CAIP 2015, Part I, LNCS 9256, pp. 312–324, 2015.
DOI: 10.1007/978-3-319-23192-1_26

target skull to produce the reconstructed skull. In some applications, such as face recognition and camera self-calibration, a set of sparse correspondences is sufficient. Skulls, on the other hand, have very complex shape and usually have more than 10000 mesh vertices. Therefore, dense correspondence is required.

Despite the popularity of ASM, the accuracy of skull reconstruction based on ASM has not been well investigated in existing literature such as [10,15,21]. It is unknown whether dense correspondence or ASM fitting contributes more error to skull reconstruction. With two sources of error, it is also unknown how to estimate the error of skull reconstruction without ground truth.

This paper aims to investigate the source of error of ASM skull reconstruction and to develop a method for estimating reconstruction error of deformed skulls without ground truth. Our investigation thus contributes to practical application of ASM reconstruction by providing good error estimates.

Note that bones have measurable thickness. Therefore 3D skull models have inner and outer surfaces. In applications such as surgery planning, forensic investigation and anthropology, only the outer surfaces are important because they define the shape appearance of faces. So, this paper focuses on the outer surfaces, which can be easily extracted from the skull models.

2   Related Work

2.1   Reconstruction of Deformed Skulls

Several approaches have been developed for skull reconstruction. A commonly used approach is symmetric-based reconstruction [7,9,14], which reflects the normal bones on one side of a skull about the lateral symmetric plane to serve as the reconstruction of the defective parts on the opposite side. When both sides are defective, which is common in practice, this approach cannot be applied.

Geometric reconstruction [2,11,20] deforms a reference skull model to register to the normal parts of a deformed skull, and outputs the registered reference model as the reconstructed model. The accuracy of this approach depends highly on the similarity between the reference and deformed skulls as well as the correlation between the normal and defective parts.

Statistical reconstruction [10,15,21] overcomes the weaknesses of the other approaches. Instead of using a single reference skull model, this approach constructs a statistical model of possible variations of human skulls. Given a target deformed skull, this approach fits the statistical model to the normal parts of the target skull, and outputs the fitted model as the reconstructed skull. In this paper, we adopt the active shape model in a way similar to [10,15,21].

2.2   Dense Correspondence

There are three approaches for computing dense correspondence between two shape models. Among them, non-rigid mesh registration is the predominant approach. Non-rigid registration such as [4,5,17,18,22] can achieve close matching but needs landmarks to guide the deformation and matching process. Methods that use manually labeled landmarks [5,6] are accurate, but manual labeling is too tedious for the entire skull. On the other hand, methods that automatically detect correspondence based on local geometric features [19] are easy to apply but are sensitive to noise and outliers, which can adversely affect their accuracy.

Surface parameterization [3,8] and group representation [13] are two other approaches for computing dense correspondence. Although they have good theoretical foundation, they are applicable only to simple shapes without holes. It is technically very difficult to apply them to complex shapes such as skulls.

In this paper, we adopt the Thin-Plate Spline (TPS) method developed in our previous work [22] for dense correspondence. Unlike existing TPS methods, our method combines both hard and soft constraints to ensure anatomically consistent correspondence and close matching between the reference and target.

3   Skull Reconstruction Method

Our method consists of three main algorithms: (1) establishing dense correspondence among skull models, (2) building active shape model (ASM) from normal training samples, and (3) fitting ASM to target skull model, which may be fractured and incomplete, to reconstruct a normal model.

3.1   Dense Correspondence

In [22], we propose a method that performs non-rigid registration of a reference model to a target model using Thin-Plate Spline (TPS). The method uses anatomical landmarks as hard constraints to ensure **anatomically consistent correspondence**, and samples control points on skull surfaces to serve as soft constraints, which provide local shape constraints for **close matching** of reference and target surfaces. For normal skulls, it can automatically detect the anatomical landmarks required. For deformed skulls, it requires manually labeled landmarks because the automatic algorithm is not accurate enough for severely deformed skulls. The method adopts a multi-stage coarse-to-fine approach, which consists of the following steps:

1. Apply fractional iterative closest point (FICP) algorithm [16] to register the reference mesh to the target mesh. FICP is more robust than ICP in handling meshes with noise and outliers.
2. Identify anatomical landmarks on the target by manual labeling or automatic detection.
3. Apply TPS to register the reference to the target with anatomical landmarks as hard constraints.
4. Sample control points on reference mesh surfaces and map them to the closest target mesh surfaces.

5. Apply TPS with anatomical landmarks as hard constraints and control points as soft constraints.
6. Resample target mesh by mapping reference mesh vertices and mesh connectivity to the target.

Step 6 ensures that the resampled target has the same number of mesh vertices and mesh connectivity as the reference. For each vertex on the reference mesh, its nearest point on the target mesh within a fixed distance and with a sufficiently similar surface normal is selected as the corresponding point. In the current implementation, the fixed distance is set to 10 mm and the surface normals are similar enough if the cosine of the angle between them is larger than 0.86. For a normal target mesh, if a corresponding point that satisfies these criteria cannot be found, then the nearest target point is used as the corresponding point because there should be no missing correspondence in normal skulls. On the other hand, for a deformed target mesh, if a corresponding point that satisfies these criteria cannot be found, then the corresponding point is regarded as a *missing vertex*. Test results [22] show that our method is more accurate than other TPS methods that use only hard constraints or soft constraints but not both.

3.2 Building Active Shape Model

After establishing dense correspondence between the training samples, they are arranged as column vectors called *shape vectors* in a matrix. Principal Component Analysis is applied to the matrix to compute the *mean shape* $\bar{s}$ and identify the major components which form the *model matrix* Φ. In our study (Section 4), we used 34 normal skulls as training samples, and 25 components were enough to achieve an unaccounted variance of less than 3%.

3.3 Active Shape Skull Reconstruction

Skull reconstruction is achieved by fitting the skull ASM to a target skull. For a normal target skull, standard ASM fitting is appropriate. For a deformed target skull, the skull ASM is fitted only to the normal parts of the target because the defective parts are either missing or fractured, which distort the skull shape. This approach is similar to those of [10,15], but is different from that of [21], which fits ASM to the whole skull including the defective parts.

After resampling, the shape vector of the target skull r is prepared. Let s' denote the target shape vector whose coordinates of the defective parts, identified as missing mesh vertices, are set to $(0,0,0)$. Let $\bar{s}'$ and Φ' denote the mean shape and model matrix of ASM whose corresponding rows are set to 0 to remove unnecessary constraints on the defective parts. Then the reconstruction problem is formulated as one of recovering the shape parameters b that best fit s':

$$s' = \bar{s}' + \Phi'b. \tag{1}$$

Since Φ' may not have an inverse, the shape parameter b is recovered using the pseudo-inverse of Φ':

$$b = (\Phi'^{\top}\Phi')^{-1}\Phi'^{\top}(s' - \bar{s}'). \tag{2}$$

Finally, the reconstructed complete skull **s** is recovered using the complete mean shape $\bar{\mathbf{s}}$ and model matrix $\boldsymbol{\Phi}$:

$$\mathbf{s} = \bar{\mathbf{s}} + \boldsymbol{\Phi}\mathbf{b}. \tag{3}$$

In practice, the target skull **r** may not be spatially aligned to the model represented by the mean shape $\bar{\mathbf{s}}'$. So, it is necessary to recover the similarity transformation T that best aligns **r** to $\mathbf{s}'$, giving

$$T(\mathbf{r}) = \mathbf{s}' = \bar{\mathbf{s}}' + \boldsymbol{\Phi}'\mathbf{b}. \tag{4}$$

Thus, the reconstruction of **r** is formulated as the problem of determining the similarity transformation T and shape parameters **b** that minimize the error E:

$$E = \left\| \bar{\mathbf{s}}' + \boldsymbol{\Phi}'\mathbf{b} - T(\mathbf{r}) \right\|^2. \tag{5}$$

Equation 5 is minimized using an iterative algorithm adapted from [1]:

ASM Fitting Algorithm

1. Initialize shape parameters **b** to zero, and set the reconstructed shape **s** as the mean shape $\bar{\mathbf{s}}$ (Eq. 3).
2. Repeat until convergence:
   (a) Compute the similarity transformation T that best aligns **r** to **s** by minimizing $\|T(\mathbf{r}) - \mathbf{s}\|^2$.
   (b) Compute shape parameters $\mathbf{b} = (\boldsymbol{\Phi}'^{T}\boldsymbol{\Phi}')^{-1}\boldsymbol{\Phi}'^{T}(T(\mathbf{r}) - \bar{\mathbf{s}}')$ (Eq. 2).
   (c) Compute the reconstructed shape $\mathbf{s} = \bar{\mathbf{s}} + \boldsymbol{\Phi}\mathbf{b}$ (Eq. 3).

4   Experiments and Discussions

4.1   Data Preparation and Test Procedure

A comprehensive set of experiments was conducted to evaluate the skull reconstruction algorithm. ASM of skull was constructed using 34 normal, complete skulls. 8 other normal, complete skulls were used as testing samples (Fig. 1(1; a–b)). They were flipped about their lateral symmetric planes to create additional test samples. As human skulls are not exactly left-right symmetric, the number of complete, normal test samples were doubled in this way to 16.

The 16 complete, normal testing samples were used to generate synthetic fractured, incomplete testing samples. To study how the severity of defects affects reconstruction result, synthetic skulls with four levels of severity were created: mild, moderate, severe, and very severe. The first three levels were either fractured or incomplete. For each of the first three levels, the skulls were manually fractured at three places: cranial, facial, and jaw bones (Fig. 1(2–4; a–c)), in a manner similar to real fractures. Incomplete skull samples were created by removing the fractured bone fragments (Fig. 1(2–4; d–f)). These incomplete cases may occur in forensic investigation due to criminal acts and surgery due to

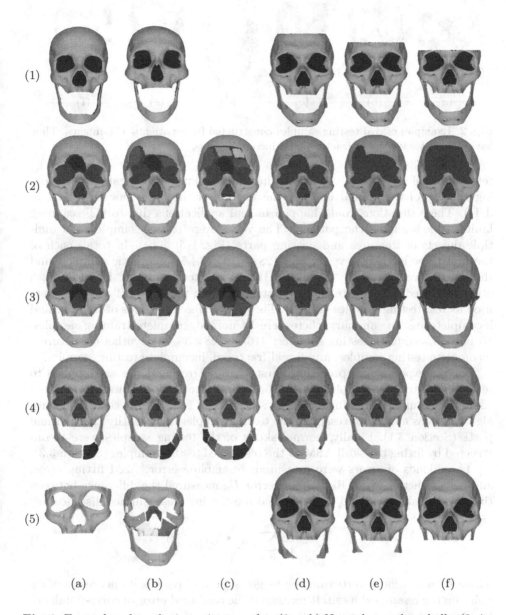

Fig. 1. Examples of synthetic testing samples. (1; a–b) Normal, complete skulls. (2–4; a–c) Skulls with mild, moderate, and severe fractures at different locations. (1–5; d–f) Skulls with mild, moderate, and severe missing parts at different locations. (1, 5; d–f) Incompleteness due to scan limits. (2–4; d–f) Incompleteness due to fractures. (5; a–b) Very severe cases with multiple defects.

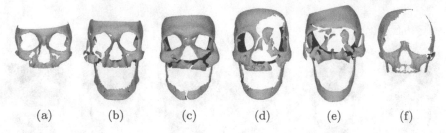

(a)   (b)   (c)   (d)   (e)   (f)

Fig. 2. Examples of real testing samples constructed from patients' CT images. They have different severities of fractures and incompleteness.

removal of defective parts. Additional incomplete skulls were created by removing the top of the cranial bone or the bottom of the lower jaw (Fig. 1(1, 5; d–f)). These situations could happen in real applications due to CT scanning limits while scanning the patients. The very severe testing samples had multiple defects of fractures and missing parts (Fig. 1(5; a–b)). In total, each of the first three levels of severity had 128 ($= 16 \times (3+5)$) synthetic samples, and the fourth level of severity had 32 ($= 16 \times 2$) synthetic samples. In addition, 6 other fractured, incomplete skulls constructed from patients' CT volumes were used as real testing samples (Fig. 2). They had different degrees of fracture and incompleteness. In summary, there were 34 normal, complete training samples; 16 normal, complete testing samples; 416 ($= 128 \times 3 + 32$) synthetic fractured, incomplete testing samples; and 6 real fractured, incomplete testing samples.

For the experimental procedure, first, dense correspondence was applied to resample the training samples (Section 3.1). Next, the skull ASM was constructed using the resampled training samples (Section 3.2). Next, dense correspondence algorithm was applied to resample the testing samples and identify their normal parts (Section 3.1). Finally, normal skulls of the testing samples were reconstructed by fitting the skull ASM to the resampled testing samples (Section 3.3).

Three kinds of errors were measured: resampling error, ASM fitting error, and reconstruction error. Resampling error E_S measured the difference between the target skull model and its resampled mesh using mean surface distance:

$$E_S = \frac{1}{m} \sum_{j=1}^{m} \|\mathbf{u}_j - \mathbf{p}_j\|, \qquad (6)$$

where $\mathbf{u}_j$ was a mesh vertex on the target skull and $\mathbf{p}_j$ was its nearest surface point on the resampled mesh. It measured the combined error of correspondence building and mesh resampling. Resampling errors of the defective and normal parts of a target skull were measured separately because the defective parts were expected to have larger resampling error compared to the normal parts.

ASM fitting error measured the difference between the resampled mesh and the mesh reconstructed by ASM fitting. Two measurement methods were adopted. The first method measured the mean displacement of mesh vertices:

$$E_F = \frac{1}{n} \sum_{i=1}^{n} \|\mathbf{v}_i - \mathbf{v}'_i\|, \tag{7}$$

where $\mathbf{v}_i$ was a mesh vertex on the resampled mesh and $\mathbf{v}'_i$ was its corresponding vertex on the reconstructed mesh. This formulation of ASM fitting error measured the average mesh vertex displacement as a result of ASM fitting. So, it evaluated the amount of shape change incurred in the ASM fitting process.

The second method measured the mean surface distance:

$$E_G = \frac{1}{n} \sum_{i=1}^{n} \|\mathbf{v}_i - \mathbf{p}'_i\|, \tag{8}$$

where $\mathbf{v}_i$ was a mesh vertex on the resampled mesh and $\mathbf{p}'_i$ was its nearest surface point on the reconstructed mesh. This formulation was appropriate since it was consistent and thus comparable to the resampling error and reconstruction error.

Reconstruction error was computed as the mean surface distance between the ground truth and the reconstructed mesh:

$$E_R = \frac{1}{n} \sum_{i=1}^{n} \|\mathbf{v}_i^* - \mathbf{q}'_i\|, \tag{9}$$

where $\mathbf{v}_i^*$ was a mesh vertex in the ground truth and $\mathbf{q}'_i$ was its nearest surface point on the reconstructed mesh.

4.2   Test Results

Figure 3 shows that the resampling error of the training samples and the testing samples is very small, mostly ranging from 0.1 mm to 0.34 mm. Moreover, it is not correlated to the severity of skull defects and reconstruction error E_R. When measured separately, test results show that the resampling error of the fractured parts is generally larger than that of the normal parts of the same skull, and it ranges from 0.2 mm to 2.3 mm (not shown in Fig. 3). Nevertheless, it is still uncorrelated to the severity of defects.

On the other hand, ASM fitting errors are correlated to the severity of defects (Fig. 4). In particular, training samples have the smallest ASM fitting errors ($E_F < 1.2$ mm, $E_G < 0.5$ mm) as expected. Synthetic testing samples with mild, moderate, and severe defects have E_F ranging from 2.2 mm to 5.3 mm and E_G between 0.9 mm and 1.7 mm, whereas those with very severe defects have E_F of 4.5 mm to 8.0 mm and E_G of 1.4 mm to 2.8 mm. For all samples, E_F, which measures average shape change, is higher than E_G, which measures mean surface distance. This shows that mean surface distance, while easy to measure and commonly used, under-estimates actual shape difference.

ASM fitting error is also strongly correlated to reconstruction error E_R (Fig. 4). Except for some outliers, there is a strong linear relationship between ASM fitting errors (E_F, E_G) and reconstruction error E_R. On the other hand,

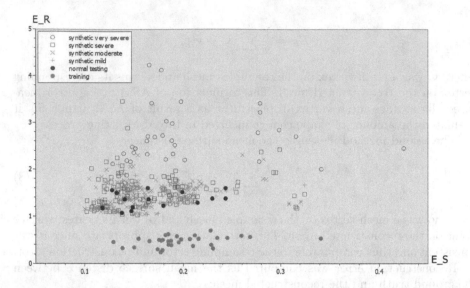

Fig. 3. A plot of resampling error E_S vs. reconstruction error E_R measured in mm

resampling error E_S is not correlated to reconstruction error E_R and is very small (about 10%) compared to E_R. So, its contribution to E_R can be omitted.

In practice, the reconstruction errors of real deformed samples are unknown because of the absence of ground truth. To the best of our knowledge, nobody has attempted to estimate the reconstruction error of real skulls. The linear relationship observed between ASM fitting error and reconstruction error makes it possible to estimate reconstruction error based on ASM fitting error. Using a robust regression method [12], the ASM fitting errors and the reconstruction error of all samples can be fitted to a line. This robust regression method iteratively re-weights each sample and minimizes the weighted sum of squared distance. The weight of each sample ranges from 0 to 1 depending on its distance to the fitted line. With a smaller weight, the sample is more likely to be an outlier.

With two ASM fitting errors E_F and E_G, three lines can be fitted: E_F vs. E_R, E_G vs. E_R, and E_F and E_G vs. E_R. The first two are single-fits whereas the third line is a dual-fit. Since we have no real testing samples with ground truth to determine which of these three methods is the best, all of them are presented in this paper. These fitted lines are evaluated on two criteria: fitting error and possibility of outlier. Fitting error computes the averaged weighted sum of absolute distances of all samples. The possibility of outlier is computed as 1 minus the averaged weight of the samples. Note that this possibility measurement is not strictly a probability. Compared to single-fit with E_F, single-fit with E_G and dual-fit have smaller fitting error but larger possibility of outlier (Table 1). This implies that E_F contributes less than E_G to dual-fit. Further study should be performed to investigate which one of these three fitting methods is better in estimating reconstruction error in real applications.

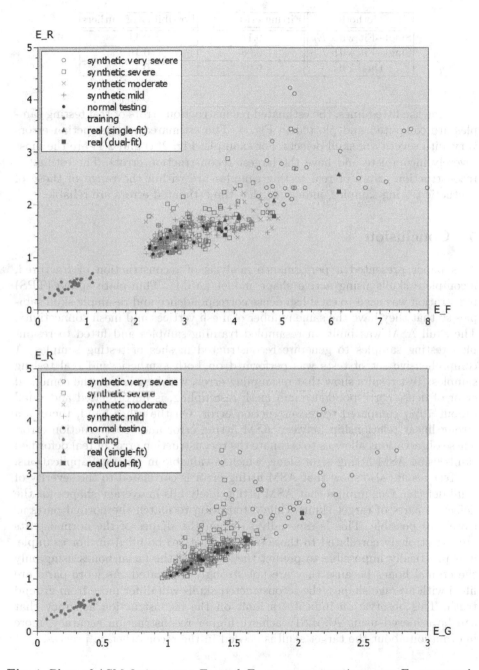

Fig. 4. Plots of ASM fitting error E_F and E_G vs. reconstruction error E_R measured in mm.

Table 1. Evaluation of fitted lines.

Methods	Fitting error (mm)	Possibility of outliers
Single-Fit with E_F	0.14	0.11
Single-Fit with E_G	0.08	0.16
Dual-Fit	0.07	0.16

Using the fitted lines, the estimated reconstruction errors of real testing samples are computed and plotted in Fig. 4. The estimated reconstruction errors vary with severity of skull defects. For example, Fig. 2(a) and 2(f) are the most severely incomplete and have the largest reconstruction errors. The estimated reconstruction errors of real testing samples are within the range of those of synthetic testing samples, indicating that the estimated errors are reliable.

5   Conclusion

This paper presented a performance analysis of reconstruction of fractured, incomplete skulls using active shape model (ASM). Thin-plate spline (TPS) registration was used to establish dense correspondence and resample skull samples so that they have the same number of mesh vertices and mesh connectivity. The skull ASM was built on resampled training samples and fitted to resampled testing samples to generate reconstructed meshes of testing samples. A comprehensive set of tests was performed on both synthetic and real testing samples. Test results show that resampling error, which measures the combined error of dense correspondence and mesh resampling, is uncorrelated and small (about 10%) compared to reconstruction error. On the other hand, there is a strong linear relationship between ASM fitting error and reconstruction error. These observations allow us to estimate the reconstruction error of real deformed skulls using ASM fitting error alone, which is valuable in practical applications.

Test results also show that ASM fitting error is correlated to the severity of skull defects. This implies that ASM fitting likely fills in average shapes for the defective parts of target skulls while attempting to match the normal parts as closely as possible. This is especially so when the shapes of the normal parts are not strongly correlated to those of the targets to be filled in. For example, it is practically impossible to predict the shapes of the facial bones using only the cranial bones because they are not strongly correlated. As more parts are filled with average shapes, the reconstructed skulls will differ more from ground truth. This observation indicates a limit on the reconstruction accuracy that can be achieved using ASM. To achieve higher reconstruction accuracy, more information about the target skull is needed in the reconstruction process.

References

1. Baldock, E.R., Graham, J.: Image Processing and Analysis: A Practical Approach. Oxford University Press (2000)
2. Benazzi, S., Stansfield, E., Milani, C., Gruppioni, G.: Geometric morphometric methods for three-dimensional virtual reconstruction of a fragmented cranium: The case of Angelo Poliziano. Int. Journal on Legal Medicine **123**(4), 333–344 (2009)
3. Bennis, C.: Piecewise surface flattening for non-distorted texture mapping. Computer Graphics **25**(4), 237–246 (1991)
4. Berar, M., Desvignes, M., Bailly, G., Payan, Y.: 3D meshes registration : application to statistical skull model. In: Campilho, A.C., Kamel, M.S. (eds.) ICIAR 2004. LNCS, vol. 3212, pp. 100–107. Springer, Heidelberg (2004)
5. Chui, H., Rangarajan, A.: A new algorithm for non-rigid point matching. In: Proc. IEEE Conf. Computer Vision and Pattern Recognition (2000)
6. Deng, Q., Zhou, M., Shui, W., Wu, Z., Ji, Y., Bai, R.: A novel skull registration based on global and local deformations for craniofacial reconstruction. Forensic Science Int. **208**, 95–102 (2011)
7. Elena, D.M., Chapuis, J., Pappas, I., Ferrigno, G., Hallermann, W., Schramm, A., Caversaccio, M.: Automatic extraction of the mid-facial plane for cranio-maxillofacial surgery planning. Int. J. Oral and Maxillofacial Surgery **35**(7), 636–642 (2006)
8. Floater, M.S., Hormann, K.: Surface parameterization: a tutorial and survey. In: Advances in Multiresolution for Geometric Modelling, pp. 157–186 (2005)
9. Gumprecht, H.K., Widenka, D.C., Lumenta, C.B.: BrainLab VectorVision Neuronavigation System: Technology and clinical experiences in 131 cases. Neurosurgery **44**(1) (1999)
10. Gunz, P.: Statistical and Geometric Reconstruction of Hominid Crania: Reconstructing Australopithecine Ontogeny. Universität Wien (2005)
11. Gunz, P., Mitteroecker, P., Bookstein, F., Weber, G.: Computer aided reconstruction of human crania. In: Proc. Computer Applications and Quantitative Methods in Archaeology (2004)
12. Holland, P.W., Welsch, R.E.: Robust regression using iteratively reweighted least-squares. Comm. in Statistics: Theory and Methods **6**(9), 813–827 (1977)
13. Kotcheff, A.C.W., Taylor, C.J.: Automatic construction of eigenshapemodels by direct optimization. Medical Image Analysis **2**(4), 303–314 (1998)
14. Lee, M.Y., Chang, C.C., Lin, C.C., Lo, L.J., Chen, Y.R.: Medical rapid prototyping in custom implant design for craniofacial reconstruction. IEEE Trans. Systems, Man and Cybernetics **3**, 2903–2908 (2003)
15. Lüthi, M., Albrecht, T., Vetter, T.: Building shape models from lousy data. In: Yang, G.-Z., Hawkes, D., Rueckert, D., Noble, A., Taylor, C. (eds.) MICCAI 2009, Part II. LNCS, vol. 5762, pp. 1–8. Springer, Heidelberg (2009)
16. Phillips, J.M., Liu, R., Tomasi, C.: Outlier robust ICP for minimizing fractional RMSD. In: Proc. Int. Conf. 3-D Digital Imaging and Modeling (2007)
17. Seo, H., Thalmann, N.M.: An automatic modeling of human bodies from sizing parameters. In: Proc. ACM SIGGRAPH (2003)
18. Souza, A., Udupa, J.K.: Automatic landmark selection for active shape models. In: Proc. SPIE Medical Imaging (2005)
19. Turner, W.D., Brown, R.E., Kelliher, T.P., Tu, P.H., Taister, M.A., Miller, K.W.: A novel method of automated skull registration for forensic facial approximation. Forensic Science Int. **154**, 149–158 (2005)

20. Wei, L., Yu, W., Li, M., Li, X.: Skull assembly and completion using template-based surface matching. In: Proc. of Int. Conf. 3D Imaging, Modeling, Processing, Visualization and Transmission (2011)
21. Zachow, S., Lamecker, H., Elsholtz, B., Stiller, M.: Reconstruction of mandibular dysplasia using a statistical 3D shape model. In: Computer Assisted Radiology and Surgery, pp. 1238–1243 (2005)
22. Zhang, K., Cheng, Y., Leow, W.K.: Dense Correspondence of skull models by automatic detection of anatomical landmarks. In: Wilson, R., Hancock, E., Bors, A., Smith, W. (eds.) CAIP 2013, Part I. LNCS, vol. 8047, pp. 229–236. Springer, Heidelberg (2013)

Content Extraction from Marketing Flyers

Ignazio Gallo(✉), Alessandro Zamberletti, and Lucia Noce

Department of Theoretical and Applied Science, University of Insubria,
Via Mazzini, 5, 21100 Varese, Italy
{ignazio.gallo,a.zamberletti,lucia.noce}@uninsubria.it
http://artelab.dicom.uninsubria.it/

Abstract. The rise of online shopping has hurt physical retailers, which struggle to persuade customers to buy products in physical stores rather than online. Marketing flyers are a great mean to increase the visibility of physical retailers, but the unstructured offers appearing in those documents cannot be easily compared with similar online deals, making it hard for a customer to understand whether it is more convenient to order a product online or to buy it from the physical shop. In this work we tackle this problem, introducing a content extraction algorithm that automatically extracts structured data from flyers. Unlike competing approaches that mainly focus on textual content or simply analyze font type, color and text positioning, we propose novel and more advanced visual features that capture the properties of graphic elements typically used in marketing materials to attract the attention of readers towards specific deals, obtaining excellent results and a high language and genre independence.

Keywords: Content extraction · Portable document format · Visual features · Marketing flyers

1 Introduction

Although e-commerce has been increasing in popularity in recent years, unstructured documents such as marketing flyers and advertising emails are still effective ways to promote products and special offers. In this study we propose a novel content extraction algorithm to automatically extract entities of interest from marketing flyers containing commercial product offers.

Most of the deals appearing within commercial flyers refer to physical retailers, and the data that can be gathered from those marketing documents is particularly appealing to online price comparison shopping engines to fill the existing gap between online and physical shopping. In fact, a searchable collection containing both physical deals extracted from marketing flyers and offers gathered from online listings would allow customers to determine whether it is more convenient to order a product online and wait for order preparation, shipping and delivery, or to physically drive to the retailer location and buy it straight from the shelf. This represents a great opportunity for physical retailers to compete against online marketplaces.

© Springer International Publishing Switzerland 2015
G. Azzopardi and N. Petkov (Eds.): CAIP 2015, Part I, LNCS 9256, pp. 325–336, 2015.
DOI: 10.1007/978-3-319-23192-1_27

The PDF standard is increasingly being used by physical retailers to create marketing materials that maintain the same visual characteristics on every different device. This is particularly important, as commercial flyers typically contain many graphic elements specifically designed to let customers quickly understand the positions of relevant offers within the pages or to attract their attention towards particular deals or sections. Most content extraction works in literature extract entities of interest from structured or semi-structured documents relying exclusively on textual features, ignoring the visual characteristics of the processed documents [1–5]. While these approaches may obtain satisfying results when processing heavily structured or plain text documents, recent works have shown that, when dealing with less structured documents containing lots of graphic elements, textual features are not discriminative enough to accurately identify all the entities of interest [6,7]. In fact, visual characteristics are typically used to highlight and categorize paragraphs of text, and therefore represent a large amount of information that can and should be used to more accurately distinguish entities of interest having low discriminative textual contents.

Casting the problem to PDF documents, existing studies transform the processed PDF content streams into raw text, wasting the visual formatting information contained within the documents, such as font type, size, color and text positioning [4,5]. If we delve even deeper into the world of PDF documents and we focus on PDF marketing flyers, it has been proved that combining textual information with additional features describing the visual characteristics of the deals in the processed documents increases classification performances [6].

Similarly to [6], the goal of this study is to underline the important role that visual features have in distinguishing different entities of interest within highly unstructured but visually rich documents. Unlike other works in literature, we propose novel and more complex visual features, *e.g.* font type frequency, markup density, xObject presence, *etc.*, that capture a wider set of visual characteristics of the processed documents and extract them directly from the PDF content streams to avoid visual distortions that may arise when converting PDF to other formats such as HTML. The use of a limited set of textual features, combined with highly discriminative visual features, enables our system to obtain satisfying results on visually dissimilar marketing flyers, while also maintaining a high language and genre independence. Although in this study we focus exclusively on marketing materials, the proposed visual features are not handcrafted for that specific domain; as such, they can be used in a wide variety of contexts in which the visual characteristics of the processed documents are discriminative for the entities that need to be identified.

2 Related Works

In the following paragraphs we introduce some recent works on content extraction that combine textual features with visual features describing the visual elements that typically help humans to quickly understand the different entities within the analyzed documents.

(a) Original   (b) Converted

Fig. 1. The conversion of a PDF file (a) to an HTML format (b) may generate formatting alterations that substantially change the visual characteristics of the original document. Conversion tool: PDF2HTML [6].

Radek *et al.* [8,9] propose a HTML content extraction method based on a page segmentation algorithm that splits rendered HTML pages into multiple basic areas that are visually separated from each other due to different background colors, frames or markup separators. Areas having similar visual characteristics are then clustered together into semantically correlated blocks which are assigned to different classes of interest on the basis of their font, spatial, text and color features.

Sun *et al.* [10] use Content Extraction via Text Density (CETD) to detect entities of interest within web pages, based on the observation that content text typically contains long and simply formatted sentences, while noise (navigation panels, advertisements, copyright information, disclaimer notices, *etc.*) is highly formatted, contain less text and shorter sentences. Statistical information about hyperlinks within the HTML Document Object Model (DOM) tree are also taken into account during the classification process. Even though CETD is completely language independent, it achieves and outperforms several competing content extraction algorithms, showing that an analysis of the lexicon used in the processed documents is not mandatory to obtain state-of-the-art results.

The idea that is possible to identify entities of interest in a language independent way is further inspected in [7]. In this work, the authors propose an automated system for content extraction from HTML web pages; the algorithm requires no user interaction and it relies exclusively on visual features extracted from both HTML tags and CSS style sheets.

Apostolova and Tomuro [6] use visual features like font size, font color and text y coordinate to detect entities of interest from online PDF flyers of real estate offerings, obtaining significant improvements over the detection results achieved using standard textual features. To extract visual attributes, PDF flyers are firstly automatically converted to HTML by analyzing PDF format operators

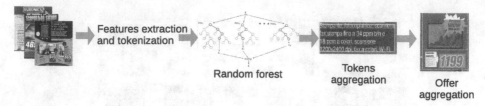

Fig. 2. Pipeline of the proposed method.

in the PDF content stream; style attributes are then dynamically extracted from the document by rendering the page with Google Chrome browser.[1]

The quality of the HTML document automatically generated when converting a PDF document depends on the degree of accordance between the PDF that is being converted and the ISO 32000-1/32000 specifications published by Adobe, *e.g.* as shown in Figure 1, when *BeginText* (BT), *EndText* (ET) and other format operators are misused in the PDF content stream, the HTML page resulting from the automatic conversion is flawed; the same holds when the processed PDF has been generated using a distiller which does not comply to the published ISO 32000-1/32000 specifications.[2]

Although none of the aforementioned algorithms extract content directly from PDF documents, it is possible to compute visual features from PDF content streams without having to convert them into HTML documents, thus avoiding the risk to alter the original document visual formatting style. In this study, multiple visual feature planes conforming with the formatting style of the original processed PDF document are automatically built by processing the format operators found in the content stream. Figure 3 shows how those visual features maintain the correct visual formatting style even for a PDF marketing flyer that cannot be automatically and correctly converted to HTML.

3   Proposed Method

The processing pipeline of the proposed approach is presented in this section: (i) feature planes and textual information are extracted from the processed marketing flyer; (ii) visual information gathered from feature planes are used to classify each word within the processed flyers using a properly trained random forest classifier; (iii) neighbouring words having similar visual characteristics are merged into semantically correlated paragraphs; (iv) paragraphs representing correlated product titles, descriptions and prices are further merged together to identify the deals contained within the processed flyer. The whole pipeline is summarized in Fig. 2 and described in detail in the remainder of this section.

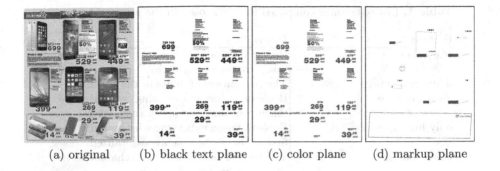

(a) original   (b) black text plane   (c) color plane   (d) markup plane

Fig. 3. Feature planes (b,c,d) automatically computed for a given flyer (a).

3.1 Visual Features

Given a PDF document, we compute the following visual feature planes: *black text*, *colored text* and *markup* (examples are provided in Fig. 3).

The *black text* plane isolates all the selectable text elements, and it is obtained by removing all but font, position and begin/end text PDF format operators from the original PDF content stream. As shown in Fig. 3b, all the selectable text elements are black and placed on a plain white background. Text position and formatting are preserved as in the starting document.

The *black text* plane is used to recognize text characters that are not readable due to missing font character maps (CMAP). In fact, when a font CMAP is missing, it is not possible to obtain the unicode representation of the fonts glyphs unless they are visually recognized using an appropriate OCR engine [11].

The *colored text* plane is obtained by removing all the following PDF format operators from the PDF content stream: b, B, b*, B*, BDC, BI, BMC, BX, c, d, Do, DP, EI, EMC, EX, f, F, f*, G, g, h, i, ID, j, J, l, m, M, MP, n, re, ri, s, S, sh, v, w, W, W*, y. Detailed information of the meaning of each PDF format operator are available in the ISO 32000-1/32000 specification document. As shown in Fig. 3c, the resulting plane is a copy of the original document, in which all the text components have been isolated from other PDF elements such as images, markup and background patterns. Unlike the *black text* plane, in the *colored text* plane text components maintain their original color, shadow, opacity and line style properties.

The *markup* plane contains exclusively all the markup and geometric elements used in the original document. As shown in Fig. 3d, this includes both text overlays (highlight, strikethrough, underline, *etc.*) and geometric figures drawn using PDF format operators, such as re and v (rectangles and lines respectively). In visually rich marketing documents, these geometric elements are particularly

---

[1] http://pdftohtml.sourceforge.net/
[2] http://www.adobe.com/devnet/pdf/pdf_reference.html

Table 1. List of features computed for each token in the processed flyer.

Feature	Description
is_number	Boolean value representing whether the token contains only digits.
digits_percentage	The percentage of digits in the token.
all_upper_case	Boolean value representing whether the token contains only upper case letters.
only_first_upper_case	Boolean value indicating whether only the first letter of the token is capitalized.
token_font_size	The largest font size of text characters in the token, measured in pixels.
token_angle	The average orientation angle of text characters in the token, measured in degrees.
token_position	The normalized position (x, y) relative to the page size.
token_color	The 3 most recurring RGB values in the region occupied by the token within the *colored text* plane.
token_font_frequency	The frequency of a specified font F_i in a specified page.
token_color_frequency	The frequency of token_color within the current document page.
token_markup_color_frequency	The frequency of the most recurring RGB value in the region occupied by the token within the *markup* plane.
token_font_page_frequency	The frequency of the token font measured over all the pages in the current document.

important as they are typically used to isolate semantically correlated text elements and draw the attention of customers towards relevant deals.

The previously described visual feature planes are used to compute the salient visual aspects of each token, or word, within the processed document. In many languages using Latin alphabet, word space may be used as a good approximation of a word divider. Unfortunately, using the space character as a delimiter to extract words from a PDF file does not always lead to optimal results. In fact, unlike other types of structured documents, PDF files do not always store word spaces, *e.g.* in some PDF documents, multiple BT/ET blocks (*begin text* and *end text* respectively) may be used within the same paragraph of text with different transformation matrix; in these cases, even though the appearance of the resulting PDF files is correct, some spaces between words are missing in the plain text stream extracted from the PDF content stream. To overcome this issue, in our method we compute the average width of text characters within the processed PDF, and use that as a metric to split text into tokens/words.

For each token we compute the set of visual features described in Table 1. Simple features such as font size, orientation, *etc.*, can be computed directly for

Table 2. Relevant entities for the extraction of offers from marketing flyers.

Entity	Description
Title	The insertion/offer title. It is usually composed of the brand name, the product name and some product specifications.
Description	The description of the object specified in the title. It gives additional details about the item.
Price	The final item price. All the strikethrough prices that may be associated with the same item need to be ignored, only the definitive price tag has to be taken into account.
Other	Content that is not related to offers or deals. This may include, but is not limited to, the flyer's title, expiration date, disclaimers and product tags.

each token, without having to analyze the entire document. On the other hand, the computation of more advanced features such as token font, color and markup frequencies require to analyze the entire content of the processed document.

More in detail, given a token/word t with its font f_t in a page p, the Token Font Frequency TFF of t in p is computed as follows:

$$TFF_{t,p} = \frac{n_{f_t}}{|p|} \tag{1}$$

where n_{f_t} is the number of tokens having font f_t in p, and $|p|$ is the total number of tokens in p.

Similarly, the Token Color Frequency TCF of a token t having font color c_t in p is computed as follows:

$$TCF_{t,p} = \frac{n_{c_t}}{|p|} \tag{2}$$

where n_{c_t} is the number of tokens having font color c_t in the page p.

Due to shadows, opacities and different text characters colors, a token/word may have multiple colors within the processed document. In our pipeline, for each token, we exploit the *colored text* plane to identify the most recurring RGB color appearing within the visual region that the token occupies in the page p, and use that RGB value as c_t.

A smilar process is used to compute the Token Markup Color Frequency $TMCF$ of the token t within the page p:

$$TMCF_{t,p} = \frac{n_{m_t}}{|p|} \tag{3}$$

where n_{m_t} is the number of tokens having markup color m_t in p. The value of m_t is computed as the most recurring RGB color in the region occupied by t in the *markup* plane for p. Please note that during the computation of token color c_t and markup color m_t, the white background on which all the elements are placed on the 3 feature planes is ignored.

Marketing flyers may have multiple pages, in these cases it is interesting to analyze the Font Page Frequency FPF of a token t in the whole document d:

$$FPF_{t,d} = \frac{|\{p_i : f_t \in p_i\}|}{|d|} \tag{4}$$

where $|\{p_i : f_t \in p_i\}|$ is the number of pages containing the font f_t in the marketing flyer d, and $|d|$ is the total number of pages in d.

Font Page Frequency is particularly relevant when processing marketing documents having multiple pages, as the fonts used to denote entities of interest typically do not change from page to page. This means that fonts having a high Font Page Frequency value are typically associated with interesting content, while low frequency fonts are usually associated with noise content, such as footnotes or disclaimers.

3.2   Token Classification and Aggregation

Tokens extracted from the processed flyers are classified as belonging to one of the entities of interest listed in Table 2. The classification task is carried out using a Random Forest classifier from Waikato Environment for Knowledge Analysis (WEKA) [12] library. Random Forest classifiers perform as well as SVM or NN classifiers when trained using a sufficient amount of data, while also being significantly faster to train [13].

Once every token in the page has been assigned to a class of interest, they need to be aggregated to form products titles, descriptions and prices. This aggregation task is carried out using an ad-hoc clustering algorithm that takes into account both the class and the position of tokens within the processed flyer.

At its first iteration, the algorithm selects the bounding box of a random seed token classified as belonging to either Title, Price or Description class, and tries to join that bounding box with all the other neighbouring bounding boxes of tokens classified as belonging to the same class c that are located at a distance $d < \epsilon$. This newly formed bounding box is then added to the page in place of all the joined bounding boxes. At each iteration a new seed token, that has not been previously selected, is chosen. The algorithm stops when all the tokens have been aggregated.

The result of this merging phase is a set of bounding boxes that represent titles, descriptions and prices of all the offers available on the flyer (see Fig. 4).

3.3   Offer Aggregation

The offers extraction process from each flyer is the last step of the presented method. This is not a trivial task as it cannot be carried out simply by considering the minimum distance between the various elements that form an offer.

Fig. 4. Examples of flyers manually tagged by experts. The relevant entities listed in Table 2 are highlighted as coloured rectangles (Title, Description and Price).

In fact, there are many cases in which one or more of the bounding boxes for the 3 relevant elements that make up an offer (Price, Title and Description) are visually closer to the bounding boxes of elements from another offer. In such cases, clustering exclusively on the basis of the distance between different bounding boxes does not lead to optimal results.

A better approach consists in clustering the bounding boxes in such way that the coverage provided by the final clusters over the processed page is maximized. This approach is motivated by the fact that marketing documents do not usually have many void areas, because retailers typically try to lower printing costs by adding as many offers as they can within each page to reduce the total size of the final flyer. As such, each offer within a page is usually localized in a particular area, and its bounding box has a minimal overlap with the other offers.

The textual information associated with an offer O is a triple (T, D, P) composed of a Title T, a Description D and a Price P. In this work, product images are not taken into account because finding the correct association between an image and its respective textual description requires a specific study, which is out of the focus of this work.

As previously stated, our offer aggregation algorithm tries to minimize the intersection area between all the bounding boxes for the offers in the processed page. The algorithm starts by selecting the bounding box of a random Price P_i and merges it with its closest Description D_i and Title T_i bounding boxes to form an offer hypothesis O_i. The same process is repeated for all the remaining Prices in the page to form a finite set of hypotheses $H_{P_i} = \{O_0, \ldots, O_n\}$. The sum $S_{H_{P_i}}$ of the intersection areas between the bounding boxes for the offers in H_{P_i} is then calculated as follows:

$$S_{H_{P_i}} = \sum_{j \neq k} O_j \cap O_k, \; j, k \in \{0, \ldots, n\} \tag{5}$$

This whole process is repeated multiple times, each time changing the starting seed Price, until all the Prices in the flyer have been selected as initial seeds. The set of offer hypotheses having minimum intra-intersection area is then selected as the best one.

4   Experiments

In the remainder of this section we present the experimental results obtained testing the proposed method on marketing flyers randomly collected from different retailers. Throughout our experimental activity we evaluate quantitatively the accuracy of the method both at identifying and classifying entities of interest within the processed flyers; and at aggregating the detected entities into offers.

4.1   Dataset

In order to evaluate the proposed approach, a total number of 1194 product offers have been gathered from 197 marketing flyers produced by 12 different retailers. The collected documents come from heterogeneous domains (electronics, gardening, clothing, *etc.*) and present substantially different design styles.

Each flyer has been manually labelled by a team of 4 experts using a specially designed GUI. As shown in Fig. 4, the experts were instructed to provide both the coordinates of all the product Titles, Descriptions and Prices in the pages, and the associations between those bounding boxes and the different offers within the pages. The information gathered from the different experts has been averaged to obtain the final ground-truth data used to evaluate the proposed method.

4.2   Evaluation Metrics

We evaluate the accuracy of the method both at classifying/aggregating individual tokens, and at aggregating the merged tokens into product offers.

Since our ground-truth data is composed of labelled bounding boxes manually drawn by experts over the different flyers, we measure the accuracy of the proposed approach by evaluating the intersection-over-union (IoU) [14] score between the bounding boxes detected by the proposed approach and the respective ground-truth information.

Each entity is evaluated independently from the others. Given a page with its ground-truth data for one of the entities from Table 2, and the aggregated predictions provided by the model for the same entity class; the evaluation process for the token classification/aggregation phase is carried out as follows: we compare the IoU score between each ground-truth bounding box and the predictions provided by the model; if one of the predicted bounding boxes achieves an IoU score greater than 0.5 with the ground-truth bounding box, the prediction is considered correct. For every ground-truth bounding box at most one predicted bounding box might be considered correct. Given the number of correct predictions, we compute the classic Precision, Recall and F-measure values.

Given a page with its ground-truth offer data, and the offer hypotheses generated as in Sec. 3.3, the evaluation process for the offer aggregation phase is carried out as follows: we compare the IoU score between each component of a ground-truth offer (Title, Description and Price) and the bounding boxes for the same component in the offer hypotheses; if every predicted component for a given offer hypothesis has an IoU that is greater than 0.5 with its respective ground-truth offer component, then the predicted offer is considered correct. For every ground-truth offer at most one hypothesis might be considered correct.

4.3 Results

Starting from a total number of 51045 tokens extracted from the dataset, 70% are used for training the classifier and the remaining 30% for testing. For each token, we compute the features listed in Table 1 using a 3×1 contextual sliding window centered on the token. As such, each token is classified on the basis of both its attributes and the attributes of its left and right neighbours.

The first step in the evaluation process aims at detecting the importance of the features listed in Table 1 using Information Gain [12]. The first 20 features selected by Information Gain in order of importance, are: font frequency, font size, font frequency right, font frequency left, font size left, font size right, y position, y position left, 1st RGB color left, 1st RGB color right, font page frequency, font page frequency right, font page frequency left, 2nd RGB color, 3rd RGB color, digit percentage, all upper case, 2nd RGB color left. Using Information Gain, only 2 among the top 20 ranked features are textual, underlining the importance of visual features.

The second experiment aims at measuring the goodness of the proposed Random Forest classifier. As listed in Table 2, tokens may belong to one of four possible classes: Title, Description, Price and Other In our experiment the classifier may contain a maximum of 10 trees; no limitations are posed on the depth of each tree; each tree considers 6 random features. The confusion matrix is presented in Table 3, 93.36% of the patterns are correctly classified, with a k-value of 0.89.

Table 3. Evaluation of the proposed method. On the left, the confusion matrix for the Random Forest classifier (k-value: 0.89). On the right, the results of both the token classification/aggregation (Descr., Title and Price) phase, and the offer aggregation phase (Aggr. offers). The best results were obtained by setting the token aggregation threshold to $\epsilon = 2 \cdot$ token_height.

	Descr.	Title	Price	Other		Precision	Recall	F-measure
Descr.	95.39%	5.57%	3.70%	3.27%	Description	0.740	0.655	0.695
Title	2.70%	91.51%	2.94%	3.51%	Title	0.789	0.837	0.812
Price	0.19%	0.67%	87.31%	2.04%	Price	0.815	0.916	0.862
Other	1.72%	2.25%	6.05%	91.18%	Aggr. offers	0.487	0.547	0.515

With the last experiment we evaluate the phases described in Sec. 3.2 and 3.3: the aggregation of tokens, and the subsequent aggregation of merged tokens into product offers. We measure Precision, Recall and F-measure values achieved on test set, while varying the token aggregation threshold ϵ from $0.1 \cdot$ token_height to $10 \cdot$ token_height. We report the best obtained results in Table 3; they have been obtained setting $\epsilon = (2 \cdot$ token_height$)$. The accuracy of the offer aggregation phase is influenced by the errors committed during the previous token classification/aggregation phase. Since the proposed method is structured as a waterfall of steps, this accuracy decreasement is inevitable.

5   Conclusion

An ad-hoc method for the automatic extraction of structured product offers from marketing flyers has been proposed. The presented approach heavily relies on novel visual features that capture the formatting details typically used in marketing documents to accurately distinguish relevant entities within the processed flyer's pages. The method has been evaluated over a collection of randomly collected flyers, achieving satisfying results while also maintaining an excellent language and genre independence due to the limited use of classical textual features.

References

1. Nadeau, D., Sekine, S.: A survey of named entity recognition and classification. Linguisticae Investigationes **30**, 3–26 (2007)
2. Ratinov, L., Roth, D.: Design challenges and misconceptions in named entity recognition. In: CoNNL, pp. 147–155 (2009)
3. Ling, X., Weld, D.: Fine-grained entity recognition. In: AAAI (2012)
4. Yuan, F., Liu, B., Yu, G.: A study on information extraction from PDF files. In: Yeung, D.S., Liu, Z.-Q., Wang, X.-Z., Yan, H. (eds.) ICMLC 2005. LNCS (LNAI), vol. 3930, pp. 258–267. Springer, Heidelberg (2006)
5. Prokofyev, R., Demartini, G., Cudré-Mauroux, P.: Effective named entity recognition for idiosyncratic web collections. In: WWW, pp. 397–408 (2014)
6. Apostolova, E., Tomuro, N.: Combining visual and textual features for information extraction from online flyers. In: EMNLP, pp. 1924–1929 (2014)
7. Zhou, Z., Mashuq, M., Sun, L.: Web content extraction through machine learning (2014)
8. Burget, R.: Layout based information extraction from html documents. In: ICDAR, pp. 624–628 (2007)
9. Burget, R., Rudolfova, I.: Web page element classification based on visual features. In: ACIIDS, pp. 67–72 (2009)
10. Sun, F., Song, D., Liao, L.: Dom based content extraction via text density. In: SIGIR, pp. 245–254 (2011)
11. Smith, R.: An overview of the tesseract ocr engine. In: ICDAR, pp. 629–6332 (2007)
12. Hall, M., Frank, E., Holmes, G., Pfahringer, B., Reutemann, P., Witten, I.H.: The weka data mining software: An update. SIGKDD Explorations **11**, 10–18 (2009)
13. Bosch, A., Zisserman, A., Munoz, X.: Image classification using random forests and ferns. In: ICCV, pp. 1–8 (2007)
14. Everingham, M., Van Gool, L., Williams, C.K.I., Winn, J., Zisserman, A.: The pascal visual object classes challenge. Computer Vision **88**, 303–338 (2010)

Puzzle Approach to Pose Tracking of a Rigid Object in a Multi Camera System

Sönke Schmid[1,2,3]([✉]), Xiaoyi Jiang[1,2,3], and Klaus Schäfers[2,3]

[1] Department of Mathematics and Computer Science,
University of Münster, Münster, Germany
soenke.schmid@uni-muenster.de
[2] European Institute for Molecular Imaging,
University of Münster, Münster, Germany
[3] Cluster of Excellence EXC 1003, Cells in Motion, CiM, Münster, Germany

Abstract. Optical tracking is a large field of research with countless sophisticated methods for a multitude of applications. However, there always exist tasks with special requirements and constraints that are not covered by traditional methods. This work presents a puzzle-based approach to tackle the problem of tracking all 6 degrees of freedom of a rigid object with few trackable features using a multi camera system. The presented algorithm capitalizes on non-sequential processing to assemble tracking information bit by bit. Validation shows that it achieves very high accuracy on real data.

Keywords: High accuracy tracking · Rigid body · Offline processing

1 Introduction

General optical tracking is a very large field of research that has already produced countless sophisticated methods for different applications [6,10]. However, special applications especially in the areas of biology and medical imaging provide extraordinary challenges that necessitate to adapt existing methods or even use uncommon approaches to yield reasonable results.

Tracking the absolute 3D position of objects using a multi camera system presents several additional challenges compared to tracking in 2D. Besides the video data further information of the scene geometry has to be considered and kept in accordance to the 2D tracking. For example, when tracking freely flying flies their 3D position has to be triangulated after finding the corresponding point pairs in the camera images. Although several possible point correspondences can be eliminated due to the epipolar geometry of the camera system this task is a form of the multi assignment problem proven to be *NP*-hard [5].

When tracking the absolute position of a single rigid object a typical approach would be automatic feature detection combined with RANSAC to determine the relative transformation. However, when the object provides only very few and poorly distinguishable features, this is bound to become instable. In that case

© Springer International Publishing Switzerland 2015
G. Azzopardi and N. Petkov (Eds.): CAIP 2015, Part I, LNCS 9256, pp. 337–349, 2015.
DOI: 10.1007/978-3-319-23192-1_28

the additional constraint provided by the rigidity can be incorporated into a standard tracking approach of single feature points. This increases the complexity of the dependencies between tracked features but it provides the opportunity to increase the tracking accuracy and reduce false positive results.

In this work we present a puzzle-based approach to tracking a rigid object that tries to incorporate every bit of information previously determined to improve the tracking result even further. Although this approach is restricted to offline processing due to its non-sequential nature, this has the potential to achieve better tracking results than realtime methods by returning to difficult passages at a later stage when more information is available. This property of offline tracking is capitalized on for example in the approach of bidirectional tracking [8].

Our algorithm starts from an arbitrary number of manually annotated frames expanding the tracking information in every direction. This is realized by using small independent tasks searching for the next fitting "puzzle piece". Depending on the result of a task it can queue up subsequent tasks completing the puzzle as much as possible. The advantage of this approach is the high tracking accuracy and the good scalability of the tracking framework on multi-core processors to deal with huge amounts of video data in reasonable time.

In Section 2 we give a short introduction to the project motivating our work. In Sections 3 and 4 we present our tracking framework in detail discussing the underlying data structure (Section 3.1), its dependencies (Section 3.2),the actual algorithm (Section 3.3), and the applied post-processing (Section 4). In Section 5 we discuss a few crucial details of the implementation. Finally, we show validation results of our tracking framework in Section 6 based on real data provided by our application.

2   Motivation and Project Description

Positron emission tomography (PET) plays an important role in today's medical imaging to study and visualize metabolism in living animals and humans. During the 15 to 45 minutes necessary for a PET scan the patient has to lie still and therefore animals are anesthetized during the scan. Since anesthesia influences the metabolism the resulting PET images of animals are biased.

In our project we try to avoid anesthetizing the animals and just place them inside a transparent cage within the PET scanner so that they can move freely during the scan [9]. To deal with the motion we use an optical camera system to track the pose and position of the head with very high accuracy. This information can be used to correct the data acquired by the PET scanner to generate a sharp PET image of the head of the animal.

Since the small animal PET-scanner has a spacial resolution of about 1 mm, this is the upper limit of the necessary tracking accuracy. However, smaller tracking errors still degrades the resulting image quality reducing the sharpness. Therefore, any improvements of the tracking accuracy below 1 mm are highly favored. Measured data from not trackable time periods can be discarded

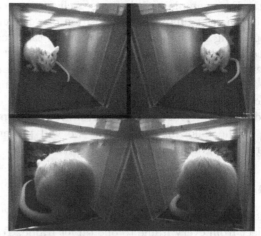

(a) Tracking Hardware   (b) Composed snapshot of all cameras during a rat experiment

Fig. 1. (a) Top: Side view of the animal cage with two of the four cameras attached. Bottom: Hardware System placed half way into the PET scanner. (b) Composed snapshot of all cameras during a PET scan of a rat. On the head of the rat a pattern of black marks was painted using a black marker pen to be used as additional trackable feature points.

for the PET reconstruction, however this reduces the statistics and therefore the image quality of the PET scan. Still, the explicit rejection of frames by the tracking system is much preferred to false positive tracking results.

The optical tracking system consists of four synchronized cameras placed around the animal chamber divided into two pairs of stereo cameras on each small side of the chamber (see Figure 1(a)). The cameras acquire images of 659×494 pixels (8-bit monochrome) at 100 Hz resolving even the fastest movements of the animals with a change of only a few pixels per frame. The illumination is realized by an infrared LED array above a diffusional layer. Due to the close range between the cameras and the cage wide angle lenses are used and their distortion is corrected for with a highly accurate method [1]. Applying highly accurate calibration tests showed that the 3D position of a checkerboard marker inside the cage could be determined with a mean accuracy of 0.125 mm [7].

3   Tracking Framework

The tracking framework presented in this paper is based on a puzzle approach. The puzzle refers to the data structure that has to be filled containing amongst other things the 3D positions of tracked feature points, their sightings in the 2D images, and descriptions of those feature points.

The data structure is initialized by few manual annotations and then filled bit by bit by small tasks working on the data already determined and the video data. For example a task can search for a specific feature point in one frame or it can triangulate the 3D position of a feature point given two 2D positions. Depending on the outcome subsequent tasks can be queued up to update the data structure or find even more information. The algorithm ends when the queue is empty and the last task executed was not able to find new information.

This course of action promises to gain as much out of the data as possible since whenever a new information is found all connected data informations are updated recursively and checked if even more puzzle pieces can be found.

In the following subsections we will present our data structure and task workflow in detail and discuss its architecture.

3.1 Data Structure

The goal of the tracking algorithm is to find the transformation of the rigid object from every frame to one target frame. To achieve this at least three pairs of feature points for each frame and the target frame are necessary to determine the rigid transformation in between. For that the 3D positions of the feature points have to be known. They can be determined by triangulating their position from the visual position in at least two of the camera images. Therefore, there exists three levels of complexity in the data: 2D, 3D, and rigid transformations. These levels of information are linked by various constraints.

An overview of the full data structure can be seen in Figure 2.

2D: For a fixed number of feature points the data structure for each frame and each camera contains the 2D position where this feature point is seen. For practical purposes for each of these positions a probability value is saved together with the local descriptions of the feature point in the corresponding camera image. Additionally, each of these entries contains a flag if this information was successfully confirmed by fulfilling all enforced constraints.

3D: On the next level of complexity for each of the feature points and for each frame the 3D position of the point is deposited together with a probability value and a confirmation flag as in the 2D case.

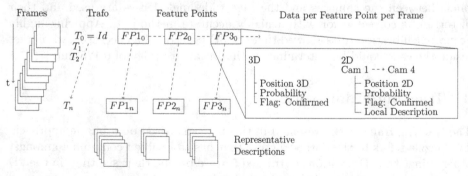

Fig. 2. Overview of the data structure of the tracking framework.

Transformations: At the highest level of complexity for each frame the transformation to the target frame is saved. On this level no more information is needed because the transformation is only determined after the information on the lower complexity levels was successfully checked against all constraints.

Feature Point Descriptions: In addition to the hierarchical data the data structure manages a list of representative descriptions of its 2D occurrences for each feature point that can be used to detect that point in the camera images.

3.2   Data Constraints

When filling the data structure several constraints have to be respected either due to pure geometry or to the plausibility given the experimental setup.

Rigid Transformations: On the level of the rigid transformations and the 3D positions the rigidity of the object poses a very hard constraint. A transformation is a rigid body transformation T if it preserves the distance of all point pairs

$$\forall_{P_1, P_2 \in \mathbb{R}^3} \|P_1 - P_2\| = \|T(P_1) - T(P_2)\| \tag{1}$$

and conserves the cross product of vectors to exclude mirroring.

   In our framework we use this strong constraint purely for confirmation to reject false positive tracking results. The constraint to conserve the scalar products is ignored in our algorithm since the method used for determining rigid transformations from point pairs returns only not mirrored rigid transformations [2].

Epiolar Geometry: Between the data level of 3D and 2D positions of the feature points the scene geometry has to be be obeyed. This means that the 2D positions p_{2D} have to accord with the projection of the 3D position P_{3D} onto the image plane given the projection matrix C of the calibrated camera:

$$p_{2D} = C(P_{3D}) \tag{2}$$

This implies the epipolar constraint between two 2D positions p_1, p_2 in different camera images

$$p_2^t F p_1 = 0 \tag{3}$$

with p_1, p_2 being the homogeneous image coordinates and F the fundamental matrix describing the epipolar geometry of the corresponding cameras [3].

   Just as the rigidity constraint, the tracking framework uses the epipolar geometry only for confirmation and filtering out false tracking results. Since this constraint is only valid for perfect data it is not checked directly but instead the total squared reprojection error of the triangulated 3D position is compared to a threshold.

$$E_{proj}(P_{3D}) = \sum_i \|C_i(P_{3D}) - p_i\|^2 \tag{4}$$

with p_i as the 2D position of the feature point of the camera image with corresponding projection function C_i.

Stability of Feature Point Description: Last but not least, the image data at the 2D position should show a tight resemblance to the known representative feature descriptions of the corresponding feature point. Depending on the actual video data and type of feature point any similarity measurement could be chosen such as histogram of orientated gradients or local binary patterns. This requirement is capitalized on to track feature points over time and then check the results against the more strict geometric constraints.

Temporal Smoothness: In addition to the spacial constraints there exist temporal dependencies. Experiments showed that mice or rats can move quite fast from one frame to the next. However, the high acquisition rate of 100 fps limits the maximal actual displacement of feature points from one frame to the next to only a few millimeters and therefore to position changes in the camera images in the one digit range. For the 3D positions of the feature points this high sampling rate allows for expecting a smooth curve over time.

3.3   Tracking Algorithm (Task Workflow)

The task workflow is the central part of the tracking framework and is in the usual understanding the tracking algorithm. It consists of several small tasks that try to fill the data structure while obeying the constraints. Figure 3 shows the full applied workflow for our project. The single tasks and their interactions are described in more detail in the following paragraphs. However, due to the partitioning of the whole tracking algorithm into small, linked tasks, this framework is highly modular and can easily be adapted to other applications.

Initialization of the Tracking Framework: The framework is initialized by a few manually annotated frames. At least the target frame has to be annotated. Any more information will improve the performance of the tracking framework.

The manual informations are inserted into the data by the task "Add Manual Point 2D". It sets the 2D position of one feature point in one camera image and gives it the maximal probability value of 1.0. In addition, the local description of the feature point in that frame is added to the list of representative descriptions. As a follow-up the task to determine the 3D position of the feature point is scheduled. Using the maximal known motion constraint the feature point is searched for in an area of 10×10 pixels in the previous and in the subsequent frame using the representative descriptions given by the current frame.

Triangulation of the 3D Position of a Feature Point: The tasks for determining the position of the 3D position of a feature point checks in the data structure if this feature point was seen in at least two camera images and if they fulfill the constraints provided by the epipolar geometry. For the actual triangulation a numerical gradient descent optimization is used for minimizing the quadratic reprojection error.

$$P_{3D}^* = \operatorname*{argmin}_{P_{3D} \in \mathbb{R}^3} \sum_i \|C_i(P_{3D}) - p_i\|^2 \tag{5}$$

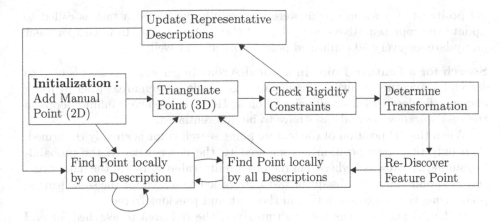

Fig. 3. Workflow of the tracking framework consisting of linked small tasks. The Algorithm is initialized by some manually determined position informations of feature points in the video frames. These informations are propagated in every direction either to the data on a higher level by triangulation of positions or sequentially by searching for the same point in subsequent frames. Each new found information updates the data structure recursively and initializes tasks to capitalize on this information.

with p_i as the 2D position of the feature point in the camera image with corresponding projection function C_i. This general approach is independent of the number of cameras and provides the possibility to use nonlinear projection functions to incorporate distortion or - in our project - the barely significant light refractions at the glass wall of the animal cage. If the triangulation was successful and the mean reprojection error is below 1.5 pixels the 3D position is accepted as quite possible and submitted into the data structure. Subsequently, a task is queued up to check for the rigidity constraints of all feature points in the frame.

Check of the Rigidity Constraint: For checking the rigidity constraint the 3D positions of the feature points in the target frame are determined once on initialization. This is done by using all manually annotated data to determine the 3D positions of the feature points in the annotated frames and the rigid transformation to the target frame. Then the 3D positions in each annotated frame are mapped to the target frame resulting in a point cloud for each feature point. The centers of these point clouds are used as the geometric model.

In the task for checking the rigidity constraint the RANSAC algorithm is applied to find the best rigid transformation between the 3D positions in the current frame to the geometric model. Then all feature points of the current frame are mapped to the model. For points that have a distance below 1 mm to the model it is assumed that their 3D position is correct. This position and the corresponding 2D positions in the camera images are marked as confirmed.

If at least one point could be marked as confirmed during this check a subsequent task is added to the queue to determine the transformation using all confirmed point correspondences. Additionally, every time a certain number of

2D positions of a feature point were successfully confirmed a task is called to update the representative descriptions of the feature point. In our experiment an update for every 50 confirmed points worked very well.

Search for a Feature Point in a Local Area: In general, this task is used to search for a feature point in an camera image inside a given area either by using one specific description or all existing ones. However, to avoid infinite loops in the task workflow several cases have to be differentiated.

When the 2D position of the feature point searched for is already confirmed, then only that very position is compared to the description. If the probability/similarity value is higher than the probability value stored in the data structure it is updated and subsequent tasks are called to search for the same feature point using the same description in the next and previous frame.

If the 2D position was not confirmed yet, the full area is searched for and the probability value of the best match is compared to the probability value already stored in the data structure. If the new search turned out a higher probability value the data is updated accordingly. If this probability surpasses a certain threshold subsequent tasks are called to triangulate the 3D position and to search for the feature point in the next and previous frame as done by the task "Add Manual Point 2D". If the threshold is not surpassed and the feature point was searched for using only a single description this task is repeated using all available representative descriptions for this feature point.

Re-Detection of Lost Feature Points: When a transformation was successfully determined for one frame the 3D position of all feature points is known theoretically. This task checks the data structure for all feature points in that frame whose 3D position was not confirmed yet. That position is projected onto the camera images and subsequent tasks are called to search for that feature point in a very small area of 3×3 pixels using all known descriptions.

Update of the Representative Descriptions of a Feature Point: Since descriptions of the feature points in the initial marked frames do not cover all possible view angles and lighting conditions it is obvious to update the descriptions using confirmed 2D sightings. When deciding which confirmed occurrence to add to the representative descriptions it would be pointless to add a very similar description to the already existing ones. On the other hand, adding an extremum could lead to a drift over time or totally false results since it is possible to be a false positive.

To address these problems we apply k-means clustering. In a first step the confirmed sightings are searched for the one with the largest distance to all existing representative descriptions. Then this extremum and the existing representative descriptions initialize a k-means clustering of all confirmed 2D-sightings of the feature point. For each resulting cluster center the nearest representative is checked against the existing descriptions. If the minimal distance surpasses a threshold it is added to the list of representative descriptions.

The probability values in the data structure are updated by searching for the newly added description in their original frame automatically propagating this information by the workflow.

Limitations of the Tracking Algorithm: The presented task workflow performs very well as can be seen in Section 6. However, in its current form it contains a significant limitation. The tracking spreads out from the manually marked key frames. If there are single frames where tracking is not possible (e.g. due to occlusion of all feature points) the tracking algorithm cannot overcome these frames. The only possibility to continue is to add another manually marked frame when tracking is possible again. If this limitation is a serious problem for the application it could be lessened in two ways. Either more cameras can be added reducing not trackable time periods or after a full run of the algorithm additional manual marked frames can be inserted where needed without restarting the whole program.

4   Post-Processing: Smoothing and Gap Filling of Rigid Transformations

When the task workflow has finished transformations were determined successfully for many frames. Up to now the time dependency was only used restricting the area to search for a feature point in a subsequent frame. As the validation shows (see Section 6) practically no false positive tracking results occurred although the stricter time dependent constraints in 3D were not used at all. They can now be applied for post-processing to smooth the results and fill small gaps.

The 3D positions of the feature points and the rigid transformation can be seen as a time series of measurements and for typical data in $\mathbb{R}^n$ smoothing and interpolation for gap filling are standard operations. In this case this is not trivial. The time series of the 3D positions could be processed in this way, however relative distances between the feature points are not necessarily conserved. In addition single time series of 3D positions exhibit a much higher number of gaps that would have to be interpolated than the series of rigid transformations.

For the set of rigid transformation no metric exists that concurs with the physical interpretation of motion. Therefore, we apply a method proposed by Park and Ravani [4] that is based on the algorithm of de Casteljau and is able to perform smoothing and gap filling at the same time.

The original algorithm of de Casteljau is used to render Bézier-curves. This method can also be employed for smoothing of sequential data using the values together with their time value as control points for the Bézier-curve. As the smoothed value of a point the corresponding point on the Bézier curve is taken. Park and Ravani translate this algorithm to the group of rigid transformations using the unique screw motions with constant speed as linear interpolation.

In our application a smoothing kernel of 15 transformations worked very well.

5   Implementation Details

5.1   Thread-Safe Data Structure

Since the amount and types of information necessary is known from the very start the actual implementation is straightforward. However, the data should be accessed from multiple threads. Therefore, the implementation has to ensure that two threads may not manipulate the same object simultaneously leaving it in an inconsistent state. This can be achieved by encapsulating the data structure and using mutual exclusion operations (mutex) in all data access operations.

We chose to safeguard each time series of information (transformations, 3D positions for each feature point, 2D positions for each feature point and camera) with its own mutex. This proved to be a good trade-off since a single mutex for the whole data structure would limit the scalability of the system and more mutexes would be unnecessary overhead.

The feature point descriptions are managed as an abstract class allowing to exchange the actual applied feature description like histogram of oriented gradients or local binary patterns. Depending on the application data the interface can be subclassed with the appropriate method.

5.2 Thread Pool Pattern for Algorithm

The processing of all tasks is implemented in the well-known thread pool pattern. A control thread manages a FIFO-queue of tasks to be executed. These are stored as an object containing their parameters and the reference to the function call. The control thread manages a pool of worker threads. Whenever a worker thread is idle it is used to execute the next task in the queue.

A problematic bottleneck proved to be the access of the video data, since it cannot be fully loaded into memory at the same time. However, a buffered data management in conjunction with smart preloading of few subsequent frames around a newly requested frame fully dissolved this bottleneck.

6 Validation

6.1 Experimental Setup

The tracking framework was tested and validated on real data using the full 45 minutes of a video from a rat experiment. To have more unique features some points and strokes were drawn on the fur of the forehead of the rat. A screenshot can be seen in Figure 1(b). With 100 fps the full video comprises 269000 frames for each camera resulting in 326 GB of raw video data. In every 200th frame 8 feature points were marked manually providing 1345 control frames in a 2 second interval. The tracking framework was initialized with 89 of them, one every 30 seconds. The remaining 1256 annotated frames were used for validation.

As feature descriptors normalized histograms of oriented gradients were used with 3×3 areas around the feature point with each 5×5 pixels. The directions of the gradients were sorted into 9 bins. As distance function basically the $L2$-norm was used but adapted to get a value between 0 and 1 with a maximum of 1 for equal descriptors. The actual applied distance function was:

$$D(d_1, d_2) = e^{-\|d_1 - d_2\|_{L2}^2} \tag{6}$$

6.2   Validation Results

The tracking framework achieved to track the head position of the rat in 199243 frames (74,07% of the total scan time). This is sufficient for the PET reconstruction and considering that there are multiple time periods when the rat washes itself and all tracked feature points are occluded, this percentage is very good.

In the manually marked frames that were not used for initializing the algorithm the confirmed 2D positions of the tracking result were compared to the manually marked positions. As a remarkable result no false positive detections of the feature points occurred and the mean distance to the manual markings was with 0.70 pixels very accurate. Figure 4(a) shows the histogram of the tracking error in pixels.

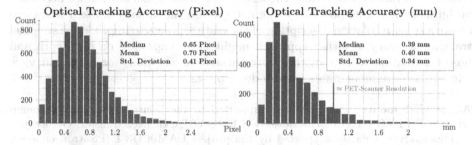

(a) Tracking accuracy in video data measured in pixels

(b) Tracking accuracy of the absolute 3D position measured in mm

Fig. 4. Validation of the tracking accuracy of the framework using 1256 manually annotated frames.

Since the tracking error in 3D is the essential value for the project the confirmed 3D positions of the feature points from the algorithm were compared to the 3D positions resulting from triangulating the manual marked positions. The tracking framework achieved a mean tracking accuracy of 0.4 mm which is by far better than the upper limit required for the application. The histogram of the tracking error in 3D can be seen in Figure 4(b).

6.3   Runtime Performance

The tracking framework was run on a server with 4 Intel Xeon CPU E5-4620 providing in sum 32 physical cores (64 virtual cores) and 384 GB main memory. The thread pool of our framework was set to 40 parallel executed tasks and the buffer size for video data in main memory was set to 10000 frames ($\approx$ 30 GB).

With these settings our algorithm needed a total runtime of about 7 hours with an average CPU load of 37 cores proving the scalability of the system. Although the algorithm does not seem very fast, it has to be considered that the runtime is reasonable and the accuracy has higher priority. Additionally, about one third of the total computational effort is located in the frameloader transforming the raw data into undistorted images using tricubic interpolation.

7   Conclusions and Future Work

In this work we presented a framework for tracking a rigid object using a puzzle based approach to achieve optimal tracking results by nonlinear processing of the video data. With only a few manual annotated frames it was possible to track the object for a high percentage of the full video with high accuracy and without false positive results. The presented framework is very modular due to its architecture consisting of linked basic operations and can be easily modified.

For future work we plan to adapt the task workflow to improve the tracking results even further and reduce the amount of manual marked frames necessary on initialization. One possibility might be to use the already tracked frames to create a super resolution description of the feature points to improve the subpixel tracking accuracy. Another approach might be to capitalize on the depth and pose information to correct the representative descriptions for scale and view angle to achieve more stable feature descriptions.

Acknowledgments. This work was supported by the Deutsche Forschungsgemein-schaft, DFG EXC 1003 Cells in Motion – Cluster of Excellence, Münster, Germany.

This study was partly supported by the project DA 1064/3-1 (Positron emission tomography of non-anesthetized freely-moving mice) of the Deutsche Forschungsge-meinschaft (DFG).

References

1. Schmid, S., Jiang, X., Schäfers, K.: High-precision lens distortion correction using smoothed thin plate splines. In: Wilson, R., Hancock, E., Bors, A., Smith, W. (eds.) CAIP 2013, Part II. LNCS, vol. 8048, pp. 432–439. Springer, Heidelberg (2013)
2. Walker, M.W., Shao, L., Volz, R.A.: Estimating 3-D Location Parameters Using Dual Number Quaternions. CVGIP: Image Underst. **54**, 358–367 (1991)
3. Hartley, R.I., Zisserman, A.: Multiple View Geometry in Computer Vision. Cambridge University Press (2004)
4. Park, F.C., Ravani, B.: Bézier Curves on Riemannian Manifolds and Lie Groups with Kinematic Applications. Trans. ASME, Journal of Mechanical Design **117**, 36–40 (1995)
5. Risse, B., Berh, D., Tao, J., Jiang, X.: Comparison of two 3D Tracking Paradigms for Freely Flying Insects. EURASIP Journal on Image and Video Processing **57** (2013)
6. Yilmaz, A., Javed, O., Shah, M.: Object Tracking: A Survey. ACM Comput. Surv. **38** (2006)
7. Schmid, S., Dawood, M., Frohwein, L., Jiang, X., Schäfers, K.P.: Camera-based high accuracy tracking system for freely moving mice inside the quadHIDAC pet scanner. In: Medical Imaging Conference, Anaheim, CA, USA (2012)
8. Caljon, T., Enescu, V., Schelkens, P., Sahli, H.: An offline bidirectional tracking scheme. In: Blanc-Talon, J., Philips, W., Popescu, D.C., Scheunders, P. (eds.) ACIVS 2005. LNCS, vol. 3708, pp. 587–594. Springer, Heidelberg (2005)

9. Jiang, X., Dawood, M., Gigengack, F., Risse, B., Schmid, S., Tenbrinck, D., Schäfers, K.: Biomedical imaging: a computer vision perspective. In: Wilson, R., Hancock, E., Bors, A., Smith, W. (eds.) CAIP 2013, Part I. LNCS, vol. 8047, pp. 1–19. Springer, Heidelberg (2013)
10. Smeulders, A.W.M., et al.: Visual Tracking: An Experimental Survey. IEEE Trans. on Pattern Analysis and Machine Intelligence **36**, 1442–1468 (2014)

Adaptive Information Selection in Images: Efficient Naive Bayes Nearest Neighbor Classification

Thomas Reineking$^{(\boxtimes)}$, Tobias Kluth, and David Nakath

Cognitive Neuroinformatics, University of Bremen,
Enrique-Schmidt-Str. 5, 28359 Bremen, Germany
{trking,tkluth,dnakath}@cs.uni-bremen.de

Abstract. We propose different methods for adaptively selecting information in images during object recognition. In contrast to standard feature selection, we consider this problem in a Bayesian framework where features are sequentially selected based on the current belief distribution over object classes. We define three different selection criteria and provide efficient Monte Carlo algorithms for the selection. In particular, we extend the successful Naive Bayes Nearest Neighbor (NBNN) classification approach, which is very costly to compute in its original form. We show that the proposed information selection methods result in a significant speed-up because only a small number of features needs to be extracted for accurate classification. In addition to adaptive methods based on the current belief distribution, we also consider image-based selection methods and we evaluate the performance of the different methods on a standard object recognition data set.

Keywords: Object recognition · Classification · Information selection · Bayesian inference · Information gain

1 Introduction

Selecting relevant information from a high-dimensional input is a fundamental problem pertaining many different areas ranging from computer vision to robotics. An effective selection strategy uses only a small subset of the available information without negatively impacting the task performance. An example of a successful selection strategy is the processing of visual information in humans where eye movements are performed in order to extract the relevant information from a scene in a very efficient manner [11]. A key feature of this selection is its adaptivity because the selection is strongly influenced by the current belief about the scene [17].

In this paper, we follow the idea of an adaptive belief-based information selection and we investigate it in the context of object recognition. While object recognition is usually viewed as a static pattern recognition problem, we model the recognition as an information gathering process unfolding in time, which is

© Springer International Publishing Switzerland 2015
G. Azzopardi and N. Petkov (Eds.): CAIP 2015, Part I, LNCS 9256, pp. 350–361, 2015.
DOI: 10.1007/978-3-319-23192-1_29

more akin to visual processing in humans. In this case, recognition becomes a problem of Bayesian information fusion where the selection of relevant information is done adaptively with regard to the current belief distribution (in contrast to classical feature selection methods, e.g. [4,7]). We propose different criteria for optimal information selection and provide efficient algorithms for their application. In addition to belief-based selection methods, we also consider an image-based method that uses a saliency operator to identify relevant locations in an image.

We combine the information selection methods with the successful NBNN object recognition approach presented in [1]. We use NBNN because it is a probabilistic approach where local image features are sequentially processed in order to update a belief distribution over possible object classes.[1] For each extracted feature, multiple expensive nearest neighbor searches have to be performed, which is why selecting a small subset of relevant features greatly reduces the computational costs of NBNN classification (for making the nearest neighbor search itself more efficient, see [9]). Note that while we focus on object recognition in this paper, the proposed belief-based information selection methods are very versatile and could therefore also be applied in other contexts.

The paper is structured as follows. In the next section, the basics of the NBNN approach are introduced. In Sect. 3, the information selection methods are described in detail. In Sect. 4, the different selection methods are combined with the NBNN approach and compared empirically on a standard object recognition data set. The paper concludes with a short discussion of the proposed methods and possible extensions.

2 Naive Bayes Nearest Neighbor

For NBNN, a set of local image descriptors is extracted from the query image (e.g. SIFT descriptors [8]) which is then used to compute the posterior probability distribution over object classes. Let $\mathcal{C}$ denote the set of object classes, and let $d_{1:N}$ denote all descriptors extracted from the query image[2] where N is the total number of descriptors found in the image. By applying Bayes' rule and by making a naive Bayes assumption regarding the conditional independence of descriptors, the posterior is given by

$$P(c|d_{1:N}) \propto P(c) \prod_{i=1}^{N} p(d_i|c) \text{ with } c \in \mathcal{C}. \tag{1}$$

The likelihood $p(d_i|c)$ for the i-th descriptor is approximated using kernel density estimation (KDE). This avoids the severe errors caused by quantizing descriptors like in bag-of-words models [2]. To reduce computational complexity and in contrast to typical KDE, only the nearest neighbor (NN) of d_i in the

---

[1] Other state-of-the-art classification approaches like deep networks [6] are not suited here because they do not allow for an incremental processing of features.

[2] We use the shorthand notation $d_{1:N} = d_1, \ldots, d_N$.

training set is considered because the density contributions of descriptors that are farther away tend to be negligible. Using a Gaussian kernel, the likelihood is approximated by

$$p(d_i|c) = \frac{1}{|\mathcal{D}_c|} \sum_{d^{(j)} \in \mathcal{D}_c} \frac{1}{\sqrt{2\pi}\sigma} \exp(-\frac{||d_i - d^{(j)}||^2}{2\sigma^2}) \tag{2}$$

$$\approx \frac{1}{\sqrt{2\pi}\sigma|\mathcal{D}_c|} \exp(-\frac{||d_i - NN_c(d_i)||^2}{2\sigma^2}) \tag{3}$$

with

$$NN_c(d_i) = \arg\min_{d^{(j)} \in \mathcal{D}_c} ||d_i - d^{(j)}|| \tag{4}$$

where σ denotes the (class-independent) KDE bandwidth, $\mathcal{D}_c$ denotes the set of descriptors in the training set belonging to class c, and $NN_c(d_i)$ denotes the NN of d_i in $\mathcal{D}_c$. The posterior is thus given by

$$P(c|d_{1:N}) \propto P(c) \prod_{i=1}^{N} p(d_i|c) \propto P(c) \exp\left(-\frac{1}{2\sigma^2} \sum_{i=1}^{N} ||d_i - NN_c(d_i)||^2\right). \tag{5}$$

Note that we ignore the descriptor count $|\mathcal{D}_c|$ for the posterior because its influence is very limited and it simplifies the derivations below. Assuming a uniform class prior, the most probable class c^* can be found using the simple decision rule

$$c^* = \arg\max_{c \in \mathcal{C}} \log P(c|d_{1:N}) = \arg\min_{c \in \mathcal{C}} \sum_{i=1}^{N} ||d_i - NN_c(d_i)||^2. \tag{6}$$

Though the decision rule in Eq. (6) is independent of σ (it is therefore ignored in the original NBNN approach), the bandwidth turns out to be relevant for the selection of optimal descriptors in the next section. We determine the optimal bandwidth σ^* by maximizing the log-likelihood of all training set descriptors $\mathcal{D} = \cup_{c \in \mathcal{C}} \mathcal{D}_c$ according to

$$\sigma^* = \arg\max_{\sigma} \log p(\mathcal{D}|\sigma) = \sqrt{\frac{\sum_{c \in \mathcal{C}} \sum_{d^{(i)} \in \mathcal{D}_c} ||d^{(i)} - NN_c(d^{(i)})||^2}{|\mathcal{D}|}}. \tag{7}$$

3   Information Selection

For selecting the most relevant descriptors, we distinguish between belief-based selection methods and image-based ones. For belief-based selection, the probabilistic model introduced in the previous section is used to predict the effect of extracting a descriptor at a particular location in the image on the current belief distribution. In contrast, for image-based selection, the image information itself is used to determine which regions in the image are most relevant without considering the training data.

We model the information selection problem as one of finding the most promising *absolute* location in an image where the object is assumed to be depicted at the center of the image. This simplification allows us to ignore the problem of object detection, which would be necessary in case of more complex scenes with variable object locations. Let l_t denote the location of a descriptor d_{l_t} in an image at the t-th extraction step after already having extracted the first $t-1$ descriptors $d_{l_1:l_{t-1}}$. To select the next optimal location, we compute a score $S(l_t)$ for each location and choose the maximum

$$l_t^* = \arg\max_{l_t \in \mathcal{L}_t} S(l_t). \tag{8}$$

To limit the number of locations, we put a grid over each image where a location represents a grid cell. Because of the naive Bayes assumption, the likelihoods of the descriptors within a cell can simply be combined by multiplying them, i.e., each likelihood $p(d_{l_t}|c)$ represents a product of the likelihoods of individual descriptors located within the same grid cell.

In the remainder of this section, we first present two belief-based information selection methods and then an image-based one.

3.1   Maximum Expected Probability

For classification it is useful to select the descriptor that maximizes the expected posterior probability (MEP) of the true class. Because the value of the next descriptor is unknown prior to extracting it, it has to be modeled as a random variable D_{l_t}. The same applies to the value of the true object class of the query image, which is modeled as a random variable $C_{\text{true}} \in \mathcal{C}$. The score S_{MEP} is the conditional expectation of the true class posterior probability

$$S_{\text{MEP}}(l_t) = E[P(C_{\text{true}}|d_{l_1:l_{t-1}}, D_{l_t})|d_{l_1:l_{t-1}}] \tag{9}$$

$$= \int \sum_{c_{\text{true}} \in \mathcal{C}} p(c_{\text{true}}, d_{l_t}|d_{l_1:l_{t-1}}) \, P(c_{\text{true}}|d_{l_1:l_t}) \, dd_{l_t} \tag{10}$$

$$= \int \sum_{c_{\text{true}} \in \mathcal{C}} p(c_{\text{true}}, d_{l_t}) \frac{P(c_{\text{true}}|d_{l_1:l_{t-1}})}{P(c_{\text{true}})} \, P(c_{\text{true}}|d_{l_1:l_t}) \, dd_{l_t} \tag{11}$$

$$\approx \frac{1}{M} \sum_{i=1}^{M} \frac{P(c^{(i)}|d_{l_1:l_{t-1}})}{P(c^{(i)})} \, P(c^{(i)}|d_{l_1:l_{t-1}}, d_{l_t}^{(i)}) \tag{12}$$

with respect to C_{true} and D_{l_t} given the previous descriptors $d_{l_1:l_{t-1}}$. Because the training samples are assumed to represent i.i.d. samples from the joint distribution $p(c_{\text{true}}, d_{l_t})$, the score can be approximated by a Monte Carlo estimate computed over the training set in Eq. (12) where $c^{(i)}$ denotes the class of the i-th image in the training set, $d_{l_t}^{(i)}$ denotes the descriptor in the i-th training image at location l_t, and M denotes the total number of images in the training set. All the posterior probabilities can be obtained using Eq. (5).

Computing the Monte Carlo estimate can be time-consuming because all descriptors in the training set have to be considered. However, the NN distances required for the likelihoods can be computed in advance so that the overall score computation is still significantly faster than having to process all descriptors from the query image. In addition, it would be possible to only use a subset of the training samples where each sample would be drawn with a probability given by the current belief distribution.

For the special case where no descriptors have been extracted ($t = 1$) or where one chooses to ignore previously extracted descriptors, we can compute a score that ignores the current belief distribution and only maximizes the normalized expected likelihood (MEL). Plugging in $P(c^{(i)})$ for the current belief distribution in Eq. (12) results in

$$S_{\text{MEL}}(l_t) = E[P(C_{\text{true}}|D_{l_t})] \tag{13}$$

$$\approx \frac{1}{M} \sum_{i=1}^{M} \frac{P(c^{(i)})}{P(c^{(i)})} P(c^{(i)}|d_{l_t}^{(i)}) \tag{14}$$

$$= \frac{1}{M} \sum_{i=1}^{M} \frac{P(c^{(i)}) \, p(d_{l_t}^{(i)}|c^{(i)})}{\sum_{c \in \mathcal{C}} P(c) \, p(d_{l_t}^{(i)}|c)}. \tag{15}$$

Because this score is independent of previous descriptors, it can be computed offline and is thus extremely fast.

3.2   Maximum Expected Information Gain

A popular method for feature selection is the maximum expected information gain (MIG) [18]. Here we consider a "dynamic" information gain version that takes previous descriptors into account during the recognition process [12,15]. It is given by the expected uncertainty/entropy reduction resulting from observing a new descriptor d_{l_t}. The information gain score S_{MIG} is the conditional expectation of this reduction with respect to D_{l_t} given the previous descriptors $d_{l_1:l_{t-1}}$:

$$S_{\text{MIG}}(l_t) = H(C|d_{l_1:l_{t-1}}) - E[H(C|d_{l_1:l_{t-1}}, D_{l_t})|d_{l_1:l_{t-1}}] \tag{16}$$

$$= H(C|d_{l_1:l_{t-1}}) - \int \sum_{c_{\text{true}} \in \mathcal{C}} p(c_{\text{true}}, d_{l_t}|d_{l_1:l_{t-1}}) H(C|d_{l_1:l_t}) \, dd_{l_t} \tag{17}$$

$$\approx H(C|d_{l_1:l_{t-1}}) - \frac{1}{M} \sum_{i=1}^{M} \frac{P(c^{(i)}|d_{l_1:l_{t-1}})}{P(c^{(i)})} H(C|d_{l_1:l_{t-1}}, d_{l_t}^{(i)}) \tag{18}$$

with entropy

$$H(X) = -\sum_{x \in \mathcal{X}} P(x) \log P(x). \tag{19}$$

Like for S_{MEP}, the expected value is approximated by a Monte Carlo estimate using samples from the training set in Eq. (18). Note that the information gain is independent of the true class, meaning that a high MIG score only requires the resulting posterior distribution to be "non-uniform", thus completely ignoring how probable the true class is.

3.3 Intrinsically Two-Dimensional Signals

The following image-based selection method uses a saliency operator which detects intrinsically two-dimensional ($I2D$) signals [19]. The intrinsic dimensionality of a signal $u(x,y)$ is defined as $I0D$ for all signals that are constant and as $I1D$ for all signals that can be written as a function of one variable in an appropriately rotated coordinate system (e.g. an image of an oriented straight edge). In contrast, $I2D$-signals make full use of the two degrees of freedom (e.g. an image of a corner or crossing lines). The $I2D$-saliency also appears to play an important role in the control of saccadic eye movements [5,16] which motivates its use as a score function within the context of this work. In order to identify the interesting $I2D$-points, we make use of the generalized curvature operator introduced in [19]: The generalized curvature operator $T_n : C^2(\Omega) \rightarrow C(\Omega)$ with compact $\Omega \subset \mathbb{R}^2$ is defined for $n \in \mathbb{N}$ by

$$T_n(u)(x) = \frac{1}{4}\left((\Delta u)^2 - \epsilon_n(u)^2\right) = \frac{1}{4}\underbrace{(\Delta u + |\epsilon_n(u)|)}_{=\lambda_1(u)}\underbrace{(\Delta u - |\epsilon_n(u)|)}_{=\lambda_2(u)} \qquad (20)$$

with eccentricity $\epsilon_n(u)^2 = (c_n * u)^2 + (s_n * u)^2$. The convolution kernels c_n and s_n are defined by their Fourier transform in polar coordinates ($x_1 = r\cos(\phi)$, $x_2 = r\sin(\phi)$) by

$$\mathcal{F}(c_n)(r,\phi) = (i)^n f(r)\cos(n\phi)$$
$$\text{and } \mathcal{F}(s_n)(r,\phi) = (i)^n f(r)\sin(n\phi).$$

f is a continuous function of the radius r given by $f(r) = 2\pi r^2 e^{\frac{1}{2}\frac{r^2}{\sigma_r^2}}$. λ_1 and λ_2 are the eigenvalues of the Hessian matrix of u in the case of $n = 2$ where the generalized curvature becomes the Gaussian curvature. The Gaussian curvature allows a distinction between elliptic, hyperbolic, and parabolic regions on the curved surface $\{(x, y, u(x, y))^T | (x, y)^T \in \mathbb{R}^2\}$. Using the eigenvalues, the clipped eigenvalue is defined by

$$CE(u) = |\min(0, \lambda_1(u))| - |\max(0, \lambda_2(u))|. \qquad (21)$$

In contrast to directly using generalized curvature as a score function, the advantage of the clipped eigenvalue is that it can distinguish between positive elliptic and negative elliptic points, i.e., both eigenvalues are positive or negative. Furthermore, the clipped eigenvalue does not respond to hyperbolic regions. The latter is useful because hyperbolic regions are often found right next to elliptic ones, in which case the hyperbolic regions would only provide redundant

(a) Original   (b) $I2D$-saliency

Fig. 1. Extracted $I2D$-saliency (b) of the image shown in (a). The extracted $I2D$-score is the clipped eigenvalue computed with the following parameters: $n = 6$, $\sigma_r = 0.2$. Positive elliptically curved regions are light and negative elliptically curved regions are dark.

information. The score function is then defined with respect to the luminance function u of the grid cell $\Omega(l_t)$ at location l_t by

$$S_{I2D}(l_t) = \frac{1}{|\Omega(l_t)|} \int_{\Omega(l_t)} |CE(u)(x)|\, dx. \tag{22}$$

In contrast to belief-based score functions, the $I2D$-saliency is a purely image-based method. Consequently, it does not require any training data. The $I2D$-score function of an example image is illustrated in Fig. 1.

4   Evaluation

We evaluate the proposed information selection methods on the Caltech 101 data set [3]. We use 15 randomly selected images from each of the 101 object classes for training and 10 for testing. All images are scaled such that they have a maximum width or height of 300 pixels. Afterwards, densely-sampled SIFT descriptors are extracted (several thousands for each image depending on the size) and the NN distances are computed.[3]

Fig. 2 shows the mean accuracy over time for the different selection methods using a 5×5 grid and 10-fold cross validation. The MEP and MEL methods result in the quickest increase in accuracy and only require extracting descriptors from less than 6 grid cells on average for reliable classification (even though the MEL method ignores the current belief distribution). The MIG and I2D methods perform only slightly worse and all of the considered methods significantly outperform the baseline methods where descriptors are either selected randomly

---

[3] We use the code provided at https://github.com/sanchom/sjm for SIFT descriptor extraction and the FLANN library [10] for fast NN matches.

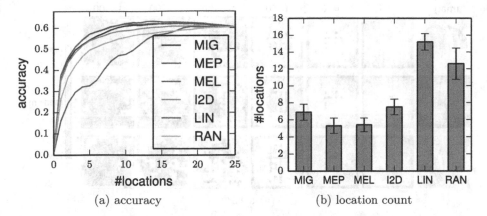

(a) accuracy (b) location count

Fig. 2. (a) Mean accuracy on the entire Caltech data set plotted for different time steps/location counts using different selection methods. (b) Mean number of time steps/location counts required for reaching at least 90% of the final accuracy where all descriptors have been extracted. The indicated standard deviation is computed with respect to the different folds.

("RAN") or line by line starting at the top of the image ("LIN"). The final accuracy after having extracted *all* descriptors is identical for each method because the extraction order is irrelevant for the classification model. Interestingly, the accuracy is highest after having extracted about half of all descriptors (except for the baseline methods), showing that the remaining descriptors tend to only decrease the recognition performance.

To illustrate the process of sequentially selecting descriptors, Fig. 3 shows score distributions over time using a 20×20 grid for three example images. For the belief-based MEP and MIG selection methods shown in (a) and (b), the score distributions change significantly over time and adapt themselves to the query image based on the current belief distribution. The I2D score distribution remains constant over time aside from setting the score of previously selected locations to 0 (the apparent change in other locations is due to scaling in the visualization). At $t = 1$, both the MEP and the MIG scores are independent of the query image and only the I2D method uses the image information. Over time, the MEP and MIG scores adapt themselves to the current belief distribution over object classes, whereas the I2D score remains unchanged. The visible "grid pattern" (especially for $t \leq 10$) is an artifact resulting from some grid cells containing more descriptors than others (this could be avoided if all cells contained roughly the same number of descriptors).

Perhaps surprisingly, the MEP score is highest at the center while the MIG score is initially highest in the periphery. One possible explanation for this effect is that the MEP method can be interpreted as a "confirmation strategy" whereas the MIG method can be interpreted as a "discriminative strategy". For MEP, extracting descriptors from the center of an object usually increases the probability of the true class without necessarily resulting in a unique classification

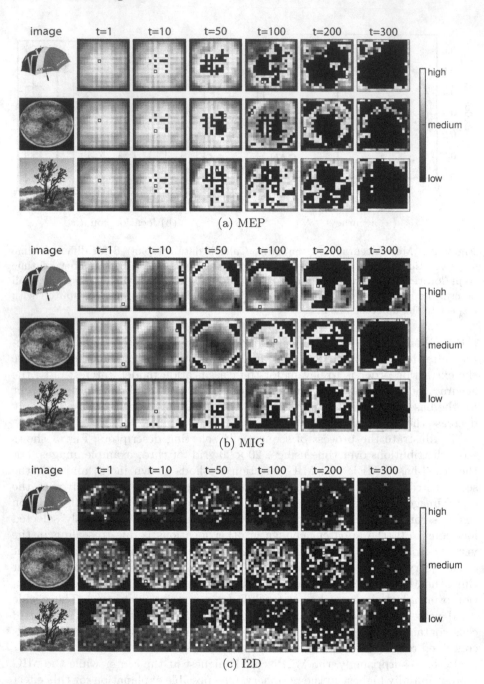

Fig. 3. Examples of score distributions over time using a 20×20 grid for different selection methods and query images. The small blue square indicates the cell with the highest score from which the next descriptor(s) are extracted. Cells that have already been selected have a score value of 0 (black).

(i.e. the overall belief distribution can still be very uniform). In contrast, the MIG method is agnostic with respect to the true class and only seeks to reduce uncertainty (e.g. by ruling out large numbers of classes). This could be accomplished by analyzing the "context" of objects, which is why the MIG method might first focus on the background.

5 Conclusion

We have proposed different methods for adaptive information selection from images where the current belief distribution directly determines which image locations should be considered next. In addition, we have also considered an image-based selection method that does not require any training data. Using these methods, we have extended the NBNN approach and we have shown that the selection methods make it possible to only consider a small subset of the available information while maintaining the original recognition performance. In particular for NBNN, where computing the NN distances for each descriptor is very time-consuming, the result is a significantly reduced computation time.

One of the problems not addressed in this paper is the fact that features in close proximity to each other are highly correlated. While the naive Bayes assumption can be justified for inference by the greatly reduced computational complexity, for the information selection it would be possible to use a more sophisticated model where correlations are explicitly considered. As a result, there would be a penalty for extracting features located very closely to each other, thus avoiding processing of redundant information.

In this paper, we have considered belief-based selection strategies (MEP, MIG) and image-based strategies (I2D) separately. A more promising approach could be a combination of both strategies [16] because the belief-based strategy completely ignores what is readily available in the image while a purely image-based strategy has difficulties selecting the relevant information because it ignores the training data. Due to the complementary nature of these strategies, a hybrid strategy could further improve the selection process.

We believe that the proposed selection methods can also be useful for problems beyond recognizing single objects. Especially for complex scenes containing many objects, an adaptive information selection strategy could predict the likely locations of objects and thereby facilitate understanding of the entire scene.

Finally, the general nature of the proposed information selection approaches allows for the application to systems which must perform actions to obtain new information from their environments (e.g. an autonomous spacecraft [14] or a melting probe [13]). These actions can cause high costs in terms of, for example, energy consumption or execution time. In these situations, it is thus highly desirable to avoid non-informative actions by using adaptive selection strategies.

Acknowledgments. This work was supported by the German Federal Ministry for Economic Affairs and Energy (DLR project "KaNaRiA", funding no. 50 NA 1318, and DLR project "CAUSE", funding no. 50 NA 1505).

References

1. Boiman, O., Shechtman, E., Irani, M.: In defense of nearest-neighbor based image classification. In: IEEE Conference on Computer Vision and Pattern Recognition, CVPR 2008, pp. 1–8. IEEE (2008)
2. Csurka, G., Dance, C., Fan, L., Willamowski, J., Bray, C.: Visual categorization with bags of keypoints. In: Workshop on Statistical Learning in Computer Vision, ECCV, vol. 1, pp. 1–2 (2004)
3. Fei-Fei, L., Fergus, R., Perona, P.: Learning generative visual models from few training examples: An incremental bayesian approach tested on 101 object categories. Computer Vision and Image Understanding **106**(1), 59–70 (2007); special issue on Generative Model Based Vision
4. Guyon, I., Elisseeff, A.: An introduction to variable and feature selection. J. Mach. Learn. Res. **3**, 1157–1182 (2003)
5. Krieger, G., Rentschler, I., Hauske, G., Schill, K., Zetzsche, C.: Object and scene analysis by saccadic eye-movements: An investigation with higher-order statistics. Spatial Vision **13**(2–3), 201–214 (2000)
6. Krizhevsky, A., Sutskever, I., Hinton, G.: Imagenet classification with deep convolutional neural networks. In: Advances in Neural Information Processing Systems, pp. 1097–1105 (2012)
7. Liu, H., Sun, J., Liu, L., Zhang, H.: Feature selection with dynamic mutual information. Pattern Recognition **42**(7), 1330–1339 (2009)
8. Lowe, D.G.: Object recognition from local scale-invariant features. In: The Proceedings of the Seventh IEEE International Conference on Computer vision, 1999, vol. 2, pp. 1150–1157. IEEE (1999)
9. McCann, S., Lowe, D.G.: Local naive Bayes nearest neighbor for image classification. In: 2012 IEEE Conference on Computer Vision and Pattern Recognition (CVPR), pp. 3650–3656. IEEE (2012)
10. Muja, M., Lowe, D.G.: Scalable nearest neighbor algorithms for high dimensional data. IEEE Transactions on Pattern Analysis and Machine Intelligence **36** (2014)
11. Najemnik, J., Geisler, W.S.: Optimal eye movement strategies in visual search. Nature **434**(7031), 387–391 (2005)
12. Kluth, T., Reineking, T., Nakath, D., Zetzsche, C., Schill, K.: Active sensorimotor object recognition in three-dimensional space. In: Freksa, C., Nebel, B., Hegarty, M., Barkowsky, T. (eds.) Spatial Cognition 2014. LNCS, vol. 8684, pp. 312–324. Springer, Heidelberg (2014)
13. Niedermeier, H., Clemens, J., Kowalski, J., Macht, S., Heinen, D., Hoffmann, R., Linder, P.: Navigation system for a research ice probe for antarctic glaciers. In: IEEE/ION PLANS 2014, pp. 959–975. IEEE (2014)
14. Pavone, M., Acikmese, B., Nesnas, I.A., Starek, J.: Spacecraft autonomy challenges for next generation space missions (2013), online (to appear in Lecture Notes in Control and Information Systems). http://goo.gl/nU8xG0
15. Reineking, T., Schill, K.: Evidential object recognition based on information gain maximization. In: Cuzzolin, F. (ed.) BELIEF 2014. LNCS, vol. 8764, pp. 227–236. Springer, Heidelberg (2014)
16. Schill, K., Umkehrer, E., Beinlich, S., Krieger, G., Zetzsche, C.: Scene analysis with saccadic eye movements: Top-down and bottom-up modeling. Journal of Electronic Imaging **10**(1), 152–160 (2001)

17. Torralba, A., Oliva, A., Castelhano, M.S., Henderson, J.M.: Contextual guidance of eye movements and attention in real-world scenes: the role of global features in object search. Psychological Review **113**(4), 766 (2006)
18. Yang, Y., Pedersen, J.O.: A comparative study on feature selection in text categorization. In: ICML, vol. 97, pp. 412–420 (1997)
19. Zetzsche, C., Barth, E.: Image surface predicates and the neural encoding of two-dimensional signal variations. In: SC-DL tentative, pp. 160–177. International Society for Optics and Photonics (1990)

The Brightness Clustering Transform and Locally Contrasting Keypoints

J. Lomeli-R.[✉] and Mark S. Nixon

Electronics and Computer Sciences, University of Southampton,
Southampton, England
jlr2g12@ecs.soton.ac.uk

Abstract. In recent years a new wave of feature descriptors has been presented to the computer vision community, ORB, BRISK and FREAK amongst others. These new descriptors allow reduced time and memory consumption on the processing and storage stages of tasks such as image matching or visual odometry, enabling real time applications. The problem is now the lack of fast interest point detectors with good repeatability to use with these new descriptors. We present a new blob-detector which can be implemented in real time and is faster than most of the currently used feature-detectors. The detection is achieved with an innovative non-deterministic low-level operator called the *Brightness Clustering Transform* (BCT). The BCT can be thought as a coarse-to-fine search through scale spaces for the true derivative of the image; it also mimics trans-saccadic perception of human vision. We call the new algorithm *Locally Contrasting Keypoints* detector or *LOCKY*. Showing good repeatability and robustness to image transformations included in the Oxford dataset, LOCKY is amongst the fastest affine-covariant feature detectors.

1 Introduction

In 2008, Tuytelaars and Mikolajczyk presented a survey on local invariant feature detectors discussing many of their characteristics [1]. Perhaps the most important topic is the criterion used to decide which features are more appropriate for particular applications. Nevertheless, it was shown that some features are more appropriate for different tasks.

Features can be categorised into three general groups, corners, blobs and regions. For instance, corner detection has long been researched and therefore, many approaches to solve this problem exist. The *Harris corner detector* [2] is arguably the most well known feature detector, based on the eigenvalues of the second order moment matrix; corners can be detected with rotation invariance. In need of faster algorithms other solutions were proposed, *SUSAN* [3], *FAST* [4], and more recently *AGAST* [5] amongst others.

The main problem with corner points is that, because of their persistence through changes in scale, they are ill-suited for describing the size of keypoint they represent; one solution to this problem is the use of blobs. The fact that

© Springer International Publishing Switzerland 2015
G. Azzopardi and N. Petkov (Eds.): CAIP 2015, Part I, LNCS 9256, pp. 362–373, 2015.
DOI: 10.1007/978-3-319-23192-1_30

blobs are contrasting regions implies that their shape carries information about both the scale and affine transformations. Moreover blobs are known to be more robust to noise and blurring than corners.

The use of such features is limited nowadays because of the lack of efficient algorithms that can find and extract information from blobs in real time. Recently a new set of descriptors was introduced, ORB [14], BRISK [15] and FREAK [16] amongst others; these descriptors can be implemented in real time in mobile processors. In [18], Heinly et al. presented a comparison of detectors and descriptors, it is left clear that the area of feature detection has not received as much attention as description in the last decade.

Some of the most well known blob detectors are the *Laplacian of Gaussian* [17] (and its approximation by *difference of Gaussians*) and, the *determinant of Hessian*. A fast implementation of the Hessian approach was presented in [11], this algorithm is well known as *Speeded up Robust Features* (SURF). More recently, Agrawal et al. presented in [7] an algorithm known as *CenSurE*; this algorithm, using integral and rotated-integral images, sets a polygon in every pixel and calculates an approximation of the Laplacian of Gaussian.

Detectors are called *invariant* to some transformations, Tuytelaars and Mikolajczyk suggests the term should be *covariant* when they change covariantly with the image transformation [1]. Mikolajczyk et al. [12] present an affine-covariant solution that, based on the second order moments of the regions surrounding the detected points, the features are affine-normalised; their solution is robust and elegant but very slow. The *Maximally Stable Extremal Regions* (MSER) [6] is an affine-covariant interest region detector that improves the computation time over Mikolajczyk's work, although it lacks robustness against blurring and noise. The use of affine features is related to the intention of making detectors robust to perspective changes. Human vision is very robust to image transformations like blurring, rotation and scaling, and also to changes in perspective. Although perspective transformations are different from affine transformations, affine-covariant local feature detectors are good approximations due to their local nature. We introduce a rapid novel affine-covariant blob detector in response to the wave of new binary descriptors; figure 1 shows some of the keypoints detected with the proposed algorithm.

This paper is divided in two main sections. First, we present the *Brightness Clustering Transform*. The BCT is an efficient algorithm that can be used to create both blob maps and ridge maps. It benefits from the use of integral images to perform a fast search through different scale spaces. Secondly, information from the blob maps is extracted; the detected blobs are called *Locally Contrasting Keypoints* (LOCKY). These keypoints contain information about the scale and affine transformations of the detected blobs and, are up to three times faster to detect than the MSER regions.

2   The Brightness Clustering Transform

Most of the complex human visual activities require alternations between eye fixations and significantly rapid eye movements known as saccades. The information

Fig. 1. LOCKY blobs detected on an image of daisies.

humans extract from a scene is a series of *snapshots* (fixations), however, we perceive scenes as single views [19]. There exist a temporal memory which integrates those *snapshots* into one *memory image*, preserving the extracted information from the fixations; the process is known as *trans-saccadic integration*.

The BCT is a non-deterministic algorithm that employs a voting scheme using rectangles on the integral image space. Each vote is randomly initialised, then it extracts information from the region being attended resembling eye fixations. When the next vote is initialised, the algorithm changes the location of attention, this is a saccade.

2.1 Blob Detection

The integral image as presented in [10], is a very useful tool to calculate the sum of rectangular areas of pixels in only three operations disregarding the size of the rectangles; it is widely used because it allows to make calculations at different scales without added computational cost.

$$ii(x,y) = \sum_{x' \leq x, y' \leq y} Im(x', y'). \tag{1}$$

$$s(x,y) = s(x, y-1) + i(x,y). \tag{2}$$

$$ii(x,y) = ii(x-1, y) + s(x,y). \tag{3}$$

Equation 1, shows the definition of the integral image. The recurrences in equations 2 and 3 allow the calculation of $ii(x, y)$ in one pass over the image ($s(x, y)$ is the cumulative row sum, $s(x, -1) = 0$ and $ii(-1, y) = 0$).

The BCT is initialised as a null-matrix of the same size as the input image (the output *memory image*). A vote means incrementing the value of a matrix element in the BCT by one; each vote is obtained in three steps. First, a rectangle with random position and size is initialised within the image. For finding blobs, we select the width and the height of the rectangle to be a power of two *i.e.* $width = 2^n$ and $height = 2^m$ $\{n, m \in \mathbb{N}\}$. The second step is to divide the rectangle in four smaller sub-regions, the sub-region with the biggest sum is now considered to be the initial rectangle; the sum is calculated using the integral image. Consider the rectangle R_t where $t = 0$ for the initial position and size, and its subregions r_0, r_1, r_2 and r_3; the next region will have an initial rectangle R_{t+1}. The second step is repeated until R_t has either $width = 2$ or $height = 2$.

$$R_{t+1} = \arg\max_{r_i} \sum_{x,y \in r_i} Im(x,y), \quad i = 0, 1, 2, 3. \tag{4}$$

Suppose the last R_t is situated in (x_f, y_f), has $width = w_f$ and $height = h_f$; in the third step, the pixel in $loc = (round(x_f + w_f/2), round(y_f + h_f/2))$ is voted. This sequence of steps is graphically presented in figure 2, algorithm 1 shows the pseudocode for the BCT.

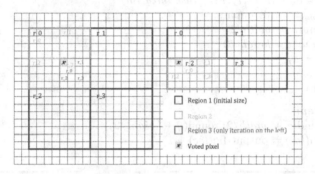

Fig. 2. A squared vote on the left and a rectangular vote on the right. R_0 in blue, R_1 in green and R_2 in red. The subregions of every step are marked as r_i with the same colour as the step they belong to.

After a user-defined number of votes, the BCT is smoothed with a small Gaussian kernel with $\sigma = 2$ and then normalised. Smoothing the BCT removes the effects of noise in the voting process and helps to find the true shape of the extracted blobs. As mentioned in [20], intermediate shape priors can yield discriminative shape structures; these structures can improve recognition tasks.

The BCT can be thought as a coarse-to-fine search through scale spaces for the true derivative of the image. Every sub-division of a rectangle is in the next smaller octave and thus, the votes start at a big scale and refine until they get to the smallest scale possible on the image. The use of rectancles benefits affine locallity; for example, a horizontal rectangle discards some information in the y axis and operates in the same scale in the x axis, this allows an improvement on the detection of oval blobs. Suppose a vote lies in (x_v, y_v) with an initial rectangle in (x_0, y_0), another vote will most likely lie in $(x_v + 1, y_v)$ if a rectangle of the same size is set in $(x_0 + 1, y_0)$. This property clusters votes around the centre of blobs, and so the shape of the blobs is extracted.

Algorithm 1. The Brightness Clustering Transform

integ_Im   = calculate integral of input_Im
output_Im = initialise output image

for $vote = 1$ **to** max_votes **do**

    First Step:
    Init region R:
        $width = 2^{rand(rangeMin, rangeMax)}$
        $height = 2^{rand(rangeMin, rangeMax)}$
        $x = rand(0, imWidth - width)$
        $y = rand(0, imHeight - height)$

    Second Step:
    while $width > 2$ & $height > 2$ **do**

        divide R in 4 subregions r_0, r_1, r_2 and r_3
        $r_{max} = \max(r_0, r_1, r_2, r_3)$ *(use integ_Im)*
        $R = r_{max}$ this implies:
            $width = width/2$
            $height = height/2$
            $x = x_{r_{max}}$
            $y = y_{r_{max}}$
    end while

    Third Step:
    $loc = (\text{round}(x + width/2), \text{round}(y + height/2))$
    $output\_Im(loc) = output\_Im(loc) + 1$

end for

In our experiments we discovered that amounts ranging from 5×10^4 to 1×10^5 votes are enough to extract the blobs in a 1024×768 image. We also noted that amounts as small as 2×10^4 votes can extract most of the significant blobs on the same image. The most commonly used values for the width and height of the rectangles range from 2^3 to 2^7; this range may be modified depending on the size of the image and the size of the blobs to be extracted.

So far the bright blobs are extracted by finding the sub-regions with the biggest sum of pixels; if we want to find dark blobs we could either modify equation 4 to be

$$R_{t+1} = \arg\min_{r_i} \sum_{x,y \in r_i} Im(x,y), \quad i = 0, 1, 2, 3, \tag{5}$$

or, find the bright blobs of the inverted image *i.e.* considering the image is an 8-bits representation, we do $Im' = 255 - Im(x, y)$ or $Im' = \text{not}(Im(x, y))$.

2.2   Ridge Detection

Ridges are one-dimensional blobs. The BCT can be modified to extract this kind of features. Half of the votes are obtained with the width set constant and equal to two, and the height again set to a power of two; this time, the rectangles are only divided in two parts along the height. The other half of the votes are obtained in the same manner, but setting the height to be constant and equal to two and varying only the width.

This operator yields a new fast ridge detector that can be used for any kind of applications from matching to extraction and segmentation.

2.3   Operator Invariance

The scale invariance of the BCT, is related to the size of the initial rectangles; as the voting process goes on, the centres of the blobs are found. The random aspect ratio of the rectangles helps to disperse the votes near the centre of the features and not only cluster them at the exact centre.

Changes in illumination are considered as multiplicative noise. We modify equation 4 as follows.

$$R_{t+1} = \arg\max_{r_i} \sum_{x,y \in r_i} K(x,y) Im(x,y). \tag{6}$$

Here, $K(x,y)$ is the illumination function. If the illumination function can be considered to be approximately constant *i.e.* $K(x,y) \approx k$ in the region covered by R_0, then k can be extracted from the equation and we see that the operator is invariant to approximately constant changes in illumination.

From the same logic we obtain that the BCT is invariant to noise with zero-mean distributions as it cancels itself in the sub-regions r_i.

3   Locally Contrasting Keypoints

The Locally Contrasting Keypoints (LOCKY) are blob keypoints extracted directly from the BCT of an image. After the normalisation process, the BCT is thresholded; the set of all the connected components in the binary image, are the detected blobs. Figure 3 describes the process for detecting the LOCKY blobs in an image.

Finding the ellipse with the same second order moments as the connected components is a fast way of extracting information from them. If F is a $2 \times N$ matrix ($N > 1$) containing the coordinates of the pixels in a connected component $(f_1, f_2, \ldots, f_N)$; the mean is the centre of the feature (eq. 8).

$$Q = \frac{1}{N-1} \sum_{n=1}^{N} (f_n - \bar{F})(f_n - \bar{F})^T. \tag{7}$$

$$\bar{F} = \begin{bmatrix} \mu_x \\ \mu_y \end{bmatrix}. \tag{8}$$

The eigenvalues of the sample covariance matrix Q (eq. 7) represent the size of the axes of the ellipse with the same second order moments; the eigenvectors

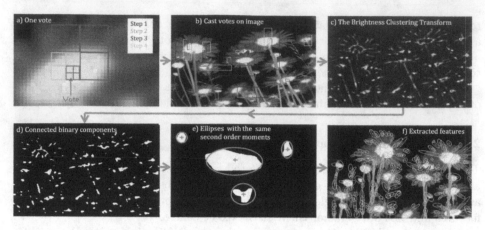

Fig. 3. The process for extracting the LOCKY features starts with the voting process to obtain the BCT. The transform is thresholded and the set of connected components is then extracted. The LOCKY features are the ellipses with the same second order moments as the connected binary components.

define the direction of the axes. In practice, the eigenvalues of Q are scaled up by a factor of five to enlarge the size of the features.

This step is similar to the ellipses of the Maximally Stable Extremal Regions. The advantages of this method are that one can detect the scale of the features by the size of the axes and, it is also possible to extract information about affine transformations and rotation of the blobs.

4   Results

The Oxford dataset [9] (figure 4) presents a good challenge for interest point detection and it is now widely used for evaluation; eight sequences composed of six images each with increasing image transformations including decreasing illumination, change in perspective, blurring, jpeg compression and a mix of scale and rotation. We use the measure of *Repeatability* defined in the same paper to compare LOCKY with both, affine-covariant and non-affine-covariant interest point detectors. In the affine-covariant group we use as comparison the *Harris-Affine* and *Hessian-Affine* detectors [12] and, the *Maximally Stable Extremal Regions* [6]. In the non-affine-covariant group, we use the BRISK detector [15], the SURF (fast-Hessian) detector [11] and, CenSurE [7] (known as the STAR detector in *openCV*). LOCKY-1 uses 1×10^5 rectangles of size ranging from 2^3 to 2^5 and a threshold of 24%; LOCKY-2 uses 1×10^6 rectangles of the same characteristics.

The measure of repeatability consists of projecting the detected features to the same basis as the original image (the first image of the sequence) using an homography matrix; comparing correspondences of features and measuring how well the region detected on the images overlap. For more information on this

Fig. 4. The first images of the sequences in the Oxford Dataset [9].

measure see [9]. We use the correspondences with 40% overlap. To be able to compare LOCKY with non-affine-covariant detectors we "disable" the measure by using a circle with a radius equal to half the size of the major axis of the ellipses.

Table 1. The average factor of time for a set of 127 images. The images were converted to grayscale with 1024×768 pixels.

Detector	Time Factor	Type	Affine
Fast-Hessian [11]	4.53	Blobs	✗
BRISK [15]	0.98	Corners	✗
CenSurE [7]	0.72	Blobs	✗
LOCKY1	1	Blobs	✓
LOCKY2	4.93	Blobs	✓
MSER [6]	3.26	Regions	✓
Hessian-Affine [12]	6.04	Blobs	✓
Harris-Affine [12]	8.53	Corners	✓

The timing results shown in table 1, were obtained using the OpenCV implementations of the algorithms (using mex files in MATLAB) in a computer with a 2 GHz $i7$ processor. Note that BRISK uses a multi-scale version of the AGAST detector which is a faster implementation of the FAST detector; LOCKY has similar timings while being able to provide information on affine transformations of the features.

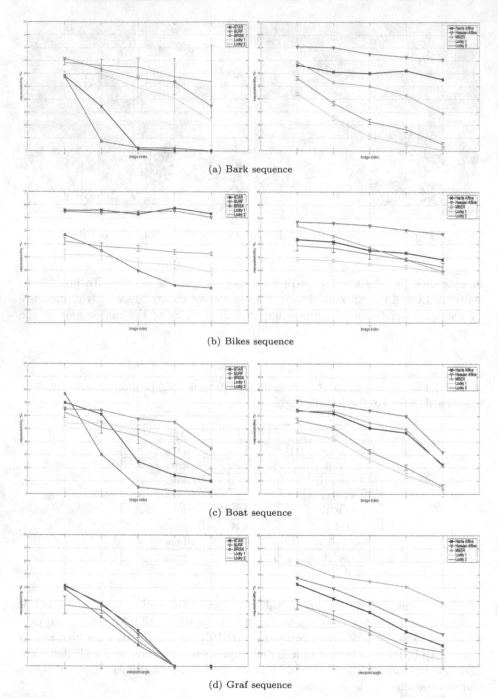

(a) Bark sequence

(b) Bikes sequence

(c) Boat sequence

(d) Graf sequence

Fig. 5. The repeatability test presented in [9]. Figures on the left column present the results of the repeatability test with no affine-covariance (features are circles); the right column shows the figures with the results using affine-covariance (features are ellipses). LOCKY-1 uses 1×10^5 rectangles of size ranging from 2^3 to 2^5 and a threshold of 24%; LOCKY-2 uses 1×10^6 rectangles of the same characteristics.

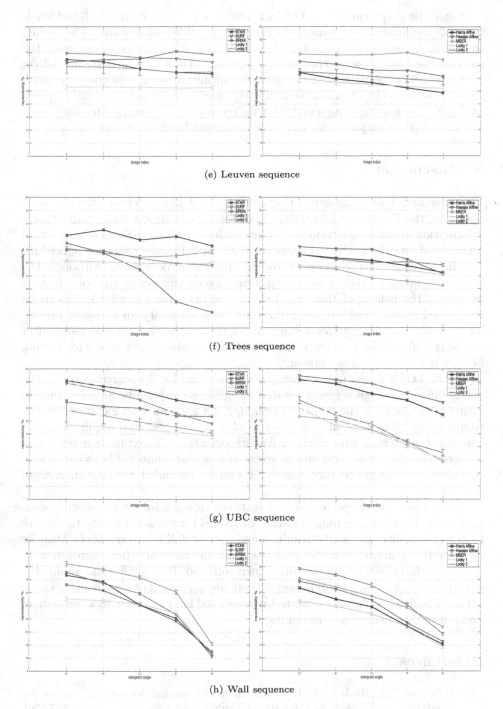

(e) Leuven sequence

(f) Trees sequence

(g) UBC sequence

(h) Wall sequence

Fig. 5. (*Continued*)

Since the detection of the LOCKY features is based in the BCT which is a non-deterministic transform every run matches different features. The results shown in Figure 5 (at the bottom) include the mean and variance over 100 runs of the test, showing that on average the LOCKY approach can deliver excellent performance: it is not dependent on initialisation and competes with those techniques already available and with its own advantages, especially speed. LOCKY detector might appear better on rectilinear structures (the wall) than on objects (the boat) and this can be investigated further.

5 Discussion

We presented a new algorithm that (via a novel non-deterministic low level operator, the Brightness Clustering Transform), can detect blobs and extract information about image transformations including affine changes in very small amounts of time. From the results we conclude that non-deterministic algorithms can help accelerate the search through different scale spaces. Although the literature contains a good amount of information on affine-covariant local feature detectors, the pairing of these with the set of descriptors available, has to be researched in more depth to reach the robustness necessary for real-world tasks. The term *invariant* imposes a hard restriction on perfect measurement after image transformations; on the other hand, the term *covariant* allows for a more flexible definition of measurement.

While LOCKY uses only rectangles as the shape for the search of blobs, the use of different polygons (using rotated integral images) can be an advantage in terms of precision on the detection although it could cause an increment in the running time. The detection of ridges is shown as a potential application and can also be extended and used for feature detection. A texture is a repetitive pattern, therefore, two votes will progress in a similar manner if both are wholly contained in a single texture; the BCT can be extended for fast analysis of textures.

Robustness means persistance of features through image transformations. Although the non-deterministic nature of LOCKY causes a dificulty to achieve high repeatability scores, the results show that LOCKY is consistent. Also, its repeatability score tends to decay slower than the score of other approaches.

Shape is an important factor, Dickinson and Pizlo [20] talk about the perception of shape and explain how objects are composed of intermediate shape priors. The detection of shape has to be researched in more depth to achieve more domain-independent object recognition.

References

1. Tuytelaars, T., Mikolajczyk, K.: Local invariant feature detectors: a survey. In: Foundations and Trends in Computer Graphics and Vision, vol. 3, pp. 177–280. Now Publishers Inc. (2008)

2. Harris, C., Stephens, M.: A combined corner and edge detector. In: Alvey Vision Conference, vol. 15, p. 50 (1988)
3. Smith, S.M., Brady, J.M.: SUSAN-a new approach to low level image processing. IJCV **23**, 45–78 (1997)
4. Rosten, E., Drummond, T.W.: Machine learning for high-speed corner detection. In: Leonardis, A., Bischof, H., Pinz, A. (eds.) ECCV 2006, Part I. LNCS, vol. 3951, pp. 430–443. Springer, Heidelberg (2006)
5. Mair, E., Hager, G.D., Burschka, D., Suppa, M., Hirzinger, G.: Adaptive and generic corner detection based on the accelerated segment test. In: Daniilidis, K., Maragos, P., Paragios, N. (eds.) ECCV 2010, Part II. LNCS, vol. 6312, pp. 183–196. Springer, Heidelberg (2010)
6. Matas, J., Chum, O., Urban, M., Pajdla, T.: Robust wide-baseline stereo from maximally stable extremal regions. In: Image and Vision Computing, vol. 22, pp. 761–767. Elsevier (2004)
7. Agrawal, M., Konolige, K., Blas, M.R.: CenSurE: Center surround extremas for realtime feature detection and matching. In: Forsyth, D., Torr, P., Zisserman, A. (eds.) ECCV 2008, Part IV. LNCS, vol. 5305, pp. 102–115. Springer, Heidelberg (2008)
8. Gunn, S.R.: On the discrete representation of the laplacian of gaussian. In: Pattern Recognition, vol. 32, pp. 1463–1472. Elsevier (1999)
9. Mikolajczyk, K., Tuytelaars, T., Schmid, C., Zisserman, A., Matas, J., Schaffalitzky, F., Kadir, T., Van Gool, L.: A comparison of affine region detectors. IJCV **65**, 43–72 (2005)
10. Viola, P., Jones, M.: Robust real-time object detection. IJCV **4**, 34–47 (2001)
11. Bay, H., Tuytelaars, T., Van Gool, L.: SURF: speeded up robust features. In: Leonardis, A., Bischof, H., Pinz, A. (eds.) ECCV 2006, Part I. LNCS, vol. 3951, pp. 404–417. Springer, Heidelberg (2006)
12. Mikolajczyk, K., Schmid, C.: An affine invariant interest point detector. In: Heyden, A., Sparr, G., Nielsen, M., Johansen, P. (eds.) ECCV 2002, Part I. LNCS, vol. 2350, pp. 128–142. Springer, Heidelberg (2002)
13. Calonder, M., Lepetit, V., Strecha, C., Fua, P.: BRIEF: binary robust independent elementary features. In: Daniilidis, K., Maragos, P., Paragios, N. (eds.) ECCV 2010, Part IV. LNCS, vol. 6314, pp. 778–792. Springer, Heidelberg (2010)
14. Rublee, E., Rabaud, V., Konolige, K., Bradski, G.: ORB: an efficient alternative to SIFT or SURF. In: ICCV, pp. 2564–2571. IEEE (2011)
15. Leutenegger, S., Chli, M., Siegwart, R.Y.: BRISK: Binary robust invariant scalable keypoints. In: ICCV, pp. 2548–2555. IEEE (2011)
16. Alahi, A., Ortiz, R., Vandergheynst, P.: Freak: fast retina keypoint. In: CVPR, pp. 510–517. IEEE (2012)
17. Marr, D., Hildreth, E.: Theory of edge detection. In: Proceedings of the Royal Society of London. Series B. Biological Sciences, vol. 207, pp. 187–217. The Royal Soc. (1980)
18. Heinly, J., Dunn, E., Frahm, J.-M.: Comparative evaluation of binary features. In: Fitzgibbon, A., Lazebnik, S., Perona, P., Sato, Y., Schmid, C. (eds.) ECCV 2012, Part II. LNCS, vol. 7573, pp. 759–773. Springer, Heidelberg (2012)
19. Jonides, J., Irwin, D.E., Yantis, S.: Integrating visual information from successive fixations. Science **215**, 192–194 (1982)
20. Dickinson, S.J., Pizlo, Z.: Shape perception in human and computer vision. Springer (2013)

Feature Evaluation with High-Resolution Images

Kai Cordes[✉], Lukas Grundmann, and Jörn Ostermann

Leibniz Universität Hannover, Hanover, Germany
{cordes,grundmann,ostermann}@tnt.uni-hannover.de

Abstract. The extraction of scale invariant image features is a fundamental task for many computer vision applications. Features are localized in the scale space of the image. A descriptor is build for each feature which is used to determine the correspondence to a second feature, usually extracted from a second image. For the evaluation of detectors and descriptors, benchmark image sets are used. The benchmarks consist of image sequences and homographies which determine the ground truth for the mapping between the images. The repeatability criterion evaluates the detection accuracy of the detectors while precision and recall measure the quality of the descriptors.

Current data sets provide images with resolutions of less than one megapixel. A recent data set provides challenging images and highly accurate homographies. It allows for the evaluation at different image resolutions with the same scene content. Thus, the scale invariant properties of the extracted features can be examined. This paper presents a comprehensive evaluation of state of the art detectors and descriptors on this data set. The results show significant differences compared to the standard benchmark. Furthermore, it is shown that some detectors perform differently on different resolutions. It follows that high resolution images should be considered for future feature evaluations.

1 Introduction

Scale invariant features play an important role in many computer vision applications, such as object recognition or scene reconstruction. These applications require discriminative and accurate features on images with large changes in illumination and perspective [9,18].

New approaches in feature detection [2,3,11,14,16,17] and description [1–3,7,11,15,16] usually use the reference test set and the evaluation protocols provided in [14,15]. It contains sequences of still images (800 × 640 pixel resolution) with changes in illumination, rotation, perspective, and scale. Only two out of eight sequences provide perspectively distorted images. The mapping from one image to the next is restricted to a homography. For the benchmark test, the ground truth homography matrices are provided. The most important criterion for the accuracy of the detectors is the repeatability criterion. The descriptors are evaluated with precision and recall curves.

Nowadays, high resolution images become more and more important. Resolutions of 4K (4000×3000 pixels) are required for the digital cinema. Even current

© Springer International Publishing Switzerland 2015
G. Azzopardi and N. Petkov (Eds.): CAIP 2015, Part I, LNCS 9256, pp. 374–386, 2015.
DOI: 10.1007/978-3-319-23192-1_31

smartphones provide large resolutions, such as the iPhone 6 with eight megapixels. However, feature evaluations are performed on images with resolutions of less than one megapixel. An evaluation of state-of-the-art feature detectors and descriptors on high resolution images is still missing. Recently, a high resolution benchmark data set was published[1]. It provides image resolution of up to 8 megapixels [6] (a first step towards 4K) and focuses on the scenario of perspectively distorted images, which is demanded by scene reconstruction applications like in [9,18]. Our contribution is the evaluation of state-of-the-art feature detectors and descriptors on the benchmark [6] compared to [14]. We examine which of the detectors and descriptors are able to transfer their performance to large resolutions.

In the following Section 2, the feature detectors and descriptors are introduced. In Section 3, the experimental setup is presented. Section 4 shows the results and Section 5 gives the conclusions.

2 Overview

Several publications give informative overviews on scale invariant feature detectors and descriptors, e.g. [8,12]. Since we concentrate on the evaluation, we just give a short overview of the competitors. The evaluated detectors are Wave [17], A-KAZE [2], ORB [16], BRISK [11], SURF [3], and SIFT [13] (cf. Table 1). The evaluation criterion is the repeatability using the matlab script provided by the authors of [14]. The resulting best detector is used in the descriptor evaluation. The evaluated descriptors are A-KAZE [2], LIOP [19], MROGH [7], GLOH [15], and SIFT [13] (cf. Table 2). In our evaluation, we exclude the descriptors ORB, BRISK, and FREAK. These approaches concentrate on fast computation, and their performance in accuracy is to our experience equal to or lower than SIFT (cf. [4,8]).

Our evaluation aims at finding the most accurate detector together with the best possible descriptor. The implementations are taken as they are provided by the authors (cf. Table 1 and 2) using default parameters. For comparison, we added the computation times found in our experiments in milliseconds per feature, computed on i7 CPU, 3.50 GHz.

3 Experimental Setup

Most evaluations employ the benchmark provided in [14]. We mainly use the recently published benchmark data set [6] for two reasons: (1) it provides higher accuracy [5] and image resolution (even different resolutions for the same scenes), (2) it concentrates on the *perspective change* scenario which is in the focus of this evaluation. For comparison, we include the most popular perspective change sequence *Graffiti* of [14]. The first images of the sequences are shown in Figure 1.

We use the repeatability criterion for the detectors evaluation while precision and recall determines the quality of the descriptors. The overlap error parameter is set to 0.4 [14].

---

[1] http://www.tnt.uni-hannover.de/project/feature_evaluation/

Table 1. The detectors which are compared in the results section.

detector	implementation	year published	computation time [ms]
SIFT [13]	Hess code [10]	2004	4.38
SURF [3]	Author's binary	2006	0.54
BRISK [11]	OpenCV 2.4	2011	0.99
ORB [16]	OpenCV 2.4	2011	0.47
A-KAZE [2]	Author's code	2013	1.04
Wave [17]	Author's binary	2013	5.58

Table 2. The descriptors with their default descriptor lengths d_l which are used for the comparisons in the results section.

descriptors	implementation	d_l	year published	computation time [ms]
SIFT [13]	Oxford binary	128	2004	1.74
GLOH [15]	Oxford binary	128	2005	1.87
MROGH [7]	Author's code	192	2011	2.35
LIOP [19]	Author's binary	144	2011	1.43
A-KAZE [2]	Author's code	61	2013	7.97

3.1 Feature Detection

The detectors provide a surprisingly large variation in extracted numbers of features. The numbers of features heavily dependent on texture, perspective, and resolution of the considered image. The detectors provided by OpenCV (ORB, BRISK) tend to extract many more features (sometimes more than 40000) than the others. Thus, we have to limit the number of detected points. For this purpose, the attribute *response* is used for each feature in OpenCV. For the evaluation, we sort the features by their response and choose the first n_f features. The number n_f is determined by the maximum of detected features by the others (A-KAZE, Wave, SURF, SIFT). In most cases, A-KAZE provides the largest number of features. The results for the repeatability are shown in Section 4.1.

3.2 Feature Descriptors

Since the A-KAZE detector provides the highest accuracy (cf. Section 4.1) and appropriate numbers of features for all of the sequences it is used for the detection task. Then, the descriptors are calculated by all methods as shown in Table 2. We use only original implementations from the authors (source code or binaries). For each detector, default parameters are used. Note, that for the descriptors different lengths d_l are provided by default (cf. Table 2). The results for precision and recall of the descriptors are shown in Chapter 4.2.

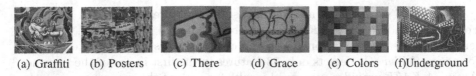

(a) Graffiti   (b) Posters   (c) There   (d) Grace   (e) Colors   (f)Underground

Fig. 1. First images of the input image sequences. The resolution is 800×640 for (a) *Graffiti* and up to 3456×2304 for the sequences (b) - (f).

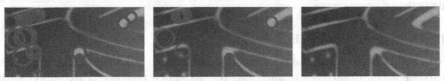

(a) *Underground* 1365×1024 (b) *Underground* 2048×1365 (c) *Underground* 3456×2304

Fig. 2. Feature detection of the *Wave* detector on different resolutions.

4   Experimental Results

The results for the detector evaluation is demonstrated in Section 4.1 while the results for descriptors is shown in Section 4.2. The approaches are subsumed in Table 1 and Table 2, respectively.

4.1   Detector Evaluation

The results for the repeatability are demonstrated in two sets:

1. A comparison between low-resolution and high-resolution for the same scenes in Figure 3 and Figure 4. (*Grace, Underground*, and *Colors*). Here, different performances are shown for some competitors.
2. The results for low-resolution input images (*Graffiti, Posters*, and *There*) in Figure 5. For these sequences, the results for higher resolution show no significant differences (*Graffiti* and *There*).

The first set shows that the performance decreases in general when using larger image resolutions. There are some examples, where the performance drops drastically. One example is the result of the *Wave* detector for the *Underground* sequence (cf. Figure 3). Here, the numbers of valid feature pairs for 8 megapixels are even smaller than the numbers for 1.5 megapixels. In Figure 2, the detection result of *Wave* is demonstrated on a part of the first image of *Underground*. On the full image, 7735 points are detected on resolution 1365×1024, 6821 on 2048×1365, and only 3282 on 3456×2304. On the contrary, *Wave* shows good performance on the *Colors* sequence. The *Colors* sequence provides a second example for a differing performance of a detector. The repeatability of *ORB* is significantly lower for 8 megapixels than for 1.5 megapixels. The *BRISK* detector gives poor results for the large resolution compared to the low resolution versions. The best results are provided by the *A-KAZE* detector.

The second set demonstrates results using smaller resolutions (cf. Figure 5). For *Graffiti* and *Posters*, *ORB* performs best, followed by *A-KAZE*. The challenging *There* sequence (strong viewpoint change) shows very low detection performance of *Wave*. It detects only 23 features in the first image of the sequence. Again, *A-KAZE* provides very good results for each of the sequences.

The overall results are subsumed in Table 3. The best results are achieved with the *A-KAZE* detector. *ORB* provides surprisingly good results for most sequences.

4.2   Descriptor Evaluation

Since *A-KAZE* provides the best results for feature detection, this approach is used. For the descriptor evaluation, the sequence test set is extended with the sequences *Wall*, *Boat*, and *Bikes* [14]. The results are shown in Figure 6 (*Graffiti* and *Wall*) and in Figure 7 (*Boat* and *Bikes*) for the lower resolution images (0.5 megapixels). The comparisons with different resolution (1.5 megapixels and 8 megapixels) of the same scene are demonstrated Figure 8 (*Grace*), in Figure 9 (*Underground*), in Figure 10 (*Colors*), and in Figure 11 (*There*). For the *Posters* sequence, too many features are extracted for the large resolution version (> 45000) to evaluate with the matlab script. We show the results of the 1.5 megapixels sequence in Figure 12. The overall results are subsumed in Table 4.

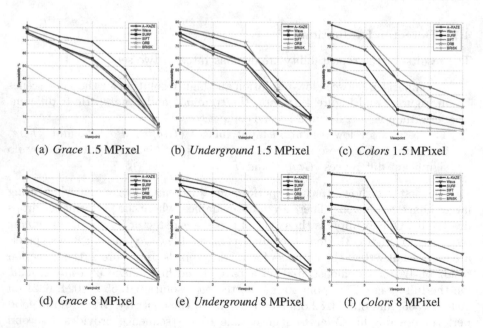

(a) *Grace* 1.5 MPixel   (b) *Underground* 1.5 MPixel   (c) *Colors* 1.5 MPixel

(d) *Grace* 8 MPixel   (e) *Underground* 8 MPixel   (f) *Colors* 8 MPixel

Fig. 3. Repeatability results for 1.5 megapixels (top row, 1365×1024) and 8 megapixels (bottom row, 3456 × 2304) for the sequences *Grace*, *Underground*, and *Colors*.

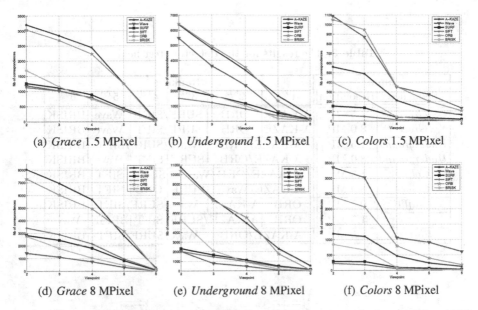

Fig. 4. Absolute numbers or valid feature pairs for 1.5 megapixels (top, 1365 × 1024) and 8 megapixels (bottom, 3456 × 2304) for *Grace*, *Underground*, and *Colors*.

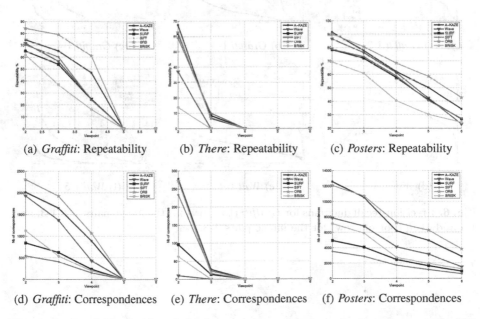

Fig. 5. Repeatability (top) and absolute numbers of features for the sequences *Graffiti* (0.5 megapixels), *There*, and *Posters* (1.5 megapixels).

Table 3. The results for the detectors test field.

| Input | | Ranking | | | | | |
Sequence	Resolution	1ST	2ND	3RD	4TH	5TH	6TH
Grace	1.5 MP	A-KAZE	ORB	SURF/SIFT		Wave	BRISK
Grace	8.0 MP	A-KAZE	ORB	SURF/SIFT		Wave	BRISK
Underground	1.5 MP	A-KAZE/ORB		Wave/SURF/SIFT			BRISK
Underground	8.0 MP	A-KAZE/ORB		SURF	SIFT	Wave	BRISK
Colors	1.5 MP	A-KAZE/ORB/Wave			SURF	SIFT	BRISK
Colors	8.0 MP	A-KAZE/Wave		SURF	ORB	SIFT	BRISK
Graffiti	0.5 MP	ORB	A-KAZE	Wave/SURF/SIFT			BRISK
There	1.5 MP	ORB	A-KAZE/SURF		SIFT	BRISK	Wave
Posters	1.5 MP	A-KAZE/ORB		Wave/SURF/SIFT			BRISK

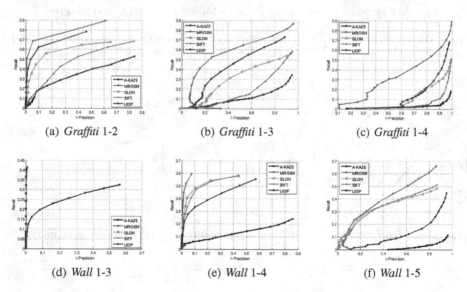

(a) *Graffiti* 1-2   (b) *Graffiti* 1-3   (c) *Graffiti* 1-4

(d) *Wall* 1-3   (e) *Wall* 1-4   (f) *Wall* 1-5

Fig. 6. Precision-recall diagrams for *Graffiti* (top row) for the image pairs 1-2, 1-3, and 1-4 and *Wall* (bottom row) for the image pairs 1-3, 1-4, 1-5.

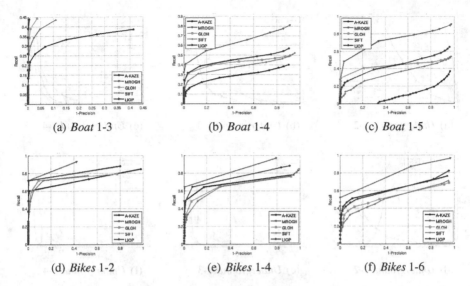

Fig. 7. Precision-recall diagrams for *Boat* (top row, image pairs 1-3, 1-4, 1-5) and *Bikes* (bottom row, image pairs 1-2, 1-4, and 1-6). The *Boat* sequence shows scale and rotation change. The *Bikes* shows differences in image blur.

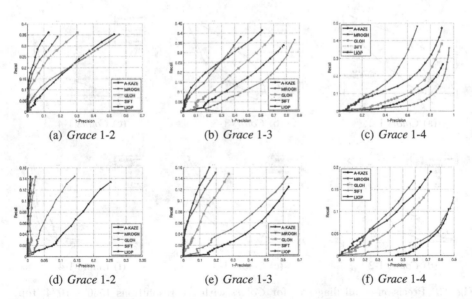

Fig. 8. Precision-recall diagrams for *Grace* with the resolutions 1536 × 1024 (top) and 3456 × 2304 (bottom).

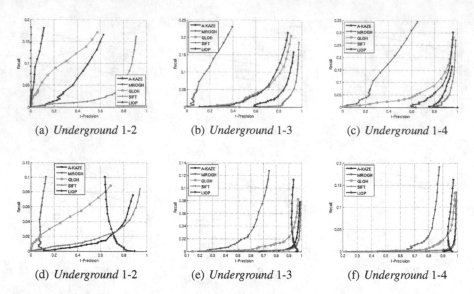

Fig. 9. Precision-recall diagrams for *Grace* with the resolutions 1536 × 1024 (top) and 3456 × 2304 (bottom).

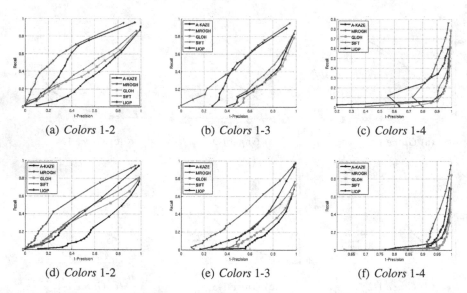

Fig. 10. Precision-recall diagrams for *Colors* with the resolutions 1536 × 1024 (top) and 3456 × 2304 (bottom).

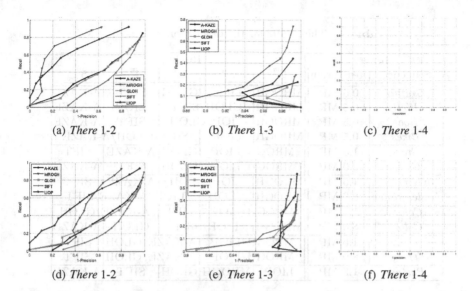

(a) *There* 1-2   (b) *There* 1-3   (c) *There* 1-4

(d) *There* 1-2   (e) *There* 1-3   (f) *There* 1-4

Fig. 11. Precision-recall diagrams for *There* with the resolutions 1536×1024 (top) and 3456×2304 (bottom). For this challenging sequence, none of the descriptors provide a result for the pair 1-4.

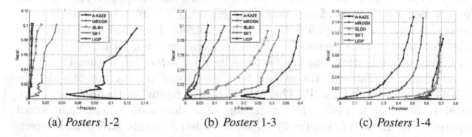

(a) *Posters* 1-2   (b) *Posters* 1-3   (c) *Posters* 1-4

Fig. 12. Precision-recall diagrams for *Posters* with the resolutions 1536×1024.

Table 4. The results for the descriptors test field.

Input		Ranking				
Sequence	Resolution	1ST	2ND	3RD	4TH	5TH
Graffiti	0.5 MP	MROGH	LIOP	GLOH	SIFT	A-KAZE
Wall	0.5 MP	MROGH	GLOH/SIFT		LIOP	A-KAZE
Boat	0.5 MP	MROGH	LIOP/GLOH		SIFT	A-KAZE
Bikes	0.5 MP	MROGH	LIOP	SIFT/GLOH/A-KAZE		
Grace	1.5 MP	MROGH/LIOP		GLOH	A-KAZE	SIFT
Grace	8.0 MP	MROGH/LIOP		GLOH	SIFT	A-KAZE
Underground	1.5 MP	MROGH	LIOP/GLOH		A-KAZE	SIFT
Underground	8.0 MP	MROGH	GLOH	LIOP/A-KAZE/SIFT		
Colors	1.5 MP	MROGH/LIOP		SIFT	A-KAZE/GLOH	
Colors	8.0 MP	MROGH	LIOP/SIFT		GLOH	A-KAZE
There	1.5 MP	MROGH/LIOP		A-KAZE/GLOH		SIFT
There	8.0 MP	MROGH/LIOP		A-KAZE/GLOH		SIFT
Posters	1.5 MP	LIOP	MROGH	GLOH	SIFT	A-KAZE

Like in the detectors evaluation, there are several examples with varying performances of descriptors on different resolutions but the same scene. For the *Grace* sequence, the *A-KAZE* descriptor provides better results than SIFT for 1.5 megapixels while being worse than SIFT for 8 megapixels (cf. Figure 8). A second example is the LIOP descriptor on the *Underground* sequence(cf. Figure 9). For 1.5 megapixels, it performs very good (ranking 2ND in the test field) while the performance drops significantly for 8 megapixels. The LIOP descriptor provides the most varying result for different sequences. For *Wall*, it ranks 4TH (cf. Figure 6) while providing the best results for *Posters* (cf. Figure 12).

As shown in Table 4, the overall best descriptor results are provided by MROGH, followed by LIOP. The MROGH descriptor is theoretically rotational invariant [7]. Thus, the estimation of a dominant orientation is not required. The *Boat* (cf. Figure 7) sequence illustrates this strength. Interestingly, MROGH provides the best results for nearly every sequence tested in this evaluation. Although the A-KAZE detector provides the most accurate features (cf. Section 4.1), its descriptor is only ranked 6TH in this test field. As expected, GLOH is slightly better than SIFT, ranking 3RD and 4TH.

5   Conclusions

A recent benchmark data set [6] allows for the evaluation of scale invariant feature detectors and descriptors on high resolution images. The benchmark enables the comparison of the approaches on different resolutions of the same scene. The evaluation presented in this paper concentrates on the accuracy of detectors and descriptors at different image resolutions. It is shown that different resolutions can lead to significantly different results for detectors (Wave, ORB) and descriptors (LIOP, A-KAZE). The most accurate detector is the A-KAZE detector. The A-KAZE regions are used for the evaluation of state of the art descriptors. Here, the MROGH descriptor leads to the best results.

The evaluation shows that the benchmark [6] offers new and interesting results regarding accuracy and high image resolutions. Furthermore, it offers the unique possibility to examine the behavior of the detectors and descriptors on different resolutions of the same scene.

References

1. Alahi, A., Ortiz, R., Vandergheynst, P.: Freak: Fast retina keypoint. In: IEEE Conference on Computer Vision and Pattern Recognition (CVPR), pp. 510–517 (2012)
2. Alcantarilla, P., Nuevo, J., Bartoli, A.: Fast explicit diffusion for accelerated features in nonlinear scale spaces. In: British Machine Vision Conference (BMVC) (2013)
3. Bay, H., Tuytelaars, T., Van Gool, L.: SURF: speeded up robust features. In: Leonardis, A., Bischof, H., Pinz, A. (eds.) ECCV 2006, Part I. LNCS, vol. 3951, pp. 404–417. Springer, Heidelberg (2006)
4. BloodAxe: OpenCV Features Comparison (2014). https://github.com/BloodAxe/OpenCV-Features-Comparison (Online; accessed February 20, 2015)
5. Cordes, K., Rosenhahn, B., Ostermann, J.: Increasing the accuracy of feature evaluation benchmarks using differential evolution. In: IEEE Symposium Series on Computational Intelligence (SSCI) - IEEE Symposium on Differential Evolution (SDE) (2011)
6. Cordes, K., Rosenhahn, B., Ostermann, J.: High-Resolution feature evaluation benchmark. In: Wilson, R., Hancock, E., Bors, A., Smith, W. (eds.) CAIP 2013, Part I. LNCS, vol. 8047, pp. 327–334. Springer, Heidelberg (2013)
7. Fan, B., Wu, F., Hu, Z.: Aggregating gradient distributions into intensity orders: A novel local image descriptor. In: IEEE Conference on Computer Vision and Pattern Recognition (CVPR), pp. 2377–2384 (2011)
8. Figat, J., Kornuta, T., Kasprzak, W.: Performance evaluation of binary descriptors of local features. In: Chmielewski, L.J., Kozera, R., Shin, B.-S., Wojciechowski, K. (eds.) ICCVG 2014. LNCS, vol. 8671, pp. 187–194. Springer, Heidelberg (2014)
9. Frahm, J.-M., Fite-Georgel, P., Gallup, D., Johnson, T., Raguram, R., Wu, C., Jen, Y.-H., Dunn, E., Clipp, B., Lazebnik, S., Pollefeys, M.: Building Rome on a cloudless day. In: Daniilidis, K., Maragos, P., Paragios, N. (eds.) ECCV 2010, Part IV. LNCS, vol. 6314, pp. 368–381. Springer, Heidelberg (2010)
10. Hess, R.: An open-source siftlibrary. In: Proceedings of the International Conference on Multimedia, MM 2010, pp. 1493–1496. ACM, New York (2010)
11. Leutenegger, S., Chli, M., Siegwart, R.: BRISK: Binary robust invariant scalable keypoints. In: IEEE International Conference on Computer Vision (ICCV), pp. 2548–2555 (2011)
12. Li, Y., Wang, S., Tian, Q., Ding, X.: A survey of recent advances in visual feature detection. Neurocomputing 149(pt. B), 736–751 (2015)
13. Lowe, D.G.: Distinctive image features from scale-invariant keypoints. International Journal of Computer Vision (IJCV) 60(2), 91–110 (2004)

14. Mikolajczyk, K., Tuytelaars, T., Schmid, C., Zisserman, A., Matas, J., Schaffalitzky, F., Kadir, T., Gool, L.V.: A comparison of affine region detectors. International Journal of Computer Vision (IJCV) **65**(1–2), 43–72 (2005)
15. Mikolajczyk, K., Schmid, C.: A performance evaluation of local descriptors. IEEE Transactions on Pattern Analysis and Machine Intelligence (PAMI) **27**(10), 1615–1630 (2005)
16. Rublee, E., Rabaud, V., Konolige, K., Bradski, G.: Orb: An efficient alternative to sift or surf. In: IEEE International Conference on Computer Vision (ICCV), pp. 2564–2571 (2011)
17. Salti, S., Lanza, A., Di Stefano, L.: Keypoints from symmetries by wave propagation. In: IEEE Conference on Computer Vision and Pattern Recognition (CVPR), pp. 2898–2905 (2013)
18. Snavely, N., Seitz, S.M., Szeliski, R.: Modeling the world from internet photo collections. International Journal of Computer Vision (IJCV) **80**, 189–210 (2008)
19. Wang, Z., Fan, B., Wu, F.: Local intensity order pattern for feature description. In: IEEE International Conference on Computer Vision (ICCV), pp. 603–610 (2011)

Fast Re-ranking of Visual Search Results by Example Selection

John Schavemaker[1]([✉]), Martijn Spitters[1], Gijs Koot[1], and Maaike de Boer[1,2]

[1] TNO Technical Sciences, The Hague, The Netherlands
[2] Radboud University, Nijmegen, The Netherlands
john.schavemaker@tno.nl

Abstract. In this paper we present a simple, novel method to use state-of-the-art image concept detectors and publicly available image search engines to retrieve images for semantically more complex queries from local databases without re-indexing of the database. Our low-key, data-driven method for associative recognition of unknown, or more elaborate, concepts in images allows user selection of visual examples to tailor query results to the typical preferences of the user. The method is compared with a baseline approach using ConceptNet-based semantic expansion of the query phrase to known concepts, as set by the concepts of the image concept detectors. Using the output of the image concept detector as index for all images in the local image database, a quick nearest-neighbor matching scheme is presented that can match queries swiftly via concept output vectors. We show preliminary results for a number of query phrases followed by a general discussion.

Keywords: Image retrieval · Concept detectors · Query expansion

1 Introduction

Internet statistics show that visual information becomes more and more important online. All major social media applications, such as FaceBook and Twitter, allow sharing of photos and videos or are centered around photos, e.g., Instagram, Flickr, and Pinterest. Smart access to this ever expanding set of visual information has therefore become essential. One of the ways to provide smart access is through annotation of the material by adding tags. These tags can be used for search. Manually annotated tags, such as in Flickr, are not accurate because because they are often subjective. One way to automatically create tags is by concept detection based on deep-learning approaches such as in Google Image Captioning [16].

An issue with annotation is that people will expect different annotations of images depending on their interpretation of the world. For example, for the query 'dangerous animals' one may think that certain animals are dangerous while others think they are not. Traditional query-expansion techniques based on semantics may not be the solution for this issue since semantic databases are typically not contextual since they provide a general interpretation of the world.

© Springer International Publishing Switzerland 2015
G. Azzopardi and N. Petkov (Eds.): CAIP 2015, Part I, LNCS 9256, pp. 387–398, 2015.
DOI: 10.1007/978-3-319-23192-1_32

The main contribution of this work is that we demonstrate a new, easy way to quickly retrieve results on a local image database by selecting visual examples as returned by popular web-based image search engines such as Bing. It provides an intuitive, visual interaction mode for the user to tailor and re-rank results to her/his preferences. Furthermore, it offers a simple way to get retrieval results for more complex queries even with concepts or adjectives for which the images are not annotated and indexed. This can be done without re-indexing of the database and without the use of semantic expansion of the query. We will illustrate that the use of image search as a means of 'visual query expansion' is an interesting alternative to semantic expansion solutions based on ConceptNet [14] allowing a fully functional image retrieval system for local databases that can deliver personalized answers to complex query phrases.

Our method is part of a larger application system, which is proposed in [11]. The application system is called GOOgle^{TM} for Sensors (GOOSE) system and it is a general-purpose search engine conceived to enable any type of user to retrieve images and videos in real-time from multiple and heterogeneous sources and sensors. The proposed system especially focuses on cameras as sensors and aims at bridging the semantic gap between natural language queries that can be posed by a user and concepts that can be recognized by the concept detectors. The search engine allows users to pose natural language queries to retrieve corresponding images. User queries are interpreted using the Stanford Parser, semantic rules and the Linked Open Data source ConceptNet and further explained in [1]. The process of on-the-fly training of concept detectors is explained in [2]. This paper focuses only on the ranking and retrieval algorithm.

The outline of this paper is as follows. In the next section related work on the topic is discussed, Section 3 introduces our method for image retrieval based on examples. In Section 4 we show results of experiments we conducted, followed by conclusions and a discussion in Section 5.

2   Related Work

Semantic search in visual data often depends on pre-trained classifiers and object detectors for ranking the target data given the query. These pre-trained classifiers and object detectors are trained with annotations from various internet resources, such as image sharing platforms, e.g., Flickr [12], large-scale manually constructed image ontologies, e.g., ImageNet [5,10] or public image search engines [6,8].

With the explosive growth of digitally available visual data and countless possible labels of interest, the expensive process of annotating and training tailored detectors for unknown concepts does not seem sustainable. Several ways have been explored to automatically annotate images based on co-occurrence of visual and textual information on the internet [13,15,17,18]. An example of a general-purpose large-scale system which learns new objects and relations from images is called NEIL [4]. This *Never Ending Image Learner* (NEIL) aims at developing the world's largest visual stuctured knowledge base with minimal human effort. NEIL queries Google Image Search to gather training examples for the objects, scenes and attributes in its ontology. The learned detectors and classifiers are subsequently applied to millions of images found on the web to learn relationships based on co-occurrence statistics.

Another relevant system is described in [3] and uses images sourced from Google to learn models for new objects on-the-fly. However, whereas their method actually computes descriptors for the retrieved images using well-known image encoding techniques like SIFT, and trains a linear SVM against a fixed set of negatives, we apply a much more basic method for *associative recognition* of unknown (or more elaborate) concepts in images. Therefore, our method can be considered as a low-key, scalable, data-driven way of retrieving images: we let our system look at examples of unknown concepts based on association with the concepts it knows.

Our approach is comparable to retraining strategies using one of the layers in a pretrained neural network, such as in [2]. Compared to using the abstract features in these layers, it has the advantage that the expansion is easily interpretable by the user, allowing the user to understand the search results and adjust the expansion, which can be very useful in real-life applications.

3 Method Description

In this section we describe in more detail how our proposed image retrieval system works. This section is divided into two parts. In Section 3.1 we describe image indexing, and Section 3.2 goes into detail about our retrieval approach. Figure 1 shows a system overview.

3.1 Image Representation and Indexing

In order to retrieve images from a database, images need to be annotated and indexed. For that purpose we use the Python implementation of the Berkeley Caffe deep-learning framework [7] trained on the ILSVRC 2012 training set with 1000 image classes. For every image in the image database a 1×1000 concept support vector with detection scores for the different concepts is calculated and used as index key for future database retrieval. The support vector represents the support ($[0,1]$) for every hypothesis that one of the $1,000$ concepts is presented in the image. Result of database indexing is an index that couples images to their corresponding support vectors.

3.2 Image Database Retrieval

Our approach for retrieving results for queries on the image database consists of the following steps:

1. Send natural language query as-is to a web-based image search engine such as Microsoft Bing, Google, or Yahoo by means of the API. In the experiments we use Bing because its API is easier to use in automatic scripts.

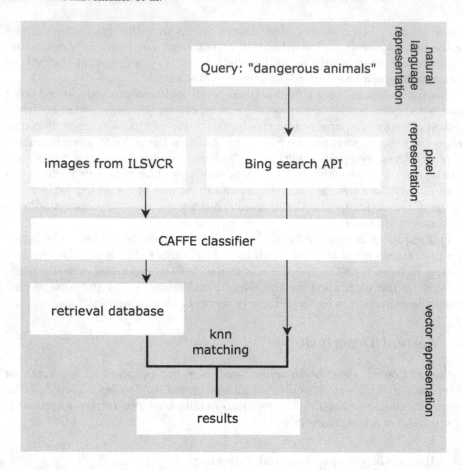

Fig. 1. System overview with in color marked the different representation layers: natural language, pixel, and concept vectors. The left path of the overview constitutes the image representation and indexing of Section 3.1, the right path is the retrieval path from Section 3.2 (steps 1 to 7).

2. Retrieve image search results by downloading the top N results, in our experiments we use $N = 20$;
3. Let user interactively select the appropriate images from the downloaded search results (this step is optional);
4. Compute the concept support vector for every image in the user image selection;
5. Match the query set of concept support vectors with the local image database index using Euclidean nearest-neighbor (k-NN, with $k = 2$);
6. Rank matching results based on Euclidean matching distance;
7. Remove duplicate matching results stemming from different visual examples.

The user selection of visual examples may range from one to many images. More examples provide better coverage of variety in the query interpretation.

The K nearest-neighbor matching with the database index can be done brute force or with tree-based approximate nearest neighbor algorithms. The parameter K is set to $K = 2$ to make sure that not one example dominates the results by limiting results of one example to at most 2 matches. For example, for the query 'angry cats' in Figure 3, higher values of K would probably lead to more similar results of Siamese cats as example #1, with a high support for the concept of Siamese Cat (0.97), may have many results close in distance.

Furthermore, steps $3 - 7$ can be repeated with alterations to user selection to quickly re-rank or renew search results. Note that only the nearest neighbor search in step 4 requires computing time that scales with the number of images in the database. This is an instance of the nearest neighbor problem, for which many optimizations are available, notably GPU implementations and approximation techniques [9]. With these algorithms, a neighbor search is still feasible within a second for tens of example images.

4 Experiments

In our experiments, we compare our 'visual query expansion' method with a 'textual query expansion' method. Our image retrieval system uses the web-based image search engine Bing to find the top 20 images relevant to the query and matches the support vectors for each of these images to the images in the database with the Euclidean nearest-neighbor distance metric. The results are displayed to the user and re-ranking is possible. An example of the Bing image search results on 'dangerous animals' is shown in Figure 2 and an example of the result of our visual query expansion method is in Figure 3. The 'textual query expansion' method uses ConceptNet to expand the query, as explained further in the next subsection.

Fig. 2. Microsoft Bing image search results for query 'dangerous animals'.

In the experiments we use the following query phrases: 'angry cats', 'beautiful dogs', 'cool old cars', 'dangerous animals','healthy food', and 'ugly modern buildings'. These phrases are intentionally chosen because they emphasize subjectivity, while at the same time being a close enough generalization or specialization of one of the categories recognized by our instance of the Caffe classifier. For example, these categories include 'snow leopard' and 'great white shark', arguably related to the 'dangerous animals' query, but also some potentially 'healthy foods', such as 'broccoli' and 'bananas'.

Fig. 3. Angry cats query: the first row shows the top 10 examples of the Bing search results. Every example shows the top 3 firing concepts of the concept detector. The second row shows the sorted database search results with their matching distance to one of the 10 examples. In addition the top 3 of concepts of the index is listed.

Evaluation is done on the evaluation set (named 'val') of ILSVRC 2012. This set is used as an example local image database. This set consists of 50,000 images with different types of objects.

4.1   Textual Query Expansion

ConceptNet 5.3 [14] is used to find relevant concept detectors for the query. ConceptNet is automatically accessed through the REST API. First, the spaces between the words are replaced with a comma. Second, the association value between a concept detector label and the query is captured using

```
"http://conceptnet5.media.mit.edu/data/5.3/assoc/c/en/"
    + query + "?filter=/c/en/"
    + detectorLabel + "\&limit=1"
```

The association value between the query and the concept detector label is used as an indication of the relevance of the concept detector for the query. If the concept detector label could not be found in ConceptNet, the more general word, which is the last word in the label (*shark* in *white_shark*), is used to assign an association value. The association value between the query and the concept detector label is used as an indication of the relevance of the concept detector for the query. The captured concepts are converted to concept support vectors by creating a 1×1000 vector where the value of the corresponding concept is set to 1.0. In the Appendix, Table 1 lists for each query the concepts in the first expansion.

4.2 Results

In the Appendix, Figures 4 and 5 present database retrieval results for all example queries using our proposed method and results using textual query expansion.

For the 'angry cats' query, the visual query expansion shows results with only cats that mainly include Siamese, Tabby, and Tiger cats, just as the user-selected examples do. The textual query expansion results show mostly cats as well with the exception of some 'Madagascar cats' and cougars that both do not match the domestic cats from the user-selected examples. In general, the cats do not look that angry with the exception of the last cougar in the textual query expansion results.

A similar picture is shown for the query 'beautiful dogs'. Again, visual query expansion results are a good match and cover the user-selected examples of Samoyed, Pomeranian, Golden retriever and Maltese dogs. The textual query expansion results start with African hunting dogs, not resembling the domestic dogs in the user-selected examples, but include Maltese dogs as well.

The results for query 'cool old cars' show some more discrepancies between our proposed method and the textual query expansion. The concept 'car' is too ambiguous for expansion: the top results include 'freight car' and 'passenger car' or 'train' as well as car parts like car mirrors. The search results of our method show better results: mainly cool old cars with the exception of two modern race cars, due to example 'racer', and two modern convertibles, due to example 'convertible'.

The results of the textual query expansion of 'dangerous animals' show some errors including an amphibious vehicle, house finch and sea slug (see also Table 1). The results of our method capture better the concept of dangerous animals as selected in the examples including tiger and three of the the African big five, i.e., lion, buffalo and elephant.

The query 'healthy food' is also hard to expand correctly: the textual expansion includes food but pizza, bagel and meat loaf are in general not considered healthy. Our method results show for the first 6 ranked results good result that mimic the fruit and vegetables from the examples including the photo composition. The feather boa results are in error of course; these are examples that in an interactive session can be omitted by the user to re-rank better search results.

The last query 'ugly modern buildings' is the hardest one for both methods. The results in Figure 5 show Bing search examples that have low concept scores, except for library and mobile home, for most selected example and as a result some mediocre results for our method. Textual query expansions is mainly into household appliances and computer hardware and are completely off.

5 Conclusions and Discussion

In this paper, we presented a novel and easy way to quickly access image databases by means of indexing images by concept detectors and finding good visual examples by querying web-based image search for examples. In this way the user has easy control on 'query expansion'. We have shown preliminary results that look promising for our proposed method. The experiments, however, are limited to a few queries and do not include a full quantitative evaluation of the method. One must also note that our queries have good coverage in the 1000 concepts of ILSVRC that include among others many cat and dog breeds. Queries that fall outside these pretrained concepts will probably be handled less well. The choice for Microsoft Bing as our primary search engine for the visual examples is also a pragmatic one (the search API is easier to script), other search engines may behave differently and are not investigated in this paper.

In future work, a full user study with an appropriate evaluation is necessary. An interesting point for the future would also be to provide both visual query expansion and textual query expansion data to the user and find out in which type of queries the visual method is preferred over the textual method and the other way around. Furthermore, it would be interesting to investigate whether one of the hidden layers of the pretrained Caffe ILSVRC neural network can be used to index images instead of the 1×1000 concept support vector. The hidden layer may contain more information that is relevant for the subjective part of the query. Retraining strategies such as [2] also use hidden layers as input.

Acknowledgments. This research was performed in the GOOSE project, which is jointly funded by the MIST research program of the Dutch Ministry of Defense and the AMSN enabling technology program.

References

1. de Boer, M.H.T., Daniele, L., Brandt, P., Sappelli, M.: Applying semantic reasoning in image retrieval. In: ALLDATA 2015, The First International Conference on Big Data, Small Data, Linked Data and Open Data, pp. 69–74. IARIA (2015)
2. Bouma, H., Eendebak, P.T., Schutte, K., Azzopardi, G., Burghouts, G.J.: Incremental concept learning with few training examples and hierarchical classification. In: Proc. SPIE, vol. 9652 (2015)
3. Chatfield, K., Zisserman, A.: VISOR: towards on-the-fly large-scale object category retrieval. In: Lee, K.M., Matsushita, Y., Rehg, J.M., Hu, Z. (eds.) ACCV 2012, Part II. LNCS, vol. 7725, pp. 432–446. Springer, Heidelberg (2013)
4. Chen, X., Shrivastava, A., Gupta, A.: Neil: Extracting visual knowledge from web data. In: 2013 IEEE International Conference on Computer Vision (ICCV), pp. 1409–1416. IEEE (2013)
5. Deng, J., Dong, W., Socher, R., Li, L.J., Li, K., Fei-Fei, L.: ImageNet: a large-scale hierarchical image database. In: CVPR 2009 (2009)
6. Fergus, R., Fei-Fei, L., Perona, P., Zisserman, A.: Learning object categories from google's image search. In: Tenth IEEE International Conference on Computer Vision, ICCV 2005, vol. 2, pp. 1816–1823. IEEE (2005)

7. Jia, Y., Shelhamer, E., Donahue, J., Karayev, S., Long, J., Girshick, R., Guadarrama, S., Darrell, T.: Caffe: Convolutional architecture for fast feature embedding. arXiv preprint 1408.5093 (2014)
8. Li, L.J., Fei-Fei, L.: Optimol: automatic online picture collection via incremental model learning. International Journal of Computer Vision 88(2), 147–168 (2010)
9. Muja, M., Lowe, D.G.: Flann, fast library for approximate nearest neighbors (2009)
10. Russakovsky, O., Deng, J., Su, H., Krause, J., Satheesh, S., Ma, S., Huang, Z., Karpathy, A., Khosla, A., Bernstein, M., Berg, A.C., Fei-Fei, L.: ImageNet Large Scale Visual Recognition Challenge (2014)
11. Schutte, K., Bouma, H., Schavemaker, J., Daniele, L., Sappelli, M., Koot, G., Eendebak, P., Azzopardi, G., Spitters, M., de Boer, M., Brandt, P.: Interactive detection of incrementally learned concepts in images with ranking and semantic query interpretation. In: Proc. of 13th International Workshop on Content-Based Multimedia Indexing (CBMI) (2015)
12. Shi, Z., Yang, Y., Hospedales, T.M., Xiang, T.: Weakly supervised learning of objects, attributes and their associations. In: Fleet, D., Pajdla, T., Schiele, B., Tuytelaars, T. (eds.) ECCV 2014, Part II. LNCS, vol. 8690, pp. 472–487. Springer, Heidelberg (2014)
13. Snoek, C.G.M., Worring, M., Koelma, D.C., Arnold, W.M., Smeulders, M.: A learned lexicon-driven paradigm for interactive video retrieval. IEEE Transactions on Multimedia 9(2) (2007)
14. Speer, R., Havasi, C.: Representing general relational knowledge in ConceptNet 5. In: LREC, pp. 3679–3686 (2012)
15. Torralba, A., Fergus, R., Freeman, W.T.: 80 million tiny images: A large data set for nonparametric object and scene recognition. IEEE Transactions on Pattern Analysis and Machine Intelligence 30(11), 1958–1970 (2008)
16. Vinyals, O., Toshev, A., Bengio, S., Erhan, D.: Show and tell: A neural image caption generator. CoRR abs/1411.4555 (2014). http://arxiv.org/abs/1411.4555
17. Wang, X.J., Zhang, L., Jing, F., Ma, W.Y.: Annosearch: Image auto-annotation by search. In: 2006 IEEE Computer Society Conference on Computer Vision and Pattern Recognition, vol. 2, pp. 1483–1490. IEEE (2006)
18. Zhang, R., Zhang, Z., Li, M., Ma, W.Y., Zhang, H.J.: A probabilistic semantic model for image annotation and multimodal image retrieval. In: Tenth IEEE International Conference on Computer Vision, ICCV 2005, vol. 1, pp. 846–851. IEEE (2005)

Appendix: Query Results

In this appendix the results for the textual query expansion from Section 4.1 is presented in Table 1. The ranking results for the six different queries from Section 4 are presented in Figures 4 and 5. These results include results for our proposed method and results using textual query expansion.

Table 1. Textual query expansion, for every query the top 10 concepts are shown with associated weights.

angry cats	Egyptian cat (1.0), Persian cat (1.0), Madagascar cat (1.0), Siamese cat (1.0), tiger cat (1.0), tabby (0.97), lynx (0.94), claw (0.89), cougar (0.81), jaguar (0.74)
beautiful dogs	Eskimo dog (1.0), Maltese dog (1.0), Bernese mountain dog (1.0), Greater Swiss Mountain dog (1.0), African hunting dog (1.0), toy poodle (0.98), standard poodle (0.98), miniature poodle (0.98), Walker hound (0.98), Afghan hound (0.98)
cool old cars	passenger car (1.0), sports car (1.0), freight car (1.0), car mirror (0.93), limousine (0.93), minivan (0.93), beach wagon (0.91), moving van (0.88), police van (0.88), fire engine (0.88)
dangerous animals	amphibious vehicle (0.94), great grey owl (0.93), sea slug (0.92), house finch (0.91), hippopotamus (0.91), red-backed sandpiper (0.89), little blue heron (0.89), echidna (0.87), gorilla (0.87), sulphur-crested cockatoo (0.87)
healthy food	pizza (0.86), bagel (0.75) meat loaf (0.74), French loaf (0.74), eggnog (0.74), corn (0.68), refrigerator (0.65), bakery (0.65), cheeseburger (0.64), chocolate sauce (0.63)
ugly modern buildings	monitor (0.60), desktop computer (0.51), hand-held computer (0.51), photocopier (0.51), sewing machine (0.50), cash machine (0.50), vending machine (0.50), electric fan (0.50), laptop (0.49), joystick (0.47)

Fig. 4. From top to bottom: retrieval results on ILSVRC 2012 val set for queries 'angry cats', 'beautiful dogs', and 'cool old cars '. Top row shows the Bing search results (as selected by the user). Middle row shows the top 10 ranked results for the proposed method. Bottom row shows the top 10 ranked results using textual query expansion.

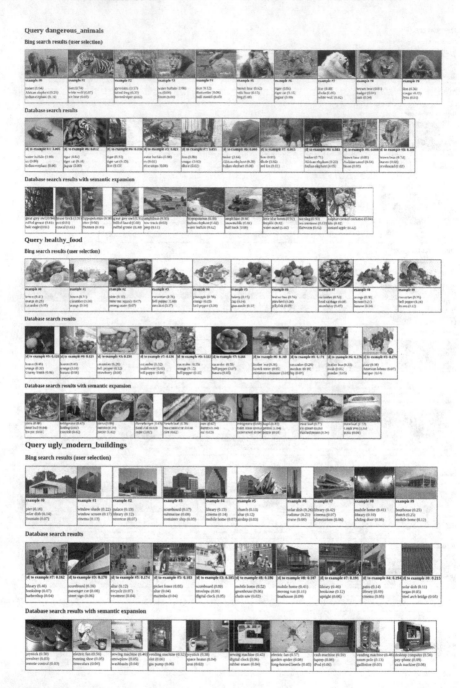

Fig. 5. Retrieval results on ILSVRC 2012 val set for query 'dangerous animals', 'healthy food', and 'ugly modern buildings'. Top row shows the Bing search results (as selected by the user). Middle row shows the top 10 ranked results for the proposed method. Bottom row shows the top 10 ranked results using textual query expansion.

Egomotion Estimation and Reconstruction with Kalman Filters and GPS Integration

Haokun Geng[1](✉), Hsiang-Jen Chien[2], Radu Nicolescu[1], and Reinhard Klette[2]

[1] Department of Computer Science, The University of Auckland,
Auckland, New Zealand
[2] School of Engineering, Auckland University of Technology, Auckland, New Zealand
hgen001@aucklanduni.ac.nz

Abstract. This paper presents an approach for egomotion estimation over stereo image sequences combined with extra GPS data. The accuracy of the estimated motion data is tested with 3D roadside reconstruction. Our proposed method follows the traditional flowchart of many visual odometry algorithms: it firstly establishes the correspondences between the keypoints of every two frames, then it uses the depth information from the stereo matching algorithms, and it finally computes the best description of the cameras' motion. However, instead of simply using keypoints from consecutive frames, we propose a novel technique that uses a set of augmented and selected keypoints, which are carefully tracked by a Kalman filter fusion. We also propose to use the GPS data for each key frame in the input sequence, in order to reduce the positioning errors of the estimations, so that the drift errors could be corrected at each key frame. Finally, the overall growth of the build-up errors can be bounded within a certain range. A least-squares process is used to minimise the reprojection error and to ensure a good pair of translation and rotation measures, frame by frame. Experiments are carried out for trajectory estimation, or combined trajectory and 3D scene reconstruction, using various stereo-image sequences.

Keywords: Egomotion estimation · Visual odometry · Kalman filter · GPS input · Roadside reconstruction

1 Introduction

Egomotion estimation (also known as visual odometry) is typically referred to determine the rotation and translation of the camera-set within a dynamic environment using image sequences taken by the cameras [21]. Motion data can be obtained by different sensors, including *light detection and ranging* (LiDAR) sensors, *inertial measurement units* (IMU), *global positioning system* (GPS) units, and optical cameras. Because of the nature of image data, the camera-based methodology generally provides reliability, robustness, and cost-effectiveness, which suits the needs and requirements of many computer-vision applications in both academic and industrial fields. Accurate egomotion estimation can be applied for navigation or route planning, for example, the vision-based navigation system used on the Mars Exploration rovers [11] is one successful demonstration of such applications.

© Springer International Publishing Switzerland 2015
G. Azzopardi and N. Petkov (Eds.): CAIP 2015, Part I, LNCS 9256, pp. 399–410, 2015.
DOI: 10.1007/978-3-319-23192-1_33

Scaramuzza et al. [17] indicated that visual odometry methods can provide accurate trajectory estimations with a small error range from 0.1% to 2% of the actual motion. Olson et al. [15] suggested that the error of egomotion estimation with only image data is achievable to less than 1% of the distance travelled. The estimated motion data is considered compulsory information to many other applications, such as speed and direction monitoring, 3D roadside reconstruction, and so forth. Because egomotion estimation has a long processing pipeline, the errors caused by noise in the input data would build-up at each phase.

In our research we started to realise that the integration of different types of sensors could lead to an optimal solution for many cases. In this paper we propose an approach that allows accurate egomotion estimation over stereo image sequences, also using GPS data. This proposed method focuses on calculating the cameras' movements between every two frames within a small time interval. We employ a set of linear Kalman filters to track a small set of selected features, in order to find the best feature candidates for motion analysis. Moreover, the proposed method can handle the additional GPS data, in order to reduce the drift errors in the actual motion. An extended Kalman filter is applied for the overall cameras' motion tracking.

The rest of the paper is structured as follows: Section 2 reviews previous work in this problem domain. Section 3 discusses our proposed approach and its mathematical theories. Section 4 shows how the additional GPS data can be used to bound the build-up error within in a certain range over a long distance. Section 6 explains the design and metrics of the experiments and their evaluations. A summary of our proposed method is given in Section 7.

2   Related Literature

Existing vision-based ego-motion algorithms take image data either from monocular cameras, stereo cameras, or omnidirectional cameras. Matthies et al. [12,13] provided a solid foundation for stereo-vision-based egomotion estimation methods. They described how to compute the error model from the input image data, and its importance for the error modelling in stereo-vision systems. The experimental results proved that the stereo systems mostly lead to better estimations than monocular systems, since the triangulation phase of the monocular system could bring more errors. Following this, numerous work has been done related to stereo-vision systems. A method for 3D rigid motion estimation, using the typical output of stereo cameras (i.e. disparity images), is presented in [5].

We choose to focus on stereo-vision methods. However, the methodology of a stereo-vision-based system could not be suitable for all situations; omnidirectional camera systems became also a popular research direction in robotics and computer vision. For example, Shakernia et al. [18] demonstrated a method for omnidirectional cameras; the presented algorithm uses the geometry of the central panoramic camera's intrinsics to create a virtual curved retina, and calculates the optical flow for the back-projected image points onto that retina. In addition, most of the existing egomotion-estimation algorithms can be adapted to work with this method.

Kalman filters are generally used to deal with noise and errors that are introduced by the input data. Julier et al. [8] introduced the unscented Kalman filter for nonlinear transformations in 2004. Franke et al. [6] proposed a novel approach of using the means of Kalman filters to track the 3D position and motion for a large number of image points, which effectively distinguishes foreground and background features. Badino et al. [1] continued to use a fusion of Kalman filters to track stereo features in 3D Euclidean space, and used a least-squares formulation to minimize the projection error between the corresponding clouds of static points from two consecutive frames. As a result, the accuracy of the overall visual odometry estimation was improved. Based on this work, Badino et al. demonstrated a head-wearable stereo system for real time ego-motion estimation; see [2], and they further improved this work in [3].

Rather than using 2D image features to solve the *Perspective-n-Point* (PnP) problem, the rigid transformation between every two consecutive image pairs could be calculated with pure 3D data. Milella et al. [14] introduced a method using the *Iterated Closest Point* (*ICP*) algorithm (Besl et al. [4]) to estimate the motion data between two sets of 3D point clouds of the static scenes.

Another popular approach for filtering out noise and input errors is called *Random Sample Consensus* (RANSAC). Kitt et al. [9] employed an *Iterative Sigma Point Kalman Filter* (ISPKF), which was implemented in [19], with a RANSAC-based outlier rejection schema, and it demonstrated its ability of improving the estimations for frame-to-frame motion in dynamic environments.

Since features are the key to all egomotion estimation algorithms, a good feature detector is critical. Song et al. [20] evaluated and compared a number of major feature detectors with respect to invariance and efficiency matrices; see also [10]. Rublee et al. [16] proposed a new *Oriented BRIEF* (ORB) detector, which appeared to be a reasonable option, because of its "reasonable" rotation invariance, noise resistant properties, and time efficiency.

3 Visual Odometry Estimation

A trinocular-camera system is mounted inside our test vehicle; it records image sequences as 12-bit RGB images at 30 Hz with a dimension of 2046×1080 pixels for every camera, as shown in Fig. 1. The real-time GPS data is also collected synchronously for each frame. We obtain the RGB value of each pixel by using the

Fig. 1. An example of a rectified trinocular frame for an outdoor environment

colour image from the left camera. Our proposed method consists of five major phases: (1) feature matching and projecting in 3D Euclidean space, (2) remove outliers of the tracked features with a fusion of Kalman filters, (3) stereo-vision based visual odometry, (4) trajectory correction with an extended Kalman filter, and (5) GPS integration. The pseudo-code of our proposed method is shown in Alg. 1.

To construct the 3D world for our experiments, we decided to use the left-handed Cartesian coordinate system where the origin is the mid-point on the

---

Input: A sequence of stereo images, $\{I_k\}_{k \geq 1}$
Additional input: Corresponding sequence of GPS data, $\{G_k\}_{k \geq 1}$
Output: Rotation $\mathbf{R}$ and translation $\mathbf{t}$ of the camera's motion
$k \leftarrow 1$ # Initialise frame index
$C_1 \leftarrow (0,0,0)$ # Initialise camera position
while *more frames* **do**

    # **Phase 1:** feature matching and projecting in 3D Euclidean space
    $\{p_i\}_{i \in F_k} \leftarrow$ all features on image I_k
    $\{p_i'\}_{i \in F_{k+1}} \leftarrow$ all features on image I_{k+1}
    $\{P_i'\}_{i \in F_{k+1}} \leftarrow$ 3D projection of $\{p_i'\}_{k+1}$

    # **Phase 2:** remove outliers of matched features with Kalman filters fusion
    $F_k' \leftarrow$ indices of filtered matching features
    $||d|| \leftarrow \sum_{i \in F_k'} \sqrt{(p_i - p_i')^2}$
    $||d_{gps}|| \leftarrow \sqrt{(G_k - G_{k+1})^2}$
    if $||d|| \leq \sigma_{(noise\ tolerance)}$ **and** $||d_{gps}|| = 0$ **then**
       | $\mathbf{R} \leftarrow \mathbf{I}_3$ and $\mathbf{t} \leftarrow [0\ 0\ 0]^\top$
    else
       # **Phase 3:** stereo-vision based visual odometry
       $(\mathbf{R}, \mathbf{t}) \leftarrow$ camera pose from $\{(p_i, P_i')\}_{i \in F_k'}$
       # **Phase 4:** trajectory correction with EKF
       $(\mathbf{R}_{ekf}, \mathbf{t}_{ekf}) \leftarrow$ rotation and translation from EKF
       # **Phase 5:** GPS integration (dynamic weighted mean)
       $(\mathbf{R}_{gps}, \mathbf{t}_{gps}) \leftarrow$ rotation and translation from GPS
       if $\mathbf{R}_{ekf} \cdot C_k + \mathbf{t}_{ekf} \leq \sigma_{gps\_window}$ **then**
           $(\mathbf{R}_{int}, \mathbf{t}_{int}) \leftarrow \alpha \cdot (\mathbf{R}_{gps}, \mathbf{t}_{gps}) + (1 - \alpha) \cdot (\mathbf{R}_{ekf}, \mathbf{t}_{ekf})$
           where $\alpha \leftarrow ||d'|| / (||d'|| + \sigma_{gps\_window})$
           and $||d'|| \leftarrow \sqrt{(X_{cam} - X_{gps})^2 + (Y_{cam} - Y_{gps})^2 + (Z_{cam} - Z_{gps})^2}$
           ,
       else
           | $(\mathbf{R}_{int}, \mathbf{t}_{int}) \leftarrow (\mathbf{R}_{ekf}, \mathbf{t}_{ekf})$
       end
    end
    $k \leftarrow k + 1$ # next frame pair
end

Algorithm 1. The proposed egomotion estimation algorithm with GPS input

road in the first frame. The z-axis is pointing to the camera's facing direction at the origin from the first frame to the second frame. The x-axis represents the distance shifts from the origin to the left. The y-axis indicates the change in height. In the 3D world coordinate, we assume that the camera is at a pre-defined position $[x\ y\ z]^\top = [\text{left height } 0]^\top$ at the beginning.

4   Error Handling and Kalman Filters

The ideal environment for egomotion estimation is that all the features from a static scene are matched and tracked perfectly, and the corresponding disparity maps should also provide 100% accurate depth information. However, our world is never perfect, every aspects of the input data will bring a certain level of noise (e.g. noise from stereo matching, errors in feature matching). Noise filtering is an essential step for any further processing.

In our approach, we use a fusion of linear Kalman filters for augmented feature tracking, in order to filter outliers with wrong disparity information, and to eliminate any miss-matched correspondences. We also propose an extended Kalman filter for tracking the rotation (Euler angles) and translation of the vehicle's motion. Julier et al. [8] suggested that the EKF is reliable for solving nonlinear problems that are almost linear. In our proposed method, we use the EKF for tracking changes of the egomotion transformation frame by frame, where the gaps (i.e. the time intervals) between every two frames are relatively small. Therefore, tracking and correcting the camera's trajectory and pose can be considered an almost linear problem, solvable with EKF.

4.1   Local Kalman Filter Fusion

The concepts of Kalman filter fusion for tracking features' 3D positions were firstly introduced by Franke et al. [6]. Our experiments have convinced us the quality of the tracked features could greatly influence the accuracy of the egomotion estimation, so we would like to select a subset of the static features with a rule-based scheme. Since the disparity maps are a major input, and we assume the disparity values contain normal-distributed noise, we could use a set of linear Kalman filters to track the change in 3D positions of the features, and build up the confidence of the selected features. Therefore, we can discard features that appear at unpredictable positions, for example a sudden change in depth, those are considered outliers. In this way, the overall accuracy of egomotion estimation can be improved.

State Vector. The state vector is a 6×1 vector, it contains the 3D positional data and its velocity:

$$\mathbf{x}_k = [x\ y\ z\ x'\ y'\ z']^\top \tag{1}$$

Process Model. The process model relates to the state vector; it describes the state vector change from the previous moment $k-1$ to the present moment k:

$$\mathbf{x}_k = \mathbf{A}_k \cdot \mathbf{x}_{k-1} + \mathbf{b}_k^\top + \mathbf{n}_k \tag{2}$$

$$\text{where} \quad \mathbf{A}_k = \begin{bmatrix} \mathbf{I}_3 & \Delta t \cdot \mathbf{I}_3 \\ 0_3 & \mathbf{I}_3 \end{bmatrix}$$

$\mathbf{A}_k$ is the state transition matrix and $\mathbf{b}_k$ is the input-control vector.

Measure Model. The measurement is obtained by the mean of the two transformations $T_{k-1|k}$(from Frame $k - 1$ to Frame k) and $T_{k|k+1}$(from Frame k to Frame $k + 1$). The measurement model only observes the position data of the current state of the tracked image features:

$$\begin{bmatrix} x_k \ y_k \ z_k \end{bmatrix}^\top = \mathbf{H} \cdot \mathbf{x}_k + \mathbf{n}_k \tag{3}$$

$$\text{where} \quad \mathbf{H} = \begin{bmatrix} 1 & 0 & 0 & 0 & 0 & 0 \\ 0 & 1 & 0 & 0 & 0 & 0 \\ 0 & 0 & 1 & 0 & 0 & 0 \end{bmatrix} \quad \text{and} \quad \mathbf{x}_k = \begin{bmatrix} x_k \ y_k \ z_k \ x'_k \ y'_k \ z'_k \end{bmatrix}^\top$$

$\mathbf{H}$ is the observation model matrix, and $\mathbf{n}_k$ is the Gaussian noise.

4.2 Global Kalman Filter

The global Kalman filter is designed to correct the errors in the camera's motion estimation. The term 'global' refers to the overall transformation matrix of the egomotion estimation. It firstly estimates the possible transformation for the 'next' state. If the difference between the predicted and measured coordinates of the vehicle is larger than a pre-defined threshold, it will then use the relative GPS data (if the GPS is active for the frame) as the new input of the measurement, and provide the corrected coordinates of the vehicle, in order to minimise the drift errors in the total travelled distance.

Process Model. The process model of our method follows the general form of a Kalman filter:

$$\mathbf{x}_k = \mathbf{A}_k \cdot \mathbf{x}_{k-1} + \mathbf{b}_k^\top + \mathbf{n}_k \tag{4}$$

where the state vector $\mathbf{x}_k$ is a 6×1 vector that contains the camera's world coordinates (X, Y, Z), with its direction vector that contains the three relevant Euler angles (i.e., 'pitch', 'roll', and 'yaw' angles). Combining the positional and directional data in state vector $\mathbf{x}_k = [X_k \ Y_k \ Z_k \ \varphi_k \ \theta_k \ \psi_k]^\top$, we obtain the state-transformation matrix:

$$\mathbf{A}_k = \begin{bmatrix} \mathbf{R}'_k & 0_{3 \times 3} \\ 0_{3 \times 3} & \mathbf{I}_3 \end{bmatrix}$$

The transition input vector of the Kalman filter is as follows:

$$\mathbf{b}_k = [t_k | \triangle \varphi_k \ \triangle \theta_k \ \triangle \psi_k]^\top$$

Measure Model. The measurement can be defined as the 3D position of the camera's GPS reading in our VO Cartesian coordinate system. A function is used to convert the latitude and longitude to $[X_{gps}, Y_{gps}, Z_{gps}]$. The relevant elevation information of the current frame can be either collected from the GPS altitude readings (with a possible large error), or it can be gathered from a road surface measurement database. The current state vector $\mathbf{x}_k$ has a relation with the measurement state vector $\mathbf{z}_k$ that is described as follows:

$$\mathbf{z}_k = \mathbf{H} \cdot \mathbf{x}_k + \mathbf{n}_k = [X_{gps}\ Y_{gps}\ Z_{gps}\ 0\ 0\ 0]^\top \tag{5}$$

and noise $\mathbf{n}_k$ is the assumed white (Gaussian) noise. Then, the measurement matrix $\mathbf{H}$ can be formed as follows:

$$\mathbf{H} = \begin{bmatrix} \mathbf{R}'_k & 0_{3\times3} \\ 0_{3\times3} & 0_{3\times3} \end{bmatrix} \tag{6}$$

where $\quad \mathbf{R}'_k = \mathbf{R}_z \cdot \mathbf{R}_y \cdot \mathbf{R}_x$

the three sub-rotations $\mathbf{R}_x$, $\mathbf{R}_y$, and $\mathbf{R}_z$ are the rotation matrices along the $x-$, $y-$, and $z-$axis directions, they are derived from the corresponding Euler angles.

Prediction. It is required to estimate an *a-priori* state vector $\tilde{\mathbf{x}}_{k+1|k}$ from Frame k to Frame $k+1$:

$$\tilde{\mathbf{x}}_{k+1|k} = \mathbf{A}_k \cdot \tilde{\mathbf{x}}_k + \mathbf{b}_k \tag{7}$$

and an *a-priori* projection noise covariance matrix $\mathbf{P}_{k+1|k}$ with its relative state measurement uncertainty $\mathbf{Q}_k$:

$$\mathbf{P}_{k+1|k} = \mathbf{A}_k \cdot \mathbf{P}_k \cdot \mathbf{A}_k^\top + \mathbf{Q}_k \tag{8}$$

Correction. First we calculate the Kalman gain

$$\mathbf{K}_{k+1} = \mathbf{P}_{k+1|k} \cdot \mathbf{H}_{k+1}^\top \cdot (\mathbf{H}_{k+1} \cdot \mathbf{P}_{k+1|k} \cdot \mathbf{H}_{k+1}^\top + \mathbf{R}_k)^{-1} \tag{9}$$

for the next state based on Eq. (5). The residual covariance $\tilde{\mathbf{n}}_{k+1}$ can be measured as follows:

$$\tilde{\mathbf{n}}_{k+1} = \mathbf{z}_{k+1} - \mathbf{H}_{k+1} \cdot \tilde{\mathbf{x}}_{k+1|k} \tag{10}$$

Finally, we update the *posteriori* state vector:

$$\tilde{\mathbf{x}}_{k+1|k+1} = \tilde{\mathbf{x}}_{k+1|k} + \mathbf{K}_{k+1} \cdot \tilde{\mathbf{n}}_{k+1} \tag{11}$$

and the *posteriori* projection noise covariance matrix:

$$\mathbf{P}_{k+1|k+1} = (\mathbf{I} - \mathbf{K}_{k+1} \cdot \mathbf{H}_{k+1}) \cdot \mathbf{P}_{k+1|k} \tag{12}$$

$\mathbf{R}_k$ is the covariance of the observation white noise $\mathbf{n}_k$, and $\mathbf{Q}_k$ is the covariance of the predicted estimation error.

5   Stereo Vision and GPS Sensor Integration

Multi-sensor integration is a key to solve many problems in the field of egomotion estimation. It brings multiple layers of input data, so that the different types of input could provide evaluations of the estimations. With additional GPS data input, we propose a multi-sensor (stereo-vision cameras and GPS unit) integration approach.

Figure 2 shows a sketch of the proposed integration approach. We use the GPS data as an evaluation supplement when the estimated vehicle's position is in the 'tolerance' window of the GPS coordinates; in this case, we trust visual odometry estimation over the GPS data. However, if the calculated trajectory (by visual odometry) is out of the 'tolerance window' according to the GPS data, then the GPS coordinates will be used as the measurement of the current frame in the extended Kalman filter. The calculated trajectory will be then corrected according to the GPS coordinates and the history of the previous improved trajectory by the EFK.

Based on the GPS data and the Kalman filter fusion, we propose a feature integration approach. It uses the GPS reading as a guidance vector for each frame to calculate the supposed positions of tracked features. Next, we use the Kalman filters to predict the estimated positions. Then we can calculate the integrated feature positions by taking the mean of the supposed and estimated positions. Finally, we use the improved feature set to calculate more accurate estimations of egomotion.

A GPS unit is used in our testing vehicle to collect real-time geodetic coordinate data (under the 'WGS 84' standard), including latitude ϕ, longitude λ, and altitude α for every frame. First, we convert this corresponding GPS data into an *Universal Transverse Mercator* (UTM) coordinate system. After the conversion, all the coordinates should be able to shift into our primary 'local' reconstruction coordinate system of the roadside reconstruction experiments. We assumed that the GPS readings contain a certain error (0.5%) due to a number of approximations, irregularities of the Earth surface, and deviations in the GPS signal readings in our formulae.

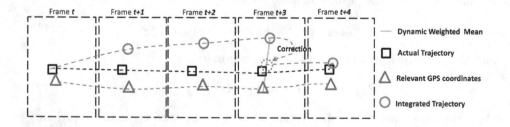

Fig. 2. A sketch for drift-error correction by GPS integration

6   Results and Evaluation

The experiments were carried out under the following assumptions: the camera's intrinsic parameters are known, and the stereo image pairs are time-synchronised and well rectified. In this paper we report about experiments with our proposed method on KITTI data [7], and also on our own data. We could not make a submission to the KITTI benchmark website because the KITTI sequences do not use the GPS data as an input, they use the GPS with IMU data for the ground truth; we would like to experience how the multi-sensor integration approach works, even if it is just a basic GPS unit with inaccurate readings.

The proposed method is implemented in C++ with OpenCV and PCL libraries. We use the 'FAST' feature detector and the 'BRISK' descriptor to ensure promising results. The 3D roadside reconstruction is used here as a part of the evaluation process.

Figure 3 illustrates a dense 3D roadside reconstruction using the KITTI data. The blue dots show the camera's trajectory in the scene estimated by our feature-matching-based visual odometry method. The green dots indicate the 'corrected' trajectory by the extended Kalman filter, being an essential element of our approach.

Figure 4 shows results using our own image sequences with additional GPS data. The 3D scene is reconstructed using sparse and filtered feature points. The red dots are the coordinates of the converted GPS signal. This figure also shows the 'discontinuous' nature of the GPS data. Therefore, the corrections of the EFK will only take place when the GPS data is active and clear. When the GPS data is missing, the EFK will still track the camera's motion, but will not rely on the guidance of the GPS signals. The green dots show the improved trajectory of the camera positions.

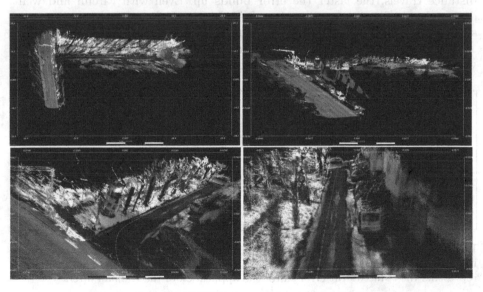

Fig. 3. Result on KITTI data without using GPS data

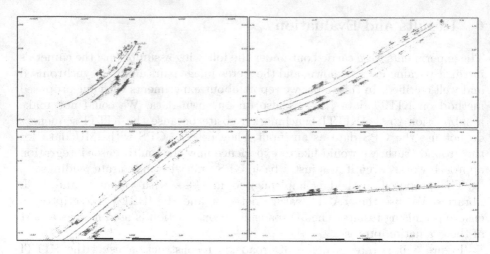

Fig. 4. Egomotion estimation with additional GPS input. The roadside is reconstructed using filtered features. The green dots show the camera positions in each frame. The red dots show the GPS coordinates for each frame

Figure 5 shows comparisons of drift errors before and after applying the Kalman filter fusion for two test sequences. It clearly indicates that the Kalman filter fusion can provide more stable and reliable results. Each test sequence contains more than 700 stereo image pairs.

The experimental results show that the additional GPS input is a valuable supplement for any stand-alone visual odometry application. It provides useful and live measurements for evaluating the calculated pose and motion data. In general, the drift error builds up over the travelled distance, the longer the distance travels, the faster the error builds up. Even with careful and well-designed noise filtering functions (e.g. RANSAC, or Kalman filters), some errors still remain occasionally, since the pipeline is complex and long.

Moreover, the multi-sensor integration enriches the input data. The resulting visual odometry supports improved reconstruction; it helps to combine street

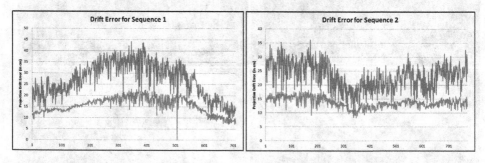

Fig. 5. Comparisons of drift errors in 3D reconstruction scenes. The red curve represents the errors before the application of the Kalman filter fusion. The blue curve represents the reduced drift errors after the application of the Kalman filters

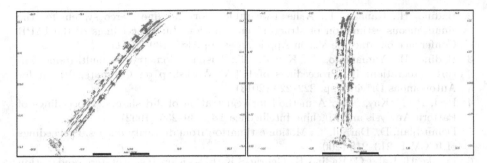

Fig. 6. The proposed multi-sensor integration demonstrates the ability of solving the *multi-run problem*: Combine 3D reconstructions obtained by multiple runs through the same street. Red and blue point clouds are the features; green and yellow lines are the camera trajectories; red or blue dotted lines are the GPS trajectories of the first or second sequence, respectively

segments according to the GPS data. Therefore, the 3D scene reconstruction can be done at a larger scale (i.e. in different sections in a large area). Figure 6 shows result for a multi-run scenario without using any ICP or 3D features. This demonstrates an alternative methodology for solving such kind of problems, compared to other traditional VO methods. However, it also heavily relies on the accuracy of the GPS input. Another benefit is that our method can bound the build-up of the drift error within a small range, which means that the overall VO drift error will not increase anymore according to the distance travelled.

7   Conclusions

In this paper, we proposed a method for egomotion estimation. It firstly calculates the visual odometry over stereo image sequences, and then integrates the motion data with additional GPS signals. For complex dynamic environments, the stereo cameras might only capture features on moving objects (e.g. when following a truck), in this case, the visual odometry can lead to wrong results, and errors can build up quickly. Since there is no way to distinguish static features from the dynamic scene in this scenario, we believe that multi-sensor integration can be a proper solution for such problems.

In our proposed approach, the reason why we choose to use feature matching rather than the traditional optical flow method at Phase 2 in our algorithm is that the feature matching method gives more reliable and stable results under many circumstances, whereas the optical flow methods could not provide such results when the displacement between every two input frames is getting larger (e.g. the vehicle speeds up).

References

1. Badino, H., Franke, U., Rabe, C., Gehrig, S.: Stereo vision-based detection of moving objects under strong camera motion. In: Proceedings of Computer Vision Theory and Applications, vol. 2, pp. 253–260 (2006)

2. Badino, H., Kanade, T.: A head-wearable short-baseline stereo system for the simultaneous estimation of structure and motion. In: Proceedings of the IAPR Conference on Machine Vision Applications, pp. 185–189 (2011)
3. Badino, H., Yamamoto, A., Kanade, T.: Visual odometry by multi-frame feature integration. In: Proceedings of ICCV Workshop on Computer Vision for Autonomous Driving, pp. 222–229 (2013)
4. Besl, P., McKay, N.D.: A method for registration of 3-d shapes. Proceedings of Pattern Analysis and Machine Intelligence **14**, 239–256 (1992)
5. Demirdjian, D., Darrell, T.: Motion estimation from disparity images. Proceedings of ICCV **1**, 213–218 (2001)
6. Franke, U., Rabe, C., Badino, H., Gehrig, S.K.: 6D-Vision: fusion of stereo and motion for robust environment perception. In: Kropatsch, W.G., Sablatnig, R., Hanbury, A. (eds.) DAGM 2005. LNCS, vol. 3663, pp. 216–223. Springer, Heidelberg (2005)
7. Geiger, A., Lenz, P., Stiller, C., Urtasun, R.: Vision meets robotics: The kitti dataset. International Journal of Robotics Research **32**(11), 1231–1237 (2013)
8. Julier, S., Uhlmann, J.: Unscented filtering and nonlinear estimation. Proceedings of the IEEE **92**(3), 401–422 (2004)
9. Kitt, B., Geiger, A., Lategahn, H.: Visual odometry based on stereo image sequences with ransac-based outlier rejection scheme. In: Proceedings of Intelligent Vehicles Symposium, pp. 486–492 (2010)
10. Klette, R.: Concise Computer Vision. Springer, London (2014)
11. Maimone, M., Cheng, Y., Matthies, L.: Two years of visual odometry on the mars exploration rovers. Journal of Field Robotics **24**, 169–186 (2007)
12. Matthies, L.: Dynamic stereo vision. Ph.D. dissertation, Carnegie Mellon University (1989)
13. Matthies, L., Shafer, S.A.: Error modeling in stereo navigation. IEEE Journal of Robotics and Automation **3**, 239–250 (1987)
14. Milella, A., Siegwart, R.: Stereo-based ego-motion estimation using pixel tracking and iterative closest point. In: Proceedings of IEEE International Conference on Computer Vision Systems, pp. 21–21 (2006)
15. Olson, C., Matthies, L., Schoppers, M., Maimone, M.: Stereo ego-motion improvements for robust rover navigation. In: Proceedings of IEEE International Conference on Robotics and Automation, vol. 2, pp. 1099–1104 (2001)
16. Rublee, E., Rabaud, V., Konolige, K., Bradski, G.: Orb: An efficient alternative to sift or surf. In: Proceedings of ICCV, pp. 2564–2571 (2011)
17. Scaramuzza, D., Fraundorfer, F.: Visual odometry tutorial. Robotics Automation Magazine **18**(4), 80–92 (2011)
18. Shakernia, O., Vidal, R., Sastry, S.: Omnidirectional egomotion estimation from back-projection flow. In: Proceedings of CVPR Workshop, vol. 7, pp. 82–82 (2003)
19. Sibley, G., Sukhatme, G.S., Matthies, L.: The iterated sigma point kalman filter with applications to long range stereo. In: Proceedings of Robotics: Science and Systems (2006)
20. Song, Z., Klette, R.: Robustness of point feature detection. In: Wilson, R., Hancock, E., Bors, A., Smith, W. (eds.) CAIP 2013, Part II. LNCS, vol. 8048, pp. 91–99. Springer, Heidelberg (2013)
21. Tian, T.Y., Tomasi, C., Heeger, D.J.: Comparison of approaches to egomotion computation. In: Proceedings of CVPR, pp. 315–320 (1996)

Bundle Adjustment with Implicit Structure Modeling Using a Direct Linear Transform

Hsiang-Jen Chien[1]([✉]), Haokun Geng[2], and Reinhard Klette[1]

[1] School of Engineering, Auckland University of Technology, Auckland, New Zealand
jchien@aut.ac.nz
[2] Department of Computer Science, University of Auckland, Auckland, New Zealand

Abstract. Bundle adjustment (BA) is considered to be the "golden standard" optimisation technique for multiple-view reconstruction over decades of research. The technique simultaneously tunes camera parameters and scene structure to fit a nonlinear function, in a way that the discrepancy between the observed scene points and their reprojections are minimised in a least-squares manner. Computational feasibility and numerical conditioning are two major concerns of todays BA implementations, and choosing a proper parametrization of structure in 3D space could dramatically improve numerical stability, convergence speed, and cost of evaluating Jacobian matrices. In this paper we study several alternative representations of 3D structure and propose an implicit modeling approach based on a Direct Linear Transform (DLT) estimation. The performances of a variety of parametrization techniques are evaluated using simulated visual odometry scenarios. Experimental results show that the computational cost and convergence speed is further improved to achieve similar accuracy without explicit adjustment over the structure parameters.

Keywords: Bundle adjustment · Multiple view reconstruction · Nonlinear optimisation · Direct linear transform

1 Introduction

Finding maximum-likelihood estimations of camera parameters and 3D structure has been the desire for long in the discipline of multiple-view reconstruction; see [1–3]. Using repetitive observations of sparse scene points in different viewing directions, bundle adjustment (BA) provides an optimal solution to the reconstruction problem by nonlinearly minimising the reprojection error function. Given that the imaging error of a tracked scene point follows a Gaussian, the optimal solution of BA is proven to be the maximum-likelihood estimation. Due to its successes, BA has been used historically in photogrammetry (e.g. [4,5]), and more recently in structure-from-motion (SfM) [6–8], simultaneous localisation and mapping (SLAM), and visual odometry (VO) [9–14].

The formulation of the BA problem is simple, its implementation, in practice, is not. Like many inverse problems, the adjoined recovery of camera parameters

© Springer International Publishing Switzerland 2015
G. Azzopardi and N. Petkov (Eds.): CAIP 2015, Part I, LNCS 9256, pp. 411–422, 2015.
DOI: 10.1007/978-3-319-23192-1_34

and scene structure is an ill-posed problem. Due to the existence of multiple local minima, a good initial guess is required to guarantee a successful convergence to a globally optimal state. The computational cost and convergence speed are also important issues when it comes to online applications. All these factors are inherently dominated by the choice of how the problem is parametrised [1,15].

In the context of VO, the canonical way to parametrise a BA problem is to use 6 parameters to represent each camera pose (3-dof location plus 3-dof direction), and 3 parameters to denote Euclidean coordinates of each scene point, assuming that intrinsic parameters are already known and remain fixed through the adjustment. Although such representation is adopted by many off-the-shelf software packages (e.g. [16–18]), recent research pointed out that choosing an alternative representation of camera's position and scene structure can lead to greatly improved numerical stability, convergence speed, and computational cost [11–15,19,20]. Therefore it is very important to investigate how different parameterizations perform under various VO scenarios.

In this paper we review and test 5 scene parametrization methods, namely the Euclidean, homogeneous, inverse depth, parallax angle, and implicit modeling method. Numerical experiments are designed to test these representations in terms of accuracy, robustness, and time efficiency.

The rest of this paper is organised as follows. In Sec. 2 we go through the formulation of BA and review two novel parameterizations. The DLT implicit modeling approach is described in Sec. 3. These parameterizations are evaluated in Sec. 4. Section 5 concludes this paper.

2   Bundle Adjustment: A Literature Review

2.1   Problem Formulation

Given n_a cameras and n_b observed scene points, the objective function specific to the BA problem is defined as follows:

$$\phi(\mathbf{a}, \mathbf{b}) = \sum_{i=1}^{n_a} \sum_{j=1}^{n_b} v_{ij} \| y_{ij} - f(\mathbf{a_i}, \mathbf{b_j}) \|^2 \tag{1}$$

where y_{ij} are the image coordinates of the j-th point observed by the i-th camera, $\mathbf{a_i} \in \mathbb{V_a}$ and $\mathbf{b_j} \in \mathbb{V}_b$ are, respectively, parametric forms of a camera and a 3D point in parameter spaces $\mathbb{V}_a$ and $\mathbb{V}_b$, v_{ij} is a binary function denoting visibility of scene points, and f is the imaging function. In particular, it defines

$$v_{i,j} = \begin{cases} 1, & \text{if the } j\text{-th point is imaged by the } i\text{-th camera} \\ 0, & \text{otherwise} \end{cases} \tag{2}$$

and

$$f(\mathbf{a_i}, \mathbf{b_j}) = \pi[R(\mathbf{a_i})g(\mathbf{b_j}) + \tau(\mathbf{a_i})] \tag{3}$$

where $\pi : \mathbb{R}^3 \to \mathbb{R}^2$ denotes the perspective projection function, $g : \mathbb{V}_a \to \mathbb{R}^3$ is a mapping that restores Euclidean coordinates of a point from its parametric form, and $R : \mathbb{V}_b \to SO(3)$ together with $\tau : \mathbb{V}_b \to \mathbb{R}^3$ rigidly transform a point from its original coordinate system into the space of camera i.

The definition slightly varies from context to context. In structure-from-motion (SfM) problems, each image is considered to be captured by a physically unique camera, therefore the intrinsic parameters need to be stored individually in **a**. In the context of monocular visual odometry, on the other hand, all the images are captured by the same camera, hence a stores only camera motion while the intrinsic parameters are considered to be known, fixed, and therefore "hard-coded" by π. Binocular or multi-camera visual odometry represent a mixture of these two cases; this requires a minor modification on the generic model.

2.2 Sparse Solution Using the Levenberg-Marquardt Algorithm

The objective function of Eq. (1) is in the sum-of-square form, hence can be minimised using the Levenberg-Marquardt (LM) algorithm [21]. Let $\mathbf{x} \in \mathbb{R}^n$ where $n = dim_{\mathbb{R}}(\mathbb{V}_a) \cdot n_a + dim_{\mathbb{R}}(\mathbb{V}_b) \cdot n_b$ be the state vector that vectorises **a** and **b**. Then, for m nonzero components Eq. (1) can be represented by a vector function $\varepsilon : \mathbb{R}^n \to \mathbb{R}^m$ where each entry $\varepsilon_i(\mathbf{x})$ denotes the residual of the observation i and its projection. This way minimising ϕ is equivalent to minimising L_2-norm of ε (i.e. $\|\varepsilon\|^2$).

The LM algorithm uses the Jacobian-approximated second-order derivative of ε to update x iteratively. For each iteration the update is decided by

$$\Delta \mathbf{x} = (\mathbf{J}^\top \mathbf{J} + \lambda \mathbf{I})^{-1} \mathbf{J}^\top \varepsilon(\mathbf{x}) \tag{4}$$

where $\mathbf{J}_{ij} = \frac{\partial \varepsilon_i}{\partial x_j}$ is the Jacobian matrix, and $\lambda \in \mathbb{R}$ the damping factor. If $\mathbf{x}' = \mathbf{x} + \Delta \mathbf{x}$ lowers $\|\varepsilon\|^2$, then the update is accepted and λ is decreased, leading to a Gauss-Newton-like behavior. Otherwise λ is increased to resemble a descent-gradient approach, and a new $\Delta \mathbf{x}$ is solved and tried repeatedly, until it attains a better solution.

An interesting sparsity pattern exists in the linear system $\mathbf{A} = \mathbf{J}^\top \mathbf{J} + \lambda \mathbf{I}$ due to mutually irrelevant structure parameters. By splitting up the camera and structure components from the linear system

$$\begin{bmatrix} \mathbf{U} & \mathbf{W} \\ \mathbf{W}^\top & \mathbf{V} \end{bmatrix} \begin{bmatrix} \Delta \mathbf{x_a} \\ \Delta \mathbf{x_b} \end{bmatrix} = \begin{bmatrix} \mathbf{J}_a^\top \\ \mathbf{J}_b^\top \end{bmatrix} \varepsilon(\mathbf{x}) \tag{5}$$

one will find that the matrix $\mathbf{V}$ contains nonzero entries only in its diagonal $dim_{\mathbb{R}}(\mathbb{V}_b) \times dim_{\mathbb{R}}(\mathbb{V}_b)$ sub-matrices. Multiplying Eq. (5) by the matrix

$$\begin{bmatrix} \mathbf{I} & -\mathbf{W}\mathbf{V}^{-1} \\ \mathbf{0} & \mathbf{I} \end{bmatrix} \tag{6}$$

yields

$$\begin{bmatrix} \mathbf{U} - \mathbf{W}\mathbf{V}^{-1}\mathbf{W}^\top & \mathbf{0} \\ \mathbf{W}^\top & \mathbf{V} \end{bmatrix} \begin{bmatrix} \Delta \mathbf{x_a} \\ \Delta \mathbf{x_b} \end{bmatrix} = \begin{bmatrix} \mathbf{J}_a^\top - \mathbf{W}\mathbf{V}^{-1}\mathbf{W}^\top \mathbf{J}_b^\top \\ \mathbf{J}_b^\top \end{bmatrix} \varepsilon(\mathbf{x}) \tag{7}$$

where $\Delta\mathbf{x_a}$ is first solved and then $\Delta\mathbf{x_b}$. By exploiting the blocky sparse structure of $\mathbf{V}$, its inverse can be quickly computed in time $O(n_b)$, where n_b is the number of scene points. Solving $\Delta\mathbf{x}$ in this two-stage fashion greatly alleviates computational complexity of BA, since $\mathbf{A}$ is typically a giant matrix that involves a huge number of scene points but only few camera parameters [16,17].

Despite that BA is typically solved using the LM algorithm, it is not specifically bound to any optimisation method. Some alternative least-squares solver such as the Gauss-Newton method [14], conjugate gradient method [22], or the dogleg algorithm [23] were reported to outperform LM in particular cases.

2.3 Parametrization Matters

Euclidean coordinates (x, y, z) are intuitively the most convenient and straightforward way to represent 3D geometry (also called *structure*). For an instance involving n_a cameras and n_b points, the solution lies in a $(6n_a+3n_b)$-dimensional manifold. Considering that a moderately feasible BA problem usually has $n_b > 10^3 \gg n_a$, the evaluation of Jacobian matrices with respect to the geometry parameters soon occupies significant time cost as Eq. (1) takes more scene points into account. Such tendency is clearly depicted by Fig. 1.

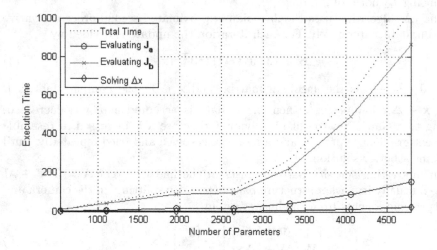

Fig. 1. BA execution time for different problem sizes

The badly scaled nature of BA has inspired some simplification strategies, which fall into two categories. Methods in the first category try to maintain a feasible problem size. Local-scope adjustment [9], or skeletal formation and parameter marginalisation [10] are popular strategies in this category. The second category attempts to simplify the representation of scene geometry using less parameters. The depth-only representation [11] reduces the geometry parameters to one-third, the line representation [6] reduces points to a more compact form, [20] studies the minimum parameters required, and radical methods further remove the structure from being explicitly adjusted, using either an embedding optimisation technique [9], or implicit modeling [24].

Ill-conditioned Jacobians are yet another reason to seek alternative geometry parameterizations. It is not rare to see a bundle adjuster move few scene points towards a numerically infinite far location, and then back to their optimal positions before the system can converge successfully [1]. In VO and SLAM applications, such singular behavior happens more often due to the presence of either far or low parallax scene points. While discarding those "problematic" points is considered a rugged solution, as they are robust features for rotation estimation, novel research recommends to adopt an appropriate parametrization to avoid the singularity caused by the fact that a point at infinity cannot be properly expressed in inhomogeneous Euclidean coordinates. Homogeneous coordinates naturally solve the singularity [1,13]. The inverse-depth representation [11] provides a numerically stable and computationally cheap solution. In [14], the geometry parameters are encoded completely in angular spaces; therefore the scaling singularity is avoided.

2.4   Inverse Depth Parametrization

Inverse depth is a concept closely related to the disparity representation in stereo vision, and has been deployed in extended Kalman filter (EKF) enabled SLAM applications (e.g. [11]). For a 3D scene point, the 6 parameters required in inverse-depth form are $(x, y, z, \theta, \phi, \rho)$, where $x, y, z \in \mathbb{R}$ specify the "anchor" position (i.e. the position of the camera where the point was first observed), $\theta \in [-\pi, \pi)$ and $\alpha \in [-\frac{4}{2}, \frac{4}{2}]$ respectively denote the azimuth and elevation angles of its observed image coordinates, and $\rho \in \mathbb{R}_0^+$ is the inverse depth. The mapping on Euclidean coordinates is achieved by

$$
\mathbf{x} = \frac{1}{\rho} \begin{bmatrix} \cos \alpha \sin \theta \\ \sin \alpha \\ \cos \alpha \cos \theta \end{bmatrix} + \begin{bmatrix} x \\ y \\ z \end{bmatrix} \tag{8}
$$

In Eq. (8), the position of each scene point is modeled as a back-projection ray originating at the anchor point and pointing toward $(\cos \alpha \sin \theta, \sin \alpha, \cos \alpha \cos \theta)$. The representation allows points at infinity to be properly handled. Despite that there are 6 parameters involved in the representation, the anchor parameters (x, y, z) are already included in the camera's motion parameters. Therefore, only geometry-specific parameters (θ, α, ρ) need to be stored.

2.5   Parallax Angle Parametrization

Parallax angle parametrization has recently been proposed to overcome the singularity of inverse depth parametrization encountered when the camera is moving toward close points [14]. It drops out the distance component of the inverse-depth parametrization and uses one more view to derive the depth.

The three angles encoding a scene point are (θ, α, ω), where the added third component $\omega \in [0, \pi)$ denotes the parallax angle defined among two views.

Let $\mathbf{x_i}$ and $\mathbf{x_j}$ be the Euclidean coordinates of a scene point transformed to its anchor views i and j, respectively, the parallax angle is defined as

$$\omega = \arccos \frac{\mathbf{x_i}^\top \mathbf{x_j}}{\|\mathbf{x_i}\|\|\mathbf{x_j}\|} \tag{9}$$

which can be used to decide the distance from the first anchor view's centre to the point, using the sine law. Let τ_{ij} be the vector connecting the anchor views in the first anchor's coordinate system and ψ the angle enclosed by $\mathbf{x_i}$ and τ_{ij}, the distance is measured as

$$\|\mathbf{x_i}\| = \frac{\sin \omega + \psi}{\sin \omega} \|\tau_{ij}\| \tag{10}$$

according to the sine law. The 3D coordinates can then be recovered using Eq. (8). The parallax-angle parametrization is illustrated in Fig. 2.

By anchoring each scene point by the pair of views that maximises ω, the parallax parametrization is useful in avoiding a numerically unstable adjustment of the 3D geometry in cases where the observed parallax angle is very small (i.e. between some of the observing positions).

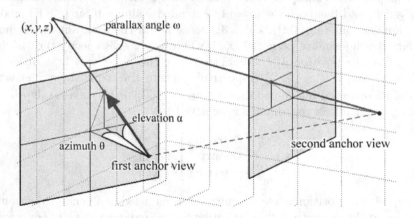

Fig. 2. Parallax representation of a 3D point using azimuth angle θ, elevation angle α, and parallax angle ω defined among two chosen anchor views

3   Implicit Geometry Modeling

The central projection model relates motion and geometry linearly in the projective space. Given a 3-by-4 projection matrix $\mathbf{P}$, a scene point $\mathbf{x}$ and its image $\mathbf{y}$, both in homogeneous coordinates, follow

$$\mathbf{y} \sim \mathbf{P}\mathbf{x} = \begin{bmatrix} \mathbf{p_1} & \mathbf{p_2} & \mathbf{p_3} \end{bmatrix}^\top \mathbf{x} \tag{11}$$

where $\sim$ denotes the equality up to a scale. The scale ambiguity can be cancelled by dividing the first and the second rows of Eq. (11) by the third, which yields a homogeneous form

$$\begin{bmatrix} y_3 \mathbf{P}_1^\top \mathbf{x} - y_1 \mathbf{P}_3^\top \mathbf{x} \\ y_3 \mathbf{P}_2^\top \mathbf{x} - y_2 \mathbf{P}_3^\top \mathbf{x} \end{bmatrix} = 0 \qquad (12)$$

Given that $\mathbf{P} = \mathbf{K} \begin{bmatrix} \mathbf{R} \ \mathbf{t} \end{bmatrix}$, where $\mathbf{K}$ is the intrinsic matrix and $[\mathbf{R} \ \mathbf{t}]$ the camera's motion, Eq. (12) poses a linear duality between the structure (i.e. geometry) and the motion. That is, when the number of constraints is sufficient that allows an over-determined homogeneous system to be built, the motion can be immediately solved in a least-squares form once the structure is determined and vice versa. Estimating either projection parameters or 3D geometry in this way is known as the direct linear transform (DLT) technique, and has been widely used in camera calibration, homography estimation, and surface triangulation [2].

Using the duality, we embed the estimation of structure in the estimation of motion during the BA process. This not only eliminates the time-consuming construction of $\mathbf{J_b}$, but also removes the impact of a structure-measurement error. However, solving Eq. (12) requires a singular value decomposition (SVD), which is computational more expensive than any of the aforementioned parameter-conversion formulas. Table 1 summarises the structure-parametrization methods studied in this paper.

Table 1. Comparison of structure-parameterization methods

Method	# Parameters	Required views	Structure computation
Euclidean	3	1	Fastest
Homogeneous	4	1	Fast
Inverse depth	3	1	Fast
Parallax angle	3	2	Fair
Implicit DLT	0	≥ 2	Slowest

4 Numerical Experiments

4.1 Motion Kinetic Model

We designed a nonlinear acceleration and deceleration kinetic model to render the motion of a vehicle. The model simulates realistic motion, better than placing camera views on an equally-spaced synthetic trajectory as shown in some previous work.

The camera is assumed to start with initial speed v_a and continuously accelerates in t_a seconds to reach its peak speed v_c, at which speed it moves steadily for t_c seconds, then starts to decelerate to the final speed v_d in t_d seconds, as depicted in Fig. 3.

We model the time-speed relation using a nonlinear continuous piece-wise function

$$v(t) = \begin{cases} \frac{v_c - v_a}{2} \left[1 + \cos \pi (1 + \frac{t}{t_a}) \right] + v_a, & t < t_a \\ \frac{v_d - v_c}{2} \left[1 + \cos \pi (1 + \frac{t}{t_d}) \right] + v_c, & t > t_c \\ v_c, & \text{otherwise} \end{cases} \tag{13}$$

The cosine-approximated linear acceleration model allows the camera's position to be determined in a handy way. Let $x_a(t)$ be the travelled distance at time t in the acceleration period; it shows that

$$x_a(t) = \int_0^t \frac{v_c - v_a}{2} \left[1 + \cos \pi (1 + \frac{x}{t_a}) \right] + v_a \, dx \tag{14}$$

Rewriting the definite integral term we have that

$$x_a(t) = \frac{v_c - v_a}{2} \left[\frac{t_a}{\pi} \sin \pi (1 + \frac{x}{t_a}) \Big|_0^t + t \right] + v_a t \tag{15}$$

The travelled distance in the deceleration period $x_d(t)$ can be derived by analogy. During the constant movement, the distance is simply $x_c(t) = v_c t$.

The parameters of the kinetic model are t_a, t_c, t_d, v_a, and v_d. Given x_Σ, the length of the motion segment, the peak speed is determined as

$$v_c = \frac{2x_\Sigma - v_a t_a - v_d t_d}{2t_c + t_a + t_d} \tag{16}$$

since $x_\Sigma = x_a(t_a) + x_c(t_c) + x_d(t_d)$.

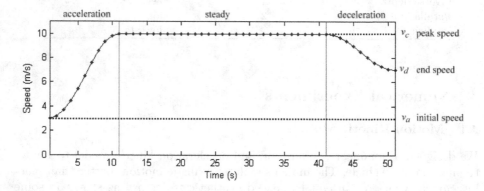

Fig. 3. Nonlinear acceleration and deceleration model used to simulate realistic camera motion. There are three periods of a motion segment. During the acceleration period, the camera first accelerates from initial speed v_a to v_c. Through the steady movement period, the camera maintains a constant speed v_c, until entering the deceleration period, in which the the velocity decreases nonlinearly to the end speed v_d

4.2   Test Data Generation

Three VO scenarios (see Fig. 4) have been designed to study the performance of different structure parametrization methods, in terms of accuracy, convergence, robustness, and time-efficiency. For each scenario, 500 scene points are generated in the camera's field of view ($\cong 50°$), within a range from 5 to 100 metres. The random generation follows the uniform distribution model. In all of the test scenarios, the camera is mounted 1.8 metres above the road surface.

To study the robustness of the parameterisation methods, the generated scene points are corrupted by various noise levels. To model the error of vision-based 3D measurement, the second camera is added to perform triangulation. The image resolution of both cameras is 640×480, and the baseline is 12 cm. For each frame, visible scene points are projected onto the left and the right cameras' image planes, in a way that 3D coordinates are transformed into the disparity space. The obtained disparity values are then contaminated by an additive Gaussian error.

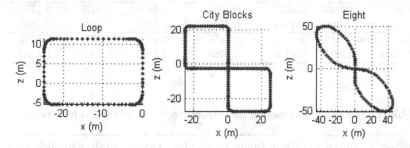

Fig. 4. Simulated VO scenarios. The Loop scenario contains 105 frames, 503 scene points and 10,341 image projections, the City Blocks scenario contains 200 frames, 506 scene points and 18,823 image projections, while the Eight scenario contains 101 frames, 500 scene points and 21,346 image projections. The camera travelled 79.69, 192.47 and 301.22 metres respectively.

4.3   Experimental Results

We implemented the sparse bundle adjustment in MATLAB. The initial motion is calculated using 3D-to-2D correspondences between consecutive frames. The 2D observations are contaminated by an additive Gaussian error. Neither sliding window BA nor data filtering is performed. The results are tabulated in Tables 2, 3 and 4. In all scenarios the optimised rotational errors are lower than $0.01°$ hence not reported in these tables.

The proposed DLT method is able to attain results above the average. In the simple Loop scenario, all parameterisations excluding the parallax angle with $\sigma = 0.5$ are able to achieve an optimised motion error within 1%. The City Blocks scenario poses a more complicated problem structure, and the initial motion

Table 2. The optimised motion and structure errors of the Loop scenario

σ	Error	Initial	Euclidean	Homogeneous	Inv. Depth	Parallax	Implicit DLT
0.1	Motion	0.09%	0.09%	0.07%	0.07%	0.07%	0.07%
	Structure	2.04m	0.23m	0.23m	0.23m	0.22m	0.19m
0.2	Motion	0.41%	0.07%	0.36%	0.36%	0.37%	0.23%
	Structure	2.32m	0.43m	0.69m	0.69m	0.69m	0.43m
0.5	Motion	0.90%	0.75%	0.54%	0.86%	2.66%	0.67%
	Structure	1.49m	1.52m	1.12m	1.57m	11.40m	1.20m

Table 3. The optimised motion and structure errors of the City Blocks scenario

σ	Error	Initial	Euclidean	Homogeneous	Inv. Depth	Parallax	Implicit DLT
0.1	Motion	1.47%	0.74%	0.24%	1.49%	4.02%	0.18%
	Structure	2.54m	2.91m	0.36m	3.06m	6.96m	0.36m
0.2	Motion	0.36%	0.06%	0.28%	0.38%	0.32%	0.17%
	Structure	2.26m	0.13m	0.48m	1.56m	0.54m	0.28m
0.5	Translation	2.61%	0.28%	1.77%	1.51%	2.76%	0.67%
	Motion	1.49m	0.61m	3.02m	2.58m	2.99m	1.14m

Table 4. The optimised motion and structure errors of the Eight scenario

σ	Error	Initial	Euclidean	Homogeneous	Inv. Depth	Parallax	Implicit DLT
0.1	Motion	0.32%	0.09%	0.71%	0.33%	0.71%	0.12%
	Structure	2.28m	0.19m	1.53m	0.61m	1.32m	0.22m
0.2	Motion	0.48%	0.04%	0.97%	0.04%	0.51%	0.23%
	Structure	1.84m	0.15m	1.93m	0.12m	0.96m	0.46m
0.5	Motion	1.67%	0.07%	4.48%	1.88%	1.67%	1.46%
	Structure	1.12m	0.29m	8.99m	3.90m	4.08m	2.94m

Table 5. Accumulated execution time after finishing all scenarios

	Euclidean	Homogeneous	Inverse depth	Parallax	Implicit DLT
Evaluating J_a	16,451s	17,422s	9,566s	17,646s	15,231s
Evaluating J_b	27,623s	36,526s	17,318s	29,960s	0.000s
Solving for x	22.58s	30.19s	13.90s	23.16s	0.88s
Total	44,097s	53,978s	26,898s	47,629s	15,214s
Iterations	118	102	81	120	35
Average per Iteration	373.70s	529.19s	332.06s	396.91s	434.69s

error is higher due to the propagation along long path. It shows that, under a significant noise level of $\sigma = 0.5$ the proposed method still converged to results comparable or better than the Euclidean parameterisation, and outperforms all other methods. In the longest test scenario Eight, the implicit modeling performs best at low noise level $\sigma = 0.1$ over other methods. As the noise level increases the Euclidaen parameterisation converges to the better estimates, and the implicit method still achieves second-best restuls. In all scenarios an accuracy within 1.5% is achieved without explicit adjustment on the scene structure.

Time analysis and convergence speed are depicted in Table 5. Implicit modeling is found to converge faster. The optimal solution is achieved within 3 iterations in average. Because of the convergence speed and the saving of time evaluating the Jacobian of structure parameters, a speed-up by a factor of three is attainable despite the expensive SVD computation.

5 Conclusions

In this paper we reviewed the structure-parameterisation problem in BA. We proposed DLT-based implicit modeling to improve the adjustment, and compared this method with two conventional methods and two novel approaches published elsewhere. The numerical experiments indicate that the proposed method is able to achieve comparative accuracy. The computational cost, however, is greatly reduced due to the absense of explicit adjustments of structure parameters.

A drawback of the DLT method is that the estimated structure minimises algebraic errors, and this optimisation process is geometrical meaningless. A nonlinear optimisation process is required. In future we aim at developing a heuristic technique that is able to automatically switch between different structure parameterisation approaches.

References

1. Triggs, B., McLauchlan, P.F., Hartley, R.I., Fitzgibbon, A.W.: Bundle adjustment – a modern synthesis. In: Triggs, B., Zisserman, A., Szeliski, R. (eds.) ICCV-WS 1999. LNCS, vol. 1883, pp. 298–372. Springer, Heidelberg (2000)
2. Hartley, R.I., Zisserman, A.: Multiple View Geometry in Computer Vision, 2nd edn. Cambridge University Press, Cambridge (2004)
3. Engels, C., Stewenius, H., Nister, D.: Bundle adjustment rules. In: Proc. Photogrammetric Computer Vision (2006)
4. Brown, D.C.: The bundle adjustment - progress and prospects. Int. Archives Photogrammetry 21(3), 3:3–3:35 (1976)
5. Granshaw, S.I.: Bundle adjustment methods in engineering photogrammetry. The Photogrammetric Record 10(56), 181–207 (1980)
6. Bartoli, A., Sturm, P.: Structure-from-motion using lines: Representation, triangulation, and bundle adjustment. Computer Vision Image Understanding 100(3), 416–441 (2005)
7. Zhang, J., Boutin, M., Aliaga, D.G.: Robust bundle adjustment for structure from motion. In: Proc. IEEE Image Processing 2006, pp. 2185–2188 (2006)

8. Snavely, N., Seitz, S.M., Szeliski, R.: Modeling the world from internet photo collections. Int. J. Computer Vision **80**(2), 189–210 (2008)
9. Zhang, Z., Shan, Y.: Incremental motion estimation through local bundle adjustment. Technical Report MSR-TR-01-54, Microsoft (2001)
10. Konolige, K., Agrawal, M.: FrameSLAM: From bundle adjustment to real-time visual mapping. IEEE Trans. Robotics **24**(5), 1066–1077 (2008)
11. Civera, J., Davison, J., Montiel, J.M.: Inverse depth parametrization for monocular SLAM. IEEE Trans. Robotics **24**(5), 932–945 (2008)
12. Sibley, G., Mei, C., Reid, I., Newman, P.: Adaptive relative bundle adjustment. In: Proc. Robotics Science Systems Conf. (2009)
13. Schneider, J., Labe, T., Forstner, W.: Incremental real-time bundle adjustment for multi-camera systems with points at infinity. Int. Arch. Photogramm. Remote Sens. Spatial Inf. Sci. **XL–1/W2**, 355–360 (2013)
14. Zhao, L., Huang, S., Sun, Y., Yan, L.: ParallaxBA: bundle adjustment using parallax angle feature parametrization. In: Proc. Robotics Automation (ICRA) 2011, pp. 3117–3124 (2011)
15. Moore, Z., Wright, D., Schinstock, D.E., Lewis, C.: Comparison of bundle adjustment formulations. In: Proc. ASPRS Annual Conf., Baltimore, Maryland (2009)
16. Lourakis, M.I.A., Argyros, A.A.: SBA: A software package for generic sparse bundle adjustment. ACM Trans. Mathematical Software **36**(1), 2:1–2:30 (2009)
17. Konolige, K.: Sparse bundle adjustment. In: Proc. British Machine Vision Conf. (BMVC), pp. 1–11 (2010)
18. Wu, C., Agarwal, S., Curless, B., Seitz, S.M.: Multicore bundle adjustment. In: Proc. Computer Vision Pattern Recognition (CVPR) 2011, pp. 3057–3064 (2011)
19. Albl, C., Pajdla, T.: Global camera parameterization for bundle adjustment. Technical Report CTU-CMP-2013-17, Czech Technical University Prague (2013)
20. Bartoli, A., Sturm, P.: Three new algorithms for projective bundle adjustment with minumum parameters. Research Report RR-4236, INRIA (2001)
21. Levenberg, K.: A method for the solution of certain non-linear problems in least squares. The Quarterly Applied Math. **2**, 164–168 (1944)
22. Byröd, M., Åström, K.: Conjugate gradient bundle adjustment. In: Daniilidis, K., Maragos, P., Paragios, N. (eds.) ECCV 2010, Part II. LNCS, vol. 6312, pp. 114–127. Springer, Heidelberg (2010)
23. Lourakis, M.I.A., Argyros, A.A.: Is Levenberg-Marquardt the most efficient optimization algorithm for implenting bundle adjustment? In: Proc. ICCV, vol. 2, pp. 1526–1531 (2005)
24. Indelman, V.: Bundle adjustment without iterative structure estimation and its application to navigation. In: Proc. IEEE/ION Position Location Navigation Symp. (PLANS), pp. 748–756 (2012)

Efficient Extraction of Macromolecular Complexes from Electron Tomograms Based on Reduced Representation Templates

Xiao-Ping Xu, Christopher Page, and Niels Volkmann[✉]

Sanford-Burnham Medical Research Institute, La Jolla, CA, USA
{xpxu,cpage,niels}@sbmri.org

Abstract. Electron tomography is the most widely applicable method for obtaining 3D information by electron microscopy. In the field of biology it has been realized that electron tomography is capable of providing a complete, molecular resolution three-dimensional mapping of entire proteoms. However, to realize this goal, information needs to be extracted efficiently from these tomograms. Owing to extremely low signal-to-noise ratios, this task is mostly carried out manually. Standard template matching approaches tend to generate large amounts of false positives. We developed an alternative method for feature extraction in biological electron tomography based on reduced representation templates, approximating the search model by a small number of anchor points used to calculate the scoring function. Using this approach we see a reduction of about 50% false positives with matched-filter approaches to below 5%. At the same time, false negatives stay below 5%, thus essentially matching the performance one would expect from human operators.

Keywords: Electron tomography · Feature extraction · Template matching · Reduced representation · Cellular tomography · Biological systems · Ribosomes · Actin filaments

1 Introduction

Modern biology has now advanced to a stage where structural information about isolated macromolecules and assemblies must be integrated to define higher-order cellular functions. Electron tomography (ET) has become a powerful tool for revealing the molecular architecture of biological cells and tissues [1-5]. The achievable resolution (3-9 nm) is intermediate between that achievable by light microscopy and X-ray crystallography, thus capable of bridging the gap between live-cell imaging and atomic resolution structures. Approaches that can directly visualize cellular organization by defining and analyzing macromolecular arrangements and interactions at high resolution within these tomograms would have a direct and major impact on research efforts in many branches of biology and biomedicine [6-8].

Electron tomography is the most widely applicable method for obtaining 3D information by electron microscopy [1], [4]. In fact, it is the only method suitable for

© Springer International Publishing Switzerland 2015
G. Azzopardi and N. Petkov (Eds.): CAIP 2015, Part I, LNCS 9256, pp. 423–431, 2015.
DOI: 10.1007/978-3-319-23192-1_35

investigating polymorphic structures such as organelles, cells and tissue. Its principle is based on illuminating the sample from many different directions (usually a tilt series around one or two axes) and to reconstruct it from those projection images. While the principles of electron tomography have been known for decades, its use has gathered momentum only in recent years.

Electron tomography provides data that is – at least in principle – capable of connecting between high-resolution structure and function in living cells by high-resolution mapping of the entire proteome of cells and tissues. However, the lack of algorithms for reliable detection and extraction of structural features and the lack of tools for large scale and automated analysis of the extracted data pose severe barriers to progress in the field. As of today, the tasks of extracting and interpreting information from the highly complex, three-dimensional scenes that make up cellular tomograms are, for the most part, painstakingly carried out manually. Apart from the subjectivity of the process, the time consuming (and tiring) nature of this manual task all but precludes the prospects of the high throughput necessary to take full advantage of the method's potential.

For example, it took over 10 months to manually segment and interpret roughly 1% of the volume of a pancreatic beta cell at high fidelity [9]. Extrapolating this to the time it would take to segment just one entire cell at similar detail comes out to be 83 years, and 4 months. Conducting a meaningful study comparing a number of cells under disease conditions with a control set would literally take thousands of man-years. The need for computational tools to efficiently aid the process and automate the structure recognition, extraction, and interpretation process as much as possible is clearly vital for making these types of studies viable.

2   Material and Methods

The quality of cryo-tomographic reconstructions can be correlated with the electron dose. A total dose of 50-300 $e^-/Å^2$ appears to give reasonable results with a "sweet spot" around 120 $e^-/Å^2$ [10]. Because this dose needs to be spread over the whole data set, the dose for each image needs to be kept low enough as to not exceed a total dose of 120 $e^-/Å^2$. For a ±60° double tilt series with a 2° increment, the dose available for a single image is only 1 $e^-/Å^2$, which gives rise to extremely high noise levels in the individual images. The signal in the resulting 3D reconstructions is improved by the dose fractionation effect [11] but the signal-to-noise ratio for these tomograms is still well below 1 (often only 0.01-0.1). Together with complications from missing data and the electron microscope's contrast transfer, this makes noise from many other image-possessing disciplines look like "Girlie Noise" (Stephan Nickell, personal communication). Owing to the immense technical difficulties of cryo-sample sectioning [12], "conventional" electron tomography, which involves staining and plastic embedding, is often preferred in practice for samples that require sectioning [13]. While the signal-to-noise ratio is improved in these samples as compared to cryo-samples, the resulting images and reconstructions still tend to be rather noisy with signal-to-noise ratios usually well below five.

2.1   Challenges

The lack of automatic and/or objective interpretation tools for electron tomograms poses a critical barrier to progress in the field [1, 5, 14]. While there have been substantial efforts during the last few years [15-18] , progress has been much slower than in related fields. One of the prime reasons for this is that image and signal processing methods developed for other domains are not straightforward to apply to electron tomography data owing to its special characteristics:

- As a consequence of the damaging effect of the electron beam, which limits the amount of electrons available for image formation, electron tomograms tend to exhibit very high noise levels.
- The geometry of the electron tomography sample holders and the shape of the electron microscopy chamber do not allow tilting more then ~70° so about a third of data space is not accessible. This generates a "missing wedge" of data, which is best seen in Fourier space as a wedge-shaped segment that contains no information. This problem can be partially alleviated experimentally by taking a second data set after rotating the sample by 90° around the optical axis, yet some of the data space is still not accessible so that some missing data artifacts will always remain.
- The transfer function of the microscope is not well determined, especially for thick specimens where there can be a significant variance in focus. In addition, the tilting introduces a focus gradient, further obstructing the underlying signal.

Although each of these issues would probably not be completely prohibitive by itself, the combination of the three makes devising automatic and objective interpretation tools a very difficult task.

2.2   Related Work

The idea of detecting and mapping macromolecules in cellular tomograms is not new. In 2000, the first feasibility test for detecting macromolecules in tomographic reconstructions using a correlation-based template-matching approach were presented [19]. This test was later expanded by others [20-22] to demonstrate feasibility in experimental settings. This type of template matching consists of using a 'matched filter' which can be shown to be a Bayesian classifier (minimizing the probability of identification errors), as long as the template and the target are nearly identical and the noise is independent and identically distributed, Gaussian, and additive [23]. These conditions are not very well met for electron tomographic reconstructions: the noise is spatially correlated by the reconstruction process and the point spread function; the tails of the noise distribution are often quite heavy, especially in stained samples [24], making the noise distribution distinctly non-Gaussian; and the uncertainty in the magnification, the potential mix of conformations, and/or the presence of stain make it difficult to obtain sufficiently accurate templates. As a consequence, many false hits are generated by this method in areas of high density such as membranes or dense vesicles (see Figure 2A, also reference [21]).

2.3   Reduced Representation Templates

To address these challenges, we are currently developing an alternative method for feature recognition in tissue volumes, which is based on reduced representation templates. Reduced representations approximate the target by a small number of anchor points. These anchor points are then used to calculate the scoring function within the search volume. This strategy makes the approach robust against noise and against local variations such as conformational pleiomorphism. The first step of the procedure consists of the construction of suitable representations that are to be used as templates for pattern matching. This can be either done from reprojections of existing models (if available) or directly from the data. In principle, the direct use of data is preferable to the use of models because this strategy eliminates model bias and avoids possible problems connected to differences in scale or resolution.

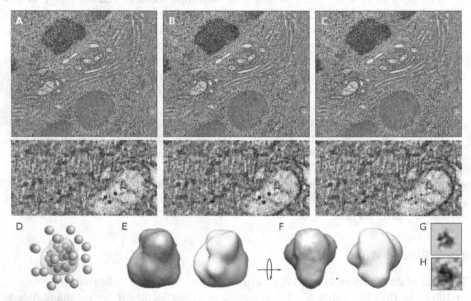

Fig. 1. Feasibility test of our detection algorithm applied to ribosome detection in a tomogram of an embedded and stained beta cell section. Hits were classified manually into true hits (red) false membrane hits (cyan), false hits in dense vesicles (green) and other false hits (blue). **A.** Hits produced using a correlation-based matched filter approach [22] using a low-pass filtered high-resolution single-particle reconstruction [25] as a template (yellow surface in E and F). This approach produces 49.3% false hits. (bottom) Enlarged area. **B.** Hits produced using the reduced representation template shown in D. 18.5% false hits. **C.** Hits after analysis of peak sphericity on the hits in B. Only 3.2% false hits remain. **D.** Reduced representation used for template matching in B. The reduced representation template consists of a sphere of 20 inside anchor points (red) surrounded by a shell of 18 outside anchor points (grey). The template used in A is overlaid as a transparent surface for reference. **E, F.** Two orthogonal views of the ribosome template used in A (yellow) and an average of 256 motifs extracted as in C (grey), calculated according to the procedure laid out in the text. The resolution estimate for the average is 62Å using the 0.5 cutoff of the Fourier shell correlation between the yellow and the gray densities. **G.** Slice through the template density used for the test in A. **H.** Slice through one of the extracted ribosomes in a similar orientation.

Macromolecules: The simplest possible representation of a density distribution is a set of points that describe the position of bright and dark spots within the motif. More complex representations that involve ranking of points with varying gray-scale can also be constructed. The speed of calculating a particular scoring function in real-space depends on the number of contributing anchor points. The fewer anchor points are used in the calculation, the faster the calculation will be finished. In addition, the idealization of the density pattern to a collection of bright and dark spots tends to be more robust than a fully detailed template in respect to minor distortions due to noise.

With the reduced representation concept, arbitrary real-space scoring functions can be used without loss of generality while still taking advantage of the corresponding speed gain. In practice, a simple expression of the form

$$score = max_{angle} \left[\Sigma(D(p_{outside}) - D(p_{inside})) \right], \tag{1}$$

where $D(p)$ denotes density sampled at anchor point p, achieves high quality results at maximum speed. Here, the sum is calculated for each Euler angle of the template the maximum is taken as the final score. *Score* will be high if at some angle all anchor points assigned 'inside' in the reduced template have relatively high intensities and – simultaneously – if all points assigned 'outside' have relatively low intensities.

Filaments: Reduced representation templates can capture arbitrary shapes. However, for the construction of reduced representation templates for filaments within cells, we can take full advantage of the filament symmetry. In fact, our tests indicate that a simple, rotationally symmetrical rod-like template works equally well as templates coding filament symmetry more accurately. The use of a rotationally symmetric template speeds up the search considerably: the template does not need to be rotated along the long axis, and only half of the search space needs to be explored because the template is also two-fold symmetrical perpendicular to its long axis. Another important consideration for filament detection is the length of the template. Optimal response will be at a length that is not too long to miss shorter segments or filament bents, and not too short to be unreasonably affected by noise in the tomogram.

2.4   Score Map Analysis

The second step of our detection approach is an analysis of the peak properties. The rationale behind this idea is that, for isolated macromolecules, a true hit should give a scoring-function peak that is compact and spherical around the correct position. For the 2D case, a step that tests for the sharpness of the peaks significantly enhances performance [26]. For the proof-of-concept 3D studies presented here, we implemented a test for the sphericity *Sph* of the peak. Here, sphericity is defined as

$$sph = (\pi^{1/3} 6V_{0.5}^{2/3})/S_{0.5}, \tag{2}$$

where $V_{0.5}$ is the peak volume at half maximum and $S_{0.5}$ is the surface area at the same cutoff.

For filaments, sphericity is not a useful criterion. Instead, we use a modified scoring function that penalizes high variance along the long axis of the reduced representation template, thus enhancing the signal when brightness is approximately the same along the filament axis. As an additional criterion we use directional coherence. Here the angle that gives the highest sum is recorded for each pixel in the density map and then compared to the angles giving the highest sum for pixels that lie along the direction of the first angle so that

$$ang = \Sigma(cos\,(\varphi_0 - \varphi_i)), \tag{3}$$

with φ_i denoting the angle at the pixel i along the axis defined by φ_0 at the central pixel.

Once filaments are detected, the score map need to be converted into parametric filament traces for further analysis. The traditional approach to achieve this task is skeletonization. However, the high noise level and the distortions due to the missing wedge in the tomograms make this approach ill-suited for extracting filament traces from score maps originating from electron tomograms.

We implemented an alternative approach that combines hierarchical watershed segmentation of the score map with classification of the segments based on the eigenvalues of the inertia tensor to identify filament-like segments. Briefly, a modified watershed transform specifically developed for electron microscopy data [27] is run directly on the score map using a conservative step size that allows separation of neighboring filament traces as well as branching filaments at the expense of slight over segmentation. The eigenvalues of the inertia tensor are then calculated for each segment. At this stage, false hits such as sheets (membranes) or star-like structures (highly intense compact contaminations) can be eliminated based on the ratios of the eigenvalues. Next, the centers of mass of slices perpendicular to the longest principal axis are determined for each segment to provide the corresponding traces. Traces are linked according to an analysis of the density between them and the directionality of the traces. This approach is significantly more robust in the presence of noise and gives much better defined traces than skeletonization approaches (Figure 2).

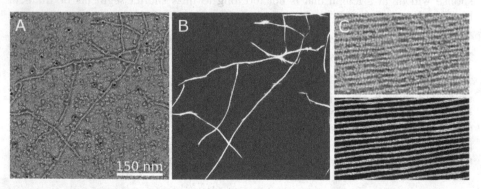

Fig. 2. Actin filament detection using reduced representation templates **A.** Slice through a tomogram of reconstituted Arp2/3 mediated actin networks [28] **B.** Filament detection performance (score map) using reduced representation templates as outlined in the text. Note the lack of interference from the heavy background. **C.** Filament detection in actin arrays cross-linked by vinculin [29]. Original data (top), and score map with overlaid filament traces (in red) are shown. Despite of the heavy cross-linking, the traces are extracted with high accuracy.

3 Results and Discussion

The reduced-representation template strategy presented here provides an approach robust against noise and against local variations such as those expected from thickness variations common in 3D biological tomograms. We recently completed two proof-of-concept applications of this algorithm (i) for detecting ribosomes in electron tomograms of high-pressure-frozen plastic embedded mammalian cell sections (Figure 1) and (ii) to trace actin filaments in reconstituted systems (Figure 2).

A study comparing performance of various algorithms for picking particles from two-dimensional cryo-micrographs showed that a 2D version of the reduced template matching approach [26] yields comparable or better results than methods using matched filters even if near-correct templates can be constructed for the matched filters [30]. Results for the implementation of a 3D version described here, using hand-annotated data, show very encouraging results for the detection of macromolecular assemblies (Figure 1) as well as for the extraction of filament traces (Figure 2).

The test for macromolecule detection was done using a hand-annotated tomogram of an embedded and stained beta cell section. Ribosomes were manually picked to provide a 'gold standard' for assignment of false positives and false negatives when using computational procedures for ribosome detection. Hits produced using a correlation-based matched filter approach [22] using a low-pass filtered high-resolution single-particle reconstruction [25] as a template produces 49.3% false positives. Application of the reduced-representation template approach produced 18.5% false positives. The reduced representation used consists of a sphere of 20 inside anchor points surrounded by a shell of 18 outside anchor points. The fact that the template is spherically symmetric, allowed a further speed-up of the calculation, which can be done within a fraction of the time required for the matched filter approach. After analysis of peak sphericity and filtering accordingly. only 3.2% of the original 18.5% false positives remain. With a percentage for missed targets of 2.6%, this is essentially the type of performance one would expect from human operators.

As an independent test of whether the extracted motifs correspond to ribosomes and not arbitrary blobs of density, we mutually aligned and averaged the extracted motifs and compared the average with the known high-resolution structure of the ribosome [25]. The analysis shows that the average and the known ribosome structure are indistinguishable at a resolution of about 6.5 nm, which is about the resolution expected for tomograms of embedded, stained sections, thus providing a strong indication that the extracted motifs are indeed ribosomes.

For testing filament detection performance, we used two sets of hand-annotated tomograms. The first consisted of tomograms of reconstituted Arp2/3 complex mediated actin networks [28], similar to those encountered at the leading edge of motile cells [31]. This is a very good test case because of the high background of particles (unbound Arp2/3 complexes), which allows testing performance in the presence of particles that potentially throw off the detection. Furthermore, Arp2/3 induces branch junctions that may also degrade performance. The second set consisted of tomograms of actin arrays cross-linked by vinculin [29], mimicking dense actin bundles similar to those encountered in stress fibers and other actin-based structures in the cell. In both cases, the performance of the detector reaches a false positive rate below 5% with the false negative rate staying below 5%, again essentially matching the performance expected for human expert operators.

4   Conclusions

Automatic feature detection for macromolecules in biological 3D tomographic data is an important and unsolved problem. This paper introduces a new approach based on the use of reduced representations and analysis of the resulting score map. The percentage of false positive for the proof-of-concept data presented here drops dramatically from about 50% to under 5% if compared to the matched filter approach.

Acknowledgments. This work was supported by National Institutes of Health grants P01 GM098412 to NV.

References

1. Frey, T.G., Perkins, G.A., Ellisman, M.H.: Electron Tomography of Membrane-Bound Cellular Organelles. Annu. Rev. Biophys. Biomol. Struct. **35**, 199–224 (2006)
2. Subramaniam, S.: Bridging the imaging gap: visualizing subcellular architecture with electron tomography. Curr. Opin. Microbiol. **8**, 316–322 (2005)
3. McIntosh, R., Nicastro, D., Mastronarde, D.: New views of cells in 3D: an introduction to electron tomography. Trends. Cell. Biol. **15**, 43–51 (2005)
4. Lucic, V., Yang, T., Schweikert, G., Forster, F., Baumeister, W.: Morphological characterization of molecular complexes present in the synaptic cleft. Structure **13**, 423–434 (2005)
5. Leis, A.P., Beck, M., Gruska, M., Best, C., Hegerl, R., Baumeister, W., Leis, J.W.: Cryoelectron tomography of biological specimens. IEEE Signal. Proc. Mag. **23**, 95–103 (2006)
6. Sali, A., Glaeser, R., Earnest, T., Baumeister, W.: From words to literature in structural proteomics. Nature **422**, 216–225 (2003)
7. Nickell, S., Kofler, C., Leis, A.P., Baumeister, W.: A visual approach to proteomics. Nat. Rev. Mol. Cell. Biol. **7**, 225–230 (2006)
8. Baumeister, W.: From proteomic inventory to architecture. FEBS Lett. **579**, 933–937 (2005)
9. Marsh, B.J., Mastronarde, D.N., Buttle, K.F., Howell, K.E., McIntosh, J.R.: Organellar relationships in the Golgi region of the pancreatic beta cell line, HIT-T15, visualized by high resolution electron tomography. Proc. Natl. Acad. Sci. USA **98**, 2399–2406 (2001)
10. Iancu, C.V., Wright, E.R., Heymann, J.B., Jensen, G.J.: A comparison of liquid nitrogen and liquid helium as cryogens for electron cryotomography. J. Struct. Biol. **153**, 231–240 (2006)
11. McEwen, B.F., Downing, K.H., Glaeser, R.M.: The relevance of dose-fractionation in tomography of radiation-sensitive specimens. Ultramicroscopy **60**, 357–373 (1995)
12. Al-Amoudi, A., Norlen, L.P., Dubochet, J.: Cryo-electron microscopy of vitreous sections of native biological cells and tissues. J. Struct. Biol. **148**, 131–135 (2004)
13. McEwen, B.F., Marko, M.: The emergence of electron tomography as an important tool for investigating cellular ultrastructure. J. Histochem. Cytochem. **49**, 553–564 (2001)

14. Marsh, B.J.: Lessons from tomographic studies of the mammalian Golgi. Biochim. Biophys. Acta. **1744**, 273–292 (2005)
15. Frangakis, A.S., Förster, F.: Computational exploration of structural information from cryo-electron tomograms. Curr. Opin. Struct. Biol. **14**, 325–331 (2004)
16. Sandberg, K., Brega, M.: Segmentation of thin structures in electron micrographs using orientation fields. J. Struct. Biol. **157**, 403–415 (2007)
17. Volkmann, N.: Methods for segmentation and interpretation of electron tomographic reconstructions. Methods. Enzymol. **483**, 31–46 (2010)
18. Volkmann, N.: Putting structure into context: fitting of atomic models into electron microscopic and electron tomographic reconstructions. Curr. Opin. Cell. Biol. **24**, 141–147 (2012)
19. Böhm, J., Frangakis, A.S., Hegerl, R., Nickell, S., Typke, D., Baumeister, W.: From the cover: toward detecting and identifying macromolecules in a cellular context: template matching applied to electron tomograms. Proc. Natl. Acad. Sci. USA **97**, 14245–14250 (2000)
20. Frangakis, A.S., Hegerl, R.: Segmentation of two- and three-dimensional data from electron microscopy using eigenvector analysis. J. Struct. Biol. **138**, 105–113 (2002)
21. Ortiz, J.O., Forster, F., Kurner, J., Linaroudis, A.A., Baumeister, W.: Mapping 70S ribosomes in intact cells by cryoelectron tomography and pattern recognition. J. Struct. Biol. **156**, 334–341 (2006)
22. Rath, B.K., Hegerl, R., Leith, A., Shaikh, T.R., Wagenknecht, T., Frank, J.: Fast 3D motif search of EM density maps using a locally normalized cross-correlation function. J. Struct. Biol. **144**, 95–103 (2003)
23. Sigworth, F.J.: Classical detection theory and the cryo-EM particle selection problem. J. Struct. Biol. **145**, 111–122 (2004)
24. van der Heide, P., Xu, X.P., Marsh, B.J., Hanein, D., Volkmann, N.: Efficient automatic noise reduction of electron tomographic reconstructions based on iterative median filtering. J. Struct. Biol. **158**, 196–204 (2007)
25. Spahn, C.M., Jan, E., Mulder, A., Grassucci, R.A., Sarnow, P., Frank, J.: Cryo-EM visualization of a viral internal ribosome entry site bound to human ribosomes: the IRES functions as an RNA-based translation factor. Cell **118**, 465–475 (2004)
26. Volkmann, N.: An approach to automated particle picking from electron micrographs based on reduced representation templates. J. Struct. Biol. **145**, 152–156 (2004)
27. Volkmann, N.: A novel three-dimensional variant of the watershed transform for segmentation of electron density maps. J. Struct. Biol. **138**, 123–129 (2002)
28. Rouiller, I., Xu, X.P., Amann, K.J., Egile, C., Nickell, S., Nicastro, D., Li, R., Pollard, T.D., Volkmann, N., Hanein, D.: The structural basis of actin filament branching by Arp2/3 complex. J. Cell. Biol. **180**, 887–895 (2008)
29. Janssen, M.E., Kim, E., Liu, H., Fujimoto, L.M., Bobkov, A., Volkmann, N., Hanein, D.: Three-dimensional structure of vinculin bound to actin filaments. Mol. Cell **21**, 271–281 (2006)
30. Zhu, Y., Carragher, B., Glaeser, R.M., Fellmann, D., Bajaj, C., Bern, M., Mouche, F., de Haas, F., Hall, R.J., Kriegman, D.J., Ludtke, S.J., Mallick, S.P., Penczek, P.A., Roseman, A.M., Sigworth, F.J., Volkmann, N., Potter, C.S.: Automatic particle selection: results of a comparative study. J. Struct. Biol. **145**, 3–14 (2004)
31. Pollard, T.D., Borisy, G.G.: Cellular motility driven by assembly and disassembly of actin filaments. Cell **112**, 453–465 (2003)

Gradients and Active Contour Models for Localization of Cell Membrane in HER2/neu Images

Marek Wdowiak[1(✉)], Tomasz Markiewicz[1,2], Stanislaw Osowski[1,3],
Janusz Patera[2], and Wojciech Kozlowski[2]

[1] Warsaw University of Technology, 1 Politechniki Sq., 00-661 Warsaw, Poland
{wdowiakm,markiewt,sto}@iem.pw.edu.pl
[2] Military Institute of Medicine, 128 Szaserow Str., 04-141 Warsaw, Poland
{jpatera,wkozlowski}@wim.mil.pl
[3] Military University of Technology,
2 Gen. S. Kaliskiego Str., 00-908 Warsaw, Poland

Abstract. The paper presents an application of the snake model to recognition of the cell membrane in the HER2 breast and kidney cancer images. It applies the modified snake to build the system recognizing the membrane and associating it with the neighboring cell. We study different forms of gradient estimation, the core point in the snake model. The particle swarm optimization algorithm is used in tuning the parameters of the snake model. On the basis of the applied procedure the estimation of the membrane continuity of cell is made. The experimental results performed on 100 cells in breast and 100 cells in kidney cancers have shown high accuracy of the membrane localizations and acceptable agreement with the expert estimations.

Keywords: Image segmentation · Object recognition · HER2/neu · Snake

1 Introduction

Recognition of the whole cells on the basis of the staining localized in the membrane is a complex task, which requires not only segmentation of the specified parts of cell, but also assigning them to the individual cells. An example of such task is in image analysis of the breast cancer created using histopathology Human Epidermal Growth Factor Receptor 2 (HER2/neu). The histopathological evaluation of a set of immunohistochemical stains is the most common task for pathologists.

The HER2/neu biomarker is recognized as a diagnostic, prognostic and predictive factor mainly in the case of breast cancer [9], but recently also discussed in kidney cancer [6]. It is indicated as an aid in assessment of breast cancer for patients for whom trastuzumab treatment is being considered. Overexpressions

© Springer International Publishing Switzerland 2015
G. Azzopardi and N. Petkov (Eds.): CAIP 2015, Part I, LNCS 9256, pp. 432–444, 2015.
DOI: 10.1007/978-3-319-23192-1_36

of HER2 protein connected with the HER2 gene amplification are diagnosed in approximately 20% of the analyzed breast cancer cases. For such patients, the trastuzumab treatment is recommended. Otherwise, HER2 is frequently expressed in normal renal tissues but rarely expressed in renal cell carcinoma (RCC) tissues [6]. Furthermore, the HER2 status of normal tissue is negatively correlated with that of the RCC tissues and the TNM stages, suggesting that HER2 is involved in RCC oncogenesis. Thus, an appropriate and reliable evaluation of HER2 status is necessary.

The HER2/neu stain is regarded as a basic step in pathomorphological evaluation of the breast cancer. This semiquantitative examination, performed on the immunostained paraffin section needs determining the presence, intensity, and continuity of membrane staining in the tumor cells. Four categories in grade scale are recognized: 0 (no membrane staining is observed or membrane staining is observed in less than 10% of the tumor cells), 1+ (a barely perceptible membrane staining is detected in more than 10% of tumor cells, the cells exhibit incomplete membrane staining), 2+ (a weak to moderate complete membrane staining observed in more than 10% of tumor cells), and 3+ (a strong complete membrane staining observed in more than 10% of tumor cells). The case 0 or 1+ indicates no HER2 gene amplification. On the other side grade 3+ indicates immediate HER2 gene amplification. The case 2+ needs additional examination using the fluorescence in situ hybridization (FISH) [9]. However, in kidney cancer there are still not clear guidelines as to how to assess HER2 status. Nevertheless, the main aspect of presented methodology is localizing and assigning the immunoreactive membrane to the individual cell. Whereas a lot of algorithms for the nuclear reactions have been developed [3,7,8], the HER2/neu membrane reaction is still treated manually or in a very rough way, not taking into account the separate cells.

In the last years some new approaches to solve this problem have been proposed. To such methods belong the application of the realtime quantitative polymerase chain reaction (PCR) using LightCycler [10], application of support vector machine [4], or fuzzy decision tree by using Mamdani and Takagi-Sugeno inference rules [13]. In spite of existing methods the new approaches are needed, because of the problems with high variability of a membrane reaction and its frequent overlapping with a cytoplasm. Such methods should deal with these difficult image analysis tasks in a more efficient way, providing higher agreement with an expert assessment.

In this paper we propose solving the problem of recognizing and assigning the membrane to the particular cell on the basis of the active contour models, called snakes, using different gradient estimations as the input attributes. We investigate the locally adaptive gradient, depending on a special relation between the cell nucleus and membrane. Our propositions are checked in the numerical experiments concerning two studied cases: the breast cancer and kidney cancer.

2   Problem Statement

An automatic evaluation of the HER2/neu membrane staining aims at the recognition of tumor cell nuclei and area of positive membrane reaction. It should specify which parts of the recognized membrane come from the specific cells and finally graduate the reaction from 0 to 3+ scale. Each of these steps requires different algorithms based on various criteria. The cell nuclei detection can be performed as a task of segmentation of the blue, rounded and generally non-touching objects. The solution of this problem was proposed by us in [15].

The main problem is a weak staining of the nuclei by the blue hematoxyline. The additional problem is their partial overlapping with the brown chromogenic substrate. The important task in this evaluation is recognition of areas with a positive membrane reaction, especially when the brown chromogenic substrate is located not only in the cell membranes, but also partially in the cell cytoplasm. In such case there is an identification problem of the appropriate membrane sections located inside the brown marked regions. Although this problem was solved by us in [15] using the hourglass shape structuring element combined with watershed algorithm there is still the problem of association of the discovered membrane segments with the proper cell, especially when the segment is touching few cells. In this paper we will solve this problem by applying the snake model of membrane [16]. On the basis of the snake results we are able to assign the membrane to the proper cell and then parametrize the localized membrane. The most important is the estimation of the continuity of the cell membrane. The continuity is defined here as the ratio of the summed lengths of membrane segments to the total length of membrane defined by the snake model.

A set of typical HER2/neu images with various grades of HER2 status are presented in Fig 1. As we can see the membrane reaction can vary from lower or higher intensity located only in a separated cell (a thin line) to a very high

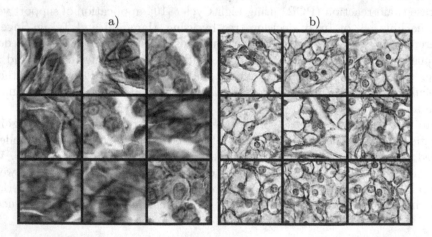

Fig. 1. The exemplary collection of cell images of breast cancer (a) and kidney cancer (b) with differences in membrane stain continuity.

intensity of the membrane location surrounded by the slightly colored cytoplasm of few touching cells. The aim of the presented study is to design method that will be able to identify any membrane positive reaction, irrespective of their intensity, different localization and character of the brown chromogenic substrate.

3   Material and Methods

The materials used in experiments come from the archive of the Pathomorphology Department in the Military Institute of Medicine in Warsaw, Poland. 125 cells of the breast and kidney cancers represented by HER2/neu preparations without any artefacts representing 1+, 2+, and 3+ grades were selected. In the case of breast cancer the analyzed data were represented by 27 cells of grade 1+, 46 cells of 2+ and 52 grades of grade 3+. The kidney cancer data were represented by 26 cells of grade 1+, 45 cells of 2+ and 54 grades of grade 3+. The paraffin embedded tissues were stained in a standard way according to the Ventana PATHWAY anti-HER-2/neu (4B5) Rabbit Monoclonal Primary Antibody protocol [1]. The specimen images were registered on the Olympus BX-61 microscope with the DP-72 colour camera under the magnification 400x and resolution 1024x768 pixels. Cells was divided in to sets: testing set with 100 cells and learning sets with 25 cells.

The quantitative analysis of the specimen needs the following steps of image processing: a) recognition of the tumor cell nuclei, b) segmentation of the immunereactive cell membranes, c) the assignment of the membrane segments to the individual cell. While the first two steps can be implemented using the set of advanced mathematical morphology transformations [11,12], the last one is very complicated due to frequent discontinuities in the membrane reaction, high variability of the cell shapes and different localizations of the cell nuclei. The classical watershed method for the individual cell separation is insufficient, as we demonstrate later.

To solve the problem, we propose to apply the snake active contour method, starting from each nucleus outline. We proceed from the nucleus to the cell contour, which is recognized on the basis of the immunoreactive membrane segments. To implement this procedure we have to select or create the most useful input image map on the basis of which we can build the gradient image, and select the most adequate parameters in the snake adaptation process. The recognized snake will represent the membrane associated with the particular cell. In the next parts of this section we introduce and compare two types of input image maps, four types of gradient and Particle Swarm Optimization method [5] for an efficient snakes parameters selection.

3.1   Input Image Map

The input map representation of the original image is crucial for a convergence of any method to an expected solution. Such map should contain the most important information about direction and distance of any pixel in the area under interest to the cell membrane. Common approach includes the selection of color components, which allow to differentiate such area in the best way. The image map formed on the basis of these colors is subject to further analysis.

We have taken into account the following color representations: RGB, CMYK, HSV, YCbCr, CIE Lab, CIE Lch, CIE uvL, CIE XYZ [2]. The ability of different pixel intensity representations to recognize the cell membranes was evaluated comparing the area (AUC) under Receiver Operating Characteristics (ROC) curve [14]. After evaluating the ability of various color space components to differentiate the immunoreactive cell membrane from nonreactive components we found that B channel (inverted) from RBG and Y channel from CMYK representation are the most useful. The input intensity map used in further analysis is created as an element-wise product of these two components.

The alternative image map can be created based on local properties of the image. Analyzing many images we have noticed that local entropy of the image reflects very well the direction and distance of any pixel to the immunoreactive membrane. These areas of the membrane regions are characterized by a higher entropy than the other tissue regions. Based on this observation we have calculated the local entropy for each pixel of the image in the neighborhood size of 5×5 pixels. It was calculated for the product of B channel (inverted) of RBG representation and Y channel of CMYK. In medical practice the images are often blurred to same degree, so the blurred image map will be also investigated in our numerical experiments.

3.2   Types of Gradient

Based on the input map, the discrete gradient arrays have to be calculated in horizontal and vertical directions to implement effectively the snake active contour algorithm [16]. In this paper we study and compare four cases: 1) directional gradient, 2) gradient vector flow (GVF) [16], 3) directional gradient radially oriented to nuclei, and 4) GVF radially oriented to nuclei. The last two modifications of gradient are proposed by us and combined with an isotropic repulsion of the contour from the nuclei in direction to the immunoreactive cell membrane.

Horizontal and Vertical Directional Gradient. The directional gradient of the gray scale image I for any pixel is calculated in both directions (horizontal and vertical) and is defined as a difference between the intensity values of the neighboring pixels in both directions, respectively. If the horizontal and vertical positions of pixel are indexed by i and j, respectively, the directional gradient values are defined by

$$\rho_x(i,j) = (I_{i,j+1} - I_{i,j-1})/2,$$
$$\rho_y(i,j) = (I_{i+1,j} - I_{i-1,j})/2 \tag{1}$$

They are compatible with the definition of the central finite difference. Their practical implementation is done using the dilation and erosion of the image by a structuring element in the form of a horizontal or vertical line segment L. In this way

$$\rho_\alpha(i,j) = (\delta_{L_\alpha} - \epsilon_{L_\alpha})/2 \tag{2}$$

where the symbols δ and ϵ represent the dilation and erosion [12], respectively, and α denotes the horizontal or vertical direction. Although different spacing of the bordering pixels can be used in selection of the length L, the value one was applied in experiments.

Gradient Vector Flow. The modulus of the directional gradient in image processing is highly dependent on the distance of pixel to the immunoreactive cell membrane. However, the input image map has nonzero elements mainly in the regions of the immunoreaction, because the cytoplasms area is almost deprived of stain. This leads to the gradient map values close to zero. Additionally, some deformations of cells in the form of boundary concavities are also observed, especially when the initial location of the nucleus in the kidney cancer cells is far from the center. This fact reduces significantly the convergence of the active contour to the cell membrane, leading in some cases to the wrong results.

For this reason, the gradient vector flow (GVF) proposed by [16], was taken into account in our investigations. The main advantages of the GVF are its insensitivity to initialization and ability of process to move into the concave boundary regions. The GVF offers higher convergence of the snake model due to better orientation of the gradient vectors with respect to edges and also larger area of attraction. Denoting by $\rho_x(i,j)$ and $\rho_y(i,j)$ the directional gradients of edge map in the point (i,j) of the image, $u_{i,j}^n$ and $v_{i,j}^n$ the GVF components of this point in nth iteration, the iterative solution of GVF can be written in the form of difference equations [16]:

$$\begin{aligned}
u_{i,j}^{n+1} &= u_{i,j}^n + \Delta t[\mu\nabla^2 u_{i,j}^n - (\rho_x^2(i,j) + \rho_y^2(i,j))(u_{i,j}^n - \rho_x(i,j))], \\
v_{i,j}^{n+1} &= v_{i,j}^n + \Delta t[\mu\nabla^2 v_{i,j}^n - (\rho_x^2(i,j) + \rho_y^2(i,j))(v_{i,j}^n - \rho_y(i,j))]
\end{aligned} \tag{3}$$

In these expressions ∇^2 is the Laplacian operator and μ a regularization parameter. After some iterations this process leads to the proper values of GVF components.

Gradient Radially Oriented to Nuclei. The direction of the mentioned above gradient formulas is related to the local maxima of the snake model. Unfortunately, the experiments have shown, that in not all cases such direction is able to find the cell membrane. The cell nuclei in kidney cancer are frequently located in an acentric position. In this case gradient points to nearest edge, all points belonging to initial contour are attracted to that edge and this leads to the wrong results of localisation of the membrane segments(only one edge detected). To solve this problem we propose here the radially oriented gradient direction, which takes into account the pixel orientation toward cell nucleus. The horizontal $\rho_{R,X}$ and vertical $\rho_{R,Y}$ components of radially oriented gradient vector for the pixel in the position (i, j) are described as follows

$$\rho_{R,X} = \sqrt{\rho_X^2 + \rho_Y^2} \cdot cos[\phi_{i_0,j_0}(i,j)],$$
$$\rho_{R,Y} = \sqrt{\rho_X^2 + \rho_Y^2} \cdot sin[\phi_{i_0,j_0}(i,j)], \qquad (4)$$

The symbol "·" denotes the point-wise multiplication of two images, $\phi_{i_0,j_0}(i,j)$ the angle direction between the pixel position (i, j) and the central point (i_0, j_0) of the nucleus. In these expressions the orientation of the vector ρ toward the nucleus of the cell is important. The same modification of the gradient direction can be applied to the GVF.

After applying this approach to either classical directional gradient or GVF we achieve two important features of the algorithm: enhancement of the information of the gradient in the edge map and the direction of the gradient oriented radially to the nuclei.

Parametric Snake Model. Snakes, or active contours, are curves defined within an image that can move under the influence of internal forces within the curve itself and external forces derived from the image data [16]. The internal and external forces are defined so that the snake will conform the desired object boundary

The internal forces coming from within the curve itself control its tension and rigidity, whereas the external forces make it fit to objects. The snake curve represented in the form of vector $\mathbf{x}(s) = [x(s), y(s)]$ for the parameter $s \in [0, 1]$ is created by minimizing the energy functional in the spatial domain of an image

$$minE = \int_0^1 \frac{1}{2}[\alpha |\mathbf{x}'(s)|^2] + E_{ext}(\mathbf{x}(s))ds \qquad (5)$$

where α and β are weighting parameters that control the snakes tension and rigidity, respectively. The first and second derivatives of snake are defined with respect to the parameter s. The external energy function E_{ext} (associated sometimes with the GVF) is taken from the input image map. In the latter case we use directly any representation of gradient map introduced above.

Particle Swarm Optimization. The proposed model of snakes requires selecting the set of seven parameters. They include a and from equation (5), the viscosity parameter, the weights of internal and external energy in the functional, and parameters corresponded with initial contours(circle) such as the radius and distance between the subsequent points that form the snakes curve [16]. Finding best solution in seven dimension space is complex task, thus optimization process is necessary. We have solved this optimization problem using the Particle Swarm Optimization (PSO) method.

PSO, originally attributed to Kennedy, Eberhart and Shi [5] and inspired by social behavior of bird flocking or fish schooling, is a computational method of optimization which applies the population (called a swarm) of candidate solutions (called particles). The particles keep track of their coordinates and also the coordinates of the entire swarm in the space. The movements of particles are guided by their own best known position in the searchspace, taking into account the entire swarm's best known position. The particle swarm optimizer tracks the best value of the objective function, obtained so far by any particle in the neighborhood of it. When better positions are being discovered they will guide the movements of the entire swarm. The process is repeated and a satisfactory solution will eventually be discovered, although there is no guarantee of finding the global optimal solution.

PSO shares many similarities with evolutionary computation techniques. The system uses a population of random solutions and searches for optima by updating generations. However, unlike evolutionary algorithms, PSO has no evolution operators such as crossover and mutation. In PSO, the particles fly through the problem space by following the current optimum particles. The advantages of PSO over evolutionary algorithm are that PSO is easier to implement and there are only few parameters to adjust. Similarly to evolutionary algorithms PSO does not require that the optimization problem be differentiable, as is required by classic optimization methods such as gradient descent or quasi-Newton methods. PSO can therefore be applicable to optimization problems that are partially irregular, noisy, change over time, etc.

Final Membrane Localization System. The complete scheme of the final membrane localization system applied by us is presented in Fig. 2. It is composed of two main parts: 1) recognition of membrane using the snake and identification of membrane parts by applying segmentation of the high intensity immunoreactive areas and 2) localization of the nucleus in the cell. Both streams are cooperating together in assigning the recognized membrane to the particular cell and assessing the continuity of the membrane. This work is concerned mainly with the first task of application of snake to the membrane localization and association with the proper cell.

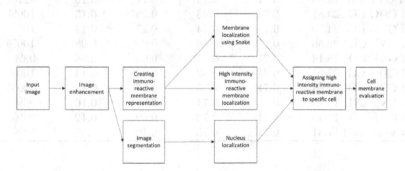

Fig. 2. The general scheme of image processing leading to the evaluation of the membrane parameters

4   Results

Aim of our work was to creating algorithm that estimates membrane continuity in the same way as an expert. To verify our approach the numerical experiments have been performed on two sets of data. The first one referred to the breast cancer and the second to the kidney cancer. Both cases required similar operations, described in the previous sections. The experiments have been performed using 100(testing set) cells representing the breast and kidney sets. The results will be presented in the numerical and graphical forms. We compare the statistical results of our automatic system (AS) to the results of an expert. The main points of comparison are the estimation of continuity of the identified membrane by AS and by an expert and also the Hausdorff distance. The Hausdorff distance represents the longest of all the distances from a point in one set to the closest point in the other set.

Table 1. The numerical results of membrane continuity estimation in breast cancer made by an expert and the automatic system

Algorithm	Hausdorf distance	Membrane continuity Expert	Membrane continuity AS	Absolute difference	Standard deviation	Accuracy of assigning membrane to a cell
CM pl CDG CG	20.90	0.71	0.59	0.14	0.11	100%
CM pl CDG RO	20.63	0.71	0.59	0.13	0.11	100%
CM pl GVF CG	22.64	0.71	0.72	0.09	0.11	97%
CM pl GVF RO	17.95	0.71	0.70	0.08	0.09	98%
CM bl CDG CG	22.26	0.71	0.61	0.13	0.12	100%
CM bl CDG RO	21.85	0.71	0.59	0.14	0.11	100%
CM bl GVF CG	22.00	0.71	0.73	0.10	0.10	98%
CM bl GVF RO	19.85	0.71	0.74	0.11	0.16	92%
EN pl CDG CG	23.81	0.71	0.43	0.28	0.15	100%
EN pl CDG RO	24.60	0.71	0.44	0.27	0.14	100%
EN pl GVF CG	22.56	0.71	0.68	0.09	0.08	100%
EN pl GVF RO	18.14	0.71	0.71	0.08	0.08	98%
EN bl CDG CG	23.21	0.71	0.52	0.20	0.14	100%
EN bl CDG RO	22.93	0.71	0.55	0.17	0.14	100%
EN bl GVF CG	19.10	0.71	0.74	0.09	0.10	96%
EN bl GVF RO	18.48	0.71	0.73	0.09	0.12	98%
Direct watershed	17.31	0.71	0.73	0.10	0.07	64%

Table 1 depicts the numerical results of experiments concerning breast cancer. They are given in the form of mean values of Hausdorff distance measure (in pixels) and membrane continuity, estimated for the set of 100 breast cancer cells at application of different versions of the algorithms. The Hausdorff distance depicts the highest distance between the membrane discovered by snake and membrane segments recognized by application of the hourglass shape structuring element combined with watershed algorithm, presented in [15]. The continuity is defined as the ratio of the summed lengths of discovered membrane segments to the total length of membrane estimated by the snake model. The next two columns of the table represent the means per cell and standard deviations regarding the absolute differences between the estimations of the membrane continuity made by AS and by an expert. The last column depicts the statistical accuracy of assigning the membrane to the proper corresponding cell. The first 8 rows present the results of direct application of color map (CM) and the last 8 the entropy (EN) approach. The last row of the table represents the direct application of watershed algorithm. We compare the efficiency of different forms of gradient generation (classical directional gradient - CDG and GVF). The radially oriented gradient estimation is denoted in the table by (RO) and the classical form of directional gradient is denoted by (CG). The results refer to the plain images (pl) and to the blurred ones (bl). The best accuracy has been obtained for an entropy map at application of radially oriented GVF gradient estimation. In this case we got full agreement of the mean value of the membrane continuity estimated by our automatic system and by an expert, at very small value of standard deviation. Direct watershed algorithm was only slightly worse than snake but only 64% were assigned.

Table 2. The numerical results of membrane continuity estimation in kidney cancer made by an expert and the automatic system

Algorithm	Hausdorf distance	Membrane continuity Expert	Membrane continuity AS	Absolute difference	Standard deviation	Accuracy of assigning membrane to a cell
CM pl CDG CG	19.34	0.70	0.56	0.16	0.13	100%
CM pl CDG RO	19.10	0.70	0.58	0.15	0.10	100%
CM pl GVF CG	22.63	0.70	0.62	0.13	0.10	99%
CM pl GVF RO	31.68	0.70	0.56	0.17	0.12	72%
CM bl CDG CG	19.56	0.70	0.53	0.19	0.13	100%
CM bl CDG RO	16.63	0.70	0.61	0.12	0.09	100%
CM bl GVF CG	19.91	0.70	0.65	0.11	0.09	99%
CM bl GVF RO	19.88	0.70	0.67	0.08	0.07	98%
EN pl CDG CG	16.90	0.70	0.52	0.19	0.12	100%
EN pl CDG RO	17.09	0.70	0.52	0.20	0.12	100%
EN pl GVF CG	16.20	0.70	0.48	0.23	0.12	100%
EN pl GVF RO	16.59	0.70	0.47	0.24	0.12	100%
EN bl CDG CG	19.99	0.70	0.46	0.25	0.13	100%
EN bl CDG RO	16.27	0.70	0.50	0.21	0.11	100%
EN bl GVF CG	18.77	0.70	0.60	0.13	0.11	100%
EN bl GVF RO	17.11	0.70	0.62	0.12	0.12	81%
Direct watershed	18.36	0.70	0.59	0.14	0.13	99%

a)   b)

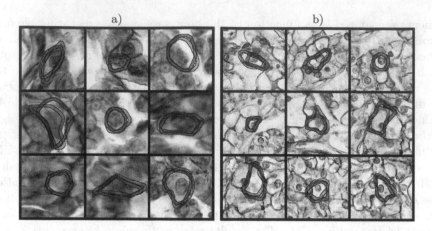

Fig. 3. The illustrative results of membrane localization in the cell images of breast cancer (a) and kidney cancer (b). The images correspond to these in Fig.1.

Table 2 presents the results concerning kidney cancer at different variants of the snake algorithm and image representation. The highest agreement of the membrane continuity (0.67 of AS against 0.70 in expert estimation) has been achieved in colour map representation of the image and radially oriented GVF gradient estimation. This time the direct application of watershed was highly inefficient (membrane continuity estimation 0.59 against the value 0.70 of an expert).

The results of image analysis are also presented in the graphical form. Fig. 3 depicts the results of membrane localizations for 9 chosen cells. They have been made by using the best snake algorithm (denoted by red color) and the expert estimation (green color) and refer to the original images of cells illustrated in Fig. 1. High similarity of the results of membrane localizations obtained by our system and expert is visible in the most cases.

5   Conclusion

The paper has presented the modified snake approach to the automatic recognition of the HER2/neu cell membrane and its association with the neighbouring cell. The main effort has been directed toward assigning the snake model of the membrane with the proper cell of the image. The work has been concentrated on comparing different methods of gradient generation and application of swarm optimization in solving the snake model in the breast and kidney cancer samples. The recognized membrane shape has enabled proposing an automatic method of the membrane continuity estimation, an important factor in the pathomorphological evaluation of breast and kidney cancers.

The experimental results have shown high efficiency of this approach to the image segmentation in the membrane localization task. The best radially oriented GVF method applied in snake model was able to generate statistical results concerning the continuity of membrane with excellent mean value agreement to the expert results and of the smallest standard deviation.

It should be noted, that our computerized system is fully automatic. Hence the recognition of the nuclei and membrane associated with the cell is done according to an automatic procedure defined within the algorithm. On the other hand the human expert selects the nuclei and membrane according to his professional knowledge, blind to the selection results of an automatic system. This is the reason of slight differences between the recognized membrane shapes observed in the segmentation results.

Acknowledgments. This work has been supported by the National Centre for Research and Development (PBS2/A9/21/2013 grant), Poland.

References

1. PATHWAY HER-2/neu (4B5) – user manual. Ventana Medical Systems, Tucson (2009)
2. Matlab Image Processing Toolbox: users guide. MathWorks, Natick (2012)
3. Grala, B., Markiewicz, T., Kozlowski, W., Osowski, S., Slodkowska, J., Papierz, W.: New automated image analysis method for the assessment of ki-67 labeling index in meningiomas. Folia Histo. Cyto. **47**(4), 587–592 (2009)
4. Kasson, P., Huppa, J., Davis, M., Brunger, A.: A hybrid machine-learning ap-proach for segmentation of protein localization data. Bioinformatics **2**(19), 3778–3786 (2005)
5. Kennedy, J., Eberhart, R.: Swarm Intelligence. Morgan Kaufmann, San Francisco (2001)
6. Latif, Z., Watters, A., Bartlet, J., Underwood, M., Aichison, M.: Gene amplification and overexpression of her2 in renal cell carcinoma. BJU Intern. **89**, 5–9 (2002)
7. Les, T., Markiewicz, T., Osowski, S., Cichowicz, M., Kozlowski, W.: Automatic evaluation system of FISH images in breast cancer. In: Elmoataz, A., Lezoray, O., Nouboud, F., Mammass, D. (eds.) ICISP 2014. LNCS, vol. 8509, pp. 332–339. Springer, Heidelberg (2014)
8. Lezoray, O., Elmoataz, A., Cardot, H., Gougeon, G., Lecluse, M., Elie, H., Revenu, M.: Segmentation of colour images from serous cytology for automated cell classification. Anal. Quant. Cytol. Histol. **22**, 311–322 (2000)
9. Littlejohns, P.: Trastuzumab for early breast cancer: evolution or revolution? Lancet Oncology **7**(1), 22–33 (2006)
10. Logan, J., Edwards, K., Saunders, N.: Real-Time PCR: Current Technology and Applications. Caister Academic Press, Norfolk (2009)
11. Naegel, B., Passat, N., Ronse, C.: Grey-level hit-or-miss transforms part i:unified theory. Pattern Recogn. **40**, 635–647 (2007)
12. Soille, P.: Morphological Image Analysis, Principles and Applications, 2nd edn. Springer, Berlin (2003)
13. Tabakov, M., Kozak, P.: Segmentation of histopathology her2/neu images with fuzzy decision tree and takagi-sugeno reasoning. Comput. Biol. Med. **49**, 19–29 (2014)

14. Tan, P., Steinbach, M., Kumar, V.: Introduction to data mining. Pearson Education Inc., Boston (2006)
15. Wdowiak, M., Markiewicz, T., Osowski, S., Swiderska, Z., Patera, J., Kozlowski, W.: Hourglass shapes in rank grey-level hit-or-miss transform for membrane segmentation in HER2/neu images. In: Benediktsson, J.A., Chanussot, J., Najman, L., Talbot, H. (eds.) Mathematical Morphology and Its Applications to Signal and Image Processing. LNCS, vol. 9082, pp. 3–14. Springer, Heidelberg (2015)
16. Xu, C., Prince, J.: Snakes, shapes, and gradient vector flow. IEEE Trans. Image Processing **7**(3), 359–369 (1998)

Combination Photometric Stereo Using Compactness of Albedo and Surface Normal in the Presence of Shadows and Specular Reflection

Naoto Ienaga[1](✉), Hideo Saito[1], Kouichi Tezuka[2], Yasumasa Iwamura[2], and Masayoshi Shimizu[2]

[1] Department of Information and Computer Science, Keio University, 3-14-1, Hiyoshi, Kohoku-ku Yokohama-shi, Kanagawa 223-8522, Japan
{ienaga,saito}@hvrl.ics.keio.ac.jp
http://www.hvrl.ics.keio.ac.jp
[2] Fujitsu Laboratories Ltd., 4-1-1, Kamikodanaka, Nakahara-ku Kawasaki-shi, Kanagawa 211-8588, Japan
{ktezuka,iwamura.yasumas,shimizu.masa}@jp.fujitsu.com
http://jp.fujitsu.com/group/labs

Abstract. We present a novel combination photometric stereo which can estimate surface normals precisely even for images including shadows and specular reflection. We can use photometric stereo if there are more than three input images. Therefore we can employ photometric stereo with $_nC_3$ combinations for n input images. We make 3D distribution of albedos and surface normals estimated from pixel intensities of $_nC_3$ pixel combinations. In the distribution, we define a novel value "compactness" to distinguish pixels which are included in neither shadows nor specular reflection from pixels which are included in shadows or specular reflection. Through experimental results, we demonstrate that the proposed method can estimate surface normals in the presence of shadows and specular reflection. Moreover the proposed method is superior to previous works in better accuracy.

Keywords: Photometric stereo · Shadow · Specular reflection · 3D shape reconstruction

1 Introduction

As found in the emergence of 3D printers, 3D shape reconstructions have recently drawn attention. Photometric stereo is the well-known effective method to obtain a 3D shape of a target object. 3D shapes are reconstructed from surface normals which are provided by photometric stereo. Photometric stereo can estimate the albedo (the ratio of incident to reflected light) and the surface normal of each pixel of some input images in which only the light direction changes. However, photometric stereo assumes that a reflection of surface of target object follows

© Springer International Publishing Switzerland 2015
G. Azzopardi and N. Petkov (Eds.): CAIP 2015, Part I, LNCS 9256, pp. 445–455, 2015.
DOI: 10.1007/978-3-319-23192-1_37

Lambertian reflectance. Therefore photometric stereo does not work properly in the presence of shadows and (or) specular reflection in which the assumption of Lambertian reflectance does not be satisfied.

Photometric stereo needs at least 3 images to estimate albedos and surface normals. When we have n images, we can employ photometric stereo with $_nC_3$ combinations. We can compute a "triplet", which has three values of p, q (a surface normal) and an albedo, from one of $_nC_3$ pixel combinations of a certain pixel of n input images. Then in the 3D space of p, q and an albedo, we can consider a distribution of $_nC_3$ triplets and we define a "compactness" of triplets. The compactness indicates the degree of concentration of triplets representing albedos and surface normals. In this paper, we propose to use the compactness so that we can remove pixels which do not obey Lambertian model.

This paper is organized as follows. In section 2, we make mention of related works. In section 3, combination photometric stereo using the compactness of albedos and surface normals is proposed. Experimental results are given in section 4 and section 5 is devoted to concluding remarks.

2   Related Works

Photometric stereo has been studied for a long time in consideration of the influence of shadows and specular reflection. Chung et al. [1] introduced an approach of estimation of parameters of Ward BRDF model by using cast shadows to overcome the influence of wide specular lobes. In [2], Hern et al. or in [3], Barsky et al. argued that methods in cases of getting 3 or 4 images. Therefore each pixel can be included in shadows or specular reflection in at most one image of n input images. However, considering a utilization of photometric stereo, it is hard to think about only less than 4 images are gained. It is rather more possible that though we can capture many images, each pixel is included in shadows or specular reflection areas in some images. For this reason, the proposed method permits shadows and specular reflection to extend plural images while the proposed method needs some input images.

Chandraker et al. [4] and Dulac et al. [5] proposed similar algorithms. Dulac et al. focus on only the shadow problem and presume the darkest pixel must be a shadow. First, they compute a surface normal from the darkest pixel, the brightest pixel and the third brightest pixel. Second, they compare observed pixel intensities with pixel intensities which are obtained from a back calculation using the surface normal obtained in the previous step. Third, they try to remove the darkest pixel if the difference is bigger than a pre-defined value. These steps are repeated until the difference will be smaller. For more details, please refer to [5].

Miyazaki et al. also tackled this challenge using graph cut in [6] and using a median value in [7]. In [7], they compute $_nC_3$ surface normals for all pixels like the proposed method. Medians of sets including surface normals of 4-connected pixels and $_nC_3$ surface normals and averages of surface normals of 4-connected pixels are used for computing conclusive surface normals. Furthermore they remove reflections of a transparent display case because the problem they addressed in [7] is a situation that an object is placed in a transparent display case like museums.

3 Proposed Method

The proposed method is performed for each pixel by starting the estimation of $_nC_3$ triplets that represent albedos and surface normals. Next, we compute the compactness to select pixels which are not included in shadows and specular reflection.

3.1 Combinations for Triplets

First of all, we summarize the basic principle of photometric stereo. We assume V represents a n dimensions vector including pixel intensities of a certain pixel of n input images, ρ is an albedo, s is a light intensity, L is a known matrix of light directions of input images and n is a surface normal. If a reflection of surface of target object follows Lambertian reflectance, V can be expressed as follow:

$$V = \rho s L n \tag{1}$$

We assume $s = 1$. Hence:

$$L^{-1}V = \rho n \tag{2}$$

n is a unit vector. Therefore the length of the left side of the equation (2) is ρ:

$$\rho = \|L^{-1}V\| \tag{3}$$

Then n is as follow:

$$n = \frac{L^{-1}V}{\|L^{-1}V\|} = (n_x, n_y, n_z)^{\mathrm{T}} \tag{4}$$

We use a x direction vector $r_x = (1, 0, p)^{\mathrm{T}}$ parallel to an object surface and a y direction vector $r_y = (0, 1, q)^{\mathrm{T}}$ to remove the redundancy of surface normals. Since p and q represent slopes of a surface in the x and the y directions respectively, they are called gradients of a surface. A surface normal can be computed by taking the cross-product of these two vectors. The relationship between these two vectors and the equation (4) is as follow.

$$n = r_x \times r_y = \begin{pmatrix} -p \\ -q \\ 1 \end{pmatrix} = \begin{pmatrix} n_x/n_z \\ n_y/n_z \\ 1 \end{pmatrix} \tag{5}$$

We compute p, q and ρ of $_nC_3$ pixel combinations of each pixel of input images according to the equation (3) and (5). We define these p,Cq,$C\rho$ as a "triplet".

3.2   Compactness

Fig. 1 shows the distribution of $_nC_3$ triplets in the 3D space of p, q and ρ for
a pixel of Fig. 7 (shown in Sec. 4.2). Circles (hereinafter referred to as "correct
triplets") are computed from pixels which are not included in shadows and specular reflection (hereinafter referred to as "correct pixels"). Meanwhile triangles
(hereinafter referred to as "wrong triplets") are computed from pixels which
are included in shadows (pixels included in shadows or specular reflection, hereinafter referred to as "wrong pixels").

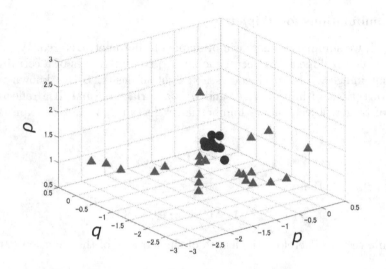

Fig. 1. Distribution of triplets of a certain pixel position. Since there are eight input
images, there are 56 ($_8C_3$) triplets of the pixel. Triplets are manually classified whether
it is correct or not. All correct triplets are almost concentrating at a particular position,
while most of wrong triplets are widely distributed.

The purpose of the proposed method is to select correct pixels, which are
not included in shadows and specular reflection. Therefore we aim to locate
correct triplets because if we can do it, what we have to do besides is only about
checking pixels constituting correct triplets. Pixels constituting correct triplets
are correct pixels (this is our definition). However, we need a value that indicates
correctness of triplets to find correct triplets.

Correct triplets are concentrating at a particular position as shown in Fig.
1 because correct triplets have similar values. Correct triplets should have same
values if all pixel intensities of input images perfectly obey Lambertian model
without any error. This property is useful to find correct triplets. Then we count
other triplets around each triplet to utilize the property. The more triplets have
others, the more it is correct.

By using this property, we propose the definition of compactness of triplet i as follow:

$$Compactness(i) = \sum_{\substack{j=1 \\ j \neq i}}^{{}_nC_3} U(i,j) \tag{6}$$

$$U(i,j) = \begin{cases} 1 & \text{if } \sqrt{(p_i - p_j)^2 + (q_i - q_j)^2} < th_{dpq} \, , \, |\rho_i - \rho_j| < th_{d\rho} \\ 0 & \text{otherwise} \end{cases} \tag{7}$$

We compute the compactness for each triplet i $(i = 1, \cdots, {}_nC_3)$. Correct triplets have a large compactness because they tend to concentrate. th_{dpq} and $th_{d\rho}$ are thresholds of surface normals and albedos. The equation (7) means that $U(i,j)$ is 1 only when triplet j is within the thresholds of triplet i. As a result, the compactness means the number of other triplets around each triplet.

Finally we vote to judge which pixels are suspected to be shadows or specular reflection instead of utilizing the surface normal of the triplet which has the maximum compactness. Because when we use constantly only three pixels though there are n pixels than when we use pixels which are not included in shadows and specular reflection as many as possible, we can calculate surface normals more accurately. We vote with only triplet(s) which have the maximum compactness. Concretely, we count pixels constituting all triplets within th_{spq} and $th_{s\rho}$ of the triplets which have the maximum compactness. For example, in the case of Fig. 2, the pixel 1 will get 2 votes, the pixel 2 will get 3 votes, the pixel 3 will not get any votes etc.

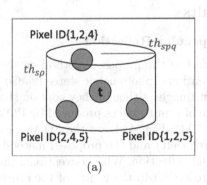

Pixel ID	Vote
1	2
2	3
3	0
4	2
5	2

(a)

Fig. 2. Example of voting. The cylinder represents the volume within th_{spq} and $th_{s\rho}$ around the target triplet denoted by "t". There are three other triplets within the cylinder volume. The right table shows that the vote of the pixels constituting those triplets.

The equations (8) and (9) must be satisfied. Because th_{dpq} and $th_{d\rho}$ should be small in order to determine the triplets which have the maximum compactness while th_{spq} and $th_{s\rho}$ should be some higher value so that more correct triplets can be extracted. Triplets which have the maximum compactness may not be one and even if so, we vote using the same table. Since correct triplets should have the maximum compactness and there should be many other correct triplets around them, votes of correct pixels should be more than votes of wrong pixels. Then we choose pixels which have votes more than $average - standard deviation$ for calculation of conclusive surface normals.

$$th_{spq} > th_{dpq} \tag{8}$$
$$th_{s\rho} > th_{d\rho} \tag{9}$$

As stated above, we have to set initially 4 thresholds th_{dpq}, $th_{d\rho}$, th_{spq}, $th_{s\rho}$ and in fact another threshold th_f. As a simple way of th_{dpq} and $th_{d\rho}$ determination, we use the following algorithm: When all triplets have less compactness than th_f with initial th_{dpq} and $th_{d\rho}$, we add the minimum distance between triplet x and triplet y outside of th_{dpq} and $th_{d\rho}$ of triplet x to initial th_{dpq} and $th_{d\rho}$ alternately. Then re-calculate the compactness. Thanks to this algorithm, setting of th_{dpq} and $th_{d\rho}$ is very easy because we just set them to small values for choosing triplets which have the maximum compactness. However, we are immune from setting th_{dpq} and $th_{d\rho}$ to too small value due to the aforesaid algorithm.

3.3   Recovering 3D Shape

After computing surface normals by using pixels selected in the previous step, we integrate surface normals and recover a 3D shape. In this process, we use Xu et al. [8]'s method.

4   Experiments and Results

4.1   Effect on Shadows and Specular Reflection

In this experiment, we show the effect of the proposed method on shadows and specular reflection, comparing conventional photometric stereo [9]. Conventional photometric stereo uses whole input images although they contain shadows and specular reflection. Fig. 3 shows one of input images produced by POV-Ray [10] and the obj file[1] downloaded from [11]. Fig. 4 shows the 3D shapes obtained from conventional photometric stereo (left) and the proposed method (right).

Fig. 5 shows the effect on specular reflection. With conventional photometric stereo (left), we can observe the projection in the center of the object because of specular reflection as shown in Fig. 3, while the projection does not appear with the proposed method (right).

The effect on shadows is shown in Fig. 6. Shadows make the form of conventional photometric stereo (left) almost a trapezoid unnaturally. While the proposed method (right) is more round and has a natural shape.

---

[1] Josea, "Clay vase garden pottery," ⟨http://artist-3d.com/free_3d_models/dnm/ model_disp.php?uid=3792⟩

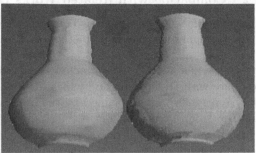

Fig. 3. One of eight input images contain shadows and specular reflection

Fig. 4. 3D shapes. Left: obtained from conventional photometric stereo [9]. Right: proposed method.

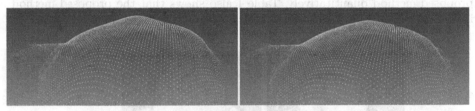

Fig. 5. Effect on specular reflection. 3D points are observed from the bottom left. Left: recovered shape by conventional photometric stereo [9]. Right: proposed method.

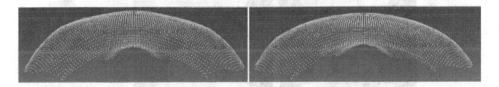

Fig. 6. Effect on shadows. 3D points are observed from the bottom. Left: recovered shape by conventional photometric stereo [9]. Right: proposed method.

Fig. 7. Three of eight input images do not contain specular reflection but shadows.

4.2   Comparing with Related Works Using Actual Images

This experiment has been carried out using Xiong et al. [12]'s data[2] shown in Fig. 7. We compare the proposed method with conventional photometric stereo [9], Miyazaki et al. [7] and Dulac et al. [5]. Seeing Fig. 7, input images do not contain much specular reflection but include many shadows. We chose these images to compare with Dulac's method which focuses only shadows.

We compare angles defined by the obtained surface normal of each method and the ground truth. In Fig. 8, black pixels indicate more than 15 degrees and white pixels indicate 0 degrees (equal to the ground truth). Top left is conventional photometric stereo. The most of the regions with shadows are black. Top right and bottom left are Miyazaki's and Dulac's respectively. The black regions are less than those of conventional photometric stereo. However, their methods could not eliminate the black regions enough. Bottom right is the proposed method in which there are the fewest black regions. We also evaluate the proposed method quantitatively. Table 1 also shows that the proposed method is more effective than the other methods.

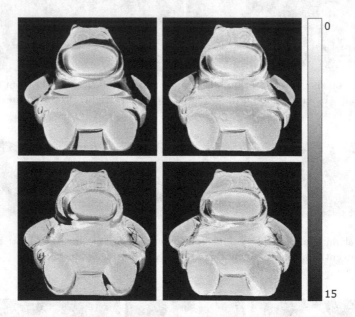

Fig. 8. Gray scale images. Angles 0-15 and pixel intensities 255-0 correspond. Top left: conventional photometric stereo [9]. Top right: Miyazaki et al. [7]. Bottom left: Dulac et al. [5]. Bottom right: proposed method.

Fig. 9 shows the 3D shapes of conventional photometric stereo (left) and the proposed method (right). Conventional photometric stereo couldn't compute

---

[2] The information to download is here, ⟨http://vision.seas.harvard.edu/qsfs/Data.html⟩

surface normals accurately because of shadows. As a result, the hollow of the eyes and the nose swells out. Then we can conclude that 3D shapes tend to swell out in the process of integrating inaccurate surface normals.

Table 1. Root mean squared error (here, error means degrees).

Conventional photometric stereo [9]	Miyazaki et al. [7]	Dulac et al. [5]	proposed method
7.76	4.97	4.93	3.93

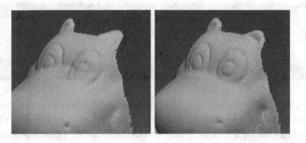

Fig. 9. 3D shapes. Left: conventional photometric stereo [9]. Right: proposed method.

4.3   Demonstration of Practical Use

In the end, we show experimental results using actual images we captured to demonstrate a practical use. We have developed the small device which supplies

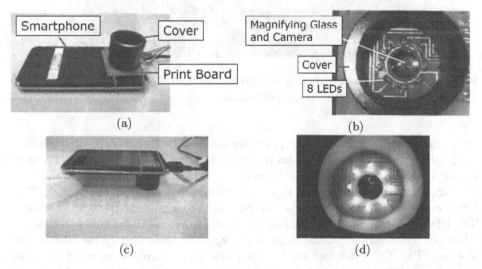

Fig. 10. Device we have developed: (a) (b) The details of the device. The LEDs turn on in turn and the camera captures eight images; (c) The state at the time of capturing; (d) The figure when all the LEDs turn on.

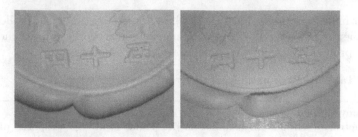

Fig. 11. Two of eight input images.

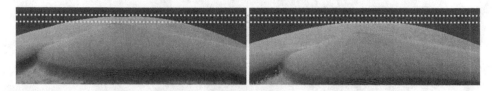

Fig. 12. 3D shapes. Left: obtained from conventional photometric stereo [9]. Right: proposed method. The yellow dotted lines are parallel to the images. The upper line and the lower line are as high as the center of the 3D shape of conventional photometric stereo and the bulge of the edge of the 3D shape of conventional photometric stereo. However, two lines are higher than those of proposed method.

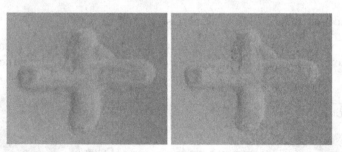

Fig. 13. Chinese character "Ten" of the 3D shapes. Left: obtained from conventional photometric stereo [9]. Right: proposed method.

eight images varying in the light positions and can be attached to smartphones (Fig. 10). Fig. 11 shows the silicon replica of the Japanese 50 yen coin captured by our device. The images include specular reflection and some shadows.

Fig. 12 are the figures of the 3D shapes which looked at from the bottom. The left is conventional photometric stereo [9] and the right is the proposed method. The left is sweller than the right like Fig. 9. It also seems that Chinese character "Ten" of conventional photometric stereo spreads more largely because of the swelling (Fig. 13). Therefore we can say our surface normals are more accurate than those of conventional photometric stereo from the conclusion of Fig. 9.

5   Conclusion

We have proposed an approach for the removal of the impact of shadows and specular reflection in photometric stereo. We utilize $_nC_3$ combinations of each pixel of n input images and define the novel value "compactness" based on the considerations of triplets which are comprised of pixels which are included in neither shadows nor specular reflection. Experimental results demonstrated that the proposed technique removes the impact of shadows and specular reflection, leads to the better results than previous works and shows the possibility of a practical use.

References

1. Chung, H., Jia, J.: Efficient photometric stereo on glossy surface with wide specular lobes. In: Proc. 2008 IEEE Computer Society Conference on Computer Vision and Pattern Recognition (CVPR 2008), June 2008
2. Hernández, C., Vogiatzis, G., Cipolla, R.: Overcoming shadows in 3-source photometric stereo. IEEE Trans. Pattern Analysis and Machine Intelligence **33**(2), 419–426 (2011)
3. Barsky, S., Petrou, M.: The 4-source photometric stereo technique for three-dimensional surface in the presence of highlights and shadows. IEEE Trans. Pattern Analysis and Machine Intelligence **25**(10), 1239–1252 (2003)
4. Chandraker, M., Agarwal, S., Kriegman, D.: Shadowcuts: photometric stereo with shadows. In: Proc. 2007 IEEE Computer Society Conference on Computer Vision and Pattern Recognition (CVPR 2007), June 2007
5. Dulac, A., Martedi, S., Saito, H., Tezuka, K., Shimizu, M.: Combination method: photometric stereo with shadows. In: Proc. 2014 Irish Machine Vision and Image Processing (IMVIP2014), pp. 137–142, August 2014
6. Miyazaki, D., Ikeuchi, K.: Photometric stereo using graph cut and m-estimation for a virtual tumulus in the presence of highlights and shadows. In: Proc. Workshop on Applications of Computer Vision in Archaeology (ACVA2010), pp. 70–77, June 2010
7. Miyazaki, D., Hara, K., Ikeuchi, K.: Median photometric stereo as applied to the segonko tumulus and museum objects. International Journal of Computer Vision **86**(2–3), 229–242 (2010)
8. Xu, J., Pachauri, D.: Project 3: photometric stereo, January 17, 2015. http://pages.cs.wisc.edu/~jiaxu/projects/Stereo/
9. Woodham, R.J.: Photometric method for determining surface orientation from multiple images. Optical Engineering **19**(1), 139–144 (1980)
10. POV-Ray, January 21, 2015. http://www.povray.org/
11. ARTIST-3D.COM, January 21, 2015. http://artist-3d.com/
12. Xiong, Y., Chakrabarti, A., Basri, R., Gortler, S.J., Jacobs, D.W., Zickler, T.: From shading to local shape. IEEE Trans. Pattern Analysis and Machine Intelligence **37**(1), 67–79 (2015)
13. Horn, B.K.P.: Robot Vision. The MIT Press, Massachusetts (1986)

Craniofacial Reconstruction Using Gaussian Process Latent Variable Models

Zedong Xiao[1], Junli Zhao[1,2], Xuejun Qiao[3], and Fuqing Duan[1(✉)]

[1] College of Information Science and Technology, Beijing Normal University,
Beijing 100875, People's Republic of China
zd.xiao@mail.bnu.edu.cn, zhaojl@yeah.net, fqduan@bnu.edu.cn
[2] College of Software and Technology, Qingdao University,
Qingdao 266071, People's Republic of China
[3] School of Science, Xian University of Architecture and Technology,
Xi'an 710055, People's Republic of China
xjqiao1@sina.com

Abstract. Craniofacial reconstruction aims at estimating the facial outlook associated to a skull. It can be applied in victim identification, forensic medicine and archaeology. In this paper, we propose a craniofacial reconstruction method using Gaussian Process Latent Variable Models (GP-LVM). GP-LVM is used to represent the skull and face skin data in a low dimensional latent space respectively. The mapping from the skull to face skin is built in the latent spaces by using least square support vector machine (LSSVM) regression model. Experimental results show that the GP-LVM latent space improves the representation of craniofacial data and boosts the reconstruction results compared with the methods in literature.

Keywords: GP-LVM · LSSVM · Craniofacial reconstruction

1 Introduction

In forensic medicine, craniofacial reconstruction (CFR) refers to the process that aims to approximate the morphology of face skin from the shape of the skull [1, 2]. It is usually considered when an unrecognizable corpse is confronted with and no other identification evidence is available. All facial reconstruction techniques are based on the assumed relationship between the soft tissue envelope and the underlying skull substrate [3]. Traditional methods are based on manual reconstruction by physically modeling a face on a skull replica with clay or plasticine [2]. However, all of them are subjective and time-consuming. With the progress in computer science and medical imaging in recent years, computer-assisted techniques have been developed for craniofacial reconstruction [1–5]. where the consistent (given the same input data, the same result is obtained) and objective (the modeling assumptions are explicit and verifiable) [3] results could be given.

© Springer International Publishing Switzerland 2015
G. Azzopardi and N. Petkov (Eds.): CAIP 2015, Part I, LNCS 9256, pp. 456–464, 2015.
DOI: 10.1007/978-3-319-23192-1_38

Computer-assisted CFR techniques can be divided into two categories: template deformation method [6,7], and statistical deformation model methods [4,5,8–11]. Template deformation methods generally deform a craniofacial template according to shape attributes of the unknown skull. They assume the corresponding faces should have main characteristics in common if skulls have similar shape attributes. Usually a suitable template is unavailable due to the diversity of craniofacial morphology, and the used smooth deformation generates the reconstructed results of large biases. Statistical deformation model methods learn the relationship between skulls and face skins by using statistical models. The models are constructed from a 3D head database, which contains skulls and their corresponding face skins. The statistical methods can reduce the model biases in template deformation methods due to multiple references. For example, Claes et al. [3] built a statistical deformable model of dense facial surface points combined with 52 associated skull land marks, and the reconstruction was obtained by fitting the model skull landmarks to the corresponding landmarks on the target skull. However, the model representation using sparse set of landmarks or semi-landmarks in these methods is far less than enough to show the variation of the craniofacial morphology.

Recent years regression techniques were used to learn the relationship between skulls and face skins. Berar et al. [1] use Latent Root Regression method to predict the face shape from a set of skull landmarks, where the face is represented as a sparse mesh. The reconstruction is highly affected by the quantity and localization accuracy of the landmarks. Paysan et al. [12] build the regression model on skull and face skin by ridge regression, and add age and weight as the impact factors. We also paid lots attention to using regression techniques to learn the relationship between skulls and face skins [5,9,10]. Duan et al. [10] took the multi-linear subspace analysis to extract the craniofacial subspace features, and established the mapping from the skull subspace to face skin subspace using the partial least squares regression. Li et al. [5] studied the craniofacial reconstruction by using least square support vector regression, where the mapping from the skull to face skin is established in Principal Component Analysis (PCA) subspace. All these works established the regression model in the linear subspaces, which cannot extract complex nonlinear craniofacial features.

In this paper, we map the skull data and skin face data to latent spaces using Gaussian Process Latent Variable Models (GP-LVM) [13], and take the least square support vector machine (LSSVM) to build the mapping from skull latent to face skin latent space. As a dimensional reduction algorithm, the GP-LVM is an effective method to represent high dimensional data through non-linear mapping [14,15]. Experimental results show that the GP-LVM latent space can represent the craniofacial data better and boost the craniofacial reconstruction. The rest of the paper is organized as follows. The materials for the craniofacial reconstruction are given in Section 2. Section 3 gives a brief introduction to the GP-LVM. Section 4 presents the method for craniofacial reconstruction. The experimental results and analysis are shown in Section 5, and the conclusion is made in Section 6.

2   Material

The used data are 208 CT head scans of individuals from 19 to 75 years old. The CT images were obtained by a clinical multi-slice CT scanner system in the Xianyang hospital located in western China. There are 81 females and 127 males. The marching cubes algorithm [16] is used to construct the polygonal mesh surfaces of the 3D skull and skin of each individual. The original skull and skin meshes have different size and pose. Since statistical methods need to build the correspondence across the data set, the data normalization is done as follows. Firstly, all samples are transformed into a uniform coordinate system, i.e. the Frankfurt coordinate system [17]. The Frankfurt system is determined by four skull landmarks, i.e. left porion, right porion, left orbitale and glabella (denoted by L_p, R_p, L_o, G, respectively). Secondly, all samples are normalized by $\frac{1}{|L_p - R_p|}$. Finally, the dense point surface registration method [4] is used to establish the dense correspondence between all skull and skin samples. The original skull and skin have more than 100,000 vertices. For convenience of computation, we remove the back parts of the head since the front part contain most features of the face, as shown in Fig. 1. Thus, all of the skin and skull samples have uniform point clouds representation, 40,969 and 41,059 vertices for skins and skulls, respectively.

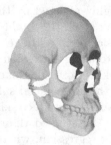 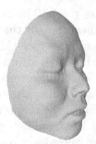

Fig. 1. The skull and face after the above processing

3   The GP-LVM

Gaussian Process Latent Variable Models (GP-LVM) [13] is a dimensional reduction algorithm using Gaussian Process. It is a generative model where each observed data point, $\mathbf{y}_i \in \mathbb{R}^D$, is generated through a noisy process form latent variable $\mathbf{x}_i \in \mathbb{R}^q$ [14],

$$\mathbf{y}_i = f(\mathbf{x}_i) + \epsilon, \tag{1}$$

where $\epsilon \sim N(\mathbf{0}, \beta^{-1}\mathbf{I})$ and the mean of GP-prior on the generative function f is zero, the marginal likelihood can be formulated by integration f,

$$P(\mathbf{Y}|\mathbf{X}, \Phi) = \prod_{j=1}^{D} \frac{1}{(2\pi)^{\frac{N}{2}}|\mathbf{K}|^{\frac{1}{2}}} exp(-\frac{1}{2}\mathbf{y}_{:,j}^T \mathbf{K}^{-1} \mathbf{y}_{:,j}) , \tag{2}$$

where $\mathbf{y}_{:,j}$ is the jth column of observed data matrix, $\mathbf{Y} = [\mathbf{y}_1 \ldots \mathbf{y}_N]^T$. Latent variable matrix, $\mathbf{X} = [\mathbf{x}_1 \ldots \mathbf{x}_N]^T$, $\mathbf{K}$ is the covariance function and linear covariance function is given by $\alpha \mathbf{X}\mathbf{X}^T + \beta^{-1}\mathbf{I}$. Φ is the hyper-parameter of the covariance function.

There are many non-linear covariance functions can be chosen to generate a non-linear mapping. In this paper, the 'RBF kernel' is taken as a non-linear function,

$$k_{n,m} = \alpha \cdot exp(-\frac{\gamma}{2}(\mathbf{x}_n - \mathbf{x}_m)) + \delta_{nm}\beta^{-1} , \tag{3}$$

where $k_{n,m}$ is the element in the nth row and mth column of $\mathbf{K}$, γ is a scale parameter and δ_{nm} denotes the Kronecker delta. The GP-LVM maximizes the marginal likelihood (2) with respect to both the latent points $\mathbf{X}$ and the hyper-parameters Φ,

$$\{\hat{\mathbf{X}}, \hat{\Phi}\} = argmax_{\mathbf{X},\Phi} P(\mathbf{X}|\mathbf{Y}, \Phi) . \tag{4}$$

Eq.(4) does not has a close-form solution, except the linear form of the covariance function. The gradient based optimization is taken, where the dimensionality of the latent space is not known a priori and must be pre-set [14].

A new point $\mathbf{x}^*$ in the latent space, can be projected into the data space as a Gaussian distribution [13]

$$p(\mathbf{y}^*|\mathbf{x}^*, \alpha, \beta, \gamma) = N(\mu^*, \delta^{*2}) , \tag{5}$$

where the mean and variance are

$$\mu^* = \mathbf{Y}^T \mathbf{K}_{I,I}^{-1} \mathbf{k}_{I,j} , $$
$$\delta^{*2} = k(\mathbf{x}^*, \mathbf{x}^*) - \mathbf{k}_{I,j}^T \mathbf{K}_{I,I}^{-1} \mathbf{k}_{I,j} , \tag{6}$$

where $\mathbf{K}_{I,I}$ denote the kernel matrix developed from the "active set" in the kernel method [13]. The $\mathbf{k}_{I,j}$ is a vector with the elements $k(x^*, x_i)$.

4 Face Reconstruction from Skull

The aim of our model is to establish a mapping from skull data $\mathbf{X} = [\mathbf{x}_1, \ldots, \mathbf{x}_N]^T$ to skin data $\mathbf{Y} = [\mathbf{y}_1, \ldots, \mathbf{y}_N]^T$. We first represent craniofacial data in low dimensional latent spaces, and then build the mapping in the latent spaces.

4.1 Representing Craniofacial Data in Latent Spaces

In order to simplify the computation, we use GP-LVM to represent skull and skin data in latent space firstly, which is to extract the non-linear feature in the skull and skin data. The proper dimensionality of latent space should be determined through the experiment. The result can be denoted as skull latent space data $\mathbf{X}' = [\mathbf{x}'_1, \ldots, \mathbf{x}'_N]^T$, skin latent space data $\mathbf{Y}' = [\mathbf{y}'_1, \ldots, \mathbf{y}'_N]^T$. Just as (4) the processing can be rewritten by,

$$\{\hat{\mathbf{X}}', \hat{\Phi_X}\} = argmax_{\mathbf{X}', \Phi_X} P(\mathbf{X}|\mathbf{X}', \Phi_X) ,$$

$$\{\hat{\mathbf{Y}}', \hat{\Phi_Y}\} = argmax_{\mathbf{Y}', \Phi_Y} P(\mathbf{Y}|\mathbf{Y}', \Phi_Y) .$$

$$(7)$$

The the gradient based optimization [13] can be taken for the solution.

4.2 Mapping in Latent Spaces

We build the regression model from skull latent space X' to skin latent space Y' by using LSSVM [18]. Compared with some linear modeling approach, such as partial least squares regression and ridge regression, LSSVM has the flexibility for extracting nonlinear relationships between variables. At the training phase, we have the following optimization,

$$\text{minimize} \quad \tfrac{1}{2} \| \boldsymbol{\omega}_j \|^2 + C \sum_{i=1}^{n} \xi_{ij}^2 ,$$

$$\text{subject to} \quad y_{ij} - (<\boldsymbol{\omega}_j, \mathbf{x}'_i> + b_j) = \xi_{ij} ,$$

$$(8)$$

where j denotes the jth dimension (j^{th} column) in skin latent space data $\mathbf{Y}'$, and i denotes the ith sample (i^{th} row) in skull and skin latent space $\mathbf{X}', \mathbf{Y}'$. C denotes the regularization parameter and ξ_i is the slack variable. Using Lagrange function to solve this equation, we obtain the optimal model parameter $\boldsymbol{\omega}_j$ and b_j.

4.3 Craniofacial Reconstruction

For an unknown 3D skull $\mathbf{x}^*$, the method proposed in this paper reconstruct the face skin $\mathbf{y}^*$ by the following steps.

Step 1. Transform $\mathbf{x}^*$ into the Frankfurt coordinate system, normalize and register $\mathbf{x}^*$ using the method in [4].
Step 2. Map $\mathbf{x}^*$ to GP-LVM latent space $\mathbf{x}^{*'}$ by using the trained GP-LVM model and parameter Φ_X and Φ_Y in (7).
Step 3. Take the trained LSSVM regression model and parameter $\boldsymbol{\omega}_j$ and b_j in (8), to map $\mathbf{x}^{*'}$ into the estimated skin GP-LVM latent space data $\hat{\mathbf{y}}^{*'}$.
Step 4. Obtain the estimated face skin $\hat{\mathbf{y}}^*$ by GP-LVM projecting $\hat{\mathbf{y}}^{*'}$ to data space $\hat{\mathbf{y}}^*$, in (5), (6).

5 Experimental Results

The experiments data are the 208 head CT scans given in Section 2. We use 150 samples (72%) as the training set, including 58 females and 92 males. The other 58 samples (28%), including 23 females and 35 males, are used as the test data. Each person contains a skull data and face skin data, all the data are represented as dense point clouds.

5.1   Reconstruction Results

In our experiment, since the dimensionality of dense point clouds representation of skull and skin is larger than 100,000, which means at least 50 GB computer RAM is required for the GP-LVM to store the covariance matrix $\mathbf{K}_c = \mathbf{X}^T\mathbf{X}$, with more than $100,000$ rows $\times$ $100,000$ columns elements. Therefore, we take PCA for dimensionality reduction firstly, and let PCA subspace dimensionality be $N - 1$ (149).

The dimensionality of skin and skull in the GP-LVM latent space are 30. In LSSVM regression model, the regularization parameter C is set to 1000, and the parameter of RBF kernel δ^2 is 300. In Fig. 2, several craniofacial reconstructed results in the test set are illustrated. The first column is the given skulls in the test set for craniofacial reconstruction, the second column is the reconstructed results, and the third column is the ground truth, the last column is the comparison of the reconstructed results and the ground truth for each person. A rainbow is used to show the difference between each corresponding point. Blue represents zero distance, and red represents maximal distance. It is shown that the proposed algorithm can obtain good craniofacial reconstructed results.

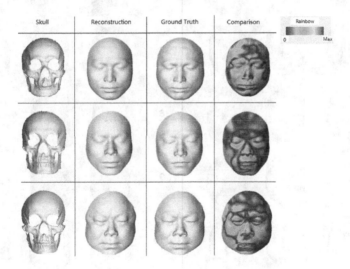

Fig. 2. Reconstruction Results

5.2   Error Analysis and Comparison

The reconstruction error can be defined as [19]

$$\varepsilon = \frac{1}{n} \sum_{i=1}^{n} |D_r(i) - D_t(i)|, \qquad (9)$$

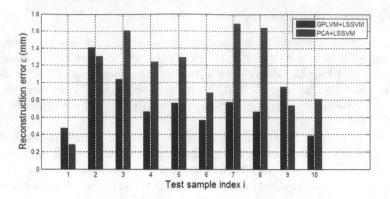

Fig. 3. Reconstruction Error Comparison

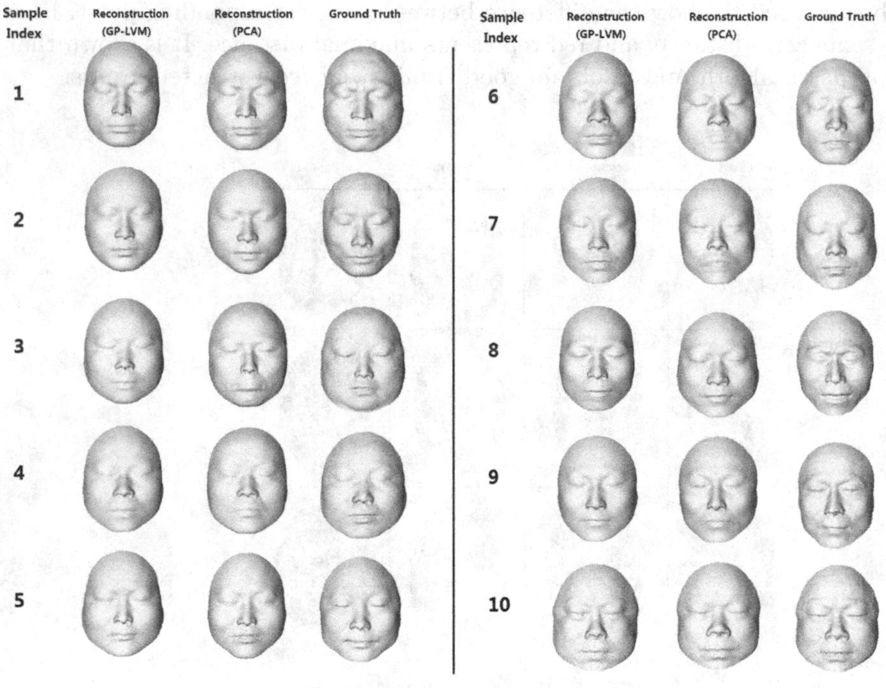

Fig. 4. Reconstruction Comparison

where D_r is the recovered shape (reconstructed face skin) and D_t is the true shape (true face skin), and n is the number of vertices in the shape. The error comparison with the method in [5] is shown in Fig. 3. From Fig. 3, we can see the construction error of our method is less than the other one for 70% of the test data. Fig. 4 shows the corresponding reconstruction faces of the cases in Fig. 3. In Fig. 4, from sample 3, 4 and 6 we can find the reconstruction results of our method is much better than the method (PCA+LSSVM) visually. All those show that the presented GP-LVM latent space (non-linear mapping) improves the representation of the craniofacial data and boosts the craniofacial reconstruction.

6   Conclusions

Craniofacial reconstruction aims to estimate the facial appearance from an unkown skull, and can be applied in victim identification, forensic medicine and archaeology. In this paper, GP-LVM is used to represent the skull and face skin data in a low dimensional latent space respectively. Compared with PCA, which is usually used in craniofacial reconstruction, GP-LVM can extract the nonlinear craniofacial features. The mapping from the skull to face skin is built in the latent spaces by using least square support vector machine (LSSVM) regression model. Experimental results validate the proposed method, and show that the GP-LVM latent space improves the representation of craniofacial data and boosts the reconstruction results.

Acknowledgments. This work was partially supported by the National Natural Science Foundation of China (Grant No.61272363), Program for New Century Excellent Talents in University (NCET-13-0051) and the Fundamental Research Funds for the Central Universities No.2013YB70.

References

1. Berar, M., Tilotta, F.M., Glaunès, J.A., Rozenholc, Y.: Craniofacial reconstruction as a prediction problem using a latent root regression model. Forensic Science International **210**(1), 228–236 (2011)
2. Claes, P., Vandermeulen, D., De Greef, S., Willems, G., Clement, J.G., Suetens, P.: Computerized craniofacial reconstruction: conceptual framework and review. Forensic Science International **201**(1), 138–145 (2010)
3. Claes, P., Vandermeulen, D., De Greef, S., Willems, G., Clement, J.G., Suetens, P.: Bayesian estimation of optimal craniofacial reconstructions. Forensic Science International **201**(1), 146–152 (2010)
4. Hu, Y., Duan, F., Zhou, M., Sun, Y., Yin, B.: Craniofacial reconstruction based on a hierarchical dense deformable model. EURASIP Journal on Advances in Signal Processing **2012**(1), 1–14 (2012)
5. Li, Y., Chang, L., Qiao, X., Liu, R., Duan, F.: Craniofacial reconstruction based on least square support vector regression. In: 2014 IEEE International Conference on Systems, Man and Cybernetics (SMC), pp. 1147–1151. IEEE (2014)
6. Kermi, A., Laskri, M.T.: A 3D deformable model constrained by anthropometric knowledge for computerized facial reconstructions. In: 2012 11th International Conference on Information Science, Signal Processing and their Applications (ISSPA), pp. 924–929. IEEE (2012)

7. Quatrehomme, G., Cotin, S., Subsol, G., Delingette, H., Garidel, Y., Grévin, G., Fidrich, M., Bailet, P., Ollier, A., et al.: A fully three-dimensional method for facial reconstruction based on deformable models. Journal of Forensic Sciences **42**(4), 649–652 (1997)

8. Berar, M., Desvignes, M., Bailly, G., Payan, Y.: 3D statistical facial reconstruction. In: Proceedings of the 4th International Symposium on Image and Signal Processing and Analysis, ISPA 2005, pp. 365–370. IEEE (2005)

9. Duan, F., Huang, D., Tian, Y., Lu, K., Wu, Z., Zhou, M.: 3D face reconstruction from skull by regression modeling in shape parameter spaces. Neurocomputing **151**, 674–682 (2015) ·

10. Duan, F., Yang, S., Huang, D., Hu, Y., Wu, Z., Zhou, M.: Craniofacial reconstruction based on multi-linear subspace analysis. Multimedia Tools and Applications **73**(2), 809–823 (2014)

11. Suetens, P., Willems, G., Vandermeulen, D., De Greef, S., Claes, P.: Statistically deformable face models for cranio-facial reconstruction. CIT. Journal of Computing and Information Technology **14**(1), 21–30 (2006)

12. Paysan, P., Lüthi, M., Albrecht, T., Lerch, A., Amberg, B., Santini, F., Vetter, T.: Face reconstruction from skull shapes and physical attributes. In: Denzler, J., Notni, G., Süße, H. (eds.) Pattern Recognition. LNCS, vol. 5748, pp. 232–241. Springer, Heidelberg (2009)

13. Lawrence, N.D.: Gaussian process latent variable models for visualisation of high dimensional data. Advances in Neural Information Processing Systems **16**, 329–336 (2004)

14. Ek, C.H., Torr, P., Lawrence, N.D.: Gaussian process latent variable models for human pose estimation. In: Popescu-Belis, A., Renals, S., Bourlard, H. (eds.) MLMI 2007. LNCS, vol. 4892, pp. 132–143. Springer, Heidelberg (2008)

15. Grochow, K., Martin, S.L., Hertzmann, A., Popović, Z.: Style-based inverse kinematics. ACM Transactions on Graphics (TOG) **23**, 522–531 (2004)

16. Lorensen, W.E., Cline, H.E.: Marching cubes: A high resolution 3D surface construction algorithm. ACM Siggraph Computer Graphics **21**, 163–169 (1987)

17. Frankfurt plane. http://en.wikipedia.org/w/index.php?title=Frankfurt_plane&redirect=no (accessed January 21, 2015)

18. Smola, A.J., Schölkopf, B.: A tutorial on support vector regression. Statistics and Computing **14**(3), 199–222 (2004)

19. Wang, X., Yang, R.: Learning 3D shape from a single facial image via non-linear manifold embedding and alignment. In: 2010 IEEE Conference on Computer Vision and Pattern Recognition (CVPR), pp. 414–421. IEEE (2010)

A High-Order Depth-Based Graph Matching Method

Lu Bai[1], Zhihong Zhang[2]([✉]), Peng Ren[3], and Edwin R. Hancock[4]

[1] School of Information, Central University of Finance and Economics, Beijing, China
[2] Software School, Xiamen University, Xiamen, Fujian, China
`zhihong@xmu.edu.cn`
[3] College of Information and Control Engineering, China University of Petroleum,
Beijing, China
[4] Department of Computer Science, University of York, York, UK

Abstract. We recently proposed a novel depth-based graph matching method by aligning the depth-based representations of vertices. One drawback of the new method is that it only considers the structural co-relations, and the spatial co-relations of vertices are discarded. This drawback limits the performance of the method on graph-based image matching problems. To overcome the shortcoming, we develop a new high-order depth-based matching method, by incorporating the spatial coordinate information of vertices (i.e., the pixel coordinates of vertices in original images). The new matching method is based on a high order dominant cluster analysis [1]. We use the new high-order matching method to identify the mismatches in the original first-order depth-based matching results, and remove the incorrect matches. Experiments on real world image databases demonstrate the effectiveness of our new high-order DB matching method.

Keywords: Depth-based representations · Graph matching · High-order depth-based matching

1 Introduction

In computer vision, graph-based image matching has been proven more robust and accurate than point pattern (pixel) matching [2]. The reason for this is that the graph structure can provide us more information about the neighborhood for each feature point, i.e., the graph structure can reflect rich structural co-relations between feature points of images [3].

Generally speaking, most existing graph matching methods can be categorized into three classes. The first of these is based on defining a measure of relational (dis)similarities between vertices and edges [4,5]. The second is based on developing more principled statistical measures of similarity [6,7]. The third one is based on optimization. Recently, an alternative graph matching method has been introduced in our previous work [8]. The key idea is to compute the depth-based representations of vertices as point coordinates, and to compute the

© Springer International Publishing Switzerland 2015
G. Azzopardi and N. Petkov (Eds.): CAIP 2015, Part I, LNCS 9256, pp. 465–476, 2015.
DOI: 10.1007/978-3-319-23192-1_39

distance measures between the point coordinates of pairwise vertices to establish the affinity matrix. Furthermore, we use the method as a means of developing a novel graph matching kernel that counts the matched vertex pairs. Since the matching method can encapsulate rich structural information in terms of an entropy measure [9,10], the matching kernel can reflect precise similarity measure between a pair of graphs and easily outperform state-of-the-art graph kernels on classification problems [10]. Unfortunately, the matching method only considers the structural co-relations, and the spatial co-relations of vertices are discarded. This drawback limits the performance of the matching method on graph-based image matching problem. This is because any slight transformation on an image plane may change the graph structure abstracted from the image radically, and the matching method may identify incorrect correspondences.

The aim of this paper is to overcome the shortcoming of our previous method, by developing a novel high-order depth-based matching method for images. We commence by refining our previous matching method, by incorporating spatial coordinate information for vertices (i.e., the pixel coordinates of vertices in original images). We refer to the refined method as the first-order depth-based matching. For a pair of graphs abstracted from two images under matching, we use the first-order matching method to construct initial uniform hypergraphs, (i.e., the orders of the hyperedges are the same). In this work, we only consider the 3-order hyperedges that encompasse three vertices. For each graph, the hyperedge weight of its hypergraph is computed through either a) the Jensen-Shannon divergence measure between the depth-based representations of the vertices forming the hyperedge or b) the similarity between the pixel coordinates of the vertices in the original images. Using the hypergraphs, we develop a new high-order graph matching method, namely the high-order depth-based matching. This is done by using high-order dominant cluster analysis [1]. We use the new high-order matching method to identify the mismatches in the coarse first-order matching results, and remove the incorrect matches. Experiments on real world image databases demonstrate the effectiveness of our new high-order matching method.

This paper is organized as follows. Section 2 introduces some preliminary concepts that will be used in this work. Section 3 defines a new high-order depth-based matching method for graph-based image matching problems. Section 4 provides the experimental evaluations. Finally, Section 5 provides the conclusion and future work.

2   Preliminary Concepts

In this section, we introduce some preliminary concepts that will be used in this work. We commence by introducing the Jensen-Shannon divergence measure for a set of graphs. Furthermore, we review the concept of the h-layer depth-based representation rooted at a vertex. Finally, we develop a new dissimilarity measure for a set of vertices by measuring the Jensen-Shannon between the h-layer depth-based representations of the vertices.

2.1   The Jensen-Shannon Divergence Measure for Graphs

In this work, we require the Jensen-Shannon divergence measure for graphs. In mutual information, the Jensen-Shannon divergence is a dissimilarity measure for probability distributions in terms of the entropy difference associated with the distributions [3]. In [3,11,12], Bai et al. have extended the divergence measure to graphs for the purpose of computing the information theoretic graph kernels. In their work, the Jensen-Shannon divergence between a pair of graphs is computed by measuring the entropy difference between the entropies of the graphs and those of a composite graph (e.g., the disjoint union graph [11]) formed by the graphs. In this subsection, we generalize their work in [11] and give the concept of measuring the Jensen-Shannon divergence for a set of graphs. Let $\mathbf{G} = \{G_n | n = 1, 2, \ldots, N\}$ denote a set of N graphs, and $G_n(V_n, E_n)$ is a sample graph in $\mathbf{G}$ with vertex set V_n and edge set E_n. The Jensen-Shannon divergence measure $\mathcal{D}$ for the set of graphs $\mathbf{G}$ is

$$\mathcal{D}(\mathbf{G}) = H_S(G_{DU}) - \frac{\sum_{n=1}^{N} H_S(G_n)}{N}, \tag{1}$$

where $H_S(G_n)$ is the Shannon entropy for G_n associated with steady state random walks [3] and is defined as

$$H_S(G_n) = - \sum_{v \in V_n} P_{G_n}(v) \log P_{G_n}(v), \tag{2}$$

where $P_{G_n}(v) = D_n(v, v) / \sum_{u \in V} D_n(u, u)$ is the probability of the steady state random walk visiting the vertex $v \in V_n$, and D is the diagonal degree matrix of G_n. Moreover, in Eq.(1) G_{DU} is the disjoint union graph formed by all the graphs in $\mathbf{G}$, and $H_S(G_{DU})$ is the Shannon entropy of the union graph. Based on the definition in [11], the entropy of the disjoint union graph is defined as

$$H_S(G_{DU}) = \frac{\sum_{n=1}^{N} |V_n| H_S(G_n)}{\sum_{n=1}^{N} |V_n|}, \tag{3}$$

where $|V_n|$ is the number of vertices of G_n. Eq.(1) and Eq.(3) indicate that the Jensen-Shannon divergence measure for a pair of graphs can be directly computed from their vertex numbers and entropy values. Thus, the divergence measure can be efficiently computed.

2.2   The Depth-Based Representation for a Graph

In this subsection, we introduce the concept of the h-layer depth-based representation around a vertex. This has been previously introduced by Bai et al. [10], by generalizing the depth-based complexity trace around the centroid vertex [9]. For an undirected graph $G(V, E)$ and a vertex $v \in V$, let a vertex set N_v^K be defined as $N_v^K = \{u \in V \mid S_G(v, u) \leq K\}$, where S_G is the shortest path matrix of G and $S_G(v, u)$ is the shortest path length between v and u. For G, the K-layer expansion subgraph $\mathcal{G}_v^K(\mathcal{V}_v^K; \mathcal{E}_v^K)$ around v is

$$
\begin{cases}
\mathcal{V}_v^K = \{u \in N_v^K\}; \\
\mathcal{E}_v^K = \{u, v \in N_v^K, \ (u, v) \in E\}.
\end{cases}
\tag{4}
$$

For the graph G, the h-layer depth-based representation around v is

$$
DB_G^h(v) = [H_S(\mathcal{G}_v^1), \cdots, H_S(\mathcal{G}_v^K), \cdots, H_S(\mathcal{G}_v^h)]^T,
\tag{5}
$$

where $(K \leq h)$, $\mathcal{G}_v^K$ is the K-layer expansion subgraph around v, and $H_S(\mathcal{G}_v^K)$ is the Shannon entropy of $\mathcal{G}_v^K$ and is defined in Eq.(2). Note that, if L_{max} is the greatest length of the shortest paths from v to the remaining vertices and $K \geq L_{max}$, the K-layer expansion subgraph is G itself.

Clearly, the h-layer depth-based representation $DB_G^h(v)$ reflects an entropy-based information content flow through the family of K-layer expansion subgraphs rooted at v, and thus can be seen as a vectorial representation of the vertex v.

2.3   Vertex Dissimilarities from the Jensen-Shannon Divergence

We measure the dissimilarity of vertices by computing the Jensen-Shannon divergence between the h-layer depth-based representations of the vertices. For a vertex set $\hat{V}$, we define the Jensen-Shannon divergence based dissimilarity measure of the vertices in $\hat{V}$ as

$$
\mathcal{D}_{JSD}(\hat{V}) = \sum_{k=1}^{h} \mathcal{D}(\mathbf{G}_{\hat{V}}^K),
\tag{6}
$$

where $\mathbf{G}_{\hat{V}}^K$ is a graph set and consists of the K-layer expansion subgraphs around the vertices in $\hat{V}$.

3   A High-Order Depth-Based Matching Method

In this section, we develop a new high-order graph-based image matching algorithm, namely the high-order depth-based matching. We commence by refining our previous matching method [10], as the first-order depth-based matching. Unlike our previous matching method that ignores the spatial information of vertices, the new matching method incorporates either the coordinate information of original images or the structural information of graph structures in the process of vertex alignments. Third, we use the matching results from the first-order depth-based matching method to construct the initial hypergraph. Finally, we use the new high-order depth-based matching method to refine the initial first-order matching results.

3.1   First-Order Depth-Based Graph Matching

In this subsection, we refine our previous matching method [10] as the first-order depth-based matching. Our method is similar to that previously introduced by Scott et al. in [2,13] for point set matching, that computes an affinity matrix in terms of the distances between points (i.e., for a pair of graphs, we compute the vectorial signature for each vertex as its point coordinate, and compute the distance measures between the point coordinates of pairwise vertices to establish the affinity matrix). For a pair of Delaunay graphs $G_p(V_p, E_p)$ and $G_q(V_q, E_q)$ abstracted from two images, we first use the h-layer depth-based representations $D^h_{G_p}(v_i)$ and $D^h_{G_q}(v_j)$ as the structural point coordinates for the vertices $v_i \in V_p$ and $u_j \in V_q$, respectively. Furthermore, we also use the pixel coordinates c_{v_i} and c_{u_j} of $v_i \in V_p$ and $u_j \in V_q$ in the original images as the spatial point coordinates for $v_i \in V_p$ and $u_j \in V_q$, respectively. For G_p and G_q, we compute the element $R(i,j)$ of their affinity matrix R by summing the Euclidean distance between $D^h_{G_p}(v_i)$ and $D^h_{G_q}(u_j)$, and that between c_i and c_j. The element $R(i,j)$ is defined as

$$R(i,j) = \{\|D^h_{G_p}(v_i) - D^h_{G_q}(u_j)\|_2\} \times \{\|c_{v_i} - c_{u_j}\|_2\}. \tag{7}$$

where R is a $|V_p| \times |V_q|$ matrix. The element $R(i,j)$ represents the dissimilarity between the vertex v_i in $G_p(V_p, E_p)$ and the vertex u_j in $G_q(V_q, E_q)$. The rows of $R(i,j)$ index the vertices of $G_p(V_p, E_p)$, and the columns index the vertices of $G_q(V_q, E_q)$. If $R(i,j)$ is the smallest element both in row i and in column j, there should be a one-to-one correspondence between the vertex v_i of G_p and the vertex u_j of G_q. We record the state of correspondence using the correspondence matrix $C \in \{0,1\}^{|V_p||V_q|}$ satisfying

$$C(i,j) = \begin{cases} 1 \text{ if } R(i,j) \text{ is the smallest element} \\ \quad \text{both in row } i \text{ and in column } j; \\ 0 \text{ otherwise.} \end{cases} \tag{8}$$

Eq.(8) implies that if $C(i,j) = 1$, the vertices v_i and v_j are matched.

Note that, unlike the matching method introduced in our previous work [10], Eq.(7) incorporates the spatial coordinate information of vertices (i.e., the pixel coordinates of vertices in original images). As a result, the new first-order depth-based matching overcomes the shortcoming of ignoring spatial information of vertices. However, like our previous matching method, for a pair of graphs, the new first-order depth-based matching may also assign a vertex from a graph more than one matched vertices from the other graph. In our work, we propose to assign a vertex one matched vertex at most. One way to achieve this is to update the matrix $C^{(m;h)}$ by adopting the Hungarian algorithm that can solve the assignment problem, following the strategy proposed in [10]. Here, the matrix $C^{(m;h)} \in \{0,1\}^{|V_p| \times |V_q|}$ can be seen as the incidence matrix of a bipartite graph $G_{pq}(V_p, V_q, E_{pq})$, where V_p and V_q are the two sets of partition parts and E_{pq} is the edge set. By performing the Hungarian algorithm on the matrix $C^{(m;h)}$, we can assign each vertex from the partition part V_p or V_q at most one matched vertex from the other partition part V_q or V_p.

3.2 A High-Order Depth-Based Matching Method

In this subsection, we aim to present a new high-order depth-based matching algorithm (referred to as hypergraph matching) for refining the feature correspondences from the first-order depth-based matching between two images. Unlike the first-order matching method that establishes consistent correspondences between features using pairwise relationships, i.e., the relational order between vertices is two. The high-order matching method, on the other hand, is concerned with high-order structural matching, i.e., the relational orders are not restricted to two. We use the new high-order matching method to identify the mismatches in the coarse first-order depth-based matching results, and reject the resulting inconsistent matches.

For a pair of graphs $G_p(V_p, E_p)$ and $G_q(V_q, E_q)$ abstracted from two sample images I_p and I_q, we commence by computing the correspondence matrix C using the first-order depth-based matching defined in Section 3.1. The matrix C records the matched vertex pairs between G_p and G_q. Assume we identify M pairs of vertices between G_p and G_q through the matrix C. We denote the M vertices of G_p as $V_p^M = \{v_1, \ldots, v_M\}$, and the M vertices of G_q as $V_q^M = \{u_1, \ldots, u_M\}$. The vertices $v_1, \ldots, v_M$ are matched with the vertices $u_1, \ldots, u_M$, respectively. With the M vertex matching results to hand, we exploit a new hypergraph matching strategy for refining the matching results. For G_p, we use the vertices $v_1, \ldots, v_M$ of G_p to form an uniform hypergraph HG_p. HG_p is a 3-order uniform hypergraph, and each hyperedge consists of three vertices. For each hyperedge of HG_p formed by three vertices $v_i, v_j, v_k \in V_p^M$, we compute its weight by measuring both the spatial similarity and the structural similarity between $v_i, v_j, v_k \in V_p^M$. Let $\mathcal{A}$ be the adjacency tensor for HG_p, its (i, j, k)-th entry $a_{i,j,k}$ represents the weight of the hyperedge formed by $v_i, v_j, v_k \in V_p^M$ and is determined by

$$a_{i,j,k} = W_C(v_i, v_j, v_k) \cdot W_{DB}(v_i, v_j, v_k), \tag{9}$$

where $W_C(v_i, v_j, v_k)$ is the spatial similarity based on the pixel coordinates of $v_i, v_j, v_k \in V_p^M$ in the original image I_p, and is defined as

$$W_C(v_i, v_j, v_k) = \det([c_i - c_k, c_j - c_k]) \cdot \sum_{i,j,k} \frac{1}{\sqrt{||c_i - c_k|| \cdot ||c_j - c_k||}}, \tag{10}$$

where c_i, c_j, c_k are all two dimensional column vectors representing the pixel coordinates of $v_i, v_j, v_k \in V_p^M$ separately, and $W_{DB}(v_i, v_j, v_k)$ is the structural similarity based on the Jensen-Shannon divergence measure between the h-layer depth-based representations of $v_i, v_j, v_k \in V_p^M$ computed from the original graph G_p, and is defined as

$$W_{DB}(v_i, v_j, v_k) = \exp(-\mathcal{D}_{JSD}(V_p^M)). \tag{11}$$

where $\mathcal{D}_{JSD}(V_p^M)$ is the dissimilarity measure of $v_i, v_j, v_k \in V_p^M$ through the Jensen-Shannon divergence, and is defined in Eq.(6).

Eq.(9), Eq.(10) and Eq.(11) indicates that $a_{i,j,k}$ not only encapsulates the spatial co-relation of v_i, v_j, v_k in the original image I_p, but also reflects the structural co-realtion of v_i, v_j, v_k in the graph G_p abstracted from I_p. Note that, the value of $a_{i,j,k}$ equals to zero if there is no hyperedge encompassing v_i, v_j, v_k. Moreover, the value of $a_{i,j,k}$ is great when the three vertices are geometrically and structurally similar, and is small if these vertices are geometrically and structurally different. Similarly, for the graph G_q, we also use the vertices u_1, ..., u_M of G_q to form an uniform hypergraph HG_q. Let the adjacency tensor for HG_q be denoted as $\mathcal{B}$. The (i,j,k)-th entry $b_{i,j,k}$ represents the weight of the hyperedge formed by $u_i, u_j, u_k \in V_q^M$.

Through the hypergraphs HG_p and HG_q, we establish the associated hypergraph HG, whose M vertices represent the possible matching pairs between the images I_p and I_q, and the weight on its hyperedge measures the similarity of the potential correspondences. We construct the adjacency tensor $\mathcal{S}$ of HG. The (i,j,k)-th entry $s_{i,j,k}$ of $\mathcal{S}$ represents the corresponding hyperedge weight and is defined as

$$S_{i,j,k} = \exp[-\frac{\|a_{i,j,k} - b_{i,j,k}\|_2^2}{\sigma}]   \tag{12}$$

where σ is a scaling parameter. Eq.(12) characterizes the structural consistency between the hypergraphs HG_p and HG_q, which are constructed by the graph G_p and G_q from the images I_p and I_q.

3.3 Structural Refinement for First-Order Depth-Based Matching Results

The task of structurally refining the first-order feature point matching results can be transformed into removing outliers, i.e., the incorrect matching results, from a tight cluster in the subspace spanned by the adjacency tensor $\mathcal{S}$ of the association hypergraph HG. According to Ren et al. [1], we apply the variation of dominant cluster analysis (DCA), the High Order Dominant Cluster Analysis (HO-DCA), to removing the outliers. Hence, we denote the column vector $\mathbf{x}$ to record the matching score, whose nth entry x_n ($n=1, \ldots, M$) indicates the degree of the structural consistency for the potential matching pairs $\{v_n, u_n\}$. Let $\mathbf{T}$ denote the subset of vertices in HG with vertices represent the correct matching pairs for HG_p and HG_q. As a result, the nth entry x_n of $\mathbf{x}$ also represent the probability for the nth vertex in HG belong to $\mathbf{T}$. For our three-dimensional tensor by using these ingredients, the optimal model can be formulate as

$$\hat{\mathbf{x}} = \arg\max_{\mathbf{x}} \sum_{i=1}^{M}\sum_{j=1}^{M}\sum_{k=1}^{M} S_{i,j,k} \prod_{n=i,j,k} x_n   \tag{13}$$

subject to the constraints $\forall n$, $x_n \geq 0$ and $\sum_{i=1}^{M} x_i = 1$.

According to Eq.(13), if the initial matching pair $\{v_n, u_n\}$ is an incorrect matching pair of $\mathbf{T}$, then the n-th entry x_n of $\mathbf{x}$ will be much less than 1. We refer to the nonzero value x_n of $\mathbf{x}$ satisfying the optimality condition in Eq.(13)

as the association degree for the matching pair $\{p_n, q_n\}$. Therefore, the problem of the moving outliers can be solved as a constraint optimization problem. Based on [1], we adopt the following iterative formula to reach the convergence of x_i

$$x_i(t+1) = x_i(t) \frac{\sum_{j=1}^{M}\sum_{k=1}^{M} S_{i,j,k} \prod_{n=j,k} x_n(t)}{\sum_{i=1}^{M}\sum_{j=1}^{M}\sum_{k=1}^{M} S_{i,j,k} \prod_{n=i,j,k} x_n(t)} \tag{14}$$

where t indicate the t-th iteration. The rest M-1 entries of $\mathbf{x}$ can be computed in the same iterative formula (14).

In this work, we use Eq.(14) to update the score vector $\mathbf{x}$ until we reach convergence. At convergence the score vector $\mathbf{x}$ is the optimal solution to Eq.(13) and the nonzero elements in $\mathbf{x}$ corresponds to correct matches.

4   Experiments

4.1   Delaunay Graphs Abstracted from Images

In this paper, we represent each image as a graph structure for the objective of structural matching. To this end, for an image, we commence by extracting its corner points using the SIFT detector [14]. We establish the Delaunay graph for the image by using the corner points as vertices. Here, each vertex is used as the seed of a Voronoi region, which expands radially with a constant speed. The linear collision fronts of the regions delineate the image plane into polygons, and the resulting Delaunay graph is the region adjacency graph for the Voronoi polygons. Examples of two images and their Delaunay graphs are shown in Fig. 1.

Fig. 1. Delaunay graph examples from COIL images.

4.2   Matching Results

To demonstrate the performance on image matching problems using our high-order depth-based matching method, we perform some real-world data experiments. We apply our matching method on the COIL image database. The COIL image database consists of images of 100 3D objects. For each object, there are 72 images that are taken from different viewing directions spaced at intervals of 5 degrees around the object. In the experiment, we use the images from four

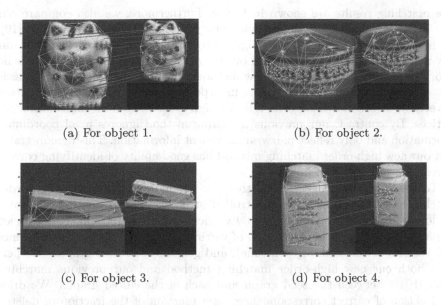

(a) For object 1.   (b) For object 2.

(c) For object 3.   (d) For object 4.

Fig. 2. High-order depth-based matching results.

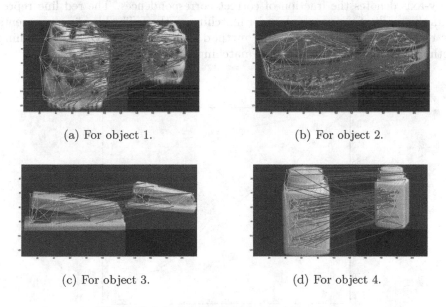

(a) For object 1.   (b) For object 2.

(c) For object 3.   (d) For object 4.

Fig. 3. Original depth-based matching results.

randomly selected objects. For each object, we select a pair of images taken from 0 degree and 15 degrees respectively. For each pair of images from an object, we establish the pair of Delaunay graphs based on the method described in Section 4.1 and perform the high-order depth-based matching method for the graphs.

The matching results are shown in Fig. 2. Furthermore, we also compare our new high-order matching method with our previous matching method in [10], the matching results are shown in Fig. 3. From these results, it is clear that our new matching method is better than our previous matching method. There is no incorrect matching result for our new method. The reason of the effectiveness is that our new matching method either incorporates pixel coordinate information of vertices in original images or reflects high-order alignment information for vertices. By contrast, our previous matching method ignores pixel coordinate information and only reflect pairwise alignment information. This demonstrates that our new high-order matching method has good ability of identifying correct correspondences between images.

To take our study one step further, we evaluate how the new high-order matching method works under controlled structural corruption. We utilize a randomly generated graph having 400 vertices as the seed graph. For the seed graph, we randomly delete a fraction of vertices. We delete the vertices 10 times (1% vertices are deleted for each time), and generate 10 edited graphs. We perform both our new high-order matching method and our previous matching method [10] between the seed graph and each of the edited graphs. We draw the fraction of correct correspondences as a function of the fraction of deleted vertices in Fig. 4. In Fig. 4, the x-axis denotes the fraction of vertices deleted and the y-axis denotes the fraction of correct correspondences. The red line represents the result of our new high-order matching method. The blue line represents the result of our previous matching method. It is clear that our new matching method is better than our previous matching method.

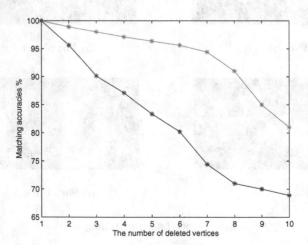

(a) Matching evaluations under graph corruption.

Fig. 4. Matching evaluations on synthetic data.

5   Conclusion

In this paper, we have developed a novel high-order depth-based matching method for graph based image matching problems. We commence by refining our previous depth-based matching method as a new first-order depth-based matching method, by incorporating the pixel coordinates of vertices in original images. Furthermore, we develop a new high-order depth-based matching method. We use the new high-order matching method to identify the mismatches in the first-order matching results, and remove the incorrect matches. Experiments on real world image databases demonstrate the effectiveness of our new high-order matching method.

Our future plans are to extend the new high-order matching method in a number of ways. First, the required Shannon entropy for the depth-based representation is computed associated with the steady state random walk. Since the random walk is based on the vertex degree which is structural simple, the Shannon entropy cannot reflect complicated information of graphs. In future work, we may consider to develop a new Shannon entropy that can encapsulate richer structural information. Second, in our previous work [15], we have developed a novel quantum Jensen-Shannon kernel using the quantum Jensen-Shannon divergence and the continuous-time quantum walk. In our feature work, we may also to consider to use the quantum Jensen-Shannon divergence as a means of computing the hyperedge weight, instead of the classical Jensen-Shannon divergence used in this work.

Acknowledgments. This work is supported by program for innovation research in Central University of Finance and Economics, and National Natural Science Foundation of China (Grant No. 61402389 and 61272398). Edwin R. Hancock is supported by a Royal Society Wolfson Research Merit Award.

References

1. Ren, P., Wilson, R.C., Hancock, E.R.: High order structural matching using dominant cluster analysis. In: Maino, G., Foresti, G.L. (eds.) ICIAP 2011, Part I. LNCS, vol. 6978, pp. 1–8. Springer, Heidelberg (2011)
2. Bai, X., Yu, H., Hancock, E.R.: Graph matching using spectral embedding and semidefinite programming. In: Proceedings of the British Machine Vision Conference, BMVC 2004, Kingston, UK, pp. 1–10, September 7–9, 2004
3. Bai, L., Hancock, E.R.: Graph kernels from the jensen-shannon divergence. Journal of Mathematical Imaging and Vision **47**, 60–69 (2013)
4. Bunke, H., Shearer, K.: A graph distance metric based on the maximal common subgraph. Pattern Recognition Letters **19**, 255–259 (1998)
5. Shapiro, L.G., Haralick, R.M.: A metric for comparing relational descriptions. IEEE Trans. Pattern Anal. Mach. Intell. **7**, 90–94 (1985)
6. Christmas, W.J., Kittler, J., Petrou, M.: Structural matching in computer vision using probabilistic relaxation. IEEE Trans. Pattern Anal. Mach. Intell. **17**, 749–764 (1995)

7. Emms, D., Wilson, R.C., Hancock, E.R.: Graph matching using the interference of discrete-time quantum walks. Image Vision Comput. **27**, 934–949 (2009)
8. Solé-Ribalta, A., Serratosa, F.: Graduated assignment algorithm for multiple graph matching based on a common labeling. IJPRAI **27** (2013)
9. Bai, L., Hancock, E.R.: Depth-based complexity traces of graphs. Pattern Recognition **47**, 1172–1186 (2014)
10. Bai, L., Ren, P., Bai, X., Hancock, E.R.: A graph kernel from the depth-based representation. In: Fränti, P., Brown, G., Loog, M., Escolano, F., Pelillo, M. (eds.) S+SSPR 2014. LNCS, vol. 8621, pp. 1–11. Springer, Heidelberg (2014)
11. Bai, L., Hancock, E.R., Ren, P.: Jensen-shannon graph kernel using information functionals. In: Proceedings of the 21st International Conference on Pattern Recognition, ICPR 2012, Tsukuba, Japan, pp. 2877–2880, November 11–15, 2012
12. Bai, L., Hancock, E.R.: A fast jensen-shannon subgraph kernel. In: Petrosino, A. (ed.) ICIAP 2013, Part I. LNCS, vol. 8156, pp. 181–190. Springer, Heidelberg (2013)
13. Scott, G.L., Longuett-Higgins, E.C.: An algorithm to associating the features of two images. In: Proceedings of the Royal Society of London B, pp. 313–320 (1991)
14. Kupfer, B., Netanyahu, N.S., Shimshoni, I.: An efficient sift-based mode-seeking algorithm for sub-pixel registration of remotely sensed images. IEEE Geosci. Remote Sensing Lett. **12**, 379–383 (2015)
15. Bai, L., Rossi, L., Torsello, A., Hancock, E.R.: A quantum jensen-shannon graph kernel for unattributed graphs. Pattern Recognition **48**, 344–355 (2015)

On Different Colour Spaces for Medical Colour Image Classification

Cecilia Di Ruberto, Giuseppe Fodde, and Lorenzo Putzu[✉]

Department of Mathematics and Computer Science, University of Cagliari,
via Ospedale 72, 09124 Cagliari, Italy
{dirubert,giufodde,lorenzo.putzu}@unica.it

Abstract. Analysis of cells and tissues allow the evaluation and diagnosis of a vast number of diseases. Nowadays this analysis is still performed manually, involving numerous drawbacks, in particular the results accuracy heavily depends on the operator skills. Differently, the automated analysis by computer is performed quickly, requires only one image of the sample and provides precise results. In this work we investigate different texture descriptors extracted from medical images in different colour spaces. We compare these features in order to identify the features set able to properly classify medical images presenting different classification problems. Furthermore, we investigate different colour spaces to identify most suitable for this purpose. The feature sets tested are based on a generalization of some existent grey scale approaches for feature extraction to colour images. The generalization has been applied to the calculation of Grey-Level Co-Occurrence Matrix, Grey-Level Difference Matrix and Grey-Level Run-Length Matrix. Furthermore, we calculate Grey-Level Run-Length Matrix starting from the Grey-Level Difference Matrix. The resulting feature sets performances have been compared using the Support Vector Machine model. To validate our method we have used three different databases, HistologyDS, Pap-smear and Lymphoma, that present different medical problems and so they represent different classification problems. The obtained experimental results have showed that in general features extracted from the HSV colour space perform better than the other and that the best feature subset has been obtained from the generalized Grey-Level Co-Occurrence Matrix, demonstrating excellent performances for this purpose.

Keywords: Medical image analysis · Features extraction · Machine learning · Colour texture classification

1 Introduction

Histology is the study of the microscopic structure of cells and tissues of organisms. The knowledge of biological microscopic structures and their functions at the sub-cellular, cellular, tissue and organ levels is essential for the study of grading and prognosis of disease. Image analysis involves complex algorithms which identify and characterize cellular colour, shape and quantity of the tissue sample using

© Springer International Publishing Switzerland 2015
G. Azzopardi and N. Petkov (Eds.): CAIP 2015, Part I, LNCS 9256, pp. 477–488, 2015.
DOI: 10.1007/978-3-319-23192-1_40

image pattern recognition technology. Tissue image analysis could be used to measure the cancer cells in a biopsy of a cancerous tumour taken from a patient and it can significantly reduce uncertainty in characterizing tumours compared to evaluations done by histologists, or improve the prediction rate of recurrence of some cancers. For example, in [1] global features are used to automatically discriminate lymphoma, in [2] image texture informations are used to automatically discriminate polyps in colonscopy images and in [3] wavelet features are used for the detection of tumours in endoscopic images. These different applications share similar computer techniques to support clinicians in automatic extraction of histological image features and classification. A typical system for histology image analysis consists of conventional image processing and analysis tools, including preprocessing, image segmentation, feature extraction and classification. For this system, traditional features include morphometrics with object size and shape, intensity and colour features and in particular texture features. Although there is not a specific definition of texture accepted by all, it can be viewed as a global descriptor generated from the repetition of local patterns. Texture is an any and repetitive geometric arrangement of the grey levels of an image. It provides important information about the spatial disposition of the grey levels and the relationship with their neighbourhood. Human visual system determines and recognizes easily different types of textures but although for a human observer it is very simple to associate a surface with a texture, to give a rigorous definition for this is very complex. Typically a qualitative definition is used to describe textures. It can be easily guessed that the quantitative analysis of texture is obtained through statistical and structural relations among the basic elements of what we call just texture. The most important aspect of texture analysis is classification that concerns the search for a particular texture among different predefined classes of texture. Classification is carried out using statistical methods that define the descriptors of the texture. Many different methods for managing texture have been developed that are based on the various ways texture can be characterized. Although there are many powerful methods reported in the literature for texture analysis, including the scale-invariant feature transform (SIFT) [4], speeded up robust feature (SURF) [5], histogram of oriented gradients (HOG) [6], local binary patterns (LBP) [7], Gabor filters [8] and others, in this work we focus on improving some of the earliest methods used for the analysis of grey level texture based on statistical approaches, that are: grey level co-occurrence matrix (GLCM), grey level difference matrix (GLDM), grey level run-length matrix (GLRLM). Motivated by the wide diffusion of these methods and by the increasing numbers of medical datasets presenting colour images we wished to investigate the possibility to improve the accuracy of these methods using the colour information. Some interesting methods have been presented in order to extend the original implementation of GLCM. In [9] the authors evaluated different values for the distance parameter that influence the matrices computation, in [10] the GLCM descriptors are extracted by calculating the weighted sum of GLCM elements, in [11] the GLCM features are calculated by using the local gradient of the matrix. In [12] to calculate the features, the grey levels and the edge orientation of the image are considered. In [13] the authors proposed to use a variable window size by multiple scales to extract descriptors by GLCM. The method in [14] uses the colour gradient to extract from GLCM statistical features. In [15] various types of GLCM descriptors (classical Haralick features and features from 3D co-occurrence matrix) and grey-level run-length features are extracted. Although the colour information to extract GLCM has already been used by other authors such as [16], one of the goals of this work is to evaluate the performance improvement that can arise from the computation and integration of many statistical features using the colour information, in particular we wish to investigate which colour space leads to better performances. The classification accuracy of each feature subsets have been compared using the Support Vector Machine (SVM), that we consider as the best classification model for biomedical application, as we showed in [17]. To validate our method we have used three different databases, HistologyDS [18], Pap-smear [19] and Lymphoma [20], that present different medical problems and so they represent different classification problems. So, our main goal is to find a set of features able to properly classify medical images presenting different classification problem. In [21] an exhaustive comparison of colour texture features and classification methods for medical image has been made, but the authors validated their method using only one database dealing with only one medical problem, that consists on discrimination of cells categories in histological images of fish ovary. The rest of the paper is organized as follows. In section 2 we report some background information necessary to introduce the existing methods used. Section 3 shows the approach proposed for the inclusion of colour information to the existent methods. Section 4 presents the experimentations realised to asses the classification performances. Finally, in section 5 we present our conclusions and some possible future works.

2 Background

A feature is defined as a function of one or more measurements, specifying some quantifiable property of an object. Features are classified into two distinct groups:

- general features: application independent features such as colour, texture and shape. They can be further divided into features calculated at each pixel, like colour and location (*pixel-level features*), features calculated over the results of segmentation or edge detection (*local features*) and features calculated over the entire image or sub-image (*global features*).
- domain-specific features: application dependent features such as human faces, fingerprints and conceptual features.

Moreover, all features can be coarsely classified into low-level features and high-level features. Low-level features can be extracted directly from the original images, whereas high-level feature extraction must be based on low-level features. There are various methods for features extraction and texture classification and the most important are based on statistical approach. In our work, to analyse a texture present in an image we use a statistical approach that provides the features extraction at various levels: co-occurrence and difference matrices, related to the low-level features, and run-length matrix related to the high-level ones.

2.1   Grey Level Co-Occurrence Matrix

One of the most powerful model for texture analysis was proposed by Haralick [22]. His method involves the creation of the grey level co-occurrence matrices GLCMs from which features that represent some image aspects, can be calculated. A GLCM represents the probability of finding two pixels i and j with distance d and orientation θ and it is denoted with $p_{d,\theta}(i,j)$. Obviously, the d and θ values can assume different values, but the most used are $d = 1$ and $\theta = [0°, 45°, 90°, 135°]$. A GLCM for an image of size N x M with N_g grey levels is a 2D array of size Ng x Ng. Haralick proposed thirteen descriptors that can be extracted from these matrices: *Angular Second Moment, Contrast, Correlation, Variance, Inverse Difference Moment, Sum Average, Sum Variance, Sum Entropy, Entropy, Difference Variance, Difference Entropy, Measure of correlation 1 and 2.*

2.2   Grey Level Difference Matrix

Another useful tool for texture analysis is the grey level difference matrix (GLDM) [23], that is a particular type of matrix originated by the absolute differences between pairs of grey levels. Actually, the GLDM is defined in a manner very similar to the GLCM, using the same notions of distance and orientation to find the pairs of grey levels. The main difference arises in the construction and dimension of the matrix. In fact, the GLDM preserves the size of the original image N x M (and not Ng x Ng), collecting the absolute difference between pairs of pixel values (and not the occurrences of two grey levels). This matrix is used to calculate the histogram $h(d)$ that denotes the number of differences with value d. The histogram is then normalized $h_N(d) = h(d)/N$ with $N = \sum_d h(d)$ in order to compute easily nine descriptors: *Mean, Angular Second Moment, Contrast, Variance, Inverse Difference Moment, Entropy, Product Moment, Cluster Shade* and *Cluster Prominence.*

2.3   Grey Level Run-Length Matrix

A different tool for texture analysis is based on information of higher order statistics that uses the grey level run-length matrices (GLRLMs) [24]. In this approach the GLRLM contains information on a particular number of equal grey levels (run) in a given direction. So, a run-length matrix is defined as a set of consecutive pixels having the same grey level. The element (i,j) of a run-length matrix specifies the number of times that the image contains a run of length j composed by all pixels with grey level i. The creation of the run-length matrices is very simple and the number of operations to be done is directly proportional to the number of image points. A coarse texture will be characterized by a long run while a finer texture will be characterized by shorter run. Also, the GLRLMs are calculated by considering the main four orientations and for each matrix eleven descriptors can be extracted: *Short Run Emphasis, Long Run Emphasis, Grey Level Non-uniformity, Run Length Non-uniformity, Run Percentage, Low*

Grey Level Run Emphasis, High Grey Level Run Emphasis, Short Run Low Grey Level Emphasis, Short Run High Grey Level Emphasis, Long Run Low Grey Level Emphasis, Long Run High Grey Level Emphasis.

3   Our Proposed System

In order to extend the classical grey level texture features to colour texture features we start by decomposing the colour image into the three channels Ch_1, Ch_2 and Ch_3, obtaining three different images, as we proposed in [25]. The most intuitive way to take into account colour information for the computation of texture feature is to use the classical implementation and pass to them every time a different colour channel. This approach could be very useful thanks to a higher number of significant descriptors extracted and passed to the classifier. An improvement to this approach belongs to the combination of the colour channels in pairs $(Ch_k, Ch_{k'})$ with $k, k' = [1, 2, 3]$. This improvement is necessary in order to take into account not only repeated pattern inside the same colour channel, but also the correlation between the colour channels. The results of this combination is a feature vector nine time longer than the classical feature vector, composed by three intra-channel feature vector (Ch_1, Ch_1), (Ch_2, Ch_2) and (Ch_3, Ch_3) and six extra-channels feature vector (Ch_1, Ch_2), (Ch_2, Ch_1), (Ch_1, Ch_3), (Ch_3, Ch_1), (Ch_2, Ch_3) and (Ch_3, Ch_2).

3.1   Features Extraction

However, not all these combinations make sense. In fact for features like GLCM and GLDM combining the channels in pairs means that the occurrences and differences for $(Ch_k, Ch_{k'})$ are calculated by storing on each (i, j) the number of occurrences (differences) of $i \epsilon Ch_k$ and $j \epsilon Ch_{k'}$ having distance=d and orientation=θ and the number of occurrences (differences) of $i \epsilon Ch_{k'}$ and $j \epsilon Ch_k$ having distance=d and orientation=θ. So, the vice versa produces the same result. Thus, for GLCM and GLDM only three extra-channels combination have been used, that are (Ch_1, Ch_2), (Ch_1, Ch_3) and (Ch_2, Ch_3). So, from these six combinations we compute the occurrences with $d = 1$ and $\theta = [0°, 45°, 90°, 135°]$ producing 24 GLCMs and 312 features. In the same way we compute the 24 GLDMs and a total number of 216 features. Obviously, the GLRLMs can be computed by using the three classical bands only, but in order to consider also repetitive pattern belonging to different colour bands we have decided to extract also run-lengths starting from the difference matrix. This brings to 36 GLRMs considering the three colour bands that we have used to compute run-lengths in the four main directions (12 GLRMs) and the 24 GLDMS already computed, that we have used to compute run-lengths in the four main directions (96 GLRLMs). From all these matrices we have extracted their respective features, for a total of 1188 descriptors (see Fig. 1).

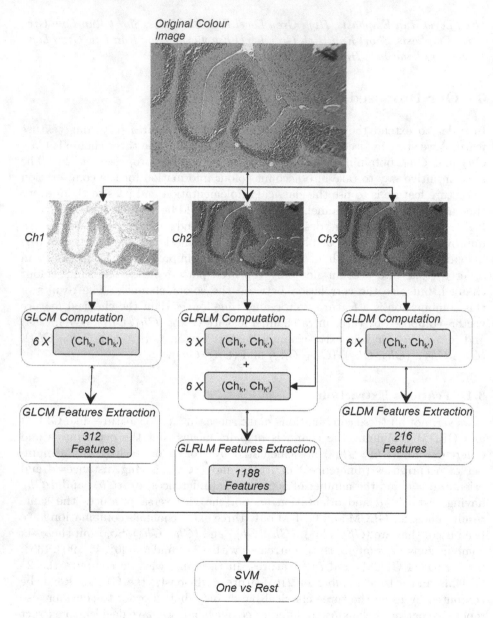

Fig. 1. Diagram of the system for colour medical image analysis.

3.2 Classification

Each extracted feature subset has been used to train a Support Vector Machine (SVM), that we consider as the best classification model for biomedical application, as we showed in [17], where we compared different classification model performances for classification of white blood cells affected by leukaemia.

The SVM classifier is trained using the *one VS rest* approach because it is the fastest to create our classification model. During our experimentations we have tested various kernels and parameters and after a process of cross-validation we have selected the one leading to better results. For each kernel function the parameters have been tuned through optimization techniques in order to find the maximum accuracy value. The selected kernel function is the RBF that uses a Gaussian radial basis function, with c parameter equal to $1e3$ and γ equal to $1e2$. Given the variable size of the datasets we have decided to perform the validation of our method using a 5 time repeated stratified holdout, which guarantees that each class is properly represented both in the training set and in the test set and at the same time it averages the roles of each subset. In our experiments training and test sets are represented respectively by the 80% and the 20% of the samples. The performances of the classification models have been evaluated by calculating the accuracy, which gives us a good indication of the performance since it considers each class of equal importance.

4   Experimental Evaluation

The experimentation has been carried out on three of the most famous colour medical image databases, HistologyDS, Pap-smear and Lymphoma, that represent three very different computer vision problems.

4.1   HystologyDS

HystologyDS database (HIS) is a collection of 20,000 images of histology for the study of fundamental tissues [18]. It is provided in a subset of 2828 images annotated by four fundamental tissues: connective, epithelial, muscular and nervous. Each tissue is captured in a 24-bit RGB image of size 720x480. Some tissue images from HIS database are showed in Fig. 2. The database is available at the following link: $http://168.176.61.90/histologyDS/$

4.2   Pap-Smear

Pap-smear database (PAP) is a collection of pap-smear images acquired from healthy and cancerous smears coming from the Herlev University Hospital (Denmark) [19]. This database is composed by 917 images containing cells, annotated

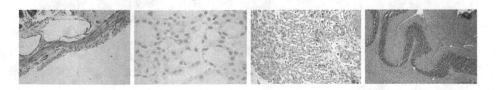

Fig. 2. Four different tissues from HistologyDS database.

into seven classes, four representing abnormal cells and three representing normal cases. Nevertheless, from the medical diagnosis viewpoint the most important requirement corresponds to the general two-class problem of correct separation between normal and abnormal cells. For this reason in our experiments we have tested only the binary case. Each cell is captured in a 24-bit RGB image without a fixed size that ranges from about 50x50 to about 300x300. Some examples are showed in Fig. 3. The database is available at the following link: $http://labs.fme.aegean.gr/decision/downloads$

4.3 Lymphoma

Lymphoma database (LYM) [20] is a collection of tissues affected by malignant lymphoma, a cancer affecting lymph nodes. Three types of malignant lymphoma are represented in the set: Chronic Lymphocytic Leukemia (CLL), Follicular Lymphoma (FL) and Mantle Cell Lymphoma (MCL). This dataset presents a collection of samples from biopses sectioned and stained by different pathologists at different sites. Only the most expert pathologists specialised in these types of lymphomas are able to consistently and accurately classify these three lymphoma types. This slide collection contains significant variation in sectioning and staining and for this reason it is more representative of slides commonly encountered in a clinical setting. This database contains a collection of 374 slides captured in a 24-bit RGB image of size 1380×1040. The database is available at the following link: $http://ome.grc.nia.nih.gov/iicbu2008/$. Some examples are showed in Fig. 4.

4.4 Numerical Results

As said previously, our aim was to compare all the feature subsets extracted with our approach in order to individuate the colour space that leads to better performances. The colour spaces considered for our experiments are: RGB, HSV , L*a*b*, Luv and Ycbcr, that are representative of the three colour space families, the primary spaces, the luminance-chrominance spaces and the perceptual spaces. So, we have tested the original features subsets separately on

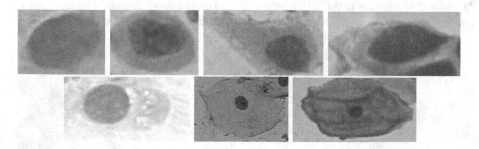

Fig. 3. The seven classes of cells belonging to Pap-smear database: first four abnormal and last three normal.

each database to asses its classification performance applied on different medical problems. The results are reported in Table 1.

As it can be seen from the table, the results are not so in favour of one of the colour space, but it is interesting to see how all the features subsets extracted from the other colour spaces outperform the feature subsets extracted using the RGB colour space. In the last column we report an overall evaluation in order to better identify the colour space who leads to better performances. In general, we can confirm that the HSV is the colour space that outperforms the others, considering all the database. Furthermore, it can be noted that the best results have been obtained using the feature subset created with the generalised co-occurrence matrix extracted from the Ycbcr. For comparison purpose we realised the same test for all the databases and the different colour spaces using the opposite colour LBP based classification as proposed in [26]. The results are reported in Table 2. Differently from the other descriptors, LBP performs better

Fig. 4. Three different kinds of lymphoma belonging to Lymphoma database.

Table 1. Accuracy values after testing each feature subset with each colour space.

Colour Space	Database	GLCM features	GLDM features	GLRL features	GLDMRL features	Overall evaluation
RGB	HIS	89.65 ± 1.6	81.43 ± 1.8	76.18 ± 1.9	86.67 ± 1.7	83.48 ± 5.3
	PAP	93.61 ± 2.1	85.36 ± 2.5	83.93 ± 2.7	89.95 ± 2.3	88,21 ± 3.8
	LYM	92.77 ± 1.5	79.13 ± 1.3	71.87 ± 1.7	87.07 ± 1.6	82,71 ± 7.9
HSV	HIS	93.14 ± 0.7	**86.87** ± 1.2	89.80 ± 1.5	**91.18** ± 1.5	90,24 ± 2.3
	PAP	**94.95** ± 1.5	**88.85** ± 2.3	90.05 ± 1.9	**90.71** ± 1.5	**91,14** ± 2.3
	LYM	95.63 ± 1.3	**88.67** ± 1.8	85.6 ± 2.1	83.33 ± 1.9	88,30 ± 4.6
Lab	HIS	93.21 ± 1.1	86.8 ± 0.6	90.63 ± 1.1	90.1 ± 1.1	90,18 ± 2.3
	PAP	93.99 ± 1.4	87.76 ± 1.8	90.16 ± 1.8	89.78 ± 2.0	90,42 ± 2.2
	LYM	94.27 ± 1.4	84.4 ± 1.9	87.2 ± 2.2	83.73 ± 1.8	87,4 ± 4.1
Luv	HIS	92.84 ± 0.9	84.54 ± 1.4	90.12 ± 1.7	90.61 ± 1.4	89,52 ± 3
	PAP	94.92 ± 1.7	83,64 ± 2.4	90.55 ± 1.5	88.9 ± 2.2	89,5 ± 4.1
	LYM	95.2 ± 1.7	82.0 ± 1.6	**89.6** ± 1.8	**87.47** ± 1.3	**88,56** ± 4.7
Ycbcr	HIS	**93.86** ± 1.0	85.95 ± 1.1	**91.16** ± 1.3	90.79 ± 1.4	**90,4** ± 2.8
	PAP	94.15 ± 2.3	85.52 ± 2.1	**90.49** ± 1.2	89.89 ± 1.5	90 ± 3
	LYM	**96.4** ± 1.6	83.32 ± 1.4	87.6 ± 1.9	86.53 ± 1.2	88,46 ± 4.8

Table 2. Accuracy values with opposite colour LBP.

Dataset	RGB	HSV	LAB	LUV	YCBCR
HIS	88.6 ± 1.3	88.6 ± 1.6	88.6 ± 1.0	81.1 ± 0.9	86.7 ± 1.0
PAP	86.0 ± 2.0	84.9 ± 2.2	86.7 ± 1.7	85.8 ± 1.2	86.7 ± 2.4
LYM	95.9 ± 2.5	94.0 ± 2.1	93.7 ± 2.7	84.7 ± 4.2	94.1 ± 2.6

Table 3. Summary table with our results compared to LBP and the state of the art.

Database	GLCM (Ycbcr)	LBP (RGB)	Previous Best
HIS	93.86 ± 1.0	88.6 ± 1.3	92.4 [15]
PAP	94.15 ± 2.3	86.0 ± 2.0	92.5 [15]
LYM	96.4 ± 1.6	95.9 ± 2.5	85 [20]

using the RGB colour spaces, but as it can be noted their performances are good only for one of the dataset taken into account. To summarise, we report the experimentation results in Table 3. The best feature subset tested is the GLCM extracted from the Ycbcr colour space, the best results obtained with opposite colour LBP using the RGB colour space and the previous best results for each database obtained by other authors.

5 Conclusions

In this work we have proposed a successful comparison of statistical texture features in order to classify colour medical images. The feature set has been obtained by generalizing the existent grey scale approaches to colour images, by decomposing the original colour image in separated bands and then recombining the bands in pairs. This approach has permitted to extract more meaningful descriptors useful for colour texture classification. Furthermore, we investigated different colour spaces in order to identify which one leads the better results. All the resulting feature subset has been compared in classification accuracy using to train a Support Vector Machine model. The classification results obtained by testing each feature subset separately on three different databases, HistologyDS, Pap-smear and Lymphoma, have showed that the HSV colour space outperforms the others and that the co-occurrence matrix features extracted using the colour information are the best features in recognizing different types of tissues and classifying diseases, outperforming the existing methods present in literature for all the database tested. The next step for this work will include the extension of our approach to LBP and trying to combine this local descriptor with the tested global descriptors. Another issue will consist in a further reduction of the feature set used in order to decrease the training time, being able to apply our approach on bigger databases with other significant medical problems, including the possibility to study different stages of pathology, if present. Further research will be devoted to improve robustness and accuracy of the method in rotation invariant classification task, which is an important issue especially for medical images that can occur in different and uncontrolled rotation angles.

Acknowledgments. This work has been funded by Regione Autonoma della Sardegna (R.A.S.) Project CRP-17615 DENIS: Dataspace Enhancing Next Internet in Sardinia. Lorenzo Putzu gratefully acknowledges Sardinia Regional Government for the financial support of his PhD scholarship (P.O.R. Sardegna F.S.E. Operational Programme of the Autonomous Region of Sardinia, European Social Fund 2007-2013 - Axis IV Human Resources, Objective 1.3, Line of Activity 1.3.1.).

References

1. Orlov, N.V., Chen, W., Eckley, D.M., Macura, T., Shamir, L., Jaffe, E.S., Goldberg, I.G.: Automatic Classification of Lymphoma Images with Transform-based Global Features. IEEE Transactions on Information Technology in Biomedicine **14**(4), 1003–1013 (2010)
2. Ameling, S., Wirth, S., Paulus, D., Lacey, G., Vilarino, F.: Texture-based polyp detection in colonoscopy. Bildverarbeitung fr die Medizin, pp. 346–350 (2009)
3. Karkanis, S.A., Iakovidis, D.K., Maroulis, D.E., Karras, D.A., Tzivras, M.: Computer-aided tumor detection in endoscopic video using color wavelet features. IEEE Transaction on Information Technology in Biomedicine **7**(3), 141–152 (2003)
4. Lowe, D.G.: Distinctive image features from scale-invariant keypoints. International Journal of Computer Vision **60**(2), 91–110 (2004)
5. Bay, H., Tuytelaars, T., Van Gool, L.: SURF: speeded up robust features. In: Leonardis, A., Bischof, H., Pinz, A. (eds.) ECCV 2006, Part I. LNCS, vol. 3951, pp. 404–417. Springer, Heidelberg (2006)
6. Dalal, N., Triggs, B.: Histograms of oriented gradients for human detection. IEEE Computer Society Conference on Conference on Computer Vision and Pattern Recognition (CVPR) **1**, 886–893 (2005)
7. Ojala, T., Pietikinen, M., Harwood, D.: A comparative study of texture measures with classification based on featured distributions. Pattern Recognition **29**(1), 51–59 (1996)
8. Jain, A.K., Farrokhnia, F.: Unsupervised texture segmentation using Gabor filters. In: IEEE International Conference on Systems, Man and Cybernetics, pp. 14–19 (1990)
9. Gelzinis, A., Verikas, A., Bacauskiene, M.: Increasing the discrimination power of the co-occurrence matrix-based features. Pattern Recognition **40**(9), 2367–2372 (2007)
10. Walker, R., Jackway, P., Longstaff, D.: Genetic algorithm optimization of adaptive multi-scale GLCM features. International Journal of Pattern Recognition and Artificial Intelligence **17**(1), 17–39 (2003)
11. Chen, S., Chengdong, W., Chen, D., Tan, W.: Scene classification based on gray level-gradient co-occurrence matrix in the neighborhood of interest points. IEEE International Conference on Intelligent Computing and Intelligent Systems (ICIS), pp. 482–485 (2009)
12. Mitrea, D., Mitrea, P., Nedevschi, S., Badea, R., Lupsor, M.: Abdominal tumor characterization and recognition using superior-order cooccurrence matrices, based on ultrasound images. Computational and Mathematical Methods in Medicine **2012** (2012)

13. Hu, Y.: Unsupervised texture classification by combining multi-scale features and k-means classifier. In: Chinese Conference on Pattern Recognition, pp. 1–5 (2009)
14. Gong, R., Wang, H.: Steganalysis for GIF images based on colors-gradient co-occurrence matrix. Optics Communications **285**(24), 4961–4965 (2012)
15. Nanni, L., Brahnam, S., Ghidoni, S., Menegatti, E., Barrier, T.: Different Approaches for Extracting Information from the Co-Occurrence Matrix. PLoS One **8**(12) (2013)
16. Benco, M., Hudec, R.: Novel method for color textures features extraction based on GLCM. Radioengineering **4**(16), 64–67 (2007)
17. Putzu, L., Di Ruberto, C.: Investigation of different classification models to determine the presence of leukemia in peripheral blood image. In: Petrosino, A. (ed.) ICIAP 2013, Part I. LNCS, vol. 8156, pp. 612–621. Springer, Heidelberg (2013)
18. Cruz-Roa, A., Caicedo, J.C., Gonzlez, F.A.: Visual Pattern Mining in Histology Image Collections Using Bag of Features. Artificial Intelligence in Medicine **52**(2), 91–106 (2011)
19. Jantzen, J., Dounias, G.: Analysis of pap-smear data. In: NISIS 2006, Puerto de la Cruz, Tenerife, Spain (2006)
20. Shamir, L., Orlov, N., Eckley, D.M., Macura, T., Goldberg, I.G.: A Proposed Benchmark Suite for Biological Image Analysis. Medical and Biological Engineering and Computing **46**(9), 943–947 (2008)
21. Gonzlez-Rufino, E., Carrin, P., Cernadas, E., Fernndez-Delgado, M., Domnguez-Petit, R.: Exhaustive comparison of colour texture features and classification methods to discriminate cells categories in histological images of fish ovary. Pattern Recognition **46**(9), 2391–2407 (2013)
22. Haralick, R.M., Shanmugam, K., Dinstein, I.: Textural Features for Image Classification. IEEE Transactions on Systems, Man and Cybernetics **3**(6), 610–621 (1973)
23. Conners, R.W., Harlow, C.A.: A Theoretical Comparison of Texture Algorithms. IEEE Transactions on Pattern Analysis and Machine Intelligence (PAMI) (3), 204–222 (1980)
24. Tang, X.: Texture Information in Run-Length Matrices. IEEE Transactions Image Processing **7**(11), 1602–1609 (1998)
25. Di Ruberto, C., Fodde, G., Putzu, L.: Comparison of statistical features for medical colour image classification. In: Nalpantidis, L., Krüger, V., Eklundh, J.-O., Gasteratos, A. (eds.) ICVS 2015. LNCS, vol. 9163, pp. 3–13. Springer, Heidelberg (2015)
26. Porebski, A., Vandenbroucke, N., Hamad, D.: LBP histogram selection for supervised color texture classification. In: IEEE International Conference on Image Processing (ICIP), pp. 3239–3243 (2013)

SIFT Descriptor for Binary Shape Discrimination, Classification and Matching

Insaf Setitra[1,2] and Slimane Larabi[2]([✉])

[1] Research Center on Scientific and Technical Information Cerist,
Ben Aknoun, Algeria
[2] University of Science and Technology Houari Boumediene, Bab Ezzouar, Algeria
isetitra@cerist.dz, slarabi@usthb.dz

Abstract. In this work, we study efficiency of SIFT descriptor in discrimination of binary shapes. We also analyze how the use of $2-tuples$ of SIFT keypoints can affect discrimination of shapes. The study is divided into two parts, the first part serves as a primary analysis where we propose to compute overlap of classes using SIFT and a majority vote of keypoints. In the second part, we analyze both classification and matching of binary shapes using SIFT and Bag of Features. Our empirical study shows that SIFT although being considered as a texture feature, can be used to distinguish shapes in binary images and can be applied to the classification of foreground's silhouettes.

Keywords: SIFT · Shape description · Classification · Image retrieval

1 Introduction

Scale Invariant Feature Transform (SIFT) proposed by David Lowe (2004) [1] is an approach for detecting and extracting local feature descriptors invariant to rotation and scaling and becomes a useful feature for image representation. Invariance of SIFT is insured by filtering and subsampling an original image so that only strong keypoints of the image are kept. To do so, difference of Gaussian is computed by differentiating each two consecutive filtered images by a Gaussian filter at different scales and repeating the process by subsampling the original image on different octaves. The final descriptor is then a histogram of gradient magnitude and orientation of each keypoint detected. Advantages of SIFT are then primarily its invariance to scale and rotation. Moreover, its strength resides in its locality. Since its introduction, SIFT received a high popularity and has been largely used in many applications [3], [4], [5], [6],[7]. However, since the descriptor is local and based on gradient magnitude and orientation of keypoints, it was considered a texture feature [2] and has received very few interest when applied to binary images. Instead, state of the art on binary image classification and matching use more shape features than texture features [18], [8], [9], [10], [11]. The most relevant work dealing with SIFT on binary images is devoted to hand gestures classification [12] by the use of SIFT feature applied to binary

© Springer International Publishing Switzerland 2015
G. Azzopardi and N. Petkov (Eds.): CAIP 2015, Part I, LNCS 9256, pp. 489–500, 2015.
DOI: 10.1007/978-3-319-23192-1_41

masks. Authors claim to improve accuracy of classification and to decrease time processing since the descriptor is not sensitive to illumination changes and less information is needed to quantify the keypoints. In this work, we study the discrimination of SIFT feature on binary images which has no texture. The classification of shapes and their matching is also studied using one keypoint or $2 - tuples$ keypoints. While the descriptor is local and represented by a set of keypoints, and number keypoints is different from an image to another, supervised classification algorithms might fall. In order to overcome this issue, we follow same rationale as in [21] i.e. we use Bag of Features approach to make a new representation of the features which simplify the task of classification.

This paper is organized as follows: we present in section 2 an approach based on a majority vote of keypoints to compute overlap of SIFT over different classes to study discrimination of SIFT on binary images. Section 3 is devoted to to classification of binary images using SIFT and Bag of Features. We present our results in section 4. We conclude this paper by some future works.

2   Class Overlap Analysis: Approach and Results

2.1   The Approach

In order to analyze discrimination of SIFT feature applied to binary images for classification, we first perform an empirical study of overlap between classes using SIFT. In a first study, we consider each keypoint independently of its neighbors. In a second study, we add the notion of neighboring where, instead of considering each keypoint independently, we consider 2 neighboring tuples of SIFT keypoints and compute the overlap of classes. SIFT descriptor is computed in the same way as in [1] and results in a set of keypoints each of which is a 128 dimensional vector of gradient orientations and a 3 dimensional vector of row coordinate, column coordinate and radius of the keypoint. Neigboring $2 - tuples$ of SIFT is a set of 256 dimensional vector (128×2), where the first 128 values are gradient orientation of the first keypoint and the second 128 values are gradient orientation of the neighboring keypoint. The neighbor of a keypoint is chosen so that its row and column coordinates are the closest to its neighbor.

To compute overlap between classes, we choose m objects from each class and compute their SIFT features. To each SIFT (respectively 2-tuples SIFT) keypoint is assigned a label which represents the class of the image to which it belongs to. Overlap between all classes is initialized to 0. Each keypoint of each image is then compared to all keypoints of all images, and the keypoint which gave the minimum distance is chosen. Overlap between the keypoint class to be compared and the class of keypoint which gave the minimum distance is incremented. Finally, overlap percentage is computed. The same process is applied for $2 - tuples$ of keypoints. The following algorithm gives an insight of the process.

Algorithm 1 sorting keypoints

1: BEGIN
2: $Overlap(C_i, C_j) = 0$, $i, j = 1..numberClasses$
3: **for** each image I of the dataset **do**
4:     C_i is the class of I;
5:     **for** Each Keypoint K of image I **do**
6:         **for** all keypoints K' of all images of the dataset different than I including also images of class C_i **do**
7:             Compute Euclidean Distance between K and K'
8:         **end for**
9:         Get K'^* the keypoint form all K' which gave the minimum distance
10:        Get C_j class of image to which belong K'^*
11:        $Overlap(C_i, C_j) + +$;
12:    **end for**
13: **end for**
14: $Overlap(C_i, C_j) = \dfrac{Ovelap(C_i, C_j)}{\sum\limits_{i=1}^{numberClasses} Ovelap(C_{i,i})}$
15: END

2.2 Overlap Accuracy of the Dataset ETH-80

Overlap experiments are performed over 100 images from each of the 8 classes of ETH-80 which is a dataset composed of 400 images of 8 classes: apple, car, cow, cup, dog, horse, pear and tomato. Each of the 400 images of each class are obtained using 10 distinct objects of the same class taken using a spherical rotation of the camera around the object while keeping the same distance from the camera and the object being pictured. Table 1 shows that SIFT keypoints always reflect the true class label. Indeed, the highest percentage of keypoints on classes is always relative to the true class label. However, some keypoints still vote for a different class. The highest the percentage is for another class different than the real one, the most similar are the classes. For example, in the first line, the highest overlap of keypoints for the class 1 is 58.52% with the class 1 which represents the class apple. The second highest overlap percentage is given to class 8 which is the class tomato. This means that, 22.92% of keypoints present in the class apple are also present in the class tomato which is true when we look at their two shapes. The same happens to the class 3 (cow) with the class 5 and 6 (dog and horse) in the third line of the table. With high percentage of overlap for the class 3 with the class 5 (13%) and the class 6 (18%) while few percentages are observed on other classes. The table, although reflects some overlaps between classes, can prove discrimination of SIFT feature on binary images.

In the second experiment, comparison between overlap of classes using independent SIFT keypoints and $2 - tuples$ of SIFT keypoints is performed. Experiment is performed over 80 images where 10 images of each class are chosen to compute the overlap. Table 1 shows that, although $2 - tuples$ of SIFT is still discriminating as percentages in the diagonal are still the highest, discrimination is decreased compared to overlap when using SIFT keypoints independently. Only three classes where discrimination is improved are class 3 (cow), class 4 (cup) and class 5 (dog) with improvement of 10.62%, 13.75% and 0.90% respectively. These percentages are presented in table 2 where posotive values represent increase in discrimination and negative values represent decrease in discrimination. Overall improvement using $n-tuples$ of SIFT is 1.08% which is negligible knowing that time processing is highly increased. At this point, we put the hypothesis that $2-tuples$ SIFT do not improve discrimination between shapes and perform more experiments below to verify this hypothesis.

Table 1. Overlap computed using SIFT, $2-tuples$ of SIFT and $2-tuples$ of SIFT descriptor respectively over 100, 10 and 10 images respectively of each of the classes: C_1 ='apple' , C_2 ='car' , C_3 ='cow' , C_4 ='cup', C_5 ='dog', C_6 ='horse', C_7 ='pear' , and C_8 ='tomato'

	$O_1\%$	$O_2\%$	$O_3\%$	$O_4\%$	$O_5\%$	$O_6\%$	$O_7\%$	$O_8\%$
C_1	**58.52**	3.63	1.04	4.93	1.06	0.62	7.27	22.92
C_2	10.53	**47.86**	6.23	8.16	4.93	5.72	6.80	9.77
C_3	4.46	8.40	**43.76**	6.12	13.48	18.05	2.90	2.84
C_4	5.43	2.39	1.33	**76.84**	2.01	1.36	5.12	5.53
C_5	4.70	6.82	13.38	7.89	**42.13**	16.45	4.99	3.65
C_6	4.41	6.21	17.58	5.18	15.57	**43.21**	4.88	2.96
C_7	14.95	2.92	0.85	7.32	1.14	1.64	**58.55**	12.63
C_8	25.68	3.85	1.29	5.65	1.17	1.26	6.75	**54.35**
	$O_1\%$	$O_2\%$	$O_3\%$	$O_4\%$	$O_5\%$	$O_6\%$	$O_7\%$	$O_8\%$
C_1	**51.10**	3.40	0.47	4.55	0.60	0.66	7.38	31.84
C_2	14.05	**30.18**	3.96	12.12	5.15	3.61	12.41	18.51
C_3	5.52	7.85	**38.25**	8.41	11.37	21.37	4.55	2.69
C_4	4.91	3.53	1.67	**77.80**	2.03	1.58	3.23	5.25
C_5	6.72	8.03	14.51	10.03	**30.11**	18.01	7.98	4.60
C_6	8.00	5.44	23.21	7.57	15.86	**30.33**	5.68	3.91
C_7	17.89	6.18	1.04	3.45	1.16	1.63	**51.35**	17.30
C_8	33.62	4.07	0.39	5.32	0.97	0.72	8.27	**46.63**
	$O_1\%$	$O_2\%$	$O_3\%$	$O_4\%$	$O_5\%$	$O_6\%$	$O_7\%$	$O_8\%$
C_1	**60.59**	5.40	0.90	5.40	1.26	0.42	5.76	20.25
C_2	18.61	**31.40**	4.31	11.64	7.29	3.50	8.46	14.80
C_3	7.13	8.55	**27.63**	11.59	16.85	20.02	3.85	4.38
C_4	8.95	4.33	2.92	**64.06**	2.96	1.53	4.94	10.32
C_5	5.87	10.81	18.46	9.86	**29.21**	15.88	5.93	3.99
C_6	6.75	5.69	18.75	7.05	14.96	**35.59**	8.94	2.27
C_7	16.37	4.50	1.60	6.81	1.74	3.49	**52.96**	12.54
C_8	25.90	5.44	1.62	9.67	0.83	0.82	6.16	**49.55**

Table 2. Overlap Difference between $2-tuples$ SIFT overlap (table 1 part 2) and SIFT overlap (table 1 part 3) for classes: C_1 ='apple' , C_2 ='car' , C_3 ='cow' , C_4 ='cup', C_5 ='dog', C_6 ='horse', C_7 ='pear' , and C_8 ='tomato'

	$O_1\%$	$O_2\%$	$O_3\%$	$O_4\%$	$O_5\%$	$O_6\%$	$O_7\%$	$O_8\%$
C_1	-9.49	**2.01**	**0.43**	**0.85**	**0.66**	-0.23	-1.62	-11.59
C_2	**4.56**	-1.21	**0.34**	-0.47	**2.14**	-0.11	-3.95	-3.70
C_3	**1.61**	-0.70	**10.62**	**3.18**	**5.48**	-1.35	-0.70	**1.70**
C_4	**4.04**	-0.80	**1.25**	**13.75**	**0.93**	-0.06	**1.71**	**5.08**
C_5	-0.85	-2.78	**3.95**	-0.17	**0.90**	-2.13	-2.06	-0.62
C_6	-1.25	-0.25	-4.46	-0.52	-0.90	-5.26	**3.26**	-1.64
C_7	-1.53	**1.68**	**0.55**	**3.36**	**0.58**	**1.86**	-1.61	-4.75
C_8	-7.72	-1.37	**1.22**	**4.35**	-0.14	**0.09**	-2.10	-2.92

3 Classification of Binary Images Using SIFT and Bag of Features

Classification of images using SIFT is very difficult because of the high dimensionality of SIFT feature and the non-fixed feature representation. We use the Bag of Features method [19] to overcome this issue and present it in what follows.

3.1 Image Representation Using Bag of Features

After computed, SIFT features for all images of the training set are concatenated into one matrix $M(n \times 128)$ where $n = \sum_{i-1}^{m} n_i$ and n_i is number of keypoints of image I_i and m is the number of images of the training set. Rows of the matrix M are then clustered using K-means clustering algorithm. K-means is an iterative algorithm which starts by defining l centers of clusters randomly from the set of n features. Then, the centers are updated by calculating distance between the center and remaining features. Once features are assigned to a center, the mean of the cluster is chosen as the new center. Update is repeated until one of two conditions: either maximum number of iterations is reached or centers are stable (means of clusters converge). Result of clustering is then l stabilized clusters, each cluster is represented by its center which is one of the 128 dimensional vector of keypoints. Let c_i be center of the cluster i. Visual vocabulary is then the matrix $VC = c_1, c_2...c_l$. The following step consists of representing each image of the dataset (training and test) with its Bag of Features using visual vocabulary. To do so, for each keypoint of each image, we compute the Euclidean distance with each Center of the Visual Vocabulary. The minimum Euclidean distance reflects the center chosen for the keypoint. Number of occurrences of a center is computed and represented by a normalized histogram of dimension k (number of features in the visual Vocabulary). Each image is then represented by its histogram of visual Features also referred as Bag of Features.

3.2   Training and Classification Using Bag of Features

After describing training and test images by their Bag of Features, the following step consists of attributing a class label to each image of the test set. The class label is given to the nearest neighbor of the test image and the training image. In other words, for an image I of the test set, the distance between its Bag of Features and Bag of Features of all images in the training set is computed. The Bag of Features which gave the minimum distance is chosen and its class label is given to the image I. Nearest Neighbor is one of the simplest supervised classification algorithms but is still accurate. We use χ^2 distance as it showed to give better results. χ^2 distance between two histograms is described as follows:

$$\chi^2 = \sum_{i=1}^{l} \frac{(HI_i - HT_i)^2}{HT_i} \tag{1}$$

where l is the dimension of the feature vector (number of bins), HI_i the Bag of Features of image I_i and HT_i Bag of Features of an image T in the training set.

4   Experimental Results

In this section we evaluate effectiveness of bag of SIFT features applied to binary images for object classification and matching. We present the quantitative analysis of the method applied to binary images on both ETH-80 [15] and MPEG-7 Core Experiment CE-Shape-1 data set [16] datasets. MPEG-7 dataset consists of 1,400 images grouped into 70 classes. Each class has 20 different shapes.

Difference between ETH-80 and MPEG-7 datasets is that the latter contains only binary images while the former contains both binary and RGB images of the same objects. We use this property in order to enhance our experiments and prove effectiveness of SIFT feature on binary images and compare accuracy of our classifier on binary and same RGB images. Besides, we divided the MPEG-7 data set into two sets: training set and test set. For each class, 10 shapes are chosen as the training samples and the remaining 10 shapes are then used for testing. We do the same for ETH-80, however, since this dataset contains much more images of the same class than MPEG-7, we vary size of the training and analyze accuracy at each time. Finally, we analyze matching using SIFT. To do so, we extend our Nearest Neighbor Classification algorithm to make it return instead of a class label, the m nearest neighboring images of a query image. We compare then resulting matching with some state of the art techniques: Inner Distance (IDSC) [13] and Graph Transduction [18], shape Context (SC) and partial matching [11]). For the qualitative analysis of matching, we input to our system the same query images as the ones of methods we compared with and display our results with their ones. We present in following subsection experiments done on both datasets. For the quantitative analysis of matching, we compute the bull's eye score of matching.

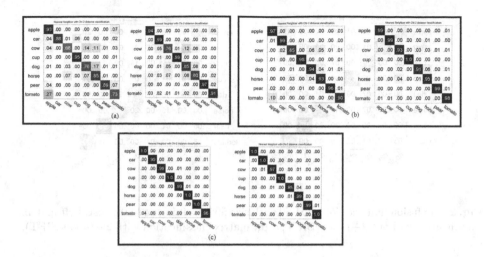

Fig. 1. Confusion matrices for ETH-80 with : (a) (20% and 80%), (b) (40% and 60%), (c) (60% and 40%) (training and test set size) respectively (left matrices binary images, right matrices RGB images)

4.1   Classification Accuracy of the Dataset ETH-80

For classification accuracy analysis, extensive experiments of ETH-80 are done by dividing the whole dataset into training and classification. Division is done following several percentages from 10 to 70% where this percentage represents ratio of training set with the whole dataset. In a first experiment, we vary size of both training and test set where sum of their two ratios is equal to 100% (upper part of table 3). By doing this, we insure not to include images of the training set into the test set. In a second experiment, we choose a small ratio of the test set (30%) and fix it for all percentages of training. Size of the training set in both cases do not exceed 70% which represent the classical percentage used in most classification experiments (2/3 training and 1/3 test). We analyze classification accuracy of RGB images and their binary masks (binary images) using the same parameters of the code book (same number of iterations of K-means clustering, same number of features in the visual vocabulary, same distance measure). Table 3 shows that classification accuracy of RGB images in most cases outperforms the one of binary images of the original RGB images. However, the difference is slight and in one case, classification of binary images outperformed classification of RGB images. In order to analyze more deeply the classification results, we moreover generate for each ratio confusion matrices. We generate more than 60 confusion matrices by varying the size of both training and test set, however, we kept only the most significant ones which correspond to ratios of table 3. Confusion matrices show that classification accuracy is enhanced in RGB images compared to binary images, however, the difference is still slight. Some interesting points can be seen in the confusion matrices: Confusion of RGB images can occur even when the shape is different, example of such a confusion can be

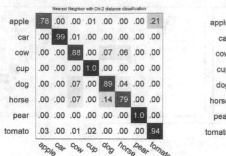 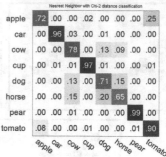

Fig. 2. Confusion matrices for ETH-80 with size 50% training and 50% test. Left matrix classification without $2-tuples$ SIFT, right matrix classification with $2-tuples$ SIFT).

seen in figure 1 where horses have been confused with cows. This confusion is less apparent in the binary images and accuracy of horse classification can reach 100% for binary images while it does not for RGB images. Such errors occurred for horses with same colors as cows and dogs and when some animals have same skin (texture). The same observation can be made for classes "Dog" and "Cow". For all other classes, classification accuracy of RGB images is slightly higher than classification accuracy of the same binary images.

The last experiment performed on ETH-80 is done in order to analyze the contribution of $2-tuples$ SIFT. Experiment emphasizes hypothesis posed in 2.1 where figure 2 shows that considering 2-tuples of SIFT decreases the classification accuracy. Overall accuracy using SIFT keypoints independently is 90.19% while it decreases when using neighboring 2-tuples of SIFT to 82.82%. Indeed, when considering neighboring keypoints, no a priori information about the contour is considered. Also, processing time when processing $2-tuples$ is increased compared to independent SIFT keypoints. We do not perform more experiments on $2-tuples$ SIFT as primary experiments show decrease in accuracy.

4.2   Classification and Matching Accuracy of the Dataset MPEG-7

For MPEG-7 dataset, 10 images from each of the 70 classes of MPEG-7 are used for training and 10 images are used for tests. As Nearest Neighbor does not need any cross validation, we directly compute classification after training. Confusion matrix is presented in figure 3. The confusion matrix is less comprehensible because number of classes is very high, however, we can see from blue rectangles in the diagonal classes that are confused the most. These classes are: 11 (camel), 28 (device_8), 69(turtle), 70 (watch). Overall classification was 78%. Figure 4 (left) shows that worst results of SIFT were obtained with the query "bird" and "lizzard". For the class "lizzard", confusion due to the presence of keypoints of these two classes in many other classes. Confusion of "bird" can be explained by the presence of very few keypoints in shapes of that class while shapes of other

Table 3. Overall accuracy on ETH-80 dataset by varying size of training set and test set

Training %	Test %	Accuracy %	
		Binary	RGB
20	80	83.01	90.22
40	60	93.91	96.79
60	40	99.03	98.71
10	30	77.77	84.61
20	30	84.82	88.35
30	30	90.49	93.05
40	30	92.20	94.87
50	30	94.23	95.51
60	30	96.68	97.75
70	30	99.14	99.25

classes have much more keypoints including the ones present in the class "bird". Right part of figure 4 in another hand is way much encouraging, where SIFT present competing results compared to state of the art methods.

Table 4 presents retrieval rate for the MPEG-7 database. Retrieval rate is measured by the so-called bullseye score which counts all matching objects within the 40 most similar candidates [20]. While some classes give perfect retrieval results (100%), some other classes reach a minimum rate of 15%.

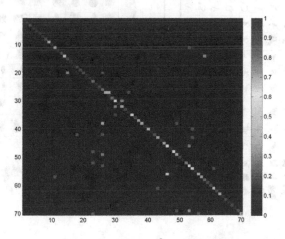

Fig. 3. Confusion matrix plot for MPEG-7 dataset with training size 1/2, test size 1/2

Table 4. Bull's score for MPEG-7 dataset

Bone: 95%	bird: 15%	children: 100%	device4:40%
flatfish: 90%	jar: 60%	snake: 20%	Comma: 90%
bottle: 55%	chopper: 100%	device5: 45%	fly: 65%
key: 30%	shoe: 100%	Glas: 90%	brick: 75%
classic: 50%	device6: 55%	fork: 20%	lizzard: 60%
spoon: 20%	HCircle: 100%	butterfly: 40%	crown: 95%
device7: 40%	fountain: 100%	lmfish: 30%	spring: 65%
Heart: 100%	camel: 60%	cup: 90%	device8: 40%
frog: 30%	octopus: 25%	stef: 55%	Misk: 100%
car: 95%	deer: 50%	device9: 45%	guitar: 30%
pencil: 20%	teddy: 100%	apple: 95%	carriage: 100%
device0: 50%	dog: 35%	hammer: 30%	car: 40%
tree: 80%	bat :45%	cattle: 50%	device1: 30%
elephant: 45%	hat: 75%	pocket: 90%	truck: 100%
beetle: 35%	cellular: 100%	device2: 30%	face:100%
horse: 35%	rat: 95%	turtle: 15%	bell: 95%
chicken: 20%	device3: 35%	fish: 35%	horseshoe: 85%
ray: 45%	watch: 80%		

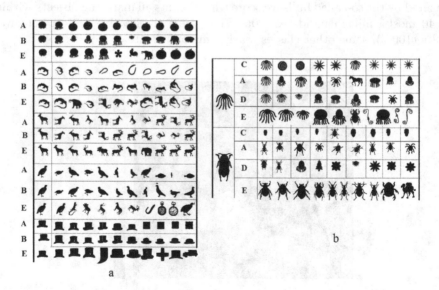

Fig. 4. (a) Matching comparison of our proposed study (E in the figure) with Inner Distance (IDSC) (A in the figure) [13] and Graph Transduction (B in the figure) [18], (b)Matching comparison of our proposed study (E in the figure) with Inner Distance (IDSC) (A in the figure) [13], Shape Conext (SC) (C in the figure) and partial matching (D in the figure) [11]

5   Conclusion

We have presented in this work an empirical study of usefulness of SIFT feature applied to binary images. Experiments show that although SIFT is most often dedicated to be applied on texture images, it can still be applied on binary images and can sometimes outperform results obtained using RGB and grey level images. We aim in further works to apply SIFT to classify directly masks derived from background subtraction [14].

References

1. Lowe, D.G.: Distinctive Image Features from Scale-Invariant Keypoints. Int. J. Comput. Vision **60**(2), 91–110 (2004)
2. Wang, X.: Intelligent Multi-camera Video Surveillance: A Review. Pattern Recogn. Lett. **34**(1), 3–19 (2013)
3. Tsuchiya, M., Fujiyoshi, H.: Evaluating feature importance for object classification in visual surveillance. In: 18th International Conference on Pattern Recognition, ICPR 2006
4. Song, Z., Chen, Q., Huang, Z., Hua, Y., Yan, S.: Contextualizing object detection and classification. In: IEEE Conference on Computer Vision and Pattern Recognition (CVPR) (2011)
5. Zhang, Z., Li, M., Huang, K., Tan, T.: Boosting local feature descriptors for automatic objects classification in traffic scene surveillance. In: 19th International Conference on Pattern Recognition, ICPR 2008
6. Deselaers, T., Heigold, G., Ney, H.: Object Classification by Fusing SVMs and Gaussian Mixtures. Pattern Recogn. **43**(7), 2476–2484 (2010)
7. Conde, C., Moctezuma, D., De Diego, I.M., Cabello, E.: HoGG: Gabor and HoG-based human detection for surveillance in non-controlled environments. Neurocomputing **100**, 19–30 (2013)
8. Chahooki, M.A.Z., Charkari, N.M.: Shape Classification by Manifold Learning in Multiple Observation Spaces. Inf. Sci. **262**, 46–61 (2014)
9. Nanni, L., Lumini, A., Brahnam, S.: Ensemble of different local descriptors, codebook generation methods and subwindow configurations for building a reliable computer vision system. Inf. Sci. **26**(2), 89–100 (2014)
10. Torresani, L., Szummer, M., Fitzgibbon, A.: Efficient object category recognition using classemes. In: Daniilidis, K., Maragos, P., Paragios, N. (eds.) ECCV 2010, Part I. LNCS, vol. 6311, pp. 776–789. Springer, Heidelberg (2010)
11. Bouagar, S., Larabi, S.: Efficient descriptor for full and partial shape matching. Multimedia Tools and Applications, 1–23 (2014). doi:10.1007/s11042-014-2417-0
12. Lin, W.-S., Wu, Y.-L., Hung, W.-C., Tang, C.-Y.: A Study of Real-Time Hand Gesture Recognition Using SIFT on Binary Images. Advances in Intelligent Systems and Applications **2**, 235–246
13. Ling, H., Jacobs, D.W.: Shape Classification Using the Inner-Distance. IEEE Transactions on Pattern Analysis and Machine Intelligence **29**(2), 286–299
14. Setitra, I., Larabi, S.: Background subtraction algorithms with post-processing: a review. In: 22nd International Conference on Pattern Recognition (ICPR) (2014)
15. Leibe, B., Schiele, B.: Analyzing appearance and contour based methods for object categorization. In: IEEE Computer Society Conference on Computer Vision and Pattern Recognition (2003)

16. Latecki, L.J., Lakmper, R., Eckhardt, U.: Shape Descriptors for non-rigid shapes with a single closed contour. In: Proc. IEEE Conf. Computer Vision and Pattern Recognition (2000)
17. Bai, X., Rao, C., Wang, X., Vocabulary, S.: A Robust and Efficient Shape Representation for Shape Matching. IEEE Transactions on Image Processing **23**(9), 3935–3949 (2014)
18. Bai, X., Yang, X., Latecki, L.J., Liu, W., Tu, Z.: Learning Context-Sensitive Shape Similarity by Graph Transduction. IEEE Transactions on Pattern Analysis and Machine Intelligence **32**(5), 861–874 (2010)
19. Seidenari, L., Serra, G., Bagdanov, A.D., Del Bimbo, A.: Local Pyramidal Descriptors for Image Recognition. IEEE Transactions on Pattern Analysis and Machine Intelligence, 2014 **36**(5), 1033–1040 (2013)
20. Kontschieder, P., Donoser, M., Bischof, H.: Beyond pairwise shape similarity analysis. In: Zha, H., Taniguchi, R., Maybank, S. (eds.) ACCV 2009, Part III. LNCS, vol. 5996, pp. 655–666. Springer, Heidelberg (2010)
21. Ramesh Peter, B., Xiand, C., Lee, T.H.: Shape classification using invariant features and contextual information in the bag-of-words model. Pattern Recognition **48**(3), 894–906 (2015)

Where is My Cup? - Fully Automatic Detection and Recognition of Textureless Objects in Real-World Images

Joanna Isabelle Olszewska$^{(\boxtimes)}$

University of Gloucestershire, Cheltenham GL50 2RH, UK
jolszewska@glos.ac.uk

Abstract. In this work, we propose a new method for fully automatic detection and recognition of textureless objects present in complex visual scenes. While most approaches only deal with shape matching, our approach considers objects both in terms of low-level features and high-level information, and represents objects' view-based templates as trees. Multi-level matching increases algorithm robustness, while the new tree structure of the template reduces its computational burden. We have evaluated our algorithm on the CMU dataset consisting of objects under arbitrary viewpoints and in cluttered environment. Our proposed approach has shown excellent performance, outperforming state-of-the-art methods.

Keywords: Object detection · Object recognition · Template · Tree · Active contours · Automatic scene understanding · Robotics

1 Introduction

Fully automatic detection and recognition of objects in images are of prime importance for applications such as robotics, scene content analysis or image understanding [4].

For this purpose, a lot of research has involved local-feature detection, and consisted in the extraction of LBP texture features [19] or distribution-based descriptors such as SIFT [18] from an object and their matching with a candidate image in order to detect the presence of the object in this image [28]. Despite very good results, these approaches are not appropriate for textureless objects which present large uniform areas. Hence, textureless object detection under arbitrary viewpoint is a challenging problem we focus on in this paper.

Most of the existing approaches to detect textureless objects are based on shape matching. In [24], object shape is defined in terms of contour fragments, but does not take into account the edge connectivity. To refine the object shape representation, [25] pieces together contours to match the object shape using shape context [5], i.e. the spatial distribution of all points relative to one point on the shape. However, these methods require a costly learning of the model or a stable edge detection [3].

© Springer International Publishing Switzerland 2015
G. Azzopardi and N. Petkov (Eds.): CAIP 2015, Part I, LNCS 9256, pp. 501–512, 2015.
DOI: 10.1007/978-3-319-23192-1_42

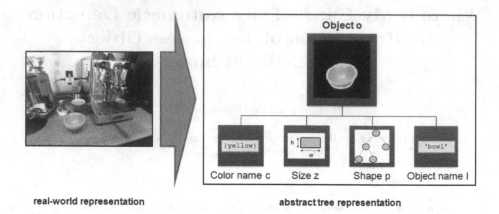

Fig. 1. Proposed representation of an object to detect and recognize. The concept is here illustrated for the case of the object 'bowl'.

As object appearance may drastically vary with the viewpoint, object detection may involve the use of an important amount of views [12]. On the other hand, robustness to intra-class shape deformations may require high-volume training sets [1]. To overcome these issues, methods such as [8] compute an average shape and the associated deformation model or soft/hard models like in [11]. Alternatively, [9] and its variant [10] use templates of sampled edge points from different viewpoints, each with a quantized orientation. These methods are very effective, but they suffer in case of object occlusions or do not allow multiple object detection.

Other methods to detect an object of interest in real-world images rely on sole color descriptors [15] or color names [26]. However, the resulting detected object is then only defined by a boundary box.

In this work, we propose to detect and recognize textureless objects accurately, i.e. by finding their boundaries, and in a fully automatic way. For that, we define objects both in terms of low-level features such as edges and color descriptors and high-level information such as shape, size, color name, and object name, as presented in Fig. 1. Object shape is computed based on low-level features and then refined using active contours [14], which automatically delineate object's boundaries. In this way, our approach does not present the major problems of the state-of-the-art object detection methods such as the loss of edge connectivity or the need of stable edge map [12].

Our approach does not require a 3D model learning, thus increasing computationally efficiency [12].

Moreover, the computational burden associated with the usually large number of view template [12] is reduced in this work by using a tree structure for the different views, while the use of color names deduced from the color descriptors enhances object detection robustness [26].

In this paper, the main contributions are a new objet representation in terms of both low and high-level attributes, including a new shape template representation following a tree structure, and innovative algorithms to perform multi-object detection and recognition. Our object representation is generic and, once matched with any candidate image, allows a fully automatic detection and recognition of textureless objects under arbitrary viewpoint in complex and cluttered environment. Our proposed method could be applied in parallel for different objects of a same image and thus leads to multiple object detection.

The paper is structured as follows. In Section 2, we present our tree representation of objects defined by visual and semantic features such as object's color set name, object's size, object's current shape, and object's name. Based on this abstract representation of a real-world object, our approach to detect and recognize it is described in Section 3. The performance of our object detection and recognition approach successfully tested on a challenging, publicly-available database containing real-world images are reported and discussed in Section 4. Conclusions are drawn up in Section 5.

2   Proposed Object Representation

In order to efficiently and robustly perform the detection and recognition of i textureless objects o under arbitrary viewpoint, we introduce a generic, tree-structured object representation as shown in Fig. 1. The proposed object representation consists of photometric, geometric, and semantic properties, all providing complementary information about the object, while leading to a unique description of the object. Based on that, an object o is characterized by four high-level attributes, namely, its color name c, its size z, its shape p, and its name l, computed as follows.

Color name $c = \{c_n\}$ consists of the main color descriptor names c_n of its n subparts calculated based on (R, G, B) values and according to SVG standard [21].

Object shape $p = \{p_j\}$ is defined by a template of different views of an object as illustrated in Fig. 2. The object in each view is then represented by active contours [14] rather than by a deformable model [27].

Hence, active contours, as displayed in Figs. 3 (3rd-6th columns) and Fig. 4 (d), are two-dimensional closed curves that evolve in the image plane from a given initial position to the foreground boundaries, characterizing thus the shape and the position of the object of interest [20]. More specifically, in this work, active contours are represented by a parametric plane curve $\mathcal{C}(s) : [0, 1] \rightarrow \mathbb{R}^2$ whose modeling involves a B-Spline formalism, while its evolution is guided by internal forces (α: elasticity, β: rigidity) described by the curves mechanical properties and the external force $\boldsymbol{\Gamma}$ resulting from characteristics of the image under study, computed by the dynamic equation as follows:

$$\mathcal{C}_t(s,t) = \alpha\, \mathcal{C}_{ss}(s,t) - \beta\, \mathcal{C}_{ssss}(s,t) + \boldsymbol{\Gamma}. \tag{1}$$

with C_{ss} and C_{ssss}, the second and the fourth derivative with respect to the curve parameter s.

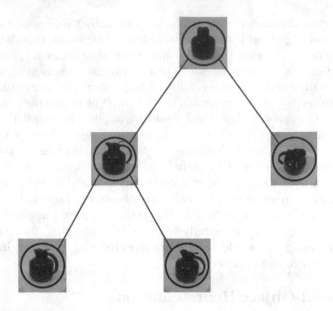

Fig. 2. Example of the proposed tree structure of the template for the object 'pitcher'

The external force $\boldsymbol{\Gamma}$ is obtained by computing the Speeded-Up Gradient Vector Flow (SUGVFB) [22] from the image edge map. This resulting force has a large capture range as well as a bidirectional convergence, leading to a precise delineation of the object's boundaries.

The object shape is itself structured as a rooted binary tree (see Fig. 2) containing j different template views of the object, with v_j active contours, computed each by Eq. (1) for the instance j of the object o. Since each active contour v_j is represented in a parametric way, it could be stored for matching purpose as a finite set of (x, y) sample points, A. Moreover, each of the object shape has an associated size z_w.

The template tree is built offline for an object of interest according to our Algorithm 2, which maps a template list L to a template tree T in order to reach computational efficiency. This transformation of a linear structure of the template list to a non-linear structure such as the tree one is innovative and requires several design choice we automatized by means of our Algorithm 2.

The distance $d_S(A, B)$ in Algorithm 2 is the similarity distance between two objects A and B, defined as follows:

$$d_S(A, B) = \frac{\#M}{\frac{\#A + \#B}{2}}, \tag{2}$$

where A and B are the compared objects, each represented by a finite set of points; where M is the doubly matched feature set as returned by Algorithm 1; and where $\#$ represents the cardinal of the related set.

Algorithm 1. Embedded Matching

Given $A' = A, B' = B, M = \emptyset,$
for all $a_i \in A'$ **do**
  for all $b_j \in B'$ **do**
    repeat
      if

$$d_P(a_i, b_j) = \min_{b \in B'} d_P(a_i, b)$$

$$\wedge \; d_P(b_j, a_i) = \min_{a \in A'} d_P(b_j, a)$$

$$\wedge \; d_P(a_i, b_j) \leq d_H(A, B)$$

$$\wedge \; d_P(b_j, a_i) \leq d_H(A, B)$$

    then

$$(a_i, b_j) \subset M$$

$$\wedge \; A' = A \backslash \{a_i\} \wedge B' = B \backslash \{b_j\}$$

      end if
    until $A' \neq \emptyset \vee B' \neq \emptyset$
  end for
end for

---

return M

Thus, in the embedded double matching process (Algorithm 1) [2], which has been proven to be efficient compared to other ones [13], [17], [23], the Hausdorff distance $d_H(A, B)$ is computed as:

$$d_H(A, B) = max\Big(d_h(A, B), d_h(B, A)\Big), \tag{3}$$

where $d_h(A, B)$ is the directed Hausdorff distance from A to B defined as:

$$d_h(A, B) = \max_{a \in A} \min_{b \in B} d_P(a, b), \tag{4}$$

with $d_P(a, b)$, the Minkowski-form distance based on the L_P norm, and defined as:

$$d_P(a, b) = \Big(\sum_k (a_k - b_k)^P \Big)^{1/P}. \tag{5}$$

The set of points associated to each of the objects are thus matched using the Hausdorff distance (Eq. (3)). Then, these matched points are paired according to Algorithm 1, where the Hausdorff distance $d_H(A, B)$, computed in Eq. (3), is used in this case as the pairing threshold. The resulting double-matched points form the set M, used in Eq. (2) to determine if an object is the same as another one.

The main advantages of the Algorithm 1 are a robust matching technique not requiring any training as well as the removal of the usual arbitrary parameter which is the matching threshold [2].

Algorithm 2. Template Tree Building

Given $L = \{v_v\}$, the template list;
Let us define T, the template tree;
$TL = \{v_i\}$, the main instances' list with $i = [0, K]$, $i \in \mathbb{N}$;
th, the leaf threshold; and $L' = L$, $T = \emptyset$, $TL = \emptyset$;

for all $v_j \in L'$ **do**
   repeat
      if

$$d_S(v_i, v_j) > th$$

    then

$$TL = TL \cup \{v_j\}$$
$$v_i = v_j$$

    end if

$$L' = L' \backslash \{v_j\}$$
   until $L' = \emptyset$
end for

for all $k \in [0, K]$, with $k \in \mathbb{N}$ **do**

$$T_{root} = TL_k$$
$$T_{left} = TL_{2k+1}$$
$$T_{right} = TL_{2k+2}$$

end for

return T

In Algorithm 2, the leaf threshold th is set offline once for each object class. On one hand, this parameter regulates the granularity of the template. Indeed, smaller is the leaf threshold value, bigger is the number of views in the template tree. On the other hand, this parameter influences the performance of the system because greater is the view number, slower is the pre-order template tree matching algorithm, but more accurate is the resulting detection rate. Hence, a trade-off between precision and computational speed could be reached and actually, this threshold value could be automatically computed by fixing the number of views of the template tree, e.g. to a small number such as 5 (see Fig. 2).

The name l constitutes a high-level feature and contributes in filling the semantic gap between the visual and the linguistic descriptions of the object. For each of the classes, the name of the object class is set once, when the object class representation is built offline. In images under investigation, the objects are detected and labeled automatically as explained in Section 3.

3 Proposed Object Detection and Recognition

Automatic detection is performed based on both low-level and high-level attributes of the object.

The first step of our proposed process relies on the color name c feature. Hence, the detection of candidate color region names, in an image, is obtained by region growing and matching with the object's color names c_n, using the distance d_H (Eq. (3)) and a color threshold which could be set independently of the images/datasets. Indeed, its value could be fixed based on the SVG standards which color definitions provide large inter-class distances. The corresponding matched regions serve for the initialization of the active contours computed as in Eq. (1).

Then, our process involves the size z feature. Thus, sizes of the delineated regions are calculated. Extracted regions are resized compared to the object's z_w sizes.

Next, our process uses the shape p feature. Indeed, the chosen resized regions are then matched to the corresponding viewpoints, following the tree structure and according to our pre-order matching algorithm (Algorithm 3), where the distance d_S is computed using Eq. (2), while the shape threshold ts value is set equal to the leaf threshold value th to keep the same sensitivity in the entire system. All the performed matching are using the double matching process as per Algorithm 1 and occur in between the active contour of the candidate object and the active contours of the object of interest's views in the template tree.

Algorithm 3. Pre-Order Template Tree Matching

Given T, the shape template tree of the object o;
Let us define $v_{root}(T)$, the active contour of the instance at the root of the considered shape tree T; v_a, the active contour of the candidate object a; and ts, the shape threshold;

match(v_a, T) **do**

if $d_S(v_a, v_{root}(T)) < ts$
then
    shape of object a is the same as shape of object o
end if

if $(T_{left} \neq \emptyset)$
then
    match(v_a, T_{left})
end if

if $(T_{right} \neq \emptyset)$
then
    match(v_a, T_{right})
end if

end do

On the other hand, compared to traditional linear templates [12] like linked lists of instances where the operation of finding an element is of complexity $\mathcal{O}(N)$, the proposed template-tree-based matching is of complexity $\mathcal{O}(logN)$, which is also computationally much faster than state-of-art techniques such as [19]. Note that our template tree approach could be thus used beyond the object detection application, since being computationally more efficient than the traditional linear template based on a list of object instances.

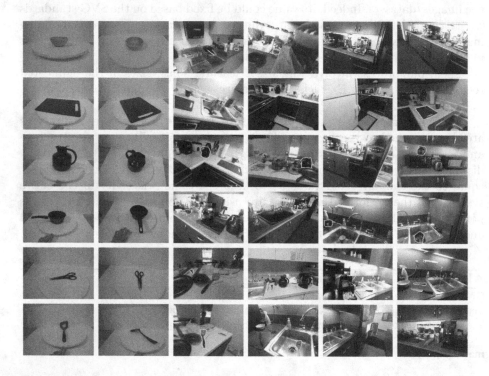

Fig. 3. Examples of results of our automatic detection and recognition approach. First and second columns: examples of the image instances under different views. Third to sixth columns: results computed by our approach. First row: 'bowl wooden' object. Second row: 'cuttingboard' object. Third row: 'pitcher' object. Fourth row: 'saucepan' object. Fifth row: 'scissors' object. Sixth row: 'spatula' object.

Finally, our process computes the name l of the detected object to finalize its recognition. Hence, once the object has been detected in an image, i.e. the color and shape attributes of the candidate object o_i match those of the object of interest, the object recognition last step associates then automatically the related object name l with the detected object o_i in the candidate image by inheritance principle.

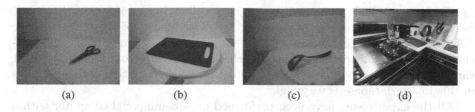

(a)   (b)   (c)   (d)

Fig. 4. Results of our detection and recognition approach in case of multiple objects: (a) example object 1; (b) example object 2; (c) example object 3; (d) results of multiple detection and recognition obtained with our approach. Best viewed in color.

The recognition process could then be repeated for any detected object within the image, and thus leads to the automatic recognition of multiple objects under arbitrary viewpoints in one image such as illustrated in Fig. 4.

Table 1. Performance of our proposed approach for the automatic detection and recognition of the objects. The detection rates are the mean average values for each of the object class.

	pitcher	saucepan	scissors
L2D	0.45	0.49	0.29
GN2	0.85	0.99	0.87
our method	0.93	0.99	0.95

4   Experimental Results

In order to test our approach, we have used the standard database CMU IKEA Kitchen Object Dataset [7] which is considered as a difficult dataset for the detection and recognition of textureless objects.

CMU-IKEA dataset contains 432 images with an average size of 640x480 pixels of non-textured kitchen objects from IKEA. These pictures in jpeg format have been captured with a GoPro Hero wearable camera mounted on the chest while performing regular household tasks to collect the dataset. Videos were collected in various kitchen environments and keyframes were automatically selected from the video sequences. So, the dataset would be as uncontrived as possible.

Objects are visible under a wide range of viewpoints, scales, illumination conditions and clutter, making this a very challenging dataset. The objects of interest could be symmetric or not, both concave and convex, owning sharp or rounded edges.

Since the dataset is unfiltered, ground truth masks for all object instances regardless of scale change, occlusion or contrast have been provided in [7], together with the scale, occlusion, and contrast statistics of each object for each image.

We have applied our system on objects called *bowl wooden, cuttingboard, pitcher, saucepan, scissors, spatula* (Fig. 3). The images of these classes have different size and resolution as well as large inter-class similarities and intra-class variations, and present additional challenges of foreground pose and light variations. Hence, the difficulty of the detection and recognition of these objects in this image database is very high.

All the experiments have been performed on a commercial computer with a processor Intel(R) Core(TM)2 Duo CPU T9300 2.50 GHz, 2 Gb RAM and using MatLab (Mathworks, Inc.) software.

In the first carried-out experiment, we have compared our algorithm's performance in terms of detection rate with two state-of-the-art methods, namely, L2D [9] and GN [11] on three classes we got data to compare with. We can observe in Table 1 that our approach outperforms the previous ones.

In Fig. 3, we presented examples of the results obtained for the 6 classes we processed with our method. Our average detection rate for all the six classes is of 95%, while our objects' detection and recognition method is computed within few milliseconds for template trees owning 5 nodes in average (as shown in Fig. 2) and using the presented object representation characterized by the four, high-level attributes.

In the second experiment, we have applied our approach to perform multiple object detection and recognition. It is worth to note that approaches such as [6] or [16] will not process in this situation.

An example of obtained results with our approach is shown in Fig. 4. Our overall detection rate for all the multiple detection of the six object types within CMU dataset is of 94%, while the computational speed of our process is compatible with online applications.

5   Conclusions

In this paper, we propose a new method for textureless object detection and recognition which is effective and fully automatic. Our approach represents any object in terms of low and high features such as its edges, color descriptors as well as color name, object size, shape and name. The proposed method extends shape matching approach by (i) considering not only object shape but also above-mentioned attributes, by (ii) applying active contours in order to extract coherent and continuous objects' boundaries, and by (iii) using an innovative tree-based shape template containing object's viewpoints. This latter structure we proposed leads to a searching algorithm we called pre-order matching algorithm which has logarithmic complexity and thus which is more computationally efficient than the standard linear search process in traditional list templates. Hence, our approach shows high computational speed and accuracy of detection and recognition of real-world objects under arbitrary viewpoint.

References

1. Alexe, B., Deselaers, T., Ferrari, V.: What is an object? In: Proceedings of the IEEE International Conference on Computer Vision and Pattern Recognition (CVPR 2010), pp. 73–80 (June 2010)
2. Alqaisi, T., Gledhill, D., Olszewska, J.I.: Embedded double matching of local descriptors for a fast automatic recognition of real-world objects. In: Proceedings of the IEEE International Conference on Image Processing (ICIP 2012), pp. 2385–2388 (October 2012)
3. Arbelaez, P., Maire, M., Fowlkes, C., Malik, J.: Contour detection and hierarchical image segmentation. IEEE Transactions on Pattern Analysis and Machine Intelligence 33(5), 898–916 (2011)
4. Azzopardi, G., Petkov, N.: Trainable COSFIRE filters for keypoint detection and pattern recognition. IEEE Transactions on Pattern Analysis and Machine Intelligence 35(2), 490–503 (2013)
5. Belongie, S., Malik, J., Puzicha, J.: Shape matching and object recognition using shape contexts. IEEE Transactions on Pattern Analysis and Machine Intelligence 24(24), 509–522 (2002)
6. Borenstein, E., Ullman, S.: Combined top-down/bottom-up segmentation. IEEE Transactions on Pattern Analysis and Machine Intelligence 30(12), 2109–2125 (2008)
7. Cmu, IKEA Kitchen Object Dataset: Carnegie Mellon University, USA (2014). http://www.cs.cmu.edu/~vmr/datasets/ikea_kitchen/
8. Ferrari, V., Jurie, F., Schmid, C.: From images to shape models for object detection. International Journal of Computer Vision 87(3), 284–303 (2010)
9. Hinterstoisser, S., Cagniart, C., Ilic, S., Sturm, P., Navab, N., Fua, P., Lepetit, V.: Gradient response maps for real-time detection of textureless objects. IEEE Transactions on Pattern Analysis and Machine Intelligence 34(5), 876–888 (2012)
10. Hsiao, E., Hebert, M.: Occlusion reasoning for object detection under arbitrary viewpoint. In: Proceedings of the IEEE International Conference on Computer Vision and Pattern Recognition (CVPR 2012) (2012)
11. Hsiao, E., Hebert, M.: Gradient networks: Explicit shape matching without extracting edges. In: Proceedings of the AAAI International Conference on Artificial Intelligence (AAAI 2013) (July 2013)
12. Hsiao, E., Hebert, M.: Shape-based instance detection under arbitrary viewpoint. In: Shape Perception in Human and Computer Vision: An Interdisciplinary Perspective, pp. 485–495. Springer (2013)
13. Huttenlocher, D.P., Klanderman, G.A., Rucklidge, W.J.: Comparing images using the Hausdorff distance. IEEE Transactions on Pattern Analysis and Machine Intelligence 15(9), 850–863 (1993)
14. Kass, M., Witkin, A., Terzopoulos, D.: Snakes: Active contour models. International Journal of Computer Vision 1(4), 321–331 (1988)
15. Khan, F.S., Anwer, R.M., van de Weijer, J., Bagdanov, A., Vanrell, M., Lopez, A.M.: Color attributes for object detection. In: Proceedings of the IEEE International Conference on Computer Vision and Pattern Recognition (CVPR 2012), pp. 3306–3313 (June 2012)
16. Levin, A., Weiss, Y.: Learning to combine bottom-up and top-down segmentation. International Journal of Computer Vision 81(1), 105–118 (2009)
17. Li, J., Lu, B.L.: An adaptive image Euclidean distance. Pattern Recognition 42(3), 349–357 (2009)

18. Lowe, D.G.: Distinctive image features from scale-invariant keypoints. International Journal of Computer Vision **60**(2), 91–110 (2004)
19. Morales-Gonzalez, A., Garcia-Reyes, E.: Simple object recognition based on spatial relations and visual features represented using irregular pyramids. Multimedia Tools Applications **63**(3), 875–897 (2013)
20. Olszewska, J.I.: Active contour based optical character recognition for automated scene understanding. Neurocomputing **161C**, 65–71 (2015)
21. Olszewska, J.I., McCluskey, T.L.: Ontology-coupled active contours for dynamic video scene understanding. In: Proceedings of the IEEE International Conference on Intelligent Engineering Systems, pp. 369–374 (June 2011)
22. Olszewska, J.I., et al.: Speeded-up gradient vector flow B-spline active contours for robust and real-time tracking. In: Proceedings of the IEEE International Conference on Acoustics, Speech and Signal Processing, pp. 905–908 (April 2007)
23. Santini, S., Jain, R.: Similarity measures. IEEE Transactions on Pattern Analysis and Machine Intelligence **21**(9), 871–883 (1999)
24. Shotton, J., Blake, A., Cipolla, R.: Multiscale categorical object recognition using contour fragments. IEEE Transactions on Pattern Analysis and Machine Intelligence **30**(7), 1270–1281 (2008)
25. Srinivasan, P., Zhu, Q., Shi, J.: Many-to-one contour matching for describing and discriminating object shape. In: Proceedings of the IEEE International Conference on Computer Vision and Pattern Recognition (CVPR 2010), pp. 1673–1680 (June 2010)
26. van de Weijer, J., Schmid, C.: Applying color names to image description. In: Proceedings of the IEEE International Conference on Image Processing (ICIP 2007), pp. III.493–III.496 (September 2007)
27. Yan, J., Lei., Z., Wen., L., Li, S.Z.: The fastest deformable part model for object detection. In: Proceedings of the IEEE International Conference on Computer Vision and Pattern Recognition (CVPR 2014), pp. 2497–2504 (June 2014)
28. Zheng, Y., Doermann, D.: Robust point matching for non-rigid shapes by preserving local neighbourhood structures. IEEE Transactions on Pattern Analysis and Machine Intelligence **28**(4), 643–649 (2006)

Automatic Differentiation of u- and n-serrated Patterns in Direct Immunofluorescence Images

Chenyu Shi[1]([✉]), Jiapan Guo[1], George Azzopardi[1,2], Joost M. Meijer[3],
Marcel F. Jonkman[3], and Nicolai Petkov[1]

[1] Johann Bernoulli Institute for Mathematics and Computer Science,
University of Groningen, Groningen, The Netherlands
{c.shi,j.guo,g.azzopardi,n.petkov}@rug.nl
[2] Intelligent Computer Systems, University of Malta, Msida, Malta
[3] Dermatology for Medical Sciences, University Medical Center Groningen (UMCG),
University of Groningen, Groningen, The Netherlands
{j.m.meijer01,m.f.jonkman}@umcg.nl

Abstract. Epidermolysis bullosa acquisita (EBA) is a subepidermal autoimmune blistering disease of the skin. Manual u- and n-serrated patterns analysis in direct immunofluorescence (DIF) images is used in medical practice to differentiate EBA from other forms of pemphigoid. The manual analysis of serration patterns in DIF images is very challenging, mainly due to noise and lack of training of the immunofluorescence (IF) microscopists. There are no automatic techniques to distinguish these two types of serration patterns. We propose an algorithm for the automatic recognition of such a disease. We first locate a region where u- and n-serrated patterns are typically found. Then, we apply a bank of B-COSFIRE filters to the identified region of interest in the DIF image in order to detect ridge contours. This is followed by the construction of a normalized histogram of orientations. Finally, we classify an image by using the nearest neighbors algorithm that compares its normalized histogram of orientations with all the images in the dataset. The best results that we achieve on the UMCG publicly available data set is 84.6% correct classification, which is comparable to the results of medical experts.

Keywords: Serration patterns analysis · Direct immunofluorescence image · COSFIRE filter · Ridge detection · Skin disease

1 Introduction

Epidermolysis bullosa acquisita (EBA) is a subepidermal autoimmune blistering disease of the skin which shares similar clinical features with other types of pemphigoid [14]. To differentiate EBA from these other types, serration pattern analysis in direct immunofluorescence (DIF) images is used by clinical experts [4,10,11,13]. Such analysis concerns two types of serrated patterns, named u- and n-serrated patterns. Fig. 1(a-b) show examples of u-serrated and n-serrated pattern images. These two types of patterns are typically located along the boundary

© Springer International Publishing Switzerland 2015
G. Azzopardi and N. Petkov (Eds.): CAIP 2015, Part I, LNCS 9256, pp. 513–521, 2015.
DOI: 10.1007/978-3-319-23192-1_43

between the green and dark regions, which are marked by red dashed lines in Fig. 1. We refer to this boundary as the region of interest. Fig. 1c shows an example of a u-serrated pattern, characteristic are the finger-like shapes pointing upwards. The presence of such a pattern is an indication for EBA. Fig. 1d shows an n-serrated pattern that contains undulating n-shapes. Such patterns are found in other types of pemphigoid. The manual analysis of serration patterns in DIF images is very challenging, mainly due to noise and lack of training of the immunofluorescence (IF) microscopists [6,10]. So far there are no automatic techniques to distinguish between these two types of serration patterns.

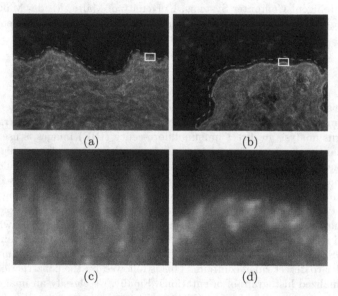

Fig. 1. Example of (a) a u-serrated and (b) an n-serrated pattern image. The areas marked by the red dashed lines indicate the regions of interest. (c-d) Enlargement of the enframed u- and n-serrated patterns in (a-b), respectively.

We propose an automatic method to recognize u- and n-serrated patterns. We apply a bank of B-COSFIRE filters [3], based on the existing COSFIRE approach [2], to the automatically identified regions of interest in DIF images in order to detect ridges and determine their orientations. Every image is then represented by a normalized histogram of orientations. We classify a test image by comparing its normalized histogram of orientations with those of the training images using a nearest neighbor approach.

The rest of the paper is organized as follows. In Section 2 we explain the proposed method. We report experiments in Section 3. Section 4 contains a discussion about certain aspects of the proposed method and we draw conclusions in Section 5.

2   Proposed Method

2.1   Overview

Here we explain the main idea of the proposed method and subsequently we provide a detailed description of each step. First, we identify the region of interest in a DIF image, which is the wavy green boundary. For this region, we enhance the contrast and detect the ridges by applying B-COSFIRE filters [3] selective for six orientations (in intervals of 30 degrees). Finally, we compare the normalized histogram of orientations of a given test image to those of the training images and assign a label according to the nearest neighbors rule.

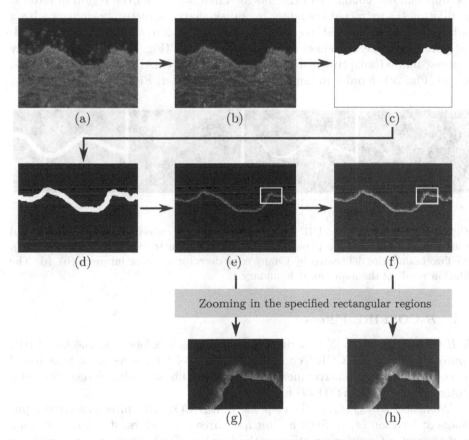

Fig. 2. Step-by-step illustration of the segmentation and enhancement of the region of interest. (a) Original RGB DIF image (of size 1392×1040 pixels) and (b) its green channel. (c) Result of the application of a morphological closing by a disk-shaped structuring element (with radius of 30 pixels) to the green channel. (d) Result of broadening the boundary obtained in (c) by means of a morphological dilation by a disk-shaped structuring element (with radius of 30 pixels). (e) The product of the green channel image and the mask. (f) Contrast-limited adaptive histogram equalization (CLAHE) of the result image. (g-h) Enlargement of the respective enframed regions.

2.2   Segmentation of the Region of Interest

Fig. 2 illustrates the main steps of the segmentation and enhancement of the region of interest. Fig. 2a shows a RGB direct immunofluorescence image. We first perform morphological closing by a disk-shaped structuring element (radius of 30 pixels) to the green channel of the DIF image (Fig. 2b), the result of which is shown in Fig. 2c. If there are more than one connected components, we only consider the one with the largest area. Subsequently, we apply the Canny edge detector[1] [5] to delineate the region boundaries. As shown in Fig. 1 some images are characterized by one boundary between the green region and the background. Others are, however, characterized by two boundaries, Fig. 3. We only consider the upper-most[2] boundary in the image. Then, we obtain the region of interest by dilating the extracted boundary by a disk-shaped structuring element with a radius of 30 pixels, Fig. 2d. We use the resulting mask to extract the corresponding part of the green channel of the original image (Fig. 2e). Finally, we apply contrast-limited adaptive histogram equalization (CLAHE) to the segmented image (Fig. 2e) in order to improve the local contrast, Fig. 2f.

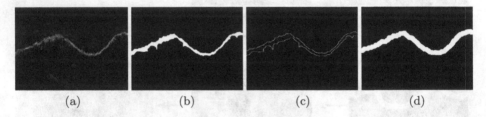

(a)   (b)   (c)   (d)

Fig. 3. (a) An example of a DIF image. (b) The largest connected component selected from the results of the morphological closing operation to the green channel of (a). (c) Two boundaries delineated by Canny edge detector from the image in (b). (d) The dilation result of the upper-most boundary.

2.3   *B*-COSFIRE Filters

A *B*-COSFIRE filter[3] [3] is a ridge detector, which is based on the COSFIRE approach [2] and the CORF computational model [1]. Its response is achieved by computing the geometric mean of a group of linearly aligned responses of a Difference-of-Gaussians (DoG) filter.

We denote by $r_{\sigma,l,\theta}(x,y)$ the response of a *B*-COSFIRE filter to a given input image at location (x,y). Such a filter has three parameters: standard deviation σ of the outer Gaussian function in the involved DoG filter[4], radius l and orientation θ. The radius l is the farthest distance from the center of the filter

---

[1] We use the following parameters: standard deviation of $\sqrt{2}$, high threshold of 0.02 and low threshold of 0.01.

[2] We choose the upper-most boundary by comparing the mean of the y-coordinates of the two boundaries

[3] Matlab scripts: http://www.mathworks.com/matlabcentral/fileexchange/49172

[4] The standard deviation of the inner Gaussian function is 0.5σ

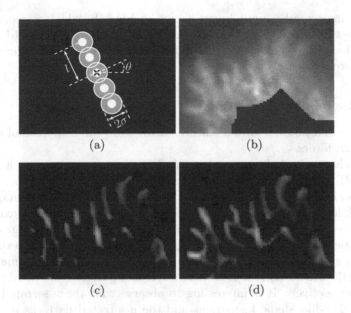

Fig. 4. (a) Structure of a B-COSFIRE filter selective for vertical ridges (orientation preference $\theta = 30$). Its area of support has a radius l of 4 pixels and it takes as input five responses from a center-on DoG filter with $\sigma = 1.2$. For illustration clarity the diameter of the outer Gaussian functions here is 2σ pixels. The afferent inputs are equally spaced in intervals of 2 pixels. The cross marker indicates the central position of the filter support and the concentric circles represent the area of support of the DoG function at the considered locations. (b) An input image and (c) the corresponding B-COSFIRE response map. (d) Superposition of the responses of a bank of B-COSFIRE filters selective for six different orientations: $\theta \in \{0, \pi/6, \ldots, 5\pi/6\}$.

at which DoG responses are considered as input to a B-COSFIRE filter in a specific position, Fig. 4a. The original B-COSFIRE filters use a blurring function to allow for some tolerance with respect to the preferred position of DoG responses. Given the small size of the ridges in DIF images it was not necessary to blur[5] the DoG responses for this application. The responses of a B-COSFIRE filter are thresholded at a given fraction t $(0 \leq t \leq 1)$ of the maximum response of $r_{\sigma,l,\theta}(x,y)$ across all the combinations of values (σ, l, θ) and all the positions (x,y) in the image. For this application, we use a fixed threshold of 0.001. We comment on the choice of the values of σ and l in Sections 3 and 4. For further technical details we refer to [1–3,7–9] and to an online implementation[6].

Fig. 4a shows the structure of a B-COSFIRE filter with a standard deviation $\sigma = 1.2$, radius $l = 4$ and orientation $\theta = 30$. The cross marker indicates the center of the area of support of the B-COSFIRE filter. As an illustration we

---

[5] We set $\sigma_0 = 0$ and $\alpha = 0$ in the B-COSFIRE implementation.

[6] http://matlabserver.cs.rug.nl

apply this filter to the input image shown in Fig. 4b, which is cropped from Fig. 2f. The thresholded filter response map is shown in Fig. 4c. Fig. 4d shows the superposition of thresholded responses of a bank of B-COSFIRE filters selective for six different orientations.

2.4   Histogram of Orientations

Here, we explain how we form a feature vector from the responses of a bank of B-COSFIRE filters.

For each segmented and enhanced DIF image, we apply a bank of B-COSFIRE filters that are selective for six orientations: $\theta \in (0, \pi/6, \ldots, 5\pi/6)$. This results in six response maps. Next, we create an orientation map by taking at each location the orientation of the B-COSFIRE filter that exhibits the maximum response. Finally, we construct the L1-normalized histogram of the resulting orientation map within the segmented region and use it as the feature vector of a given DIF image. Fig. 5(a-c) and Fig. 5(d-f) show normalized histograms of the orientation maps of three u-serrated patterns and three n-serrated patterns, respectively. It is interesting to observe that the u-serrated patterns result in valley-like shape histograms and the n-serrated patterns in a hill-like shape histograms.

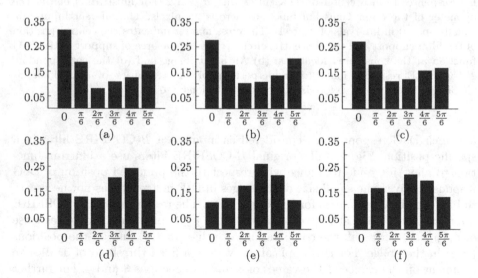

Fig. 5. Normalized histograms of orientation maps of (a-c) the three u-serrated patterns and (d-f) the three n-serrated patterns in Fig. 6, respectively

3   Evaluation

3.1   Data Set

We use a data set from an image-based online test [12] provided by the University Medical Center Groningen (UMCG). It comprises 26 DIF images from different pemphigoid patients, 11 of which contain u-serrated patterns and the rest contain n-serrated patterns. All images are taken with magnifications of ×40 and ×63. We only consider the ones with ×40 magnification as they are the most commonly used in hospitals. Fig. 6(a-f) show six examples of gray scale DIF images which are described by the histograms in Fig. 5(a-f).

3.2   Experiments

We apply the methods proposed in Section 2 to the 26 DIF images and compute for every DIF image a normalized histogram of orientations. For the evaluation of the proposed method, we use the nearest neighbor algorithm to classify each image as u-serration or n-serration pattern by comparing its normalized histogram of orientations with the ones of the remaining 25 DIF images in the dataset. Considering that a B-COSFIRE filter uses parameters σ and l, we run various experiments by systematically changing the values of the parameters σ ($\sigma \in \{0.5, 1, \ldots, 5\}$ and l ($l \in \{2, 4, 6\}$. Fig. 7 shows the experimental results with the highest correct classification rate being 84.6% (22 out of 26), which we achieve by using leave-one-out cross-validation. We achieve this result with two pairs of parameters, $\sigma = 1.5$, $l = 2$ and $\sigma = 2.5$, $l = 4$, which are indicated by the large star and circle markers in Fig. 7, respectively.

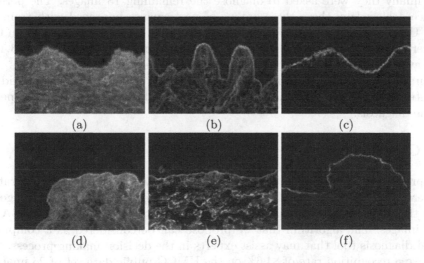

(a)   (b)   (c)

(d)   (e)   (f)

Fig. 6. The green channels of (a-c) three u-serrated and (d-f) three n-serrated patterns.

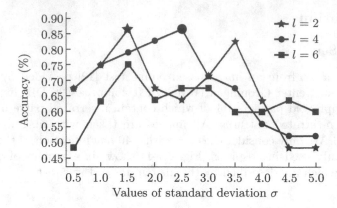

Fig. 7. Results achieved on the UMCG data set with different values of $\sigma \in \{0.5, 1, \ldots, 5\}$ and $l \in \{2, 4, 6\}$ of the involved B-COSFIRE filters. The large star and circle indicate the highest classification rate we achieve.

4   Discussion

The classification rate of 84.6% which we achieve is comparable to the results obtained by trained medical experts in an online test [10]. In that test, there were three categories of experts with a priori knowledge on the subject; namely dermatology residents at the UMCG, dermatologists and pathologists who had participated in the annual Dutch blistering course in Groningen during 2005-2012, and international experts in blistering diseases. They were first asked to diagnose 13 DIF images. Then, they were given more information on the subject by means of an online instruction video[7] about n- and u-serrated patterns, and finally they were asked to diagnose the remaining 13 images. The performance achieved by these three groups of participants improved with training [10]. UMCG experts reached a performance of 82.1%, the participants from the blistering course achieved 72.8% and the international experts achieved 83.4%. The average recognition rate for all participants was 78.6%.

In future work, we aim to develop an algorithm that localizes the n- and u-serrated patterns in a DIF image, which is also useful to aide the medical experts in the diagnosis.

5   Conclusions

We propose an approach for the automatic classification of u- and n-serrated patterns in DIF images to distinguish EBA from other forms of pemphigoid. It is the first one that addresses the challenging problem of detecting EBA in DIF images. The algorithm that we propose can be considered as a computer aided diagnosis tool that may assist experts in the decision making process. We achieve a recognition rate of 84.6% on the UMCG public data set of 26 images, which is comparable to the performance of medical experts.

---

[7] Online training: http://www.nversusu.umcg.nl

Acknowledgment. We wish to thanks to the photographer and data manager of the dermatology department of UMCG for their valuable help.

References

1. Azzopardi, G., Petkov, N.: A CORF computational model of a simple cell that relies on LGN input outperforms the Gabor function model. Biological Cybernetics **106**(3), 177–189 (2012)
2. Azzopardi, G., Petkov, N.: Trainable COSFIRE Filters for Keypoint Detection and Pattern Recognition. IEEE Transactions on Pattern Analysis and Machine Intelligence **35**(2), 490–503 (2013)
3. Azzopardi, G., Strisciuglio, N., Vento, M., Petkov, N.: Trainable COSFIRE filters for vessel delineation with application to retinal images. Medical Image Analysis **19**(1), 46–57 (2015)
4. Buijsrogge, J.J.A., Diercks, G.F.H., Pas, H.H., Jonkman, M.F.: The many faces of epidermolysis bullosa acquisita after serration pattern analysis by direct immunofluorescence microscopy. British Journal of Dermatology **165**(1), 92–98 (2011)
5. Canny, J.: A Computational Approach to Edge Detection. IEEE Transactions on Pattern Analysis and Machine Intelligence **8**(6), 679–698 (1986)
6. Gammon, W., Kowalewski, C., Chorzelski, T., Kumar, V., Briggaman, R., Beutner, E.: Direct immunofluorescence studies of sodium chloride-separated skin in the differential diagnosis of bullous pemphigoid and epidermolysis bullosa acquisita. Journal of the American Academy of Dermatology **22**(4), 664–670 (1990)
7. Petkov, N.: Biologically motivated computationally intensive approaches to image pattern-recognition. Future Generation Computer Systems **11**(4–5), 451–465 (1995). 1994 Europe Conference on High Performance Computing and Networking (HPCN Europe 94), Munich, Germany, 1994
8. Petkov, N., Kruizinga, P.: Computational models of visual neurons specialised in the detection of periodic and aperiodic oriented visual stimuli: Bar and grating cells. Biological Cybernetics **76**(2), 83–96 (1997)
9. Petkov, N., Westenberg, M.: Suppression of contour perception by band-limited noise and its relation to non-classical receptive field inhibition. Biological Cybernetics **88**(10), 236–246 (2003)
10. Terra, J.B., Meijer, J.M., Jonkman, M.F., Diercks, G.F.H.: The n- vs. u-serration is a learnable criterion to differentiate pemphigoid from epidermolysis bullosa acquisita in direct immunofluorescence serration pattern analysis. British Journal of Dermatology **169**(1), 100–105 (2013)
11. Terra, J.B., Pas, H.H., Hertl, M., Dikkers, F.G., Kamminga, N., Jonkman, M.F.: Immunofluorescence serration pattern analysis as a diagnostic criterion in antilaminin-332 mucous membrane pemphigoid: immunopathological findings and clinical experience in 10 Dutch patients. British Journal of Dermatology **165**(4), 815–822 (2011)
12. UMCG: UMCG online test (2013). http://www.nversusu.umcg.nl/
13. Vodegel, R., Jonkman, M., Pas, H., De Jong, M.: U-serrated immunodeposition pattern differentiates type VII collagen targeting bullous diseases from other subepidermal bullous autoimmune diseases. British Journal of Dermatology **151**(1), 112–118 (2004)
14. Woodley, D.T., Briggaman, R.A., O'Keefe, E.J., Inman, A.O., Queen, L.L., Gammon, W.R.: Identification of the skin basement-membrane autoantigen in epidermolysis bullosa acquisita. New England Journal of Medicine **310**(16), 1007–1013 (1984)

Means of 2D and 3D Shapes and Their Application in Anatomical Atlas Building

Juan Domingo[1]([✉]), Esther Dura[1], Guillermo Ayala[2], and Silvia Ruiz-España[3]

[1] Dpto. de Informática, Escuela de Ingenierías, University of Valencia,
Avda. de la Universidad, S/n, 46100 Burjasot, Spain
{Juan.Domingo,Esther.Dura}@uv.es
[2] Dpto. de Estadística e I.O., Facultad de Matemáticas,
University of Valencia, Valencia, Spain
Guillermo.Ayala@uv.es
[3] Center of Biomaterials and Tissue Engineering,
Polytechnic University of Valencia, Valencia, Spain
silviaruiz.es@gmail.com

Abstract. This works deals with the concept of mean when applied to 2D or 3D shapes and with its applicability to the construction of digital atlases to be used in digital anatomy. Unlike numerical data, there are several possible definitions of the mean of a shape distribution and procedures for its estimation from a sample of shapes. Most popular definitions are based in the distance function or in the coverage function, each with its strengths and limitations. Closely related to the concept of mean shape is the concept of atlas, here understood as a probability or membership map that tells how likely is that a point belongs to a shape drawn from the shape distribution at hand. We devise a procedure to build probabilistic atlases from a sample of similar segmented shapes using information simultaneously from both functions: the distance and the coverage. Applications of the method in digital anatomy are provided as well as experiments to show the advantages of the proposed method regarding state of the art techniques based on the coverage function.

Keywords: Probabilistic atlas · Mean shapes · Medical image segmentation

1 Introduction and Previous Work

The statistical concept of mean is clearly defined for univariate numerical distributions and many extensions have been proposed to deal with multivariate and/or categorical data. Nevertheless, it is in general much more difficult to extend this concept to 2D or 3D shapes. First of all, shapes should be aligned (in the language of medical image, registered) to a common spatial reference frame. Later, some kind of summary that preserves the structural properties that define the shape, independently of individual variations, must be found. If only the mean shape or the mean besides some kind of variation intervals are

© Springer International Publishing Switzerland 2015
G. Azzopardi and N. Petkov (Eds.): CAIP 2015, Part I, LNCS 9256, pp. 522–533, 2015.
DOI: 10.1007/978-3-319-23192-1_44

kept, we have a binary atlas. On the other hand, if the mean shape or some of the intermediate steps for its calculation are used to get a measure of belonging of each point to the shape, we have a probabilistic atlas.

We are mainly interested in probabilistic atlases, however obtaining the mean shape and confidence intervals is an interesting task with applications in multiple fields like morphometry, living organism classification, industrial inspection and what it is our main goal: digital anatomy. In this area, the mean shape can be useful to determine the deviation of an organ from its normal or expected shape. However for some medical imaging procedures, such as organ segmentation, the mean alone may be insufficient and here is where an anatomical atlas plays a major role. An interesting example can be found in [1]. The atlas, if given as a set of possible modes of shape variation, provides a valuable help for identification of structures, quantitative analysis and coregistration. If given as a probabilistic map can provide a priori information (prior probabilities) that can guide segmentation algorithms based on Bayesian classifiers. Also, it can serve as initial function that evolves according to actual data in level-set based methods.

As stated before, the samples (input shapes used for atlas construction) must be registered. The influence of the registration process in the final atlas is crucial. Some registration methods are based on principal components (PCA, see below) through the use of automatic of manually provided landmarks like [8] or in diffeomorphic registration to a reference shape, like [11]. A problem is that different geometric transformations (and therefore, different atlases) can arise depending on the chosen reference shape and coregistration method. As stated in [12], "a registration method removes all variation in the data by matching the structures exactly and the probabilities should have only two values: zero or one..." (provided, of course, a perfect registration method). What we argue here is that the use of a very good registration method (for instance: one which allows local deformations) removes the real variations of shape and size that exists in the sample data, and therefore the resulting atlas is biased and less useful for segmenting a new, unknown case. This is why we only allowed using a registration procedure that involves rigid transformations (translation, rotation and scaling at most) to take into account later the shape variation by morphological methods. A consequence of that is that, apart from the mean shape and probabilistic atlas, minimal and maximal shapes roughly equivalent to tolerance intervals could be obtained, as well.

Most of the methods proposed to get prototypical shapes are based on the use of principal component analysis, either to align the shape (rotation to get the main inertia axes aligned for all individuals) and later to extract its modes of variation along each principal direction. The main drawback of this approach arises when shapes are quite irregular and over all, when the values of the eigenvalues of the PCA matrix, or at least two of them, are not too different, even a good way to cope with these problems is the decomposition using appropriate functions like spherical harmonics (see [10]). Alternative proposals for alignment include the use the directions of minimal projection area (see [6]) or the sides of the minimal enclosing box (MEB), as in [2]. Moreover, the result of the prototype obtained by these approaches from a set of binary shapes is also a binary shape, not the probability map we are interested in.

Completely different ways to obtain the mean set are based on the concepts of distance function and coverage function. The initial problem of correct registration arises here too, and must be solved by any of the formerly mentioned methods. Once the shapes have been registered, coverage function gives the probability of a point to be covered by a shape of the shape distribution; there are simple estimators for it, assuming we have access to a sample of shapes. Indeed, all the procedures for building probabilistic atlas in digital anatomy use, up to our knowledge, the coverage function or transformations of it even most of them use non-rigid registration methods on the input shapes before doing coverage estimation. Examples include the seminal paper of Park ([8]) and others like [13] or the interesting idea of weighting the voxels to reduce estimation bias ([14]).

Nevertheless, not only the coverage function can be used; distance function is defined as the distance from a point in space to the closest point in the boundary of a given shape (can be defined as unsigned, or signed, getting inner points with its negative distance to the boundary. See eq. 1). From it, the concept of mean distance function can be defined and its value estimated from a sample of shapes. Going from mean coverage or mean distance functions to a binary mean shape can be done simply by thresholding, being the natural threshold 0 for the signed mean distance. Complete definitions and more sophisticated ways to obtain the mean shapes can be seen in [5]. The previous reference most similar to our approach is the work of Pohl ([9]) that transforms a signed distance map into a log-odds map via a logistic link function; the authors show how the log-odds can be efficiently combined, either from samples taken along time or samples segmented by different observers. The main difference with this work is that they assume statistical independence among voxels whereas in this work the global dependence is managed by the fitting of a generalized linear model.

Our approach follows the ideas based on distance and coverage functions and the main point is that, instead of thresholding the coverage or the distance function to get a binary mean, information of both functions can be simultaneously used to build a probabilistic map. This will be done by assuming that coverage is related with distance by means of a generalized linear model (GLM) that can be estimated from the data. The linear model also provides confidence intervals for the result of the estimation at each point.

2   Description of the Approach

From now on, we will work with random compact sets denoted as Φ. The realizations of a random compact set are binary shapes: sets of points of $\mathbb{R}^2$ or $\mathbb{R}^3$ (in general, $\mathbb{R}^d$) with the only restriction of being compact (but not necessarily convex). For a fixed shape S, and for any point $x \in \mathbb{R}^d$, $1_S(x)$ will stand for the set indicator function, i.e.:

$$1_S(x) = \begin{cases} 1 & \text{if } x \in S \\ 0 & \text{if } x \notin S \end{cases}$$

For a random compact set Φ the value $1_\Phi(x)$ is a random variable with values in $\{0, 1\}$.

In a similar way, $d_S(x)$ will be the signed distance function to S:

$$d_S(x) = \begin{cases} \min_{y \in \partial S} d(x, y) & \text{if } x \notin S \\ 0 & \text{if } x \in \partial S \\ -\min_{y \in \partial S} d(x, y) & \text{if } x \in int(S), \end{cases} \tag{1}$$

being $d(x, y)$ the Euclidean distance between points x and y, ∂S the boundary of S and $int(S)$ the interior of the set S. $d_\Phi(x)$ is a random variable. Since $1_\Phi(x) = 0 \iff d(x) > 0$ and $1_\Phi(x) = 1 \iff d(x) \leq 0$, it is clear that, given $d(x)$, $1_\Phi(x)$ is known. Let

$$p(x) = E\left(1_\Phi(x)\right) = P(x \in \Phi), \tag{2}$$

being E the expectation over all sets in Φ and let the mean distance function $d_\Phi^*(x)$ be defined as

$$d_\Phi^*(x) = Ed(x, \Phi). \tag{3}$$

Our idea is to interpret $p(x)$ as playing the role of an atlas, indicating where it is most likely to find a point that belongs to Φ. If we have a random sample of Φ i.e. independent and identically distributed (as Φ) random compact sets $\Phi_1, \ldots, \Phi_n$, where $\phi_1, \ldots, \phi_n$ are the corresponding realizations. The unbiased estimator for $d_\Phi^*(x)$ would be

$$\hat{d}^*(x) = \sum_{i=1}^n \frac{d_{\Phi_i}(x)}{n}, \tag{4}$$

and similarly, the unbiased estimator for the function $p(x)$:

$$\hat{p}_1(x) = \sum_{i=1}^n \frac{1_{\Phi_i}(x)}{n}. \tag{5}$$

Nevertheless, we will not attempt such simple possibility for estimation of p because it only uses local information (that attached to a single location x). On the contrary, mean distance function is much smoother and embodies to some extent the global shape of the random set. This is why we will attempt to estimate the function $p(x)$ using information about the mean distance function.

Assuming that $p(x) = f(d^*(x))$ (i.e.: the probability is a function of the mean distance function) the goal is to find a sensible link between both. But $d^*(x)$ can take positive and negative values. We will resort to the usual approach in generalized linear models: link input and output through a cumulative distribution function, a non-decreasing function $F : \mathbb{R} \longrightarrow [0, 1]$. From the value $d^*(x)$ its transformations using a basis functions denoted as $v(x) = (1, v_1(d^*(x)), \ldots, v_{p-1}(d^*(x)))'$ will be considered, being t' is the transpose of the vector t. We will assume the following model.

$$p(x) = F(\beta' v(x))$$

with $\beta' = (\beta_0, \beta_1, \ldots, \beta_{p-1})$. The two usual choices for the link function F are the cumulative distribution functions corresponding either to the standard logistic distribution or the standard normal distribution. In particular, we will use the logistic distribution so

$$p(x) = \frac{e^{\beta' v(x)}}{1 + e^{\beta' v(x)}}.$$

Let us consider a given point x_0. If $p(x)$ is a smooth function then a constant value for $p(x)$ in a ball centered at x, $B(x_0, h)$ with $h > 0$, can be assumed. If $(x_j, 1_{\phi_i}(x_j))$ with $j = 1, \ldots, J$ denote the points located within $B(x_0, h)$, the local pseudo-likelihood function for the i-th realization ϕ_i is given by

$$\prod_{j=1}^{J} w(x_j, x_0) p(x_j)^{1_{\phi_i}(x_j)} (1 - p(x_j))^{1 - 1_{\phi_i}(x_j)}, \tag{6}$$

where $w(x, x_0) = K(\| x - x_0 \| / h)$ being K a kernel function and h the bandwidth. But we have a random sample of Φ so the whole likelihood function can be written as:

$$L(\beta) = \prod_{i=1}^{n} \prod_{j=1}^{J} w(x_j, x_0) p(x_j)^{1_{\phi_i}(x_j)} (1 - p(x_j))^{1 - 1_{\phi_i}(x_j)},$$

whose log-likelihood is

$$l(\beta) = \log L(\beta) =$$

$$\sum_{i=1}^{n} \sum_{j=1}^{J} \Bigg(\log(w(x_j, x_o)) + 1_{\Phi_i}(x_j) \log(p(x_j)) +$$

$$+ (1 - 1_{\Phi_i}(x_j)) \log(1 - p(x_j)) \Bigg). \tag{7}$$

Let $\hat{\beta}(x_0)$ be the vector of parameters that maximize this global likelihood, i.e.:

$$\hat{\beta}(x_0) = argmax_\beta \, l(\beta).$$

$\hat{\beta}$ will be found using appropriate optimization methods. The estimator proposed for the probability function $p(x)$ is finally:

$$\hat{p}(x_0) = \frac{e^{\hat{\beta}(x_0)' v(x)}}{1 + e^{\hat{\beta}(x_0)' v(x)}}. \tag{8}$$

whose value at each location x_0 constitutes our atlas.

The assumed linear model also gives the possibility of estimating simultaneous confidence bands, i.e. a 95% confidence interval around each estimated value. The width of this interval is related with the degree of confidence we can put on the estimation at each point; this can be a valuable help when relying on the atlas values for a real task of anatomical segmentation.

3   Implementation

In practical terms we really use the shape representation in digital form, i.e., as sets of pixels/voxels in the sampled space $\mathbb{Z}^2$ or $\mathbb{Z}^3$ with a binary value assigned, 1 meaning that the point belongs to the shape and 0 that it is empty space. The shapes available will be either generated from simulation programs or obtained by segmenting real images to extract the pixels/voxels that fulfill a property, normally extracted from local visual features of the image like gray level, color, texture or similar. In our case the synthetic examples have been generated with a program in C++ using the ITK libraries ([4]) and the anatomical real examples have been manually segmented by a radiologist. The coverage functions and signed distance functions were obtained from the binary images also with C++ programs, again using the ITK, as long as the final estimation of the probabilistic atlas. The optimization step required a call to a function included in the *locfit* package ([7]) of the statistical software R done from inside the C++ program using the *Rcpp* and *RInside* packages ([3]). The linear model has been set up to use the simplest possible predictor (i.e.: $v(x) = (1, \bar{d}(x))$) and the kernel function K and bandwidth h used in equation 6 have been left to the default values provided by the *locfit* package.

4   Examples

4.1   Simulation Example

A set of 20 four-sided polygons were generated as a test sample. Their vertexes were randomly placed around the points in $\mathbb{R}^2$ $\{(-100, -100), (-100, 100), (100, 100), (100, -100)\}$ moved in each coordinate by Gaussian noise with 0 mean and standard deviation $\sigma = 10$, as shown in figure 1 (left). The same figure shows in its right-half, upper-left part the generated probabilistic atlas (color scale with red for higher values and blue for lower values), in its upper-right the atlas thresholded at 0.5, and in the lower row the thresholded normalized coverage function (threshold 0.5) and the thresholded mean distance function (threshold 0).

4.2   Liver and Vertebra Atlas

The anatomical example starts from 40 shapes obtained by manual segmentation of the liver done by a radiologist from a set of perfusion magnetic resonance (MR) images of the abdominal cavity taken from 21 different patients (in some cases two or three different shapes of the same patient were used, taken at different times). As an illustration, the mean shape (using only the signed mean distance function thresholded at 0) of each patient, or the only shape for the cases of only one shape per patient, are shown in figure 2.

The coregistration of the cases was done assuming only a rigid transformation (translation plus rotation) using the method of minimal enclosing box alignment described in [2].

Fig. 1. Polygons with random vertexes generated as a synthetic sample and result of probabilistic atlas (upper-left), its thresholding (upper-right), thresholded coverage function (lower-left) and thresholded mean distance function (lower-right)

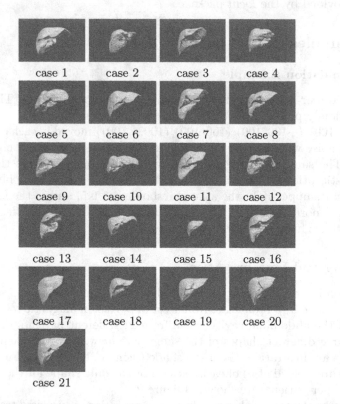

Fig. 2. 3D mean liver for each of the 21 different patients

In a similar way, 25 shapes of the lumbar vertebra L1, each of a different patient, were manually segmented from MRI images; as an illustration, 16 of them are shown in figure 3.

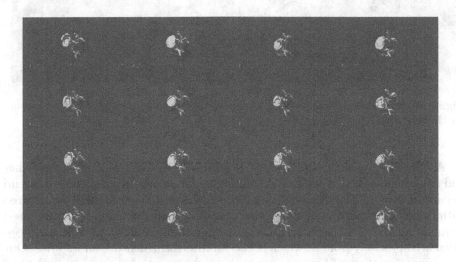

Fig. 3. 3D lumbar vertebra of 16 of the 25 different patients

Figure 4 shows the mean shapes obtained by thresholding the normalized coverage function (eq. 5) at 0.5 and the mean signed distance function (eq. 4) at 0, for the liver (left side) and the same representation for the vertebra (right side).

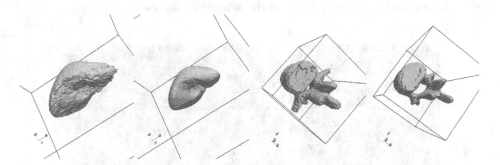

Fig. 4. Mean shapes by thresholding of coverage function and mean distance function for the liver (left) and vertebra (right).

Figure 5 shows in its left side a slice of the probability map (color scaled with blue for lower values, red for higher ones) superimposed to a cut of the thresholded atlas (binary shape) for the liver and in the same representation for the vertebra (right side).

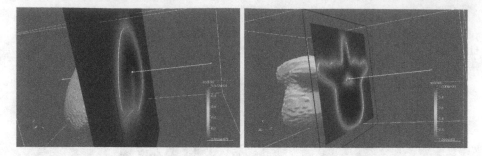

Fig. 5. A slice of the probabilistic atlas superimposed to its own thresholded version for the liver (left) and vertebra (right).

As it can be appreciated in figure 4, mean-based distance function is smoother and more regular, which is a desirable property for an atlas since we do not intend to capture individual variations but a representative shape that can be compared with or deformed to match any specific case. On the other hand, coverage-based mean is rougher but more accurate in terms of probability since it has been calculated precisely from it, which is also an interesting feature for an atlas. Our approximation (figure 5) aims to get both good properties by combining the two sources of information in a judicious manner.

Finally, figure 6 shows a color representation of the confidence of the probability estimator measured as the width of the confidence interval for the liver and vertebra, this time being blue the higher confidence (lower interval width) and red the lower confidence. It is clear that the estimation is more precise in the inner and outer part of the shapes and less precise at its limits, even in the case of the liver the confidence is lower inside the organ, particularly at the lower part, due to the greater variability of the sample of shapes.

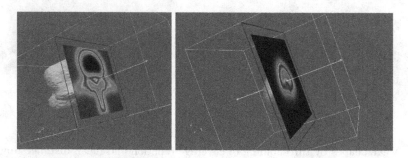

Fig. 6. Representation of the confidence interval width for the GLM estimation of the probability map.

5   Experiments

Objective evaluation of the proposed method will be done with an experiment performed equally in both of the studied cases, liver and vertebra. The experiment aims to compare the usual atlas built with the coverage function (simple estimation of the probability of coverage) with the improvement through the use of the GLM. The comparison will use a leave-one-out: for each of the N available cases of the sample, from now on the test case, an atlas is built with both methods using all the other $N-1$ cases, and then compared with the test case. This is to show the ability to generalize and adapt to a new case, the intended property of an atlas. The comparison will be done in terms of four matching measures: the total mass of probability given by the atlas enclosed in the test case, and some measures of distance between binary shapes: Haussdorf distance, Dice coefficient and Jaccard index. Since the atlas is not a binary shape, it will be thresholded by 0.5 before measuring the three last quantities; the choice of 0.5 as threshold is not critical for comparison, if used for both atlas types.

Given a binary shape S we will call $V(S)$ to its volume. Let $P(x) \in [0..1])\forall x \in \mathbb{R}^3$ be the probabilistic atlas; let P_t be the binary shape obtained by thresholding (i.e.: $x \in P_t \iff P(x) \geq 0.5$) and let T be the test shape. The total mass of probability $Int_p(P, T)$ is defined as

$$Int_p(P, T) = \frac{1}{V(T)} \int_T P(x)dx$$

The Haussdorf distance $H_d(P_t, T)$ is

$$H_d(P_t, T) = \max \left\{ \sup_{x \in P_t} \inf_{y \subset T} d(x, y), \sup_{y \in T} \inf_{x \in P_t} d(x, y) \right\}$$

being $d(x, y)$ the Euclidean distance between the point x and y. The Dice (or Sorensen-Dice) coefficient and the Jaccard index are respectively defined as

$$Dice(P_t, T) = \frac{2V(P_t \cap T)}{V(P_t) + V(T)} \qquad Jac(P_t, T) = \frac{V(P_t \cap T)}{V(P_t \cup T)}$$

To have an atlas as similar as possible to a shape the Int_p should be high (close to 1). Between binary shapes, $Dice$ and $Jaccard$ (both also in $[0..1]$) should be high whereas Haussdorf distance (a positive value) should be small. Results for the liver atlases are shown in table 1 and for the vertebra in table 2. The first column shows the mean of the corresponding index (each different measure in a row) for the coverage-based atlas and the second column the paired results for our proposed GLM atlas. A t-test for the difference of means was applied in all cases with the null hypothesis of equality of means. The third column shows the p-value of the t-test and the fourth and fifth columns the 95% confidence interval for the difference of means.

Both tables show that for all the proposed measures our atlas shows better performance (integral of the probability, Dice similarity and Jaccard index

Table 1. Comparison between coverage-based atlas and the proposed GLM atlas for the live-one-out test with 40 liver shapes. See text for detailed explanation.

	Coverage	GLM	p-value	CI-lower	CI-upper
Int_p	0.73	0.84	0.00	-0.12	-0.10
H_d	43.53	34.84	0.00	8.18	9.21
$Dice$	0.71	0.79	0.00	-0.10	-0.06
Jac	0.56	0.66	0.00	-0.13	-0.07

Table 2. Comparison between coverage-based atlas and the proposed GLM atlas for the live-one-out test with 25 vertebra shapes. See text for detailed explanation.

	Coverage	GLM	p-value	CI-lower	CI-upper
Int_p	0.80	0.91	0.00	-0.12	-0.10
H_d	11.39	8.42	0.00	2.48	3.45
$Dice$	0.74	0.76	0.03	-0.03	0.00
Jac	0.59	0.62	0.03	-0.04	0.00

increase whereas Hausdorff distance decrease) always with a significance level below 0.05 (p-values are rounded to two decimal places and when given as 0.0 they were all below 10^{-9}); the only exceptions are the Dice and Jaccard in the case of the vertebra which are not so low (0.03) but still below 0.05.

6   Conclusions and Further Work

A probabilistic atlas has been defined as a map of $\mathbb{R}^d$ in $[0..1]$ that gives the probability that each point has to belong to a class of similar shapes. This work has proposed a method to estimate it from examples taking into account both the coverage function and the distance function, in an aim to capture the best properties of each approach. Also, we purposely renounce to use a too precise registration method that could reduce the variability of the sample, a feature that we consider important for an atlas. We argue that a probabilistic atlas may provide some advantages to alternative methods like those based on PCA and principal modes for certain applications like guided segmentation algorithms that need a-priori information or may improve if such information is available. A drawback of the method is the need to have a sufficiently abundant sample of cases obtained by mean of manual segmentation programs, a process usually tedious and cumbersome.

Further work will include more experiments with other organs or bones (in particular, the whole vertebral spine) and ways to find a more precise estimation of probability with two possible improvements: try with other generalized linear models and doing local regression taking into account not only distance intervals but also spatial location. This would be a way to take into account the differences in precision between points of the space without sacrificing the variability due to the intrinsic differences between shapes.

Acknowledgments. This work has been supported by project DPI2013-45742-R from the Spanish Ministry of Economy and Innovation.

References

1. Bauer, S., Seiler, C., Bardyn, T., Buechler, P., Reyes, M.: Atlas-based segmentation of brain tumor images using a markov random field-based tumor growth model and non-rigid registration. In: Annual Intl. Conf. of the IEEE Engineering in Medicine and Biology Society (EMBC), pp. 4080–4083, September 2010
2. Dura, E., Domingo, J.: Alternative method for binary shape alignment of non-symmetrical shapes based on minimal enclosing box. Electronics Letters **48**(22), 1401–1402 (2012)
3. Eddelbuettel, D., Francoisloader, R.: Rinside R package: C++ classes to embed R in C++ applications (2014). http://cran.r-project.org/web/packages/RInside
4. Ibañez, M.V., Schroeder, W., Cates, L.: Insight Software Consortium The ITK Software Guide. http://www.itk.org/ItkSoftwareGuide.pdf
5. Jankowski, H., Stanberry, L.: Expectations of random sets and their boundaries using oriented distance functions. Journal of Mathematical Imaging and Vision **36**, 291–303 (2010)
6. Johan, H., Li, B., Wei, Y., Iskandarsyah, Y.W.: 3D model alignment based on minimum projection area. The Visual Computer **27**(6–8), 565–574 (2011)
7. Loader, C.: locfit R package: Local regression, likelihood and density estimation (2013). http://cran.r-project.org/web/packages/locfit
8. Park, H., Bland, P.H., Meyer, C.R.: Construction of an abdominal probabilistic atlas and its application in segmentation. IEEE Transactions on Medical Imaging **22**(4), 483–492 (2003)
9. Pohl, K., Fisher, J., Bouix, S., Shenton, M., et al.: Using the logarithm of odds to define a vector space on probabilistic atlases. Medical Image Analysis **11**(5), 465–477 (2007)
10. Tateyama, T., Okegawa, M., Uetani, M., Tanaka, H., Kohara, S., Han, X., et al.: Efficient shape representation and statistical shape modeling of the liver using spherical harmonic functions (SPHARM). In: 13th Intl. Symp. on Advanced Intelligent Systems (ISIS) Soft Computing and Intelligent Systems (SCIS), pp. 428–431, November 2012
11. Xiong, W., Ong, S.H., Tian, Q., Guozhen, X., Zhou, J., Liu, J., Venkatash, S.K.: Construction of a linear unbiased diffeomorphic probabilistic liver atlas from CT images. In: 16th IEEE Intl. Conference on Image Processing Image Processing (ICIP), pp. 1773–1776, November 2009
12. Lötjönen, L., Wolz, R., Koikkalainen, J., Thurfiell, L., et al.: Improved generation of probabilistic atlases for the expectation maximization classification. In: IEEE Intl. Symp. on Biomedical Imaging: From Nano to Macro, pp. 1839–1842 (2011)
13. Park, H., Hero, A., Bland, P., Kessler, M., Seo, J., Meyer, C.: Construction of Abdominal Probabilistic Atlases and Their Value in Segmentation of Normal Organs in Abdominal CT Scans. IEICE Transactions on Information and Systems **E93.D**(8), 2291–2301 (2011)
14. Wolz, R., Chu, C., Misawa, K., Fujiwara, M., Mori, K., Ruecket, D.: Automated Abdominal Multi-Organ Segmentation with Subject-specific Atlas Generation. IEEE Transactions on Medical Imaging **32**(9), 1723–1730 (2013)

Optimized NURBS Curves Modelling Using Genetic Algorithm for Mobile Robot Navigation

Sawssen Jalel[1,2]([⊠]), Philippe Marthon[2], and Atef Hamouda[1]

[1] LIPAH Research Laboratory, Faculty of Sciences of Tunis,
Tunis El Manar University, 2092 Tunis, Tunisia
atef_hammouda@yahoo.fr
[2] Site ENSEEIHT de l'Institut de Recherche en Informatique de Toulouse (IRIT),
University of Toulouse, 2 rue Charles Camichel BP, 7122 Toulouse, France
{sawssen.jalel,philippe.marthon}@enseeiht.fr

Abstract. This paper presents a new approach for solving one of the crucial robotic tasks: the global path planning problem. It consists in calculating the existing optimal path, for a non-point, non-holonomic robot, from start to goal position in terms of Non Uniform Rational B-Spline (NURBS) curve. With a priori knowledge of the environment and the robot characteristics (size and radius of curvature), the algorithm begins by selecting a set of control points derived from the shortest, collision-free polyline path. Then, an optimized NURBS curve modelling using Genetic Algorithm (GA) is introduced to replace that polyline path by a smooth curvature-constrained curve which avoids obstacles. Computer simulation studies demonstrate the effectiveness of the proposed method.

Keywords: NURBS curves parameterization · Robot path planning · Path smoothing · Curvature constraint · Genetic algorithm

1 Introduction

The autonomous mobile robotics aim, more specifically, to develop systems able to move independently. Direct applications are particularly in the fields of automotive, planetary exploration and service robotics, which is why path planning for mobile robots is one of the most important aspects in robot navigation that has been extensively studied over the last decade.

The path planning environment can be categorized into two major classes which are Static and Dynamic. In the static environment, the whole solution must be found before starting execution. However, for dynamic or partially observable environments replannings are required frequently, with more update time. Depending on environment type, path planning algorithms are divided into two categories, which are Local and Global methods. They might also be divided into Traditional and Intelligent methods. Eminent traditional path planning methods include potential field, visibility graph and cell decomposition approaches. As to intelligent methods, they include particle swarm optimization, neural networks, ant clony algorithms, fuzzy logic, memetic algorithm and

© Springer International Publishing Switzerland 2015
G. Azzopardi and N. Petkov (Eds.): CAIP 2015, Part I, LNCS 9256, pp. 534–545, 2015.
DOI: 10.1007/978-3-319-23192-1_45

genetic algorithms [1], [2]. Obviously, each one of them has its own strengths and limits which encourage researchers to search for alternative and more efficient methods.

In the last decade, genetic algorithms have been widely used to generate the optimum path thanks to their strong optimization ability. Although it has rapid and high search quality, GA has some limits such as the premature convergence and local optimum. To overcome this, many GA-based path planning methods have been implemented by means of customizing genetic operators and defining new operators [3]-[10].

We note that these algorithms does not take the size of the robot into consideration since it is regarded as a point-sized which could produce unsafe paths. Although these methods provide paths essentially trying to minimize their length, most fail to take into account the continuity of curvature as a parameter of the fitness function. Thus, the resulted path is made up of connected segments which makes the robot needing additional energy to change its direction. Motivated by the increase demand of prominent path planner for mobile robot, we aim to introduce a new approach based on an optimized NURBS curves modelling using genetic algorithm.

The remainder of the paper is organized as follows: Section 2 introduces the proposed approach, while the experimental evaluation of the system is described in Section 3. Conclusions are finally presented in Section 4.

2 Algorithm Description

2.1 Overview

This paper proposes a path planning scheme for a mobile robot in static environment. The robot's work area Ω is represented by a two-dimensional map cluttered with static rectangular obstacles of arbitrary size and position ($\Omega = \Omega_{free} \cup \Omega_{obst}$). The robot is modeled as a circle of diameter d, taking into account its dimensions, and a minimum radius of curvature ρ_{min}.

The objective is to find the existing shortest collision-free path from a starting point S to a target point T that satisfies the curvature-constraint. Our algorithm starts by selecting a set of waypoints which will be used as control points for the NURBS curve representing the planned path. Both traditional and intelligent methods are employed. In fact, the guiding polyline is determined using techniques of skeletonization, mathematical morphology and a shortest path algorithm. Then, GA is used to set the weight parameter of the NURBS curve.

2.2 Path's Control Points Selection

Algorithm 1 describes the procedure of control points computation. This algorithm starts by extracting the skeleton of the obstacle-free space Ω_{free}, to which, it connects the start and target point giving, accordingly, the extended skeleton X upon which the robot may move. Then, a morphological process is applied to classify the pixels of X into End Points (EP), Junction Points (JP), Critical Curve Points (CCP) and Curve Points (CP). Afterward, a weighted graph is constructed by associating $EP(X)$, $JP(X)$ and $CCP(X)$ with the vertices, and the set of $CP(X)$ with the edges. The weights of edges are generated by considering the Euclidean distances between vertices. Before applying Bellman Ford Algorithm to calculate the shortest path between S and T, the algorithm applies a graph reduction step to remove the edges that represent inaccessible corridors by the robot [11]. Finally, the set of control points P is calculated as the union of end points, junction points and critical curve points belonging to the shortest polyline path S_{opt}.

Algorithm 1. Control Points Selection

Input: Ω, S, T, d
Output: Control Point Sequence $P = \{P_1, P_2, ..., P_n\}$
1 **begin**
2     $X = SkeletonExtraction(\Omega_{free}, S, T)$;
3     $EP(X) = [\bigcup_i \epsilon_{\theta_i(\overline{A})}(\overline{X})] \cap X$;
4     $JP(X) = [\bigcup_i \epsilon_{\theta_i(B)}(X)] \cup [\bigcup_i \epsilon_{\theta_i(C)}(X)]$;
5     $CCP(X) = CurveCriticalPoint(X)$;
6     $CP(X) = X \backslash (EP(X) \cup JP(X) \cup CCP(X))$;
7     $G = GraphConstruction(EP(X), JP(X), CCP(X), CP(X))$;
8     $G' = GraphReduction(G, d, \Omega)$;
9     $S_{opt} = BellmanFordAlgorithm(G', S, T)$;
10    $P = EP(S_{opt}) \cup JP(S_{opt}) \cup CCP(S_{opt})$;
11   **return** (P);

2.3 Path Generation Using GA-Based NURBS Curves

NURBS curves are chosen to model the robot's path because of their flexibility and geometric properties, combined with the fact that NURBS algorithms are fast and numerically stable. They allow representation of geometrical shapes in a compact form [12]. A pth degree NURBS curve is a vector valued piecewise rational polynomial function of the form:

$$C(u) = \frac{\sum_{i=0}^n N_{i,p}(u) w_i P_i}{\sum_{i=0}^n N_{i,p}(u) w_i} \qquad a \leq u < b \qquad (1)$$

Where $\{P_i\}$ are the n control points, $\{w_i\}$ are the corresponding weights and the $\{N_{i,p}(u)\}$ are the pth B-spline basis functions defined on the non-uniform knot vector U, by DeBoor-Cox Calculation as follows :

$$N_{i,p}(u) = \frac{u - u_i}{u_{i+p} - u_i} N_{i,p-1}(u) + \frac{u_{i+p+1} - u}{u_{i+p+1} - u_{i+1}} N_{i+1,p-1}(u) \qquad (2)$$

Where

$$N_{i,0}(u) = \begin{cases} 1 & \text{if } u_i \leq u < u_{i+1} \\ 0 & \text{else} \end{cases}$$

A considerable amount of research has been carried out in the parametriza-tion domain. Indeed, finding a correct parameterization and the weight of the control points when calculating the curve have been the main issues in curve fit-ting techniques. Many evolutionary optimization techniques have been success-fully applied [13], [14]. In this paper, we aim to exploit the influence of the weight factor. In fact, the weight of a point P_k determines its influence on the associated curve. Thus, increasing (decreasing) w_k pulls (pushes) the curve toward (away from) this point. Also, we note that the weight parameter is inversely propor-tional to the radius of curvature and, accordingly, proportional to the curvature value (Fig. 1).

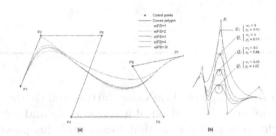

Fig. 1. (a)NURBS curve with w(P2) varying (b) Variation Weight vs radius of curva-ture

Let $P_1, P_2, ..., P_n$ be an ordered control point sequence. We want to calculate a NURBS curve which approximates this set while taking into account the system constraints related to the environment and the robot's characteristics (size and radius of curvature). The problem, therefore, is to find the right parametrization of the weight parameter. For this purpose, we propose a GA-based NURBS curve parametrization procedure which, for given control parameters (number of iterations, population size, rates of crossover and mutation), finds an optimal path. Algorithm 2 describes our adaptation of GA to robot path generation in terms of NURBS curves.

This algorithm begins by creating the initial population by assigning ran-dom weight values ($w_i \in [0.1; MaxWeight]$) to control points. Then, it cycles until a fixed number of iterations. A cycle has five main stages: (i) evaluation of the population based on a multi-objective fitness function, (ii) selection of parents, (iii) performing crossover operation, (iv) performing mutation opera-tion and finally updating the current population by removing some individuals to maintain the population size unchanged. The algorithm ends by selecting the best chromosome of the last population which represents the optimal path.

Individual Representation. The chromosome structure must have sufficient information about the entire path from the start to the end point in order to be able to represent it. In our context, an individual is a NURBS curve representing a path candidate. Such a curve is defined by a set of n weighted points as shown

---

Algorithm 2. GA-based NURBS curve parameterization

Input: Ω, P, p, ρ_{min}, d, $MaxWeight$, n_iter, $PopSize$, c_rate, m_rate

Output: Planned path C

1 **begin**
2     $P_w = InitPopulation(P, PopSize, MaxWeight)$;
3     $it = 1$;
4   **while** $it \le n\_iter$ **do**
5         $Evaluation(P_w, \Omega, \rho_{min}, d)$;
6         $Parents = Selection(P_w, c\_rate)$;
7         $CrossoverOp(P_w, Parents)$;
8         $MutationOp(P_w, m\_rate)$;
9         $UpdatePop(P_w, PopSize)$;
10         $it = it + 1$;
11   **return** $(Best(P_w))$;

---

in Fig. 2, for which P_1 and P_n are always the starting and destination configurations. Each gene represents the location of a waypoint (x and y coordinate) and its associated weight. It is noteworthy that location of this point is fixed while its associated weight is varying.

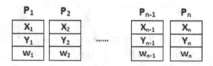

Fig. 2. Chromosome Representation

Evaluation Function. During each generation, the population of paths is evaluated to quantify their degree of elitism which depends on how suitable the solution (path) is according to the problem. Consequently, an individual's fitness value should be proportional to its survival ability. Most GA-based path planning existing methods consider the path length as fitness function to minimize and neglect feasibility. Consequently, the resulted path may not be followed by the robot if it does not respect the curvature limit related to its minimum radius of curvature. In addition, having low variation of curvatures along the path is of considerable importance.

In this study, we propose an accurate evaluation function that depends on four parameters: the safety, the feasibility, the length and the curvatures standard deviation of the path. The objective function for a path C is then defined as:

$$f(C) = \alpha . P_{safety}(C) + \beta . P_{feasibility}(C) + \gamma . \frac{1}{P_{length}(C)} + \delta . P_\sigma(C) \qquad (3)$$

Where $P_{safety}(C)$ is the path safety constraint and denotes the number of collisions:

$$P_{safety}(C) = |P_{col}| \tag{4}$$

Where:

$$P_{col} = \{p_i \in C, i = 1..k1\} = C \cap \Omega_{obst} \tag{5}$$

$P_{feasibility}(C)$ is the path feasibility related to the robot's minimum radius of curvature and determined as the number of curve points that exceeds the absolute value of the curvature limit:

$$P_{feasibility}(C) = |P_{cur}| \tag{6}$$

Where:

$$P_{cur} = \{p_j \in C, j = 1..k2 ||curvature(p_j)| > \frac{1}{\rho_{min}}\} \tag{7}$$

$P_{length}(C)$ is the path length, determined as:

$$P_{length}(C) = \int_0^1 \|C'(u)\| \, du \tag{8}$$

Where $C'(u)$ is the derivative of $C(u)$. Finally $P_\sigma(C)$ denotes the standard deviation of curvatures along the path which measures the dispersion of the curvatures values around their arithmetical mean c_{mean}:

$$P_\sigma(C) = \sqrt{\frac{1}{m} \sum_{i=1}^m (c_i - c_{mean})^2} \tag{9}$$

α, β, γ and δ are weighting factors. It is abvious, in our method, that the best individual will have the minimum fitness value.

Selection Method. The probability of survival of an individual is directly related to its relative potency in the population. There are many selection strategies such as rank-based selection, roulette wheel selection, elitist selection and tournament selection. In this study, the rank-based fitness assignment is employed.

Crossover Operator. The fundamental role of crossover is to allow the recombination of information in the genetic heritage of the population by combining the features of two parents to form two offsprings. Conventional crossover methods include single-point crossover and two-point crossover which is proven more effective. To enhance the population diversity, an n-point crossover is used where n is the number of crossing points. The number and sites of the crossover are randomly generated in each iteration. Therefore, the two offsprings are obtained by copying in the first offspring the genes of $Parent1$ up to the first crosspoint then supplementing with the genes of $Parent2$ up to the second crosspoint and so on until the nth crosspoint as shown in Fig. 3, where n equals 3 and the crossover sites are 2, 5 and 7.

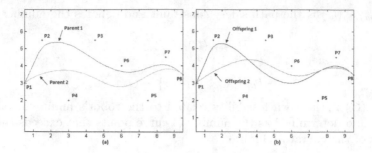

Fig. 3. (a) Two chromosomes (NURBS curves approximation of 7 control points) before the crossover: weight vector of Parent 1(0.1, 3.4, 4.5, 1.2, 2.3, 3, 4, 2), weight vector of Parent 2(5.2, 0.4, 3.2, 3.6, 5.1, 2, 2, 2) (b) Generated offsprings after the crossover: weight vector of offspring 1(0.1, 3.4, 3.2, 3.6, 5.1, 3, 4, 2), weight vector of offspring 2(5.2, 0.4, 4.5, 1.2, 2.3, 2, 2, 2).

Mutation Operator. For the purpose of increasing the population's diversity, mutation operation is required in genetic algorithms despite its low probability. In conventional genetic algorithms, random mutation is employed. However, random mutation can cause infeasible paths. To obviate this, we propose a new mutation operator which modifies a particular gene (nonrandom), with a guided manner and with the aim of optimizing the fitness value of the selected individual for mutation by exploiting the influence of the weight parameter of NURBS curves (as previously described). In fact, obstacle avoidance can be ensured by increasing the weight factor of some control points. Likewise, the curvature constraint can be ensured by decreasing some control points' weights.

Algorithm 3 describes the proposed mutation operator. Indeed, the mutation process starts by checking the feasibility of the path. Thus, two cases may arise: For an infeasible path, which could either has collisions with obstacles or has inadmissible values of curvature, if it intersects obstacles ($P_{col} \neq \emptyset$) then the algorithm consists in randomly selecting a path's point that collides with obstacles. Subsequently, determining its closest control point (in terms of Euclidean Distance) and, finally, increasing the weight value of the corresponding gene which result in the reduction of the cardinality of P_{col}. Else, the algorithm involves selecting a random point of the set P_{cur} which exceeds the limit of curvature. Then, decreasing the weight value of the gene corresponding to its closest control point. Thereby reducing the cardinality of P_{cur}. Thus, for an unfeasible path, the mutation operator will either reduce the number of points intersecting the obstacles, or decrease the number of path points that does not satisfy the curvature constraint. Therefore the mutated individual will be improved after this operation. In the case of a feasible path, the algorithm attempts to decrease the maximum value of curvature, reducing thereby the measure of curvatures dispersion. In fact, after determining the path's point having the maximum curvature value, the modification consists in decreasing the weight value of the gene corresponding to its closest control point.

Algorithm 3. Proposed Mutation Operator

Input: Selected path for mutation (Cs)
Output: Mutated path Cs

1 **begin**
2   **if** ($P_{safety}(Cs) = 0$ & $P_{feasibility}(Cs) = 0$) **then**
3       $x = SelectMaxCurvature(C_s)$;
4       $P_m = NearestPoint(P, x)$;
5       $DecreaseWeight(P_m)$;
6   **else if** ($P_{safety}(Cs) = 0$) **then**
7       $x = RandomSelect(P_{cur})$;
8       $P_m = NearestPoint(P, x)$;
9       $DecreaseWeight(P_m)$;
10   **else**
11       $x = RandomSelect(P_{col})$;
12       $P_m = NearestPoint(P, x)$;
13       $IncreaseWeight(P_m)$;
14    $RegenerateNURBScurve(C_s, P_m)$;
15   **return** (C_s);

3   Simulation Studies and Discussion

To investigate the effectiveness of the proposed algorithm, Three simulation experiments were conducted. Various input parameters related to the environment and the robot are summarized in Table 1. Likewise, different values of the GA parameters are considered as listed in Table 2. In the experiments, we notice that Blue denotes an accessible area while Red denotes an impenetrable area. S and T represent the start and the goal point, respectively. All generated NURBS curves are of degree 4.

For Map I, after computing the shortest polyline path from S to T, a set of 16 control points (red points in Fig. 4(a)) is determined. Initial population is created by generating randomly values of weights between 0.1 and 5. This population is evolved generation by generation to calculate the optimum path with respect to the system requirements. GA is run one by one with the methods of random mutation and the mutation proposed in this research.

Table 1. Input parameters of environment and robot

Parameters	$N * M$	S	T	d	ρ_{min}
Map I	140*140	(128,17)	(11,127)	3	2.5
Map II	100*100	(76,73)	(91,7)	2	0.66
Map III	80*80	(40,74)	(29,9)	1	2

Table 2. Input parameters of GA

Parameters	Chromosome length	Population size	Crossover probability	Mutation probability	Max generations
Map I	16	50	0.5	0.03	70
Map II	12	80	0.6	0.1	100
Map III	16	50	0.65	0.05	40

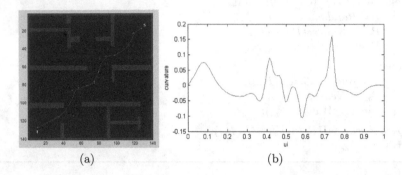

(a)   (b)

Fig. 4. (a) Planned path under Map I. (b) Distribution of curvatures along computed path.

Fig. 5 shows the convergences of these methods. We note that a GA with the proposed mutation operator converges more rapidly and gives better solution than random mutation based GA which can produce more infeasible paths.

With crossover probability equal to 0.5 and a mutation probability of 0.03, the algorithm succeeded to provide, within 18 iterations (red curve in Fig. 5), the best solution. In fact, the best individual of the first generation has a fitness value of 0.0319, a length equal to 173.14 and a standard deviation of curvatures equal to 0.05. As seen in Table 4, these values have been optimized to provide an

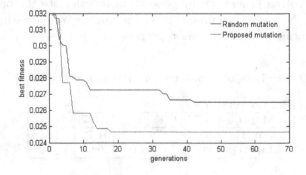

Fig. 5. Comparison of mutation operators' convergences for Map I.

optimal path of length equal to 168.95, with 0.0246 as fitness value and 0.04 as final measure of curvatures dispersion. The weight vector of the computed path is $W = (2.53, 2.27, 2.33, 3.15, 3.99, 1.31, 0.55, 4.46, 1.45, 1.14, 2.92, 0.35, 0.46, 0.54, 4.09, 4.81)$.

As the robot's minimum radius of curvature of the first experiment was set to 2.5, the generated path must have 0.4 as the maximum allowable value of curvature. This constraint was ensured and the maximum value of curvature is 0.16 (Fig. 4(b)).

The generated paths in [9] are made up of connected segments, consequently the robot following it has to stop and restart frequently which causes extra waste of energy. Figures 6 and 7 show the simulation results obtained, for the same environments (Map II and Map III), by the algorithm proposed in this paper.

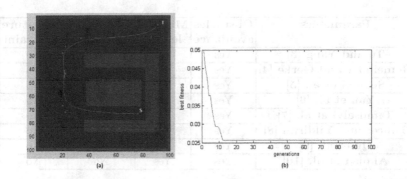

Fig. 6. Simulation results under Map II (Epsilon-type environment): (a) Planned path. (b) Evolution procedure of the proposed GA based mobile robot path planning algorithm.

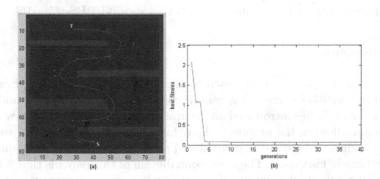

Fig. 7. Simulation results under Map III (Z-type environment): (a) Planned path. (b) Evolution procedure of the proposed GA based mobile robot path planning algorithm.

Table 3. Experimental results

Parameters	Best fitness	$P_\sigma(C)$	$P_{length}(C)$	|Max curvature|
Map I	0.0246	0.04	168.95	0.16
Map II	0.0256	0.04	166.66	0.13
Map III	0.0635	0.12	157.9	0.32

We note that the low value of the standard deviation of curvatures indicates that the data points tend to be very close to the mean, proving the homogeneity of the distribution of curvatures and consequently the smoothness criterion. Experimental results are summarized in Table 4.

Table 4. Output Specifications for Genetic Algorithm Based Robot Path Planning

Parameters	Obstacles avoidance	Minimal length	Curvature continuity	Curvature constraint
Tu and Yang [3]	Yes	Yes	No	No
Gemeinder and Gerke [4]	Yes	No	No	No
Sedighi et al. [5]	Yes	Yes	No	No
Yun et al. [6]	Yes	Yes	No	No
Tamilselvi et al. [7]	Yes	Yes	No	No
Tuncer and Yildirim [8]	Yes	Yes	No	No
Qu et al. [9]	Yes	Yes	No	No
Ahmed et al. [10]	Yes	Yes	No	No

Unlike the methods given in Table 4, the proposed algorithm not only ensures the properties of safety and minimal length but also respects the limit of allowable curvature along the computed curve. The main idea is to exploit the geometric effect of the weight parameter of NURBS curves while generating the optimal path, contrary to existing methods that uses NURBS [15], [16].

4   Conclusion

This paper has proposed an approach to the path planning problem, based on an optimized NURBS curve using genetic algorithm, for a non-point and non-holonomic robot. It has introduced an accurate fitness function and a new mutation operator allowing the proposed algorithm to efficiently generate a smooth, obstacle avoiding and curvature-constrained path with minimal length and minimal variations of curvature. The main contribution of this paper is that NURBS curves are not only used as means of smoothing but also are involved in meeting the system constraints via a suitable parameterization, using genetic algorithm, of the weights of control points which allows better benefit from the influence and the geometrical effect of this parameter, which has not been well exploited in previous works.

Future studies include investigating the path planning task with different optimization methods. Furthermore, it will be interesting to adopt our algorithms into real world applications, and to involve the research for the path planning problem in dynamic environments.

References

1. Khatib, O.: Real time obstacle avoidance for manipulators and mobile robots. International Journal of Robotics Research **5**, 90–98 (1986)
2. Bigaj, P., Kacprzyk, J.: A memetic algorithm based procedure for a global path planning of a movement constrained mobile robot. In: Proceedings of the IEEE Congress on Evolutionary Computation, CEC, pp. 135–141 (2013)
3. Tu, J., Yang, S.X.: Genetic algorithm based path planning for a mobile robot. In: IEEE International Conference on Robotics and Automation (ICRA), pp. 1221–1226 (2003)
4. Gemeinder, M., Gerke, M.: GA-based path planning for mobile robot systems employing an active search algorithm. Appl. Soft Comput. **3**, 149–158 (2003)
5. Sedighi, K.H., Ashenayi, K., Manikas, T.W., Wainwright, R.L., Tai, H.M.: Autonomous local path planning for a mobile robot using a genetic algorithm. In: IEEE Congress on Evolutionary Computation (CEC), pp. 1338–1345 (2004)
6. Yun, S.C., Ganapathy, V., Chong, L.O.: Improved genetic algorithms based optimum path planning for mobile robot. In: 11th International Conference on Control, Automation, Robotics and Vision(ICARCV), pp. 1565–1570 (2010)
7. Tamilselvi, D., Shalinie, S.M., Thasneem, A.F., Sundari, S.G.: Optimal path selection for mobile robot navigation using genetic algorithm in an indoor environment. In: Thilagam, P.S., Pais, A.R., Chandrasekaran, K., Balakrishnan, N. (eds.) ADCONS 2011. LNCS, vol. 7135, pp. 263–269. Springer, Heidelberg (2012)
8. Tuncer, A., Yildirim, A.: Dynamic path planning of mobile robots with improved genetic algorithm. Computers & Electrical Engineering **38**, 1564–1572 (2012)
9. Qu, H., Xing, K., Alexander, T.: An improved genetic algorithm with co-evolutionary strategy for global path planning of multiple mobile robots. Neurocomputing. **120**, 509–517 (2013)
10. Ahmed, F., Deb, K.: Multi-objective optimal path planning using elitist non-dominated sorting genetic algorithms. Soft Comput. **17**, 1283–1299 (2013)
11. Jalel, S., Marthon, P., Hamouda, A.: Optimum path planning for mobile robots in static environments using graph modelling and NURBS curves. In:12th WSEAS International Conference on Signal Processing, Robotics and Automation(ISPRA), pp. 216–221 (2013)
12. Piegl, L., Tiller, W.: The NURBS book, 2nd edn. Springer, Heidelberg (1997)
13. Adi, D.I.S., Shamsuddin, S.M., Ali, A.: Particle swarm optimization for NURBS curve fitting. In: Sixth International Conference on Computer Graphics, Imaging and Visualization: New Advances and Trends(CGIV), pp. 259–263 (2009)
14. Jing, Z., Shaowei, F., Hanguo, C., Optimized NURBS curve and surface modelling using simulated evolution algorithm. In: Second International Workshop on Computer Science and Engineering (WCSE), pp. 435–439 (2009)
15. Singh, A.K., Aggarwal, A., Vashisht, M., Siddavatam, R.: Robot motion planning in a dynamic environment using offset non-uniform rational B-splines (NURBS). In: ICIT, pp. 312–317. IEEE (2011)
16. Xidias, E.K., Aspragathos, N.A.: Continuous curvature constrained shortest path for a car-like robot using S-Roadmaps. In: MED, pp. 13–18. IEEE (2013)

Robust Learning from Ortho-Diffusion Decompositions

Sravan Gudivada and Adrian G. Bors[✉]

Department of Computer Science, University of York, York YO10 5GH, UK
adrian.bors@york.ac.uk

Abstract. This paper describes a new classification method based on modeling data by embedding diffusions into orthonormal decompositions of graph-based data representations. The training data is represented by an adjacency matrix calculated using either the correlation or the covariance of the training set. The application of the modified Gram-Schmidt orthonormal decomposition alternating with diffusion and data reduction stages, is applied recursively at each scale level. The diffusion process is strengthening the representation pattern of representative features. Meanwhile, noise is removed together with non-essential detail during the data reduction stage. The proposed methodology is shown to be robust when applied to face recognition considering low image resolution and corruption by various types of noise.

Keywords: Ortho-diffusion decompositions · Gram-schmidt algorithm · Robust face recognition

1 Introduction

A challenge in complex data analysis problems is when we have to recover a low dimensional intrinsic manifold which manifests itself through a very complex representation in the observable space. Spectral graph theory was used for representing data structures on graphs by using singular value decomposition of the Laplacian matrix of a given data set [10]. Diffusion distances, can be used to represent the local data structure in order to reveal relational properties of the data set at different scales [3,12,16]. Magioni and Mahadevan proposed the diffusion wavelet methodology allowing the study of data at different scales as generated by the geometry of their underlying manifold [11]. This approach recursively splits the data space into orthonormal subspaces. A framework for handling non-symmetric neighborhoods in diffusion wavelets was defined in [15]. Diffusion wavelets have been used in image segmentation [5], for texture synthesis [9], image sequence analysis in [7,17].

Face representations on a lower intrinsic manifold has been considered in various face recognition algorithms. Principal component analysis (PCA) was used for decomposing the covariance matrix of the training set of faces producing a set of eigenfaces [14]. Other face recognition algorithms are using Fisher's linear discriminant analysis (LDA) as in Fisherfaces [1], independent component

© Springer International Publishing Switzerland 2015
G. Azzopardi and N. Petkov (Eds.): CAIP 2015, Part I, LNCS 9256, pp. 546–557, 2015.
DOI: 10.1007/978-3-319-23192-1_46

analysis [4], kernel PCA [19], and the locality-preserving projection as in Laplacianfaces (LPA) [8], orthogonal Laplacianfaces (OLPP) [2] and the multilinear discriminant analysis [18].

In this paper we propose a new ortho-diffusion methodology for face recognition. The training set of faces is represented by using either the correlation weighted by the graph transition matrix or by using the covariance of training set as in [14]. In the proposed methodology the graph-based representation of faces is decomposed recursively using the modified Gram-Schmidt algorithm with pivoting the columns [13]. This decomposition produces at each scale a set of orthonormal bases functions and a set of residual diffusion wavelets modeling small features and the detail with respect to the given scale. This is followed by a sparsing procedure and then by graph-diffusion. Images of faces are projected onto the resulting ortho-diffusion space and they are classified according to the minimal distance to the ortho-diffusion weights associated with faces from the training set. The diffusion analysis framework is provided in Section 2 and the proposed ortho-diffusion methodology is described in Section 3. The classification in the ortho-diffusion space is detailed in Section 4. In Section 5 we provide the experimental results, when the proposed methodology is applied in four different face databases, while the conclusions are given in Section 6.

2   Graph Representation of the Data

Let us consider a training set of M images $\{\mathbf{I}_i|, i = 1, \ldots, M\}$, considered in the experiments as representing faces, of size $m \times n$. In the following we consider that each face image is represented as a column in a matrix of size $mn \times M$. An adjacency matrix $\mathbf{K}$, is formed by using the similarity kernel for two entries x_i and x_k from $\mathbf{I}$ as:

$$K(\mathbf{x}_i, \mathbf{x}_k) = \exp[-(\mathbf{x}_i - \mathbf{x}_k)^\tau(\mathbf{x}_i - \mathbf{x}_k)/\sigma^2] \tag{1}$$

where σ is the scale of the diffusion kernel and represents a weighting for the data similarity measure. The random walk for t time steps is calculated by means of the transition matrix $\mathbf{P_I} = (\mathbf{D}^{-1}\mathbf{K})^t$, where $\mathbf{D}$ is a diagonal matrix with each diagonal element representing the degree of a node, defined for $\mathbf{x}_i$ as $d(\mathbf{x}_i) = \sum_{k=1}^{n} K(\mathbf{x}_i, \mathbf{x}_k)$ and we consider $t = 1$.

The correlation of the training set weighted by the transition matrix is evaluated as :

$$\mathbf{C}_r = \mathbf{I} \, \mathbf{P_I} \, \mathbf{I}^\tau. \tag{2}$$

The second face representation relies on the inter-variation of face images derived from their covariance matrix as in the eigenfaces approach [14]. Firstly, the mean face and the deviation of each face from the mean face is evaluated as $\bar{\mathbf{I}} = \frac{1}{M} \sum_{i=1}^{M} \mathbf{I}_i$ and $\mathbf{S}_i = \mathbf{I}_i - \bar{\mathbf{I}}$. Each $\mathbf{S}_i$ makes up a column in a matrix $\mathbf{A}$ of size $mn \times M$. The spread of the face variation within the training set is modeled by the covariance matrix:

$$\mathbf{C}_v = \mathbf{A}^\tau \mathbf{A}, \tag{3}$$

where matrix $\mathbf{C}_v$, represents the covariance matrix of the training set.

3   The Ortho-Diffusion Decomposition

In the following we consider a new methodology which embeds diffusion into ortho-normal decompositions on adjacent matrices at various scales. A diffusion wavelet tree is produced by the recursive orthogonal decomposition of the data matrix $\mathbf{C}$ into a set of diffusion scaling functions, denoted for each recursion step j as $\mathbf{\Phi}_j$ and their orthogonal wavelet functions $\mathbf{\Psi}_j$, [11,15]. The scaling functions $\mathbf{\Phi}_j$ span the subspace $\mathcal{V}_j$, which holds the property of inclusion for successive recursions $\mathcal{V}_j \subseteq \mathcal{V}_{j-1}$, while the wavelets $\mathbf{\Psi}_j$ span the complementary orthogonal space $\mathcal{W}_j$:

$$\mathcal{V}_{j-1} = \mathcal{V}_j \oplus^{\perp} \mathcal{W}_j. \tag{4}$$

Each recursion step j corresponds to a different data representation scale. The ortho-diffusion decomposition consists of four processing stages at each recursion j: orthonormalization, data reduction and diffusion. In the case of graph-based image data representations, the basis functions model image features at scale j, while the diffusion wavelets represent mostly noise and small features (small with respect to the given scale j).

The orthonormal decomposition of the given graph-based data representation is performed by the modified Gram-Schmidt with pivoting the columns ($\mathcal{QR}$ algorithm) [11,15]. The $\mathcal{QR}$ algorithm decomposes a given matrix into an orthogonal matrix $\mathbf{Q}$ whose columns are orthonormal bases functions and a triangular matrix $\mathbf{R}$, [13]. In the following we use the notation $[\mathbf{\Phi}_b]_{\mathbf{\Phi}_a}$ for a matrix representing the base $\mathbf{\Phi}_b$ with respect to $\mathbf{\Phi}_a$. We denote the triangular matrix by $[\mathbf{C}]_{\mathbf{\Phi}_a}^{\mathbf{\Phi}_b}$ whose column space is represented using bases $\mathbf{\Phi}_a$ at scale a, while the row space is represented using bases $\mathbf{\Phi}_b$ at scale b. The matrix $\mathbf{C}$ is represented initially at the scale $j = 0$ on the basis set $\mathbf{\Phi}_0$ as $[\mathbf{\Phi}_0]_{\mathbf{\Phi}_0}$. Let us consider its columns as the set of functions $\tilde{\mathbf{\Phi}}_0 = \{[\mathbf{\Phi}_0]_{\mathbf{\Phi}_0}\delta_k\}_k$ on the given graph, where δ_k is a set of Dirac functions. The $\mathcal{QR}$ procedure decomposes $[\mathbf{C}]_{\mathbf{\Phi}_0}^{\mathbf{\Phi}_0}$ at the first level $j = 0$ as:

$$([\mathbf{\Phi}_1]_{\mathbf{\Phi}_0}, [\mathbf{C}]_{\mathbf{\Phi}_0}^{\mathbf{\Phi}_1}) \leftarrow \mathcal{QR}([\mathbf{C}]_{\mathbf{\Phi}_0}^{\mathbf{\Phi}_0}, \epsilon, \theta) \tag{5}$$

where $\mathbf{Q}$ matrix is represented as $[\mathbf{\Phi}_1]_{\mathbf{\Phi}_0}$, while the triangular matrix $\mathbf{R}$ is $[\mathbf{C}]_{\mathbf{\Phi}_0}^{\mathbf{\Phi}_1}$ and where we assume a data reduction mechanism defined by the precision ϵ and the reduction parameter θ.

The $\mathcal{QR}$ algorithm proceeds with the orthonormalization of columns of the given matrix, starting from the first column. From the invariant subspace theory, the product of $\mathbf{R}$ and $\mathbf{Q}$ is the new representation of $\mathbf{C}$ with respect to the space spanned by the columns of $\mathbf{Q}$:

$$[\mathbf{C}]_{\mathbf{\Phi}_0}^{\mathbf{\Phi}_0} = [\mathbf{C}]_{\mathbf{\Phi}_0}^{\mathbf{\Phi}_1}[\mathbf{\Phi}_1]_{\mathbf{\Phi}_0}. \tag{6}$$

We obtain a linear transformation represented through the triangular matrix $[\mathbf{C}]_{\mathbf{\Phi}_0}^{\mathbf{\Phi}_1}$, which is the transformation of the matrix $\mathbf{C}$ whose columns are represented with respect to the new base $\mathbf{\Phi}_1$, while the rows are represented with respect to $\mathbf{\Phi}_0$, and the orthonormal matrix $[\mathbf{\Phi}_1]_{\mathbf{\Phi}_0}$ representing the base $[\mathbf{\Phi}_1]$ with respect to $[\mathbf{\Phi}_0]$, [13].

The $\mathcal{QR}$ decomposition is applied recursively, where at each scale j, a new base Φ_{j+1} replaces Φ_j, starting with $j = 0$, as in equation (6). The orthonormal bases functions spanning Φ_j and representing columns in $[\Phi_j]_{\Phi_j}$ represent characteristic features of the given image set. At each recursion stage j, the $\mathcal{QR}$ decomposition results into an orthonormal matrix $[\Phi_{j+1}]_{\Phi_j}$ and a triangular matrix $[\mathbf{C}^{2^{j+1}}]_{\Phi_j}^{\Phi_{j+1}}$. $\mathcal{QR}$ decomposition is reversible and at after each recursion j we can obtain back the matrix representation from the product of $\mathbf{R}$ and $\mathbf{Q}$:

$$[\mathbf{C}]_{\Phi_j}^{\Phi_j} = [\mathbf{C}]_{\Phi_j}^{\Phi_{j+1}}[\Phi_{j+1}]_{\Phi_j}. \tag{7}$$

While so far we have a perfect data preservation transformation, the following processing steps ensure a compact and robust approximation of the data representation on the given manifold.

The $\mathcal{QR}$ decomposition is followed by a data reduction step. Henceforth, we consider for further processing only the columns representing bases functions characterizing the underlying graph data:

$$\tilde{\Phi}_j = \{\|[\Phi_{j+1}]_{\Phi_j}\delta_k\| > \epsilon\}_k, \tag{8}$$

where ϵ represents a set precision, $\|\cdot\|$ represents the norm of the column extracted by the Dirac function δ_k. When removing a column from $[\Phi_{j+1}]_{\Phi_j}$, we remove its corresponding row from $[\mathbf{C}^{2^{j+1}}]_{\Phi_j}^{\Phi_{j+1}}$, as well. By removing the columns with low norms we eliminate low level feature representation as well as noise which are deemed non-essential for further data representation. For enforcing the sparseness of the triangular matrix $[\mathbf{C}^{2^{j+1}}]_{\Phi_j}^{\Phi_{j+1}}$ we neglect all entries which are smaller than a threshold θ and consider them as zero henceforth. These data reduction procedures ensure that only the essential data characteristics are retained while compressing the given data representation space. The precision ϵ and sparseness threshold θ should be chosen such that we achieve an appropriate representation of the data space by means of a compact set of vectors.

Column pivoting is employed in the matrix $\mathbf{Q}$ when the given matrix is nearly rank deficient and in this case the columns with higher norms are interchanged with those that have smaller norms, bringing them forward in the ranking of orthonormal basis functions [13]. This results into a grouping of significant orthonormal bases functions in the leading set of columns from the matrix $[\Phi_1]_{\Phi_0}$.

The decomposition and data reduction stages described above are followed by a data representation diffusion processing step on the graph representation as $[\mathbf{C}^{2^j}]_{\Phi_j}^{\Phi_{j+1}}$ for scale j. The diffusion process is implemented as a dilation of the features modeled by the existing ortho-diffusion bases from the existing scale j to a new scale $j + 1$. At scale $j + 1$, the dilation is applied by squaring the operator $[\mathbf{C}^{2^{j+1}}]_{\Phi_{j+1}}^{\Phi_{j+1}}$ such that:

$$[\mathbf{C}^{2^{j+1}}]_{\Phi_{j+1}}^{\Phi_{j+1}} = ([\mathbf{C}^{2^j}]_{\Phi_j}^{\Phi_{j+1}}[\Phi_{j+1}]_{\Phi_j})^2 = [\mathbf{C}^{2^j}]_{\Phi_j}^{\Phi_{j+1}}([\mathbf{C}^{2^j}]_{\Phi_j}^{\Phi_{j+1}})^\tau, \tag{9}$$

where we used the property of orthonormality for the matrices involved. This corresponds to implementing a diffusion on the data representation at the scale

j and reprojecting the given data to the scale $j+1$, strengthening the main data features, while removing noise and any non-essential smaller features (small relative to the given scale). The representation on the scale base $\mathbf{\Phi}_{j+1}$ corresponds to analyzing the data on larger neighborhoods than when considering the analysis on the previous scale base $\mathbf{\Phi}_j$. The graph-based representation at scale $j+1$ models coarser data features, while the representation at scale j would represent smaller features and noise.

A set of extended bases functions $[\mathbf{\Phi}_{j+1}]_{\Phi_0}$ are calculated at each recursion $j+1$ with respect to the initial bases $\mathbf{\Phi}_0$ as in the following:

$$[\mathbf{\Phi}_{j+1}]_{\Phi_0} = [\mathbf{\Phi}_{j+1}]_{\Phi_j}[\mathbf{\Phi}_j]_{\Phi_0}. \tag{10}$$

Because with each scale $j+1$ the number of bases functions decreases due to the data reduction step, the matrix $[\mathbf{\Phi}_{j+1}]_{\Phi_j}$ becomes ever smaller, while $[\mathbf{\Phi}_{j+1}]_{\Phi_0}$ is formed by a number of columns recording the essential image information with respect to the initial base $\mathbf{\Phi}_0$. Consequently, the dimension of the extended bases function vectors of $[\mathbf{\Phi}_{j+1}]_{\Phi_0}$ becomes equal to that of the columns of the initial data matrix $\mathbf{C}$ represented as $[\mathbf{\Phi}_0]_{\Phi_0}$. Each basis function, representing columns of $[\mathbf{\Phi}_{j+1}]_{\Phi_j}$ can be used to represent image features in a low resolution image, while the extended basis function representing columns of $[\mathbf{\Phi}_{j+1}]_{\Phi_0}$ map these features to the size of the original training set images. At scale $j+1$, the representation of $\mathbf{C}^{2^{j+1}}$ is compressed, depending on the value of precision ϵ and on the sparse matrix threshold θ. The algorithm will terminate when all bases functions fulfil the condition (8) for the given maximum scaling level, j_{max}.

Wavelet bases $[\mathbf{\Psi}_{j+1}]_{\Phi_j}$, defining the space $\mathcal{W}_j$, represent the complementary of the basis functions space according to (4), and are evaluated using sparse factorization as:

$$[\mathbf{W}]_{\Phi_j}^{\Phi_j} = \mathbf{I}_j - [\mathbf{\Phi}_j]_{\Phi_{j-1}} \cdot [\mathbf{\Phi}_j]^{\tau}_{\Phi_{j-1}} \tag{11}$$

where $\mathbf{I}_j$ is the identity matrix of identical size with the matrix $[\mathbf{\Phi}_j]_{\Phi_j}$. We apply the orthonormal $\mathcal{QR}$ decomposition on the resulting matrix $[\mathbf{W}]_{\Phi_j}^{\Phi_j}$ in a similar way as in (5) using the same precision ϵ and sparse matrix threshold θ:

$$([\mathbf{\Psi}_{j+1}]_{\Phi_j}, [\mathbf{W}_R]_{\Phi_j}^{\Phi_{j+1}}) \leftarrow \mathcal{QR}([\mathbf{W}]_{\Phi_j}^{\Phi_j}, \epsilon, \theta) \tag{12}$$

where $[\mathbf{W}_R]_{\Phi_j}^{\Phi_{j+1}}$ represents the corresponding triangular matrix. The wavelets represent the high frequency information, corresponding to small features and noise in the data and are not considered for further processing. Nevertheless, the calculation of diffusion wavelets ensures that the ortho-diffusion decomposition is reversible at each recursion stage j according to equation (4) [7].

4   Face Recognition Using Ortho-Diffusion Bases

A set of ortho-diffusion faces, each corresponding to an extended ortho-diffusion basis from (10) are obtained by using a similar approach to the diffusion maps from [12,16], but by using orthonormal extended bases functions instead of the eigenvectors of the Laplacian matrix [6]. The diffusion distance metric calculated based on the extended basis functions at the level j between two image pixels at locations i and k is given by:

$$D_{\Phi_j}(i,k) = \sqrt{(\Phi_j(i) - \Phi_j(k))^\tau (\Phi_j(i) - \Phi_j(k))} \qquad (13)$$

where we consider all the extended bases functions defined on the graph between the two given pixels. The ortho-diffusion face is obtained by calculating the feature representation at a certain image location by summing up the diffusion distances from all the other image pixels:

$$\Delta_{i,j} = \sum_{k=1}^{mn} D_{\Phi_j}(i,k). \qquad (14)$$

Each face from the training set can be approximated using the most significant ortho-diffusion faces. In the following we consider a set of leading N extended bases functions from the orthonormal matrix $[\Phi_j]_{\Phi_0}$. Let us denote by $\mathbf{Y} = \{[\Phi_j]_{\Phi_0}\delta_k\}_k$ for $k = 1, \ldots, N$ and so $\mathbf{Y}$ is a subset of $\tilde{\Phi}_j$ from (8) for a characteristic scale j. We calculate the corresponding weights Ω_i of the given face image $\mathbf{I}_i$, when using either the correlation (2), or the covariance (3), by:

$$\Omega_i = \mathbf{Y}^\tau \mathbf{S}_i \qquad (15)$$

where $i = 1, \ldots, M$. Consequently, the face images can be approximately reconstructed.

For a given face image $\mathbf{I}_t$, which is not in the training set, we can calculate its projection weights in the given N ortho-diffusion vector space and obtain its characteristic weights as Ω_t. Face recognition is decided according to the minimum Euclidean distance in the space defined by the ortho-normal faces:

$$\arg\min_{k=1}^{M}[(\Omega_t - \Omega_k)^\tau(\Omega_t - \Omega_k)] \qquad (16)$$

where the size of vectors Ω_k and Ω_t is N.

5   Experimental Results

In the following we provide the results when using the proposed ortho-diffusion face representation methodology, described in Section 4, for face recognition on the Yale and GeorgiaTech (GT) databases. For determining the robustness of face recognition methodology we test on both downsampled original face databases as well as when adding noise. Each face image is resized to 56×46 pixels. We consider three types of noise, each defined by different characteristics: Gaussian, Salt and Pepper, and Speckle noise. Gaussian noise simulates thermal noise in sensors. Salt and Pepper noise is an impulsive type of noise which can

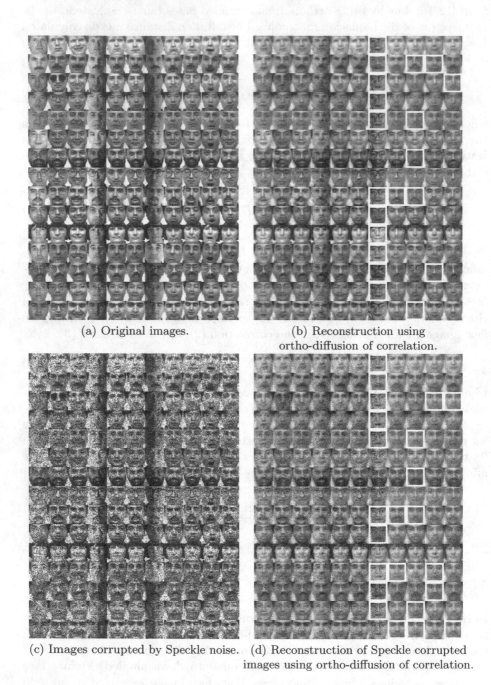

(a) Original images.

(b) Reconstruction using ortho-diffusion of correlation.

(c) Images corrupted by Speckle noise.

(d) Reconstruction of Speckle corrupted images using ortho-diffusion of correlation.

Fig. 1. Face images from Yale database.

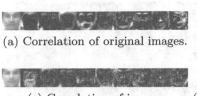

(a) Correlation of original images.

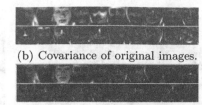

(b) Covariance of original images.

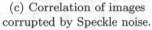

(c) Correlation of images
corrupted by Speckle noise.

(d) Covariance of noise corrupted images.
corrupted by Speckle noise.

Fig. 2. Images representing ortho-diffusion bases functions for the Yale face database.

be caused by analog-to-digital converter errors, bit errors in transmission, etc. This type of noise is characterized by its probability of occurring, considered as equal for values of 0 and 255. This can simulate loss of information in data transmission and could destroy radically the face features. Speckle noise is a multiplicative type of noise, characterized by a parameter determining its intensity level, which can be used to simulate atmospheric conditions such as rain, snow or mist interfering with the image acquisition process. We consider face representation using either the correlation, as in equation (2) or the covariance as in equation (3). In all the experiments we consider the scaling parameter for calculating the pairwise data similarity as $\sigma = 0.03$ in equation (1), while the precision for pivoting the column in the $\mathcal{QR}$ algorithm is $\epsilon = 10^{-6}$, and the sparseness threshold for the elements from the triangular matrix $[\mathbf{C}^{2^{j+1}}]_{\Phi_j}^{\Phi_{j+1}}$ in the $\mathcal{QR}$ algorithm is $\theta = 2.22 \times 10^{-16}$.

Yale database contains 165 images of 15 subjects, which are shown in Figure 1a. In this database there are 11 images per subject with varying facial expressions, with or without glasses and a wide variations of lighting. We can observe that the 4th and the 7th sample face image for each individual has significant lighting variation. Figures 2a and b display 10 and 20, respectively, ortho-diffusion bases when modeling either the correlation or the covariance matrix. The reconstructed faces from the Yale database using the ortho-diffusion faces modeling the covariance matrix are shown in Figure 1(b). Yale database faces corrupted by Speckle noise characterized by a scattering parameter of 0.2 are shown in Figure 1c and reconstructed using ortho-diffusion bases of the correlation matrix in Figure 1d. The representation of the ortho-diffusion bases modeling the correlation, as in equation (2), and the covariance matrix, as in equation (3), of the Speckle corrupted Yale database are shown as "ghost faces" in Figures 2c and d, respectively.

Georgia Tech (GT) database contains 15 images for 50 subjects and 15. Most of face images were acquired under varying illumination conditions, facial expression, and appearance captured at different scales and orientations. We consider a training set of eight faces for each person. 11 images of 12 subjects from GT database, when corrupted by Salt and Pepper noise of probability 8% are shown in Figure 3a. We reconstruct the whole database of 750 faces and the same images as in Figure 3a reconstructed using ortho-diffusion bases of

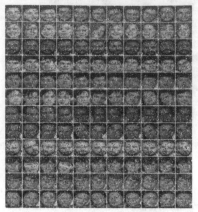
(a) Images corrupted by Salt and Pepper noise.

(b) Reconstructed when modelling image correlation with ortho-diffusion bases.

Fig. 3. Image faces from Georgia Tech database.

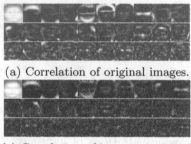
(a) Correlation of original images.

(b) Covariance of original images.

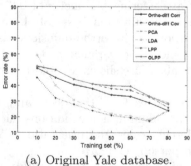
(c) Correlation of images corrupted by Salt and Pepper noise.

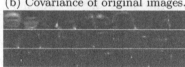
(d) Covariance of images corrupted by Salt and Pepper noise.

Fig. 4. Images representing ortho-diffusion bases functions for GT database.

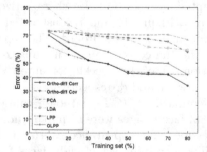
(a) Original Yale database.

(b) Yale faces corrupted by Speckle noise.

Fig. 5. Face recognition rates for Yale database when increasing the training dataset.

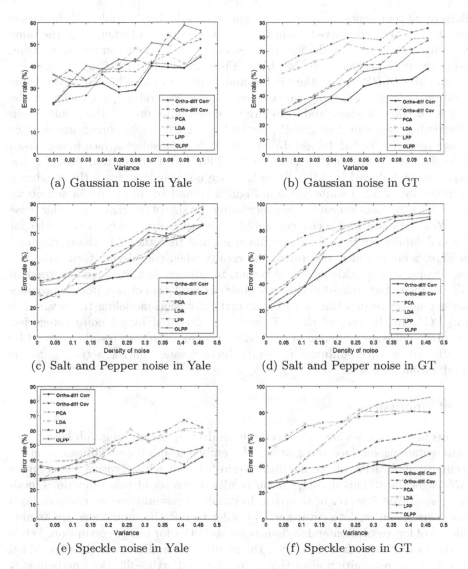

Fig. 6. Face recognition rates when considering various noise statistics for Yale in a, c, e, and GT database in b, d and f.

the correlation matrix are shown in Figure 3b. The representation of 30 ortho-diffusion bases modeling the correlation and covariance matrix of the Georgia Tech database, when free of noise, are shown in Figures 4a and b and when corrupted by Salt and Pepper noise in Figure 4c and d, respectively.

For the statistical estimation of the classification results for both proposed approaches by using the modeling of the correlation as in equation (2) and the covariance according to equation (3) by using the mean face are considered.

Each result represents the average recognition results for 20 trials. All the experiments have been conducted under the same conditions and when using the same rescaling for all faces at the size of 56×46 pixels. We consider for comparison using the PCA (Eigenfaces) [14], LDA (Fisherfaces) [1], LPP (Laplacian faces) [8] and the OLPP, called the Orthogonal Laplacian faces [2] under the same conditions. In the following we consider 6 faces for training set and 5 in the test set in Yale database and in Figure 6a, c and e, we present the results when considering Gaussian, Salt and Pepper and Speckle noise for corrupting the face image from the Yale database. In all cases, when considering face images from Yale database corrupted by noise, ortho-diffusion of correlation provides the best results, followed by LPP. Faces that are not classified correctly are shown individually within a white frame in Figures 1b and 1d. In Figure 5a and 5b we provide the recognition rates when increasing the size of the training set for noise free Yale data and for Speckle corrupted image set, respectively. We consider for the GT database 8 faces for the training set and the other 7 in the testing and in Figures 6b, d and f, we present the results when considering Gaussian, Salt and Pepper and Speckle noises, of various intensities. In the case of the original GT database, the ortho-diffusion modeling of correlation of face images provides slightly better results than OLPP, the ortho-diffusion modeling the covariance and PCA. In the case of the GT database corrupted by all noise categories, the ortho-diffusion modeling of correlation provides the best results followed by OLPP and the ortho-diffusion modeling the covariance matrix, according to the results from Figure 6.

6   Conclusion

In this paper we describe an ortho-diffusion decomposition on graph based data representations for face recognition. We embed graph-based diffusions into a recursive application of the modified Gram-Schmidt with pivoting the columns ($\mathcal{QR}$ algorithm). This decomposition results into a set of bases functions modeling significant features of the data. In graph representations we consider both data correlation or data covariance. In order to test the robustness, we assume images of low resolution and various noise statistics for image corruption. While in the case of noise free data sets, the results are similar with those provided by other face recognition algorithms, the proposed ortho-diffusion methodology applied on correlation matrices provides the best results when considering face images corrupted by noise. The proposed methodology can be applied on 3D face data or in other applications as well.

References

1. Belhumeur, P., Hespanha, J., Kriegman, D.: Eigenfaces vs. fisherfaces: Recognition using class specific linear projection. IEEE Trans. on Pattern Analysis and Machine Intelligence **19**(7), 711–720 (1997)
2. Cai, D., He, X., Han, J., Zhang, H.J.: Orthogonal laplacianfaces for face recognition. IEEE Trans. on Image Processing **15**(11), 3608–3614 (2006)

3. Coifman, R.R., Lafon, S.: Diffusion maps. Applied Comput. Harmon. Anal. **21**(1), 5–30 (2006)
4. Draper, B., Baek, K., Bartlett, M., Beveridge, R.: Recognizing faces with PCA and ICA. Computer Vision and Image Understanding **91**(1–2), 115–137 (2003)
5. Essafi, S., Langs, G., Paragios, N.: Hierarchical 3d diffusion wavelet shape priors. In: Proc. of IEEE Int. Conf. on Computer Vision, pp. 1717–1724 (2009)
6. Gudivada, S., Bors, A.G.: Face recognition using ortho-diffusion bases. In: Proc. 20th European Signal Processing Conference, pp. 1578–1582 (2012)
7. Gudivada, S., Bors, A.G.: Ortho-diffusion decompositions of graph-based representation of images. Pattern Recognition (2015)
8. He, X., Yan, S., Hu, Y., Niyogi, P., Zhang, H.J.: Face recognition using laplacianfaces. IEEE Trans. on Pattern Analysis and Machine Intelligence **27**(3), 328–340 (2005)
9. Lu, J., Dorsey, J., Rushmeier, H.: Dominant texture and diffusion distance manifolds. Proc. Eurographics Computer Graphics Forum **28**(2), 667–676 (2009)
10. Luxburg, U.: A tutorial on spectral clustering. J. of Statistics and Computing **17**(4), 395–416 (2007)
11. Magioni, M., Mahadevan, S.: Fast direct policy evaluation using multiscale analysis of markov diffusion processes. In: Proc. of the 23rd International Conference on Machine Learning, pp. 601–608 (2005)
12. Singer, A., Coifman, R.R.: Non-linear independent component analysis with diffusion maps. Applied and Computational Harmonic Analysis **25**(1), 226–239 (2008)
13. Trefethen, L.N., Bau, D.: Numerical Linear Algebra. SIAM (1997)
14. Turk, M., Pentland, A.: Eigenfaces for recognition. J. Cognitive Neuroscience **3**(1), 71–86 (1991)
15. Wang, C., Mahadevan, S.: Multiscale dimensionality reduction based on diffusion wavelets. Tech. rep., Univ. of Massachusetts (2009)
16. Wartak, S, Bors, A.G.: Optical flow estimation using diffusion distances. In: Proc. Int. Conf on Pattern Recognition, pp. 189–192 (2010)
17. Wild, M.: Nonlinear approximation of spatiotemporal data using diffusion wavelets. In: Kropatsch, W.G., Kampel, M., Hanbury, A. (eds.) CAIP 2007. LNCS, vol. 4673, pp. 886–894. Springer, Heidelberg (2007)
18. Yan, S., Yu, D., Yang, Q., Zhang, L., Tang, X., Zhang, H.: Multilinear discriminant analysis for face recognition. IEEE Trans on Image Processing **16**(1), 212–220 (2007)
19. Zhang, B.C., Shan, S.G., Chen, X., Gao, W.: Histogram of gabor phase patterns: A novel object representation approach for face recognition. IEEE Trans. on Image Processing **16**(1), 504–516 (2007)

Filter-Based Approach for Ornamentation Detection and Recognition in Singing Folk Music

Andreas Neocleous[1,2]($\boxtimes$), George Azzopardi[2,3], Christos N. Schizas[1], and Nicolai Petkov[2]

[1] Department of Computer Science, University of Cyprus, Nicosia, Cyprus
neocleous.andreas@gmail.com
[2] Johann Bernoulli Institute for Mathematics and Computer Science, University of Groningen, Groningen, The Netherlands
[3] Intelligent Computer Systems, University of Malta, Msida, Malta

Abstract. Ornamentations in music play a significant role for the emotion whilch a performer or a composer aims to create. The automated identification of ornamentations enhances the understanding of music, which can be used as a feature for tasks such as performer identification or mood classification. Existing methods rely on a pre-processing step that performs note segmentation. We propose an alternative method by adapting the existing two-dimensional COSFIRE filter approach to one-dimension (1D) for the automatic identification of ornamentations in monophonic folk songs. We construct a set of 1D COSFIRE filters that are selective for the 12 notes of the Western music theory. The response of a 1D COSFIRE filter is computed as the geometric mean of the differences between the fundamental frequency values in a local neighbourhood and the preferred values at the corresponding positions. We apply the proposed 1D COSFIRE filters to the pitch tracks of a song at every position along the entire signal, which in turn give response values in the range [0,1]. The 1D COSFIRE filters that we propose are effective to recognize meaningful musical information which can be transformed into symbolic representations and used for further analysis. We demonstrate the effectiveness of the proposed methodology in a new data set that we introduce, which comprises five monophonic Cypriot folk tunes consisting of 428 ornamentations. The proposed method is effective for the detection and recognition of ornamentations in singing folk music.

Keywords: Signal processing · Folk music analysis · Computational ethnomusicology · Performer classification · Mood classification · Ornamentation detection · Ornamentation recognition · COSFIRE

1 Introduction

A common technique for expressing emotions in music performance is the addition of short notes to the main melody. These notes are called ornamentations and can be arbitrarily or systematically inserted. A glissando, also known as

© Springer International Publishing Switzerland 2015
G. Azzopardi and N. Petkov (Eds.): CAIP 2015, Part I, LNCS 9256, pp. 558–569, 2015.
DOI: 10.1007/978-3-319-23192-1_47

vibrato, for instance, is a rapid alteration of a series of consecutive notes. It is one of the most frequent ornamentations. Several other ornamentations are also used such as amplitude variation called tremolo and stretching or shortening the duration of notes, among others. In Fig. 1a we present the audio signal of the song Syrinx for solo flute by Claude Debussy. The vertical lines indicate a note with a tremolo ornamentation, which is shown enlarged in Fig. 1b.

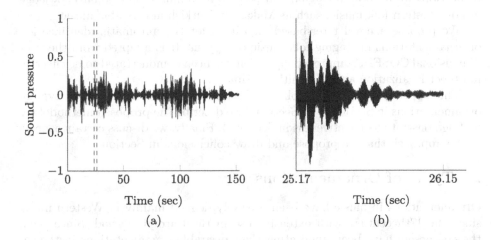

Fig. 1. (a) The sound pressure signal of the song Syrinx for solo flute by Claude Debussy. (b) Tremolo ornamentation that is characterized by amplitude modulation.

The importance of ornamentations in music has been researched and described by music theorists [1]. They are related to the feeling which a performer or a composer aims to create. In the field of music information retrieval (MIR), it has been shown that musicians have a unique way to perform their ornamentations and that it is a distinctive feature for performer identification [2–4].

The majority of these related studies are focused on applications in Western music and they mainly analyse ornamentations of musical instruments rather than singing voice [5–7]. Furthermore, the methodology of these studies require note segmentation. This creates additional computational difficulties since note segmentation is still a challenging problem in MIR.

In [8] the authors initially attempt to segment notes in traditional flute performances. Then they explore knowledge about ornamentations within a segmented note. They propose to separate ornamentations into two categories namely single-note and multi-note, which in turn are composed of two and three-sub categories, respectively.

In this work we are interested in ornamentation detection and recognition of folk music of the Eastern countries. It is generally harder to process Eastern folk songs than Western music from a signal processing point of view. Since folk music is frequently recorded in an environment such as a public place, which may cause low quality recordings covered with background noise. Also, the singers in folk music are usually not professionals and therefore they may sing out of tune, forgetting melodies and others. One major difference between Eastern and Western music is the frequency distance between consecutive notes. In Western music this difference is strictly logarithmically equal into twelve notes per octave. In Eastern music and especially in Makam this distance between notes is not equally distributed. An automated system that will be able to capture ornamentations from an audio signal will help to accumulate additional knowledge of non-Western folk music, such as Makam in Turkish and Arabic music.

We propose a novel filter-based algorithm for the automatic identification of ornamentations in singing folk music of Cyprus. It is adapted from the two-dimensional COSFIRE approach [9], which has been demonstrated to be effective in object localization and recognition in images.

This paper is organized as follows. First we introduce the proposed type of ornamentations in Section 2. In Section 3 we describe the proposed methodology and demonstrate its effectiveness in Section 4. Finally, we discuss certain aspects of the approach that we propose and draw conclusions in Section 5.

2   Types of Ornamentations

Ornamentations in music have been precisely defined mainly in Western music since the 17th century with extensive use in the Baroque period. Since then, the composers have been annotating their desirable ornamentations in the so-called musical score. A musicological study can gather significant information from such transcriptions such as note frequency and duration, rhythm, tempo and others.

In folk music usually the composer is not known, hence there is no written score or any similar information about a song. The music is transmitted orally and mutates over time. Therefore, significant information about ornamentations is stored in the available recordings.

In this paper we make an attempt to create meaningful categories that describe the type of each ornament. We adopt the terms "single-note" and "multi-note" ornamentations from [8] and we introduce some additional sub-categories based on the music theory. We propose the following sub-categories within the single-note category: linear positive, linear negative, glissando positive and glissando negative (Fig. 2a). The major feature of this category is that only one alteration of a small note is done. A multi-note consists of alterations of more than one note and comprises two sub-categories: the vibrato positive and vibrato negative (Fig. 2b).

3   Methods

In this section we present the three main steps of the proposed methodology: feature extraction, configuration and application of the proposed 1D COSFIRE filters for ornamentation detection, followed by detection and recognition. In Fig. 3 we present the main steps of our methodology.

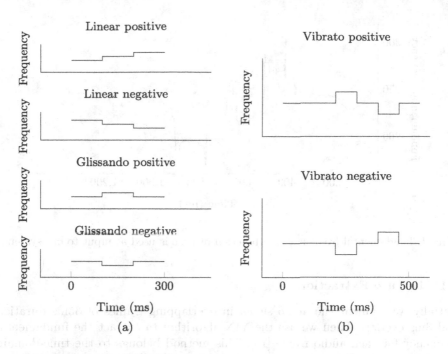

Fig. 2. Ornamentations which belong to (a) single-note and (b) multi-note subcategories. The frequencies can take any values in the range of singing voice.

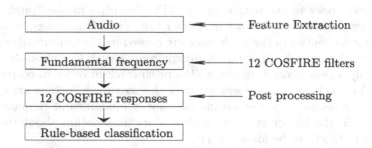

Fig. 3. The main steps of our proposed method. The audio signal is converted in to its fundamental frequency (pitch track). 12 COSFIRE filters are configured using the frequencies of the 12 western notes. The COSFIRE filters are applied to the pitch track, returning 12 responses, one for each COSFIRE filter. The responses are then binarized and post processed. Rule-based approach is used to identify and classify ornamentations.

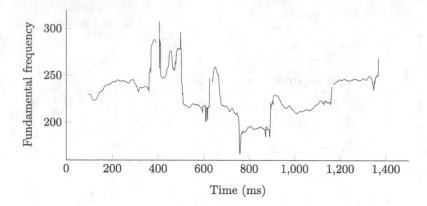

Fig. 4. Fundamental frequency as a function of time is used as input to our system.

3.1   Feature Extraction

Initially we segment the audio signal in overlapping frames of 33ms duration and 3ms overlap. Then we use the YIN algorithm to extract the fundamental frequency for each audio frame [10]. This method belongs to the time-domain based algorithms. First, the Autocorrelation function (ACF) is computed in each frame. Some of the peaks in the output of the ACF represent multiples of the period of the input signal. The repeating pattern of the audio signal is identified by choosing the highest non-zero-lag peaks of the ACF output, and process them with a number of modifications to return a candidate for the fundamental frequency. We refer to the output of the YIN algorithm as the "pitch track". In Fig. 4 we show the pitch track extracted from one of the songs in our data set. The discontinuities in the pitch track are caused by the inharmonicity of the signal at vocal pauses or other non harmonic sounds such as consonants.

We apply a post-processing step to the pitch track in order to correct some errors of YIN. The most frequent error is the so called "octave error". The algorithm erroneously chooses a candidate for a fundamental frequency that has a value in the higher or lower octave. More information about this post-processing method can be found in [11].

3.2   Configuration of a COSFIRE Filter

Originally COSFIRE filters were proposed as trainable filters for computer vision applications. Here we adopt that idea to 1D pitch tracks. A 1D COSFIRE filter uses as input the frequency values at certain positions around a specific point in time of an audio signal. The preferred frequency values and positions for which the resulting filter achieves a maximum value of 1 are determined in manual configuration process. In theory, a note has a single frequency that is constant over time. In practice however, the frequencies of a singing note vary slightly over time as illustrated by an example in Fig. 6a and the shape of the

C C# D D# E F F# G G# A A# B

Do Di Re Ri Mi Fa Fi Sol Sil La Li Si

Fig. 5. The twelve notes of the Western music theory. The Western classical notation is shown first below the notes and the Spanish notation is shown second.

frequency signal is different every time the note is performed. Since one note has a specific duration and the theoretical fundamental frequency of a note is constant over time, we consider the same frequency value for a set of n points and we call this vector a prototype. The parameter n is set experimentally. We choose to configure prototypes with shorter durations as compared to the usual durations of performed notes. A COSFIRE filter which is configured with such a prototype, will return multiple strong responses along a note. This fact increases the chances of getting a strong response to the desirable position which in this case is a performed note.

We denote by $P = \{(f_i, \rho_i) \mid i = 1, \ldots, n\}$ a COSFIRE filter that is selective for a given prototype of n points. Each point i of the prototype is described by a pair (f_i, ρ_i), where f_i is the frequency of the note at position (temporal shift) ρ_i with respect to the midpoint of the prototype, where $\rho_i = i - (n+1)/2$. For instance, the COSFIRE filter that is configured by the note "A" of ($n=$) 5 points, results in the following set P:

$$P = \begin{cases} (f_1 = 220, \ \rho_1 = \text{-}2), \\ (f_2 = 220, \ \rho_2 = \text{-}1), \\ (f_3 = 220, \ \rho_3 = 0), \\ (f_4 = 220, \ \rho_4 = 1), \\ (f_5 = 220, \ \rho_5 = 2) \end{cases}$$

We configure 12 COSFIRE filters that are selective for the third octave of the 12 notes of the Western music theory as illustrated in Fig. 5. The frequencies in Hz of those 12 notes are the following: 130.8, 138.6, 146.8, 155.6, 164.8, 174.6, 185, 196, 207.7, 220, 233.1, 246.9, 261.6, 277.2, 293.7, 311.1, 329.6, 349.2.

3.3 Response of a COSFIRE Filter

We denote by $r_P(t)$ the response of a COSFIRE filter to a signal S at time t. We compute it by taking the geometric mean of the similarity values, which we obtain by a Gaussian kernel function, between the preferred fundamental frequencies f_i and the corresponding frequencies in the concerned neighbourhood.

$$r_P(t) = \left(\prod_{i=1}^{|P|} \exp \frac{-(f_i - S_{t+\rho_i})^2}{2\sigma^2} \right)^{\frac{1}{|P|}} , \sigma = \sigma_0 + \alpha(|\rho_i|) \qquad (1)$$

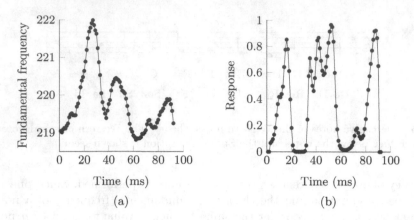

Fig. 6. (a) Fundamental frequency of an original ornamented note that is used as a test signal. (b) The response of the A-selective COSFIRE filter when applied to the test signal.

where $\sigma_0 = 0.5$ and $\alpha = 0.1$ are constant values that we set experimentally. In this way, the tolerance with respect to the preferred frequency increases with increasing distance from the support center of the COSFIRE filter at hand.

The signal in Fig. 6b shows the fundamental frequency of an original note "A" of 92 audio frames covering frequencies in the range between 218 and 222 Hz and we use it as a test signal. The COSFIRE filter P is applied in every position of the test signal and the response is shown in 6b. The maximum value of the response is achieved only at the point where the original note has the same values as the prototype. High responses are also achieved for signals that are similar to the prototype.

3.4 Post Processing

In Fig. 7a we show a part of a pitch track that was extracted from one of the songs in our data set. Below it, we illustrate the responses of three COSFIRE filters that are selective for the notes B, C and C# and are shown with thin solid lines.

Then, we binarize the responses using an absolute threshold of 0.01. We call a unit the consecutive binarized responses that have responses of 1. Such units are shown Fig. 7 (b-d) with dashed lines. In case during a time interval between two units there are no responses from other COSFIRE filters, we set all responses between those two units to 1. There is only one such an example in Fig. 7 which is obtained by the C-selective filter. If there is temporal overlap between units of different filters we only keep the unit with the longest duration.

Then we transform the binarized responses signals for an input audio signal into a symbolic representation of the sequence that every unit appears. In the example presented in Fig. 7 the symbolic sequence is [C.217, B.16, C.6, C#.13, C.6, B.11, C.5 C#.4]. The letters represent the names of the notes of the Western

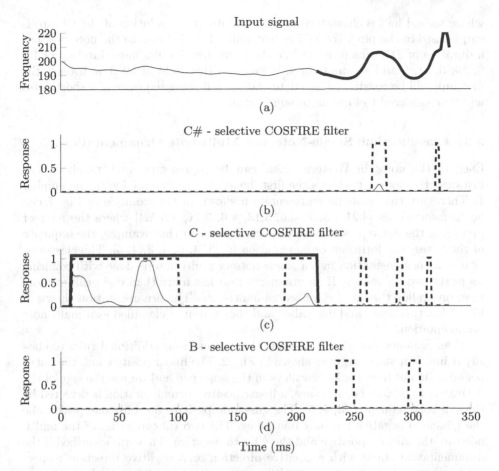

Fig. 7. Post processing procedure. (a) A part of a pitch track. The automatic detection and recognition of an ornamentation is emphasized in the second half of the signal. (b-d) The responses of three filters that were configured to be selective for the three Western notes C#, C and B. The binarized responses are shown with dashed lines. The thick line in (c) shows how consecutive units of a filter response are connected.

music and the number following the dot is the duration of each unit in number of frames. A vibrato is present at the second half with an alteration of short semitones around the note "C" and it is emphasized in Fig.7a.

3.5 Ornamentation Detection

In order to detect any type of ornamentation we first set a time threshold on the duration of every unit of the symbolic representation. The units that exceed the threshold are considered as notes and the remaining units are marked as parts of ornamentations. Typically, there is a sequence of such short units that consists of the entire ornamentation. In the example shown in Fig. 7 we present a note whose second half is characterized by a vibrato. The evolution of the vibrato is emphasised in the pitch track. The first unit which belongs to the note "C" has a duration of 217 time frames while the remaining 7 units have duration of 16, 6, 13, 6, 11, 5 and 4 time frames. If we set a threshold of 30 time frames, the first unit will be considered as a note and the following sequence of 7 short notes will be considered to form an ornamentation.

3.6   Classification: Single-Note and Multi-note Ornamentations.

Each of the notes in Western music can be represented with numbers. For instance, the note A is always the first, hence it is represented with the number 1. Therefore, the symbolic representation shown in the example in Fig. 7 can be transformed as [4.217, 3.16, 4.6, 5.13, 4.6, 3.11, 4.5 5.4] where the number preceding the dot represents the respective note. In this example, the sequence of the notes that forms an ornamentation is: [3, 4, 5, 4, 3, 4, 5]. The classification of an ornamentation into a single-note or multi note is done with counting its peaks and its valleys. If an ornamentation has more than one peak or more than one valley then it is classified as multi-note. The ornamentation shown in Fig. 7 has two peaks and one valley and therefore it is classified as a multi-note ornamentation.

If an ornamentation is single-note, then we use four additional rules to classify it into four sub-categories shown in Fig. 2. The linear positive and the linear negative do not have peaks or valleys in the sequence and we use the sign of the derivative to decide. For instance, a linear positive ornamentation is detected by the symbolic sequence: [3, 4, 5]. The glissando positive has only one peak while the glissando negative has only one valley. The two subcategories of the multi-note are the vibrato positive and the vibrato negative. They are identified if the ornamentation starts with a positive direction or a negative direction respectively. For example, a vibrato positive is described by the symbolic sequence: [3, 4, 3].

4   Experiments and Results

4.1   Data Set

We created a data set of five Cypriot folk songs with total duration of 403 seconds containing 428 ornamentations. They are monophonic singing voice recordings encoded with 44.1kHz sampling frequency. We refer as the ground truth data the positions that are around in the middle of an ornamentation. They are manually annotated by the first author of this paper who is an experienced musician. The list of the songs used to validate our method is given in Table 1. From the 428 ornamentations, 270 are single-note and 158 are multi-note. The data set is available online[1].

---

[1] https://www.cs.ucy.ac.cy/projects/folk/

Table 1. The list of songs used for the validation of our method. Information about the duration, the number of ornamentations and their type is included.

	Manes	Agapisa	Panw xorio	Giallourika	Sousa	Sum
Duration (ms)	84.6	112.3	78.7	74.9	53.3	403.8
Ornamentations (#)	84	123	81	85	55	428
Single-note	56	85	46	50	33	270
Linear positive	9	24	20	10	6	50
Linear negative	7	14	6	17	6	50
Glissando positive	32	42	15	20	16	131
Glissando negative	2	5	5	3	2	17
Multi note	28	38	35	35	22	158
Vibrato positive	23	29	20	32	12	116
Vibrato neg	5	8	15	3	10	41

4.2 Results

The results are summarised in Table 2 in terms of precision, recall and F-measure. The manual annotation was done by setting a marker in the middle of every ornamentation. Then, we consider a true positive when this marker lies anywhere between the predicted start and end positions of an ornamentation. The false positives are considered when there is no pre-annotated marker between the predicted start and end positions and we count the false negatives when there is a marker with no predictions around it.

In Fig. 8 we illustrate a precision-recall plot by changing the time threshold that is used to identify ornamentations from notes. The value of the precision and recall when F-measure reaches maximum is indicated with a dot marker and it has a value of 0.76. We obtain the same results when we used COSFRE filters selective for note signals of length 5, 11, 15, 19 and 21ms.

Table 2. Results. The Ornamentation in row 1 contain results that are made of the results in subsequent lines.

	P	R	F-Score
Ornamentations	0.83	0.71	0.76
Single	0.7	0.56	0.63
Single 1	0.7	0.4	0.52
Single 2	0.63	0.62	0.62
Single 3	0.71	0.45	0.55
Single 4	0.29	0.65	0.4
Multi	0.61	0.35	0.45
Multi 1	0.61	0.48	0.54
Multi 2	0.32	0.76	0.45

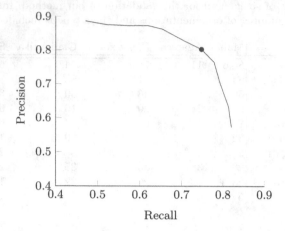

Fig. 8. Precision-recall plot obtained by varying the time threshold used to distinguish notes from parts of ornamentations.

5   Discussion and Conclusions

The COSFIRE filters are sensitive to amplitude tolerance, which is essential for non-stationary signals such as the singing voice. They are conceptually simple and easy to implement. They have been successful in pattern recognition of images in several applications including traffic sign detection and recognition [9]. They can be used for other applications such as note segmentation since they are able to capture note changes. The modelling of the pitch track with COSFIRE filters can also be used for the identification of repeating melodies.

In order to compare the proposed 1D COSFIRE filters with an already established method for the identification of similar signals, we cross correlate the same 12 prototypes with the pitch tracks of our data set. We observe that this system returns similar values for all the 12 prototypes and therefore it is not effective for ornamentation detection. Also, the results shown in Table 2 are comparable to the ones reported in [6]. Even though the database used in [6] is different than the one used in this study, we consider that our method is less complex since we avoid the note segmentation which is a challenging task itself. This study is a preliminary work on the ornamentation detection and classification. The classification of the multi ornamentations did not yield significant results, although this is due to the complexity of the problem. We aim to improve the classification stage that is currently rule-based to more sophisticated machine learning techniques. In future work we will attempt to compare our method with other databases used in previous work of other people. The results will be reported in another study. The above, demonstrate that there is a lot of work to be done in this research topic.

The contribution of our work is three-fold. First, it avoids note segmentation which is still a challenging and complex problem. Second, it uses only one feature, the fundamental frequency and third it is effective with complex musical signals such as singing voice. The use of the pitch track as the main input feature to our method contributes to a system that is fast and less complex as compared to other methods [6–8]. The results that we obtain for the ornamentation detection and recognition are promising and a validation of additional folk music will be done in another study.

Acknowledgments. This research was funded from the Republic of Cyprus through the Cyprus research promotion foundation and also supported by the University of Cyprus by the research grant ΑΝΘΡΩΠΙΣΤΙΚΕΣ / ΑΝΘΡΩ / 0311(BE) / 19.

References

1. Taylor, E.: The AB guide to music. The Associate Board of the Royal Schools of Music (Publishing), London (1989)
2. Ramrez, R., Maestre, E., Pertusa, A., Gmez, E., Serra, X.: Performance-based Interpreter Identification in Saxophone Audio Recordings. IEEE Transactions on Circuits and Systems for Video Technology **17**, 356–364 (2007)
3. Ramrez, R., Prez A., Kersten S., Maestre E.: Performer identification in celtic violin recordings. In: International Conference on Music Information Retrieval (2008)
4. Ramrez, R., Maestre E.: A framework for performer identification in audio recordings. In: International Workshop on Machine Learning and Music - ECML-PKDD (2009)
5. Boenn, G.: Automated quantisation and transcription of musical ornaments from audio recordings. In: Proc. of the Int. Computer Music Conf. (ICMC), pp. 236–239 (2007)
6. Casey, M., Crawford, T.: Automatic location and measurement of ornaments in audio recording. In: Proc. of the 5th Int. Conf. on Music Information Retrieval (ISMIR), pp. 311–317 (2004)
7. Gainza, M., Coyle, E.: Automating ornamentation transcription. In: IEEE Int. Conf. on Acoustics, Speech and Signal Processing (2007)
8. Kokuer, M., Jancovic, P., Ali-MacLachlan, I., Athwal, C.: Automated detection of single - and multi-note ornaments in irish traditional flute playing. In: 15th International Society for Music Information Retrieval Conference (ISMIR) (2014)
9. Azzopardi, G., Petkov, N.: Trainable COSFIRE filters for keypoint detection and pattern recognition. IEEE Transactions on Pattern Analysis and Machine Intelligence **35**, 490–503 (2012)
10. Cheveigne, A., Kawahara, H.: Yin, a fundamental frequency estimator for speech and music. Journal of the Acoustical Society of America **111**(4), 1917–1930 (2002)
11. Panteli M.: Pitch Patterns of Cypriot Folk Music between Byzantine and Ottoman Influence. Master thesis. University of Pompeu Fabra (2011)

Vision-Based System for Automatic Detection of Suspicious Objects on ATM

Wirat Rattanapitak$^{(\boxtimes)}$ and Somkiat Wangsiripitak

Faculty of Information Technology, King Mongkut's Institute of Technology
Ladkrabang, 1 Chalongkrung Road Ladkrabang, Bankok 10520, Thailand
rattanapitak@gmail.com

Abstract. Most skimming devices attached to an automatic teller machine (ATM) are similar in color and shape to the host machine, vision-based detection of such things is therefore difficult. A background subtraction method may be used to detect changes in a normal situation. However, without human detection, its background model is sometimes polluted by the ATM user, and the method cannot detect suspicious objects left in the scene. This paper proposes a real-time system which integrates (i) a simple image subtraction for detection of user arrival and departure, and (ii) an automatic detection of suspicious objects left on the ATM. The background model is updated only when no user is found, and used to detect suspicious objects based on a *guided* adaptive threshold. To avoid a detection miss, nonlinear enhancement is applied to amplify the intensity differences between foreign objects and host machine. Experimental results show that the proposed system increases correctly detected area by 13.21% compared with the fixed threshold method. It has no detection miss and false alarm either.

Keywords: Skimming · Automated teller machine · Suspicious objects · Objects detection · Video surveillance

1 Introduction

An automated teller machine (ATM) is always a target of fraudulent attack, such as a card theft device, a skimmer, a trapping in front of the dispense point, a magnetic card reader, a wireless camera, and a fake keypad [1–3,9,13,14]. Most are equipments attached illegally to the ATM front panel, in order to steal money, ATM cards, or some data (e.g. PIN codes and data in the card), which are then used to illegally withdraw and/or transfer money from the victim's account. In general, ATMs are not equipped with a self-defense system, so they cannot detect those illegal devices. Vision based surveillance systems have been proposed also for detection of changes in the scene, but they often fail in detection of suspicious objects on ATM due to a strong resemblance between illegal objects and the ATM. To successfully detect such foreign objects, image frames are normally captured such that the ATM front panel fills the entire frame. Therefore most area of image frame is regularly covered by a user's body during his ATM

© Springer International Publishing Switzerland 2015
G. Azzopardi and N. Petkov (Eds.): CAIP 2015, Part I, LNCS 9256, pp. 570–581, 2015.
DOI: 10.1007/978-3-319-23192-1_48

transaction, and most background based methods per se (without detection of users) cannot detect foreign objects as expected.

This paper proposes an automatic detection system which uses a camera as the only sensor to detect suspicious objects on the ATM. The system integrates (i) a simple detection of an ATM user (entry and exit), and (ii) an automatic detection of foreign objects on the ATM after the user leaves. In this paper, we also propose two modifications so as to improve the detection rate. One is an additional step of image enhancement which helps increase the background-subtracted values of suspicious pixels. The other is the method of adaptively determining (*guided*) threshold based on intensity differences of selected subregion. This threshold will be used later in extraction of suspicious objects.

The remainder of this paper is organized as follows: some related works on detection of the ATM fraud are described in the next section. Then the proposed method is detailed in Sect. 3. In Sect. 4, experimental results are shown. Conclusions and future works are drawn at the end.

2 Related Works

There exist some related works which address the problem of ATM criminal and fraud. Some analyze an ATM usage pattern in order to detect the counterfeit ATM card, helping stop further illegal transactions as soon as possible [11,13]. These methods however do not detect the skimming device but the illegal activities after the ATM card is skimmed. A method of secure cash withdrawal using an additional device is also proposed to make it more secure, e.g. the one that allows a user to use his/her mobile phone to securely withdraw cash from ATM [1]. Although it seems to be secure, it requires users to perform an additional step for each transaction. To make the ATM more intelligent, the self-defense technology for ATM is proposed in the design frameworks of an advanced intelligent ATM. This enables many secure activities on ATM such as banknote validation, user identification, form and character recognition, and foreign objects detection [14]. The method employs image processing and pattern recognition techniques together with multiple types of sensors, resulting in a high cost of investment.

Many video surveillance methods [6,17,18] are developed for human and object detection, so that the criminal attempts on ATM can be stopped or detected as soon as possible. One of them uses a CCTV, which is separated from the ATM body, to monitoring the ATM and its surrounding and to detecting abnormal events or suspicious acts by human, such as a robbery attempt [6,17]. Some researchers do use the camera already installed inside the ATM to detect irregular behavior of ATM's user, e.g. face-hiding, peeping and wandering [18].

Examples of vision-based systems which detect suspicious objects (including skimming devices) on the ATM are the self-defense ATM of [14] and the automatic alarm system of [17]. The former however suffers from light reflection and cannot apply, without machine modification, to the old machine type. The latter needs an authorized person to reset the alarm each time it is triggered.

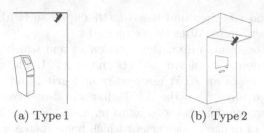

(a) Type 1   (b) Type 2

Fig. 1. Camera position in the purposed system.

Some methods report that they can detect abandoned objects (such as [16]), but those objects must be obvious and easily perceived otherwise the detection fails. Some (such as [10,15]) are adaptive such that they can detect even a slight change in the scene, but when applied to the closeup images of ATM, they struggle with the intermittent appearance of ATM user which covers most parts of the frames. Without modification, they cannot apply to detection of illegal objects on ATM.

3   Approach

The automatic detection of foreign objects on ATM using a camera is proposed here. The camera is set at the position where most parts of ATM panel are visible. Any suspicious objects in the current image frame are discovered by removing the background using background subtraction and a simple background model. Here only the frame in which the user does not exist will be used for strange object detection, avoiding a miss detection during user appearance. The background model, here, is an image frame selected from the frames before the current ATM user gets into and after the previous user leaves the scene, allowing an automatic update of background model. Therefore our proposed system requires a detection of ATM users, which also proposed here. Details of each step are as follows.

3.1   Camera Location

While all parts of ATM front panel must be visible to the camera (so that all possible suspicious objects, including the small one, can be detected), the camera should not be in the position where the user's private information, e.g. ATM card's PIN being pushed by the user, is recorded. The camera in the proposed system is therefore set at the location behind the ATM user such that transaction details are hidden by his/her body and kept secret. Fig.1 illustrates the position and orientation of camera in our proposed system.

3.2   Detection of User Entry

When the ATM user comes into the scene, most contents in image frame will change rapidly. The sudden changes of image content between adjacent frames are detected here to notify the system that there is the ATM user getting in.

First, a pixel-wise image subtraction of "current image frame F_n of size $M \times N$" and "previous image frame F_{n-1} of the same size" is performed based on their intensities $F(i,j)$. Then the number of pixel pairs of which absolute differences are greater than the threshold T (here is zero) is counted and stored as the variation score $C_{n,n-1}$ of frame F_n, i.e.

$$C_{n,n-1} = \sum_{i=1}^{M} \sum_{j=1}^{N} d_{n,n-1}(i,j) , \tag{1}$$

$$d_{n,n-1}(i,j) = \begin{cases} 1, & \text{if } |F_n(i,j) - F_{n-1}(i,j)| > T \\ 0, & \text{otherwise} . \end{cases} \tag{2}$$

In theory, when there is no change in the scene, the variation score $C_{n,n-1}$ of frame F_n should be approximately equal to zero ($C_{n,n-1} \approx 0$), but in practice it has some values (here about $200,000$). Some causes of that phenomenon are that an image sensor itself is unstable and/or illumination always changes.

A fluctuation and a spike (called "outliers") in the values of $C_{n,n-1}$ while no one in the scene are also the consequence of those incidents. In order to eliminate the outliers, we apply RANSAC [8] and averaging filter with the sliding window of size 7 frames. The jitters between variation score of adjacent frames are removed by a maximum filter with the sliding window of size 120 frames.

The entrance of ATM user is detected by comparing the variation score $C_{n,n-1}$ of current frame with the score $C_{n-1,n-2}$ of previous frame. If the difference is greater than 25% of the variation score in the previous frame , i.e.

$$C_{n,n-1} - C_{n-1,n-2} > (0.25) \cdot C_{n-1,n-2} , \tag{3}$$

the system will judge that there is someone coming into the scene.

3.3 Detection of User Exit

When the user leaves the scene, the variation score (degree of changes in image content) of current frame will decrease to the value approximately the same as those of the frames before the user enters. However, we cannot use this criterion to detect a user exit because such low value of variation score is also obtained when the user stands still in the scene.

In this paper, user's leaving is therefore detected by examining two criteria. The first one is to compare the variation score $C_{n,n-1}$ of the current frame with the score $C_{s,s-1}$ of the (background) frame F_s (which is selected from images before user coming in), and then verify if it is within $C_{s,s-1} \pm 10\%$, i.e.

$$|C_{n,n-1} - C_{s,s-1}| < (0.1) \cdot C_{s,s-1} . \tag{4}$$

The other one is to directly verify if image contents of current frames F_n are similar to those of F_s which is the frame before user entry. To examine this criterion, (1) and (2) are first applied to calculating the variation score $C_{n,s}$

(which indicates how many pixels in the current frame F_n are changed when comparing it with the selected background frame F_s). However the score $C_{n,s}$ contains some erroneous values caused by unstableness of illumination and image sensor, therefore the score $C_{n,s}$ is subtracted by $C_{s,s-1}$ so as to remove those errors. Since the total area of suspicious objects is assumed in this paper to be less than 20% of the image area, the second criterion is satisfied if

$$|C_{n,s} - C_{s,s-1}| < (0.2) \cdot (M \times N) \tag{5}$$

Note that only when (4) and (5) are fulfilled, the system will judge that the ATM user has been out of the scene.

Now we will explain how and which image frame is selected as the background model. The background image F_s (used here and in subsection 3.4) is selected automatically and randomly from 30 frames taken 2 seconds before the ATM user entering the scene. It is selected (updated) again when new ATM user comes in. Note that the constants used in (3) - (5) have been verified by experiments. The sizes of suspicious objects and the ATM user (large and small body) are also taken into account when the system is designed .

3.4   Suspicious Object Detection

A basic method of suspicious objects detection starts from subtraction of two gray scale images – one is a normal image frame of ATM (later called "clean frame" or "background frame") and the other with illegal objects attached on it (later called "polluted frame"). The image frame of absolute difference (later called 'difference frame') is then binarized by a threshold determined one way or another (e.g. [5]), and suspicious objects are finally extracted.

Based on the above-mentioned method, an adaptive or a flexible background model (e.g. [4,10,15]) may be used with some modification, e.g. excluding the frames of which most image areas are covered by the body of user. Here, we propose a simpler adaptive background subtraction approach. In general, a quality of detection heavily depends on the value of threshold. If the distribution of pixels in "difference frame" is ideally bimodal (solid curve in Fig.2a) with a low mode representing background area and a high mode the pixels of suspicious objects (dotted curve and dashed curve), the optimum threshold may be obtained by Otsu's method [12] and used to separate the two groups of pixels with some errors in shaded area. However, in practice, the distribution becomes unimodal if the absolute differences of suspicious pixels are relatively equal to those of clean area (Fig.2b). In addition, due to different degrees of intensity changes on various surfaces (many different normal vectors) of ATM panel, the distribution can be more complex as shown in Fig.3a. These cause Otsu's method fail in object extraction. Here, we presents the solution to these problems as follows.

Increasing Intensity Difference of Suspicious Pixels. Due to the similarity of suspicious objects and their underneath ATM part, the intensity differences between "clean frame" and "polluted frame" at the position of illegal objects do

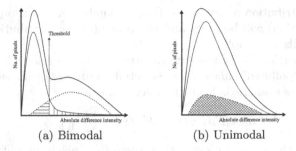

(a) Bimodal   (b) Unimodal

Fig. 2. Distribution of absolute difference for whole image (solid), background area (dotted) and object area (dashed).

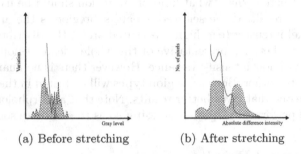

(a) Before stretching   (b) After stretching

Fig. 3. Distribution of absolute difference for background area (dotted) and object area (dashed, shaded).

not differ much from those at the "clean area". To enhance the differences at the "polluted area", histogram stretching (here histogram equalization is used) is first applied as the preprocessing step to the 'clean' and the 'polluted' frames individually. The image of absolute difference between the two frames is then created. Since two stretching functions (one for each frame) are different, the degree of pixel intensity shift on one frame is distinct from that on the other frame. As a result, pixel intensity at the polluted position in both frames will become more distinct – i.e. the absolute difference of polluted area is amplified (shaded area in Fig.3a→b) – which helps increase the detection rate (see experimental results in Sect. 4).

Thresholding Guided by Subregion. When the absolute difference image of two enhanced image frames is obtained, it is transformed to binary image by thresholding method. The histogram of difference image is not always bimodal, therefore Otsu's method sometimes fails to classify suspicious objects area from background. If these distributions of "clean area" (dotted curve in Fig.2) and that of "polluted area" (dashed curve) are known, the optimum threshold for foreign object extraction can be determined (with some false positives included), but this is not the case in real world. In this paper, we present that careful selection of (known) 'clean' subregion in the difference image can be used to provide the distribution of all 'clean' (background) area – although the height (of the distribution) will be lower and the range (of the distribution) is usually narrower. Details are as follows.

First, the distribution of absolute difference between selected "background" image F_s and "polluted" image F_p in selected 'clean' area (of size $a \times b$, where $a = 25, b = 15$) is examined. Then the maximum value,

$$\max |F_s(i, j) - F_p(i, j)|_{i=1..a, j=1..b} ,\qquad(6)$$

is used as the threshold for extracting suspicious pixels in difference image, allowing illegal objects to be extracted from background. Note that the size $a \times b$ of 'clean' sub-area is empirically determined.

The question here is that "what kind of subregion should be used?" in order to obtain a good result. If the selected 'clean' subregion is the area with high variation of pixel intensity (e.g. highly textured area), the distribution range is considered to be a better representative of the whole 'clean' region, rather than using the area with low intensity variance. However there is no guarantee that it will outperform the other. Both subregion types will be tested in the experiments so as to find the one that gives better results. Note that a morphological opening and closing are performed as post-processing so as to eliminate some errors.

4   Experimental Results

The proposed system runs on an Intel Pentium Core 2 Duo Core 2.26 GHz Processor. Grey level images of size 1920×1080 pixels are provided at 30 Hz from a CMOS camera over a USB link, but the region of interest (ROI) used in processing is of size 405 × 720 pixels. Four types of ATM located outdoors are used in the experiments. The LCD display area is masked out. Image sequences are captured during the afternoon (noon-3pm) and in the evening (4pm-6pm). The processing time is about 0.24 seconds/frame, allowing the system to run at 4 fps. Note that the time can be reduced by optimizing the code.

4.1   Results of Foreign Object Extraction

Figs. 4a and 5a show the images of 'clean' ATMs, type B and type C respectively, while Figs. 4b and 5b show the same ATMs with illegal objects attached on them. The ground truth of suspicious objects is shown in Figs. 4c (one object) and 5c (two objects). Extraction results are shown as binary images in Figs. 4d~4i and Figs. 5d~5i. Note that if the ATM user does not know in advance that there are suspicious objects attached on the ATM, it may be difficult to find them.

As shown in the figures, better results are obtained by applying a histogram stretching to image frame prior to subtraction. Without the stretching, results are undesirable (Figs. 4d~4f and 5d~5f). When histogram stretching is applied (Figs. 4g~4i and 5g~5i), the thresholding guided by subregion of low intensity variance is more efficient than the other two methods, in terms of no detection

Fig. 4. ATM type B with one suspicious object. (a-b) image without and with suspicious object. (c) ground truth. Middle and bottom rows show extraction results without and with histogram stretching, respectively. Thresholding used in binarization is determined by Otsu's method (d,g), guided by subregion of high (e,h) and low (f,i) intensity variation.

miss. It outperforms Otsu's method which could detect only one foreign object in Fig. 5g. It is also superior to the thresholding guided by sub-area of high intensity variance that could not detect anything in Fig. 4h and missed one foreign object in Fig. 5h. Although there are few small areas of false positive appeared in the result of thresholding guided by low variance subregion, they are very small and easy to remove.

4.2   Sensitivity and Specificity

Efficiency of additional preprocessing step and new thresholding method proposed in Sect. 3 is verified by measuring the sensitivity (true positive rate,

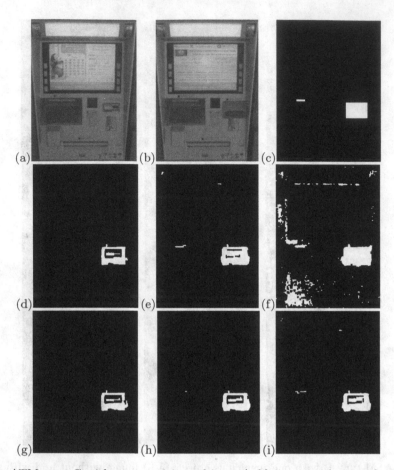

Fig. 5. ATM type C with two suspicious objects. (a-b) image without and with suspicious objects. (c) ground truth. Middle and bottom rows show extraction results without and with histogram stretching, respectively. Thresholding used in binarization is determined by Otsu's method (d,g), guided by subregion of high (e,h) and low (f,i) intensity variation.

abbreviated as TPR) and specificity (true negative rate, abbreviated as TNR) [7], and comparing them to that of Otsu's method. Note that a false positive rate is abbreviated as FPR and a false negative rate as FNR.

Tables 1-2 show the results of examining 10800 image frames in the afternoon and in the evening – all with one or two foreign objects. In the tables, a thresholding guided by subregion of high and low-intensity variance are abbreviated as 'Hi.' and 'Lo.', respectively. In terms of security, 'high TPR' and 'no detection miss (with low FNR)' are preferable – histogram stretching and thresholding guided by subregion of low intensity variance are therefore the best combination. However, as for an annoying false alarm, the smaller the FPR is, the better the results are. Although thresholding guided by low variance sub-image is not

Table 1. Accuracy and error rates of foreign object detection in pixels (afternoon). The best rates are underlined. Value with asterisk (*) indicates that there is a detection miss.

Type	True Positive (%)			True Negative (%)			False Positive (%)			False Negative (%)			Accuracy (%)		
	Otsu	Hi.	Lo.	Otsu	Hi.	Lo.	Otsu	Hi.	Lo.	Otsu	Hi.	Lo.	Otsu	Hi.	Lo.
Without histogram stretching															
A	88.447	0	76.222	71.413	100	98.374	28.587	0.000	1.626	11.553	100*	23.778	79.930	50	87.298
B	1.211	0	0	75.050	99.998	99.814	24.950	0.002	0.186	98.789*	100*	100*	38.130	49.999	49.907
C	69.626	0	93.879	99.990	100	98.993	.010	0.000	1.007	30.374	100*	6.121	84.808	50	96.436
D	99.607	0	99.645	88.194	100	84.566	11.806	0.000	15.434	0.393	100*	0.355	93.900	50	92.106
Avg.	64.723	0	67.436	83.662	100	95.437	16.338	0.000	4.563	35.277	100*	32.564	74.192	50	81.437
With histogram stretching															
A	73.039	0	69.319	99.302	100	99.515	0.698	0	0.485	26.961	100*	30.681	86.170	50	84.417
B	62.182	1.692	51.498	98.778	100	99.838	1.222	0	0.162	37.818	98.308*	48.502	80.480	50.846	75.668
C	41.480	0	91.302	99.953	100	97.278	0.047	0	2.722	58.520	100*	8.698	70.717	50	94.290
D	99.373	0.774	99.896	99.668	100	99.059	0.332	0	0.941	0.627	99.226*	0.104	99.520	50.387	99.477
Avg.	69.018	0.616	78.004	99.425	100	98.023	0.575	0	1.077	30.982	99.384*	21.996	84.222	50.308	88.463

Table 2. Accuracy and error rates of foreign object detection, in pixels (evening). The best rates are underlined. Value with asterisk (*) indicates that there is a detection miss.

Type	True Positive (%)			True Negative (%)			False Positive (%)			False Negative (%)			Accuracy (%)		
	Otsu	Hi.	Lo.	Otsu	Hi.	Lo.	Otsu	Hi.	Lo.	Otsu	Hi.	Lo.	Otsu	Hi.	Lo.
Without histogram stretching															
A	83.197	82.017	94.962	99.687	99.711	98.583	0.313	0.289	1.417	16.803	17.983	5.038	91.442	90.864	96.772
B	62.656	56.467	79.391	99.923	99.962	97.051	0.077	0.038	2.949	37.344*	43.533*	20.609	81.290	78.215	88.221
C	63.057	86.300	97.321	99.949	99.575	98.524	0.051	0.425	1.476	36.943*	13.700	2.679	81.503	92.938	97.923
D	28.568	71.016	94.162	100	99.464	95.644	0.000	0.536	4.356	71.432*	28.984	5.838	64.284	85.240	94.903
Avg.	59.370	73.950	91.459	99.890	99.678	97.451	0.110	0.322	2.549	40.630	26.050	8.541	79.630	86.814	94.455
With histogram stretching															
A	68.818	65.031	85.546	99.756	99.825	99.026	0.244	0.175	0.974	31.182	34.969	14.454	84.287	82.428	92.286
B	73.813	54.855	90.411	99.755	99.997	95.088	0.245	0.003	4.912	26.187*	45.145*	9.589	86.784	77.426	92.749
C	60.504	66.451	85.642	99.948	99.828	98.531	0.052	0.172	1.469	39.496	33.549	14.358	80.226	83.130	02.087
D	65.428	65.534	90.185	99.440	99.669	98.605	0.560	0.331	1.395	34.572	34.466	9.815	82.434	82.601	94.395
Avg.	67.141	62.967	87.946	99.725	99.829	97.812	0.275	0.171	2.188	32.859	37.033	12.054	83.433	81.398	92.879

the best (compared with results of thresholding guided by the high one), the false positive pixels do not cluster in a big size such that they are misinterpreted as suspicious objects. Therefore 'low variance subregion based thresholding' and 'image stretching' are desirable techniques for detection of foreign objects on ATM, with the accuracy (in pixels) increased by 13.21% on average (2.15% for stretching and 11.06% for proposed thresholding).

4.3 Verification of False Alarm on 'Clean' Image

The false alarm on 'clean' image (the frame without illegal objects) is also verified here, by illustrating the binary image of detection result (one example is shown in Fig. 6) and by examining the FPR. As shown in the figure, thresholding by Otsu's method gives the worst result with 32.36% of FPR on average (most results obtained by Otsu's are worse than that shown in Fig. 6a). The proposed thresholding which is guided by subregion (Figs. 6b~6c) provides superior results with FPR=0.003% and 0.01% for the guide by subregion of high and low intensity

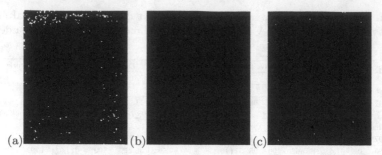

Fig. 6. ATM type B without illegal objects (with stretching). (a) Otsu's method. (b-c) thresholding guided by subregion of high & low intensity variation.

variation, respectively. This level of false alarm (small in pixel number and cluster size) can be easily eliminated by post-processing.

5   Conclusion

The paper presented the integrated vision-based system for automatic detection of suspicious objects on ATM. The system could detect an ATM user, and allowed the proposed background-subtraction to extract stationary foreign objects, which are attached on the ATM front panel, from their host machine. The method proposed here transformed image histograms (of both background and incoming images *individually*) before image differencing so as to enhance the subtracted value in the area of illegal objects — allowing successful detection of them even though they are quite similar to the host. New thresholding method guided by selected subregion also helped determine the optimum threshold – it is used later for successful object extraction – though the distribution of difference image is not bimodal. Experiments on outdoor ATM image sequences in the afternoon and evening showed its success in detection of suspiciously attached object, including those similar in color to the host ATM, without 'detection miss' and 'false alarm'. The detection could also run continuously without intervention by a system admin, because the background frame was automatically updated each time a new user came in (using the frames just before user's entry). Testing the method with night scene is planned next. Automatic and dynamic selection of sub-area used in guided thresholding will be implemented as well, so that the good results are maintained. An automatic segmentation of static and dynamic background (such as the area of LCD monitor) will be implemented next to allow easier system setup.

Acknowledgments. The research is partially supported by Faculty of Information Technology, King Mongkuts Institute of Technology Ladkrabang.

References

1. Arabo, A.: Secure cash withdrawal through mobile phone/device. In: International Conference on Computer and Communication Engineering, ICCCE 2008, pp. 818–822, May 2008

2. Batiz-Lazo, B., Reid, R.: The development of cash-dispensing technology in the UK. IEEE Annals of the History of Computing **33**(3), 32–45 (2011)
3. Bradbury, D.: A hole in the security wall: ATM hacking. Network Security **2010**(6), 12–15 (2010)
4. Bruzzone, L., Prieto, D.: Automatic analysis of the difference image for unsupervised change detection. IEEE Transactions on Geoscience and Remote Sensing **38**(3), 1171–1182 (2000)
5. Cooke, T.: Background subtraction using global textures. In: 2012 International Conference on Digital Image Computing Techniques and Applications (DICTA), pp. 1–7, December 2012
6. Ding, N., Chen, Y., Zhong, Z., Xu, Y.: Energy-based surveillance systems for ATM machines. In: 2010 8th World Congress on Intelligent Control and Automation (WCICA), pp. 2880–2887, July 2010
7. Fawcett, T.: An introduction to ROC analysis. Pattern Recognition Letters **27**(8), 861–874 (2006)
8. Fischler, M.A., Bolles, R.C.: Random sample consensus: A paradigm for model fitting with applications to image analysis and automated cartography. Commun. ACM **24**(6), 381–395 (1981)
9. Guo, H., Jin, B.: Forensic analysis of skimming devices for credit fraud detection. In: 2010 2nd IEEE International Conference on Information and Financial Engineering (ICIFE), pp. 542–546, September 2010
10. Hofmann, M., Tiefenbacher, P., Rigoll, G.: Background segmentation with feedback: the pixel-based adaptive segmenter. In: 2012 IEEE Computer Society Conference on Computer Vision and Pattern Recognition Workshops (CVPRW), pp. 38–43, June 2012
11. Krivko, M.: A hybrid model for plastic card fraud detection systems. Expert Systems with Applications **37**(8), 6070–6076 (2010)
12. Otsu, N.: A threshold selection method from gray-level histograms. IEEE Transactions on Systems, Man and Cybernetics **9**(1), 62–66 (1979)
13. Reardon, B., Nance, K., McCombie, S.: Visualization of ATM usage patterns to detect counterfeit cards usage. In: 2012 45th Hawaii International Conference on System Science (HICSS), pp. 3081–3088, January 2012
14. Sako, H., Watanabe, T., Nagayoshi, H., Kagehiro, T.: Self-defense-technologies for automated teller machines. In: International Machine Vision and Image Processing Conference, IMVIP 2007, pp. 177–184, September 2007
15. St-Charles, P.L., Bilodeau, G.A., Bergevin, R.: Flexible background subtraction with self-balanced local sensitivity. In: 2014 IEEE Conference on Computer Vision and Pattern Recognition Workshops (CVPRW), pp. 414–419, June 2014
16. Zin, T.T., Tin, P., Toriu, T., Hama, H.: A novel probabilistic video analysis for stationary object detection in video surveillance systems. IAENG International Journal of Computer Science **39**(3), 295–306 (2012)
17. Yi, H., Liu, J., Wang, X.: Automatic alarm system for self-service bank based on image comparation. In: 2011 International Symposium on Computer Science and Society (ISCCS), pp. 48–50, July 2011
18. Yi, M.: Abnormal event detection method for ATM video and its application. In: Lin, S., Huang, X. (eds.) CESM 2011, Part II. CCIS, vol. 176, pp. 186–192. Springer, Heidelberg (2011)

Towards Ubiquitous Autonomous Driving: The CCSAD Dataset

Roberto Guzmán[1], Jean-Bernard Hayet[1]([✉]), and Reinhard Klette[2]

[1] Centro de Investigación En Matemáticas, Guanajuato, Mexico
jbhayet@cimat.mx
[2] Auckland University of Technology, Auckland, New Zealand

Abstract. Several online real-world stereo datasets exist for the development and testing of algorithms in the fields of perception and navigation of autonomous vehicles. However, none of them was recorded in developing countries, and therefore they lack the particular challenges that can be found on their streets and roads, like abundant potholes, irregular speed bumpers, and peculiar flows of pedestrians. We introduce a novel dataset that possesses such characteristics. The stereo dataset was recorded in Mexico from a moving vehicle. It contains high-resolution stereo images which are complemented with direction and acceleration data obtained from an IMU, GPS data, and data from the car computer. This paper describes the structure and contents of our dataset files and presents reconstruction experiments that we performed on the data.

1 Introduction

The advances in the field of autonomous cars in recent years have been significant. Even though autonomous driving on highways has been possible since the 1990s [16], it was until recent years that several teams accomplished autonomous driving in real-world urban environments [17]. Despite these achievements, reliable driving in urban environments is still an unsolved problem, mainly because busy urban environments are complex and unpredictable, and they lack the "simple structure" that can be found in highway scenarios.

To be able to provide safe and comfortable autonomous driving in urban traffic, a precise and comprehensive perception of the environment is fundamental. In autonomous vehicles, several types of sensors are used together to provide a rich view of the surroundings and compensate for each other's weaknesses. Among them, stereo cameras are a popular choice, as they can provide both 3D and texture information, and in some cases, color information, too. Also, compared to other sensors, like laser scanners, they are cheap and consume less power. To obtain 3D information from the acquired images, heavy processing is required. Besides, because of the nature of the applications, algorithms are required to run in real-time. Although stereo vision [11] is a very active research topic, with new stereo algorithms introduced every year, and with existing real-time hardware implementations e.g. [6], further developments are still needed.

© Springer International Publishing Switzerland 2015
G. Azzopardi and N. Petkov (Eds.): CAIP 2015, Part I, LNCS 9256, pp. 582–593, 2015.
DOI: 10.1007/978-3-319-23192-1_49

Several stereo vision datasets are available to boost the development of the perception capabilities of autonomous vehicles. The Rawseeds project [5] provides a high-quality benchmarking toolkit for autonomous robotics, suitable for evaluating and comparing algorithms for localization, mapping, or SLAM. They used many sensors, including binocular and trinocular camera systems. EISATS [1] offers several synthetic and real-world sequences captured under various weather and lighting conditions. Some of the sequences include ego-motion data and ground truth from a laser scanner. The HCI/Bosch Robust Vision Challenge [9] provides several hand-picked challenging high-resolution outdoor scenes recorded under diverse weather conditions. The provided scenes demonstrate that common assumptions of stereo matching algorithms, like brightness constancy, fail in the real world. The Daimler Stereo Dataset [3] provides stereo data of bad weather highway scenes with partial ground truth for the so called *stixels*. Also, in [14], the authors augmented a stereo sequence with manually labeled ground truth based on polygonal areas. Finally, the popular KITTI Dataset [7] features 6 hours of diverse traffic scenarios recorded using high-resolution stereo cameras with ground truth from a laser scanner.

To the best of our knowledge, no dataset exists with the particular characteristics of the streets and roads of developing countries. They offer challenges not common on the roads of developed countries, where most of the existing datasets have been recorded. First, lane marking and road signaling are sometimes either absent, insufficient, or ignored by others. Also, the pedestrian flow is less structured, as pedestrians often share the road with cars and may cross roads anywhere. Besides, the road quality is often poor, with many irregular speed bumps or potholes. All these challenges increase the complexity of driving in urban scenarios. In the introduced *CIMAT Challenging Sequences for Autonomous Driving* (CCSAD), we compiled sequences recorded on Mexican roads with the aforementioned features. We equipped a vehicle with a stereo pair of high-resolution greyscale cameras and complemented the image data with acceleration and direction data from an IMU, GPS data obtained from a smartphone, and vehicle speed and RPM readings from the car computer. To enrich our dataset, we also recorded sequences in a Mexican colonial town with challenging scenarios like very narrow streets or a subterraneous tunnel network.

The rest of the paper is organized as follows. The sensor setup is presented in Section 2. The dataset contents is described in Section 3. Stereo reconstruction experiments performed over the data are described in Section 4. Finally, Section 5 contains the conclusions and the description of our future work.

2   Sensor Setup Description

The sensors we used to acquire the dataset are enlisted below:

- 2 × Basler Scout scA1300-32fm Firewire greyscale cameras, with up to 1.2 Megapixels resolution. The imaging sensor is a 1/3" Sony ICX445 CCD, with progressive scan and a frame rate up to 33 fps.

Fig. 1. Vehicle sensor setup. The coordinate frames of the cameras and the IMU are shown in blue and green, respectively.

- 2 × Computar lenses, 8 mm, with a horizontal field of view of ∼ 28°, and a vertical field of view of ∼ 21°.
- 1 × XSens MTi miniature MEMS-based Attitude and Heading Reference System, with a Gyro bias stability of 20° per hour, a dynamic accuracy of 2° RMS, and an angular resolution of 0.05°.
- 1 × GPS-enabled Android-based smartphone.

To retrieve data from the car computer, we attached a bluetooth interface based on the ELM-327 chip to the SAE J1962 OBD-II port of the car. We used a mobile workstation and a NI sbRIO-9632 embedded real-time controller to acquire and log the data. The mobile workstation acquires the car, GPS and image data while the real-time controller acquires the data from the MTi IMU. Both computers clocks are synchronized using the NTP protocol. The real-time controller also generates the triggering pulses to the cameras, so that they are hardware synchronized. The stereo rig has a baseline of approximately 50 cm and is mounted on top of the vehicle. The MTi IMU is mounted approximately in the middle point between the two cameras. A picture of this setup is shown in Fig. 1.

3   Dataset Description

We acquired around 500 GB of data which correspond to more than 96,000 stereo pairs distributed in 42 sequences, which amounts to approximately 1 h and 20 minutes of stereo sequences. The longest sequence comprises 3,162 pairs whereas the shortest one is made of 1,201 pairs. The sequences were recorded in 3 different sessions. For each recorded sequence, we provide a ZIP file with a common structure. The file contains, besides all the acquired data, a video of the full sequence for quick visualization of its contents. All the timestamps correspond to the milliseconds elapsed since the start of the recording day. In the following subsections, we describe in detail the data provided by each type of sensor.

We classified our sequences into four categories: 'Colonial Town Streets', 'Urban Streets', 'Avenues and Small Roads', and 'Tunnel Network'. Some example frames are shown in Fig. 2. All sequences were recorded in daytime with

| Urban Streets | Avenues & Small Roads | Colonial Town Streets | Tunnel Network |

Fig. 2. Image Samples. The figure shows four examples for each category (along each column). The images shown correspond to the left camera.

varying lighting conditions, except for the sequences corresponding to the 'Tunnel network' category; they are recorded at night. One can observe that they offer the typical challenges for stereo-matching algorithms present in real-world scenarios like shadowing and solar/lens flares.

3.1 Image Data

We acquired the stereo pairs at 20 fps, using a radiometric depth of 12 bits per pixel. The image resolution was 1096×822. The raw images are saved using 16 bits per pixel, thus the 4 most significant bits are set to be zero.

At night, when the pixel intensities are low and the signal-to-noise ratio is reduced, it is important to take measures to reduce the amount of noise affecting the image. Therefore, right before we started to record the sequences corresponding to the '*Tunnel Network*' category, we acquired 100 images with the lens cap closed, and averaged them to obtain the so-called *dark frame*, in which the intensities are generated only by noise. Then, we subtracted the dark frame from the acquired images, in order to reduce the effects of noise in the images.

For convenience, we also provide rectified images with 8-bit pixel depth. Because of the effect of lens distortion and mechanical misalignment, the rectified images are slightly smaller than the raw ones. We also provide the original calibration images and the dark frames; see Section 3.2 for more details. All images are saved in PNG files with loss-less compression. The timestamps corresponding to the images are provided in the file image_timestamps.txt.

3.2   Camera Calibration Data

We used Zhang's technique [19] as implemented in OpenCV [15] to calibrate the cameras, using a symmetrical circle grid pattern, visible to the two cameras. To rectify the images, we used the algorithm proposed by Bouguet, which is also available in OpenCV. Results of the calibration and rectification processes are provided in text files intrinsics_selected.yml and extrinsics_selected.yml. They are compliant with OpenCV's FileStorage format. The provided calibration data is calculated considering that 3D points in the world are expressed in a coordinate system O_w aligned with the rectified left camera coordinate system, but centered in the left camera's center of projection.

The file intrinsics_selected.yml contains $\mathbf{K}_i \in \mathbb{R}^{3\times3}$, the camera calibration matrix (unrectified), and $\mathbf{D}_i \in \mathbb{R}^8$, the distortion coefficients (unrectified).

The file extrinsics_selected.yml includes $\mathbf{R} \in \mathbb{R}^{3\times3}$, the rotation matrix that, before rectification, aligns the right and left cameras coordinate systems; $\mathsf{T} \in \mathbb{R}^3$, the translation vector that, before rectification, brings the origin of the right-camera coordinate system into the left one; $\mathbf{R}_i \in \mathbb{R}^{3\times3}$, the rectifying rotation matrix for the i-th camera; $\mathbf{P}_i \in \mathbb{R}^{3\times4}$, the projection matrix for the i-th camera; $\mathbf{Q} \in \mathbb{R}^{3\times4}$, the reprojection matrix for points in the rectified left camera. It maps an image point and its disparity to a 3D point in O_w.

In both files, we use $i \in \{0,1\}$ where 0 represents the left image and 1 represents the right image. The projection matrices have the form:

$$\mathbf{P}_i = \begin{bmatrix} \alpha & 0 & u_0 & \alpha T_i \\ 0 & \alpha & v_0 & 0 \\ 0 & 0 & 1 & 0 \end{bmatrix} \qquad (1)$$

where α is the focal length in pixels, and T_i is the baseline with respect to the left camera, expressed in the i-th camera frame. They map homogeneous 3D points $\mathbf{X} = \begin{bmatrix} X\ Y\ Z\ 1 \end{bmatrix}^T$ to homogeneous 2D points $\mathbf{x} = \begin{bmatrix} x\ y\ w \end{bmatrix}^T$ through $\mathbf{P}_i\mathbf{X} = \mathbf{x}$. The reprojection matrix $\mathbf{Q}$ has the form:

$$\mathbf{Q} = \begin{bmatrix} 1 & 0 & 0 & -u_0 \\ 0 & 1 & 0 & -v_0 \\ 0 & 0 & 0 & \alpha \\ 0 & 0 & \frac{1}{T} & 0 \end{bmatrix} \qquad (2)$$

and can be used to obtain the 3D coordinates expressed in O_w of an image point $[u, v]$ in the rectified left camera, given its associated disparity d.

Thus, given the coordinates $[u, v]$ of an image point and its disparity d, a homogeneous point $[u, v, d, 1]^T$ can be constructed and mapped to 3 dimensions:

$$\mathbf{Q} \cdot \begin{bmatrix} u \\ v \\ d \\ 1 \end{bmatrix} = \begin{bmatrix} x \\ y \\ z \\ w \end{bmatrix} \qquad (3)$$

The 3D coordinates of the point are then $[\frac{x}{w}, \frac{y}{w}, \frac{z}{w}]$.

Additionally to the image calibration data previously described, we provide for each recording session a ZIP file named calib_imgs_session_i.zip, where i represents the session number, containing all of the calibration images that were taken and an XML file that enlists which of the images were actually used in the calibration and rectification process.

3.3 IMU, GPS, and Car Computer Data

The IMU we used can provide data for acceleration (m/s^2), direction $(degrees)$, rate of turn $(degrees/s)$, and earth magnetic field $(a.u.)$. The IMU data we acquired is provided in the text file IMU_data.csv. The data is stored in a tabular format, where each row corresponds to an IMU reading and the individual fields are separated by commas. Initially we acquired data from the IMU at 50 Hz and acquired only acceleration and direction data. Later improvements of the software allowed us to increase the acquisition rate to 100 Hz, and to include also the rate of turn and earth magnetic field data. When this data is available, the corresponding fields appear in the IMU data file.

The fields are the following, and are delivered in the order specified: 'Timestamp', 'Roll', 'Pitch', 'Yaw', 'MagX', 'MagY', 'MagZ', 'GyroX', 'GyroY', 'GyroZ','AccX', 'AccY', 'AccZ'. Note that, to estimate the acceleration due to the vehicle motion, the gravity must be subtracted from the readings.

The GPS data was recorded at approximately 1 Hz. It is provided in the CSV file gps_data.csv. The provided fields are 'Timestamp', 'Latitude' and 'Longitude'. We also provide the GPS data in GPX format in the file gps_data.txt to allow a review of the data in a compatible application such as Google Earth.

The data acquired from the car computer is provided in the file car_data.csv which shares the basic format with the IMU and GPS data files. The car data was recorded with an approximate frequency of 3 Hz. The provided fields are the following: 'Timestamp', 'Speed' and 'RPM'. The speed units are km/h.

4 Experiments

Many stereo pairs from our recorded dataset offer challenges that are not easily handled by current stereo matching algorithms. Lens flares, reflections, motion blur, and projective distortion resulting from a wide baseline, are some of the challenges that can be found in the acquired images. We evaluated the performance of several stereo matchers on our real-world imagery, and the results of the performed evaluation are presented in this section.

Fig. 3. Selected pairs. The figure shows 8 stereo pairs selected for the evaluation discussion (of stereo matchers) in this paper.

4.1 Disparity Map Generation

For illustrating the discussion of performance of stereo matching algorithms, we present 8 representative stereo pairs from our dataset in Fig. 3. We selected those pairs because they feature different challenges that can potentially show a particular weaknesses of a stereo matching algorithm. We also provide a brief description of those stereo pairs:

- *"Big avenue"* (Fig. 3-a): A big avenue with a relatively untextured road surface, which complicates the matching process. The lane markers are not clearly visible in some regions, and the roadwork ahead is poorly signaled.
- *"Street with potholes 1"* (Fig. 3-b): Urban street with a very poor road surface. Many potholes appear, and are filled with water from a recent downpour. The reflections on the water may affect the matching process.
- *"Pocitos street"* (Fig. 3-c): Urban scene with shadows from a building. The road slope magnifies the distortion caused by the horizontal displacement of the cameras. Also, some pixels (road and sidewalk) are saturated.
- *"Lens flare 1"* (Fig. 3-d): Scene affected by lens flare. This results in a violation of the intensity constancy assumption (ICA) for corresponding pixels; see also [11] for ICA.

- *"Tunnel crossing"* (Fig. 3-e): Crossing in a tunnel network. Low-light conditions and reflections caused by water on the road are particularly challenging.
- *"Street with potholes 2"* (Fig. 3-f): Another urban street with deplorable road surface. The road looks relatively untextured, and there is a speed bumper which in some places is difficult to distinguish from the road surface.
- *"Lens flare 2"* (Fig. 3-g): Lens flare affecting the scene. The left frame is more affected than the right frame, violating the ICA. Because of the bending of the road, the number of occluded pixels is significant.
- *"Columns in tunnel"* (Fig. 3-h): Tunnel network scene. It is affected by low-light conditions, and by motion-blur, caused by the increased exposure time.

Selected Stereo Matching Algorithms. We evaluated five algorithms, namely *block matching, semi-global matching, belief propagation matching, graph cut matching*, and the ELAS stereo matching approach [8].

In the case of block-matching (BM), we used its OpenCV implementation [13,15]. A post-filtering stage is performed on the obtained disparity map where a left-right consistency check is performed, and non-confident disparities are removed. Also, a *"speckle"* filter is optionally run over the disparity map to remove small patches of disparity values inconsistent with its surroundings.

For semi-global matching, we also used the OpenCV implementation, based on [10], with several differences: The used data cost is the Birchfield-Tomasi (BT) measure [2] instead of the mutual information measure. The data cost is aggregated in a window, and not pixel-wise as in the original paper. This is why the algorithm is called *Semi-Global Block Matching* (SGBM). The number of directions used is normally 5, but can be increased to 8 (instead of 16 as in [10]).

For belief propagation (BP), we used the implementation from [4]. They use a scaled and truncated version of the absolute difference (AD) data cost, which does not perform well in practice. We included the sum of absolute differences (SAD), its zero-mean version ($ZSAD$) and the *census*(CEN) data costs, but only obtained good results when using ZSAD and CEN. See [11] for definitions. The smoothness term is a linear truncated cost. For both cost functions, we used 7 iterations and 7 scale levels.

In the case of graph cut (GC), we used the authors implementation of [12]. The original data cost is BT, extended to include also the vertical direction. In our tests, this data cost did not perform well, even when aggregated on a window, so we adapted the SAD, $ZSAD$ and CEN data costs. In practice, we obtained good results only with the CEN data cost. Referring to the original paper, if $a_1 = \langle \mathbf{p}, \mathbf{q} \rangle$ and $a_2 = \langle \mathbf{r}, \mathbf{s} \rangle$, the penalty V_{a_1, a_2} is defined as follows:

$$V_{a_1, a_2} = \begin{cases} 3\lambda & \text{if } \max(|I(\mathbf{p}) - I(\mathbf{r})|, |I(\mathbf{q}) - I(\mathbf{s})|) < 5 \\ \lambda & \text{otherwise} \end{cases} \tag{4}$$

where $I(\mathbf{p})$ is the intensity at pixel $\mathbf{p}$. The occlusion penalty is defined as 10λ, so that all the penalties are expressed in terms of only λ. Our best results were obtained using $\lambda = 3$, 7×7 windows, and $t = 6$ iterations. No significant improvement on the quality of the disparity maps was noticeable using more iterations.

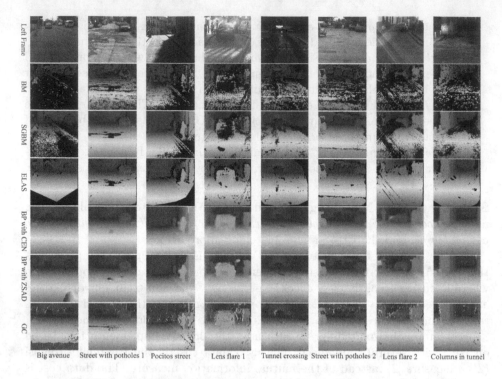

Fig. 4. Disparity maps obtained for the 8 selected pairs

Pixels that end up labeled as being occluded, are filled with the disparity from the left-closest non-occluded pixel along the same epipolar line.

In the case of ELAS, we used the authors implementation, with the parameter set `ROBOTICS` as specified by the authors. We modified the original code to generate disparity maps with no scaling.

For all the stereo matchers but ELAS, the maximum disparity d_{max} is set to be 240. ELAS automatically detects the disparity range.

4.2 Qualitative Evaluation

Even though we have no disparity ground-truth, we can offer an analysis of the perceived quality of the disparity maps (d-maps). Attributes such as density, presence of noise, coherence with scene information, smoothness, object border definition have been considered here. The obtained d-maps are shown in Fig. 4.

D-maps are shown with a color code for better visualization. Red is for to the closest objects and violet is for objects far away. Pixels in black have unassigned disparities, because either the left-right consistency check failed, or the confidence on the assigned disparity was not high enough.

The BM algorithm produced sparser d-maps than the others, because it failed to find disparity values for low-textured regions, where image information alone is not enough to find a reliable disparity; see for example the BM d-map for

"*Big avenue*" and to a less extent the d-map for "*Columns in tunnel*". The lack of smoothness constraints penalizes the performance of the algorithm.

The SGBM results are a clear improvement over the observed performance of BM. This is obvious while comparing the d-maps for "*Big avenue*" and "*Street with potholes 2*" obtained with BM and SGBM. Although SGBM also fails to determine disparities with high confidence on some low-textured regions, the d-maps it delivers are denser and would allow a better scene understanding. As we show in 4.3, SGBM is by far the fastest among global/semi-global matchers.

The d-maps obtained by ELAS are slightly denser than with SGBM. Also, they look "edgy", because of the underlying triangulation. In some pairs it failed to determine the disparities in the closest regions, see for example "*Big avenue*" and "*Pocitos street*". The algorithm performs poorly, as for the previous two, in absence of texture. In some cases, such as in the far road section of "*Columns in tunnel*", it manages to estimate the disparity, when BM and SGBM fail.

BP gave the highest quality d-maps, especially using the *CEN* data cost. Even with missing texture, it found dense, coherent disparity estimates, even though no post-filtering step, like speckle filtering, was done. The object boundaries look a bit over-smoothed in some pairs. Comparing the *ZSAD* and *CEN* data costs, the d-maps with *CEN* are of better quality than the ones with *ZSAD*. For example, for "*Big avenue*", an artifact in the road surface can be seen in the BP d-map obtained with *ZSAD* that is not present in the one obtained using *CEN*.

GC in general obtained d-maps with good quality, even with missing texture. However, in contrast to BP, smooth changes in depth, such as on the road surface, sometimes do not translate into smooth changes in disparity, see for example "*Tunnel crossing*'. Also, the d-maps obtained with GC are affected by noise, and several small patches of miscalculated disparities can be seen. The GC approach failed to assign correct disparities to the closest region in "*Big avenue*".

Among the challenges present in the selected pairs, the reflections of water on the road were the ones that especially caused issues for all the correspondence algorithms. BP with *CEN* data cost was the best in this situation; see the d-maps corresponding to "*Street with potholes 1*" and "*Tunnel crossing*". Surprisingly, GC and especially BP could deal with the artifacts introduced by lens flares, as in "*Lens flare 1*" and "*Lens flare 2*". ELAS also delivered reasonably good results, although artifacts caused by the lens flares can be observed. BM and SGBM struggled more with this condition. Regarding the dark conditions in "*Tunnel crossing*" and "*Columns in tunnel*", BP was the best matcher, followed by GC, although the d-maps obtained with the latter technique are more affected with noise. ELAS was slightly better than SGBM, both offering d-maps with an acceptable density, but in general ELAS dealt better with the low-texture regions.

BP offers the best overall performance, dealing with most of the presented challenges and delivering the d-maps with the highest quality, ahead of GC. However, both may be affected by noise and by the lack of smoothness. ELAS and SGBM offer similar performances, with far from perfect d-maps, but useful enough to allow basic scene understanding. Their performance is low in regions with scarce image texture and cannot handle easily the most difficult challenges. Finally, the d-maps from BM are the ones with the lowest quality. This was expected because of the simplicity of the algorithm. However, in most cases, the d- maps are still offering valuable information about the general scene geometry.

4.3   Runtime Comparison

To compare the runtime of the selected stereo matchers, we calculated 30 d-maps, including the 8 input pairs discussed above, on a mobile workstation running Linux Mint 64 Bit, equipped with a Core i7 processor running at 2.20 Ghz and 8 GB of RAM. We used the frames at full resolution. The BM and SGBM implementations use the SSE2 instruction set, and ELAS exploits the SSE3 instruction set. The BP and GC implementations do not exploit any performance-enhancing library.

Table 1. Average run times of the selected algorithms

	BM	SGBM	ELAS	BP-ZSAD	BP-CEN	GC
Run time (s)	0.11	1.29	0.43	40.91	43.51	2118.14

For autonomous driving, it is important to update several times a second the environment representation, to navigate safely. A comparison of the mean run-time of each algorithm is presented in Table 1. Among the used implementations, only BM allows a reasonable update time, with 100 ms on average. Furthermore, it is highly parallelizable and can be implemented very efficiently in parallel hardware. The runtimes of ELAS and SGBM are within the same order of magnitude, with average run-times around 0.5 and 1 s respectively, and could be used in autonomous driving after some algorithmic improvement or adaptation to specialized hardware, such as FPGAs or GPUs. Actually, for SGBM, several real-time implementations have already been developed, e.g. [6]. The execution times for BP, and specially GC, exceeding more than half an hour, are orders of magnitude above the desired runtime, so it will require more work before they can be used in real-time applications. In the case of BP, there are some results [18], where GPUs allow close to real-time performance on low-resolution imagery. Finally, we observed a memory usage of more than 4 GB for BP, which is a lot, especially considering that in autonomous driving the hardware platforms should be low-power embedded systems, with restricted memory.

5   Conclusions

We presented in this paper a novel dataset that shows a wide variety of challenging scenarios for autonomous driving that can be found on the roads of developing countries. We release it online for further improvements of stereo-matchers for *robust* environment perception and scene understanding, used in autonomous vehicles. The dataset may help to bring the technology also closer to everyday use in both developing and developed countries. In the future, we plan to include 2D annotations to objects of interest presented in the recorded scenes, and to provide software utilities to make it easier to work with the data. The dataset can be found at camaron.cimat.mx/Personal/jbhayet/ccsad-dataset.

References

1. Auckland U. of Technology: The.enpeda. Image Sequence Analysis Test Site (EISATS). www.cerv.aut.ac.nz/EISATS
2. Birchfield, S., Tomasi, C.: A pixel dissimilarity measure that is insensitive to image sampling. IEEE Trans. Pattern Anal. Mach. Intell. **20**, 401–406 (1998)
3. Daimler A.G.: Ground truth stixel dataset. www.6d-vision.com/ground-truth-stixel-dataset
4. Felzenszwalb, P., Huttenlocher, D.: Efficient belief propagation for early vision. Int. J. Comput. Vision **70**, 41–54 (2006)
5. Fontana, G., Matteucci, M., Sorrenti, D.: Methods and experimental techniques in computer engineering, chap. 4, pp. 55–68. Springer Briefs in Applied Sciences and Technology, Springer (2014)
6. Gehrig, S., Rabe, C.: Real-time semi-global matching on the CPU. In: Proc. ICVPR Workshops, pp. 85–92 (2010)
7. Geiger, A., Lenz, P., Stiller, C., Urtasun, R.: Vision meets robotics: The KITTI dataset. Int. J. Robotics Research (2013)
8. Geiger, A., Roser, M., Urtasun, R.: Efficient large-scale stereo matching. In: Kimmel, R., Klette, R., Sugimoto, A. (eds.) ACCV 2010, Part I. LNCS, vol. 6492, pp. 25–38. Springer, Heidelberg (2011)
9. Heidelberg Collaboratory for Image Processing: Robust vision challenge. www.hci.iwr.uniheidelberg.de/Static/challenge2012/
10. Hirschmüller, H.: Stereo processing by semiglobal matching and mutual information. IEEE Trans. Pattern Anal. Mach. Intell. **30**, 328–341 (2008)
11. Klette, R.: Concise Computer Vision. Springer, London (2014)
12. Kolmogorov, V., Zabih, R.: Computing visual correspondence with occlusions using graph cuts. In: Proc. ICCV, pp. 508–515 (2001)
13. Konolige, K.: Small vision system: hardware and implementation. In: Proc. ISRR, pp. 111–116 (1997)
14. Ladicky, L., Sturgess, P., Russell, C., Sengupta, S., Bastanlar, Y., Clocksin, W.F., Torr, P.H.S.: Joint optimization for object class segmentation and dense stereo reconstruction. Int. J. Computer Vision **100**, 122–133 (2012)
15. OpenCV: Open Source Computer Vision Library. www.opencv.org
16. Pomerleau, D., Jochem, T.: Rapidly adapting machine vision for automated vehicle steering. IEEE Expert: Intelligent Systems Their Applications **11**, 19–27 (1996)
17. U. of Parma: Public ROad Urban Driverless-Car Test 2013. www.vislab.it/proud-en/
18. Xiang, X., Zhang, M., Li, G., He, Y., Pan, Z.: Real-time stereo matching based on fast belief propagation. Machine Vision Applications **23**, 1219–1227 (2012)
19. Zhang, Z.: A flexible new technique for camera calibration. IEEE Trans. Pattern Anal. Mach. Intell. **22**, 1330–1334 (2000)

Discriminative Local Binary Pattern
for Image Feature Extraction

Takumi Kobayashi[✉]

National Institute of Advanced Industrial Science and Technology,
1-1-1 Umezono, Tsukuba, Japan
takumi.kobayashi@aist.go.jp

Abstract. Local binary pattern (LBP) is widely used to extract image features in various visual recognition tasks. LBP is formulated in quite a simple form and thus enables us to extract effective image features with a low computational cost. There, however, are some limitations mainly regarding sensitivity to noise and loss of image contrast information. In this paper, we propose a novel LBP-based image feature to remedy those drawbacks without degrading the simplicity of the original LBP formulation. Encoding local pixel intensities into binary patterns can be regarded as separating them into two modes (clusters). We introduce Fisher discriminant criterion to optimize the LBP coding for exploiting binary patterns stably and discriminatively with robustness to noise. Besides, image contrast information is incorporated in a unified way by leveraging the discriminant score as a weight on the corresponding binary pattern; thereby, the prominent patterns are emphasized. In the experiments on pedestrian detection, the proposed method exhibits superior performance compared to the ordinary LBP and the other methods, especially in the case of lower-dimensional features.

Keywords: Visual recognition · Image feature · Local binary pattern · Discriminant criterion

1 Introduction

In visual recognition, it is a fundamental procedure to extract features from images, which is followed by classification. While various types of image feature have been proposed so far [3,11,21,24], local binary pattern (LBP) [15,20] is one of the commonly used features due to its simple formulation and high performance. The LBP method has been mainly applied to measure texture characteristics [6,7,15–17], and in recent years it is shown to be favorably applicable to various kinds of visual recognition tasks besides texture classification, such as face recognition [1,22], face detection [8], pedestrian detection [24] and sound classification [10].

The LBP method encodes local pixel intensities into binary patterns on the basis of the center pixel intensity in the local region. There are some limitations in LBP, mainly regarding sensitivity to noise and loss of local textual information, *i.e.*, image contrast. In the last two decades, considerable research effort has been

© Springer International Publishing Switzerland 2015
G. Azzopardi and N. Petkov (Eds.): CAIP 2015, Part I, LNCS 9256, pp. 594–605, 2015.
DOI: 10.1007/978-3-319-23192-1_50

made to address those drawbacks of LBP leading to variants of LBP. In [17], the image contrast information is separately extracted by computing variance of local pixel intensities and joint distribution of the contrast feature and LBP is employed. The contrast information, local variance, is also naturally incorporated into LBP formulation via weighting binary patterns in [6]. LBP can be combined with HOG features [3] to compensate such information loss [24]. The robustness to noise is improved by developing binary patterns to ternary patterns [22] which are further extended to quinary ones [14], though the number of patterns corresponding to the feature dimensionality is significantly increased. It is also possible to build noise-robust LBP by simply considering local statistics, mean [8] or median [7], as a threshold instead of the center pixel intensity in coding. To further improve robustness, we have recently extended LBP to fully incorporate statistical information, mean and variance, in the processes both of coding and weighting. For more elaborated review of LBP, refer to [20].

In this paper, we propose a novel method to extract LBP-based image features with retaining simplicity of the original LBP formulation as well as remedying the limitations of LBP. We first generalize the LBP formulation by focusing on the two fundamental processes of coding and weighting, and then along the line of [6–8,10], propose *discriminative LBP* by providing a discriminative approach to determine those two fundamentals. In the discriminative approach, LBP coding is regarded as separating local pixel intensity distribution into two modes (clusters) and from that viewpoint, a threshold is optimized by maximizing the Fisher discriminant score which is further utilized in weighting. Thereby, the discriminative LBP stably encodes the local pixel intensities into binary patterns via the optimization with high robustness to noise, also incorporating image contrast information in a unified manner. Due to simplicity as in the ordinary LBP, the proposed method can be easily integrated with the sophisticated extension which has been applied to LBP, such as uniform pattern [16] and combination with the other image features [24].

2   Discriminative Local Binary Pattern

In this section, we detail the proposed method, called *discriminative LBP*. We first give a general formulation for extracting local binary patterns (LBP) [15] with review of the LBP variants based on that formulation. Then, the discriminative perspective is introduced into the processes of coding and weighting which are fundamental in the general formulation.

2.1   General Formulation for LBP

Let $r = (x, y)$ be a spatial position in a two-dimensional image I and $I(r)$ indicates the pixel intensity at that position. In LBP [15], local pixel intensities are focused on and encoded by binarizing individual pixel intensities as follows;

$$\texttt{code}(\mathcal{L}_c; \tau_c) = \sum_{j=1}^{N} 2^{j-1} \llbracket I(r_i) > \tau_c \rrbracket \quad \in \{0, \cdots, 2^N - 1\}, \qquad (1)$$

Table 1. Comparison in variants of LBP

method	τ	w
ordinary LBP [20]	$I(c)$	1
median LBP (MBP) [7]	$\mathtt{median}(I)$	1
improved LBP [8]	μ	1
LBP variance [6]	$I(c)$	σ^2
statistics-based LBP [10]	μ	σ
discriminative LBP (proposed)	$\arg\max \sigma_B$	$\sqrt{\frac{\max \sigma_B^2}{\sigma^2 + C}}$

where $[\![\cdot]\!]$ indicates the Iverson bracket that equals to 1 if the condition in the brackets is satisfied and 0 otherwise. $\mathcal{L}_c = \{r_i\}_{i=1}^N$ denotes a local pixel configuration centered at $c \in \mathbb{R}^2$, comprising N spatial positions r_i close to c. For example, the simplest and widely used configuration consists of $N = 8$ surrounding pixels in a 3×3 local patch and it is further extended in a multi-scale setting [17]. Though the number of codes (binary patterns) is exponentially increased according to N, it is also possible to suppress the pattern variation by considering uniform patterns [16]. As shown in (1), the local image pattern on $\mathcal{L}_c$ is encoded into a N-bit code by means of binarization of pixel intensities with a threshold τ_c. Finally, LBP codes computed by (1) are aggregated to LBP features $x \in \mathbb{R}^{2^N}$ over a region of interest $\mathbb{D}$,

$$x_i = \sum_{c \in \mathbb{D}} w_c [\![\mathtt{code}(\mathcal{L}_c; \tau_c) = i - 1]\!], \quad i \in \{1, \cdots, 2^N\}, \tag{2}$$

where w_c is a voting weight which indicates significance of the local binary pattern.

LBP variants can be placed in this general formulation as shown in Table 1. As to coding, an ordinary LBP [20] is established by setting $\tau = I(c)$ and in [7,8] it is modified by local statistics, $\tau = \mu = \frac{1}{N}\sum_i I(r_i)$ and $\tau = \mathtt{median}_i[I(r_i)]$, respectively. On the other hand, the local variance, $\sigma^2 = \frac{1}{N}\sum_i(I(r_i) - \mu)^2$, which is separately employed as local image contrast in [17], is incorporated as the weight w in [6], and very recently, we have proposed statistics-based LBP [10] by effectively applying those simple statistics to both coding and weighting as $\tau = \mu$ and $w = \sigma$; it should be noted that most methods simply employ *hard* voting weights, *i.e.*, $w = 1$. Thus, we can say that the LBP method generally contains two essential parameters τ and w to be designed a priori for extracting effective image features.

2.2 Discriminative Coding

We propose a novel coding method which optimizes the threshold τ and the voting weight w in (1, 2) based on a discriminative criterion.

The LBP coding (1) can be viewed as approximating local pixel intensity distribution in $\mathcal{L}_c$ by two modes separated by the threshold τ. In a least squares sense, which also means to fit Gaussian models from a probabilistic viewpoint, we can measure *quality* of the code by the following residual error,

$$\epsilon(\tau) = \frac{1}{N} \left\{ \sum_{i|I(r_i) \leq \tau} (I(r_i) - \mu_0)^2 + \sum_{i|I(r_i) > \tau} (I(r_i) - \mu_1)^2 \right\}, \tag{3}$$

where $\quad \mu_0 = \dfrac{1}{N_0} \sum_{i|I(r_i) \leq \tau} I(r_i), \quad N_0 = \sum_i [\![I(r_i) \leq \tau]\!], \tag{4}$

$$\mu_1 = \frac{1}{N_1} \sum_{i|I(r_i) > \tau} I(r_i), \quad N_1 = \sum_i [\![I(r_i) > \tau]\!]. \tag{5}$$

Here, we represent two modes with the mean μ_0 and μ_1, respectively. The residual error ϵ corresponds to within-class variance σ_W^2 for the classes which are partitioned by the threshold τ. Minimizing ϵ coincides with maximization of Fisher discriminant score [4], actually maximization of between-class variance σ_B^2;

$$\sigma_B^2(\tau) = \frac{N_0}{N}(\mu_0 - \mu)^2 + \frac{N_1}{N}(\mu_1 - \mu)^2 = \frac{N_0 N_1}{N^2}(\mu_1 - \mu_0)^2. \tag{6}$$

Thus, the threshold τ is optimized by

$$\gamma^* = \arg \max_{\tau \in \{I(r_i)\}_{i=1}^N} \sigma_B^2(\tau). \tag{7}$$

Thereby, the proposed discriminative coding with γ^* reduces the error (ϵ) in assigning binary codes (1) as well as enhances the discriminativity (σ_B) between two modes partitioned by γ^*. This procedure is performed in the same way as Otsu's auto-thresholding method [18] applied to pixel intensities $\{I(r_i)\}_{i=1}^N$.

Next, we can accordingly determine the voting weight w as the (square root of) discriminant score;

$$w = \sqrt{\frac{\sigma_B^2(\gamma^*)}{\sigma^2 + C}}, \tag{8}$$

where C is a small constant to avoid numerical instability for smaller σ, especially in the case that local pixel intensities are close to uniform; in this study, we set $C = 0.01^2$ for pixel intensity scale $[0, 1]$. This weight reflects how far the two modes are separated by γ^* and therefore is considered to measure significance of the corresponding binary pattern.

The proposed coding is built on the optimization (7), while the other methods employ hard coding [7,8,15] and soft coding with simple statistics [6,10]. The computational cost for the optimization is negligible due to a small number of pixels N to be focused on in $\mathcal{L}_c$; a brute-force approach optimizes (7) with computational complexity $O(N^2)$, but N is empirically quite small, *e.g.*, $N = 8$ or 9 in most cases.

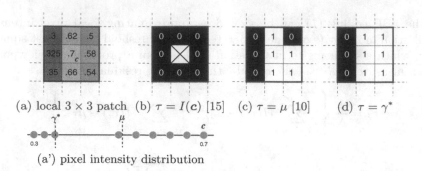

(a) local 3×3 patch (b) $\tau = I(c)$ [15] (c) $\tau = \mu$ [10] (d) $\tau = \gamma^*$

(a') pixel intensity distribution

Fig. 1. Examples of LBP codes by various thresholds. A local patch (a) of pixel intensity distribution (a') is encoded into binary codes by ordinary LBP $\tau = I(c)$ [15] (b), statistics-based LBP $\tau = \mu$ [10] (c) and the proposed method $\tau = \gamma^*$ (d). In (c, d), $\mathcal{L}_c$ includes the center pixel c. The proposed method produces a stable code with a large margin which is hardly affected by noise.

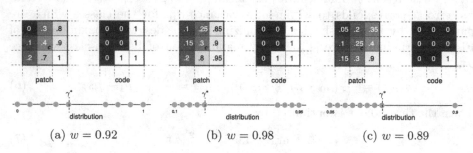

(a) $w = 0.92$ (b) $w = 0.98$ (c) $w = 0.89$

Fig. 2. Examples of weights in the proposed method. In each figure, the input local patch, its pixel intensity distribution and the resultant binary pattern (code) are shown in top-left, bottom and top-right, respectively. Details are in the text.

2.3   Characteristics of Discriminative Coding

The ordinary LBP [15] of $\tau = I(c)$ and $w = 1$ always assigns a local image pattern with one of the LBP codes, no matter how the image pattern is less significant, such as being close to uniform. The LBP coding takes into account only magnitude relationships between the pixel intensities of neighborhoods and that of a center pixel, $I(c)$, in disregard of the margin. Thus, even a small fluctuation on the pixels whose intensities are close to $I(c)$ easily degenerates the LBP code by breaking up the magnitude relationships, which results in totally different features. In other words, the binary codes on the pixel intensities of a small margin from $I(c)$ are vulnerable to noise, causing unstable LBP features.

On the other hand, the proposed coding (Section 2.2) extracts a discriminative structure of a local pixel intensity distribution, exhibiting high robustness to noise. In the structure, two modes endowed by the threshold γ^* are discriminatively separated with a statistically large margin due to maximizing Fisher discriminant score in (7), which exhibits stable patterns as shown in Figure 1.

Besides, for weighting, the significance of the local pattern is effectively measured by Fisher discriminant score (8) as shown in Figure 2. Even for the similar image patches resulting in the same code, the patch of sharply separated pixel intensities gets the larger weight than that of blurred intensities (Figure 2ab). On the other hand, smaller weight is assigned to the patch of which distribution is highly biased (Figure 2c), even though it is sharply separated. Such a biased distribution can be regarded as a noisy pattern containing a outlier and thus it is favorable that such code contributes less to the feature.

It should be noted that the proposed LBP is invariant to affine transformation of pixel intensities, $aI(r) + b$, in terms of coding and weighting as in the ordinary LBP, while the statistics-based LBP [10] is affected by scaling a in the weight $w = \sigma$.

The proposed method effectively extracts the geometrical characteristics in an image, various patterns of gradients and curvatures which are considered to be fundamental local geometries for describing an image structure. Those essential characteristics are represented by the local binary patterns which reflect discriminative structures of the pixel intensity distributions with high robustness to noise. Through weighting by Fisher discriminant scores, the patches of less texture are ignored, contributing less to the feature, while distinctive ones, such as around object edges, are highly focused on by large weights.

3   Techniques for Image Feature

We mention some practically useful techniques for extracting effective image features [24].

Normalization. The discriminative LBP produces features in a histogram form which is regarded as a discrete probability distribution over the LBP codes. The Hellinger (Bhattacharya) kernel can be effectively applied to measure the similarity between those probability distributions [2], and it is possible to embed the kernel in a (linear) dot product of the feature vectors by normalizing the features in the following form [19]; $\hat{x} = \sqrt{\frac{x}{\|x\|_1}}$. This normalization enhances the discriminative power of features by enhancing difference on smaller feature values while suppressing it on larger values via the square root function.

Cell-Structured Feature. In the case of object classification, it is demanded to extract features related to *parts* which compose the target objects. Those part-based features are naively extracted by partitioning the object image into subregions, called *cells*, on which the features are computed [3,11]. The final feature is built by simply concatenating all cell-wise features. Note that in this study, the above-mentioned normalization is applied to respective cell-wise feature vectors before concatenation.

Binary Pattern Reduction. The dimensionality of the LBP-based feature is exponentially increased according to the number of pixels N in the local patch $\mathcal{L}_c$. If one wants to reduce the feature dimensionality such as due to memory limitation, binary patterns can be reduced by considering *uniform patterns* [16]. Uniform patterns are constructed by allowing only a few times 0/1 transitions on the neighborhood pixels surrounding the center c; 256-dimensional features of $N = 8$ are reduced to 58-dimensional ones by uniform patterns allowing only two times 0/1 transitions and 512-dimensional features of $N = 9$ including the center become 114-dimensional ones as well[1].

4   Experimental Results

We apply the proposed method to pedestrian detection tasks using the Daimler Chrysler pedestrian benchmark dataset [13] for evaluating the performance from various aspects and INRIA person dataset [3].

In feature extraction, the local patch $\mathcal{L}_c$ is restricted within 3×3 pixels since the larger patch degrades performance as reported in [24], and we apply L_2-Hellinger normalization to LBP-based feature vectors.

4.1   Performance Analysis on Daimler Chrysler Dataset

The Daimler Chrysler pedestrian dataset is composed of five disjoint sets, three for training and two for test. Each set has 4,800 pedestrian and 5,000 pedestrian-free images of 18×36 pixels. For constructing cell-structured features, we consider cells of 6×6 pixels, producing 3×6 cells over an image. We follow the standard evaluation protocol on this dataset, in which the linear classifier is trained on two out of three training sets by using liblinear [5] and is tested on each of the test sets, producing six evaluation results. We measure the average of accuracies at equal error rate across the six results.

In the following, we analyze in detail the proposed method in terms of coding by τ, weighting with w and feature dimensionality controlled by a local patch $\mathcal{L}_c$ and pattern reduction (Section 3). Performance results in various settings are shown in Table 2.

Coding and Weighting. Compared to the ordinary LBP (the first row in Table 2), the proposed method (the last row) significantly improves the performance with and without uniform patterns (Table 2ab). Under the condition of the same feature dimensionality, the method is still largely superior to ordinary LBP as shown in lines 1 and 5 of Table 2, though only weighting and coding are modified to discriminative ones (Section 2.2). In addition, our method outperforms the statistics-based LBP [10] in all feature dimensionalities; see lines 3, 5, 7 and 9 in Table 2. We further set the weighting as $w = 1$ in both statistics-based

---

[1] 58 patterns for $N = 8$ consist of 1 flat pattern for zero 0/1 transition, 56 moderate patterns for less than or equal to twice transitions and 1 messy pattern for greater than twice transitions. In $N = 9$, we consider 1 flat and 1 messy patterns no matter what the center pixel is, and $112 = 56 \times 2$ moderate patterns according to the center pixel state.

Table 2. Performance analysis on Daimler Chrysler dataset for various settings in LBP formulation. The local patch $\mathcal{L}_c$ of $N = 8$ excludes the center pixel. The number of dimensionality of cell-wise features is shown in the column of 'Dim.'. The performances of the proposed method are underlined.

	(a) Full binary pattern					(b) Uniform pattern			
	$\mathcal{L}_c$	τ	w	Dim.	Acc. (%)	$\mathcal{L}_c$	τ	w	Dim.	Acc. (%)
1.	$N=8$	$I(c)$	1	256	92.29	$N=8$ $I(c)$		1	58	91.32
2.	$N=8$	μ	1	256	94.04	$N=8$ μ		1	58	93.42
3.	$N=8$	μ	σ	256	94.32	$N=8$ μ		σ	58	93.64
4.	$N=8$	γ^*	1	256	95.02	$N=8$ γ^*		1	58	94.71
5.	$N=8$	γ^*	$\sqrt{\frac{\sigma_B^2}{\sigma^2+C}}$	256	$\underline{95.11}$	$N=8$ γ^*		$\sqrt{\frac{\sigma_B^2}{\sigma^2+C}}$	58	$\underline{94.77}$
6.	$N=9$	μ	1	512	94.62	$N=9$ μ		1	114	94.23
7.	$N=9$	μ	σ	512	94.87	$N=9$ μ		σ	114	94.40
8.	$N=9$	γ^*	1	512	95.12	$N=9$ γ^*		1	114	94.93
9.	$N=9$	γ^*	$\sqrt{\frac{\sigma_B^2}{\sigma^2+C}}$	512	$\underline{95.25}$	$N=9$ γ^*		$\sqrt{\frac{\sigma_B^2}{\sigma^2+C}}$	114	$\underline{95.16}$

LBP and our method in order to give light on the effectiveness of the discriminative coding with threshold γ^*. A threshold in coding is crucial to encode the local pixel intensities into a binary pattern, while weighting works just for assigning significance to those patterns. Comparing the methods of $w = 1$, thresholds μ and γ^* are superior to the ordinary threshold $I(c)$ and in particular, our discriminative threshold γ^* significantly outperforms both of μ and $I(c)$. Thus, it is confirmed that the proposed method which discriminatively optimizes the threshold can effectively work in constructing local binary patterns for image features. By incorporating discriminative weights, the performance is further improved as shown in lines 4-5 and 8-9.

Dimensionality. By controlling a local patch $\mathcal{L}_c$ and applying the uniform pattern (Section 3), the feature dimensionality is halved, accordingly causing a little performance degeneration; compare (a) with (b), and lines 2-5 with 6-9 in Table 2. Note that in the case that a local patch $\mathcal{L}_c$ is of $N = 8$, the proposed and statistics-based methods do not take into account the center pixel intensity $I(c)$ at all in coding and weighting. Figure 3 graphically summarizes the performance results from the viewpoint of the feature dimensionalities. The performance gain achieved by the proposed method is larger in the lower dimensional features. This is because the discriminative power per feature element (binary pattern) is higher in the proposed method due to the discriminative coding and thus even lower dimensional features work well in classification. Thus, we can say that the proposed method is effective especially for lower dimensional LBP features

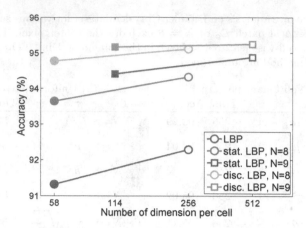

Fig. 3. Performance analysis on the Daimler Chrysler dataset in terms of feature dimensionality. Empty and filled markers indicate the performances of full binary patterns and uniform patterns, respectively. The horizontal axis shows dimensionality in log scale. This figure is best viewed in color.

Table 3. Performance comparison to the other methods.

Method	Ours, $N=9$, full	Ours, $N=9$, uniform	HOG [3]	[12]	[23]	[9]
Acc. (%)	**95.25**	**95.16**	86.41	89.25	91.10	94.32

such as by applying the uniform pattern, which is practically useful by saving memory usage for features. Based on the trade-off between performance and dimensionality, we recommend to apply the proposed method with the uniform pattern and $N = 9$ local patch including the center pixel.

Comparison to the Other Methods. The proposed method is compared to the other methods than LBP; HOG [3], additive kernel based feature maps [12, 23] and higher-order co-occurrence [9]. Although our method is quite simple, the performance is superior to those methods; note that even the method of $N = 9$ with the uniform pattern outperforms those state-of-the-arts.

4.2 INRIA Person Dataset

Next, the proposed method is tested on the INRIA person dataset [3]. It contains 2,416 person annotations and 1,218 person-free images for training, and 1,132 person annotations and 453 person-free images for test; the person annotations (bounding boxes) are scaled into a fixed size of 64 × 128 pixels. Cell-structured features are computed on cells of 8 × 8 or 16 × 16 pixels, producing 8 × 16 or 4 × 8 cells on a detection window of 64 × 128 pixels. In each cell, LBP-based features with *uniform patterns* of $N = 9$ are extracted to reduce the feature dimensionality. The performance is shown in Figure 4 where for quantifying and

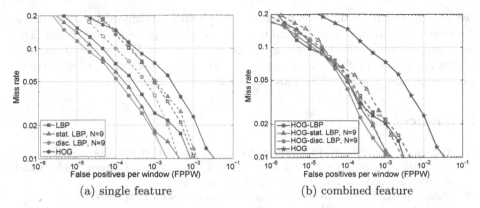

(a) single feature   (b) combined feature

Fig. 4. Performance comparison on the INRIA dataset. The solid lines show the performance of LBP-based features with cells of 8 × 8 pixels while the dashed lines are for cells of 16 × 16 pixels. Note that the uniform patterns are applied to LBP-based features. The performance of single type of feature is shown in (a), while that of combined features with HOG is in (b). The ordinary HOG-LBP method [24] is denoted by HOG-LBP.

comparing methods, we plotted detection error trade-off curves by calculating miss rate and false positive rate per detection window.

As shown in Figure 4a, the proposed method outperforms LBP-related methods [10,15] and HOG [3] in both cases of 8 × 8 and 16 × 16 px cells. Note that the method with cells of 16 × 16 pixels produces 3648-dimensional feature vector which is close to HOG dimensionality (3780 dimension). The larger cell of 16 × 16 pixels contains a substantial number of pixels, *i.e.*, LBP codes, to construct features, which statistically contributes to increase robustness of noise-sensitive LBP features; the LBP method becomes even comparable to the statistics-based LBP method [10] as shown in Figure 4a (comparing dashed lines for 16 × 16 px cells with solid ones for 8 × 8 px cells). In contrast, the proposed method is superior to the LBP method in any cases due to discriminative coding.

Finally, the LBP-based features are combined with HOG as proposed in [24]; Figure 4b shows the performance results. The performance is improved by the combination and the proposed method again outperforms the ordinary HOG-LBP [24].

5 Conclusion

In this paper, we have proposed a novel LBP-based method to extract effective image features. We generalize the LBP formulation by focusing on the two fundamental processes of coding and weighting, and the proposed method provides a discriminative approach to determine those two fundamentals. In the discriminative approach, LBP coding which actually binarizes pixel intensities by a threshold is regarded as separating a local pixel intensity distribution into two modes, and from that viewpoint the threshold is optimized by maximizing the Fisher discriminant score which is subsequently employed in weighting. The experimental results on pedestrian detection show that the proposed method exhibits favorable performance compared to the other methods, and in particular, the method works well for lower-dimensional features.

References

1. Ahonen, T., Hadid, A., Pietikäinen, M.: Face description with local binary patterns: Application to face recognition. IEEE Transaction on Pattern Analysis and Machine Intelligence **28**(12), 2037–2041 (2006)
2. Bishop, C.M.: Pattern Recognition and Machine Learning. Springer (2007)
3. Dalal, N., Triggs, B.: Histograms of oriented gradients for human detection. In: IEEE Conference on Computer Vision and Pattern Recognition, pp. 886–893 (2005)
4. Duda, R.O., Hart, P.E., Stork, D.G.: Pattern Classification, 2 edn. Wiley-Interscience (2001)
5. Fan, R.E., Chang, K.W., Hsieh, C.J., Wang, X.R., Lin, C.J.: Liblinear: A library for large linear classification. Journal of Machine Learning Research **9**, 1871–1874 (2008)
6. Guo, Z., Zhang, L., Zhang, D.: Rotation invariant texture classification using lbp variance (lbpv) with global matching. Pattern Recognition **43**(3), 706–719 (2010)
7. Hafiane, A., Seetharaman, G., Zavidovique, B.: Median binary pattern for textures classification. In: Kamel, M.S., Campilho, A. (eds.) ICIAR 2007. LNCS, vol. 4633, pp. 387–398. Springer, Heidelberg (2007)
8. Jin, H., Liu, Q., Lu, H., Tong, X.: Face detection using improved lbp under bayesian framework. In: International Conference on Image and Graphics, pp. 306–309 (2004)
9. Kobayashi, T.: Khigher-order co-occurrence features based on discriminative co-clusters for image classification. In: British Machine Vision Conference, pp. 64.1-64.11
10. Kobayashi, T., Ye, J.: Acoustic feature extraction by statistics based local binary pattern for environmental sound classification. In: International Conference on Acoustic, Speech and Signal Processing, pp. 3076–3080 (2014)
11. Lowe, D.: Distinctive image features from scale invariant features. International Journal of Computer Vision **60**, 91–110 (2004)
12. Maji, S., Berg, A.: Max-margin additive classifiers for detection. In: International Conference on Computer Vision, pp. 40–47 (2009)
13. Munder, S., Gavrila, D.M.: An experimental study on pedestrian classification. IEEE Transactions on Pattern Analysis and Machine Intelligence **28**(11), 1863–1868 (2006)
14. Nanni, L., Lumini, A., Brahnam, S.: Local binary patterns variants as texture descriptors for medical image analysis. Artificial Intelligence in Medicine **49**(2), 117–125 (2010)
15. Ojala, T., Pietikäinen, M., Harwood, D.: Performance evaluation of texture measures with classification based on kullback discrimination of distributions. In: International Conference on Pattern Recognition, pp. 582–585 (1994)
16. Ojala, T., Pietikäinen, M., Harwood, D.: A comparative study of texture measures with classification based on feature distributions. Pattern Recognition **29**(1), 51–59 (1998)

17. Ojala, T., Pietikäinen, M., Mäenpää, T.: Multiresolution gray-scale and rotation invariant texture classification with local binary patterns. IEEE Transaction on Pattern Analysis and Machine Intelligence 24(7), 971–987 (2002)
18. Otsu, N.: Discriminant and least squares threshold selection. In: International Conference on Pattern Recognition, pp. 592–596 (1978)
19. Perronnin, F., Sánchez, J., Mensink, T.: Improving the fisher kernel for large-scale image classification. In: European Conference on Computer Vision, pp. 143–156 (2010)
20. Pietikäinen, M., Zhao, G., Hadid, A., Ahonen, T.: Computer Vision Using Local Binary Pattern. Springer (2011)
21. Szeliski, R.: Computer Vision: Algorithms and Applications. Springer (2011)
22. Tan, X., Triggs, B.: Enhanced local texture feature sets for face recognition under difficult lighting conditions. IEEE Transactions on Image Processing 19(6), 1635–1650 (2010)
23. Vedaldi, A., Zisserman, A.: Efficient additive kernels via explicit feature maps. In: IEEE Conference on Computer Vision and Pattern Recognition (2010)
24. Wang, X., Han, T.X., Yan, S.: An hog-lbp human detector with partial occlusion handling. In: International Conference on Computer Vision, pp. 32–39 (2009)

A Homologically Persistent Skeleton is a Fast and Robust Descriptor of Interest Points in 2D Images

Vitaliy Kurlin[1,2]([✉])

[1] Microsoft Research Cambridge, 21 Station Road, Cambridge CB1 2FB, UK
[2] Department of Mathematical Sciences, Durham University, Durham DH1 3LE, UK
vitaliy.kurlin@gmail.com
http://kurlin.org

Abstract. 2D images often contain irregular salient features and interest points with non-integer coordinates. Our skeletonization problem for such a noisy sparse cloud is to summarize the topology of a given 2D cloud across all scales in the form of a graph, which can be used for combining local features into a more powerful object-wide descriptor.

We extend a classical Minimum Spanning Tree of a cloud to a Homologically Persistent Skeleton, which is scale-and-rotation invariant and depends only on the cloud without extra parameters. This graph

(1) is computable in time $O(n \log n)$ for any n points in the plane;
(2) has the minimum total length among all graphs that span a 2D cloud at any scale and also have most persistent 1-dimensional cycles;
(3) is geometrically stable for noisy samples around planar graphs.

Keywords: Skeleton · Delaunay triangulation · Persistent homology

1 Introduction: Problem and Overview

Pixel-based 2D images often contain *salient features* represented as points with non-integer coordinates. The resulting unstructured set is an example of a point *cloud* C, formally a finite metric space with pairwise distances between points.

The important problem in low level vision is to extract a meaningful structure from a given irregular cloud C. The traditional approach is to select a scale parameter, say a radius or the number of neighbors, and build a neighborhood graph. However, a real image may not have a single suitable scale parameter and we need to combine features found at multiple scales. This paper solves the skeletonization problem in its hardest form without any input parameters.

Parameterless Skeletonization for Sparse Clouds. Given only an unstructured cloud $C \subset \mathbb{R}^2$ of points with any real coordinates, find a quickly computable structure that provably represents the topology of C at all scales.

© Springer International Publishing Switzerland 2015
G. Azzopardi and N. Petkov (Eds.): CAIP 2015, Part I, LNCS 9256, pp. 606–617, 2015.
DOI: 10.1007/978-3-319-23192-1_51

Our solution is a 'homological' extension of a classical Minimum Spanning Tree MST(C) of a cloud C to a *Homologically Persistent Skeleton* HoPeS(C) that describes 1-dimensional cycles hidden in C over all possible scales α.

In section 2 we explain motivations for building HoPeS(C) and give a high level description of our contributions. In section 3 we compare our method with related work. In sections 4–5 we prove that HoPeS(C) or its subgraphs are
- **computable** in time $O(n \log n)$ for a cloud $C \subset \mathbb{R}^2$ of n points (Lemma 3)
- **invariant** up to rotations and uniform scale transformations (Lemma 4)
- **optimal** among all graphs capturing cycles of C at any scale (Theorem 5)
- **stable** under perturbations of samples C of graphs $G \subset \mathbb{R}^2$ (Corollary 8).

Fig. 1. Top: a cloud C of feature points. Bottom: HoPeS$'(C)$ and its simplification.

Fig. 1 shows the cloud C of $n = 7830$ feature points obtained by thresholding a real image in the top row, see details in section 6. The cloud C is the *only input* for producing the derived skeleton HoPeS$'(C)$ in the bottom row, where we kept only the most persistent cycle. The last picture of Fig. 1 is a simplified version of HoPeS$'(C)$ after removing short branches, see Definition 6. So HoPeS$'(C)$ provides a best 'guess' about the global topology of C in time $O(n \log n)$.

2   Our Contributions and Motivations of HoPeS(C)

Our parameterless skeletonization is based on *persistent homology*, which is the flagship method of Topological Data Analysis [10]. The key idea is to summarize topological features of data over all possible scales. A topological invariant that persists over a long interval of the scale is a true feature of the data, while noisy features have a short life span (a low persistence). The resulting persistent invariants are provably stable under noise, see [14, Appendix A]

Fig. 2 shows a cloud C on the integer lattice for simplicity, though our constructions work for any real coordinates. For any set $C \subset \mathbb{R}^2$ and $\alpha > 0$, the *α-offset* C^α consists of all points in $\mathbb{R}^2$ that are at most α away from C. Here α is the scale parameter (radius or width) of the α-offset $C^\alpha \subset \mathbb{R}^2$ around C.

We may gradually shrink a disk within itself to its center by making the radius smaller. We can not deform a circle to its center, because a smaller circle

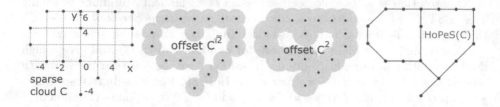

Fig. 2. A cloud C, α-offsets C^α and Homologically Persistent Skeleton HoPeS(C)

would be outside the original circle. So a circle is topologically non-trivial, while any closed loop in a disk is contractible. Spaces connected by such continuous deformations have the same *homotopy type*. We now formalize our problem.

Multi-scale Topological Skeletonization: given a cloud $C \subset \mathbb{R}^2$, find a graph whose vertices are all points of C and whose suitable subgraphs have the homotopy type of the α-offset C^α for any α. A Homologically Persistent Skeleton HoPeS(C) is an optimal and stable skeleton satisfying the above requirements.

A cloud C is an ε-*sample* of (ε-*close* to) a graph $G \subset \mathbb{R}^2$ if $G \subset C^\varepsilon$ and $C \subset G^\varepsilon$. So any point of C is at most ε away from a point of G and any point of G is at most ε away from a point of C. The maximum possible value of ε is the upper bound of noise (the *Hausdorff* distance between G and its sample C).

Here is a high-level description of our contributions to skeletonization.
• Definition 2 introduces a Homologically Persistent Skeleton HoPeS(C) of a cloud $C \subset \mathbb{R}^2$ summarizing the persistence of 1-dimensional cycles in all C^α.
• Lemma 3 proves that, for a cloud $C \subset \mathbb{R}^2$ of any n points, HoPeS(C) has the size $O(n)$ and is computed in time $O(n \log n)$ without any extra parameters.
• Lemma 4 shows that HoPeS(C) is a scale-and-rotation invariant of $C \subset \mathbb{R}^2$.
• Theorem 5 proves that the reduced graph HoPeS($C; \alpha$) at any scale $\alpha > 0$ has the minimum length among all graphs that have the homotopy type of C^α.
• Theorem 7 guarantees that for any ε-sample of a simple enough graph $G \subset \mathbb{R}^2$, HoPeS$'(C)$ is a correct topological reconstruction of G in the 2ε-offset $G^{2\varepsilon}$.
• Corollary 8 implies that the derived subgraph HoPeS$'(C)$ is stable for any δ-perturbation of a cloud C that was ε-sampled around a planar graph G.

The Novelty of this Paper is not the fast algorithm for 1-dimensional persistence, but the new fundamental concept of a Homologically Persistent Skeleton HoPeS(C) that depends only a cloud $C \subset \mathbb{R}^2$ and solves the skeletonization problem without extra parameters and with guarantees in Theorems 5 and 7.

A graph without cycles is a *forest*. A connected forest is a *tree*. For a cloud $C \subset \mathbb{R}^2$, a *Minimum Spanning Tree* MST(C) is a tree that has the vertex set C and the minimum total length of edges, see Fig. 3. The *reduced forest* MST($C; \alpha$) is obtained from MST(C) by removing all open edges longer than 2α.

A connected graph G *spans* a cloud C if C is the vertex set of G. A graph G *spans* a possibly disconnected α-offset C^α if G has vertices at all points of the

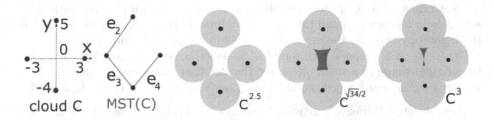

Fig. 3. Cloud C, minimum spanning tree MST(C) and α-offsets $C^{2.5}$, $C^{\sqrt{34}/2}$, C^3.

cloud C and any vertices of G are in the same connected component of G if and only if these vertices are in the same connected component of the α-offset C^{α}.

Points $p, q \in C$ are in the same *single-edge cluster* of C if $d(p, q) \leq 2\alpha$. Lemma 1 says that MST(C) is a universal optimal object that describes the 0-dimensional topology (all single-edge clusters) of C across all scales α.

Lemma 1. *For a cloud C and any scale $\alpha \geq 0$, the reduced forest MST$(C; \alpha)$ has the minimum total length of edges among all graphs that span C^{α} at the same scale α. Hence all connected components of the reduced forest MST$(C; \alpha)$ are in a 1-1 correspondence with all single-edge clusters of the cloud C.*

Lemma 1 and all later results are proved in [14, Appendix B]. Theorem 5 extends the optimality of MST(C) in Lemma 1 for clusters (dimension 0 approximation of C) to HoPeS(C) for cycles (dimension 1 approximation of C).

3   Comparison with Related Past Skeletonization Work

Our approach may look similar to the well-known scale-space theory [17] that suggests how to find a suitable scale. However, we do not choose any scale, we find topological features with longest life spans, which may not overlap. For instance, if one feature lives over the scale interval $1 \leq \alpha \leq 2$ and another over $3 \leq \alpha \leq 4$, then both features can not be captured at any fixed scale α. We can capture both features only by analyzing their life spans among all features.

The classical scale selection relies on analyzing data at discrete scales, usually proportional to powers of 2. The persistent homology works over the continuous scale so that all critical scales are found only from a given cloud, not by manually selecting a step size for incrementing the scale. Though we wouldn't say that persistent homology is 'perpendicular' to scale-space theory, our method is at least 'diagonal' to a scale selection, see diagonal gaps in Definiton 6.

To the best of our knowledge, all known skeletonization algorithms for clouds need extra parameters such as a scale α or a noise bound ε, e.g. [4]. Hence all these algorithms can not run on our minimal input, which is only a cloud C. Since a manual choice of parameters can be unfair, the experimental comparison with the past work seems impossible and we can compare only theoretical aspects.

N. Cornea et al. [6] stated the following requirements for skeletonization.

- *Topology*: a skeleton found from a noisy sample C is homeomorphic to (or has the homotopy type of) the original shape as in Theorem 7 from section 5.
- *Centering*: if a shape is well-sampled, a skeleton geometrically approximates the original shape in a small offset, see the 2ε-offset guarantee in Theorem 7.
- *Efficiency*: a near linear time in the number n of points as in our Lemma 3.

Our skeleton HoPeS(C) satisfies the extra conditions: independence of extra parameters, rotation-and-scale invariance and stability under bounded noise.

R. Singh et al. [18] approximated a skeleton of a shape by a subgraph of a Delaunay triangulation based on 2nd order Voronoi regions. The algorithm has 3 threshold parameters: K for the minimum number of edges in a cycle and $\delta_{min}, \delta_{max}$ for inserting and merging Voronoi regions. M. Aanjaneya et al. [1] solved a related problem approximating a metric on a large input graph by a metric on a small output graph. So the input is a graph, not a cloud of points.

Starting from a noisy sample of an unknown graph G with a scale parameter, X. Ge et al. [11] produced the Reeb graph with the same number of loops as the graph G. This output is an abstract graph of a simplicial complex on a cloud C and is not intrinsically embedded into any space even if $C \subset \mathbb{R}^2$. [11, section 3.3] reported 'spurious branches or loops in the Reeb graph constructed no matter how we choose a radius or a number of neighbours to decide the scale'.

F. Chazal et al. [3] introduced a new α-Reeb graph for a graph reconstruction in different settings. The distance between points in a noisy sample C is measured geodesically within a given neighborhood graph on C, while we consider offsets of C with respect to the ambient distance in $\mathbb{R}^2$. Their algorithm has the same fast time $O(n \log n)$ and they also gave conditions when the reconstructed graph has a required homotopy type.

T. Dey et al. [8] built a complex depending on a user-defined graph that spans a cloud C of n points. This Graph Induced Complex GIC has the same homology H_1 as the Rips complex of a cloud C at a suitable scale α. The 2D skeleton of GIC needed for computing H_1 has the size $O(n^3)$ in a worst case.

For image segmentation, α-offsets were similarly used in [16] (with 2 extra parameters) and in [13] (without parameters). A Homologically Persistent Skeleton can be defined for arbitrary filtrations on a cloud in any metric space [15].

The discussion in [2, section 13] proposed to select features by persistence [10] and led us to the new concept of HoPeS(C) in Definition 2. The key advantage of our approach over the past work is the *absence of any user-defined parameters*.

- HoPeS(C) of a cloud C has no extra input parameters (such as ε or α) that are needed in all past skeletonization algorithms for an unstructured cloud C.

Table 1. Comparison of similar skeletonization methods for unstructured clouds.

Papers	[11], 2011	[1], 2012	[8], 2013	[3], 2014	this paper
Extra input	radius r	radius r, noise ε	graph spanning C	scale α	no parameters
Complexity	$O(n \log n)$	$O(n^2)$	at least $O(n^3)$	$O(n \log n)$	$O(n \log n)$

• For a cloud $C \subset \mathbb{R}^2$ of any n points, the skeleton HoPeS(C) with $O(n)$ edges can be found in time $O(n \log n)$, which is comparable only with [3], [11], [18].

• HoPeS(C) is the *first universal structure* on a cloud C that summarizes all cycles of C^α and has a subgraph HoPeS$'(C)$ stable under perturbations of C.

• HoPeS$'(C)$ for an ε-sample C of G approximates G in the thin offset $G^{2\varepsilon} \subset \mathbb{R}^2$. [3] has guarantees for the abstract Gromov-Hausdorff distance, not in $\mathbb{R}^2$.

• Theorem 5 gives guarantees only in simple terms of a graph $G \subset \mathbb{R}^2$ and its noisy ε-sample $C \subset \mathbb{R}^2$, while [11, Theorem 3.1] needs a complex K with a homotopy equivalence $h : K \to G$ that ε-approximates the metrics of K and G.

4 A Homologically Persistent Skeleton and Its Optimality

Here we give a rather intuitive introduction into homology theory using only α-offsets C^α as typical spaces, see rigorous definitions in [14, Appendix Λ].

The *0-dimensional homology* H_0 counts connected components. Formally, $H_0(C^\alpha)$ is the group (or vector space of linear combinations with coeffiecients in $\mathbb{Z}_2 = \{0,1\}$) generated by the components of C^α. For instance, the offset $C^{2.5}$ in Fig. 3 has 2 components. Hence $H_0(C^{2.5}) = \mathbb{Z}_2 \oplus \mathbb{Z}_2$ has rank (*dimension*) 2.

The *1-dimensional homology* H_1 of $C^\alpha \subset \mathbb{R}^2$ similarly counts *holes* in C^α (bounded regions in the complement $\mathbb{R}^2 - C^\alpha$). For example, the offset $C^{\sqrt{34}/2}$ in Fig. 3 has 1 red hole, so $H_1(C^{\sqrt{34}/2}) = \mathbb{Z}_2$. This hole splits into 2 holes at $\alpha = 3$, hence $H_1(C^3) = \mathbb{Z}_2 \oplus \mathbb{Z}_2$. The smaller of the 2 holes disappears when $\alpha = \frac{25}{8}$ is the circumradius of the triangle on vertices $(\pm 3, 0)$ and $(0, -4)$, so $H_1(C^{25/8}) = \mathbb{Z}_2$. The remaining hole dies when $\alpha = \frac{17}{5}$ is the circumradius of the triangle on vertices $(\pm 3, 0)$ and $(0, 5)$, hence $H_1(C^{17/5}) = 0$ is trivial.

All α-offsets form an ascending *filtration* (a nested sequence of spaces) $C = C^0 \subset \cdots \subset C^\alpha \subset \cdots \subset C^{+\infty} = \mathbb{R}^2$. These inclusions induce linear maps in H_1:

$$C^{2.5} \subset C^{\sqrt{34}/2} \subset C^3 \subset C^{25/8} \subset C^{17/5} \text{ induce } 0 \to \mathbb{Z}_2 \to \mathbb{Z}_2 \oplus \mathbb{Z}_2 \to \mathbb{Z}_2 \to 0.$$

The sequence of the linear maps in H_1 above splits into 2 simpler sequences: hole 1 lives over the interval $\frac{\sqrt{34}}{2} \leq \alpha < \frac{17}{5}$, namely $0 \to \mathbb{Z}_2 \to \mathbb{Z}_2 \to \mathbb{Z}_2 \to 0$, hole 2 lives over the short interval $3 \leq \alpha < \frac{25}{8}$, namely $0 \to 0 \to \mathbb{Z}_2 \to 0 \to 0$.

At $\alpha = 3$ when the initial hole splits into 2 smaller holes, we assume that one of the holes 'inherits' (continues the life of) the previous hole, while another hole is 'newborn' at the splitting moment. The standard convention is to give preference to a longer living hole. So the life spans (the *barcode*) of the filtration $\{C^\alpha\}$ are $[\frac{\sqrt{34}}{2}, \frac{17}{5})$ and $[3, \frac{25}{8})$. We plot the endpoints of these bars as red dots with coordinates (birth, death) in the *persistence diagram* PD$\{C^\alpha\}$, see Fig. 4.

This diagram is a summary of life spans of holes (1-dimensional homology classes) of C^α across all scales α. The key result of persistent homology is the Stability Theorem [5] roughly saying that any small perturbation of the cloud C gives rise to a similar small perturbation of the diagram PD$\{C^\alpha\}$ in the plane.

If a hole of C^α is born, then this hole becomes enclosed by a cycle through points of C. The last longest edge in this enclosing cycle is added at the *birth* time α of the hole and is *critical* for the hole in question. Hole 1 born at $\alpha = \frac{\sqrt{34}}{2}$ has the critical edge e_1, see Fig. 4. Hole 2 born at $\alpha = 3$ has the critical edge e_5.

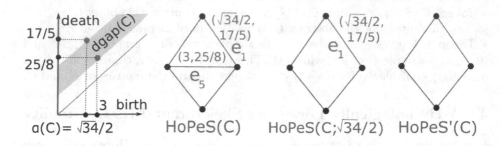

Fig. 4. Diagram $\mathrm{PD}\{C^\alpha\}$ for the cloud C in Fig. 3 and skeletons from Definitions 2, 6.

For any filtration $\{C^\alpha\}$, each red dot in $\mathrm{PD}\{C^\alpha\}$ has a corresponding critical edge e (between points of C) with the label $(\mathrm{birth}(e), \mathrm{death}(e))$. Our Definition 2 transforms the diagram $\mathrm{PD}\{C^\alpha\}$ of disconnected points into a universal structure on the data cloud C summarizing the persistence of holes in $\{C^\alpha\}$ for all α.

Definition 2. *For a cloud C, a* Homologically Persistent Skeleton HoPeS(C) *is the union of* MST(C) *and all critical edges with their labels* $(\mathrm{birth}, \mathrm{death})$, *see Fig. 4. The* reduced *skeleton* HoPeS(C; α) *is obtained from* HoPeS(C) *by removing all edges longer than* 2α *and all critical edges e with* $\mathrm{death}(e) \leq \alpha$.

If $\alpha = 0$, then HoPeS(C; 0) $= C$ is the given cloud. By Definition 2 a critical edge e belongs to the reduced skeleton HoPeS(C; α) if and only if $\mathrm{birth}(e) \leq \alpha < \mathrm{death}(e)$. So a critical edge e is added to HoPeS(C; α) at $\alpha = \mathrm{birth}(e)$ and is later removed at the larger scale $\alpha = \mathrm{death}(e)$. The cloud C in Fig. 3 has HoPeS(C; $\frac{\sqrt{34}}{2}$) $=$ MST(C) $\cup\, e_1$, but HoPeS(C; 3) coincides with HoPeS(C).

The filtration $\{$HoPeS(C; α)$\}$ may not be monotone with respect to the scale α. But if HoPeS(C; α) has become connected, it will stay connected for all larger α. Indeed, removing a critical edge destroys only a cycle, not connectivity.

Similarly to MST(C), a Homologically Persistent Skeleton HoPeS(C) is unique in a general position when the distances between all points of C are different.

Lemma 3. *For any cloud $C \subset \mathbb{R}^2$ of n points, a Homologically Persistent Skeleton* HoPeS(C) *has the size $O(n)$ and is computable in time $O(n \log n)$.*

Lemma 4 below help visualize the 1-dimensional persistence diagram $\mathrm{PD}\{C^\alpha\}$ directly on the cloud C. Lemma 4 justifies that HoPeS(C) is suitable for Computer Vision applications where a scale-and-rotation invariance is important.

Lemma 4. *For a cloud $C \subset \mathbb{R}^2$, the 1-dimensional persistence diagram* PD$\{C^\alpha\}$ *of the filtration of α-offsets C^α can be reconstructed from a Homologically Persistent Skeleton* HoPeS(C). *The topological structure of* HoPeS(C) *is invariant under any affine transformation whose 2×2 matrix has equal eigenvalues.*

Our first main Theorem 5 says that HoPeS(C) is an optimal graph that extends MST(C) and captures the persistence of all holes in the filtration $\{C^\alpha\}$.

Theorem 5. *For any cloud $C \subset \mathbb{R}^2$ and any $\alpha > 0$, the graph* HoPeS$(C; \alpha)$ *has the minimum total length of edges over all graphs $G \subset C^\alpha$ that span the α-offset C^α and induce an isomorphism in 1-dimensional homology $H_1(G) \to H_1(C^\alpha)$.*

A graph G *spans* C^α if $G \subset C^\alpha$ induces an isomorphism $H_0(G) \cong H_0(C^\alpha)$. An isomorphism $H_1(G) \cong H_1(C^\alpha)$ means that the graph G has the homotopy type of the α-offset $C^\alpha \subset \mathbb{R}^2$. Hence our Homologically Persistent Skeleton $G =$ HoPeS(C) solves the multi-scale skeletonization problem stated in sections 1–2.

5 The Reconstruction Theorem and Stability of HoPeS(C)

A Homologically Persistent Skeleton HoPeS(C) contains all 1-dimensional cycles in the offsets C^α across the full range of α. It is natural to select cycles with highest persistence to get a smaller subgraph HoPeS$'(C) \subset$ HoPeS(C). So we select not a scale as in scale-space theory, but a widest diagonal gap in the persistence diagram PD$\{C^\alpha\}$. This widest gap makes sense for finite sets C and for any *compact* set $S \subset \mathbb{R}^2$ that is a finite union of closed topological disks.

Definition 6. *For a compact set $S \subset \mathbb{R}^2$ and the ascending filtration of offsets S^α, a diagonal gap in the persistence diagram* PD$\{S^\alpha\}$ *is a largest (by inclusion) strip $\{0 \leq a < y - x < b\}$ that has no points from the diagram, see Fig. 3.*

The widest diagonal gap dgap(S) *has the largest width $|\text{dgap}(S)| = b - a$. Let the subdiagram* PD$'\{S^\alpha\} \subset$ PD$\{S^\alpha\}$ *have only the points above* dgap(S). *The* critical scale $\alpha(S)$ *is the maximum birth over all* (birth, death) $\in$ PD$'\{S^\alpha\}$.

For a cloud $C = S$, the derived skeleton HoPeS$'(C)$ *is obtained from* HoPeS(C) *by removing (1) all edges longer than $2\alpha(C)$, and (2) all critical edges either with* death $\leq \alpha(C)$ *or with* (birth, death) *below the widest diagonal gap* dgap(C).

In Definition 6 if there are different gaps with the same width, we say that the gap with largest values along the vertical death axis has the largest width. The cloud C in Fig. 3 has the widest gap dgap(C) between the points $(\frac{\sqrt{34}}{2}, \frac{17}{5})$ and $(3, \frac{25}{8})$ in PD$\{C(\alpha)\}$, so the critical scale is $\alpha(C) = \frac{\sqrt{34}}{2}$, see Fig. 4.

Condition (1) above guarantees that HoPeS$'(C) \subset$ HoPeS$(C; \alpha(C))$, because all long critical edges e with birth$(e) > \alpha(C)$ are removed, see [14, Appendix B]. Condition (2) filters out cycles with early deaths and low persistence, but

HoPeS$'(C) \neq$ HoPeS$(C; \alpha(C))$. Instead of selecting a fixed scale as in scale-space theory, we select cycles by their persistence across all scales α.

We define concepts needed for Theorem 7. A non-self-intersecting cycle L in a graph $G \subset \mathbb{R}^2$ is *basic* if L encloses a bounded region of $\mathbb{R}^2 - G$. When α is increasing, the hole enclosed by the α-offset L^α is born at $\alpha = 0$ and dies at the scale $\alpha = \rho(L)$ that is called the *radius* of the cycle L. So the initial hole enclosed by L has the life span $[0, \rho(L))$. The heart-shaped hole in the first picture of Fig. 5 completely dies at $\alpha = \rho(L)$, which holds for any convex hole.

In general, when α is increasing new holes can be born in G^α, let they be enclosed by $L_1, \ldots, L_k$ at their birth times. The *thickness* $\theta(G) = \max\limits_{j=1,\ldots,k} \rho(L_j)$ is the maximum persistence of these smaller holes born during the evolution of offsets G^α. If no such holes appear, then $\theta = 0$, otherwise $\theta > 0$, see Fig. 5.

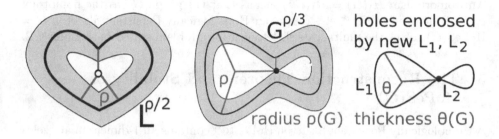

Fig. 5. The 'heart' graph has thickness $\theta = 0$. The 'figure-eight' graph has $\theta > 0$.

Theorem 7 says that HoPeS$'(C)$ is a close approximation to a graph G from any its ε-sample C. The homotopy type of a connected graph G is determined by its $H_1(G)$. Namely, G continuously deforms to a wedge of dim $H_1(G)$ loops.

Theorem 7. *Let C be any ε-sample of a connected graph $G \subset \mathbb{R}^2$ with a thickness $\theta(G) \geq 0$ and $m \geq 1$ basic cycles having ordered radii $\rho_1 \leq \cdots \leq \rho_m$. If $\rho_1 > 7\varepsilon + \theta(G) + \max\limits_{i=1,\ldots,m-1} \{\rho_{i+1} - \rho_i\}$, then the critical scale $\alpha(C) \leq \varepsilon$, and the derived skeleton HoPeS$'(C)$ is 2ε-close to G and has the homotopy type of G.*

The inequality above means that the cycles of the graph G have 'comparable' sizes, i.e. the smallest radius ρ_1 is larger by a good margin than any gap $\rho_{i+1} - \rho_i$ between the ordered radii. Hence the diagonal gap $\{\theta(G) < \text{death} - \text{birth} < \rho_1\}$ in the diagram PD$\{G^\alpha\}$ of the graph G will remain wide enough to be automatically recognized in the perturbed diagram PD$\{C^\alpha\}$ for any ε-sample C of G.

Theorem 7 is stronger than any estimate of homology from noisy samples. In addition we build on a sample C an actual skeleton HoPeS$'(C)$ that is 2ε-close to an unknown graph G. Theorem 7 extends simpler [13, Theorem 32], which works only for a much smaller class of graphs $G \subset \mathbb{R}^2$ with thickness $\theta = 0$.

Corollary 8. *In the conditions of Theorem 7 if another cloud $\tilde{C}$ is δ-close to C, then the perturbed derived skeleton HoPeS$'(\tilde{C})$ is $(2\delta + 4\varepsilon)$-close to HoPeS$'(C)$.*

We can't expect that HoPeS$'(C)$ is locally stable for any cloud C, because a minimum spanning tree MST(C) is sensitive to perturbations of C. However, Corollary 8 guarantees the overall stability of the derived skeleton (within a small offset) in the most practical case for noisy sample of graphs.

6 Algorithm, Experiments and Practical Applications

[14, Appendix A] justifies that complicated α-offsets C^α can be replaced by simpler α-complexes $C(\alpha)$, which filter a Delaunay triangulation Del(C). Starting from a cloud $C \subset \mathbb{R}^2$ of n points, we build Del(C) in time $O(n \log n)$ with $O(n)$ space. Regions in the complement $\mathbb{R}^2 - C(\alpha)$ are dual to their boundaries. This duality [15] reduces 1-dimensional persistence of cycles in the filtration $\{C(\alpha)\}$ to 0-dimensional persistence of connected components in $\mathbb{R}^2 - C(\alpha)$.

Fig. 6. A sample C of O45, diagram PD$\{C(\alpha)\}$, HoPeS$'(C)$ and its simplification.

The 0-dimensional persistence is computed in time $O(n\Lambda^{-1}(n))$ using a union-find structure [10], where $\Lambda^{-1}(n)$ is the slow growing inverse Ackermann function. We extend this algorithm by recording a critical edge along which regions of $\mathbb{R}^2 - C(\alpha)$ merge when α is decreasing, see [14, AppendixC].

Fig. 7. A sample C of D33, diagram PD$\{C(\alpha)\}$, HoPeS$'(C)$ and its simplification.

Fig. 6 shows 121 random points sampled from a real image of hieroglyph O45. The second picture of Fig. 6 is the diagram PD$\{C(\alpha)\}$ with a widest diagonal gap

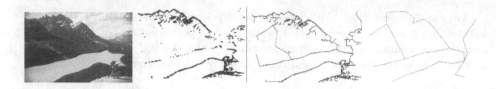

Fig. 8. Image BSD176035, cloud C of 3603 points, HoPeS′(C) and its simplification.

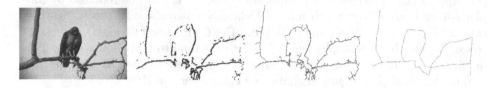

Fig. 9. Image BSD42049, cloud C of 1763 points, HoPeS′(C) and its simplification.

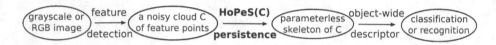

Fig. 10. Pipeline for building an object-wide descriptor from noisy local features

clearly separating the noise near the diagonal from 2 red points corresponding to 2 cycles in the derived graph HoPeS′(C). Theorem 7 gives the lower bound $\alpha(C)$ for the unknown noise level ε. We use this intrinsic critical scale $\alpha(C)$ for pruning short branches and collapsing short edges to get a simplified version of HoPeS′(C) in the last picture of Fig. 6, see details in [14, Appendix C]. Fig. 7 has similar results for 321 points sampled from another hieroglyph D33.

In Fig. 8 we selected feature points from a challenging image by simply comparing the color of each pixel with the average in 5×5 neighborhood. The threshold for the normal deviation in the 3-dimensional RGB space was 65 as in Fig. 1. Fig. 9 shows similar results for the normal deviation 100 of the color.

Table 2 has the running time in milliseconds for the database BSD500, where all images have 481×321 pixels and we used 2 thresholds in each image, see details in [14, Appendix D]. We used a small laptop with 1.33GHz RAM 2GB to show that the algorithm is fast for embedded systems. The C++ code is on author's page http://kurlin.org/projects/persistent-skeletons.php.

Table 2. Time for extracting C from images in BSD500 and computing HoPeS′(C).

Images from BSD500	42049	42049	176035	176035	175083	175083	134049	134049
Time for a cloud C, ms	1022	1336	1017	1038	1066	1015	1051	1165
Points in the cloud C	2664	3604	3603	4249	3928	4950	4396	6767
Time for HoPeS′(C), ms	969	1789	1898	2629	2143	3602	3780	6259

We have demonstrated the following practical applications of HoPeS(C).
• Robust recognition of low quality scans in Fig. 6, 7, see more results in [14].
Such visual markers [7] can replace shop barcodes not readable by humans.
• A fast topological summary of images, see Fig. 1, 8 and more details in [14].

References

1. Aanjaneya, M., Chazal, F., Chen, D., Glisse, M., Guibas, L., Morozov, D.: Metric graph reconstruction from noisy data. IJCGA **22**, 305–325 (2012)
2. Attali, D., Boissonnat, J.-D., Edelsbrunner, H.: Stability and computation of medial axes – a state-of-the-art report. In: Math. Foundations of Visualization, Computer Graphics, and Massive Data Exploration, pp. 109–125. Springer (2009)
3. Chazal, F., Huang, R., Sun, J.: Gromov-Hausdorff approximation of filament structure using Reeb-type graph. Discrete Comp. Geometry **53**, 621–649 (2015)
4. Chernov, A., Kurlin, V.: Reconstructing persistent graph structures from noisy images. Image-A **3**, 19–22 (2013)
5. Cohen-Steiner, D., Edelsbrunner, H., Harer, J.: Stability of persistence diagrams. Discrete and Computational Geometry **37**, 103–130 (2007)
6. Cornea, N., Silver, D., Min, P.: Curve-Skeleton Properties, Applications, and Algorithms IEEE Trans. Visualization Comp. Graphics **13**, 530–548 (2007)
7. Costanza, E., Huang, J.: Designable visual markers. In: Proceedings of SIGCHI 2009: Special Interest Group on Computer-Human Interaction, pp. 1879–1888 (2009)
8. Dey, T., Fan, F., Wang, Y.: Graph induced complex on data points. In: Proceedings of SoCG 2013: Symposium on Computational Geometry, pp. 107–116 (2013)
9. Edelsbrunner, H.: The union of balls and its dual shape. Discrete Computational Geometry **13**, 415–440 (1995)
10. Edelsbrunner, H., Harer, J.: Computational topology: an introduction. AMS
11. Ge, X., Safa, I., Belkin, M., Wang, Y.: Data skeletonization via Reeb graphs. In: Proceedings of NIPS 2011, pp. 837–845 (2011)
12. Kurlin, V.: A fast and robust algorithm to count topologically persistent holes in noisy clouds. In: Proceedings of CVPR 2014, pp. 1458–1463 (2014)
13. Kurlin, V.: Auto-completion of contours in sketches, maps and sparse 2D images based on topological persistence. In: Proceedings of CTIC 2014, pp. 594–601 (2014)
14. Kurlin, V.: A Homologically Persistent Skeleton is a fast and robust descriptor of interest points in 2D images (full version of this paper). http://kurlin.org
15. Kurlin, V.: A one-dimensional Homologically Persistent Skeleton of an unstructured point cloud in any metric space. Computer Graphics Forum **34**(5), 253–262 (2015)
16. Letscher, D., Fritts, J.: Image segmentation using topological persistence. In: Kropatsch, W.G., Kampel, M., Hanbury, A. (eds.) CAIP 2007. LNCS, vol. 4673, pp. 587–595. Springer, Heidelberg (2007)
17. Lindeberg, T.: Scale-Space Theory in Computer Vision. Kluwer Publishers (1994)
18. Singh, R., Cherkassky, V., Papanikolopoulos, N.: Self-organizing maps for the skeletonization of sparse shapes. Tran. Neural Networks **11**, 241–248 (2000)

A k-max Geodesic Distance and Its Application in Image Segmentation

Michael Holuša[⊠] and Eduard Sojka

Department of Computer Science, FEECS, VŠB - Technical University of Ostrava,
17. Listopadu 15, 708 33 Ostrava-poruba, Czech Republic
{michael.holusa,eduard.sojka}@vsb.cz

Abstract. The geodesic distance is commonly used when solving image processing problems. In noisy images, unfortunately, it often gives unsatisfactory results. In this paper, we propose a new k-max geodesic distance. The length of path is defined as the sum of the k maximum edge weights along the path. The distance is defined as the length of the path that is the shortest one in this sense. With an appropriate choice of the value of k, the influence of noise can be reduced substantially. The positive properties are demonstrated on the problem of seeded image segmentation. The results are compared with the results of geodesic distance and with the results of the random walker segmentation algorithm. The influence of k value is also discussed.

Keywords: Geodesic distance · Shortest path problem · Image segmentation

1 Introduction

Finding the distance between two points is an important task in computer science with many applications in robotics, data clustering, or in image processing [3,7]. The geodesic distance [10] is a commonly used distance measure in many tasks of image processing [4]. It is defined as the shortest path on the surface that is defined by the image function. In the discrete case, it is the shortest path in the weighted graph that corresponds to the image (the weights of edges reflect the brightness differences between the endpoints of edges).

Many image segmentation methods are based on the geodesic distance. A framework for interactive image segmentation based on the distance computing from the user-provided seeds is presented in [1]. The geodesic distance is also used as an unary term in the graph cut method [9], or as a part of the CRF model that combines the graph cut method and geodesic distance [12]. In [11], the authors improved the geodesic distance segmentation algorithm by incorporating the shape priors. In [5], the author introduced a k-shortest path algorithm that finds k distinct paths between two points. This approach uses the usual geodesic distance determining the k shortest paths between the points. The k-shortest paths method is used, for example, in object tracking [2].

Although the geodesic distance is frequently used, it is also known that it is sensitive to noise in image, which negatively influences the results. This was

G. Azzopardi and N. Petkov (Eds.): CAIP 2015, Part I, LNCS 9256, pp. 618–629, 2015.
DOI: 10.1007/978-3-319-23192-1_52

a motivation to find a distance that ignores the noise if possible and takes into account only the important brightness changes, such as edges. If we assume that the noise is reflected by the low-weighted edges, while the relevant image information is in the edges with higher weights, the sensitivity to noise may decrease by considering only few edges on each path with the highest weights.

In this paper, we propose a new k-max geodesic distance. The length of path is defined as the sum of the k maximum edge weights along the path. The k-max geodesic distance is defined as the length of the path that is the shortest one in this sense. For illustrating the properties of the k-max geodesic distance and for its comparison with the geodesic distance, the seeded segmentation is used. The seeded segmentation uses a priori user-provided seeds scribbled into the particular segment areas. The distance is computed from the seeds to all image points. In the binary image segmentation, an image point is labeled as an object, if the distance from the object seed is lower than the distance from the background seed. Otherwise, the image point is labeled as a background.

We also compare our method with the random walker segmentation method proposed in [6]. This method was chosen since it has a similar approach as the distance-based methods; it determines the probabilities that a random walk from an image point reaches one of the seed points.

The paper is organized as follows. The problems of geodesic distance are presented in Section 2. In Section 3, the k-max geodesic distance is introduced. Section 4 contains the description of the algorithm for computing the k-max geodesic distance. The experimental results and the comparisons are presented in Section 5. Section 6 is a conclusion. We note that in the rest of the paper, we will simply say k-max distance instead of the long name k-max geodesic distance.

2   Geodesic Distance and Its Problems

In this section, we focus on the geodesic distance and its behavior in images. Consider a graph and two nodes in it, denoted by A and B, respectively. Let P be a path connecting A and B; $P = (v_{p_1}, v_{p_2}, v_{p_3}, \ldots, v_{p_n})$, where v_{p_i} are the nodes through which the path is running; $v_{p_1} \equiv A$, $v_{p_n} \equiv B$. The geodesic length of path is the sum of the weights of all its edges, i.e., $l_{\mathrm{g}}(P) = \sum_{i=1}^{n-1} w_{(p_i, p_{i+1})}$. Let $\mathcal{P}_{AB}$ be the set of all existing paths between A and B in the graph. The geodesic distance between A and B is then defined as $d_{\mathrm{g}}(A, B) = \min_{P \in \mathcal{P}_{AB}} l_{\mathrm{g}}(P)$.

In image processing, the weight of edge is often determined by the equation

$$w_{i,j} = 1.0 - e^{-\frac{(b_i - b_j)^2}{2\sigma_w}} + \beta, \tag{1}$$

where b_i, b_j are the values of brightness at the v_i and v_j node, respectively; σ_w is a constant. The value of β determines the price for using the edge regardless how big the brightness difference between its endpoints is. It can also be $\beta = 0$, which reflects the fact that the pixels with the same brightness are regarded as close to each other; the points may be geometrically distant in the xy plane but they should create one segment. Although this setting does not satisfy the

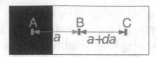

Fig. 1. The synthetic test image (it is shown without noise here) with the points depicted between which the distance is to be measured. We would expect that $d_g(A, B) > d_g(B, C)$ (especially for $da = 0$). Due to noise, the opposite incorrect result is often reported by the geodesic distance (Table 2).

identity of indiscernibles condition of the metric, it can be useful to keep small or even zero distances in the areas with a constant brightness. In the rest of the paper, we consider $\beta = 0$.

We tested the geodesic distance on the synthetic images containing the unit brightness step (Fig. 1) with Gaussian noise added ($\sigma = \frac{1}{3}$) into the image. The geodesic distances $d_g(A, B)$ and $d_g(B, C)$ were measured (see Fig. 1). Since A and B are in different image segments, and B and C are both in the same segment, we expect that $d_g(A, B)$ should always be greater than $d_g(B, C)$. The results in Table 1 show that it is not necessarily true if noise is present. The error rate stated in the table tells how many times the geodesic distance erroneously answered that $d_g(A, B) < d_g(B, C)$. It can be seen that the geodesic distance has a high error rate even in the cases when B is placed directly into the center of AC ($da = 0$).

Table 1. The error rate computed for the geodesic distances from Fig. 1, $\sigma = \frac{1}{3}$ (see text for further explanation). All the values were computed from 10^5 samples.

	$da = 0$	$da = 2$	$da = 5$	$da = 10$
$a = 10$	14.5 %	22.0 %	36.5 %	61.0 %
$a = 20$	18.0 %	25.5 %	37.5 %	60.0 %

Let us now illustrate how this problem influences image segmentation (Fig. 2). Consider an image with two segments: the object and the background. Let O and B denote the object and the background seed, respectively. Let x measure the coordinates of points along the shortest path between O and B; $I(x)$ stands for brightness at x; $d_g(O, x)$ is the distance between the object seed and the point whose coordinate is x. Similarly, $d_g(B, x)$ is the distance from the background seed. The big change of $I(x)$ shows the place where the edge separates the object and the background, which is also the place where the diagrams of the functions $d_g(O, x)$ and $d_g(B, x)$ should intersect if segmentation is done on the basis of distance. Fig. 2 shows how the situation may turn out in the real-life (i.e. noisy) images. The equality of distances may occur at other place than the edge, which leads to incorrect segmentation. Informally speaking, this problem is caused by summing many small and unimportant values, which may overshadow the values that are important.

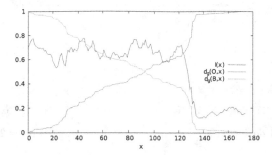

Fig. 2. The diagram of the distances along a path between the object seed and the background seed; x measures the coordinate along the path (for the object seed, we have $x = 0$); $d_g(O, x)$ stands for the distance between the object seed and the point whose coordinate along the path is x. Similarly, $d_g(B, x)$ is the distance from the background seed. $I(x)$ stands for the brightness at x. See text for further explanation.

3 k-max Geodesic Distance

In this section, we introduce the new k-max distance. Let $\sum_{\text{top}_k}(.)$ stand for the sum of the k highest values in a collection of nonnegative real numbers (the edge weights in our case). We define the length of path as a sum of the k highest weights on it, i.e., $l_{km}(P) = \sum_{\text{top}_k}(w_{(p_1,p_2)}, w_{(p_2,p_3)}, \ldots, w_{(p_{n-1},p_n)})$, where P is a path. Let $\mathcal{P}_{AB}$ be the set of all paths between A and B. The k-max distance between A and B is then defined as $d_{km}(A, B) = \min_{P \in \mathcal{P}_{AB}}\{l_{km}(P)\}$.

The behavior of the k-max distance was tested on the same images as in the case of the geodesic distance in the previous section. Firstly, we have measured the distances $d_{km}(A, B)$ and $d_{km}(B, C)$ between the points in Fig. 1 and evaluated the error rates in the same way as in the previous section. The results for $k \in \langle 1, 20 \rangle$ are visualized in Fig. 3. For clarity, we also show the corresponding error rates of the geodesic distance from Table 1, which are visualized as the straight horizontal lines in the diagrams. The results show that, for almost every k, the error rate is much better than it is in the case of geodesic distance. The k-max distance performs worse only for $k = 1$ combined with a low value of da. For the high values of k, the error rate of the new distance approaches (from the bottom) to the error rate of the geodesic distance, which is expected since for $k = \infty$, $d_g(A, B) \equiv d_{km}(A, B)$.

We also tested how the k-max distance behaves along the shortest path between the object and background seed, similarly as we did for the geodesic distance in the previous section (Fig. 2). The result is shown in Fig. 4. It can be seen that the k-max distance is much less sensitive to noise and the edge position is detected correctly. (We explain that the range on the x axis is bigger than in the case of geodesic distance since it happened here that the shortest k-max path is longer in the xy plane than it was for the geodesic distance in Fig. 2. This conforms with the expectation since we have $\beta = 0$ in Eq. (1)).

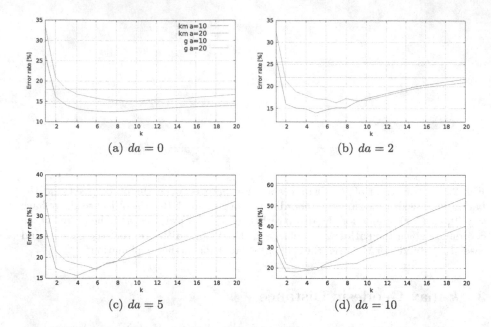

(a) $da = 0$ (b) $da = 2$

(c) $da = 5$ (d) $da = 10$

Fig. 3. The error rates of the k-max distance for various values of k, a and da (see Fig. 1). For a wide range of k values, the k-max distance reaches much better error rates than the geodesic distance. The explanation of colors presented in (a) is valid also for all remaining images; km stands for the k-max distance, g stands for the geodesic distance.

4   The Algorithm

In this section, we present how the algorithm for computing the k-max distance is constructed. Taking into account the fact that the distances in graph are computed from the shortest to the longest, the algorithm may be regarded as similar to the well-known Dijkstra algorithm. On the other hand, substantial modifications are required so that the distance whose definition was presented in Section 3 could be computed. When computing the geodesic distance, only one value is stored in each node. During the updates, it is changed into the distance that has been found to this node. When computing the k-max distance, a list of vectors containing k maximum weights has to be associated with each node. The following example shows the need for storing such a list.

Consider three nodes in a graph (Fig. 5), denoted by A, B, and C, respectively. Say that we have $k = 2$ and that two paths exist from A to B. Let $\boldsymbol{m}_{B_1} = (4, 3)$ and $\boldsymbol{m}_{B_2} = (5, 1)$, respectively, be the vectors of maximum values (*max vectors* briefly) corresponding to both paths from A to B (Fig. 5). The vectors contain two (since $k = 2$) maximum weights found along the corresponding path (for simplicity, we now suppose that the weights are integer numbers). It follows that the distance between A and B is $d_{km}(A, B) = 5 + 1 = 6$. Let

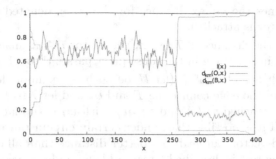

Fig. 4. The diagram of the k-max distances along the path between the object seed and the background seed. In contrast with the geodesic distance (see Fig. 2 for comparison and further explanation), the position of edge is indicated correctly.

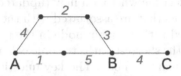

Fig. 5. An example of weighted graph on which the k-max distance algorithm is illustrated.

us now say that B and C are connected with an edge whose cost is $w_{B,C} = 4$. The first mentioned path from A to B leads to the vector $m_{C_1} = (4,4)$ at C (the value of 3 in m_{B_1} is replaced with the value of 4), which gives the distance $d_{km}(A,C) = 4 + 4 = 8$. Surprisingly, the second path from A to B with the vector $m_{B_2} = (5,1)$ that determined the k-max distance $d_{km}(A,B)$ gives the vector $m_{C_2} = (5,4)$ that does not determine the distance $d_{km}(A,C)$ since $5+4 > 4+4$. In spite of the fact that the vector m_{B_2} was decisive for determining the distance between A and B, another vector that was not the best one at B was needed at B for determining the distance $d_{km}(A,C)$. It was necessary to have at B not only the vector m_{B_2}, but also the vector m_{B_1}, i.e. a list of vectors is generally needed at each node. The algorithm can now be formulated as follows.

Algorithm THE k-MAX DISTANCE IN GRAPH
Input: The graph and its node S from which the distances should be computed.
Output: The k-max distances to all the nodes in the graph.

1. For all nodes in the graph, clear the list of the attached max vectors.
2. Attach the max vector $m_{S_1} = (0,0,\dots,0)$ to S and mark this vector as active.
3. **while** an active vector exists in any node in the graph **do**
4.   Among all active vectors (attached to all nodes of the graph), find the vector, denoted by m_T^*, whose sum of values is minimal. The sum

determines the k-max distance for the node, denoted by T, to which this vector is attached.

5. Output the distance of T. Mark the vector m_T^* as inactive; it will not be used in searching in the subsequent passes through the while cycle.

6. For each neighbor of T (let U be such a neighbor, let $w_{T,U}$ be the weight of the edge connecting T and U, and let $\mathcal{M}_U$ be the list of the vectors attached to U) update m_T^* with $w_{T,U}$ (updating is described later). If it is possible that, under certain circumstances in future, the updated vector can lead to a better distance than all other vectors in $\mathcal{M}_U$ (the test is described later), add the updated vector into $\mathcal{M}_U$.

The operation of updating m_T^* with $w_{T,U}$ is carried out as follows. Find the minimum value in m_T^*. If the minimum value is greater then $w_{T,U}$, m_T^* remains unchanged. Otherwise, the minimum value in m_T^* is replaced with $w_{T,U}$.

Now we focus on the decision whether a new (updated) max vector should be added into the list of vectors that are associated with the node. Say that we have two max vectors associated with a certain node in the graph (like the B node in Fig. 5). It is possible that the shortest paths to some other nodes (like to the node C in Fig. 5) will run through this node. The key question now is: Are both the vectors important for generating the possible shortest paths to other nodes? Is it possible to say, for example, that some of them will never be used in any shortest path and, therefore, it is not necessary to store it? The answer is given in the following observation: Consider two max vectors $m_1 = (m_{1,1}, m_{1,2}, \ldots, m_{1,k})$ and $m_2 = (m_{2,1}, m_{2,2}, \ldots, m_{2,k})$. Suppose that the values in the vectors are sorted from the biggest to the smallest, i.e. $m_{1,1} \geq m_{1,2} \geq \cdots \geq m_{1,k}$ and similarly also for the second vector. If the inequality $\sum_{j=1}^{q} m_{1,j} \leq \sum_{j=1}^{q} m_{2,j}$ holds for all q, $1 \leq q \leq k$, then the vector m_2 will never be used in any shortest path to some other node, i.e. there is no need for storing it.

In order to show this decision method, say that we measure the length of path from A through B to C (see Fig. 5, contrary to Fig. 5, the common subpath from B to C has generally more than one edge). We have two max vectors m_1 and m_2 at B. Say that r values are replaced in m_1 and s values are replaced in m_2 on the way from B to C. For simplicity, we firstly explore the case $r = s$. We compare the sums of $k - r$ maximum values in both vectors. If $\sum_{j=1}^{k-r} m_{1,j} \leq \sum_{j=1}^{k-r} m_{2,j}$, m_2 cannot give a shorter path length to C (for the BC subpath that is being considered). The lengths of the particular whole paths (that are different between A and B) are given by the above mentioned sums plus the sum of the newly included costs. These, however, are the same for both paths since they are the maximum costs on the considered common subpath from B to C. Now we consider the case $r > s$ (the case $r < s$ may be explained by interchanging the vectors). From the fact that $r > s$, it follows that $r - s$ entries from r smallest entries in m_2 were greater than $r - s$ smallest entries that modified m_1 on the subpath from B to C. Again, if $\sum_{j=1}^{k-r} m_{1,j} \leq \sum_{j=1}^{k-r} m_{2,j}$, m_2 cannot give a shorter path length to C. The lengths of the whole paths are obtained by adding the sum of the weights of s new elements that are the same in both cases (s maximum weights on the common subpath from B to C) and by adding the sum of the remaining $r - s$ elements that is greater for

m_2. This consideration is valid for all values of r, $0 \leq r \leq k$, which corresponds to various subpaths between B and C and various weights of edges along these subpaths.

5   Experiments

The efficiency of the k-max distance is evaluated on the seeded image segmentation. At the beginning of this section, we show how the choice of the value of k influences the quality of segmentation. Then, we focus on the relationship between the segmentation results and the positions of seeds. After that, we will test the methods on the real-life image segmentation. We will compare the results obtained from the k-max distance, the geodesic distance, and the random walker segmentation. In the experiments, we set the parameters from Eq. (1) to $\sigma = \frac{1}{3}$ and $\beta = 0$ for the distance-based methods. In the case of random walker, we experimentally found σ that achieves the best result for each image. The seeds were defined manually.

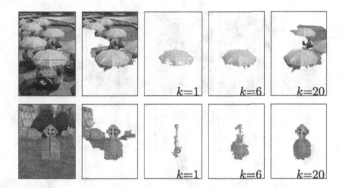

Fig. 6. On the influence of the k value on the segmentation result. The input images with the seeds (the first column), the results of seeded segmentation based on the geodesic distance (the second column), and the results of seeded segmentation based on the k-max distance for various values of k (the columns 3-5).

As was demonstrated in Fig. 3, the error rate of the k-max distance varies with the value of k. In the first experiment, we show that the value of k also affects the result of segmentation. In Fig. 6, the results of segmentation are presented for the geodesic distance (column 2) and for the k-max distance for several k values ($k = 1$, $k = 6$, and $k = 20$; column 3-5). In the first image (row 1), the goal is to segment only the yellow umbrella into which the object seed is scribbled. The segmentation based on the geodesic distance is apparently bad (Fig. 6). In the case of the k-max distance, the segmentation is close to the desired result if low values of k (even $k = 1$) are used. For $k = 20$, the object segment that is detected "overflows" from the true object, and the result becomes similar to the result of the geodesic distance (as was explained before, this behavior

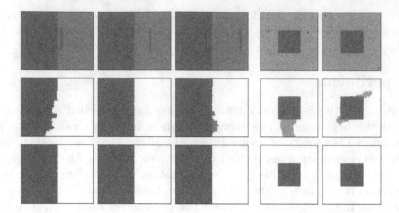

Fig. 7. The sensitivity to the seed positions. The input images with the seeds (first row), the results of segmentation using the geodesic distance (second row), the results of segmentation using the k-max distance, $k = 2$ (third row).

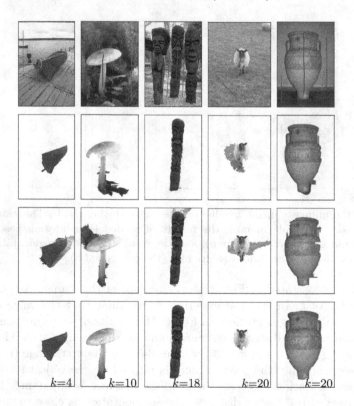

Fig. 8. The results of segmentation based on the geodesic distance, the k-max distance and the random walker technique. The input images with the seeds (first row), the results for the random walker (second row), the results for the geodesic distance (third row), the results for the k-max distance (fourth row).

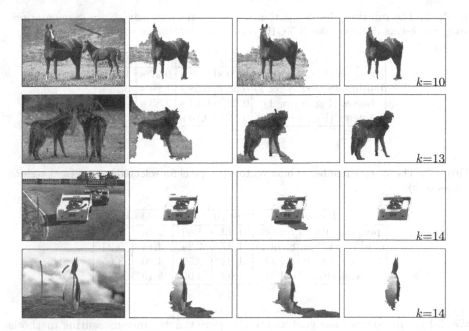

Fig. 9. The results of segmentation based on the geodesic distance, the k-max distance and the random walker technique. The input images with the seeds (first column), the results for the random walker (second column), the results for the geodesic distance (third column), the results for the k-max distance (fourth column).

is expected). On the other hand, a good segmentation of the gravestone in the second image (row 2) is achieved with a relatively high value of k ($k = 20$); lower values of k lead to an incomplete object. We can conclude that the choice of the k value is not universal, but it depends on image properties.

In the next experiment, we explore how the positions of seeds influence the result of segmentation (Fig. 7). It can be seen that the results of geodesic distance (row 2) are dependent on the seed positions, which is undesirable. The k-max distance provides much better results (row 3), which again, simply speaking, is mainly due to the fact that it does not sum the noise values that are unimportant. In both cases, the results are as expected; the roots of the behavior that can be seen in the figure were explained sufficiently in Sections 2 and 3.

Finally, we test and compare the methods on the images obtained from the Berkeley segmentation dataset [8]. In addition, we compare the distance-based methods with the random walker segmentation algorithm. The results are shown in Fig. 8 and Fig. 9 (in the case of k-max distance, the value of k was chosen to give the visually best segmentation). It can be seen again that the k-max distance outperforms the geodesic distance, and also outperforms the random walker method. Naturally, the results could be improved by adding new seeds.

Table 2. The run times for computing the selected previously shown segmentations using the k-max distance (one 2.5 GHz core computer, image size $= 450 \times 300$).

image	$k = 1$	$k = 10$	$k = 30$	$k = 50$
penguin (Fig. 9 row 4)	0.29 s	0.48 s	0.97 s	1.90 s
mushroom (Fig. 8 col 2)	0.28 s	0.58 s	1.96 s	5.73 s
horses (Fig. 9 row 1)	0.29 s	0.64 s	2.83 s	15.04 s
totems (Fig. 8 col 3)	0.30 s	0.70 s	3.57 s	17.47 s

Table 3. The average number of max vectors per pixel for selected images (and various values of k).

image	$k = 10$	$k = 20$	$k = 30$	$k = 50$
penguin (Fig. 9 row 4)	1.22	1.46	1.76	2.29
mushroom (Fig. 8 col 2)	1.47	2.34	3.18	6.23
horses (Fig. 9 row 1)	1.63	2.58	4.00	8.65
totems (Fig. 8 col 3)	1.63	3.02	5.19	12.08

We did not do so since our goal was to compare the distance measuring methods under the same and difficult circumstances that can be expected in practice.

From the algorithm description in Section 4, it is obvious that computing the k-max distance is more complicated than computing the geodesic distance. This is reflected in a bigger time complexity. Table 2 shows the run times that were needed for computing the segmentations of particular previously shown images; various values of k were considered.

In Section 4, we also explained the need for storing more than one max vector in each graph node, which slows down the algorithm and increases the memory consumption. Table 3 shows the average number of max vectors per a node for a set of selected images and for various values of k. It can be seen from the table that the number of vectors increases with k. Fortunately, according to our experience, good segmentation results are usually achieved with $k < 30$; the number of max vectors remains acceptable for these values of k.

6 Conclusion

In this paper, we introduced a new distance in graphs, called the k-max geodesic distance. The length of path is defined as the sum of the k maximum edge weights along the path. The distance is defined as the length of the path that is the shortest one in this sense. We also presented the algorithm for computing the new distance. We demonstrated the problems of geodesic distance and we showed that the k-max distance has a chance to overcome them. The new distance measure was tested by using it in seeded image segmentation; the geodesic distance was used for comparison, and also the random walker method, which is a recognized algorithm in the seeded segmentation area. According to the results, the k-max geodesic distance achieves the best results. On the other hand, its computation requires more time and memory than the computation of the geodesic distance, which is caused by the need for storing (at each graph node) a certain number of vectors containing k maximum weights along the possible paths to the node. Therefore, our future goal is to try to further reduce the number of stored vectors by improving the method that decides about keeping or discarding the vectors. This should reduce the time and memory requirements of the algorithm.

Acknowledgments. This work was supported by the grant SP2015/141 of VŠB - TU Ostrava, Faculty of Electrical Engineering and Computer Science.

References

1. Bai, X., Sapiro, G.: Geodesic matting: A framework for fast interactive image and video segmentation and matting. Int. J. Comput. Vision **82**(2), 113–132 (2009)
2. Berclaz, J., Turetken, E., Fleuret, F., Fua, P.: Multiple object tracking using k-shortest paths optimization. IEEE Trans. Pattern Anal. Mach. Intell. (2011)
3. Borgefors, G.: Distance transformations in arbitrary dimensions. Computer Vision, Graphics, and Image Processing **27**(3), 321–345 (1984)
4. Criminisi, A., Sharp, T., Blake, A.: GeoS: geodesic image segmentation. In: Forsyth, D., Torr, P., Zisserman, A. (eds.) ECCV 2008, Part I. LNCS, vol. 5302, pp. 99–112. Springer, Heidelberg (2008)
5. Eppstein, D.: Finding the k shortest paths. SIAM J. Comp. **28**(2), 652–673 (1998)
6. Grady, L.: Random walks for image segmentation. IEEE Trans. Pattern Anal. Mach. Intell. **28**(11), 1768–1783 (2006)
7. Kormos, A., Kormos, J., Nagy, B., Zrg, Z.: Choosing appropriate distance measurement in digital image segmentation. Annales Univ. Sci. Budapest. Sect. Comp. **24**, 193–208 (2004)
8. Martin, D., Fowlkes, C., Tal, D., Malik, J.: A database of human segmented natural images and its application to evaluating segmentation algorithms and measuring ecological statistics. In: Proc. 8th Int'l Conf. Computer Vision, vol. 2, pp. 416–423 (2001)
9. Price, B.L., Morse, B.S., Cohen, S.: Geodesic graph cut for interactive image segmentation. In: CVPR, pp. 3161–3168. IEEE (2010)
10. Toivanen, P.J.: New geodesic distance transforms for gray-scale images. Pattern Recogn. Lett. **17**(5), 437–450 (1996)
11. Wang, J., Yagi, Y.: Shape priors extraction and application for geodesic distance transforms in images and videos. Pattern Recogn. Lett. **34**(12), 1386–1393 (2013)
12. Zhou, L., Qiao, Y., Yang, J., He, X.: Learning geodesic CRF model for image segmentation. In: 2012 19th IEEE International Conference on Image Processing (ICIP) (2012)

Ground Level Recovery from Terrestrial Laser Scanning Data with the Variably Randomized Iterated Hierarchical Hough Transform

Leszek J. Chmielewski[✉] and Arkadiusz Orłowski

Faculty of Applied Informatics and Mathematics (WZIM), Warsaw University of Life
Sciences (SGGW), Ul. Nowoursynowska 159, 02-775 Warsaw, Poland
{leszek_chmielewski,arkadiusz_orlowski}@sggw.pl
http://www.wzim.sggw.pl

Abstract. The planar digital terrain model to be used in the analysis of
forest measurements made with terrestrial LIDAR scanning is proposed
for regions dominated by plains. The structure of the data suggests that
the iterated version of the Hough transform is a suitable method. This
makes it possible to reduce the time and memory requirements of the
method. Randomization with the fraction of data used varying with distance to the scanner is proposed to address the biasing of the result
towards the measurements which are made with higher density in the
central part of the stand. Using this method instead of weighted voting reduces the time of analysis. Hierarchical approach leads to further
reduction of time. The method can be extended to models formed from
more than one plane.

Keywords: Digital terrain model · DTM · Ground level · LIDAR ·
TLS · Hough transform · HT · Randomized · Iterated · Hierarchical

1 Introduction

In the measurements of forest, the modeling of the terrain level (ground level) is
one of the fundamental tasks. Much has been done towards calculating the digital
terrain model (DTM) from the airborne laser scanning (ALS) data, e.g. [1], see [2]
for a literature survey. The errors of such models reported in literature exceed
0.5 m [3]. According to our knowledge, finding the DTM from the terrestrial laser
scanning (TLS) data was rarely or not at all reported in the literature until quite
recently. Costantino and Angelini [4] developed a method based on least squares
estimation and interpolation for enhancing the DTM found for TLS and other
data for a road-type area using commercial systems. Eltner et al. [5] investigated
soil erosion with the use of a very precise DTM found from TLS and unmanned
aerial vehicle data. Puttonen [6] proposed a method of finding the DTM from
TLS, which is one of the first literature reports on the analysis of forest TLS
data aimed at finding the DTM. At the same time, in some publications on
the measurement of forest parameters, the terrain model is found from ALS,

© Springer International Publishing Switzerland 2015
G. Azzopardi and N. Petkov (Eds.): CAIP 2015, Part I, LNCS 9256, pp. 630–641, 2015.
DOI: 10.1007/978-3-319-23192-1_53

like in [7], or is not explicitly mentioned at all, like for example in [8]. In our previous works [9,10,11] we have made an implicit simplifying assumption that the ground is a horizontal plane. In this paper we shall consider a tilted plane.

As stated above, the errors of the DTMs, for regions vegetated by forests, found from ALS data exceed 0.5 m. In geographical regions dominated by plains, large areas comparable in size to single forest stands, typically analyzed with TLS in one measurement run, can be approximated with a single plane well within the error bounds of corresponding size.

Finding the terrain model is the first step in the analysis, so as the data the measurement points without information on whether they belong to the terrain, to the trees or to other objects should be used. Therefore, the method to be applied should be robust against the presence of data which do not belong to the object to be modeled. The terrain model will be the plane, so it is expected that those data which are consistent with the most apparent plane should be taken into account. This suggests to use one of the robust methods belonging to the family of Hough transforms (HT) originated by P.V.C. Hough in [12] and further developed in innumerable studies. Besides that this transform was applied to many problems, there is little literature on the detection of planes with HT. The classical HT is considered in [16] for detecting a plane in 3D parameter space, but its large time and memory consumption lead to a conclusion that another method of plane detection should be chosen. In [17] a number of different Hough space concepts is analyzed and a new ball-shaped architecture is proposed which assures uniform accuracy and rotation invariance of the solutions. The voting subset consists of three points randomly chosen from the set of measurement points, which makes it possible to find three parameters of the plane in each vote. The classical HT is used in [18], while the emphasis of that paper is laid upon the problem of manipulating the plane representation within the frames of the conformal geometric algebra. In [19] the curved shape of the LIDAR scans which follow the shape of conics is utilized to organize the accumulation more efficiently. In [20] the data used are structured in such a way that it is possible to find the local direction of the postulated plane. This direction is used to decouple the calculations of direction and distance. In [21] the clustering of points is possible, so the centroids and the directional structure of clusters can be used to organize the accumulation.

In this paper we shall not utilize any ordering in the data set. To avoid the use of a 3D accumulator for the 3D problem of detection of the plane we shall apply the Iterated HT introduced in the photogrammetry setting by Habib and Schenk [13]. This will solve the problem of large memory consumption. The excessive time requirements resulting from the large number of data and the relatively high required accuracy of the plane parameters will be overcome with the use of a hierarchical version of the HT.

The TLS data for the forest stands contain very large numbers of measurement points. It will be shown further that it is justified to state that the majority of these data pertain to the ground. The volume of data is much more than necessary to calculate the result; therefore, using a randomized HT approach [14,15] will be applied. The distribution of ground data points along the radius from the LIDAR is highly non-uniform, so the fraction of points selected by a random procedure can be made dependent on this distribution. This will fulfil the need for weighting the votes coming from regions with different data densities.

The remainder of this paper is organized as follows. The data sets used and the problem to be solved will be described in Sect. 2. The description of the method proposed to find the DTM will be divided between Sect. 3.1, in which the basic method will be introduced and its drawbacks as well as potential for improvements will be assessed, and Sect. 3.2 in which two improvements – randomization and hierarchy – will be proposed and justified. Typical results for some of the data will be shown and discussed in Sect. 4 and the paper will be concluded in Sect. 5.

2   Data and Problem Statement

The data were scanned at 15 stands near Głuchów in the Grójec Forest District, Mazovian Voivodship (Central Poland), with the terrestrial LIDAR scanner FARO LS HE880. A stand is a square area of the forest established for measurement purposes ($\approx 30 \times 30$ m). The stands will be further denoted as G01-G15. For each stand, between 12 and 22 millions of measurement points were collected, from one LIDAR position in a stand.

Calculations were carried out for all the stands; however, in this paper the results for stands G01 and G13 will be shown, as these stands were characteristic for two reasons. The first is that the stand G13 is a good example of the small density of vegetation at the low level. This can be seen in Fig. 1b: the majority of measurement points come from the ground (range approx. $\langle -2.0, -0.8 \rangle$ m), the second large subset comes from the tree crowns (range $\langle 7.5, 14.0 \rangle$ m), and the intermediate interval of heights corresponding to the tree trunks has a lower density of measurements. On the contrary, for G01 shown in Fig. 1a, the lower level of vegetation gives rise to an additional set of local maxima between the ground level and the crowns (range approx. $\langle -1.0, 6.0 \rangle$ m). The second reason is that the results for G13 exhibited the largest variability with the changing fraction of data selected in the randomized HT (Sect. 3.2).

The plane will be described in the coordinate system $Oxyz$, with Oz pointing vertically upwards, by an equation in the form

$$(x - x_0)n'_x + (y - y_0)n'_y + (z - z_0)n'_z = 0 \ , \tag{1}$$

where the six parameters are as follows: $[n'_x, n'_y, n'_z]$ is the unit normal vector and (x_0, y_0, z_0) is a reference point belonging to the plane. From these parameters three are independent. We shall assume that the normal vector is not unit, but that its vertical component is unit. This will make it impossible to represent vertical planes, but such planes do not appear in plain regions. Further, we shall use the fact that the data are LIDAR-centered which means that they are expressed in a coordinate system with Oz axis located in the LIDAR's axis of

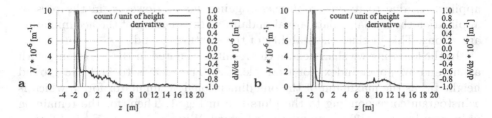

Fig. 1. Vertical profiles of the counts of measurement points of two stands: (a) G01; (b) G13. Derivative shown to underline that the maximum indicates the ground level. Truncated maxima amount to around 66×10^6 for (a) and 111×10^6 for (b).

rotation which is vertical. Therefore, if the reference point is chosen somewhere along this axis, then both x_0 and y_0 will be zero. Equation (1) will become

$$x\,n_x + y\,n_y + z - z_0 = 0 \tag{2}$$

and will explicitly have three parameters. These three unknown parameters have to be estimated with the use of given measurement points $P_i = (x_i, y_i, z_i)$, $i = 1, \ldots, M$, where $M \gg 3$. From these points, some belong to the ground which is planar only approximately, some belong to the trees, other vegetation and possibly to other overground objects, which are out from interest in this problem, and some are under the ground level due to scanning errors.

3   Method

Let us start from an observation that a large part, if not a majority, of measurement points belong to the ground. This can be seen in vertical profiles of the data for practically every stand, as shown in Fig. 1 for G01 and G13. The peak near $z = -1.3\,\mathrm{m}$ dominates the plots (it is a common custom that the measuring heads of the LIDARs are placed at the breast height (1.30 m) from the ground).

This observation suggests that the vertical coordinate of the ground can be found from the LIDAR data in a stable way independently from the estimation of the inclination. Moderate inclination of the ground surface should not disturb due to that, as we shall see further in Sec. 3.2, a dominating part of the ground points are located near to the scanner.

3.1   Basic Method

If a classical one-to-many version of the Hough transform is used with (2) then for each measurement point $P(x_i, y_i, z_i)$ the plane according to (2) with (x, y, z) set to the components of P should be plotted in a 3D accumulator for (n_x, n_y, z_0). This would require large memory for such an accumulator and considerable time for plotting the planes.

Instead of this, we shall use an iterative algorithm. The iterated HT proposed by Habib et al. [13] was critically assessed by Chmielewski [22] in a different application, due to its low robustness against noise. However, in the present application the available data are abundant, so the maxima of the accumulators are strong. This justifies the stability of the solutions found.

In the following we shall denote the results estimated in the iteration j with a hat and an upper index, for example, $\widehat{z_0}^j$. The idea is to find the ground height $\widehat{z_0}^1$ as the maximum of the one-dimensional accumulator for z_0 which is a histogram corresponding to the plots like in Fig. 1. Then, for the remaining unknowns $[n_x, n_y]$, a 2D accumulator is formed. When z_0 is set to $\widehat{z_0}^1$ in (2) then in this accumulator for each measurement point the line expressing the relation between n_x and n_y is plotted according to

$$x_i n_x + y_i n_y + z_i - \widehat{z_0}^1 = 0 \ . \tag{3}$$

The maximum in this accumulator corresponds to $[\widehat{n_x}, \widehat{n_y}]^1$. Forming and analyzing the two accumulators is repeated until the results stabilize (see Alg. 1).

Algorithm 1.

1. Read the data.
2. Iterate for j staring from 1:
   (a) Form and analyze the accumulator for z_0 to find $\widehat{z_0}^j$.
   (b) If $j > 1$ and result did not change: $\widehat{z_0}^j = \widehat{z_0}^{j-1}$ go to 3.
   (c) Form and analyze the accumulator for $[n_x, n_y]$ to find $[\widehat{n_x}, \widehat{n_y}]^j$.
   (d) If $j > 1$ and result did not change: $[\widehat{n_x}, \widehat{n_y}]^j = [\widehat{n_x}, \widehat{n_y}]^{j-1}$ go to 3.
   (e) Set $j := j + 1$.
3. Save the results and stop.

The dimensions of the 1D accumulator for z_0 will be from 1 to Z, and for the 2D accumulator for $[n_x, n_y]$ from 1 to A thus forming a square matrix of size $A \times A$. To assure the sufficient accuracy, the sizes will be chosen as follows. For the range of z_i found in the data, Z is chosen so that one accumulator element corresponds to 0.01 m. For the ranges of n_x and $n_y \in \langle -1, 1 \rangle$, parameter A is set to 2000, so that the normal vector components are found with the accuracy up to 0.001 which corresponds to $\tan^{-1}(0.001) \approx 0.057°$ for small angles and increasing up to $\tan^{-1}(1) - \tan^{-1}(0.999) \approx 0.029°$ for angles close to 45°. This range is enough in plains and assures the accuracy of 0.02 m height at the distance of 20 m which is more than the practical limit for such measurements.

An example of how the calculations proceed is shown in Fig. 2. It is characteristic that the maxima in the accumulators are clearly distinguishable.

Execution time depends linearly on the number of measurement points M, linearly on the size Z of the accumulator for height z_0, linearly on the size A of the square accumulator for $[n_x, n_y]$ when its formation is considered and quadratically when its analysis is considered. The complexity can be expressed as

$$C(M, Z, A) = aM + MT(b + cZ + dA) + TeA^2 = O(MA) \ , \tag{4}$$

where T is the number of iterations, and the constants $a - e$ are related, respectively: a to reading the data, b to forming and c to analyzing the accumulator

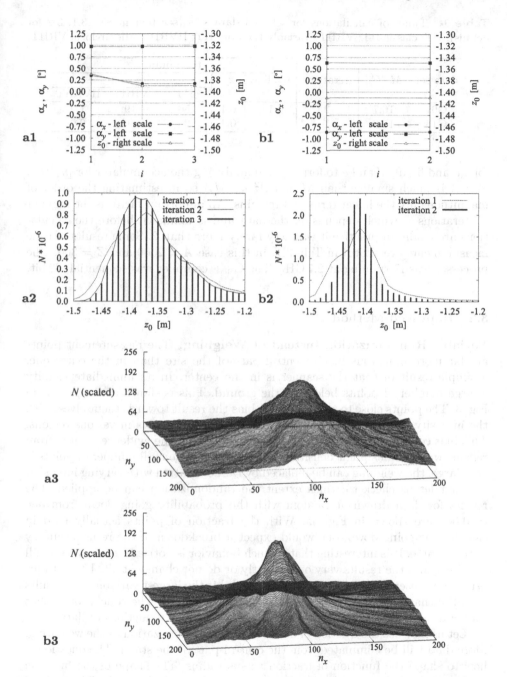

Fig. 2. Chosen results for two stands: (**a**) G01, (**b**) G13. Subfigures (**a1, b1**): results of iterations (components of the normal transformed to angles); (**a2, b2**): accumulators of height z_0 for all iterations; (**a3, b3**): accumulator of normal vector $[n_x, n_y]$ for last iteration (scaled into $\langle 0, 255 \rangle$ for visualization), only central parts of tables shown.

Table 1. Times of calculations for selected data sets (see text in Sec. 3.1, 3.2 for details). HT: classic HT; VRHT: Variably Random HT; HVRHT: Hierarchical VRHT.

data set	$M[10^6]$	iterations	reading	z_0	time [min]		
						$[n_x, n_y]$	
					HT	VRHT	HVRHT
G01	16.7	2	1	0.1	56	19	1.9
G13	15.8	1	1	0.1	28	9	0.9

for z_0, and finally d and e to forming and analyzing the accumulator for $[n_x, n_y]$. Size A is much smaller than M and $A^2 \ll MA$ so in estimating the order of magnitude only the linear term MA remains. An important factor is the number of iterations T which depends on the data and is unknown before the calculations are made. In practice it was very rarely more than 2. Some results of time measurements are shown in Tab. 3.1. In this case $A = 2000$ and $Z = 300$. The processor was i7 running at 2.7 GHz. The C++ compiler was sequential, 32 bit.

3.2 Improved Method

Variable Randomization Instead of Weighing. The measurement points are far more numerous in the central part of the site than in the outer one, a simple result of that the scanner is in the center. In its immediate vicinity a large number of points belong to the ground. This is shown in the graphs in Fig. 3. The points close to the center can bias the result towards themselves, with the intensity proportional to the ratio of densities of points in various regions. This bias could be reduced by appropriately weighing the evidence coming from regions with various point densities. Due to that the general number of points is very large, the weighing can be replaced by randomization with varying intensity.

First let us check to which extent the randomization can be applied. The results for data drawn at random with the probability going down from one to 0.001 are shown in Fig. 4a. With the fraction of points actually used in calculations going down, one would expect a breakdown of the result accuracy at some value. It is interesting that no such behavior is noticed even at very small fractions, and the results vary only slightly or do not change at all. The data for G13 were chosen for display because they exhibit the largest variability of results with the changing fraction, among the sets investigated. The conclusion is that randomization can be safely used even with important reductions of data.

Let us now use the fraction of data chosen by randomization as the weighting. More data will be eliminated from the central part of the stand. The question is how to shape the function of fraction versus radius. The shape of the function of the number of points along radius is close to linear in log scale. The ratio of ground data goes down in some stands and is close to constant in others. Neither of these shapes seem to give clue on the proper shape of fraction versus radius. Therefore, a linear change of the fraction going up from a given value for zero radius to one for a radius r_{lim} which corresponds to a state *far from the center* is

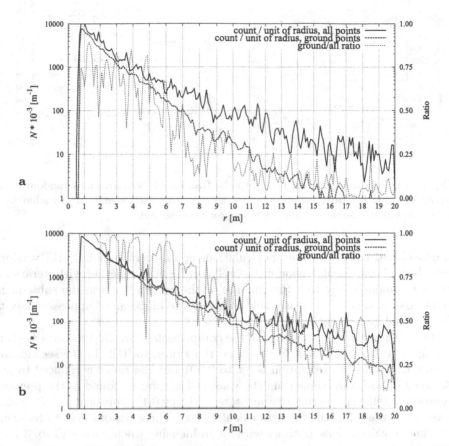

Fig. 3. Horizontal profiles of the counts of measurement points of two stands: (**a**) C01; (**b**) G13. Note the logarithmic scale for the axes of point counts. Points not farther from the ground level than 5 cm considered as ground points.

postulated. Let us assume arbitrarily that *far* means half the way from zero to a distance corresponding to *the farthest possible*. To establish this distance let us recall that due to occlusion, in stands having simple structure the radius should be limited to approximately 15 m if low errors are expected from the results from TLS [23]. Therefore, $r_{lim} = 7.5$ m.

The results for fractions depending on radius are shown in Fig. 4b. Some of the results switch to a different, but still close value and further they remain stable for the fraction of drawn measurement points going down. The calculation time decreases linearly together with the actual fraction of data used. In the calculations with constant fraction it actually went down to one minute and for variable fraction to one third of the original time.

A cautious conclusion is that variable randomization can be used to reduce the calculation time, while the bias caused by the large number of central results on the terrain model seems not to be significant.

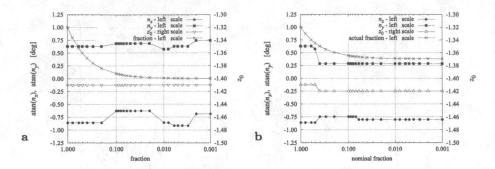

Fig. 4. Changes of results for G13 with the fraction of data drawn at random going down. Versions for randomization: (**a**) constant with radius and (**b**) variable with radius. In either case no breakdown point can be observed.

Hierarchical HT. The time of calculations is considerable in both HT versions described. Hierarchical version of the HT can be used together with iterations, which is supported by that the changes of the results between the subsequent iterations are small. It is reasonable to apply the hierarchical approach only to the accumulation of the normal vector.

In the first iteration the range of the components of $[n_x, n_y]$ remains $\langle -1, 1 \rangle$ but the resolution can be safely reduced ten times, to 0.01. In the second and further iterations the resolution is set to 0.001 but the range is reduced to 100 elements in both directions from the values of n_x and n_y found in the previous iterations, giving the room for parameter change by 0.1 (equivalent to 5.7°, a step never encountered in the hitherto calculations). These actions lead to reducing the time of calculations 10 times without influencing the accuracy (Tab. 3.1).

4   Results and Discussion

An example of results for stand G13, variably randomized with the reference fraction 0.01, is shown in Fig. 5.

At this stage, the quality of results can be estimated by simple observation. The ground is not planar in general. The distances from the planar model to ground points which can be seen in visualizations amount to less than 0.5 m (except the places where the terrain clearly depart from the planar model). Therefore, the accuracy is acceptable, in comparison with the errors of DTMs found in literature, for forest conditions [2]. A strong indication that the surface is optimal in the sense of matching the evidence contained in the data is the shape of the vote densities in the accumulators. The functions have clear, easily distinguishable global maxima (Fig. 2a2-b3).

The similar methodology can be used to find more than one plane to represent the terrain having a more complex structure. Successful experiments with reducing the number of data indicates that positive results can be obtained also in regions where the data points are available in smaller numbers.

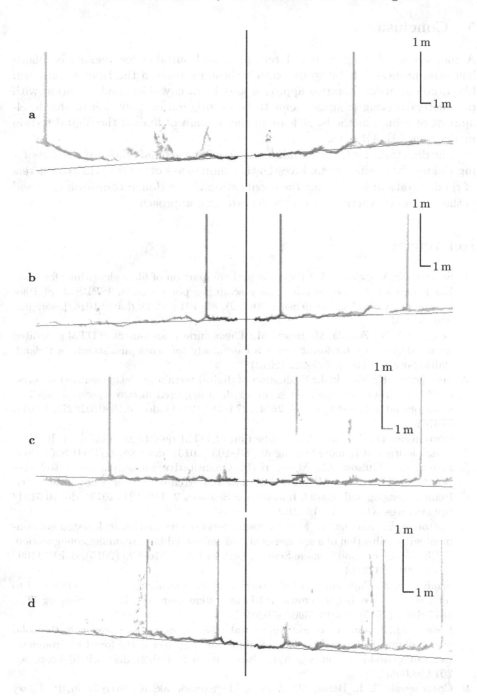

Fig. 5. Results for G13, variable randomization with parameter 0.01. Cross-sections plotted for 5° wide sectors for angles (**a**) 0°, (**b**) 45°, (**c**) 90°, (**d**) 135° from Ox. Black line represents Oz. Estimated ground level shown in red. Red arrow in (c) represents ≈ 16 cm. Maximum distance from center is 20 m. Each sector contains $\approx 300\,000$ points. Darkness level proportional to density of points.

5 Conclusions

A method for finding a digital terrain model suitable for regions of plains has been proposed. It integrates such techniques used in the Hough transform like randomization, iterative approach and hierarchy. The randomization with parameters varying in space seems to be an original contribution to the development of robust methods, at least in the domain of finding the digital terrain model from LIDAR data.

The directions for further studies are: acquiring ground truth data and verifying the results against them; investigating more ways of varying the parameters of randomization; introducing the fuzzification in the Hough transform used and gathering more experience with the hierarchical approach.

References

1. Sithole, G., Vosselman, G.: Experimental comparison of filter algorithms for bare-Earth extraction from airborne laser scanning point clouds. ISPRS J. of Photogrammetry and Remote Sensing **59**(1–2), 85–101 (2004). doi:10.1016/j.isprsjprs. 2004.05.004
2. Stereńczak, K., Zasada, M., Brach, M.: The accuracy assessment of DTM generated from LIDAR data for forest area - a case study for scots pine stands in Poland. Baltic Forestry **19**(2), 252–262 (2013)
3. Stereńczak, K., Kozak, J.: Evaluation of digital terrain models generated in forest conditions from airborne laser scanning data acquired in two seasons. Scandinavian Journal of Forest Research **26**(4), 374–384 (2011). doi:10.1080/02827581.2011. 570781
4. Costantino, D., Angelini, M.: Production of DTM quality by TLS data. International Journal of Remote Sensing **46**, 80–103 (2013). doi:10.5721/EuJRS20134606
5. Eltner, A., Mulsow, C., Maas, H.G.: Quantitative measurement of soil erosion from TLS and UAV data. International Archives of the Photogrammetry, Remote Sensing and Spatial. Information Sciences **2**, 119–124 (2013). doi:10.5194/ isprsarchives-XL-1-W2-119-2013
6. Puttonen, E., Krooks, A., et al.: Ground level determination in forested environment with utilization of a scanner-centered terrestrial laser scanning configuration. IEEE Geoscience and Remote Sensing Letters **12**(3), 616–620 (2015). doi:10.1109/ LGRS.2014.2353414
7. Srinivasan, S., Popescu, S., et al.: Terrestrial laser scanning as an effective tool to retrieve tree level height, crown width, and stem diameter. Remote Sensing **7**(2), 1877–1896 (2015). doi:10.3390/rs70201877
8. Dassot, M., Colin, A., et al.: Terrestrial laser scanning for measuring the solid wood volume, including branches, of adult standing trees in the forest environment. Computers and Electronics in Agriculture **89**, 86–93 (2012). doi:10.1016/j.compag. 2012.08.005
9. Chmielewski, L.J., Bator, M., Zasada, M., Stereńczak, K., Strzeliński, P.: Fuzzy hough transform-based methods for extraction and measurements of single trees in large-volume 3D terrestrial LIDAR data. In: Bolc, L., Tadeusiewicz, R., Chmielewski, L.J., Wojciechowski, K. (eds.) ICCVG 2010, Part I. LNCS, vol. 6374, pp. 265–274. Springer, Heidelberg (2010)

10. Chmielewski, L.J., Bator, M.: Hough transform for opaque circles measured from outside and fuzzy voting for and against. In: Bolc, L., Tadeusiewicz, R., Chmielewski, L.J., Wojciechowski, K. (eds.) ICCVG 2012. LNCS, vol. 7594, pp. 313–320. Springer, Heidelberg (2012)

11. Chmielewski, L.J., Bator, M., Olejniczak, M.: Advantages of using object-specific knowledge at an early processing stage in the detection of trees in LIDAR data. In: Chmielewski, L.J., Kozera, R., Shin, B.-S., Wojciechowski, K. (eds.) ICCVG 2014. LNCS, vol. 8671, pp. 145–154. Springer, Heidelberg (2014)

12. Hough, P.: Machine analysis of bubble chamber pictures. In: Proc. Int. Conf. on High Energy Accelerators and Instrumentation, CERN (1959)

13. Habib, A., Schenk, T.: New approach for matching surfaces from laser scanners and optical sensors. In: Csatho, B.M., (ed.) Proc. Joint Workshop of ISPRS III/5 and III/2 on Mapping Surface Structure and Topography by Air-borne and Space-borne Lasers, La Jolla, San Diego, CA, Nov 9–11, 1999

14. Xu, L., Oja, E., Kultanen, P.: A new curve detection method: Randomized Hough transform (RHT). Pattern Recognition Letters **11**(5), 331–338 (1990)

15. Kälviäinen, H., Hirvonen, P., et al.: Probabilistic and non-probabilistic Hough transforms: overview and comparisons. Image and Vision Computing **13**(4), 239–252 (1995). doi:10.1016/0262-8856(95)99713-B

16. Tarsha-Kurdi, F., Grussenmeyer, P.: Hough-transform and extended RANSAC algorithms for automatic detection of 3D building roof planes from Lidar data. In: Proc. ISPRS Workshop on Laser Scanning 2007 and SilviLaser 2007, vol. XXXVI-3/W52, Espoo, Finland, pp. 407–412, September 2007

17. Borrmann, D., Elseberg, J., et al.: The 3d hough transform for plane detection in point clouds: A review and a new accumulator design. 3D Research **2**(2) (2011). doi:10.1007/3DRes.02(2011)3

18. Bernal-Marin, M., Bayro-Corrochano, E.: Integration of Hough Transform of lines and planes in the framework of conformal geometric algebra for 2D and 3D robot vision. Pattern Recognition Letters **32**(16), 2213–2223 (2011). doi:10.1016/j.patrec. 2011.05.014

19. Grant, W., Voorhies, R., Itti, L.: Finding planes in LiDAR point clouds for real-time registration. In: IEEE/RSJ Int. Conf. Intelligent Robots and Systems IROS 2013, pp. 4347–4354, November 2013. doi:10.1109/IROS.2013.6696980

20. Hulik, R., et al.: Continuous plane detection in point-cloud data based on 3D Hough Transform. Journal of Visual Communication and Image Representation **25**(1), 86–97 (2014). doi:10.1016/j.jvcir.2013.04.001

21. Limberger, F.A., Oliveira, M.M.: Real-time detection of planar regions in unorganized point clouds. Pattern Recognition **48**(6), 2043–2053 (2015). doi:10.1016/j. patcog.2014.12.020

22. Chmielewski, L.: Choice of the Hough transform for image registration. Proc. SPIE. **5505**, 122–134 (2004). doi:10.1117/12.577912

23. Zasada, M., Stereńczak, K., et al.: Horizon visibility and accuracy of stocking determination on circular sample plots using automated remote measurement techniques. Forest Ecology and Management **302**, 171–177 (2013). doi:10.1016/j.foreco. 2013.03.041

U3PT: A New Dataset for Unconstrained 3D Pose Tracking Evaluation

Ngoc-Trung Tran[1,2]([✉]), Fakhreddine Ababsa[2], and Maurice Charbit[1]

[1] LTCI-CNRS, Telecom ParisTECH, 37-39, Rue Dareau, 75014 Paris, France
trung-ngoc.tran@telecom-paristech.fr
[2] IBISC, University of Evry, 40, Rue du Pelvoux, 91020 Evry, France

Abstract. 3D pose tracking using monocular cameras is an important topic, which has been receiving a great attention since last decades. It is useful in many domains such as: Video Surveillance, Human-Computer Interface, Biometrics, etc. The problem gets much challenging if occurring, for example, fast motion, out-of-plane rotation, the illumination changes, expression, or occlusions. In the literature, there are some datasets reported for 3D pose tracking evaluation, however, all of them retains simple background, no-expression, slow motion, frontal rotation, or no-occlusion. It is not enough to test advances of in-the-wild tracking. Indeed, collecting accurate ground-truth of 3D pose is difficult because some special devices or sensors are required. In addition, the magnetic sensors usually used for 3D pose ground-truth, is uncomfortable to wear and move because of their wires. In this paper, we propose a new recording system that allows people move more comfortable. We create a new challenging dataset, named U3PT (Unconstrained 3D Pose Tracking). It could be considered as a benchmark to evaluate and compare the robustness and precision of state-of-the-art methods that aims to work in-the-wild. This paper will also present the performances of two well-known state-of-the-art methods compared to our method on face tracking when applied to this database. We have carried out several experiments and have reported advantages and some limitations to be improved in the future.

Keywords: 3D pose tracking · 3D head tracking · Pose estimation · Unconstrained pose tracking · Pose tracking dataset · Synthetic data

1 Introduction

The main goal of head pose tracking is to estimate the 6 Degrees-of-Freedom (DoF) - consists of 3D translation and three axial rotations - of a person's head relative to the camera view. As commonly-use in the literature, we adopt three terms Yaw (or Pan), Pitch (Tilt) and Roll for three axial rotations. The detail related to pose estimation in general could be found in this interesting survey (Murphy-Chutorian and Trivedi [2009]), whereas we just consider the pose estimation via tracking approaches because it is much more accurate and applicable to many applications nowadays.

© Springer International Publishing Switzerland 2015
G. Azzopardi and N. Petkov (Eds.): CAIP 2015, Part I, LNCS 9256, pp. 642–653, 2015.
DOI: 10.1007/978-3-319-23192-1_54

In the field of face tracking, a lot of studies over the last decade has provided significant progress, such as: i) using template models, e.g, Active Appearance Model (Cootes et al. [2001], Xiao et al. [2004], Matthews and Baker [2004]), Cylinder (Cascia et al. [2000], Xiao et al. [2003]) or Candide (Alonso et al. [2007]), ii) using local matching, e.g, (Vacchetti et al. [2004], Jang and Kanade [2008], Wang et al. [2012]), iii) using local discriminative classifiers, e.g, Constrained Local Model (Cristinacce and Cootes [2006], Wang et al. [2008], Saragih et al. [2011]). In recent years, cascaded regression has become the leading approach for accurate and robust face alignment, in which most of them has achieved state-of-the-art performance. The basic idea is to use a sequence of weak regressors, which are learned sequentially. The pioneer works of cascaded regression have been proposed in (Dollar et al. [2010], Valstar et al. [2010]) for object alignment, then be applied in (Cao et al. [2012]; Xiong and la Torre Frade [2013]) successfully for face alignment and tracking. Many methods were proposed using cascaded regression to improve performances in terms of accuracy, speed, or occlusion (Burgos-Artizzu et al. [2013], Ren et al. [2014], Kazemi and Sullivan [2014], Zhang et al. [2014], Sun et al. [2013]). Cascaded regression based methods have shown the high accuracy and real-time speed, merely it is restricted between (-45°,45°). This problem happens because of two reasons: First, the acquisition of ground-truth for unconstrained views is too expensive in practice. Second, annotating hidden landmarks at invisible side is difficult. In this paper, we will base on this approach and propose a solution to make it work at larger poses.

In the literature, some datasets were reported for pose estimation evaluation in video sequences. The most popular one is Boston University Face Tracking (BUFT) dataset (Cascia et al. [2000]). Its ground-truth of 3D pose is captured by magnetic sensors *"Flock and Birds"* with an accuracy of less than 1°. It has two subsets: uniform-light set and varying-light set. The uniform-light set has a total of 45 video sequences (320×240 resolution) for 5 subjects (9 videos per subject) with available ground-truth of pose consisting of three directions: Yaw, Pitch and Roll. The varying-light set contains 27 sequences of 3 subjects recorded under same condition like the first set except fast-changing lighting conditions. So far, this is no longer a challenging dataset, because all subjects in this dataset always kept their faces neural while moving their heads slowly and no occlusion happens, the background is not too cluttered and the angles of three direction is mostly not larger than 40°. Many works reported high performance on this dataset (Xiao et al. [2003], Jang and Kanade [2008], Wang et al. [2012]). CLEAR07 (Stiefelhagen et al. [2007]) contains multi-view video recordings of a seminar room. It consists of 15 videos with four-synchronized cameras with frame rate at 15fps. This dataset provides both pose data from single view and multi-view. However, the subject captured for head pose is just seating in the same place. IDIAP Head Pose (Ba and Odobez [2007]) is an another source of LEAR07, and the values of Yaw, Pitch and Roll range only between (-60,60), (-60,15) and (-30,30) respectively for the single view. Methods evaluated on this dataset not fully automatic because the bounding-box is provided.

(Murphy-Chutorian and Trivedi [2008]) created a dataset recording drivers while driving in daytime and night-time lighting conditions. The drivers faces are usually neutral at mostly frontal views. There are other datasets reviewed in the survey (Murphy-Chutorian and Trivedi [2009]), but they are not much more challenging than above-mentioned datasets because of simple background, slow motion or frontal. Most of datasets reported used the magnetic sensors not comfortable to wear and move around because of wires connecting between them and the computer. In this work, we will propose a new way of recording 3D ground-truth that enables people to move around more comfortably. By this, we create a new database to evaluate in-the-wild pose tracking methods efficiently and more detail.

So, our contributions in this paper consists of two folds: i) We implement the state-of-the-art face tracking method and then propose a new way that allows to able to work with extreme poses or in-the-wild conditions. ii) We propose a new recording system to do recording accurately and more comfortable. Our new database contains challenging conditions that enable to evaluate advances of 3D pose tracking. The remaining of this paper is organized as follows: Section 2 describes the background of the face tracking method we want to improve. Section 3 discusses about our recording system. Experimental results and analysis are presented in Section 4. Finally, we provide in Section 5 some conclusions and further perspectives.

2   Towards to In-the-wild Tracking

Cascaded regression approach is now a promising approach which has shown the reliable capability of in-the-wild face tracking, but one of its limitations is out-of-plane tracking. In this study, we base on this approach and propose a new way to let it work at larger rotation.

2.1   Cascaded Regression

Let the shape $\mathbf{S} \in R^{2p \times 1}$ be the coordinate vector of p facial landmarks. Let $\widehat{\mathbf{S}}$ be true shape. The goal of face alignment is to align the shape $\mathbf{S}$ as closely as the true shape by minimizing $\|\widehat{\mathbf{S}} - \mathbf{S}\|$. To estimate the shape, we use a sequence of T weak regressors $(r(1), r(2), ..., r(T))$, $r(t) \in R^{2p \times D}$, D is the dimension of feature $\Phi \in R^{D \times 1}$ extracted from the image:

$$\mathbf{S}(t) = \mathbf{S}(t-1) + r(t)\Phi(I, \mathbf{S}(t-1)), \quad t = 1, ..., T \tag{1}$$

Given the facial image I and the initial face shape $\mathbf{S}(0)$, one weak regressor $r(t)$ estimates the new shape at time t $\mathbf{S}(t)$ from image features $\Phi(I, \mathbf{S}(t-1))$ computed using the previous shape $\mathbf{S}(t-1)$ on the image I. The sequentially training of the weak regressors $r(t)$ is based on N examples $\{(I_i, \widehat{\mathbf{S}}_i)\}_{i=1}^{N}$ by minimization as:

$$\arg\min_{r(t)} \sum_{i=1}^{N} \left\| \widehat{\mathbf{S}}_i - (\mathbf{S}_i(t-1) + r(t)\Phi(I_i, \mathbf{S}_i(t-1))) \right\|_2^2 \tag{2}$$

Φ is the vector concatenating local descriptors of p landmarks $\Phi = [\phi_1^T \ldots \phi_p^T]^T$. Hence, the local descriptor $\phi_i \in R^{d \times 1}$ is SIFT descriptor extracted in local region of i-th landmark. The initial shape $\mathbf{S}(0)$ is simply the mean shape aligned in the area detected by the face detectors. This minimization is a linear regression problem whose solution is in closed-form. We use the same way like (Xiong and la Torre Frade [2013]) to train the sequence of weak regressors. The parameters of our implementation, such as: patch size, the number of regressors,... is similar to (Xiong and la Torre Frade [2013]) and we obtained the same performance as in this paper.

2.2   Synthetic Data for Out-of-plane Tracking

Although cascaded regression approach is just considered for frontal face tracking so far, we believe that it is possible to work at out-of-plane rotations if a good training dataset of such conditions is provided. In the literature, two relevant datasets can be mentioned: AFLW (Koestinger et al. [2011]) and Multi-PIE (Gross et al. [2010]). The main limitation of these datasets are no information of hidden landmark annotation on large Yaw images. So, the number of landmarks among views is different that makes a gap of tracking and pose estimation, for example, from frontal to profile views. Indeed, the view-based models like using mixture of trees as (Zhu and Ramanan [2012]) could be a solution, otherwise pose detectors are required. It turns out that most of methods usually solve this profile problem by adaptive ways. The state-of-the-art, Intraface (Xiong and la Torre Frade [2013]), was only capable to handle restricted ranges, e.g, Yaw $\in$ [-45° 45°]. (Saragih et al. [2011]) developed a tracker tracking larger Yaw but not too robust. In addition, Pitch and Roll are not well-considered in current datasets.

In contrast, the synthetic data is a cheaper solution to create a high pose variation database. Thanks to 3D face models, the landmark number are the same among views because 2D projection of hidden landmarks could still be located. So, the gap of multi-view tracking could be bridged. In this study, we propose to use 3D face reconstruction to create extreme poses and combine with real data. We suppose that the real dataset is good for frontal tracking while the synthetic dataset is for other views. The extra mount of synthetic images will be included to the current datasets for training. We implemented 3D Morphable Model (3DMM) (Blanz and Vetter [1999]) to create our own synthetic data. We annotated once 51 inner landmarks similar to 300-W dataset (Sagonas et al. [2013]). The boundary landmarks are not considered because textures of two face sides are not good in our implementation of 3D face reconstruction. {Fig. 1} are some examples of 51 annotated landmarks and its rendering in different poses. In detail, we generate randomly about 3000 synthetic data using 3DMM for extreme poses. For real data, we use about 2000 images of training subsets of LFPW and Helen from 300-W dataset like (Ren et al. [2014]). In fact, this algorithm is originally developed for 2D face alignment, but it could be extended easily for tracking by using the aligned face at previous frame as the initial for the current one. The 3D pose is estimated by using POSIT (Dementhon and Davis [1995])

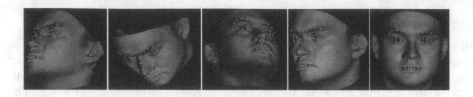

Fig. 1. The annotation of 51 landmarks in synthetic images and its rendering.

aligning a 3D model into 2D shape in this study. Indeed, the pose estimation would be improved more if using Bayesian tracking techniques, e.g. (Ababsa [2009]; Ababsa and Mallem [2006])

3 Recording System for Unconstrained 3D Pose Tracking

To build one dataset, the most importance is the ground-truth. We propose to use one stereo-infrared system to capture the 3D pose. The system enables to capture the ground-truth accurately while the face pose is unconstrained. For the recording campaign, three things need to be well-prepared: the setup of recording system, the calibration of cameras, and the definition of recording protocols.

Recording System. The proposed system consists of one RGB camera and one stereo-infrared device (SMARTTRACK) installed as {Fig. 2}. SMARTTRACK could detect five markers of the fly-stick from a distance and estimate accurately its 6 DOF. To use the fly-stick for the head pose ground-truth, we design a fly-stick hat people can wear on as {Fig. 2} while moving around. The system is installed as follows: The infrared device is located about 50cm higher than the RGB camera to be able to always detect all markers. The tripod enables to change the system height respect to people being recorded. These cameras are kept fixed vertically during the recording process and connected to one computer via the wire cable. For the infrared device, the driver is available on the website of the provider SMARTTRACK and it provides also the C/C++ API and the software Dtrack2 to connect and control. Notice that the infrared device and RGB camera need to be synchronized (we developed a function for this purpose) to capture at the same frame rate. The RGB camera and the infrared system also needs to be calibrated to get the correct 3D ground-truth in the coordinate of RGB camera. The calibration process of two devices is presented in following section.

Calibration. The calibration is first performed for each device. The traditional calibration using the check-board 7×9 via the Matlab toolbox (Bouguet [2003]) for RGB camera. The Dtrack2 supports the automatic calibration process for infrared device. For stereo calibration, we do annotation the 2D location of

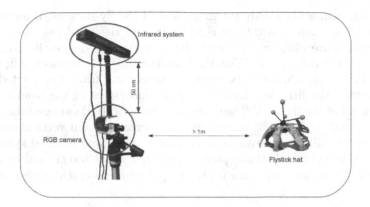

Fig. 2. The installation of recording system.

reference origin (red point in {Fig. 3}) on 2D images responding to 3D location detected by infrared cameras. So, 45 frames are collected to annotate the origin of the fly-sticks with available 3D ground-truth of infrared device. The {Fig. 3} shows the stereo-calibration to estimate the rotation $\mathbf{R}_{ic}$ and translation $\mathbf{T}_{ic}$ from the infrared to RGB cameras. Let denote that the i-th frame has 2D position of origin is $\mathbf{l}_i$ corresponding to the its known 3D coordinates $\mathbf{L}_i$ estimated by the infrared device. The transformation matrices are estimated through the least square problem:

$$\{\hat{\mathbf{R}}_{ic}, \hat{\mathbf{T}}_{ic}\} = \arg \min_{\mathbf{R}_{ic}, \mathbf{T}_{ic}} \sum_{i=1}^{N} \left(\mathbf{l}^i - \mathscr{P}([\hat{\mathbf{R}}_{ic}\hat{\mathbf{T}}_{ic}]\mathbf{L}^i) \right)^2 \tag{3}$$

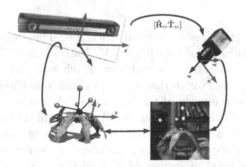

Fig. 3. The calibration diagram of RGB and infrared cameras.

where $\mathscr{P}$ is the projection of 3D position of fly-stick after transforming it from the infrared device to the RGB camera's coordinates. However, the location and rotation estimated is only the movement of the fly-stick worn on the head. It is difficult to have exactly the rigid motion of the head because the head sizes of people are different. To solve this problem, we define the pose of the first frame as the reference of (Yaw,Pitch,Roll)=(0,0,0). It means the first frame needs to make sure always to be frontal. The coming frames computed as the difference from the first one. By this way, the movement of the head is exactly the movement of the fly-stick. The calibration error of RGB camera using Matlab calibration toolbox is (0.162, 0.161) pixels in horizontal and vertical directions, and the stereo-calibration error between RGB camera and infrared system that we proposed is 3 pixels. It is acceptable value that is not too critical because we use the first frame as a reference for to compute ground-truth of next ones.

Recording. Our dataset consists of 50 videos of 10 subjects. One subject is recorded five videos during 20-40 seconds/video with the resolution 768×576. The first frame is always the frontal respect to the camera view. We set up the recording protocol to capture videos in challenging conditions: illumination, wide rotation, expression, occlusion, fast motion and complex movements. The dataset is recorded in the office environment with the cluttered background. Videos are recorded as the following protocols in raising up the difficult levels gradually for each subject from video 1 to 5:

- The 1st video (frontal): Subjects stay in front of the camera system and then walk around in the view of camera while keeping looking at it.
- The 2nd video (near-frontal + expression): Like the first one; except subjects sometimes change their expression or rotate a little bit head directions.
- The 3rd video (profile): Subjects stay in front of the camera system, then walk around and change its head direction, possibly wide rotations.
- The 4th video (profile + expression + occlusion): Like the third one, except subjects sometimes change expression or make some occlusions.
- The 5th video (in-the-wild): Subjects move comfortably in the view of camera.

As result, one video has its ground-truth file. The format of each line in ground-truth consists of 6 values $[V_x\ V_y\ V_z\ \text{Yaw Pitch Roll}]$. V_x, V_y, V_z: 3D coordinates of three axis of x, y, z and Yaw, Pitch and Roll are angles of three orientations respectively. Notice that V_x, V_y, V_z and Yaw Pitch Roll is computed corresponding to the reference of the first frame. At some frames, the infrared camera could not find out the fly-stick, so all the field of rotation and translation are set to -1 at these frames. For evaluation, we propose two measures: robustness and accuracy. The robustness P is the percentage of the number of well-detected frames N_s over the total of frames of ground-truth N_{total} (excluding frames having no ground-truth): $P = \frac{N_s}{N_{total}}100\%$. One frame is well-detected if the distance of the 2D position (projection) between our estimation and ground-truth is smaller than a threshold, and we fix this threshold be 40 pixels in our experiments. Notice that to be robust with scale problem, we normalize the distance by the factor $\frac{V_z}{F_{focal}}$, where F_{local} is the focal length of RGB camera.

Fig. 4. Some sample video sequences in our datasets.

The accuracy is the Mean Absolute Error (MAE) between the estimation and the ground-truth of head pose. For example, the error of Yaw (similarly for the Pitch and Roll) are computed as follows:

$$E_{yaw} = \frac{1}{N_s} \sum_{i \in S_s} |\Theta_{yaw}^i - \widehat{\Theta}_{yaw}^i| \tag{4}$$

where N_s is the number of well-detected frames and S_s is the set of frames Θ_{yaw}^i and $\widehat{\Theta}_{yaw}^i$ is the estimation and the ground-truth of Yaw. The error of the dataset is the average of all videos. {Fig. 5} shows sample frames of our database.

4   Experiments

4.1   Public Datasets

Before testing methods on own recordings, we report their performance on uniform-light set of BUFT. Our purpose is to make sure that state-of-the-art methods chosen to investigate our recordings later are good enough. In {Table 1}, although we are not better than some methods reported on this dataset, we have the more or less the same performance; especially, the Yaw and Pitch precision compared to fully-automatic method ("*" is fully automatic, otherwise semi-automatic). Among methods that can estimate simultaneously rigid and non-rigid parameters ("+" is able to estimate the non-rigid parameters), we are much better than FaceTracker (Saragih et al. [2011]). It demonstrates the efficiency of our tracking approach. Intraface (Xiong and la Torre Frade [2013]) is the best among fully-automatic methods. In fact, it is similar to ours except it is trained on much more real data than ours (but no detail is reported). Notice that the results of FaceTracker and Intraface on BUFT are performed by us.

To verify the in-the-wild and extreme pose tracking of our approach, two datasets are chosen: a) YouTube Celebrities dataset (Kim et al. [2008]), a challenging dataset as for in-the-wild conditions, b) Honda/UCSD (Lee et al. [2003]) with the complex motion patterns and extreme poses. This video[1] shows the results on some videos that our method is robust with these challenging videos.

---

[1] http://goo.gl/PL11JC

Table 1. The tracking performance on the uniform-light set of BUFT dataset.

Approach	E_{yaw}	E_{pitch}	E_{roll}	E_m
Wang et al., 2012	3.8	2.7	1.9	2.8
Xiao et al., 2003	3.8	3.2	1.4	2.8
Intraface (*,+)	4.1	3.0	2.2	3.1
Lefevre and Odobez, 2009 (+)	4.4	3.3	2.0	3.2
Jang and Kanade, 2008 (*)	4.6	3.7	2.1	3.5
Asteriadis et al., 2014 (*)	4.3	3.8	2.6	3.5
Morency et al., 2008 (*)	5.0	3.7	2.9	3.9
Facetracker (*,+)	4.3	4.8	2.6	3.9
Our method (*,+)	**4.4**	**3.3**	**3.0**	**3.6**

4.2   Unconstrained 3D Pose Tracking (U3PT) Dataset

In this section, we will use our own dataset (U3PT) to evaluate our tracker and two other trackers: FaceTracker and Intraface, two fully-automatic methods, that have good results on BUFT. Intraface based on the frontal face detectors to align the face, so they are only good for near-frontal views. FaceTracker can track the profile but be not really robust. Otherwise, our method can track well the high number of frames compared to other methods. The results in {Table 2} show performances of considered methods. We have the best results for the robustness but we are worse than Intraface for precision.

Table 2. The performance of methods on our own U3PT dataset.

Approach	P	E_{yaw}	E_{pitch}	E_{roll}	E_m
FaceTracker	30.6%	9.9	10.3	8.9	9.7
IntraFace	52.1%	6.2	6.4	7.0	6.5
Our method	**54.2%**	**8.4**	**7.8**	**6.3**	**7.5**

To be more detail, we evaluate considered methods on each specific groups of our database. Each group has a similar head movement patterns as reported in the earlier section. It enables us to see more detail the capability of methods on challenging cases. {Fig. 5} shows the accuracy and robustness of methods on each group. FaceTracker is the worst in the comparison at both robustness and precision in all groups. Two first groups, we have best performances on both accuracy and robustness. It means that our methods are more robust with frontal and expression tracking compared to other methods. However, we have only better robustness at three remaining groups compared to Intraface. It is because three groups have profile rotation that seems our estimation of profile views are not really good. Although our method has a better robustness but lower accuracy compared to Intraface.

The performance let us know about the difficulty of our recordings. Only about a half of number frames can be well-tracked, while the accuracy is low. Our method could work well with out-of-plane rotation on UCSD/Honda dataset, but it is impossible to do the same on U3PT because likely the background of this dataset is too cluttered. Whereas, our synthetic training data is completely black.

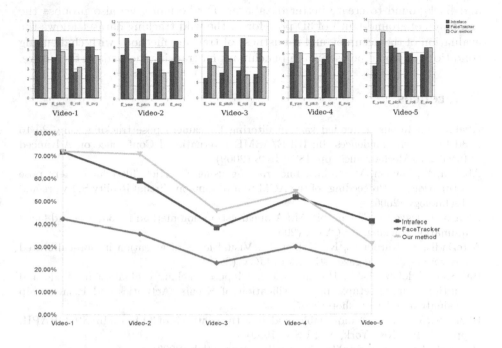

Fig. 5. The accuracies and robustness on each video group.

Intraface detects only a half of number frames because it bases on the frontal face detection to align 3D face. Although, the number of our real training data is only about 2000 images too small compared to Intraface, but with the support of synthetic data could make our method comparable to it. We believe if 3DMM is implemented better (background and expression), our method will be much better.

5   Conclusion

We proposed a new approach using cascaded regression for efficient tracking using the combination of synthetic and real dataset. The real dataset is good for frontal view, otherwise, the synthetic data makes the system robust with the large of rotations such as: Yaw or Pitch. The result shows the possibility of using synthetic data to by-pass the difficulties of lack of training data for such situations as Honda/UCSD video demo. By the combination of two kind of datasets, the robustness with large rotation tracking is more robust. However, when using on cluttered background, our synthetic images is not useful because its background is completely black. In addition, the facial animation of our 3DMM model haven't yet implemented to make the face tracking more reliable. In the future work, we aims to develop 3DMM with facial expression and background to create better databases. Furthermore, we also propose the campaign of ground-truth of 3D pose for in-the-wild tracking dataset allows the evaluation of the accuracy and robustness of tracking methods with challenging conditions. It would be useful as a benchmark for tracking methods in the future.

References

Ababsa, F.: Robust extended kalman filtering for camera pose tracking using 2d to 3d lines correspondences. In: IEEE/ASME International Conference on Advanced Intelligent Mechatronics, pp. 1834–1838 (2009)

Ababsa, F., Mallem, M.: Robust line tracking using a particle filter for camera pose estimation. In: Proceedings of the ACM Symposium on Virtual Reality Software and Technology (2006)

Alonso, J., Davoine, F., Charbit, M.: A linear estimation method for 3d pose and facial animation tracking. In: CVPR (2007)

Asteriadis, S., Karpouzis, K., Kollias, S.: Visual focus of attention in non-calibrated environments using gaze estimation. IJCV (2014)

Ba, S.O., Odobez, J.-M.: Probabilistic head pose tracking evaluation in single and multiple camera setups. In: Classification of Events, Activities and Relationship Evaluation and Workshop (2007)

Blanz, V., Vetter, T.: A morphable model for the synthesis of 3d faces. In: SIGGRAPH, pp. 187–194, New York, NY, USA (1999)

Bouguet, J.Y.: Camera calibration toolbox for matlab (2003)

Burgos-Artizzu, X., Perona, P., Dollár, P.: Robust face landmark estimation under occlusion. In: ICCV (2013)

Cao, X., Wei, Y., Wen, F., Sun, J.: Face alignment by explicit shape regression. In: CVPR (2012)

Cascia, M.L., Sclaroff, S., Athitsos, V.: Fast, reliable head tracking under varying illumination: An approach based on registration of texture-mapped 3d models. TPAMI **22**(4), 322–336 (2000)

Cootes, T.F., Edwards, G.J., Taylor, C.J.: Active appearance models. TPAMI **23**(6), 681–685 (2001)

Cristinacce, D., Cootes, T.F.: Feature detection and tracking with constrained local models. In: BMVC (2006)

Dementhon, D.F., Davis, L.S.: Model-based object pose in 25 lines of code. IJCV **15**, 123–141 (1995)

Dollar, P., Welinder, P., Perona, P.: Cascaded pose regression. In: CVPR (2010)

Gross, R., Matthews, I., Cohn, J.F., Kanade, T., Baker, S.: Multi-pie. IVC **28**(5), 807–813 (2010)

Jang, J.-S., Kanade, T.: Robust 3d head tracking by online feature registration. In: FG (2008)

Kazemi, V., Sullivan, J.: One millisecond face alignment with an ensemble of regression trees. In: CVPR (2014)

Kim, M., Kumar, S., Pavlovic, V., Rowley, H.A.: Face tracking and recognition with visual constraints in real-world videos. In: CVPR (2008)

Koestinger, M., Wohlhart, P., Roth, P.M., Bischof, H.: Annotated facial landmarks in the wild: a large-scale, real-world database for facial landmark localization. In: First IEEE International Workshop on Benchmarking Facial Image Analysis Technologies (2011)

Lee, K., Ho, J., Yang, M., Kriegman, D.: Video-based face recognition using probabilistic appearance manifolds 1, 313–320 (2003)

Lefevre, S., Odobez, J.-M.: Structure and appearance features for robust 3d facial
actions tracking. In: ICME (2009)

Valstar, M.F., Martinez, X.B., Pantic, M.: Facial point detection using boosted regression and graph models. In: CVPR, pp. 2729–2736 (2010)

Matthews, I., Baker, S.: Active appearance models revisited. IJCV 60(2), 135–164
(2004)

Morency, L.-P., Whitehill, J., Movellan, J.R.: Generalized adaptive view-based appearance model: integrated framework for monocular head pose estimation. In: FG (2008)

Murphy-Chutorian, E., Trivedi, M.M.: HyHOPE: Hybrid Head Orientation and
Position Estimation for Vision-based Driver Head Tracking. IEEE Intelligent Vehicles Symposium (2008)

Murphy-Chutorian, E., Trivedi, M.M.: Head pose estimation in computer vision: A
survey. PAMI 31(4) (2009)

Ren, S., Cao, X., Wei, Y., Sun, J.: Face alignment at 3000 fps via regressing local
binary features (2014)

Sagonas, C., Tzimiropoulos, G., Zafeiriou, S., Pantic, M.: 300 faces in-the-wild challenge: the first facial landmark localization challenge. In: ICCV Workshops (2013)

Saragih, J.M., Lucey, S., Cohn, J.F.: Deformable model fitting by regularized landmark
mean-shift. IJCV 91, 200–215 (2011)

Stiefelhagen, R., Bernardin, K., Bowers, R., Rose, R.T., Michel, M., Garofolo, J.S.:
The CLEAR 2007 evaluation. In: Stiefelhagen, R., Bowers, R., Fiscus, J.G. (eds.)
RT 2007 and CLEAR 2007. LNCS, vol. 4625, pp. 3–34. Springer, Heidelberg (2008)

Sun, Y., Wang, X., Tang, X.: Deep convolutional network cascade for facial point
detection. In: CVPR (2013)

Vacchetti, L., Lepetit, V., Fua, P.: Stable real-time 3d tracking using online and offline
information. TPAMI 26(10), 1385–1391 (2004)

Wang, H., Davoine, F., Lepetit, V., Chaillou, C., Pan, C.: 3-d head tracking via invariant keypoint learning. IEEE Transactions on Circuits and Systems for Video Technology 22(8), 1113–1126 (2012)

Wang, Y., Lucey, S., Cohn, J.: Enforcing convexity for improved alignment with constrained local models. In: CVPR (2008)

Zhu, X., Ramanan, D.: Face detection, pose estimation, and landmark localization in
the wild. In: CVPR (2012)

Xiao, J., Baker, S., Matthews, I., Kanade, T.: Real-time combined 2d+3d active appearance models. CVPR 2, 535–542 (2004)

Xiao, J., Moriyama, T., Kanade, T., Cohn, J.: Robust full-motion recovery of head by
dynamic templates and re-registration techniques. International Journal of Imaging
Systems and Technology 13, 85–94 (2003)

Xiong, X., la Torre Frade, F.D.: Supervised descent method and its applications to face
alignment. In: CVPR (2013)

Zhang, J., Shan, S., Kan, M., Chen, X.: Coarse-to-Fine Auto-Encoder Networks
(CFAN) for real-time face alignment. In: Fleet, D., Pajdla, T., Schiele, B., Tuytelaars, T. (eds.) ECCV 2014, Part II. LNCS, vol. 8690, pp. 1–16. Springer, Heidelberg
(2014)

Characterization and Distinction Between Closely Related South Slavic Languages on the Example of Serbian and Croatian

Darko Brodić[1]([✉]), Alessia Amelio[2], and Zoran N. Milivojević[3]

[1] Technical Faculty in Bor, University of Belgrade, V.J. 12, 19210 Bor, Serbia
dbrodic@tf.bor.ac.rs
[2] Institute for High Performance Computing and Networking, National Research
Council of Italy, CNR-ICAR, Via P. Bucci 41C, 87036 Rende (CS), Italy
amelio@icar.cnr.it
[3] College of Applied Technical Sciences, Aleksandra Medvedeva 20, 18000 Niš, Serbia
zoran.milivojevic@vtsnis.edu.rs

Abstract. The paper proposes a new method for characterization and distinction between closely related languages on the example of Serbian and Croatian languages. In the first step, the method transforms the text in different languages into the uniformly coded text. It is carried out in accordance to the position of each sign of the script in the text line and its height. Then, the coded text given as 1-D image is subjected to the texture analysis. According to that analysis, a feature vector of 28 elements is established. These 28 elements are extracted from co-occurrence texture and adjacent local binary pattern analysis. The feature vector is a starting point for classification by an extension of a state of the art method, called GA-ICDA. As a result, the distinction between the closely related languages is correctly accomplished. The method is tested on a database of documents in Serbian and Croatian languages. The experiments give promising results.

Keywords: Closely related languages · Coding · Co-occurrence analysis · Information retrieval · Language recognition · Local binary pattern

1 Introduction

The South Slavic languages are one of three branches of the Slavic languages, [13]. South Slavic group of languages is adopted by Balkan nations, speaking by approximately 30 million speakers. This group of languages is divided into western and eastern parts. Western South Slavic languages include the following languages: Slovenian, Croatian, Bosnian, Serbian and Montenegrin, while Eastern South Slavic languages are Macedonian and Bulgarian. Obviously, the criterion for discrimination of these languages is the script that they use for writing, i.e. Latin (Western) and Cyrillic (Eastern).

© Springer International Publishing Switzerland 2015
G. Azzopardi and N. Petkov (Eds.): CAIP 2015, Part I, LNCS 9256, pp. 654–666, 2015.
DOI: 10.1007/978-3-319-23192-1_55

We have to point out that some authors mean that the Montenegrin is a sub-Serbian language [17]. Unlike the other languages, Serbian and Montenegrin languages support live synchronic diagraphia allowing the use of Latin and Cyrillic scripts [14]. Although same researchers point out that the division of the Bosnian, Croatian and Serbian languages is political [16], the others consider them as closely related languages [15].

From all aforementioned, it is obvious that the differences between these languages are minimal. It is confirmed by the fact that Serbs, Croats, Bosniacs and Montenegrins can easily understand each others. Furthermore, the researching of differences between these closely related languages is a real challenge.

In this paper, we propose a new approach to the characterization and distinction between closely related languages on the example of Serbian and Croatian languages, which were previously known as Serbo-Croatian or Croatian-Serbian language (up to the political division of Yugoslavia). This approach extended our previous works related to script recognition [19][18] by introducing new extracted features from the text. In this way, the feature extraction vector obtained by co-occurrence analysis of the coded text numbering up to 12 elements was enlarged by adding new 16 elements obtained by adjacent local binary pattern analysis [20]. At the end, the feature classification process carried out by an extension of a state of the art method called *Genetic Algorithms Image Clustering for Document Analysis* (GA-ICDA) was efficiently leading to adequate characterization of Serbian and Croatian languages and establishing their distinction.

Organization of the paper is as follows. Section 2 explains the proposed multi-stage algorithm. Section 3 describes the experiment. Section 4 gives the results and makes a discussion. Section 5 states the concluding remarks.

2   The Proposed Algorithm

The proposed algorithm is a multi-stage method. It includes feature extraction, feature classification, and characterization and distinction of closely related languages on the example of Serbian and Croatian languages. Feature extraction includes script mapping, co-occurrence first and second level feature extraction and adjacent local binary pattern extraction. According to the obtained results, the feature classification by GA-ICDA is carried out. The method is tested on training and test sets of Serbian and Croatian documents included in a custom oriented database. Classification of the results establishes the characterization of each language. According to that, the discrimination between closely related languages is efficiently established using GA-ICDA tool. The detailed block scheme of proposed method is given in Fig. 1.

2.1   Script Mapping

Currently, Croatian language can be written in Latin script, while Serbian language according to synchronic diagraphia can use both Latin and Cyrillic scripts.

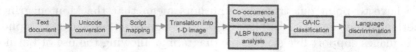

Fig. 1. Detailed block scheme of the proposed method.

In this paper, we assume that Croatian and Serbian languages are written in Latin script. Taking into account the printed text characteristics [21], each letter in Latin script can be classified in accordance with its position in text line and its height. Each text line can be divided into three different non-overlapping zones. These zones that spread out from bottom to top are: (i) lower, (ii) middle and (iii) upper zones [21]. Corresponding to aforementioned zones all letters are classified as: (i) short, (ii) ascender, (ii) descendent and (iv) full. Short letter is a sign in an alphabet, which has so-called x-height one [22]. It is present in the middle zone. Ascender letter represents each sign that precedes in both the upper and middle zones. Descendent letter corresponds to a sign which includes the areas of lower and middle zones. At the end, the full letter is a sign that outspreads over upper, middle and lower zones. This division is called script type classification. Corresponding to aforementioned classification, each letter from the alphabet is replaced with the equivalent code [19][18]. It is built in the following manner:

$$f(x) = y, \text{ where } x \in X \text{ and } y \in Y. \tag{1}$$

In our example, X includes all letters from Croatian and Serbian alphabets (30 different letters in small and capital variation), while Y represents their classification in accordance to script type classification:

$$Y = \{1, 2, 3, 4\}, \tag{2}$$

where 1, 2, 3, and 4 are assigned to short, ascender, descendent and full letter.

Currently, each text is transformed into the "coded" text containing only numbers 1, 2, 3, 4 instead of all letters or other signs. Such a text contains only numbers. Hence, it looks like a long 1-D set of four different numbers. However, we can imagine that it can represent the image containing only four different levels of gray. If it is so, then we can treat it as an image. Fig. 2 shows an example of text mapping into the coded text that corresponds to a gray-level image.

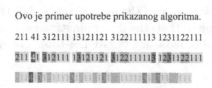

Fig. 2. The procedure of initial text mapping into the coded text and correspondent gray-scale 1-D image.

Then, the image can be subjected to different texture analysis.

2.2 Co-occurrence Texture Analysis

The texture of the image shows the information on the spatial arrangement of the colors or intensities in an image. It contains some statistical properties of the image, and can register the similar structures and degree of randomness in the image. Hence, the texture is very important in identifying similar or different regions in an image. Co-occurrence texture analysis is one of the earliest methods for texture feature extraction [23]. We use this method to create a part of our feature vector.

The image under consideration is $\mathbf{I}$. It is a gray scale image featuring M rows, N columns, and T number of grays. The spatial relationship of gray levels in the given image is the co-occurrence matrix $\mathbf{C}$. Co-occurrence matrix $\mathbf{C}$ is a square matrix, whose dimension is determined by the number of gray levels T, i.e. $T \times T$. To compute $\mathbf{C}$, a central pixel of the image $I(x, y)$ with a neighborhood defined by the window of interest (WOI) has been taken. Window of interest commonly called WOI is defined by inter-pixel distance d and orientation θ. Typically d is set to 1, which means the first neighbor pixel. Furthermore, the 8-connected neighborhood is considered. Hence, the following values of $\theta = 0°, 45°, 90°, 135°$ are possible. Co-occurrence matrix $\mathbf{C}$ for the image $\mathbf{I}$ is calculated as [24]:

$$C(i, j) = \sum_{x=1}^{M} \sum_{y=1}^{N} \begin{cases} 1 \text{ if } I(x, y) = i, \text{and } I(x + \Delta x, y + \Delta y) = j \\ 0 \qquad \text{otherwise} \end{cases} \quad (3)$$

where i and j are the intensity values of the image $\mathbf{I}$, x and y are the spatial positions in the image $\mathbf{I}$, the offset $(\Delta x, \Delta y)$ is the distance between the pixel-of-interest and its neighbor. At this point, it is important to note that offset heavily depends on the used direction θ and the distance d. In our example, the calculation is much simpler. Because text represents 1-D image, the neighborhood that exists is 2-connected, and the only feasible θ is $0°$. Normalized matrix $\mathbf{P}$ obtained from the GLCM $\mathbf{C}$ is calculated as [25]:

$$P(i, j) = \frac{C(i, j)}{\sum_{i}^{N} \sum_{j}^{N} C(i, j)} \quad (4)$$

All extracted texture features are divided into the first and the second order statistical features. The first order texture features represent the first four elements of our feature vector. The feature vector is enlarged with additional eight elements proposed in [23]. These elements represent the second order texture features. They are given below in Table 1.

2.3 Script Type Local Binary Pattern Analysis

Local binary pattern (LBP) represents a simple methodology which extracts the features according to local binary partition. For each pixel $I(x, y)$ in the image, its eight neighbors are examined in order to find out if their intensity is greater than that of the pixel under consideration. Then, new values of neighbor pixels are calculated by thresholding them according to the intensity of the pixel $I(x, y)$. The results from the eight neighbors are used to create an eight-digit binary number. When the whole image is analyzed, a histogram of obtained eight-digit numbers is used to represent the texture of the image. As a starting point of the method, the initial image is given by the vector $\mathbf{I}$, and $\mathbf{r} = (x, y)^T$ is a position vector in $\mathbf{I}$. The LBP is defined as:

Table 1. First and second order texture statistics.

First order	$\mu_x = \sum_{i=1}^{N} i \sum_{j=1}^{N} P(i,j),$
	$\mu_y = \sum_{j=1}^{N} j \sum_{i=1}^{N} P(i,j),$
	$\sigma_x = \sqrt{\sum_{i=1}^{N} (i - \mu_x)^2 \sum_{j=1}^{N} P(i,j)},$
	$\sigma_y = \sqrt{\sum_{j=1}^{N} (j - \mu_y)^2 \sum_{i=1}^{N} P(i,j)}.$
Second order	$\text{Correlation} = \sum_{i=1}^{N} \sum_{j=1}^{N} \frac{(i \cdot j) \cdot P(i,j) - (\mu_x \cdot \mu_y)}{\sigma_x \cdot \sigma_y},$
	$\text{Energy} = \sum_{i=1}^{N} \sum_{j=1}^{N} P(i,j)^2,$
	$\text{Entropy} = -\sum_{i=1}^{N} \sum_{j=1}^{N} P(i,j) \cdot \log P(i,j),$
	$\text{Maximum} = \max\{P(i,j)\},$
	$\text{Dissimilarity} = \sum_{i=1}^{N} \sum_{j=1}^{N} P(i,j) \cdot |i - j|,$
	$\text{Contrast} = \sum_{i=1}^{N} \sum_{j=1}^{N} P(i,j) \cdot (i - j)^2,$
	$\text{Invdmoment} = \sum_{i=1}^{N} \sum_{j=1}^{N} \frac{1}{1 + (i - j)^2} P(i,j),$
	$\text{Homogeneity} = \sum_{i=1}^{N} \sum_{j=1}^{N} \frac{P(i,j)}{1 + |i - j|}.$

$$b_i(r) = \begin{cases} 1, & I(r) \leq I(r + \Delta r_i) \\ 0, & \text{otherwise} \end{cases}, \tag{5}$$

where $i = 1, ..., N_n$. N_n is the number of neighbor pixels, while Δr_i are displacement vectors from the position of center pixel r to neighbor pixels [20]. For 8-connected neighborhood, N_n is equal to 8, while the displacement distance $d(\Delta r_i)$ is equal to 1 (pixel). Next, LBP $b(r)$ is converted into a decimal number. The histogram of LBPs is generated by considering the decimals as labels.

Fig.3 shows an example of a micro pattern and LBP corresponding to it.

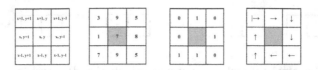

Fig. 3. LBP of the image. From left to right: WOI (3×3), the example, thresholding in respect to center pixel, and direction of the patterns (most to least important).

Fig. 4. LBP for text. From left to right: WOI (1×3), the example, thresholding in respect to center pixel, and and direction of the patterns (most to least important).

From Fig. 3 we obtained LBP as '01010110'. In our example the coded text is represented as 1-D image. Hence, WOI is reduced to 1×3 subimage with only two neighbor pixels around the center pixel. It leads to a total number of all LBP micro patterns of $2^2 = 4$. Fig. 4 shows calculation of the LBP micro patterns applied to the text example and resultant LBP equal to '10'.

2.4   Script Type Adjacent Local Binary Pattern Analysis

As an extension to LBP, the adjacent local binary patterns (ALBP) are proposed in [20]. They can be described as the co-occurrence LBP. In the first step, the LBP is modified in order to obtain two subset LBPs [20]: (i) LBP(+) and (ii) LBP(×). LBP(+) considers only the direction given by sign +, i.e. two horizontal and two vertical pixels in the neighborhood of the center pixel. LBP(×) considers only the direction given by sign ×, i.e. the four diagonal pixels in the neighborhood of the center pixel. Fig. 5 illustrates both subset micro patterns.

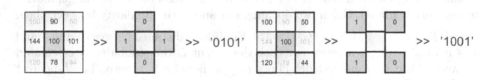

Fig. 5. LBP (+) and (×) example of image (8-connected neighborhood): (Left) Local image block (+), Local binary pattern block (+), and Binary label (+), (Right) Local image block (×), Local binary pattern block (×), and Binary label (×).

Then, the combination of adjacent LBP(+) and LBP(×) creates ALBP. LBP (+) can be connected to another LBP (+) horizontally or vertically. In contrast, LBP(×) can be connected to another LBP(×) diagonally (two diagonal directions)[20]. However, it is not important in our case, because LBP(+) for

Fig. 6. ALBP example of text (2-connected neighborhood). From left to right: First local text block (+), Second local text block (+), First local binary pattern block (+), Second local binary pattern block (+), and Binary label.

us only matters. It is valid due to the nature of text (1-D), because ALBP is formed by the co-occurrence of two adjacent LBP(+). It is shown in Fig. 6.

In our case the combination of two local 2-digit binary labels creates a 4-bit binary label, which represents a total number of $2^4 = 16$ micro patterns. In this way, we obtain additional 16 features added to our feature vector establishing a total of 28 scalar values for characterization and distinction between closely related languages.

2.5   Feature Classification

Classification of text documents is performed by *Genetic Algorithms Image Clustering for Document Analysis* (GA-ICDA), an extension of the Genetic Algorithms Image Clustering (GA-IC) framework [2]. GA-IC is an evolutionary-based framework for clustering an image database. Four meaningful modifications are introduced in GA-ICDA for discrimination of documents written in closely related languages. The first difference is in the feature representation. Each document is represented as the vector of 28 values combining the aforementioned GLCM and ALBP features. The second modification is in the graph construction procedure. Text documents are modeled as a weighted graph $G = (V, E, W)$, with $n = |V|$ nodes, $m = |E|$ edges and a set W of edge weights. Each text document is a graph node.

G is built in multiple steps. Differently from [2] where the L_1 norm is used, the distance matrix of the documents is obtained by computing the Euclidean distance (L_2) for each pair of document feature vectors. Then, the similarity scores are calculated. Given two documents i and j, the similarity between them is $w(i, j) = e^{-\frac{d(i,j)^2}{a^2}}$, where $d(i, j)$ is the Euclidean distance between i and j and a is a local scale parameter. For each document i, the similarity is calculated between i and its h-nearest neighbors nn_i^h, otherwise it is zero. The h-nearest neighbors of a document i are those documents with the h-lowest Euclidean distance values from i inside the distance matrix, where h is a parameter. Recall from [2] that the number of h-nearest neighbors can be greater than h. The obtained document similarity matrix represents the adjacency matrix M of G as computed in GA-IC framework. Now, let f be the node ordering induced by the adjacency matrix M. It is a one-to-one function associating the graph nodes to integers $f : V \rightarrow \{1, 2, ...n\}$. Let $f(i)$ be the label of the node $i \in V$, where a different label is assigned to each node. Mimicking [9], for each node $i \in V$, we calculate the difference between $f(i)$ and the labels $F = \{f(nn_i^h(1)),$

$f(nn_i^h(2)),...$, $f(nn_i^h(k))\}$ of its k h-nearest neighbors $nn_i^h = \{nn_i^h(1), nn_i^h(2),$ ..., $nn_i^h(k)\}$. This difference is expressed as:

$$\forall i \in V, \left| f(i) - f(nn_i^h(j)) \right|, 1 \leq j \leq k \tag{6}$$

Then, for each node i, we eliminate from M the edges between i and its h-nearest neighbors whose label difference from i is greater than a threshold T. Consequently, in GA-ICDA an element $w_{i,j}$ of the new adjacency matrix M' is defined as:

$$w_{i,j} = \begin{cases} e^{-\frac{d(i,j)^2}{a^2}} & \text{if } j \in nn_i^h, i \neq j, |f(i) - f(j)| \leq T \\ 0 & \text{otherwise.} \end{cases} \tag{7}$$

Thus, if the documents i and j have a high Euclidean distance $d(i,j)$ to each other, the similarity score $w_{i,j}$ between them will be quite low. On the contrary, if the two documents have a small Euclidean distance $d(i,j)$ between them, provided that their corresponding nodes are near to each other with respect to the given node ordering ($|f(i) - f(j)| \leq T$), their similarity score $w_{i,j}$ will be high. Fig. 7 shows an example of graph construction.

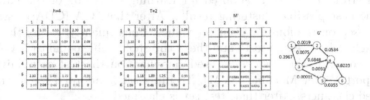

Fig. 7. Example of graph construction. From left to right: for each node in the distance matrix, detection of the 4-nearest neighbors (in red), for each node, detection of the neighbors with label difference smaller or equal to T=2 with respect to the label of that node (in blue), creation of the graph G' from the obtained adjacency matrix M'.

Document clustering is realized by the genetic algorithm used in [2]. The difference is that the output of the genetic algorithm is only a raw partitioning of the graph in node clusters. In fact, starting from them, a merging of cluster pairs is performed until a fixed number is obtained. Specifically, let $C = \{c_1, ...c_d\}$ be the d clusters found from the genetic algorithm. Given a cluster $c_p \in C$, the distance between c_p and the other clusters $\{c_q\}, q = 1...d, q \neq p$, is evaluated. Then, merging is performed between c_p and the cluster $c_h \in C$ having the minimum distance from it. Let $c_p = \{c_p^1, ..., c_p^a\}$ and $c_h = \{c_h^1, ..., c_h^b\}$ be two clusters with respectively a and b number of document feature vectors. The distance $D(c_p, c_h)$ between them is the L_1 norm between those two feature vectors, one for each cluster, which are the farthest away from each other:

$$D(c_p, c_h) = max_{c_p^x, c_h^y} \{d(c_p^x, c_h^y) | c_p^x \in c_p, c_h^y \in c_h\} \tag{8}$$

where $d(c_p^x, c_h^y)$ is the L_1 norm between two document feature vectors c_p^x and c_h^y.

3   Experiment

For testing of the proposed method, an experiment is conducted on a custom oriented database. The database is composed of a training and test set. Training set includes Serbian and Croatian documents extracted mainly from newspapers and the web. The training set of database contains 45 documents given in Serbian and Croatian languages, where 32 out of 45 are Serbian documents and 13 are Croatian documents. Documents count from 500 to 5000 characters. The co-occurrence analysis is sensitive to the low number of samples, which in our case are the characters. Hence, the documents of more than 500 characters can be successfully adopted for valid statistical analysis, which is a premise of the factor analysis. The test set contains 20 documents, where 10 out of 20 are Serbian documents and 10 out of 20 are Croatian documents. The documents count from 500 to 5000 characters.

4   Results and Discussion

First of all, the training set is used for tuning the parameters of GA-ICDA. A trial and error procedure is adopted for learning the value of the parameters giving the best possible clustering results. After that, GA-ICDA classifies the test set based on the found parameter values. Consequently, we fix the h value of the neighborhood equal to 15 and the T threshold value equal to 7. GA-ICDA is compared with other two supervised classifiers on the test set: Naive-Bayes and Support Vector Machine (SVM). Training set is adopted for learning the supervised classifiers. After that, test set is classified.

Secondly, GA-ICDA classifies the training set in an unsupervised manner. Obtained results are compared with results of other three unsupervised classifiers: Complete Linkage Hierarchical Clustering, Expectation Maximization (EM) and Self Organizing Map (SOM). The same values of 15 and 7 are adopted respectively for the h neighborhood and the T threshold.

We chose to compare GA-ICDA with hierarchical, EM, SOM, Naive-Bayes and SVM because they are well-known in literature for document classification [6],[12],[10],[8],[1]. Also, to demonstrate the effectiveness of the modifications introduced in GA-ICDA, clustering is performed also by GA-IC on both the training and test set. The same value of the h neighborhood equal to 15 has been fixed for GA-IC classifier. All the classifiers (unsupervised and supervised) use the same document feature representation of GA-ICDA: 4 GLCM semi-features, 8 GLCM full texture features and 16 ALBP features. Fig. 8 depicts the feature distribution of the training set by using statistical analysis.

In particular, the median (continuous line) and the quartiles, 25% and 75% points, (dotted lines) are plotted for each feature (co-occurrence and ALBP along the x-axis). The y-axis defines the value of such statistical measures, computed for each document class (Serbian in blue and Croatian in red). It is worth to observe as the typical differences and similarities between the Serbian and Croatian languages are easier to distinguish. Although the median value between the

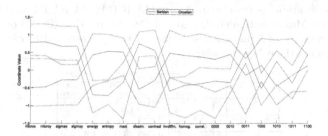

Fig. 8. Feature distribution of the training set for the two document classes Serbian and Croatian languages in terms of median value (continuous line) and quartiles, 25% and 75% points, (dotted lines).

corresponding features shows a differentiation between the two classes, the two languages are strictly correlated and the problem appears as complex.

Four performance measures for document classification validation, *F-Measure*, *Purity*, *Entropy* and *Normalized Mutual Information (NMI)*, [3],[11],[5] are adopted for results evaluation. They are the weighted sum on the fraction of documents of the measures computed for each language class. In the supervised classifiers, these measures are used for comparing the results obtained from classification with the true language classes on the test set.

Each classification algorithm has been executed 100 times on a quad-core desktop computer with 8 Gbyte of RAM and Windows 7. The average values of the performance measures together with the standard deviation have been computed on these runs. Table 2 shows the performance measures obtained from the execution of GA-ICDA, GA-IC, hierarchical clustering, EM and SOM on the training set. Table 3 illustrates the performance measures obtained from the execution of GA-ICDA, GA-IC, Naive-Bayes and SVM on the test set. Standard deviation is reported in parenthesis. Values in bold correspond to cases when GA-ICDA outperforms the other classifiers.

It is worth to observe as GA-ICDA is superior to the other classifiers perfectly recognizing the two correct classes of documents in Serbian and Croatian languages for both the training and test sets. GA-IC without modifications is not able to correctly classify the two languages. In fact, it performs poorly, finding 3 classes of languages out of 2, an F-Measure value of 0.58, a Purity value of 0.71, a Entropy value of 0.34 and a NMI value of 0.25.

Although the hierarchical clustering in Table 1 obtains better performances than EM and SOM, it doesn't outperform GA-ICDA. In fact, hierarchical clustering has a F-Measure and a Purity values of 0.87, a Entropy value of 0.40 and a NMI value of 0.41. It is also interesting to observe as the combination of the bottom-up hierarchical merging procedure together with the evolutionary method is able to overcome in terms of clustering results the pure bottom-up hierarchical approach. SOM reaches a good Purity value of 0.83, however the number of detected clusters is 4 against the real number of classes which is 2.

Table 2. Classification results obtained from GA-ICDA, GA-IC, Hierarchical Clustering, Expectation Maximization (EM) and Self Organizing Map (SOM) on the training set. nc is the number of found classes. Values in bold correspond to cases when GA-ICDA outperforms the other classifiers.

Algorithm	nc	F-measure	Purity	Entropy	NMI
GA-ICDA	2	**1.0000**	**1.0000**	**0.0000**	**1.0000**
		(0.0000)	(0.0000)	(0.0000)	(0.0000)
GA-IC	3	0.5800	0.7105	0.3362	0.2504
		(0.0000)	(0.0000)	(0.0000)	(0.0000)
Hierarchical	2	0.8695	0.8684	0.3980	0.4150
		(0.0000)	(0.0000)	(0.0000)	(0.0000)
EM	2	0.6992	0.7284	0.3974	0.2344
		(0.1012)	(0.0757)	(0.0870)	(0.1007)
SOM	4	0.6046	0.8332	0.5830	0.2866
		(0.0376)	(0.0228)	(0.0886)	(0.0205)

Table 3. Classification results obtained from GA-ICDA, GA-IC, Naive-Bayes and Support Vector Machine (SVM) on the test set. nc is the number of found classes. Values in bold correspond to cases when GA-ICDA outperforms the other classifiers.

Algorithm	nc	F-measure	Purity	Entropy	NMI
GA-ICDA	2	**1.0000**	**1.0000**	**0.0000**	**1.0000**
		(0.0000)	(0.0000)	(0.0000)	(0.0000)
GA-IC	2	0.5652	0.6500	0.9122	0.0756
		(0.0000)	(0.0000)	(0.0000)	(0.0000)
Naive-Bayes	2	0.6491	0.6500	0.9320	0.0669
		(0.0000)	(0.0000)	(0.0000)	(0.0000)
SVM	2	0.5489	0.5500	0.9926	0.0073
		(0.0000)	(0.0000)	(0.0000)	(0.0000)

In Table 2, it is interesting to note as GA-ICDA, although it is an unsupervised approach, outperforms Naive-Bayes and SVM on the test set, for which a learning phase by the training set is required. The real difference is that Naive-Bayes and SVM "know" the class labels of the training documents and use them for learning the classifier, while GA-ICDA learns the parameter values without this information. In any case, Naive-Bayes overcomes SVM, reaching a F-Measure and a Purity values of 0.65, a Entropy value of 0.93 and a very low NMI value of 0.07. On the other hand, the base version of GA-IC, which is also unsupervised, has a F-Measure value of 0.56, a Purity value of 0.65, a Entropy value of 0.91 and a NMI value of 0.07 on the test set, results comparable with those obtained by the Naive-Bayes and SVM supervised approaches.

The best classification result of the closely related Slavic languages, i.e. Serbian and Croatian is obtained in [26]. Their method received the language discrimination result between 0.857 and 0.902. If we compare it with our results, it is obvious that our method has advantage in the domain of language discrimination correctness. Furthermore, the proposed method reduces the number of variables, which makes it computer time non-intensive.

5 Conclusions

The manuscript proposed an efficient methodology for the characterization and distinction between closely related languages on the example of Serbian and Croatian languages. It was based on the baseline status of each script sign by creating uniformly coded text. The statistical analysis of the coded text was performed by the co-occurrence matrix calculation and adjacent local binary patterns. The extracted feature vectors obtained by statistical analysis showed dissimilarity, which was efficiently captured by the classification tool GA-ICDA. The results of experiments showed very positive results. Hence, a future application and extension of the proposed method is promising in the area of the automatic language translation, language recognition, in preprocessing steps of OCR, and for video text recognition.

Acknowledgments. This work was partially supported by the Grant of the Ministry of Science of the Republic Serbia within the project TR33037.

References

1. Aggarwal, C., Zhai, C.: A survey of text clustering algorithms. Mining Text Data, pp. 77–128. Springer (2012)
2. Amelio, A., Pizzuti, C.: A new evolutionary-based clustering framework for image databases. In: Elmoataz, A., Lezoray, O., Nouboud, F., Mammass, D. (eds.) ICISP 2014. LNCS, vol. 8509, pp. 322–331. Springer, Heidelberg (2014)
3. Andrews, N.O., Fox, E.A.: Recent Developments in Document Clustering. Technical report, Computer Science, Virginia Tec. (2009)
4. Diem, M., Kleber, F., Fiel, S., Sablatnig, R.: Semi-automated document image clustering and retrieval (2013)
5. Hu, X., Yoo, I.: A comprehensive comparison study of document clustering for a biomedical digital library medline. In: Proc. 6th ACM/IEEE-CS Joint Conference, pp. 220–229 (2006)
6. Ji, J., Zhao, Q.: Applying naive bayes classifier to document clustering. JACIII **14**(6), 624–630 (2010)
7. Liu, X., Gong, Y., Xu, W., Zhu, S.: Document clustering with cluster refinement and model selection capabilities. In: Proc. 25th Ann. Int. ACM SIGIR Conf. on Research and Devel. in Inf. Retr., SIGIR 102, NY, USA, pp. 191–198 (2002)
8. Marinai, S., Marino, E., Soda, G.: Self-organizing maps for clustering in document image analysis. In: Marinai, S., Fujisawa, H. (eds.) Mach. Learn. in Doc. Anal. and Recogn. SCI, vol. 90, pp. 193–219. Springer, Heidelberg (2008)
9. Mart, R., Laguna, M., Glover, F., Campos, V.: Reducing the bandwidth of a sparse matrix with tabu search. Europ. J. Oper. Res. **135**(2), 450–459 (2001)
10. Pu, Y., Shi, J., Guo, L.: A hierarchical method for clustering binary text image. In: Yuan, Y., Wu, X., Lu, Y. (eds.) ISCTCS 2012. CCIS, vol. 320, pp. 388–396. Springer, Heidelberg (2013)
11. De Vries, C.M., Geva, S., Trotman, A.: Document clustering evaluation: Divergence from a random baseline. CoRR, abs/1208.5654 (2012)
12. Yang, C., Yi, Z.: Document clustering using locality preserving indexing and support vector machines. Soft Comp. **12**(7), 677–683 (2008)
13. Ronelle, A.: In honor of diversity: the linguistic resources of the Balkans. In: Kenneth, E. (ed.) Naylor Memorial Lecture Series in South Slavic Linguistics, vol. 2, Ohio State University, Dept. of Slavic and East European Languages and Literatures (2000)
14. Dale, I.R.H.: Digraphia. Int. J. of the Soc. of Lang. **26**, 5–13 (1980)

15. Miller, B.: Translating Between Closely Related Languages in Statistical Machine Translation. Master of Science by Research, School of Informatics, University of Edinburg (2008)

16. Kordic, S.: Pro und kontra: "Serbokroatisch heute". In: Slavistische Linguistik 2002: Referate des XXVIII. Konstanzer Slavistischen Arbeitstreffens, Bochum 2002. Slavistishe Beitrage, vol. 434, p. 141. Otto Sagner, Munich (2002)

17. Greenberg, R.D.: Language and identity in the Balkans: Serbo-Croatian and its disintegration. Oxford University Press (2004)

18. Brodić, D., Milivojević, Z.N., Maluckov, Č.A.: An approach to the script discrimination in the Slavic documents. Soft Comp. (in press) (online). doi:10. 1007/s00500-014-1435-1

19. Brodić, D., Milivojević, Z.N., Maluckov, Č.A.: Recognition of the Script in Serbian Documents using Frequency Occurrence and Co-occurrence Analysis. The Scient. World J. **2013**(896328), 1–14 (2013)

20. Nosaka, R., Ohkawa, Y., Fukui, K.: Feature extraction based on co-occurrence of adjacent local binary patterns. In: Ho, Y.-S. (ed.) PSIVT 2011, Part II. LNCS, vol. 7088, pp. 82–91. Springer, Heidelberg (2011)

21. Zramdini, A.W., Ingold, R.: Optical Font Recognition Using Typographical Features. IEEE T. Pattern Anal. **20**(8), 877–882 (1998)

22. Yi, L.: Machine printed character segmentation An overview. Patt. Rec. **28**(1), 67–80 (1995)

23. Haralick, R.M., Shanmugan, K., Dinstein, I.: Textural features for image classification. IEEE T. Sys., Man, and Cyber. **3**(6), 610–621 (1973)

24. Eleyan, A., Demirel, H.: Co-occurrence matrix and its statistical features as a new approach for face recognition. Turkish J. Electr. Engin. and Comp. Sci. **19**(1), 97–107 (2011)

25. Clausi, D.A.: An analysis of co-occurrence texture statistics as a function of grey level quantization. Canadian J. Remote Sens. **28**(1), 45–62 (2002)

26. Tiedemann, J., Ljubesic, N.: Efficient discrimination between closely related languages. In: Proceedings of COLING 2012, Mumbai, India, pp. 2619–2634 (2012)

Few-Views Image Reconstruction with SMART and an Allowance for Contrast Structure Shadows

Vitaly V. Vlasov, Alexander B. Konovalov$^{(\boxtimes)}$, and Alexander S. Uglov

Russian Federal Nuclear Center – Zababakhin Institute of Applied Physics, Snezhinsk, Russia
vitaly.vlasov.v@gmail.com, a_konov@mail.vega-int.ru,
a.s.uglov@vniitf.ru

Abstract. The paper describes an original algorithm for reconstructing tomographic images from a few views. The algorithm is based on the known iterative Simultaneous Multiplicative Algebraic Reconstruction Technique (SMART). It is peculiar in that corrections for different zones of the reconstruction area are calculated differently with allowance for the distribution of shadows from contrast structures. The algorithm we call SMART-SA (SMART with Shadow Allowance) is implemented in 2D and tested for two numerical models with an air cavity and a material interface with 10% contrast. Reconstruction results are evaluated visually and quantitatively with such characteristics as correlation coefficient and deviation factor. It is shown that SMART-SA is capable of reconstructing the images that are free of artifacts typical of few-views tomography, and it performs especially well in combination with the MART-AP algorithm we published earlier.

Keywords: Few-views tomography · Shadow allowance · SMART-SA · Discrete tomography · MART-AP · Correlation coefficient · Deviation factor

1 Introduction

In the recent 15-20 years we have observed increasingly growing interest to the methods and algorithms of few-views computed tomography [1]. A need to reconstruct the inner structure of an object in conditions when a few projections (usually less than 10) are only registered arises in many areas of tomography applications. These are, for example, nondestructive testing in industry [2], plasma emission tomography [3], electron tomography of nanomaterials [4], tomography of explosion-compressed metal shells [5], fast detonation research [6] and other. The main problem of few-views tomography is high-intensity artifacts which are present on the images reconstructed with the standard iterative algorithms such as, for example, the algebraic reconstruction technique (ART) [7], the simultaneous algebraic reconstruction technique (SART) [8,9] or the maximum entropy technique (MENT) [10] because of strongly incomplete data. These artifacts are usually seen as streaks tangent to contrast structures, causing severe difficulty in the reproduction and recognition of fine details and low-contrast structures. Lots of methods and algorithms for dealing the artifacts have been developed in recent decades, but few are really effective. So, the recognition and compensation of artifacts with the

© Springer International Publishing Switzerland 2015
G. Azzopardi and N. Petkov (Eds.): CAIP 2015, Part I, LNCS 9256, pp. 667–677, 2015.
DOI: 10.1007/978-3-319-23192-1_56

well-known adaptive filtration method of Rangayyan and Gordon [11] is not always a success. Only a limited class of objects can be treated successfully with our modification of the multiplicative algebraic reconstruction technique (MART) which allows for the non-uniform distribution of weighting coefficient sums and solution correction numbers over the cells of the reconstruction area [12,13]. The list of algorithms that provide only local success can be extended.

Now, perhaps the most effective methods of artifact compensation in few-views tomography are those that use a priori information about the object. The leaders are Bayesian reconstruction methods [6], [14] and discrete tomography methods [15,16]. The former use a priori information on the distribution law of the object function being reconstructed, and the latter use information on its discrete values. Examples of successful discrete tomography algorithms include the discrete algebraic reconstruction technique (DART) [4], [17,18] and MART which uses a priori information (MART-AP) [19,20]. Our algorithm MART-AP organizes a loop of "external" iterations each with the standard MART and its "internal" iterations. But corrections to the solution approximation are made with account for a so-called "mask of a priori values" which bears a priori information on the discrete values of the object function. This mask is synthesized through threshold segmentation and adjusted with respect to the results of each "external" iteration. We showed in [20] that MART-AP not only successfully treats simple binary objects with low-frequency structures, but also reconstructs contrast high-frequency structures with submillimeter resolution. Unfortunately, MART-AP is not always as efficient as desired. It is rather sensitive to errors in the selection of values for the object function which are used as a priori information. Also, it is not always a success in the accurate reproduction of interfaces between low-contrast structures if high-contrast structures are near. This effect is excellently demonstrated by Fig. 1 which shows two numerical 2D models and results of their reconstruction with MART-AP. The first model has a wavy interface with 10% contrast (Fig. 1(a)), and the second has the same interface plus an air cavity (Fig. 1(c)). Hereafter all reconstructions are done from nine views in fan beam geometry with magnification 5. The sources were set within a 192-degree sector at equal angular steps. It is seen from Fig. 1 that MART-AP performs excellently for the first model (Fig. 1(b)) and very badly for the second (Fig. 1(d)). These results of reconstruction confirm that still in need are the artifact preventive methods and algorithms that would become alternatives or complements to the method and algorithms of discrete tomography.

This paper presents one of such algorithms. It is a modification of the multiplicative SART and we called it SMART-SA (SMART with shadow allowance). Our algorithm is based on the use of weighted corrections in the cells which are "shadowed" by high-contrast structures. The weights in each particular case are found from a "shadow mask" which is generated with a special algorithm. The paper is organized as follows. Section 2 justifies and describes SMART-SA. Section 3 gives examples of reconstruction with the new algorithm for two numerical models and quantitatively evaluates quality of tomograms. The conclusion provides inferences on prospects for the algorithm and the relevance of its further improvement for the soonest adaptation to real experiment.

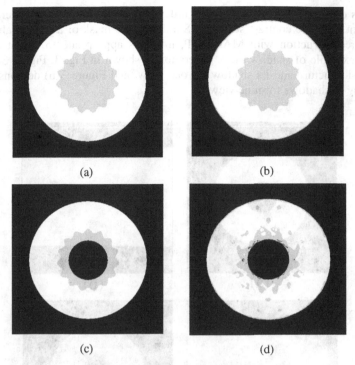

Fig. 1. Examples of MART-AP reproduced interfaces of low-contrast structures

2   SMART-SA Justification and Description

In order to recognize and compensate artifacts from few-views imaging we need first to understand the mechanism of their formation. The example of Fig. 1 suggests that high-contrast structures play the most important role. The mechanism that governs the formation of artifacts from high-contrast structures can be seen from the analysis of the iterative process inherent in the algebraic reconstruction techniques. Each algebraic technique, additive or multiplicative ART, additive or multiplicative SART, or MENT, distributes the residual uniformly in the entire reconstruction area if the initial distribution of the sought object function is uniform. But if an object has a high-contrast difference, the difference smears along the beam and forms a streak. In this case the contrast structure of the object "shadows" the other structures. For next view, the iterative reconstruction procedure produces another streak which "overlays" the first. Thus the streaks on previous views affect the reproduction of structures on the tomogram, forming large networked artifacts. The formation of artifacts is clearly seen in Fig. 2 which shows the model with a contrast structure in the form of cavity (Fig. 2(a)) and its reconstruction from one (Fig. 2(b)), two (Fig. 2(c)) and nine (Fig. 2(d)) views with MART. It is seen from Fig. 2(d) that the contrast structure (cavity) is reproduced with no distinct artifacts. This conveys the suggestion that corrections in a manner other than traditional need to be done only in the cells that are shadowed by the contrast structure. Ultimately, we can try to exclude corrections in these cells of the view involved. But in order to do that, we need to generate a shadow pattern from the contrast structure. Similar to the mask of a priori values in the multistep reconstruction with MART-AP, it seems appropriate to call it a shadow mask. An example of shadow mask generation is shown in Fig. 3. Figure 3(a) shows the contrast structure and its shadow for one view, and Figure 3(b) demonstrates the overlapping of shadows for nine views.

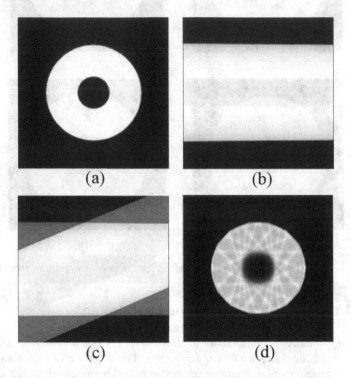

Fig. 2. Model with cavity (a) and its MART reconstruction from one (b), two (c) and nine (d) views

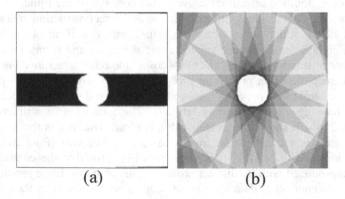

Fig. 3. An example of shadow mask generation for the contrast structure in the form of cavity

For contrast structure identification, we use an interactive segmentation method implemented by an algorithm whose steps are described below.

When searching the way in which we should do corrections in the cells shadowed by the contrast structures, we should take into account that simply excluding the cells in a view from consideration we will come to a non-uniform distribution of correction numbers on the reconstruction area, which will add artifacts. For the first time we investigated this effect in [15,16] where we studied the photon average trajectory method [21] for the reconstruction of diffuse optical tomograms. It was proposed that the effect could be smoothed by doing corrections in the same manner as it is done in SART, SMART and MENT, but with allowance for the generated shadow mask (Fig. 3(b)). Recall that these algorithms, unlike ART and MART, do not adjust corrections obtained for the previous view but save them and then calculate the arithmetic mean over all views. It is seen from the Fig. 3(b) that the shadow mask determines regions with cells in white and black, and cells in gray of different tones. The region where cells are white is the high-contrast structure. All nine views will be accounted for in corrections for these cells. Corrections in cells in half-tone shadow regions will be done with account for fewer views. Some of the few black cells adjacent to the contrast structure will be corrected only once. It should be noted here that when we were studying this method of correction, we saw that single correction is sometimes insufficient for the adequate reproduction of the boundary of a high-contrast structure. That is why it seems wise to do an adaptive smoothing near the boundary.

If the object has several contrast structures, we must search them sequentially, and create an integral mask by means of logical multiplication of all shadow masks generated for each structure. With all the above taken into account, we can describe our algorithm of reconstruction with shadows from contrast structures by the following steps:

__Algorithm of reconstruction with shadows from contrast structures__

Step 1: Reconstruct the image with a standard algebraic technique (for example, MART or SMART).

Step 2: Identify all contrast structures from the reconstructed image and create the list C of the contrast structures.

Step 3: Choose the next structure from the list C.

Step 4: Do interactive segmentation in the region of the contrast structure.

Step 5: Generate the shadow mask for the contrast structure.

Step 6: Remove the contrast structure being consideration from the list C.

Step 7: If C is not empty, go to *Step 3*, otherwise go to *Step 8*.

Step 8: Create the integral mask by means of logical multiplication of all shadow masks generated.

Step 9: Reconstruct the image with SART-type algorithm with account for that many views in each region of cells as defined by the integral mask.

Step 10: On each iteration, do adaptive smoothing in the regions where corrections are done once.

Step 11: End.

Step 4 includes interactive segmentation based on a simple algorithm of binarization from the threshold of image intensity in the selected pixel. In effect, this algorithm is a basic region growing algorithm (see, for example, [22,23]). Let $\mathbf{f} = \{f_i\}_1^I$ be a vector that describes the sought object function, I is the number of pixels in the reconstruction area. Then the interactive segmentation algorithm can be described by the following steps:

Algorithm of interactive segmentation of contrast structure

Step 1: Choose pixel n within the contrast structure.

Step 2: Choose a threshold δ which characterizes the structure.

Step 3: Initiate the list of pixels L_n near pixel n for the analysis.

Step 4: Initiate the list of pixels S which belong to the sought segment. Initially the list is empty: $S = \{\ \}$.

Step 5: Choose the next pixel l from the list L_n.

Step 6: If $|f_l - f_n| \leq \delta$,

- add pixel l to the list S,
- add the neighbor pixels of pixel l to the list L_n,
- remove pixel l from the list L_n.

Step 7: If L_n is not empty, go to *Step 5*, otherwise go to *Step 8*.

Step 8: End. The list S includes the pixels that belong to the sought segment.

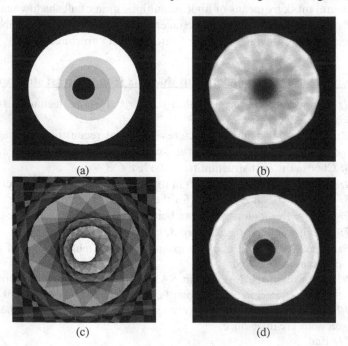

(a)   (b)

(c)   (d)

Fig. 4. Model with cavity and two interfaces (a), its MART reconstruction (b), shadow mask (c) and reconstruction with the proposed algorithm (d)

The threshold δ (*Step 2*) is chosen and if necessary adjusted interactively in such a way as to allow the contrast structure to be identified most correctly in the operator's view.

For adaptive smoothing (*Step 10* of the reconstruction algorithm), we use the classical moving mean method (see, for example, [23]).

An example which demonstrates how our reconstruction algorithm works is shown in Fig. 4. The model (Fig. 4(a)) has a cavity and two spherical (circular in 2D) interfaces. The contrast jump on both the interfaces is 10%. Figure 4(b) demonstrates the MART reconstruction of the model; Figure 4(c) shows the shadow mask, and Figure 4(d) shows the final result of reconstruction with shadow allowance. In this case, as well in all cases below, corrections on *Step 9* were done multiplicatively, i.e., with SMART. That is why it seems appropriate to refer to the algorithm as SMART with shadow allowance (SMART-SA).

The qualitative analysis of Fig. 4 clearly shows that the result is quite encouraging despite that the initial model is not reproduced ideally. Indeed, the level of artifacts on the tomogram of Fig. 4(d) is much lower than in Fig. 4(b), and such much as to allow the resolution of both interfaces.

The next section gives other examples demonstrating SMART-SA effectiveness. It also contains the quantitative analysis of reconstructed images.

3   Reconstruction Results and Their Analysis

It was mentioned in the introduction that the reason for our development of SMART-SA was the need to develop either an effective alternative, or an effective complement to the MART-AP algorithm of discrete tomography, which is also aimed to remove artifacts from lacking data. In this context it is of interest to compare these algorithms and consider their combination. Below we provide and analyze results from the reconstruction of two numerical models with the following algorithms: 1) MART, 2) SMART-SA and 3) combined SMART-SA and MART-AP: SMART-SA+MART-AP. Last case assumes the successive work of the two algorithms. The two models we chose for testing are typical of studies into the fast explosive processes [6]. The first model is the model of Fig. 1(c), and the second is the model with cavity and two interfaces, which is similar to the model of Fig. 4(a). The difference is that one of the interfaces has an additional displacement along the ordinate axis. The results of reconstruction of the models from nine projections are presented in Fig. 5.

The qualitative analysis of Fig. 5 shows that SMART-SA is, in principle, capable of solving the artifact compensation problem. However, the accuracy of low-contrast structure reproduction with SMART-SA is not very high (see Fig. 5(e) and 5(f)). As for the combination of SMART-SA and MART-AP, it is seen to give best results. Especially it is related to the model with wavy interface which is reproduced almost ideally (Fig. 5(g)).

For the quantitative analysis of our results we use the following characteristics (see, for example, [24]):

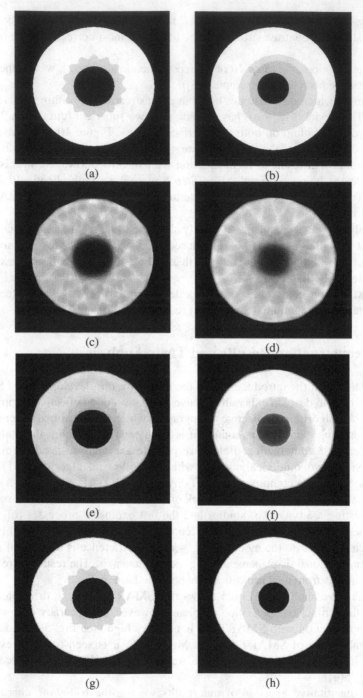

Fig. 5. Models ((a) and (b)) and their reconstructions with MART ((c) and (d)), SMART-SA ((e) and (f)), SMART-SA+MART-AP ((g) and (h))

1. Correlation coefficient

$$k_c = \frac{\sum_{i=1}^{I}\left(f_i^t - \overline{f}^t\right)\left(f_i^m - \overline{f}^m\right)}{(I-1)\Delta f^t \Delta f^m},$$

(1)

where $\overline{f}$ and Δf are the mean value and the root-mean-square deviation which are calculated over all I cells; the indices m and t bear relation to the initial model and the reconstructed image, respectively.

2. Deviation factor

$$k_d = \frac{\sqrt{\frac{1}{I}\sum_{i=1}^{I}\left(f_i^t - f_i^m\right)^2}}{\Delta f^m}.$$

(2)

A large value of k_c shows a high correlation between the reconstructed image and the initial model and indicates a high level of reconstruction accuracy. Conversely, a small value of k_d shows a good coincidence of two images and is also indicative of high reconstruction accuracy. The correlation coefficient and the deviation factor for all reconstructed images presented in Fig. 5 are shown in table 1.

Table 1. The quantitative characteristics of reconstructed images

Model	Reconstruction algorithm	k_c	k_d
Model with cavity and wavy interface	MART	0.9895	0.1448
	SMART-SA	0.9956	0.0949
	SMART-SA+MART-AP	**0.9963**	**0.0862**
Model with cavity and two circular interfaces	MART	0.9850	0.1726
	SMART-SA	0.9927	0.1206
	SMART-SA+MART-AP	**0.9960**	**0.0893**

The data of table 1 justify the inferences made from the visual analysis of the reconstructed images. The best result is obtained with the use of the combination of SMART-SA and MART-AP. Thus the SMART-SA algorithm can be an effective complement to the MART-AP algorithm of discrete tomography when we need to compensate streak artifacts from high-contrast structures.

We believe that SMART-SA has a good prospect for improvement. Now it uses a very simple scheme of weighted corrections in the cells which are shadowed by high-contrast structures. Corrections are calculated with no account for the "bad" views that are responsible for artifacts. In other words the weighting coefficients for these views are equal to zero. It is clear that the weighting scheme can be done more adaptable to compensate for SMART-SA shortcomings, such as the presence of regions where correction is done once.

Our codes are written in MATLAB. Calculations are done on a 1.7-GHz Pentium 4, 512-Mb RAM Intel PC. The solution correction procedure without interactive manipulations onto a 500×500 grid takes approximately 5 minutes. We can say that shadow mask synthesis is almost of no effect on the time required for reconstruction, but interactive segmentation does take considerable time. So, the segmentation of one contrast structure in our calculations took about 10-15 minutes. In further work it seems appropriate to implement automatic or semiautomatic segmentation as described, for example, in [25].

4   Conclusion

We have presented an original algorithm SMART-SA for image reconstruction in few-views tomography. The algorithm involves generation of an artifact shadow pattern we refer to as shadow mask. The mask defines the regions where corrections are made selectively excluding the views responsible for artifacts. Currently SMART-SA is implemented for 2D and tested for two numerical models. One of them has a cavity and a wavy interface with 10% contrast jump and the other has a cavity and two circular boundaries each with 10% contrast jump too. Reconstruction results were subjected to qualitative and quantitative analysis with use of such characteristics of image quality as correlation coefficient and deviation factor. Results of testing show that SMART-SA which implements the proposed method of artifact compensation helps getting tomograms without artifacts. It is also shown that SMART-SA works more effectively in combination with the MART-AP algorithm of discrete tomography.

The authors believe that results of their research allow them to infer that SMART-SA seems quite promising, at least, for the reconstruction of models similar to those presented. The further development of the algorithm includes improvements in the scheme of weighted corrections.

References

1. Herman, G.T.: Fundamentals of Computerized Tomography: Image Reconstruction from Projections. Springer-Verlag, London (2009)
2. Scott, D.M., Williams, R.A. (eds.) Frontiers in Industrial Process Tomography. Engineering Foundation, New York (1996)
3. Pickalov, V.V., Melnikova, T.S.: Plasma Tomography. Nauka, Novosibirsk (1995). (in Russian)
4. Batenburg, K.J., Bals, S., Sijbers, J., Kübel, C., Midgley, P.A., Hernandez, J.C., Kaiser, U., Encina, E.R., Coronado, E.A., Van Tendeloo, G.: 3D Imaging of Nanomaterials by Discrete Tomography. Ultramicroscopy **109**, 730–740 (2009)
5. Konovalov, A.B., Mogilenskikh, D.V., Kozlov, E.A., Vlasov, V.V., Kiselev, A.N., Kovalev, E.V., Zakharov, M.N., Povyshev, V.N., Stavrietskii, V.I.: Few-View Gamma Tomography Used to Monitor Scabbing and Shear Fracture in a Spherical Iron Shell Compressed by Explosion. Russ. J. Nondestruct. Testing **44**(1), 15–24 (2008)

6. Pang, T.F.: AWE multi-axis radiographic facility: a review of 3D-reconstructions from limited data. In: Mohammad-Djafari, A. (ed.) AIP Conference Proceedings, vol. 568, pp. 521–530. AIP Publ., New York (2001)
7. Gordon, R., Bender, R., Herman, G.T.: Algebraic Reconstruction Techniques (ART) for Three-Dimensional Electron Microscopy and X-Ray Photography. J. Theor. Biol. **29**, 471–481 (1970)
8. Anderson, A., Kak, A.: Simultaneous Algebraic Reconstruction Technique (SART): A Superior Implementation of the ART Algorithm. Ultrason. Imaging **6**, 81–94 (1984)
9. Byrne, C.L.: Iterative Image Reconstruction Algorithms Based on Cross-Entropy Minimization. IEEE Trans. Image Process. **2**, 96–103 (1993)
10. Minerbo, G.: MENT: A Maximum Entropy Algorithm for Reconstructing a Source from Projection Data. Comput. Graph. Image Process. **10**, 48–68 (1979)
11. Rangayyan, R.M., Gordon, R.: Streak Preventive Image Reconstruction with ART and Adaptive Filtering. IEEE Trans. Med. Imaging **1**, 173–178 (1982)
12. Konovalov, A.B., Vlasov, V.V., Kalintsev, A.G., Kravtsenyuk, O.V., Lyubimov, V.V.: Time-Domain Diffuse Optical Tomography Using Analytic Statistical Characteristics of Photon Trajectories. Quantum Electronics **36**, 1048–1055 (2006)
13. Konovalov, A.B., Mogilenskikh, D.V., Vlasov, V.V., Kiselev, A.N.: Algebraic reconstruction and post-processing in incomplete data computed tomography: from X-rays to laser beams. In: Obinata, G., Dutta, A. (eds.) Vision Systems: Applications, pp. 487–518. I-Tech Education and Publishing, Vienna (2007)
14. Siltanen, S., Kolehmainen, V., Jaervenpaa, S., Kaipio, J.P., Koistinen, P., Lassas, M., Pirttila, J., Somersalo, E.: Statistical Inversion for X-Ray Tomography with Few Radiographs. I. General Theory. Phys. Med. Biol. **48**, 1437–1463 (2003)
15. Herman, G.T., Kuba, A. (eds.): Discrete Tomography: Foundations, Algorithms and Applications. Birkhauser, Boston (1999)
16. Herman, G.T., Kuba, A. (eds.): Advances in Discrete Tomography and its Applications. Birkhauser, Boston (2007)
17. Batenburg, K.J., Sijbers, J.: DART: A Practical Reconstruction Algorithm for Discrete Tomography. IEEE Trans. Image Process. **20**, 2542–2553 (2011)
18. Batenburg, K.J., Sijbers, J., Poulsen, H.F., Knudsen, E.: DART: A Robust Algorithm for Fast Reconstruction of Three-Dimensional Grain Maps. J. Appl. Crystalogr. **43**, 1464–1473 (2010)
19. Vlasov, V.V., Konovalov, A.B., Uglov, A.S.: An a priori information based algorithm for artifact preventive reconstruction in few-view computed tomography. In: 5th International Symposium on Communications, Control and Signal Processing, paper 042. University Roma Tre, Roma (2012)
20. Konovalov, A.B., Vlasov, V.V.: Spatial Resolution Analysis for Few-Views Discrete Tomography Based on MART-AP Algorithm. ISRN Sign. Process. **2013**, 356291 (2013)
21. Konovalov, A.B.: Time-Domain Diffuse Optical Mammotomography. The Photon Average Trajectory Method. Lambert Academic Publishing, Saarbrüken (2014). (in Russian)
22. Zucker, S.W.: Region Growing: Childhood and Adolescence. Comput. Graphics Image Process. **5**, 382–399 (1976)
23. Gonzalez, R.C., Woods, R.E.: Digital Image Processing. Prentice-Hall, New Jersey (2002)
24. Klose, A.D., Hielscher, A.H.: Quasi-Newton Methods in Optical Tomographic Image Reconstruction. Inverse Problems **19**, 387–409 (2003)
25. Batenburg, K.J., Van Aarle, W., Sijbers, J.: A Semi-Automatic Algorithm for Grey Level Estimation in Tomography. Pattern Recognit. Lett. **32**, 1395–1405 (2011)

Gaussian Mixture Model Selection
Using Multiple Random Subsampling
with Initialization

Josef V. Psutka[1,2][✉]

[1] New Technologies for the Information Society, Pilsen, Czech Republic
[2] Department of Cybernetics, University of West Bohemia,
Pilsen, Czech Republic
psutka_j@kky.zcu.cz

Abstract. Selecting optimal number of components in Gaussian Mixture Model (GMM) is of interest to many researchers in the last few decades. Most current approaches are based on information criterion, which was introduced by Akaike (1974) and modified by many other researchers. The standard approach uses the EM algorithm, which fits model parameters to training data and determines log-likelihood functions for increasing number of components. Penalized forms of log-like- lihood function are then used for selecting number of components. Just searching for new or modified forms of penalty function is subject of permanent effort how to improve or do robust these methods for various type of distributed data. Our new technique for selection of optimal number of GMM components is based on **M**ultiple **R**andom **S**ubsampling of training data with **I**nitialization of the EM algorithm (MuRSI). Results of many performed experiments demonstrate the advantages of this method.

Keywords: Gaussian mixture models · Model selection · Model parameters

1 Introduction

Mixture modeling is a widely accepted technique for powerful and flexible modeling heterogeneous data coming from various populations. Such data can be typically met in tasks of computer vision, speech recognition, machine learning, but also in completely different areas, such as biology, medicine, economics and others. It is well known that for such purposes the Gaussian Mixture Models (GMMs) are very suitable. Any continuous distribution can be approximated sufficiently well by a weighted sum of Gaussian distributions [5]. However, while parameters of this model structure (e.g. means, covariance matrices and mixture weights) are usually estimated by EM algorithm, then determining the number

---

This paper was supported by the project no. P103/12/G084 of the Grant Agency of the Czech Republic.

G. Azzopardi and N. Petkov (Eds.): CAIP 2015, Part I, LNCS 9256, pp. 678–689, 2015.
DOI: 10.1007/978-3-319-23192-1_57

of components is still widely discussed issue [2], [3], [9],[10]. The reasons are often different objectives to be achieved using the GMM. Other goals are pursued in cluster analysis (unsupervised learning), where priority interest is to identify the probable number of clusters. Different goals are tracked in the case of supervised estimation of statistical GMM that fits data with sufficient accuracy. In the first case, the accuracy (in simulation tasks) is assessed comparing true vs. estimated number of components, while the second task should be evaluated in another way. In such a case it should be measured how accurately an estimated model fits the data. Since the EM algorithm is preferably used for estimation model parameters we have to mention, in addition to its outstanding features, also some negative, e.g. estimated parameters are strongly affected by initial positions of Gaussian mixture means. The results of our extensive simulation experiments have shown that the level of model quality does not always depend on whether the number of true components corresponds to the number of estimated ones. In many published studies (articles) discussing this issue (i.e. clustering and/or modelling) the both problems are mixed and the only criterion in simulation tasks is a consent of the true and estimated number of components. However, even here is true, that too many components in mixture may overfit the data and provide model with poor interpretation, while too few components may not prepare flexible model, which approximate the true underlying data structure [6]. The question of course is, what is the optimal number of components for the given task, and when the estimated model is under- or over- fitted.

Most current approaches estimating the optimal number of components are based on information criterion, which was introduced by Akaike [1] and modified by Schwartz [7] and many other researchers [8], [9]. The standard access uses the EM algorithm, which fits model parameters to training data and successively determines corresponding log-likelihood functions for increasing number of components. Then log-likelihood functions with a penalized form are considered to estimate the recommended number of components. Just searching for new or modified forms of penalty function is subject of permanent improvements of these methods. This effort is often caused by not so good behavior of estimated mixture models for various types of tasks and distributed data.

Our approach to determine the number of components in GMM that fit training data sufficiently well is relatively simple in tasks with large number of training data, where the one part of training data is used for estimating model parameters while the second part (validation data) is used for determining number of GMM components. However, in real applications only a finite set of training data is available so it is most advisable to use all the training data for the estimation of model parameters (i.e. means, covariance matrices and mixture weights). To determine an "optimal" number of GMM components in these cases we developed new technique based on **Multiple Random Subsampling** of training data with **Initialization** of the EM algorithm (MuRSI). Random subsampling performs data split of the entire training data on to development and validation datasets. Splitting procedure is performed S times. In each of S runs this procedure randomly selects a fixed number of development samples (without replacement), the rest of samples creates the validation dataset. For each of the S development datasets we train GMMs, which are initialized by the "best" final parameters of the GMMs trained on the whole training dataset. For each of the S splitting the corresponding validation samples are used to determine the number of GMM components. Note, that the start of the EM algorithm initialized with the "best" estimated parameters usually results in fast retrained model, which have only slightly modified parameters compared with the "parent" model.

To objectively measure the quality of estimated GMMs (with various number of components) and/or to compare a performance of several models trained by different approaches (e.g. by information criteria), the measures based on the mean square error (MSE) and log-likelihood ratio (LLR) were used. Results of many performed experiments demonstrate the advantages of the developed method.

2   Model Selection Based on Information Criterion

The methods based on information criterion have a basis in the likelihood-ratio test, which is used to compare the fit of two models provided the simpler model is a special case of more complex model, known as nested model. A standard computing likelihood-ratio test uses logarithm and the corresponding statistics called log-likelihood ratio statistics is defined as

$$\Lambda = -2 \log \left(\frac{L(\Theta_1| X)}{L(\Theta_0| X)} \right) = -2 \log L(\Theta_1| X) + 2 \log(L(\Theta_0| X), \tag{1}$$

where $L(\Theta_0|X)$ is the likelihood function of the more complex model parameterized by the set of parameters Θ_0, the $L(\Theta_1| X)$ is the likelihood function of the competing simpler model parameterized by Θ_1, and X is set of samples for which we assume for simplicity that are independent and identically distributed (i.i.d.) random variables. Note that the test statistic is approximately a χ^2 distribution with degrees of freedom equal $fp_0 - fp_1$, where fp_0 and fp_1 denote the number of free parameters of models 0 and 1, respectively.

Based on this analysis the information criterion uses log-likelihood function – whose value grows (from principle) for increasing number of GMM components (which gradually leads to overfitting on training data) – and tries to penalize an increase of this function by a penalty derived from the number of estimated parameters. Setting of the penalty is essentially a solution to the dilemma between under- and over-fitting, i.e. the optimization of model complexity.

If the training data and the set of candidate models are available, the model selection criterion (MSC) selects a model that minimizes a loss function MSC that is defined as

$$MSC = -2 \log L \left(\hat{\Theta}|X \right) + f(N, m), \tag{2}$$

where $L(\hat{\Theta}|X)$ is the likelihood function, X the set of training samples, $\hat{\Theta}$ the maximum likelihood estimate of Θ, N the number of training samples and m the number of freely adjusted parameters (degree of freedom) in Θ, which is in the case of the GMM a function of both the dimension n and the number of GMM components k. While the first term is a measure of the quality of fit of candidate model to the data, then the second one plays the role of penalty term against overfitting. If the object of our search is model with an optimum number of components k, then such a model can be found by solving the equation

$$k^* = \min_k MSC(k) = -2 \log L\left(\hat{\Theta}_{(k)}|X\right) + f(N, n, k), \qquad (3)$$

where $\hat{\Theta}_{(k)}$ is the maximum likelihood estimate of Θ for the GMM with k components.

In Akaike criterion (AIC), the penalty function is formed only of free parameters m

$$AIC(k) = -2 \log L\left(\hat{\Theta}_{(k)}|X\right) + 2m, \qquad (4)$$

where $m = k\left[n(n+1)/2 + n\right] + k - 1$, n is the space dimension and k the number of GMM components. It was shown that Akaike criterion exhibits asymptotic behavior, i.e. it asymptotically leads to a strict overparameterization of the model order [6], [8]. In order to alleviate inconsistencies in Akaike's criterion Schwarz proposed the penalty function in (2) based also on the number of samples N [7]. This new criterion is called Bayesian information criterion (BIC) and is of the form

$$BIC(k) = -2 \log L\left(\hat{\Theta}_{(k)}|X\right) + m \log N. \qquad (5)$$

Note that this criterion is asymptotically convergent and is better suited to search for models with large N ($N \to \infty$).

3   Measures for Assessment of Model Quality

In order to objectively compare the quality of the newly proposed method MuRSI with the classical information criteria AIC and BIC (note that both are the standard functions of Statistics Toolbox in MATLAB) in the task of GMM estimation with "optimal" number of components, we performed a large number of simulation experiments. For this purpose, we created a generator of random samples, which is controlled by the GMM with the parameters $\Theta^G = \{c_r^G, \mu_r^G, C_r^G\}_{r=1,\dots,R}$, where c_r is the positive weight of r-th mixture component ($\sum_{r=1}^R c_r = 1$), μ_r the mean vector and C_r the covariance matrix both for r-th mixture component. Now suppose that this GMM source generated dataset X of N samples $\{x_1, x_2, \dots, x_N\}$, which belong to a n-dimensional Euclidean space and are of course identically distributed. Now we can define the likelihood function for dataset X and Θ^G as

$$L(\Theta^G|X) = \prod_{i=1}^N p\left(x_i|\Theta^G\right) = \prod_{i=1}^N \sum_{r=1}^R c_r^G\, p\left(x_i\,|\,\mu_r^G, C_r^G\right), \qquad (6)$$

where

$$p(x\,|\,\mu_r, C_r) = (2\pi)^{-n/2}(\det C_r)^{-1/2}\exp\left\{-\frac{1}{2}(x-\mu_r)^T C_r^{-1}(x-\mu_r)\right\}. \qquad (7)$$

The selection of the appropriate measure for evaluating the quality of the estimated model is affected by the objective, which we pursue. Recall that our priority is not to estimate from the training data the true number of components of the Gaussian mixture model, which was in the simulation experiments the source of the training data, but to find the GMM that best fits this data. For this purpose we chose two measures. The first is based on a log-likelihood ratio (LLR) test comparing the model of source generator Θ^G and the model $\hat{\Theta}$, which was estimated using training data

$$\Lambda_{\mathrm{LLR}} = -2\log\left[\frac{L(\hat{\Theta}|X)}{L(\Theta^G|X)}\right] = 2\left[\sum_{i=1}^{N}\log p(x_i|\Theta^G) - \sum_{i=1}^{N}\log p(x_i|\hat{\Theta})\right] =$$

$$= \sum_{i=1}^{N}\log\left[\frac{p(x_i|\Theta^G)}{p(x_i|\hat{\Theta})}\right]^2 \tag{8}$$

The second measure is the mean square error (MSE) calculated for log-likelihoods of individual data

$$\Delta_{\mathrm{MSE}}^2 = \frac{1}{N}\sum_{i=1}^{N}\left[\log p(x_i|\Theta^G) - \log p(x_i|\hat{\Theta})\right]^2 = \frac{1}{N}\sum_{i=1}^{N}\left[\log\frac{p(x_i|\Theta^G)}{p(x_i|\hat{\Theta})}\right]^2 \tag{9}$$

Analyzing both equations we find that the MSE is much rigorous measure, because it sums up the square of errors (i.e. the square of log-likelihood differences) for each individual sample in the dataset, while the LLR calculates differences of a sum of both log-likelihood functions for the whole dataset.

4   Data Preparation for Experiments

In order to objectively compare the newly proposed approach to determine the number of GMM components that best fit data coming from experimental tasks, we conducted a large number of experiments with synthetically generated data. The source for data generation in our experiments was Gaussian mixture model (GMM) with parameters $\Theta^G = \{c_r^G, \mu_r^G, C_r^G\}_{r=1,\dots,R}$, where R is the number of mixture components, c_r the weight of r-th mixture component, μ_r the mean vector and C_r the covariance matrix both for r-th mixture component. The source model for generating data has been designed with the following parameters:

$$c_r^G = rand_r(1)/\sum_{i=1}^{R}rand_i(1), \qquad r = 1,\dots,R, \tag{10}$$

$$\mu_r^G = [\,1 - 2rand_r(1,n)\,]\,q\,, \qquad r = 1,\dots,R, \tag{11}$$

$$C_r^G = A_r A_r^{\mathrm{T}}, \quad \text{where } A_r = rand_r(n,n), \qquad r = 1,\dots,R, \tag{12}$$

where $rand(.)$ function returns uniformly distributed pseudorandom numbers (same as in MATLAB notation), $\sum_{r=1}^{R} c_r^G = 1$, q is a multiplicative factor, n space dimension, A is randomly generated matrix of dimension n.

All parameters of the source model are thus generated randomly. Location of mean values of individual components of GMM is randomly situated in the n-dimensional cube and coefficient q can this cube increase/decrease. Each of the many realized experiments was conducted always with new data created by the randomly generated model Θ^G. In a generator of data was possible to set $\{N, R, n, q\}$, where N is the number of generated data, R is the number of mixture components in the source GMM, n the space dimension, and q the multiplicative factor. For each experiment the set X of random n-dimensional vectors $X = \{x_1, x_2, ..., x_N\}$ was generated.

5   Using Validation Data for Determining the Number of Components

Our approach to determine the number of GMM components that optimally fit a set of training data $\Phi = \{t_1, ..., t_T\}$ is based on the idea that with gradually increasing number k of GMM components the log-likelihood $\log L(\hat{\Theta}_{(k)}|\Phi) = \sum_{i=1}^{T} \log p(t_i | \hat{\Theta}_{(k)})$ will continuously increase, however from a certain number of components it will lead to overfitting model on the training data. This means that if we postponed a set of validation data $\Psi = \{v_1, ..., v_V\}$, which was randomly selected from the same distribution (same source) as training data, then the log-likelihood $\log L(\hat{\Theta}_{(k)}|V) = \sum_{i=1}^{V} \log p(v_i | \hat{\Theta}_{(k)})$ calculated for the validation data V should first grow and essentially copy $\log L(\hat{\Theta}_{(k)}|\Phi)$ and at the moment of overfitting the increase of $\log L(\hat{\Theta}_{(k)}|V)$ should stop and gradually decline. This idea is also possible to support by the analysis of the relationship of log-likelihood ratio (8), where the goal is to find such a model, which minimizes Λ_{LLR}. Estimating the optimal number of components $\hat{k}_{VAL}$ for validation data is then defined by

$$\hat{k}_{VAL} = \min_{k}\{\Lambda_{LLR-VAL}\} = \min_{k} 2 \left[\sum_{i=1}^{V} \log p(v_i|\Theta^G) - \sum_{i=1}^{V} \log p(v_i|\hat{\Theta}_{(k)})\right].$$
(13)

Since the first sum in brackets does not depend on k (it has for all k the same value), the (13) can be rewritten to the form

$$\hat{k}_{VAL} = \max_{k} \sum_{i=1}^{V} \log p\left(v_i|\hat{\Theta}_{(k)}\right), \qquad k = 1, 2, ...,$$
(14)

where the model parameters $\hat{\Theta}_{(k)}$ were estimated on the basis of training data Φ and using the EM algorithm. The $\hat{k}_{VAL}$ has an advantage that it can be determined even in real experiments, where attributes of data source are not usually known. As will be shown below $\hat{k}_{\text{VAL}}$ has the power to find a very good estimate of the number of GMM components and to minimize both Λ_{LLR}, and $\Delta^2_{\text{MSE}}(9)$. For completeness only recall that based on (3), (4), (5) the $\hat{k}_{\text{AIC}}$ and $\hat{k}_{\text{BIC}}$ may be written in the similar form as $\hat{k}_{\text{VAL}}$

$$\hat{k}_{\text{AIC}} = \min_{k} \left[-2 \sum_{i=1}^{T} \log p\left(t_i | \hat{\Theta}_{(k)} \right) + 2m \right], \qquad k = 1, 2, \dots, \qquad (15)$$

$$\hat{k}_{\text{BIC}} = \min_{k} \left[-2 \sum_{i=1}^{T} \log p(t_i | \hat{\Theta}_{(k)}) + m \log N \right], \qquad k = 1, 2, \dots \qquad (16)$$

where $m = k \left[n(n+1)/2 + n \right] + k - 1$, n is the space dimension and k the number of GMM components.

The resulting procedure:

1. Data generator, which is controlled by the model Θ^G with adjustable parameters R (number of components), n (space dimension), N (number of generated data), and q (multiplicative factor), generates a set X of N vectors x, $X = \{x_1, \dots, x_N\}$.
2. From the set X we select randomly (without replacement) training $\Phi = \{t_1, \dots, t_T\}$, validation $\Psi = \{v_1, \dots, v_V\}$ and test $\Omega = \{z_1, \dots, z_Z\}$ subsets. In our experiments we set $T = V = Z = N/3$, the reason for such data division is discussed in the footnote[1].
3. For $k = 1, 2, \dots$ we gradually estimate from the training set Φ the parameters $\hat{\Theta}_{(k)}$.
4. We determine $\hat{k}_{\text{VAL}}(14)$, $\hat{k}_{\text{AIC}}(15)$ and $\hat{k}_{\text{BIC}}(16)$. If we ensure for individual estimates of EM algorithm to be $\log L\left(\hat{\Theta}_{(k+1)} | \Phi \right) > \log L\left(\hat{\Theta}_{(k)} | \Phi \right)$, then searching $\hat{k}$ in (14), (15) and (16) can be stopped 2-3 steps after finding (mostly the first) extreme in the above equations.
5. To compare all three methods (VAL, AIC and BIC) we performed several experiments with the set of test data $\Omega = \{z_1, \dots, z_Z\}$. We were interested in results of $\Delta^2_{\text{MSE}-\Omega}$ and $\Lambda_{\text{LLR}-\Omega}$

$$\Delta^2_{\text{MSE}-\Omega} = \frac{1}{Z} \sum_{i=1}^{Z} \left[\log p\left(z_i | \Theta^G \right) - \log p\left(z_i | \hat{\Theta}_{(\hat{k})} \right) \right]^2, \qquad (17)$$

$$\Lambda_{\text{LLR}-\Omega} = 2 \left[\sum_{i=1}^{Z} \log p\left(z_i | \Theta^G \right) - \sum_{i=1}^{Z} \log p\left(z_i | \hat{\Theta}_{(\hat{k})} \right) \right], \qquad (18)$$

where $\hat{k}$ are $\hat{k}_{\text{VAL}}$, $\hat{k}_{\text{AIC}}$ and $\hat{k}_{\text{BIC}}$.

Experiments no.1-6:

For our initial experiments, we set $N = 300\ 000$, i.e. $T = V = Z = 10^5$, $n = 2$, $R = 5$, $q = 10$; 5; 1; 0.5; 0.1; 0.05. Each experiment, i.e. for $q = 10$; 5 etc, we run at least

100 times. Because the model parameters are generated randomly, we got (at least) 100 different results. Average values $\Delta^2_{\text{MSE}-\Omega}$ and $\Lambda_{\text{LLR}-\Omega}$ obtained in these experiments are shown in Table 1, 2, and 3.

From the results shown in Table 1, 2 and 3 is evident that the method using validation data outperformed the classical AIC and BIC particularly in cases where the mean values of the GMM components were situated in a square (2-dimensional cube) with decreasing side of square.

The method of estimating the number of components based on the simple utilization of postponed validation data is useful in tasks where there is plenty of annotated data for which we want to create a model. The thing is that with the increasing number of training data significantly decreases the absolute value of the approximation error (e.g. $\Delta^2_{\text{MSE}-\Omega}$) of the estimated model. This means that a model estimated from a large number of training data selected from the same population is more accurate. It should therefore be an effort especially in tasks with fewer training data to use the full set of this data to determine the parameters $\hat{\Theta}$.

Table 1. Results of experiments ($q=10$ and 5)

	$q=10$; $T=V=Z=10^5$; $R=5$; $n=2$				$q=5$; $T=V=Z=10^5$; $R=5$; $n=2$			
	rank	$\Delta^2_{\text{MSE}-\Omega}$ $[10^{-4}]$	rank	$\Lambda_{\text{LLR}-\Omega}$ $[10^{-5}]$	rank	$\Delta^2_{\text{MSE}-\Omega}$ $[10^{-4}]$	rank	$\Lambda_{\text{LLR}-\Omega}$ $[10^{-5}]$
VAL	2	3.06	2	7.26	1	3.07	1	6.86
AIC	3	4.12	3	7.66	3	3.61	3	7.82
BIC	1	3.04	1	7.19	2	3.12	2	7.42

Table 2. Results of experiments ($q=1$ and 0.5)

	$q=1$; $T=V=Z=10^5$; $R=5$; $n=2$				$q=0.5$; $T=V=Z=10^5$; $R=5$; $n=2$			
	rank	$\Delta^2_{\text{MSE}-\Omega}$ $[10^{-4}]$	rank	$\Lambda_{\text{LLR}-\Omega}$ $[10^{-5}]$	rank	$\Delta^2_{\text{MSE}-\Omega}$ $[10^{-4}]$	rank	$\Lambda_{\text{LLR}-\Omega}$ $[10^{-5}]$
VAL	1	3.75	1	9.66	1	4.19	1	10.98
AIC	3	4.23	2	10.66	2	4.38	2	11.83
BIC	2	4.04	3	11.57	3	4.61	3	13.97

Table 3. Results of experiments ($q=0.1$ and 0.05)

	$q=0.1$; $T=V=Z=10^5$; $R=5$; $n=2$				$q=0.05$; $T=V=Z=10^5$; $R=5$; $n=2$			
	rank	$\Delta^2_{\text{MSE}-\Omega}$ $[10^{-4}]$	rank	$\Lambda_{\text{LLR}-\Omega}$ $[10^{-5}]$	rank	$\Delta^2_{\text{MSE}-\Omega}$ $[10^{-4}]$	rank	$\Lambda_{\text{LLR}-\Omega}$ $[10^{-5}]$
VAL	1	4.39	1	10.87	1	4.51	1	10.98
AIC	2	4.88	2	12.79	2	4.99	2	12.03
BIC	3	5.09	3	15.54	3	5.15	3	14.73

6 Using MuRSI for Determining the Number of Components

The developed technique based on multiple random subsampling of training data with initialization (MuRSI) is primarily useful for estimating the optimal number of the GMM components, if there is little training data. MuRSI technique performs randomly a split of the entire training data $\Phi = \{t_1, \ldots, t_T\}$ on the development $\Gamma = \{d_1, \ldots, d_D\}$ and validation $\Psi = \{v_1, \ldots, v_V\}$ datasets. Splitting procedure is performed S-times while each data split randomly selects (without replacement) a fixed number D of development samples, the rest (the second part) of samples creates the validation dataset. The resulting value of optimal number of components is obtained as the average of results of S resamplings.

The resulting procedure:

1. Data generator, which is controlled by the model Θ^G with adjustable parameters R (the number of components), n (the space dimension), N (the number of generated data), and q (the multiplicative factor), generates set X of N vectors x, $X = \{x_1, \ldots, x_N\}$.
2. From the set X we select randomly (without replacement) training $\Phi = \{t_1, \ldots, t_T\}$, and test $\Omega = \{z_1, \ldots, z_Z\}$ subsets. In our experiments we set $T = Z = N/2$. The reason for such data division is discussed in the footnote[1].
3. For $k = 1, 2, \ldots$ we gradually estimate from the training set Φ the model parameters $\hat{\Theta}_{(k)}$. We ensure for individual estimates of EM algorithm to be $\log L\left(\hat{\Theta}_{(k+1)} | \Phi\right) > \log L\left(\hat{\Theta}_{(k)} | \Phi\right)$.
4. We randomly select (without replacement) from Φ a fixed number of development data $\Gamma = \{d_1, \ldots, d_D\}$, the rest of samples $V (=T\text{-}D)$ creates the validation dataset $\Psi = \{v_1, \ldots, v_V\}$. We set $D = V = T/2$ [1]. The point 4 is performed S-times always with a new splitting.

---

[1] The reason for such partitioning the training dataset Φ into the development Γ and validation Ψ datasets is a result of many experiments performed with the MuRSI algorithm. The best results were achieved when the training data was divided into two approximately equal parts, i.e. $D \approx V$, where D is the number of development data and V is the number of validation data. Other methods, such as K-fold cross-validation and its degenerate case Leave-one-out cross validation ($D = T - 1$ and $V = 1$), did not provide so good results. To avoid a drawback of data partitioning method used, namely that some observations could never be selected in the development set, or in the validation set, we performed always the next experiment with the replaced development and validation datasets. In case that there is a large amount of annotated data, it may not be a validation set selected by random subsampling as in the MuRSI algorithm, but it may be allocated as an independent dataset Φ. The choice of sizes Φ and Ψ is not critical here, however, to set the same conditions as in MuRSI, we chose $T = V$, which was a good solution. Selecting the number of training data is not crucial, we chose $Z = T$ in both methods. Consequently resulting partitioning data into training/development/ validation/test subsets is: for the first method (Chapter 5) $T = V = Z = N/3$, for MuRSI $D = V = T/2$ and $Z = T$.

5. For each of the S development datasets we estimate using EM algorithm parameters $\hat{\Theta}^{\Gamma}_{(k)}(s)$ of GMM. The start of the EM algorithm is initialized by the "best" final parameters of corresponding GMM, which was estimated on the whole training dataset.

6. We determine $\hat{k}_{\text{MuRSI}}$ as

$$\hat{k}_{\text{MuRSI}} = \max_{k} \sum_{s=1}^{S} \sum_{i=1}^{V} \log p \left[v_i | \hat{\Theta}^{\Gamma}_{(k)}(s) \right], \qquad k = 1, 2, \ldots\ldots \qquad (19)$$

Searching $\hat{k}_{\text{MuRSI}}$ can be stopped 2-3 steps after finding maximum.

7. To compare MuRSI technique with AIC and BIC we performed several experiments with the test dataset Ω. Again, we are interested in resulting values $\Delta^2_{\text{MSE}-\Omega}$ and $\Lambda_{\text{LLR}-\Omega}$, which can be computed from (17) and (18). As $\hat{k}$ we used in these equations $\hat{k}_{\text{MuRSI}}$, $\hat{k}_{\text{AIC}}$, and $\hat{k}_{\text{BIC}}$. Note that $\hat{k}_{\text{AIC}}$ and $\hat{k}_{\text{BIC}}$ has been estimated on the basis of the entire training set Φ, i.e. from (15) and (16).

Experiments no.7-12:

We tested the MuRSI technique in the following experiments: We set N=4000, (i.e. T=2000, D=V=1000 and Z=2000), n=2, R=5, q=10; 5; 1; 0.5; 0.1; 0.05. Each experiment, i.e. for q=10; 5; ... etc, we run at least 100 times, always with new randomly generated data. To assess how many times it should be repeated random resampling of individual training set, we computed (19) for S=1, 5, 10, 20 and 50. Average values $\Delta^2_{\text{MSE}-\Omega}$ and $\Lambda_{\text{LLR}-\Omega}$ obtained for these experiments are shown in Table 4, 5, and 6.

The results show that the MuRSI technique outperforms in all experiments the established AIC and BIC techniques. Analyzing results for individual S=1, 5, 10, 20, and 50 we can see, that in experiments with S=10 or 20 is sufficient number of repetitions of resampling process.

Table 4. Results of experiments (q=10 and 5)

	\multicolumn{4}{c}{q=10; D=Z=2000; R=5; n=2}				\multicolumn{4}{c}{q=5; D=Z=2000; R=5; n=2}		
	rank	$\Delta^2_{\text{MSE}-\Omega}$ $[10^{-2}]$	rank	$\Lambda_{\text{LLR}-\Omega}$ $[10^{-3}]$	rank	$\Delta^2_{\text{MSE}-\Omega}$ $[10^{-2}]$	rank	$\Lambda_{\text{LLR}-\Omega}$ $[10^{-3}]$
MuRSI$_{50}$	1	1.47	1	7.77	1	1.75	1	8.18
MuRSI$_{20}$	1	1.47	1	7.77	(1)	1.77	(1)	8.31
MuRSI$_{10}$	1	1.47	1	7.77	(1)	1.80	(1)	8.39
MuRSI$_{5}$	-	1.49	-	7.96	(1)	1.84	(1)	8.50
MuRSI$_{1}$	-	1.89	-	9.74	-	2.08	-	9.63
AIC	3	2.34	3	12.35	3	2.89	2	12.21
BIC	2	1.48	1	7.77	2	1.85	3	8.63

Table 5. Results of experiments ($q=1$ and 0.5)

	$q=1;\ D=Z=2000;\ R=5;\ n=2$				$q=0.5;\ D=Z=2000;\ R=5;\ n=2$			
	rank	$\Delta^2_{\mathrm{MSE}-\Omega}$ $[10^{-2}]$	rank	$\Lambda_{\mathrm{LLR}-\Omega}$ $[10^{-3}]$	rank	$\Delta^2_{\mathrm{MSE}-\Omega}$ $[10^{-2}]$	rank	$\Lambda_{\mathrm{LLR}-\Omega}$ $[10^{-3}]$
MuRSI$_{50}$	1	2.02	1	9.51	(1)	1.89	(1)	9.19
MuRSI$_{20}$	(1)	2.06	(1)	9.62	(1)	1.91	(1)	9.33
MuRSI$_{10}$	(1)	2.05	(1)	9.60	1	1.84	1	9.17
MuRSI$_{5}$	(1)	2.05	(1)	9.62	(1)	2.04	(1)	10.01
MuRSI$_{1}$	-	2.38	-	11.16	(1)	2.19	(1)	10.12
AIC	3	3.28	3	13.94	3	2.76	3	13.22
BIC	2	2.33	2	10.96	2	2.39	2	10.76

Table 6. Results of experiments ($q=0.1$ and 0.05)

	$q=0.1;\ D=Z=2000;\ R=5;\ n=2$				$q=0.05;\ D=Z=2000;\ R=5;\ n=2$			
	rank	$\Delta^2_{\mathrm{MSE}-\Omega}$ $[10^{-2}]$	rank	$\Lambda_{\mathrm{LLR}-\Omega}$ $[10^{-3}]$	rank	$\Delta^2_{\mathrm{MSE}-\Omega}$ $[10^{-2}]$	rank	$\Lambda_{\mathrm{LLR}-\Omega}$ $[10^{-3}]$
MuRSI$_{50}$	1	1.90	(1)	8.96	(1)	1.66	1	9.15
MuRSI$_{20}$	(1)	1.96	(1)	9.30	(1)	1.66	(1)	9.15
MuRSI$_{10}$	(1)	1.96	(1)	9.30	1	1.59	1	7.90
MuRSI$_{5}$	(1)	2.11	(1)	9.72	1	1.59	(1)	7.90
MuRSI$_{1}$	(1)	2.45	(1)	11.23	(1)	1.94	(1)	9.33
AIC	3	2.99	3	13.95	3	3.30	3	16.04
BIC	2	2.73	2	11.34	2	2.20	2	9.38

7   Conclusions

The presented paper describes a new approach to determine the optimal number of GMM components in tasks where the goal is to find the model that best fits the given data. The proposed approaches are not based on the information criterion as currently used methods, but use the techniques of validation or cross-validation based on multiple random subsampling of training data with initialization. The advantage of the proposed methods is their robustness, i.e. they provide very good results for the sets of training data with various properties. Because the researcher typically does not know the characteristics of the data for which he looks for a model, the proposed methods provide some assurance, that the solution will be the best or very close to the best, while a priory choice of BIC or AIC can end (and often ends) in a model with lower accuracy. It can be clearly seen from the results of experiments, where during mutual approaching the means of individual components of the GMM lose some methods their accuracy.

Although MuRSI is particularly attractive for tasks with smaller amounts of training data, the proposed method can be equally well used for larger datasets.

It should be expected, however, the increase of computation time, which is not (due to the initialization step of the EM algorithm) fatal. Since the main objective of this study was to introduce the functionality of the new algorithms (especially MuRSI) for estimation the number of components of GMM in statistical modeling, we will focus our attention in further research also on optimization of time requirements, especially in applications with higher dimension of space and a larger number of components.

References

1. Akaike, H.: A new look at the statistical model identification. IEEE Transactions on Automatic Control **AC–19**, 716–723 (1974)
2. Bulteel, K., Wilderjans, T.F., Tuerlinckx, F., Ceulemans, E.: CHull as an alternative to AIC and BIC in the context of mixtures of factor analyzers. Behav. Res. **45**, 782–791 (2013)
3. Chen, P., Wu, T.J., Yang, J.: A comparative study of model selection criteria for the number of signals. IET Radar Sonar Navig. **2**(3), 180–188 (2008)
4. Huang, T., Peng, H., Zhang, K.: Model Selection for Gaussian Mixture Models. Cornell University Library (2013). http://arxiv.org/abs/1301.3558v1
5. McLachlan, G., Peel, D.: Finite Mixture Models. John Wiley & Sons, New York (2000)
6. Oliver, Ch., Jouzel, F., El Matouat, A.: Choice of the number of component clusters in mixture models by information criteria. In: Vision Interface 1999, Trois-Riveres, Canada (1999)
7. Schwarz, G.: Estimating the dimension of a model. Ann. Stat. **6**, 461–464 (1978)
8. Shibata, R.: Selection of the order of an autoregressive model by Akaik's information criterion. Biometrika **52**(3), 333–345 (1976)
9. Vrieze, S.I.: Model selection and psychological theory: A discussion of the differences between the Akaike Information Criterion (AIC) and the Bayesian Information Criterion (BIC). Psychological Methods **17**(2), 228–243 (2012)
10. Xie, C., Chang, J., Liu, Y.: Estimating the Number of Components in Gaussian Mixture Models Adaptively. Journal of Information & Computational Science **10**(14), 4453–4460 (2013)

Vectorisation of Sketched Drawings Using Co-occurring Sample Circles

Alexandra Bonnici[✉] and Kenneth P. Camilleri

Department of Systems and Control Engineering, Faculty of Engineering,
University of Malta, Msida, Malta
{alexandra.bonnici,kenneth.camilleri}@um.edu.mt

Abstract. This paper presents a drawing vectorisation algorithm which
uses multiple concentric families of circles placed in a dense grid on the
image space. We show that any off-centered junction within the family
of circles can be located and hence show how these junction points may
be linked to neighbouring junction points, thereby creating a vector representation of the drawing geometry. The proposed algorithm identified
98% of the junctions in the drawings on which it was evaluated, each
within a localisation error of 4.7 ± 2.3 pixels, resulting in straight line
vectors which are well placed with respect to the drawn edges.

1 Introduction

Computer interpretation of sketches and drawings, in its simplest form, changes
the hand-drawn, raster drawings into a vector format that can be used by
computer-aided design tools [15,21]. Drawings are more than the sum of individual lines and human observers use domain knowledge to identify particular
arrangements of the line vectors and use this knowledge to interpret the drawings. These particular line arrangements may be used by drawing interpretation
algorithms to extract structures from the drawing in a similar manner as a
human expert would [3,13]. In this work, we are particularly interested in the
ability of inferring 3D shape from 2D drawings, where the structures of interest
are the junctions that form the skeletal 3D structure of the sketched objects.
Vectorisation techniques typically follow a two-tier approach, where the drawing
is first binarised, following which, lines are sampled to obtain a vector representation of the drawing [5,15,22]. Such an approach incurs the additional costs of
the binarisation step which may be problematic, particularly of the image background is of non-uniform intensity, such as what would be obtained in drawing
images digitised by means of cameras on smart-phones or tablets.

In this paper, we propose an alternative vectorisation algorithm that can
work directly on grey-level images. The image is sampled using circle samplers,
labelling each sampled point as a line or junction point, where junction points
can be further classified according to the specific junction geometry.

The rest of the paper is organised as follows: Section 2 presents a literature
review on vectorisation algorithms; Section 3 presents our proposition of using

© Springer International Publishing Switzerland 2015
G. Azzopardi and N. Petkov (Eds.): CAIP 2015, Part I, LNCS 9256, pp. 690–701, 2015.
DOI: 10.1007/978-3-319-23192-1_58

concentric circle samplers to detected off-centered junctions within the sampled region; Section 4 shows how the circle samplers can be used to vectorise the drawing; Section 5 presents the results obtained by the proposed algorithm while Section 6 concludes the paper.

2   Related Work

Converting line drawings into a vector format requires the localisation of lines from the image, discarding pixels that account for the stroke line widths retaining only those necessary to maintain the topology of the drawing, that is, the line's medial axis. This can be achieved through skeletonisation [9] which will however intoreduce distortions as the lines approach junction points [6]. To avoid these distortions, other methods can be employed to obtain the medial axis, for example, through the use of contours [22] and Delauny triangles [16] among others. Since these methods assess whether each pixel is a candidate pixel on the medial axis, they incur large computational costs which may be reduced by adapting sparse pixel tracking approaches such as that described in [1,17,18] among others. Here, lines are extracted by sampling the image using rectangles [18], squares [17] and circles [1], starting with a strategically located seed pixel which is propagated along the lines of the drawing. Since lines have a rectilinear shape, rectangular samplers have the advantage of having a similar shape as the lines being sampled [12]. However, this will also require rotating the sampler so that it is aligned with the lines in the image [12]. This alignment requirement can be avoided by taking the grey-level profile of the boundary pixels [1,17]. In such cases, circle samplers, being isotropic, are more suited samplers. Line location can also be performed by using the Hough transform, which accumulates the line parameters in an accumulator array [19]. Peaks in the accumulation array correspond to the image line parameters which must then be localised in the image space [19]. The grey-level image is typically pre-processed to obtain an edge-map, such that the peak localisation is dependent on the accuracy of the edge detection. Thus research is invested in more robust edge localisation [4].

Vectorization by sparse pixel tracking and the Hough transform techniques can extract lines in their entirety even in the presence of intersections with other lines. However, these intersections are valuable for the algorithmic, 3D interpretation of the drawing, since such intersections form the junctions which define the 3D geometry of the object. For example, line-labelling algorithms such as [14] among others, require the identification of the geometry of the junction points in order to provide meaningful line labels. To this extent, additional post-processing is often performed to detect line intersections [8,10].

Sampling the grey-level profile of the image around a given line can potentially provide for the detection of junction points without the requirement of additional post-processing. In particular, the isomorphic nature of circle samplers allows the sampling of a line pixel neighbours in a locus of points equidistant from the line point, hence sampling any other line that can potentially intersect with the line being sampled. Sparse pixel tracking however requires sequential tracking of the image, starting from some seed pixel centred on the line [17,18], incurring additional computational overheads to locate a suitable seed and maintain the path propagation.

We hypothesise that the grey-level profile of the circle sampler can be used to deduce the orientations of lines passing through the circle as well as the location of a junction point within the circle such that the image can be sampled simultaneously, in its entirety by multiple circles strategically placed across the image.

3   Junction Localisation from Sampling Circles

Consider a binary image containing a junction point P with position vector $\boldsymbol{J}_P$. The junction is formed when thin line segments with unknown orientations θ, $\theta = [0, 2\pi)$ intersect at P. In the particular case, the junction has N line segments emerging from it, each with orientation θ_n, $n = 1 \cdots N$. A pixel position on any of the line segments may be expressed as:

$$\mathbf{x}_n(r) = \mathbf{J}_P + r\mathbf{k}_{\theta_n} \tag{1}$$

where $\mathbf{x}_n(r)$ is the pixel coordinates of a point on the nth line segment forming the junction, r is the displacement from the junction point and $\mathbf{k}_{\theta_n} = [\cos\theta_n, \sin\theta_n]^T$. If $\theta \in [0, 2\pi)$, then (1) describes a single point on the circumference of such a circle, specifically the point at which the line segment emerging from the junction point intersects with the circle circumference. Such a circle can be used to sample the image around the junction, in which case, the grey-level profile of the circle circumference can be ideally modelled by:

$$I_r(\beta(\theta)) = \begin{cases} 1 & \text{when } \beta(\theta) = \theta_n \\ 0 & \text{otherwise} \end{cases} \tag{2}$$

where $\beta(\theta) = [0, 2\pi)$ is the angle on the circle circumference at which the line segment intersects with the circle circumference. This sampling circle can therefore be used to determine the line orientation of the line segments at the junction. Repeating the sampling by using concentric sampling circles increases the confidence in the estimated line orientations. Moreover, junctions consist of two or more line pairs which have an angular separation $\Delta\theta$ such that we may define a co-occurrence matrix $S(\theta, \Delta\theta)$ as:

$$S(\theta, \Delta\theta) = \frac{1}{M} \sum_m I_{r_m}(\beta(\theta)) I_{r_m}(\beta(\theta + \Delta\theta)) \tag{3}$$

where r_m is the radius of the mth circle, $m = 1 \cdots M$ and M is the total number of concentric sampling circles. This allows for further discrimination between line segments that are part of the centered junction and others that are accidental intersections with the sampling circles. In this particular case, with the circles centred on the junction, $\beta(\theta) = \theta$ and the concentric circles centered on P will have identical grey-level profiles $I_r(\beta(\theta))$.

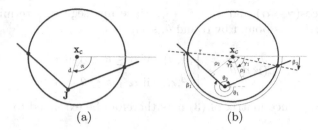

(a)   (b)

Fig. 1. A sampling circle containing an off-centred L-Junction showing (a) the junction parameters and (b) the line parameters and intersecting angles.

Lemma 1. *The line orientations at a junction may be estimated from $[\hat{\theta}, \Delta\hat{\theta}] = \arg\{\max\{S(\theta, \Delta\theta)\}\}$*

Proof. Following from (2), $I_{r_m}(\beta(\theta))I_{r_m}(\beta(\theta + \Delta\theta)) = 1$ if and only if the sampling circle intersects with two line segments with some orientation θ and $\theta + \Delta\theta$. If these line segments form part of a centred junction, then for all M concentric sampling circles, $\beta(\theta) = \theta_n$ and $\beta(\theta + \Delta\theta) = \theta_n + \Delta\theta$. If however the line segments do not form part of the centred junction and are just accidental intersections between the sampling circles, then $\beta(\theta) \neq \theta_n$ and $\beta(\theta + \Delta\theta) \neq \theta_n + \Delta\theta$. Moreover, the angle of intersection between the sampling circles and the lines will be different for all sampling circles and hence, $S(\theta, \Delta\theta) = \frac{1}{M}$. Thus, as $M \to \infty$, $S(\theta, \Delta\theta) \to \mathbf{E}[I_r(\beta(\theta))I_r(\beta(\theta + \Delta\theta))]$ and hence, $[\hat{\theta}, \Delta\hat{\theta}] = \arg\{\max\{S(\theta, \Delta\theta)\}\}$ is a consistent estimator of the line orientations of the line segments at a centred junction.   ⊓

3.1   Localisation of Off-centered Junction Points

Although Lemma 1 shows that circle samplers can be used to determine the line orientations of all line segments at a junction, the circle samplers must be centered on the junction point, thus incurring computational overheads required to select suitable seed pixels to act as circle centres. In order to bypass this, it is desirable to locate the junction point when it occurs anywhere within the sampling circle, relaxing the requirement of having the set of concentric circle samplers centered on the junction point.

Consider the centre C of the circle sampler as a local point of reference. As shown in Fig. 1(a), the junction point P can be referred to C using the parameters $\boldsymbol{d} = (d, \alpha)$. Similarly, each junction line segment can be referred to the circle centre using the polar coordinates (ρ, γ) as shown in Fig. 1(b). The angle on the circumference at which the line segments intersect with the circle circumference is now a function of the junction position, the radius and the line orientations such that (2) may be re-written as:

$$I_r(\beta(r; \boldsymbol{d}, \theta)) = \begin{cases} 1 & \text{when } \beta(r; \boldsymbol{d}, \theta) = \gamma \pm \cos^{-1}\left(\frac{\rho}{r}\right) \\ 0 & \text{otherwise} \end{cases} \tag{4}$$

where $\rho = d\cos(\gamma - \alpha)$ and $\gamma = \theta + \frac{\pi}{2}$. Since line segments terminate at the junction, $\beta(r; \boldsymbol{d}, \theta)$ is bound by α and θ, such that

$$\beta(r; \boldsymbol{d}, \theta) \mapsto \begin{cases} [\alpha, \theta) & \text{if } \alpha \leq \theta < \alpha + \pi \\ (\theta, \alpha] & \text{if } \alpha + \pi \leq \theta < \alpha \end{cases} \tag{5}$$

The co-occurrence matrix of (3) may therefore be extended to

$$S(\boldsymbol{d}, \theta, \Delta\theta) = \frac{1}{M} \sum_m I_{r_m}(\beta(r_m; \boldsymbol{d}, \theta)) I_{r_m}(\beta(r_m; \boldsymbol{d}, \theta + \Delta\theta)) \tag{6}$$

Lemma 2. *The junction position and line orientations may be estimated from* $[\hat{\boldsymbol{d}}, \hat{\theta}, \hat{\Delta\theta}] = \arg\{\max\{S(\boldsymbol{d}, \theta, \Delta\theta)\}\}$.

Proof. Given any sampling circle of radius r_m, there will be an infinite number of combinations of the parameters $(\boldsymbol{d}, \theta, \Delta\theta)$ for which $\beta(r; \boldsymbol{d}, \theta)$ corresponds to the intersecting angle between the line segment and the circle circumference. However, only if $(\boldsymbol{d}, \theta, \Delta\theta)$ correspond to the junction position and line orientations will $I(r_m, \beta(r_m; \boldsymbol{d}, \theta)) = 1$ for all $m = 1, \cdots, M$. Otherwise, $I_{r_m}(\beta(r_m; \boldsymbol{d}, \theta)) = 1$ only for specific sampling circles.
Hence, as $M \to \infty$, $S(\boldsymbol{d}, \theta, \Delta\theta) \to \mathbf{E}_r[I_r(\beta(r; \boldsymbol{d}, \theta)) I_r(\beta(r; \boldsymbol{d}, \theta + \Delta\theta))]$ and thus, $\arg\{\max\{S(\boldsymbol{d}, \theta, \Delta\theta)\}\}$ is a consistent estimator of the junction position and line segment orientation. $\qquad\square$

Note that in the particular case when the junction is centered on the circle samplers, $\boldsymbol{d} = 0$ so that $S(\boldsymbol{d}, \theta, \Delta\theta) = S(0, \theta, \Delta\theta) = S(\theta, \Delta\theta)$ as represented in (3).

3.2   Localisation of Junctions with Thick Line Segments

The discussion thus far assumes that the drawing consists of thin line segments. In practice, this is not the case since the resolution of the scanning device and the pen thickness introduce some finite line width w to the strokes. If we model the stroke segments as rectangular strips of length l and width w, as shown in Fig. 2(a), then it can be easily observed that the orientation resolution of the line segment is reduced to $\theta \pm \delta\theta$ where $\delta\theta = \tan^{-1}(\frac{w}{l})$, corresponding to the lines passing through the diagonals of the rectangular segment. Thus, for a given junction position, there will be a range of values of $\beta(r; \boldsymbol{d}, \theta)$ for which $I_r(\beta(r; \boldsymbol{d}, \theta)) = 1$, corresponding to an arc on the circumference of the sampling circle. Consequently, for some junction position vector $\boldsymbol{d}$, $S(\boldsymbol{d}, \theta, \Delta\theta)$ will contain regions of maximal values, centered on $(\theta, \Delta\theta)$ and whose size is dependent on $\delta\theta$.

The thickness of the line segments will also reduce the localisation resolution of the junction point to a parallelogram region which can be described as the locus of points common to both line segments as shown in Fig. 2(b). The size and aspect ratio of this area are dependent on the line widths as well as the angular separation $\Delta\theta$ between the lines at the junction. The diagonals of this junction region will correspond to the true junction point and thus, for some value of $(\theta, \Delta\theta)$, $S(\boldsymbol{d}, \theta, \Delta\theta)$ will contain regions of maximal values centered on

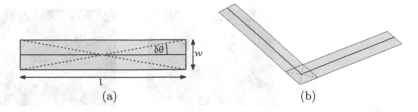

Fig. 2. (a) Thick lines can be modelled as rectangular segments of width w and length l. (b) The junction area formed by the two thick line segments. This can be described as the loci of points common to both line segments. Diagonals of the junction area intersect at the true junction point.

the junction point specified by d that correspond to the junction location in the sampling circle. Thus $\arg\{\max\{S(d,\theta,\Delta\theta)\}\}$ will contain groups of $(\hat{d},\hat{\theta},\Delta\hat{\theta})$ values, each centred on the true values of $(d,\theta,\Delta\theta)$ such that the group centroid can be used as estimates for the line orientations and junction location estimates.

3.3   Junction and Line Estimates from Grey-Level Images

Scanned images of drawings are often grey-level images rather than binary images and therefore the co-occurrence of the line stroke intersections with the circle sampler will be affected by the grey-level distribution of the line strokes. Apart from the anti-aliasing effect introduced by the digitising medium, resulting in image blur, the grey-level distribution at the sampling circle will also be affected by the nature of the pencil used to make the drawing strokes as well as the paper upon which the drawing is made. In general, a pencil can be characterised by the degree of hardness, the mixture of graphite, clay and wax particles in the writing core, the shape of the pencil tip and the pressure distribution of the tip [7, 20]. The shape of the tip can be modelled by polygons, with the area of the tip in contact with the paper will vary depending on the angle at which the pencil is held to the paper. In general, the midpoint of the polygonal shape can be considered as the main pressure distribution point, that is, the pencil will distribute most graphite onto the paper at the centre of the pencil tip and hence, the strokes produced by the typical pencil will be darker towards the centre of the stroke [20]. This can be observed in Figure 3.3 which shows the average stroke grey-level obtained from 30 strokes taken from 6 sample drawings.

Thus, line and junction parameters corresponding to line segments passing through the periphery of the stroke will not have co-occurrence values which are as strong as for those that correspond to line segments passing through the stroke centre. Consequently, the region of maximal values in $S(d,\theta,\Delta\theta)$ will be smaller than for crisp, binary strokes. These regions are still centered around the line and junction parameters in $S(d,\theta,\Delta\theta)$ such that the parameter estimation is not affected by the grey-level images. This is advantageous to the vectorisation problem since the algorithm does not require prior binarisation.

Fig. 3. (a) The grey profile of a line stroke and the co-occurrence values for (b) a binary image with thick lines, (c) a pencil sketch of the image

3.4 Sampling Long, Straight Line Segments

When sampling circles are placed at random locations within the image, it may be possible that although a line segment emerging from a junction passes through the circle area, the junction itself lies beyond the sampling circle. In such cases, junction point specified by d that falls on the line segment, $S(d, \theta, \Delta\theta)$ will be a maximum when θ corresponds to the line orientation and $\Delta\theta = \pi$. Thus, while $\arg\{\max\{S(d, \theta, \Delta\theta)\}\}$ will consist of a compact set for $\theta, \delta\theta$, there will be a wider range of possible values for d parameter values, spanning the entire length of the line segment. The mean of these values will correspond to a point at the centre of the line segment and we define such a point as a *virtual* junction point.

4   Using Concentric Sampling Circles for Vectorisation

In order to vectorise the drawing, circle samplers should cover the whole image such that all junction points are sampled. These junction points must then be connected to obtain the topological structure of the drawing. Straight line segments are used between the detected junctions making up the topological structure to approximate the line drawing segments between the junctions. To ensure that the drawing is sampled completely, sampling circles are placed on an equidistant grid of centre points covering the entire image. The size of the grid is set such that it corresponds to the size of the largest inscribed square in the circle sampler, that is, the grid size is set at $\sqrt{2}r_M$, where r_M is the radius of the largest circle in the concentric set of sampling circles. This ensures that every junction point in the image will be sampled by at least one circle as shown in Fig. 4(a).

Within such a grid system, each sampling circle has eight neighbours to which it can be connected with a straight line vector. However, not all these circles necessarily contain line strokes and if a sampling circle samples only the image background, this can be discarded, removing the vector link that connects such a circle to its neighbours as shown in Fig. 4(b). The remaining circles are centred on the junction point, refining the resolution of the line vectors. Moreover, since

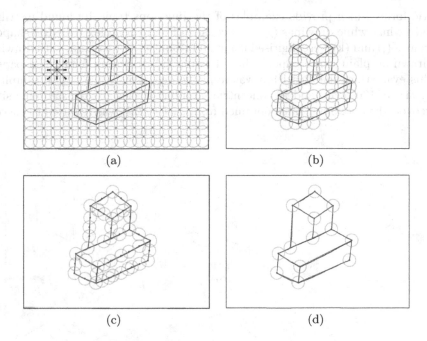

Fig. 4. Using sampling circles for vectorisation. (a) sampling circles are placed on an evenly spaced grid, allowing the sampling circles to overlap such that the entire image space is sampled. Each circle can be linked to eight neighbouring circles. (b) Sampling circles that fall on the image background can be removed, deleting redundant links accordingly. (c) Remaining circles can be aligned to the junction points located within the circles, merging samplers that correspond to the same junction point. (d) Virtual junction points may be removed, retaining only the true junction points and hence obtaining a vector representation of the drawing.

there is a degree of overlap between the sampling circles, circles that sample the same junction point are merged into a single circle which inherits the vector links of the parent samplers as shown in Fig. 4(c).

In this way, the topology of the drawing may be refined until all circles are centred on the junction points or the virtual junction points on the line medial axis. All circles corresponding to virtual junction points can then be removed, retaining the topological structure of the drawing by creating direct links between sampling circles that were initially linked through the virtual junction point. Thus, the resulting topology contains only junction points and vector links which correspond to the edges linking these junction points as shown in Fig. 4(d).

5   Results

The algorithm was evaluated on sample drawings such as those shown in Fig 5. These drawings vary in complexity, with drawings (a) - (f) showing simple geometric forms which provide examples of the junctions typically found in trihedral drawings while drawings (g) - (h) consist of more complex trihedral shapes. Drawings (j) and (k) were digitised using an in-built tablet camera, with drawing (j) drawn on plain white paper, while drawing (k) drawn on feint-ruled paper. In this evaluation, the algorithm was implemented using a maximum sampling circle size of 100 pixels and 70 concentric sampling circles at each sampling site. Moreover, the maximum value obtained from $S(d, \theta, \Delta\theta)$ was required to exceed

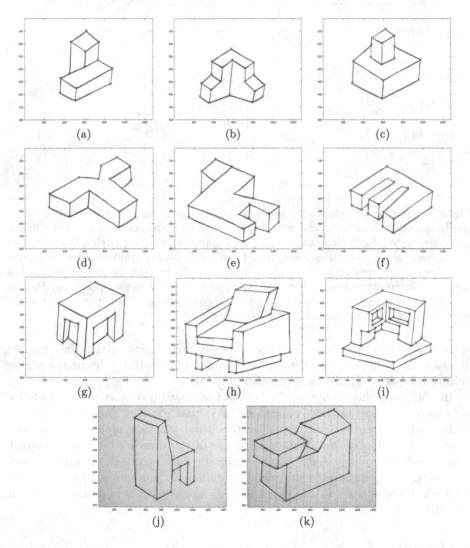

Fig. 5. The vectors obtained from the vectorisation algorithm superimposed on the drawings

a maximum value of 0.8 in order to identify and discard sampling circles that fall on the image background.

The proposed vectorisation algorithm identifies 306 of the 310 junctions present in these test drawings, with a mean localisation error of 4.7 ± 2.3 pixels, resulting in straight line vectors which are well placed with respect to the drawn edges. The algorithm fails to identify two junctions in drawing (f) and another junction in drawings (g) and (k). This is due to the fact that in these drawings, the length of the segments at the junction are smaller than the size of the circle samplers, lowering the co-occurrence value of these lines since they do not co-occur across all circles in the family of concentric circle samplers.

The performance of the proposed vectorisation algorithm was compared with that obtained by the Sparse Pixel Vectorisation (SPV) algorithm described in [2]. The performance was measured using the pixel recovery index (PRI) proposed in the vectorisation evaluation protocol of [11]. This measures the degree of overlap between the detected vectors and the ground-truth representation of the drawings and consists of two components, namely the true detection rate D_p and the false detection rate F_p such that $PRI = 0.5D_p + 0.5(1 - F_p)$. Ideally, the true detection rate $D_p = 1$ while the false detection rate $F_p = 0$ such that $PRI = 1$. The results obtained are given in Table 1. Here we can note that the SPV algorithm has high PRI values for drawings (a) - (j), as expected from the results reported in [2]. We can also observe that the performance of the proposed circle-based vectorisation is at an equal level as the SPV algorithm for these drawings. Performance differs for Drawing (k), where, due to the required binarisation of the drawing, the SPV also vectorises the feint lines of the paper background, resulting in a large number of false detections, since these lines do not form part of the sketched drawing. Using the proposed circle-based vectorisation algorithm, these lines do not provide a significant accumulation value in the

Table 1. Comparison of the performance of the circle-based vectorisation algorithm with the sparse pixel vectorisation algorithm, showing the pixel detection rate, D_p, the false detection rate F_p and the pixel recovery index PRI

Drawing	SPV			Circle-based vectorisation		
	D_p	F_p	PRI	D_p	F_p	PRI
(a)	0.90	0.06	**0.92**	0.91	0.11	**0.90**
(b)	0.89	0.06	**0.92**	0.86	0.10	**0.88**
(c)	0.91	0.05	**0.93**	0.92	0.09	**0.91**
(d)	0.88	0.09	**0.90**	0.91	0.11	**0.90**
(e)	0.90	0.13	**0.89**	0.92	0.09	**0.91**
(f)	0.86	0.11	**0.87**	0.78	0.10	**0.84**
(g)	0.89	0.06	**0.92**	0.86	0.10	**0.88**
(h)	0.85	0.11	**0.87**	0.90	0.11	**0.89**
(i)	0.88	0.11	**0.89**	0.87	0.11	**0.88**
(j)	0.88	0.08	**0.90**	0.82	0.20	**0.81**
(k)	0.72	0.75	**0.48**	0.77	0.10	**0.84**

co-occurrence matrix $S(\mathbf{d}, \theta, \Delta\theta)$ and thus are not represented as vectors, such that only vectors representing the sketched drawing are retained by the proposed algorithm, as desired. Moreover, the proposed circle-vectorisation algorithm can identify and label the junction points while obtaining the vector representation of the drawing.

6   Conclusion

In this paper, we present the hypothesis that junction points may be localised within some sampling circle by noting the co-occurrences of the intersecting angles between the circle samples and the line strokes that form the junction. Hence, we show that the drawing can be vectorised using multiple circles without the need for path following, selection of suitable located seed pixels or image binarisation. The algorithm detected 98% of the junctions from the drawings on which it was evaluated.

The algorithm requires that sampling circles are placed on a dense grid in order to ensure that each junction point appears in at least one sampling circle. While this ensures that all junctions can be sampled, the circle samplers may occasionally fail to locate a junction point. This is mainly due to the fixed size of the sampling circles while the drawing may contain regions of mixed resolution. Thus, the vectorisation may be further improved by allowing the size of the family of concentric sampling circles to adjust according to the local drawing detail resolution.

References

1. Bonnici, A., Camilleri, K.: A circle-based vectorization algorithm for drawings with shadows. In: Proceedings of the International Symposium on Sketch-Based Interfaces and Modelling, pp. 69–77 (2013)
2. Dori, D., Wenyin, L.: Automated cad conversion with the machine drawing understanding system: concepts, algorithms, and performance. IEEE Transactions on Systems, Man and Cybernetics, Part A: Systems and Humans **29**(4), 411–416 (1999)
3. Gennari, L., Kara, L.B., Stahovich, T.F., Shimada, K.: Combining geometry and domain knowledge to interpret hand-drawn diagrams. Computers & Graphics **29**(4), 547–562 (2005)
4. Guerreiro, R.F.C., Aguiar, P.M.Q.: Extraction of line segments in cluttered images via multiscale edges. In: Proceedings of the 2013 IEEE International Conference of Image Processing (2013)
5. Hasson, N., Aljunid, S., Ahmad, R.: Extract dominant elements and shapes from raster images. In: International Conference on Electronic Design, ICED 2008, pp. 1–4 (2008)
6. Hilaire, X., Tombre, K.: Robust and accurate vectorization of line drawings. IEEE Transactions on Pattern Analysis and Machine Interpretation **28**(6), 890–904 (2006)
7. Jin, W., Hujun, B., Weihua, Z., Qunsheng, P., Yingqing, X.: Automatic image-based pencil sketch rendering. J. Comput. Sci. Technol. **17**(3), 347–355 (2002)

8. Kang, S.K., Choung, Y.C., Park, J.A.: Image corner detection using hough transform. In: Marques, J.S., de la Blanca, N.P., Pina, P. (eds.) IbPRIA 2005. LNCS, vol. 3523, pp. 279–286. Springer, Heidelberg (2005)
9. Katz, R.A., Pizer, S.M.: Untangling the blum medial axis transform. International Journal of Computer Vision **55**(2–3), 139–153 (2004)
10. Liu, J., Chen, Y., Tang, X.: Decomposition of complex line drawings with hidden lines for 3d planar-faced manifold object reconstruction. IEEE Transactions on Pattern Analysis and Machine Intelligence **33**(1), 3–15 (2011)
11. Liu, W., Dori, D.: A protocol for Performance Evaluation of Line Detection Algorithms. Machine Vision Applications **9**, 240–250 (1997)
12. Liu, W., Dori, D.: Sparse pixel vectorisation: An algorithm and its performance evaluation. IEEE Transactions of Pattern Analysis and Machine Intelligence **21**(3), 202–215 (1999)
13. Lu, T., Yang, Y., Yang, R., Cai, S.: Knowledge extraction from structured engineering drawings. In: Fifth International Conference on Fuzzy Systems and Knowledge Discovery, FSKD 2008, vol. 2, pp. 415–419 (2008)
14. Myers, R., Hancock, E.R.: Genetic algorithms for ambiguous labelling problems. Pattern Recognition **33**(4), 685–704 (2000)
15. Nagy, G.: Twenty years of document image analysis in pami. IEEE Transactions on Pattern Analysis and Machine Intelligence **22**(1), 38–62 (2000)
16. Naouai, M., Narjess, M., Hamouda, A.: Line extraction algorithm based on image vectorization. In: 2010 International Conference on Mechatronics and Automation (ICMA), pp. 470–476 (2010)
17. Nidelea, M., Alexei, A.: Method of the square - a new algorithm for image vectorization. In: 2012 9th International Conference on Communications (COMM), pp. 115–118 (2012)
18. Song, J., Su, F., Chen, J., Tai, C., Cai, S.: An object-oriented progressive-simplification-based vectorization system for engineering drawings: Model, algorithm, and performance. IEEE Transactions of Pattern Analysis and Machine Intelligence **24**(8) (2002)
19. Song, J., Lyu, M.R.: A hough transform based line recognition method utilizing both parameter space and image space. Pattern Recognition **38**(4), 539–552 (2005)
20. Sousa, M.C., Buchanan, J.W.: Observational models of graphite pencil materials. Computer Graphics Forum **19**(1), 27–49 (2000)
21. Tombre, K., Ah-Soon, C., Dosch, P., Masini, G., Tabbone, S.: Stable and robust vectorization: how to make the right choices. In: Chhabra, A.K., Dori, D. (eds.) GREC 1999. LNCS, vol. 1941, pp. 3–18. Springer, Heidelberg (2000)
22. Wei, J., Li, M., Wang, Y., Chen, C., Hong, W., Chen, Z.: Parallel algorithm designed for polygon vectorization. In: 20th International Conference on Geoinformatics (GEOINFORMATICS), 2012, pp. 1–4 (2012)

Robust Contact Lens Detection Using Local Phase Quantization and Binary Gabor Pattern

Lovish[1]($\boxtimes$), Aditya Nigam[1,2], Balender Kumar[1], and Phalguni Gupta[1,3]

[1] Department of Computer Science and Engineering,
Indian Institute of Technology Kanpur, Kanpur 208016, UP, India
{lovishc,naditya,balendk,pg}@cse.iitk.ac.in
[2] School of Computing and Electrical Engineering,
Indian Institute of Technology Mandi, Mandi 175001, HP, India
aditya@iitmandi.ac.in
[3] National Institute of Technical Teacher's and Research,
Salt Lake, Kolkata 700106, India

Abstract. Due to its resistance to circumvention, iris has been used as a prime biometric trait in border crossings and identity related civil projects. However, sensor level spoofing attacks such as the use of printed iris, plastic eyeballs and contact lens pose a challenge by helping intruders to sidestep security in iris based biometric systems. Attacks through contact lenses are most challenging to detect as they obfuscate the iris partially and part of original iris remains visible through them. In this paper, we present a contact lens dataset containing 12823 images acquired from 50 subjects. Each subject has images pertaining to no lens, soft lens and cosmetic lens class. Verification results with three different techniques on three datasets suggest an average degradation of 3.10% in EER when subject is wearing soft lens and 17.34% when subject is wearing cosmetic lens. Further we propose a cosmetic lens detection approach based on Local Phase Quantization(LPQ) and Binary Gabor Pattern(BGP). Experiments conducted on publicly available IIITD Vista, IIITD Cogent, ND_2010 and self-collected dataset indicate that our method outperforms previous lens detection techniques in terms of Correct Classification Rate and false Acceptance Rate. The results suggest that a comprehensive texture descriptor having blur tolerance of LPQ and robustness of BGP is suitable for cosmetic lens detection.

1 Introduction

Iris has emerged as a prime biometric trait in the past decade. It has been deployed in large scale biometric identification programs such as UIDAI in India [6], RIC in Brazil [5] and EIDA in UAE [2]. One of the reason behind use of iris is its resistance to circumvention. Unfortunately sensor level spoofing attacks such as use of printed iris, artificial eyeballs and contact lenses have raised the issue of iris liveness detection in the biometric community.

Broadly, contact lenses can be classified into two categories based on their appearance - soft lens and cosmetic lens. Soft lenses are transparent in nature

© Springer International Publishing Switzerland 2015
G. Azzopardi and N. Petkov (Eds.): CAIP 2015, Part I, LNCS 9256, pp. 702–714, 2015.
DOI: 10.1007/978-3-319-23192-1_59

and are used to correct vision problems such as myopia, hypertropia and astigmatism. Cosmetic contact lenses have a pattern printed on them that changes the appearance of human iris apart from correcting vision of the subject. The texture printed on the cosmetic contact lens partially obfuscates the original iris pattern. Although it has been shown experimentally that the use of cosmetic contact lens leads to decrease in both identification and verification accuracy [18,26], a rigorous study using multiple recognition schemes on multiple datasets has not been been carried out yet. This is of utmost importance as an increase in false Rejection Rate can assist a criminal in eluding detection. Moreover, an impostor may also be able to impersonate iris of another subject by wearing a custom made cosmetic contact lens.

Among various sensor level attacks on iris biometric systems, detection of cosmetic contact lens is most challenging. As lens covers the iris partially, dilation and constriction of pupil is visible through the lens. Hence pupilary response based on lighting changes cannot be used to determine the presence of the lens accurately. Moreover, printed pattern on cosmetic lens differs depending on the manucturer as shown in Figure 1.

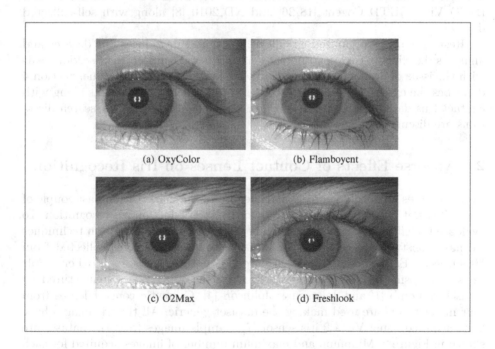

(a) OxyColor   (b) Flamboyent

(c) O2Max   (d) Freshlook

Fig. 1. Cosmetic Lens from Different manucturers

Several hardware and software based cosmetic lens detection schemes have been proposed in past decade. Hardware based schemes are based on purkinje image formation [20] and stereo imaging [15]. Despite being accurate, these schemes require additional equipment to function. Textural feature based methods utilizing Grey Level Co-occurence Matrix (GLCM) [13], Local Binary Patterns (LBP) [23] and Binary Statistical Image Features (BSIF) [17] have also been proposed. GLCM based features have been used in Wei et al [25] with a Correct Classification Rate (CCR) of 94.1% on a 960 image dataset. He et al [14] used multi-resolution LBP for feature extraction step and AdaBoost for learning most discriminative features. They have also employed kernel density estimation to counter class imbalance in the dataset. On a dataset of 600 cosmetic contact lens images they obtain a false accept rate of 0.67%. LBP weighted through SIFT descriptor has been used in [27]. A correct classification accuracy of 99.14% is achieved over an experimental dataset containing images from 72 subjects. In [19] Komulainen et al have suggested the use of BSIF features for generalizing lens detection over unseen cosmetic lens patterns. However, they have conducted experiments only on a single dataset.

In this paper, we show the effect of contact lenses on iris recognition process using three techniques. Finally we propose a robust cosmetic lens detection technique based on the fusion of two texture descriptors. The proposed contact lens detection technique is tested over three publicly available benchmark dataset IIITD Vista, IIITD Cogent [18,26] and ND_2010 [8] along with self-collected dataset.

Rest of paper is organized as follows. Section 2 introduces our dataset and analyzes the effect of cosmetic contact lens on iris recognition. Next section deals with the issue of designing a robust cosmetic lens detection technique. Section 4 describes the experiments performed over three benchmark datasets along with contact lens dataset collected at our lab. Conclusion and future research directions are discussed in Section 5.

2   Adverse Effects of Contact Lenses on Iris Recognition

Contact lenses are available freely and cheaply in the market from past couple of years. Thus, it becomes important to quantify their effect on iris recognition. To evaluate the effect of contact lenses on some existing iris recognition techniques we have constructed a contact lens dataset containing images collected from 50 subjects. Each subject has been enrolled in three classes - No Lens, Soft Lens and Cosmetic Lens. Soft lenses used by the subjects are manuctured by Bausch & Lomb [1] and Johnson & Johnson [4]. Cosmetic contact lenses from four manucturers are used making the dataset generic. All the iris images have been acquired using Vista 2 iris sensor [7]. Sample images from the dataset are shown in Figure 2. Minimum and maximum number of images acquired for each iris class are 20 and 50 respectively. To the best of our knowledge, it is the largest contact lens dataset in terms of number of acquired images. The database has been uploaded and is available for research purposes under mutual agreement. Table 1 summarizes the dataset.

Unlike in [18], where matching has been carried out through a commercial matcher we have used three iris recognition techniques to quantify the performance

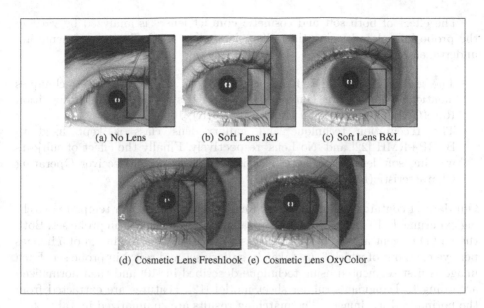

Fig. 2. Example Images from the Our Contact Lens dataset. Right side contains a magnified version of part shown in black box.

Table 1. Summary of Our Contact Lens dataset

Class of Images	Cosmetic lens, Soft lens, No lens
Cosmetic Lens Manucturers	O2Max, Flaymboyent, Oxycolor, Freshlook [3]
Cosmetic Lens Color	Hazel, Green, Blue, Gray
Soft Lens Manucturers	Bausch & Lomb [1], Johnson & Johnson [4]
Iris Sensor	Vista Imaging 2 [7]
Images per class	Cosmetic Lens:4218 No Lens:4551 Soft Lens:4054
Minimum/Maximum number of images per eye class	20/50
Total Images	12823

of iris recognition systems. These include techniques proposed by Masek [21], Daugman [12] and Nigam et al [22]. Log-Gabor and Gabor filtering based approach have been used by Masek and Daugman respectively while Nigam et al have used fusion of a block level variant of local binary patterns and relational measures to extract features from a normalized iris template.

The effect of both soft and cosmetic contact lenses is analyzed by varying the probe lens class keeping the gallery lens class fixed. Two experiments are undertaken in this regard:-

- The gallery lens class is fixed as 'No Lens'. Iris recognition techniques mentioned above are compared on the basis of Correct Recognition Rate(CRR) [16] and Equal Error Rate(EER) [16].
- The recognition technique and gallery lens class is kept fixed to BLBP+RMH [22] and 'No Lens' respectively. Finally the effect of subjects wearing soft lens or cosmetic lens is visualized using Receiver Operating Characteristic(ROC) [16].

Our dataset contains a minimum of 20 images per eye class. For template matching experiments 10 images are taken in gallery set and the rest in probe set. Both the IIITD Cogent and IIITD Vista dataset [18,26] have a minimum of 5 images per eye class out of which 3 are taken in gallery set and rest 2 in probe set. Each image is first segmented using technique described in [10] and then normalized according to Daugman's rubber sheet model [12]. Features are extracted from the normalized iris images. The matching results are summarized in Table 2.

Table 2. Performance Degradation due to use of Contact Lens. GC and PC stand for gallery class and probe class respectively. CRR and EER in %. Avg. Degn. stands for D_{CRR} and D_{EER} averaged over the three datasets.

Dataset	Technique	Masek [21]				Gabor [12]				BLBP+RMH [22]			
	GC-PC	CRR	D_{CRR}	EER	D_{EER}	CRR	D_{CRR}	EER	D_{EER}	CRR	D_{CRR}	EER	D_{EER}
IIITD Cogent [18,26]	No-No	96.76	-	4.56	-	95.27	-	6.51	-	98.75	-	**3.14**	-
	No-Soft	96.25	0.51	5.41	0.85	92.75	2.52	6.49	0.02	97.50	1.25	**4.17**	1.03
	No-Cosmetic	57.03	39.73	**17.16**	12.60	35.92	59.35	23.80	17.29	68.34	30.41	18.43	15.29
IIITD Vista [18,26]	No-No	99.75	-	2.27	-	99.75	-	2.35	-	100	-	**1.16**	-
	No-Soft	91.50	8.25	8.04	5.77	92.75	7.00	6.87	4.52	93.75	7.25	**5.31**	4.15
	No-Cosmetic	58.79	40.96	26.11	23.84	48.74	51.01	21.17	18.82	70.85	29.15	**12.62**	11.46
Our Dataset	No-No	99.79	-	3.34	-	99.69	-	3.81	-	99.89	-	**1.43**	-
	No-Soft	95.00	4.79	7.36	4.02	95.59	4.10	7.99	4.18	96.66	3.23	**4.86**	3.43
	No-Cosmetic	66.81	32.98	21.31	17.97	52.50	47.19	24.54	20.73	67.38	32.51	**19.59**	18.16
Avg Degdn	No-Soft	-	4.51	-	3.54	-	4.54	-	2.90	-	3.91	-	2.87
	No-Cosmetic	-	37.89	-	18.13	-	52.51	-	18.94	-	30.69	-	14.97

ROC curves in Figure 3 illustrates the comparison between iris recognition techniques. For each dataset, EER is minimum when recognition is carried out using BLBP+RMH approach except in the case when cosmetic lens images from IIITD Cogent dataset are matched with no lens images. Although BLBP+RMH

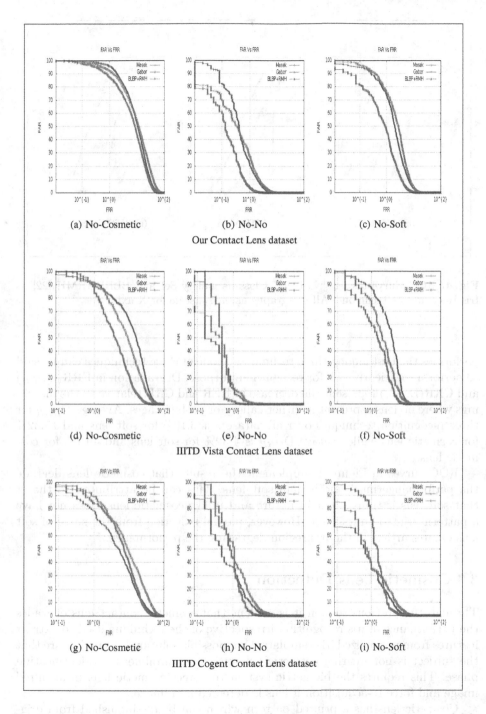

Fig. 3. Receiver Operating Characteristic(ROC) curves comparing performance of different iris recognition techniques. All the graphs use $\log_{10}$ scale for X-axis

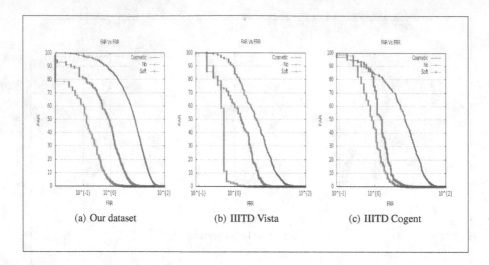

(a) Our dataset   (b) IIITD Vista   (c) IIITD Cogent

Fig. 4. ROC Curve taking "No-Lens" Class as gallery Set and BLBP+RMH [22] as Iris Recognition Technique. All the graphs use $\log_{10}$ scale for X-axis

performes the best among three techniques, none of these techniques can be said to perform sufficiently well for recognition purpose. Degradation in ERR(D_{EER}) and CRR(D_{CRR}) represent the decrease in EER and CRR relative to the matchings where no lens is present in either gallery or probe images. Average D_{EER} for three recognition techniques over all datasets is 3.10% for soft lens and 17.32% for cosmetic lens while average D_{CRR} is 4.32% for soft lens and 49.7% for cosmetic lens.

ROC curves in Figure 4 supplement the results that cosmetic lens degrade the performance much more than soft lens. This can be attributed to the ct that soft lens is transparent in nature and unlike cosmetic lens, does not have a pattern printed on its surce. However, partial reflection from the surce of soft lens creates articts in the iris region degrading the performance.

3   Cosmetic Lens Detection

Through the previous section it is evident that cosmetic contact lens degrades the performance of iris recognition irrespective of the technique used to extract features from normalized iris template. One possible solution is to make sure that the subject is not wearing cosmetic lens either in enrollment or identification phase. This requires the biometric system to detect cosmetic lens in acquired image and force re-acquisition if lens is detected in a image.

Cosmetic lens has a printed pattern which can be distinguished from original iris using texture classification techniques. Previous works addressing cosmetic lens detection have proposed the use of Grey Level Co-occurrence Matrix

(GLCM) [25], Local Binary Patterns (LBP) [14,26,27] and Binary Statistical Image Features (BSIF) [19] as texture descriptors for this task. LBP is considered as a reasonable descriptor under illumination variation whereas BSIF uses Independent Component Analysis (ICA) to arrive at a more general texture descriptor. However, none of these descriptors are robust to image blurring, which is frequently encountered during image acquisition.

A possible solution lies in deblurring the image but most of the deblurring techniques introduce new articts making further analysis more cumbersome. Local Phase Quantization [24] based texture descriptor has been proven to be robust to both motion as well as focus blur. Spatial blur is represented as a convolution of original image with a blur function which results in multiplication in the frequency domain. Let I,B and L be the original image, blur function and blurred image in frequency domain. The relation between their phase can be represented as:-

$$\angle L = \angle I + \angle B$$

Assuming that the point spread function(PSF) causing the blur is centrally symmetric, its Fourier transform B possess phase of either 0 or π depending on the sign of B. Thus if $B > 0$, $\angle B = 0$ else $\angle B = \pi$. Considering the ct that PSF is rectangular for motion and focus blur and has some positive values of B for small values of frequencies [9], it makes use of Discrete Fourier Transform (DFT) to extract phase information from four low frequency components. The phase information from both real and imaginary part of the components is de-correlated for statistical independence and quantized to values between 0-255 using binary coding. Finally a 256-bin histogram is constructed from the quantized values over all the spatial image positions.

Binary Gabor Pattern [28] uses difference between image regions rather than difference between two pixels as in LBP to make the descriptor more robust to noise. Gabor filters are used to find the difference between regions. The real and complex part of Gabor filter are represented in Equation 1 and Equation 2 respectively. DC component from both real and imaginary parts of Gabor filter is removed before convolving the filters with image to guarantee.

$$g(x, y) = \exp(-\frac{1}{2}(\frac{(x')^2}{\sigma^2} + \frac{(y')^2}{(\gamma\sigma)^2})) \cos(\frac{2\pi}{\lambda}x') \tag{1}$$

$$h(x, y) = \exp(-\frac{1}{2}(\frac{(x')^2}{\sigma^2} + \frac{(y')^2}{(\gamma\sigma)^2})) \sin(\frac{2\pi}{\lambda}x') \tag{2}$$

where $x' = x\cos(\theta) + y\sin(\theta)$ and $y' = -x\sin(\theta) + y\cos(\theta)$. θ represents the orientation of the Gabor filter with respect to the normal, γ denotes the spatial aspect ratio, $sigma$ denotes the sigma of Gaussian and λ is the wavelength of the sinusoidal function.

Binary Gabor Pattern combines the benefits of both LBP and Gabor filters. The BGP descriptor for an image is obtained by first convolving the patches in the image by a filter bank containing Gabor filters at 8 different orientations say

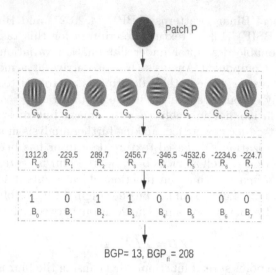

Fig. 5. Calculation of BGP for a particular patch P

(G_0 to G_7) as shown in Figure 5. Vector containing the convolved responses R is thresholded on the basis of the sign of response and binarized to obtain vector B . The binarized vector is transformed to a unique number by assigning a binomial ctor 2^i for each value of i in $B = B_i | i = 0..7$ and converting it into its decimal equivalent. Hence the BGP value for a give patch P can be given as:-

$$BGP = \sum_{i=0}^{7} B_i . 2^i \qquad (3)$$

From the Equation 3 it evident that there are 2^8 unique values possible from 8 bits of B. In order to address rotation invariance, BGP is re-defined as:-

$$BGP_{ri} = MAX(RSFT(BGP, i) | i = 0..7) \qquad (4)$$

where RSFT performs a circular bitwise right shift on the 8-bit number 7 times and MAX takes the maximum of these values. For B_{ri}, 36 distinct values are possible. B_{ri} values extracted from both real and complex part of Gabor filter are concatenated to form a 72-bit histogram. Figure 5 shows the complete process of determining BGP descriptor from an image region.

In our contact lens detection scheme, the acquired iris image is segmented and normalized. LPQ histogram is extracted for the normalized iris image. Three Gabor filter banks differing in value of wavelength and scale are initialized. BGP histograms using the filter banks are concatenated to form a 216-bin histogram. Both the LPQ and BGP histograms are concatenated to form a 472 bit feature vector. The feature vector is passed onto a trained SVM classifier which assigns labels for or against the presence of cosmetic lens

4   Experimental Results

Apart from the three datasets mentioned in Section 2 we have also used ND_2010 [8] which contains 1400 images each for no Lens and cosmetic lens class. In all the experiments, 66% of the subjects are used as training set and rest of the subjects as test set.

We have compared the result of LPQ+BGP approach with GLCM [25], LBP [14] and BSIF [19] approach. For GLCM, we have used the mean and range of inverse difference moment (f_{idm}), sum average (f_{sa}) and sum entropy (f_{se}) as feature vector mentioned in [25]. For LBP, we concatenated histograms for two LBP operators $LBP_{8,1}^{riu2}$ and $LBP_{16,3}^{riu2}$ together to form the feature vector. The radius and size of features learnt in BSIF are taken to be 3 units and 12 bits respectively because it provided consistent results to the authors in [19]. For BGP, three resolutions $(\lambda_i, \sigma_i)_{i=1..3}$ set as (1.3,0.7),(5.2,2.5) and (22,4.5) are taken to construct three BGP histograms which are concatenated to form a 216 bit feature vector.

We have used Support Vector Machine (SVM) [11] with radial basis kernel for classification purpose. The correct classification rate and false Acceptance Rate for different lens detection techniques is shown in Table 3. Performance of our method is marginally better for IIITD Vista and IIITD Cogent while significantly better for ND_2010 dataset which contains significant number of blurred images. BSIF slightly outperforms our method over our dataset due to its generalizing property as it contains four varieties of cosmetic contact lens.

Figure 6 shows some correctly classified images by the proposed BGP+LPQ approach which were falsely accepted as genuine by other approaches. Note that some adequately blurred images are classified correctly by our approach but not through GLCM,LBP or BSIF features.

Table 3. CCR and R across different Texture Description Techniques. R represents % of cosmetic lens images accepted as genuine.

Descriptor	GLCM [25]		LBP [14]		BSIF [19]		LPQ+BGP	
Dataset	CCR	R	CCR	R	CCR	R	CCR	R
Our dataset	57.05	30.02	97.54	0.55	98.44	**0.55**	**98.91**	0.86
IIITD Vista	50.00	55.88	99.70	0.58	99.70	0.58	**99.85**	**0.29**
IIITD Cogent	36.86	46.07	89.54	12.91	**98.21**	3.29	96.81	**2.82**
ND_2010	56.59	31.11	95.82	6.22	85.93	28.44	**99.12**	**1.55**

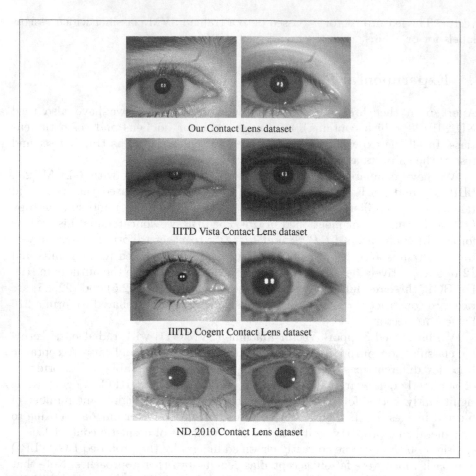

Fig. 6. Images pertaining to Contact Lens class falsely accepted as No Lens by GLCM,LBP and BSIF but correctly classified by our approach.

5   Conclusion

In this paper, we have evaluated the effect of soft and cosmetic lens on IIITD Vista, IIITD Cogent and cosmetic lens dataset acquired in our lab. Three iris recognition techniques have been used to quantify and firmly establish the degradation of recognition performance both in the case of soft and cosmetic contact lens. Further we compared existing cosmetic lens detection techniques with the proposed technique that uses fusion of LPQ and BGP texture descriptors. Our technique outperformed LBP, GLCM and BSIF for IIITD Vista, IIITD Cogent and ND_2010 datasets. BSIF performed slightly better than BGP+LPQ over our dataset as there were four different cosmetic lens classes present in the dataset. However, our approach performs significantly better that BSIF for ND_2010 dataset which contain blurred images.

Lot of research has been carried out in countering the sensor level spoofing attacks on iris based recognition systems, most of it is towards exploring new hard-coded texture descriptors. A full proof technique addressing all the challenges like illumination variation, image blurring, sensor interoperability and adaptation to new textures is yet to be discovered.

References

1. Baush and Lomb Iconnect lenses. http://www.bausch.in/our-products/contact-lenses/lenses-for-short-sighted-long-sighted/iconnect/ (accessed: 2014–12-1)
2. Emirates Identity Authority. http://www.id.gov.ae/en/ (accessed: 2014–12-1)
3. Freshlook Contact Lenses. http://www.freshlookcontacts.com/ (accessed: 2014–12-1)
4. Johnson and Johnson Acuvue Contact Lenses. http://www.acuvue.co.in/ (accessed: 2014–12-1)
5. RIC. https://www.planalto.gov.br/ccivil_03/decreto/d89250.htm (accessed: 2014–12-1)
6. Unique Identification Authority of India. http://uidai.gov.in/about-uidai.html (accessed: 2014–12-1)
7. Vista Imaging FA2 Sensor. http://www.vistaimaging.com/FA2_product.html (accessed: 2014–12-1)
8. Baker, S.E., Hentz, A., Bowyer, K.W., Flynn, P.J.: Degradation of iris recognition performance due to non-cosmetic prescription contact lenses. Computer Vision and Image Understanding **114**(9), 1030–1044 (2010)
9. Banham, M.R., Katsaggelos, A.K.: Digital image restoration. IEEE Signal Processing Magazine **14**(2), 24–41 (1997)
10. Bendale, A., Nigam, A., Prakash, S., Gupta, P.: Iris segmentation using improved hough transform. In: Emerging Intelligent Computing Technology and Applications, pp. 408–415. Springer (2012)
11. Cristianini, N., Shawe-Taylor, J.: An introduction to support vector machines and other kernel-based learning methods. Cambridge University Press (2000)
12. Daugman, J.: How iris recognition works. In: Proceedings of International Conference on Image Processing (ICIP 2002), pp. 33–36 (2002)
13. Haralick, R.M., Shanmugam, K., Dinstein, I.H.: Textural features for image classification. IEEE Transactions on Systems, Man and Cybernetics **6**, 610–621 (1973)
14. He, Z., Sun, Z., Tan, T., Wei, Z.: Efficient iris spoof detection via boosted local binary patterns. In: Tistarelli, M., Nixon, M.S. (eds.) ICB 2009. LNCS, vol. 5558, pp. 1080–1090. Springer, Heidelberg (2009)
15. Hughes, K., Bowyer, K.W.: Detection of contact-lens-based iris biometric spoofs using stereo imaging. In: Proc. 46th Hawaii International Conference on System Sciences (HICSS), pp. 1763–1772. IEEE (2013)
16. Jain, A.K., Flynn, P., Ross, A.A.: Handbook of biometrics. Springer (2007)
17. Kannala, J., Rahtu, E.: BSIF: Binarized statistical image features. In: Proc. 21st International Conference on Pattern Recognition (ICPR), pp. 1363–1366. IEEE (2012)
18. Kohli, N., Yadav, D., Vatsa, M., Singh, R.: Revisiting iris recognition with color cosmetic contact lenses. In: Proc. International Conference on Biometrics (ICB), pp. 1–7. IEEE (2013)

19. Komulainen J., Hadid A, Pietikäinen M.: Generalized textured contact lens detection by extracting BSIF description from cartesian iris images. In: Proc. International Joint Conference on Biometrics (IJCB 2014), Clearwater, Fl (2014)

20. Lee, E.C., Park, K.R., Kim, J.: Fake iris detection by using purkinje image. In: Zhang, H., Jain, A.K. (eds.) ICB 2006. LNCS, vol. 3832, pp. 397–403. Springer, Heidelberg (2005)

21. Masek, L., et al.: Recognition of human iris patterns for biometric identification. M.Tech Thesis, The University of Western Australia (2003)

22. Nigam, A., Krishna G, V., Gupta, P.: Iris recognition using block local binary patterns and relational measures. In: Proceeding of International Joint Conference on Biometrics, pp. 1–7. IEEE (2014)

23. Ojala, T., Pietikäinen, M., Mäenpää, T.: Multiresolution gray-scale and rotation invariant texture classification with local binary patterns. IEEE Transactions on Pattern Analysis and Machine Intelligence 24(7), 971–987 (2002)

24. Ojansivu, V., Heikkilä, J.: Blur insensitive texture classification using local phase quantization. In: Elmoataz, A., Lezoray, O., Nouboud, F., Mammass, D. (eds.) ICISP 2008 2008. LNCS, vol. 5099, pp. 236–243. Springer, Heidelberg (2008)

25. Wei, Z., Qiu, X., Sun, Z., Tan, T.: Counterfeit iris detection based on texture analysis. In: Proc. 19th International Conference on Pattern Recognition, pp. 1–4. IEEE (2008)

26. Yadav, D., Kohli, N., Doyle, J., Singh, R., Vatsa, M., Bowyer, K.W.: Unraveling the effect of textured contact lenses on iris recognition. In: Proc. IEEE Transactions on Information Forensics and Security (2014)

27. Zhang, H., Sun, Z., Tan, T.: Contact lens detection based on weighted LBP. In: Proc. 20th International Conference on Pattern Recognition (ICPR), pp. 4279–4282. IEEE (2010)

28. Zhang, L., Zhou, Z., Li, H.: Binary gabor pattern: an efficient and robust descriptor for texture classification. In: Proc. 19th IEEE International Conference on Image Processing (ICIP), pp. 81–84. IEEE (2012)

Low-Dimensional Tensor Principle Component Analysis

Hayato Itoh[1]([✉]), Atsushi Imiya[2], and Tomoya Sakai[3]

[1] School of Advanced Integration Science, Chiba University, Chiba, Japan
hayato-itoh@graduate.chiba-u.jp
[2] Institute of Management and Information Technologies, Chiba University,
Chiba, Japan
[3] Graduate School of Engineering, Nagasaki University, Nagasaki, Japan

Abstract. We clarify the equivalence between second-order tensor principal component analysis and two-dimensional singular value decomposition. Furthermore, we show that the two-dimensional discrete cosine transform is a good approximation to two-dimensional singular value decomposition and classical principal component analysis. Moreover, for the practical computation in two-dimensional singular value decomposition, we introduce the marginal eigenvector method, which was proposed for image compression. To evaluate the performances of the marginal eigenvector method and two-dimensional discrete cosine transform for dimension reduction, we compute recognition rates for image patterns. The results show that the marginal eigenvector method and two-dimensional discrete cosine transform have almost the same recognition rates for images in six datasets.

1 Introduction

In this paper, we clarify the equivalence between the second-order tensor principal component analysis (TPCA) and the two-dimensional singular value decomposition (2DSVD). Furthermore, we show that the 2DSVD is theoretically equivalent to the classical principal component analysis using vector representation. We call the classical PCA for vectors the vector PCA. Moreover, for the practical computation of the 2DSVD, we introduce the marginal eigenvector (MEV) method that was proposed for an image compression in 1981 by Otsu.

Digitised spatiotemporal images in video analysis and volumetric data in medical image analysis are expressed as the third order tensors, since digitised spatiotemporal images and volumetric data are three dimensional arrays. For the compact representation of these spatiotemporal data and volumetric data, tensors are a useful mathematical tool. For fast image pattern recognition, compact representation of these image data is desired. The principal component analysis (PCA) method is a traditional method for data compression. The PCA method is extended to the higher dimensional array data [1,2], as the tensor PCA methods that construct a small size tensor using the orthogonal decomposition of tensor, while the classical PCA (the vector PCA) estimates a low dimensional linear subspace using principal component analysis.

© Springer International Publishing Switzerland 2015
G. Azzopardi and N. Petkov (Eds.): CAIP 2015, Part I, LNCS 9256, pp. 715–726, 2015.
DOI: 10.1007/978-3-319-23192-1_60

The second-order TPCA, which directly decomposes an image matrix, is the tensor PCA method [1,2] for two-dimensional images. A survey presented [2] shows that there are three basic projections for a tensor. The second-order TPCA uses the tensor-to-tensor projection consists of 1- and 2-mode projections that act to columns and rows of images, respectively.

The two-dimensional principal component analysis (2DPCA) [3] is proposed for image representation. However, the projection method in the 2DPCA is not a bilinear form since the 2DPCA uses only the 2-mode projection. The MEV method [4] that is based on both 1- and 2-mode projections is proposed for compression of an image compression. The 2DSVD [5,6] that is also based on both 1- and 2-mode projections is proposed for compression of an image compression as an extension of the singular value decomposition [7] The projections in the MEV and the 2DSVD are equivalent to the tensor-to-tensor projection for a second-order tensor. This mathematical property implies that the 2DSVD is a special case of TPCA. However, the compression rate of the 2DSVD is smaller than the 2DDCT [5] for a same reconstruction quality. The iterative algorithm for the second-order TPCA [8] is proposed. This iterative algorithm method is two-dimensional version of the iterative algorithm for the SVD [9,10].

The two-dimensional tensor subspace method (2DTSM) [11], that measures a similarity between an input image and tensor subspace of a class, is proposed as extension of the subspace method [12] for image pattern recognition. The 2DTSM adopts the MEV to construct each tensor subspace of a class.

In order to evaluate the performances of the MEV and the 2DDCT for dimension reduction, we compute recognition rates for image patterns. The results show that the marginal eigenvector method and the two-dimensional discrete cosine transform establish almost same performances to recognition rates for images in 6 datasets.

The 2DDCT-II is used for the coding in MPEG. In the MPEG, firstly, a digital image of $n \times n$ pixels is partitioned to $N \times N$ blocks. Usually, the size of block is 8×8 pixels. Then, each $N \times N$ block is transformed to frequency domain using the 2DDCT-II. Finally the each transformed value in each block is encoded.

2 Tensor Projection for Images

We briefly summarise the multilinear projection for two-dimensional arrays from ref. [2]. The Nth-order tensor is defined by

$$\mathcal{X} \in \mathbb{R}^{I_1 \times I_2 \times \cdots \times I_N}, \tag{1}$$

which is denoted by N indices i_n with each subscript n denoting the n-mode of $\mathcal{X}$. For the outer products of N vectors, if the tensor $\mathcal{X}$ satisfies the condition

$$\mathcal{X} = \boldsymbol{u}^{(1)} \circ \boldsymbol{u}^{(2)} \circ \cdots \circ \boldsymbol{u}^{(N)}, \tag{2}$$

where $\circ$ denotes the outer product, we call this tensor $\mathcal{X}$ a rank-one tensor. For $\mathcal{X}$, the n-mode vectors, $n = 1, 2, \ldots, N$, are defined as the I_n-dimensional vectors

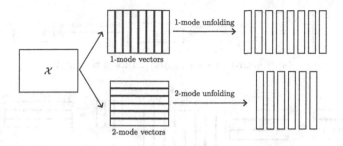

Fig. 1. 1- and 2-mode unfoldings of a second order tensor $\mathcal{X} \in \mathbb{R}^{6 \times 8}$.

obtained from $\mathcal{X}$ by varying this index i_n while fixing all the other indices. The unfolding of $\mathcal{X}$ along the n-mode vectors of $\mathcal{X}$ is defined as

$$\mathcal{X}_{(n)} \in \mathbb{R}^{I_n \times (I_1 \times I_2 \times \ldots I_{n-1} \times I_{n+1} \times \cdots \times I_N)}, \tag{3}$$

where the column vectors of $\mathcal{X}_{(n)}$ are the n-mode vectors of $\mathcal{X}$. Figure 1 shows an example of n-mode unfolding for a second-order tensor. The n-mode product of a tensor $\mathcal{X}$ and a matrix $U \in \mathbb{R}^{I_1 \times I_2 \times \ldots, \times I_{n-1} \times I_{n+1} \times I_n}$, denoted as $\mathcal{X} \times_n U$, is the tensor with entries

$$(\mathcal{X} \times_n U)(i_1, i_2, \ldots, j_n, i_{n+1}, \ldots, i_N) = \sum_{i_n} \mathcal{X}(i_1, \ldots, i_n, \ldots, i_N) \cdot U(j_n, i_n). \tag{4}$$

We define the inner product of two tensors $\mathcal{X}_1, \mathcal{X}_2 \in \mathbb{R}^{I_1 \times I_2 \times \cdots \times I_N}$ by

$$\langle \mathcal{X}_1, \mathcal{X}_2 \rangle = \sum_{i_1} \sum_{i_2} \cdots \sum_{i_N} \mathcal{X}_1(i_1, i_2, \ldots, i_N) \cdot \mathcal{X}_2(i_1, i_2, \ldots, i_N). \tag{5}$$

Using this inner product, we have the Frobenius norm of a tensor $\mathcal{X}$ as

$$\|\mathcal{X}\|_{\mathrm{F}} = \sqrt{\langle \mathcal{X}, \mathcal{X} \rangle}. \tag{6}$$

For the two tensors $\mathcal{X}_1$ and $\mathcal{X}_2$, we define the distance between them as

$$d(\mathcal{X}_1, \mathcal{X}_2) = \|\mathcal{X}_1 - \mathcal{X}_2\|_{\mathrm{F}}. \tag{7}$$

Although this definition is a tensor-based measure, this distance is equivalent to the Euclidean distance between the vectorised tensors $\mathcal{X}_1$ and $\mathcal{X}_2$.

For a tensor, a multilinear projection maps the input tensor data from one space to another space. We have three basic multilinear projections, that is, the vector-to-vector projection (VVP), tensor-to-vector projection (TVP) and tensor-to-tensor projection (TTP). The VVP is a linear projection from a vector to another vector. To use the VVP for tensors, we need to reshape tensors into vectors before the projection. The TVP, which is also referred to as the rank-one projection [13–15], consists of elementary multilinear projections (EMPs).

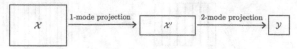

(a) Tensor-to-tensor projection for a tensor $\mathcal{X}$

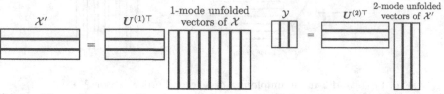

(b) 1-mode projection for $\mathcal{X}$ represented by a linear projection

(c) 2-mode projection for $\mathcal{X}$ represented by a linear projection

Fig. 2. Tensor-tensor projection of a tensor $\mathcal{X} \in \mathbb{R}^{6 \times 8}$ to a lower-dimensional tensor $\mathcal{Y} \in \mathbb{R}^3$.

The EMP projects a tensor to a scalar. Using d EMPs, the TVP obtains a d-dimensional vector projected from a tensor. The TTP projects a tensor to another tensor of the same order. In this paper, we focus on methods to find the optimal projection for the TTP.

As the tensor $\mathcal{X}$ is in the tensor space $\mathbb{R}^{I_1} \otimes \mathbb{R}^{I_2} \otimes \ldots \mathbb{R}^{I_N}$, the tensor space can be interpreted as the Kronecker product of N vector spaces $\mathbb{R}^{I_1}, \mathbb{R}^{I_2}, \ldots, \mathbb{R}^{I_N}$. To project $\mathcal{X} \in \mathbb{R}^{I_1} \otimes \mathbb{R}^{I_2} \otimes \ldots \mathbb{R}^{I_N}$ to another tensor $\mathcal{Y}$ in a lower-dimensional tensor space $\mathbb{R}^{P_1} \otimes \mathbb{R}^{P_2} \otimes \ldots \mathbb{R}^{P_N}$, where $P_n \leq I_n$ for $n = 1, 2, \ldots, N$, we need N projection matrices $\{U^{(n)} \in \mathbb{R}^{I_n \times P_n}\}_{n=1}^N$. Using the N projection matrices, we have the TTP given by

$$\mathcal{Y} = \mathcal{X} \times_1 U^{(1)\top} \times_2 U^{(2)\top} \cdots \times_N U^{(N)\top}. \tag{8}$$

This projection is established in N steps, where in the nth step, each n-mode vector is projected to a P_n-dimensional space by U^n.

A second-order tensor $\mathcal{X} \in \mathbb{R}^{I_1 \times I_2}$, which is the matrix $X \in \mathbb{R}^{I_1 \times I_2}$, is denoted as a pair of indices (i_1, i_2). For the Kronecker product of two vectors $u^{(1)}$ and $u^{(2)}$, if the tensor $\mathcal{X}$ satisfies the condition

$$\mathcal{X} = u^{(1)} \otimes u^{(2)}, \tag{9}$$

we call this tensor $\mathcal{X}$ a rank-one tensor. For a tensor $\mathcal{X}$, the unfolding of $\mathcal{X}$ is defined by

$$\mathcal{X}_{(1)} = X \in \mathbb{R}^{I_1 \times I_2}, \quad \mathcal{X}_{(2)} = X^\top \in \mathbb{R}^{I_2 \times I_1}. \tag{10}$$

The 1- and 2-mode products of a tensor by a matrix $U^\top$ are given by

$$\mathcal{X} \times_1 U^\top = U^\top X, \quad \mathcal{X} \times_2 U^\top = U^\top X^\top, \tag{11}$$

respectively. For a tensor $\mathcal{X}$ in the tensor space $\mathbb{R}^{I_1} \otimes \mathbb{R}^{I_2}$, using 2-projection matrices, we have the TTP

$$\mathcal{Y} = \mathcal{X} \times_1 U^{(1)} \times_2 U^{(2)}, \tag{12}$$

which projects $\mathcal{X}$ to a lower-dimensional tensor space. Figure 2(a) shows the two steps for the projection of a second order tensor to a lower-dimensional tensor. Figures 2(b) and (c) show the procedures used to project a tensor in the first and second steps, respectively. Replacing the tensor $\mathcal{X}$ with a matrix $\boldsymbol{X} \in \mathbb{R}^{m \times n}$, we have the TTP

$$Y = U^{(1)\top} X U^{(2)} \tag{13}$$

for the second-order tensor as a matrix representation. From the reduced matrix $\boldsymbol{Y}$, we have the reconstruction given by

$$X = U^{(1)} Y U^{(2)\top}. \tag{14}$$

3 Two-Dimensional Singular Value Decomposition

For a collection of matrices $\{\boldsymbol{X}_i\}_{i=1}^{N} \in \mathbb{R}^{m \times n}$ satisfying zero expectation condition $\mathrm{E}(\boldsymbol{X}_i) = 0$, the orthogonal-projection-based data reduction

$$\hat{X}_i = U^\top X_i V, \tag{15}$$

where $U = [u_1, \ldots, u_m]$ and $V = [v_1, \ldots, v_n]$, is performed by minimising the criterion

$$J_- = \mathrm{E}\left(\|\boldsymbol{X}_i - \boldsymbol{U}\hat{\boldsymbol{X}}_i \boldsymbol{V}^\top\|_{\mathrm{F}}^2 \right) \tag{16}$$

and maximising the criteria

$$J_+ = \mathrm{E}\left(\|\boldsymbol{U}^\top \boldsymbol{X}_i \boldsymbol{V}\|_{\mathrm{F}}^2 \right) \tag{17}$$

$$J_V = \mathrm{E}\left(\|\boldsymbol{U}^\top \boldsymbol{X}_i^\top \boldsymbol{X}_i \boldsymbol{V}\|_{\mathrm{F}}^2 \right) \tag{18}$$

$$J_U = \mathrm{E}\left(\|\boldsymbol{U}^\top \boldsymbol{X}_i \boldsymbol{X}_i^\top \boldsymbol{U}\|_{\mathrm{F}}^2 \right) \tag{19}$$

with respect to the conditions

$$U^\top U = I_m \text{ and } V^\top V = I_n, \tag{20}$$

where $\boldsymbol{I}_m$ and $\boldsymbol{I}_n$ are the identity matrices in $\mathbb{R}^{m \times m}$ and $\mathbb{R}^{n \times n}$, respectively.

The eigendecomposition problems are derived by computing the extremals of

$$E_- = J_- + tr(\boldsymbol{I} - \boldsymbol{V}^\top \boldsymbol{V})\boldsymbol{\Lambda}) + tr(\boldsymbol{I} - \boldsymbol{U}^\top \boldsymbol{U})\boldsymbol{\Sigma}), \tag{21}$$

$$E_+ = J_+ + tr(\boldsymbol{I} - \boldsymbol{V}^\top \boldsymbol{V})\boldsymbol{\Lambda}) + tr(\boldsymbol{I} - \boldsymbol{U}^\top \boldsymbol{U})\boldsymbol{\Sigma}), \tag{22}$$

$$E_V = J_V + tr(\boldsymbol{I} - \boldsymbol{V}^\top \boldsymbol{V})\boldsymbol{\Lambda}), \tag{23}$$

$$E_U = J_U + tr(\boldsymbol{I} - \boldsymbol{U}^\top \boldsymbol{U})\boldsymbol{\Sigma}). \tag{24}$$

The optimisation of J_- and J_+ derive the SVD

$$MV = V\Lambda \text{ and } NU = U\Sigma, \tag{25}$$

where $\Sigma \in \mathbb{R}^{m \times m}$ and $\Lambda \in \mathbb{R}^{n \times n}$ are diagonal matrices satisfying the relationships $\lambda_i = \sigma_i$ for

$$\Sigma = \text{diag}(\sigma_1, \sigma_2 \cdots, \sigma_K, 0 \cdots, 0) \text{ and } \Lambda = \text{diag}(\lambda_1, \lambda_2 \cdots, \lambda_K, 0 \cdots, 0). \tag{26}$$

The optimisation of J_V and J_U derive the eigendecomposition problems in eq. 25.[1]. For $p_{1j} \in \{e_j\}_{j=1}^K$ and $p_{2j} \in \{e_k\}_{k=1}^K$, $e_i^\top e_j = \delta_{ij}$, we set orthogonal projection matrices $P_1 = \sum_{j=1}^{k_1} p_{1j} p_{1j}^\top$ and $P_2 = \sum_{j=1}^{k_2} p_{2j} p_{2j}^\top$. Using these P_1 and P_2, the low-rank matrix approximation [16,17] is achieved by

$$Y_i = (P_1 U)^\top X_i (P_2 V) = L^\top X_i R, \tag{27}$$

where P_1 and P_2 are k_1 and k_2 selected bases of projection matrices U and V, respectively. The low-rank approximation using eq. (27) is called the 2DSVD method in the context of image compression [5,6]. Moreover, the method based on the transform

$$Y_i = X_i R \tag{28}$$

is called 2DPCA [3].

For 2DSVD, we have the following theorem.

Theorem 1. *The 2DSVD method is equivalent to the vector PCA method.*

(*Proof*) The equation

$$(P_1 U)^\top X (P_2 V) = Y \tag{29}$$

is equivalent to

$$(P_2 V \otimes P_1 U)\text{vec} X = \text{vec} Y. \tag{30}$$

(Q.E.D.)

Furthermore, 2DDCT is a good approximation of 2DSVD since 2DDCT is a good approximation of PCA for reduction of images [11]. Moreover, the projection that selects $K = k_1 k_2$ bases of the tensor space spanned by $u_i \otimes v_j$, $i = 1, 2, \ldots, m$ and $j = 1, 2, \ldots, n$, is

$$(P_2 V \otimes P_1 U) = (P_2 \otimes P_1)(V \otimes U) = PW, \tag{31}$$

where W and P are a unitary matrix and the projection matrix, respectively. Therefore, 2DSVD is equivalent to TPCA for matrices because matrices are second-order tensors. In our application, a $n \times n$ digital array is directly compressed by the 2DDCT-II with order $\mathcal{O}(n^2)$. If we apply the fast Fourier transform to the computaiton of the 2DDCT-II, the computational complexity is $\mathcal{O}(n \log n)$.

---

[1] For an iterative method [9,10] for SVD see the Appendix.

4 Two-Dimensional Tensor Subspace Method

As an extension of the subspace method for vector data, we introduced a new linear tensor subspace method for a matrix called the 2DTSM [11]. For a matrix $\boldsymbol{X}$, setting P_{L} and P_{R} to be orthogonal projections, we call the operation

$$\boldsymbol{Y} = P_{\mathrm{L}}^{\top} \boldsymbol{X} P_{\mathrm{R}} \tag{32}$$

the orthogonal projection of $\boldsymbol{X}$ to $\boldsymbol{Y}$. Therefore, using this expression for a collection of matrices $\{\boldsymbol{X}_i\}_{i=1}^{N}$, such that $\boldsymbol{X}_i \in \mathbb{R}^{m \times n}$ and $\mathrm{E}(\boldsymbol{X}_i) = 0$, the solutions of

$$(P_{\mathrm{L}}, P_R) = \arg \max \mathrm{E} \left(\frac{\|P_{\mathrm{L}}^{\top} \boldsymbol{X}_i P_{\mathrm{R}}\|_{\mathrm{F}}}{\|\boldsymbol{X}_i\|_{\mathrm{F}}} \right) \; w.r.t. \; P_{\mathrm{L}}^{\top} P_{\mathrm{L}} = \boldsymbol{I}, \; P_{\mathrm{R}}^{\top} P_{\mathrm{R}} = \boldsymbol{I} \tag{33}$$

define a bilinear subspace that approximates $\{\boldsymbol{X}_i\}_{i=1}^{N}$. Here, the norm $\|\boldsymbol{X}\|_{\mathrm{F}}$ for matrix $\boldsymbol{X}$ represents the Frobenius norm. Therefore, using the solutions of eq. (33), if a query matrix $\boldsymbol{G}$ satisfies the condition

$$\arg \left(\max_i \frac{\|P_{\mathrm{L},i}^{\top} \boldsymbol{G} P_{\mathrm{R},i}\|_{\mathrm{F}}}{\|\boldsymbol{G}\|_{\mathrm{F}}} \right) = \{P_{\mathrm{L},k}, P_{\mathrm{R},k}\}, \tag{34}$$

we conclude that $\boldsymbol{G} \in \mathcal{C}_k(\delta)$ when $\mathcal{C}_k(\delta) = \{\boldsymbol{X} \mid \|P_{\mathrm{L},k}^{\top} \boldsymbol{X} P_{\mathrm{R},k} - \boldsymbol{X}\|_{\mathrm{F}} \ll \delta\}$, $k = 1, 2, \ldots, N_{\mathcal{C}}$.

In practical computation to find the projections P_{L} and P_{R} in eq. (33), we adopt the MEV [4]. This is a projection considering the distributions of column and row vectors of sampled images. We define two matrices

$$M_{\mathrm{r}} = \frac{1}{N} \sum_{i=1}^{N} \boldsymbol{X}_i \boldsymbol{X}_i^{\top} \in \mathbb{R}^{m \times m} \quad \text{and} \quad M_{\mathrm{c}} = \frac{1}{N} \sum_{i=1}^{N} \boldsymbol{X}_i^{\top} \boldsymbol{X}_i \in \mathbb{R}^{n \times n}. \tag{35}$$

Using these two matrices, we have

$$\mathrm{E} \left(\|P_{\mathrm{L}}^{\top} \boldsymbol{X}_i P_{\mathrm{R}}\|_{\mathrm{F}}^2 \right) = \frac{1}{N} \sum_{i=1}^{N} \left(P_{\mathrm{L}}^{\top} \boldsymbol{X}_i P_{\mathrm{R}} \right) \left(P_{\mathrm{L}}^{\top} \boldsymbol{X}_i P_{\mathrm{R}} \right)^{\top} = P_{\mathrm{L}}^{\top} M_{\mathrm{r}} P_{\mathrm{L}},$$

and

$$\mathrm{E} \left(\|P_{\mathrm{L}}^{\top} \boldsymbol{X}_i P_{\mathrm{R}}\|_{\mathrm{F}}^2 \right) = \frac{1}{N} \sum_{i=1}^{N} \left(P_{\mathrm{L}}^{\top} \boldsymbol{X}_i P_{\mathrm{R}} \right)^{\top} \left(P_{\mathrm{L}}^{\top} \boldsymbol{X}_i P_{\mathrm{R}} \right) = P_{\mathrm{R}}^{\top} M_{\mathrm{c}} P_{\mathrm{R}}.$$

Furthermore, for the two matrices M_{r} and M_{c}, using the Lagrange multipliers Λ_{r} and Λ_{c}, we find projections satisfying

$$J(P_{\mathrm{L}}) = tr \left(P_{\mathrm{L}}^{\top} M_{\mathrm{r}} P_{\mathrm{L}} \right) - tr \left(\left(P_{\mathrm{L}}^{\top} P_{\mathrm{L}} - \boldsymbol{I} \right) \Lambda_{\mathrm{r}} \right), \tag{36}$$

$$J(P_Y) = tr \left(P_{\mathrm{R}}^{\top} M_{\mathrm{c}} P_{\mathrm{R}} \right) - tr \left(\left(P_{\mathrm{R}}^{\top} P_{\mathrm{R}} - \boldsymbol{I} \right) \Lambda_{\mathrm{c}} \right), \tag{37}$$

where I is the identity matrix. The solutions of eqs. (36) and (37) are given as the solutions of the eigenproblems of M_r and M_c, respectively. We set $\{u_j\}_{j=1}^{k_1}$ and $\{v_j\}_{j=1}^{k_2}$ as the eigenvectors of M_r and M_c, respectively. We define the eigenvectors of M_r and M_c as $\|u_j\|_2 = 1$ and $\|v_j\|_2 = 1$ for eigenvalues $\lambda_1^r \geq \lambda_2^r \geq \cdots \geq \lambda_j^r \geq \cdots \geq \lambda_n^r$ and $\lambda_1^c \geq \lambda_2^c \geq \cdots \geq \lambda_j^c \geq \cdots \geq \lambda_n^c$, respectively. Therefore, for given numbers $k_1 \leq m$ and $k_2 \leq n$, the operators P_L and P_R are defined as $P_{L,k_1} = [u_1, u_2, \ldots, u_m]$ and $P_{R,k_2} = [v_1, v_2, \ldots, v_n]$ as the matrices consist of each set of eigenfunctions, respectively. These obtained projections are equivalent to the projections obtained by 2DSVD [5] using eq. (28). Practically, the computational complexity of solving the eigendecomposition problem for $n \times n$-matrix is $\mathcal{O}(n^3)$.

5   Numerical Examples

To validate the relation between the MEV method (2DSVD and 2DTSM) and the 2DDCT, we compute the recognition rate using six image datasets: cropped versions of the extended YaleB dataset [18], ORL face dataset [19], ETH80 dataset [20], NEC animal dataset [21], MNIST dataset [22] and ETL9G character dataset [23]. Figure 3 shows examples of images belonging to the same class in each dataset. For the validation, we compress images in these datasets by the MEV method and 2DDCT. Table 1 shows details of each dataset and parameters used in the compression.

Using the compressed images belonging to the same class in each dataset, we compute the cumulative contribution ratio (CCR) for the eigenvalues of the covariance matrices of the 1- and 2-modes for the images.

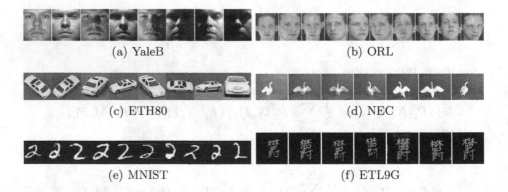

(a) YaleB   (b) ORL

(c) ETH80   (d) NEC

(e) MNIST   (f) ETL9G

Fig. 3. Examples of images belonging to the same class in each dataset. (a) Face images of the same person with different conditions of illumination. (b) Face images of the same person with different camera positions. (c) Images of the same object with different camera positions, where the number of degrees of freedom is two. (d) Images of the same object with different camera positions, where the number of degrees of freedom is one. (e) Images of the same handwritten digit. (f) Images of the same handwritten Chinese character written by different people.

Table 1. Details of each dataset. ♯class and ♯data/class represent the number of classes and the number of data in each class, respectively. The image size is the original size of the images in each dataset. The reduced image size is the size of the images after image-representation-based dimension reduction.

	#class	#data /class	image size [pixel]	reduced image size [pixel]
YaleB	38	64	192×168	32×32
ORL	40	10	112×92	32×32
ETH80	30	41	128×128	32×32
NEC	60	72	480×580	32×32
MNIST	10	7,000	28×28	15×15
ETL9G	152	200	127×128	32×32

Figure 4 shows the CCRs for the six datasets. In Figs. 4(a)-(f), we define the compression ratio as d/k for the case of using k eigenvectors, corre-

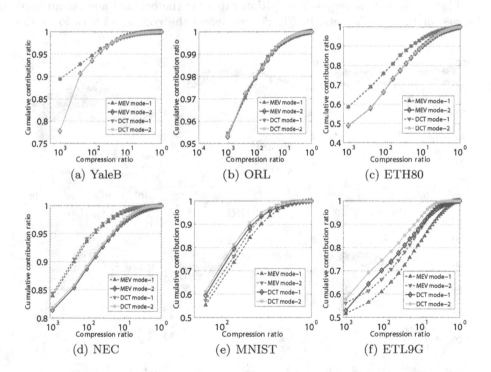

Fig. 4. Cumulative contribution ratios for he six datasets. The vertical and horizontal axes represent the cumulative contribution ratio and the compression ratio, respectively. Upward triangles and diamonds represent the cumulative contribution ratios of the eigenvalues of the covariance matrices for the 1- and 2-modes, respectively, of the images compressed by the MEV method. Downward triangles and squares represent the cumulative contribution ratios of the eigenvalues of the covariance matrices for the 1- and 2-modes, respectively, of the images compressed by the 2DDCT.

sponding to k major eigenvalues, in d-dimensional space to construct the linear subspace. As shown in Figs. 4(a)-(d), the CCR curves for the MEV method and 2DDCT are coincident. In Figs. 4(b), the CCR curves for the 1- and 2-modes are coincident for the MEV method and 2DDCT. This means that the eigenvalues of the 1- and 2-modes are coincident. In Figs. 4(a),(d),(e) and (f), the CCR curves are approximately the same except for a few of the largest eigenvalues.

For the validation, we compute the recognition rate using the original and dimension-reduced images of the six datasets with the 2DTSM as the classifier. The MNIST dataset is predivided into training and test data before it is distributed. For the YaleB, ORL, ETH80 and NEC datasets, images labeled with even numbers are used as training data and the other images are used as test data. The recognition ratio is defined as the successful label-estimation ratio for 1000 label estimations. In each estimation of a label for a query, queries are randomly chosen from the test data. For both the 1- and 2-modes, we evaluated the results for linear subspaces with from one to 32 dimensions.

Figures 5(a)-(f) show the recognition rates for the original and compressed images in the six datasets. In Fig. 5, we define the compression ratio as the

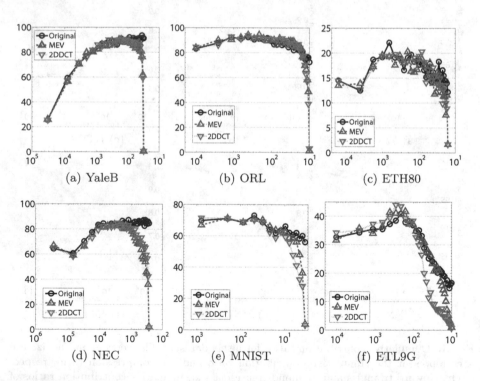

Fig. 5. Recognition rates for original and compressed images. The vertical and horizontal axes represent the recognition rate and compression ratio, respectively. Circles, upward triangles and downward triangles show the recognition rates for the original dimension, the MEV method and the 2DDCT, respectively.

original dimension divided by k^2, where k is the number of selected principal axes for both the 1- and 2-modes. According to those results, the MEV method and 2DDCT give almost the same recognition rate.

6 Conclusions

We first clarified equivalence between second-order tensor principal component analysis and two-dimensional singular value decomposition. Second, we introduced the marginal eigenvalue method as a practical computation method for two-dimensional singular value decomposition. Finally, to compare the effects of the marginal eigenvalue method and the two-dimensional discrete cosine transform on image pattern recognition, we presented two numerical examples. In the first example, using images compressed by the marginal eigenvalue method and two-dimensional discrete cosine transform, we computed the cumulative contribution ratio of the eigenvalues for a tensor subspace. In the second example, we computed the accuracy of image pattern recognition for images compressed by the marginal eigenvalue method and two-dimensional discrete cosine transform All the results in these two numerical examples demonstrated the equivalent performance of the two methods for image pattern recognition.

Appendix

The pair of dynamic equations

$$\frac{d}{dt}V = [V[MV]] \tag{38}$$

$$\frac{d}{dt}U = [U[NU]] \tag{39}$$

is used to compute a pair of sequences that satisfy the conditions

$$\lim_{t \to \infty} V_t = V, \ \lim_{t \to \infty} U_t = U, \tag{40}$$

to obtain the solutions in eq. (25). These dynamic equations derive an iterative method for the achievement of 2D-SVD. See also refs. [9] and [10].

References

1. Lu, H., Plataniotis, K., Venetsanopoulos, A.: Multilinear principal component analysis of tensor objects for recognition. In: Proc. International Conference on Pattern Recognition, vol. 2, pp. 776–779 (2006)
2. Lu, H., Plataniotis, K.N., Venetsanopoulos, A.N.: A survey of multilinear subspace learning for tensor data. Pattern Recognition 44, 1540–1551 (2011)
3. Yang, J., Zhang, D., Frangi, A.F., Yang, J.Y.: Two-dimensional PCA: a new approach to appearance-based face representation and recognition. IEEE Trans. Pattern Analysis and Machine Intelligence 26, 131–137 (2004)

4. Otsu, N.: Mathematical Studies on Feature Extraction in Pattern Recognition. PhD thesis, Electrotechnical Laboratory (1981)
5. Aase, S., Husoy, J., Waldemar, P.: A critique of SVD-based image coding systems. In: Proc. IEEE International Symposium on Circuits and Systems, vol. 4, pp. 13–16 (1999)
6. Ding, C., Ye, J.: Two-dimensional singular value decomposition (2DSVD) for 2D maps and images. In: Proc. SIAM International Conference on Data Mining, pp. 32–43 (2005)
7. Golub, G.H., Van Loan, C.F.: Matrix Computations. The Johns Hopkins University Press (1996)
8. Ye, J., Janardan, R., Qi, L.: GPCA: an efficient dimension reduction scheme for image compression and retrieval. In: Proc. ACM SIGKDD International Conference on Knowledge Discovery and Data Mining, pp. 354–363 (2004)
9. Helmke, U., Moore, J.: Singular-value decomposition via gradient and self-equivalent flows. Linear Algebra and Its Applications **169**, 223–248 (1992)
10. Moore, J.B., Mahony, R.E., Helmke, U.: Numerical gradient algorithms for eigenvalue and singular value calculations. SIAM Journal on Matrix Analysis and Applications **15**, 881–902 (1994)
11. Itoh, H., Sakai, T., Kawamoto, K., Imiya, A.: Topology-preserving dimension-reduction methods for image pattern recognition. In: Kämäräinen, J.-K., Koskela, M. (eds.) SCIA 2013. LNCS, vol. 7944, pp. 195–204. Springer, Heidelberg (2013)
12. Oja, E.: Subspace Methods of Pattern Recognition. Research Studies Press (1983)
13. Wang, Y., Gong, S.: Tensor discriminant analysis for view-based object recognition. In: Proc. International Conference on Pattern Recognition, vol. 3, pp. 33–36 (2006)
14. Tao, D., Li, X., Wu, X., Maybank, S.: Elapsed time in human gait recognition: a new approach. In: Proc. International Conference on Acoustics, Speech and Signal Processing, vol. 2 (2006)
15. Hua, G., Viola, P.A., Drucker, S.M.: Face recognition using discriminatively trained orthogonal rank one tensor projections. In: Proc. IEEE Conference on Computer Vision and Pattern Recognition (2007)
16. Ye, J.: Generalized low rank approximations of matrices. In: Proc. International Conference on Machine Learning (2004)
17. Liang, Z., Shi, P.: An analytical algorithm for generalized low-rank approximations of matrices. Pattern Recognition **38**, 2213–2216 (2005)
18. Georghiades, A.S., Belhumeur, P.N., Kriegman, D.J.: From few to many: Illumination cone models for face recognition under variable lighting and pose. IEEE Trans. Pattern Analysis and Machine Intelligence **23**, 643–660 (2001)
19. Samaria, F., Harter, A.: Parameterisation of a stochastic model for human face identification. In: Proc. IEEE Workshop on Applications of Computer Vision (1994)
20. Leibe, B., Schiele, B.: Analyzing appearance and contour based methods for object categorization. In: Proc. Computer Vision and Pattern Recognition, vol. 2, pp. 409–415 (2003)
21. Mobahi, H., Collobert, R., Weston, J.: Deep learning from temporal coherence in video. In: Proc. International Conference on Machine Learning (2009)
22. LeCun, Y., Bottou, L., Bengio, Y., Haffner, P.: Gradient-based learning applied to document recognition. Proc. IEEE **86**, 2278–2324 (1998)
23. Saito, T., Yamada, H., Yamada, K.: On the data base ETL9 of handprinted characters in JIS Chinese characters and its analysis. IEEJ Journal of Industry Applications, 757–764 (1985)

Empirical Study of Audio-Visual Features Fusion for Gait Recognition

Francisco M. Castro[1], Manuel J. Marín-Jiménez[2]($\boxtimes$), and Nicolás Guil[1]

[1] Department of Computer Architecture, University of Malaga, Málaga, Spain
{fcastro,nguil}@uma.es
[2] Department of Computing and Numerical Analysis,
University of Cordoba, Córdoba, Spain
mjmarin@uco.es

Abstract. The goal of this paper is to evaluate how the fusion of audio and visual features can help in the challenging task of people identification based on their gait (i.e. the way they walk), or *gait recognition*. Most of previous research on gait recognition has focused on designing visual descriptors, mainly on binary silhouettes, or building sophisticated machine learning frameworks. However, little attention has been paid to audio patterns associated to the action of walking. So, we propose and evaluate here a multimodal system for gait recognition. The proposed approach is evaluated on the challenging 'TUM GAID' dataset, which contains audio recordings in addition to image sequences. The experimental results show that using late fusion to combine two kinds of tracklet-based visual features with audio features improves the state-of-the-art results on the standard experiments defined on the dataset.

Keywords: Gait · Biometrics · Audio · Video · Fusion · Dense trajectories

1 Introduction

Given a video sequence depicting people walking, the goal of this work is to identify them (i.e. assign an identity) based on the way they walk. This problem is known as *gait recognition*. Typically, gait recognition has been based on features extracted from visual information, as sequences of silhouettes [10] or dense trajectories of points [3]. However, the use of audio information has not been extensively studied. This is in part due to the lack of audio tracks associated to video sequences, as happens in the most popular databases for gait recognition (e.g. CASIA gait dataset [27]). Recently, Hofmann et al. [11] released 'TUM Gait from Audio, Image and Depth (GAID) database', or 'TUM GAID'. This is a dataset of gait sequences that contains not only image sequences, but also audio recordings and depth information provided by a Microsoft Kinect sensor. The results they present on the RGB channel are based on binary silhouettes (i.e. Gait Energy Image [10]) combined with a 1-Nearest Neighbor classifier on PCA+LDA-compressed data. They also extract

© Springer International Publishing Switzerland 2015
G. Azzopardi and N. Petkov (Eds.): CAIP 2015, Part I, LNCS 9256, pp. 727–739, 2015.
DOI: 10.1007/978-3-319-23192-1_61

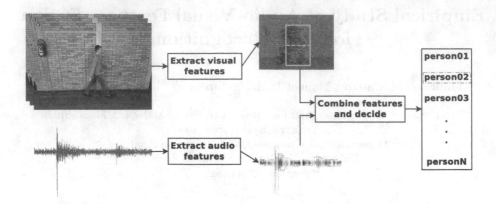

Fig. 1. Proposed pipeline for human gait recognition. Given a video sequence of people walking, audio and visual information are combined in order to assign an identity from a set of predefined ones.

diverse audio features in the time and frequency domain, training a linear SVM on top of them. Finally, they use a simple fusion method on the score domain (i.e. after classification from each modality) to take a decision – giving the sum rule the best results during fusion.

Nevertheless, most of the best results presented in [11] are based on depth information, leaving the image and audio information in a second place. In contrast, we propose in this paper a multimodal approach for gait recognition where non silhouette-based visual features take more relevance, as well as the fusion information method. Showing that by combining two sets of tracklet-based features [3] with audio features, the achieved gait recognition results outperform the ones reported in [11] by using RGB+depth+audio. In particular, the contributions of this paper are: (i) unified approach for using audio and visual information for the problem of gait recognition; (ii) thorough evaluation of the proposed approach on the challenging TUM GAID dataset; and, (iii) new state-of-the-art results on TUM GAID dataset. In addition, we will show that the late fusion method of Ye et al. in [26] – originally designed for content-based image and video retrieval using multimodal features – is able to boost the recognition results even on a single modality when it is properly applied on a 'one-vs-all' ensemble of binary classifiers.

The rest of the paper is organized as follows. After presenting the related works, Sec. 2 describes the audio-visual features proposed to describe gait. In Sec. 3, different fusion information strategies are discussed. The experiments and results are presented in Sec. 4. And, Sec. 5 contains the conclusions.

1.1 Related Works

Many research papers have been published in recent years tackling the problem of human gait recognition. For example, in [12] we can find a survey on this problem summarizing some of the most popular approaches based on video information. Some of them use explicit geometrical models of human bodies, whereas others use only image features. The most popular approach is a silhouette-based descriptor, called Gait Energy Image (GEI) [10], where the main idea is to compute a temporal averaging of the binary silhouettes of the target subject. Based on this approach, many improvements have been published like the approach of Liu et al. [17] whose key idea is to compute Histogram of Oriented Gradients (HOG) descriptors from GEI and Chrono-Gait Image (CGI). Martin-Felez and Xiang [19] propose a new ranking model for gait recognition based on GEI. This new formulation allows to leverage training data from different datasets improving the recognition performance.

Gait recognition based on audio information is a less studied problem due to its high complexity and lack of databases. The main gait dataset with audio information is the TUM-GAID dataset [11]. The authors of this dataset present a baseline method based on building a high level descriptor that is composed of a set of low level descriptors like loudness or Mel-Frequency Cepstral Coefficients (MFCC). Finally, this high level descriptor is used as input for a SVM. Geiger et al. [8] propose an improvement of the previous method by selecting the features that produce best results and removing the rest. Thus, the noise is reduced and the results are improved. Later, the same authors propose a new method based on Hidden Markov Models (HMM) [7] that outperforms the previous methods in terms of precision.

Finally, if multiple information sources are available, the natural idea is to try to combine or fuse the information from them to build a richer representation. The main strategies of fusion are early fusion and late fusion. Early fusion or feature level fusion, has been widely used and a large number of approaches have appeared in recent years [1]. The most simple early fusion strategy consists of concatenating descriptors of different sources to build a new and larger descriptor. A more complex strategy is the called Multiple Kernel Learning (MKL) [2] which learns a linear or non linear kernel combination and the associated classifier simultaneously. On the other hand, late fusion aims to combine confidence scores of features of different models. In this case, the easiest strategy is to build the new confidence scores based on weighted scores of different models according to their global accuracy. A more powerful approach is presented in [26] where the method tries to build new confidence scores by removing the possible classification error following a minimization process.

2   Audio-Visual Features

In this section we will present how we describe gait sequences both from audio and visual information, obtaining a representation from each modality that can be directly fed into a classifier.

We adopt the following pipeline to describe a gait sequence: (i) extract low-level features from each modality (i.e. audio and image); (ii) generate a mid-level representation from each modality; (iii) fuse information from the different modalities; and (iv) assign an identity. This pipeline is visually represented in Fig. 1.

2.1 Audio Descriptors

When an audio track is available for the target video sequence, we can compute a set of low-level descriptors from it, each representing different properties of the sound. The following descriptors are computed from audio frames (i.e. continuos portion of the audio track) of t seconds (e.g. $t = 0.05$) as in [18]: (i) basic statistics: zero-cross, coefficient of skewness, excess kurtosis, flatness and entropy; (ii) Mel spectrum; and, (iii) Mel-Frequency Cepstral Coefficients (MFCC).

We use 'MIR Toolbox v1.5' [15] for their computation. Then, all those low-level descriptors are concatenated into a single aural descriptor for a given audio frame. The dimensionality of the derived audio descriptor is 58 dimensions (i.e. 5 for basic statistics, 40 for Mel spectrum, 13 for MFCC).

2.2 Visual Descriptors

From all the possible visual descriptors existing in the literature for video sequences, we will choose descriptors that represent motion. Therefore, the first step to extract motion-based descriptors is to compute densely sampled trajectories (or tracklets). Those tracklets are computed by following the approach of Wang et al. [24].

The first step is to compute dense optical flow [6] $F = (u_t, v_t)$ on a dense grid (i.e. step size of 5 pixels and over 8 scales). Then, each point $p_t = (x_t, y_t)$ at frame t is tracked to the next frame by median filtering as: $p_{t+1} = (x_t, y_t) + (M * F)|_{(\bar{x}_t, \bar{y}_t)}$, where M is the kernel of median filtering and $(\bar{x}_t, \bar{y}_t)$ is the rounded position of p_t. To minimize drifting effect, the tracking is limited to L frames. We use $L = 15$ as in [13]. As a postprocessing step, uninformative and noisy trajectories (e.g. excessively short or showing sudden large displacements) are removed.

As in [3], we are only interested in those tracklets that are generated by people. Therefore, we detect people in image sequences by background subtraction [14], fit a bounding-box to each detection and remove those tracklets that do not share spatio-temporal coordinates with the person bounding-boxes. The tracklets of interest will be described as explained below.

DCS Features. Once the local trajectories are computed, one choice is to describe them with the Divergence-Curl-Shear (DCS) descriptor proposed by Jain et al. [13]. As described in [13], the divergence is related to axial motion, expansion and scaling effects, whereas the curl is related to rotation in the image plane. DCS has been already employed by Castro et al. in [3] in the problem of gait recognition with excellent results. Note that a DCS descriptor is typically composed of four parts: 2D normalized coordinates, a histogram combining Divergence and Curl, a histogram combining Curl and Shear, and a histogram combining Divergence and Shear. Using the default parameters of the software released by [13], this descriptor has 318 dimensions (2D coordinates: 30; Div+Curl: 96; Curl+Shear: 96; Div+Shear: 96).

H2M Features. An alternative descriptor commonly used in conjunction with tracklets is the concatenation of Histograms of Oriented Gradients (HOG) [4], Histograms of Optical Flow (HOF) and Motion Boundary Histograms (MBH) [5], named H2M for compactness.

We use the software of [24] to compute H2M, so the default sizes for HOG, HOF and MBH are 96, 108 and 192, respectively. These, in combination with the 30 dimensions derived from the normalized 2D coordinates of the tracklets, makes a total of 426 dimensions.

2.3 Video-Level Gait Representation

In order to build a video-level gait descriptor, we need to summarize the low-level features extracted from each modality. We use here Fisher Vectors (FV) encoding [21], as previously done for gait recognition in [3].

FV encoding, that can be seen as an extension of the Bag of Words (BOW) representation [22], builds on top of a Gaussian Mixture Model (GMM), where each Gaussian corresponds to a visual word. Whereas in BOW, an image is represented by the number of occurrences of each visual word, in FV an image is described by a gradient vector computed from a generative probabilistic model.

The dimensionality of FV is $2ND$, where N is the number of Gaussians in the GMM, and D is the dimensionality of the low-level audio or visual descriptors. In our case, a typical value for the number of Gaussians is $N = 600$. The value of D is given by the dimensionality of the low-level descriptors (e.g., $D = 318$ for DCS, $D = 426$ for H2M) or the number of dimensions obtained after applying PCA (e.g., $D = 150$).

As stated in [21], the capability of description of the FV can be improved by applying it a signed square-root followed by L2 normalization. So, we adopt this finding for our descriptors.

3   Information Fusion

When several sources of information are available, a method to fuse those sources is needed. On the one hand, we can combine those sources of information before learning a classification model. This approach is usually known as *early fusion*. A typical example of early fusion is the concatenation of descriptor vectors. On the other hand, we can train independent classifiers from each source of information, and then, define a strategy to fuse the classification or confidence scores. This is known as *late fusion*.

In this section, we start by describing the classification approach we have chosen, and, then, we present three fusion information strategies that we will evaluate later in the experimental section (Sec. 4).

3.1   Classification

Given a set of video-level descriptors, we train as many binary linear SVM classifiers [20] as different subject identities have to be learnt. For each binary classifier, the positive class is the target subject, and all the remaining subjects are labelled as negative samples. This setup is usually known as 'one-vs-all'. There-fore, given a test sample, a classification score is assigned by each classifier of the ensemble. Identity is assigned according to the binary classifier that returned the maximum score.

In practice, the Fisher Vector descriptors obtained in Sec. 2 for representing the video sequences are compressed by standard Principal Components Analysis (PCA) before being fed into the SVM. We use the implementation available in 'VLFeat library' [23] for classification.

3.2   Feature Vector Concatenation

The simplest method for information fusion is vector concatenation. Given a set of n row vectors $\{\mathbf{f}_1, \mathbf{f}_2, ..., \mathbf{f}_n\}$, each computed from a different type of feature, a new feature vector $\hat{\mathbf{f}}$ is defined as the concatenation of the n feature vectors. This approach can be considered as an early fusion method, since the combination of information is carried out before any learning/classification procedure.

3.3   Weighted Scores

Weighted scores (WS) is a late fusion method that uses the estimated accuracy of the individual models to assign a weight to each confidence score, obtaining in this way a new combined score. Given a set of n confidence score vectors $\{\mathbf{s_1}, \mathbf{s_2}, ..., \mathbf{s_n}\}$, associated to n models, and their corresponding weighting factors $\{a_1, a_2, ..., a_n\}$, the final score vector $\mathbf{s}_f$ is computed as follows:

$$\mathbf{s}_f = \sum_{i=1}^{n} \mathbf{s}_i \cdot a_i \tag{1}$$

3.4   Rank Minimization

The method proposed by Ye et al. [26], for the problems of object categoriza-tion and video event detection, can be classified into the category of late fusion methods. We will use the term *Rank Minimization* (RM) to denote this method along the paper. After obtaining classification scores from different models, usu-ally trained on different features, we want to combine those scores in order to improve the classification capability of each individual model, obtaining a (hope-fully) better score.

Let $\mathbf{s} = [s_1, s_2, ..., s_m]$ be a confidence score vector of a model on m samples. A pairwise relationship matrix T is constructed from $\mathbf{s}$ as: $T_{jk} = \text{sign}(s_j - s_k)$

Given n models, the robust late fusion method of Ye et al. aims at optimizing the following problem:

$$\min_{\hat{T}, E_i} \|\hat{T}\|_* + \lambda \sum_{i=1}^{n} \|E_i\|_1; \text{s.t. } T_i = \hat{T} + E_i, i = 1, ..., n; \hat{T} = -\hat{T}^\top \tag{2}$$

Where T_i is the pairwise relationship matrix of the i-th model, E_i is a sparse matrix associated to the i-th model, $\hat{T}$ is the estimated rank-2 pairwise relationship matrix consistent among the samples and models, and λ is a positive tradeoff parameter to be cross-validated. Such optimization problem is solved by inexact Augmented Lagrange Multiplier method [16].

As described in [26], given the estimated matrix $\hat{T}$, and assuming that $\hat{T}$ is generated from $\hat{\mathbf{s}}$ as $\hat{T} = \hat{\mathbf{s}}\mathbf{e}^\top - \mathbf{e}\hat{\mathbf{s}}^\top$, the new score vector $\hat{\mathbf{s}}$ is computed as

$$(1/m)\hat{T}\mathbf{e} = \arg\min_{\hat{\mathbf{s}}} \|\hat{T}^\top - (\hat{\mathbf{s}}\mathbf{e}^\top - \mathbf{e}\hat{\mathbf{s}}^\top)\|_F^2, \tag{3}$$

treating $(1/m)\hat{T}\mathbf{e}$ as the recovered $\hat{\mathbf{s}}$ after the late fusion of the input scores.

Adaptation of the Rank Minimization method to gait recognition. Let n be the number of sources of information we want to use in our system. In our 'one-vs-all' ensemble of binary SVMs, we have one classifier specialized in a single identity for each source of information. Let us name it c_k^i, where i represents the i-th identity and k represents the k-th source of information.

During test time, from each binary classifier c_k^i, we will obtain a vector $\mathbf{s}_k^i$ of m scores (one per test sample). So, we can compute a pairwise relationship matrix T_k^i from each $\mathbf{s}_k^i$. In other words, if $\mathcal{T}^i = \{T_1^i, T_2^i, ..., T_n^i\}$ is the set of pairwise relationship matrices for a given identity i, we can obtain from $\mathcal{T}^i$ a new vector $\hat{\mathbf{s}}^i$ of identity-specialized scores, that combines the n sources of information. This process is repeated independently for each identity-specialized classifier i, thus, obtaining a new set of scores $\mathcal{S} = \{\hat{\mathbf{s}}^1, \hat{\mathbf{s}}^2, ..., \hat{\mathbf{s}}^N\}$, where N is the number of possible identities. To decide the final identity of each test sample, we seek the maximum over its scores in $\mathcal{S}$, assigning as identity the one of the identity-specialized classifier that generated such combined score.

In the particular case where only a single modality is available, i.e. $n = 1$, the proposed approach is completely valid as well. We will show in the experimental results (Sec. 4.3) that using this strategy to re-score the outputs of the SVM ensemble improves significantly the recognition accuracy. In contrast, one limitation of this method is that it requires having available all the test samples in order to obtain the new scores.

As in [26], we could adopt an *out-of-sample* strategy when we have a new sample at test time not seen during the RM computation. Basically, [26] propose to assign a score based on the feature similarity of the new test sample with regard to the previously seen samples. The reader is referred to [26] for further details on this case.

4   Experiments and Results

We present in this section the experiments conducted to validate our proposed pipeline for gait recognition using both visual and audio information. We try to answer the following research questions: (a) *in terms of recognition accuracy, how far can we go by using each modality independently?*; (b) *can we really recognize*

Fig. 2. TUM-GAID dataset. People recorded from the same camera viewpoint walking indoors in two seasons. Three situations are included in the dataset: normal walking, walking with a bag and walking with coating shoes.

people by using their gait sound?; (c) *what fusion information strategy is the most suitable for the proposed features?*; and (d) *how much is the improvement, if any, when fusing audio and visual features in the task of gait recognition?*

We start by describing the dataset used for our experiments along with the experimental setup, and, then, we present and discuss the results.

4.1   Dataset

In TUM GAID 305 subjects perform two walking trajectories in an indoor environment. The first trajectory is performed from left to right and the second one from right to left. Therefore, both sides of the subjects are recorded. Two recording sessions were performed, one in January, where subjects wore heavy jackets and mostly winter boots, and the second in April, where subjects wore different clothes. Some examples can be seen in Fig. 2.

Hereinafter the following nomenclature is used to refer each of the four walking conditions considered: *normal* walk (N), carrying a *backpack* of approximately 5 kg (B), wearing coating *shoes* (S), as used in clean rooms for hygiene conditions, and *elapsed time* (TN-TB-TS).

Each subject of the dataset is composed of: six sequences of normal walking ($N1, N2, N3, N4, N5, N6$), two sequences carrying a bag ($B1, B2$) and two sequences wearing coating shoes ($S1, S2$). In addition, 32 subjects were recorded in both sessions (i.e. January and April) so they have 10 additional sequences ($TN1, TN2, TN3, TN4, TN5, TN6, TB1, TB2, TS1, TS2$).

The action is captured by a Microsoft Kinect sensor which provides a video stream, a depth stream and a four-channel audio. Video and depth are recorded at a resolution of 640 × 480 pixels with a frame rate of approximately 30 fps. The four-channel audio is sampled with 24 bits at 16 kHz.

In [11], Hofmann et al. designed the recommended experiments that should be performed in the database. For that purpose, they split the database in 3 partitions: 100 subjects for training and building models, 50 subjects for validation and 155 subjects for testing. Finally, a set of experiments (Sec. 4.2) are proposed for validating the robustness of the algorithms against different factors.

4.2   Experimental Setup

We describe here the experiments performed to give answer to the questions stated at Sec. 4. After the description of the experiments, the experimental results are discussed in Sec. 4.3.

Experiment A: baseline. We use each modality independently to recognize the gait. For this experiment we use DCS, H2M and Audio to obtain our baseline results that we would try to improve with fusion strategies. For DCS and H2M we use the following parameters in PFM: PCAL=150 (PCA applied at descriptor level), PCAH=256 (PCA applied at FV level), K=600 (dictionary size), and a single spatial level where the person bounding-box is vertically split into two non overlapping spatial cells (see Fig. 1) to encode coarse spatial information. For FV-Audio we use PCAL=50, PCAH=75, K=50. These parameters have been chosen through experimentation on a set of possible values and taking those that obtain best results. The results of this experiment are summarized in Tab. 1, where each row corresponds to a different method.

   Experiment B: fusion strategies. We use the fusion methods described in Sec. 3 for trying to improve the baseline results. We perform the experiments with each combination of modalities, that is, DCS+Audio, DCS+H2M, H2M+Audio and DCS+H2M+Audio. Since the obtained baseline results are nearly perfect (i.e. $\geq 99\%$) for the standard cases (N, B and S), we focus hereinafter on the temporal cases (TN, TB and TS). We cross-validate the parameters of the evaluated models on the validation set. Specifically, in Rank Minimization (Sec. 3.4) we use the following parameters: $\lambda = 1$, $\mu = 0.05$ (normalization factor), $\varepsilon = 10^{-5}$ (max error allowed), $\mu_{max} = 10^{10}$ (max μ allowed), $\rho = 1.001$ (increment factor of μ). In Weighted Scores (Sec. 3.3), the weight factors have been obtained as the average of the top five accuracies for each scenario in the training set defined in the dataset. Note that in Vector Concatenation (Sec. 3.2) there are no parameters to tune. The results of this experiment are summarized in Fig. 3.

   Experiment C: Rank Minimization method on single modality. Using as input the classification scores obtained during experiment A, we use the Rank Minimization method described in Sec. 3.4 to optimize them and obtain a better accuracy. We use the same parameters used in previous experiments. The results of this experiment are summarized in Tab. 3.

4.3   Results

The results shown in Tab. 1 correspond to *experiment A* and the state-of-the-art for visual features. Each row represents a different method. The first method (SDL) is specialized in temporal identification and the authors only report experiments for the case TN. We can see that PFM-DCS outperforms or obtains similar results in most cases. The worst case is TN where we obtain a 2.1% less than the best result (excluding SDL due to its specialization in only temporal cases). Note how our approach improves the state-of-the-art average from 88.2% to 96.0%.

Table 1. State-of-the-art on TUM GAID: visual features PFM-DCS. Percentage of correct recognition on TUM GAID for diverse methods. Each column corresponds to a different scenario. Column 'Avg' is the weighted average computed as the sum of the weighted mean scores of N, B, S and TN, TB, TS. Best results are marked in bold.

	Method	N	B	S	TN	TB	TS	Avg
Video	SDL [28]	-	-	-	**96.9**	-	-	-
	GEI [11]	99.4	27.1	52.6	44.0	6.0	9.0	56.0
	SVIM [25]	98.4	64.2	91.6	65.6	31.3	50.0	81.4
	RSM [9]	**100.0**	79.0	97.0	58.0	38.0	**57.0**	88.2
	PFM-DCS (this paper)	99.7	**99.0**	**99.0**	78.1	**62.0**	54.9	**96.0**
Audio	SVM [11]	44.5	27.4	4.8	3.0	0.0	3.0	23.4
	SVM+feat. sel. [8]	51.9	28.4	4.2	-	-	-	-
	HMM [7]	**65.5**	**36.5**	9.0	-	-	-	-
	FV-Audio (this paper)	62.3	30.3	**9.0**	**12.5**	**18.8**	**12.5**	**32.1**

In bottom part of Tab. 1 we can see the results of *experiment A* and the state-of-the-art for audio. Each row represents a different method. Note that only the work of Hofmann et al. [11] uses the temporal cases, the rest are focused in non temporal cases. If we compare our method (row 'FV-Audio') with that work, the results indicate that FV-Audio is better in temporal and non temporal cases, obtaining between a 9.5% and a 18.5% of improvement in temporal cases and between a 2.9% and a 17.8% in non temporal cases. Focusing in non temporal case, FV-Audio is close to the results of HMM and outperforms the rest of the compared methods.

Then, in Fig. 3 we can see the fusion results for *experiment B* for each evaluated fusion method and scenario. Note that 'DCS' results for PFM differ from the results shown in Tab. 1 as in those experiments we use temporal partitioning of the sequences to generate more training samples, but for audio this technique is not applicable so we use the results without temporal partitioning. According

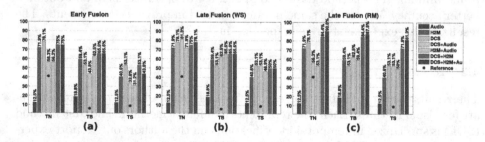

Fig. 3. Comparative recognition results: single modalities vs fusion. Each bar represents either a single modality or a combination of them. In each plot, the results are grouped per scenario. 'Reference' case refers to [11]. **(a)** Early fusion: feature concatenation. **(b)** Late fusion: Weighted Scores. **(c)** Late fusion: Rank Minimization. (Best viewed in electronic format)

to the results, Concatenation, WS and RM clearly outperform the work of Hofmann et al.[11] in all cases. Due to the low accuracy of the audio-based models, fusions 'DCS+Audio' and 'H2M+Audio' do not present important improvements by using Concatenation and RM, with the exception of *TS* where RM presents a significant improvement. On the other hand, WS is able to boost the results in all cases. Comparing fusion with our single modality results, 'DCS+H2M' presents a high improvement in case *TB*, with respect to the best single case of DCS and H2M, because of the good accuracy of both methods, obtaining a relative improvement of more than 10.4% in Concatenation and WS, and 42% in RM. This improvement is more noticeable in cases *TB* and *TS* of RM, where we obtain a relative increase of 42.1% and 35.4% respectively. Finally, in the fusion strategy 'DCS+H2M+Audio', Audio clearly contributes in RM, obtaining a relative increase of more than 3.7% in the worst case and 13% in the best case. In Concatenation and WS, this fusion does not improve the previous results. As additional information, we show rank-5 results (i.e. whether the correct identity is within the top 5) in Tab. 2.

In summary, and according to the results, the best fusion strategy is RM. Using this strategy, in the worst case we obtain improvements, with respect to using single modalities, of 16%, 47% and 53% in *TN*, *TB* and *TS* respectively.

Finally, in Tab. 3 we present the results of the *experiment C* where each row is a different scenario. As we can see, when the initial scores are good enough (in our experiments, an accuracy of 40% is enough to obtain a significant improvement), RM is able to optimize the scores matrix to improve the accuracy significantly. In our case, both visual features 'DCS' and 'H2M' show improvement. However, since Audio achieves low accuracy, the classification scores are not improved. According to our experimental results, we can achieve an improvement between 3% and 28% depending on the case tested.

Table 2. Recognition results on TUM GAID: Rank-5. Percentage of correct recognition on TUM GAID, using rank-5 measurement, for diverse fusion methods. Each column corresponds to a different fusion and a different scenario. Best results are marked in bold.

Method	DCS+Audio			DCS+H2M			H2M+Audio			DCS+H2M+Audio		
	TN	*TB*	*TS*	*TN*	*TB*	*TS*	*TN*	*TB*	*TS*	*TN*	*TB*	*TS*
Concatenation	93.8	92.2	81.3	93.8	87.5	90.6	90.6	90.6	84.4	93.8	90.6	90.6
RM	81.3	87.5	78.1	**93.8**	93.8	**96.9**	75.0	87.5	87.5	90.6	**96.9**	96.9

Table 3. Rank Minimization with single modality. Percentage of correct recognition on TUM GAID using Rank Minimization with one modality. Each column corresponds to a different scenario. Best results are marked in bold.

Scenario	Audio	H2M	DCS	Audio-RM	H2M-RM	DCS-RM
TN	12.5	71.9	**78.1**	9.4	75.0	**84.4**
TB	18.8	**59.4**	53.1	18.8	75.0	**81.3**
TS	12.5	40.6	**53.1**	12.5	62.6	**71.9**

5 Conclusions and Future Work

This paper has presented a thorough evaluation of audio-visual features for the task of person identification based on gait. The results on 'TUM GAID' dataset show that, although most of the gait information is clearly visual, some audio patterns also help to identify people. In addition, the combination of two sets of visual features (i.e. DCS and H2M) improves the recognition accuracy of the system (compared to just using one of them) in the 'temporal' scenario – people wearing different clothes in different epochs of the year – specially in the cases where people wear a backpack or coating shoes, up to 79% better. Another interesting finding is that the Rank Minimization method of Ye et al. [26] can be used on a single modality of gait descriptors combined with an ensemble of 'one-vs-all' SVM classifiers to re-score the individual classification scores, boosting the recognition accuracy up to 53% (e.g. from 53.1% to 81.3% with DCS on *TB*, Tab. 3).

As future work, we plan to extend this study to other modalities and datasets.

Acknowledgments. This work has been partially funded by project TIC-1692 (Junta de Andalucía), and the Research Projects TIN2012-32952 and BROCA, both financed by FEDER and the Spanish Ministry of Science and Technology. We also thank the reviewers for their helpful comments.

References

1. Atrey, P.K., Hossain, M.A., El Saddik, A., Kankanhalli, M.S.: Multimodal fusion for multimedia analysis: a survey. Multimedia systems **16**(6), 345–379 (2010)
2. Bach, F., Lanckriet, G., Jordan, M.: Multiple kernel learning, conic duality and the SMO algorithm. In: Proc. ICML, p. 6 (2004)
3. Castro, F.M., Marín-Jiménez, M., Medina-Carnicer, R.: Pyramidal Fisher Motion for multiview gait recognition. In: Proc. ICPR, pp. 1692–1697 (2014)
4. Dalal, N., Triggs, B.: Histograms of oriented gradients for human detection. In: CVPR, vol. 1, pp. 886–893. IEEE Computer Society, Washington (2005)
5. Dalal, N., Triggs, B., Schmid, C.: Human detection using oriented histograms of flow and appearance. In: Leonardis, A., Bischof, H., Pinz, A. (eds.) ECCV 2006. LNCS, vol. 3952, pp. 428–441. Springer, Heidelberg (2006)
6. Farnebäck, G.: Two-frame motion estimation based on polynomial expansion. In: Bigun, J., Gustavsson, T. (eds.) SCIA 2003. LNCS, vol. 2749, pp. 363–370. Springer, Heidelberg (2003)
7. Geiger, J.T., Kneißl, M., Schuller, B., Rigoll, G.: Acoustic Gait-based Person Identification using Hidden Markov Models. ArXiv e-prints (2014)
8. Geiger, J., Hofmann, M., Schuller, B., Rigoll, G.: Gait-based person identification by spectral, cepstral and energy-related audio features. In: Proc. ICASSP, pp. 458–462, May 2013
9. Guan, Y., Li, C.: A robust speed-invariant gait recognition system for walker and runner identification. In: Int. Conf. on Biometrics (ICB), pp. 1–8, June 2013
10. Han, J., Bhanu, B.: Individual recognition using gait energy image. IEEE PAMI **28**(2), 316–322 (2006)

11. Hofmann, M., Geiger, J., Bachmann, S., Schuller, B., Rigoll, G.: The TUM Gait from Audio, Image and Depth (GAID) database: Multimodal recognition of subjects and traits. J. of Visual Com. and Image Repres. **25**(1), 195–206 (2014)

12. Hu, W., Tan, T., Wang, L., Maybank, S.: A survey on visual surveillance of object motion and behaviors. IEEE Transactions on Systems, Man, and Cybernetics, Part C: Applications and Reviews **34**(3), 334–352 (2004)

13. Jain, M., Jegou, H., Bouthemy, P.: Better exploiting motion for better action recognition. In: CVPR, pp. 2555–2562 (2013)

14. KaewTraKulPong, P., Bowden, R.: An improved adaptive background mixture model for real-time tracking with shadow detection. In: Video-Based Surveillance Systems, pp. 135–144. Springer (2002)

15. Lartillot, O., Toiviainen, P.: MIR in Matlab (ii): A toolbox for musical feature extraction from audio. In: ISMIR, pp. 127–130 (2007)

16. Lin, Z., Chen, M., Ma, Y.: The augmented Lagrange multiplier method for exact recovery of corrupted low-rank matrices (2010). arXiv preprint arXiv:1009.5055

17. Liu, Y., Zhang, J., Wang, C., Wang, L.: Multiple HOG templates for gait recognition. In: Proc. ICPR, pp. 2930–2933. IEEE (2012)

18. Marín-Jiménez, M., Muñoz Salinas, R., Yeguas-Bolivar, E., Pérez de la Blanca, N.: Human interaction categorization by using audio-visual cues. Machine Vision and Applications **25**(1), 71–84 (2014)

19. Martín-Félez, R., Xiang, T.: Uncooperative gait recognition by learning to rank. Pattern Recognition **47**(12), 3793–3806 (2014)

20. Osuna, E., Freund, R., Girosi, F.: Support Vector Machines: training and applications. Tech. Rep. AI-Memo 1602, MIT, March 1997

21. Perronnin, F., Sánchez, J., Mensink, T.: Improving the fisher kernel for large-scale image classification. In: Daniilidis, K., Maragos, P., Paragios, N. (eds.) ECCV 2010, Part IV. LNCS, vol. 6314, pp. 143–156. Springer, Heidelberg (2010)

22. Sivic, J., Zisserman, A.: Video Google: A text retrieval approach to object matching in videos. ICCV **2**, 1470–1477 (2003)

23. Vedaldi, A., Fulkerson, B.: VLFeat: An open and portable library of computer vision algorithms (2008). http://www.vlfeat.org/

24. Wang, H., Kläser, A., Schmid, C., Liu, C.L.: Action Recognition by Dense Trajectories. In: CVPR, pp. 3169–3176 (2011)

25. Whytock, T., Belyaev, A., Robertson, N.: Dynamic distance-based shape features for gait recognition. J. Math. Imaging and Vision **50**(3), 314–326 (2014)

26. Ye, G., Liu, D., Jhuo, I.H., Chang, S.F.: Robust late fusion with rank minimization. In: CVPR, pp. 3021–3028 (2012)

27. Yu, S., Tan, D., Tan, T.: A framework for evaluating the effect of view angle, clothing and carrying condition on gait recognition. Proc. ICPR **4**, 441–444 (2006)

28. Zeng, W., Wang, C., Yang, F.: Silhouette-based gait recognition via deterministic learning. Pattern Recognition **47**(11), 3568–3584 (2014)

Web User Interact Task Recognition
Based on Conditional Random Fields

Anis Elbahi[⊠] and Mohamed Nazih Omri

Research Unit MARS, Computer Science Department,
Faculty of Sciences of Monastir, Monastir, Tunisia
Elbahi.anis@gmail.com, MohamedNazih.omri@fsm.rnu.tn

Abstract. Recognition activity of web users based on their navigational behavior during interaction process is an important topic of Human Computer Interaction. To improve the interaction process and interface usability, many studies have been performed for understanding how users interact with a web interface in order to perform a given activity. In this paper we apply the Conditional Random Fields approach for modeling human navigational behavior based on mouse movements to recognize web user tasks. Experimental results show the efficiency of the proposed model and confirm the superiority of Conditional Random Fields approach with respect to the Hidden Markov Models approach in human activity recognition.

Keywords: Conditional random fields · Hidden markov models · User task recognition · Cursor behavior analysis · Human computer interaction · Pattern recognition · Machine learning

1 Introduction

Inferring the activity of web users based on their navigational behavior is an important topic of HCI which are extensively studied during last decade. For years, various techniques have been used in this field, such as eye movements tracking [1], mouse tracking [2], physiological and psychological tracking [3] and click-through analysis [4]. These techniques have proven good efficiency in user behavior understanding and interfaces usability evaluation.

Understanding navigational behavior of users can help designers to improve interfaces usability, to provide assistance for users with disabilities and others applications such as e-learning. Obviously mouse pointing device is the most commonly used tool during interaction with computer interfaces. On the one hand, the activity of mouse cursor such as movements, clicks and scrolling can be easily captured and recorded during interaction process. On the other hand, analysis of cursor behavior can provide high quality clues of a spontaneous, precise, direct and unbiased trace of user behavior. Such trace can be considered as a good indicator of the user reasoning strategy during a web activity. Consequently many studies have been performed to understand users cognitive

© Springer International Publishing Switzerland 2015
G. Azzopardi and N. Petkov (Eds.): CAIP 2015, Part I, LNCS 9256, pp. 740–751, 2015.
DOI: 10.1007/978-3-319-23192-1_62

strategy based on their cursor navigational behavior. Many other researches [5], [6] have proposed different models based on possibility theory, on bayesian and semantic networks to recognize the goal of the users. In this paper, we used the Conditional Random Fields (CRF) approach [7] in order to recognize the tasks of web users, based on their navigational behavior using mouse movement data.

2   Navigational Behavior Analysis Based on Mouse Movement Tracking

During web session, users seek to perform various tasks such as logging, ordering a product and sending an email. For each task, users perform basic operations such as keyboard events, moving a cursor, selecting an option, clicking a link and pressing a button. Since early computers, the mouse has been the most commonly used device during human computer interaction process. Using a cursor pointing device during web activities, users draw their navigational behavior. For many years, the cursor activity tracking attracts much attention of researchers who are interested in user navigational behavior. Mouse movement tracking has been evaluated as an alternative to eye tracking for determining attention on the web page. Therefore, various studies have been achieved in this context such as the study of Chen et al. [8] who have found that mouse and eye movements are strongly related and that 75% of mouse saccades move to significant regions of the screen where eye gaze are moved. In the same study, it has been confirmed that mouse data can be used to infer the intent of user. Those findings have led to extend the studies of user behavior analysis using mouse tracking technique.

Mouse movements are explored to provide insights into the intention behind a web search query [2] and click prediction . Zheng et al. [9] presented a new approach for user re-authentication using behavioral biometrics provided by mouse dynamics. In a similar way, [10] analyses the interaction of users with a computer system in order to identify users only by analyzing their interaction behavior mainly based on mouse events.

Today, mouse movement tracking is a very effective technique, easy to use, freely available and that does not disturb user behavior during the interaction. Mainly based on mouse trajectory, we propose a new model using CRF approach to automatically recognize web user tasks.

3   A User Task as a Sequence of Fixed Areas of Interest

Web interfaces can be presented as a set of significant regions called interface Items Of Interest (IOI) or Areas Of Interest (AOI) which can be manually specified or automatically discovered [11].

Usually, users perform various tasks (activities) using pointing device. During a task, without being aware, users move the cursor across the web interfaces and fix various AOI. The following figure presents an example of a sequence describing fixed AOI during logging into Gmail account task.

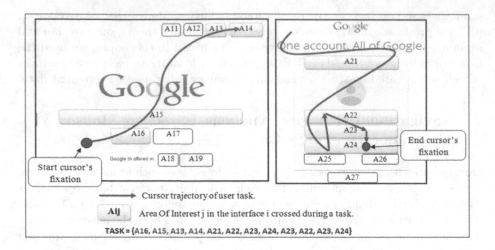

Fig. 1. Example of user task defined as a sequence of fixed AOI.

To define a task, we rely on activity theory [12] and the work of Gotz et al. [13] who characterized user behavior at four levels based on the semantic richness of the activity. The following figure presents logging into Gmail account via Google interface task based on Gotz task description.

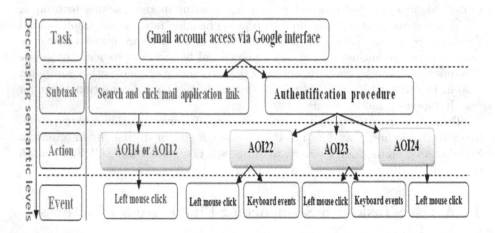

Fig. 2. Example of user task representation based on Gotz description.

As shown in figure 2, according to different levels the user task can be defined as a temporal sequence of subtasks or a succession of AOI or elementary events. In our study, we focus on mouse trajectory crossing different AOI during a web user task.

Thus, according to Gotz task representation, we define a task as a temporal sequence of fixed AOI during a period of time T. $\text{TSK}_i = \{ \text{AOI}_1, \text{AOI}_2, \ldots, \text{AOI}_T \}$. Despite this clear definition of tasks, their automatic recognition is very challenging to solve for many reasons. Firstly, a user task is a result of a complex human navigational behavior because the same user may perform the same task twice differently. Secondly, users doing a same task do not necessarily have the same succession of fixed AOI. Thirdly, same AOI can be similarly relevant to perform different tasks.

4   Utility of Task Recognition

Knowing user tasks can tell us about:

- First, second and last performed tasks: the order of tasks execution can provide insights about the user cognitive strategy.
- Tasks that consume more or less users time: the task execution time can give clues about the most attractive or ignored tasks.
- Most repeated tasks: task frequency can provide evidences about the difficulty of the task.

Thus, automatic task identification can improve the general interaction process by giving help in real time to unfamiliar users, helping users with disabilities, improving systems security and interfaces usability.

In pattern recognition applications, probabilistic graphical models have been successfully used and various studies prove that Conditional Random Fields (CRF) outperforms Hidden Markov Models (HMM) in sequence labeling tasks [14,15]. Motivated by this assumption, we propose to use a CRF model to automatically recognize a web user task based on mouse movements. Thereafter the recognition rate of our proposed model will be compared with HMM model developed by Elbahi et al.[16]. In next section, we briefly present the basics of HMM and CRF approaches in order to better understand the proposed model.

5   HMM and CRF :A Brief Presentation

For more than two decades, Hidden Markov Models [17] have been widely used in various fields for modeling and labeling stochastic sequences such as speech, object and web users activity recognition[18]. Recently, CRF theory [7], have been proposed to alleviate HMM assumptions and then have been used successfully in various fields such as the information retrieval process[19,20]. To better understand why CRF gained more power and then more popularity with respect to the HMM approach, we must have at least basics of both approaches. First, HMM are generative probabilistic directed graphical models which makes two important assumptions.

Assumption 1: Each label y_t, depends only on its previous label y_{t-1}.

Assumption 2: Each observation x_t depends on the current label y_t.

Based on these simplifications, a HMM defined over a set of N hidden states and an alphabet of discrete symbols, can be specified by $\lambda = (A, B, \Pi)$ with $A = \{a_{ij}\}$ is the matrix of transition probabilities, $B = \{b_j(k)\}$ is the matrix of observations emission probabilities and $\Pi = \{\pi_i\}$ is the initial probability distribution vector over initial states. Learning HMM parameters A, B and Π is done by maximizing the joint probability $P(Y, X)$ in the training data, using Baum-Welch algorithm.

$$P(Y, X) = \prod_{t=1}^{T} P(x_t|y_t)P(y_t|y_{t-1}) \tag{1}$$

Secondly, CRF are discriminative undirected graphical models. Due to the discriminative nature of CRF, it becomes possible to represent much more knowledge in the model using feature functions. With CRF we try to maximize a conditional probability $P(Y|X)$:

$$P(Y|X) = \frac{1}{Z(X)} \exp\left(\sum_{t=1}^{T}\sum_{k=1}^{N} \lambda_k f_k(y_{t-1}, y_t, X) + \sum_{t=1}^{T}\sum_{k=1}^{N} +\mu_k g_k(y_t, X)\right) \tag{2}$$

HMM which is based on (1) and CRF, based on (2), are very similar because $\lambda_k f_k(y_{t-1}, y_t, X)$ are similar to transition probability $P(y_t|y_{t-1})$ and $\mu_k g_k(y_t, X)$ are analogous to observation probability emission $P(x_t|y_t)$. For more details about HMM and CRF approaches, reader can see [21, 22].

6   CRF for User Task Modeling

6.1   User Task Modeling

Like presented above, a web interface can be presented as a set of items called AOI which can be pointed by mouse cursor during users tasks.

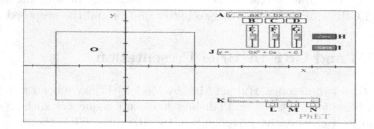

Fig. 3. Areas Of Interest in Equation Grapher interface.

Figure 3 presents the "Equation Grapher" online simulator[1] interface described as a set of 15 areas of interest AOI={A,B,C,D,E,F,G,H,I,J,K,L,M,N,O} judged by an expert as frequently pointed regions during users tasks.

---

[1] Phet available on : http://phet.colorado.edu.

Like presented previously, each task can be defined as a finite, temporal, stochastic sequence of AOI set by a user during a period of time. In order to get a sequence of fixed AOI during a task, coordinates of mouse cursor have been recorded at each time slice t. The obtained data (vector of cursor coordinates) will be provided as input for the following algorithm. In output, the vectorization algorithm provides the sequence of AOI related to the mouse movement coordinates during user task.

Algorithm 1. Vectorization algorithm

Input:
X={};
Coordinates of mouse cursor path recorded for a task;
Details of each area of interest AOI;
$T \leftarrow$ Total duration of the task;
$\Delta t \leftarrow$ Time between recordings of two cursor coordinates;
begin
    for $t \leftarrow 1$ *to* T *(with* Δt *step)* **do**
        if *(mouse cursor coordinates is in* AOI_k*)* **then**
           | $X[t] \leftarrow AOI_k$
        end
    end
end
Output:
$X = \{x_1, x_2, \ldots, x_T\}$ // the observation sequence

6.2   The Proposed Model

In this section we present the proposed CRF model.

- TASKs= {tsk_1, tsk_2,..., tsk_M} : set of M labels concerning M tasks that can be performed by users.
- AOI={aoi_1, aoi_2,..., aoi_N} : set of N AOI of the web interface that can be pointed by users during tasks.
- X={aoi_k_1,..., aoi_k_t, ..., aoi_k_T} :the sequence of observations describing AOI fixed by mouse cursor during a task, with $1 \leq k \leq N$
- Y={tsk_i_1,..., tsk_i_t, ..., tsk_i_T} : the label sequence describing the interaction process. At each time step (t) only one label is used to describe the task of user, with $1 \leq i \leq M$.

Each observation sequence X given to CRF model corresponds to a sequence of fixed AOI during only one task. So, the model is designed to infer only one task for a given observation sequence Y. Thus, each sequence of observations given to model must be entirely labeled using a single tag corresponding to performed task. Graphically, our model can be presented as follows:

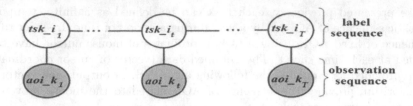

Fig. 4. Graphical representation of CRF proposed model.

Features functions are key components of any CRF model and must be well defined before model training. Let $F = \{f_1, f_2, \ldots, f_n\}$ be a set of features functions. Each function $f_j(y_{t-1}, y_t, X, t)$ looks at a pair of adjacent labels (y_{t-1} and y_t) and all the observation sequence (X) at each time step (t).

For the proposed model, y_t refers to the current task label (tsk_i_t) and x_t represents the current observation at time t (aoi_k_t).

In order to define, to train and to test the model, we used CRF++ tool[2] that implements a fast learning Newton's method LBFGS and a decoding method using Viterbi algorithm. Using CRF++ we can define templates to automatically generate a set of features functions.

Next, we present some examples of used features functions generated using CRF++ templates.

Template 1 : U00 :%x[0,0] , generate a set of functions like:
$$f_i(y_{t-1}, y_t, X, t) = \begin{cases} 1 \text{ if } y_t \in \text{TASKs and } x_t \in \text{AOI} ; \\ 0 \text{ otherwise} \end{cases}$$

For example:
$$f_1(y_{t-1}, y_t, X, t) = \begin{cases} 1 \text{ if } y_t = \text{tsk\_1 and } x_t = \text{aoi\_2} ; \\ 0 \text{ otherwise} \end{cases}$$

f_1 return 1 if the current label (y_t) is tsk_1 and the current observation (x_t) is aoi_2 else f_1 return 0.

Template 2 : U01 :%x[-1,0]/%x[0,0]/%x[1,0] , generate a set of functions like:
$$f_j(y_{t-1}, y_t, X, t) =$$
$$\begin{cases} 1 \text{ if } y_t \in \text{TASKs and } x_t \in \text{AOI and } x_{t+1} \in \text{AOI and } x_{t-1} \in \text{AOI}; \\ 0 \text{ otherwise} \end{cases}$$

For example:
$$f_2(y_{t-1}, y_t, X, t) =$$
$$\begin{cases} 1 \text{ if } y_t = \text{tsk\_2 and } x_t = \text{aoi\_1 and } x_{t+1} = \text{aoi\_2 and } x_{t-1} = \text{aoi\_4}; \\ 0 \text{ otherwise} \end{cases}$$

f_2 return 1 if the current label (y_t) is tsk_2 and the current observation (x_t) is aoi_1 and next observation (x_{t+1}) is aoi_2 and previous observation (x_{t-1}) is aoi_4 else f_2 return 0.

After defining the model structure and features functions, we train the model in order to reestimate the features functions parameters vector Θ. For the training step, we use a training set D defined by: $D = \{x^{(i)}, y^{(i)}\}_{i=1}^{|D|}$ and containing

---

[2] CRF++ available on: http://crfpp.googlecode.com/svn/trunk/doc/index.html.

labeled observation sequences. Each one corresponds to a single task and entirely labeled using a single tag.

7 Experiments and Discussion

7.1 Experimental Settings

Once, the structure of the CRF model and the set of features functions have been defined as previously described, we prepared a "training and test" set to validate the proposed model. The prepared data set is based on real manipulations, which consists of three different tasks performed by 51 students of secondary school using the "equation grapher" interface. The three tasks are:

Task1 = called "DEG2": during this task a student is asked to perform a graphical representation of a quadratic equation of the form $ax^2 + bx + c = 0$ (a, b and c $\neq 0$) and to keep in memory the shape of the drawn curve.

Task2 = called "DEG1": student is asked to perform a graphical representation of a quadratic equation of the form $ax^2 + bx + c = 0$ (a=0 and b, c $\neq 0$) and to keep in memory the shape of the drawn curve.

Task3 = called "INT", during this task a student is asked to discover (and keep in memory) intersection coordinates of a quadratic equation of the form $ax^2 + bx + c = 0$ (a,b,c $\neq 0$) and the same quadratic equation $ax^2 + bx + c = 0$ (a,c=0). Like described below, the three tasks are very similar and complex to distinguish based only on cursor trajectory. The properties of used training set are summarized in the following table:

Table 1. Characteristics of used training set

Characteristics	Number
Interface number	1
Areas Of Interest in used interface	15
Sentences (Performed tasks)	51
Task 1 (DEG2)	17
Task 2 (DEG1)	17
Task 3 (INT)	17
Words (AOI pointed during all tasks)	79304
Used tags	3

Once, different AOI have been defined as described by figure 3. In order to obtain a sequence of observations, we asked each user to perform only one task (among three mentioned above) and we use OGAMA tool[3] for recording mouse cursor coordinates at each time slice (1 centisecond) during a task. The obtained data are given to a vectorization algorithm to produce an observation sequence corresponding to the performed task. Once, the 51 observation sequences are

---

[3] OGAMA available on : http://www.ogama.net/.

prepared and labeled, we estimate the parameters of the CRF model. The used sampling technique is LOOCV (Leave One Out Cross Validation) consisting of taking, at each time, one single task (labeled sequence of observations) from the "training and test" set for testing .The remaining tasks are used for training. Obtained results are shown and discussed in the next section.

7.2   Experimental Results and Discussion

Although, three tasks are quite similar as described above, experimental results, presented in table 2, showed that HMM model recognize 76.47% of users tasks while CRF model make out 88.23%.These results show that CRF proposed model have better ability than the HMM model developed by Elbahi et al. [16].

Table 2. Recognition rate of CRF and HMM models

Task Type	HMM			CRF		
	Samples	Errors	Recognition rate	Samples	Errors	Recognition rate
Task1(DEG2)	17	8	52,94%	17	3	82,35%
Task2 (DEG1)	17	0	100%	17	2	88,23%
Task3(INT)	17	4	76,47%	17	1	94,11%
Total	51	12	**76,47%**	51	6	**88,23%**

To explain why CRF outperforms HMM approach in user task recognition, remember that a task is defined as a finite, temporal, stochastic sequence of AOI manipulated during a period of time T. Each task is described by a sequence of observations X={$aoi\_k_1,\ldots, aoi\_k_t, \ldots, aoi\_k_T$}. Therefore, in order to recognize a given task, it is necessary to take into consideration all focused AOI during a given task. HMM models are founded on the independence assumption which says that variables do not depend on each other and they do not affect each other in any way except as allowed by the Markov property. Consequently, each used AOI at time t depends only on AOI at time t-1, and each label at time t depends only on the current observation at time t. This is not always the case in real applications such as web user tasks. Due to primary advantage of CRF approach which is the relaxation of the independence assumption, CRF models can take into account more complex dependencies between variables. Therefore, all focused AOI during a task can be taken into consideration by CRF models. For this reason, CRF outperforms HMM model in users tasks recognition.

As shown in table 2, for task DEG1 HMM performed better than CRF, because when performing task DEG1, users unconsciously spend more time pointing at some AOIs that are more relevant for task DEG2 and task INT. This bad annotation has a bigger impact on the accuracy of discriminative models because during learning step, classes compete to find the best discriminative fit, while in generative model the parameters for each class are learned separately.

Table 3 shows the average cursor fixations in each AOI for tasks DEG2, DEG1 and INT. The same table also presents average cursor fixations in each AOI two tasks, the first called TASKX and the second called TASKY. TASKX is INT task and correctly recognized by both models while TASKY is INT task and judged by CRF and HMM models as DEG2 task. Likewise, Table 3 shows that areas A, H, K, L and N are rarely fixed during three tasks, therefore they can be considered as unimportant areas [23] which do not attract the user cursor during interaction. Such ignored areas do not have a great impact on user strategy during tasks. As shown in table3, task DEG2 is too dependent on areas E (28.84%) and B(15.18%) and task DEG1 is too dependent on areas G(21.84%) , F(18.57%), D(14.91%) and C(14.74%) while most used AOI for task INT are O(24.51%) and E(13.64%). These results show that each type of task attracts user attention into well defined regions in the interface. Therefore, during each task mouse movements draw the user behavior in a well defined order. This trajectory can be used to describe the strategy of user during interaction process [24].

Table 3. Mouse fixations rate per AOI during tasks

AOIs	A	B	C	D	E	F	G	H	I	J	K	L	M	N	O
DEG2	1,81	15,18	6,33	6,47	28,84	11,05	4,57	0,84	7,45	4,96	1,45	1,04	1,04	1,04	7,93
DEG1	1,02	2,57	14,74	14,91	3,61	18,57	21,84	2,05	11,25	3,45	0,69	1,39	0,17	0,03	3,71
INT	0,00	10,60	9,14	10,03	13,64	6,83	7,82	0,82	4,84	1,49	1,40	0,80	7,66	0,43	24,51
TASKX	0,00	6,91	16,31	6,01	9,85	4,93	6,33	0,00	2,11	3,33	0,45	0,13	9,60	0,00	34,04
TASKY	0,00	18,86	6,93	21,24	29,51	2,84	0,53	2,51	9,30	1,58	1,12	1,12	0,00	0,00	4,47

TASKX which is INT task was correctly recognized by CRF and HMM models, in fact, mouse fixations rate of TASKX show that user focuses on areas E(9.85%), M(9.60%) and O(34.04%) which are more relevant for INT task than DEG1 and DEG2 tasks. During TASKY which is of type INT, but recognized by both models as DEG2, the user usually focuses on relevant AOI for task DEG2 E(29.51%) and B(18.86%) and ignores area M (0.00%) and O(4.47%) considered as important to perform a task INT. Knowing that all users have successfully performed the required tasks, we can see that during TASKY, the user adopts a different strategy to perform an INT task. This explains the failure of two models in recognizing TASKY. CRF and HMM models estimate their parameters based on observation sequences. Each one describes the user strategy during a task based on fixed AOI. If the majority of users adopt a similar way, "strategy of group", to perform a given task, HMM and CRF models will adjust their configurations based on this strategy of the group. To perform a given task, a human may adopt a strategy which is quite different of the one adopted by the majority of users; this task may be the cause of CRF and HMM failure. In fact a normal realisation of a given task results in a normal use of important AOI which are relevant for this task and ignoring (non-use) of important areas (region, link, button), or overusing of unimportant areas, should be considered as an indicator of different user strategy during task realization.

8   Conclusion

User interaction analysis based on mouse movement tracking can tell us about the users intended task, AOIs that highly attract the user's attention and ignored AOIs. Also, the analysis of cursor behavior can give insights about the strategy adopted by the majority of users and the particular users strategy during a given task. Furthermore, HMM and CRF models present a good ability in human activity recognition with a clear superiority of CRF compared to HMM.

In this work, we used CRF approach in order to recognize tasks performed by users, based on mouse movements during interaction process with web interface. Experimental results show the good performance of the proposed model and confirm the superiority of CRF with respect to HMM in user task recognition mainly based on mouse movements. Also, results show that each task type have a great impact on mouse behavior because the cursor is more attracted by some AOI than others according to each type of task.

In spite of the effectiveness of probabilistic models, such as HMM and CRF, in labeling sequences especially in human activity recognition, there are some constraints that overwhelm the power of used approaches to model the human interaction due to the complex nature of human behavior and because during parameter estimation, CRF and HMM will be adjusted based on "the group's strategy" adopted by the majority of users during a realisation of a given task.

References

1. Bulling, A., Ward, J., Gellersen, H., Tröster, G., et al.: Eye movement analysis for activity recognition using electrooculography. IEEE Transactions on Pattern Analysis and Machine Intelligence **33**(4), 741–753 (2011)
2. Guo, Q., Agichtein, E.: Exploring mouse movements for inferring query intent. In: Proceedings of the 31st Annual International ACM SIGIR Conference on Research and Development in Information Retrieval, pp. 707–708. ACM (2008)
3. Dufresne, A., Courtemanche, F., Prom Tep, S., Senecal, S.: Physiological measures, eye tracking and task analysis to track user reactions in user generated content. In: 7th Internationcal Conference on Methods and Techniques in Behavioral Research (Measuring Behavior 2010), p. 218 (2010)
4. Huang, J., White, R.W., Dumais, S.: No clicks, no problem: using cursor movements to understand and improve search. In: Proceedings of the SIGCHI Conference on Human Factors in Computing Systems, pp. 1225–1234. ACM (2011)
5. Omri, M.N.: Fuzzy knowledge representation, learning and optimization with bayesian analysis in fuzzy semantic networks. In: 1999 Proceedings of the 6th International Conference on Neural Information Processing (ICONIP 1999), vol. 1, pp. 412–417. IEEE (1999)
6. Omri, M.N., Tijus, C.A.: Uncertain and approximative knowledge representation in fuzzy semantic networks. In: The Twelfth International Conference On Industrial & Engineering Applications of Artificial Intelligence & Expert Systems IEA/AIE 1999, Cairo, Egypt (1999)
7. Lafferty, J., McCallum, A., Pereira, F.C.N.: Probabilistic models for segmenting and labeling sequence data, Conditional random fields (2001)

8. Chen, M.C., Anderson, J.R., Sohn, M.H.: What can a mouse cursor tell us more?: correlation of eye/mouse movements on web browsing. In: CHI 2001 Extended Abstracts on Human Factors in Computing Systems, pp. 281–282. ACM (2001)

9. Zheng, N., Paloski, A., Wang, H.: An efficient user verification system via mouse movements. In: Proceedings of the 18th ACM Conference on Computer and Communications Security, pp. 139–150. ACM (2011)

10. Heimgärtner, R.: Identification of the User by Analyzing Human Computer Interaction. In: Jacko, J.A. (ed.) HCI International 2009, Part III. LNCS, vol. 5612, pp. 275–283. Springer, Heidelberg (2009)

11. Mathe, S., Sminchisescu, C.: Action from still image dataset and inverse optimal control to learn task specific visual scanpaths. In: Advances in Neural Information Processing Systems, pp. 1923–1931 (2013)

12. Nardi, B.A.: Activity theory and human-computer interaction. Context and Consciousness: Activity Theory and Human-Computer Interaction, pp. 7–16 (1996)

13. Gotz, D., Zhou, M.X.: Characterizing users' visual analytic activity for insight provenance. Information Visualization 8(1), 42–55 (2009)

14. Quattoni, A., Collins, M., Darrell, T.: Conditional random fields for object recognition. In: Advances in Neural Information Processing Systems, pp. 1097–1104 (2004)

15. Vail, D.L., Veloso, M.M., Lafferty, J.D.: Conditional random fields for activity recognition. In: Proceedings of the 6th International Joint Conference on Autonomous Agents and Multiagent Systems, p. 235. ACM (2007)

16. Elbahi, A., Mahjoub, M.A., Omri, M.N.: Hidden markov model for inferring user task using mouse movement. In: Fourth International Conference on Information and Communication Technology and Accessibility (ICTA), pp. 1–7. IEEE (2013)

17. Rabiner, L.R.: A tutorial on hidden markov models and selected applications in speech recognition. Proceedings of the IEEE 77(2), 257–286 (1989)

18. Elbahi, A., Omri, M.N., Mahjoub, M.A.: Possibilistic reasoning effects on hidden markov models effectiveness. In: IEEE International Conference on Fuzzy Systems (FUZZ-IEEE). IEEE (in press, 2015)

19. Fkih, F., Omri, M.N.: Complex terminology extraction model from unstructured web text based linguistic and statistical knowledge. International Journal of Information Retrieval Research (IJIRR) 2(3), 1–18 (2012)

20. Boughamoura, R., Omri, M.N., Youssef, H.: Use of conditional random field to extract pertinent information from web resources. In: An International Forum for Exploring e-Business and e-Government Research, Applications, and Technologies (TIGERA) (2008)

21. Rabiner, L.R., Juang, B.-H.: An introduction to hidden markov models. IEEE ASSP Magazine 3(1), 4–16 (1986)

22. Sutton, C., McCallum, A.: An introduction to conditional random fields for relational learning. Introduction to Statistical Relational Learning, pp. 93–128 (2006)

23. Poole, A., Ball, L.J.: Eye tracking in hci and usability research. Encyclopedia of Human Computer Interaction 1, 211–219 (2006)

24. Tan, D., Nijholt, A.: Brain-computer interfaces and human-computer interaction. In: Brain-Computer Interfaces, pp. 3–19. Springer (2010)

Tree Log Identification Based on Digital Cross-Section Images of Log Ends Using Fingerprint and Iris Recognition Methods

Rudolf Schraml[1]([✉]), Heinz Hofbauer[1],
Alexander Petutschnigg[2], and Andreas Uhl[1]

[1] Department of Computer Sciences, University of Salzburg, Salzburg, Austria
rudi.schraml@gmail.com
[2] Department of Forest Products Technology and Timber Construction,
University of Applied Sciences Salzburg, Salzburg, Austria

Abstract. Tree log biometrics is an approach to establish log traceability from forest to further processing companies. This work assesses if algorithms developed in the context of fingerprint and iris recognition can be transferred to log identification by means of cross-section images of log ends. Based on a test set built up on 155 tree logs the identification performances for a set of configurations and in addition the impacts of two enhancement procedures are assessed.

Results show, that fingerprint and iris recognition based approaches are suited for log identification by achieving 100% detection rate for the best configurations. In assessing the performance for a large set of tree logs this work provides substantial conclusions for the further development of log biometrics.

1 Introduction

Commonly the term biometrics stands for the study of behavioural or physiological characteristics to identify living people. But the theoretical background and the concepts of human biometrics have been carried over to the recognition of plants, vegetables, animals, industrial products and most relevant for this study to the recognition of tree logs or boards [20]. This study deals with concepts of fingerprint and iris recognition and explores their applicability to the identification of tree logs using cross-section images (CS-Images) of log ends.

In order to close the traceability gap between the forest site and the further processing companies tree log identification is an economic requirement to map the ownership of each log. Additionally, social aspects have become more important and sustainability certificates like Pan European Forest Certification (PEFC) and Forest Stewardship Council (FSC) are a must have for all end-sellers. Finally, traceability is legally bound by the European Timber Regulation (EUTR) to prohibit illegal logging in the EU [4].

This work is partially funded by the Austrian Science Fund (FWF) under Project No. TRP-254.

G. Azzopardi and N. Petkov (Eds.): CAIP 2015, Part I, LNCS 9256, pp. 752–765, 2015.
DOI: 10.1007/978-3-319-23192-1_63

State-of-the art traceability approaches rely on physically marking each log and in the past decade huge efforts were taken to push the development of new traceability approaches. For example, the final report of the Indisputable Key Project [19] promotes the usage of Radio Frequency Identification transponders to establish log traceability.

First investigations on the hypothesis that logs are separate entities on the basis of biometric log characteristics were carried out in the works of [2,3,5]. For the purpose of tracking logs within the sawmill 2D and 3D scanners were utilized to extract geometric wood properties as biometric features. Such devices are not applicable for industrial usage at forest site.

On account of the fact, that log end faces show features in terms of annual rings, pith position, shape and dimension it is assumed that CS-Images of log ends can be used as biometric characteristic to set-up a biometric system. A first work on log biometrics using CS-Images was presented by [1] as an effort to curb poaching of trees. For this purpose, pseudo Zernike moments are computed for CS-Images captured from poached tree stumps and first results were presented for a small testset. The achieved results were quite good but the extracted features more or less rely on the cutting pattern and the shape of the CS.

By superficially comparing annual ring patterns of log ends to human fingerprints one perceives their similarity. Based on this observation, [16] investigated temporal and longitudinal variances of CS-Images of a single tree log. The authors adopted the FingerCode approach [7] to compute and compare templates from CS-Images. Furthermore, in [15] the impact of different real world CS variation types on the robustness of biometric log recognition is assessed. Although the authors draw first conclusions on the identification performance, the utilized testset is too small and the results are not convincing.

In considering the identification performance for 150 different tree logs this work demonstrates that a biometric system using log end images is suited for log tracking. Additionally to the fingerprint-based approach utilized in [15,16], this work evaluates the applicability of well-known iris recognition approaches. Furthermore, it is not clear to which extent the enhancement procedure utilized in [15,16] influences the verification and identification performance. For this purpose, all approaches are evaluated with and without enhancement. Results show, that enhancement basically is beneficial to overcome issues caused by CS variations.

Section 2 introduces the computation and matching of log templates using approaches from fingerprint and iris recognition. Subsequently, the experimental evaluation is presented in Section 3 followed by the conclusions in Section 4.

2 CS-Code Computation and Matching

An exemplary enrolment and identification scheme for log biometrics is depicted in Fig. 1. Enrolment of a tree log is performed in the forest. After a tree log is cut and processed by a harvester the log end is captured by a digital camera mounted on the harvester head. Templates of logs which are computed by

means of CS-Images are
denoted as CS-Codes.
For enrolment the com-
puted CS-Code is stored
in the database. Identification can be performed
at each stage of the log
processing chain where
an appropriate captur-
ing device is available.
Typically, identification
is required when a log
is delivered to a sawmill.

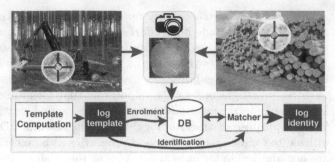

Fig. 1. Exemplary enrolment and identification schemes

Independent of the template computation approach procedure the CS-Image is
registered and enhanced preliminary. The fingerprint- and iris-based CS-Code
computation schemes are depicted in Fig. 2.

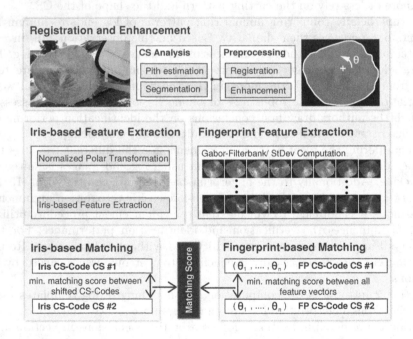

Fig. 2. Fingerprint- and iris-based template computation and matching schemes

2.1   CS Registration and Enhancement

For registration the pith position and CS boundary have to be determined in
advance. Automated approaches for pith estimation and CS segmentation were

presented in [12,18] and [17], respectively. The CS-Image is rotated around the pith position, cropped to the CS boundary box and scaled to 512 pixels in width. Rotation is performed to generate rotated versions of the input image or to align the CS to a unique rotational position.

The registered CS-Image is then utilized for the enhancement procedure. Commonly, the annual ring pattern is disturbed due to cutting and there arise different types of intraclass CS variations in real world identification scenarios [15]. The purpose of enhancement is to strengthen the annual ring pattern contrast and to compensate CS variations. Similarly to fingerprint enhancement [6], three consecutive stages are performed: Local orientation estimation, local frequency estimation and local adaptive filtering. Initially, the CS-Image is subdivided into half-overlapping blocks to reduce boundary effects caused by local filtering. On the basis of registered CS-Images which are scaled to 512 pixels in width, 32×32 pixels blocks are a good choice in terms of timing performance and capturing local annual ring pattern information.

In the first stage, the local orientation of each block is determined based on peak estimation in the Fourier Spectrum (see [18]). Next, the local orientation field is low-pass filtered with a Gaussian to correct wrong orientation estimates. Based on the orientation estimates of each block the corresponding dominant frequency in the Fourier Spectrum is determined. Therefore, the Fourier Spectrum of each block is subdivided into sub-bands and sectors and the dominating frequency is defined as the sector sub-band which shows the maximum integral of its magnitudes. If this sector sub-band does not correspond to the block orientation it is neglected and the local frequency is interpolated using a Gaussian. Finally, the Fourier Spectrum of each block is filtered with a Log-Gabor which is tuned to the block orientation and frequency. As in [16] a bandwidth of three times the variance of the Fourier Spectrum and as spread value the blocksize/4 is utilized. After filtering, the filtered spectra are inverse transformed and utilized as new block values.

In this work additionally a variant of this procedure is evaluated which differs in the local orientation estimation procedure. Initially, local orientations are computed for each block as described above. Subsequently, the pith position is used to detect wrong orientation estimates in case the angular distance between the block origin/pith position and the local orientation estimate exceeds a threshold. Thereby, the threshold for a each block is specified by $t = \lambda * log(\text{pith distance})$, where λ is an arbitrary value and the pith distance is the distance between the block origin and the pith. Thus, the threshold increases with an increasing pith distance which takes into account that annual rings close to pith are more circular. For each local orientation estimate which exceeds this threshold the estimate is replaced by the direction to the pith position. All further steps are performed like as for the first approach (exemplary enhancement results see Fig. 6).

2.2 Fingerprint-Based CS-Codes

Same as in [15,16] the FingerCode approach is adopted to compute and compare CS-Codes from CS-Images. With intent to capture different annual ring pattern frequencies the utilized Gabor filterbank is built up on six different filters and for each filter eight rotated versions are created.

CS-Code computation is performed in three stages: First, the registered and enhanced CS-Image is filtered with each filter in the filterbank. The filtered images are further subdivided into blocks (e.g. 16×16 pixels). For all blocks of each filtered image, the grey value standard deviations are computed and stored into a matrix. Values of blocks which are not within the CS border are assigned with a marker value. These markers are used to discriminate between background and CS in the matching procedure. All matrices are stored as a one-dimensional vector.

Compared to fingerprints, the rotational misalignment range of a CS-Image is not restricted to a certain range. Rotational variances are compensated by repeatedly computing features for rotated versions of the input CS-Image. All feature vectors computed for different rotations $(\Theta_1, \ldots, \Theta_n)$ compose the CS-Code of a CS-Image.

Matching Procedures. Matching between two CS-Images is performed by computing the minimum matching score (MS) between all feature vectors $(\Theta_1, \ldots, \Theta_n)$ of the CS-Codes from both CS-Images.

Three different matching procedures are evaluated to investigate the impact of including shape information. The MS is computed by:

$$MS(CS_1, CS_2) = \frac{1}{M} \sum_{i=0}^{n} D(CS_1(i), CS_2(i)) \tag{1}$$

where CS_1, CS_2 are two feature vectors of the CS-Codes which are compared, i specifies the index of the feature value in both vectors and MCS_1, MCS_2 are masks which allow to differentiate between background and CS.

The first matching procedure MS_{AP} uses a distance function which just uses feature value pairs which are in the intersection of both CSs . For normalization, M is defined by the amount of considered feature value pairs: $M = |MCS_1 \cap MCS_2|$. Thus, this procedure relies on the discriminative power of the annual ring pattern.

$$D_{AP} = \begin{cases} |CS_1(i) - CS_2(i)| & \text{if } i \in MCS_1 \cap MCS_2 \\ 0 & \text{otherwise} \end{cases} \tag{2}$$

For the second procedure $MS_{AP\&S}$ the distance function $D_{AP\&S}$ includes a penalty value $P_{AP\&S}$. The penalty is added to all feature value pairs which are in the symmetric difference of the CS masks and for normalization $M = |MCS_1 \cup MCS_2|$ is used. Hence, the MS increases for differently shaped CSs. $P_{AP\&S}$ is defined by the mean value of the feature value distributions of both feature vectors.

$$D_{AP\&S} = \begin{cases} |CS_1(i) - CS_2(i)| + P_{AP\&S} & \text{if } i \in MCS_1 \triangle MCS_2 \\ |CS_1(i) - CS_2(i)| & \text{if } i \in MCS_1 \cap MCS_2 \\ 0 & \text{otherwise} \end{cases} \tag{3}$$

Finally, the third procedure uses score level fusion of the MS_{AP} score and the False Negative Rate (F) which is computed for (MCS_1, MCS_2). F is defined as the ratio between the symmetric difference of the two masks and total amount of pixels in the smaller mask. For score level fusion MS_{AP} and F are normalized using the factors σ_{AP}, σ_F. They are precomputed based on the feature value ranges of MS_{AP} and F so that they become equally weighted in the score level fusion.

$$F = \frac{MCS_1 \triangle MCS_2}{\min(|MCS_1|, |MCS_2|)}, \quad MS_{AP,F} = MS_{AP} \cdot \sigma_{AP} + F \cdot \sigma_F \qquad (4)$$

2.3   Iris-Based CS-Codes

The pith of a cross-section is a unique feature which can be used as reference point. In combination with the CS border it is used to polar transform CS-Images. In this work polar transformed CS-Images are treated like polar iris images and it is evaluated if iris feature extractors and comparators are applicable for log biometrics.

For this purpose, the registered and enhanced CS-Image is transformed by using bi-cubic interpolation. For normalization each pixel in the polar image is stretched according to the max. pith to border radius. Two different formats for the polar-transformation are evaluated. The first is equal to the usual format demanded by many iris feature extractors: 512×64 pixels. Compared to the size of the iris, CSs are larger and the transformation is not restricted to an annular shaped ring. In case of more than 64 annual rings the common polar transformation format of 512×64 pixels causes a loss of information. Because of that and the quadratic format of the registered CS-Images, in addition a format of

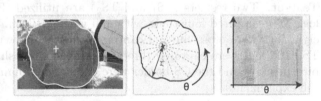

Fig. 3. CS-Image polar transformation scheme

512×512 pixels is evaluated. The polar transformation scheme is depicted in Fig. 3 and exemplary polar transformed CS-Images for both formats are shown in Fig. 6. For iris recognition based CS-Code computation and template matching the USIT package [14] is utilized.

3   Experiments

In the experiments the verification and identification performances for different configurations are assessed. Introductory, the testset is outlined and the experimental setup for the utilized configurations is described (see Section 3.1). Finally, the results are presented and discussed in Section 3.2.

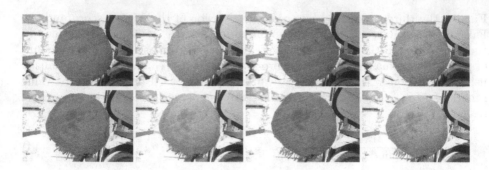

Fig. 4. Testset One (TS$_1$): Each row shows four CS-Images of a single log. The first two CS-Images illustrate the difference of capturing the log end with and without flash. The latter two images are taken after the log end was cross-cut, with and without flash.

Fig. 5. Testset Two (TS$_2$): CS-Images from 4 logs

Testset. Two testsets (TS$_1$ and TS$_2$) are utilized. For TS$_1$ 50 different tree logs were captured four times with and without flash. Additionally, the ends of eight logs were cross-cut and captured once again, with and without flash. In TS$_2$ 105 logs were captured three times without flash. For each CS-Image the pith position and the CS border were determined manually and are utilized for the experiments.

3.1 Experimental Setup

For all CS-Images of the testsets CS-Codes and MSs were computed for different configurations and enhancement procedures. Subsequently, the setup for the enhancement procedures and the different CS-Code computation approaches are outlined.

Enhancement. The first procedure, entitled as ENH$_1$, is equal to the procedure suggested in [16]. As described in Section 2.1 the second just differs in the local orientation estimation procedure and is entitled as ENH$_2$. For comparison, all configurations are additionally evaluated without enhancement ENH$_{NO}$. Exemplary results for ENH$_{NO}$ and ENH$_2$ are shown in Fig. 6.

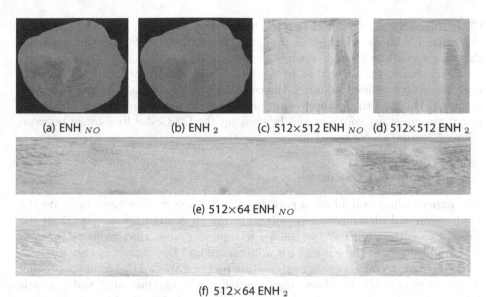

(a) ENH $_{NO}$ (b) ENH $_2$ (c) 512×512 ENH $_{NO}$ (d) 512×512 ENH $_2$

(e) 512×64 ENH $_{NO}$

(f) 512×64 ENH $_2$

Fig. 6. Illustration of the impact of enhancement for CS-Image #2 - TS$_2$. The original CS-Image is depicted in the top left image of Fig. 5.

Fingerprint (FP) Configurations. Rotational variances are compensated by computing feature vectors for rotations in the range from $-15°$ to $15°$. The CS-Codes are computed using 16×16 non-overlapping blocks and the Gabor filterbank is build up on six different filters tuned to 8 directions:

$$G(\lambda, \theta, \sigma, \gamma) = G(\lambda, \sigma) = ((1.5, 2), (2.5, 2), (3.5, 3), (4.5, 3), (5.5, 3), (6.5, 3)),$$
$$\theta = \{0, 22.5, ..., 135, 157.5\}, \gamma = 0.7$$

Iris Configurations. Different configurations based on the feature extractors and comparators provided by the USIT package [14] are utilized. Compared to iris images, the resolution of CS-Images is higher and the polar transformation is not restricted to an annular ring.

In case of 512×64 pixels we utilize the following feature extractors: lg [11], ko [8], cr [13] and qsw [9]. Except for ko which uses koc as comparator all MSs are computed using the Hamming distance (hd).

For 512×512 pixels polar CS-Images the lg algorithm was extended to formats bigger than the 512×64 in accord with the original algorithm by defining the region of interest (ROI) through a number of rows r with a height h_r. Like the original, a row is condensed into a 1-D signal which is run through the Gabor filtering process. Since it is not clear which configuration of r and h_r is best we choose to use a variance of combinations, including combinations where the ROI does not span the whole polar-transformed CS-Image. However, unlike the iris biometry case which excludes the outer iris boundary, which frequently exhibits occlusions by cilia, we choose to exclude the inner residual part of the polar

CS-Image. This part consists of a low number of pixels which are stretched to the polar CS-Image width, thus providing nearly no usable information. Note that the size of the feature vector is dependent on h_r.

Furthermore the algorithm by Ko et al. was simply adopted by allowing bigger textures without adapting the cell-size which is averaged. Note that as a result the length of the feature vector increases with the size of the texture. Rotational variances are compensated by shifting the CS-Codes in a range between -7 to 7 feature vector positions.

3.2   Results and Discussion

The experimental evaluation is performed in two stages. First, we evaluate the verification and identification performance for all configurations. Based on the Equal Error Rates (EERs) and Rank 1 recognition rates conclusions on the general applicability of the FP and iris approaches and the impact of enhancement are presented. Second, a closer examination on the intra- and interclass matching score distribution (SD) subsets points out how the enhancement and CS variations affect the intra- & interclass separability and thus the biometric system performance. Note that the intra- and interclass SDs correspond to the genuine and impostor distributions in biometrics [10].

Verification Performance Evaluation. The EERs for all configurations computed for TS_1 and TS_2 are depicted in Table 1. Most important for this work, most of the EERs are quite low and show a high degree of separability between the intra- and interclass SD for a large set of tree logs. Same as in [15] the EERs of the FP configurations show that shape information improves the verification performance.

Except MS_{AP}, all other configurations include shape information in some way, e.g. the polar transformation relies on the CS boundary. Basi-

Table 1. EERs [%] for the FP and iris configurations

Configuration		ENH_{NO}	ENH_1	ENH_2
FP	MS_{AP}	15.7	1.7	0.9
	$MS_{AP\&S}$	1.85	0.74	0.68
	$MS_{AP,F}$	1.53	0.37	0.17
IRIS 512x512	$lg, hd(16/32)$	0.21	0.68	0.82
	$lg, hd(50/10)$	0.16	0.72	0.32
	$lg, hd(64/08)$	0.16	0.76	0.51
	ko, koc	2.73	4.88	4.24
IRIS 512x64	cr, hd	5.27	3.41	4.97
	lg, hd	1.34	3.64	5.42
	qsw, hd	3.44	5.73	8.33
	ko, koc	4.95	8.09	7.35

cally, the results for MS_{AP} show the discriminative power of the annual ring pattern solely and it is very amazing that MS_{AP} and ENH_2 achieves an EER of 0.9%.

As expected, the utilized enhancement procedures improve the EERs of all FP configurations. Furthermore, the results of the FP configurations show that ENH_2 leads to better EERs than ENH_1.

For the iris configurations enhancement does not improve the EERs. This is very likely caused by the block artefacts of the enhancement procedures which are carried to the polar CS-Images. The best EERs for the iris configurations are reached using lg as feature extractor. Furthermore, the different variations for lg in terms of number of rows and row height $lg, hd(r \ / \ h_r)$ show that an increasing number of rows improves the verification performance. Overall configurations the best EERs are achieved using $lg, hd(50,10)$ and $lg, hd(64,08)$. Although $lg, hd(50,10)$ ignores 12 pixel of each image the results are equal to the second configuration. Regarding the two different polar transformation formats, the results show that the larger format improves the EERs for the feature extractors which are assessed for both formats (lg and ko).

In Fig. 7 the intra- and interclass SDs for selected FP and iris configurations are depicted in the first and second row, respectively. These charts point out a significant difference which is not recognizable when considering just the EERs. Basically, they illustrate that the intra- and interclass SDs of the depicted FP and iris configurations are statistically significantly different.

For the FP configurations the charts for the three different matching procedures (ENH$_{NO}$) illustrate that by including shape information the separability is improved. Compared to the FP configurations, the interclass SDs of the iris configurations show a low variance and are thus narrow shaped. On the other hand, the intraclass SDs show a high variance and are broad shaped. Thereby, an increasing number of rows enforces this observation and the separability increases.

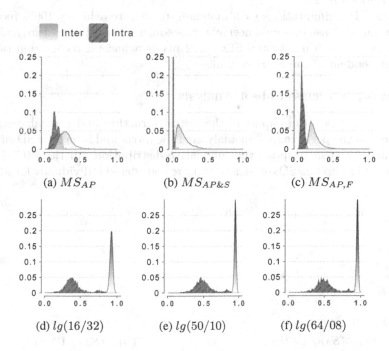

(a) MS_{AP}

(b) $MS_{AP\&S}$

(c) $MS_{AP,F}$

(d) $lg(16/32)$

(e) $lg(50/10)$

(f) $lg(64/08)$

Fig. 7. Intra-, Interclass SDs for selected FP and Iris configurations (ENH$_{NO}$). [X-Axis: Matching Score, Y-Axis: Probability]

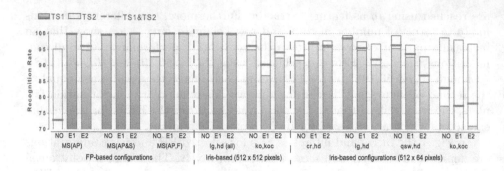

Fig. 8. Identification performance evaluation - Rank 1 detection rates.

3.3 Identification Performance Evaluation

An overview on the identification performance is depicted in Fig. 8. For each configuration, the Rank 1 recognition rates are given for TS_1, TS_2 and for the combination of both (TS_1 & TS_2). Results show, that the recognition rates for TS_1 are lower than for TS_2. The total recognition rate for TS_1 & TS_2 is somewhere in-between. The lower rates for TS_1 are caused by the higher degree of CS-variations in TS_1.

For the FP configurations each matching procedure achieves 100% recognition rate for at least one enhancement procedure. Surprisingly, nearly all iris configurations which use lg and 512×512 pixels achieve a recognition rate of 100% independent of the enhancement.

3.4 Intra-, Interclass Subset Analysis

In order to illustrate the impact of the testset structure and the enhancement procedures on the performance an analysis of the intra- and interclass SD subsets is presented. For this purpose, the cumulative distribution functions (CDFs) of the intra- and interclass SDs of each testset are considered individually for MS_{AP}

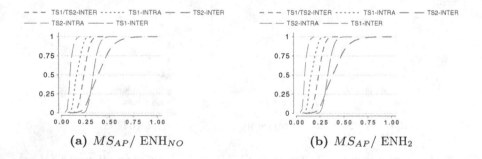

Fig. 9. CDFs for the intra-/ interclass SD subsets of two selected configurations. [X-Axis: Matching Score, Y-Axis: Probability]

(without and with enhancement). The intraclass CDFs in Fig. 9a illustrate that the intraclass MSs of TS_1 are inferior than those from TS_2. Thereby, Fig. 9b shows that ENH_2 reduces this difference and the intraclass CDFs get closer and shift to the left. Although the interclass CDFs also shift slightly to the left the overlap between the intra- and interclass CDFs decreases and thus the performance is improved. The inferior intraclass MSs of TS_1 are caused by CS variations included in TS_1.

The CDFs for all intraclass SD subsets of TS_1 computed with $MS_{AP}/$ ENH_{NO} are shown in Fig. 10. As expected, the CS-Images captured with and without flash (F, NF) are quite similar to each other. Furthermore, CS-Images of CSs captured with flash (F) are more similar to each other than those captured without flash (NF).

MSs computed between CS-Images captured without and those with flash (NF-F) show up inferior MSs. Finally, and as investigated in [15,16] the chart illustrates the impact of cross-cutting the log end on the performance. Matching scores computed between the initial log end CS-Images and the cross-cut log end CS-Images are shown in the subsets: F-CF, F-CNF, NF-CF and NF-CNF. Fig. 10 illustrates that these subsets show inferior MSs compared to the other subsets.

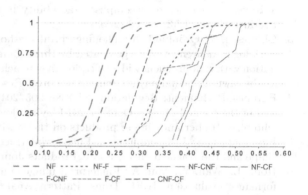

Fig. 10. Intraclass SD Subset Analysis for TS_1. NF = No Flash, F = Flash, CNF = Cut No Flash, CF = Cut Flash. [X-Axis: Matching Score, Y-Axis: Probability]

4   Conclusions

This work demonstrates that FP and iris recognition based approaches can be successfully transferred to the field of wood log tracking. Based on the variety of 155 logs the results are a first indication for the applicability of log biometrics to log identification.

In case of the FP recognition based approach the best results were achieved by including shape information in the matching procedure $MS_{AP,F}$. Furthermore, the results show that the performance of the FP configurations is significantly improved by the enhancement procedures. For the iris recognition based approaches the best results were achieved using lg features and hd as comparator. Thereby, a larger format and an increasing number of rows for the feature extraction is beneficial for the performance.

In the identification performance experiments the FP based approach and all iris configurations which use lg and 512×512 pixels achieve 100% detection rate at Rank 1. It can be concluded that Gabor features are well suited to extract discriminative annual ring pattern features.

Future research should deal with the impact of automated pith estimation and CS segmentation on the biometric system performance.

References

1. Barrett, W.: Biometrics of cut tree faces. In: Sobh, T. (ed.) Advances in Computer and Information Sciences and Engineering, pp. 562–565. Springer, Netherlands (2008)
2. Chiorescu, S., Grönlund, A.: The fingerprint approach: using data generated by a 2-axis log scanner to accomplish traceability in the sawmill's log yard. Forest Products Journal **53**, 78–86 (2003)
3. Chiorescu, S., Grönlund, A.: The fingerprint method: Using over-bark and under-bark log measurement data generated by three-dimensional log scanners in combination with radiofrequency identification tags to achieve traceability in the log yard at the sawmill. Scandinavian Journal of Forest Research **19**(4), 374–383 (2004)
4. EuropeanParliament: Regulation (EU) No 995/2010 of the European Parliament and of the council of 20th October 2010 laying down the obligations of operators who place timber and timber products on the market (2010)
5. Flodin, J., Oja, J., Grönlund, A.: Fingerprint traceability of logs using the outer shape and the tracheid effect. Forest Products Journal **58**(4), 21–27 (2008)
6. Hong, L., Wan, Y., Jain, A.: Fingerprint image enhancement: Algorithm and performance evaluation. IEEE Trans. Pattern Anal. Mach. Intell. **20**(8), 777–789 (1998)
7. Jain, A.K., Prabhakar, S., Hong, L., Pankanti, S.: Filterbank-based fingerprint matching. IEEE Transactions on Image Processing **9**(5), 846–859 (2000)
8. Ko, J.G., Gil, Y.H., Yoo, J.H., Chung, K.I.: A novel and efficient feature extraction method for iris recognition. ETRI Journal **29**(3), 399–401 (2007)
9. Ma, L., Tan, T., Wang, Y., Zhang, D.: Efficient iris recognition by characterizing key local variations. IEEE Transactions on Image Processing **13**, 739–750 (2004)
10. Maltoni, D., Maio, D., Jain, A.K., Prabhakar, S.: Handbook of fingerprint recognition. Springer, New York (2009)
11. Masek, L.: Recognition of Human Iris Patterns for Biometric Identification, Master's thesis, University of Western Australia (2003)
12. Norell, K., Borgefors, G.: Estimation of pith position in untreated log ends in sawmill environments. Computers and Electronics in Agriculture **63**(2), 155–167 (2008)
13. Rathgeb, C., Uhl, A.: Secure Iris Recognition Based on Local Intensity Variations. In: Campilho, A., Kamel, M. (eds.) ICIAR 2010, Part II. LNCS, vol. 6112, pp. 266–275. Springer, Heidelberg (2010)
14. Rathgeb, C., Uhl, A., Wild, P.: Iris Recognition: From Segmentation to Template Security, Advances in Information Security, vol. 59. Springer (2013)
15. Schraml, R., Charwat-Pessler, J., Petutschnigg, A., Uhl, A.: Robustness of biometric wood log traceability using digital log end images. Tech. rep., University of Salzburg (2014)

16. Schraml, R., Charwat-Pessler, J., Uhl, A.: Temporal and longitudinal variances in wood log cross-section image analysis. In: IEEE International Conference on Image Processing 2014 (ICIP 2014), Paris, FR (October 2014)
17. Schraml, R., Uhl, A.: Similarity Based Cross-Section Segmentation in Rough Log End Images. In: Iliadis, L. (ed.) AIAI 2014. IFIP AICT, vol. 436, pp. 614–623. Springer, Heidelberg (2014)
18. Schraml, R., Uhl, A.: Pith estimation on rough log end images using local Fourier spectrum analysis. In: Proceedings of the 14th Conference on Computer Graphics and Imaging (CGIM 2013), Innsbruck, AUT (February 2013)
19. Uusijärvi, R.: Indisputable key project. http://interop-vlab.eu/ei_public_deliverables/indisputable-key (2010) (last accessed: July 28, 2011)
20. Wayman, J., Jain, A., Maltoni, D.: Biometric Systems. Springer, Heidelberg (2005)

Detecting Human Falls: A Vision-FSM Approach

Roger Trullo[1]([✉]) and Duber Martinez[2]

[1] Laboratoire d'Informatique, Université F. Rabelais de Tours, Tours, France
roger.trulloramirez@univ-tours.fr
[2] Perception and Intelligent Systems, Universidad del Valle, Cali, Colombia
duber.martinez@correounivalle.edu.co

Abstract. In this paper, we present a computer vision based system able to detect human falls. We show in detail all the stages of our system and the considerations taken for the provided results. We propose a simple scheme for detection and tracking followed by a Finite State Machine (FSM). The proposed system presents a good performance under different environment conditions.

1 Introduction

The human falls are one of the main risks in elderly people who stay alone during a great part of time. According to [1] approximately one third of older adults over the age of 75 who live in houses present falls every year. In [2] it is mentioned that although much of the falls do not result in serious injures, 47% of these people cannot get up without assistance after such an event. On the other hand, the injures related to falls have shown to be one of the five more common causes of death in elderly people [3].

The majority of this kind of accidents take place in interior environments such as homes or offices. The systems for monitoring these environments play a key role in the opportune detection of these emergencies.

Currently there are different kind of devices or ways to detect these accidents like wearable devices; some are automatic and others require user activation [1].

For fall detection it has been used acoustic sensors trying to detect abrupt changes in the environment. In [4] for example it is shown a system based on a set up of microphones in the space and, by means of audio processing, they identify the possible occurrence of a fall.

The most used sensors however have been wearable accelerometers which detect abrupt changes in the position in the space and with this information determine if a fall has occurred [5].

This kind of devices have shown to be very precise in the detection of falls; however they result to be uncomfortable for the user who can even forget to wear it. This is one of the reasons why several computer vision researchers have studied this topic and the results obtained are very promising.

In [3] GMM (Gaussian Mixture Model) is used for human detection by background subtraction. They compute parameters like aspect ratio, the angle of the

G. Azzopardi and N. Petkov (Eds.): CAIP 2015, Part I, LNCS 9256, pp. 766–777, 2015.
DOI: 10.1007/978-3-319-23192-1_64

centroid with respect to the horizontal axis and gradients magnitudes. This data is compared with several thresholds in order to detect a fall.

In [6] the fall detection is worked by means of High Definition IP cameras using 4G wireless technology and H.264 compress video for better use of the bandwidth. In this work the movement is detected using the difference of intensities between consecutive frames and creating a movement history image. They fit an ellipse for the detected objects and compute the standard deviation of their eccentricity, orientation angle and position of the centroid. The system detects a fall if these parameters are above some thresholds followed by a very small movement detection.

In [7] the detection is inferred by the change in the human silhouette; since during a fall, the shape of the detected person changes very quickly and during normal activities its change is slow. In order to accomplish the detection, they represent the person with only three points obtained by dividing region of the person's contour by three (on the y axis) and computing the centroid of each sub-region. Based on this information they determine two lines between the superior and inferior point towards the central point, which are used to compute the orientation angle with respect to the horizontal axis of the image. With the information of the changes in these variables followed by absence of movement during some defined time, they can detect a possible fall.

In this work, we present the development of an automatic vision system for detecting and alerting emergency situations manifested by falls.

The first stage of the proposed system is the automatic extraction of objects of interest from the background; in this case we model the background using a codebook representation. The second component makes a filtering of contours trying to eliminate objects with low chances of being a person. In the next step we proceed to determine if a given contour belongs to a person based on shape and color criteria. Once a contour is accepted as a person, we perform a simple tracking in order to have information about his movement and use coherence information between frames. The last stage of the system detects the fall by means of a Finite State Machine (FSM) and an alarm is generated.

The main contribution of this paper is the proposal of a simple FSM, based on changes in the slope of the line formed by joining the centroid positions of the person's contour in consecutive frames, to detect a fall. The proposed system presents good results as it will be shown in section III.

2   System Design

This work was developed using C++ with OpenCV library for image processing. The proposed system has 6 main blocks: background subtraction; contour filtering; people identification; tracking; fall detection and an alarm block. In Fig. 1 it is possible to see the general scheme of the system.

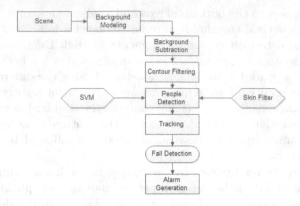

Fig. 1. System Diagram

2.1   Modeling and Background Subtraction

The background modeling is done using the codebooks technique [8] which is an extension of the work presented in [9]. This technique presents better results than a Gaussian modeling since it creates several simple models that allow to represent scenes with typical moving objects in homes like fans or curtains. The technique basically consists in build a model of the background from a long observation sequence. For each pixel a codebook is built and this is conformed by one or more codewords. Each codeword is basically a structure with a superior and inferior limit of intensity values. These limits keep growing as new observations lie inside or close to these limits; and for samples away, new codewords are created. Empirically we obtained better results by using YUV color space instead of RGB or HSV. The model of the scene was created from 300 frames. In order to determine if a pixel belongs to the background it must hold that its intensity value for each of the channels be inside the superior and inferior limits of any of the codewords belonging to that pixel. In Fig. 2 is shown the result of background subtraction using the technique.

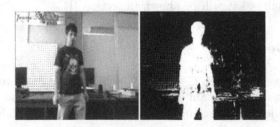

Fig. 2. Background subtraction result

2.2   Contours Filtering

In Fig. 2 is possible to see that the resulting image presents noise level relatively high. In order to improve this, we apply opening and closing morphological operations. Then the contours are found by polygonal approximation and they are filtered by perimeter $i.e.$ the contours with a perimeter value lower than some threshold are eliminated. In Fig. 3 is possible to see the result of this operation.

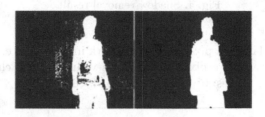

Fig. 3. Contours filtering result

On the other hand, the shadows in an image reduce the throughput of several computer vision algorithms. The elimination of the shadows is then a very important step. In this case for example, the contour of the person could appear much larger than its real size since the shadow was detected as belonging to the contour. In order to try to eliminate the shadows we used the technique presented in [10] where the following equation is presented:

$$SP_t(x,y) = \begin{cases} 1 \text{ if } \alpha \leq \frac{I_t^V}{B_t^V} \leq \beta \\ \quad \wedge \ |I_t^S(x,y) - B_t^S(x,y)| \leq \tau_S \\ \quad \wedge \ |I_t^H(x,y) - B_t^H(x,y)| \leq \tau_H \\ 0 \text{ other case} \end{cases} \tag{1}$$

Where B is the background image, I is the image with the foreground object, the super indexes V and S make reference to the channels V and S of the transformation to the HSV color space, and the sub index t is the current time. The thresholds α, β, τ_S and τ_H are found experimentally and in this case we used values of 0.4, 1, 25 and 20 respectively. In Fig. 4 is shown the result after applying the mentioned technique.

2.3   People Detection

For determining if a given contour belongs to a person, we use two criteria; the contour must have a percentage of skin color pixels over some threshold and the contour must have an omega (Ω) shape.

Fig. 4. Shadow removal result

Skin Filter. To classify a pixel as skin we work in HSV space. From the study presented in [11] we take a pixel as skin if its values for the channels H and S are in the following ranges: $0° <H< 50°$, $0.23<S<0.58$.

Shape Identification. The binary image is cropped by the third part from top to down in order to catch the omega shape formed by the head and shoulders of a person. To this sub image we compute 30 Fourier descriptors [12] which are used as feature vector. In Fig. 5a is shown one of these contours.

For the classification of a contour as a person we used a SVM [13]. In this case we used 518 images of contours of persons that were extracted manually as training set for the positive class. For the negative class we used 376 non person images like objects and noise images obtained by illumination problems. Each sample was represented by 30 Fourier descriptors as stated above. We used a Gaussian Kernel with a unit C value and $\gamma = 0.5$. The parameters were tuned by using cross validation over a coarse-grid search. In the Fig. 5b is shown the the detection of a person with the exposed method.

(a)

(b)

Fig. 5. Shape Identification (a) Omega shape of a person's contour. (b) Detection result.

2.4 Tracking

The tracking stage is very important since it is in charge of monitoring the movement of the person. In this work we use the centroid coordinates information. The tracking scheme is very simple and is based on checking the distance of the current and previous position of the centroid; if the value is lower than some threshold we assign it as belonging to the same person. The threshold was defined to be 10% of the average size of the frame; that is, for a 640x480 image the value is set to 56 pixels.If the value is above the threshold it is assumed that the detection is not correct; otherwise the system continues to the fall detection step. The proposed tracking would only work for one person and with no occlusions; however a fall detection system aims to help people living alone and this would be a valid consideration.

2.5   Fall Detection

For the fall detection we made a series of observations in test videos to the position of the centroid of the object in the y axis and the changes in the slope of the line formed by joining the y centroid positions of the person's contour in consecutive frames; trying to identify a pattern which characterizes different actions of the person like everyday activities and in particular eventual falls. In Fig. 6 we show some of the images obtained from the videos which were used to determine the thresholds that were used in the system.

Fig. 6. Everyday Activities

In Fig. 7 we show the changes in the centroid position in the y axis for situations that are considered as normal and don't require an alarm. In this case there are three behaviors shown as squares. The first one represents a regular walk from a person entering by the inferior part of the image and going away from the camera. The second square represents a person walking while holding the same depth. Finally the third square represents a person sitting down and remaining like that in the scene.

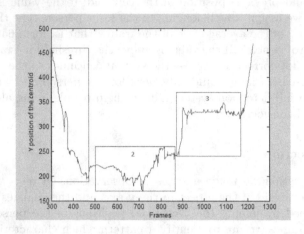

Fig. 7. y axis change of the centroid position of a person doing everyday activities

In Fig. 8a on the other hand is shown the position change during a fall(inside the rectangle). It is worth to notice that during the fall there is a characteristic profile with an abrupt change followed by an almost constant value.

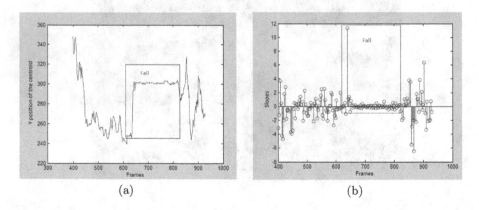

Fig. 8. An example during a fall (a) y axis change of the centroid position. (b) slope values.

Based on this observations, one can conclude that the slope of the line formed by subsequent centroid positions is a value that can characterize the falls. In Fig. 8b we show an example of different slope values; the rectangle indicates the values during a fall. It is also important to notice that this framework is dependent of the point of view of the camera. One possible solution to overcome this situation, is to have several cameras with different points of views and take into consideration the x axis as needed.

For the fall detection in this work, we propose as solution a Finite State Machine (FSM) since these kind of events present a sequence almost defined; that is, it presents a big change in the slope, followed by small variations in this value. For the design of the FSM we analyzed different sequence videos with different activities and defined empirical thresholds which worked under different conditions.

Finite State Machine. The proposed FSM is based on the slope of the position in the centroid of the detected contour. In general terms, the FSM determines a fall event if it detects a big slope value followed by very small changes; which may represent a person laying down in the ground. We define then experimentally a *threshold1* for the big change in the position, a *thereshold2* representing a person with a very small movement (probably laying down on the ground) and a minimum number of samples (*minzeros*) before activating the alarm confirming the fall. In Fig. 9 we show the FSM of the system.

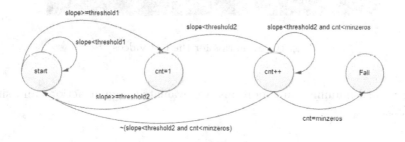

Fig. 9. FSM for fall detection

3   Experimental Results

The proposed method was tested in two scenes where there was objects with small movements like fans, and two types of illumination: normal and low; in the normal illumination the four lamps available of the room were on, and in the low, only half of them were on. This with the aim of testing the ability of the system to model real environments.

The test videos contain people making regular activities like walking, sitting and picking up objects; this with the aim of quantify the false positive rate of the system. On the other hand, the videos also contain falls, which vary in the angle with respect to the camera, in order to determine the true positive rate.

We made different tests where we have simulated falls with different positions and angles. For security reasons for obtaining simulated falls close to real ones, we used a mattress to absorb the shocks.

We defined a protocol to follow consisting in that each individual would appear in three videos, the first containing regular activities. The second, containing 8 simulated falls from different angles and distances. To achieve this the person should simulate the falls from the four sides and the four corners of the mattress. The third video was recorded with low illumination and the person simulated two falls in random positions. The scenarios are shown in the figure 10.

Fig. 10. Scenarios for the test videos

For normal illumination conditions, we evaluated regular actions and simulated falls:

3.1 Regular Activities

In order to determine the ability of the system to avoid false positives, we tested 16 sequences for 16 individuals; 9 in the scenario 1 and 7 in the scenario 2. The system presented a good performance to fast walks, reposing and picking up objects. There was not any false detection for these actions. The true negative rate obtained was 96%. All of the false positives were caused for sitting up actions, since they generate slope profiles quite similar to the falls.

3.2 Falls Simulation

The objective of this test is to determine the ability of the system to detect effectively falls situations. We tested the same number of sequences of the previous experiment with normal illumination. The number of falls per person was 8 (4 sides and 4 corners of the mattress). In Fig. 11 we show two frames of the sequences to appreciate the positions of the camera and the mattress in both scenarios.

Fig. 11. Captures of the falls sequences

In the table 1 we present the results obtained when testing the system with regular actions and simulated falls under normal illumination conditions. We compute accuracy, specificity and sensitivity.

Table 1. Results under normal illumination conditions

	Fall Accident		Accuracy	Sensitivity	Specificity
System Judgement	True	False	83,42%	75,81%	96%
Positive	94	3			
Negative	30	72			

For low illumination conditions, we evaluated falls simulations; in this case, each person simulated two falls from different angles, giving a total of 32 events. The system showed a true positive rate of 71.87%. In Fig. 12 it is shown the difference between the scene with normal illumination and the scene with low illumination.

Fig. 12. Scene under the different types of illumination

In the Table 2 we present the global results obtained, taking into account all the experiments done; that is, including normal and low illumination.

Table 2. Global results of the system

	Fall Accident		Accuracy	Sensibility	Specificity
System Judgement	True	False	81,82%	75%	96%
Positive	117	3			
Negative	39	72			

The system under normal conditions of illumination presented an accuracy of 83.42%, sensitivity of 75.81% and a specificity of 96%; if we take into account the results obtained under low illumination conditions, the system has an accuracy of 81.82%, sensitivity of 75% and a specificity of 96%, which shows that the system has a good performance in detecting and alerting falls, under different environments and illumination conditions.

4   Conclusion

In this work we have presented an automatic vision system for fall detection. For people detection we use a simple background subtraction method, color information and a SVM classifier for shape detection using Fourier descriptors as features. The next stage is in charge of the fall detection, and it is done by tracking the position of the person which is used by the proposed FSM. Once a fall has been detected, the system generates an alarm as emergency protocol.

The experimental results show that the system is able to detect and alert fall successfully under different environments conditions.

It is also important to notice, that the results presented take into account the whole process; that means that in certain occasions, the results were affected by problems in the detection of the person. One can expect then, that using a more sophisticated algorithm to detect the person, the results will improve considerably.

References

1. Willems, J., Debard, G., Bonroy, B., Vanrumste, B., Goedeme, T.: How to detect human fall in video? an overview. In: Positioning and Context-Awareness International Conference, POCA 2009, Brussels, Belgium (2009)
2. Yu, M., Yu, Y., Rhuma, A., Naqvi, S., Wang, L., Chambers, J.: An online one class support vector machine-based person-specific fall detection system for monitoring an elderly individual in a room environment. IEEE Journal of Biomedical and Health Informatics **17**, 1002–1014 (2013)
3. Vishwakarma, V., Mandal, C., Sural, S.: Automatic Detection of Human Fall in Video. In: Ghosh, A., De, R.K., Pal, S.K. (eds.) PReMI 2007. LNCS, vol. 4815, pp. 616–623. Springer, Heidelberg (2007)

4. Zhuang, X., Huang, J., Potamianos, G., Hasegawa-Johnson, M.: Acoustic fall detection using gaussian mixture models and gmm supervectors. In: IEEE International Conference on Acoustics, Speech and Signal Processing, ICASSP 2009, pp. 69–72 (2009)
5. Lindemann, U., Hock, A., Stuber, M., Keck, W., Becker, C.: Evaluation of a fall detector based on accelerometers: A pilot study. Medical and Biological Engineering and Computing **43**, 548–551 (2005)
6. Nair, R., Bing, B.: Intelligent activity detection techniques for advanced hd video surveillance systems. In: 2010 IEEE Sarnoff Symposium, pp. 1–5 (2010)
7. Chua, J.L., Chang, Y.C., Lim, W.K.: Intelligent visual based fall detection technique for home surveillance. In: 2012 International Symposium on Computer, Consumer and Control (IS3C), pp. 183–187 (2012)
8. Bradski, G., Kaehler, A.: Learning OpenCV: Computer Vision in C++ with the OpenCV Library. 2nd edn. O'Reilly Media, Inc. (2013)
9. Kim, K., Chalidabhongse, T.H., Harwood, D., Davis, L.: Real-time foreground-background segmentation using codebook model. Real-Time Imaging **11**, 172–185 (2005)
10. Cucchiara, R., Grana, C., Piccardi, M., Prati, A.: Detecting objects, shadows and ghosts in video streams by exploiting color and motion information. In: Proceedings of the 11th International Conference on Image Analysis and Processing, pp. 360–365 (2001)
11. Phung, S., Bouzerdoum, A., Chai, D.S.: Skin segmentation using color pixel classification: analysis and comparison. IEEE Transactions on Pattern Analysis and Machine Intelligence 27, 148–154 (2005)
12. Zahn, C.T., Roskies, R.Z.: Fourier descriptors for plane closed curves. IEEE Transactions on Computers C-21, 269–281 (1972)
13. Cristianini, N., Shawe-Taylor, J.: An Introduction to Support Vector Machines: And Other Kernel-based Learning Methods. Cambridge University Press, New York (2000)

Trademark Image Retrieval Using Inverse Total Feature Frequency and Multiple Detectors

Minoru Mori[✉], Xiaomeng Wu, and Kunio Kashino

NTT Communication Science Laboratories, NTT Corporation, Tokyo, Japan
mori.minoru@lab.ntt.co.jp

Abstract. Conventional similar trademark search methods have mainly handled only binary images and measured similarities globally between trademark images. Recent image retrieval methods using the bag-of-visual-words strategy can deal with the same object detection on the some various conditions like image size variation but cannot well handle vague similarity for simple shape objects in particular. However the real task for screening trademark images demands several image retrieval functions such as simultaneous validation of global and local similarities. In this paper we describe more effective methods for managing trademark image screening. Our method is twofold; One is a combination of multiple detectors for more various shape description and the other is an inverse total feature frequency that reflects extracted feature number for weighting each visual word more effectively in the bag-of-visual words strategy. Experiments with real trademark images show that our proposed method achieves higher accuracies than conventional methods.

Keywords: Trademark · Image retrieval · Multiple detectors · Feature frequency · IDF

1 Introduction

To acquire and protect intellectual property rights is becoming more important for many companies internationally, because intellectual property rights are one of keys to the business competitiveness. The applications of several intellectual properties such as patents or trademarks are gradually increasing and the officer of intellectual properties has to manage a lot of applications more promptly and precisely. These years all the information of intellectual properties are handled as digital information and several technologies such as text retrieval are, therefore, often applied for reducing costs and processing time. For managing trademark images, image retrieval techniques have been proposed [5,7–9,20]. Conventional trademark retrieval methods mainly handle binary images and validate global similarity between a query image and registered ones in database. The approach that compares images globally is not clearly enough to validate the acceptance possibility of the application. The reason is that examiners for trademark screening mainly take two viewpoints for similarity measures between images; global similarity and local one as the comparison between

© Springer International Publishing Switzerland 2015
G. Azzopardi and N. Petkov (Eds.): CAIP 2015, Part I, LNCS 9256, pp. 778–789, 2015.
DOI: 10.1007/978-3-319-23192-1_65

parts of images. Recently many image retrieval methods based on bag-of-visual-words (BoVW) technique using local key point detectors and descriptors have been proposed [2,3,10,13,14,17]. These methods enable to compare a part of a query image to a part of the registered one and detect almost same parts between images successfully, even if parts between images have different size or are rotated.

However a real task of the trademark screening is more complicated than our thought. The image retrieval for the trademark screening has different viewpoints from ordinary image retrieval researches. One is to detect not only same marks or objects but also similar ones. Similar trademarks that may cause consumers' confusion should not be registered. Therefore not only almost same images but also vaguely similar ones need to be detected. Second is that a part of interest in a query image is unclear. Examiners usually don't know which part is similar to a part of a registered image or a whole registered one. Therefore the region of interest cannot be designated in advance and size variation between parts or images or interest is sometimes very large. Third is to neglect colors but to feature shapes. The main viewpoint about similarity is based on shape. Therefore the image retrieval based on BoVW using a single detector cannot be simply applied to this task, because such methods cannot well handle vague global similarity or subtle local similarity. Figure 1 shows an example of a query image and its corresponding registered images selected by the examiners as correct results.

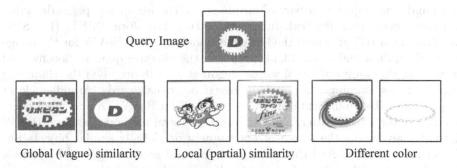

Fig. 1. Example of image pair with various similarities. Note the letter gDh and the gear-like pattern in the query. These parts are contained in the registered image on some level. Therefore all of these registered images have to be treated as correct answers.

In this paper, we propose practical approaches that satisfy conditions mentioned above and achieve higher retrieval accuracies for improving the trademark screening task. Our proposed method is twofold; One is the combination of global and local similarity measurement using multiple key point detectors. The other is an improved weighing method based on feature frequency for expressing the importance of each visual word more effectively. Experiments using trademark images show that our proposed methods provide higher search accuracies than conventional methods. The rest of this paper is organized as follows; Section 2 gives related works on trademark image retrieval and recent image retrieval methods. Section 3 describes the details of our proposed methods. Experimental results are explained and discussed in Section 4. Section 5 concludes this paper and lists future works.

2 Related Works

As mentioned in section 1, many methods have been proposed for tackling the trademark image retrieval task, e.g. [5,7–9,20]. Chen et al. [5] utilized the region orientation information entropy. Hussain and Eakins [9] exploited the topological properties of the self-organizing map. Hung et al. [8] or Wei et al. [20] treated not only global shape similarity of the contour but also interior structure difference by using features inside a trademark image. Huang et al. [7] separated an image into some components and described the shape of each part. Though conventional methods have achieved high search accuracies in their report, many of them can handle only the global shape similarity of binary images. But a lot of real trademark images consist of gray-scaled or colored part(s) and merged (no separated) parts. Therefore their methods cannot be applied to screening of such trademark images.

These ten years image retrieval methods using BoVW methodology have been proposed, e.g. [2,3,10,13,14,17], and archived good performance for the image retrieval mainly on natural scene images. These methods based on BoVW well handle an object as a part of an image by the use of key point detectors and local descriptors like Scale-Invariant Feature Transform (SIFT) [11]. Sivic and Zisserman [17] presented the basic methodology using BoVW for the image retrieval. Philbin and et al. [13,14] proposed the effective quantization method to enhance the ability of visual words. Jegou et al. [10] proposed the Hamming embedding for refining the matching based on visual words. Arandjelovic et al. presented the fundamental improved method on BoVW [2] and more effective descriptors [3]. However, many of image retrieval methods based on BoVW virtually can handle the search of not vaguely or globally similar objects but almost same objects. And they often treat natural scene images with complex structures in which enough features to describe characteristics of images can be extracted. Therefore these methods often cannot deal with the retrieval of trademark images; Some of query images and registered ones are simple-shaped and the search function needs to retrieve vaguely and globally similar images to a query image.

3 Proposed Method

3.1 Multiple Detectors for Measuring Both of Global and Local Similarities

As mentioned above, the image retrieval method for trademark screening needs to detect not only images globally similar to a query image but also images that are locally similar to a query one. Though image retrieval methods based on BoVW usually can deal with local part similarity, vague and global similarity between images are not necessarily handled well. And, contrary to natural scene images that are often used for image retrieval researchers, trademark images often consist of part(s) with simple shape. Therefore key point detectors like SIFT, which are often used for local descriptors, are not sometimes able to detect enough number of points to characterize each image shape when the use of single key point detector. Moreover, in trademark screening tasks, the difference between a part that is interested in a query image and a part that is interested in the registered image are often larger on image size than that in natural scene image retrieval tasks; Some interested parts in trademark images are very small and such parts cannot be detected by a usual single key point detector.

To deal with such problems, we exploit multiple key point detectors for obtaining more features. In this paper we use Difference of Gaussian (DoG) [11], Maximally Stable Extremal Regions (MSER) [12] and Accelerated KAZE (AKAZE) [1] as key point detectors mainly for local similarity measure. DoG is one of the most widely-used key point detectors. MSER better handles large scale local regions. AKAZE makes our method more robust as regards anisotropic distortions. In addition to these detectors, we also use the dense sampling as the feature detector for evaluating global similarity effectively and describing a small part in detail. We validate two methodologies using multiple detectors for tackling problems mentioned above; One is a single search path by the use of all the detector methods of each local detector and the dense sampling as early fusion. This is a simple procedure as conventional search methods using BoVW with multiple detected features. The other methodology is the combination of the search procedures using only local detectors for local similarity and that using the dense sampling for global similarity as late fusion. In the matching phase on the global similarity measure using the dense sampling for the combined search, we exploit the pyramid match kernel [6]. The pyramid match kernel allows us to compare shapes in a more relaxing and loose manner for the global similarity. This method provides higher accuracies for this task.

As the combination of several features or similarity values, the multi kernel learning (MKL) [4] has been proposed and some researches exploit this method, e.g. [19]. The usage of MKL is available only for supervised tasks where much labeled data can be provided beforehand. However, trademark image retrieval is virtually an unsupervised application because of few labeled data. Therefore, we use not MKL but another combination method. In this paper we use the order-based combination. The detailed procedure is as follows; Let r_l^p and r_g^p be the order given by the local similarity and that by the global similarity in the p-th registered image, respectively. The tentative combined order of the p-th registered image, r_c^p is given by

$$r_c^p = min(r_l^p, r_g^p) + \frac{(r_l^p + r_g^p)}{2N},$$ (1)

where N is the total number of images used in the database. By comparing orders given by local similarity and global one on an interested registered image, higher (more accurate) order is basically adopted for an interested registered image. If candidates with the same order exist, the candidate with smaller total order, $r_l^p + r_g^p$ is adopted first. This is applied to all the registered images (candidates) and the candidates are the re-ordered using each tentative combined order, r_c, for the final rank. Figure 2 depicts the two search flows of the single path and the combination.

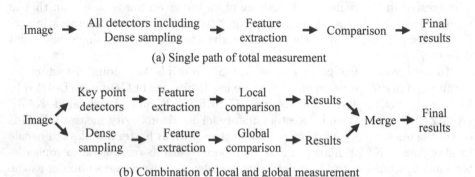

(a) Single path of total measurement

(b) Combination of local and global measurement

Fig. 2. Search flows for both of global and local similarities. (a) Single search path with all the detectors as early fusion. (b) Combination of searches for local similarity and that for global similarity as late fusion

As the feature descriptor, the SIFT descriptor [11] is used for all the kinds of the detectors including the dense sampling. Each feature is assigned to the nearest visual word (code) in the codebook built by clustering all the features extracted from all the registered images mentioned later using the k-means algorithm. And the inverted index is built by the use of all the visual words for faster search.

As the similarity measure, we exploited not the conventional cosine similarity with tf-idf but the query likelihood model [18] as the probabilistic ranking measure [15] and that is defined as follow;

$$sim(\boldsymbol{q}, \boldsymbol{r}) = \sum_k^K q_k r_k^n idf(v_k), \tag{2}$$

where, $idf(v_k)$ is Inverse Document Frequency (IDF) [16,17] for the k-th visual word v_k. $\boldsymbol{q}$ is the set of the number of the frequency of each visual word in a query image and expressed as $(q_1, q_2, \ldots, q_k, \ldots, q_K)$. $\boldsymbol{r}$, $(r_1^n, r_2^n, \ldots, r_k^n, \ldots, r_K^n)$, is the set of the existence or non-existence of each visual word in the n-th registered image in database. Therefore q_k can take any integer value more than 0 and r_k takes only 0 or 1. The conventional cosine similarity is penalized with visual words frequently extracted from the registered image and this tends to degrade search accuracies. On the other hand, the similarity value based on the query likelihood model depends on only the number of feature frequency in the query image. And each similarity value is not normalized and only the magnitude relationship among values is meaningful.

3.2   Inverse Total Feature Frequency and Thresholding

In section 3.1, we proposed the use of the multiple detectors including the dense sampling. This approach generates more number of extracted features than the conventional use of the single detector and enables to describe and characterize each image more effectively. However this tends to not only cause a lot of noisy features but also degrade the ability of IDF as the weight to strengthen the separability among images. The reason is that the conventional IDF is based on the sum of the number of images that contain an interested visual word and this number is given by summing 0 or 1 on each image. Therefore, extracting more features increases the number of images that contain an interested visual word and tends to saturate IDF values under the limited size of the codebook used. The fixed value of total number of images as the numerator used in the calculation of the IDF is also one of causes of the saturation. Moreover the little reflection of feature frequency on IDF is based on the sum of 0 or 1 given by each image that contains an interested visual word or not, and this can be regarded as one shortcoming of IDF. The reason is that an image that contains only 1 certain visual word and another image that includes a lot of same visual words are regarded as the same importance. In addition to these shortcomings of IDF, a lot of noisy features caused by the increase of feature number are becoming unable to be disregard on the calculation of similarity values and may decrease the retrieval ability because of larger similarity values caused by summing IDFs of many noisy features.

Therefore, we need to exploit not the image frequency containing each visual word but information for reflecting the importance of each visual word more effectively. In this paper we propose a new weight calculation based on the number of extracted features, called the Inverse Total Feature Frequency (ITFF). The detailed computation procedures of IDF and ITFF are described as follows; Let d_k is the number of images where the interested k-th visual word, v_k, in the size of K appears. The IDF for the k-th visual word, $idf(v_k)$, is given by

$$idf(v_k) = \log \frac{N}{d_k}. \tag{3}$$

In contrast, our ITFF based on the feature frequency, $itff(v_k)$ is defined by

$$itff(v_k) = \log \frac{\sum_n \sum_k f_k^n}{\sum_n f_k^n}, \tag{4}$$

where, f_k^n is the number of the interested k-th visual word extracted from the n-th registered image. By the use of the numerator of Eq. (4) instead of N, the proposed ITFF cannot be saturated and $\sum_n f_k^n$ can provide more variable values that reflects the feature frequency.

By our proposed ITFF, we can obtain more flexible weights that may strengthen the separability among images. However, many features, especially extracted by the dense sampling, tend to decrease the search ability even if each ITFF/IDF given by the large number of each visual word is small, because a lot of visual words with small IDF can achieve larger similarity values. To avoid such a shortcoming, we threshold ITFFs/IDFs with less values; This means that ITFFs/IDFs less than the threshold are regarded as 0 and are not used when calculating similarity values. This technique gives the possibility to not only increase the search accuracy but also decrease the search time as the side effect because of the fewer voting processes. In this paper threshold values for each method were determined in a preliminary experiment.

4   Experiments

4.1   Experimental Setup

As experimental data, we gathered Japanese trademark images. We used 100 images as query images from gathered images. And we asked experienced examiners of trademark image screening to select similar images to query images, which are to be listed as their corresponding similar trademark images as correct answers. The total number of the corresponding similar images is 314; this means that each query has averagely 3.14 correct answers. In addition to their corresponding images, we used other 5,000 images for registered database. Therefore our database consists 5,314 images with 100 query images.

Parameters used in the experiments are as follows; Each image was normalized into 512 pixels while retaining the aspect ratio. The size of the codebook is 50,000. Features using the dense sampling were extracted on every 16, 32, and 64 pixels for sub-blocks of 16×16, 32×32, and 64×64 pixels, respectively.

The recall at on the top p-th order is used as the accuracy measure for evaluating the performance of each method, because the real trademark screening task needs only higher recall rates for reducing costs and time. In this paper we validated recall rates on the top 10, 50, 100, and 500-th order.

Figure 3 shows examples of query images and their corresponding registered images selected by the examiners as correct results.

4.2   Results and Discussions

First, we compared each method for local similarity using key point detectors with no IDF and with IDF; The combinations of detectors used are DoG, multiple detectors of DoG, MSER and AKAZE (MD), and multiple detectors and the dense sampling (MD+DS), and only the dense sampling (DS) for global similarity. Table 1 shows the recall rates as the detection accuracies of each method. From table 1, more detectors used have obtained higher recall rates in the use of

Query Image   Examples of corresponding images

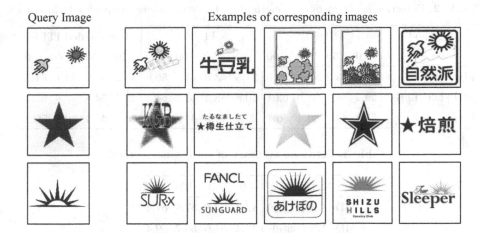

Fig. 3. Examples of query images and their corresponding registered images.

Table 1. Detection accuracy of each method with no IDF / with IDF

Method	With no IDF				With IDF			
	10	50	100	500	10	50	100	500
DoG	32.2	43.0	45.5	54.1	30.9	39.5	43.0	52.6
MD	30.6	40.1	47.5	60.5	30.9	43.0	48.1	59.6
MD+DS (Early)	35.7	43.6	47.8	59.2	39.2	48.4	51.9	63.1
DS	29.3	37.3	41.1	51.3	33.8	42.4	47.1	56.7

key point detectors. This tendency seems reasonable. Searches using IDF generally tend to provide higher accuracies and many of these results fit that. However, some results with IDF are lower than that with no IDF. The reason appears to be few number of registered images used for the IDF calculation.

Second, we tested the effectiveness of our improved weighing technique ITFF that is based on the feature frequency and thresholding. From the detector combinations presented in table 1, we selected and validated MD, MD+DS (early), and DS as the high-performance methods. Table 2 gives the recall rates on each order of these three methods. From these results, we can say that our proposed ITFF with thresholding enables to enhance the search accuracies compared to conventional IDF. ITFF itself provides higher rates on more feature frequency. The thresholding technique is effective on few feature frequency.

Finally we validated the total performance of our proposed methods using early or late fusion. The recall rates of each fusion method are tabulated in table 3. The method using fusion techniques have obtained higher rates than other simple/single search methods. But the difference of these two ways to fuse multiple local detectors into the dense sampling is not so large. Early fusion

Table 2. Detection accuracy of each method with several inverse frequency techniques

Method	IDF				ITFF				Thresholded ITFF			
	10	50	100	500	10	50	100	500	10	50	100	500
MD	30.9	43.0	48.1	59.6	31.5	43.0	47.7	59.6	34.7	43.0	48.1	61.5
MD+DS (Early)	39.2	48.4	51.9	63.1	40.8	48.4	53.2	64.3	42.4	54.8	57.6	67.4
DS	33.8	42.4	47.1	56.7	36.3	44.6	49.7	58.3	36.3	44.3	50.0	59.9

Table 3. Detection accuracy of each fusion method

Method	10	50	100	500
MD+DS (Early)	42.3	54.8	57.6	67.4
MD+DS (Late)	42.4	51.6	56.7	69.4

seems to obtain higher rates on lower orders and late fusion tends to achieve higher rates on higher orders.

Figure 4 and 5 show examples of search results improved by our proposed ITFF and that given by the fusion of multiple detectors, respectively. The numbers under each registered image show the order obtained by each method. Figure 4 indicates that our ITFF weights each visual word more effectively than the conventional IDF. Figure 5 depicts the effectiveness of the fusion of multiple detectors and the dense sampling. The query in the upper row is shaped so simply that only local multiple detectors without the dense sampling as an ordinary BoVW method cannot retrieve many of the corresponding images correctly. But both fusion methods that combine the local detectors and the dense sampling give better results. From these results, we can say that our proposed methods are superior to conventional methods for the trademark image screening task.

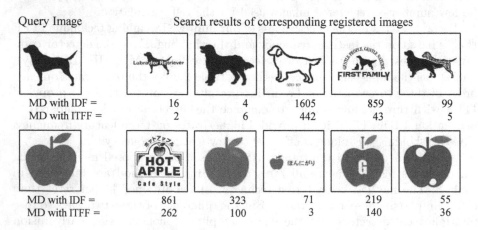

Fig. 4. Examples of search results improved by ITFF.

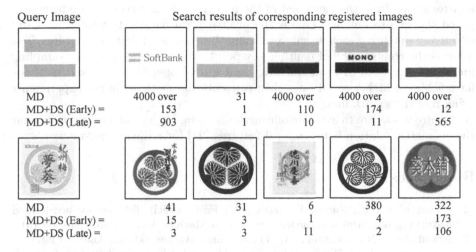

Fig. 5. Examples of search results improved by early or late fusion of multiple detectors.

Fig. 6. Examples of erroneous search results.

Figure 6 shows examples that were erroneously retrieved even by the proposed methods. These examples indicate that even our proposed method cannot well handle several types of images like an image with a simple-shaped part of interest or a conceptually similar image

5   Conclusion

In this paper we have proposed the practical image retrieval methods for screening trademark images. To evaluate similarities between a query image and a registered one from the viewpoint of the real trademark screening, we have proposed the two techniques; One is the inverse total feature frequency for more effectively weighting each visual word using the number of detected features. The other is the combination of multiple key point detectors and the dense sampling for measuring both of local similarity and global one. Our proposed methods have achieved higher recall rates than conventional methods in the experiments using real trademark images.

Future works are to evaluate our methods using bigger dataset and to exploit the geometric relation between local features [21] for reducing mis-retrievals.

References

1. Alcantarilla, P.F., Nuevo, J., Bartoli, A.: Fast explicit diffusion for accelerated features in nonlinear scale spaces. In: British Machine Vision Conference (2013)
2. Arandjelovic, R., Zisserman, A.: Three things everyone should know to improve object retrieval. In: IEEE Conference on Computer Vision and Pattern Recognition, pp. 2911–2918 (2012)
3. Arandjelovic, R., Zisserman, A.: All about vlad. In: IEEE Conference on Computer Vision and Pattern Recognition, pp. 1578–1585 (2013)
4. Bach, F.R., Lanckriet, G.R.G.: Multiple kernel learning, conic duality, and the smo algorithm. In: International Conference on Machine Learning (2004)
5. Chen, C.K., Sun, Q.Q., Yang, J.Y.: Binary trademark image retrieval using region orientation information entropy. In: International Conference on Computational Intelligence and Security Workshops, pp. 295–298 (2007)
6. Grauman, K., Darrell, T.: The pyramid match kernel: discriminative classification with sets of image features. International Conference on Computer Vision **2**, 1458–1465 (2005)
7. Huang, Y., Guo, L., Yang, J.: Binary trademark retrieval using shape and spatial feature. International Symposium on Multispectral Image Processing and Pattern Recognition **5286**, 81–84 (2003)
8. Hung, M.H., Hsieh, C.H., Kuo, C.M.: Similarity retrieval of shape images based on database classification. J. Visual Commun. Image Representation **17**(5), 970–985 (2006)
9. Hussain, M., Eakins, J.P.: Component-based visua lclustering using the self-organizing map. Neural Networks **20**(2), 260–273 (2007)
10. Jegou, H., Douze, M., Schmid, C.: Improving bag-of-features for large scale image search. International Journal on Computer Vision **87**(3), 316–336 (2010)
11. Lowe, D.G.: Distinctive image features from scale-invariant keypoints. International Journal on Computer Vision **60**(2), 91–110 (2004)
12. Matas, J., Chum, O., Urban, M., Pajdla, T.: Robust wide baseline stereo from maximally stable extremal regions. In: British Machine Vision Conference, pp. 384–393 (2002)
13. Philbin, J., Chum, O., Isard, M., Sivic, J., Zisserman, A.: Object retrieval with large vocabularies and fast spatial matching. In: IEEE Conference on Computer Vision and Pattern Recognition (2007)
14. Philbin, J., Chum, O., Isard, M., Sivic, J., Zisserman, A.: Lost in quantization: Improving particular object retrieval in large scale image databases. In: IEEE Conference on Computer Vision and Pattern Recognition (2008)

15. Ponte, J.M., Croft, W.B.: A languate modeling approach to information retrieval. In: ACM SIGIR Conference on Research and Development in Information Retrieval, pp. 275–281 (1998)
16. Salton, G.: Automatic text processing: The transformation, analysis, and retrieval of information by computer. Addison-Wesley Longman Publishing, Boston (1989)
17. Sivic, J., Zisserman, A.: Video google: A text retrieval approach to object matching in videos. In: International Conference on Computer Vision, pp. 1470–1477 (2003)
18. Song, F., Croft, W.B.: A general language model for information retrieval. In: ACM Conference on Information and Knowledge Management, pp. 316–321 (1999)
19. Varma, M., Ray, D.: Learning the discriminative power-invariance trade-off. In: International Conference on Computer Vision (2007)
20. Wei, C.H., Li, Y., Chau, W.Y., Li, C.T.: Trademark image retrieval using synthetic features for describing global shape and interior structure. Pattern Recognition **42**(3), 386–394 (2009)
21. Wu, X., Kashino, K.: Image retrieval based on anisotropic scaling and shearing invariant geometric coherence. In: International Conference on Pattern Recognition, pp. 3951–3956 (2014)

Adaptive Graph Learning for Unsupervised Feature Selection

Zhihong Zhang[1], Lu Bai[2(✉)], Yuanheng Liang[3], and Edwin R. Hancock[4]

[1] Software School, Xiamen University, Xiamen, Fujian, China
[2] School of Information, Central University of Finance and Economics, Beijing, China
bailu69@hotmail.com
[3] School of Mathematical Sciences, Xiamen University, Xiamen, Fujian, China
[4] Department of Computer Science, University of York, York, UK

Abstract. Most existing feature selection methods select features by evaluating a criterion which measures their ability to preserve the similarity structure of a data graph. However, these methods dichotomise the process of constructing or learning the underlying data graph and subsequent feature ranking. Once the graph is determined so as to characterize the structure of the similarity data, it is left fixed in the following ranking or regression steps. As a result, the performance of feature selection is largely determined by the effectiveness of graph construction step. The key to constructing an effective similarity graph is to determine a data similarity matrix. In this paper we perform the problem of estimating or learning the data similarity matrix and data-regression as simultaneous tasks, to perform unsupervised spectral feature selection. Our new method learns the data similarity matrix by optimally re-assigning the neighbors for each data point based on local distances or dis-similarities. Meanwhile, the $\ell_{2,1}$-norm is imposed to the transformation matrix to achieve row sparsity, which leads to the selection of relevant features. We derive an efficient optimization method to solve the simultaneous feature similarity graph and feature selection problems. Extensive experimental results on real-world benchmark data sets shows that our method consistently outperforms the alternative feature selection methods.

Keywords: Graph learning · Laplacian · Unsupervised feature selection

1 Introduction

Feature selection is an effective solution to pattern analysis and mchine learning problems involving high-dimensionality data, and has been exploited in a wide variety of real-world applications. Recent studies of spectral feature selection have integrated manifold learning techniques into the feature selection process. Spectral feature selection can significantly improve the performance of feature selection because it preserves the local structures of the data via manifold learning. Typical methods include: Laplacian score (LapScore) [1], spectral feature selection (SPEC) [2], multicluster feature selection (MCFS) [3] and minimum

© Springer International Publishing Switzerland 2015
G. Azzopardi and N. Petkov (Eds.): CAIP 2015, Part I, LNCS 9256, pp. 790–800, 2015.
DOI: 10.1007/978-3-319-23192-1_66

redundancy spectral feature selection (MRSF) [4]. However, these methods perform manifold learning and regression as sequential steps. For example, MCFS [3] uses a graph to characterize the manifold structure and performs locality preserving projection (LPP) in the first-step. In the second step, MCFS performs spectral regression using a single eigenvector at a time to estimate element sparsity. Finally, a new score rule is designed to rank the goodness of the features using element sparsity. MRSF [4], on the other hand, uses the $\ell_{2,1}$-norm regularizer to replace the ℓ_1-norm regularizer in MCFS which leads to row sparsity. The row sparsity used in MRSF is better fitted for feature selection than the element sparsity used in MCFS. LapScore [1] uses a k-nearest neighbor graph to model the local geometric structure of the data and then selects the features that are most consistent with the graph structure. The SPEC [2] algorithm is an extension of LapScore aimed at making it more robust to noise.

Compared with traditional unsupervised feature selection approaches, the above methods have been in many cases been demomstrated to perform better. Nevertheless, their performance can also be further improved since they each separate the problems of estimating or learning a similarity graph and feature selection. Once the graph is determined so as to characterize the data sample similarity and underlying manifold structure, it remains fixed in the subsequent feature ranking or regression steps. As a result, the feature selection performance is largely determined by the effectiveness of graph construction.

Key to constructing a data similarity graph is to determine the elements of the similarity matrix from which it is derived. In this paper, we aim to learn the data similarity matrix by adaptively and optimally assigning neighbors for each data point. This is based on local connectivity. Our main assumption is that the data points with small distances have a large probability to be neighbors. More importantly, by adding the $\ell_{2,1}$-norm regularization to the transformation matrix, our new model simultaneously learns both the data similarity matrix and a sparse transformation matrix, to achieve the optimal feature selection results. We also provide an effective algorithm to solve the proposed problem. Compared with traditional unsupervised feature selection methods, our method integrates the merits of graph learning and sparse regression. Experimental results are provided which demonstrate the effectiveness of the method.

2 Related Work

In this section, we review some well known learning-based unsupervised feature selection methods which are closely related to our proposed method.

1) MCFS and MRSF: MCFS and MRSF are learning based feature selection methods that first compute an embedding and then use regression coefficients to rank each feature. In the first step, both methods compute a low dimensional embedding represented by the co-ordinate matrix Y. One simple way to derive a low dimensional embedding is to use Laplacian Eigenmap (LE) [6], a well known dimensionality reduction method. Let $Y = [y_1, y_2, \ldots, y_n]$ and $\hat{y}_i$ be the transpose of the i-th row of Y. The idea common to both MCFS and MRSF is to

regress all x_i to $\hat{y}_i$. Their differences are used to determine sparseness constraints. MCFS uses ℓ_1-norm regularization and can be regarded as solving the following problems in sequence:

$$arg \min_{YY^T=I} tr(YLY^T)$$
$$arg \min_{W} \|W^T X - Y\|_2^2 + \alpha\|W\|_1 \qquad (1)$$

Similarly, MRSF first computes the embedding using an eigen-decomposition of the graph Laplacian and then regresses with $\ell_{2,1}$-norm regularization. In other words, MRSF can be regarded as solving the following two problems in sequence:

$$arg \min_{YY^T=I} tr(YLY^T)$$
$$arg \min_{W} \|W^T X - Y\|_2^2 + \alpha\|W\|_{2,1} \qquad (2)$$

MCFS and MRSF employ different sparseness constraints, i.e., ℓ_1 and $\ell_{2,1}$, in constructing a transformation matrix which is used for selecting features. Nevertheless, the low dimensional embedding, i.e., Y, is determined in the first step and remains fixed in the subsequent ranking or regression step. In other words, we do not consider the later requirements of feature selection in deriving the embedding Y. If they both characterized the manifold structure and also quantified the requirements of regression, then these methods would perform better.

2) JELSR [5]: Instead of simply using the graph Laplacian to characterize high dimensional data structure and then regression, JELSR (joint embedding learning and sparse regression) unifies embedding/learning and sparse regression in constructing a new framework for feature selection:

$$arg \min_{W,YY^T=I} tr(YLY^T) + \beta(\|W^T X - Y\|_2^2 + \alpha\|W\|_{2,1}) \qquad (3)$$

where α and β are balance parameters. The objective function in Eq. (3) is convex with respect to W and Y. W and Y can be updated in an alternative way. As indicated in [5], the objective of sparse regression, i.e. the value of W, also affects the low dimensional embedding, i.e., Y. Alternative methods, such as MCFS and MRSF, just minimize $tr(YLY^T)$.

3) LPP [7]: LPP (locality preserving projection) constructs a graph by incorporating neighborhood information derived from the data. Using the graph Laplacian, a transformation is computed to map the data into a subspace by optimally maintaining the local neighborhood information. LPP optimizes a linear transformation W according to

$$arg \min_{W} \sum_{i,j=1}^{n} \|W^T x_i - W^T x_j\|^2 s_{ij} \qquad (4)$$

The basic idea underlying LPP is to find a transformation matrix W, which transforms the high-dimensional data X into a low-dimensional matrix XW, so as to maximally preserve the local connectivity structure of X with XW. Minimizing (4) ensures that, if x_i and x_j are close, then as a result $W^T x_i$ and $W^T x_j$ are close too.

3 Adaptive Graph Learning

Key to constructing a graph representation of the data is determining a weight matrix S, where s_{ij} expresses the similarity between points x_i and x_j. Usually, the graph is constructed by connecting each point to its k-nearest neighbors and the weights for the connected points are computed using a Gaussian function of the interpoint distance. However, the size of the neighborhood needs to be specified in advance. In real-world applications, it is hard to estimate the neighborhood size and different data points have a different optimal neighbourhood size. In our study, the graph is constructed from the learned data similarity matrix by using an adaptive neighbourhood with optimal neighbor selection for each data point, based on the local connectivity. Specifically, denote by $X = [x_1, x_2, \ldots, x_n]^T \in \Re^{n \times d}$ the data matrix. For each data point x_i, there is an associated positive value s_{ij}, which is the probability the data point x_j connecting to x_i as a neighbor. Usually, a smaller distance $\|x_i - x_j\|_2^2$ should be assigned a larger probability s_{ij}, and so a natural method to determine the probabilities $s_{ij}|_{j=1}^n$ is by solving the following problem:

$$\min_{s_i^T 1 = 1, 0 \leq s_i \leq 1} \sum_{j=1}^n \|x_i - x_j\|_2^2 s_{ij} \tag{5}$$

where $s_i \in \Re^{n \times 1}$ is a vector with the j-th element as s_{ij}. With this local connection, only the nearest data point can be the neighbor of x_i with probability 1 and all the remianing points can not be neighbors of x_i. In order to automatically regulate the effects of distance, we introduce a regularization term into (5) which we can assign the neighbors for all the data points:

$$\min_{\forall i, s_i^T 1 = 1, 0 \leq s_i \leq 1} \sum_{i,j=1}^n (\|x_i - x_j\|_2^2 s_{ij} + \lambda s_{ij}^2) \tag{6}$$

The second term in Eq. (6) is a regularization term, whch does not involve any distance information derived from the data. In this way, all the data points can be the neighbors of x_i with the same probability $\frac{1}{n}$. This can be viewed as a maximum ignorrance prior on the neighbor assignment. From the graph partitioning perspective, the neighbor assignment has a close connection with both spectral clustering [8,9] and manifold learning [10], which considers the case when the data are drawn by sampling from a probability distribution and each data distribution (or connected component) corresponds to one cluster. Given a graph with similarity matrix S, spectral clustering aims to solve the following problem:

$$\sum_{i,j=1}^n \|f_i - f_j\|_2^2 s_{ij} = 2Tr(F^T L_S F) \tag{7}$$

where each node i is assigned a function value $f_i \in \Re^{c \times 1}$, $F \in \Re^{n \times c}$ with the i-th row formed by f_i, $L_S = D_S - \frac{S^T + S}{2}$ is the Laplacian matrix from graph theory, the degree matrix $D_S \in \Re^{n \times n}$ is defined as a diagonal matrix where the i-th diagonal element is $\sum_j (s_{ij} + s_{ji})/2$. The optimal solution of Eq. (7) is the spectral decomposition of the Laplacian matrix L_S, i.e., the optimal solution F is formed by the c smallest eigenvalues corresponding to the eigenvectors of L_S associated with the c connected components in the graph. Therefore, an ideal neighbor assignment is that the connected components in the data are the clusters in the data.

Usually the neighbor assignment with Eq. (6) can not reach the optimum for an artbitrary value of λ. In most cases, all the data points are connected as just one connected component. In order to achieve the ideal neighbor assignment, we add a constraint $rank(L_S) = n - c$ to the probabilities $s_{i,j}|_{i,j=1}^{n}$ in the problem stated in 6 such that the assignment becomes an adaptive process to make the number of connected components exactly c. Thus, our new neighbor assignment model solves the problem

$$\min_S \sum_{i,j=1}^{n} (\|x_i - x_j\|_2^2 s_{ij} + \gamma s_{ij}^2)$$
$$s.t. \quad \forall_i, s_i^T 1 = 1, 0 \leq s_i \leq 1, rank(L_S) = n - c \tag{8}$$

Because of the constraint $rank(L_S) = n-c$, the graph with the learned similarity matrix S will have exactly c connected components. However, the constraint is not easy to solve. According to Ky Fan's Theorem [11], we reformulate the problem (8) to render it more tractable as

$$\min_{S,F} \sum_{i,j=1}^{n} (\|x_i - x_j\|_2^2 s_{ij} + \gamma s_{ij}^2) + 2\lambda Tr(F^T L_S F)$$
$$s.t. \quad \forall_i, s_i^T 1 = 1, 0 \leq s_i \leq 1, F \in \Re^{n \times c}, F^T F = I \tag{9}$$

4   Graph Learning for Unsupervised Feature Selection

After adaptive graph learning, the next problem is how to extract meaningful features from the graph. As shown in Eq. (4), each row of the transformation matrix W corresponds to a feature in the original space. In order to perform feature selection, it is desirable to have some rows of the transformation matrix set to be all zeros. This in turn leads us to use the $\ell_{2,1}$-norm on the transformation matrix W, and this leads to row-sparsity of W. As a result, based on Eq. (4) and Eq. (9), we formulate joint graph learning and feature selection as follows:

$$\min_{S,W,F} \sum_{i,j=1}^{n} (\|W^T x_i - W^T x_j\|_2^2 s_{ij} + \gamma s_{ij}^2) + 2\lambda Tr(F^T L_S F) + \mu \|W\|_{2,1}$$
$$s.t. \quad \forall_i, s_i^T 1 = 1, 0 \leq s_i \leq 1, W^T S_t W = I, F \in \Re^{n \times c}, F^T F = I \tag{10}$$

Let the transformation matrix be $W \in \Re^{d \times m}$ with $m < d$ and the total scatter matrix be $S_t = X^T H X$, where $H = I - \frac{1}{n} 11^T$ is the centering matrix. We constrain the subspace with $W^T S_t W = I$ such that the data in the subspace are statistically uncorrelated.

The goal of Eq. (10) is to find a transformation matrix W which maps the data into a lower dimensional space by optimally preserving the local geometric structure or neighborhood information. The local geometric structure of the data is captured by the local neighborhood relationships and is characterized through the adaptive graph learning. Specifically, we capture local geometric structure by learning a graph in which each point is adaptively assigned the optimal number of neighbors. To make the neighbor assignment adaptive, such that the connected components in the data number exactly c, we constrain S with $Tr(F^T L_S F)$. Therefore, in the proposed objective function of Eq. (10), we learn both the transformation matrix W and the data similarity matrix S simultaneously.

5 Optimization Algorithm for the Optimisation Problem in (10)

To obtain the global minimal solution of (10), we propoase an iterative and interleaved optimization process, which can be summarized as in Algorithm 1. In each iteration step, the Laplacian matrix L_S is calculated with the current S, where $L_S = D_S - \frac{S^T + S}{2}$ and $D_S \in \Re^{n \times n}$ is a diagonal matrix with the i-th diagonal element as $\sum_j (s_{ij} + s_{ji})/2$. F is updated based just on the calculated L_S as in equation (11). The sparse matrix W is updated by (16). After obtaining W, we then update the matrix U using Eq.(14). Finally, For each i, we update the i-th row of S by solving the optimisation problem in (19) and obtain the optimal solution as Eq. (21).

We first fix S and W, then the optimisation problem in (10) becomes

$$\min_{F^T F = I, F \in \Re^{n \times c}} Tr(F^T L_S F) \tag{11}$$

the optimal solution of Eq. (11) is the spectral decomposition of the Laplacian matrix L_S, i.e., the optimal solution F is formed by the c eigenvectors of L_S corresponding to the c smallest eigenvalues.

When F is fixed, the optimisation problem in (10) becomes

$$\min_{S,W} \sum_{i,j=1}^{n} (\|W^T x_i - W^T x_j\|_2^2 s_{ij} + \gamma s_{ij}^2) + 2\lambda Tr(F^T L_S F) + \mu \|W\|_{2,1}$$

$$s.t. \quad \forall_i, s_i^T 1 = 1, 0 \le s_i \le 1, W^T S_t W = I \tag{12}$$

For the optimisation problem in (12), we then fix S and solve for W. The sub-problem then becomes

$$\min_{W} \sum_{i,j=1}^{n} (\|W^T x_i - W^T x_j\|_2^2 s_{ij} + \mu \|W\|_{2,1}$$

$$s.t. \quad W^T S_t W = I \tag{13}$$

Note that $\|W\|_{2,1}$ is convex. Nevertheless, its derivative does not exist when $\hat{w}_i = 0$ for $i = 1, 2, \ldots, d$. Therefore, we use the definition $tr(W^T U W) = \|W\|_{2,1}/2$ in [5] when $\hat{w}_i$ is not equal to 0. The matrix $U \in \Re^{d \times d}$ is diagonal with i-th diagonal element where

$$U_{ii} = \frac{1}{2\|\hat{w}_i\|_2} \tag{14}$$

Then the optimisation problem in (13) can be rewritten as the following one according to Eq. (7)

$$\min_{W,U} Tr(W^T X^T L_S X W) + \mu Tr(W^T U W)$$

$$s.t. \quad W^T S_t W = I \tag{15}$$

which can be rewritten as the following optimisation problem

$$\min_{W,U} Tr(W^T (X^T L_S X + \mu U) W)$$

$$s.t. \quad W^T S_t W = I \tag{16}$$

When the matrix U is fixed, the optimal solution to the problem in (16) is the spectral decomposition of $S_t^{-1}(X^T L_S X + \mu U)$, i.e., the optimal solution W is formed by the k eigenvectors of $S_t^{-1}(X^T L_S X + \mu U)$ corresponding to the k smallest eigenvalues (we assume the null space of the data X is removed, i.e., S_t is invertible). After that, we fix W and update U by employing the formulation in (14) directly.

For the optimisation problem in (12), if W is fixed, then according to Eq. (7), it can can be rewritten as

$$\min_{S} \sum_{i,j=1}^{n} (\|W^T x_i - W^T x_j\|_2^2 s_{ij} + \gamma s_{ij}^2) + \lambda \sum_{i,j=1}^{n} \|f_i - f_j\|_2^2 s_{ij}$$

$$s.t. \quad \forall_i, s_i^T 1 = 1, 0 \leq s_i \leq 1 \tag{17}$$

Note that the problem in (17) exhibits independence between different i, and so we can solve the following optimisation problem individually for each i:

$$\min_{s_i} \sum_{j=1}^{n} (\|W^T x_i - W^T x_j\|_2^2 s_{ij} + \gamma s_{ij}^2) + \lambda \sum_{j=1}^{n} \|f_i - f_j\|_2^2 s_{ij}$$

$$s.t. \quad \forall_i, s_i^T 1 = 1, 0 \leq s_i \leq 1 \tag{18}$$

Let $d_{ij}^{wx} = \|W^T x_i - W^T x_j\|_2^2$ and $d_{i,j}^f = \|f_i - f_j\|_2^2$, and let $d_i^w \in \Re^{n \times 1}$ be the vector with the j-th element $d_{ij}^w = d_{ij}^{wx} + \lambda d_{ij}^f$, then the optimisation problem in (18) can be written in vector form as

$$\min_{s_i} \left\| s_i + \frac{1}{2\gamma} d_i^w \right\|_2^2$$
$$s.t. \quad s_i^T 1 = 1, 0 \leq s_i \leq 1 \tag{19}$$

The Lagrangian function of the problem in (19) is

$$L(s_i, \eta, \beta_i) = \frac{1}{2} \left\| s_i + \frac{1}{2\gamma} d_i^w \right\|_2^2 - \eta(s_i^T 1 - 1) - \beta_i^T s_i \tag{20}$$

where η and $\beta_i \geq 0$ are the Lagrangian multipliers.

According to the KKT condition [12], it can be verified that the optimal solution s_i should be

$$s_{ij} = (-\frac{d_{ij}^w}{2\gamma_i} + \eta)_+ \tag{21}$$

Based on Eq. (21) and the constrain $s_i^T 1 = 1$, we have

$$\sum_{j=1}^k (-\frac{d_{ij}^w}{2\gamma_i} + \eta) = 1$$
$$\Rightarrow \quad \eta = \frac{1}{k} + \frac{1}{2k\gamma_i} \sum_{j=1}^k d_{ij}^w \tag{22}$$

In summary, we solve the optimization problem in (10) in an iterative and interleaved way. More concretely, we first update $L_S = D_S - \frac{S^T + S}{2}$, where $D_S \in$

Algorithm 1. Adaptive graph learning for unsupervised feature selection (AGLUFS)

Input: $X \in \Re^{n \times d}$, cluster number c, reduced dimension k, parameter γ, μ and a large enough λ accordingly.

Output: $S \in \Re^{n \times n}$ with exact c connected components, the optimal sparse transformation matrix $W \in \Re^{d \times k}$

1: **while** not converge **do**
2:      Update $L_S = D_S - \frac{S^T + S}{2}$, where $D_S \in \Re^{n \times n}$ is a diagonal matrix with the i-th diagonal element as $\sum_j (s_{ij} + s_{ji})/2$;
3:      Update F by (11), whose columns are the c eigenvectors of L_S corresponding to the c smallest eigenvalues;
4:      Update W by (16) whose columns are the k eigenvectors of $S_t^{-1}(X^T L_S X + \mu U)$ corresponding to the k smallest eigenvalues;
5:      Update U by Eq. (14);
6:      For each i, we update the i-th row of S by solving the problem in (19) and obtain the optimal solution as Eq. (21).
7: **end while**

$\Re^{n \times n}$ is a diagonal matrix with the i-th diagonal element as $\sum_j (s_{ij} + s_{ji})/2$. If S and W are fixed, we can solve the optimization problem in (11) to update F, whose columns are the c eigenvectors of L_S corresponding to the c smallest eigenvalues. When F is fixed, we then fix S and U. We then employ (16) to update W, whose columns are the k eigenvectors of $S_t^{-1}(X^T L_S X + \mu U)$ corresponding to the k smallest eigenvalues. After that, we fix W and update U by Eq. (14). Finally, for each i, we update the i-th row of S by solving the problem in (19) and obtain the optimal solution as Eq. (21), where $d_i^w \in \Re^{n \times 1}$ is a vector with the j-th element as $d_{ij}^w = \|W^T x_i - W^T x_j\|_2^2 + \lambda \|f_i - f_j\|_2^2$.

6   Experiments and Comparisons

To demonstrate the effectiveness of the proposed approach, we conduct experiments on three benchmark data sets with high dimension, i.e., AR face dataset, Isolet spoken data set and the MSRA50 image dataset. Table. 1 summarizes the extents and properties of the three benchmark data-sets.

Table 1. Summary of three benchmark data sets

Data-set	Sample	Features	Classes
AR	1680	2000	120
MSRA50	1799	1024	12
Isolet	7797	617	26

In order to explore the discriminative capabilities of the information captured by our method, we use the selected features for further classification. We compare the classification results from our proposed method (AGLUFS) with four representative uspervised feature selection algorithms. These methods are LapScore [1], SPEC [2], MCFS [3], JELSR [5]. A 10-fold cross-validation strategy using the C-Support Vector Machine (C-SVM) [13] is employed to evaluate the classification performance. Specifically, the entire sample is randomly partitioned into 10 subsets and then we choose one subset for test and use the remaining 9 for training, and this procedure is repeated 10 times. The final accuracy is computed by averaging of the accuracies from all experiments.

As seen from Fig. 1, from the statistical view, we can see that our proposed method (AGLUFS) achieves significantly better results comparing to the baseline algorithms in all cases. This is obviously because the proposed AGLUFS simultaneously learns the graph and a sparse transformation matrix, to achieve the optimal feature selection results, but each of the rival algorithms dichotomise the process of constructing or learning the underlying data graph and subsequent feature ranking. Although both MCFS and JELSR lead to the element sparsity, the classification performance of MCFS is worse than JELSR (see Fig. 1(a) and Fig. 1(c)). This occurs because JELSR simultaneously performs manifold learning and regression, but MCFS sequentially performs them. This demonstrated that simultaneously performing manifold learning and regression is better. Comparatively, LapScore gives the worst performance. This is because it does not

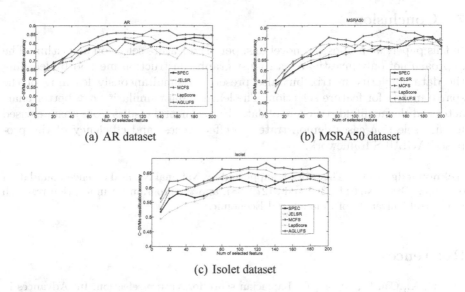

(a) AR dataset   (b) MSRA50 dataset

(c) Isolet dataset

Fig. 1. Accuracy rate vs. the number of selected features on three benchmark datasets by unsupervised learning.

Table 2. The best result of all methods and their corresponding size of selected feature subset.

Dataset	AR	MSRA50	Isolet
SPEC	83.1%(180)	75.7%(180)	64.6%(170)
JELSR	83.9%(120)	72.5%(170)	66 4%(110)
MCFS	81%(120)	74.8%(190)	65.1%(110)
LapScore	77.7%(130)	74.7%(180)	60.6%(130)
AGLUFS	**87.1%(130)**	**79.8%(140)**	**68.3%(130)**

take feature redundancy into account and is prone to selecting redundant features.

The best result for each method together with the corresponding size of the selected feature subset are shown in Table. 2. In the table, the classification accuracy is shown first and the optimal number of features selected is reported in brackets. Overall, AGLUFS achieves the highest degree of dimensionality reduction, i.e. it selects a smaller feature subset compared with those obtained by the alternative methods. For example, in the MSRA50 data set, the best result obtained by the alternative feature selection methods is 75.7% with the SPEC algorithm and 180 features. However, our proposed method AGLUFS gives a better accuracy 79.8% when only 140 features are used. The results further verify that AGLUFS can select more informative feature subset than baselines and the importance of joint graph learning and feature selection.

7   Conclusion

In this paper, we proposed a novel unsupervised feature selection algorithm. The approach not only investigates a robust graph construction method by learning the data similarity matrix but also presents a simultaneously learning of the sparse matrix for feature selection. The learned data similarity can better characterized the manifold structure of data. Experimental results from unsupervised feature selection cases demonstrate the effectiveness and efficiency of the proposed AGLUFS framework.

Acknowledgments. This work is supported by National Natural Science Foundation of China (Grant No.61402389 and 61272398), and the program for innovation research in Central University of Finance and Economics.

References

1. He, X., Cai, D., Niyogi, P.: Laplacian score for feature selection. In: Advances in Neural Information Processing Systems, pp. 507–514 (2005)
2. Zhao, Z., Liu, H.: Spectral feature selection for supervised and unsupervised learning. In: Proceedings of the 24th International Conference on Machine Learning, pp. 1151–1157 (2007)
3. Cai, D., Zhang, C., He, X.: Unsupervised feature selection for multi-cluster data. In: Proceedings of the 16th ACM SIGKDD International Conference on Knowledge Discovery and Data Mining, pp. 333–342 (2010)
4. Zhao, Z., Wang, L., Liu, H.: Efficient Spectral Feature Selection with Minimum Redundancy. In: Proceedings of AAAI, pp. 673–678 (2010)
5. Hou, C., Nie, F., Yi, D., Wu, Y.: Joint embedding learning and sparse regression: A framework for unsupervised feature selection. IEEE Transactions on Cybernetics **44**(6), 793–804 (2014)
6. Belkin, M., Niyogi, P.: Laplacian eigenmaps for dimensionality reduction and data representation. Neural Computation **15**(6), 1373–1396 (2003)
7. He, X., Niyogi, P.: Locality preserving projections, Neural information processing systems. MIT Press, Cambridge (2003)
8. Chan, P.K., Jordan, M., Weiss, Y.: Spectral k-way ratio-cut partitioning and clustering. IEEE Transactions on Computer-Aided Design of Integrated Circuits and Systems **13**(9), 1088–1096 (1994)
9. Ng, A.Y., Niyogi, P.: On spectral clustering: Analysis and an algorithm. Advances in Neural Information Processing Systems **2**, 849–856 (2002)
10. Belkin, M., Niyogi, P.: Laplacian eigenmaps and spectral techniques for embedding and clustering. Advances in Neural Information Processing Systems **14**, 585–591 (2001)
11. Fan, K.: On a theorem of Weyl concerning eigenvalues of linear transformations I. Proceedings of the National Academy of Sciences of the United States of America **35**(11), 652–655 (1949)
12. Boyd, S., Vandenberghe, L.: Convex optimization. Cambridge University Press (2004)
13. Chang, C., Lin, C.: Libsvm: a library for support vector machines. ACM Transactions on Intelligent Systems and Technology (2011)

Shot and Scene Detection via Hierarchical Clustering for Re-using Broadcast Video

Lorenzo Baraldi$^{(\boxtimes)}$, Costantino Grana, and Rita Cucchiara

Dipartimento di Ingegneria "Enzo Ferrari", Università degli Studi di Modena e Reggio Emilia, Via Vivarelli 10, 41125 Modena, MO, Italy
{lorenzo.baraldi,costantino.grana,rita.cucchiara}@unimore.it

Abstract. Video decomposition techniques are fundamental tools for allowing effective video browsing and re-using. In this work, we consider the problem of segmenting broadcast videos into coherent scenes, and propose a scene detection algorithm based on hierarchical clustering, along with a very fast state-of-the-art shot segmentation approach. Experiments are performed to demonstrate the effectiveness of our algorithms, by comparing against recent proposals for automatic shot and scene segmentation.

Keywords: Shot detection · Scene detection · Clustering · Performance measures

1 Introduction

In recent years video content has become the major source of Internet traffic, and the large availability of video has led to great interest in fields different from simple entertainment or news broadcasting, such as education. This has also caused a strong interest in the re-use of video content coming from major broadcasting networks, which have been producing high quality edited videos for popular science purposes, such as documentaries and similar programs.

Unfortunately, re-using videos is not an easy task, since it requires video editing skills and tools, on top of the difficulty of finding the parts of videos which effectively contain the specific content one is interested in. Indeed, accessing and browsing a video in an effective way is still a problematic task, especially when the length of the video makes the usage of common seek operations unfeasible to get an insight of the video content.

There is a growing need for managing video content as pieces of text, allowing significant parts to be easily identified, selected, copy and pasted, and so on. The basic unit for this task cannot be the single frame, as a letter cannot be the basic unit for copy and pasting meaningful content from text: higher level groupings are needed, such as DVD chapters. The problem is that most of the on-line reusable content is not provided with editor defined video sub units.

Scene detection has been recognized as a tool which effectively may help in this context, going beyond simple editing units, such as shots. The task is

© Springer International Publishing Switzerland 2015
G. Azzopardi and N. Petkov (Eds.): CAIP 2015, Part I, LNCS 9256, pp. 801–811, 2015.
DOI: 10.1007/978-3-319-23192-1_67

to identify coherent sequences of shots in videos, without any help from the editor or publisher. Of course, a fundamental requirement for scene detection is to accurately identify shot changes. Moreover, evaluating the performance of automatic systems for scene detection is not an easy task: techniques previously employed for different purposes are applied to newer problems, even if they do not perfectly match with the objective at hand, but are easily understood from previous experience. Often this approach leads to erroneous interpretations of the experimental evaluations.

In this paper we present a complete pipeline for scene detection, that includes a shot detection algorithm and a cluster based approach for grouping shots into coherent scenes, and that shows superior results when compared to state-of-the-art methods. We also try to tackle the problem of evaluating scene segmentation results, by proposing an improved definition of the coverage/overflow measures [10], which solves frequently observed cases in which the numeric interpretation would be quite different from the expected results. We publicly release the annotated dataset used for the evaluation as well as the source code of our shot segmentation algorithm.

2   Related Works

Video decomposition techniques aim to partition a video into sequences, like shots or scenes. Shots are elementary structural segments that are defined as sequences of images taken without interruption by a single camera. Scenes, on the contrary, are often defined as series of temporally contiguous shots characterized by overlapping links that connect shots with similar content [5].

Most of the existing shot detection techniques relies on the extraction of low level features, like pixel-wise pixel comparisons or color histograms. Other techniques exploit structural features of the frames, such as edges. After the introduction of SVM classifiers, moreover, several approaches exploited them to classify candidate transitions [6]. Recently, algorithms that rely on local descriptors (such as SIFT or SURF) were also proposed. One of the most recent approaches to shot detection, presented in [1], is indeed based on local SURF descriptors and HSV color histograms. Abrupt transitions are detected by thresholding a distance measure between frames, while longer gradual transition are detected by means of the derivative of the moving average of the aforesaid distance. A GPU-based computing framework is also proposed to allow real-time analysis. Their method, when run on a PC with an Intel i7 processor at 3.4 GHz and a NVIDIA GPU, takes one third of the video duration to run.

On a different note, semantically coherent shots which are temporally close to each other can be grouped together to create scenes. Existing works in this field can be roughly categorized into three categories: *rule-based methods*, that consider the way a scene is structured in professional movie production, *graph-based methods*, where shots are arranged in a graph representation, and *clustering-based methods*, in which a clustering algorithm is applied to features extracted from shots [2,3]. They can rely on visual, audio, and textual features.

Rule-based approaches consider the way a scene is structured in professional movie production. Of course, the drawback of this kind of methods is that they tend to fail in videos where film-editing rules are not followed, or when two adjacent scenes are similar and follow the same rules. Liu *et al.* [7], for example, propose a visual based probabilistic framework that imitates the authoring process and detects scenes by incorporating contextual dynamics and learning a scene model. In [4], shots are represented by means of key-frames, thus, the first step of this method is to extract several key-frames from each shot: frames from a shot are clustered using the spectral clustering algorithm, color histograms as features, and the euclidean distance to compute the similarity matrix. The number of clusters is selected by applying a threshold Th on the eigenvalues of the Normalized Laplacian. The distance between a pair of shots is defined as the maximum similarity between key-frames belonging to the two shots, computed using histogram intersection. Shots are clustered using again spectral clustering and the aforesaid distance measure, and then labeled according to the clusters they belong to. Scene boundaries are then detected from the alignment score of the symbolic sequences.

In graph-based methods, instead, shots are arranged in a graph representation and then clustered by partitioning the graph. The Shot Transition Graph (STG), proposed in [11], is one of the most used models in this category: here each node represents a shot and the edges between the shots are weighted by shot similarity. In [8], color and motion features are used to represent shot similarity, and the STG is then split into subgraphs by applying the normalized cuts for graph partitioning. More recently, Sidiropoulos *et al.* [9] introduced a new STG approximation that exploits features automatically extracted from the visual and the auditory channel. This method extends the Shot Transition Graph using multimodal low-level and high-level features. To this aim, multiple STGs are constructed, one for each kind of feature, and then a probabilistic merging process is used to combine their results. The used features include visual features, such as HSV histograms, outputs of visual concept detectors trained using the Bag of Words approach, and audio features, like background conditions classification results, speaker histogram, and model vectors constructed from the responses of a number of audio event detectors.

3   Scene Detection as a Clustering Problem

Since scenes are sets of contiguous shots, the first step in scene detection is to identify shot boundaries. Therefore, we propose a shot segmentation approach that assures high accuracy levels, while keeping execution times low. Our method identifies shot boundaries by computing an extended difference measure, that quantifies the change in the content of two different positions in the video, where positions can be both frames and half-frames. We iteratively compare it against experimentally specified thresholds and parameters that indicate the existence of cuts and gradual transitions.

Algorithm 1. Shot detection

$T \leftarrow \{\}$;

/* Abrupt transition detection   */
w $\leftarrow$ 0.5;
$C = \{\}$;
forall the $n \le N$ **do**
    if $M_w^n > T$ **then**
       | insert (n, n) into C
    end
end
Merge consecutive elements of C;
$T \leftarrow \{t_i \in C : Peak_w(t_i) > T_P\}$

/* Gradual transition detection   */
for $w \leftarrow 1$ **to** W **do**
    $C = \{\}$;
    forall the $n \le N$ **do**
        if $M_w^n > T$ **then**
           | insert (n, n) into C
        end
    end
    Merge consecutive elements of C;
    foreach $c \in \{t_i \in C : Peak_w(t_i) > T_P\}$ **do**
        if *distance between c and its nearest element in* $T \le T_S$ **then**
           | insert c into T
        end
    end
end

3.1 Shot Boundaries Detection

Given two consecutive shots in a video sequence, the first one ending at frame e, and the second one starting at frame s, we define the transition length as the number of frames in which the transition is visible, that is $L = s - e - 1$. An abrupt transition, therefore, is a transition with length $L = 0$. The transition center is defined as $n = (e + s)/2$ and may correspond to a non-integer value, that is an inter-frame position. This is always true in case of abrupt transitions.

Given a feature $F(i)$ describing frame i, we define the extended difference measure M_n^w, centered on frame or half-frame n, with $2n \in \mathbb{N}$, and with a frame-step $2w \in \mathbb{N}$, as

$$M_w^n = \begin{cases} d\left[F(n - w), F(n + w)\right], & \text{if } n + w \in \mathbb{N} \\ \frac{1}{2}\left(M_w^{n-\frac{1}{2}} + M_w^{n+\frac{1}{2}}\right), & \text{otherwise} \end{cases} \tag{1}$$

where $d(F(i), F(j))$ is the distance between frames i and j, computed in terms of feature F. The second term of the expression is a linear interpolation adopted for inter-frame positions. This is necessary because the feature F is relative to a single frame and cannot be directly computed at half-frames. In our case, distance $d(F(i), F(j))$ is a linear combination of the sum of squared differences of frames i and j and of the χ^2 distance of color histograms extracted from frames i and j. Both measures are normalized by the number of pixels in a frame. The selected features have the property to be almost constant immediately before and after a transition, and to have a constant derivative during a linear transition.

The algorithm starts by simple thresholding the M_w^n values at all frames and half frames positions with $w = 0.5$. This gives us a set of candidate positions for transitions. Now two operations are needed: merging and validation. Merging is simply the aggregation of adjacent candidate positions, providing a list of candidate transitions $C = \{t_i = (f_i, l_i)\}$, where f_i is the first position of the transition, and l_i is the last position. These may be real transitions (most likely hard cuts), or false positives, that is shots with high level differences due to motion. Validation is then performed by measuring the transition $Peak$ value, defined as:

$$Peak_w(t) = \max_{f \leq n \leq l}(M_w^n) - \min(M_w^{f-2w}, M_w^{l+2w}) \tag{2}$$

The $Peak_w(t)$ value measures the variation in difference values between the transition and the adjacent shots. In order to validate the transition, therefore, a significant variation must be observed on at least one side of the candidate transition.

To detect gradual transitions, we repeat the previous steps at increasing values of w. Doing so would possibly cause other positions to surpass the threshold value, thus changing and eventually invalidating previously found transitions. For this reason, every validated transition is protected by a "safe zone". This in practice makes it so that only positions between previous transitions with distance superior to a certain number of frames are further analyzed.

In total we need to setup four parameters for our algorithm: T, the threshold on the differences levels; T_P, a threshold on the $Peak$ value, which in practice was usually set to $T/2$; T_S, the number of frames before and after validated transitions, which won't be further analyzed; finally, W, the maximum value for w. A summary of the approach is presented in Algorithm 1.

3.2 Scene Detection via Hierarchical Clustering

Having detected shot boundaries, we now identify scenes by grouping adjacent shots. Shots are described by means of color histograms, hence relying on visual features only: given a video, we compute a three-dimensional histogram of each frame, by quantizing each RGB channel in eight bins, for a total of 512 bins. Then, we sum histograms from frames belonging to the same shot, thus obtaining a single L_1-normalized histogram for each shot.

In contrast to other approaches that used clustering for scene detection, we build a distance measure that jointly describes appearance similarity and temporal proximity. The generic distance between shots $\mathbf{x}_i$ and $\mathbf{x}_j$ is therefore defined as

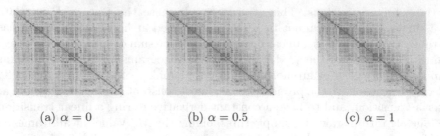

(a) $\alpha = 0$ (b) $\alpha = 0.5$ (c) $\alpha = 1$

Fig. 1. Effect of α on distance measure $d(\mathbf{x}_i, \mathbf{x}_j)$. Higher values of α enforce connections between near shots and increase the quality of the detected scenes (best viewed in color).

$$d(\mathbf{x}_i, \mathbf{x}_j) = 1 - \exp\left(-\frac{d_1^2(\psi(\mathbf{x}_i), \psi(\mathbf{x}_j)) + \alpha \cdot d_2^2(\mathbf{x}_i, \mathbf{x}_j)}{2\sigma^2}\right) \qquad (3)$$

where $\psi(\mathbf{x}_i)$ is the normalized histogram of shot $\mathbf{x}_i$, d_1^2 is the Bhattacharyya distance and $d_2^2(\mathbf{x}_i, \mathbf{x}_j)$ is the normalized temporal distance between shot $\mathbf{x}_i$ and shot $\mathbf{x}_j$, while the parameter α tunes the relative importance of color similarity and temporal distance. To describe temporal distance between frames, $d_2^2(\mathbf{x}_i, \mathbf{x}_j)$ is defined as

$$d_2^2(\mathbf{x}_i, \mathbf{x}_j) = \frac{|m_i - m_j|}{l} \qquad (4)$$

where m_i is the index of the central frame of shot $\mathbf{x}_i$, and l is the total number of frames in the video. As shown in Fig. 1, the effect of applying increasing values of α to d is to raise the similarities of adjacent shots, therefore boosting the temporal consistency of the resulting groups.

We then cluster shots using hierarchical clustering methods based on complete linkage, where the dissimilarity between two clusters C_x and C_y is defined as the maximum distance of their elements

$$d(C_x, C_y) = \max_{\mathbf{x}_i \in C_x, \mathbf{x}_j \in C_y} d(\mathbf{x}_i, \mathbf{x}_j) \qquad (5)$$

To cluster N shots, we start with N clusters, each containing a single shot, then we iteratively find the least dissimilar pair of clusters, according to Eq. 5, and merge them together, until everything is merged in a single cluster. This process generates a hierarchy of shots, with N levels and i clusters at level i, and each level represents a clustering of the input shots.

Once a particular level is selected, our definition of distance does not guarantee a completely temporal consistent clustering (i.e. some clusters may still contain non-adjacent shots); at the same time, too high values of α would lead to a segmentation that ignores color dissimilarity. The final scene boundaries are created between adjacent shots that do not belong to the same cluster.

4   Experiments

We firstly describe the measures used to evaluate scene segmentation techniques, then, we assess the effectiveness of our shot detection and scene approaches by comparing them against recent methods. We also address two drawbacks of the existing measures.

4.1   Performance Measures

We adopt the Coverage, Overflow and F-Score measures, proposed in [10], to evaluate our scene detection results. Coverage $\mathcal{C}$ measures the quantity of shots belonging to the same scene correctly grouped together, while Overflow $\mathcal{O}$ evaluates to what extent shots not belonging to the same scene are erroneously grouped together. Formally, given the set of automatically detected scenes $\mathbf{s} = [\mathbf{s}_1, \mathbf{s}_2, ..., \mathbf{s}_m]$, and the ground truth $\tilde{\mathbf{s}} = [\tilde{\mathbf{s}}_1, \tilde{\mathbf{s}}_2, ..., \tilde{\mathbf{s}}_n]$, where each element of $\mathbf{s}$ and $\tilde{\mathbf{s}}$ is a set of shot indexes, the coverage $\mathcal{C}_t$ of scene $\tilde{\mathbf{s}}_t$ is proportional to the longest overlap between $\mathbf{s}_i$ and $\tilde{\mathbf{s}}_t$:

$$\mathcal{C}_t = \frac{\max_{i=1...,m} \#(\mathbf{s}_i \cap \tilde{\mathbf{s}}_t)}{\#(\tilde{\mathbf{s}}_t)} \tag{6}$$

where $\#(\mathbf{s}_i)$ is the number of shots in scene $\mathbf{s}_i$. The overflow of a scene $\tilde{\mathbf{s}}_t$, $\mathcal{O}_t$, is the amount of overlap of every $\mathbf{s}_i$ corresponding to $\tilde{\mathbf{s}}_t$ with the two surrounding scenes $\tilde{\mathbf{s}}_{t-1}$ and $\tilde{\mathbf{s}}_{t+1}$:

$$\mathcal{O}_t = \frac{\sum_{i=1}^{m} \#(\mathbf{s}_i \setminus \tilde{\mathbf{s}}_t) \cdot \min(1, \#(\mathbf{s}_i \cap \tilde{\mathbf{s}}_t))}{\#(\tilde{\mathbf{s}}_{t-1}) + \#(\tilde{\mathbf{s}}_{t+1})} \tag{7}$$

The computed per-scene measures can then be aggregated into values for an entire video as follows:

$$\mathcal{C} = \sum_{t=1}^{n} \mathcal{C}_t \cdot \frac{\#(\tilde{\mathbf{s}}_t)}{\sum \#(\tilde{\mathbf{s}}_i)}, \quad \mathcal{O} = \sum_{t=1}^{n} \mathcal{O}_t \cdot \frac{\#(\tilde{\mathbf{s}}_t)}{\sum \#(\tilde{\mathbf{s}}_i)} \tag{8}$$

finally, an F-Score metric can be defined to combine Coverage and Overflow in a single measure, by taking the harmonic mean of $\mathcal{C}$ and $1 - \mathcal{O}$.

We identify two inconveniences of these measures, hence we propose an improved definition. The first one is that, being computed at the shot level, an error on a short shot is given the same importance of an error on a very long shot. On the other hand, we propose to normalize $\mathcal{O}_t$ with respect to the length of $\tilde{\mathbf{s}}_t$ instead of that of $\tilde{\mathbf{s}}_{t-1}$ and $\tilde{\mathbf{s}}_{t+1}$, since we believe that the amount of error due to overflowing should be related to the current scene length, instead of its two neighbors. As an example, consider a ground truth segmentation where a long scene is surrounded by two short scenes: if the detected scene is the union of all three, the actual amount of overflow for the middle scene is quite small, while the usage of the original measures would result in a 100% overflow.

Fig. 2. Two consecutive scenes from the RAI dataset.

Therefore, we propose the Coverage* and Overflow* measures, where the cardinality operator $\#$ is replaced with the number of frames of a scene, $l(\mathbf{s}_i)$, and overflow is redefined as follows:

$$O_t^* = \min\left(1, \frac{\sum_{i=1}^m l(\mathbf{s}_i \setminus \tilde{\mathbf{s}}_t) \cdot \min(1, l(\mathbf{s}_i \cap \tilde{\mathbf{s}}_t))}{l(\tilde{\mathbf{s}}_t)}\right) \tag{9}$$

Note that we limit the amount of overflow to one: this also assures that our coverage and overflow belong to $[0, 1]$, a property which was not guaranteed in Eq. 7. The corresponding $\mathcal{C}^*$ and $\mathcal{O}^*$ for an entire video can be obtained in the same way of Eq. 8, using the newly defined cardinality operator.

4.2 Evaluation

We evaluate our shot and scene detection approach on a collection of ten randomly selected broadcasting videos from the Rai Scuola video archive[1], mainly documentaries and talk shows (see Figure 2). Shots and scenes have been manually annotated by a set of human experts to define the ground truth. Our dataset

---

[1] http://www.scuola.rai.it

Table 1. Characteristics of the RAI Dataset and shot detection performance in terms of F-measure.

Video	% of gradual	Avg. trans. duration
V_1	0.21	3.82
V_2	0.07	1.58
V_3	0.09	1.41
V_4	0.45	14.10
V_5	0.89	19.48
V_6	0.06	0.74
V_7	0.04	0.49
V_8	0.09	1.65
V_9	0.58	12.64
V_{10}	0.44	10.53

Video	Method in [1]	Our method
V_1	0.92	**0.97**
V_2	0.92	**0.97**
V_3	0.94	**0.95**
V_4	**0.82**	0.78
V_5	**0.55**	0.38
V_6	0.93	**0.96**
V_7	0.89	**0.94**
V_8	0.94	0.94
V_9	0.75	**0.76**
V_{10}	0.77	0.77
Average	0.84	0.84

Table 2. Performance comparison on the RAI dataset using the Coverage, Overflow and F-Score measures.

Video	Chasanis et al. [4]			Sidiropoulos et al. [9]			Our method		
	F-Score	C	O	F-Score	C	O	F-Score	C	O
V_1	0.70	0.64	0.24	0.72	0.84	0.37	**0.73**	0.61	0.11
V_2	0.36	0.80	0.77	0.59	0.85	0.55	**0.73**	0.59	0.06
V_3	0.58	0.73	0.52	0.58	0.90	0.57	**0.60**	0.79	0.51
V_4	0.50	0.65	0.60	0.33	0.94	0.80	**0.77**	0.78	0.23
V_5	0.25	0.93	0.86	0.66	0.76	0.41	**0.76**	0.72	0.19
V_6	0.18	0.89	0.90	0.71	0.77	0.34	**0.73**	0.74	0.28
V_7	0.37	0.70	0.75	0.51	0.78	0.62	**0.70**	0.72	0.31
V_8	**0.62**	0.57	0.32	0.45	0.88	0.70	0.60	0.65	0.44
V_9	0.27	0.87	0.84	0.43	0.92	0.72	**0.83**	0.85	0.19
V_{10}	0.54	0.91	0.62	0.44	0.94	0.71	**0.61**	0.49	0.20
Average	0.44	0.77	0.64	0.54	0.86	0.58	**0.70**	0.69	0.25

and the corresponding annotations, together with the code of our shot detection algorithm, are available for download at http://imagelab.ing.unimore.it

For the shot detection task, our dataset contains 987 shot boundaries, 724 of them being hard cuts and 263 gradual transitions. The percentage of gradual transitions greatly varies from video to video, with V_4, V_5, V_9 and V_{10} having a percentage of gradual transitions superior to 44%, and the rest having a mean of 9%.

The performance of the proposed approach was evaluated and compared against the recent proposal of Apostolidis et al. [1], using the executable provided by the authors. Threshold T was set to 80, while the safe zone T_S was fixed to 20 frames, and we repeated our gradual transitions search routine up to $w = 2.5$. As it can be seen from the experimental results summarized in Table 1, our approach performs considerably well, achieving high levels of F-measure on all videos, except in videos with lots of gradual transitions. Indeed, it shows very good performances on abrupt and short gradual transitions, while it tends to

Table 3. Performance comparison on the RAI dataset using the Coverage*, Overflow* and F-Score* measures.

Video	Chasanis et al. [4]			Sidiropoulos et al. [9]			Our method		
	F-Score*	C^*	O^*	F-Score*	C^*	O^*	F-Score*	C^*	O^*
V_1	0.70	0.65	0.24	0.70	0.63	0.20	**0.82**	0.75	0.10
V_2	0.60	0.91	0.55	0.61	0.73	0.47	**0.67**	0.55	0.15
V_3	0.51	0.87	0.64	0.51	0.89	0.64	**0.60**	0.84	0.54
V_4	0.54	0.70	0.56	0.22	0.95	0.88	**0.73**	0.79	0.33
V_5	0.34	0.92	0.79	0.57	0.66	0.50	**0.79**	0.73	0.14
V_6	0.20	0.89	0.88	**0.74**	0.72	0.24	0.68	0.67	0.31
V_7	0.37	0.75	0.76	0.56	0.69	0.53	**0.80**	0.78	0.17
V_8	0.59	0.65	0.47	0.15	0.89	0.92	**0.62**	0.66	0.42
V_9	0.07	0.83	0.96	0.15	0.94	0.92	**0.85**	0.91	0.20
V_{10}	0.50	0.93	0.66	0.11	0.93	0.94	**0.67**	0.57	0.20
Average	0.44	0.81	0.65	0.43	0.80	0.63	**0.72**	0.73	0.26

fail on very long transitions. Overall, our method achieves competitive results when compared to [1]. Regarding time performance, the running time of a CPU-based single-thread implementation of our algorithm is about 13% of the video duration on a PC with Intel i7 processor at 3.6 GHz, which is more than twice faster than [1].

To evaluate our scene detection approach, instead, we compare our method against the multimodal approach presented in [9] and that of [4]. We use the executable of [9] provided by the authors[2] and reimplement the method in [4]. Parameters of [4] were selected to maximize the performance on our dataset.

The overall results on the dataset are shown in Table 2, using Vendrig's measures (Coverage, Overflow and F-Score), and in Table 3, using our improved definitions (Score*, Overflow* and F-Score*). Our method achieves competitive results, using both measures, when compared to recent and state-of-the-art methods like [9], and features a considerably reduced overflow. When shot duration is taken into account, using our measures, the improvement of our method over the others is even clearer.

5   Conclusions

We described a novel approach to video re-use by means of shot and scene detection, which is motivated by the need of accessing and re-using the existing footage in more effective ways. We presented a shot detection approach that relies on an extended distance measure and that is capable of detecting abrupt and gradual transitions, with very low execution times, and a scene detection model that jointly considers temporal proximity and color similarity. Our scene detection results outperform the state-of-the-art algorithms by a large margin on the RAI dataset.

---

[2] http://mklab.iti.gr/project/video-shot-segm

Acknowledgments. This work was carried out within the project "Città educante" (CTN01_00034_393801) of the National Technological Cluster on Smart Communities cofunded by the Italian Ministry of Education, University and Research - MIUR.

References

1. Apostolidis, E., Mezaris, V.: Fast Shot Segmentation Combining Global and Local Visual Descriptors. In: IEEE Int. Conf. Acoustics, Speech and Signal Process, pp. 6583–6587 (2014)
2. Baraldi, L., Grana, C., Cucchiara, R.: Measuring Scene Detection Performance. In: Paredes, R., Cardoso, J.S., Pardo, X.M. (eds.) IbPRIA 2015. LNCS, vol. 9117, pp. 395–403. Springer, Heidelberg (2015)
3. Baraldi, L., Grana, C., Cucchiara, R.: Scene segmentation using temporal clustering for accessing and re-using broadcast video. In: IEEE International Conference on Multimedia and Expo (IEEE ICME 2015) (2015)
4. Chasanis, V.T., Likas, C., Galatsanos, N.P.: Scene detection in videos using shot clustering and sequence alignment. IEEE Trans. Multimedia 11(1), 89–100 (2009)
5. Hanjalic, A., Lagendijk, R.L., Biemond, J.: Automated high-level movie segmentation for advanced video-retrieval systems. IEEE Trans. Circuits Syst. Video Technol. 9(4), 580–588 (1999)
6. Ling, X., Yuanxin, O., Huan, L., Zhang, X.: A method for fast shot boundary detection based on SVM. In: Congress on Image and Signal Processing, CISP 2008, vol. 2, pp. 445–449 (2008)
7. Liu, C., Wang, D., Zhu, J., Zhang, B.: Learning a Contextual Multi-Thread Model for Movie/TV Scene Segmentation. IEEE Trans. Multimedia 15(4), 884–897 (2013)
8. Rasheed, Z., Shah, M.: Detection and representation of scenes in videos. IEEE Trans. Multimedia 7(6), 1097–1105 (2005)
9. Sidiropoulos, P., Mezaris, V., Kompatsiaris, I., Meinedo, H., Bugalho, M., Trancoso, I.: Temporal video segmentation to scenes using high-level audiovisual features. IEEE Trans. Circuits Syst. Video Technol. 21(8), 1163–1177 (2011)
10. Vendrig, J., Worring, M.: Systematic evaluation of logical story unit segmentation. IEEE Trans. Multimedia 4(4), 492–499 (2002)
11. Yeung, M.M., Yeo, B.L., Wolf, W.H., Liu, B.: Video browsing using clustering and scene transitions on compressed sequences. In: IS&T/SPIE's Symposium on Electronic Imaging: Science & Technology, pp. 399–413 (1995)

Locally Adapted Gain Control for Reliable Foreground Detection

Duber Martinez[1], Alessia Saggese[2]([✉]), Mario Vento[2], Humberto Loaiza[1],
and Eduardo Caicedo[1]

[1] Department of Electrical and Electronic Engineering,
University of Valle, Cali, Colombia
`duber.martinez@correounivalle.edu.co,`
`{humberto.loaiza,eduardo.caicedo}@correounivalle.edu.co`
[2] Department of Computer Engineering and Electrical Engineering and Applied
Mathematics, University of Salerno, Fisciano, Italy
`{asaggese,mvento}@unisa.it`

Abstract. One of the first steps in video analysis systems is the detection of objects moving in the scene, namely the foreground detection. Therefore, the accuracy and precision obtained in this phase have a strong impact on the performance of the whole system. Many camera manufacturers include internal systems, such as the automatic gain control (AGC), so as to improve the image quality; although some of these options enhance the human perception, they may also introduce sudden changes in the intensity of the overall image, which risk to be wrongly interpreted as moving objects by traditional foreground detection algorithms. In this paper we propose a method able to detect the changes introduced by the AGC, and properly manage them, so as to minimize their impact on the foreground detection algorithms. The experimentation has been carried out over a wide and publicly available dataset by adopted one well known background subtraction technique and the obtained results confirm the effectiveness of the proposed approach.

1 Introduction

The proliferation of cameras spread over the territory is everyday most common due to the need for security. In consequence, the scientific community has leaded to find solutions able to automatically understand the human behaviors in video sequences [1][2]. One of the most important steps of such systems is the detection of moving objects populating the scene, usually called foreground objects [3]. This step is traditionally achieved by background subtraction algorithms, based on a reference image (the background), which does not contain any foreground object [3][4][5][6].

Most of the algorithms proposed up to now in the literature are based on images acquired in a visible spectrum [7]. The main limitations of such approach become evident in real environments as soon as weather conditions change: think, as an example, to low visibility conditions due to darkness or fog: a solution to

© Springer International Publishing Switzerland 2015
G. Azzopardi and N. Petkov (Eds.): CAIP 2015, Part I, LNCS 9256, pp. 812–823, 2015.
DOI: 10.1007/978-3-319-23192-1_68

this problem can be found using infrared images from thermal cameras [8]. Of course, in this case the conventional background subtraction algorithms fail and then more suited solutions need to be found [9][10].

Systems based on thermal cameras, in fact, have to deal with several problems: on one side, the traditional problems related to the foreground detection step, such as camouflage or environment changes [10]. On the other side, they have to manage more specific problems such as changes due to internal adjustments like the Automatic Gain Control (AGC). The AGC system is a feature introduced by the camera manufacturers to help in capturing the image with a suitable range for reception, by adjusting the sensor gain and the camera exposure time. Camera AGC improves the dynamic range and image contrast, varying the internal gain to increase or decrease the sensibility according to scene conditions [11].

Although this option allows to significantly improving the image quality, it can also affect the performance of the foreground detection algorithms. This influence is especially strong in thermal cameras, because, when hot objects such as a human body move in of the field of view, large regions of pixels get high intensity levels. As a result of these changes, the AGC system adjusts the sensor gain in an attempt to avoid saturation.

The resulting change can lead to sudden large variations of intensity even in consecutive frames. These sudden changes can result in a failure in case of most background modeling applications. For this reason, in many cases, a lot of real images with important information, but obtained in with the AGC option enabled, are discarded for testing of such algorithms.

The basic methods for background subtraction algorithms consist of a simple average or median of previous frames [12] [13][14]. However, their main limitation is that they cannot handle multi-modal background distributions. This problem is partially solved by [15] and [16] which adopt techniques based on Gaussian Mixture Model (GMM) and kernel density estimators respectively. Although they allow modeling more complex background distribution, they model the image intensity at a pixel level, thus resulting in a limitation in the exploitation of spatial correlation. This lack generates fails to compensate for AGC when it produces large variations in image intensity at a global level. Other techniques as [17] calculate optical flow on each pixel; thanks to this approach, such methods are able to detect all the changes between adjacent frames, so revealing to be particularly suited for detecting crowd movements. However, optical flow methods are very sensitive to brightness change and very expensive from a computational point of view.

In general the more complicated methods tend to lack either in terms of computation speed, or in terms of memory requirements [3],[18]. In addition, most of background subtraction algorithms require adjustment of internal parameters and thresholds, in order to achieve best adaptation to different scenarios [19]. However, even if the setting of such parameters is proper to surroundings conditions, it could be too sensitive to sudden changes by AGC.

In [20] the authors focus on thermal cameras and propose a modified version of GMM algorithm able to compensate the AGC changes. They assume that the AGC transfer function corresponds to a polynomial relation close to the line y=x, and then they introduce explicitly this transfer function for modifying the update equations of the parameters of Gaussian components. The main limitations of this method lie in the fact that is directly applicable with a particular foreground algorithm, for using with another is necessary remodeling it. In addition, the solution only allows detecting AGC changes near to the line y=x, therefore, more complex or strong changes are not compensated. In [21] the authors work with infrared images; they propose an affine model of sensor gain. They first extract a sparse set of features in each frame using the Harris corner detector in order to establish correspondences between adjacent frames. Then they find potential matching pairs using normalized correlation, and finally they estimate the parameters of a global affine alignment using an iterative method. This approach have two constraints: in fact it requires that (i) the corner detection be repeatable, so implying that many of the corners from frame t should also have corresponding corners detected in frame $t + 1$ and so on; (ii) the affine model of sensor gain describes properly the behavior of thermal sensor.

In this paper we propose a method able to increase the robustness in the foreground detection phase with respect to changes introduced by the AGC system. The main contributions of our approach respect to previous works are the following: (i) our approach differently from other methods, can potentially work with any background subtraction algorithm, without requiring any internal modifications; (ii) our approach corrects more complex AGC changes, such as found in some thermal cameras that introduce multi-valued functions to improve the dynamic range. This occurs when the AGC system applies different transformation functions to pixels with the same intensity value, but located in separate regions in the image; (iii) our method does not require to find points of correspondence in the frames, or any features extraction step. (iv) Finally, a new dataset built for validating the method is made publicly available for benchmarking purposes.

The remaining sections of the paper are organized as follows: in Sections 2 and 3, the problem that involves the AGC for the foreground detection phase and our solution are presented, respectively. In Section 4 we presented the results obtained by combining the proposed approach with five different background subtraction algorithms. Finally Section 5 draws some conclusions and further research directions.

2   Preliminaries

Most of the camera manufacturers provide some properties for increasing the images quality; one of most common properties for enhancing the contrast is the automatic gain control (AGC), which increases the intensifier gain if the scene is too dark, and decrease the gain if is too bright according to some thresholds [11]. In the case of thermal cameras, the effect is stronger if is compared with visible spectrum cameras: it is due to the impact on overall image intensity when a relatively hot object like a human appears in the scene; in fact, it can produce saturation points and thus may generate abrupt changes that are detected by the background subtraction algorithms like false foreground. An example useful to clarify this concept is shown in Figure 1: in particular, Figures 1(a) and 1(b) show two successive frames, with different internal gains adjusted by the AGC system. Figures 1(c) and 1(d) report the corresponding foreground masks obtained by a traditional background subtraction algorithm. It is evident that traditional background subtraction and updating algorithms are not able to deal with such variations.

Furthermore, the manufacturers can provide different kinds of AGC systems; in fact, in some cases the transformation function that produces changes in the intensity is nonlinear, and not necessarily univocal. It implies that it is possible to find pixels with the same intensity value, but in different regions of the image, where the AGC system performs different adjustment operations. For example, in Figure 2(a) the central pixel in the boxes red and blue have both the same intensity value of 98; with the transformation by AGC, shown in Figure 2(b), the central pixel in the box on the left is increased to 154, while the middle pixel of blue box is decreased to 53. This multi-valued behavior is shown in Figure 3, where the changes introduced by AGC have been mapped. In particular, the curves relates the mapping between the intensities values of pixels belonging to the previous frame (Figure 2(a), horizontal axis) and the ones belonging to the current frame (Figure 2(b), vertical axis) are shown.

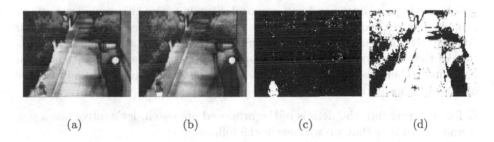

(a)   (b)   (c)   (d)

Fig. 1. An example of the effect of AGC: two successive frame (a,b) and the corresponding foreground mask (c,d) obtained by traditional background subtraction algorithms.

3   The Proposed Method

At this point it is clear that the foreground pixels detected by a background subtraction algorithm can belong to two different categories: (i) objects moving in the scene; (ii) spurious object, due for instance to changes introduced by AGC systems. In this last case, the changes follow a pattern defined by an internal transformation function which depends on the particular AGC system, and

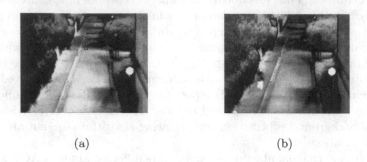

(a)   (b)

Fig. 2. Example of internal gain change

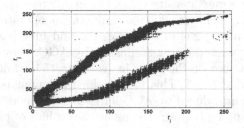

Fig. 3. Multi-valued transformation relation between the pixels belonging to the previous frame (x-axis) and the ones belonging to the current frame (y-axis).

which could be nonlinear and non-univocal. Starting from this consideration, we propose a novel two-steps method able to autonomous adapt to the particular AGC system: in particular, during a preliminary training step the change pattern of the AGC system is extracted and the related transformation relation is computed. Then, the foreground produced by the AGC is insulated and filtered of initial foreground.

Before entering into the details of the proposed approach, let's introduce a couple of symbols that we will use in the following

- I_t the image acquired at the current frame t
- p is the generic pixel at the position (x,y)
- FG_{t-1} is the foreground computed in the frame $t-1$
- I_{ref} is the reference image for AGC
- FG_{ref} is the foreground corresponding to I_{ref}
- R is the region of I_t that does not contain points which belong to FG_{t-1}.

The frequency function $f(r_i, r_j)$ can be computed as the number of points p belonging to the region R such that their value is equal to r_i in the current frame I_t while it is equal to r_j in the reference image I_{ref}:

$$f(r_i, r_j) = \sum_{p \in R} \{p : I_t(p) = r_i \wedge I_{ref}(p) = r_j\}. \tag{1}$$

r_i, r_j is a possible couple c of values into the intensity range $[0, MAX]$, being MAX the maximum value of intensity for a given representation of the colors. Given the different combinations of the c value, we can define two sets C^1 and C^2 including the upper and lower points of the line $y = x$, respectively:

$$C^1 = \{c : r_j \geq r_i \wedge f(r_i, r_j) > Fmin\} \tag{2}$$

$$C^2 = \{c : r_j < r_i \wedge f(r_i, r_j) > Fmin\} \tag{3}$$

$Fmin$ represents the minimum frequency, used to reduce the noise effect. In this work we experimentally set this value to 5 by data sampling.

For each set C^k, $k = 1, 2$ we can associate a transformation function T^k aiming to minimize the estimation error of the new values of intensity generated by the AGC system. Given the generic transformation $T_k(r_i)$, the best transformation $T^*(r_i)$ can be computed as:

$$T^*(r_i) = \underset{T^k}{\mathrm{argmin}} \left\{ \sum_{c \in C^k} \|T^k(r_i) - r_j\| \right\}; \quad k = 1, 2 \tag{4}$$

Each transformation $T^k = \sum_{n=0}^{3} a_n r_i^n$ is modeled as a polynomial function of degree 3.

It implies that for the pixels $p \in R$ the following condition holds:

$$T^*[I_t(p)] \approx I_{ref}(p); \quad k = 1, 2 \tag{5}$$

Starting from the above assumptions, let consider a traditional background subtraction algorithm BGS which is able to obtain a basic foreground FGB_t by analyzing the current image I_t:

$$FGB_t = BGS[I_t] \tag{6}$$

Three different regions can be identified in FGB_t: R_O, which contains foreground pixels due to moving objects; R_A, due to changes introduced by AGC systems and finally R_N due to the noise.

This partition implies that the current image can be considered composed by the following regions:

$$I_t = \{I_t(p)|_{p \in R_B}\} \cup \{I_t(p)|_{p \in R_A}\} \cup \{I_t(p)|_{p \in R_O}\} \cup \{I_t(p)|_{p \in R_N}\}, \tag{7}$$

where R_B encodes all those points which do not belong to the foreground image.

Since these are mutually exclusive partitions, they are non-overlapping regions, therefore, it is possible to apply the transformation function T^* separately for each region of the image I_t. Thus, starting from Eq. (7), we can obtain:

$$T^*[I_t] = \{T^*[I_t(p)|_{p \in R_B}]\} \cup \{T^*[I_t(p)|_{p \in R_A}]\}$$
$$\cup \{T^*[I_t(p)|_{p \in R_O}]\} \cup \{T^*[I_t(p)|_{p \in R_n}]\} \tag{8}$$

The application of the transformation function to R_A and R_B, as shown in Eq. 5, implies that such points of the image become equivalent to the reference image I_{ref}:

$$T^* [I_t(p)|_{p\in R_B}] \approx I_{ref}(p)|_{p\in R_B} \tag{9}$$

$$T^* [I_t(p)|_{p\in R_A}] \approx I_{ref}(p)|_{p\in R_A} \tag{10}$$

Thus, Eq. 8 can be re written as follow:

$$T^* [I_t] \approx \{I_{ref}(p)|_{p\in R_B}\} \cup \{I_{ref}(p)|_{p\in R_A}\}$$
$$\cup \{T^* [I_t(p)|_{p\in R_O}]\} \cup \{T^* [I_t(p)|_{p\in R_n}]\} \tag{11}$$

We can note that the negative effects introduced by the AGC system have been completely neglected. Thus, the subtraction between the current frame and the reference image $T^* [I_t] - I_{ref}$ implies that only those pixels associated to noise and moving objects (regions R_O and R_N, respectively) are taken into account:

$$T^* [I_t] - I_{ref} = \{(T^k [I_t(p)] - I_{ref}(p)) |_{p\in R_O}\}$$
$$\cup \{(T^k [I_t(p)] - I_{ref}(p)) |_{p\in R_n}\} \tag{12}$$

In conclusion, the foreground mask FG_t computed by the proposed approach in order to deal with AGC system can be evaluated by filtering FGB_t, extracted by traditional background subtraction algorithm, as follows:

$$FG_t = \{p: \ p \in FGB_t \wedge T^* [I_t(p)] - I_{ref}(p) > Th\} \tag{13}$$

The threshold Th is calculated according to Eq. 14 and corresponds to the mean of standard deviations along of the curves C^k associated to the chosen transformation, and weighted by a factor of 4. This value is chosen so as to eliminate statistically distant points, around 4 time the standard deviations.

$$Th^k = \frac{4}{N_i} \sum_{i=1}^{N_i} \sqrt{\frac{1}{N_j^i} \sum_{j=1}^{N_j^i} (r_j - \mu_j^i)^2}$$
$$\forall j : (r_i, r_j) \in C^k \tag{14}$$

N_i is the number of different values of r_i, being $N_i \leq L$; N_j^i is the number of different value of r_j for the same value of r_i, with $N_j^i << N_i$; finally μ_j^i is the mean value of N_j^i values of r_j.

Starting from the obtained foreground mask, the reference frame I_{ref} and the related foreground mask FG_{ref} can be finally updated as follows:

$$I_{ref} = \begin{cases} I_t, & \text{if } |FG_t| \leq |FG_{ref}| \\ I_{ref}, & \text{otherwise} \end{cases} \tag{15}$$

$$FG_{ref} = \begin{cases} FG_t, & \text{if } |FG_t| \le |FG_{ref}| \\ FG_{ref}, & \text{otherwise} \end{cases} \tag{16}$$

where $|X|$ corresponds to the number of pixels belonging to the related image X.

4 System Validation

In this section is described the methodology to evaluate the method proposed for the AGC compensation; the background subtraction algorithm used for test, the dataset characteristics, the performance metric used, and finally the experimental result obtained and their discussion.

4.1 The Dataset

At the best of our knowledge, no publicly available datasets for this purpose have been released up to now. For this reason, we constructed a data set composed by four video sequences in different scenarios. The sequences introduce variations of camera distance, and diverse distributions of static elements present in the scene like: grass, trees, asphalt, walls, etc. Figure 4 shows images for each view: each video sequence has been obtained with a thermal camera Axis Q1910 with the AGC option enabled, and image resolution of 360 x 288. More details are provided in Table 1.

The dataset, together with the ground truth hand made by an expert, is publicly available for benchmarking purposes and can be downloaded at the following link: http://mivia.unisa.it/database/AGC_dataset.zip.

Table 1. Details of the acquired dataset, in terms of number of frames, frame rate and number of objects populating the scene.

Figure	Sequence	# of frames	frame rate	# of objects
4(a)	S1	312	4	33
4(b)	S2	81	4	20
4(c)	S3	218	4	31
4(d)	S4	263	4	10

4.2 Performance Metrics

In order to evaluate the impact on the background subtraction algorithms performance, we used the standard set of metrics proposed in [22]. In particular, the considered indicators are the following:

Multiple Object Detection Accuracy (MODA) considers the accuracy aspect of system performance. To this end, is used the missed detection and

(a)   (b)   (c)   (d)

Fig. 4. An example of the four views of the considered dataset.

false positive counts. The maximum value is 1, which implies that there are not missed objects, or false positives in the sequence. MODA value equal to 0 indicates that the number of missed objects and false positives is equal to the number of ground truth objects. Negative values indicate a high number of missed objects and/or false positives; for example a value of -1 indicates that the number of missed objects and/or false positives is the double of the number of ground truth objects.

Multiple Object Detection Precision (MODP) highlights the precision aspect of system performance. It is used the spatial overlap information between the ground truth and the system output. $MODP = 1$ indicates perfect correspondence between the ground truth and detected objects.

4.3   Analysis of the Achieved Results

In this section we report the impact of our AGC correction method over the well-known background subtraction algorithm ***Gaussian Mixture Model (GMM)*** [15], which is one of the most used algorithms for object detection. Each pixel is modeled separately as a mixture of K Gaussians. A pixel from a new image is considered to be a background pixel if its new value is well described by its probability density function.

In Figure 5 we show an example of foreground detected for specific frames in the four test video sequences, where take place sudden changes by AGC. Figures $(a, b, c$ and $d)$ correspond to foreground detected by the basic GMM algorithm, and $(e, f, g$ and $h)$ the respective foreground after applying the proposed method.

In Table 2 we report the numeric performance indicators for this example. The columns GMM correspond to basic algorithm, and columns $AGCC$ to the AGC Correction algorithm proposed. In table 3 we finally report the performance indicators for the overall set of test video sequences (S1, S2, S3 and S4).

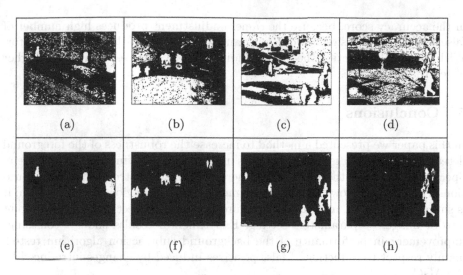

Fig. 5. Foreground before (a,b,c,d) and after (e,f,g,h) the proposed AGC compensation.

Table 2. Performance improvement for the frames considered in Figure 5.

Frames	MODP GMM	MODP AGCC	MODA GMM	MODA AGCC
(a, e)	0.813	0.828	-17.667	1.000
(b, f)	0.857	0.825	-1.800	0.800
(c, g)	0.789	0.778	-1.2857	0.857
(d, h)	0.672	0.695	-0.500	0.667
$Avg.$	**0.784**	0.782	-5.313	**0.831**
$Std.$	0.075	0.062	8.253	0.138

Table 3. Performance improvement for the whole considered dataset.

Sequence	MODP GMM	MODP AGCC	MODA GMM	MODA AGCC
$S1$	0.759	0.766	0.561	0.782
$S2$	0.930	0.958	-0.283	0.902
$S3$	0.788	0.790	0.637	0.909
$S4$	0.773	0.826	-0.611	0.889
$Avg.$	0.812	**0.835**	0.076	**0.870**
$Std.$	0.079	0.086	0.619	0.059

The obtained results show that thanks to the proposed method, we are able to achieve a significant improvement in the foreground detection performance. The MODP indicator shows similar values in both cases, this means that our method do not produce additional lost objects. The main impact is obtained in the accuracy score, because the camera adjustment produces high number of false positives. This is reflected in low or negative values of the MODA indicator. With the AGC correction the MODA indicator shows an average increase higher of ten times its value.

5   Conclusions

In this paper we presented a method to increase the robustness of the foreground detection phase, with respect to changes introduced by the internal AGC system. Specifically, we used thermal images where the impact is stronger due to saturation. The method allows compensating multi-valued behavior of AGC system; it is simple of applying, and does not require automatic detection of interest point into of image, or parameters setting. Experimental results show a consistent improvement in performance of the background subtraction algorithm tested, mainly respect to reduction of false positives induced by changes introduced by the AGC.

In future works we are planning to include additional background subtraction algorithms to demonstrate the robustness and generality of our method. In addition, we are considering to introduce a sensitivity analysis that indicates how is affected the performance with respect to changes by AGC, when is varied the setting of internal parameters in the basic background subtraction algorithms.

References

1. Brun, L., Saggese, A., Vento, M.: Dynamic scene understanding for behavior analysis based on string kernels. IEEE Transactions on Circuits and Systems for Video Technology **24**, 1669–1681 (2014)
2. Acampora, G., Foggia, P., Saggese, A., Vento, M.: A hierarchical neuro-fuzzy architecture for human behavior analysis. Information Sciences **310**, 130–148 (2015)
3. Piccardi, M.: Background subtraction techniques: a review. IEEE Int. Conf. on Systems, Man and Cybernetics, vol. 4, pp. 3099–3104 (2004)
4. Bouwmans, T.: Recent Advanced Statistical Background Modeling for Foreground Detection: A Systematic Survey. Recent Patents on Computer Science **4**, 147–176 (2011)
5. Ramya, A., Raviraj, P.: A Survey and Comparative Analysis of Moving Object Detection and Tracking. International Journal of Engineering Research and Technology **2**, 147–176 (2013)
6. Conte, D., Foggia, P., Percannella, G., Tufano, F., Vento, M.: An experimental evaluation of foreground detection algorithms in real scenes. EURASIP J. Adv. Sig. Proc. **2010** (2010)
7. Chaquet, E.J., Carmona, J.M., Fernndez, A.: A survey of video datasets for human action and activity recognition. Comput. Vis. Image Underst., 117(6), 633–659 (2013)
8. tao Wang, J., bao Chen, D., yan Chen, H., yu Yang, J.: On pedestrian detection and tracking in infrared videos. Pattern Recognition Letters 33(6), 775–785 (2012)
9. Davis, J.W., Sharma, V.: Background-subtraction using contour-based fusion of thermal and visible imagery. Comput. Vis. Image Underst. **106**, 162–182 (2007)

10. Davis, J.W., Sharma, V.: Robust background-subtraction for person detection in thermal imagery. In: Conference on Computer Vision and Pattern Recognition Workshop, vol. 8(8), 128–135 (2004)
11. Fowler, K.R.: Automatic gain control for image-intensified camera. IEEE T. Instrumentation and Measurement **53**(4), 1057–1064 (2004)
12. Cucchiara, R., Grana, C., Prati, A., Piccardi, M.: Detecting objects, shadows and ghosts in video streams by exploiting color and motion information. IEEE Transactions on Pattern Analysis and Machine Intelligence, 360–365 (2001)
13. Lo, B., Velastin, S.: Automatic congestion detection system for underground platforms. In: Proc. of 2001 Int. Symp. on Intell. Multimedia, Video and Speech Processing, pp. 158–161 (May 2001)
14. Lee, B., Hedley, M.: Background Estimation for Video Surveillance. In: Image and Vision Computing New Zealand 2002, IVCNZ 2002, pp. 315–320 (2002)
15. Gaber, M.M., Stahl, F., Gomes, J.B.: Background. In: Pocket Data Mining. SBD, vol. 2, pp. 7–22. Springer, Heidelberg (2014)
16. Elgammal, A., Duraiswami, R., Harwood, D., Davis, L.S.: Background and foreground modeling using nonparametric kernel density estimation for visual surveillance. Proceedings of the IEEE **90**, 1151–1163 (2002)
17. Suganya Devi., Malmurugan, A.K., Sivakumar, R.: Efficient foreground extraction based on optical flow and smed for road traffic analysis, vol. 4(4), pp. 177–182 (2012)
18. Shahbaz, J., Hariyono, A., Jo, K.-H.: Evaluation of background subtraction algorithms for video surveillance. In: 21st Korea-Japan Joint Workshop on Frontiers of Computer Vision (FCV), pp. 1–4 (2015)
19. Gandhama, I., Nanded, A., Talbar, S.: Evaluation of Background Subtraction Algorithms for Object Extraction. In: International Conference on Pervasive Computing (ICPC), p. 8–10 (2015)
20. Kumar, V., Bhargava, N., Chaudhuri, S., Seetharaman, G.: Fast compensation of illumination changes for background subtraction. In: IEEE AIPR, pp. 1–7 (2013)
21. Yalcin, H., Collins, R., Hebert, M.: Background estimation under rapid gain change in thermal imagery. Comput. Vis. Image Underst. **106**, 148–161 (2007)
22. Kasturi, R., Goldgof, D., Soundararajan, P., Manohar, V., Garofolo, J., Bowers, R., Boonstra, M., Korzhova, V., Zhang, J.: Framework for performance evaluation of face, text, and vehicle detection and tracking in video: Data, metrics, and protocol. IEEE Trans on PAMI **31**(2), 319–336 (2009)

Fourier Features For Person Detection
in Depth Data

Viktor Seib$^{(\boxtimes)}$, Guido Schmidt, Michael Kusenbach, and Dietrich Paulus

Active Vision Group (AGAS), University of Koblenz-Landau,
Universitätsstr. 1, 56070 Koblenz, Germany
{vseib,guidoschmidt,mkusenbach,paulus}@uni-koblenz.de
http://agas.uni-koblenz.de

Abstract. A robust and reliable person detection is crucial for many applications. In the domain of service robots that we focus on, knowing the location of a person is an essential requirement for any meaningful human-robot interaction. In this work we present a people detection algorithm exploiting RGB-D data from Kinect-like cameras. Two features are obtained from the data representing the geometrical properties of a person. These features are transformed into the frequency domain using Discrete Fourier Transform (DFT) and used to train a Support Vector Machine (SVM) for classification. Additionally, we present a hand detection algorithm based on the extracted silhouette of a person. We evaluate the proposed method on real world data from the Cornell Activity Dataset and on a dataset created in our laboratory.

Keywords: People detection · Silhouette detection · Hand detection · Fourier features · Service robots

1 Introduction

The ability of service robots to properly react to the commands given by a user highly depends on the robot's capability to reliable detect the position of the interacting person. Apart from the position of the person itself, also the position of its hands is of large interest for a natural interaction. This comes from the customary practice of people to use gestures for interaction. Important gestures that a service robot needs to be aware of in its daily routine is pointing to a position or object of interest, raising a hand to call for attention or waving the hand to call the robot.

With the availability of affordable RGB-D cameras the problem of person detection can be addressed by the combination of RGB camera data, as well as geometrical information based on depth data (figure 1). We propose an approach that exploits these information by calculating 2 novel features. In the first step, a model-based search is performed on the input data to find possible person candidates. For each candidate, 2 features are computed: the *Frontal Feature* and the *Width Feature*. To obtain a low dimensional feature vector, the computed features are transformed to the frequency domain using Discrete Fourier Transform

© Springer International Publishing Switzerland 2015
G. Azzopardi and N. Petkov (Eds.): CAIP 2015, Part I, LNCS 9256, pp. 824–836, 2015.
DOI: 10.1007/978-3-319-23192-1_69

(a)   (b)

Fig. 1. Example RGB image (a) and the corresponding depth image (b) taken from the Cornell Activity Dataset [14].

(DFT) and a Support Vector Machine (SVM) is trained on the obtained Fourier coefficients. The presented approach enables us to detect standing and sitting persons in different poses and orientations towards the camera. Additionally, for frontal facing persons hands are detected using skin color extraction from the face and distances between possible hand candidates on the previously detected person's silhouette. The presented approach is successfully applied on the service robot *Lisa* in our lab.

In the following section 2 we briefly review related work on people detection and especially people detection on depth data. The section 3 and section 4 describe our proposed approach in detail and introduce the proposed features. Finally, section 5 presents evaluation results obtained from the Cornell Activity Dataset [14] and a dataset acquired in our lab and discusses the obtained results. This paper is concluded by section 6 where a summary and an outlook to future work is presented.

2   Related Work

In the past years, several approaches for person detection and tracking using depth data were proposed. However, the actual devices that data stems from are changing. A few years ago, laser sensors or costly stereo camera systems were used. For instance, Bertozzi et al. [1] use a combination of an RGB stereo setup combined with infrared stereo cameras. They extract histograms of oriented gradients (HOG) for classification. The HOG feature is not only used for RGB data, as for example by Dalal and Triggs [5]. It was also adapted to depth data, resulting in the histograms of oriented depths (HOD) detector introduced by Spinello and Arras [13]. Also combinations of HOG and HOD are used as for instance demonstrated in [7].

Machine learning approaches are also exploited for shape matching e.g. the approach described by Xia et al. [11]. Xia et al. use chamfer distance matching to find candidate regions for people locations and examine these with a three

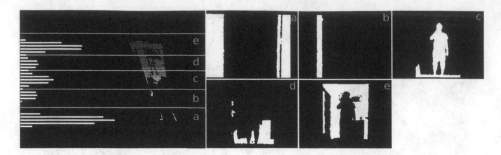

Fig. 2. The resulting depth histogram and the corresponding extracted depth slices are represented as binary images.

dimensional head model. Other approaches use distance transformations and extract a joint representation of detected people, as Lee et al. show in [10].

Paisitkriangkrai et al. [12] introduce spatial pooling on a set of covariance descriptors for feature extraction. Choi et al. [4] introduce a Monte Carlo based Particle Filter. The applied descriptor is based on HOG and on a shape vector is derived from the upper body part of a person candidate. This approach is capable of handling dynamic scenes.

Similar to the approach of Choi et al., our algorithm is also based on shape extraction of the shoulder region and the head. However, we use 2 features specifically designed to detect silhouettes from depth data. As proposed by Hordern and Kirchner [8], we also transform the features with DFT before using them for SVM training and classification.

3 Person Detection

In this section we describe our algorithm for silhouette detection. In the following, we employ a right-handed coordinate system, where the x-axis points forward, the y-axis to the left and the z-axis to the top.

3.1 Candidate Detection

To find candidates for person detection, we first compute a point histogram along the depth axis (x-axis) and then perform a model based search. The input point cloud is divided into equally thick slices along the depth axis. In our experiments we use a thickness of $a = 0.1m$ for each slice. Each slice corresponds to a histogram bin, holding the number of points in that slice. The idea behind this histogram is that potential objects form local point clusters in the scene. To find these objects local minima inside the histogram are found. The objects are expected to be located between these extracted local minima.

In the following step, the point cloud is resliced at locations corresponding to minima in the histogram as shown in figure 2. For every depth slice, a binary image I is generated by only considering points located inside the corresponding

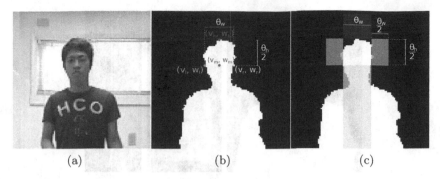

Fig. 3. The RGB data of a person's silhouette (a) and the corresponding binary image (b and c) is shown. The head model assumptions are illustrated in (b), whereas the occupancy of test regions is shown in (c).

slice. A model-based search is performed on the set of binary images $I_0 \dots I_n$ to find person candidates.

First, local maxima $I_i(v_h, w_h)$ on the vertical axis in each binary images I_i are extracted. These are possible head positions, which need to be validated against our model assumptions. Since the binary images were created from point clouds, a 3D point is known for every valid (i.e. "white") pixel $I_i(v, w)$. This permits us to define model parameters in metric space rather than in pixels. In the following, the function $\mathcal{P}(I(v, w))$ is used to obtain the corresponding 3D point $p = (x, y, z)^T$ from a pixel $I(v, w)$ in the binary image. Further, the inverse function $\mathcal{Q}(p)$ is used to obtain the pixel in the binary image corresponding to a 3D point p in the organized point cloud. The actual mapping of a color pixel to a depth pixel (and vice-versa) depends on the dataset (see section 5).

Our model assumption consists of a typical head width θ_w and height θ_h (given in a range of minimal and maximal valid sizes) and includes the approximated calculation of the possible head dimensions, as shown in figure 3. For a local maximum $I_i(v_h, w_h)$ to be selected as candidate, the following propositions must hold. First, there has to be a valid pixel $I(v_m, w_m)$ (middle point), defined as

$$I(v_m, w_m) = \mathcal{Q}(p_{v_m, w_m}) = \mathcal{Q}(p_{v_h, w_h} - (0, 0, \frac{\theta_h}{2})^T). \qquad (1)$$

in the binary image, corresponding to a point $\frac{\theta_h}{2}$ below the maximum. Equation 1 requires that at least the upper half of the head must be visible.

Two other points, the left and the right border point of the head, $I(v_l, w_l)$ and $I(v_r, w_r)$, have to be set in the binary image at the same height as the middle point $I(v_m, w_m)$, fulfilling the constraint

$$\theta_{h,min} < ||\mathcal{P}(I(v_l, w_l)) - \mathcal{P}(I(v_r, w_r))|| < \theta_{h,max}. \qquad (2)$$

The found value $\theta_w = ||\mathcal{P}(I(v_l, w_l)) - \mathcal{P}(I(v_r, w_r))||$ is the hypothetical head width. As a result of processing every binary image according to this model-based search, a set of object hypotheses is obtained possessing human head-like

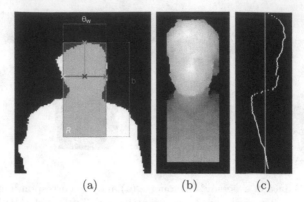

(a)   (b)   (c)

Fig. 4. The image section R used to extract the frontal feature is shown in (a). The contained part of the silhouette is shown in (b). Image (c) shows the frontal silhouette from the side. The horizontal line in (c) is the mean distance value in region R.

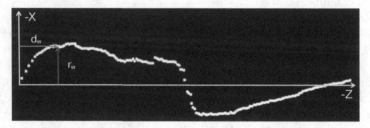

Fig. 5. The extracted values d_w and r_w for the frontal features are shown. This figure corresponds to figure 4 (c) rotated by 90° to the left. The axes are labeled according to the same coordinate system used for feature extraction. The resulting curve is the input data for the DFT.

characteristics at their highest position. Note that this model-based approximation of a head is computationally faster than fitting a circle around local maxima of the binary images.

This set of hypotheses is further refined by calculating the percentage of filled pixels in the binary image in four test regions around the detected hypothetical head (figure 3). The first region represents the area above the highest point of the head with a height of $\frac{\theta_h}{2}$ and the width θ_w. Further, 2 equal regions, one located on the left the other located to the right of the head, are examined. The fourth and last region is located below the head and extends to the bottom of the corresponding binary image. For every region, the percentage of filled pixels in the binary image is calculated. Ideally, the areas above, left and right of the head should be empty. On the other hand, the area below the head should be completely filled, representing a hypothetical torso and legs of a person. Because of possible occlusions by objects in front of the torso, pixels from depth slices in front of the detected candidate are also considered when determining the ratio of filled pixels in the bottom area. After applying these model-based rules, the search space for possible persons is reduced from the whole input point cloud to a set of person candidates.

3.2   Features

For further classification, we propose to extract 2 features for each candidate: the *Frontal Feature* and the *Width Feature*. Both features are well suited to differentiate between persons and objects and are described in the following.

Frontal Feature. The idea of our *Frontal Feature* is to encode the frontal depth contour of the face and upper body of a person. This feature is computed using the previously extracted binary image of the head and the torso and the corresponding point cloud. Therefore, the position, width and height of the head are known. We extract an image section R which is horizontally centered at the head. Vertically, R starts at $I_i(v_h, w_h)$ being the highest point, with the parameter b determining the sections height (figure 4). We obtained best results with $b = 0.5m$ in our experiments. The resulting region covers the candidate's head and upper body. For each pixel row w inside the binary image section R, the mean depth value r_w of all points in this row is computed as

$$r_w = \frac{\sum_{v=0}^{V} \mathcal{P}_x(R(v, w))}{V} \tag{3}$$

where V is the width of R in pixels, $R(v, w)$ is a pixel in R and $\mathcal{P}_x(R(v, w))$ is a function that returns the x-value (i.e. the value on the forward axis) of the point at pixel $R(v, w)$. This provides some stability against rotations and side movements of the head, as well as sensor noise. Further, we calculate the distance d_w of each row w to the highest point $I(v_h, w_h)$ as

$$d_w = \frac{\sum_{v=0}^{V} \mathcal{P}_z(R(v, w))}{V} - \mathcal{P}_z(I(v_h, w_h)) \tag{4}$$

where $\mathcal{P}_z$ is defined similar to $\mathcal{P}_x$, but returning the z-value (i.e. the vertical coordinate). Now we have obtained a mean depth value r_w and a vertical distance d_w to the top point for each row. The resulting frontal contour of a person is visualized in figure 4 for a person facing the camera. The computed values r_w and d_w from R are shown in figure 5. Depending on the person's orientation towards the camera, this feature provides different profiles.

Width Feature. This feature benefits from the fact that persons facing the sensor will have a broader shoulder section compared to their head width. Again we use $b = 0.5m$ for the height of the section of interest R, its width is set to the width of the binary image. We now extract the leftmost $\mathcal{P}(R(v_l, w_l))$ and the rightmost $\mathcal{P}(R(v_r, w_r))$ valid point in each row of the binary image, obtaining the row width b_w from

$$b_w = ||\mathcal{P}_y(I(v_l, w_l)) - \mathcal{P}_y(I(v_r, w_r))||, \tag{5}$$

where $\mathcal{P}_y$ returns the value on the horizontal axis. Further, we again use the vertical distance d_w of each row to the highest point of the head $I(v_h, w_h)$.

3.3 Fourier Feature Vectors

Both features can be seen as functions of the distance d_w from the top point of the candidate head. In case of the *Frontal Feature* function values are the average depth values r_w and in case of the *Width Feature* the width b_w of the candidate silhouette. These two features are computed for each candidate and transformed into the frequency domain using the Fourier transform. Since we have discrete functions (discretized by the lines of the binary images), we use the Discrete Fourier transform (DFT). The actual feature vector is composed of the resulting Fourier coefficients. We can adapt the length of the feature vector by omitting high frequency Fourier coefficients. While the computed features originally had a length of 50, after the Fourier transform we retain only the first 6 coefficients. Figure 7 depicts several sinusoids corresponding to the first Fourier coefficient. Unlike in the work of Hordern et al. [8], where the feature vector is divided by the constant component and therefore is scale invariant, we

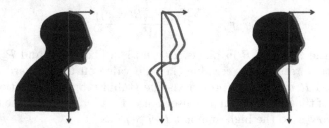

Fig. 6. Omitting the constant component of the Fourier Transform results in a distance independent feature vector sinusoid (shown in red), in contrast to the distance dependent sinusoid with the constant component (shown in green).

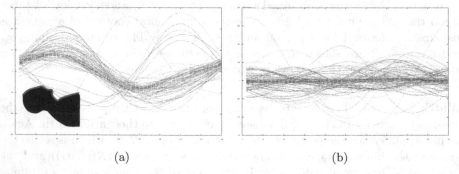

(a)   (b)

Fig. 7. The sinusoids corresponding to the first Fourier coefficient of several human silhouettes are depicted in (a). The outliers stem from partially visible silhouettes at image borders. Image (b) shows the first sinusoids of different objects.

omit the constant component from the feature vector without division. In our case this leads to the feature vector being invariant to the distance of the person to the sensor (figure 6). Our features are based on metric data and scale is an important factor in the process of people detection. We therefore do not want to have a scale invariant feature in order not to detect e.g. toys like dolls that have a similar silhouette, but different size as a human. The resulting feature vector is used to train a support vector machine (SVM) with a radial basis function kernel (RBF).

4   Hand Detection

Since we are interested in interacting with people, we focus on detecting hands of upraised and outstretched arms. These are signs of calling for attentions and thus should be recognized by a service robot.

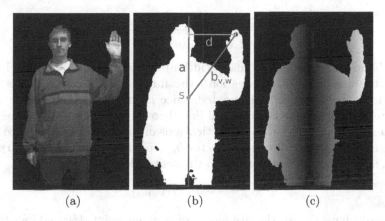

(a)   (b)   (c)

Fig. 8. Illustration of the geometric model to determine the distance between any silhouette point $\mathcal{P}(M(v, w))$ and the centroid s. Image (a) shows the RGB data of the silhouette, while (b) shows the binary image. In image (c) the distance matrix D is depicted.

Starting from the already known highest pixel $I(v_h, w_h)$ of a detected person, a region growing is performed on the binary image. We use the 4-neighborhood for region growing. For 2 neighboring pixels $I(v_a, w_a)$ and $I(v_b, w_b)$, with $I(v_a, w_a)$ being part of the region, $I(v_b, w_b)$ has to fulfill 2 criteria to be added to the region. First, its corresponding 3D point $\mathcal{P}(I(v_b, w_b))$ must not be farther away from the 3D point of a point in the region $\mathcal{P}(I(v_a, w_a))$ than the threshold value c_1:

$$\|\mathcal{P}(I(v_a, w_a)) - \mathcal{P}(I(v_b, w_b))\| < c_1. \tag{6}$$

Additionally, it has to be within the range c_2 of the corresponding 3D point of the highest point of the head, $\mathcal{P}(I(v_h, w_h))$:

$$\|\mathcal{P}(I(v_h, w_h)) - \mathcal{P}(I(v_b, w_b))\| < c_2. \tag{7}$$

In contrast to the initial binary image I, the resulting binary image M contains only the silhouette of the person (without possible background clutter). In the following, the hand is detected using two cues: by taking into account the distance of the hand from the body and exploiting skin color.

4.1   Distance Cue

To exploit the distance cue, the detected body in the silhouette binary image M is reduced to a single vertical line through the centroid of the silhouette. The centroid is calculated from all 3D points of the silhouette using the points p as

$$p = \begin{cases} \mathcal{P}(M(v,w)) & \text{if } M(v,w) = 1 \\ (0,0,0)^T & \text{else} \end{cases}.$$ (8)

The centroid s is then computed as the mean of all points

$$s = \frac{\sum_{v=0}^{V} \sum_{w=0}^{W} \mathcal{P}(M(v,w))}{\sum_{v=0}^{V} \sum_{w=0}^{W} M(v,w)}$$ (9)

where V and W represent the image width and image height, respectively. Note that in the denominator of equation 9 the number of the valid pixels in the silhouette binary image M is computed, since all pixels in M are either 1 or 0. We represent the silhouette's centroid line through the point s by a directional vector $\boldsymbol{a} = (0,0,1)^T$ parallel to the vertical axis of the coordinate reference frame. Now we can calculate a directional vector $\boldsymbol{b}_{v,w}$ pointing from an arbitrary point $\mathcal{P}(M(v,w))$ in the silhouette image to the centroid s as

$$\boldsymbol{b}_{v,w} = s - \mathcal{P}(M(v,w)).$$ (10)

As shown in figure 8 (b), the distance d of a given point $M(v,w)$ can then be calculated by the cross product

$$d_{vw} = ||\boldsymbol{a} \times \boldsymbol{b}_{v,w}||$$ (11)

and a distance matrix D created according to

$$D(v,w) = \begin{cases} d_{vw} & \text{if } \mathcal{P}(M(v,w)) = 1 \\ 0 & \text{else} \end{cases}.$$ (12)

4.2   Skin Color

We use the skin color as the second cue for hand detection. The detected person's face color is used as a reference color. Please note that at this point the person's silhouette is already segmented. The skin color detection is thus not influenced by clutter in the environment.

To extract a representing skin color, we convert the RGB-data of the face region to HSV and then create a color histogram. The HSV color space has

Table 1. Dataset samples from the Cornell Activity Dataset [14] used to evaluate the people detection algorithm

Person 1				Person 2			
subset	action	pose	# images	subset	action	pose	# images
(A)	brushing teeth	standing	1351	(A)	still	standing	482
(B)	drinking water	standing	1746	(C)	drinking water	standing	508
(C)	wearing contact lenses	standing	440	(F)	opening pill container	standing	210
(E)	working on laptop	sitting	1265	(I)	cooking (stirring)	standing	442
(H)	talking on the phone	standing	1442	(L)	writing on white board	standing	609
Person 3				Person 4			
subset	action	pose	# images	subset	action	pose	# images
(A)	still	standing	374	(A)	still	standing	276
(D)	still	sitting	474	(F)	opening pill container	standing	215
(H)	opening pill container	standing	245	(G)	opening pill container	standing	346
(M)	walk around	standing	511	(J)	cooking (choping)	standing	390
(Q)	wearing contact lenses	standing	447	(K)	working on computer	sitting	411

been proved to be a reliable color space for skin and hand detection [9], [3], [6]. However, the exact choice of the color space is not critical, since we are not actually *detecting* skin color, but rather comparing the face color with possible hand locations on the segmented silhouette.

The generated histogram will show a clustering of the skin color. To clean the histogram from colors originating from the hair, eyebrows, eyes or lips, only the high-valued classes of the histogram are used. Starting with the highest valued class, further high-valued classes are added, until the number of pixels in the valid classes exceeds a predefined threshold. During detection, each pixel with a color inside the valid histogram classes will be regarded as skin color. The resulting colors and the corresponding pixels are stored in a separate binary image S. Both cues are combined to a hand confidence map M as shown in the following Equation:

$$M_{hand}(v, w) = \alpha \cdot D(v, w) + \beta \cdot \frac{S(v, w)}{max(S)} \tag{13}$$

with the 2 weights α and β and the normalization value $max(S)$ with the maximum histogram value. Note that no separate normalization for the distance value is needed, since it is already in metric space. For a validation of possible hands the maximum inside M_{hand} is computed. Regions in the neighborhood of the first maximum, as well as the maximum itself are excluded and the remaining values are used to compute a second maximum, resulting in both hands of a person.

5   Evaluation and Results

The people detection algorithm was evaluated with sample sets from the Cornell Activity Dataset [14]. The dataset was recorded with the Microsoft Kinect. The provided RGB and depth images are aligned, so no manual alignment is

Table 2. Person detection results with different features applied

Frontal Feature				
	Person 1	Person 2	Person 3	Person 4
Precision	0.679	0.958	0.606	0.887
Recall	0.999	0.904	0.940	0.960
Width Feature				
	Person 1	Person 2	Person 3	Person 4
Precision	0.684	0.887	0.468	0.973
Recall	0.976	0.904	0.996	0.955
Frontal & Width Feature				
	Person 1	Person 2	Person 3	Person 4
Precision	0.684	0.983	0.575	0.973
Recall	0.977	0.860	0.885	0.964

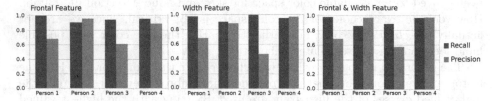

Fig. 9. Precision and recall results on the three different configurations

necessary. We used the CAD-60 subset, which originally consists of 60 RGB-D videos of 4 humans (2 male, 2 female) performing different home activities. For the evaluation, 5 subsets of each person from the dataset were used as indicated in table 1. Since the tested dataset was provided to evaluate action recognition, we had to manually annotate the different images with the correct locations of the persons. This dataset was used to evaluate only the people detection, because the dataset does not provide sufficient hand gestures. We used 60% of the images for training and the remaining 40% for testing. The evaluation was performed 3 times: using only the *Frontal Feature*, only the *Width Feature* and finally using both features. The results are reported in table 2 and figure 9.

As can be seen from table 2 the recall for the *Frontal Features* as well as for the *Width Feature* is in all cases above 90%. However, based on the results it can not be definitely decided which features is best. On the other hand, when both features are combined the recall decreases, which speaks in favor of only using one of the proposed features. In general, the precision is below the recall in all cases. This means that our algorithm rather oversees a person instead of detecting a person where there is none. This behavior is largely due the parameterization of the candidate detection step as described in section 3 and can be changed by adjusting the parameters. Still, certain poses could not be detected by our algorithm. Mainly, persons standing close to high objects or bending over objects have a low recognition rate. Further, problems occurred when the head was occluded.

To evaluate the hand detection, we used our own dataset with 457 test images. The sensor was calibrated using well established techniques [15], [2] to provide accurate RGB and depth image alignment to create the dataset. The hand detection performed with a recall of 73% and a precision of 79%. In this case, main problems arose due to complicated lighting situations, where skin colors differ between hand and face and therefore hands cannot be detected properly.

6   Conclusions and Outlook

In this work we proposed a system for people detection based on RGB-D data. Person candidates are extracted from the input point cloud. Two novel Fourier features are computed on the candidate silhouettes and used for classification. The experiments indicate that using only one of the features at a time leads to better results than using a combination of both features. When only one feature is used, recall is above 90% in all cases, while precision is lower, but still at a high value. The hand detection algorithms achieves a recall and precision above 70%. These promising results support our approach for silhouette and hand detection.

In its current state, our algorithm is challenged by people bending over, since the resulting pose does not support our model of a head being directly above the torso. Our future work will concentrate on further improving the algorithm and adjust our geometric human model. We will extend it to not only check the test areas below the head, but also in a diagonal direction to be able to detect bending people.

References

1. Bertozzi, M., Broggi, A., Del Rose, M., Felisa, M., Rakotomamonjy, A., Suard, F.: A pedestrian detector using histograms of oriented gradients and a support vector machine classifier. In: Intelligent Transportation Systems Conference, ITSC 2007, pp. 143–148. IEEE (2007)
2. Brown, L.G.: A survey of image registration techniques. ACM Computing Surveys (CSUR) **24**(4), 325–376 (1992)
3. Cerlinca, T.L., Pentiuc, S.G., Vatavu, R.D., Cerlinca, M.C.: Hand posture recognition for human-robot interaction. In: Proceedings of the 2007 Workshop on Multimodal Interfaces in Semantic Interaction, pp. 47–50. ACM (2007)
4. Choi, W., Pantofaru, C., Savarese, S.: Detecting and tracking people using an rgb-d camera via multiple detector fusion. In: 2011 IEEE International Conference on Computer Vision Workshops (ICCV Workshops), pp. 1076–1083. IEEE (2011)
5. Dalal, N., Triggs, B.: Histograms of oriented gradients for human detection. In: IEEE Computer Society Conference on Computer Vision and Pattern Recognition, CVPR 2005, vol. 1, pp. 886–893 (June 2005)
6. Ghosh, S., Zheng, J., Chen, W., Zhang, J., Cai, Y.: Real-time 3d markerless multiple hand detection and tracking for human computer interaction applications. In: Proceedings of the 9th ACM SIGGRAPH Conference on Virtual-Reality Continuum and its Applications in Industry, pp. 323–330. ACM (2010)

7. González, D.I.R., Hayet, J.-B.: Fast Human Detection in RGB-D Images with Progressive SVM-Classification. In: Klette, R., Rivera, M., Satoh, S. (eds.) PSIVT 2013. LNCS, vol. 8333, pp. 337–348. Springer, Heidelberg (2014)

8. Hordern, D., Kirchner, N.: Robust and efficient people detection with 3-d range data using shape matching. In: Australasian Conference on Robotics and Automation (2010)

9. Kakumanu, P., Makrogiannis, S., Bourbakis, N.: A survey of skin-color modeling and detection methods. Pattern Recognition 40(3), 1106–1122 (2007)

10. Lee, S.J., Nguyen, D.D., Jeon, J.W.: Design and Implementation of Depth Image Based Real-Time Human Detection. Journal of Semiconductor Technology and Science 14(2), 212–226 (2014)

11. Xia, L., Chen, C.-C., Aggarwal, J.K.: Human Detection Using Depth Information by Kinect. In: International Workshop on Human Activity Understanding from 3D Data in Conjunction with CVPR (HAU3D) (2011)

12. Paisitkriangkrai, S., Shen, C., van den Hengel, A.: Strengthening the Effectiveness of Pedestrian Detection with Spatially Pooled Features. CoRR, abs/1407.0786 (2014)

13. Spinello, L., Arras, K.O.: People detection in RGB-D data. In: IEEE/RSJ Int. Conf. on (2011)

14. Sung, J., Ponce, C., Selman, B., Saxena, A.: Human activity detection from rgbd images. plan, activity, and intent recognition, 64 (2011)

15. Zhang, Z.: A flexible new technique for camera calibration. IEEE Transactions on Pattern Analysis and Machine Intelligence 22(11), 1330–1334 (2000)

Author Index

Ababsa, Fakhreddine I-642
Afzal, Hassan II-712
Aghdam, Hamed Habibi II-242
Aguirre, Hernán E. II-566
Akimoto, Youhei II-566
Alatrista-Salas, Hugo II-664
Alegre, Enrique II-336
Alimi, Adel M. II-725
Allegra, Dario II-604
Amelio, Alessia I-654
Amengual, Xesca I-64
Aouada, Djamila II-712
Aribi, Yassine II-725
Ayala, Guillermo I-522
Azzopardi, George I-513, I-558, II-300,
    II-336, II-348

Bac, Alexandra II-616
Badawi, Ahmed II-737
Bai, Lu I-465, I-790, II-85
Baldacci, Fabien II-277
Baluja, Shumeet II-96
Barakova, Emilia I. I-274
Baraldi, Lorenzo I-801
Barbarar, Jonathan I-235
Barrat, Sabine II-579
Baumann, F. I-1
Beltrán-Castañón, Cesar II-326, II-664
Betancourt, Alejandro I-274
Biehl, Michael II-760, II-772
Bonnici, Alexandra I-690
Borg, Mark II-207
Bors, Adrian G. I-137, I-546
Bosch, Anna I-64
Bouzaieni, Abdessalem II-554, II-579
Bräuer-Burchardt, Christian II-49, II-61
Brodić, Darko I-654
Buyssens, Pierre I-149
Byna, Surendra II-426

Caarls, Wouter I-174
Caicedo, Eduardo I-812
Calcagno, Salvatore II-494

Camilleri, Kenneth P. I-288, I-690, II-207,
    II-628
Camilleri, Tracey A. I-288
Casaca, Wallace II-675
Castro, Francisco M. I-727
Cerman, Martin II-687
Charbit, Maurice I-642
Cheng, Yuan I-312, II-640
Chien, Hsiang-Jen I-399, I-411
Chmielewski, Leszek J. I-630
Cinque, Luigi II-541
Cointault, Frédéric II-134
Collins, William D. II-426
Colnago, Marilaine II-675
Cordes, Kai I-374
Cortés, Xavier I-113
Cossu, Rossella II-541
Covell, Michele II-96
Cristina, Stefania II-628
Cucchiara, Rita I-801

D'Orazio, T. II-591
Daisy, Maxime I-149
Dart, Eli II-426
de Boer, Maaike I-387
de la Rosa, Josep Lluís I-64
De Marsico, Maria II-195
de Vries, Gert-Jan II-760
Destelle, François II-712
Devy, Michel I-52
Di Ruberto, Cecilia I-477, II-415
Diem, Markus II-109
Diep, Daniel I-161
Domingo, Juan I-522
Dong, Junyu II-518
Duan, Fuqing I-456
Dura, Esther I-522
Dusik, Jan I-27

Effenberg, A.O. I-1
Ehlers, A. I-1
Elbahi, Anis I-740

Elleuch, Mohamed   II-371
Enzweiler, Markus   I-14
Ewerth, Ralph   II-359

Fabri, Simon G.   I-288
Farinella, Giovanni M.   II-604
Farokhi, Sajad   I-88
Farrugia, Reuben A.   II-700
Farrugia, Trevor   I-235
Fernández-Robles, Laura   II-336
Fiel, Stefan   II-26
Filip, Jiří   II-289
Flusser, Jan   I-88
Fodde, Giuseppe   I-477
Forczmański, Paweł   I-77, II-529
Franke, Uwe   I-14
Freisleben, Bernd   II-359
Fuchs, Christian   II-38
Fuhl, Wolfgang   I-39
Fukushima, Atsushi   II-184
Fusiello, Andrea   II-13

Galea, Christian   II-700
Gallo, Ignazio   I-325
Gavrilova, Marina L.   I-211
Geng, Haokun   I-399, I-411
Ghorbel, Faouzi   II-230
Giordano, Daniela   I-100, II-383
Gonzalez-Diaz, Rocio   II-687
Gonzalez-Lorenzo, Aldo   II-616
Goumeidane, Aicha Baya   II-554
Grala, Bartlomiej   II-1
Grana, Costantino   I-801
Granell, Emilio   I-246
Grélard, Florent   II-277
Grundmann, Lukas   I-374
Gudivada, Sravan   I-546
Guil, Nicolás   I-727
Guo, Jiapan   I-513, II-348
Gupta, Phalguni   I-702, II-506
Guzmán, Roberto   I-582
Guzmán-Masías, Luis   II-664

Haeusler, Ralf   II-394
Haindl, Michal   I-261, I-300
Hammer, Barbara   II-437
Hamouda, Atef   I-534
Han, Simeng   II-134
Hancock, Edwin R.   I-465, I-790, II-85

Hanocka, Rana   II-313
Hayet, Jean-Bernard   I-582
Heidemann, Gunther   II-450
Heikkilä, Janne   II-158, II-171
Heravi, Elnaz Jahani   II-242
Hirano, Yuta   I-186
Hödlmoser, Michael   II-482
Hofbauer, Heinz   I-752
Hollaus, Fabian   II-109
Holuša, Michael   I-618
Höschl, Cyril IV   I-88
Hoyoux, Thomas   II-403

Ienaga, Naoto   I-445
Ignat, Anca   II-220
Imiya, Atsushi   I-186, I-223, I-715, II-749
Inagaki, Shun   II-749
Islam, Muhammad   II-737
Itoh, Hayato   I-223, I-715, II-749
Iwamura, Yasumasa   I-445

Jalel, Sawssen   I-534
Jia, Lei   II-470
Jiang, Weiming   II-470
Jiang, Xiaoyi   I-337, II-266
Jonker, Pieter   I-174
Jonkman, Marcel F.   I-513
Jribi, Majdi   II-230
Juarez-Chambi, Ronald   II-326

Kaden, Marika   II-772
Kampel, Martin   II-482
Kannala, Juho   II-158, II-171
Kashino, Kunio   I-778
Kasneci, Enkelejda   I-39
Kato, Tomoya   I-223
Kavasidis, Isaak   I-100, II-383
Kherallah, Monji   II-371
Khlebnikov-Núñez, Sofía   II-326
Kiryati, Nahum   II-313
Klette, Reinhard   I-14, I-198, I-399, I-411,
    I-582, II-394
Kluth, Tobias   I-350
Kobayashi, Takumi   I-594
Koga, Hisashi   II-73
Konovalov, Alexander B.   I-667
Koot, Gijs   I-387
Kozlowski, Wojciech   I-432, II-1
Kropatsch, Walter   II-687

Kubek, Mario M.   I-27
Kübler, Thomas   I-39
Kudo, Mineichi   I-261
Kühmstedt, Peter   II-49, II-61
Kumar, Balender   I-702, II-506
Kurlin, Vitaliy   I-606
Kusenbach, Michael   I-824

Lachaud, Jacques-Olivier   II-277
Lai, Jian   II-652
Larabi, Slimane   I-489
Lenseigne, Boris   I-174
Leow, Wee Kheng   I-312, II-640, II-652
Lézoray, Olivier   I-149
Li, Fanzhang   II-470
Liang, Yuanheng   I-790
Liu, Dongwei   I-198
Loaiza, Humberto   I-812
Loddo, Andrea   II-415
Lomeli-R., J.   I-362
Lovish   I-702

Magnier, Baptiste   I-161
Magri, Luca   II-13
Maleika, Wojciech   I-77
Manfredi, Guido   I-52
Mao, Xin   II-518
Marani, R.   II-591
Marcenaro, Lucio   I-274
Mari, Jean-Luc   II-616
Marín-Jimenez, Manuel J.   I-727
Markiewicz, Andrzej   II-529
Markiewicz, Tomasz   I-432, II-1
Marthon, Philippe   I-534
Martinez, Duber   I-766, I-812
Martínez-Hinarejos, Carlos-D.   I-246
McGuire, Kimberly   I-174
Medina-Rodríguez, Rosario   II-664
Meijer, Joost M.   I-513
Mikeš, Stanislav   I-261
Milivojević, Zoran N.   I-654
Milotta, Filippo L.M.   II-604
Mirbach, Bruno   II-712
Montesinos, Philippe   I-161
Moorfield, Bradley   II-394
Morabito, Francesco Carlo   II-494
Moreno-García, Carlos Francisco   I-113
Morerio, Pietro   I-274
Mori, Minoru   I-778
Moschini, Ugo   II-121

Mühling, Markus   II-359
Mühlpforte, N.   I-1
Mustaniemi, Janne   II-158

Nacereddine, Nafaa   II-554
Nakath, David   I-350
Nappi, Michele   II-195
Nebel, David   II-772
Neocleous, Andreas   I-558
Neuhaus, Frank   II-38
Nicolescu, Radu   I-198, I-399
Nigam, Aditya   I-702, II-506
Nixon, Mark S.   I-362
Noce, Lucia   I-325
Nonato, Luis Gustavo   II-675
Notni, Gunther   II-49, II-61

Okabe, Takahiro   II-184
Olszewska, Joanna Isabelle   I-501
Omri, Mohamed Nazih   I-740
Oncevay-Marcos, Arturo   II-326
Orłowski, Arkadiusz   I-630
Osowski, Stanislaw   I-432
Ostermann, Jörn   I-374
Ottersten, Björn   II-712

Pagani, Alain   II-254
Page, Christopher   I-423
Palazzo, Simone   I-100
Papushoy, Alex   I-137
Patera, Janusz   I-432
Paulus, Dietrich   I-824, II-38
Pauws, Steffen   II-760
Pedrini, Helio   II-146
Percannella, Gennaro   II-266
Petkov, Nicolai   I-513, I-558, II-300, II-336, II-348
Petutschnigg, Alexander   I-752
Pfeiffer, David   I-14
Piater, Justus H.   II-403
Prabhat   II-426
Psutka, Josef V.   I-678, II-462
Puig, Domenec   II-242
Putzu, Lorenzo   I-477, II-415

Qiao, Xuejun   I-456

Rattanapitak, Wirat   I-570
Rauterberg, Matthias   I-274
Real, Pedro   II-616

Regazzoni, Carlo S.   I-274
Reinders, C.   I-1
Reineking, Thomas   I-350
Ren, Peng   I-465
Renò, V.   II-591
Riccio, Daniel   II-195
Rodríguez-Sánchez, Antonio J.   II-403
Rosenhahn, B.   I-1
Rosenstiel, Wolfgang   I-39
Ruiz-España, Silvia   I-522
Rushdi, Muhammad   II-737

Sablatnig, Robert   II-26, II-109
Saggese, Alessia   I-812
Saito, Hideo   I-445
Sakai, Tomoya   I-715
Salon, Christophe   II-134
Santos, Anderson   II-146
Schäfers, Klaus   I-337
Schavemaker, John   I-387
Scheuermann, B.   I-1
Schizas, Christos N.   I-558
Schmid, Sönke   I-337
Schmidt, Guido   I-824
Schöning, Julius   II-450
Schraml, Rudolf   I-752
Schulz, Alexander   II-437
Seib, Viktor   I-824
Selim, Mohamed   II-254
Serratosa, Francesc   I-113
Setitra, Insaf   I-489
Seychell, Dylan   I-125
Shi, Chenyu   I-513, II-348
Shi, Yaxin   II-518
Shimizu, Masayoshi   I-445
Sidobre, Daniel   I-52
Sim, Terence   II-652
Simon, Jean-Claude   II-134
Sippel, Katrin   I-39
Sojka, Eduard   I-618
Somol, Petr   II-289
Spampinato, Concetto   I-100, II-383
Spitters, Martijn   I-387
Stanco, Filippo   II-604
Stella, E.   II-591
Stricker, Didier   II-254
Strisciuglio, Nicola   II-300
Suk, Tomáš   I-88

Sukthankar, Rahul   II-96
Swiderska, Zaneta   II-1
Szedmak, Sandor   II-403

Tabbone, Salvatore   II-554, II-579
Tabone, Wilbert   I-125
Tagougui, Najiba   II-371
Taher, Hamed   II-737
Talebi, Hossein   I-211
Tanaka, Kiyoshi   II-566
Tao, Junli   I-14
Teeninga, Paul   II-121
Tezuka, Kouichi   I-445
Toda, Masato   I-174
Trager, Scott C.   II-121
Tran, Ngoc-Trung   I-642
Triyar, Jyoti   II-506
Trullo, Roger   I-766
Tschumperlé, David   I-149
Tsukada, Masato   I-174

Uglov, Alexander S.   I-667
Uhl, Andreas   I-752
Unger, Herwig   I-27

Vácha, Pavel   I-300
van de Gronde, Jasper J.   II-783
Venkatrayappa, Darshan   I-161
Vento, Mario   I-812, II-266, II-300
Versaci, Mario   II-494
Vialard, Anne   II-277
Villmann, Thomas   II-772
Vishwanath, Venkatram   II-426
Vlasov, Vitaly V.   I-667
Volkmann, Niels   I-423

Wali, Ali   II-725
Wang, Chaoyan   II-85
Wangsiripitak, Somkiat   I-570
Wdowiak, Marek   I-432
Wehner, Michael   II-426
Wilkinson, Michael H.F.   II-121
Winkens, Christian   II-38
Wolf, Patrick   II-482
Wu, Xiaomeng   I-778

Xiao, Zedong   I-456
Xie, Shudong   II-640
Xu, Xiao-Ping   I-423

Yeoh, Tze Wei   II-566
Ylimäki, Markus   II-171

Zamberletti, Alessandro   I-325
Zapotecas-Martínez, Saúl   II-566
Zhang, Kun   I-312, II-640
Zhang, Li   II-470

Zhang, Zhao   II-470
Zhang, Zhihong   I-465, I-790
    II-85
Zhao, Junli   I-456
Zhao, Mingbo   II-470
Zhong, Guoqiang   II-518
Zou, Zijun   II-73

Printed in the United States
By Bookmasters